Dear Reader

This 18th edition of the Michelin Guide Europe offers the latest selection of hotels and restaurants.

This Spring, 11 European countries (Austria, Belgium, Finland, France, Germany, Republic of Ireland, Italy, Luxembourg, Netherlands, Portugal, and Spain) will begin preparations for a single common currency, the EURO, to be in place for the year 2002.

Currently the EURO is in use, particularly for hotel and restaurant prices, where a customer may choose to settle the bill by cheque or credit card. These establishments will therefore accept payment in either EUROS or in the local currency.

The implementation is however still under development, and we have therefore decided to continue to include prices in this Guide in local currency.

We hope that you will enjoy your travels with the Michelin Guide and thank you for your comments which are always appreciated.

Bon voyage !

Contents

*In addition to those situated in the main cities,
restaurants renowned for their excellent cuisine
will be found in the towns printed
in light type in the list above.*

Dear Reader

*With the aim of giving the maximum amount
of information in a limited number of pages
Michelin has adopted a system of symbols
which is renowned the world over.
Failing this system the present publication would run
to six volumes.
Judge for yourselves by comparing the descriptive text below
with the equivalent extract from the Guide in symbol form.*

La Résidence (Paul) , ✆ 09 18 21 32 43,
❀❀ *Fax 09 18 21 32 49*, ≼ lake, « Flowered garden »,
🔲 ✗ - ✗ ☎ 🚗. AE E JCB   **BX a**
March-November - **Meals** *(closed Sunday)* 350/650 –
⌣ 75 – **25 rm** 500/800.
Spec. Goujonnettes de sole. Poulet aux écrevisses. Profiteroles.
Wines. Vouvray, Bourgueil.

---

*This demonstration
clearly shows that each
entry contains a great
deal of information.
The symbols are easily
learnt and knowing
them will enable
you to understand
the Guide and to choose
those establishments
that you require.*

*A very comfortable hotel where you will enjoy
a pleasant stay and be tempted to prolong your visit.
The excellence of the cuisine, which is personally
supervised by the proprietor Mr Paul, is worth a detour
on your journey.
The hotel is in a quiet secluded setting, away
from built-up areas.
To reserve phone 09 18 21 32 43 ; the Fax number
is 09 18 21 32 49.
The hotel affords a fine view of the lake ;
in good weather it is possible to eat outdoors.
The hotel is enhanced by an attractive flowered garden
and has an indoor swimming pool and a private tennis
court. Smoking is not allowed in certain areas
of the hotel. Direct dialling telephone in room.
Parking facilities, under cover, are available to hotel guests.
The hotel accepts payment by American Express,
Eurocard and Japan Credit Bureau credit cards.
Letters giving the location of the hotel
on the town plan :* BX a.
*The hotel is open from March to November
but the restaurant closes every Sunday.
The set meal prices range from 350 F for the lowest
to 650 F for the highest.
The cost of continental breakfast served in the bedroom
is 75 F.
25 bedroomed hotel. The charges vary from 500 F for a
single to 800 F for the best double or twin bedded room.
Included for the gourmet are some culinary specialities,
recommended by the hotelier : Strips of deep-fried sole
fillets, Chicken with crayfish, Choux pastry balls filled
with ice cream and covered with chocolate sauce.
In addition to the best quality wines you will find many
of the local wines worth sampling : Vouvray, Bourgueil.*

Hotels, Restaurants

Categories, standard of comfort

⛪⛪⛪	XXXXX	*Luxury in the traditional style*
⛪⛪	XXXX	*Top class comfort*
⛪	XXX	*Very comfortable*
⛪	XX	*Comfortable*
⛪	X	*Quite comfortable*
		Traditional pubs serving food
M		*In its class, hotel with modern amenities*

Atmosphere and setting

⛪⛪⛪ ... ⛪	*Pleasant hotels*
XXXXX ... X	*Pleasant restaurants*
« Park »	*Particularly attractive feature*
	Very quiet or quiet secluded hotel
	Quiet hotel
⩽ sea, ※	*Exceptional view, Panoramic view*
⩽	*Interesting or extensive view*

Cuisine

❀❀❀	*Exceptional cuisine in the country,* *worth a special journey*
❀❀	*Excellent cooking : worth a detour*
❀	*A very good restaurant in its category*
Meals	*The* **"Bib Gourmand"** *:* *Good food at moderate prices*

Hotel facilities

30 rm	*Number of rooms*
⊟ **TV**	*Lift (elevator) – Television in room*
	Non-smoking areas
	Air conditioning
☎	*Telephone in room: direct dialling for outside calls*
	Minitel – modem point in the bedrooms
	Tennis court(s) – Outdoor or indoor swimming pool
	Sauna – Exercise room
	Garden – Beach with bathing facilities
	Meals served in garden or on terrace
⚓	*Landing stage*
Ⓟ **Ⓟ** **Ⓟ**	*Garage – Car park*
♿	*Bedrooms accessible to disabled people*
150	*Equipped conference room : maximum capacity*
	Dogs are not allowed
without rest.	*The hotel has no restaurant*

Prices

*These prices are given in the currency of the country
in question. Valid for 1999 the rates shown should
only vary if the cost of living changes
to any great extent.*

Meals

Meals 130/260	*Set meal prices*
Meals a la carte 160/290	*"a la carte" meal prices*
b.i.	*House wine included*
	Table wine available by the carafe

Hotels

30 rm 305/500	*Lowest price for a comfortable single and highest price for the best double room.*
30 rm � 345/580	*Price includes breakfast*

Breakfast

� 55	*Price of breakfast*

Credit cards

Credit cards accepted

Service and Taxes

*Except in Finland, Greece, Hungary, Poland and Spain,
prices shown are inclusive, that is to say service
and V.A.T. included. In the U.K. and Ireland,
s = service only included, t = V.A.T. only included.
In Italy, when not included, a percentage
for service is shown after the meal prices, eg. (16 %).*

Town Plans

Main conventional signs

Tourist Information Centre
Hotel, restaurant – Reference letter on the town plan
Place of interest and its main entrance } *Reference letter*
Interesting church or chapel } *on the town plan*
Shopping street – Public car park
Tram
Underground station
One-way street
Church or chapel
Poste restante, telegraph – Telephone
Public buildings located by letters :
Police (in large towns police headquaters) – Theatre – Museum
Coach station – Airport – Hospital – Covered market
Ruins – Monument, statue – Fountain
Garden, park, wood – Cemetery, Jewish cemetery
Outdoor or indoor swimming pool – Racecourse
Golf course
Cable-car – Funicular
Sports ground, stadium – View – Panorama

Names shown on the street plans are in the language of the country to conform to local signposting.

Sights

★★★ *Worth a journey*
★★ *Worth a detour*
★ *Interesting*

Ami lecteur

Cette 18ᵉ édition du Guide Michelin Europe vous propose une sélection d'hôtels et de restaurants des principales villes d'Europe.

En ce printemps 1999, onze pays d'Europe (Allemagne, Autriche, Belgique, Espagne, Finlande, France, République d' Irlande, Italie, Luxembourg, Pays-Bas et Portugal) s'apprêtent à disposer pour 2002 d'une monnaie commune et unique, l'EURO.

Dès à présent, son usage est admis, en particulier dans l'affichage des prix comme dans le règlement (par chèque ou carte bancaire) des notes d'hôtels et de restaurants.
Les professionnels sont donc tenus d'accepter indifféremment les paiements en EUROS ou dans la devise du pays.

Toutefois, cette mise en oeuvre étant progressive, nous avons choisi d'indiquer dans notre ouvrage les prix dans la monnaie nationale de chaque pays.
Nous vous souhaitons d'agréables séjours et vous remercions de vos commentaires toujours très appréciés.

Bon voyage avec Michelin. ———————

Hôtels, Restaurants

Classe et confort

⛫⛫⛫	XXXXX	*Grand luxe et tradition*
⛫⛫⛫	XXXX	*Grand confort*
⛫⛫	XXX	*Très confortable*
⛫⛫	XX	*Bon confort*
⛫	X	*Assez confortable*
	℡	*Traditionnel "pub" anglais servant des repas*
M		*Dans sa catégorie, hôtel d'équipement moderne*

L'agrément

⛫⛫⛫ ... ⛫	*Hôtels agréables*
XXXXX ... X	*Restaurants agréables*
« Park »	*Élément particulièrement agréable*
🐾	*Hôtel très tranquille, ou isolé et tranquille*
🐾	*Hôtel tranquille*
⇐ sea, ⁂	*Vue exceptionnelle, panorama*
⇐	*Vue intéressante ou étendue*

La table

✿✿✿	*Une des meilleures tables du pays, vaut le voyage*
✿✿	*Table excellente, mérite un détour*
✿	*Une très bonne table dans sa catégorie*
😋 Meals	*Le* **"Bib Gourmand"** *:*
	Repas soignés à prix modérés

L'installation

30 rm	*Nombre de chambres*
	Ascenseur – Télévision dans la chambre
	Non-fumeurs
	Air conditionné
	Téléphone dans la chambre direct avec l'extérieur
	Prise Modem – Minitel dans la chambre
	Tennis – Piscine : de plein air ou couverte
	Sauna – Salle de remise en forme
	Jardin – Plage aménagée
	Repas servis au jardin ou en terrasse
	Ponton d'amarrage
	Garage – Parc à voitures
	Chambres accessibles aux handicapés physiques
150	*Salles de conférences : capacité maximum*
	Accès interdit aux chiens
without rest.	*L'hôtel n'a pas de restaurant*

Les prix

Les prix sont indiqués dans la monnaie du pays. Établis pour l'année 1999, ils ne doivent être modifiés que si le coût de la vie subit des variations importantes.

Au restaurant

Meals 130/260	*Prix des repas à prix fixes*
Meals à la carte 160/290	*Prix des repas à la carte*
b.i.	*Boisson comprise*
	Vin de table en carafe

A l'hôtel

30 rm 305/500	*Prix minimum pour une chambre d'une personne et maximum pour la plus belle chambre occupée par deux personnes*
30 rm 345/580	*Prix des chambres petit déjeuner compris*

Petit déjeuner

55	*Prix du petit déjeuner*

Cartes de crédit

Cartes de crédit acceptées

Service et taxes

A l'exception de la Finlande, de la Grèce, de la Hongrie, de la Pologne et de l'Espagne, les prix indiqués sont nets. Au Royaume Uni et en Irlande, s = service compris, t = T.V.A. comprise. En Italie, le service est parfois compté en supplément aux prix des repas. Ex. : (16 %).

Les Plans

Principaux signes conventionnels ___________

 Information touristique

Hôtel, restaurant – Lettre les repérant sur le plan

Monument intéressant et entrée principale ⎱ Lettre les repérant
Église ou chapelle intéressante ⎰ sur le plan

 Rue commerçante – Parc de stationnement public

Tramway

Station de métro

Sens unique

Église ou chapelle

Poste restante, télégraphe – Téléphone

 Édifices publics repérés par des lettres :

Police (dans les grandes villes commissariat central) –
Théâtre – Musée

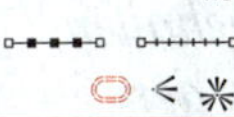 Gare routière – Aéroport – Hôpital – Marché couvert

Ruines – Monument, statue – Fontaine

 Jardin, parc, bois – Cimetière, Cimetière israélite

Piscine de plein air, couverte – Hippodrome –

Golf

Téléphérique – Funiculaire

Stade – Vue – Panorama

*Les indications portées sur les plans
sont dans la langue du pays,
en conformité avec la dénomination locale.*

Les curiosités ___________

 Vaut le voyage

★★ Mérite un détour

★ Intéressante

Lieber Leser

Die vorliegende 18. Ausgabe des Roten Michelin-Führers Europa bietet Ihnen eine aktuelle Auswahl an Hotels und Restaurants in den wichtigsten Städten Europas.

Jetzt im Frühjahr 1999 bereiten sich elf europäische Länder (Belgien, Deutschland, Finnland, Frankreich, Irland, Italien, Luxemburg, die Niederlande, Österreich, Portugal und Spanien) darauf vor, daß sie ab dem Jahr 2002 eine gemeinsame, einheitliche Währung haben werden, den EURO.

Schon jetzt darf der EURO verwendet werden, vor allem bei der Preisauszeichnung oder bei der (bargeldlosen) Begleichung von Hotel-und Gaststättenrechnungen. Geschäftsinhaber sind also gehalten, Zahlungen in EURO oder in der Landeswährung gleichermaßen zu akzeptieren.

Da sich diese Umstellung aber nach und nach vollzieht, haben wir uns entschieden, in der vorliegenden Ausgabe die Preise noch in der jeweiligen Landeswährung anzugeben.

Wir wünschen Ihnen überall einen angenehmen Aufenthalt und danken Ihnen für Ihre Anregungen und Hinweise, die uns stets willkommen sind.

Gute Reise mit Michelin.

Hotels, Restaurants

Klasseneinteilung und Komfort

🏨	XXXXX	*Großer Luxus und Tradition*
🏨	XXXX	*Großer Komfort*
🏨	XXX	*Sehr komfortabel*
🏨	XX	*Mit gutem Komfort*
🏠	X	*Mit Standard-Komfort*
	🍺	*Traditionelle Pubs die Spiesen anbieten*
M		*Moderne Einrichtung*

Annehmlichkeiten

🏨 ... 🏠	*Angenehme Hotels*
XXXXX ... X	*Angenehme Restaurants*
« Park »	*Besondere Annehmlichkeit*
⊗	*Sehr ruhiges oder abgelegenes und ruhiges Hotel*
⊗	*Ruhiges Hotel*
≤ sea, ☀	*Reizvolle Aussicht, Rundblick*
≤	*Interessante oder weite Sicht*

Küche

❀❀❀	*Eine der besten Küchen des Landes : eine Reise wert*
❀❀	*Eine hervorragende Küche : verdient einen Umweg*
❀	*Eine sehr gute Küche : verdient Ihre besondere Beachtung*
😋 **Meals**	*Der "Bib Gourmand" :*
	Sorgfältig zubereitete preiswerte Mahlzeiten

Einrichtung

30 rm	*Anzahl der Zimmer*
🛗 📺	*Fahrstuhl – Fernsehen im Zimmer*
🚭	*Nichtraucher – Klimaanlage*
☎	*Zimmertelefon mit direkter Außenverbindung*
	Minitel Anschluß im Zimmer
	Tennis – Freibad – Hallenbad
	Sauna – Fitneßraum
	Garten – Strandbad
	Garten-, Terrassenrestaurant
⚓	*Bootssteg*
🚗 Ⓟ	*Garage – Parkplatz*
♿	*Für Körperbehinderte leicht zugängliche Zimmer*
150	*Konferenzräume mit Höchstkapazität*
	Hunde sind unerwünscht
without rest.	*Hotel ohne Restaurant*

Die Preise

Die Preise sind in der jeweiligen Landeswährung angegeben. Sie gelten für das Jahr 1999 und ändern sich nur bei starken Veränderungen der Lebenshaltungskosten.

Im Restaurant

Meals 130/260	*Feste Menupreise*
Meals à la carte 160/290	*Mahlzeiten "a la carte"*
b.i.	*Getränke inbegriffen*
	Preiswerter Wein in Karaffen

Im Hotel

30 rm 305/500	*Mindestpreis für ein Einzelzimmer und Höchstpreis für das schönste Doppelzimmer für zwei Personen.*
30 rm 345/580	*Zimmerpreis inkl. Frühstück*

Frühstück

55	*Preis des Frühstücks*

Kreditkarten

Akzeptierte Kreditkarten

Bedienungsgeld und Gebühren

Mit Ausnahme von Finnland, Griechenland, Ungarn, Polen und Spanien sind die angegebenen Preise Inklusivpreise. In den Kapiteln über Großbritannien und Irland bedeutet s = Bedienungsgeld inbegriffen, t = MWSt inbegriffen. In Italien wird für die Bedienung gelegentlich ein Zuschlag zum Preis der Mahlzeit erhoben, zB (16 %).

Stadtpläne

Erklärung der wichtigsten Zeichen

Informationsstelle

Hotel, Restaurant – Referenzbuchstabe auf dem Plan

Sehenswertes Gebäude mit Haupteingang } *Referenzbuchstabe*

Sehenswerte Kirche oder Kapelle } *auf dem Plan*

Einkaufsstraße – Parkplatz, Parkhaus

Straßenbahn

U-Bahnstation

Einbahnstraße

Kirche oder Kapelle

Postlagernde Sendungen, Telegraph – Telefon

Öffentliche Gebäude, durch Buchstaben gekennzeichnet :

Polizei (in größeren Städten Polizeipräsidium) – Theater – Museum

Autobusbahnhof – Flughafen

Krankenhaus – Markthalle

Ruine – Denkmal, Statue – Brunnen

Garten, Park, Wald – Friedhof, Jüd. Friedhof

Freibad – Hallenbad – Pferderennbahn

Golfplatz und Lochzahl

Seilschwebebahn – Standseilbahn

Sportplatz – Aussicht – Rundblick

Die Angaben auf den Stadtplänen erfolgen, übereinstimmend mit der örtlichen Beschilderung, in der Landessprache.

Sehenswürdigkeiten

★★★ *Eine Reise wert*

★★ *Verdient einen Umweg*

★ *Sehenswert*

読者のみなさまへ

この第18版では、ヨーロッパ主要都市のホテルとレストランを選んで紹介してあります。

1999年の春、ヨーロッパ11カ国（アイルランド共和国、イタリア、オーストリア、オランダ、スペイン、ドイツ、フィンランド、フランス、ベルギー、ポルトガル、ルクセンブルク）は、2002年からのヨーロッパ共通・単一通貨ユーロEURO流通の準備に入ります。

すでに、ホテル、レストランでの支払いも価格表示も、ユーロ単位の使用が認められています。
ホテル、レストラン側は、その国の通貨でもユーロ単位による支払いでも区別することなく受け取らなくてはなりません。

しかし、この移行は段階的におこなわれているため、本書では、価格表示を現在の各国の基準通貨で表示してあります。

よい旅をお楽しみください。
ボン・ボワイヤージュ。

ホテル　レストラン

等級と快適さ

豪華で伝統的様式
トップクラス
たいへん快適
快適
割に快適
食事もできる伝統的なパブ
等級内での近代的設備のホテル

居心地

居心地よいホテル
居心地よいレストラン
《 Park 》　特に魅力的な特徴
大変静かなホテルまたは人里離れた静かなホテル
静かなホテル
≤ sea, ※　見晴らしがよい展望（例：海）、パノラマ
素晴らしい風景

料理

※※※　最上の料理、出かける価値あり
※※　素晴らしい料理、寄り道の価値あり
※　等級内では大変おいしい料理
Meals　**"Bib Gourmand"!**：手頃な値段でおいしい料理

設備

30 rm　部屋数
エレベーター　室内テレビ
禁煙
空調設備
室内に電話あり　外線直通
ミニテル／モデムの回線付き
テニスコート　屋外プール　屋内プール
サウナ　トレーニングルーム
くつろげる庭　整備された海水浴場
食事が庭またはテラスでできる
専用桟橋
駐車場　パーキング
体の不自由な方のための設備あり
150　会議または研修会の出来るホテル
犬の連れ込みおことわり
without rest.　レストランのないホテル

料金

料金は1999年のその国の貨幣単位で示してありますが、物価の変動などで変わる場合もあります。

レストラン

Meals 130/260
Meals à la carte 160/290
定食、ア・ラ・カルトそれぞれの最低料金と最高料金
b.i.　飲みもの付き
デカンター入りテーブルワインあり

ホテル

30 rm 305/500
30 rm
一人部屋の最低料金と二人部屋の最高料金
345/580　朝食料金

朝食

55　朝食料金

クレジット・カード

MC AE GB S
D E JCB VISA
クレジット・カード使用可

サービス料と税金

フィンランド、ギリシャ、スペイン以外の国に関しては正価料金。イギリス及びアイルランドでは、s.：サービス料込み、t.：付加価値税込み、を意味する。イタリアでは、サービス料が料金に加算されることがある。例：（16%）

地図

主な記号

ツーリスト・インフォメーション

ホテル・レストラン－地図上での目印番号

興味深い歴史的建造物とその中央入口 ｝ 地図上での

興味深い教会または聖堂　目印番号

Thiers (R.) 商店街　公共駐車場

路面電車

地下鉄駅

一方通行路

教会または聖堂－局留郵便、電報－電話

公共建造物、記号は下記の通り

警察（大都市では、中央警察署）－劇場－美術館、博物館

バス・ターミナル－空港－病院－屋内市場

遣跡－歴史的建造物、像－泉

庭園、公園、森林－墓地－ユダヤ教の墓地

屋外プール、屋内プール－競馬場－ゴルフ場

ロープウェイ－ケーブルカー

スタジアム－展望－パノラマ

地図上の名称は、地方の標識に合わせてその国の言葉で表記されています。

名所

★★★　ぜひ訪ねたいところ

★★　その次に訪ねたいところ

★　おすすめのところ

NEW YORK
UTC − 5
DIRECT DAILY FLIGHTS
Total time of journey
(in hours)
Amsterdam 9 1/4
Athens 12
Barcelona 9 1/4
Berlin 12 3/4
Brussels 10 3/4
Budapest 11
Copenhagen 9 3/4
Dublin 8 3/4
Düsseldorf 9 1/4
Frankfurt 9 3/4
Geneva 9 1/2
Glasgow 10
Hamburg 11
Helsinki 12
Lisbon 8 3/4
London 9 1/2
Luxembourg 11 1/2
Madrid 9 1/4
Milan 9 3/4
Munich 11 3/4
Oslo 9 1/2
Paris 9 3/4
Rome 10 1/2
Stockholm 11 1/2
Vienna 10 1/2
Warsaw 12 1/2
Zürich 9 3/4
J.F. KENNEDY
AIRPORT
IRL
DUBLIN
UTC
UTC + 1
Glasgow
Edinburgh
GB
Liverpool
Leeds
Manchester
Birmingham
London
Amsterdam
The Hague
NL
Rotterdam
Bruges
Antwerp
Brussels
Lille
B
Liège
Luxembourg
L
Paris
Valley
of the Loire
F
Geneva
Lyons
Bordeaux
Bilbao
Nice
Marseilles
Cannes
Barcelona
P
Madrid
E
Lisbon
Valencia
Sevilla
Málaga

FIN
UTC + 2
Helsinki
N
Oslo
S
Stockholm
Gothenburg
DK
Copenhagen
Hamburg
Berlin
Warsaw
Hanover
Leipzig
PL
Düsseldorf
Dresden
Cologne
D
Prague
CZ
Frankfurt
Stuttgart
Vienna
Strasbourg
Munich
Salzburg
Budapest
Basle
Zurich
Innsbruck
A
H
CH
Berne
Venice
Milan
Turin
Florence
Monaco
I
Rome
Naples
GR
Athens
Palermo
Taormina
A   Austria
B   Belgium
CH   Switzerland
CZ   Czech Republic
D   Germany
DK   Denmark
E   Spain
F   France
FIN Finland
GB   United Kingdom
GR   Greece
H   Hungary
I   Italy
IRL Ireland
L   Luxembourg
N   Norway
NL   Netherlands
PL   Poland
P   Portugal
S   Sweden

DISTANCES BY ROAD

(in kilometres)

The chart is a triangular distance matrix; the highlighted Helsinki row/column and the **1286** callout show the Helsinki–Strasbourg distance (1286 km).

	Amsterdam	Athens	Barcelona	Berlin	Berne	Bordeaux	Brussels	Budapest	Cologne	Copenhagen	Dublin	Edinburgh	Frankfurt	Geneva	Hamburg	Helsinki	Lisbon	London	Luxembourg	Lyons	Madrid	Manchester	Marseilles	Milan	Munich	Oslo	Paris	Prague	Rome	Stockholm	Strasbourg	Stuttgart	Venice	Vienna	Warsaw
Athens	2837																																		
Barcelona	1562	3091																																	
Berlin	665	2584	1863																																
Berne	840	3316	925	913																															
Bordeaux	1080	3240	567	1631	849																														
Brussels	205	2793	1366	774	648	892																													
Budapest	1388	1510	1916	852	1107	2045	1347																												
Cologne	256	2579	1360	566	588	1068	211	1137																											
Copenhagen	778	2938	2095	391	1222	1797	886	1252	732																										
Dublin	954	3587	1972	1538	1368	1164	796	2151	1015	1679																									
Edinburgh	1101	3823	2119	1686	1515	1608	943	2298	1162	488	391																								
Frankfurt	441	2396	1331	537	429	1149	399	955	189	798	1203	1350																							
Geneva	913	2446	762	1072	164	684	718	1268	748	1381	1335	1483	588																						
Hamburg	465	2780	1782	284	913	1483	573	1145	418	321	1365	1512	489	1072																					
Helsinki	1205	2540	2389	505	1883	2182	1317	1630	1110	795	2154	2390	1101	1656	776																				
Lisbon	2278	4320	1238	2829	2146	1193	2091	3136	2266	2995	2361	2806	2347	1983	2681	3423																			
London	479	3253	1496	1055	892	985	320	1672	536	1195	467	643	724	860	881	1820	2182																		
Luxembourg	379	2637	1155	765	436	928	215	1170	193	927	1004	1152	235	506	614	1303	2125	529																	
Lyons	929	2560	635	1231	315	537	734	1419	728	1463	1341	1488	699	152	1149	1758	1855	865	522																
Madrid	1775	3761	618	2326	1526	690	1588	2516	1763	2492	1858	2303	1844	1362	2178	2913	619	1680	1623	1235															
Manchester	820	3478	1837	1404	1233	1029	661	2016	880	1544	212	351	1068	1201	1231	2045	2226	333	870	1205	1723														
Marseilles	1241	2622	504	1542	605	654	1046	1444	1039	1774	1652	1799	1010	441	1461	2070	1725	1177	833	314	1104	1518													
Milan	1085	2128	981	1033	357	1130	892	950	833	1426	1612	1760	674	317	1117	1575	2202	1137	680	445	1581	1478	509												
Munich	831	2063	1378	585	434	1246	729	636	580	944	1541	1688	398	594	789	1120	2599	1065	514	745	1978	1406	1003	498											
Oslo	1047	3521	2363	970	1502	2065	1155	1833	1000	557	1000	728	1078	1662	591	690	3262	456	1196	1731	2759	768	2044	1707	1525										
Paris	497	2913	1092	1048	551	581	309	1473	484	1213	877	1024	576	500	900	1605	1778	402	355	460	1275	743	773	846	822	1482									
Prague	847	2110	1706	338	756	1598	870	514	654	732	1674	1821	499	915	625	1095	2795	1199	722	1074	2306	1539	1386	868	379	1313	1025								
Rome	1653	2389	1351	1494	925	1500	1460	1204	1401	1853	2180	2328	1242	871	1698	2041	2572	1705	1248	963	1951	2046	879	564	905	2434	1401	1288							
Stockholm	1386	3568	2702	998	1829	2404	1494	1861	1339	585	1056	965	1405	1989	928	165	3601	1799	1535	2070	3098	868	2383	2033	1553	538	1821	1341	2462						
Strasbourg	588	2438	1129	753	243	1063	432	998	348	1007	1207	1355	214	402	698	1286	2260	732	220	497	1729	1073	810	488	361	1288	490	596	1056	1615					
Stuttgart	600	2302	1230	629	286	1182	515	858	348	968	1327	1474	189	445	659	1166	2450	851	300	596	1830	1192	888	477	220	1248	609	472	1045	1575	148				
Venice	1243	1878	1235	1060	611	1384	1146	698	992	1420	1866	2013	874	579	1264	1615	2456	1391	933	707	1835	1731	763	269	472	2001	1109	810	523	2029	743	634			
Vienna	1146	1862	1788	623	865	1803	1105	243	895	1017	1909	2056	713	1024	910	924	3009	1433	928	1175	2389	1774	1316	823	394	1598	1231	285	1076	1626	758	617	571		
Warsaw	1221	2249	2325	591	1375	2187	1330	670	1122	981	2094	2241	1093	1535	874	346	3384	1607	1321	1693	2881	1960	2006	1512	995	1401	1604	612	1766	852	1216	1087	1260	684	
Zurich	807	2417	1047	835	126	938	635	997	556	1174	1355	1502	396	286	865	1388	2268	879	422	437	1648	1220	728	280	313	1454	592	678	848	1781	232	208	533	757	1293

AIR LINKS *(in hours)*

3½ not daily

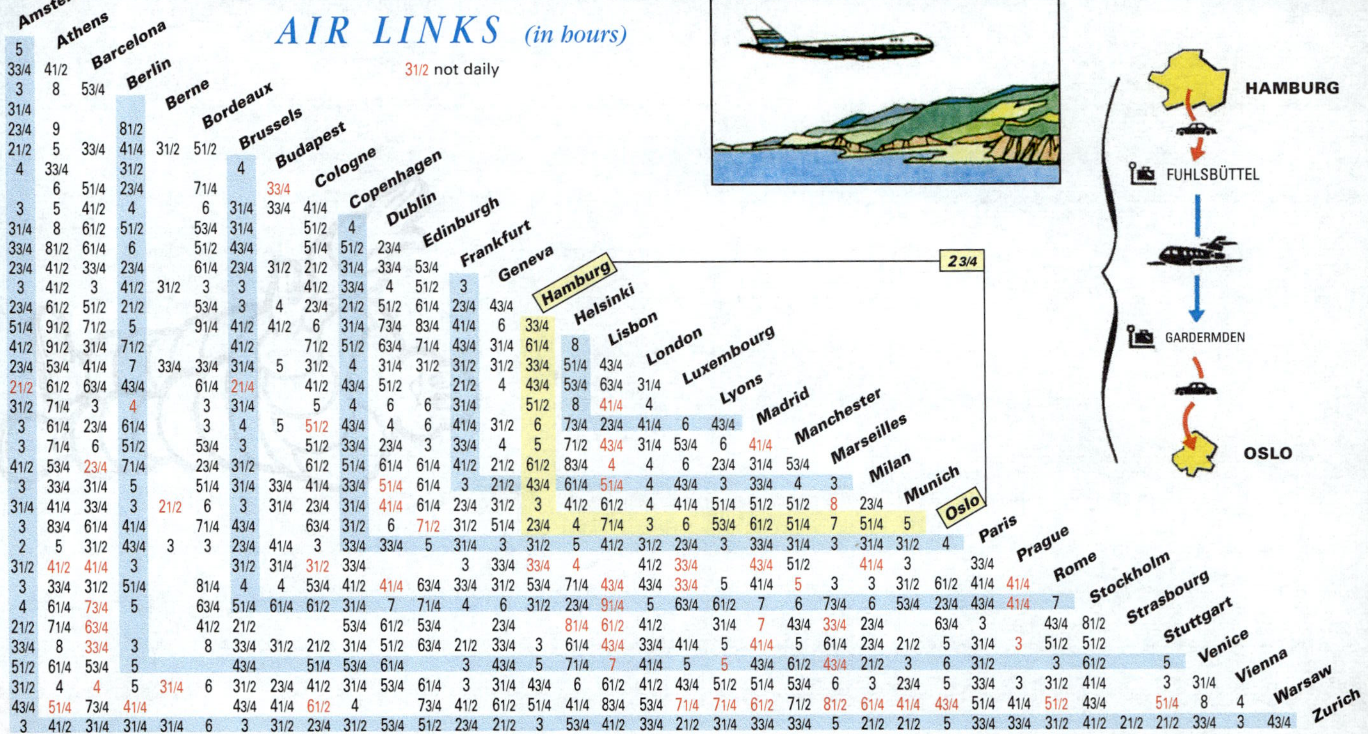

The chart is a triangular flight-time matrix between European cities (times in hours). It is reproduced below as three column-blocks; the left "From" column is repeated in each block, and empty cells indicate no listed value.

Block 1 — destinations Amsterdam to Edinburgh

From	Amsterdam	Athens	Barcelona	Berlin	Berne	Bordeaux	Brussels	Budapest	Cologne	Copenhagen	Dublin	Edinburgh
Athens	5											
Barcelona	3¾	4½										
Berlin	3	8	5¾									
Berne	3¼											
Bordeaux	2¾	9		8½								
Brussels	2½	5	3¾	4¼	3½	5½						
Budapest	4	3¾		3½			4					
Cologne	6	5¼	2¾		7¼	3¾	3¾	4¼				
Copenhagen	3	5	4½	4		6	3¼	3¾	4¼			
Dublin	3¼	8	6½	5½		5¾	3¼		5½	4		
Edinburgh	3¾	8½	6¼	6		5½	4¾		5¼	5½	2¾	
Frankfurt	2¾	4½	3¾	2¾		6¼	2¾	3½	2½	3¼	3¾	5¾
Geneva	3	4½	3	4½	3½	3	3		4½	3¾	4	5½
Hamburg	2¾	6½	5½	2½		5¾	3	4	2¾	2½	5½	6¼
Helsinki	5¼	9½	7½	5		9¼	4½	4½	6	3¼	7¾	8¾
Lisbon	4½	9½	3¼	7½			4½		7½	5½	6¾	7¼
London	2¾	5¾	4¼	7	3¾	3¾	3¼	5	3½	4	3¼	3½
Luxembourg	2½	6½	6¾	4¾		6¼	2¼		4½	4¾	5½	
Lyons	3½	7¼	3	4		3	3¼		5	4	6	6
Madrid	3	6¼	2¾	6¼		3	4	5	5½	4¾	4	6
Manchester	3	7¼	6	5½		5¾	3		5½	3¾	2¾	3
Marseilles	4½	5¾	2¾	7¼		2¾	3½		6½	5¼	6¼	6¼
Milan	3	3¾	3¼	5		5¼	3¼	3¾	4¼	3¾	5¼	6¼
Munich	3¼	4¼	3¾	3	2½	6	3	3¼	2¾	3¼	4¼	6¼
Oslo	3	8¾	6¼	4¼		7¼	4¾		6¾	3½	6	7½
Paris	2	5	3½	4¾	3	3	2¾	4¼	3	3¾	3¾	5
Prague	3½	4½	4¼	3			3½	3¼	3½	3¾		
Rome	3	3¾	3½	5¼		8¼	4	4	5¾	4½	4¼	6¾
Stockholm	4	6¼	7¾	5		6¾	5¼	6¼	6½	3¼	7	7¼
Strasbourg	2½	7¼	6¾			4½	2½				5¾	6½
Stuttgart	3¾	8	3¾	3		8	3¾	3½	2½	3¼	5½	6¾
Venice	5½	6¼	5¾	5			4¾		5¼	5¾	6¼	
Vienna	3½	4	4	5	3¼	6	3½	2¾	4½	3¼	5¾	6¼
Warsaw	4¾	5¼	7¾	4¼			4¾	4¼	6½	4		
Zurich	3	4½	3¼	3¼	3¼	6	3	3½	2¾	3½	5¾	5½

Block 2 — destinations Frankfurt to Milan

From	Frankfurt	Geneva	Hamburg	Helsinki	Lisbon	London	Luxembourg	Lyons	Madrid	Manchester	Marseilles	Milan
Geneva	3											
Hamburg	2¾	4¾										
Helsinki	4¼	6	3¾									
Lisbon	4¾	3¼	6¼	8								
London	3½	3½	3¾	5¼	4¾							
Luxembourg	2½	4	4¾	5¾	6¾	3¼						
Lyons	3¼		5½	8	4¼	4	4					
Madrid	4¼	3½	6	7¾	2¾	4¼	6	4¾				
Manchester	3¾	4	5	7½	4¾	3¼	5¾	6	4¼			
Marseilles	4½	2½	6½	8¾	4	4	6	2¾	3¼	5¾		
Milan	3	2½	4¾	6¼	5¼	4	4¾	3	3¾	4	3	
Munich	2¾	3½	3	4½	6½	4	4¼	5¼	5½	5½	8	2¾
Oslo	3½	5¼	2¾	4	7¼	3	6	5¾	6½	5¼	7	5¼
Paris	3¼	3			4½	3½	2¾	3	3¾	3¼	3	3¼
Prague	3	3¾			4½	3¾			4¾	5½		4¼
Rome	3¾	3½			4¾	4¾	3¾	5	4¼	5	3	3
Stockholm	4	6			9¼	5	6¾	6½	7	6	7¾	6
Strasbourg	5¾				6½	4½		3¼	7	4¾	3¾	2¾
Stuttgart	2½	3¾			4¾	3¾	4¼	5	4¼	5	6¼	2¾
Venice	3	4¾				7	4¼	5	5	4¾	6½	4¾
Vienna	3	3¼				6½	4½	4¾	5½	5¼	5¾	6
Warsaw	7¾	4½				3¾	5¾	7¼	7¼	6½	7½	8½
Zurich	2¾	2½	3	5¾	4½	3¾	2½	3¼	3¾	3¾	5	2½

Block 3 — destinations Munich to Warsaw

From	Munich	Oslo	Paris	Prague	Rome	Stockholm	Strasbourg	Stuttgart	Venice	Vienna	Warsaw
Oslo	5										
Paris	3½	4									
Prague	3		3¾								
Rome	3½	6½	4¼	4¼							
Stockholm	5¾	2¾	4¾	4¼	7						
Strasbourg		6¾	3		4¾	8½					
Stuttgart	2½	5	3¼	3	5½	5½					
Venice	2½	3	6	3½	3	6½		5			
Vienna	3	2¾	5	3¾	3	3½	4¼	3	3¼		
Warsaw	6¼	4¼	4¾	5¼	4¼	5½	4¾	5¼	8	4	
Zurich	2½	5	3¾	3¾	3½	4½	2½	2½	3¾	3	4¾

Austria

Österreich

PRACTICAL INFORMATION

LOCAL CURRENCY

Austrian Schilling; *100 ATS = 7,27 Euros (€)*

TOURIST INFORMATION

In Vienna: *Österreich-Information, 1040 Wien, Margaretenstr. 1, ℰ (01) 587 20 00, Fax (01) 588 66 20*
Niederösterreich Touristik-Information, 1010 Wien, Walfischgasse 6, ℰ (01) 513 80 220, Fax (01) 513 80 22 30

Austrian National Holiday: *26 October*

AIRLINES

Austrian-Swissair-Sabena: *1010 Wien, Kärntner Ring 18, ℰ (01) 17 66 76 00, Fax (01) 17 66 76 99*

Air France: *1010 Wien, Kärntner Str. 49, ℰ (01) 51 41 80, Fax (01) 513 94 26*

British Airways: *1010 Wien, Kärntner Ring 10, ℰ (01) 505 76 91, Fax (01) 504 20 84*

Japan Airlines: *1010 Wien, Kärntner Str. 11, ℰ (01) 79 56 75 67, Fax (01) 512 75 54*

Lufthansa City Center: *1010 Wien, Kärntner Str. 42, ℰ (01) 589 140, Fax (01) 589 14 10*

FOREIGN EXCHANGE

Hotels, restaurants and shops do not always accept foreign currencies and it is wise, therefore, to change money and cheques at the banks and exchange offices which are found in the larger stations, airports and at the border.

SHOPPING and BANK HOURS

Shops are open from 9am to 6pm, but often close for a lunch break. They are closed Sunday and Bank Holidays (except the shops in railway stations).
Branch offices of banks are open from Monday to Friday between 8am and 12.30pm (in Salzburg 12am) and from 1.30pm to 3pm (in Salzburg 2pm to 4.30pm), Thursday to 5.30pm (only in Vienna).
In the index of street names, those printed in red are where the principal shops are found.

BREAKDOWN SERVICE

ÖAMTC: *See addresses in the text of each city.*
ARBÖ: *in Vienna: Mariahilfer Str. 180, ℰ (01) 89 12 17, Fax (01) 89 12 12 36*
in Salzburg: Münchner Bundesstr. 9, ℰ (0662) 43 83 81, in Innsbruck: Stadlweg 7, ℰ (0512) 34 51 23
In Austria the ÖAMTC (emergency number ℰ 120) and the ARBÖ (emergency number ℰ 123) make a special point of assisting foreign motorists. They have motor patrols covering main roads.

TIPPING

Service is generally included in hotel and restaurant bills. But in Austria, it is usual to give more than the expected tip in hotels, restaurants and cafés. Taxi-drivers, porters, barbers and theatre attendants also expect tips.

SPEED LIMITS

The speed limit in built up areas (indicated by place name signs at the beginning and end of such areas) is 50 km/h - 31 mph; on motorways 130 km/h - 80 mph and on all other roads 100 km/h - 62 mph. Driving on Austrian motorways is subject to the purchase of a road tax obtainable from border posts and ÖAMTC.

SEAT BELTS

The wearing of seat belts in Austria is compulsory for drivers and all passengers.

VIENNA

(WIEN) *Austria* 🄨🄧🄦 ⑩ 🄤🄥🄦 ⑫ – *pop. 1 640 000 – alt. 156 m.*

Budapest 208 ④ – München 435 ⑦ – Praha 292 ① – Salzburg 292 ⑦ – Zagreb 362 ⑥.

🅩 *Tourist-information,* ✉ *A-1010, Kärtner Str. 38,* ☏ *(01) 513 88 92*
ÖAMTC, ✉ *A-1010, Schubertring 1,* ☏ *(01) 71 19 90, Fax (01) 7 13 18 07.*

🛈 *Freudenau 65a,* ☏ *(01) 728 95 64,*
🛈 *Weingartenallee 22,* ☏ *(01) 250 72*
🛈 *At Wienerberg* ☏ *(01) 661 23 70 00*
🛩 *Wien-Schwechat by* ③, ☏ *(01) 70 07 22 31, Air Terminal, at Stadtpark* (HY)
☏ *(01) 58 00 23 00.*
🚗 ☏ *(01) 58 00 29 89. – Exhibition Centre (Wiener Messe), Messeplatz 1,* ☏ *(01) 727 20.*

SIGHTS

THE HOFBURG★★★ AND SOUVENIRS OF THE HABSBURGS

Around the Hofburg JR: *St Michael's Square (Michaelerplatz)★ – St Michael's Gate (Michael-zrtor)★ – Swiss Gate (Schweizertor)★ – Josefsplatz★ – Heroe's Square (Heldenplatz)★* HJR
Souvenirs of the Habsburgs; Imperial Apartments (Kaiserappartments)★ – Imperial porcelain and silver collection. Milan centerpiece★★ – Imperial Treasury★★★; Rudolf Imperial Crown★★★; Insignia and regalia of the Holy Roman Germanic Empire★★★ – Spanish Riding School★★ – Austrian National Library★ – Albertina Collection of Graphic Art★★ JR
Church of the Capucins (Kapuzinerkirche): Imperial Crypt of the Habqburg pantheon (Kaisergruft)★★ JR
*Other Museums in the Hofburg; Ephesos-Museum★★ (Frieze from the Parthian momument★★)
Museum of Ancient Musical Instruments★★ – Collection of Arms Armour★ – Ethnographic Museum★*

SCHÖNBRUNN★★★

Schloss Schönbrunn AZ; *Tour of the Palace★★ – Carriage Museum★ – Park★★ ⩽★ of the Gloriette★★ – Zoo★*

BUILDINGS AND MONUMENTS

St. Stephen's Cathedral (Stephansdom)★★★ KR *– Stephansplatz★★ – Cathedral Museum (Dom-und DiözesanMuseum)★★* KR **M**¹⁹
Unters Belvedere★★ CY *Museum of Austrian Medieval Art (Museum für mittelalterliche Österreichische Kunst)★ – Museum of Austrian Baroque Art (Barockmuseum)★★
Oberes Belvedere★* CY: *19 and 20C Austrian and International Art (Galerie des 19. und 20. Jahrhunderts)★★ – Staatsoper★★* JS *– Church of Charles Borromero (Karlskirche)★★* CY *– Burgtheater★* HR *– St. Peter's Church (Peterskirche)★* JR *– Church of the Jesuits (Jesuitenkirche)★* KLR *– Maria am Gestade★* JP *– Abbey of the Scots (Schottenstift)★, Scotsaltar★★* JPR

JUGENDSTIL AND SECESSION

Post Office Savings Bank (Postsparkasse)★ KLR *– Wagner-Pavillons★* JS *– Secession Pavilion (Secessionsgebäude)★★* JS *– Buildings★ by Wagner on Linke Wienzeile – Wagner Villas★ (in Penzing)* BYZ *– St. Leopold's Church in Penzing (Kirche am Steinhof)★★* AY

STREETS, SQUARES AND PARKS

The Tour of the Ring (Rundfahrt über den Ring)★★ – Graben★ (Plague Pillar★★) JR *– Donner Brunner★★* JR *– Volksgarten★* HR *– Spittelberg Quarter★* HS *– Prater★ (Riesenrad★★)* CY

MUSICAL VIENNA

Pasquamatihaus★ (Beethoven) HP **85** *– Figaro-Haus★ (Mozart)* KR *Schubert-Museum★* BY **M**⁵ *– Haydn-Museum★* BYZ **M**¹⁰ *– Strausshaus★* LP

IMPORTANT MUSEUMS

Museum of Art History (Kunsthistorisches Museum)★★★ HS *– Art Gallery of the Academy of Fine Arts (Gemäldegalerie der Akademie der Bildenden Künste)★★* JS *– Austrian Museum of Applied and Decorative Arts (Österreichische Museum für Angewandte Kunst)★★* LR *– Historical Museum of the City of Vienna (Historisches Museum der Stadt Wien)★* KS *Natural History Museum (Naturhistorisches Museum)★* HS *– City of Vienna Jewish Museum (Jüdisches Museum der Stadt Wien)★* JR *– Museum of Military History (Heeresgeschichtliches Museum)★* CZ **M**²³ *Ṫ Treasure Chamber of the Grand Masters (Schatzkammer des Deutschen Ordens)★* KR *– Josephinum★* BY *– **M**²⁴ – Sigmund Freud Museum★* BY **M**²⁵ *– Tram Museum (Wiener Strassenbahnmuseum)★* CY **M**³ *– Clock and Watch Museum (Uhrenmuseum der Stadt Wien)★* JR **M**¹⁷

EXCURSIONS

UNO-City★ CY *– Donaupark★* CX *– Donauturm ⩽★★* CX *– Leopoldsberg★★ ⩽★★* BX *– Klosterneuburg Abbey (Stift Klosterneuburg)★ (Altarpiece by Nicolas of Verdun★★) N: 13km – Heiligenkreuz★ SW: 32 km by ⑥ – Grinzing★* BX *– Wienerwald★ SW by ⑥ – Heiligenstadt★ (Karl-Marx-Hof★)* BX.

Write us...

If you have any comments on the contents of this Guide.

Your praise as well as your criticisms will receive careful consideration and, with your assistance, we will be able to add to our stock of information and, where necessary, amend our judgments.

Thank you in advance!

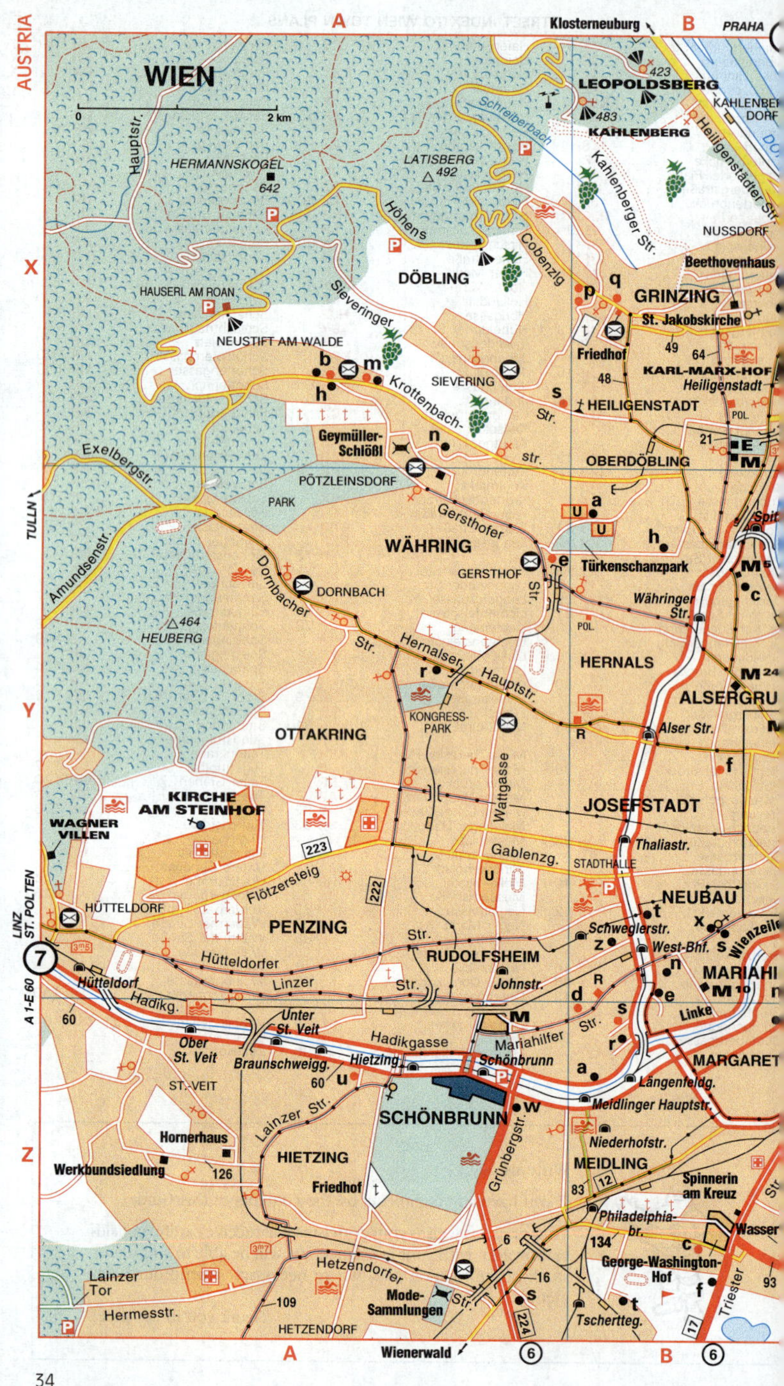
AUSTRIA
WIEN
0   2 km
Klosterneuburg
PRAHA
LEOPOLDSBERG
423
483
KAHLENBERG
KAHLENBERG
DORF
Heiligenstädter Str.
Schreiberbach
HERMANNSKOGEL
642
LATISBERG
492
Höhens
Cobenzlg
Kahlenberger Str.
NUSSDORF
DÖBLING
Beethovenhaus
p
q
GRINZING
HAUSERL AM ROAN
Sieveringer
St. Jakobskirche
Friedhof
49
64
KARL-MARX-HOF
Heiligenstadt
NEUSTIFT AM WALDE
b
m
SIEVERING
48
s
HEILIGENSTADT
h
Krottenbach-
POL
Geymüller-
Schlößl
n
str.
OBERDÖBLING
21
E
M.
Exelbergstr.
PÖTZLEINSDORF
U
a
U
TULLN
PARK
Gersthofer
h
Spit
Amundsenstr.
WÄHRING
e
Türkenschanzpark
M
Dornbacher
GERSTHOF
Währinger
c
DORNBACH
Str.
Str.
464
POL
HEUBERG
Hernalser
Hauptstr.
HERNALS
M 24
r
ALSERGRU
OTTAKRING
Kongress-
PARK
R
Alser Str.
M
f
KIRCHE
AM STEINHOF
Wattgasse
JOSEFSTADT
WAGNER
VILLEN
223
Thaliastr.
Gablenzg.
STADTHALLE
Flötzersteig
U
NEUBAU
222
t
x
HÜTTELDORF
Schweglerstr.
z
West-Bhf.
s
Wienzeile
PENZING
Str.
RUDOLFSHEIM
n
MARIAHI
LINZ
ST. PÖLTEN
Hütteldorfer
Johnstr.
R
M 10
7
Hütteldorf
Linzer
Str.
d
s
e
A 1-E 60
60
Hadikg.
R
Linke
MARGARET
Unter
St. Veit
Hadikgasse
M
r
Ober
St. Veit
Hietzing
Mariahilfer
Braunschweigg.
Schönbrunn
a
Längenfeldg.
ST.-VEIT
60
u
Meidlinger Hauptstr.
SCHÖNBRUNN
w
Hornerhaus
Niederhofstr.
Grünbergstr.
HIETZING
MEIDLING
Werkbundsiedlung
126
Friedhof
83
12
Spinnerin
am Kreuz
3m7
134
Philadelphia-
br.
c
Wasser
George-Washington-
Hof
Lainzer
Tor
109
Hetzendorfer
Str.
f
93
Hermesstr.
Mode-
Sammlungen
s
t
17
HETZENDORF
Tschertteg.
224
Wienerwald
6
6

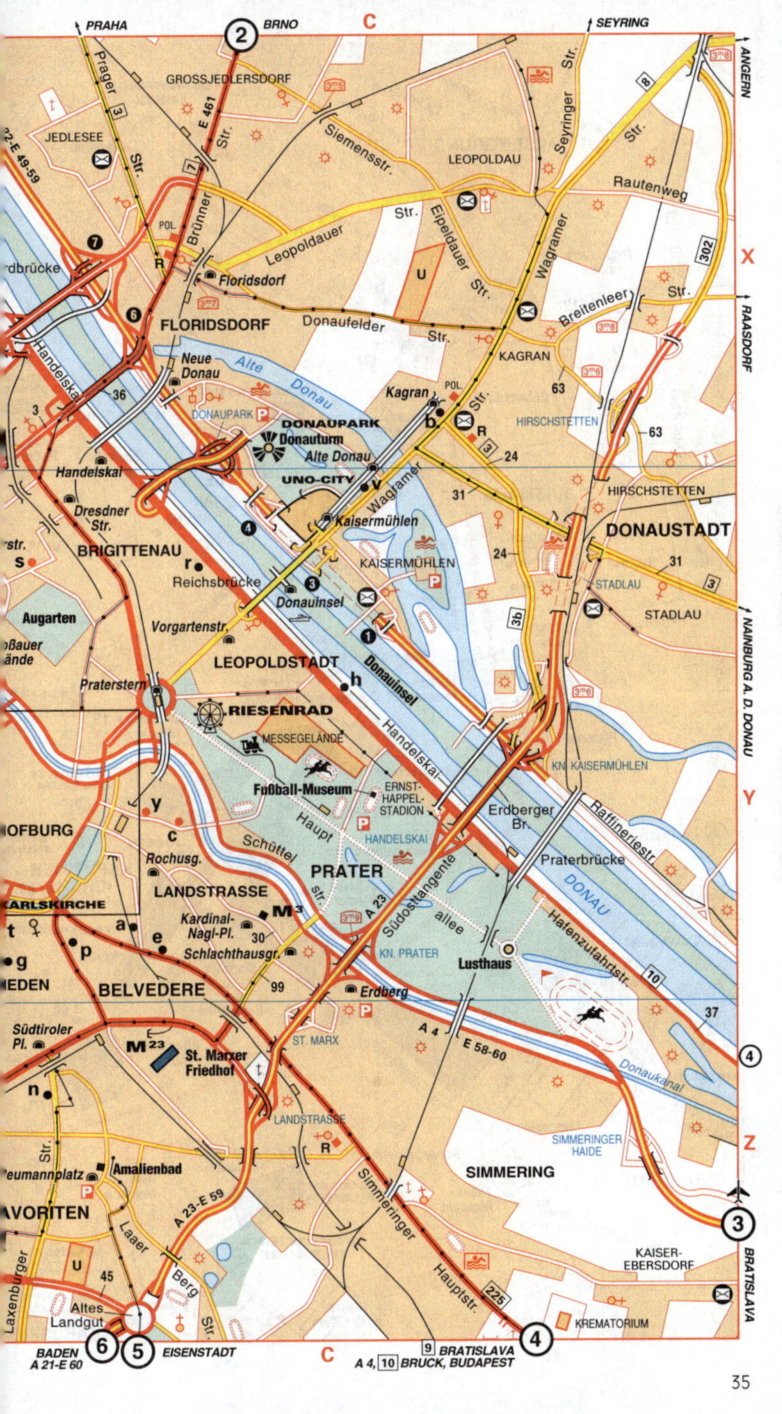
PRAHA
BRNO
C
SEYRING
ANGERN
2
GROSSJEDLERSDORF
Prager
Str.
E 461
Brünner
Str.
7
Siemensstr.
LEOPOLDAU
Seyringer
Str.
Rautenweg
JEDLESEE
A2-E 49-59
POL.
Str.
Leopoldauer
Str.
U
Eipeldauer Str.
Wagramer Str.
302
X
RAASDORF
7
R
Floridsdorf
FLORIDSDORF
Donaufelder
Str.
Breitenleer
Str.
6
Handelskai
Neue
Donau
Alte Donau
Kagran
POL.
KAGRAN
63
HIRSCHSTETTEN
36
DONAUPARK
DONAUPARK
Donauturm
Alte Donau
UNO-CITY
Kagran
b
R
Str.
24
63
3
Handelskai
V
Wagramer
31
HIRSCHSTETTEN
Dresdner
Str.
Kaisermühlen
KAISERMÜHLEN
24
DONAUSTADT
BRIGITTENAU
4
31
STADLAU
3
s
r
Reichsbrücke
3
Donauinsel
STADLAU
Augarten
Vorgartenstr.
1
3b
ßauer
ände
LEOPOLDSTADT
Donauinsel
Praterstern
h
Handelskai
KN KAISERMÜHLEN
RIESENRAD
MESSEGELÄNDE
Fußball-Museum
ERNST-
HAPPEL-
STADION
Erdberger
Br.
Raffineriestr.
Y
OFBURG
y
Haupt
Praterbrücke
c
HANDELSKAI
DONAU
Rochusg.
Schüttel
str.
PRATER
LANDSTRASSE
M 3
KARLSKIRCHE
t
a
Kardinal-
Nagl-Pl.
30
A 23
Südosttangente
allee
KN. PRATER
Hafenzufahrtstr.
g
e
Schlachthausgr.
Lusthaus
10
EDEN
p
BELVEDERE
99
Erdberg
37
Südtiroler
Pl.
A 4
E 58-60
M 23
St. Marxer
Friedhof
ST. MARX
Donaukanal
4
n
LANDSTRASSE
Z
R
SIMMERINGER
HAIDE
eumannplatz
Str.
Amalienbad
Simmeringer
SIMMERING
A 23-E 59
Laxenburger Str.
AVORITEN
U
45
Laaer
Berg
Str.
Hauptstr.
225
3
BRATISLAVA
Altes
Landgut
KAISER-
EBERSDORF
6
5
EISENSTADT
C
9
BRATISLAVA
4
BADEN
A 21-E 60
A 4, 10 BRUCK, BUDAPEST
KREMATORIUM

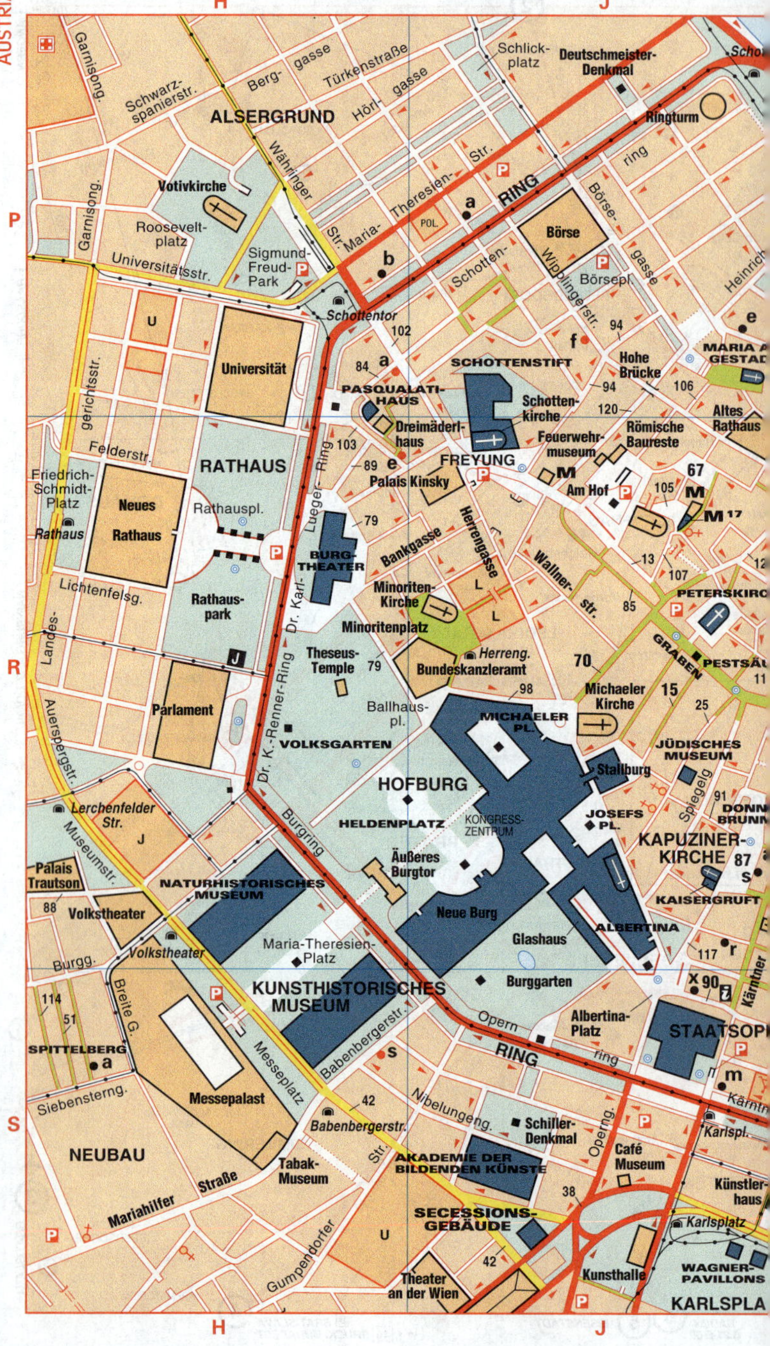
H
J
Garnisong.
Schwarz-spanierstr.
Berg- gasse
Türkenstraße
Hörl- gasse
Schlick-platz
Deutschmeister-Denkmal
Scho
ALSERGRUND
Währinger
Ringturm
Votivkirche
Maria-
Theresien-
Str.
a
RING
Börse- gasse
Börse
Roosevelt-platz
POL.
Schotten-
Börsepl.
Wipplingerstr.
Heinrich
Universitätsstr.
Sigmund-Freud-Park
b
94
e
Schottentor
MARIA A
GESTAD
U
102
f
SCHOTTENSTIFT
Hohe Brücke
84
a
94
106
Universität
PASQUALATI-HAUS
Schotten-kirche
Römische Baureste
Altes Rathaus
gerichtsstr.
Dreimäderl-haus
Feuerwehr-museum
120
Felderstr.
103
e
FREYUNG
Am Hof
M
67
RATHAUS
89
Palais Kinsky
105
M
M 17
Friedrich-Schmidt-Platz
Rathauspl.
Lueger-Ring
79
Bankgasse
Herrengasse
13
Neues Rathaus
Wallner- str.
107
PETERSKIRC
Rathaus
BURG-THEATER
Minoriten-Kirche
85
12
Lichtenfelsg.
L
1050
Rathaus-park
Minoritenplatz
L
70
GRABEN
PESTSÄU
Landes-
J
Theseus-Temple
79
Herreng.
15
11
Auerspergstr.
Dr. K.-Renner-Ring
Dr. Karl-
Bundeskanzleramt
Michaeler Kirche
25
Parlament
98
VOLKSGARTEN
MICHAELER PL.
JÜDISCHES MUSEUM
Lerchenfelder Str.
Burgring
HOFBURG
Stallburg
91
DONN BRUNN
Museumstr.
J
HELDENPLATZ
KONGRESS-ZENTRUM
JOSEFS PL.
KAPUZINER-KIRCHE
Palais Trautson
Äußeres Burgtor
87
88
Volkstheater
NATURHISTORISCHES MUSEUM
S
Volkstheater
Neue Burg
KAISERGRUFT
Burgg.
Maria-Theresien-Platz
Glashaus
ALBERTINA
117
r
Breite G.
KUNSTHISTORISCHES MUSEUM
Burggarten
X 90
114
Babenbergerstr.
Opern
Kärntner
51
Messeplatz
Albertina-Platz
STAATSOP
SPITTELBERG
a
s
RING
m
Siebensterng.
42
ring
Kärntn
Babenbergerstr.
Nibelungeng.
Schiller-Denkmal
Karlspl.
NEUBAU
Str.
AKADEMIE DER BILDENDEN KÜNSTE
Operng.
Café Museum
Tabak-Museum
38
Künstler-haus
Mariahilfer
Straße
U
SECESSIONS-GEBÄUDE
Karlsplatz
Gumpendorfer
42
Theater an der Wien
Kunsthalle
WAGNER-PAVILLONS
KARLSPLA
H
J
P
R
S

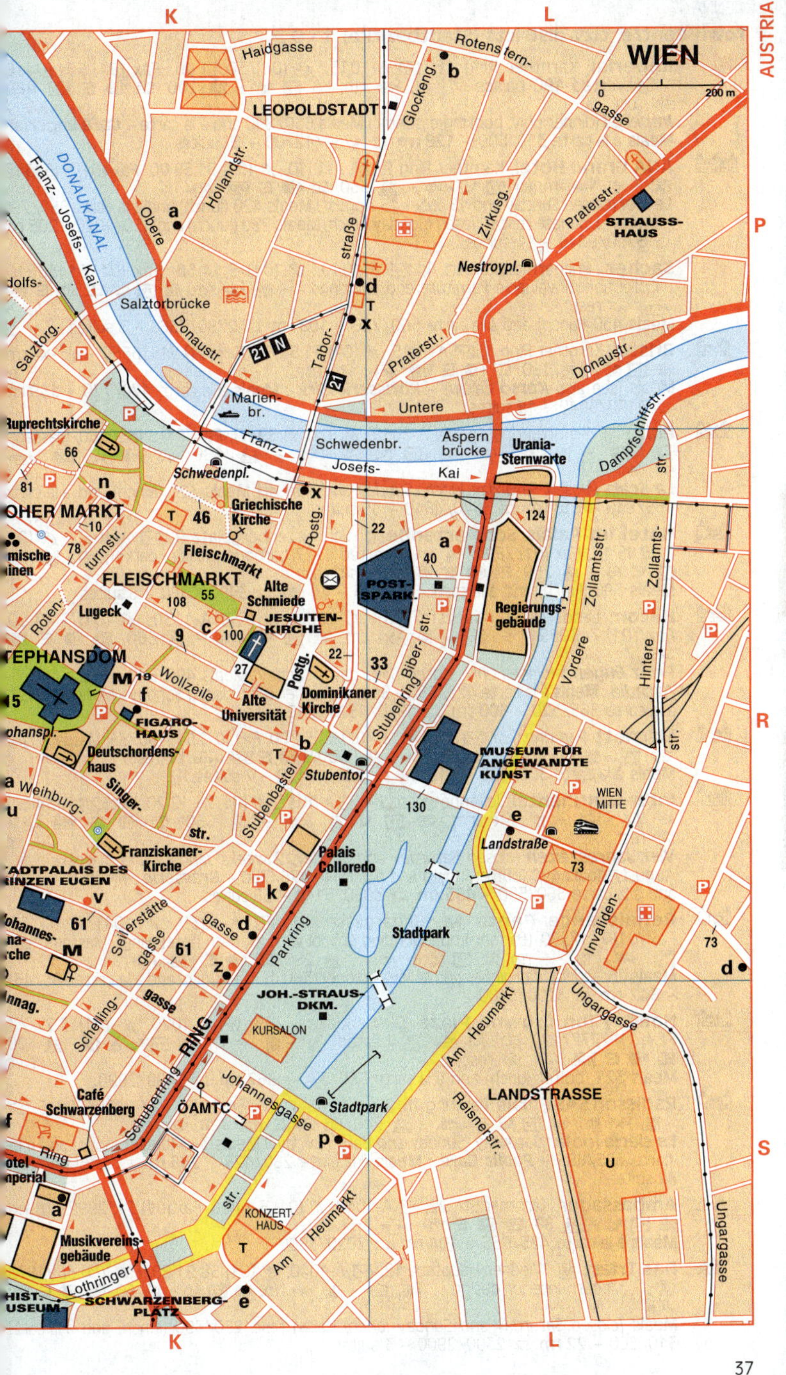

AUSTRIA
K
L
WIEN
Haidgasse
Rotenstern-
gasse
LEOPOLDSTADT
Glockeng.
b
0   200 m
Hollandstr.
straße
Zirkusg.
Praterstr.
STRAUSS-
HAUS
P
Obere
a
Donaukanal
Franz- Josefs- Kai
Nestroypl.
dolfs-
Salzgr.
Salztorbrücke
Donaustr.
Praterstr.
Donaustr.
d
T
x
21 N
Tabor-
21
Untere
P
Marien-
br.
Schwedenbr.
Aspern-
brücke
Urania-
Sternwarte
Dampfschiffstr.
str.
Ruprechtskirche
Franz-
Josefs-
Kai
66
P
81
Schwedenpl.
x
Postg.
124
OHER MARKT
n
Griechische
Kirche
22
Zollamtsstr.
Zollamts-
T
46
a
mische
10
turmstr.
Fleischmarkt
40
Regierungs-
gebäude
str.
P
Hintere
inen
78
Roten-
FLEISCHMARKT
Alte
Schmiede
POST-
SPARK.
Vordere
Biber-
P
Lugeck
108
55
JESUITEN-
KIRCHE
P
9
c
100
22
33
TEPHANSDOM
27
Postg.
Dominikaner
Kirche
Stubenring
MUSEUM FÜR
ANGEWANDTE
KUNST
5
M
19
Wollzeile
Alte
Universität
WIEN
MITTE
f
FIGARO-
HAUS
b
130
e
ohanspl.
Deutschordens-
haus
T
Stubentor
Landstraße
a
Weihburg-
Stubenbastei
P
73
u
Singer-
str.
P
Franziskaner-
Kirche
Palais
Colloredo
k
Parkring
TADTPALAIS DES
RINZEN EUGEN
P
73
V
d
Johannes-
61
Sellerstätte
gasse
gasse
Stadtpark
d
che
M
61
nnag.
Z
Schelling-
gasse
JOH.-STRAUS-
DKM.
RING
Am Heumarkt
Ungargasse
LANDSTRASSE
KURSALON
Johannesgasse
Café
Schwarzenberg
Schubertring
ÖAMTC
P
Stadtpark
Reisnerstr.
f
p
P
Ring
Ungargasse
otel
perial
U
a
str.
KONZERT-
HAUS
Am Heumarkt
Musikvereins-
gebäude
T
Lothringer-
HIST.
USEUM
SCHWARZENBERG-
PLATZ
e
K
L
S
P
R

AUSTRIA

Town Centre, city districts (Stadtbezirke) 1 - 9 :

Imperial, Kärntner Ring 16, ⊠ A-1015, ℘ (01) 50 11 00, *Fax (01) 5011041C*
« Converted 19C palace » – |‡|, ⇔ rm, ▤ TV ℂ – 200. AE ⓞ E VISA JCB
⅍ rest
KS
Imperial (dinner only, booking essential) **Meals** 630/890 and à la carte – **Café Imperial**
Meals à la carte 350/600 – **128 rm** ⌸ 4750/12700 – 27 suites.

ANA Grand Hotel, Kärntner Ring 9, ⊠ A-1010, ℘ (01) 51 58 00, *Fax (01) 5151313*
⇔ – |‡|, ⇔ rm, ▤ TV ℂ ⇔ – 350. AE ⓞ E VISA JCB
KS
Le ciel (closed Sunday and 15 July - 15 August) **Meals** 420 (lunch) and à la carte 650/79C
– *Unkai* (Japanese rest.) (closed Monday lunch) **Meals** 220 (lunch) and 450/1020 – **205 rn**
⌸ 3790/6040 – 11 suites.

Sacher, Philharmonikerstr. 4, ⊠ A-1010, ℘ (01) 5 14 56, *Fax (01) 5145681C*
« Collection of valuable furniture and paintings » – |‡|, ⇔ rm, ▤ TV ℂ. AE ⓞ E VISA
JCB. ⅍ rest
JS
Meals 450 (lunch) and à la carte 560/720 – **108 rm** ⌸ 2780/7560 – 3 suites.

Bristol, Kärntner Ring 1, ⊠ A-1015, ℘ (01) 51 51 60, *Fax (01) 51516550* – |‡|, ⇔ rm
▤ TV ℂ – 180. AE ⓞ E VISA JCB. ⅍ rest
JS
Meals (see also **Korso** below) – **Rôtisserie Sirk** : **Meals** à la carte 470/770 – **139 rn**
⌸ 4170/6040 – 11 suites.

Plaza Ⓜ, Schottenring 11, ⊠ A-1010, ℘ (01) 31 39 00, *Fax (01) 31390160*, Massage
↥⑤, ⇔s – |‡|, ⇔ rm, ▤ TV ℂ ⑤ ⇔ – 180. AE ⓞ E VISA JCB
⅍ rest
JP
La Scala (closed Saturday lunch, Sunday and August) **Meals** 320 (lunch) and à la carte
455/830 – **218 rm** ⌸ 3670/4840 – 35 suites.

Hotel im Palais Schwarzenberg, Schwarzenbergplatz 9, ⊠ A-1030, ℘ (01)
7 98 45 15, *Fax (01) 7894714*, « Converted 1727 baroque palace ; park », ⇔, ⅋ – |‡|
TV ℂ Ⓟ – 250. AE ⓞ E VISA JCB. ⅍ rest
CY
Meals 390 (lunch) and à la carte 660/855 – **44 rm** ⌸ 3490/6380 – 6 suites.

Hilton, Landstraßer Hauptstr. 2 (near Stadtpark), ⊠ A-1030, ℘ (01) 7 17 00
Fax (01) 7130691, ≤, ⇔ – |‡|, ⇔ rm, ▤ TV ℂ ⇔ – 660. AE ⓞ E VISA
JCB
LR
Prinz Eugen : (dinner only, closed Saturday - Sunday) **Meals** 490/640 and à la carte –
Arcadia : **Meals** à la carte 425/580 – **Sam's** : (dinner only, closed Sunday - Monday) **Meals**
à la carte 365/520 – **600 rm** ⌸ 4060/4820 – 19 suites.

Marriott, Parkring 12a, ⊠ A-1010, ℘ (01) 51 51 80, *Fax (01) 515186736*, Massage, ↥⑤
⇔s, ⬚ – |‡|, ⇔ rm, ▤ TV ℂ ⑤ ⇔ – 500. AE ⓞ E VISA JCB. ⅍ rest
KR
Meals à la carte 300/600 – **313 rm** ⌸ 3860/4120 – 7 suites.

Inter-Continental, Johannesgasse 28, ⊠ A-1037, ℘ (01) 71 12 20, *Fax (01) 7134489*
≤, ↥⑤, ⇔s – |‡|, ⇔ rm, ▤ TV ℂ ⑤ ⇔ – 560. AE ⓞ E VISA JCB
⅍ rest
KS
Vier Jahreszeiten (closed Saturday and Sunday, 2 weeks January and 3 weeks July -
August) **Meals** 490 (buffet lunch) and à la carte 475/750 – **Brasserie** : **Meals** 220 lunch
and à la carte 380/500 – **453 rm** ⌸ 3030/5140 – 58 suites.

Renaissance Penta Ⓜ, Ungargasse 60, ⊠ A-1030, ℘ (01) 71 17 50,
Fax (01) 7117590, (former imperial riding school with modern hotel wing), Massage, ⇔s
⬚, ⇔ – |‡|, ⇔ rm, ▤ TV ℂ ⑤ ⇔ – 280. AE ⓞ E VISA JCB
CY
Meals (closed Sunday dinner and Monday dinner) 360 (buffet lunch) and à la carte 285/435
– **342 rm** ⌸ 3200/3400.

Holiday Inn Crowne Plaza Ⓜ, Handelskai 269, ⊠ A-1020, ℘ (01) 7 27 77,
Fax (01) 72777199, ⇔, ↥⑤, ⇔s, ⬚ (heated), ⅋ – |‡|, ⇔ rm, ▤ TV ℂ ⑤ Ⓟ – 300
AE ⓞ E VISA JCB. ⅍ rest
CY
Meals 325 (buffet lunch) and à la carte 380/570 – **367 rm** ⌸ 2190/2990.

Radisson SAS Palais, Parkring 16, ⊠ A-1010, ℘ (01) 51 51 70, *Fax (01) 5122216*, ⇔s
– |‡|, ⇔ rm, ▤ TV ℂ ⑤ ⇔ – 240. AE ⓞ E VISA JCB. ⅍ rest
KR
Le siècle (closed Saturday, Sunday and Bank Holidays) **Meals** 340 (buffet lunch) and à la
carte 395/685 – **Palais Café** : **Meals** à la carte 280/425 – **246 rm** ⌸ 2560/4420 –
42 suites.

Ambassador, Kärntner Str. 22, ⊠ A-1010, ℘ (01) 5 14 66, *Fax (01) 5132999* – |‡| ⇔
▤ TV ℂ – 80. AE ⓞ E VISA JCB
JR
Meals à la carte 425/635 – **104 rm** ⌸ 2020/3800.

Das Triest Ⓜ, Wiedner Hauptstr. 12, ⊠ A-1040, ℘ (01) 58 91 80, *Fax (01) 5891818*
⇔, « Modern interior design », ↥⑤, ⇔s – |‡|, ⇔ rm, ▤ TV ℂ – 60. AE ⓞ E VISA
JCB
CY
Meals (closed Saturday and Sunday lunch) Italian rest. 290/390 (lunch) and à la carte
310/560 – **72 rm** ⌸ 2300/2900 – 3 suites.

Hotel de France, Schottenring 3, ⊠ A-1010, ℰ (01) 31 36 80, *Fax (01) 3195969*, ⇌s – ⃒🛗⃒, ✲ rm, ▤ rest, TV ☎ & – 🛎 120. AE ⓪ E VISA JCB. ✖ rest — HP b
Meals *(closed Saturday)* 295 (buffet lunch) and à la carte 420/610 – **216 rm** ⊑ 1950/3900 – 7 suites.

Arcotel Hotel Wimberger M, Neubaugürtel 34, ⊠ A-1070, ℰ (01) 52 16 50, *Fax (01) 52165810*, 🗚, ⇌s – 🛗⃒, ✲ rm, ▤ rm, TV 📞 & 🚗 – 🛎 400. AE ⓪ E VISA — BY t
Meals 325 (buffet lunch) à la carte 340/480 – **225 rm** ⊑ 2100/2800 – 7 suites.

Rogner-Dorint Hotel Biedermeier, Landstraßer Hauptstr. 28 (at Sünnhof), ⊠ A-1030, ℰ (01) 71 67 10, *Fax (01) 71671503*, 🏖, « Bedrooms furnished in the Biedermeier style » – 🛗⃒, ✲ rm, TV ☎ 📞 🚗 – 🛎 60. AE ⓪ E VISA. ✖ rm — LR d
Meals à la carte 380/485 – **203 rm** ⊑ 1950/2530 – 12 suites.

Kaiserin Elisabeth without rest, Weihburggasse 3, ⊠ A-1010, ℰ (01) 51 52 60, *Fax (01) 515267* – 🛗⃒ TV ☎. AE ⓪ E VISA JCB — KR a
63 rm ⊑ 1500/2550.

City-Central without rest, Taborstr. 8, ⊠ A-1020, ℰ (01) 21 10 50, *Fax (01) 21105140* – 🛗⃒ ✲ ▤ TV ☎ 📞 & P. AE ⓪ E VISA JCB. ✖ rest — KP x
58 rm ⊑ 1700/2540.

Stefanie, Taborstr. 12, ⊠ A-1020, ℰ (01) 21 15 00, *Fax (01) 21150160*, 🏖 – 🛗⃒ ✲, ▤ rm, TV ☎ 📞 🚗 – 🛎 70. AE ⓪ E VISA JCB — KLP d
Meals 245/500 and à la carte 320/430 – **131 rm** ⊑ 1520/2540.

K. u. K. Hotel Maria Theresia without rest, Kirchberggasse 6, ⊠ A-1070, ℰ (01) 5 21 23, *Fax (01) 5212370* – 🛗⃒, ✲ rm, ▤ TV ☎ 📞 🚗 – 🛎 40. AE ⓪ E VISA JCB — HS a
123 rm ⊑ 1820/2420.

Starlight Suiten M without rest, Salzgries 12, ⊠ A-1010, ℰ (01) 5 35 92 22, *Fax (01) 535922211*, 🗚, ⇌s – 🛗⃒ ✲ ▤ TV ☎ 📞 🚗. AE ⓪ E VISA — JP e
49 suites ⊑ 1680/2080.

Sofitel Belvedere, Am Heumarkt 35, ⊠ A-1030, ℰ (01) 71 61 60, *Fax (01) 71616844* – 🛗⃒, ✲ rm, TV ☎ 📞 🚗 – 🛎 150. AE ⓪ E VISA — KS e
Meals à la carte 235/490 – **211 rm** ⊑ 2120/3040.

K. u. K. Palais Hotel without rest, Rudolfsplatz 11, ⊠ A-1010, ℰ (01) 5 33 13 53, *Fax (01) 533135370* – 🛗⃒, ✲ rm, ▤ TV ☎ 📞. AE ⓪ E VISA JCB — JP h
66 rm ⊑ 1820/2420.

Astron Suite Hotel M without rest, Mariahilfer Str. 78, ⊠ A-1070, ℰ (01) 5 24 56 00, *Fax (01) 524560015*, 🗚, ⇌s – 🛗⃒ ✲ ▤ TV ☎ 📞 & 🚗. AE ⓪ E VISA JCB BY x
73 suites ⊑ 1820/2860.

Kummer, Mariahilfer Str. 71a, ⊠ A-1060, ℰ (01) 5 88 95, *Fax (01) 5878133* – 🛗⃒, ✲ rm, TV ☎ 📞. AE ⓪ E VISA JCB. ✖ rest — BY s
Meals à la carte 280/400 – **100 rm** ⊑ 1595/2400.

Erzherzog Rainer, Wiedner Hauptstr. 27, ⊠ A-1040, ℰ (01) 50 11 10, *Fax (01) 50111350* – 🛗⃒, ✲ rm, ▤ rest, TV ☎ – 🛎 30. AE ⓪ E VISA — CY g
Meals à la carte 215/420 – **84 rm** ⊑ 1720/2230.

Astoria, Kärntner Str. 32, ⊠ A-1015, ℰ (01) 51 57 70, *Fax (01) 5157782*, 19C house with period interior – 🛗⃒, ✲ rm, TV ☎ – 🛎 20. AE ⓪ E VISA JCB — JR r
Meals *(closed Saturday and Sunday)* à la carte 300/600 – **108 rm** ⊑ 1700/2800.

Lassalle M without rest, Engerthstr. 173, ⊠ A-1020, ℰ (01) 21 31 50, *Fax (01) 21315100*, ⇌s, 🏊 – 🛗⃒ ✲ TV ☎ 📞 & 🚗 – 🛎 40. AE ⓪ E VISA JCB — CY r
140 rm ⊑ 1460/1900 – 4 suites.

Mercure Nestroy M without rest, Rotensterngasse 12, ⊠ A-1020, ℰ (01) 21 14 00, *Fax (01) 211407*, ⇌s – 🛗⃒ ✲ TV ☎ 📞 🚗 – 🛎 70. AE ⓪ E VISA — LP b
62 rm ⊑ 1670/2080 – 7 suites.

Holiday Inn M, Margaretenstr. 53, ⊠ A-1050, ℰ (01) 58 85 00, *Fax (01) 58850899*, 🏖 – 🛗⃒ TV ☎ 📞 & 🚗. AE ⓪ E VISA JCB — BY m
Meals à la carte 285/360 – **101 rm** ⊑ 1800/2200.

Arkadenhof M without rest, Viriotgasse 5, ⊠ A-1090, ℰ (01) 3 10 08 37, *Fax (01) 3107678* – 🛗⃒ ✲ ▤ TV ☎ 🚗 – 🛎 20. AE ⓪ E VISA — BY c
45 rm ⊑ 1380/1880.

Falkensteiner Hotel Palace, Margaretenstr. 92, ⊠ A-1050, ℰ (01) 54 68 60, *Fax (01) 5468686*, ⇌s – 🛗⃒ ▤ TV ☎ 🚗 – 🛎 60. AE ⓪ E VISA. ✖ rest — BZ b
Meals à la carte 260/380 – **117 rm** ⊑ 1430/1990.

Amadeus without rest, Wildpretmarkt 5, ⊠ A-1010, ℰ (01) 5 33 87 38, *Fax (01) 533873838* – 🛗⃒ ▤ TV ☎ 📞. AE ⓪ E VISA — JR y
closed 21 to 27 December – **30 rm** ⊑ 1130/2100.

🏨 **Mercure Europaplatz** Ⓜ, Matrosengasse 6, ✉ A-1060, 𝄖 (01) 59 90 1
Fax (01) 5976900 – 🛗, ⇥ rm, 🖩 📺 ☎ 🕻 & 🚗 – 🔒 40. 🅰🅴 ⓞ 🄴 𝗩𝗜𝗦𝗔 🄹🄲🄱   BY
Meals à la carte 240/445 – **210 rm** ☕ 1790/2190 – 5 suites.

🏨 **Europa**, Kärntner Str. 18, ✉ A-1015, 𝄖 (01) 51 59 40, Fax (01) 51594888 – 🛗 🖩 [
☎. 🅰🅴 ⓞ 🄴 𝗩𝗜𝗦𝗔 🄹🄲🄱. ⌘ rest   JR
Meals à la carte 320/420 – **113 rm** ☕ 1800/2800.

🏨 **Am Parkring**, Parkring 12, ✉ A-1015, 𝄖 (01) 51 48 00, Fax (01) 5148040, ≼ Vien
– 🛗, ⇥ rm, 🖩 📺 ☎ 🚗. 🅰🅴 ⓞ 🄴 𝗩𝗜𝗦𝗔 🄹🄲🄱. ⌘ rest   KR
Meals (closed Sunday dinner, Monday dinner and mid July - mid August) à la carte 360/5[
– **64 rm** ☕ 1820/2650 – 8 suites.

🏨 **König von Ungarn**, Schulerstr. 10, ✉ A-1010, 𝄖 (01) 51 58 40, Fax (01) 515848, [
– 🛗, 🖩 rm, 📺 ☎ & – 🔒 15. 🅰🅴 ⓞ 🄴 𝗩𝗜𝗦𝗔 🄹🄲🄱   KR
Meals (closed Saturday) à la carte 390/510 – **33 rm** ☕ 1650/2350 – 8 suites.

🏨 **Mercure Wien Zentrum**, Fleischmarkt 1a, ✉ A-1010, 𝄖 (01) 53 46 0[
Fax (01) 53460232 – 🛗, ⇥ rm, 🖩 📺 ☎ 🕻 &. 🅰🅴 ⓞ 🄴 𝗩𝗜𝗦𝗔   KR
Meals à la carte 260/360 – **154 rm** ☕ 1790/2190.

🏨 **Capricorno** without rest, Schwedenplatz 3, ✉ A-1010, 𝄖 (01) 53 33 10 4[
Fax (01) 53376714 – 🛗 📺 ☎ 🕻 🚗 🅿. 🅰🅴 ⓞ 🄴 𝗩𝗜𝗦𝗔   KR
46 rm ☕ 1420/2360.

🏨 **Mercure Wien City** without rest, Hollandstr. 3, ✉ A-1020, 𝄖 (01) 21 31 3[
Fax (01) 21313230 – 🛗, ⇥ rm, 🖩 📺 ☎ 🕻 & 🚗. 🅰🅴 ⓞ 🄴 𝗩𝗜𝗦𝗔 🄹🄲🄱. ⌘ rest   KP
63 rm ☕ 1670/2080.

🏨 **Artis**, Rennweg 51, ✉ A-1030, 𝄖 (01) 7 13 25 21, Fax (01) 7145930 – 🛗, ⇥ rm, [
☎ 🚗 – 🔒 50. 🅰🅴 ⓞ 🄴 𝗩𝗜𝗦𝗔 🄹🄲🄱   CY
Meals à la carte 225/380 – **168 rm** ☕ 1500/2100.

🏨 **Ibis Wien Mariahilf**, Mariahilfer Gürtel 22, ✉ A-1060, 𝄖 (01) 5 99 9[
Fax (01) 5979090 – 🛗, ⇥ rm, 🖩 📺 ☎ & 🚗 – 🔒 120. 🅰🅴 ⓞ 🄴 𝗩𝗜𝗦𝗔   BY
Meals à la carte 220 – **341 rm** ☕ 1010/1330.

XXXX **Steirereck**, Rasumofskygasse 2/Ecke Weißgerberlände, ✉ A-1030, 𝄖 (01) 7 13 31 6[
❀❀ Fax (01) 71351682 – 🖩. 🅰🅴 ⓞ 🄴 𝗩𝗜𝗦𝗔   CY
closed Saturday, Sunday and Bank Holidays – **Meals** (outstanding wine list, tour of th[
wine-cellar possible) (booking essential) 395 (lunch) and à la carte 630/835
Spec. Spargelsulz auf Schalottenvinaigrette (spring). Rehrücken auf Linsenpörkö[
(autumn). Geeistes Zimtparfait mit Vogelbeersauce.

XXXX **Korso** - Hotel Bristol, Kärntner Ring 1, ✉ A-1015, 𝄖 (01) 51 51 65 46, Fax (01) 5151655
❀ – 🖩. 🅰🅴 ⓞ 🄴 𝗩𝗜𝗦𝗔 🄹🄲🄱. ⌘   JS
closed Saturday lunch – **Meals** 380 (lunch) and à la carte 690/885
Spec. Rieslingkalbsbeuschel. Wurzelrostbraten mit Krennockerln. Topfennockerl in Kürbi[
Krokant mit Eierliköreis.

XXX **Drei Husaren**, Weihburggasse 4, ✉ A-1010, 𝄖 (01) 51 21 09 20, Fax (01) 5121092[
– 🅰🅴 ⓞ 🄴 𝗩𝗜𝗦𝗔 🄹🄲🄱   KR
Meals 440 (lunch) and à la carte 510/898.

XXX **Academie**, Untere Viaduktgasse 45/Marxergasse, ✉ A-1030, 𝄖 (01) 7 13 82 5[
❀ Fax (01) 7138257 – 🅰🅴 ⓞ 🄴 𝗩𝗜𝗦𝗔 🄹🄲🄱   CY
closed Saturday, Sunday, Bank Holidays and 3 weeks August – **Meals** (booking essentia[
(outstanding wine list) 330 (lunch) and à la carte 435/650
Spec. Hummer im Bohnenkrautgelée und Pastinaksalat. Gerösteter Kalbsfuß mit Ölpaprik[
Buttermandelschaum mit Kokosnußschokolade.

XXX **Selina**, Laudongasse 13, ✉ A-1080, 𝄖 (01) 4 05 64 04, Fax (01) 4080459 – 🅰🅴 ⓞ [
❀ 𝗩𝗜𝗦𝗔 🄹🄲🄱   BY
closed Sunday and Bank Holidays – **Meals** and à la carte 420/660
Spec. Schaumsuppe von Teigtaschen mit Rindfleisch, Bohnen und Kürbiskern-Rahm. Kalb[
rahmbeuscherl mit Griessknöderln. Schokolade-Schupfnudeln in Nußkrokant-Brösel.

XXX **Grotta Azzurra** (Italian rest.), Babenbergerstr. 5, ✉ A-1010, 𝄖 (01) 5 86 10 4[
Fax (01) 586104415 – 🅰🅴 ⓞ 🄴 𝗩𝗜𝗦𝗔 🄹🄲🄱   HS
closed 24 to 26 December – **Meals** 275 (lunch) and à la carte 410/570.

XXX **Steirer Stub'n**, Wiedner Hauptstr. 111, ✉ A-1050, 𝄖 (01) 5 44 43 49
Fax (01) 5440888 – 🖩. 🅰🅴 ⓞ 🄴 𝗩𝗜𝗦𝗔   BZ
closed Sunday and Bank Holidays – **Meals** (booking essential) à la carte 310/490.

XX **Walter Bauer**, Sonnenfelsgasse 17, ✉ A-1010, 𝄖 (01) 5 12 98 71, Fax (01) 512987
– 🅰🅴   KR
closed Saturday lunch, Sunday, Monday, Bank Holidays, 1 week Easter and mid July - m[
August – **Meals** (booking essential) 295 and à la carte 380/680.

XX **Kupferdachl**, Schottengasse 7 (first floor, entrance Mölker Bastei), ✉ A-1010, 𝄖 (0[
5 33 93 81 14, Fax (01) 53393814 – 🅰🅴 ⓞ 🄴 𝗩𝗜𝗦𝗔 🄹🄲🄱   HP
closed Saturday lunch, Sunday and Bank Holidays – **Meals** à la carte 345/560.

XX **Schubertstüberln**, Schreyvogelgasse 4, A-1010, (01) 5 33 71 87, Fax (01) 5353546, – AE ◑ E VISA JCB   HR e
closed Saturday and Sunday – **Meals** à la carte 330/580.

XX **Salut**, Wildpretmarkt 3, A-1010, (01) 5 33 13 22, Fax (01) 5331322 – AE ◑ E VISA   JR y
closed Sunday and Bank Holidays – **Meals** à la carte 445/580.

XX **Plachutta**, Wollzeile 38, A-1010, (01) 5 12 15 77, Fax (01) 512157720, – . ◑ E VISA   KR b
closed 2 weeks July – **Meals** (booking essential) à la carte 410/550.

XX **Cantinetta Antinori**, Jasomirgottstrasse 3, A-1010, (01) 5 33 77 22, Fax (01) 533772211 – AE ◑ E VISA   KR s
Meals (Italian rest.) (booking essential) 260 (lunch) and à la carte 325/520.

X **Fadinger**, Wipplingerstr. 29, A-1010, (01) 5 33 43 41 – VISA   JP f
closed Saturday and Sunday – **Meals** (booking essential) 150/440 (lunch) and à la carte 230/560
Spec. Gänselebervariationen. Gefüllte Perlhuhnbrust mit Pilzen. Steinbutt mit Kräuter gebraten.

X **Zum Kuckuck**, Himmelpfortgasse 15, A-1010, (01) 5 12 84 70, Fax (01) 7741855 – AE ◑ E VISA JCB   KR v
closed Sunday – **Meals** 255 (lunch) and à la carte 350/550.

X **Hedrich**, Stubenring 2, A-1010, (01) 5 12 95 88   LR a
open 11am - 9pm, closed Friday to Sunday, Bank Holidays and August – **Meals** à la carte 280/495.

City districts (Stadtbezirke) 10 - 15 :

Holiday Inn M, Triester Str. 72, A-1100, (01) 6 05 30, Fax (01) 60530580, ≤, – , rm, TV car – 420. AE ◑ E VISA JCB.   BZ f
Meals 320 (buffet lunch) and à la carte – **176 rm** 2560/2970 – 4 suites.

Renaissance Wien, Ullmannstr. 71, A-1150, (01) 89 10 20, Fax (01) 89102100, , s, – , rm, TV car – 200. AE ◑ E VISA JCB   BZ a
– **Orangerie** : Meals à la carte 355/765 – **Allegro** : Meals 385/480 (buffet only) – **309 rm** 3015/3540 – 3 suites.

Gartenhotel Altmannsdorf , Hoffingergasse 26, A-1120, (01) 8 04 75 27, Fax (01) 804752751, , Park, s – , rm, TV car – 60. AE ◑ E VISA   AZ s
Meals à la carte 345/495 – **95 rm** 1500/1900.

Bosei M , Gutheil-Schoder-Gasse 9, A-1100, (01) 66 10 60, Fax (01) 6610699 – , rm, TV P – 200. AE ◑ E VISA JCB   BZ t
Meals à la carte 315/420 – **193 rm** 1360/1690 – 8 suites.

Favorita M without rest, Laxenburger Str. 8, A-1100, (01) 60 14 60, Fax (01) 60146720, s – TV car – 150. AE ◑ E VISA JCB. rest   CZ n
161 rm 1360/1690 – 3 suites.

Kaiserpark-Schönbrunn, Grünbergstr. 11, A-1120, (01) 8 13 86 10, Fax (01) 8138183 – , rm,, rest, TV – 20. AE ◑ E VISA   AZ w
Meals à la carte 210/410 – **50 rm** 1200/1700.

Dorint Budget Hotel, Felberstr. 4, A-1150, (01) 98 11 10, Fax (01) 98111930, s – , rm, TV car – 280. AE ◑ E VISA   BY z
Meals 200/300 and à la carte 280/450 – **252 rm** 1950/2600.

Reither without rest, Graumanngasse 16, A-1150, (01) 8 93 68 41, Fax (01) 8936835, s, – TV car. AE ◑ E VISA   BZ r
closed 23 to 27 December – **50 rm** 1080/1680.

XXX **Altwienerhof** with rm, Herklotzgasse 6, A-1150, (01) 8 92 60 00, Fax (01) 89260008, « Winter garden, courtyard-terrace » – TV . AE ◑ E VISA   BZ s
closed 1 to 24 January – **Meals** (closed Saturday lunch and Sunday) (outstanding wine list) 298 (lunch) and à la carte 480/695 – **23 rm** 700/1400.

XX **Windows of Vienna**, Wienerbergstr. 7 (22th floor), A-1100, (01) 6 07 94 80, Fax (01) 6072267, Vienna – car. ◑ VISA   BZ c
Meals à la carte 490/570.

XX **Vikerl's Lokal**, Würfelgasse 4, A-1150, (01) 8 94 34 30   BYZ d
closed Sunday dinner and Monday, 3 weeks July to August – **Meals** 245/365 and à la carte 335/480.

XX **Hietzinger Bräu**, Auhofstr. 1, A-1130, (01) 87 77 08 70, Fax (01) 877708722, – . ◑ E VISA   AZ u
closed mid July - mid August and 24 to 26 December – **Meals** (mainly boiled beef dishes) (booking essential) à la carte 370/570.

City districts (Stadtbezirke) 16 - 19 :

Modul, Peter-Jordan-Str. 78, ⊠ A-1190, ℘ (01) 47 66 00, Fax (01) 47660117, 🌿 –
🖥 TV ☎ 🚗 – 🏋 500. AE ⓪ E VISA JCB
Meals 180/280 and à la carte 310/470 – **40 rm** ⊑ 1450/1750 – 8 suites.
BY

Landhaus Fuhrgassl-Huber 🦢 without rest, Rathstr. 24, ⊠ A-1190, ℘ (01)
4 40 30 33, Fax (01) 4402714, « Country house atmosphere », 🌿 – 🛗 TV ☎ 🚗
E VISA
AX
closed last week January - first week February – **22 rm** ⊑ 960/1470.

Gartenhotel Glanzing 🦢 without rest, Glanzinggasse 23, ⊠ A-1190, ℘ (01)
47 04 27 20, Fax (01) 470427214, 🛴, ⇌s, 🌿 – 🛗 TV ☎. AE ⓪ E VISA
AX
18 rm ⊑ 980/1880.

Jäger without rest, Hernalser Hauptstr. 187, ⊠ A-1170, ℘ (01) 48 66 62 00
Fax (01) 48666208 – 🛗 TV ☎. AE ⓪ E VISA
AY
18 rm ⊑ 980/1700.

Celtes without rest, Celtesgasse 1a, ⊠ A-1190, ℘ (01) 4 40 41 51
Fax (01) 4404152116 – 🛗 TV ☎. AE ⓪ E VISA JCB
AX
16 rm ⊑ 850/1400.

Park-Villa without rest, Hasenauerstr. 12, ⊠ A-1190, ℘ (01) 3 67 57 00
Fax (01) 319100541, ⇌s, 🌿 – 🛗 ✂ TV ☎. AE ⓪ E VISA JCB
BY
21 rm ⊑ 1280/1800.

Schild without rest, Neustift am Walde 97, ⊠ A-1190, ℘ (01) 44 04 04 40
Fax (01) 4404000, 🌿 – 🛗 TV ☎ Ⓟ. AE E VISA
AX
32 rm ⊑ 860/1580.

Eckel, Sieveringer Str. 46, ⊠ A-1190, ℘ (01) 3 20 32 18, Fax (01) 3206660, 🌿 –
⓪ VISA – *closed Sunday, Monday, 8 to 23 August and 24 December - 17 January* – **Mea**
à la carte 320/685.
AX

Plachutta with rm, Heiligenstädter Str. 179, ⊠ A-1190, ℘ (01) 3 70 41 25
Fax (01) 37412520, 🌿 – TV ☎. E VISA
BX
closed 22 July - 11 August – **Meals** *(mainly boiled beef dishes)* à la carte 370/590 – **4 rm**
⊑ 760/1180.

Sailer, Gersthofer Str. 14, ⊠ A-1180, ℘ (01) 47 92 12 10, Fax (01) 479212118, 🌿
AE ⓪ E VISA
AY
Meals à la carte 400/585.

City district (Stadtbezirk) 22 :

Forum M, Wagramer Str. 21, ⊠ A-1220, ℘ (01) 26 02 00, Fax (01) 2602020, 🌿,
⇌s – 🛗, ✂ rm, 🖥 TV 📞 🚗 – 🏋 400. AE ⓪ E VISA JCB. 🚫 rest
CY
Meals à la carte 260/470 – **252 rm** ⊑ 2890/3450 – 3 suites.

Donauzentrum M without rest, Wagramer Str. 83, ⊠ A-1220, ℘ (01) 20 35 54 50
Fax (01) 2035545183, ⇌s – 🛗 ✂ 🖥 TV ☎ 🚗 – 🏋 40. AE ⓪ E VISA
CX
137 rm ⊑ 1460/1900.

Mraz u. Sohn, Wallensteinstr. 59, ⊠ A-1200, ℘ (01) 3 30 45 94, Fax (01) 3501536, 🌿
– Ⓟ. VISA
CY
closed Saturday, Sunday, 3 weeks August and 24 December to 6 January – **Meals** *(bookin*
essential) 690/1150 and à la carte 475/655
Spec. Langustinencremesuppe mit Tomatenratatouille. Stelze und Rücken vom Milchkal
mit zweierlei Sellerie. Mille feuille vom Bauerntopfen mit Passionsfruchtjoghurt.

Heurigen and Buschen-Schänken (wine gardens) – *(mostly self-service, hot and co*
dishes from buffet, prices according to weight of chosen meals, therefore not show
below. Buschen-Schänken sell their own wines only) :

Oppolzer, Himmelstr. 22, ⊠ A-1190, ℘ (01) 3 20 24 16, Fax (01) 3202416, « Garden »
closed Sunday, Christmas and New Year – **Meals** *(buffet only) (dinner only).*
BX

Altes Preßhaus, Cobenzlgasse 15, ⊠ A-1190, ℘ (01) 3 20 02 03, Fax (01) 32002032
🌿, « Old vaulted wine cellar with wine press » – AE ⓪ E VISA JCB
BX
closed January - February and 1 week Christmas – **Meals** *(dinner only)* à la carte 190/45

Wolff, Rathstr. 44, ⊠ A-1190, ℘ (01) 4 40 23 35, Fax (01) 4401403, « Terrace
garden » – **Meals** *(buffet only).*
AX

Fuhrgassl Huber, Neustift am Walde 68, ⊠ A-1190, ℘ (01) 4 40 14 05
Fax (01) 4402730, *(wine-garden with Viennese Schrammelmusik),* « Courtyard-terrace »
– E VISA
AX
open from 2pm – **Meals** *(buffet only).*

Grinzinger Hauermandl, Cobenzlgasse 20, ⊠ A-1190, ℘ (01) 3 20 89 49
Fax (01) 320571322, 🌿 – AE ⓪ E VISA JCB
BX
closed Sunday – **Meals** *(dinner only)* à la carte 260/380.

at Auhof motorway station *West : 8 km by* ⑦ :

🏨 **Novotel Wien-West**, Am Auhof, ✉ A-1140, *ℰ (01) 97 92 54 20, Fax (01) 9794140,*
☄, ⤳ (heated), ⇒ – ▮, ⟲ rm, ▤ ▣ ☎ & Ⓟ – 🛌 180. AE ① E VISA
Meals à la carte 200/410 – **114 rm** ⊇ 1275/1450.

at Perchtoldsdorf *South-West : 13 km by B12 and Breitenfurter Str.* AZ :

XXX **Jahreszeiten**, Hochstr. 17, ✉ A-2380, *ℰ (01) 8 65 31 29, Fax (01) 865312973* – ▤.
❀ AE ① VISA
*closed Saturday lunch, Sunday dinner, Monday, Bank Holidays, 1st week April and 25 July
- 15 August* – **Meals** 330 (lunch) and à la carte 560/695
Spec. Hausgebeizter Lachs auf Trüffelnudeln. Zanderfilet auf Thai-Sun-Sauce. Nougat-
knöderl auf Karamelsauce.

at Vienna-Schwechat Airport ③ : *20 km* :

🏨 **Sofitel** Ⓜ, at the airport, ✉ A-1300, *ℰ (01) 70 15 10, Fax (01) 7062828* – ▮, ⟲ rm,
▣ & Ⓟ – 🛌 30. AE ① E VISA JCB. ℠ rest
Meals Italian rest. 250 (lunch) and à la carte 360/400 – **142 rm** ⊇ 3140/3780.

🏨 **Novotel**, at the airport, ✉ A-1300, *ℰ (01) 70 10 70, Fax (01) 7073239,* ⇌ – ▮, ⟲ rm,
▣ ☎ & Ⓟ – 🛌 30. AE ① E VISA JCB. ℠ rest
Meals à la carte 170/370 – **183 rm** ⊇ 1750/2170.

INNSBRUCK *Austria* 426 *G 7,* 987 ④⓪ – *pop. 120 000 – alt. 580 m – Wintersport : 580/2300 m*
🚠 *3* 🚡 *7* – **See :** *Maria-Theresien-Strasse* ★ *CZ* ≤ ★★ *on the Nordkette, Belfry (Stadtturm)
CZ B* ❀ ★ *over the city – Little Golden Roof (Goldenes Dachl)* ★ *CZ – Helblinghaus* ★ *CZ – Hof-
burg* ★ *CZ – Hofkirche CZ (Maximilian's Mausoleum* ★, *Silver Chapel* ★★ *) – Tyrol Museum of
Popular Art (Tiroler Volkskunstmuseum)* ★★ *CDZ – "Ferdinandeum" Tyrol Museum (Tiroler
Landesmuseum "Ferdinandeum")* ★ *DZ* M² *– Wilten Basilica* ★ *AY –* **Envir. :** *Hafelekar* ❀ ★★ *–
Upland Tour (Mittelgebirge)* ★★ *(Hall in Tirol* ★, *Volders* ★, *Igls* ★, *– Elbögen road* ★★ *) – The Stu-
baital* ★.

🏌 *Innsbruck-Igls, Lans (0512) 37 71 65 ;* 🏌 *Innsbruck-Igls, Rinn (05223) 81 77.*
🛈 *Innsbruck Information, Burggraben 3,* ✉ *A-6020,* *ℰ (0512) 53 56, Fax (0512) 535643.*
ÖAMTC, Andechsstr. 81, *ℰ (0512) 3 32 01 20, Fax (0512) 391612.*
Wien 733 – München 140 – Salzburg 164.

Plans on following pages

🏨 **Europa-Tyrol**, Südtiroler Platz 2, ✉ A-6020, *ℰ (0512) 59 31, Fax (0512) 587800,* ⇌
– ▮, ⟲ rm, ▤ rest, ▣ ☎ 🚗 – 🛌 200. AE ① E VISA JCB   DZ **a**
Meals 380/780 and à la carte – **122 rm** ⊇ 1900/2850 – 6 suites.

🏨 **Holiday Inn**, Salurner Str. 15, ✉ A-6010, *ℰ (0512) 5 93 50, Fax (0512) 5935220,* ⇌
– ▮, ⟲ rm, ▤ ▣ ☎ – 🛌 250. AE ① E VISA JCB. ℠ rest   CDZ **b**
– *Guggeryllis :* **Meals** à la carte 305/490 – **176 rm** ⊇ 1600/2800 – 4 suites.

🏨 **Goldener Adler** ⊗, Herzog-Friedrich-Str. 6, ✉ A-6020, *ℰ (0512) 57 11 11,
Fax (0512) 584409,* ☄, « *14C Tyrolian inn* » – ▮ ▣ ☎. AE ① E VISA   CZ **c**
Meals à la carte 315/580 – **33 rm** ⊇ 1080/2100.

🏨 **Central**, Gilmstr. 5, ✉ A-6020, *ℰ (0512) 59 20, Fax (0512) 580310,* 🛦, ⇌ – ▮, ⟲ rm,
▣ ☎ – 🛌 30. AE ① E VISA   DZ **d**
Meals à la carte 195/442 – **87 rm** ⊇ 1290/2100.

🏨 **Maria Theresia** without rest, Maria Theresienstr. 31, ✉ A-6020, *ℰ (0512) 59 33,
Fax (0512) 575619* – ▮ ⟲ ▣ ☎ 🚗 – 🛌 20. AE ① E VISA JCB   CZ **g**
103 rm ⊇ 1350/2200.

🏨 **Romantik Hotel Schwarzer Adler**, Kaiserjägerstr. 2, ✉ A-6020, *ℰ (0512) 58 71 09,
Fax (0512) 561697* – ▮, ⟲ rm, ▣ ☎ 🚗 – 🛌 40. AE ① E VISA   DZ **e**
closed February - 15 March – **Meals** *(closed Sunday and Bank Holidays)* à la carte 310/550
– **40 rm** ⊇ 1200/2300.

🏨 **Neue Post**, Maximilianstr. 15, ✉ A-6020, *ℰ (0512) 5 94 76, Fax (0512) 581818* – ▮,
⟲ rm, ▣ ☎ ℰ Ⓟ. AE ① E VISA JCB   CZ **v**
Meals *(closed Sunday)* à la carte 215/400 – **60 rm** ⊇ 1100/2600.

🏨 **Alpotel Tirol**, Innrain 13, ✉ A-6020, *ℰ (0512) 57 79 31, Fax (0512) 57793115,* ⇌
– ▮, ▤ rest, ▣ ☎ & 🚗 – 🛌 50. AE ① E VISA – **Meals** *(closed Saturday lunch, Sunday
and Bank Holidays)* à la carte 290/540 – **73 rm** ⊇ 1060/1700.   CZ **f**

🏨 **Grauer Bär**, Universitätsstr. 7, ✉ A-6020, *ℰ (0512) 5 92 40, Fax (0512) 574535,* ⇌
– ▮ ▣ ☎ Ⓟ – 🛌 180. AE ① E VISA JCB. ℠ rest   DZ **k**
Meals à la carte 265/465 – **100 rm** ⊇ 1100/1900.

🏨 **Sporthotel Penz**, Fürstenweg 183, ✉ A-6020, *ℰ (0512) 2 25 14,
Fax (0512) 22514124* – ▮ ▣ ☎ Ⓟ – 🛌 50. AE E VISA. ℠   by Fürstenweg   AY
Meals à la carte 195/410 – **70 rm** ⊇ 780/1380.

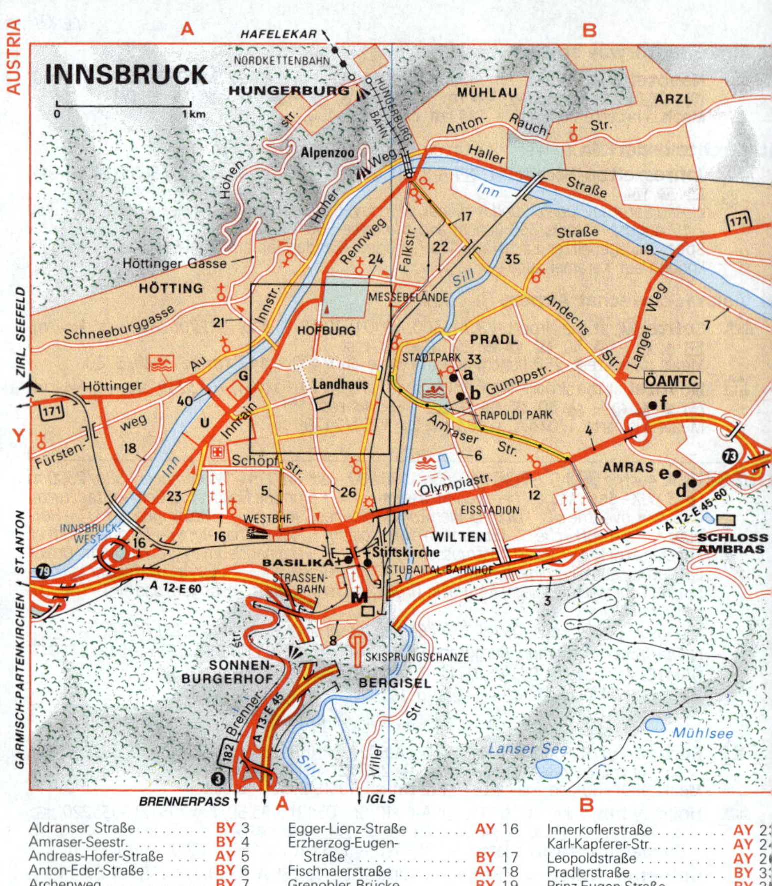

Aldranser Straße	BY	3
Amraser-Seestr.	BY	4
Andreas-Hofer-Straße	AY	5
Anton-Eder-Straße	BY	6
Archenweg	BY	7
Bergiselweg	AY	8
Burgenland-Straße	BY	12
Egger-Lienz-Straße	AY	16
Erzherzog-Eugen-Straße	BY	17
Fischnalerstraße	AY	18
Grenobler Brücke	BY	19
Höttinger Gasse	AY	21
Ingenieur-Etzel-Straße	BY	22
Innerkoflerstraße	AY	23
Karl-Kapferer-Str.	AY	24
Leopoldstraße	AY	26
Pradlerstraße	BY	33
Prinz-Eugen-Straße	BY	35
Universitäts-Brücke	AY	40

Maximilian without rest, Marktgraben 7, ✉ A-6020, ☎ (0512) 5 99 67, Fax (0512) 577450 – ▯ TV ☎. AE ⑩ E VISA. ⁂   CZ
40 rm ☕ 1250/1800.

Innsbruck, Innrain 3, ✉ A-6020, ☎ (0512) 5 98 68, Fax (0512) 572280, ≘s, ☒ – ▯ ▤ TV ☎ 🚗. AE ⑩ E VISA   CZ
Meals (dinner only) (residents only) – **91 rm** ☕ 1200/1690.

Zach without rest, Wilhelm-Greil-Str. 11, ✉ A-6020, ☎ (0512) 58 96 67, Fax (0512) 5896677 – ▯ TV ☎. AE ⑩ E VISA. ⁂   DZ
24 rm ☕ 850/1350.

Tourotel Breinössl, Maria Theresien Str. 12, ✉ A-6020, ☎ (0512) 58 41 65, Fax (0512) 58416526, beer garden – ▯, ⁌ rm, TV ☎ Ⓟ. AE ⑩ E VISA JCB   CZ
Meals à la carte 170/300 – **40 rm** ☕ 960/1540.

Weißes Rößl ⁂, Kiebachgasse 8, ✉ A-6020, ☎ (0512) 58 30 57, Fax (0512) 5830575, ⁂ – ▯ TV ☎. AE E VISA JCB   CZ
closed 2 weeks April and November – **Meals** (closed Sunday and Bank Holidays) à la carte 210/410 – **14 rm** ☕ 850/1500.

Weisses Kreuz ⁂, Herzog-Friedrich-Str. 31, ✉ A-6020, ☎ (0512) 5 94 79, Fax (0512) 5947990, ⁂, « 15C Tyrolian inn » – TV ☎. AE E VISA   CZ
Meals à la carte 210/430 – **40 rm** ☕ 730/1400.

INNSBRUCK

AUSTRIA

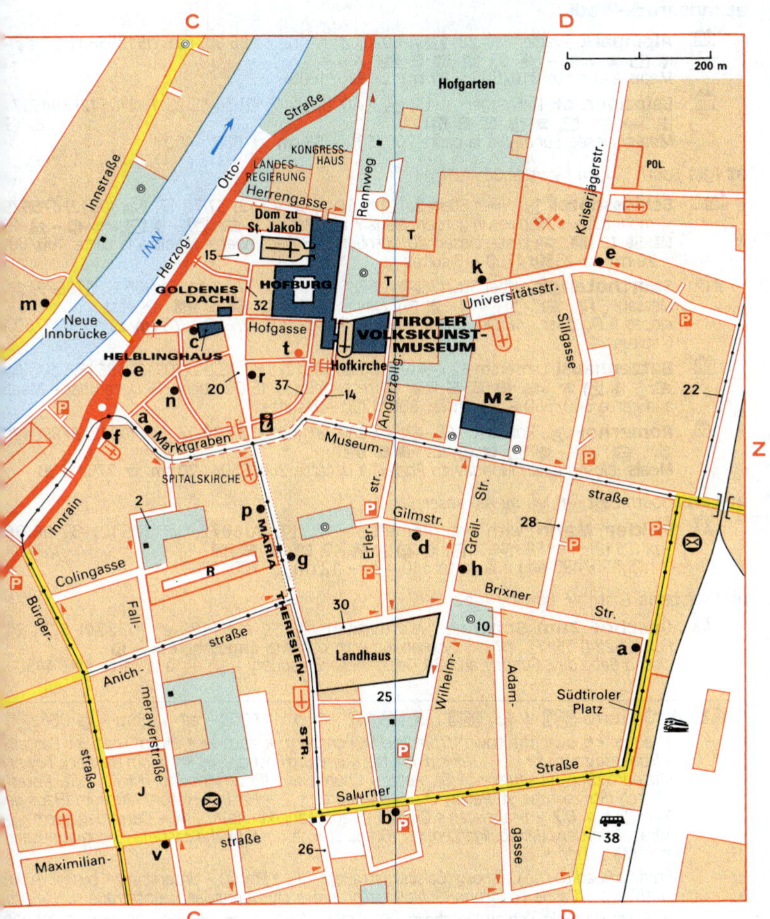

at Innsbruck-Amras :

Bierwirt, Bichlweg 2, A-6020, (0512) 34 21 43, Fax (0512) 3421435,
« Comfortable, rustic lounge in typical Bavarian style », – rm,
80. VISA   BY
Meals *(closed Sunday)* à la carte 185/415 – **47 rm** 750/1400.

at Innsbruck-Pradl :

Alpinpark, Pradler Str. 28, A-6020, (0512) 34 86 00, Fax (0512) 364172,
– 30. AE E VISA JCB   BY
Meals à la carte 210/500 – **87 rm** 980/1600.

Leipzigerhof, Defreggerstr. 13, A-6020, (0512) 34 35 25, Fax (0512) 394357,
rm, TV AE E VISA   BY
Meals *(closed Sunday)* à la carte 200/390 – **55 rm** 800/1400.

at Igls *South : 4 km by Viller Str.* AB :

Schlosshotel , Viller Steig 2, A-6080, (0512) 37 72 17, Fax (0512) 378679
 mountains, « Mansion in garden, elegant installation », , – TV P – 15
AE E VISA. rest– *closed 20 October - 18 December* – **Meals** à la carte 400/600
– **20 rm** 2550/4700 – 6 suites.

Sporthotel Igls, Hilber Str. 17, A-6080, (0512) 37 72 41, Fax (0512) 378679,
Massage, , , , – TV – 50. AE E VISA. rest
closed 9 October - 18 December – **Meals** à la carte 350/600 – **78 rm** 1430/2760
6 suites.

Batzenhäusl, Lanserstr. 12, A-6080, (0512) 3 86 18, Fax (0512) 386187, ,
– TV P. AE E VISA. rest – *closed 15 October - 15 December* – **Meals**
à la carte 300/560 – **30 rm** 800/1700 – 3 suites.

Römerhof , Römerstr. 62, A-6080, (0512) 37 89 02, Fax (0512) 3789042C
, , – TV P. AE E VISA
Meals *(closed lunch Monday to Friday)* à la carte 260/650 – **20 rm** 770/1280.

at Lans *South-East : 6 km by Aldranser Str.* BY :

XX **Wilder Mann** with rm, Römerstr. 12, A-6072, (0512) 37 96 96
Fax (0512) 379139, – TV P – 40. AE E VISA
Meals 350/480 and à la carte 310/470 – **12 rm** 700/1700.

at Wattens *East : 16 km : by A 12* BY :

XX **Gasthof Zum Schwan**, Swarovskistr. 2, A-6112, (05224) 5 21 21
Fax (05224) 55175, , « Tyrolian inn with convivial atmosphere » – P
closed Saturday, Sunday and 24 December - 6 January – **Meals** à la carte 320/445.

SALZBURG *Austria* 420 W 23, 426 L 5, 987 ④① – *pop. 147000 – alt. 425 m –* 0662.

See : ★★ *over the town (from the Mönchsberg)* X *and* ★★ *(from Hettwer Bastei)*
– Hohensalzburg ★★ X, Z : ★★ *(from the Kuenburg Bastion),* ★★ *(from the Reck Tower)*
Museum (Burgmuseum)★ – St. Peter's Churchyard (Petersfriedhof)★★ Z *– St. Peter's*
Church (Stiftskirche St. Peter)★★ Z *– Residenz*★★ Z *– Natural History Museum (Haus de*
Natur)★★ Y M2 *– Franciscan's Church (Franziskanerkirche)★* Z A *– Getreidegasse★* Y
Mirabell Gardens (Mirabellgarten)★ V *(Grand Staircase ★★ of the castle) – Baroquemuseun*
★ V M3 *– Dom★* Z.

Envir. : *Road to the Gaisberg (Gaisbergstraße)*★★ *(★) by* ① *– Untersberg★ by* ② : 10 kn
(with) *– Castle Hellbrunn (Schloß Hellbrunn)* ★ *by Nonntaler Hauptstraße* X.

 Salzburg-Wals, Schloß Klessheim, (0662) 85 08 51 ; *Hof (*① : 20 km), (06229
23 90 ; *St. Lorenz (*① : 29 km), (06232) 38 35.

 Innsbrucker Bundesstr. 95 (by ③), (0662) 85 12 23 - *City Air Terminal(Autobu*
Station), Südtiroler Platz V.

 Lastenstraße V.

Exhibition Centre (Messegelände), Linke Glanzeile 65, (0662) 3 45 66.

 Tourist Information, Mozartplatz 5, A-5020, (0662) 88 98 73 30.

ÖAMTC, Alpenstr. 102 (by ②), (0662) 63 99 90, Fax (0662) 6399945.

Wien 292 ① *– Innsbruck 177* ③ *– München 140* ③

Plans on following pages

Österreichischer Hof, Schwarzstr. 5, A-5020, (0662) 8 89 77
Fax (0662) 8897714, « Salzach-side setting, terrace with old town and castle » –
rm, TV – 70. AE E VISA JCB   Y
***Zirbelzimmer* :** Meals à la carte 465/730 – ***Salzach-Grill* :** Meals à la carte 280/500
120 rm 1850/5900 – 7 suites.

SALZBURG

Erzabt-Klotz-Str. . . . . X 9	Nonntaler Hauptstr. . . . . . . X 29	
Gstättengasse . . . . X 12	Rainerstraße . . . . V V 29	
Kaiserschützenstr. . . . . . . V 20	Schießstattstr. . . . . V V 33	
uerspergstraße . . . . V 3	Lindhofstr. . . . . V 22	Schwarzstr. . . . . V V 34
rglsteinstraße . . . . X 5	Mirabellplatz . . . . V 26	Späthgasse . . . . X 37

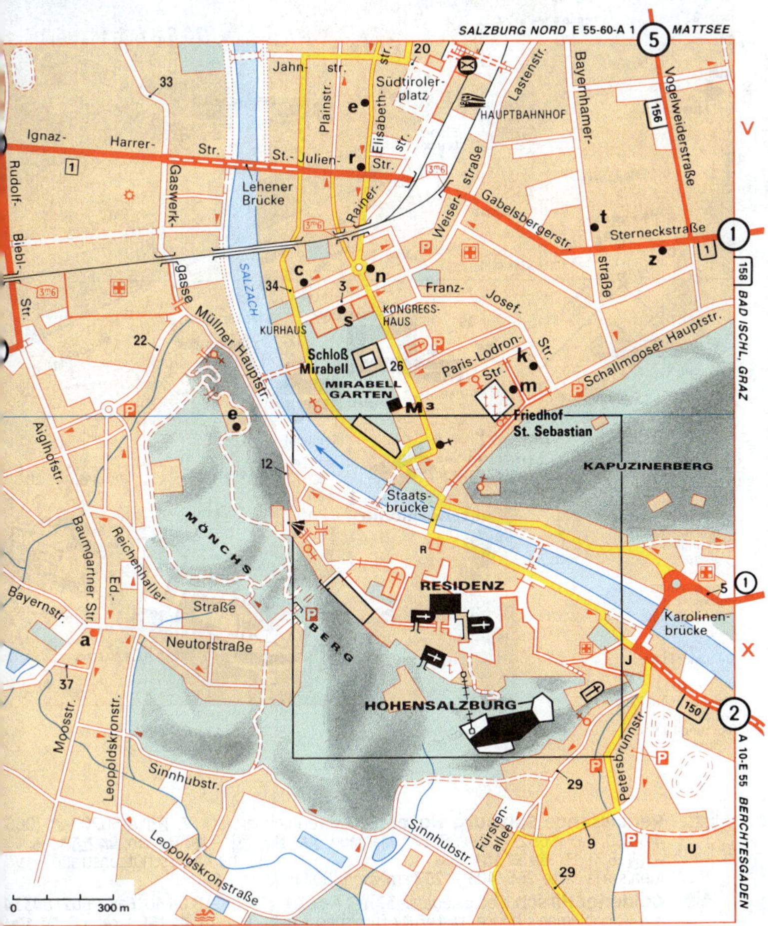

Sheraton Ⓜ, Auerspergstr. 4, ✉ A-5020, ☏ (0662) 88 99 90, *Fax (0662) 881776*, « Terrace in spa gardens », entrance to the spa facilities – ☷, ⇷ rm, ▤ TV ☏ ♿ 🚗 – ⚕ 120. AE Ⓞ E VISA JCB – **Meals** *(closed Sunday and Monday dinner)* à la carte 336/574 – **163 rm** ☕ 2100/5285 – 9 suites
V s

Altstadt Radisson SAS, Judengasse 15, ✉ A-5020, ☏ (0662) 8 48 57 10, *Fax (0662) 8485716*, « Modernised 14C nobleman's house, antique furnishings » – ☷, ⇷ rm, ▤ TV 🚗 – ⚕ 35. AE Ⓞ E VISA JCB. ⚕ rest
Y s
Meals à la carte 370/550 – **60 rm** ☕ 3465/6600 – 13 suites

Bristol, Makartplatz 4, ✉ A-5020, ☏ (0662) 87 35 57, *Fax (0662) 8735576* – ☷, ⇷ rm, ▤ TV ☏ – ⚕ 60. AE Ⓞ E VISA JCB
Y a
closed 2 February - 25 March - see **Bei Bruno** below – **62 rm** ☕ 2800/5300 – 8 suites

Crowne Plaza-Pitter Ⓜ, Rainerstr. 6, ✉ A-5020, ☏ (0662) 8 89 78, *Fax (0662) 878893*, ⇌ – ☷, ⇷ rm, ▤ TV ☏ ♿ – ⚕ 160. AE Ⓞ E VISA JCB. ⚕ rest
Rainerstube *(dinner only)* **Meals** à la carte 360/510 – **Auersperg** *(lunch only)* **Meals** à la carte 265/400 – **186 rm** ☕ 1900/4800 – 6 suites

Renaissance Salzburg Hotel, Fanny-von-Lehnert-Str. 7, ⌧ A-5020, ℰ (0662) 4 68 80, *Fax (0662) 4688298*, Massage, – rm, TV – 800. AE ⓪ E VISA JCB   by Kaiserschützenstraße   V
Meals à la carte 265/403 – **257 rm** ⌚ 1650/1950

Goldener Hirsch, Getreidegasse 37, ⌧ A-5020, ℰ (0662) 8 08 40, *Fax (0662) 84334.* « 15C nobleman's house, tastefully furnished » – , – rm, TV – m0. AE ⓪ VISA JCB   Y
Meals à la carte 500/630 – **70 rm** ⌚ 2600/7540 – 3 suites

Schloß Mönchstein , Mönchsberg Park 26, ⌧ A-5020, ℰ (0662) 8 48 55 5 *Fax (0662) 848559,* < Salzburg and surroundings, « Small castle with elegant, stylis furnishings, wedding chapel, park », – TV P. AE ⓪ E VISA JC rest   X
closed early February - mid March – **Meals** à la carte 500/1150 – **17 rm** ⌚ 2900/650

Rosenberger, Bessarabierstr. 94, ⌧ A-5020, ℰ (0662) 4 35 54 6 *Fax (0662) 43951095,* – rm, TV P – 360. AE ⓪ E VISA   by (
Meals à la carte 250/410 – **120 rm** ⌚ 1350/1850

Dorint Rogner Hotel, Sterneckstr. 20, ⌧ A-5020, ℰ (0662) 88 20 3 *Fax (0662) 8820319,* – rm, TV ☎ – 160. AE ⓪ E VIS rest   V
Meals à la carte 231/430 – **139 rm** ⌚ 1530/2500 – 4 suites

Carlton without rest, Markus-Sittikus-Str. 3, ⌧ A-5020, ℰ (0662) 88 21 9 *Fax (0662) 87478447,* – TV ☎ P. AE ⓪ E VISA JCB   V
39 rm ⌚ 1370/2560 – 11 suites

Mercure, Bayerhamerstr. 14, ⊠ A-5020, ℰ (0662) 8 81 43 80, Fax (0662) 871111411,
🌳 – 🕽, 🐆 rm, TV ☎ & 🚗 ℗ – 🛆 100. AE ⓘ E VISA JCB V t
Meals à la carte 220/490 – **121 rm** ☕ 1295/1990

Novotel Salzburg City, Franz-Josef-Str. 26, ⊠ A-5020, ℰ (0662) 88 20 41,
Fax (0662) 874240, ⊆s – 🕽, 🐆 rm, TV ☎ & 🚗 ℗ – 🛆 75. AE ⓘ E
VISA V k
Meals à la carte 206/480 – **140 rm** ☕ 1390/1710

Zum Hirschen, St.-Julien-Str. 21, ⊠ A-5020, ℰ (0662) 88 90 30, Fax (0662) 8890358,
Massage, ⊆s – 🕽 🐆 TV ☎ ℗. AE ⓘ E VISA JCB V r
Meals à la carte 200/405 – **64 rm** ☕ 845/1750

Schaffenrath, Alpenstr. 115, ⊠ A-5020, ℰ (0662) 63 90 00, Fax (0662) 639005,
🌳, Massage, ⊆s – 🕽, 🐆 rm, TV ☎ ✆ ℗ – 🛆 90. AE ⓘ E VISA JCB. 🗙 rest by ②
Meals à la carte 185/370 – **51 rm** ☕ 990/1680

Kasererhof without rest, Alpenstr. 6, ⊠ A-5020, ℰ (0662) 6 39 65,
Fax (0662) 6396550, 🚙 – 🕽 🐆 TV ☎ ℗. AE ⓘ E VISA JCB by ②
closed 8 to 28 March – **51 rm** ☕ 1225/3560

Wolf-Dietrich, Wolf-Dietrich-Str. 7, ⊠ A-5020, ℰ (0662) 87 12 75, Fax (0662) 882320,
⊆s, 🖾 – 🕽 TV ☎ 🚗. AE ⓘ E VISA JCB V m
closed early February - mid March – **Meals** (closed Sunday) (dinner only) à la carte 255/395
– **29 rm** ☕ 950/2100

Hohenstauffen without rest, Elisabethstr. 19, ⊠ A-5020, ℰ (0662) 8 77 66 90,
Fax (0662) 87219351 – 🕽 🐆 TV ☎ 🚗 ℗. AE ⓘ E VISA JCB V e
27 rm ☕ 790/2065

Fuggerhof without rest, Eberhard-Fugger-Str. 9, ⊠ A-5020, ℰ (0662) 6 41 29 00,
Fax (0662) 6412904, ≼, ⊆s, 🖾, 🚙 – 🕽 TV ☎ & 🚗 ℗. 🗙by Bürglsteinstr. X
closed 20 to 26 December – **20 rm** ☕ 980/2800

Gablerbräu, Linzer Gasse 9, ⊠ A-5020, ℰ (0662) 8 89 65, Fax (0662) 8896555, 🌳
– 🕽 TV ☎ – 🛆 25. AE ⓘ E VISA JCB Y d
Meals à la carte 180/390 – **52 rm** ☕ 950/1900

XX **Alt Salzburg**, Bürgerspitalgasse 2, ⊠ A-5020, ℰ (0662) 84 14 76, Fax (0662) 841477
– AE ⓘ E VISA JCB Y c
closed Sunday - Monday lunch, except festival period – **Meals** à la carte 300/490

XX **Bei Bruno** -Hotel Bristol, Makartplatz 4, ⊠ A-5020, ℰ (0662) 87 84 17 – AE ⓘ E VISA
JCB Y a
closed Sunday and 3 weeks March except festival period – **Meals** à la carte 285/560

XX **K+K Restaurant am Waagplatz**, Waagplatz 2 (1st floor), ⊠ A-5020, ℰ (0662)
84 21 56, Fax (0662) 84215633, 🌳, « Medieval dinner with period performance in the
Freysauff-Keller (by arrangement) » – AE ⓘ E VISA JCB Z h
Meals (booking essential) à la carte 320/510

XX **Riedenburg**, Neutorstr. 31, ⊠ A-5020, ℰ (0662) 83 08 15, Fax (0662) 8443529, 🌳
– ℗. AE ⓘ E VISA X a
closed Monday lunch and Sunday – **Meals** à la carte 375/530

X **Zum Mohren**, Judengasse 9, ⊠ A-5020, ℰ (0662) 84 23 87, Fax (0662) 85814222 –
AE ⓘ E VISA JCB Y g
closed mid June - mid July and Sunday except August and December – **Meals** (booking
essential) à la carte 240/450

at Salzburg-Aigen by Bürglsteinstr. X :

Rosenvilla without rest, Höfelgasse 4, ⊠ A-5026, ℰ (0662) 62 17 65,
Fax (0662) 6252308 – TV ☎ ℗. AE
15 rm ☕ 1190/2270

Doktorwirt, Glaser Str. 9, ⊠ A-5026, ℰ (0662) 62 29 73, Fax (0662) 62171724,
🌳, ⊆s, 🖾 (heated), 🚙 – TV ☎ 🚗 ℗ – 🛆 25. AE ⓘ E VISA JCB.
🗙 rest
closed 10 to 26 February and mid October - late November – **Meals** (closed Monday)
à la carte 200/410 – **39 rm** ☕ 840/1900

XX **Gasthof Schloß Aigen**, Schwarzenbergpromenade 37, ⊠ A-5026, ℰ (0662)
62 12 84, Fax (0662) 621284, 🌳 – ℗. AE ⓘ E VISA
closed Wednesday - Thursday lunch and 3 weeks January - February – **Meals** à la carte
315/495

at Salzburg-Gnigl by ① :

XX **Pomodoro**, Eichstr. 54, ⊠ A-5023, ℰ (0662) 64 04 38, 🌳 – AE E VISA
closed Monday - Tuesday, Christmas to 6 January and mid July - late August – **Meals**
(booking essential) (Italian rest.) à la carte 350/480

at Salzburg-Liefering *by* ④ :

Brandstätter, Münchner Bundesstr. 69, ⊠ A-5020, ℰ (0662) 43 45 3
Fax (0662) 43453590, 🏡, ⇌s, 🏊, 🌿 – 🛗, 🍴 rest, TV ☎ 🅿 – 🛄 3
🍴 rest
closed 22 to 27 December – **Meals** *(closed 2 to 16 January, 1 week May and Sunday excep
in season)* (booking essential) à la carte 295/600 – **35 rm** ⊋ 980/1960
Spec. Lauwarmer Kalbsbrustsalat mit Gemüsevinaigrette. Bauernente in Rohr gebrate
Rehrücken mit Pilzen und Selleriepüree

at Salzburg-Maria Plain *by Plainstr.* V :

Maria Plain 🦅, Plainbergweg 41, ⊠ A-5101, ℰ (0662) 4 50 70 1
Fax (0662) 45070119, (17C inn), « Garden with ⩻ », 🌿 – 🛗 TV ☎ 🚗 🅿 – 🛄 40.
OD E VISA
closed 1 week July – **Meals** *(closed Tuesday - Wednesday except festival period)* à la cart
270/380 – **27 rm** ⊋ 880/1500 – 5 suites

at Salzburg-Nonntal :

Purzelbaum, Zugallistr. 7, ⊠ A-5020, ℰ (0662) 84 88 43, *Fax (0662) 8443529*, 🌿
(Bistro rest.) – AE OD E VISA
closed Monday lunch and Sunday – **Meals** (booking essential for dinner) à la cart
445/580

on the Heuberg *North-East : 3 km by* ① – *alt. 565 m*

Schöne Aussicht 🦅, Heuberg 3, ⊠ A-5023 *Salzburg*, ℰ (0662) 64 06 08
Fax (0662) 6406082, « Garden with ⩻ Salzburg and Alps », ⇌s, 🏊, 🌿, 🍴 – TV ☎ (
– 🛄 30. AE OD E VISA. 🍴 rest
March - October – **Meals** (dinner only) à la carte 265/480 – **28 rm** ⊋ 700/1800

on the Gaisberg *by* ① :

Vitalhotel Kobenzl 🦅, Gaisberg 11, *alt. 730 m*, ⊠ A-5020 *Salzburg*, ℰ (066
64 15 10, *Fax (0662) 642238*, 🏡, « Beautiful panoramic location with ⩻ Salzbur
and Alps », Massage, 🎿, ⇌s, 🏊, 🌿 – 🛗, 🍴 rm, TV 🅿 – 🛄 40. AE OD E VIS
🍴 rest
closed 6 January - 6 March – **Meals** à la carte 427/735 – **40 rm** ⊋ 1650/4300 – 15 suite

Romantik-Hotel Gersberg Alm 🦅, Gersberg 37, *alt. 800 m*, ⊠ A-5023 *Salzbur
Gnigl*, ℰ (0662) 64 12 57, *Fax (0662) 644278*, 🏡, ⇌s, 🏊, 🌿, 🍴 – TV ☎ 🅿 – 🛄 4
AE OD E VISA
Meals (booking essential) à la carte 350/485 – **45 rm** ⊋ 1078/3185

near Airport *by* ③ :

Radisson-SAS-Airport-Center-Hotel, Bundesstr. 4, ⊠ A-5073 *Salzburg-Wal
ℰ (0662) 8 58 10, *Fax (0662) 85814000* – 🛗, 🍴 rm, 🍽 TV ☎ 📞 ♿ 🚗 – 🛄 90. A
OD E VISA
Meals à la carte 230/455 – **152 rm** ⊋ 1300/2050 – 7 suites

Airporthotel, Dr.-M.-Laireiter-Str. 9, ⊠ A-5020 *Salzburg-Loig*, ℰ (0662) 85 00 2
Fax (0662) 85002044, ⇌s, 🏊 – 🛗, 🍴 rm, TV ☎ 🚗 🅿 – 🛄 20. AE OD E VIS
JCB
Meals (residents only) – **37 rm** ⊋ 990/1960

at Anif ② : *7 km*

Friesacher, ⊠ A-5081, ℰ (06246) 89 77, *Fax (06246) 897749*, 🏡, Massage, ⇌s,
– 🛗 TV ☎ 🅿 – 🛄 25
closed 2 to 22 January – **Meals** *(closed Wednesday except Festival period)* à la cart
220/400 🍷 – **52 rm** ⊋ 840/1960

at Elixhausen *North : 8 km by* ⑤ :

Romantik-Hotel Gmachl, Dorfstr. 14, ⊠ A-5161, ℰ (0662) 4 80 21 2
Fax (0662) 48021272, 🏡, ⇌s, 🏊 (heated), 🌿, 🍴(indoor), 🐎 (indoor) – 🛗 TV ☎ (
– 🛄 40. AE OD E VISA
closed mid June - early July – *(closed Sunday dinner and Monday lunch)* à la carte 270/50
– **34 rm** ⊋ 1260/2800 – 3 suites

at Hallwang-Söllheim *by* ①, *and Linzer Bundesstraße : 7 km :*

Pfefferschiff, Söllheim 3, ⊠ A-5300, ℰ (0662) 66 12 42, *Fax (0662) 661841*, 🏡
🅿. 🍴
closed Sunday - Monday, late June - mid July and 1 week September – **Meals** à la cart
435/680
Spec. Blunzenguglhupf auf Linsenkraut. Rehrückenfilet mit Apfelkruste. Marillenschmarre
mit Kürbiskernparfait

at Hof *by ① : 20 km :*

🏨 **Schloß Fuschl** ⚘, ✉ A-5322, ☎ (06229) 2 25 30, Fax (06229) 2253531, ≤, 🏕,
(former 15C hunting seat with 3 guesthouses), Massage, ≘s, 🅂, 🐾, ✕, ▸9 – 🛗 📺
🚗 🅿 – 🛎 100. 🆎 ⓪ Ⓔ 𝗩𝗜𝗦𝗔 🄹🄲🄱. ⍋ rest
Meals à la carte 480/745 – **84 rm** ⌓ 3100/4000 – 12 suites

🏠 **Jagdhof am Fuschlsee**, ✉ A-5322, ☎ (06229) 2 37 20, Fax (06229) 2372413, ≤,
(former 18C farmhouse with guesthouse), ≘s, 🅂, 🌿 – 🛗 📺 ☎ 🅿 – 🛎 90. 🆎 ⓪
Ⓔ 𝗩𝗜𝗦𝗔 🄹🄲🄱
Meals à la carte 260/440 – **57 rm** ⌓ 950/1600

at Fuschl am See ① : *26 km :*

🏠 **Ebner's Waldhof** ⚘, Seepromenade, ✉ A-5330, ☎ (06226) 82 64, Fax (06226) 8644,
≤, 🏕, Massage, ≘s, 🅂, 🐾, 🌿, ✕ – 🛗 📺 🅿 – 🛎 60. ⍋ rest
closed 15 March - April and November - 15 December – **Meals** (booking essential) à la carte
320/465 – **75 rm** ⌓ 1035/2640

at Mondsee ① : *28 km (by motorway A 1)*

🏨 **Seehof** ⚘, (South-East : 7 km), ✉ A-5311 *Loibichl*, ☎ (06232) 50 31,
Fax (06232) 503151, ≤, « Garden-terrace », Massage, ≘s, 🐾, 🌿, ✕ – ⍋ rest, 📺
🚗 🅿 – 🛎 15. ⍋
mid May - mid September – **Meals** à la carte 350/540 – **35 rm** ⌓ 3600/5720 – 4 suites

at Werfen *South : 42 km by ② and A 10 :*

✕✕✕ **Karl-Rudolf Obauer** with rm, Markt 46, ✉ A-5450, ☎ (06468) 5 21 20,
❀❀ Fax (06468) 521212 – 🍽 📺 ☎ 🅿. 🆎
Meals (booking essential) 380/790 and à la carte 480/835 – **8 rm** ⌓ 980/1800
Spec. Forellenstrudel "Obauer". Gefüllte Zucchiniblüten mit Schwammerl und Thymian
(season). Grapefruitsnocken mit Safrankompott

Benelux

Belgium

BRUSSELS – ANTWERP – BRUGES – LIÈGE

Grand Duchy of Luxembourg

LUXEMBOURG

Netherlands

AMSTERDAM – The HAGUE – ROTTERDAM

PRACTICAL INFORMATION

LOCAL CURRENCY

Belgian Franc: *100 BEF = 2,48 euros (€) can also be used in Luxembourg*
Dutch Florin: *100 NLG = 45,38 euros (€)*

TOURIST INFORMATION

Telephone numbers and addresses of Tourist Offices are given in the text of each city under 🛈.
National Holiday: *Belgium: 21 July; Netherlands: 30 April; Luxembourg: 23 June.*

AIRLINES

SABENA : *rue Marché-aux-Herbes 110, 1000 Bruxelles, ☎ (02) 723 23 23, Airport Findel – Terminal, L-1110 Luxembourg, ☎ 432 42 41, Strawinskylaan 813, 1077 XX Amsterdam, ☎ (020) 470 14 70.*

LUXAIR : *Luxembourg Airport, L-2987 Luxembourg, ☎ 4 79 81.*

KLM : *rue Maurice Charlent 53, 1160 Bruxelles, ☎ (02) 717 20 70, Luxembourg Airport, L-2987 Luxembourg, ☎ 4 79 81, Amsterdamseweg 55, 1182 GP Amstelveen, ☎ (020) 649 34 56.*

FOREIGN EXCHANGE

In Belgium, *banks close at 4.30pm and weekends;*
in the Netherlands, *banks close at 5.00pm and weekends, Schiphol Airport exchange offices open daily from 6.30am to 11.30pm.*

TRANSPORT

Taxis: *may be hailed in the street, at taxi ranks or called by telephone.*
Bus, tramway: *practical for long and short distances and good for sightseeing.*
*Brussels has a **Métro** (subway) network. In each station complete information and plans will be found.*

POSTAL SERVICES – SHOPPING

Post offices open Monday to Friday from 9am to 5pm in Benelux.
Shops and boutiques are generally open from 9am to 7pm in Belgium and Luxembourg, and from 9am to 6pm in the Netherlands. The main shopping areas are:

in Brussels: *Rue Neuve, Porte de Namur, Avenue Louise, Avenue de la Toison d'Or, Boulevard de Waterloo, Rue de Namur - Also Brussels antique market on Saturday from 9am to 3pm, and Sunday from 9am to 1pm (around Place du Grand-Sablon) - Flower and Bird market (Grand-Place) on Sunday morning - Flea Market (Place du Jeu de Balles) – Shopping Centres: Basilix, Westland Shopping Center, Woluwé Shopping Center, City 2, Galerie Louise.*

in Luxembourg: *Grand'Rue and around Place d'Armes - Station Quarter.*

in Amsterdam: *Kalverstraat, Leidsestraat, Nieuwendijk, P.C. Hoofstraat, Beethovenstraat, Van Baerlestraat and Utrechtsestraat – Shopping Center, Magna Plaza – Secondhand goods and antiques (around Rijksmuseum and Spiegelgracht) – Flower Market – Amsterdam Flea Market (near Waterlooplein).*

BREAKDOWN SERVICE *24 hour assistance:*

Belgium: *TCB, Brussels ☎ (02) 233 22 11 – VTB-VAB, Antwerp ☎ (03) 253 63 63 – RACB, Brussels ☎ (02) 287 09 00.*

Luxembourg: *ACL ☎ 45 00 451.*

Netherlands: *ANWB, The Hague ☎ (070) 314 71 47 – KNAC, The Hague ☎ (070) 383 16 12.*

TIPPING *In Benelux, prices include service and taxes.*

SPEED LIMITS – SEAT BELTS

In Belgium and Luxembourg, the maximum speed limits are 120 km/h-74 mph on motorways and dual carriageways, 90 km/h-56 mph on all other roads and 50 km/h-31 mph in built-up areas. In the Netherlands, 100/120 km/h-62/74 mph on motorways and "autowegen", 80 km/h-50 mph on other roads and 50 km/h-31 mph in built-up areas. In each country, the wearing of seat belts is compulsory for drivers and passengers.

BRUSSELS

(BRUXELLES – BRUSSEL) *1000 Région de Bruxelles-Capitale – Brussels Hoofdstedelijk Gewest* **213** ⑱ *and* **909** G 3 – ㉑ S – *Pop. 950 597.*

Paris 308 – Amsterdam 204 – Düsseldorf 222 – Lille 116 – Luxembourg 219.

TOURIST OFFICES

TIB Hôtel de Ville, Grand'Place, ✉ 1000, ✆ (02) 513 89 40, Fax (02) 514 45 38.
Office de Promotion du Tourisme (OPT), r. Marché-aux-Herbes 61, ✉ 1000, ✆ (02) 504 02 00, Fax (02) 513 69 50.
Toerisme Vlaanderen, Grasmarkt 61, ✉ 1000, ✆ (02) 504 03 00, Fax (02) 513 88 03.

For more information on tourist attractions consult our Green Guide to Brussels.

BRUXELLES
BRUSSEL

E F

Q R S T

G
H
Q
R
S
T
SCHAERBEEK
SCHAARBEEK
Av. L. Bertrand
Av. Deschanel
Av. Rogier
Paul
PARC JOSAPHAT
Av. des Azalées
Bd Lambermont
Bd Gal Wahis
Rue
Av. H. Dunant
Bd Léopold III
102
R. H. Chomé
de Genève
108
133
21
Av. Artan
Rue Dailly
Chazal
Av. Rogier
k
Chée de Louvain
Pl. Colonel Bremer
Av. Clays
Pl. Dailly
Chée de Louvain
Bd A. Reyers
R.T.B.F. B.R.T.N.
T-JOSSE-TEN-NOODE
T.-JOOST-TEN-NODE
Louvain
R. de Pavie
28
de
Av. du
v
Plasky
Eug.
Diamant
Av. de Roodebeek
18
E 40
Av. des Cerisiers
R
187
171
Square Ambiorix
R. des Patriotes
Diamant
118
Square Vergote
Joseph II
a
k
s
e
y
z
c
Av. de Cortenbergh
Rue
de
Bd Brand Whitlock
u
G. Henri
P
de Maelbeek
d
la
Centre Berlaymont
Av. de la Renaissance
Av. de
Loi Schuman
PARC DU
M
c
Linthout
INSTITUTIONS
Secteur en travaux
CINQUANTENAIRE
de Trèves
Espace Léopold
EUROPÉENNES
R. Belliard
106
Av.
181
M 11
M 3
Mérode
Avenue de Tervuren
k
b
d
Parc Léopold
M 26
R. du Cornet
f
K 1
Av. des Celtes
Sq. Mar. Montgomery
S
Wavre
M
a
r
Hap
Louis
Av. de la Chasse
ETTERBEEK
72
Rue
d'Auderghem
St-Michel
P Thieffry
M 12
R. du Sceptre
R. Gray
R. de
Chée de l'Orient
Chée de Wavre
216
Boileau
Av. E. Messens
R. Philippe Baucq
220
R. Gray
T
G
0   500 m

BRUXELLES
BRUSSEL

Américaine (R.)	**FU**	8
Auguste Rodin (Av.)	**GU**	12
Besme (Av.)	**EV**	18
Boondael (Drève de)	**GX**	22
Cambre (Bd de la)	**GV**	33
Coccinelles (Av. des)	**HX**	40
Congo (Av. du)	**GV**	48
Copernic (R.)	**FX**	51
Dodonée (R.)	**FV**	61
Dries	**HX**	63
Emile de Beco (Av.)	**GU**	79
Emile De Mot (Av.)	**GV**	81
Eperons d'Or (Av. des)	**GU**	85
Everard (av.)	**EV**	91
Hippodrome (Av. de l')	**GU**	120

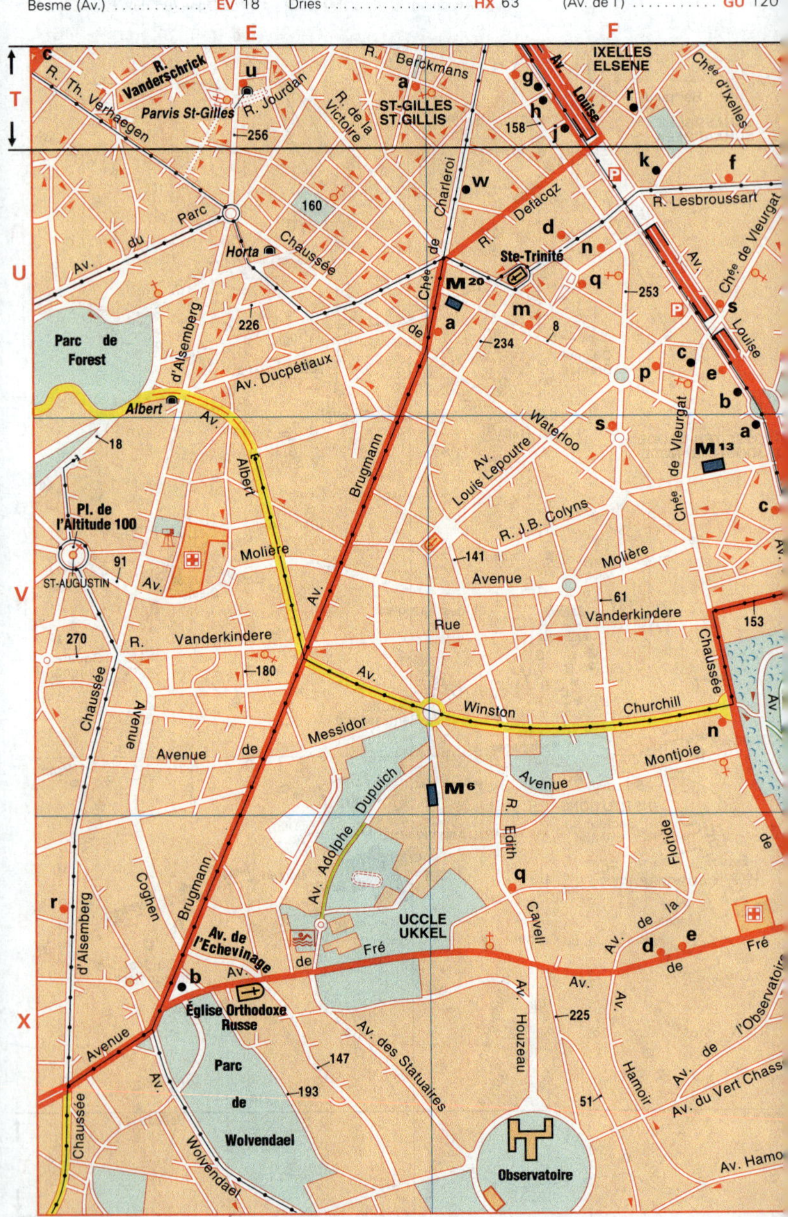

BELGIUM

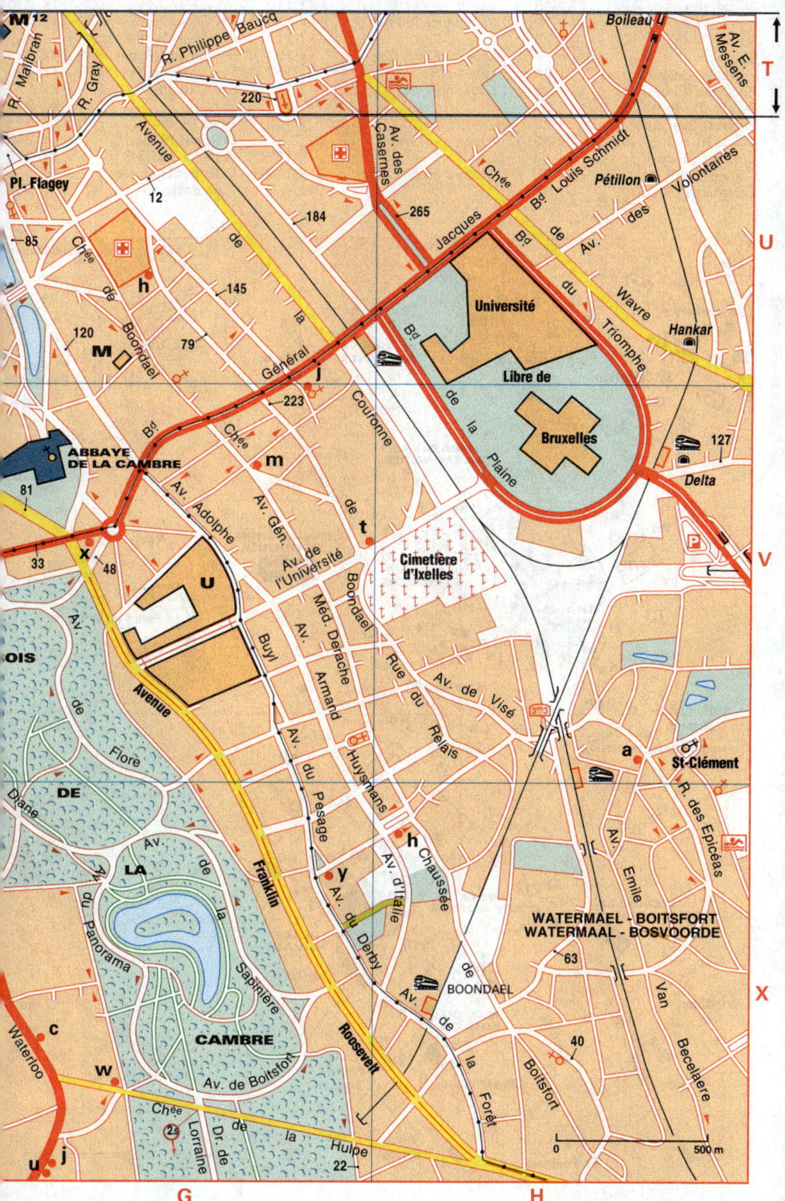

BRUXELLES
BRUSSEL

GOLF COURSES

▮18 ▮9 at Tervuren SE : 14 km, Château de Ravenstein ✆ (02) 767 58 01, Fax (02) 767 28 41 – ▮18 at Melsbroek NE : 14 km, Steenwagenstraat 11 ✆ (02) 751 82 05, Fax (02) 751 84 25 – ▮18 at Anderlecht, Sports Area of la Pede, r. Scholle 1 ✆ (02) 521 16 87, Fax (02) 521 51 56 – ▮9 at Watermael-Boitsfort, chaussée de la Hulpe 53a ✆ (02) 672 22 22, Fax (02) 675 34 81 – ▮9 at Overijse SE : 16 km, Gemslaan 55 ✆ (02) 687 50 30, Fax (02) 687 37 68 – ▮9 at Itterbeek W : 8 km, J.M. Van Lierdestraat 24 ✆ (02) 567 00 38, Fax (02) 567 02 23 – ▮18 at Kampenhout NE : 20 km, Wildersedreef 56 ✆ (0 16) 65 12 16, Fax (0 16) 65 16 80 – ▮9 at Duisburg E : 18 km, Hertswegenstraat 59 ✆ (02) 769 45 82, Fax (02) 767 97 52.

PLACES OF INTEREST

BRUSSELS SEEN FROM ABOVE

Atomium★ – Basilica of the Sacred Heart★ – Arcades of the Royal Museum of the Army and Military History★ HS M25.

FAMOUS VIEWS OF BRUSSELS

The Law Courts ES J – Administrative sections of the City of Brussels KY – Place Royale★ KZ.

GREEN AREAS

Parks : Bruxelles, Wolvendael, Woluwé, Laeken, Cinquantenaire, Duden, Bois de la Cambre, Forêt de Soignes.

HISTORICAL MONUMENTS

Grand-Place★★★ JY – Monnaie Theatre★ JY – St Hubert Arcades★★ JKY – Erasmus' House (Anderlecht)★★ – Castle and park (Gaasbeek)★★ (SW : 12 km) – Royal Greenhouses (Laeken)★★.

CHURCHES

Sts-Michael's and Gudule's Cathedral★★ KY – Church of N.-D. de la Chapelle★ JZ – Church of N.-D. du Sablon★ KZ – Abbey of la-Cambre (Ixelles)★★ FGV – Church of Sts-Pierre and Guidon (Anderlecht)★.

MUSEUMS

Museum of Ancient Art★★★ KZ – Museum of the Cinquantenaire★★★ HS M11 – Museum of Modern Art★★ KZ M2 – Belgian Centre for Comic Strip Art★★ KY M8 – Autoworld★★ HS M3 – Natural Science Museum★★ GS M26 – Museum of Musical Instruments★★ KZ M21 – Meunier Museum (Ixelles)★ FV M13 – Ixelles Community Museum (Ixelles)★★ GT M12 – Charlier Museum★ FR M9 – Bibliotheca Wittockiana (Woluwé-St-Pierre)★ – Royal Museum of Central Africa (Tervuren/district)★★ – Horta Museum (St-Gilles)★★ EFU M20 – Van Buuren Museum (Uccle) EFV M6.

MODERN ARCHITECTURE

Atomium★ – Berlaymont Centre GR – European Parliament GS – Arts Centre KZ Q1 – Administrative sections of the City of Brussels KY – Garden-Cities Le Logis and Floréal (Watermael-Boitsfort) – Garden-Cities Kapelleveld (Woluwé-St-Lambert) – UCL Campus (Woluwé-St-Lambert) – Stoclet Palace (Tervuren/district)★ – Swift (La Hulpe/district) – Shop-front P. Hanker★ KY W – Ixelles council building FS K2 – Van Eetvelde Hotel★ GR 187 – Old England★ KZ N – Cauchie House (Etterbeek)★ HS K1.

SCENIC AREAS

Grand-Place★★★ JY – Grand and Petit Sablon★★ JZ – St Hubert Arcades★★ JKY – Place du Musée KZ – Place Ste-Catherine JY – The Old Town (Halles St-Géry – vault of the Senne – Church of Riches Claires) ER – Rue des Bouchers★ JY – Manneken Pis★★ JZ – The Marolles District JZ – Galerie Bortier JY.

Alphabetical listing of hotels and restaurants

Starred establishments

✿✿✿

| 21 | XXXX | Bruneau | 15 | XXX | Comme Chez Soi |

✿✿

| 26 | XXXXX | Bijgaarden (De) | 21 | XXX | Claude Dupont |
| 14 | XXXX | Sea Grill (at Radisson SAS H.) | 17 | XXX | Écailler du Palais Royal (L') |

✿

27	XXXX	Barbizon	19	XXX	Saint Guidon
18	XXXX	Maison du Bœuf (at Hilton H.)	19	XXX	Truffe Noire (La)
16	XXXX	Maison du Cygne (La)	26	XX	Aloyse Kloos
19	XXXX	Villa Lorraine	19	XX	Baguettes Impériales (Les)
26	XXXX	Michel	20	XX	Grignotière (La)
25	XXX	Des 3 Couleurs	20	XX	Stirwen
27	XXX	Pyramid	17	XX	Trente rue de la Paille
			24	XX	Vieux Boitsfort (Au)

Establishments according to style of cuisine

Buffets

15   Atelier (L') *Q. de l'Europe*
18   Café Wiltcher's (at Conrad H.)
     Q. Louise
19   Crescendo (at Sheraton Towers H.)
     Q. Botanique, Gare du Nord

Grill

21   Aub. de Boendael (L')
     Ixelles Q. Boondael
27   Aub. Napoléon *Env. at Meise*
24   Grill (Le) *Watermael-Boitsfort*
24   Hoef (De) *Uccle*

Pub rest – Brasseries

14   Arenberg
23   Art H. Siru *St-Josse Q. Botanique*
22   Atelier de la Truffe Noire (L')
     Ixelles Q. Louise
21   Brasserie Marebœuf (La)
     Ixelles Q. Boondael
24   Brasseries Georges *Uccle*
28   Clarine *Env. at Strombeek-Bever*
24   Entre-Temps (L')
     Watermael-Boitsfort
19   Erasme *Anderlecht*
27   Istas *Env. at Overijse*
26   Kasteel Gravenhof *Env. at Dworp*
28   Lindbergh Taverne
     (at Sheraton Airport H.)
     Env. at Zaventem
16   Matignon *Q. Grand'Place*
28   Met (De) *Env. at Vilvoorde*
20   Paix (La) *Anderlecht*
16   Roue d'Or (La) *Q. Grand'Place*
28   Stockmansmolen *Env. at Zaventem*
25   Vignoble de Margot (Le)
     Woluwé-St-Pierre

Regional

15   In 't Spinnekopke
16   Kelderke ('t) *Q. Grand'Place*

Seafood – Oyster bar

17   Belle Maraîchère (La)
     Q. Ste-Catherine
21   Brasserie Mareboeuf (La)
     Ixelles Q. Boondael

24   Brasseries Georges *Uccle*
23   Cadre Noir (Le)
     Schaerbeek Q. Meiser
17   Écailler du Palais Royal (L')
     Q. des Sablons
17   François *Q. Ste-Catherine*
14   Sea Grill (at Radisson SAS H.)
17   Sirène d'Or (La) *Q. Ste-Catherine*
28   Stoveke ('t)
     Env. at Strombeek-Bever
17   Truite d'Argent and
     H. Welcome (La)
     Q. Ste-Catherine
25   Vignoble de Margot (Le)
     Woluwé-St-Pierre

Basque

21   fils de Jules (Le) *Ixelles Q. Bascule*

Chinese

24   Cité du Dragon (La) *Uccle*
19   Lychee *Q. Atomium*
19   Ming Dynasty *Q. Atomium*
20   New Asia *Auderghem*

Indian

24   Chutney *Uccle*
18   Palais des Indes (Au) *Q. Louise*
18   Porte des Indes (La) *Q. Louise*
24   Rives du Gange (Les)
     Watermael-Boitsfort

Indonesian

23   Zinneke (Le) *Schaerbeek Q. Meiser*

Italian

23   Amici miei *Schaerbeek Q. Meiser*
27   Arlecchino (L')
     (at Aub. de Waterloo H.)
     Env. at Sint-Genesius-Rode
17   Castello Banfi *Q. des Sablons*
19   Frascati (Le) *Q. Atomium*
23   I Trulli *St-Gilles Q. Louise*
25   Mucha (Le) *Woluwé-St-Pierre*
15   Pappa e Citti *Q. de l'Europe*
15   Roma
21   San Daniele *Ganshoren*
23   Senza Nome *Schaerbeek*
22   Tutto Pepe *Ixelles Q. Louise*

Japanese

20 Momotaro Etterbeek
    Q. Cinquantenaire
15 Samourai
18 Tagawa *Q. Louise*
18 Taishin (at Mayfair H.)
    Q. Louise
15 Take Sushi *Q. de l'Europe*

Moroccan

20 Khaïma (La) *Auderghem*
22 Mamounia (La) *St-Gilles*

Portuguese

22 Forcado (Le) *St-Gilles*

Scandinavian

14 Atrium *(at Radisson SAS H.)*

Spanish

20 Grillange *Etterbeek*
15 Jardín de España (El)
    Q. de l'Europe

Thaï

24 Blue Elephant *Uccle*
27 Bois Savanes
    Env. at Sint-Genesius-Rode
18 Larmes du Tigre (Les)
    Q. Palais de Justice
24 Maison de Thaïlande (La)
    Watermael-Boitsfort
22 Perles de Pluie (Les) *Ixelles Q. Louise*

Vietnamese

19 Baguettes Impériales (Les)
    Q. Atomium
20 Citronnelle (La) *Auderghem*
21 Pagode d'Or (La) *Ixelles Q. Boondael*
21 Yen *Ixelles*

BRUXELLES (BRUSSEL)

Radisson SAS, r. Fossé-aux-Loups 47, ✉ 1000, ✆ (0 2) 219 28 28 and 227 31 20 (rest), *Fax (0 2) 219 62 62,* « Patio with remains of 12C City enclosure wall », ↕, ⇌s – ⇕ ⤬ ▤ TV ☎ ⇋ – 益 25-380. AE Ⓞ Ⓔ VISA JCB   KY   f
Meals see rest *Sea Grill* below – *Atrium* (partly Scandinavian cuisine) *Lunch 975* - a la carte 1150/1900 – ☕ 850 – **275 rm** 12000/15000, 6 suites.

Astoria, r. Royale 103, ✉ 1000, ✆ (0 2) 227 05 05, *Fax (0 2) 217 11 50,* « Early 20C residence, Belle Epoque style », ↕, ⇌s – ⇕ ⤬ ▤ TV ☎ ⇋ Ⓟ – 益 25-180. AE Ⓞ Ⓔ VISA. ⋇ rest   KY   b
Meals *Le Palais Royal* (closed Saturday lunch and Sunday dinner) *Lunch 1150* - 1600 – ☕ 850 – **104 rm** 5000/13000, 14 suites.

Le Plaza, bd. A. Max 118, ✉ 1000, ✆ (0 2) 227 67 00, *Fax (0 2) 227 67 20* – ⇕ ⤬ ▤ TV ☎ ⇋ – 益 25-800. AE Ⓞ Ⓔ VISA JCB   FQ
Meals (closed Saturday and Sunday) – a la carte 1250/1550 – ☕ 750 – **187 rm** ☕ 11700/12700, 6 suites.

Métropole, pl. de Brouckère 31, ✉ 1000, ✆ (0 2) 217 23 00, *Telex 21234, Fax (0 2) 218 02 20,* « Late 19C hall and lounges », ↕, ⇌s – ⇕ ⤬ ▤ TV ☎ – 益 25-400. AE Ⓞ Ⓔ VISA JCB. ⋇ rest   JY   c
Meals see rest *L'Alban Chambon* below – **370 rm** ☕ 10500/12500, 5 suites.

Bedford, r. Midi 135, ✉ 1000, ✆ (0 2) 512 78 40, *Fax (0 2) 514 17 59* – ⇕ ⤬ ▤ TV ☎ ⇋ – 益 25-250. AE Ⓞ Ⓔ VISA JCB. ⋇   ER   k
Meals *Lunch 795* – a la carte approx. 1100 – **302 rm** ☕ 7100/8500.

Jolly Atlanta, bd A. Max 7, ✉ 1000, ✆ (0 2) 217 01 20, *Fax (0 2) 217 37 58* – ⇕ ⤬ ▤ rest, TV ☎ ⇋ – 益 25-50. AE Ⓞ Ⓔ VISA JCB. ⋇   JY   d
Meals (residents only) – **235 rm** ☕ 8650/9300, 6 suites.

Président Centre without rest, r. Royale 160, ✉ 1000, ✆ (0 2) 219 00 65, *Telex 26784, Fax (0 2) 218 09 10* – ⇕ ⤬ ▤ TV ☎ ⇋. AE Ⓞ Ⓔ VISA JCB. ⋇   KY   a
73 rm ☕ 5750/6800.

Arctia without rest, r. Arenberg 18, ✉ 1000, ✆ (0 2) 548 18 11, *Fax (0 2) 548 18 20,* ⇌s – ⇕ ⤬ ▤ TV ☎ ⅙ – 益 25-80. AE Ⓞ Ⓔ VISA   KY   r
100 rm ☕ 6000/7300.

Royal Embassy without rest, bd Anspach 159, ✉ 1000, ✆ (0 2) 512 81 00, *Fax (0 2) 514 30 97,* ⇌s – ⇕ ⤬ TV ☎. AE Ⓞ Ⓔ VISA   ER   e
54 rm ☕ 5750/6800.

Arenberg, r. Assaut 15, ✉ 1000, ✆ (0 2) 501 16 16, *Fax (0 2) 501 18 18,* ↕ – ⇕ ⤬, ▤ rest, TV ☎ ⇋ – 益 25-75. AE Ⓞ Ⓔ VISA JCB. ⋇ rest   KY   g
Meals (Pub rest) (lunch only July-August) (closed Saturday and Sunday lunch) *Lunch 695* – a la carte approx. 900 – **155 rm** ☕ 4700/12000.

Chambord without rest, r. Namur 82, ✉ 1000, ✆ (0 2) 548 99 10, *Fax (0 2) 514 08 47* – ⇕ TV ☎. AE Ⓞ Ⓔ VISA JCB   KZ   u
☕ 650 – **69 rm** 4900.

Queen Anne without rest, bd E. Jacqmain 110, ✉ 1000, ✆ (0 2) 217 16 00, *Fax (0 2) 217 18 38* – ⇕ TV ☎. AE Ⓞ Ⓔ VISA   EFQ   a
60 rm ☕ 2900/3400.

George V without rest, r. 't Kint 23, ✉ 1000, ✆ (0 2) 513 50 93, *Fax (0 2) 513 44 93* – ⇕ TV ☎ Ⓟ. AE Ⓔ VISA   ER   c
16 rm ☕ 2300/2500.

Sabina without rest, r. Nord 78, ✉ 1000, ✆ (0 2) 218 26 37, *Fax (0 2) 219 32 39* – ⇕ TV ☎. AE Ⓞ Ⓔ VISA JCB   KY   c
24 rm ☕ 2250/2500.

Sea Grill - (at Radisson SAS H.), r. Fossé-aux-Loups 47, ✉ 1000, ✆ (0 2) 227 31 20, *Telex 22202, Fax (0 2) 219 62 62,* Seafood – ▤ Ⓟ. AE Ⓞ Ⓔ VISA JCB   KY   i
❀❀ *closed Saturday lunch, Sunday, Bank Holidays, 4 to 11 April and 18 July-15 August* – **Meals** *Lunch 2450 b.i.* – 2550, a la carte 2200/2950
Spec. St-Jacques à la vapeur d'algues, crème légère au cresson (15 September-15 April). Manchons de crabe royal tièdis au beurre de persil plat. Homard à la presse.

L'Alban Chambon - (at Métropole H.), pl. de Brouckère 31, ✉ 1000, ✆ (0 2) 217 76 50, *Telex 21234, Fax (0 2) 218 02 20,* « Late 19C atmosphere » – ▤. AE Ⓞ Ⓔ VISA JCB. ⋇   JY   c
closed Saturday, Sunday, Bank Holidays and 19 July-13 August – **Meals** 1450 b.i./1990.

Comme Chez Soi (Wynants), pl. Rouppe 23, ✉ 1000, ℰ (0 2) 512 29 21, *Fax (0 2) 511 80 52*, **«** Belle Epoque atmosphere with Horta decor **»** – 🔲 **🅿. AE ⓪ E VISA**   ES m
closed Sunday, Monday, 4 July-2 August, 24 December and 30 December-11 January – **Meals** (booking essential) *Lunch 2150* – 3550/4850, – a la carte 2800/3500
Spec. Filets de sole, mousseline au Riesling et aux crevettes grises. Noisettes de cochon de lait à l'huile de truffes blanches, croustillant de fins légumes. Mousse légère à la badiane, gelée de fruits rouges et languettes de gaufre de Bruxelles.

Roma, r. Princes 14, ✉ 1000, ℰ (0 2) 219 01 94, *Fax (0 2) 218 34 30*, Italian cuisine –
🔲. **AE ⓪ E VISA**   JY e
closed Saturday lunch, Sunday and 20 July-20 August – **Meals** *Lunch 950* – a la carte 1300/1650.

Astrid "Chez Pierrot", r. Presse 21, ✉ 1000, ℰ (0 2) 217 38 31, *Fax (0 2) 217 38 31*
– **AE ⓪ E VISA JCB**   KY e
closed Sunday, Easter week and 15 July-15 August – **Meals** *Lunch 750* – 950/1350.

J and B, r. Baudet 5, ✉ 1000, ℰ (0 2) 512 04 84, *Fax (0 2) 511 79 30* – 🔲. **AE ⓪ E**
VISA JCB   KZ z
closed Saturday lunch, Sunday, Bank Holidays and 21 July-15 August – **Meals** *Lunch 695* – 995.

Samourai, r. Fossé-aux-Loups 28, ✉ 1000, ℰ (0 2) 217 56 39, *Fax (0 2) 230 46 90*, Japanese cuisine – 🔲. **AE ⓪ E VISA JCB. ⅍**   JY e
closed Tuesday, Sunday lunch and 15 July-15 August – **Meals** *Lunch 590* – a la carte 1250/1750.

In 't Spinnekopke, pl. du Jardin aux Fleurs 1, ✉ 1000, ℰ (0 2) 511 86 95, *Fax (0 2) 513 24 97*, 🌦, Partly regional cuisine, open until 11 p.m., **«** Typical ancient Brussels pub **»** – 🔲. **AE ⓪ E VISA**   ER d
closed Saturday lunch, Sunday and Bank Holidays – **Meals** *Lunch 295* – a la carte 850/1350.

Quartier de l'Europe

Dorint Ⓜ, bd Charlemange 11, ✉ 1000, ℰ (0 2) 231 09 09, *Fax (0 2) 230 33 71*, **«** Contemporary photography exhibition **»**, ↕, ≦s – 🛗 ⅍ 🔲 📺 ☎ & 🚗 – 🛎 25-150. **AE ⓪ E VISA. ⅍** rest   GR c
Meals (closed lunch Saturday and Sunday) *Lunch 1090* – a la carte 900/1550 – ☕ 700 – **206 rm** 9600, 2 suites.

Europa Inter.Continental, r. Loi 107, ✉ 1040, ℰ (0 2) 230 13 33, *Telex 26310, Fax (0 2) 280 09 67*, ↕, ≦s – 🛗 ⅍ 🔲 📺 ☎ 🚗 🅿 – 🛎 25-350. **AE ⓪ E VISA JCB. ⅍**   GR d
Meals 990/1650 – ☕ 700 – **236 rm** 9500/10500, 4 suites.

Eurovillage, bd Charlemagne 80, ✉ 1000, ℰ (0 2) 230 85 55, *Fax (0 2) 230 56 35*, 🌦, ↕, ≦s – 🛗 ⅍ 🔲 📺 ☎ 🚗 – 🛎 25-120. **AE ⓪ E VISA JCB**   GR a
Meals (closed Saturday, Sunday lunch and August) *Lunch 750* – a la carte 1000/1350 – ☕ 600 – **80 rm** 6000/8000.

New Hotel Charlemagne without rest, bd Charlemagne 25, ✉ 1000, ℰ (0 2) 230 21 35, *Fax (0 2) 230 25 10* – 🛗 ⅍ 📺 ☎ 🚗 – 🛎 30-60. **AE ⓪ E VISA**   GR k
☕ 550 – **66 rm** 3400/5900.

El Jardín de España, r. Archimède 65, ✉ 1000, ℰ (0 2) 736 34 49, *Fax (0 2) 735 17 45*, 🌦, Spanish cuisine with tapas-bar – **AE ⓪ E VISA**   GR s
closed Saturday lunch and Sunday – **Meals** *Lunch 420* – a la carte approx. 1300.

Pappa e Citti, r. Franklin 18, ✉ 1000, ℰ (0 2) 732 61 10, *Fax (0 2) 732 57 40*, 🌦, Italian cuisine – **AE ⓪ E VISA. ⅍**   GR e
closed Saturday, Sunday, Bank Holidays, August and 23 December-5 January – **Meals** *Lunch 1050* – a la carte 1200/1750.

L'Atelier, r. Franklin 28, ✉ 1000, ℰ (0 2) 734 91 40, *Fax (0 2) 735 35 98*, 🌦, Partly buffets – **AE ⓪ E VISA**   GR y
closed weekends, Bank Holidays and August – **Meals** *Lunch 850* – 1050 b.i./1200.

Take Sushi, bd Charlemagne 21, ✉ 1000, ℰ (0 2) 230 56 27, 🌦, Japanese cuisine – **AE ⓪ E VISA**   GR z
closed Saturday and Sunday lunch – **Meals** *Lunch 480* – 850/1350.

Quartier Grand'Place (Ilot Sacré)

Royal Windsor, r. Duquesnoy 5, ✉ 1000, ℰ (0 2) 505 55 55, *Fax (0 2) 505 55 00*, ↕, ≦s – 🛗 ⅍ 🔲 📺 ☎ 🚗 – 🛎 25-350. **AE ⓪ E VISA JCB**   JYZ f
Meals see rest **Les 4 Saisons** below – ☕ 880 – **260 rm** 12000, 15 suites.

Le Méridien Ⓜ ⅍, Carrefour de l'Europe 3, ✉ 1000, ℰ (0 2) 548 42 11 and 548 47 16 (rest), *Fax (0 2) 548 40 80*, ≤, ↕ – 🛗 ⅍ 🔲 📺 ☎ & 🚗 – 🛎 25-200. **AE ⓪ E VISA JCB. ⅍** rm   KZ h
Meals (closed Saturday lunch) *Lunch 1095* – a la carte 1650/2200 – ☕ 850 – **217 rm** 12000/13000, 7 suites.

BELGIUM

Amigo, r. Amigo 1, ⊠ 1000, ℘ (0 2) 547 47 47, *Telex 21618, Fax (0 2) 547 47 47*
« Collection of works of art » – |≜| ✳ ▤ TV ☎ ⇔ – 🔬 25-200. AE ① E *VISA* JCB
✳ rest   JY x
Meals a la carte 1200/1750 – **178 rm** ⊒ 6700/11500, 7 suites.

Carrefour de l'Europe, r. Marché-aux-Herbes 110, ⊠ 1000, ℘ (0 2) 504 94 00
Fax (0 2) 504 95 00 – |≜| ✳ ▤ TV ☎ – 🔬 25-150. AE ① E *VISA* JCB. ✳   JKY r
Meals *(closed Saturday and Sunday)* a la carte approx. 1200 – ⊒ 850 – **58 rm**
9100/10100, 5 suites.

Le Dixseptième without rest, r. Madeleine 25, ⊠ 1000, ℘ (0 2) 502 57 44, *Fax (0 2)*
502 64 24, « Elegant town house » – |≜| TV ☎ – 🔬 25. AE ① E *VISA* JCB. ✳ JY
17 rm ⊒ 6300/7100, 7 suites.

Novotel off Grand'Place, r. Marché-aux-Herbes 120, ⊠ 1000, ℘ (0 2) 514 33 33
Fax (0 2) 511 77 23 – |≜| ✳ ▤ TV ☎ – 🔬 25. AE ① E *VISA* JCB   JKY r
Meals – a la carte approx. 1000 – ⊒ 500 – **136 rm** 5800/6500.

Aris M without rest, r. Marché-aux-Herbes 78, ⊠ 1000, ℘ (0 2) 514 43 00, *Fax (0 2)*
514 01 19 – |≜| ▤ TV ☎ 🕭. ① E *VISA*. ✳   JY g
53 rm ⊒ 5500/6500.

Ibis off Grand'Place without rest, r. Marché-aux-Herbes 100, ⊠ 1000, ℘ (0 2)
514 40 40, *Fax (0 2) 514 50 67* – |≜| ✳ ▤ TV ☎. AE ① E *VISA* JCB   JKY v
⊒ 300 – **180 rm** 4200/4700.

Matignon, r. Bourse 10, ⊠ 1000, ℘ (0 2) 511 08 88, *Fax (0 2) 513 69 27* – |≜| TV ☎
AE ① E *VISA*   JY c
Meals (Pub rest, open until 11 p.m.) *(closed Monday and 15 January-25 February)* Lunch 650
– 850 – **37 rm** ⊒ 2600/3300.

Sema without rest, r. Harengs 6, ⊠ 1000, ℘ (0 2) 514 07 60, *Fax (0 2) 548 90 39* – |≜|
TV ☎. AE E *VISA*   JY s
10 rm ⊒ 3825/4250, 1 suite.

La Maison du Cygne, Grand'Place 9, ⊠ 1000, ℘ (0 2) 511 82 44, *Fax (0 2) 514 31 48*
« Former 17C guildhouse » – ▤ P. AE ① E *VISA* JCB. ✳   JY w
closed Saturday lunch, Sunday, first 3 weeks August and late December – **Meals** Lunch 1450
– 2400/2650, – a la carte 2100/2900
Spec. Foie d'oie en tous ses habits. Gibiers en saison. Chartreuse de St-Jacques, nage de
légumes et moules.

Les 4 Saisons - (at Royal Windsor H.), 1st floor, r. Homme Chrétien 2, ⊠ 1000, ℘ (0 2)
505 55 55, *Fax (0 2) 505 55 00* – ▤ P. AE ① E *VISA* JCB. ✳   JYZ n
closed Saturday lunch, Sunday and mid July-mid August – **Meals** Lunch 1490 – a la carte
1750/2450.

Aux Armes de Bruxelles, r. Bouchers 13, ⊠ 1000, ℘ (0 2) 511 55 98, *Fax (0 2)*
514 33 81, Open until 11 p.m., « Brussels atmosphere » – ▤. AE ① E *VISA* JCB JY
closed Monday except Bank Holidays and 15 June-12 July – **Meals** Lunch 895 b.i. – 1100/1695

La Tête d'Or, r. Tête d'Or 9, ⊠ 1000, ℘ (0 2) 511 02 01, *Fax (0 2) 502 44 91,* « Ancient
Brussels residence » – AE ① E *VISA*. ✳   JY u
Meals Lunch 950 – 1395/1495.

Le Cerf, Grand'Place 20, ⊠ 1000, ℘ (0 2) 511 47 91, *Fax (0 2) 546 09 59*   JY z
closed Sunday – **Meals** (dinner only until 11 p.m. except Wednesday) a la carte 1250/1700

Falstaff Gourmand, r. Pierres 38, ⊠ 1000, ℘ (0 2) 512 17 61 – ▤. AE ① E *VISA*
closed Sunday dinner, Monday and last 2 weeks July-first week August – **Meals** Lunch 595
– 950/1250.   JY m

L'Ogenblik, Galerie des Princes 1, ⊠ 1000, ℘ (0 2) 511 61 51, *Fax (0 2) 513 41 58,*
Open until midnight, « Ancient pub interior » – AE ① E *VISA* JCB   JY p
closed Sunday – **Meals** – a la carte 1700/2400.

La Roue d'Or, r. Chapeliers 26, ⊠ 1000, ℘ (0 2) 514 25 54, *Fax (0 2) 512 30 81,* Open
until midnight, « Typical ancient Brussels pub with surrealist murals » – AE ① E *VISA* JY y
closed August – **Meals** – a la carte approx. 1400.

't Kelderke, Grand'Place 15, ⊠ 1000, ℘ (0 2) 513 73 44, *Fax (0 2) 512 30 81,* « Pub
in a vaulted cellar, Brussels atmosphere », Regional cooking, open until 2 a.m. – AE ①
VISA   JY
Meals Lunch 275 – a la carte 850/1200.

Quartier Ste-Catherine (Marché-aux-Poissons)

Atlas ⊗ without rest, r. Vieux Marché-aux-Grains 30, ⊠ 1000, ℘ (0 2) 502 60 06
Fax (0 2) 502 69 35 – |≜| TV ☎ ⇔ – 🔬 40. AE ① E *VISA*   ER a
83 rm ⊒ 2900/5350, 5 suites.

Astrid without rest, pl. du Samedi 11, ⊠ 1000, ℘ (0 2) 219 31 19, *Fax (0 2) 219 31 70*
– |≜| TV ☎ 🕭 ⇔ – 🔬 25-120. ① E *VISA*   JY b
100 rm ⊒ 5500/6500.

BELGIUM

Ibis Brussels City without rest, r. Joseph Plateau 2, ✉ 1000, ℘ (0 2) 513 76 20, *Fax (0 2) 514 22 14* – ▯ ✇ TV ☎ ♿ – 🛆 25-80. AE ⓪ E VISA JCB JY a
☕ 300 – **235 rm** 3600.

La Sirène d'Or, pl. Ste-Catherine 1a, ✉ 1000, ℘ (0 2) 513 51 98, *Fax (0 2) 502 13 05*, Seafood – ▭ Ⓟ. AE ⓪ E VISA ER g
closed Sunday, Monday and first 3 weeks August – **Meals** – 800/1350.

François, quai aux Briques 2, ✉ 1000, ℘ (0 2) 511 60 89, *Fax (0 2) 512 06 67*, 🌿, Oyster bar, seafood – ▭. AE ⓪ E VISA JCB JY k
closed Monday – **Meals** *Lunch 995* – a la carte 1600/1950.

La Belle Maraîchère, pl. Ste-Catherine 11, ✉ 1000, ℘ (0 2) 512 97 59, *Fax (0 2) 513 76 91*, Seafood – ▭ Ⓟ. AE ⓪ E VISA JY k
closed Wednesday and Thursday – **Meals** – 995/1750.

La Truite d'Argent and H. Welcome with rm, quai au Bois-à-Brûler 23, ✉ 1000, ℘ (0 2) 219 95 46, *Fax (0 2) 217 18 87*, 🌿 – ▯, ▭ rest, TV ☎. ⓪ E VISA JY h
Meals (Seafood) *(closed Saturday lunch, Sunday, Bank Holidays, 1 week August and 20 December-15 January) Lunch 1000 b.i.* – 1080/1540 – ☕ 350 – **10 rm** 2300/3200.

Le Loup-Galant, quai aux Barques 4, ✉ 1000, ℘ (0 2) 219 99 98, *Fax (0 2) 219 99 98* – AE ⓪ E VISA EQ a
closed Sunday, Monday, Bank Holidays, 1 week Easter, 1 to 15 August and 24 to 31 December – **Meals** *Lunch 490* – 960/1390.

Quartier des Sablons

Jolly du Grand Sablon Ⓜ, r. Bodenbroek 2, ✉ 1000, ℘ (0 2) 512 88 00, *Telex 20397, Fax (0 2) 512 67 66* – ▯ ✇ ▭ TV ☎ 🚗 – 🛆 25-100. AE ⓪ E VISA JCB. 🌿 KZ p
Meals a la carte 1650/1950 – **195 rm** ☕ 9500/10600, 6 suites.

L'Écailler du Palais Royal (Basso), r. Bodenbroek 18, ✉ 1000, ℘ (0 2) 512 87 51, *Fax (0 2) 511 99 50*, Seafood – ▭. AE ⓪ E VISA JCB KZ r
closed Sunday, Bank Holidays, 2 to 10 April and 2 to 31 August – **Meals** – a la carte 2650/3400
Spec. Soufflé d'oursins (November-February). Grenadin de saumon d'Écosse. Turbot rôti à l'arête.

Au Duc d'Arenberg, pl. du Petit Sablon 9, ✉ 1000, ℘ (0 2) 511 14 75, *Fax (0 2) 512 92 92*, 🌿, « Collection of modern paintings » – E VISA KZ a
closed Sunday, Bank Holidays and last week December – **Meals** *Lunch 1600* – 2100.

Castello Banfi, r. Bodenbroek 12, ✉ 1000, ℘ (0 2) 512 87 94, *Fax (0 2) 512 87 94*, Partly Italian cuisine – ▭. AE ⓪ E VISA KZ q
closed Sunday lunch June-July, Sunday dinner, Monday, 1 week Easter, last 3 weeks August and late December – **Meals** *Lunch 995* – 1695.

"Chez Marius" En Provence, pl. du Petit Sablon 1, ✉ 1000, ℘ (0 2) 511 12 08, *Fax (0 2) 512 27 89* – AE ⓪ E VISA KZ s
closed Sunday and Bank Holidays – **Meals** *Lunch 850* – 1100/2000.

Trente rue de la Paille (Martiny), r. Paille 30, ✉ 1000, ℘ (0 2) 512 07 15, *Fax (0 2) 514 23 33*, Open until 11.30 p.m. – ▭. AE ⓪ E VISA JZ x
closed Saturday, Sunday, Bank Holidays, mid July-mid August and Christmas-New Year – **Meals** *Lunch 1250* – a la carte 1700/2350
Spec. Carpaccio de saumon mariné au citron vert et poivre rose. Filet de veau aux girolles. Panaché de fondants aux chocolats noir et blanc.

La Clef des Champs, r. Rollebeek 23, ✉ 1000, ℘ (0 2) 512 11 93, *Fax (0 2) 513 89 49*, 🌿 – ▭. AE ⓪ E VISA JZ k
closed Sunday, Monday and Bank Holidays – **Meals** – 1050/1290.

La Tortue du Zoute, r. Rollebeek 31, ✉ 1000, ℘ (0 2) 513 10 62, *Fax (0 2) 381 02 90*, 🌿 – AE ⓪ E VISA JCB JZ k
closed Tuesday, Sunday dinner, carnival holiday and 22 December-5 January – **Meals** *Lunch 650* – 890/1590.

Lola, pl. du Grand Sablon 33, ✉ 1000, ℘ (0 2) 514 24 60, Open until 11.30 p.m. – ▭. AE E VISA JZ c
Meals – a la carte approx. 1100.

Quartier Palais de Justice

Hilton, bd de Waterloo 38, ✉ 1000, ℘ (0 2) 504 11 11, *Fax (0 2) 504 21 11*, ≤ town, 🏋 ⚖ – ▯ ✇ ▭ TV ☎ ♿ 🚗 – 🛆 45-600. AE ⓪ E VISA JCB FS s
Meals see rest **Maison du Bœuf** below – **Café d'Egmont** 1090 – ☕ 925 – **422 rm** 9500/12900, 7 suites.

XXXX **Maison du Bœuf** - (at Hilton H.), 1st floor, bd de Waterloo 38, ✉ 1000, ℰ (0 2) 504 11 11, *Telex 22744, Fax (0 2) 504 21 11*, ≤ – ▤ Ⓟ AE ⓞ E VISA JCB — FS s
Meals *Lunch 1750* – a la carte approx. 3300
Spec. Poêlée de langoustines aux épices douces, bisque au Beaumes-de-Venise. Coffre de pigeonneau et foie gras chaud au cacao et salsifis. Tartare maison au caviar.

X **L'Idiot du village,** r. Notre Seigneur 19, ✉ 1000, ℰ (0 2) 502 55 82, Open until 11 p.m. – AE ⓞ E VISA — JZ a
closed Saturday, Sunday, 21 July-15 August and 24 December-3 January – **Meals** *Lunch 500* – a la carte 1200/1650.

X **Les Larmes du Tigre,** r. Wynants 21, ✉ 1000, ℰ (0 2) 512 18 77, *Fax (0 2) 502 10 03*, 😗, Thaï cuisine – AE ⓞ E VISA — ES p
closed Saturday lunch – **Meals** *Lunch 395* – a la carte 900/1300.

Quartier Léopold *(see also at Ixelles)*

AÎÎA **Stanhope,** r. Commerce 9, ✉ 1000, ℰ (0 2) 506 91 11, *Fax (0 2) 512 17 08*, « Town house with walled terrace », ∱, ≘s – ⧢ ▤ TV ☎ ⇔. AE ⓞ E VISA JCB. ⚒ — KZ v
Meals see rest **Brighton** below – ⚏ 750 – **35 rm** ⚏ 6500/14900, 15 suites.

AÎÎA **Swissôtel** Ⓜ, r. Parnasse 19, ✉ 1050, ℰ (0 2) 505 29 29, *Fax (0 2) 505 25 55*, ∱, ≘s, ⊠ – ⧢ ⇚ ▤ TV ☎ & ⇔ – ⚐ 25-360. AE ⓞ E VISA JCB. ⚒ — FS e
Meals (open until 11 p.m.) *(closed Sunday) Lunch 1100* – 1150/1350 – ⚏ 700 – **238 rm** 8300/9300, 19 suites.

XXX **Brighton** - (at Stanhope H.), r. Commerce 9, ✉ 1000, ℰ (0 2) 506 91 11, *Fax (0 2) 512 17 08*, 😗 – ▤. AE ⓞ E VISA JCB. ⚒ — KZ v
closed Saturday, Sunday, Christmas and New Year – **Meals** 1350/2100.

Quartier Louise *(see also at Ixelles and at St-Gilles)*

AÎÎÎA **Conrad** ⚘, av. Louise 71, ✉ 1050, ℰ (0 2) 542 42 42 and 542 48 50 (rest), *Fax (0 2) 542 42 00 and 542 48 42 (rest)*, 😗, « Hotel complex around an early 20C mansion », ∱ – ⧢ ⇚ ▤ TV ☎ & ⇔ – ⚐ 25-650. AE ⓞ E VISA. ⚒ rest — FS f
Meals see rest **La Maison de Maître** below – **Café Wiltcher's** (Buffet)*Lunch 1100* - a la carte 1450/1850 – ⚏ 950 – **254 rm** 14000/17000, 15 suites.

AÎÎA **Bristol Stephanie** Ⓜ, av. Louise 91, ✉ 1050, ℰ (0 2) 543 33 11, *Fax (0 2) 538 03 07*, ∱, ≘s, ⊠ – ⧢ ⇚ ▤ TV ☎ ⇔ – ⚐ 25-215. AE ⓞ E VISA. ⚒ rest — FT g
Meals *(closed Saturday, Sunday, 17 July-15 August and 23 December-3 January) Lunch 950* – a la carte approx. 1400 – ⚏ 780 – **140 rm** 9200/10200, 2 suites.

AÎA **Mayfair,** av. Louise 381, ✉ 1050, ℰ (0 2) 649 98 00, *Fax (0 2) 649 22 49* – ⧢ ⇚ ▤ TV ☎ ⇔ – ⚐ 30-60. AE ⓞ E VISA JCB. ⚒ — FV a
Meals see rest **Taishin** below – **Louis XVI** *(closed Saturday) Lunch 580* - a la carte 1150/1800 – ⚏ 580 – **97 rm** 7200/8200, 2 suites.

ⒷA **Clubhouse** without rest, r. Blanche 4, ✉ 1000, ℰ (0 2) 542 58 00, *Fax (0 2) 537 00 18* – ⧢ ⇚ TV ☎ ⇔ – ⚐ 30. AE ⓞ E VISA JCB. ⚒ — FT h
⚏ 750 – **80 rm** 7200/9400.

ⒷA **Brussels** without rest, av. Louise 315, ✉ 1050, ℰ (0 2) 640 24 15, *Fax (0 2) 647 34 63* – ⧢ ⇚ TV ☎ ⇔ – ⚐ 30. AE ⓞ E VISA JCB — FU b
49 rm ⚏ 3000/5450, 1 suite.

ⒷA **Agenda Louise** without rest, r. Florence 6, ✉ 1000, ℰ (0 2) 539 00 31, *Fax (0 2) 539 00 63* – ⧢ TV ☎ ⇔. AE ⓞ E VISA JCB — FT j
⚏ 300 – **38 rm** 3800/4300.

XXXX **La Maison de Maître** - (at Conrad H.), av. Louise 71, ✉ 1050, ℰ (0 2) 542 47 16, *Fax (0 2) 542 48 42* – ▤ Ⓟ. AE ⓞ E VISA — FS f
closed Saturday lunch, Sunday, Bank Holidays and August – **Meals** *Lunch 1400* – 1950/2850.

XX **La Porte des Indes,** av. Louise 455, ✉ 1050, ℰ (0 2) 647 86 51, *Fax (0 2) 640 30 59*, Indian cuisine, « Exotic decor » – ▤. AE ⓞ E VISA — FV c
closed Sunday lunch – **Meals** *Lunch 650* – a la carte 1250/1700.

XX **Au Palais des Indes,** av. Louise 263, ✉ 1050, ℰ (0 2) 646 09 41, *Fax (0 2) 646 33 05*, Indian cuisine, open until 11 p.m., « Collection of Indian guitars » – ▤. AE ⓞ E VISA JCB
closed lunch Saturday and Sunday – **Meals** *Lunch 695* – a la carte 950/1300. — FU h

XX **Taishin** - (at Mayfair H.), av. Louise 381, ✉ 1050, ℰ (0 2) 649 98 00, *Fax (0 2) 649 22 49*, Japanese cuisine – ▤ Ⓟ. AE ⓞ E VISA JCB. ⚒ — FV v
closed Sunday and Monday – **Meals** *Lunch 450* – 1200/3000.

XX **Tagawa,** av. Louise 279, ✉ 1050, ℰ (0 2) 640 50 95, *Fax (0 2) 648 41 36*, Japanese cuisine – ▤ Ⓟ. AE ⓞ E VISA JCB. ⚒ — FU e
closed Saturday lunch, Sunday and 23 December-3 January – **Meals** 1100/3200.

Quartier Bois de la Cambre

Villa Lorraine (Van de Casserie), av. du Vivier d'Oie 75, ⊠ 1000, ℰ (0 2) 374 31 63, *Fax (0 2) 372 01 95*, ❀, « Shaded terrace » – Ⓟ. AE ⓪ E VISA JCB   GX w
closed Sunday and 3 weeks July – **Meals** *Lunch 1750* – 3000, a la carte 3250/3750
Spec. Chaud-froid de rouget et foie de canard au vinaigre balsamique. Suprème de turbotin au beurre de homard. Coucou de Malines au vin jaune et morilles (April-August).

La Truffe Noire, bd de la Cambre 12, ⊠ 1000, ℰ (0 2) 640 44 22, *Fax (0 2) 647 97 04*, « Elegant interior » – ▤. AE ⓪ E VISA   GV x
closed Saturday lunch, Sunday, last 3 weeks August and first week January – **Meals** *Lunch 1975 b.i.* – 2100, a la carte 3300/3700
Spec. Carpaccio aux truffes. St-Pierre aux poireaux et truffes. Truffe au chocolat noir en cage de sucre.

Quartier Botanique, Gare du Nord *(see also at St-Josse-ten-Noode)*

Sheraton Towers, pl. Rogier 3, ⊠ 1210, ℰ (0 2) 224 31 11, *Fax (0 2) 224 34 56*, ⊬₆, ⊜s, ▨ – ⋕ ⋉ ▤ TV ☎ & ☞ – 🏊 25-600. AE ⓪ E VISA JCB   FQ n
Meals *Crescendo* (Partly buffets, open until 11 p.m.) a la carte 900/1400 – ☲ 840 – 464 rm 11000/13000, 43 suites.

Président World Trade Center, bd E. Jacqmain 180, ⊠ 1000, ℰ (0 2) 203 20 20, *Fax (0 2) 203 24 40*, ⊬₆, ⊜s, 🥢 – ⋕ ⋉ TV ☎ ☞ – 🏊 25-350. AE ⓪ E VISA JCB
Meals *Lunch 990* – a la carte 850/2000 – **286 rm** ☲ 8500/9500, 16 suites.   FQ d

Le Dome with annex Le Dome II Ⓜ, bd du Jardin Botanique 12, ⊠ 1000, ℰ (0 2) 218 06 80, *Fax (0 2) 218 41 12*, ❀ – ⋕ ⋉ ▤ TV ☎ – 🏊 25-100. AE ⓪ E VISA. ❄ rm
Meals *Lunch 650* – a la carte approx. 1100 – **125 rm** ☲ 3000/3500.   FQ m

Président Nord without rest, bd A. Max 107, ⊠ 1000, ℰ (0 2) 219 00 60, *Fax (0 2) 218 12 69* – ⋕ ▤ TV ☎. AE ⓪ E VISA JCB. ❄   FQ k
63 rm ☲ 3900/4900.

Quartier Atomium (Centenaire - Trade Mart - Laeken)

Holiday Inn Garden Court, Parc des Expositions - av. Impératrice Charlotte 6, ⊠ 1020, ℰ (0 2) 478 70 80, *Fax (0 2) 478 10 00*, ❀ – ⋕ ⋉ TV ☎ Ⓟ – 🏊 25-200. AE ⓪ E VISA   BK e
Meals *Lunch 680* – a la carte 1100/1400 – **79 rm** ☲ 4350/4750.

Les Baguettes Impériales (Mme Ma), av. J. Sobieski 70, ⊠ 1020, ℰ (0 2) 479 67 32, *Fax (0 2) 479 67 32*, ❀, Partly Vietnamese cuisine, « Terrace » – ▤. AE ⓪ E VISA. ❄
closed Tuesday, Sunday dinner, 2 weeks Easter and August – **Meals** a la carte 1800/2500
Spec. Mï au homard. Crêpe croustillante au homard. Pigeonneau farci aux nids d'hirondelle.

Ming Dynasty, Parc des Expositions - av. de l'Esplanade BP 9, ⊠ 1020, ℰ (0 2) 475 23 45, *Fax (0 2) 475 23 50*, Chinese cuisine, open until 11 p.m. – ▤ Ⓟ. AE ⓪ E VISA
closed Saturday lunch, Sunday and 19 July-15 August – **Meals** *Lunch 750* – a la carte approx. 1000.

Lychee, r. De Wand 118, ⊠ 1020, ℰ (0 2) 268 19 14, *Fax (0 2) 268 19 14*, Chinese cuisine, open until midnight – ▤. AE ⓪ E VISA
closed 15 July-15 August – **Meals** *Lunch 325* – a la carte approx. 1000.

Le Frascati, bd E. Bockstael 201, ⊠ 1020, ℰ (0 2) 426 52 73, *Fax (0 2) 426 52 73*, Italian cuisine, with trattoria, open until 11 p.m. – ▤. AE ⓪ E VISA JCB
closed Saturday lunch, Sunday and 1 to 20 August – **Meals** *Lunch 1200 b.i.* – a la carte approx. 1900.

ANDERLECHT

Le Prince de Liège, chaussée de Ninove 664, ⊠ 1070, ℰ (0 2) 522 16 00, *Fax (0 2) 520 81 85* – ⋕ TV ☎ ☞ – 🏊 25. AE ⓪ E VISA
Meals *(closed Sunday dinner and 9 July-7 August)* *Lunch 545* – 850/1395 – **32 rm** ☲ 1950/3250.

Ustel, Square de l'Aviation 6, ⊠ 1070, ℰ (0 2) 520 60 53 and 522 30 25 (rest), *Fax (0 2) 520 33 28*, ❀ – ⋕ ⋉ TV ☎ ☞ – 🏊 25-60. AE ⓪ E VISA. ❄
Meals *La Grande Écluse* « In the machinery room of a lock » (open until 11 p.m.) *(closed lunch Saturday and Sunday)* *Lunch 450* - 1190 – **94 rm** ☲ 3600/4300.

Erasme, rte de Lennik 790, ⊠ 1070, ℰ (0 2) 523 62 82, *Fax (0 2) 523 62 83*, ❀ – ⋕ ⋉, ▤ rest, TV ☎ & Ⓟ – 🏊 25-80. AE ⓪ E VISA JCB
Meals (Pub rest) *(closed 1 to 15 August)* *Lunch 425* – 655 – **52 rm** ☲ 2850.

Saint Guidon 2nd floor, in the R.S.C. Anderlecht football stadium, av. Théo Verbeeck 2, ⊠ 1070, ℰ (0 2) 520 55 36, *Fax (0 2) 523 38 27* – ▤ Ⓟ – 🏊 25-500. ⓪ E VISA JCB
closed Saturday, Sunday, Bank Holidays, first league match days and 15 June-15 July – **Meals** (lunch only) 995/2100 b.i. – a la carte approx. 2500
Spec. Matelote persillée d'anguilles en terrine. Sole meunière, purée de pommes de terre et carottes au cerfeuil. Nougat glacé.

XX **Alain Cornelis,** av. Paul Janson 82, ⊠ 1070, ✆ (0 2) 523 20 83, Fax (0 2) 523 20 83,
😶 – AE ① E VISA. ✱
*closed Wednesday dinner, Saturday lunch, Sunday, Bank Holidays, Easter week, first 2
weeks August and Christmas-New Year* – **Meals** a la carte 1450/2000.

XX **La Brouette,** bd Prince de Liège 61, ⊠ 1070, ✆ (0 2) 522 51 69, Fax (0 2) 522 51 69
– AE ① E VISA
closed Saturday lunch, Sunday dinner, Monday and July – **Meals** Lunch 750 – 1300.

X **La Paix,** r. Ropsy-Chaudron 49 (opposite the slaughterhouse), ⊠ 1070, ✆ (0 2)
523 09 58, Fax (0 2) 520 10 39, Pub rest – AE ① E VISA. ✱
closed Saturday, Sunday and last 3 weeks July – **Meals** (lunch only except Friday) a la carte
1000/1400.

AUDERGHEM (OUDERGEM)

XX **La Grignotière** (Chanson), chaussée de Wavre 2041, ⊠ 1160, ✆ (0 2) 672 81 85,
❀ Fax (0 2) 672 81 85 – AE ① E VISA
closed Sunday, Monday and August – **Meals** – 1750/2000
Spec. Langoustines à la vapeur de verveine, ragoût de girolles. Noix de ris de veau rôties
sur bois de réglisse, ragoût de champignons. Turbotin rôti et émulsion de cerfeuil.

XX **L'Abbaye de Rouge Cloître,** r. Rouge Cloître 8, ⊠ 1160, ✆ (0 2) 672 45 25, Fax (0 2)
660 12 01, 😶, « On the edge of a forest » – Ⓟ – ▲ 25-45. AE ① E VISA
closed Tuesday, after 8 p.m. and 1 to 15 January – **Meals** Lunch 550 – a la carte approx
1100.

X **La Citronnelle,** chaussée de Wavre 1377, ⊠ 1160, ✆ (0 2) 672 98 43, Fax (0 2)
672 98 43, 😶, Vietnamese cuisine – AE ① E VISA
closed Monday, Saturday lunch and last 2 weeks August – Meals Lunch 420 – a la carte
approx. 1000.

X **New Asia,** chaussée de Wavre 1240, ⊠ 1160, ✆ (0 2) 660 62 06, Fax (0 2) 673 40 54,
😶, Chinese cuisine, « Shaded terrace » – ▤. AE ① E VISA. ✱　　　　　　　　　HU a
closed Monday except Bank Holidays and last 3 weeks July – **Meals** Lunch 290 – 480/920

X **La Khaïma,** chaussée de Wavre 1390, ⊠ 1160, ✆ (0 2) 675 00 04, Fax (0 2) 675 00 04,
Moroccan cuisine, open until 11 p.m., « Berber tent interior theme » – ✱
closed August – **Meals** 995.

ETTERBEEK

XX **Stirwen** (Troubat), chaussée St-Pierre 15, ⊠ 1040, ✆ (0 2) 640 85 41, Fax (0 2)
❀ 648 43 08 – AE ① E VISA JCB　　　　　　　　　　　　　　　　　　　GS a
*closed Saturday dinner in July-August, Saturday lunch, Sunday, 2 weeks August and late
December* – **Meals** Lunch 1050 – a la carte approx. 1700
Spec. Tête de veau ravigote. Désossé de pieds de porc façon Ste-Menehould. Joue de
boeuf braisée à la bourguignonne.

XX **Grillange** 1st floor, av. Eudore Pirmez 7, ⊠ 1040, ✆ (0 2) 649 26 85, Fax (0 2)
649 26 85, Spanish cuisine – AE ① E VISA. ✱　　　　　　　　　　　　　GT a
closed Sunday, Monday and 15 July-20 August – **Meals** Lunch 500 – 1200/1500.

Quartier Cinquantenaire (Montgomery)

🏠 **Clubhouse Park** without rest, av. de l'Yser 21, ⊠ 1040, ✆ (0 2) 735 74 00, Fax (0 2)
735 19 67, 🛁, 🚭, 🏊 – 📶 ✦ TV ☎ – ▲ 25-50. AE ① E VISA JCB　　　　HS c
☕ 750 – 51 rm ☕ 7200/8400.

XX **Le Serpolet,** av. de Tervuren 59, ⊠ 1040, ✆ (0 2) 736 17 01, Fax (0 2) 736 67 85, 😶
– ▤. AE ① E VISA　　　　　　　　　　　　　　　　　　　　　　　HS b
closed Saturday lunch and Sunday dinner – **Meals** Lunch 695 – 995.

X **Momotaro,** av. d'Auderghem 106, ⊠ 1040, ✆ (0 2) 734 06 64, Fax (0 2) 734 64 18,
Japanese cuisine with Sushi-bar – AE ① E VISA. ✱　　　　　　　　　　GS t
closed lunch Saturday and Sunday and first 2 weeks August – **Meals** Lunch 395 – 850/1850

EVERE

🏠 **Belson** without rest, chaussée de Louvain 805, ⊠ 1140, ✆ (0 2) 705 20 30, Fax (0 2)
705 20 43, 🛁 – 📶 ✦ ▤ TV ☎ 🚗 – ▲ 25. AE ① E VISA. ✱
☕ 700 – **131 rm** 2990/9650, 3 suites.

🏠 **Mercure,** av. J. Bordet 74, ⊠ 1140, ✆ (0 2) 726 73 35, Fax (0 2) 726 82 95, 😶 – 📶
✦ TV ☎ 🚫 🚗 – ▲ 25-120. AE ① E VISA
Meals (*closed lunch Saturday and Sunday*) – a la carte 1000/1400 – ☕ 600 – **113 rm**
4500/5950, 7 suites.

🏠 **Evergreen** without rest, av. V. Day 1, ⊠ 1140, ✆ (0 2) 726 70 15, Fax (0 2) 726 62 60
– TV ☎. AE ① E VISA
20 rm ☕ 2000/3150.

FOREST (VORST)

De Fierlant without rest, r. De Fierlant 67, ⊠ 1190, ℘ (0 2) 538 60 70, Fax (0 2) 538 91 99 – 🛗 TV ☎. AE ① E VISA
closed 23 July-16 August and 24 December-3 January – **40 rm** ⊒ 2300/2600.

GANSHOREN

Bruneau, av. Broustin 75, ⊠ 1083, ℘ (0 2) 427 69 78, Fax (0 2) 425 97 26, 🌳, « Terrace » – 🗐. AE ① E VISA
closed holiday Thursdays, Tuesday dinner, Wednesday, August and 1 to 10 February – **Meals** *Lunch 1750* – 3245/4675, – a la carte 2750/3400
Spec. Ravioles de céleri aux truffes. Dos de cabillaud à la royale. Suprème de coucou de Malines arlequin.

Claude Dupont, av. Vital Riethuisen 46, ⊠ 1083, ℘ (0 2) 426 00 00, Fax (0 2) 426 65 40 – AE ① E VISA
closed Monday, Tuesday and July – **Meals** *Lunch 1775* – 2175/3250, – a la carte 2100/3000
Spec. Cassolette d'écrevisses Nantua (July-January). Canette des bois au cidre bouché. Selle de chevreuil rôtie au thym (October-December).

San Daniele, av. Charles-Quint 6, ⊠ 1083, ℘ (0 2) 426 79 23, Fax (0 2) 426 92 14, Partly Italian cuisine – 🗐. AE ① E VISA
closed Sunday, Monday dinner and 15 July-20 August – **Meals** – a la carte 1200/2100.

Cambrils 1st floor, av. Charles-Quint 365, ⊠ 1083, ℘ (0 2) 465 35 82, Fax (0 2) 465 76 63, 🌳 – 🗐. AE E VISA
closed dinner Monday and Thursday, Sunday, and 15 July-15 August – **Meals** *Lunch 890* – 1090/1230.

IXELLES (ELSENE)

Yen, r. Lesbroussart 49, ⊠ 1050, ℘ (0 2) 649 07 47, 🌳, Vietnamese cuisine, open until 11 p.m. – AE ① E VISA. ⌀   FU f
closed Sunday – **Meals** *Lunch 320* – a la carte 850/1150.

Quartier Boondael (University)

Le Couvert d'Argent, pl. Marie-José 9, ⊠ 1050, ℘ (0 2) 648 45 45, Fax (0 2) 648 22 28, 🌳, « Elegant pavilion in garden » – 🅟. AE ① E VISA JCB   GX y
closed Sunday, Monday, 1 week Easter and last 2 weeks August – **Meals** – 1050/2250.

L'Aub. de Boendael, square du Vieux Tilleul 12, ⊠ 1050, ℘ (0 2) 672 70 55, Fax (0 2) 660 75 82, 🌳, Grill rest, « Rustic » – 🗐 🅟. AE ① E VISA   HX h
closed Saturday, Sunday, Bank Holidays, 17 July-15 August and 25 December-2 January – **Meals** – 1375 b.i..

La Pagode d'Or, chaussée de Boondael 332, ⊠ 1050, ℘ (0 2) 649 06 56, Fax (0 2) 649 06 56, 🌳, Vietnamese cuisine, open until 11 p.m. – AE ① E VISA. ⌀   GV m
closed Monday – **Meals** *Lunch 350* – 890/1350.

La Brasserie Marebœuf, av. de la Couronne 445, ⊠ 1050, ℘ (0 2) 648 99 06, Fax (0 2) 648 38 30, Oyster bar, open until midnight – 🗐. AE ① E VISA   GHV t
closed Sunday and Bank Holidays – **Meals** *Lunch 590* – 895.

Quartier Bascule

Capital, chaussée de Vleurgat 191, ⊠ 1050, ℘ (0 2) 646 64 20, Fax (0 2) 646 33 14, 🌳 – 🛗 ✂, 🗐 rest, TV ☎ 🚗 – 🕍 25-40. AE ① E VISA JCB. ⌀   FU c
Meals *(closed Saturday) Lunch 590* – a la carte 1000/1300 – **62 rm** ⊒ 3900/4300.

La Mosaïque, r. Forestière 23, ⊠ 1050, ℘ (0 2) 649 02 35, Fax (0 2) 649 02 35, 🌳 – 🅟. AE ① E VISA   FU p
closed Saturday lunch, Sunday, Bank Holidays, 5 to 7 April, 24 to 26 May, 16 August-5 September and 24 December-1 January – **Meals** *Lunch 1200 b.i.* – 1500 b.i./2500 b.i..

Maison Félix 1st floor, r. Washington 149 (square Henri Michaux), ⊠ 1050, ℘ (0 2) 345 66 93, Fax (0 2) 344 92 85 – AE ① E VISA   FV s
closed Sunday, Monday and last 2 weeks July – **Meals** – 1290.

Le fils de Jules, r. Page 35, ⊠ 1050, ℘ (0 2) 534 00 57, Fax (0 2) 534 52 00, Basque and Landes cuisine, open until 11 p.m. – AE ① E VISA   FU m
closed lunch Saturday and Sunday, 1 to 16 August and 24 December-2 January – **Meals** *Lunch 395* – 890/1200.

Quartier Léopold *(see also at Bruxelles)*

Leopold, r. Luxembourg 35, ⊠ 1050, ℘ (0 2) 511 18 28, Fax (0 2) 514 19 39, 🌳, 🌳 – 🛗 🗐 TV ☎ 🚗 – 🕍 25-60. AE ① E VISA JCB. ⌀ rest   FS y
Meals *(closed Sunday) Lunch 1095* – a la carte 1350/2000 – ⊒ 400 – **88 rm** 3400/5650.

Quartier Louise *(see also at Bruxelles and at St-Gilles)*

Sofitel without rest, av. de la Toison d'Or 40, ⊠ 1050, ℘ (0 2) 514 22 00, Fax (0 2) 514 57 44, ⅃ᵌ – 🛗 ⤬ ▤ TV ☎ – 🛎 25-120. AE ⓞ Ε VISA JCB
☕ 800 – **165 rm** 12000, 5 suites.
FS

Four Points Sheraton M, r. Paul Spaak 15, ⊠ 1000, ℘ (0 2) 645 61 11, Fax (0 2) 646 63 44, 🌿, ⇆s, 🚣 – 🛗 ⤬ ▤ TV ☎ ⅙ 🚗 – 🛎 25-40. AE ⓞ Ε VISA
Meals (dinner only until 11 p.m.) *(closed 15 July-15 August)* a la carte approx. 1100 – ☕ 550 – **128 rm** 3350/6250.
FU

Beau-Site without rest, r. Longue Haie 76, ⊠ 1000, ℘ (0 2) 640 88 89, Fax (0 2) 640 16 11 – 🛗 TV ☎. AE ⓞ Ε VISA
38 rm ☕ 3000.
FT

Argus without rest, r. Capitaine Crespel 6, ⊠ 1050, ℘ (0 2) 514 07 70, Fax (0 2) 514 12 22 – 🛗 TV ☎. AE ⓞ Ε VISA
41 rm ☕ 3300/3600.
FS

O' comme 3 Pommes, pl. du Châtelain 40, ⊠ 1050, ℘ (0 2) 644 03 23, Fax (0 2) 644 03 23, 🌿 – AE Ε VISA
closed lunch Saturday and Monday, Sunday, 15 to 28 February and 15 to 31 August – **Meals** *Lunch* 480 – 1690.
FU

L'Atelier de la Truffe Noire, av. Louise 300, ⊠ 1050, ℘ (0 2) 640 54 55, Fax (0 2) 648 11 44, « Modern brasserie » – AE ⓞ Ε VISA
closed Sunday, last 3 weeks August and first week January – **Meals** (lunch only) a la carte 1200/1700.
FU

Les Perles de Pluie, r. Châtelain 25, ⊠ 1050, ℘ (0 2) 649 67 23, Fax (0 2) 644 07 60, Thaï cuisine, open until 11 p.m. – AE ⓞ Ε VISA
closed Saturday lunch and Monday – **Meals** *Lunch* 460 – 850/1750.
FU

Tutto Pepe, r. Faider 123, ⊠ 1050, ℘ (0 2) 534 96 19, Fax (0 2) 534 96 19, Italian cuisine, open until 11.30 p.m. – AE Ε VISA ⤬
closed Saturday lunch and Sunday – **Meals** a la carte 1000/1750.
FU

MOLENBEEK-ST-JEAN (SINT-JANS-MOLENBEEK)

Le Béarnais, bd Louis Mettewie 318, ⊠ 1080, ℘ (0 2) 411 51 51, Fax (0 2) 410 70 81 – ▤. AE ⓞ Ε VISA JCB
closed Sunday, Monday dinner and 21 July-5 August – **Meals** *Lunch* 1090 – 1600/2500.

ST-GILLES (SINT-GILLIS)

Cascade M without rest, r. Berckmans 128, ⊠ 1060, ℘ (0 2) 538 88 30, Fax (0 2) 538 92 79 – 🛗 ⤬ ▤ TV ☎ 🚗 – 🛎 25. AE ⓞ Ε VISA JCB
80 rm ☕ 6000/6400.
ES

Inada, r. Source 73, ⊠ 1060, ℘ (0 2) 538 01 13, Fax (0 2) 538 01 13 – AE ⓞ Ε VISA
closed Saturday lunch, Sunday, Monday and 16 to 31 July – **Meals** *Lunch* 850 – a la carte 1700/2400.
ET

Le Forcado, chaussée de Charleroi 192, ⊠ 1060, ℘ (0 2) 537 92 20, Fax (0 2) 537 92 20, Portuguese cuisine – ▤. AE ⓞ Ε VISA
closed Sunday, Monday, Bank Holidays and August – **Meals** – a la carte approx. 1300.
EFU

La Mamounia, av. Porte de Hal 9, ⊠ 1060, ℘ (0 2) 537 73 22, Fax (0 2) 539 39 59, Moroccan cuisine, open until 11 p.m. – AE ⓞ Ε VISA JCB
closed Monday except Bank Holidays and mid July-mid August – **Meals** *Lunch* 450 – 745/1295.
ES

Quartier Louise *(see also at Bruxelles and at Ixelles)*

Manos Stephanie without rest, chaussée de Charleroi 28, ⊠ 1060, ℘ (0 2) 539 02 50, Fax (0 2) 537 57 29, « Mansion with particular character » – 🛗 ▤ TV ☎ 🚗. AE ⓞ Ε VISA JCB
48 rm ☕ 6850/8250, 7 suites.
FS

Manos without rest, chaussée de Charleroi 102, ⊠ 1060, ℘ (0 2) 537 96 82, Fax (0 2) 539 36 55, « Elegant town house », 🚣 – 🛗 TV ☎ 🚗 – 🛎 25. AE ⓞ Ε VISA JCB
30 rm ☕ 6850/8250, 9 suites.
FU

Diplomat without rest, r. Jean Stas 32, ⊠ 1060, ℘ (0 2) 537 42 50, Fax (0 2) 539 33 79 – 🛗 TV ☎ 🚗 – 🛎 35. AE ⓞ Ε VISA JCB
68 rm ☕ 6500/7500.
FS

Les Capucines, r. Jourdan 22, ✉ 1060, ✆ (0 2) 538 69 24, *Fax (0 2) 538 69 24*, 🌴
– AE ① E VISA   FS u
closed Sunday, Monday dinner, Bank Holidays, 2 weeks Easter and last 2 weeks August –
Meals Lunch 595 – 995.

I Trulli, r. Jourdan 18, ✉ 1060, ✆ (0 2) 538 98 20, *Fax (0 2) 537 79 30*, 🌴, Partly Italian
cuisine, open until midnight – AE ① E VISA JCB   FS c
closed Sunday, 11 to 31 July and 22 December-4 January – **Meals** Lunch 495 – a la carte
1650/2100.

ST-JOSSE-TEN-NOODE (SINT-JOOST-TEN-NODE)

Quartier Botanique *(see also at Bruxelles)*

Royal Crown Gd H. Mercure, r. Royale 250, ✉ 1210, ✆ (0 2) 220 66 11, *Fax (0 2)*
217 84 44, 🏋, ⇆s – 🛗 ✂ ▤ TV ☎ 🚗 – 🕍 25-550. AE ① E VISA JCB   FQ r
Meals see rest *Rue Royale* below – ⌿ 650 – **310 rm** 8000, 5 suites.

Crowne Plaza, r. Gineste 3, ✉ 1210, ✆ (0 2) 203 62 00, *Fax (0 2) 203 55 55*, 🌴, 🏋,
⇆s – 🛗 ✂ ▤ TV ☎ – 🕍 25-500. AE ① E VISA JCB. ✖ rest   FQ v
Meals *Le Temps Présent* (open until 11 p.m.) Lunch 895 - a la carte 1450/1800 – ⌿ 900
– **358 rm** 7800/8800.

Art H. Siru, pl. Rogier 1, ✉ 1210, ✆ (0 2) 203 35 80 and 203 20 03 (rest), *Fax (0 2)*
203 33 03, « Each room decorated by a contemporary Belgian artist » – 🛗 ✂ TV ☎ –
🕍 25-80. AE ① E VISA. ✖   FQ p
Meals (Brasserie) *(closed Sunday)* a la carte approx. 1300 – **101 rm** ⌿ 5500/6200.

Albert Premier without rest, pl. Rogier 20, ✉ 1210, ✆ (0 2) 203 31 25, *Fax (0 2)*
203 43 31 – 🛗 TV ☎ – 🕍 25-60. ① E VISA   FQ q
285 rm ⌿ 3000/4500.

Rue Royale - (at Royal Crown Gd H. Mercure), r. Royale 250, ✉ 1210, ✆ (0 2) 220 66 11,
Fax (0 2) 217 84 44 – ▤ 🅿. AE ① E VISA JCB   FQ r
closed Sunday – **Meals** Lunch 1350 – a la carte 1900/2500.

De Ultieme Hallucinatie, r. Royale 316, ✉ 1210, ✆ (0 2) 217 06 14, *Fax (0 2)*
217 72 40, « Art Nouveau interior » – 🅿 – 🕍 40. AE ① E VISA. ✖   FQ t
closed Saturday lunch, Sunday, Bank Holidays and 18 July-16 August – **Meals** Lunch 1075
– 1450/2750 b.i..

Les Dames Tartine, chaussée de Haecht 58, ✉ 1210, ✆ (0 2) 218 45 49, *Fax (0 2)*
218 45 49 – AE ① E VISA   FQ s
closed Sunday and Monday – **Meals** Lunch 750 – 990/1395.

SCHAERBEEK (SCHAARBEEK)

Senza Nome, r. Royale Ste-Marie 22, ✉ 1030, ✆ (0 2) 223 16 17, *Fax (0 2) 223 16 17*,
Italian cuisine – ▤. E VISA. ✖   FQ u
closed Saturday lunch, Sunday and August – **Meals** a la carte 1000/1500.

Quartier Meiser

Lambermont (with annex 🏨 - 47 rm) without rest, Allée des Frésias 18, ✉ 1030,
✆ (0 2) 246 02 11, *Fax (0 2) 246 02 00*, 🏋 – 🛗 TV ☎ 🚗 – 🕍 25. AE ① E VISA
8 rm ⌿ 3600/4100, 43 suites.   GHQ c

Le Cadre Noir, av. Milcamps 158, ✉ 1030, ✆ (0 2) 734 14 45, Seafood – AE ① E
VISA   HR v
closed Saturday lunch, Sunday dinner, Monday and 15 to 31 July – **Meals** – 950/1100.

Amici miei, bd. Gén. Wahis 248, ✉ 1030, ✆ (0 2) 705 49 80, *Fax (0 2) 705 29 65*, Italian
cuisine – AE ① E VISA   HQ k
closed Saturday lunch, Sunday and Bank Holidays – **Meals** – a la carte approx. 1400.

Le Zinneke, pl. de la Patrie 26, ✉ 1030, ✆ (0 2) 216 79 50, *Fax (0 2) 245 03 22*, 🌴,
Partly Indonesian cuisine – AE ① E VISA   GHQ f
closed Tuesday, Saturday lunch and first 2 weeks September – **Meals** Lunch 495 – a la carte
850/1300.

UCCLE (UKKEL)

County House, square des Héros 2, ✉ 1180, ✆ (0 2) 375 44 20, *Fax (0 2) 375 31 22*
– 🛗, ▤ rest, TV ☎ 🚗 – 🕍 25-80. AE ① E VISA. ✖   EX b
Meals a la carte 1150/1600 – **86 rm** ⌿ 3500/6000, 16 suites.

Les Frères Romano, av. de Fré 182, ✉ 1180, ✆ (0 2) 374 70 98, *Fax (0 2) 374 04 18*
– 🅿. AE ① E VISA   FX d
closed Sunday, Bank Holidays and last 3 weeks August – **Meals** Lunch 975 – a la carte
1600/2100.

XX **Villa d'Este,** r. Etoile 142, ⊠ 1180, ℰ (0 2) 376 48 48, 🌳, « Terrace » – 🅿. 🆎 (
E VISA
closed Sunday dinner, Monday, July and late December – **Meals** 990/1750.

XX **L'Amandier,** av. de Fré 184, ⊠ 1180, ℰ (0 2) 374 03 95, Fax (0 2) 374 86 92, 🌳
« Terrace overlooking the garden » – 🅿. 🆎 ① E VISA   FX
closed Saturday lunch and Sunday – **Meals** Lunch 950 – a la carte approx. 1900.

XX **Blue Elephant,** chaussée de Waterloo 1120, ⊠ 1180, ℰ (0 2) 374 49 62, Fax (0
375 44 68, Thaï cuisine, « Exotic decor » – 🗐 🅿. 🆎 ① E VISA   GX
closed Saturday lunch – **Meals** Lunch 650 – a la carte 1050/1650.

XX **Chutney,** chaussée de Waterloo 1134, ⊠ 1180, ℰ (0 2) 375 69 46, Fax (0 2) 375 69 4
Indian cuisine – 🆎 ① E VISA JCB   GX
closed Sunday dinner and Monday – **Meals** Lunch 450 – 890/1350.

XX **Willy et Marianne,** chaussée d'Alsemberg 705, ⊠ 1180, ℰ (0 2) 343 60 09 – 🆎 (
E VISA   EX
closed Tuesday, Wednesday, late July-early August and late January-early February
Meals Lunch 450 – 995.

X **La Cité du Dragon,** chaussée de Waterloo 1024, ⊠ 1180, ℰ (0 2) 375 80 80, Fax (0
375 69 77, 🌳, Chinese cuisine, open until 11 p.m., « Exotic garden with fountains » – (
🆎 ① E VISA   GX
Meals Lunch 485 – 810/2350.

X **Le Passage,** av. J. et P. Carsoel 13, ⊠ 1180, ℰ (0 2) 374 66 94, Fax (0 2) 374 69 2
🌳 – 🅿. 🆎 ① E VISA
closed Saturday lunch, Sunday and 3 weeks July – **Meals** Lunch 550 – a la carte 1300
1800.

X **De Hoef,** r. Edith Cavell 218, ⊠ 1180, ℰ (0 2) 374 34 17, Fax (0 2) 375 30 84, 🌳, Gr
rest, « 17C inn » – 🆎 ① E VISA   FX
closed 10 to 31 July – **Meals** Lunch 395 – 795.

X **Brasseries Georges,** av. Winston Churchill 259, ⊠ 1180, ℰ (0 2) 347 21 0(
Fax (0 2) 344 02 45, 🌳, Oyster bar, open until midnight – 🗐 🅿. 🆎 ①
VISA   FV
Meals Lunch 600 – 975/1990.

WATERMAEL-BOITSFORT (WATERMAAL-BOSVOORDE)

XX **Au Vieux Boitsfort** (Gillet), pl. Bischoffsheim 9, ⊠ 1170, ℰ (0 2) 672 23 32, Fax (0
660 22 94, 🌳 – 🆎 ① E VISA JCB
closed Saturday lunch and Sunday – **Meals** (booking essential) Lunch 1590 – a la cart
1900/2400
Spec. Langoustines à la tomate confite et huile d'olives. Manchons de volaille braisés à l'a
doux et truffes. Frangipane de pommes au coulis d'abricots.

XX **Les Rives du Gange,** av. de la Fauconnerie 1, ⊠ 1170, ℰ (0 2) 672 16 01, Fax (0 2
672 43 30, 🌳, Indian cuisine – 🆎 ① E VISA JCB. 🚫
Meals Lunch 695 – 1250.

X **L'Entre-Temps,** r. Philippe Dewolfs 7, ⊠ 1170, ℰ (0 2) 672 87 20, Fax (0 2) 672 87 2(
🌳, Brasserie – 🆎 ① E VISA JCB
closed Tuesday dinner, Wednesday and 21 July-15 August – **Meals** Lunch 525
895.

X **La Maison de Thaïlande,** r. Middelbourg 22, ⊠ 1170, ℰ (0 2) 672 26 57, Fax (0 2
675 90 81, 🌳, Thaï cuisine – 🆎 ① E VISA   CN
closed lunch Saturday and Sunday and Tuesday – **Meals** – a la carte 850/1200.

X **Le Grill,** r. Trois Tilleuls 1, ⊠ 1170, ℰ (0 2) 672 95 13, Fax (0 2) 660 22 94, Grill res
– 🆎 ① E VISA JCB
closed Saturday lunch and Sunday dinner – **Meals** – 800.

WOLUWÉ-ST-LAMBERT (SINT-LAMBRECHTS-WOLUWE)

🏨 **Sodehotel La Woluwe** M 🚫, av. E. Mounier 5, ⊠ 1200, ℰ (0 2) 775 21 11, Fax (0 2
770 47 80, 🌳 – 🛗 🍴 🗐 📺 ☎ 🚼 🚗 🅿 – 🛎 25-200. 🆎 ① E VISA
🚫 rest
Meals Le Lidrus a la carte approx. 1400 – ☕ 695 – **112 rm** 8200/13200, 8 suites.

🏠 **Lambeau** M without rest, av. Lambeau 150, ⊠ 1200, ℰ (0 2) 732 51 70, Fax (0 2
732 54 90 – 🛗 📺 ☎. 🆎 ① E VISA   HR
24 rm ☕ 2600/3400.

XXX **Mon Manège à Toi,** r. Neerveld 1, ⊠ 1200, ℰ (0 2) 770 02 38, Fax (0 2) 762 95 8(
« Floral garden » – 🅿. 🆎 ① E VISA JCB. 🚫
closed Saturday lunch, Sunday and late December – **Meals** 1850.

BELGIUM

XX **Moulin Lindekemale**, av. J.-F. Debecker 6, ⊠ 1200, ℘ (0 2) 770 90 57, Fax (0 2) 762 94 57, « Former watermill » – **P**. AE ◑ E VISA. ※ *closed Saturday lunch, Sunday dinner, Monday, Easter week, last week July-first week August and Christmas week* – **Meals** *Lunch 1500 b.i.* – a la carte approx. 1500.

X **Les Amis du Cep**, r. Th. Decuyper 136, ⊠ 1200, ℘ (0 2) 762 62 95, Fax (0 2) 771 20 32, ※ – E VISA. ※ *closed Sunday and Monday* – **Meals** *Lunch 425* – 1250.

WOLUWÉ-ST-PIERRE (SINT-PIETERS-WOLUWE)

Montgomery M ※, av. de Tervuren 134, ⊠ 1150, ℘ (0 2) 741 85 11, Fax (0 2) 741 85 00, ₤₅, ≘s – ⌀ ⊁ ▤ TV ☎ ⇔ – ₤ 35. AE ◑ E VISA JCB. ※
HS k
Meals *La Duchesse* (*closed weekends and Bank Holidays*) *Lunch 1050* - 1500/1790 – ☕ 600 – **61 rm** 10400/13300, 2 suites.

XXX **Des 3 Couleurs** (Tourneur), av. de Tervuren 453, ⊠ 1150, ℘ (0 2) 770 33 21, Fax (0 2) 770 80 45, ※, « Terrace » – AE ◑ E VISA
closed Saturday lunch, Sunday dinner, Monday and 16 August-15 September – **Meals** *Lunch 1800 b.i.* – 2000, a la carte approx. 2400
Spec. Langoustines en brunoise de légumes, sauce au Champagne. Duo de ris et rognon de veau. Gibiers en saison.

XX **Le Vignoble de Margot**, av. de Tervuren 368, ⊠ 1150, ℘ (0 2) 779 23 23, Fax (0 2) 779 05 45, ≤, ※, Brasserie with oyster bar, « Surrounded by vines, overlooking park and ponds » – ▤ **P**. ◑ E VISA
closed Saturday lunch, Sunday, Bank Holidays and 24 December-3 January – **Meals** – a la carte 1700/2000.

XX **Medicis**, av. de l'Escrime 124, ⊠ 1150, ℘ (0 2) 779 07 00, Fax (0 2) 779 19 24, ※ – AE ◑ E VISA
closed Saturday lunch and Sunday – **Meals** *Lunch 525* – 950/1650.

X **Le Mucha**, av. Jules Dujardin 23, ⊠ 1150, ℘ (0 2) 770 24 14, Fax (0 2) 770 24 14, ※, Partly Italian cuisine, open until 11 p.m. – AE ◑ E VISA
closed Sunday and 1 to 22 September – **Meals** *Lunch 460* – 850/1250.

BRUSSELS ENVIRONS

at Diegem *Brussels-Zaventem motorway Diegem exit* Ⓒ *Machelen pop. 11 582* – ⊠ *1831 Diegem :*

Holiday Inn Airport, Holidaystraat 7 ℘ (0 2) 720 58 65, Fax (0 2) 720 41 45, ₤₅, ≘s, ⊠, ⅓ – ⌀ ⊁ ▤ TV ☎ **P** – ₤ 25-400. AE ◑ E VISA JCB. ※ rest
Meals (open until 11 p.m.) *Lunch 1195 b.i.* – a la carte 1000/1650 – ☕ 675 – **310 rm** 9000.

Sofitel Airport, Bessenveldstraat 15 ℘ (0 2) 713 66 66, Fax (0 2) 721 43 45, ※, ₤₅, ⅓, ⋒ – ⊁ ▤ TV ☎ **P** – ₤ 25-300. AE ◑ E VISA. ※ rest
Meals *La Pléiade* (*closed Friday dinner, Saturday and Sunday*) 1450 – ☕ 750 – **125 rm** 10000/13000.

Novotel Airport, Olmenstraat ℘ (0 2) 725 30 50, Fax (0 2) 721 39 58, ※, ₤₅, ≘s, ⅓ – ⌀ ⊁ ▤ TV ☎ **P** – ₤ 25-100. AE ◑ E VISA JCB
Meals (open until midnight) a la carte approx. 1200 – ☕ 500 – **207 rm** 5450/5650.

Rainbow Airport M, Berkenlaan 4 ℘ (0 2) 721 77 77, Fax (0 2) 721 55 96, ※ – ⌀ ⊁ ▤ TV ☎ & **P** – ₤ 25-80. AE ◑ E VISA JCB. ※
Meals (*closed Saturday, Sunday, Christmas and New Year*) *Lunch 590* – 850 – **99 rm** ☕ 5500/5900.

Holiday Inn Express M without rest, Berkenlaan 5 ℘ (0 2) 725 33 80, Fax (0 2) 725 38 10 – ⌀ ⊁ TV ☎ & **P** – ₤ 25-180. AE ◑ E VISA
79 rm ☕ 4750.

Ibis Airport, Bessenveldstraat 17 ℘ (0 2) 725 43 21, Fax (0 2) 725 40 40, ※ – ⌀ ⊁, ▤ rest, TV ☎ & **P** – ₤ 25-60. AE ◑ E VISA JCB
Meals *Lunch 450* – 850 – ☕ 300 – **96 rm** 3500.

at Dilbeek *W : 7 km* – *pop. 37 521* – ⊠ *1700 Dilbeek :*

Relais Delbeccha ※, Bodegemstraat 158 ℘ (0 2) 569 44 30, Fax (0 2) 569 75 30, ※, ⋒ – TV ☎ **P** – ₤ 25-120. AE ◑ E VISA. ※
Meals (*closed Sunday dinner*) 1025/1550 – **12 rm** ☕ 2950/4500.

XX **Host. d'Arconati** ※ with rm, d'Arconatistraat 77 ℘ (0 2) 569 35 00, Fax (0 2) 569 35 04, ※, « Floral terrace », ⋒ – TV ☎ **P** – ₤ 60. AE E VISA. ※
Meals (*closed Sunday dinner, Monday and Tuesday*) 1795 b.i. – **4 rm** ☕ 2000/3000.

at Dworp (Tourneppe) S : 16 km © Beersel pop. 22 746 – ⊠ 1653 Dworp :

Kasteel Gravenhof ⑤, Alsembergsesteenweg 676 ℘ (0 2) 380 44 99, Fax (0 2)
380 40 60, ♨, « Woodland setting, lake », ☞ – ⑤ TV ☎ P – ⚎ 25-120. AE ⓪ E VISA
⅏ rm
Meals (Pub rest) Lunch 625 – a la carte approx. 1200 – ⊑ 395 – **24 rm** 4850.

at Grimbergen N : 11 km – pop. 32 637 – ⊠ 1850 Grimbergen :

Abbey, Kerkeblokstraat 5 ℘ (0 2) 270 08 88, Fax (0 2) 270 81 88, ♬, ≋s, ☞ – ⑤
▤ rest, TV ☎ P – ⚎ 30-200. AE ⓪ E VISA. ⅏ rm
closed July – Meals **'t Wit Paard** (closed Saturday and Sunday) Lunch 1250 - a la cart
1850/2350 – ⊑ 500 – **28 rm** 4200/5500.

at Groot-Bijgaarden NW : 7 km © Dilbeek pop. 37 521 – ⊠ 1702 Groot-Bijgaarden :

Waerboom, Jozef Mertensstraat 140 ℘ (0 2) 463 15 00, Fax (0 2) 463 10 30, ≋s,
– ⑤ TV ☎ P – ⚎ 25-270. AE ⓪ E VISA. ⅏
closed mid July-mid August – Meals (residents only) – **35 rm** ⊑ 3500/4600.

Gosset Ⓜ, Alfons Gossetlaan 52 ℘ (0 2) 466 21 30, Fax (0 2) 466 18 50, ♨ – ⑤ ⅏
TV ☎ P – ⚎ 25-200. AE ⓪ E VISA. ⅏ rm
closed 23 December-4 January – Meals Lunch 350 – a la carte 1000/1450 – **48 rm**
⊑ 2000/4100.

De Bijgaarden, I. Van Beverenstraat 20 (near castle) ℘ (0 2) 466 44 85, Fax (0 2)
463 08 11, ≤, ♨ – AE ⓪ E VISA
closed Saturday lunch, Sunday, Bank Holidays, 4 to 12 April, 15 August-6 September an
2 to 4 January – Meals Lunch 2150 – 3250/4500, – a la carte 3350/4300
Spec. St-Jacques marinées aux truffes blanches du Piémont (October-December).
Turbot rôti ''château'' et béarnaise de homard. Pigeon de Vendée à la
presse.

Michel (Coppens), Schepen Gossetlaan 31 ℘ (0 2) 466 65 91, Fax (0 2) 466 90 07, ♨
– P. AE ⓪ E VISA
closed Sunday, Monday and August – Meals Lunch 1600 – 2250, a la carte approx. 2400
Spec. Foie d'oie poché sur pannequet de laitue et sirop de Porto. Saumurage de
turbot au citron confit. Saumon mariné, légèrement fumé et mousse de cour
gettes.

at Hoeilaart SE : 13 km – pop. 9 666 – ⊠ 1560 Hoeilaart :

Groenendaal, Groenendaalsesteenweg 145 (at Groenendaal) ℘ (0 2) 657 94 47
Fax (0 2) 657 20 30, ♨ – TV ☎ P. AE ⓪ E VISA JCB
Meals (closed Saturday and Sunday) – 980/1595 – **8 rm** ⊑ 3100/4500.

Aloyse Kloos, Terhulpsesteenweg 2 (at Groenendaal) ℘ (0 2) 657 37 37, ♨, « On the
edge of a forest » – P. AE ⓪ E VISA JCB
closed Sunday dinner, Monday and late July-August – Meals Lunch 1450 – 2350 b.i., a la carte
approx. 2300
Spec. Ravioles de champignons des bois aux truffes. Jambon marbré aux truffes, poché
au foin (December-March). Poulet fermier aux morilles.

at Huizingen S : 12 km © Beersel pop. 22 746 – ⊠ 1654 Huizingen :

Terborght, Oud Dorp 16 (near E 19, exit ⑮) ℘ (0 2) 380 10 10, Fax (0 2) 380 10 97
♨, « Rustic » – ▤ P. AE ⓪ E VISA. ⅏
closed dinner Sunday and Tuesday, Monday, carnival and 15 July-15 August – Meals Lunch
1500 b.i. – 1850.

at Kobbegem NW : 11 km © Asse pop. 27 442 – ⊠ 1730 Kobbegem :

De Plezanten Hof, Broekstraat 2 ℘ (0 2) 452 89 39, Fax (0 2) 452 99 11, ♨ – P
AE ⓪ E VISA
closed dinner Tuesday and Sunday, Wednesday, 1 week carnival and 21 July-13 August
– Meals Lunch 1150 – 1750/1950.

at Kraainem E : 12 km – pop. 12 934 – ⊠ 1950 Kraainem :

d'Oude Pastorie, Pastoorkesweg 1 (Park Jourdain) ℘ (0 2) 720 63 46, Fax (0 2)
720 63 46, « Lakeside setting in park » – P. AE ⓪ E VISA. ⅏
closed Monday dinner, Thursday, 5 to 12 April and 16 August-6 September – Meals Lunch
1200 – a la carte 1400/1700.

at Linkebeek S : 12 km – pop. 4 630 – ⊠ 1630 Linkebeek :

Le Saint-Sébastien, r. Station 90 ℘ (0 2) 380 54 90, Fax (0 2) 380 54 41, ♨ – P
⓪ E VISA
closed Monday and mid August-mid September – Meals Lunch 750 – 1150/1450.

at Machelen *NE : 12 km – pop. 11 582 – ⊠ 1830 Machelen :*

XXX **Pyramid** (D'Haese), Heirbaan 210 ℘ *(0 2) 252 50 72, Fax (0 2) 253 47 65,* 🍴, « *Modern interior, terrace with landscaped garden* » – 🅿. AE Ⓞ E VISA JCB. *closed Saturday lunch, Sunday, Monday dinner, 1 week after Easter, late July-early August and late December –* **Meals** *Lunch 1300 – 1750/3250 b.i., – a la carte 2000/2600* **Spec.** Confit de cailles aux épinards crus, croûtons et lardons. Soupe au pistou et homard norvégien. Ris de veau braisé à brun Zingara.

at Meise *N : 14 km – pop. 17 979 – ⊠ 1860 Meise :*

XXX **Aub. Napoléon,** Bouchoutlaan 1 ℘ *(0 2) 269 30 78, Fax (0 2) 269 79 98, Grill rest –* 🅿. AE Ⓞ E VISA *closed August –* **Meals** *Lunch 1450 – a la carte 1850/2200.*

XXX **Koen Van Loven,** Brusselsesteenweg 11 ℘ *(0 2) 270 05 77, Fax (0 2) 270 05 46,* 🍴 *–* 🔥 *25-150.* AE Ⓞ E VISA *closed Sunday dinner, Monday, carnival week, Easter holidays and first 2 weeks August –* **Meals** *Lunch 1175 – 1545/1845.*

at Melsbroek *NE : 14 km Ⓒ Steenokkerzeel pop. 10 184 – ⊠ 1820 Melsbroek :*

XXX **Boetfort,** Sellaerstraat 42 ℘ *(0 2) 751 64 00, Fax (0 2) 751 62 00,* 🍴, « *17C mansion, park* » – 🅿 – 🔥 *25-40.* AE Ⓞ E VISA. *closed Wednesday dinner, Saturday lunch, Sunday and carnival week –* **Meals** *Lunch 1200 – 1950/2400.*

at Nossegem *E : 13 km Ⓒ Zaventem pop. 26 559 – ⊠ 1930 Nossegem :*

XX **Roland Debuyst,** Leuvensesteenweg 614 ℘ *(0 2) 757 05 59, Fax (0 2) 759 50 08,* 🍴 *–* 🅿. AE Ⓞ E VISA *closed Saturday lunch, Sunday, Monday dinner and 2 weeks August –* **Meals** *Lunch 1350 – 1900.*

at Overijse *SE : 16 km – pop. 23 726 – ⊠ 3090 Overijse :*

XXXX **Barbizon** (Deluc), Welriekendedreef 95 (at Jezus-Eik) ℘ *(0 2) 657 04 62, Fax (0 2) 657 40 66,* 🍴, « *Norman style villa, terrace and garden on the edge of a forest* » – 🅿. AE E VISA *closed Tuesday, Wednesday, February and late July-early August –* **Meals** *Lunch 1425 – 1750/3250, – a la carte 2500/2900* **Spec.** Pistou de langoustines rôties, salades amères et semoule. Gibiers (September-January). Filet de rouget au thym citron et confit d'agneau aux olives et basilic.

X **Istas,** Brusselsesteenweg 652 (at Jezus-Eik) ℘ *(0 2) 657 05 11, Fax (0 2) 657 05 11,* 🍴, Pub rest – 🅿. E VISA *closed Wednesday, Thursday and August –* **Meals** *– a la carte 850/1350.*

at Sint-Genesius-Rode *(Rhode-St-Genèse) S : 13 km – pop. 18 099 – ⊠ 1640 Sint-Genesius-Rode :*

🏨 **Aub. de Waterloo,** chaussée de Waterloo 212 ℘ *(0 2) 358 35 80, Fax (0 2) 358 38 06 –* 📶 ✈ ▦ TV ☎ 🅿 *–* 🔥 *25-70.* AE Ⓞ E VISA **Meals** *see rest* **L'Arlecchino** *below – 83 rm* ☕ *2450/6800.*

XX **L'Arlecchino** - (at Aub. de Waterloo H.), chaussée de Waterloo 212 ℘ *(0 2) 358 34 16, Fax (0 2) 358 28 96,* 🍴, *Italian cuisine, with trattoria –* ▦ 🅿. AE Ⓞ E VISA. *closed August –* **Meals** *895/1280.*

XX **Michel D,** r. Station 182 ℘ *(0 2) 381 20 66, Fax (0 2) 381 20 66,* 🍴 *–* 🅿. AE Ⓞ E VISA *closed Wednesday, Saturday lunch, Sunday dinner and 20 July-15 August –* **Meals** *Lunch 690 – 1500.*

X **Bois Savanes,** chaussée de Waterloo 208 ℘ *(0 2) 358 37 78, Fax (0 2) 358 37 78,* 🍴, *Thaï cuisine –* 🅿. AE Ⓞ E VISA *closed lunch Monday and Tuesday and last 3 weeks August –* **Meals** *Lunch 495 – a la carte approx. 1100.*

at Sint-Pieters-Leeuw *SO : 13 km – pop. 29 800 – ⊠ 1600 Sint-Pieters-Leeuw :*

🏨 **Green Park** M Ꮙ, V. Nonnemanstraat 15 ℘ *(0 2) 331 19 70, Fax (0 2) 331 03 11,* 🍴, « *Lakeside setting* », 🛠, 🚗 *–* 📶 TV ☎ 🚗 🅿 *–* 🔥 *25-100.* AE Ⓞ E VISA JCB. *rest closed July –* **Meals** *(closed Friday) Lunch 450 – a la carte 1150/1550 –* **18 rm** ☕ *3850/4350.*

at Strombeek-Bever *N : 9 km Ⓒ Grimbergen pop. 32 637 – ⊠ 1853 Strombeek-Bever :*

🏨 **Alfa Rijckendael** M Ꮙ, Luitberg 1 ℘ *(0 2) 267 41 24 and 267 55 00 (rest), Fax (0 2) 267 94 01,* 🍴, ⊜ *–* 📶 TV ☎ 🚗 🅿 *–* 🔥 *25-40.* AE Ⓞ E VISA **Meals** *(closed Wednesday) Lunch 880 b.i. – a la carte 1700/2350 –* **49 rm** ☕ *4600/5100.*

Clarine, Romeinsesteenweg 572 ☎ (0 2) 461 00 21, Fax (0 2) 461 04 84 – 📶 📺 ☎
– 🛎 25-80. AE ⓞ E VISA
Meals (Pub rest) 1190 – **75 rm** ⊑ 3950/4250.

Val Joli, Leestbeekstraat 16 ☎ (0 2) 460 65 43, Fax (0 2) 460 04 00, 🌳, « Terrace an
garden » – 🅿. AE ⓞ E VISA   BK
closed Monday, Tuesday, 2 weeks June and 2 weeks November – Meals Lunch 480
995/1590.

't Stoveke, Jetsestraat 52 ☎ (0 2) 267 67 25, Fax (0 2) 267 54 89, 🌳, Seafood – E
ⓞ E VISA
closed Sunday, Monday, Bank Holidays, 3 weeks June, Christmas and New Year – Mea
Lunch 1190 – a la carte 1600/2550.

at Vilvoorde (Vilvorde) N : 17 km – pop. 33 806 – ✉ 1800 Vilvoorde :

de Rembrandt, Lange Molensstraat 60 ☎ (0 2) 251 04 72, 🌳, « In a 15
watchtower » – AE ⓞ E VISA. 🍽
closed Saturday and 21 July-15 August – Meals (lunch only except Tuesday and Thursda
a la carte 1550/2300.

De Met 1st floor, Grote Markt 7 ☎ (0 2) 253 30 00, Fax (0 2) 253 31 00, Partly pub res
« Former covered market, Art Deco style » – 🛎 25-400. AE E VISA. 🍽
closed Sunday – Meals Lunch 1375 b.i. – a la carte approx. 1900.

'T Puur Toeval, Rooseveltlaan 18 ☎ (0 2) 253 68 39, Fax (0 2) 253 68 39, 🌳 – AE ⓞ
E VISA
closed Saturday lunch, Sunday, Monday dinner, 1 week carnival and 19 July-9 August
Meals Lunch 795 – 1095/1395.

at Wemmel N : 12 km – pop. 13 773 – ✉ 1780 Wemmel :

Le Gril aux herbes d'Evan, Brusselsesteenweg 21 ☎ (0 2) 460 52 39, Fax (0 2
461 19 12, 🌳 – AE ⓞ E VISA
closed Wednesday, Saturday lunch, 1 to 20 July and 25 to 31 December – Meals Lunch 89
– 1600/1950.

Parkhof "Beverbos", Parklaan 7 ☎ (0 2) 460 42 89, Fax (0 2) 460 25 10, 🌳
« Terrace in public park » – 🅿. AE ⓞ E VISA JCB
closed Wednesday and late September-early October – Meals Lunch 950 – 1200/2000.

at Wezembeek-Oppem E : 11 km – pop. 13 680 – ✉ 1970 Wezembeek-Oppem :

L'Aub. Saint-Pierre, Sint-Pietersplein 8 ☎ (0 2) 731 21 79, Fax (0 2) 731 28 28, 🌳
– AE ⓞ E VISA
closed Saturday lunch, Sunday, Bank Holidays, 15 July-15 August and 24 December-
January – Meals Lunch 980 – a la carte 1650/2100.

at Zaventem Brussels-Zaventem airport motorway – pop. 26 559 – ✉ 1930 Zaventem :

Sheraton Airport, at airport ☎ (0 2) 725 10 00, Telex 27085, Fax (0 2) 725 11 55
🏋 – 📶 🍽 ▤ 📺 ☎ ♿ 🚗 – 🛎 25-600. AE ⓞ E VISA JCB
Meals **Concorde** Lunch 1450 - a la carte 2000/2550 – **Lindbergh Taverne** (open unt
11.30 p.m.) Lunch 770 - a la carte 850/1350 – ⊑ 840 – **297 rm** 11400/13400, 2 suites

Stockmansmolen 1st floor, H. Henneaulaan 164 ☎ (0 2) 725 34 34, Fax (0 2) 725 7:
05, Partly pub rest, « Former watermill » – ▤ 🅿. AE ⓞ E VISA
closed Saturday, Sunday, 18 July-10 August, Christmas and New Year – Meals Lunch 172
– a la carte 2400/2800.

MICHELIN GREEN GUIDES in English

Austria	Great Britain	Rome
Barcelona	Greece	San Francisco
Belgium Luxemburg	Ireland	Scandinavia Finland
Berlin	Italy	Scotland
Brussels	London	Spain
California	Mexico	Switzerland
Canada	Netherlands	Thailand
Chicago	New England	Tuscany
The West Country of	New York - New Jersey	Venice
England	- Pennsylvania	Vienna
Europe	New York City	Wales
France	Paris	Washington DC
Florida	Portugal	
Germany	Quebec	

NTWERP (ANTWERPEN) *2000* 212 ⑮ *and* 909 *G 2 -* ⑧ *S – pop. 453030.*

See : *Around the Market Square and the Cathedral*★★★ : *Market Square*★ *(Grote Markt)* FY , *Vlaaikensgang*★ FY, *Cathedral*★★★ *and its tower*★★★ FY – *Butchers' House*★ *(Vleeshuis)* : *Musical instruments*★ FY D – *Rubens' House*★★ *(Rubenshuis)* GZ – *Interior*★ *of St. James' Church (St-Jacobskerk)* GY - *Hendrik Conscience Place*★ GY – *St. Charles Borromeo's Church*★ *(St-Carolus Borromeuskerk)* GY – *St. Paul's Church (St-Pauluskerk)* : *interior*★ FY – *Zoo*★ *(Dierentuin)* DEU – *Zurenborg Quater*★ EV – *The port (Haven)* FY.

Museums : *Maritime "Steen"*★ *(Nationaal Scheepvaartmuseum Steen)* FY – *Etnographic Museum*★ FY M¹ – *Plantin-Moretus*★★★ FZ – *Mayer Van den Bergh*★★ : *Mad Meg*★★ *(Dulle Griet)* GZ – *Rockox House*★ *(Rockoxhuis)* GY M⁴ – *Royal Art Gallery*★★★ *(Koninklijk Museum voor Schone Kunsten)* CV M⁵ – *Museum of Photography*★ CV M⁶ – *Open-air Museum of Sculpture Middelheim*★ *(Openluchtmuseum voor Beeldhouwkunst)* – *Provincial Museum Sterckshof-Zilvercentrum*★.

⸬ ⸬ *at Kapellen N : 15,5 km, G. Capiaulei 2* ℘ *(0 3) 666 84 56, -* ⸬ *at Aartselaar S : 10 km, Kasteel Cleydael* ℘ *(0 3) 887 00 79 -* ⸬ ⸬ *at Wommelgem E : 10 km, Uilenbaan 15* ℘ *(0 3) 355 14 30 -* ⸬ *at Broechem E : 13 km, Kasteel Bossenstein, Moor 16* ℘ *(0 3) 485 64 46.*

🛈 *Grote Markt 15* ℘ *(0 3) 232 01 03, Fax (0 3) 231 19 37 – Tourist association of the province, Karel Oomsstraat 11,* ✉ *2018,* ℘ *(0 3) 216 28 10, Fax (0 3) 237 83 65.*

Brussels 48 – Amsterdam 159 – Luxembourg 261 – Rotterdam 103.

Plans on following pages

Old Antwerp

Hilton Ⓜ, Groenplaats ℘ (0 3) 204 12 12, Fax (0 3) 204 12 13, « Facade of an early 20C department store », ᴌᕋ, ⇔s – ‖ ✕ 🔲 TV ☎ 🚗 – 🛆 30-1000. AE ⓪ E VISA JCB   FZ m
Meals see rest ***Het Vijfde Seizoen*** below – **199 rm** ⌚ 7900/12400, 12 suites.

Alfa Theater Ⓜ, Arenbergstraat 30 ℘ (0 3) 203 54 10, Fax (0 3) 233 88 58, ⇔s – ‖ ✕ 🔲 TV ☎ 🚗 – 🛆 25-50. AE ⓪ E VISA. 🙾   GZ t
Meals *(closed Saturday lunch, Sunday and Bank Holidays)* Lunch 650 – 1350 – **122 rm** ⌚ 3400/6700, 5 suites.

De Witte Lelie 🐧 without rest, Keizerstraat 16 ℘ (0 3) 226 19 66, Fax (0 3) 234 00 19, « Typical 17C terraced houses, patio » – ‖ TV ☎ 🚗. AE ⓪ E VISA JCB   GY z
closed 22 December-3 January – **7 rm** ⌚ 6500/15000, 3 suites.

Rubens 🐧 without rest, Oude Beurs 29 ℘ (0 3) 222 48 48, Fax (0 3) 225 19 40 – ‖ TV ☎ 🚗 Ⓟ – 🛆 25-50. AE ⓪ E VISA JCB. 🙾   FY y
35 rm ⌚ 5850/6850, 1 suite.

't Sandt, Het Zand 17 ℘ (0 3) 232 93 90, Fax (0 3) 232 56 13, « 19C residence in rococo style » – ‖ TV ☎ 🚗 – 🛆 25-150. AE ⓪ E VISA. 🙾 rest   FZ w
Meals a la carte approx. 1300 – **14 rm** ⌚ 5500/6000, 1 suite.

Prinse 🐧 without rest, Keizerstraat 63 ℘ (0 3) 226 40 50, Fax (0 3) 225 11 48 – ‖ ✕ ✕ 🔲 TV ☎ 🕭 🚗 – 🛆 25-100. AE ⓪ E VISA. 🙾   GY a
34 rm ⌚ 3800/5100, 1 suite.

Villa Mozart, Handschoenmarkt 3 ℘ (0 3) 231 30 31, Fax (0 3) 231 56 85, 🏠, ⇔s – ‖ TV ☎. AE ⓪ E VISA JCB   FY e
Meals (Pub rest) Lunch 595 – a la carte 850/1350 – ⌚ 500 – **25 rm** 3500/6400.

Antigone without rest, Jordaenskaai 11 ℘ (0 3) 231 66 77, Fax (0 3) 231 37 74 – ‖ TV ☎ Ⓟ – 🛆 30. AE ⓪ E VISA. 🙾   FY a
18 rm ⌚ 3000/3500.

't Fornuis (Segers), Reyndersstraat 24 ℘ (0 3) 233 62 70, Fax (0 3) 233 99 03, « 17C residence, rustic interior » – AE ⓪ E VISA. 🙾   FZ c
closed Saturday, Sunday, last 3 weeks August and late December – **Meals** (booking essential) a la carte 2200/3150
Spec. Sandwich de crabe aux épices. Turbot poêlé sauce crèmeuse d'haricots blancs. Pain perdu d'épices aux pommes.

Huis De Colvenier, St-Antoniusstraat 8 ℘ (0 3) 226 65 73, Fax (0 3) 227 13 14, 🏠, « Late 19C residence, murals and winter garden » – ▤ Ⓟ. AE ⓪ E VISA   FZ k
closed Saturday lunch, Sunday dinner, Monday, 1 week carnival and August – **Meals** Lunch 1300 – a la carte approx. 2400.

Het Vijfde Seizoen (at Hilton H.), Groenplaats ℘ (0 3) 204 12 29, Fax (0 3) 204 12 13 – ▤. AE ⓪ E VISA JCB   FZ m
Meals – 1450/2450.

La Rade 1st floor, E. Van Dijckkaai 8 ℘ (0 3) 233 37 37, Fax (0 3) 233 49 63, « Former 19C freemason's lodge » – AE ⓪ E VISA   FY g
closed Saturday lunch, Sunday, Bank Holidays, carnival week and 12 to 31 July – **Meals** Lunch 1450 – a la carte 2050/2650.

ANTWERPEN

C
JACHT HAVEN
Charles de Costerlaan
WAASLANDTUN
LINKEROEVER
laan
Gloriant
Emile Verhaeren- laan
Halewijnlaan
Thonetlaan
Fr. Van Eedenplein
Blancefloerlaan
ST-ANNATUNNEL
(voor voetgangers)
Galgenweellaan
Pluvierstr.
Beatrijslaan
GALGENWEEL
SCHELDE
153
187
105
105
c
Kronenburg
Nationale st
M
e
r
72
36
207
P
Vlaamse Ka
67
M 6
M 5
ZUID
69
116
120
121
133
51
a
Amerikalei
Paleis
91
Ledeganckkaai
Bolivarplaats
Montignystr.
Brederodestr.
St. Laureisstr.
24
79
27
Lange Elzenstr.
16
5
5
ANTWERPEN ZUID
P
106
Binnensingel R
64
X
52
R 1
180
90
C
0   400 m
T
U
V
X

R 1
NIEUW LOBROEKDOK
Slachthuislaan
Noorderlaan
Ellermanstr.
Lange
Lobroekstr.
202
w
Schijnpoort
204
81
174
Stuivenbergplein
APARTE DOK
WILLEMDOK
4
124
K
25
148
6
3
31
u
Oranjestr.
39
55
Onderwijsstr.
58
84
Van Kerckhovenstr.
Italielei
183
181
Diepestr.
Handelsstr.
Handel
T
208
Begijnhof
p
39
Elisabeth
Lange
Beeldekensstr.
Pothoekstr.
118
b
114
Lange
142
39
Kerkstr.
St.-Jacobskerk
Nieuwstr.
c
60
175
136
CATHEDRAAL
96
f
u
T
63
e
Astrid
Carnotstr.
BORGERHOUT
123
Opera
109
d
U
Meir
103
h
t
M
138
q
Centraal Station
162
s
DIERENTUIN
Turnhoutsebaan
T
165
M
Diamant
k
154
r
H
Rubenslei
v
151
a
Kroonstr.
166
162
s Herenstr.
Frankrijklei
STADSPARK
P
178
22
127
Van Eycklei
Plantin
Plantin
Bleekhofstr.
102
b
en
Moretuslei
19
130
135
22
y
171
J
33
21
t
s
97
k
162
x
Anselmostr.
Lange Leemstr.
130
Mechelse
186
straat
Transvaalstr.
Pretoriastr.
M
37
steenweg
Lange
65
y
38
Belgielei
Leemstr.
210
V
12
WIJK ZURENBORG
Lange Lozanastr.
79
G. Vliesstr.
Mariälei
16
70
P
Lamorinière
110
KONING ALBERT PARK
Boomgaardstr.
R 1
43
Markgravelei
d
159
Grote Steenweg
Statiestr.
X
n
i
157
e
b
Gen.
Vredestraat
V. Van Rijswijcklaan
v
K. Oomsstr.
Lemanstr.
Binnensingel
R 10
z
Desguinlei
BERCHEM
66
D
E

ANTWERPEN

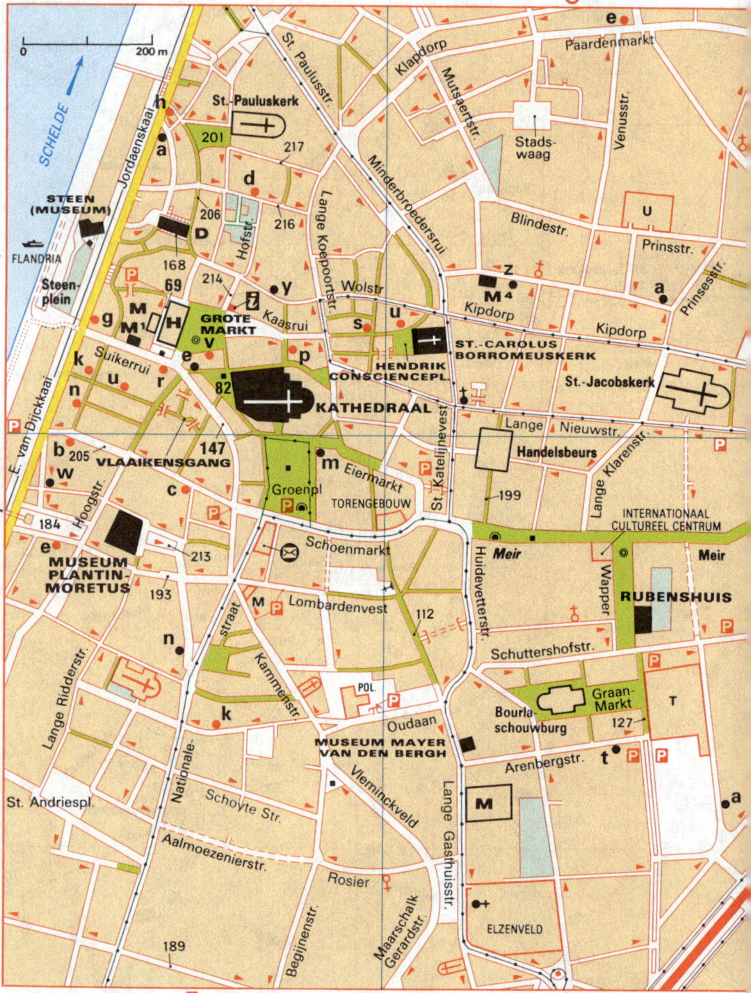

Pleasant hotels and restaurants are shown in the Guide by a red sign.
Please send us the names of any where you have enjoyed your stay.
Your Michelin Guide will be even better.

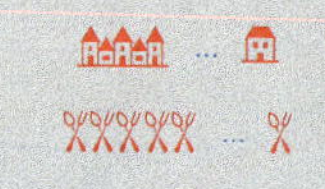

XXX **De Kerselaar** (Michiels), Grote Pieter Potstraat 22 *(0 3) 233 59 69, Fax (0 3) 233 11 49* – 🍽. AE ⑩ E VISA JCB — **FY n**
closed lunch Saturday and Monday, Sunday, 21 March-1 April and 25 July-8 August – **Meals** *Lunch 1650* – 2150, a la carte 2200/2500
Spec. Carpaccio de homard à la vinaigrette de pommes et vanille. Lotte rôtie sur un caramel d'échalotes et queues d'écrevisses. Corne d'abondance au chocolat blanc, fruits rouges et coulis de fruits sauvages.

XX **'t Silveren Claverblat,** Grote Pieter Potstraat 16 *(0 3) 231 33 88, Fax (0 3) 231 31 46* – AE ⑩ E VISA. ✗ — **FY k**
closed Tuesday and Saturday lunch – **Meals** 2000 b.i./2750 b.i..

XX **De Gulden Beer,** Grote Markt 14 *(0 3) 226 08 41, Fax (0 3) 232 52 09,* �, Partly Italian cuisine – 🍽. AE ⑩ E VISA. ✗ — **FY v**
Meals *Lunch 1500 b.i.* – 1200/2200.

XX **P. Preud'homme,** Suikerrui 28 *(0 3) 233 42 00, Fax (0 3) 226 08 96,* 🌫, Open until midnight – 🍽. AE ⑩ E VISA. ✗ — **FY r**
closed January – **Meals** *Lunch 1200* – a la carte 1500/2700.

XX **Het Nieuwe Palinghuis,** St-Jansvliet 14 *(0 3) 231 74 45, Fax (0 3) 231 50 53,* Seafood – 🍽. AE ⑩ E VISA — **FZ e**
closed Monday, Tuesday and June – **Meals** – a la carte 1500/2050.

XX **Neuze Neuze,** Wijngaardstraat 19 *(0 3) 232 27 97, Fax (0 3) 225 27 38* – AE ⑩ E VISA JCB — **FY s**
closed Saturday lunch, Sunday, 2 weeks August, 1 week Christmas and 1 week January – **Meals** *Lunch 1500 b.i.* – 1750/2600 b.i..

XX **De Matelote** (Garnich), Haarstraat 9 *(0 3) 231 32 07, Fax (0 3) 231 08 13,* Seafood – 🍽. AE ⑩ E VISA — **FY u**
closed lunch Saturday and Monday, Sunday, Bank Holidays, June and 1 to 15 January – **Meals** – a la carte 1800/2500
Spec. Cocktail de crevettes grises aux tomates confites. Raie poêlée aux fines herbes et sauce moutardée au Xérès. Palette de légumes méditerranéenne.

XX **Zirk,** Zirkstraat 29 *(0 3) 225 25 86, Fax (0 3) 226 51 77* – Ⓟ. AE ⑩ E VISA. ✗ — **FY d**
closed Saturday lunch, Sunday, Monday, 1 week February and 1 to 23 August – **Meals** *Lunch 850* – 1700/2300.

XX **De Manie,** H. Conscienceplein 3 *(0 3) 232 64 38, Fax (0 3) 232 64 38,* 🌫 – AE E VISA — **GY u**
closed Wednesday, Sunday dinner, 16 August-1 September and 15 to 27 January – **Meals** *Lunch 800* – a la carte 1000/1800.

X **De Reddende Engel,** Torfbrug 3 *(0 3) 233 66 30, Fax (0 3) 233 66 30,* 🌫 – AE ⑩ E VISA. ✗ — **FY p**
closed Wednesday, Saturday lunch, 15 to 23 February, 16 August-14 September and 2 to 5 January – Meals 975/1250.

X **Tête-à-Tête,** Vlasmarkt 14 *(0 3) 227 37 17, Fax (0 3) 227 37 17,* « Artistic pub » – AE ⑩ E VISA — **FZ b**
closed Wednesday, last 2 weeks August and last 2 weeks January – **Meals** (dinner only until 11 p.m.) a la carte 1300/1600.

X **Dock's Café,** Jordaenskaai 7 *(0 3) 226 63 30, Fax (0 3) 226 65 72,* Brasserie-Oyster bar, open until midnight – AE ⑩ E VISA JCB. ✗ — **FY h**
closed Saturday lunch – **Meals** *Lunch 650* – a la carte 1200/1600.

X **Don Carlos,** St-Michielskaai 34 *(0 3) 216 40 46,* 🌫, Partly Spanish cuisine – ✗ **CU c**
closed Monday – **Meals** (dinner only) a la carte approx. 1200.

Town Centre

🏨 **Radisson SAS Park Lane** Ⓜ, Van Eycklei 34, ✉ 2018, *(0 3) 285 85 85 and 285 85 80 (rest), Fax (0 3) 285 85 86,* ⩽, ₤ₛ, ≘ₛ, 🏊 – 🛗 ✗ 🍽 TV ☎ 🚗 – 🕍 25-500. AE ⑩ E VISA. ✗ rest — **DV y**
Meals : *Longchamps (closed Saturday lunch, Sunday dinner, Bank Holidays and mid July-mid August) Lunch 1100* - a la carte 1450/1750 – ☕ 700 – **163 rm** 6200/9500, 14 suites.

🏨 **Astrid Park Plaza** Ⓜ, Koningin Astridplein 1, ✉ 2018, *(0 3) 203 12 34, Fax (0 3) 203 12 51,* ⩽, ₤ₛ, ≘ₛ, 🏊 – 🛗 ✗ 🍽 TV ☎ 🚗 – 🕍 25-500. AE ⑩ E VISA. ✗ rest — **DEU e**
Meals *(closed Saturday lunch) Lunch 950* – a la carte approx. 1300 – ☕ 750 – **226 rm** 5100/11000, 3 suites.

🏨 **Carlton,** Quinten Matsijslei 25, ✉ 2018, *(0 3) 231 15 15, Fax (0 3) 225 30 90* – 🛗 ✗ 🍽 TV ☎ 🚗 – 🕍 25-100. AE ⑩ E VISA JCB. ✗ rest — **DU v**
Meals *(closed dinner Friday and Sunday, Saturday lunch and 26 July-13 August) Lunch 675* – a la carte 1350/1800 – **126 rm** ☕ 5950/7600, 1 suite.

Alfa De Keyser Ⓜ, De Keyserlei 66, ⊠ 2018, ℰ (0 3) 206 74 60, Fax (0 3) 232 39
ℐ, ⊆ₛ, ⊠ – ⧉ ⊁ ▤ TV ☎ – ⚐ 25-160. AE ⓘ ⴹ VISA JCB
Meals (Pub rest) (closed Saturday lunch and Sunday) Lunch 795 – a la carte 1200/2350
120 rm � 3400/5900, 3 suites.
DU

Hyllit Ⓜ, De Keyserlei 28 (access by Appelmansstraat), ⊠ 2018, ℰ (0 3) 202 68 00 a
227 44 88 (rest), Fax (0 3) 202 68 90, ⛲ – ⧉ ▤ TV ☎ ⌨ – ⚐ 30. AE ⓘ ⴹ VI
⊁
DU
Meals *Gran Duca* (partly Italian cuisine, open until 11 p.m.) Lunch 1350 - a la carte appro
1800 – ⊆ 550 – **74 rm** 3600/5500, 5 suites.

Plaza without rest, Charlottalei 43, ⊠ 2018, ℰ (0 3) 218 92 40, Fax (0 3) 218 88 23
⧉ ⊁ ▤ TV ☎ ⌨ – ⚐ 25. AE ⓘ ⴹ VISA. ⊁
80 rm ⊆ 6900/9400.
DV

Queens, Copernicuslaan 2, ⊠ 2018, ℰ (0 3) 223 40 40, Fax (0 3) 223 40 41, ℐ, ⊆
⊠, ⊁ – ⧉ ⊁ ▤ TV ☎ ⌨ – ⚐ 25-1000. AE ⓘ ⴹ VISA JCB
EU
Meals (closed lunch Saturday and Monday, Sunday and mid July-mid August) Lunch 1195
a la carte approx. 1400 – ⊆ 595 – **286 rm** 5750, 3 suites.

Residence without rest, Molenbergstraat 9 ℰ (0 3) 232 76 75, Fax (0 3) 233 73 28
⧉ TV ☎ ⌨ – ⚐ 40. AE ⓘ ⴹ VISA. ⊁
48 rm ⊆ 3400/8000.
DU

Antverpia without rest, Sint-Jacobsmarkt 85 ℰ (0 3) 231 80 80, Fax (0 3) 232 43
– ⧉ TV ☎ ⌨ – ⚐ 40. AE ⓘ ⴹ VISA JCB. ⊁
DU
⊆ 400 – **19 rm** 3500/6000.

Alfa Empire without rest, Appelmansstraat 31, ⊠ 2018, ℰ (0 3) 203 54 00, Fax (0
233 40 60 – ⧉ ⊁ ▤ TV ☎ ⌨. AE ⓘ ⴹ VISA JCB
DU
70 rm ⊆ 2900/5600.

Alfa Congress, Plantin en Moretuslei 136, ⊠ 2018, ℰ (0 3) 270 02 10, Fax (0
235 52 31 – ⧉ ⊁ ▤ TV ☎ ⌨ Ⓟ – ⚐ 25-120. AE ⓘ ⴹ VISA. ⊁
EV
Meals (closed Saturday and Sunday) Lunch 800 – a la carte 900/1300 – ⊆ 400 – **66 r**
1900/3000.

Colombus without rest, Frankrijklei 4 ℰ (0 3) 233 03 90, Fax (0 3) 226 09 46, ℐ, ⊠
– ⧉ TV ☎ ⌨. AE ⓘ ⴹ VISA JCB. ⊁
DU
32 rm ⊆ 3350/3950.

Astoria without rest, Korte Herentalsestraat 5, ⊠ 2018, ℰ (0 3) 227 31 30, Fax (0
227 31 34 – ⧉ ⊁ ▤ TV ☎ ⌨. AE ⓘ ⴹ VISA JCB
DU
66 rm ⊆ 4200/5200.

Atlanta without rest, Koningin Astridplein 14, ⊠ 2018, ℰ (0 3) 203 09 19, Fax (0
226 37 37 – ⧉ ⊁ TV ☎ – ⚐ 30. AE ⓘ ⴹ VISA. ⊁
DEU
60 rm ⊆ 2250/5000.

Ambassador without rest, Belgiëlei 8, ⊠ 2018, ℰ (0 3) 281 41 61, Fax (0 3) 239 55
– ⧉ TV ☎ ⌨. AE ⓘ ⴹ VISA. ⊁
DEV
77 rm ⊆ 2350/6000.

Eden without rest, Lange Herentalsestraat 25, ⊠ 2018, ℰ (0 3) 233 06 08, Fax (0
233 12 28 – ⧉ TV ☎ ⌨. AE ⓘ ⴹ VISA
DU
66 rm ⊆ 2600/4000.

De Barbarie, Van Breestraat 4, ⊠ 2018, ℰ (0 3) 232 81 98, Fax (0 3) 231 26 78, ⛲
– AE ⴹ VISA JCB. ⊁
DV
closed Saturday lunch, Sunday, Monday, 1 week Easter and first 2 weeks September
Meals Lunch 1450 – a la carte 2250/2850.

De Lepeleer, Lange St-Annastraat 10 ℰ (0 3) 225 19 31, Fax (0 3) 231 31 24, ⛲
« Several small houses in a 16C cul-de-sac » – ▤ Ⓟ – ⚐ 25-50. AE ⓘ ⴹ VISA
DU
closed Saturday lunch, Sunday, Bank Holidays and 21 July-17 August – **Meals** Lunch 995
2200.

De Zeste, Lange Dijkstraat 36, ⊠ 2060, ℰ (0 3) 233 45 49, Fax (0 3) 232 34 18 – ▤
AE ⓘ ⴹ VISA
DT
closed Sunday – **Meals** Lunch 1200 – 2100.

Blue Phoenix, Frankrijklei 14 ℰ (0 3) 233 33 77, Fax (0 3) 233 88 46, Chinese cuisin
– ▤. AE ⴹ VISA
DU
closed Monday, Saturday lunch and August – **Meals** Lunch 800 – 1100/1950.

La Luna, Italiëlei 177 ℰ (0 3) 232 23 44, Fax (0 3) 232 24 41, Multinational cuisines, ope
until 11 p.m. – ▤. AE ⓘ ⴹ VISA. ⊁
DT
closed Saturday lunch, Sunday, Easter, 15 July-15 August and Christmas-New Year – **Meal**
a la carte 1300/1750.

Klare Wijn, Dageraadplaats 16, ⊠ 2018, ℰ (0 3) 236 13 82, Fax (0 3) 236 13 82 – A
ⴹ VISA JCB
EV
closed Monday, Tuesday, Saturday lunch and 15 July-15 August – **Meals** Lunch 575
1350/1850.

XX **'t Peerd,** Paardenmarkt 53 ℰ (0 3) 231 98 25, Fax (0 3) 231 59 40, ☂ – ▤. AE ① E
VISA
GY e
closed Tuesday dinner, Wednesday, 2 weeks Easter and 2 weeks September – **Meals** *Lunch
1275 – a la carte 1300/2100.*

X **'t Lammeke,** Lange Lobroekstraat 51 (opposite the slaughterhouse), ✉ 2060, ℰ (0 3)
236 79 86, Fax (0 3) 271 05 16, ☂ – ▤. AE ① E VISA JCB
ET w
closed lunch Saturday and Sunday and Monday – **Meals** *Lunch 875 – 1225/1650.*

X **Yamayu Santatsu,** Ossenmarkt 19 ℰ (0 3) 234 09 49, Fax (0 3) 234 09 49, Japanese
cuisine – ▤. AE ① E VISA
DTU b
closed Sunday lunch, Monday, first 2 weeks August and last week December – **Meals** *Lunch
450 – 1500.*

South Quarter

🏨 **Holiday Inn Crowne Plaza,** G. Legrellelaan 10, ✉ 2020, ℰ (0 3) 237 29 00,
Telex 33843, Fax (0 3) 216 02 96, ☂, ₺, ☎s, ▣ – ▤ ✕ ▤ TV ☎ P – ♨ 25-800.
AE ① E VISA JCB. ✆
Meals *Lunch 950 – a la carte approx. 1500 –* ☕ *675 –* **258 rm** *6950, 4 suites.*

🏨 **Sofitel,** Desguinlei 94, ✉ 2018, ℰ (0 3) 244 82 11, Fax (0 3) 216 47 12, ₺, ☎s – ▤
✕ ▤ TV ☎ 🚗 P – ♨ 25-650. AE ① E VISA JCB. ✆ rest
DX z
Meals *Tiffany's (closed Saturday lunch and Sunday) Lunch 1300 b.i. - a la carte approx. 1400
–* ☕ *610 –* **210 rm** *3600/6500, 5 suites.*

🏠 **Firean** ✍, Karel Oomsstraat 6, ✉ 2018, ℰ (0 3) 237 02 60, Fax (0 3) 238 11 68,
« *Period residence, Art Deco style* » – ▤ ▤ TV ☎ 🚗. AE ① E VISA
DX n
closed 1 to 20 August and Christmas-New Year – **Meals** *see rest* **Minerva** *below –* **15 rm**
☕ *4200/5800.*

🏠 **Industrie** M *without rest, Emiel Banningstraat 52* ℰ (0 3) 238 66 00, Fax (0 3)
238 86 88 – TV ☎. AE ① E VISA. ✆
CV a
13 rm ☕ *2500/3500.*

XXX **Loncin,** Markgravelei 127, ✉ 2018, ℰ (0 3) 248 29 89, Fax (0 3) 248 38 66, ☂, Open
until midnight – ▤ P. AE ① E VISA
DX d
closed Saturday lunch and Sunday – **Meals** *Lunch 1350 – a la carte approx. 2400.*

XX **Liang's Garden,** Markgravelei 141, ✉ 2018, ℰ (0 3) 237 22 22, Fax (0 3) 248 38 34,
Chinese cuisine – ▤. AE ① E VISA
DX d
closed Sunday and 2 weeks August – **Meals** *Lunch 950 – a la carte 1150/1750.*

XX **De Poterne,** Desguinlei 186, ✉ 2018, ℰ (0 3) 238 28 24, Fax (0 3) 248 59 67 – AE ①
E VISA
DX u
closed Saturday lunch, Sunday, 21 July-15 August and 25 December-1 January – **Meals**
Lunch 1450 – a la carte 2050/2400.

XX **Kommilfoo,** Vlaamse Kaai 17 ℰ (0 3) 237 30 00, Fax (0 3) 237 30 00 – ▤. AE ① E
VISA. ✆
CV e
closed Saturday lunch, Sunday, Monday and last 2 weeks June – **Meals** *Lunch 1100 – a la
carte 1300/1600.*

X **Minerva** *- (at Firean H.), Karel Oomsstraat 36,* ✉ 2018, ℰ (0 3) 216 00 55, Fax (0 3)
216 00 55 – ♨ 25. AE ① E VISA. ✆
DX e
closed Sunday, Monday and last week July-first 2 weeks August – **Meals** *Lunch 1200 b.i. –
a la carte 1050/1950.*

Suburbs

North *– ✉ 2030 :*

🏨 **Novotel,** Luithagen-haven 6 (Haven 200) ℰ (0 3) 542 03 20, Fax (0 3) 541 70 93, ☂,
▨, ✕ – ▤ ✕ ▤ TV ☎ P – ♨ 25-180. AE ① E VISA JCB. ✆ rest
Meals *(open until 11 p.m.) a la carte approx. 1200 –* ☕ *475 –* **119 rm** *3600.*

at Berchem Ⓒ Antwerpen – ✉ 2600 Berchem :

XXX **De Tafeljoncker,** Frederik de Merodestraat 13 ℰ (0 3) 281 20 34, Fax (0 3) 281 20 34,
☂ – ▤ P. AE ① E VISA
DX f
closed Saturday lunch, Sunday dinner, Monday, 1 week February and 2 weeks July – **Meals**
Lunch 1900 b.i. – 2500 b.i./2950 b.i..

XX **De Troubadour,** Driekoningenstraat 72 ℰ (0 3) 239 39 16, Fax (0 3) 230 82 71 – ▤.
AE ① E VISA
DX a
closed Sunday, Monday and last 3 weeks July – **Meals** *– 795/1195.*

X **Margaux,** Terlinckstraat 2 ℰ (0 3) 230 55 99, Fax (0 3) 230 40 71, ☂ – E VISA.
✆
DX b
closed Sunday, Monday and 1 to 23 September – **Meals** *Lunch 895 – a la carte 1100/
1600.*

at Borgerhout E : 3 km © Antwerpen – ⊠ 2140 Borgerhout :

🏛 **Holiday Inn,** Luitenant Lippenslaan 66 ☎ (0 3) 235 91 91, Fax (0 3) 235 08 96, ≦s, ⬚
– ⊞ ⇔ ▤ TV ☎ P – ⚄ 25-230. AE ⓞ E VISA JCB. ⅍ rest
Meals (closed Sunday lunch) Lunch 950 – a la carte approx. 1500 – � 550 – **201 rm**
2950/7450, 3 suites.

at Deurne NE : 3 km © Antwerpen – ⊠ 2100 Deurne :

XX **De Violin,** Bosuil 1 ☎ (0 3) 324 34 04, Fax (0 3) 326 33 20, 🀆, « Small farmhouse »
– P. AE ⓞ E VISA. ⅍
closed Sunday, Monday dinner and late August-first 2 weeks September – **Meals** Lunch
1495 b.i. – a la carte approx. 2000.

at Ekeren N : 11 km © Antwerpen – ⊠ 2180 Ekeren :

XX **Hof de Bist,** Veltwijcklaan 258 ☎ (0 3) 664 61 30, Fax (0 3) 664 67 24, 🀆, « Rustic
inn » – P. AE ⓞ E VISA
closed Monday, Tuesday, August and Christmas holiday – **Meals** (dinner only) 2000.

at Merksem N : 2 km © Antwerpen – ⊠ 2170 Merksem :

XXX **Maritime,** Bredabaan 978 ☎ (0 3) 646 22 23, Fax (0 3) 646 22 71, 🀆, Seafood – P.
AE ⓞ E VISA. ⅍
closed Monday – **Meals** Lunch 995 – 1950.

Environs

at Aartselaar S : 10 km – pop. 14 380 – ⊠ 2630 Aartselaar :

🏛 **Kasteel Solhof** ⅍ without rest, Baron Van Ertbornstraat 116 ☎ (0 3) 877 30 00,
Fax (0 3) 877 31 31, « Terrace in public park », 🐎 – ⊞ TV ☎ P – ⚄ 25-50. AE ⓞ E
VISA. ⅍
closed Christmas-New Year – � 650 – **24 rm** 4800/8000.

XXXX **Host. Kasteelhoeve Groeninghe** with rm, Kontichsesteenweg 78 ☎ (0 3)
457 95 86, Fax (0 3) 458 13 68, ≼, 🀆, « Restored Flemish farm », 🐎 – TV ☎ P
⚄ 25-150. AE E VISA. ⅍
closed 20 December-4 January – **Meals** (closed Saturday lunch, Sunday and Bank Holidays)
Lunch 1500 – 2350/2950 – � 500 – **7 rm** 3900/5250.

XXX **Kasteel Cleydael** ⅍ with rm, Cleydaellaan 36 (W : direction Hemiksem) ☎ (0 3)
887 05 04, Fax (0 3) 877 20 18, « Restored moated feudal castle with golf course » – TV
☎ P – ⚄ 25-60. AE ⓞ E VISA. ⅍
closed Saturday lunch, Sunday, Monday, Bank Holidays, 18 July-18 August and 23 Decem-
ber-5 January – **Meals** Lunch 1750 b.i. – a la carte approx. 2300 – **6 rm** � 5500/6500, 1 suite

XX **Villa Verde,** Kleistraat 175 ☎ (0 3) 887 56 85, Fax (0 3) 887 22 56, ≼, 🀆, « Garden
and terrace » – P. AE ⓞ E VISA JCB. ⅍
closed Saturday lunch, Sunday dinner, Monday, carnival week, 15 July-7 August and 21
to 30 December – **Meals** Lunch 1200 – 1750/2450.

at Boechout SE : 9 km – pop. 11 744 – ⊠ 2530 Boechout :

XXX **De Schone van Boskoop** (Keersmaekers), Appelkantstraat 10 ☎ (0 3) 454 19 31,
🕸 Fax (0 3) 454 19 31, 🀆, « Interior design, ornamental pool and statues in garden » – P.
AE E VISA. ⅍
closed Sunday, Monday, 6 to 10 April, last 3 weeks August and first week January – **Meals**
Lunch 1500 – a la carte 2850/3350
Spec. Mille-feuille de St-Jacques crues aux truffes et haricots verts marinés. Coucou de
Malines au foie d'oie et truffes. Cannelloni aux deux chocolats, gelée de poires et sabayon
froid d'elixir d'Anvers.

at Kapellen N : 15,5 km – pop. 25 510 – ⊠ 2950 Kapellen :

XXX **De Bellefleur** (Buytaert), Antwerpsesteenweg 253 ☎ (0 3) 664 67 19, Fax (0 3)
🕸🕸 665 02 01, 🀆, « Veranda with pergola surrounded by floral garden » – P. AE ⓞ E VISA
closed Saturday lunch, Sunday, Monday and July – **Meals** Lunch 1850 b.i. – 3850 b.i., a la carte
2650/3750
Spec. St-Jacques poêlées aux cèpes de Bordeaux (October-February). Lotte rôtie, sauce
hollandaise à la moutarde. Lièvre des neiges au malt et aux légumes de saison (mid October-
December).

at Schilde NE : 13 km © 19 498 – ⊠ 2970 Schilde :

XX **Henri IV,** Louis Mariënlaan 5 ☎ (0 3) 383 11 49, Fax (0 3) 383 11 49, 🀆 – ▤ P. AE
ⓞ E VISA
closed Tuesday, Saturday lunch, 1 to 12 February and 30 August-23 September – **Meals**
a la carte 1400/1950.

t Schoten NE : 10 km – pop. 32 099 – ⊠ 2900 Schoten :

XX **Kleine Barreel**, Bredabaan 1147 ☎ (0 3) 645 85 84, Fax (0 3) 645 85 03 – ▤ ℗. ΑΕ
⓪ Ε 𝑉𝐼𝑆𝐴 JCB. ⌘
Meals Lunch 1175 – 1250/1675.

XX **Uilenspiegel**, Brechtsebaan 277 (3 km on N 115) ☎ (0 3) 651 61 45, Fax (0 3)
652 08 08, ☙, « Terrace and garden » – ℗. ΑΕ Ε 𝑉𝐼𝑆𝐴
closed Monday, Tuesday, 3 weeks July and 26 January-9 February – **Meals** 850/1990.

t Wijnegem E : 10 km – pop. 8 572 – ⊠ 2110 Wijnegem :

XXX **Ter Vennen**, Merksemsebaan 278 ☎ (0 3) 326 20 60, Fax (0 3) 326 38 47, ☙,
« Terrace » – ℗. ΑΕ ⓪ Ε 𝑉𝐼𝑆𝐴
Meals Lunch 1675 b.i. – 2295 b.i..

Kruiningen Zeeland (Netherlands) Ⓒ Reimerswaal pop. 20 499 𝟮𝟭𝟭 Ė 14 and 𝟵𝟬𝟴 Ḋ 7 – 56 km.

🏠 **Le Manoir** 🦢, Zandweg 2 (W : 1 km), ⊠ 4416 NA, ☎ (0 113) 38 17 53, Fax (0 113)
38 17 63, ≤, 🚣 – 📺 ☎ ℗. ΑΕ ⓪ Ε 𝑉𝐼𝑆𝐴 JCB
closed first week October and 3 weeks January – **Meals** see rest **Inter Scaldes** below –
⊡ 30 – **10 rm** 335/460, 2 suites.

XXXX **Inter Scaldes** (Mme Boudeling) - at Le Manoir H., Zandweg 2 (W : 1 km), ⊠ 4416 NA,
❀❀ ☎ (0 113) 38 17 53, Fax (0 113) 38 17 63, ☙, « Terrace-veranda overlooking an English-
style garden » – ℗. ΑΕ ⓪ Ε 𝑉𝐼𝑆𝐴 JCB
closed Monday, Tuesday, 1 week October and 3 weeks January – **Meals** Lunch 90 – 153/190,
– a la carte approx. 200
Spec. Homard fumé, sauce au caviar. Huîtres chaudes de Zélande, vinaigrette à la rose
(September-May). Turbot en robe de truffes et son beurre.

BRUGES (BRUGGE) 8000 West-Vlaanderen 𝟮𝟭𝟯 ③ and 𝟵𝟬𝟵 Ċ 2 – pop. 115 500.

See : Procession of the Holy Blood★★★ (De Heilig Bloedprocessie) – Historic centre and
canals★★★ (Historisch centrum en grachten) – Market square★★ (Markt) AU, Belfry and
Halles★★★ (Belfort en Hallen) ≤★★ from the top AU – Market-town★★ (Burg) AU – Basilica
of the Holy Blood★ (Basiliek van het Heilig Bloed) : low Chapel★ or St. Basiles Chapel (bene-
den- of St-Basiliuskapel) AU B – Chimney of the "Brugse Vrije"★ in the Palace of the
"Brugse Vrije" AU S – Rosery quay (Rozenhoedkaai) ≤★★ AU 63 – Dijver ≤★★ AU –
St. Boniface bridge (Bonifatiusbrug) : site★★ AU – Beguinage★★ (Begijnhof) AV – Trips on
the canals★★★ (Boottocht) AU – Church of Our Lady★ (O.-L.-Vrouwekerk) : tower★★, sta-
tue of the Madonna★★, tombstone★★ of Mary of Burgundy★★ AV N.
Museums : Groeninge★★★ (Stedelijk Museum voor Schone Kunsten) AU – Memling★★★
(St. John's Hospital) AV – Gruuthuse★ : bust of Charles the Fifth★ (borstbeeld van Karel-
V) AU M¹ – Brangwyn★ AU M⁴ – Folklore★ (Museum voor Volkskunde) DY M².
Envir : Zedelgem : baptismal font★ in the St. Lawrence's church SW : 10,5 km – Damme★
NE : 7 km.
📍 at Sijsele NE : 7 km, Doornstraat 16 ☎ (0 50) 33 35 72, Fax (0 50) 35 89 25.
🛈 Burg 11 ☎ (0 50) 44 86 86, Fax (0 50) 44 86 00 and at railway station, Stationsplein
– Tourist association of the province, Kasteel Tillegem ⊠ 8200 Sint-Michiels, ☎ (0 50)
38 02 96, Fax (0 50) 38 02 92.
Brussels 96 – Ghent 45 – Lille 72 – Ostend 28.

Plans on following pages

Town Centre

🏰 **Crowne Plaza** 🦢, Burg 10 ☎ (0 50) 34 58 34, Fax (0 50) 34 56 15, ≤, « Interesting
medieval remains and objects in basement », ℣ゟ, ≘s, ▨ – ▯ ⇥ ▤ 📺 ☎ ⅋ ☒ ℗
– ⚒ 25-400. ΑΕ ⓪ Ε 𝑉𝐼𝑆𝐴 JCB. ⌘   AU a
Meals : **'t Kapittel** (closed Wednesday dinner, Saturday lunch and Sunday) Lunch 995 b.i.
- 1450 b.i./2325 b.i. - **De Linde** Lunch 695 - a la carte 1000/1450 – ⊡ 800 – **93 rm**
6600/8000, 3 suites.

🏠 **de' Medici** 🦢, Potterierei 15 ☎ (0 50) 33 98 33 and 44 31 31 (rest), Fax (0 50) 33 07 64
and 33 05 71 (rest), « Modern style », ℣ゟ, ≘s – ▯ ⇥ 📺 ☎ ☒ ⅋ ℗ – ⚒ 25-80.
ΑΕ ⓪ Ε 𝑉𝐼𝑆𝐴 JCB. ⌘ rest   CX g
Meals (Japanese cuisine) (closed Monday and Tuesday lunch) Lunch 495 – 1280 – **79 rm**
⊡ 5300/6200.

🏠 **De Tuilerieën** without rest, Dijver 7 ☎ (0 50) 34 36 91, Fax (0 50) 34 04 00, ≤, ≘s
▨ – ▯ 📺 ☎ ℗ – ⚒ 25-45. ΑΕ ⓪ Ε 𝑉𝐼𝑆𝐴 JCB   AU c
closed 2 weeks December – **24 rm** ⊡ 7100/13100.

🏠 **Relais Oud Huis Amsterdam** 🦢 without rest, Spiegelrei 3 ☎ (0 50) 34 18 10,
Fax (0 50) 33 88 91, ≤, « 17C residence, former Dutch trading post », 🚣 – ▯ ⇥ 📺
☎ ☒ – ⚒ 25. ΑΕ ⓪ Ε 𝑉𝐼𝑆𝐴 JCB   AT d
34 rm ⊡ 4750/6750.

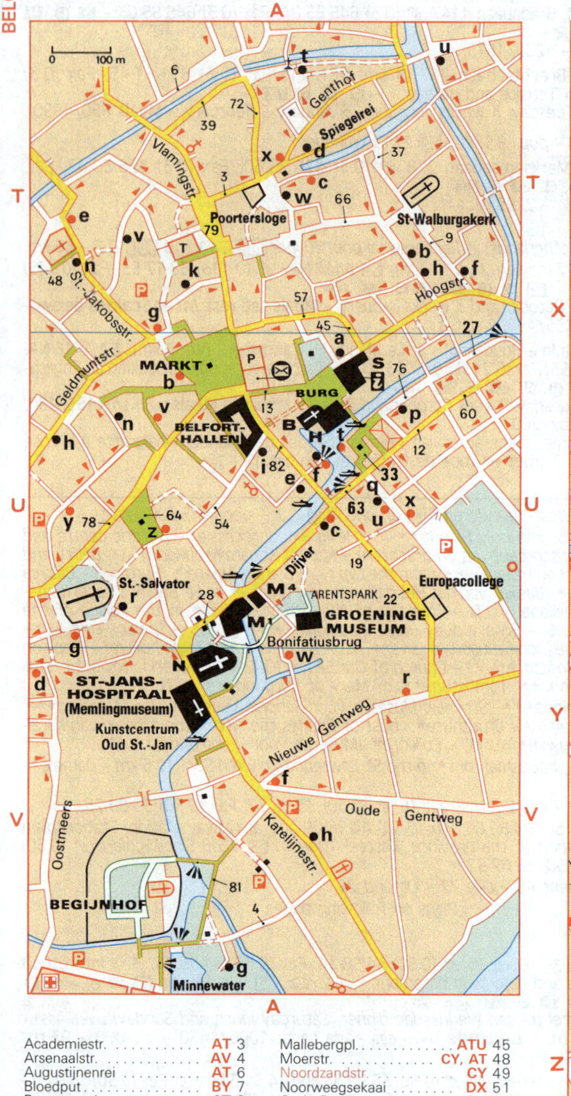
BRUGGE
0   100 m
0   300 m
Genthof
Spiegelrei
Vlamingstr.
Poortersloge
St-Walburgakerk
Hoogstr.
St.-Jakobsstr.
Geldmuntstr.
MARKT
BURG
BELFORT-HALLEN
Dijver
St.-Salvator
ARENTSPARK
Europacollege
GROENINGE MUSEUM
Bonifatiusbrug
ST-JANS-HOSPITAAL
(Memlingmuseum)
Kunstcentrum
Oud St.-Jan
Nieuwe Gentweg
Oostmeers
Katelijnestr.
Oude   Gentweg
BEGIJNHOF
Minnewater
Veemarktstr.
Sint
Leopold II
Leopold I laan
Scheepsdalelaan
Ezelpoort
Lauwerstraat
K. de Stoutelaan
Bevrijdingslaan
N 351
Guido Gezellelaan
Hoefijzer
Gulden
Smedenst.
SMEDENPOORT
Smedenst.
Hendrik
BEURSHA
POL.
N 32
Stationslaan
Consciencelaan
BOEVERIEPOORT
Kon. Albertlaan

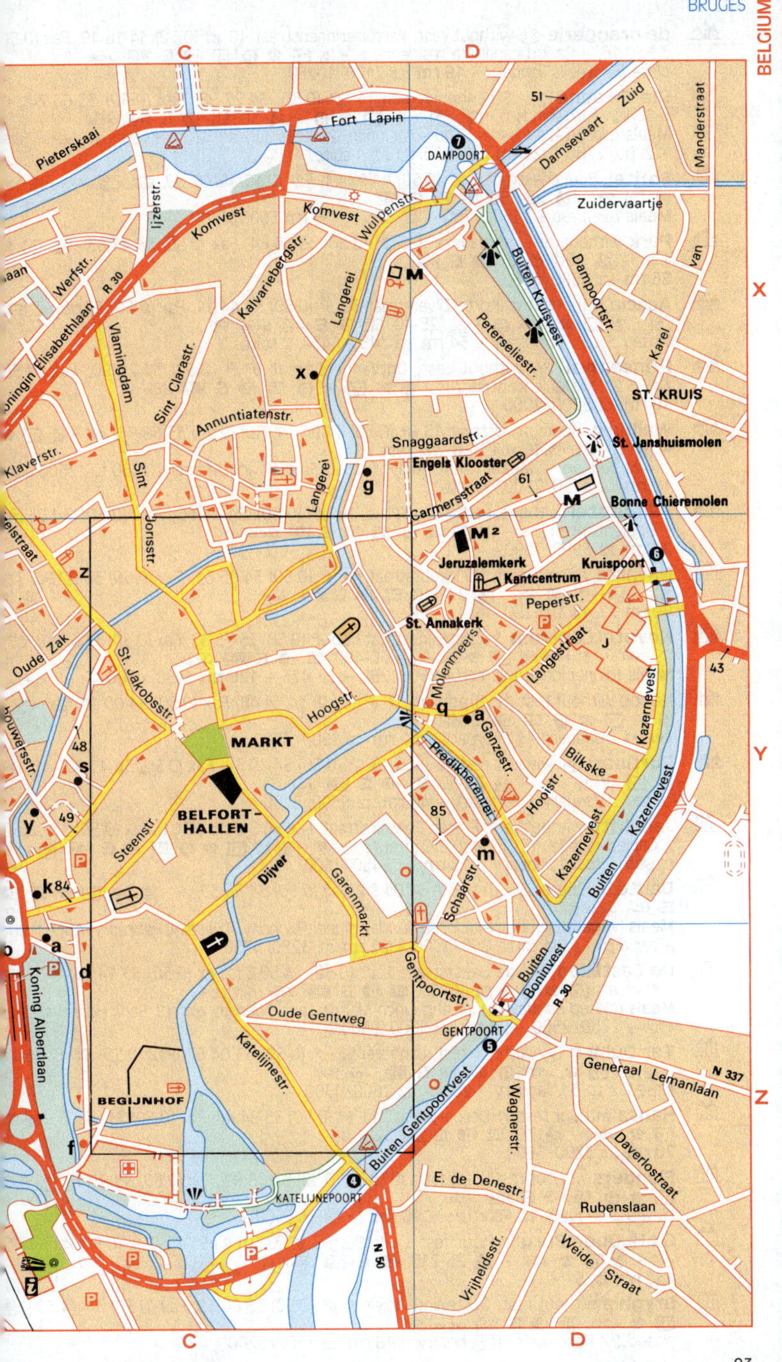
BELGIUM
Pieterskaai
Fort Lapin
51
Damsevaart
Zuid
Manderstraat
DAMPOORT
Zuidervaartje
Dampoortstr.
Komvest
Komvest
Wulpenstr.
Karel
van
Werfstr.
Kalvariebergstr.
Langerei
Buiten Kruisvest
X
Koningin Elisabethlaan
R 30
Vlamingdam
Peterseliestr.
Sint Clarastr.
ST. KRUIS
x
Annuntiatenstr.
Snaggaardstr.
St. Janshuismolen
Langerei
Engels Klooster
61
Bonne Chieremolen
Klaverstr.
g
Carmersstraat
M
Sint
Jonsstr.
Jeruzalemkerk
M²
Kantcentrum
Kruispoort
6
Peperstr.
Z
St. Annakerk
Oude Zak
Langestraat
J
Molenmeers
43
St. Jakobsstr.
Hoogstr.
q
a
Kazernevest
48
Ganzestr.
Bilkske
S
Predikherenrei
Hooistr.
Kazernevest
MARKT
y
49
85
Hooistr.
Kazernevest
Steenstr.
Buiten
k 84
BELFORT-
HALLEN
m
Buiten
Dijver
Garenmarkt
Schaarstr.
a
d
Gentpoortstr.
Buiten Boninvest
Koning Albertlaan
Oude Gentweg
R 30
Katelijnestr.
Gentpoort
5
Generaal Lemanlaan
N 337
BEGIJNHOF
Buiten Gentpoortvest
Wagnerstr.
Z
f
Daverlostraat
4
KATELIJNEPOORT
E. de Denestr.
Vrijheldsstr.
Rubenslaan
N 50
Weide
Straat
93

de orangerie ⑤ without rest, Kartuizerinnenstraat 10 ☎ (0 50) 34 16 49, Fax (0 50) 33 30 16, « Period canalside residence » – 🛗 TV ☎ 🅿. AE ① E VISA JCB
AU
closed 2 weeks January – **19 rm** ☐ 7100/10250.

Die Swaene ⑤, Steenhouwersdijk 1 ☎ (0 50) 34 27 98, Fax (0 50) 33 66 74, ≤
« Stylish furnishings », ≘s, 🏊 – 🛗 TV ☎ 🅿 – 🔬 30. AE ① E VISA JCB
AU
Meals (closed Wednesday, Thursday lunch, 2 weeks July and 2 weeks January) Lunch 125
– 2000/2700 – **21 rm** ☐ 6000/9150, 1 suite.

Sofitel, Boeveriestraat 2 ☎ (0 50) 44 97 11, Fax (0 50) 44 97 99, ≘s, 🏊, 🏏 – 🛗 ✦
🗇 TV ☎ – 🔬 25-150. AE ① E VISA JCB
CZ
Meals Lunch 550 – 1150/1750 – ☐ 575 – **155 rm** 5900/7100.

Park without rest, Vrijdagmarkt 5 ☎ (0 50) 33 33 64, Fax (0 50) 33 47 63 – 🛗 TV
🚗 – 🔬 25-250. AE ① E VISA
CY
86 rm ☐ 4580/5860.

Acacia without rest, Korte Zilverstraat 3a ☎ (0 50) 34 44 11, Fax (0 50) 33 88 17, ≘s
🏊 – 🛗 TV ☎ 🚗 🅿 – 🔬 25-40. AE ① E VISA JCB. ✱
AU
closed 3 to 20 January – **34 rm** ☐ 3450/6450, 2 suites.

Prinsenhof ⑤ without rest, Ontvangersstraat 9 ☎ (0 50) 34 26 90, Fax (0 50)
34 23 21, « Opulent interior » – 🛗 🗇 TV ☎ 🅿. AE ① E VISA JCB
CY
16 rm ☐ 3700/7000.

Walburg, Boomgaardstraat 13 ☎ (0 50) 34 94 14, Fax (0 50) 33 68 84, 🚗 – 🛗 TV
– 🔬 30. AE ① E VISA JCB. ✱ rest
AT
closed January – **Meals** (dinner only) (closed Sunday and Monday) 1650 b.i./2500 b.i. –
12 rm ☐ 4750/7500, 1 suite.

Pandhotel without rest, Pandreitje 16 ☎ (0 50) 34 06 66, Fax (0 50) 34 05 56
« Opulent interior » – 🛗 TV ☎ 🅿. AE ① E VISA JCB
AU
24 rm ☐ 3990/7990.

Navarra without rest, St-Jakobsstraat 41 ☎ (0 50) 34 05 61, Fax (0 50) 33 67 90, 🕫
≘s, 🏊 – 🛗 TV ☎ – 🔬 25-110. AE ① E VISA JCB
AT
89 rm ☐ 4500/5250.

Novotel Centrum ⑤, Katelijnestraat 65b ☎ (0 50) 33 75 33, Fax (0 50) 33 65 56, 🏡
🏊, 🚗 – 🛗 ✦ 🗇 TV ☎ 🕭 – 🔬 50-400. AE ① E VISA JCB
AV
Meals (dinner only) a la carte 850/1250 – ☐ 475 – **126 rm** 3950/4300.

Karos without rest, Hoefijzerlaan 37 ☎ (0 50) 34 14 48, Fax (0 50) 34 00 91, ≘s, 🏊
🛗 🗇 TV ☎ 🅿. AE ① E VISA
BY
closed 2 January-14 February – **60 rm** ☐ 2900/4800.

Portinari ⑤ without rest, 't Zand 15 ☎ (0 50) 34 10 34, Fax (0 50) 34 41 80 – 🛗 ✦
🗇 TV ☎ 🕭 🚗 – 🔬 25-80. AE ① E VISA JCB
CY
closed 2 January-1 February – **40 rm** ☐ 3500/5200.

Jan Brito without rest, Freren Fonteinstraat 1 ☎ (0 50) 33 06 01, Fax (0 50) 33 06 52
« Gabled façade, 16, 17 and 18C interior », 🚗 – 🛗 🗇 TV ☎ 🅿. AE ① E VISA JCB. ✱
AU
closed 3 to 21 January – **18 rm** ☐ 3450/7600.

Dante, Coupure 29a ☎ (0 50) 34 01 94, Fax (0 50) 34 35 39, ≤ – 🛗 ✦ TV ☎. AE ①
E VISA JCB. ✱
DY
Meals (vegetarian cuisine) (closed Sunday dinner, Monday, Tuesday, February, August and
after 8 p.m.) a la carte 850/1300 – **22 rm** ☐ 3250/4750.

De Castillion, Heilige Geeststraat 1 ☎ (0 50) 34 30 01, Fax (0 50) 33 94 75, 🏡, ≘s
– 🗇 rest, TV ☎ 🅿 – 🔬 25-50. AE ① E VISA JCB. ✱ rest
AU
Meals (closed Sunday dinner and lunch Monday and Tuesday except Bank Holidays) Lunch
1500 – 2250/2500 – **20 rm** ☐ 5000/9500.

Ter Duinen ⑤ without rest, Langerei 52 ☎ (0 50) 33 04 37, Fax (0 50) 34 42 16, ≤
– 🛗 🗇 TV ☎ 🚗 🅿. AE ① E VISA JCB. ✱
CX
closed 2 to 31 January – **20 rm** ☐ 2600/4500.

Hansa without rest, N. Desparsstraat 11 ☎ (0 50) 33 84 44, Fax (0 50) 33 42 05 – 🛗 🗇
TV ☎ 🚗 – 🔬 30. AE ① E VISA JCB. ✱
AT
20 rm ☐ 3200/5600.

Flanders without rest, Langestraat 38 ☎ (0 50) 33 88 89, Fax (0 50) 33 93 45, 🏊 – 🛗
TV ☎ 🅿. AE ① E VISA JCB
DY
closed 3 January-12 February – **16 rm** ☐ 3950/5500.

Gd H. Oude Burg without rest, Oude Burg 5 ☎ (0 50) 44 51 11, Fax (0 50) 44 51 00
🚗 – 🛗 TV ☎ 🚗 – 🔬 25-210. ① E VISA JCB
AU
138 rm ☐ 5750.

Bryghia without rest, Oosterlingenplein 4 ☎ (0 50) 33 80 59, Fax (0 50) 34 14 30 – 🛗
TV ☎ 🚗. AE ① E VISA JCB. ✱
AT
closed 27 December-10 February – **18 rm** ☐ 3500/5200.

Adornes without rest, St-Annarei 26 ℘ (0 50) 34 13 36, Fax (0 50) 34 20 85, ≤, « Period vaulted cellars » – |‡| TV ☎ 🅿. AE E VISA JCB
AT u
closed January-12 February – **20 rm** ⌖ 2700/3700.

Aragon without rest, Naaldenstraat 24 ℘ (0 50) 33 35 33, Fax (0 50) 34 28 05 – |‡| TV ☎ ⊂⊃. AE ① E VISA JCB
AT v
39 rm ⌖ 4000/4800.

Biskajer ≫ without rest, Biskajersplein 4 ℘ (0 50) 34 15 06, Fax (0 50) 34 39 11 – |‡| TV ☎. AE ① E VISA
AT w
17 rm ⌖ 3200/3950.

Azalea without rest, Wulfhagestraat 43 ℘ (0 50) 33 14 78, Fax (0 50) 33 97 00, « Canalside terrace » – |‡| TV ☎ ⊂⊃ 🅿. AE ① E VISA JCB
CY y
25 rm ⌖ 3200/5500.

't Putje (with annex ≫), 't Zand 31 ℘ (0 50) 33 28 47, Fax (0 50) 34 14 23, 🏵 – |‡| TV ☎ – 🔬 30. AE ① E VISA. ⊗
CZ a
Meals (Pub rest, partly grill, open until midnight) Lunch 315 – 850/995 – **24 rm** ⌖ 2250/3400.

Patritius without rest, Riddersstraat 11 ℘ (0 50) 33 84 54, Fax (0 50) 33 96 34, 🚗 |‡| TV ☎ &. ⊂⊃ 🅿 – 🔬 25. AE ① E VISA JCB
AT b
closed January-13 February – **16 rm** ⌖ 2900/4000.

Anselmus without rest, Ridderstraat 15 ℘ (0 50) 34 13 74, Fax (0 50) 34 19 16 – TV ☎. AE E VISA JCB. ⊗
AT h
closed January – **10 rm** ⌖ 2550/2950.

Ter Brughe without rest, Oost-Gistelhof 2 ℘ (0 50) 34 03 24, Fax (0 50) 33 88 73, « Ancient vaulted cellars » – TV ☎. AE ① E VISA
AT a
23 rm ⌖ 2900/5400.

Egmond ≫ without rest, Minnewater 15 ℘ (0 50) 34 14 45, Fax (0 50) 34 29 40, ≤, « Early 20C residence in garden » – TV ☎ 🅿. ⊗
AV g
closed January – **8 rm** ⌖ 3700/3950.

Gd H. du Sablon, Noordzandstraat 21 ℘ (0 50) 33 39 02, Fax (0 50) 33 39 08, « Early 20C hall with Art Deco cupola » – |‡| TV ☎ – 🔬 25-100. AE ① E VISA
AU h
Meals (residents only) – **36 rm** ⌖ 3100/3900.

Bourgoensch Hof, Wollestraat 39 ℘ (0 50) 33 16 45, Fax (0 50) 34 63 78, ≤ canals and old Flemish houses, 🏵 – |‡| TV ☎ ⊂⊃ 🅿. E VISA
AU f
closed 10 January-15 February ; 18 November-15 March open weekends only – **Meals** Lunch 985 – a la carte approx. 1400 – **15 rm** ⌖ 3350/5350.

Montovani ≫ without rest, Schouwvegerstraat 11 ℘ (0 50) 34 53 66, Fax (0 50) 34 53 67 – TV ☎. AE ① E VISA. ⊗
BY c
closed 24, 25 and 31 December, 1 January and 11 to 28 January – **13 rm** ⌖ 1600/2600.

XXXX
❀❀❀
De Karmeliet (Van Hecke), Langestraat 19 ℘ (0 50) 33 82 59, Fax (0 50) 33 10 11, 🏵, « Ancient patrician residence, terrace » – 🅿. AE ① E VISA JCB. ⊗
DY q
closed Sunday lunch June-September, Sunday dinner, Monday and 16 August-3 September – **Meals** 3400/5800 b.i., – a la carte 3050/3750
Spec. Suprêmes de pigeon rôti, ses cuisses confites et pied de porc en saucisson. Tuile sucrée et salée aux grosses langoustines et chicons confits. Ravioli à la vanille et pommes caramélisées en chaud-froid.

XXX
❀
De Snippe (Huysentruyt) ≫ with rm, Nieuwe Gentweg 53 ℘ (0 50) 33 70 70, Fax (0 50) 33 76 62, 🏵, « 18C residence with murals and shaded terrace » – |‡| TV ☎ 🅿. AE ① E VISA
AV r
closed 14 February-12 March – **Meals** (closed Sunday and Monday lunch) – 1950/3650 b.i., – a la carte approx. 2900 – **9 rm** (closed Sunday November-Easter) ⌖ 5000/5500
Spec. Filets de sole farcis aux truffes et jeunes artichauts. St-Jacques grillées à la crème de salsifis et caviar. Civet de pigeonneau aux girolles.

XXX
❀
Den Gouden Harynck (Serruys), Groeninge 25 ℘ (0 50) 33 76 37, Fax (0 50) 34 42 70 – 🅿. AE ① E VISA
AUV w
closed Sunday, Monday, 1 week after Easter, last 2 weeks July-first week August and last week December – **Meals** Lunch 1300 – 2200, a la carte approx. 2700
Spec. Langoustines grillées au curry doux et pomme verte. Homard vapeur à l'huile de noix. Canard à la fondue d'oignons, navets et aromates.

XXX
Duc de Bourgogne with rm, Huidenvettersplein 12 ℘ (0 50) 33 20 38, Fax (0 50) 34 40 37, ≤ canals, « Rustic decor and murals of late medieval style » – ▤ rest, TV ☎. AE ① E VISA JCB
AU t
closed 3 weeks July and January – **Meals** (closed Monday and Tuesday lunch) Lunch 1250 – a la carte approx. 2500 – **10 rm** ⌖ 3700/5300.

XXX
Den Braamberg, Pandreitje 11 ℘ (0 50) 33 73 70, Fax (0 50) 33 99 73 – AE E VISA
closed Thursday, Sunday, 15 to 31 July and 1 to 12 January – **Meals** Lunch 1780 b.i. – a la carte 1950/2600.
AU q

BRUGES

XXX **'t Pandreitje,** Pandreitje 6 ℘ (0 50) 33 11 90, Fax (0 50) 34 00 70 – AE ① E VISA JC
closed Wednesday, Sunday, 15 to 21 February, 5 to 21 July and 1 to 7 November – Mea
– 1750/2450.
AU

XXX **De Witte Poorte,** Jan Van Eyckplein 6 ℘ (0 50) 33 08 83, Fax (0 50) 34 55 60,
« Vaulted dining room, walled inner garden » – AE ① E VISA JCB
AT
closed Sunday, Monday, late June-early July and 2 weeks January – **Meals** *Lunch 1150*
1700/1950.

XX **De Lotteburg,** Goezeputstraat 43 ℘ (0 50) 33 75 35, Fax (0 50) 33 04 04,
« Shaded terrace » – ▣. AE ① E VISA JCB. ⚗
AV
closed Monday, Tuesday, last week January-first week February and 26 July-8 August
Meals *Lunch 1095 – 1550/1950.*

XX **'t Stil Ende,** Scheepsdalelaan 12 ℘ (0 50) 33 92 03, Fax (0 50) 33 26 22, 🌳, « Moder
interior » – ▣. AE ① E VISA. ⚗
BX
closed Saturday lunch, Sunday dinner, Monday, first week March and late July-early Augu
– **Meals** *950/1850.*

XX **'t Bourgoensche Cruyce** 🦢 with rm, Wollestraat 41 ℘ (0 50) 33 79 26, Fax (0 5
34 19 68, ≤ canals and old Flemish houses – ⊠, ▣ rest, TV ☎. AE ①
E VISA
AU
Meals *(closed Tuesday, Wednesday, 28 June-7 July and 15 November-9 December) Lun*
1750 b.i. – a la carte 2100/2800 – **8 rm** *(closed 15 November-9 December)* 🍵 *3500/490*

XX **Hermitage** (Dryepondt), Ezelstraat 18 ℘ (0 50) 34 41 73, Fax (0 50) 34 10 27 – ①
☸ VISA JCB
CY
closed Sunday, Monday and July-August – **Meals** *(dinner only) (booking essential) a la car*
approx. 2500
Spec. Buisson de filets de sole en goujonnettes. Queues de langoustines grillées à l'ail e
fines herbes. Pigeonneau rôti aux baies de cassis.

XX **Kardinaalshof,** St-Salvatorskerkhof 14 ℘ (0 50) 34 16 91, Fax (0 50) 34 20 62, Sea
food – AE ① E VISA
AUV
closed Wednesday, Thursday lunch and late June-early July – **Meals** *– 1150/1950.*

XX **Patrick Devos,** Zilverstraat 41 ℘ (0 50) 33 55 66, Fax (0 50) 33 58 67, 🌳, « Bel
Epoque interior, patio » – AE ① E VISA JCB. ⚗
AU
closed Sunday, Bank Holidays, 21 July-8 August and 24 to 31 December – **Meals** *Lun*
1100 b.i. – 1200/2400.

XX **Bhavani,** Simon Stevinplein 5 ℘ (0 50) 33 90 25, Fax (0 50) 34 89 52, 🌳, Indian cuisir
– AE ① E VISA
AU
Meals *Lunch 550 – a la carte approx. 1100.*

XX **Den Dijver,** Dijver 5 ℘ (0 50) 33 60 69, Fax (0 50) 44 62 51, 🌳, Beer cuisine – AE
VISA
AU
closed Tuesday 15 November-15 March, Wednesday, late February-early March, late June
early July and late August-early September – **Meals** *Lunch 850 – 1400 b.i..*

XX **Spinola,** Spinolarei 1 ℘ (0 50) 34 17 85, Fax (0 50) 34 13 71, « Rustic » – AE ① E VIS
closed Sunday, Monday lunch, last week January-first week February and last week June
first week July – **Meals** *– 1550/1950.*
AT

XX **Tanuki,** Oude Gentweg 1 ℘ (0 50) 34 75 12, Fax (0 50) 33 82 42, Japanese cuisine wit
Teppan-Yaki and Sushi-bar – ▣. AE E VISA JCB
AV
closed Monday, Tuesday, late July and late January – **Meals** *Lunch 480 – 1690/2100.*

X **Brasserie Raymond,** Eiermarkt 5 ℘ (0 50) 33 78 48, Fax (0 50) 33 78 48, 🌳, Ope
until 11.30 p.m. – AE ① E VISA JCB
AT
closed Monday dinner, Tuesday, 1 to 15 March and 1 to 15 July – **Meals** *Lunch 495 – 995 b*

X **Cafedraal,** Zilverstraat 38 ℘ (0 50) 34 08 45, Fax (0 50) 33 52 41, 🌳, Pub rest, ope
until 11.30 p.m., « Historical residence with inner terrace » – AE ① E VISA JCB AU
closed Sunday and Monday – **Meals** *Lunch 395 – a la carte 1300/1700.*

X **Huize Die Maene,** Markt 17 ℘ (0 50) 33 39 59, Fax (0 50) 33 44 60, Pub rest, ope
until 11 p.m. – AE ① E VISA
AU
Meals *Lunch 495 – 975.*

X **René Van Puyenbroeck,** St-Jakobsstraat 58 ℘ (0 50) 34 12 24 – AE E VISA JCB. ⚗
closed Sunday dinner, Monday and 10 July-8 August – **Meals** *975/1450.*
AT

Suburbs

North-West – ✉ *8000 :*

XX **De Gouden Korenhalm,** Oude Oostendsesteenweg 79a (Sint-Pieters) ℘ (0 50
31 33 93, Fax (0 50) 31 18 96, 🌳, « Typical Flemish farmhouse » – ℗. AE ① E VISA
closed Monday, Wednesday dinner, late February and late August-early September – Mea
Lunch 995 – 1450/1950.

South – ⊠ 8200 :

🏨 **Novotel Zuid,** Chartreuseweg 20 (Sint-Michiels) ✆ (0 50) 40 21 40, *Fax (0 50) 40 21 41,*
☂, 🛋, 🎱 – |💃| 🚭, 🍽 rest, 📺 ☎ 🔥 ℙ – 🍽 25-200. 🆎 ⓵ Ⓔ 𝘝𝘐𝘚𝘈 𝐉𝐂𝐁
Meals *Lunch 590* – 850 – ⊇ 475 – **101 rm** 3450/3850.

XX **Casserole** (Hotel school), Groene-Poortdreef 17 (Sint-Michiels) ✆ (0 50) 40 30 30,
Fax (0 50) 40 30 35, ☂, « Garden setting » – ℙ – 🍽 25. 🆎 ⓵ 𝘝𝘐𝘚𝘈. 🐾
closed Saturday, Sunday and school Holidays – **Meals** (lunch only) 950.

South-West – ⊠ 8200 :

🏨 **Host. Pannenhuis** 🐾, Zandstraat 2 ✆ (0 50) 31 19 07, *Fax (0 50) 31 77 66,* ≤, ☂,
« Terrace and garden » – 📺 ☎ 🔥 ℙ – 🍽 25. 🆎 ⓵ Ⓔ 𝘝𝘐𝘚𝘈 𝐉𝐂𝐁. 🐾 rest
Meals *(closed Tuesday dinner, Wednesday, 15 January-2 February and 2 to 19 July)* *Lunch*
1300 – 1550/1850 – **18 rm** ⊇ 3450/4250.

XX **Herborist** 🐾 with rm, De Watermolen 15 (by N 32 : 6 km, then on the right after E 40,
St-Andries) ✆ (0 50) 38 76 00, *Fax (0 50) 39 31 06,* ☂, « Inn with country atmosphere »,
🏇 – 🍽 rest, 📺 ☎ ℙ. Ⓔ 𝘝𝘐𝘚𝘈. 🐾
closed Sunday dinner, Monday, 22 March-6 April, 26 June-6 July, 26 September-6 October
and 26 December-10 January – **Meals** *Lunch 2250 b.i.* – 3350 b.i./3850 b.i. – **4 rm**
⊇ 3250/4350.

at Sint-Kruis *E : 6 km* Ⓒ *Bruges* – ⊠ 8310 Sint-Kruis :

🏨 **Wilgenhof** 🐾 without rest, Polderstraat 151 ✆ (0 50) 36 27 44, *Fax (0 50) 36 28 21,*
≤, « An area of reclaimed land (polder) », 🏇 – 📺 ☎ ℙ. 🆎 ⓵ Ⓔ 𝘝𝘐𝘚𝘈
closed last week January – **6 rm** ⊇ 2500/4100.

XXX **Ronnie Jonkman,** Maalsesteenweg 438 ✆ (0 50) 36 07 67, *Fax (0 50) 35 76 96,* ☂,
« Terraces » – ℙ. 🆎 ⓵ Ⓔ 𝘝𝘐𝘚𝘈 𝐉𝐂𝐁
closed Sunday, Monday, 1 to 15 April, 15 to 30 July and 1 to 15 October – **Meals** *Lunch*
1850 b.i. – a la carte 2000/2450.

Environs

at Hertsberge *S by N 50 : 12,5 km* Ⓒ *Oostkamp pop. 21 078* – ⊠ 8020 Hertsberge :

XXX **Manderley,** Kruisstraat 13 ✆ (0 50) 27 80 51, *Fax (0 50) 27 80 51,* ☂, « Terrace and
garden » – ℙ. 🆎 ⓵ Ⓔ 𝘝𝘐𝘚𝘈
closed Sunday dinner, Monday, first week October and last 3 weeks January – **Meals** *Lunch*
1250 – 1750/2100.

at Ruddervoorde *S by N 50 : 12 km* Ⓒ *Oostkamp pop. 21 078* – ⊠ 8020 Ruddervoorde :

XX **Host. Leegendael** with rm, Kortrijkstraat 498 (N 50) ✆ (0 50) 27 76 99, *Fax (0 50)*
27 58 80, « Period residence, country atmosphere » – 🍽 rest, 📺 ☎ ℙ. 🆎 ⓵
Ⓔ 𝘝𝘐𝘚𝘈
closed 1 week carnival and last week June-first week July – **Meals** *(closed Tuesday, Wed-*
nesday and Sunday dinner) *Lunch 990* – a la carte 1600/2000 – **6 rm** ⊇ 1750/2550.

at Varsenare *W : 6,5 km* Ⓒ *Jabbeke pop. 13 411* – ⊠ 8490 Varsenare :

XXX **Manoir Stuivenberg** (Scherrens frères) with rm, Gistelsteenweg 27 ✆ (0 50) 38 15 02,
❀ *Fax (0 50) 38 28 92,* ☂ – |💃|, 🍽 rest, 📺 ☎ ℙ – 🍽 25-400. 🆎 ⓵ Ⓔ 𝘝𝘐𝘚𝘈. 🐾
closed Sunday and Monday except Bank Holidays and 19 July-3 August – **Meals** *Lunch 1485*
– 3495 b.i., a la carte 2650/3200 – **8 rm** ⊇ 5000/6750, 1 suite
Spec. Filets de rouget à la brunoise de câpres et citron. Poitrine de pigeon en crapaudine.
Soufflé chaud à la vanille, sauce au chocolat.

at Waardamme *S by N 50 : 11 km* Ⓒ *Oostkamp pop. 21 078* – ⊠ 8020 Waardamme :

XX **Ter Talinge,** Rooiveldstraat 46 ✆ (0 50) 27 90 61, *Fax (0 50) 28 00 52,* ☂, « Terrace »
– ℙ. 🆎 Ⓔ 𝘝𝘐𝘚𝘈
closed Wednesday, Thursday, 19 February-4 March and 20 August-2 September – **Meals**
Lunch 1100 – 1725.

at Zedelgem *SW : 10,5 km* – pop. 21 681 – ⊠ 8210 Zedelgem :

🏨 **Zuidwege,** Torhoutsesteenweg 128 ✆ (0 50) 20 13 39, *Fax (0 50) 20 17 39,* ☂ – 🚭,
🍽 rm, 📺 ☎ ℙ – 🍽 25. 🆎 ⓵ Ⓔ 𝘝𝘐𝘚𝘈. 🐾 rm
Meals (Pub rest) *(closed Saturday, Sunday lunch and Christmas holiday)* a la carte 850/1300
– **16 rm** ⊇ 1900/2750.

XX **Ter Leepe,** Torhoutsesteenweg 168 ✆ (0 50) 20 01 97, *Fax (0 50) 20 88 54* – 🍽 ℙ
– 🍽 220. 🆎 ⓵ Ⓔ 𝘝𝘐𝘚𝘈
closed Wednesday dinner, Sunday and 19 July-4 August – **Meals** *Lunch 1375 b.i.* – a la carte
1200/1750.

BELGIUM

Kruishoutem 9770 Oost-Vlaanderen 213 ⑯ and 909 D 3 – pop. 7 769 – 44 km.

XXX **Hof van Cleve** (Goossens), Riemegemstraat 1 (near N 459, motorway E 17 - A 14, exi
⑥) ℰ (0 9) 383 58 48, Fax (0 9) 383 77 25, ≼, 🏡, « Farmhouse in open fields » – 🄵
AE ⓸ E VISA. 🛇 – closed Sunday, Monday, 1 week Easter, 3 weeks August and lat
December-early January – **Meals** Lunch 1850 – 2450/3750, – a la carte 2500/3350
Spec. Ravioli ouvert de girolles et joue de bœuf braisée, sabayon à l'estragon. Pigeonnea
au lard croustillant, parmentière aux truffes et Banyuls. Moelleux au chocolat, coulis d
griottes et glace au thé vert.

Waregem 8790 West-Vlaanderen 213 ⑮ and 909 D 3 – pop. 35 750 – 47 km.

XXXX **'t Oud Konijntje** (Mmes Desmedt), Bosstraat 53 (S : 2 km near E 17) ℰ (0 56) 60 19 3
Fax (0 56) 60 92 12, 🏡, « Floral terrace » – 🄿 AE ⓸ E VISA
closed dinner Thursday and Sunday, Friday, 21 July-13 August and 24 December-4 Januar
– **Meals** Lunch 1650 – 1950/3950, – a la carte 2550/3150
Spec. Gâteau de homard, pommes d'amour confites à l'huile d'olives. Poêlée de crevette
de Zeebrugge et turbotin en mousseline de pommes de terre. Raviolis de ris de veau poch
au bouillon de poule, râpée de truffes et vieux Parmesan.

Sluis Zeeland (Netherlands) © Sluis-Aardenburg pop. 6 455 211 F 15 and 908 B 8 – 21 km.

XX **Oud Sluis** (Herman), Beestenmarkt 2, ✉ 4524 EA, ℰ (0 117) 46 12 69, Fax (0 117
46 30 05, 🏡, Seafood, « Typical farmhouse » – AE ⓸ E VISA
closed Thursday, Friday, 2 weeks June, 2 weeks October and last week December – **Mea**
Lunch 80 – 110/185 b.i., – a la carte 135/165
Spec. Six préparations d'huîtres de Zélande (September-April). Pot-au-feu de turbot et d
homard de Zélande (May-August). Bar aux langoustines grillées, risotto au citron et fine
herbes (May-October).

LIÈGE 4000 213 ㉒ and 909 J 4 ⑰ N – pop. 189 510.

See : Citadel ≼★★ DW – Cointe Park ≼★ CX – Old town★★ – Palace of the Prince
Bishops★ : court of honour★★ EY – The Perron★ (market cross) EY A – Baptisma
font★★★ of St. Bartholomew's church FY – Treasury★★ of St. Paul's Cathedral : reliquar
of Charles the Bold★★ EZ – St. James church★★ : vaults of the nave★★ EZ – Altarpiece
in the St. Denis church EY – Church of St. John : Wooden Calvary statues★ EY
Aquarium★ FZ D.
Museums : Life in Wallonia★★ EY – Religious and Roman Art Museum★ FY M⁵ – Curtius an
Glass Museum★ : evangelistary of Notger★★★, collection of glassware★ FY M¹
Arms★ FY M³ – Ansembourg★ FY M² – Modern Art and Contemporary Art★ DX M⁷.
Envir : Blégny-Trembleur★★ NE : 20 km – Baptismal font★ in the church★ of St. Severi
SW : 27 km – Visé N : 17 km, Reliquary of St. Hadelin★ in the collegiate church.
🏌₉ r. Bernalmont 2 ℰ 227 44 66, Fax 227 91 92 - 🏌₁₈ at Angleur S : 7,5 km, rte du Cor
droz 541 ℰ (0 4) 336 20 21, Fax (0 4) 337 20 26 - 🏌₁₈ at Gomzé-Andoumont SE : 18 km
r. Gomzé 30 ℰ (0 4) 360 92 07, Fax (0 4) 360 92 06.
🚗 ℰ (0 4) 342 52 14.
🄱 En Féronstrée 92 ℰ (0 4) 221 92 21, Fax (0 4) 221 92 22 and Gare des Guillemin
ℰ (0 4) 252 44 19 – Tourist association of the province, bd de la Sauvenière 77 ℰ (0 4
232 65 10, Fax (0 4) 232 65 11.
Brussels 97 – Amsterdam 242 – Antwerp 119 – Cologne 122 – Luxembourg 159.

Plans on following pages

🏨 **Bedford** Ⓜ, quai St-Léonard 36 ℰ (0 4) 228 81 11, Fax (0 4) 227 45 75, 🏡, « Inne
garden » – 🛗 ✀ 🖥 TV ☎ 🚻 🚗 🄿 – 🛗 25-220. AE ⓸ E VISA   DW
Meals Lunch 990 – a la carte 950/1350 – **147 rm** 🍽 6950/8450, 2 suites.

Old town

🏨 **Mercure**, bd de la Sauvenière 100 ℰ (0 4) 221 77 11, Fax (0 4) 221 77 01 – 🛗 ✀ 🖥
TV ☎ 🚗 – 🛗 25-100. AE ⓸ E VISA   EY
Meals Lunch 590 – a la carte approx. 1300 – **105 rm** 🍽 4950/5450.

XXX **Au Vieux Liège**, quai Goffe 41 ℰ (0 4) 223 77 48, Fax (0 4) 223 78 60, « 160
residence » – 🖥. AE ⓸ E VISA   FY a
closed Wednesday dinner, Sunday and mid July-mid August – **Meals** Lunch 990 – 1350/1900

XXX **Chez Max,** pl. de la République Française 12 ℰ (0 4) 222 08 73, Fax (0 4) 222 90 02, 🏡
Oyster bar, « Elegant brasserie decorated by Luc Genot » – AE ⓸ E VISA   EY
closed Saturday lunch and Sunday – **Meals** Lunch 490 – a la carte 1350/1650.

XX **Robert Lesenne,** r. Boucherie 9 ℰ (0 4) 222 07 93, Fax (0 4) 222 92 33, « Ancien
almshouse watchtower in an atrium » – 🖥. AE ⓸ E VISA   FY n
closed Saturday lunch, Sunday and 15 July-15 August – **Meals** 1495
Spec. Foie gras de trois façons. Rognon de veau au Péket. Soufflé moelleux au chocolat

XX **Folies Gourmandes,** r. Clarisses 48 ☎ (0 4) 223 16 44, 🌿, « Early 20C house with garden-terrace » – AE ⓸ E VISA   EZ q
closed Sunday dinner, Monday, 1 week after Easter and last 2 weeks September – **Meals** – 1150.

XX **Le Shanghai** 1st floor, Galeries Cathédrale 104 ☎ (0 4) 222 22 63, *Fax (0 4) 223 00 50,* Chinese cuisine – 🍽. AE ⓸ E VISA   EZ r
closed Tuesday, 15 to 24 February and 6 to 28 July – **Meals** *Lunch 525* – a la carte approx. 1000.

X **Enoteca,** r. Casquette 5 ☎ (0 4) 222 24 64
E VISA. ✷   EY g
closed Saturday lunch and Sunday – Meals *Lunch 590* – 1090.

X **Lalo's Bar,** r. Madeleine 18 ☎ (0 4) 223 22 57, *Fax (0 4) 223 22 57,* Italian cuisine, open until 11 p.m. – 🍽. AE ⓸ E VISA   EY d
closed Saturday lunch, Sunday and 15 July-15 August – **Meals** *Lunch 690* – 850/1250.

Guillemins

🏠 **L'Univers** without rest, r. Guillemins 116 ☎ (0 4) 254 55 55, *Fax (0 4) 254 55 00* – ◫
✺ TV ☎ P – 🔼 25-80. AE ⓸ E VISA   CX a
☕ 270 – **47 rm** 1900/2200.

X **Le Duc d'Anjou,** r. Guillemins 127 ☎ (0 4) 252 28 58, Mussels in season, open until 11.30 p.m. – 🍽. AE ⓸ E VISA   CX n
Meals – 820.

Right banc (Outremeuse - Palais des Congrès)

🏨 **Holiday Inn** without rest, Esplanade de l'Europe 2, ✉ 4020, ☎ (0 4) 342 60 20, *Fax (0 4) 343 48 10,* ≤, 🏋, ≋s, 🖼 – ◫ ✺ 🍽 TV ☎ ♿ ⇔ P – 🔼 25-70. AE ⓸ E VISA
214 rm ☕ 6475/8650, 5 suites.   DX a

🏠 **Simenon,** bd de l'Est 16, ✉ 4020, ☎ (0 4) 342 86 90, *Fax (0 4) 344 26 69* – ◫ TV ☎.
AE ⓸ E VISA   FZ x
Meals (open until midnight) *(closed Wednesday and 15 December-15 January)* a la carte approx. 900 – ☕ 180 – **11 rm** 2000.

Suburbs

at Angleur *S : 4 km* © Liège – ✉ 4031 Angleur :

🏠 **Le Val d'Ourthe** without rest, rte de Tilff 412 ☎ (0 4) 365 91 71, *Fax (0 4) 365 91 71* – TV ☎ ⇔ P. AE ⓸ E VISA
☕ 300 – **12 rm** 3200/3800.

XX **L'Orchidée Blanche,** rte du Condroz 457 (N 680) ☎ (0 4) 365 11 48, *Fax (0 4) 367 09 16* – P. AE ⓸ E VISA
closed Tuesday dinner, Wednesday, 1 week February and last 3 weeks July – **Meals** – 900/1995 b.i..

at Chênée *E : 7,5 km* © Liège – ✉ 4032 Chênée :

XXX **Le Gourmet,** r. Large 91 ☎ (0 4) 365 87 97, *Fax (0 4) 365 38 12,* 🌿, « Winter garden » – P. AE ⓸ E VISA – *closed Monday dinner, Wednesday and Saturday lunch except Bank Holidays, 2 weeks July and first week January* – Meals – 980/1700.

XX **Le Vieux Chênée,** r. Gravier 45 ☎ (0 4) 367 00 92, *Fax (0 4) 367 59 15,* Mussels in season – AE ⓸ E VISA
closed Thursday except Bank Holidays – **Meals** *Lunch 890* – a la carte 1100/1550.

Environs

at Ans *NW : 4 km – pop. 27 648 –* ✉ 4430 Ans :

XX **Le Marguerite,** r. Walthère Jamar 171 ☎ (0 4) 226 43 46, *Fax (0 4) 226 38 35,* 🌿 – AE ⓸ E VISA – *closed Saturday lunch, Sunday, Monday, last 3 weeks July and late December* – **Meals** *Lunch 980* – 1450.

XX **La Fontaine de Jade,** r. Yser 321 ☎ (0 4) 246 49 72, *Fax (0 4) 263 69 53,* Chinese cuisine, open until 11 p.m. – 🍽. AE ⓸ E VISA
closed Tuesday and first 3 weeks July – **Meals** *Lunch 485* – a la carte approx. 1000.

at Flémalle *SW : 14 km* © Flémalle pop. 26 126 – ✉ 4400 Flémalle :

XXX **La Ciboulette,** chaussée de Chokier 96 ☎ (0 4) 275 19 65, *Fax (0 4) 275 05 81,* 🌿 – 🍽. AE ⓸ E VISA
closed Monday, Saturday lunch, dinner Sunday and Wednesday, 3 to 18 August and 26 December-12 January – **Meals** *Lunch 1900 b.i.* – 2590 b.i./3490 b.i..

XX **Le Gourmet Gourmand,** Grand-Route 411 ☎ (0 4) 233 07 56, *Fax (0 4) 233 19 21,* 🌿 – 🍽. AE ⓸ E VISA – *closed Saturday lunch, Monday and dinner Tuesday, Wednesday and Thursday* – **Meals** *Lunch 1100* – 1450.

LIÈGE

0   300 m

163
69
87
R. Xhovémont
Campine
de
Montagne
Ste
Walburge
R. Pierreuse
Rue
des
Glacis
Citadelle

CENTRE SPORTIF
DE XHOVEMONT

Carrefour
Fontainebleau

R. L. Fraigneux

MUSÉE DE LA
VIE WALLONNE

PALAIS DES
PRINCES ÉVÊQUES

la Batte
Meuse
Quai
des Tanneurs
B^d de la Constitution

R. Léopold

Laurent

St.

JONFOSSE

St. Paul

Sauvenière

R. de l'Université

B^d de la

OUTRE-MEUSE

Pl. du
Congrès

94
G
141
g
18
22

R.

R. Wazon

St.

156
Gilles

Av. Destenay

Q. Roosevelt

Q. van Beneden

R. J. d'Outremeuse

43
16
9
10

ST. JACQUES

Piercot

B^d

Rue

Louvrex

JARDIN
BOTANIQUE

A 602

35

R. Fabry

R. Frère Orban

PARC
D'AVROY

Quai
Marcellis

21

Rue d'Harscamp

R. Basse Wez

54
84

108

109

Quai

LONGDOZ

Grétry

GRIVEGNÉE

4^m1

R. de Joie

Av.

R. du Plan Incliné

B^d

40
15

Av. Blonden

R. de Fragnée

Pont
Albert Ier

115

a

Palais des
Congrès

B

Parc

de la

Boverie

M

M⁷

162

Mozart

Q. Mativa

POL

B^d R. Poincarré

FÉTINNE

R. de Fétinne

B^d Frankignoul

49

a
66
n

GUILLEMINS

R. de
Sclessin

R.
de Rome

Quai de

Rome

49

Vennes

148

Pl. des
Nations-Unies

3^m9

4^m3

Quai des
Ardennes

Ourthe

G.
Parc
de Cointe

Observatoire

Kleyer

Varin

Pont de
Fragnée

57

MONUMENT
INTERALLIÉ

COINTE

Académie (R. de l')	EY 4	Fétinne (Pont de)	DX 57
Amercoeur (Pont d')	DW 9	Georges Simenon (R.)	FZ 61
Amercoeur (R. d')	DW 10	Gérardrie (R.)	EY 63
Bois-l'Evêque (R.)	CX 15	Goffe (Quai de la)	FY 64
Bonaparte (Quai)	DW 16	Guillemins (R. des)	CX 66
Bonnes-Villes (R. des)	DW 18	Hauteurs (Bd des)	CW 69
Boverie (Quai de la)	DX 21	Joffre (R.)	EY 75
Bressoux (Pont de)	DW 22	Joie (R. de)	CX 78
Bruxelles (R. de)	EY 24	Lairesse (R.)	DX 84
Casquette (R. de la)	EYZ 28	Léon Philippet (Bd)	CW 87
Cathédrale (R. de la)	EZ	Léopold (R.)	EFY
Charles Magnette (R.)	EZ 31	Liberté (R. de la)	FZ 88
Churchill (Quai)	FZ 33	Longdoz (Pont de)	FZ 90
Clarisses (R. des)	EZ 34	Longdoz (Quai de)	FZ 91
Croisiers (R. des)	EZ 39	Maastricht (Quai de)	FY 93
Dartois (R.)	CX 40	Marché (Pl. du)	EY 96
Déportés (Pl. des)	FY 42	Maréchal (R. A.)	FY 97
Dérivation (Quai de la)	DW 43	Maghin (R.)	DW 94
Emile de Laveleye (Bd)	DX 49	Notger (Square)	EY 107
En Féronstrée	FY	Orban (Quai)	DX 108
Est (Bd de l')	FYZ 51	Orban ou de Huy (Pont d')	DX 109
Fer (R. du)	DX 54	Ourthe (Quai de l')	FZ 112
		Palais (R. du)	EY 114

Parc (R. du)	DX 115	Saint-Léonard (Quai)	FY 139
Pitteurs (R. des)	FZ 120	Saint-Léonard (R.)	DW 141
Pont d'Avroy (R.)	EZ 121	Saint-Pholien (R. et Pl.)	FY 142
Pont d'Île	EY 123	Serbie (R. de)	CX 148
Prémontrés (R. des)	EZ 124	Trappé (R.)	CW 156
Puits-en-Soc (R.)	FZ 126	Université (R. de l')	EYZ 157
Ransonnet (R.)	FY 127	Ursulines (Imp. des)	FY 159
Régence (R. de la)	EYZ 129	Vennes (Pont des)	DX 162
Rép. Française (Pl. de la)	EY 130	Victor-Hugo (Av.)	CW 163
Saint-Gilles (R.)	EZ	Vinâve d'Île (R.)	EZ
Saint-Hubert (R.)	EY 136	20-Août (Pl. du)	EZ 169
Saint-Lambert (Pl.)	EY 138		

at Herstal *NE : 8 km – pop. 36 626 –* ⊠ *4040 Herstal :*

🏨 **Post** ⊁, r. Hurbise 160 (by motorway E 40, exit ㉞) 𝒞 (0 4) 264 64 00, *Fax (0 4) 248 06 90*, 🍴, ⊾ – 🛗, ▤ rest, 📺 ☎ 🅿 – 🕴 *25-80*. 🆎 ⓘ Ⓔ 𝗩𝗜𝗦𝗔
Meals *Lunch 800 – a la carte 950/1450 –* **98 rm** ⊇ *4400/5900.*

at Neuville-en-Condroz *S : 18 km* © *Neupré pop. 9 406 –* ⊠ *4121 Neuville-en-Condroz :*

🍴🍴🍴🍴 **Le Chêne Madame** (Mme Tilkin), av. de la Chevauchée 70 (in Rognacs wood SE : 2 km)
𝒞 (0 4) 371 41 27, *Fax (0 4) 371 29 43*, 🍴, « *Country Inn* » – 🅿 🆎 ⓘ Ⓔ 𝗩𝗜𝗦𝗔
closed Monday, dinner Sunday and Thursday and August – **Meals** *– 1300/2900, – a la carte 1800/2200*
Spec. Poularde de Bresse au vinaigre de framboises et miel d'acacia. Truite au bleu. Gibiers en saison.

Hasselt 3500 Limburg **213** ⑨ and **909** Ì3 – pop. 67 552 – 42 km.

at Stevoort by N 2 : 5 km to Kermt, then road on the left Ⓒ Hasselt – ⊠ 3512 Stevoort :

XXXXX   **Scholteshof** (Souvereyns) ⤴ with rm, Kermtstraat 130 𝒫 (0 11) 25 02 02, Fax (0 11)
❀❀   25 43 28, ≼, 🏡, « 18C farmhouse with vines, kitchen garden, orchard and gardens ir
countryside setting », 🍴 – TV ☎ P – ⚓ 25-60. AE ① E VISA
closed 12 to 29 July and 1 to 21 January – **Meals** (closed Wednesday) Lunch 2800 b.i. – a
la carte approx. 4300 – ☕ 600 – **11 rm** 5500/6000, 7 suites
Spec. Langoustines rôties, jus de cresson et ragoût de girolles. Carpaccio de bœuf en trois
symphonies. Soufflé léger, cœur de chocolat orangé, miel et sauge.

Namur 5000 Namur **213** ⑳ **214** ⑤ and **909** Ĥ4 – pop. 105 243 – 61 km.

at Lives-sur-Meuse E : 9 km Ⓒ Namur – ⊠ 5101 Lives-sur-Meuse :

XXXX   **La Bergerie** (Lefevere), r. Mosanville 100 𝒫 (0 81) 58 06 13, Fax (0 81) 58 19 39, ≼
❀❀   « Overlooking the valley, terrace and garden with ornamental fountain » – 🍽 P. AE ①
E VISA
closed Sunday dinner in winter, Monday, Tuesday, last 2 weeks February and last 2 weeks
August – **Meals** Lunch 2000 b.i. – a la carte approx. 2600
Spec. Truite de notre vivier, soufflé homardine. Agneau rôti "Bergerie". Le gâteau de crê-
pes soufflées.

Pepinster 4860 Liège **213** ㉓ and **909** K̇4 – pop. 9 129 – 26 km.

XXX   **Host. Lafarque** ⤴ with rm, Chemin des Douys 20 (W : 4 km by N 61, locality Gof-
❀❀   fontaine) 𝒫 (0 87) 46 06 51, Fax (0 87) 46 97 28, ≼, 🏡, « Park », 🚗 – TV ☎ P. AE
① E VISA. 🚿 rm
closed Monday, Tuesday, 3 to 30 March and 1 to 15 September – **Meals** 2275 a la carte
approx. 2900 – ☕ 450 – **6 rm** 3500/5550
Spec. Langoustines aux artichauts et tomates confites à la badiane. Fantaisie de saumon
et pied de porc au sabayon de raifort. Gibiers en saison.

St-Vith 4780 Liège **214** ⑨ and **909** L̇5 – pop. 8 904 – 78 km.

XXX   **Zur Post** (Pankert) with rm, Hauptstr. 39 𝒫 (0 80) 22 80 27, Fax (0 80) 22 93 10 – TV
❀❀   ☎. AE ① E VISA
closed Sunday dinner, Monday, Tuesday lunch and first 3 weeks January – **Meals** Lunch 1450
– 1800/3500, – a la carte 2500/3000 – ☕ 500 – **8 rm** 2000/3200
Spec. Fond d'artichaut farci d'une poêlée de foie d'oie aux épinards. Bouillabaisse claire
à l'orientale, aux langoustines royales grillées. Mignonettes de chevreuil à la sauce au vir
d'Arbois et sureau (15 September-December).

Tongeren 3700 Limburg **213** ㉒ and **909** J̇3 – pop. 29 864 – 19 km.

at Vliermaal N : 5 km Ⓒ Kortessem pop. 7 943 – ⊠ 3724 Vliermaal :

XXXXX   **Clos St. Denis** (Denis), Grimmertingenstraat 24 𝒫 (0 12) 23 60 96, Fax (0 12) 26 32 07
❀❀   « 17C farmhouse manor, shaded terrace and garden » – P. AE ① E VISA. 🚿
closed Monday, Tuesday, 11 to 15 April, 30 June-15 July, 3 and 4 November and 1 to 16
January – **Meals** Lunch 1750 – 3500/4950, – a la carte 3000/4200
Spec. Rosace de pommes de terre ratte aux truffes et homard minute. Tronçon de turbot
poché, pommes de terre écrasées à l'huile d'olive, câpres et citron vert. Raviolis de foie
d'oie à la crème de truffes.

Maastricht Limburg (Netherlands) **211** Ṫ17 and **908** Ï9 – pop. 118 933 – 33 km.

XXX   **Toine Hermsen**, St-Bernardusstraat 2, ⊠ 6211 HL, 𝒫 (0 43) 325 84 00, Fax (0 43)
❀❀   325 83 73 – 🍽. AE ① E VISA JCB. 🚿   CZ b
closed Saturday lunch, Sunday, Monday, 2 weeks carnival and last week December-first
week January – **Meals** Lunch 60 – 115, /140, – a la carte approx. 115
Spec. Salade d'asperges et petits œufs pochés, vinaigrette de truffes d'été (May-June)
Queues de langoustines grillées, risotto de homard et bisque de homard à ma façon. Perdreau sauvage rôti au naturel (September-November).

Weert Limburg (Netherlands) **211** Ṫ15 and **908** Ï8 – pop. 42 328 – 90 km.

XXX   **l'Auberge** (Mertens) with rm, Wilhelminasingel 76, ⊠ 6001 GV, 𝒫 (0 495) 53 10 57
❀❀   Fax (0 495) 54 45 96, 🏡, « Terrace » – 🛗 TV ☎ 🚗 – ⚓ 25. AE ① E VISA. 🚿
closed Sunday and Monday – **Meals** Lunch 73 – 100/165, – a la carte approx. 135 – ☕ 35
– **14 rm** 150/225
Spec. Mosaïque de St-Jacques, truffes, Parmesan et queues de langoustines (October-
April). Roulade de foie d'oie fumé au ragoût de cèpes (August-November). Lièvre de la
région à la royale (October-January).

LUXEMBOURG – LËTZEBUERG

924 E 4 *and* **909** L 7 – *pop. 78 290.*

Amsterdam 391 – Bonn 190 – Brussels 219.

Plans of Luxembourg
Centre of Luxembourg .... pp. 2 and 3
List of hotels and restaurants .... pp. 4 to 7

TOURIST OFFICE

*Luxembourg City Tourist Office, pl. d'Armes, ⊠ 2011, ℘ 22 28 09, Fax 47 48 18.
Air Terminus, gare centrale ⊠ 1010, ℘ 42 82 82 20, Fax 42 82 82 38.
Airport at Findel ℘ 42 82 82 21.*

GOLF COURSE

🏴 *Hoehenhof (Senningerberg) near Airport, r. de Trèves 1, ⊠ 2633, ℘ 34 00 90,
Fax 34 83 91.*

PLACES OF INTEREST

VIEWPOINTS

*Place de la Constitution★★ F – St-Esprit★★ Plateau G – Cliff Path★★ G – The Bock★★ G
– Boulevard Victor Thorn★ G 121 – Three Acorns★ DY.*

MUSEUMS

*National Museum of History and Art★ : Gallo Roman section★ and Luxembourg Life section
(decorative arts, folk art and traditions)★★ G M[1] – Historical Museum of the City of
Luxembourg★ G M[3].*

OTHER THINGS TO SEE

*Bock Casemates★★ G – Grand Ducal Palace★ G – Cathedral of Our Lady★ F – Grand
Duchess Charlotte Bridge★ DY.*

MODERN ARCHITECTURE

Plateau de Kirchberg : European Centre DEY.

LUXEMBOURG
0   400 m
R. F. Seimetz
Square Édouard André
LIMPERTSBERG
CIMETIÈRE ISRAËLITE
Av. du Bois
Av. Henri VII
Av. Victor Pasteur
Av. de la Faïencerie
CHAMP DES GLACIS
R. des Glacis
Côte d'Eich
Rue Laurent Menager
R. St. Mathieu
Val des Bons Malades
Konrad
Cour de Justice Européenne
BANQUE EUROPÉENNE D'INVESTISSEMENT
Avenue R. Schuman
Centre
Bâtiment Tour
PONT GRANDE-DUCHESSE CHARLOTTE
Les Trois Glands
TOUR MALAKO
CLAUSEN
Royal
Porte Neuve
Av. E. Reuter
RTL
B'd Roosevelt
PALAIS G.-DUCAL
Montée de Clausen
Rue de Trèves
CATHÉDRALE N-DAME
Alzette
R. Vauban
Duchesse Charlotte
Joseph II
Av. Monterey
B'd Grande Duchesse
Av. Marie Thérèse
Boulevard d'Esch
R. E. Lavandier
Route
R. de la vallée
Pétrusse
Boulevard de la Pétrusse
Av. de la Pétrusse
Avranches
Viaduc
Pl. de la Gare
Rue d'Anvers
R. de Strasbourg
Rue Fischer
HOLLERICH
Hollerich
Rue de
Fraternité
des
B'd Charlotte
GRANDE-DUCHESSE CHARLOTTE

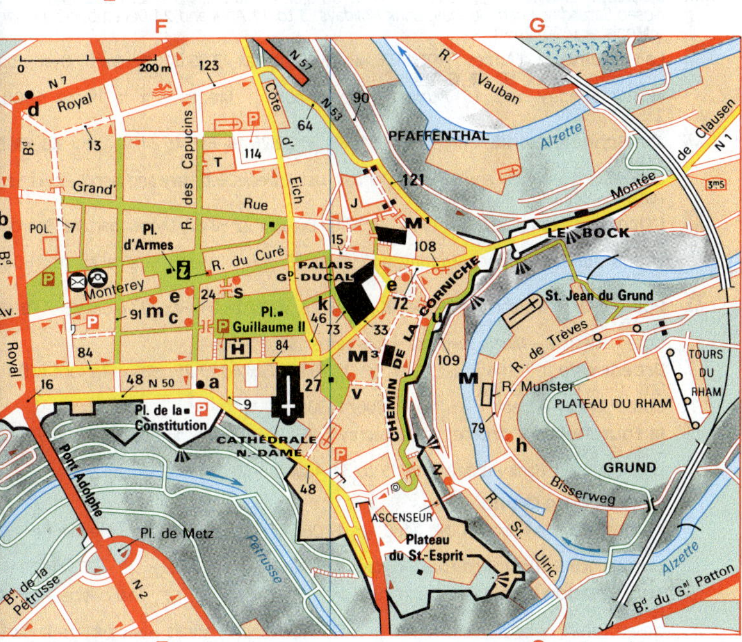

E
Rue
70
nauer
Bâtiment
J. Monnet
4
6
KIRCHBERG
Erasme
N 51
CENTRE
Kennedy
OPÉEN
P
43
67
Hémicycle
N 1
Y
de Neudorf
Rue
28
N 1ᵃ
R. de Trèves
E

F
G
0   200 m
N 7
123
d
Royal
N 57
Côte d'
64
N 53
90
R. Vauban
PFAFFENTHAL
Alzette
de Clausen
N 1
13
des Capucins
P
114
T
Eich
121
3m5
Grand'
Rue
J
b
M¹
POL.
7
Pl. d'Armes
R.
15
108
LE BOCK
Montée
B
R. du Curé
PALAIS
Gᵈ DUCAL
e
Monterey
24
S
k
e
72
CHEMIN DE LA CORNICHE
St. Jean du Grund
91 m c
Pl. Guillaume II
46
73
33
R. de Trèves
Av.
84
M³
H
84
109
M
TOURS DU RHAM
16
48 N 50
a
27
V
R. Munster
PLATEAU DU RHAM
Royal
9
79
h
Pl. de la Constitution
CATHÉDRALE N.-DAME
48
GRUND
Bisserweg
Pont Adolphe
ASCENSEUR
R. St. Ulric
Alzette
Pl. de Metz
Plateau du St-Esprit
Pétrusse
Bᵈ de la Pétrusse
N 2
Bᵈ du Gᵃˡ Patton
F
G

LUXEMBOURG (side tab)

Luxembourg-Centre

Le Royal, bd Royal 12, ✉ 2449, ✆ 241 61 61, Fax 22 59 48, 🍴, Fˢ, ⊆s, 🏊 – ⍟ ✚
🍽 📺 ☎ 🅿 – ⚎ 25-350. AE ① E VISA JCB. ✵ rest
    F c
Meals see rest *La Pomme Cannelle* below – *Le Jardin* Lunch 1080 - a la carte 1100/1700
– **185 rm** ⊇ 9500/13000, 20 suites.

Gd H. Cravat, bd Roosevelt 29, ✉ 2450, ✆ 22 19 75, Telex 2846, Fax 22 67 11 – ⍟
✚, 🍽 rest, 📺 ☎ – ⚎ 25. AE ① E VISA
    F a
Meals (Pub-rest) Lunch 490 – 950/1250 – **58 rm** ⊇ 5900/7400.

Rix without rest, bd Royal 20, ✉ 2449, ✆ 47 16 66, Fax 22 75 35 – ⍟ 📺 ☎ 🅿. E VISA
✵
    F b
closed 17 December-3 January – **21 rm** ⊇ 4480/6680.

Parc-Belle-Vue ⟋, av. Marie-Thérèse 5, ✉ 2132, ✆ 45 61 41, Fax 456 14 12 22, ⟨
🍴 – ⍟ 📺 ☎ 🅿 – ⚎ 25-400. AE ① E VISA
    CZ p
Meals Lunch 650 – a la carte 850/1550 – **58 rm** ⊇ 2950/3300.

Clairefontaine (Tintinger), pl. de Clairefontaine 9, ✉ 1341, ✆ 46 22 11, Fax 47 08 21
🍴 – ▤. AE ① E VISA
    G v
closed Sunday, Monday, 15 to 22 February and 13 to 23 August – **Meals** Lunch 1750 – 2560
a la carte approx. 2400
Spec. Foie gras d'oie et gelée au Porto. Poularde de Bresse en vessie, sauce Albufera. Pavé
de lotte, navets longs et beurre d'herbes. **Wines** Riesling, Pinot gris.

St-Michel (Glauben) 1st floor, r. Eau 32, ✉ 1449, ✆ 22 32 15, Fax 46 25 93, « In the
old city, rustic interior » – AE ① E VISA
    G e
closed Saturday lunch, Sunday, Bank Holidays, 30 July-16 August and 24 December-3
January – **Meals** Lunch 1750 – 2700/3300 b.i. – a la carte 2500/2850
Spec. Trio de foie gras à notre façon. Lotte poêlée aux langoustines et taboulé au
safran. Filet de bœuf en pot-au-feu, mousseline au raifort. **Wines** Riesling, Pinot
noir.

La Pomme Cannelle (at Le Royal H.), bd Royal 12, ✉ 2449, ✆ 241 61 61, Fax 22 59 48
« Indian Empire style interior atmosphere » – ▤ 🅿. AE ① E VISA
JCB. ✵
    F c
closed Saturday lunch, Sunday, Bank Holidays and first 3 weeks August – **Meals** a la carte
1550/2150.

Speltz, r. Chimay 8, ✉ 1333, ✆ 47 49 50, Fax 47 46 77, 🍴 – AE ① E VISA   F c
closed Saturday lunch, Sunday, Bank Holidays, 3 to 11 April and 24 December-2 January
– **Meals** – 1450/2450.

La Lorraine, pl. d'Armes 7, ✉ 1136, ✆ 47 46 20, Fax 47 09 64, 🍴, Partly Oyster bar
and Seafood – ▤. AE ① E VISA
    F e
closed Sunday and 15 August-6 September – **Meals** – a la carte 1900/
2650.

Jan Schneidewind, r. Curé 20, ✉ 1368, ✆ 22 26 18, Fax 46 24 40, 🍴 – AE ① E
VISA. ✵
    F s
closed lunch Saturday and Sunday, Monday, last 2 weeks February and last 2 weeks September – **Meals** 1380/1980 b.i..

L'Océan, r. Louvigny 7, ✉ 1946, ✆ 22 88 66, Fax 22 88 67, Oyster bar and Seafood
– AE ① E VISA
    F
closed Sunday dinner, Monday and 5 to 28 July – **Meals** – a la carte 1800/
2200.

Poêle d'Or, r. Marché-aux-Herbes 20, ✉ 1728, ✆ 22 26 06, Fax 22 26 05, 🍴 – AE ①
E VISA JCB
    G k
closed Tuesday – **Meals** Lunch 990 – a la carte 1300/1600.

Breedewee, r. Large 9, ✉ 1917, ✆ 22 26 96, Fax 46 77 20, 🍴, « Terrace with ⟨
Grund » – AE ① E VISA
    G u
closed Sunday – **Meals** Lunch 560 – 1200/1400.

la fourchette à droite, av. Monterey 5, ✉ 2163, ✆ 22 13 60, Fax 22 24 95, 🍴
– AE E VISA
    F n
closed Sunday, Bank Holidays and 15 to 31 August – **Meals** Lunch 520 – 1250.

Luxembourg-Grund

Kamakura, r. Münster 4, ✉ 2160, ✆ 47 06 04, Fax 46 73 30, Japanese cuisine – AE
① E VISA. ✵
    G k
closed lunch Saturday and Bank Holidays and Sunday – **Meals** Lunch 360 – 755/1980.

Thai Céladon, Montée du Grund 28, ✉ 1645, ✆ 47 49 34, 🍴, Thaï cuisine – AE ①
E VISA. ✵
    G
closed Saturday lunch, Sunday and 1 to 15 November – **Meals** Lunch 590 – a la carte
1100/1500.

Luxembourg-Station

Gd H. Mercure Alfa without rest, pl. de la Gare 16, ⊠ 1616, ℰ 49 01 11, *Fax 49 00 09* – |≑| ✠ 🖃 TV ☎. AE ⓞ E VISA — DZ **z**
⬜ 500 – **74 rm** 5400/6400, 1 suite.

President, pl. de la Gare 32, ⊠ 1024, ℰ 48 61 61, *Fax 48 61 80* – |≑| ✠ 🖃 TV ☎
– 🏛 40. AE ⓞ E VISA. ✠ rest — DZ **v**
Meals (dinner only) *(closed Sunday and August-10 September)* a la carte approx. 850 –
35 rm ⬜ 4000/6400.

City M without rest, r. Strasbourg 1, ⊠ 2561, ℰ 29 11 22, *Fax 29 11 33* – |≑| TV ☎
🚗 – 🏛 25-100. AE ⓞ E VISA — DZ **k**
35 rm ⬜ 3950/5350.

Christophe Colomb, r. Anvers 10, ⊠ 1130, ℰ 408 41 41, *Fax 40 84 08,* 🍴 – |≑|
🖃 rest, TV ☎ – 🏛 25. AE ⓞ E VISA — CZ **h**
Meals *(closed Saturday and Sunday)* Lunch 340 – a la carte 850/1300 – **24 rm**
⬜ 3700/4050.

International, pl. de la Gare 20, ⊠ 1616, ℰ 48 59 11, *Fax 49 32 27* – |≑| ✠, 🖃 rest,
TV ☎ – 🏛 25-50. AE ⓞ E VISA. ✠ rm — DZ **z**
Meals *(closed 22 December-8 January)* Lunch 1010 – 850/1500 – **48 rm** ⬜ 4100/5300,
1 suite.

Central Molitor, av. de la Liberté 28, ⊠ 1930, ℰ 48 99 11, *Fax 48 33 82,* 🍴 – |≑|,
🖃 rest, TV ☎ 🚗 – 🏛 35. AE ⓞ E VISA — CDZ **x**
Meals *(closed Saturday, Sunday dinner, 2 to 22 August and 20 December-9 January)* Lunch
360 – a la carte 950/1350 – **36 rm** ⬜ 3500/4500.

Arcotel without rest, 1st floor, av. de la Gare 43, ⊠ 1611, ℰ 49 40 01, *Fax 40 56 24*
– |≑| TV ☎. AE ⓞ E VISA. ✠ — DZ **a**
20 rm ⬜ 4800.

Marco Polo without rest, r. Fort Neipperg 27, ⊠ 2230, ℰ 406 41 41, *Fax 40 48 84*
– |≑| TV ☎ 🚗. AE ⓞ E VISA — DZ **d**
18 rm ⬜ 3700/4050.

Aub. Le Châtelet (annex 🏠 - 9 rm), bd de la Pétrusse 2, ⊠ 2320, ℰ 40 21 01,
Fax 40 36 66 – |≑| TV ☎ Ⓟ. AE ⓞ E VISA. ✠ rest — CZ **e**
Meals (dinner residents only) – **34 rm** ⬜ 3500/4500.

Nobilis, av. de la Gare 47, ⊠ 1611, ℰ 49 49 71, *Fax 40 31 01* – |≑| 🖃 TV ☎ Ⓟ – 🏛 50.
AE ⓞ E VISA — DZ **z**
Meals Lunch 650 – 1450/1950 – ⬜ 350 – **47 rm** 3900/4600.

XXX **Cordial** 1st floor, pl. de Paris 1, ⊠ 2314, ℰ 48 85 38, *Fax 40 77 76* –
E VISA — DZ **b**
closed Saturday lunch, Sunday dinner, Monday, 15 to 21 February and 15 July-15 August
– **Meals** – 1450/2650.

XX **Italia** with rm, r. Anvers 15, ⊠ 1130, ℰ 48 66 26, *Fax 48 08 07,* 🍴, Partly Italian cuisine
– TV ☎. AE ⓞ E VISA — CZ **f**
Meals – a la carte 950/1800 – **20 rm** ⬜ 2625/3255.

Suburbs

Airport *NE : 8 km :*

Sheraton Aérogolf ⌆, rte de Trèves 1, ⊠ 1019, ℰ 34 05 71, *Fax 34 02 17* – |≑|
✠ 🖃 TV ☎ Ⓟ – 🏛 25-120. AE ⓞ E VISA
Meals *Le Montgolfier* (open until midnight) Lunch 990 - a la carte approx. 1700 – ⬜ 630
– **144 rm** 6850/7350, 1 suite.

Ibis, rte de Trèves, ⊠ 2632, ℰ 43 88 01, *Fax 43 88 02,* ≤ – |≑| 🖃 TV ☎ Ⓟ – 🏛 25-80.
AE ⓞ E VISA
Meals Lunch 350 b.i. – 850 – ⬜ 300 – **120 rm** 2600/3100.

Trust Inn without rest, r. Neudorf 679, ⊠ 2220, ℰ 42 30 51, *Fax 42 30 56* – 🖃 TV
☎ Ⓟ. AE ⓞ E VISA
⬜ 200 – **7 rm** 1700/2500.

XX **Le Grimpereau,** r. Cents 140, ⊠ 1319, ℰ 43 67 87, *Fax 42 60 26,* 🍴 – Ⓟ. AE E VISA.
✠
*closed Tuesday July-15 September, Monday, 15 to 22 February, 2 to 24 August and 1
to 8 November* – **Meals** 850/1650.

at Belair *W : 1,5 km* ⓒ *Luxembourg :*

Parc Belair M ⌆, av. du X Septembre 109, ⊠ 2551, ℰ 44 23 23, *Fax 44 44 84,* ≤,
🍴, 🔁 – |≑| ✠, 🖃 rest, TV ☎ 🚗 – 🏛 25-400. AE ⓞ E VISA
Meals (dinner only except Sunday) a la carte 1100/1600 – **45 rm** ⬜ 6700,
7 suites.

Astoria, av. du X Septembre 44, ⊠ 2550, ℰ 44 62 23, Fax 45 82 96, ☂ – ▤ – ♨ 25.
AE ⑩ E VISA
CZ a
closed dinner Sunday and Monday – **Meals** 1080/1290.

Thailand, av. Gaston Diderich 72, ⊠ 1420, ℰ 44 27 66, Fax 44 27 66, Thaï cuisine –
AE ⑩ E VISA. ✵
closed Monday, Saturday lunch and 15 August-4 September – **Meals** *Lunch 690* – a la carte
1150/1500.

at Dommeldange *(Dummeldéng)* N : 5,5 km Ⓒ Luxembourg :

Inter.Continental ⍟, r. Jean Engling 12, ⊠ 1466, ℰ 4 37 81, Fax 43 60 95, ≤, ☂
ℐ₅, ≦s, ☒ – ⧈ ⤢ ▤ TV ☎ ℗ – ♨ 25-360. AE ⑩ E VISA JCB. ✵ rest
Meals ***Les Continents*** *(closed lunch Saturday and Sunday, August and early January) Lunch*
1450 - 2000/2950 – ***Café Stiffchen*** *Lunch 1050* - a la carte approx. 1500 – ☕ 840 – **306 rm**
7900, 31 suites.

Parc, rte d'Echternach 120, ⊠ 1453, ℰ 43 56 43, Fax 43 69 03, ☂, ℐ₅, ≦s, ☒, ⬛
✖ – ⧈, ▤ rest, TV ☎ ℗ – ♨ 25-1500. AE ⑩ E VISA
Meals (open until 11.30 p.m.) *Lunch 750* – a la carte 950/1500 – **218 rm** ☕ 3800/5600,
3 suites.

Host. du Grünewald, rte d'Echternach 10, ⊠ 1453, ℰ 43 18 82 and 42 03 14 (rest),
Fax 42 06 46 and 42 03 14 (rest), ⬛ – ⧈, ▤ rest, TV ☎ ℗ – ♨ 25-40. AE ⑩ E VISA
✵ rest
Meals *(closed Saturday lunch, Sunday and 1 to 24 January) Lunch 1590* – a la carte
1750/2500 – **23 rm** ☕ 3900/4900, 2 suites.

at Gasperich *(Gaasperech)* S : 4 km Ⓒ Luxembourg :

Inn Side Ⓜ, r. Henri Schnadt 1 (Cloche d'Or), ⊠ 2530, ℰ 490 00 61, Fax 49 06 80, ☂
« Design », ℐ₅, ≦s – ⧈ ⤢, ▤ rest, TV ☎ ♿ ⬛ – ♨ 25-200. AE ⑩ E VISA. ✵ rest
Meals (buffets) *Lunch 895* – 1350 – **158 rm** ☕ 5100/6400.

Upland of Kirchberg *(Kiirchbierg)* :

Sofitel Ⓜ ⍟, r. Fort Niedergrünewald 6 (European Centre), ⊠ 2015, ℰ 43 77 61,
Fax 42 50 91 – ⧈ ⤢ ▤ TV ☎ ♿ ⬛ ℗ – ♨ 25-75. AE ⑩ E VISA. ✵ rest EY a
Meals ***Brasserie Europa*** (open until 11 p.m.) *(closed August) Lunch 1200* - a la carte
1600/2100 – ☕ 750 – **100 rm** 8500/9000, 4 suites.

Novotel ⍟, r. Fort Niedergrünewald 6 (European Centre), ⊠ 2015, ℰ 429 84 81,
Fax 43 86 58, ☂, ≦s, ☒ – ⧈ ⤢ ▤ TV ☎ ♿ ℗ – ♨ 25-300. AE ⑩ E VISA JCB
✵ rest
EY a
Meals (open until midnight) a la carte approx. 1000 – **260 rm** ☕ 5400/5900.

at the skating-rink of Kockelscheuer *(Kockelscheier)* S by N 31 :

Patin d'Or (Berring), rte de Bettembourg 40, ⊠ 1899, ℰ 22 64 99, Fax 40 40 11 – ▤
℗. AE ⑩ E VISA. ✵
closed Saturday, Sunday, Bank Holidays, first week September and Christmas-New Year –
Meals 2000, a la carte 2200/2850
Spec. Escalope de cabillaud demi-sel poêlée sur purée aïllée. Pied de porc farci et queue
de bœuf en feuille de choux aux lentilles. Fondant moelleux au chocolat et aux agrumes.
Wines Pinot gris, Riesling Koëppchen.

at Limpertsberg *(Lampertsbierg)* NW : 1 km Ⓒ Luxembourg :

Bouzonviller, r. A. Unden 138, ⊠ 2652, ℰ 47 22 59, Fax 46 43 89, ≤, ☂ – ▤. AE
E VISA
closed Saturday, Sunday, Bank Holidays, Easter week, 3 weeks August and late December
– **Meals** *Lunch 1600* – a la carte 1800/2150.

at Rollingergrund *(Rolléngergronn)* NW : 3 km Ⓒ Luxembourg :

Sieweburen, r. Septfontaines 36, ⊠ 2534, ℰ 44 23 56, Fax 44 23 53, ≤, ☂
« Woodland setting », ⬛ – TV ☎ ℗. E VISA
closed late December-early January – **Meals** (Pub rest) *(closed Wednesday) Lunch 340* – a
la carte 900/1500 – **14 rm** ☕ 2700/3700.

Environs

at Bridel *(Briddel)* by N 12 : 7 km Ⓒ Kopstal pop. 3 002 :

Le Rondeau, r. Luxembourg 82, ⊠ 8140, ℰ 33 94 73, Fax 33 37 46, ☂ – ℗. AE ⑩
E VISA
closed Monday dinner, Tuesday, 3 weeks August and 2 weeks January – **Meals** – 980/
1900.

at Hesperange *(Hesper)* *SE : 5,5 km – pop. 10 287*

XXX **L'Agath** (Steichen), rte de Thionville 274 (Howald), ⌧ 5884, ☎ 48 86 87, Fax 48 55 05, ⊕ – 🄿 – 🛆 60. 🆎 ⓞ 🄴 *VISA*
closed Saturday lunch, Sunday dinner, Monday, 1 to 20 August and 26 December-9 January – **Meals** *Lunch 1600* – 1850, a la carte 2300/2750
Spec. Carpaccio infusé à la truffe, salade et copeaux de foie gras. St-Pierre à la crème de cèpes et truffes d'Alba. Selle d'agneau rôtie et petits farcis. **Wines** Riesling, Pinot gris.

at Strassen *(Strossen)* *W : 4 km – pop. 5 844*

🏠 **L'Olivier** with apartments, rte d'Arlon 140, ⌧ 8008, ☎ 31 36 66, Fax 31 36 27 – |‡| ✗
📺 ☎ 👍 🚗 🄿 – 🛆 25-50. 🆎 ⓞ 🄴 *VISA*
Meals see rest *La Cime* below – **42 rm** ⌸ 3990/5640, 4 suites.

XX **La Cime** - (at L'Olivier H.), rte d'Arlon 140a, ⌧ 8008, ☎ 31 88 13, Fax 31 36 27, ⊕ – 🄿. 🆎 ⓞ 🄴 *VISA*
Meals – 1090/1690.

XX **Le Nouveau Riquewihr,** rte d'Arlon 373, ⌧ 8011, ☎ 31 99 80, Fax 31 97 05, ⊕ – 🄿. 🆎 ⓞ 🄴 *VISA*
closed Sunday – **Meals** *Lunch 980* – a la carte 1400/1700.

at Walferdange *(Walfer)* *N : 5 km – pop. 6 138*

🏠 **Moris,** pl. des Martyrs, ⌧ 7201, ☎ 330 10 51, Fax 33 30 70, ⊕ – |‡|, ▤ rest, 📺 ☎ 🄿 – 🛆 50. 🆎 ⓞ 🄴 *VISA*
Meals *(closed 24 December-6 January)* *Lunch 650* – 1100/1500 – **24 rm** *(closed 24 December-1 January)* ⌸ 2900/3900.

XX **l'Etiquette,** rte de Diekirch 50, ⌧ 7220, ☎ 33 51 67, Fax 33 51 69, ⊕ – 🄿. 🆎 ⓞ 🄴 *VISA*
Meals *Lunch 630* – 780/1100.

Echternach *(lechternach)* 924 *D* 6 and 409 *M* 6 – pop. 4 367 – 35 km.

at Geyershaff *(Ceieschhaff)* *SW : 6,5 km by E 27* ⓒ *Bech pop. 872 :*

XXX **La Bergerie** (Phal), ⌧ 6251, ☎ 79 04 64, Fax 79 07 71, ≤, ⊕, « Floral country setting » – 🄿. 🆎 ⓞ 🄴 *VISA*
closed Sunday dinner, Monday and 15 January-late February – **Meals** – 2650/3450, – a la carte approx. 3000
Spec. Foie gras d'oie au naturel. Pavé de bar rôti à la réglisse. Selle d'agneau en croûte aux amandes et pistaches. **Wines** Gewürztztraminer.

Paliseul *6850 Luxembourg belge (Belgium)* 214 ⑯ *and* 909 *I* 6 – pop. 4 846 – 94 km.

XXX **Au Gastronome** (Libotte) with rm, r. Bouillon 2 (Paliseul-Gare) ☎ 53 30 64, Fax 53 38 91, « Ardennes country Inn, floral garden with 🛝 » – ▤ 📺 ☎ 🚗 🄿. 🆎 ⓞ 🄴 *VISA*
closed Sunday dinner and Monday except Bank Holidays, Tuesday lunch except Bank Holidays and July-August, January-9 February and 22 June-2 July – **Meals** *Lunch 1800 b.i.* – 1950/3100, – a la carte 2250/2850 – **9 rm** ⌸ 3300/4800
Spec. Cuisses de grenouilles au coulis de persil et croquettes d'ail. Queues d'écrevisses glacées au Champagne et pomme de terre au caviar (July-December). Dos et côtelettes de cochon de lait rôtis, sauce aux épices.

AMSTERDAM

Noord-Holland **210** *J 8 –* (28) *N,* **211** *O 8 and* **908** *G 4* (27) *S –* **27** (45) *– pop. 715 148.*

Brussels 204 – Düsseldorf 227 – The Hague 60 – Luxembourg 419 – Rotterdam 76.

TOURIST OFFICE

VVV Amsterdam, Stationsplein 10, ⊠ *1012 AB,* ℰ *0900-400 40 40, Fax (0 20) 625 28 69.*

GOLF COURSES

[18] *at Halfweg (W : 6 km) Bauduinlaan 35,* ⊠ *1047 HK,* ℰ *(0 20) 497 78 66, Fax (0 20) 497 59 66 –* [9] *at Duivendrecht (S : 5 km) Zwarte Laantje 4,* ⊠ *1099 CE,* ℰ *(0 20) 694 36 50, Fax (0 20) 663 46 21 –* [18] *Buikslotermeerdijk 141,* ⊠ *1027 AC,* ℰ *(0 20) 632 56 50, Fax (0 20) 634 35 06 –* [18] *at Holendrecht (SO) Abcouderstraatweg 46,* ⊠ *1105 AA,* ℰ *(0 294) 28 12 41, Fax (0 294) 28 63 47.*

CASINO

Holland Casino KZ*, Max Euweplein 62,* ⊠ *1017 MB (near Leidseplein),* ℰ *(0 20) 521 11 11, Fax (0 20) 521 11 10.*

PLACES OF INTEREST

VIEUWPOINTS

Keizersgracht★★ KVY – *from the sluice bridge on the Oudezijds Kolk and the Oudezijds Voorburgwal*★ LX.

HISTORICAL MONUMENTS

Dam : Royal Palace★ KX – *Beguine Convent*★★ KX – *Cromhout Houses*★ KY **A⁴** – *Westerkerk*★ KX – *Nieuwe Kerk*★ KX – *Oude Kerk*★ LX.

HISTORICAL MUSEUMS

Amsterdam Historical Museum★★ KX – *Jewish Museum*★ LY – *Allard Pierson Museum*★ : *archeological finds* LXY – *the House of Anne Frank*★★ KX – *Netherlands Maritime History Museum*★★ MX – *Tropical Museum*★ – *Van Loon Museum*★★ LY – *Willet-Holthuysen Museum*★ LY.

FAMOUS COLLECTIONS

Rijksmuseum★★★ KZ – *Van Gogh Museum*★★★ (*Rijksmuseum*) JZ – *Museum of Modern Art*★★ JZ – *Amstelkring "Our Dear Lord in the Attic"*★ (*Museum Amstelkring Ons' Lieve Heer op Solder*) : *clandestine chapel* LX – *Rembrandt's House*★ : *works by the master* LX – *Cobra (Modern Art)*.

MODERN ARCHITECTURE

Housing in the Jordaan district and around the Nieuwmarkt – Contemporary structures at Amsterdam Zuid-Oost (ING bank).

SCENIC AREAS AND PARKS

Old Amsterdam★★★ – *Herengracht* KVY – *Canals*★★★ (*Grachten*) *with hotel-boats (Amstel) – The Jordaan (Prinsengracht*★★, *Brouwersgracht*★, *Lijnbaansgracht, Looiersgracht, Egelantiersgracht*★, *Bloemgracht*★) KX – JKY – *Realeneiland – Dam* LY – *Thin Bridge*★ (*Magere Brug*) LY – *The Walletjes (red light district)* MX – LY – *Sarphatipark* LZ – *Oosterpark – Vondelpark* JZ – *Artis*★★ MY (*zoological park*) – *Singel*★★ KY.

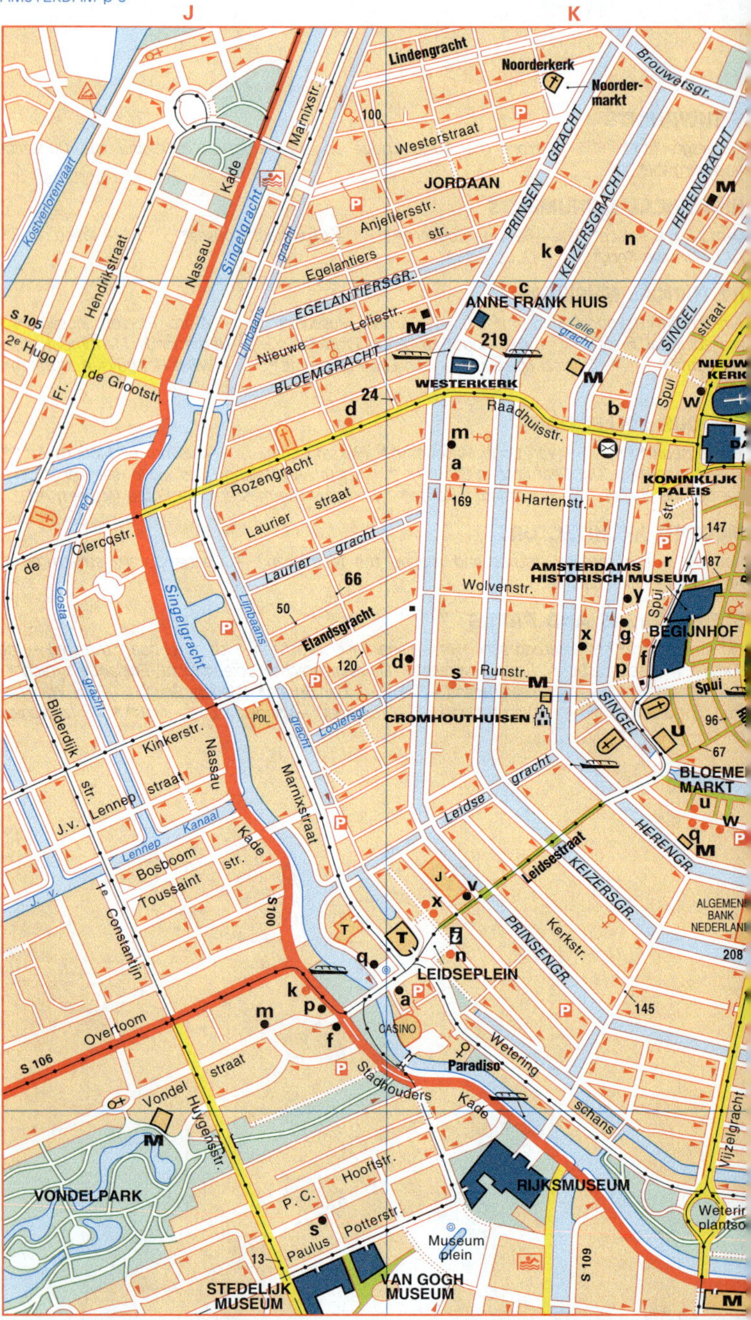

NETHERLANDS

V

X

Y

Z

J   K

Lindengracht
Noorderkerk
Noorder-
markt
Brouwersgr.
100
Westerstraat
JORDAAN
PRINSEN GRACHT
KEIZERSGRACHT
HERENGRACHT
Anjeliersstr.
str.
Egelantiers
k
n
M
Egelantiersgr.
Leliestr.
c
ANNE FRANK HUIS
Nieuwe
Lelie gracht
SINGEL
straat
BLOEMGRACHT
M
219
NIEUWE
KERK
S 105
WESTERKERK
b
2e Hugo
de Grootstr.
Fr.
d 24
Raadhuisstr.
M
Spui
w
DA
Rozengracht
m
KONINKLIJK
PALEIS
Laurier   straat
a
169
Hartenstr.
str.
de Clercqstr.
147
de
Laurier   gracht
AMSTERDAMS
HISTORISCH MUSEUM
187
r
Costa
66
Wolvenstr.
y
Spui
50
x
g
BEGIJNHOF
Singelgracht
Linbaans
P
Elandsgracht
p
f
120
d
s
Runstr.
Spui
Bilderdijk
POL
Looiersgr.
M
CROMHOUTHUISEN
96
U
67
Kinkerstr.
Nassau
Leidse   gracht
BLOEMEN
MARKT
str. Lennep   straat
Marnixstraat
SINGEL
u
w
J.v. Lennep
Kanaal
HERENGR.
q
M
Bosboom
Kade
J
ALGEMENE
BANK
NEDERLAND
Toussaint   str.
S 100
Leidsestraat
KEIZERSGR.
v
x
1e Constantijn
Kerkstr.
208
T
n
q
PRINSENGR.
Overtoom
k
LEIDSEPLEIN
a
m
p
145
f
CASINO
Wetering
P
S 106
straat
Stadhouders
Paradiso
schans
Vondel
Kade
Huygensstr.
Hooftstr.
M
RIJKSMUSEUM
VONDELPARK
P. C.
Vizelgracht
Weterin
plantso
s
Potterstr.
13
Paulus
Museum
plein
S 109
M
STEDELIJK
MUSEUM
VAN GOGH
MUSEUM

J   K

NETHERLANDS
AMSTERDAM
HET IJ
IJtunnel
S 116
0   200 m
V
PASSAGIERS-
TERMINAL
S 100
Centraal
Station
Stationspl.
de Ruijter Kade
Open
Haven
AIR
TERMINAL
Front
NIEUWE
ZIJDE
Damrak
dijk
195
105
126
69
g
j
a
47
162 POL
nieuwen
BEURS
VAN
BERLAGE
Damrak
19
OUDE KERK
OUDE
ZIJDE
215
MUSEUM
AMSTELKRING
Scheepvaart
huis
Voorburg Wal
Achterburg Wal
Zeedijk
Geldersekade
Recht Boomssloot
Waals
Eilandsgracht
Prins Hendrikkade
NEW
METROPOLIS
OOSTERDOK
156
x
22
NEDERLANDS
SCHEEPVAART
MUSEUM
M
k
40
157
159
186
142
Zuiderkerk
186
Waag
Nieuw
markt
Zijds
Zijds
Zijds
Kloveniers burgwal
Montelbaanstoren
OUDE SCHANS
Uilenburgergracht
Valkenburgerstr.
93
Entrepot
dok
rinsenhof
b
h
Oude
Oude
U
REMBRANDT
HUIS
88
Mr. Visser Plein
166
M
M
ALLARD
IERSON M.
160
141
c
Muntplein
58
AMSTEL
171
REMBRANDTPL.
172
198
d
x
h
V
T
Waterloopl.
H
T
Waterlooplein
Blauwbrug
Amstelstr.
r
Zwanenburg wal
139
JOODS
HISTORISCH
MUSEUM
Nieuwe
AMSTELHOF
Nieuwe
Keizers
Herengr.
Hortus
Botanicus
Plantage
ARTIS
PLANTAGE
Middenlaan
MUSEUM
WILLET-HOLTHUYSEN
Amstel
Utrechtsestr.
MUSEUM
AN LOON
Kerkstr.
m
MAGERE
BRUG
Nieuwe
Achter
Nieuwe
Prinsengracht
Weesperstr.
Plantage Muider
gr.
Roeters-
str.
gracht
Amstel
Kerk
9
De Duif
Reguliersg.
e
Amstelsluizen
T
Weesperplein
Sarphatistr.
Sarphatistr.
S 100
Hogesluis
Brug
Frederiksplein
Wetering   schans
a
Mauritskade
Westeinde
Oosteinde
Wibautstraat
Ruyschstr.
b
d
Singelgracht
Stadhouderskade
Amstel
L
M
X
Y
Z

STREET INDEX TO AMSTERDAM TOWN PLAN

Alphabetical listing of hotels and restaurants

A

7 Ambassade
7 American
7 Amstel
8 Amstel Botel
8 Amsterdam
8 Asterisk
10 Aujourd'hui

B

10 Barbizon Centre
7 Barbizon Palace
10 Beddington's
12 Bokkedoorms (De) (at Haarlem/Overveen)
9 Bordewijk
10 Brasserie Van Baerle

C – D

9 Café Roux (at The Grand H.)
7 Canal Crown
8 Canal House
8 Caransa
8 Christophe
11 Ciel Bleu (at Okura H.)
8 Cok City

10 Cok Hotels
7 Crowne Plaza City Centre
8 Dikker en Thijs Fenice
12 Dorint
9 Dynasty

E – F – G

8 Eden
10 Edo and Kyo (at Gd H. Krasnapolsky H.)
8 Estheréa
7 Europe
8 Excelsior (at Europe H.)
10 Fita
11 Galaxy
10 Garage (Le)
11 Garden
9 Gouden Reael (De)
11 Grand Hotel
7 Gd H. Krasnapolsky
7 Grand (The)

H

10 Haesje Claes
11 Halvemaan
12 Herbergh (De)
11 Hilton

NETHERLANDS

Establishments according to style of cuisine

Buffets

12 Greenhouse (at Hilton Schiphol H.)
Env. at Schiphol

Pub rest – Brasseries

7 American *Centre*
7 Amstel Bar and Brasserie (The)
(at Amstel H.) *Centre*
11 Brasserie Camelia (at Okura H.)
South and West Q.
7 Brasserie De Palmboom
(at Radisson SAS H.) *Centre*
7 Brasserie Reflet
(at Gd H. Krasnapolsky H.) *Centre*
10 Brasserie Van Baerle
Rijksmuseum
7 Café Barbizon
(at Barbizon Palace H.) *Centre*
9 Café Roux (at The Grand H.)
Centre
10 Garage (Le) *Rijksmuseum*
10 Keyzer *Rijksmuseum*
8 Port van Cleve (Die) *Centre*
12 Run-Way Café
(at Sheraton Schiphol H.)
Env. at Schiphol
8 Tulip Inn *Centre*

Seafood – Oyster bar

9 Oesterbar (De) *Centre*
9 Pêcheur (Le) *Centre*
12 Pescadou (Le)
Env. at Amstelveen

Asian

9 Sea Palace *Centre*

Chinese

9 Sichuan Food *Centre*

Dutch regional

7 Dorrius
(at Crowne Plaza City Centre)
Centre
8 Roode Leeuw (De)
(at Amsterdam H.) *Centre*

Indian

11 Pakistan *South and West Q.*

Indonesian

9 Indrapura *Centre*
9 Long Pura *Centre*
10 Radèn Mas *Rijksmuseum*

Italian

7 Caruso (at Jolly Carlton H.)
Centre
11 Roberto's (at Hilton H.)
South and West Q.
8 Tulip Inn *Centre*

Japanese

10 Edo and Kyo
(at Gd H. Krasnapolsky H.) *Centre*
9 Hosokawa *Centre*
11 Sazanka (at Okura H.)
South and West Q.
11 Yamazato (at Okura H.)
South and West Q.

Oriental

9 Dynasty *Centre*
9 Manchurian *Centre*

Swiss

7 Swissôtel *Centre*

Thaï

10 Tom Yam *Centre*

Centre

Amstel ⮑, Prof. Tulpplein 1, ⊠ 1018 GX, ℘ (0 20) 622 60 60, *Fax (0 20) 622 58 08,*
≤, 🏖, 🏋, ⇌s, 🏊, ⚓ – 🛗 ✗ ▤ 🅣🅥 ☎ 🅟 – 🚣 25-180. 🆀🅴 ⓪ 🄴 𝗩𝗜𝗦𝗔 🅹🅲🅱. ⛟MZ a
Meals see rest **La Rive** below – **The Amstel Bar and Brasserie** (open until 11.30 p.m.)
Lunch 60 - a la carte approx. 90 – ☕ 53 – **64 rm** 850/950, 15 suites.

The Grand ⮑, O.Z. Voorburgwal 197, ⊠ 1012 EX, ℘ (0 20) 555 31 11, *Fax (0 20)*
555 32 22, « Historic building, authentic Art Nouveau lounges, inner garden », ⇌s, 🏊,
🚗 – 🛗 ✗ ▤ 🅣🅥 ☎ 🚘 – 🚣 25-300. 🆀🅴 ⓪ 🄴 𝗩𝗜𝗦𝗔 🅹🅲🅱. ⛟ LX b
Meals see rest **Café Roux** below – ☕ 35 – **153 rm** 690/795, 13 suites.

Europe, Nieuwe Doelenstraat 2, ⊠ 1012 CP, ℘ (0 20) 531 17 77, *Fax (0 20) 531 17 78,*
≤, 🏖, « Collection of Dutch landscape paintings in late 19C lounge », 🏋, ⇌s, 🏊, ⚓
– 🛗 ▤ 🅣🅥 ☎ 🅟 – 🚣 25-80. 🆀🅴 ⓪ 🄴 𝗩𝗜𝗦𝗔 🅹🅲🅱 LY c
Meals see rest **Excelsior** below – **Le Relais** (open until midnight) *Lunch 32* - 43/59 – ☕
50 – **94 rm** 500/730, 6 suites.

Barbizon Palace, Prins Hendrikkade 59, ⊠ 1012 AD, ℘ (0 20) 556 45 64, *Fax (0 20)*
624 33 53, 🏋, ⇌s – 🛗 ✗ ▤ 🅣🅥 ☎ ♿ 🚘 – 🚣 25-300. 🆀🅴 ⓪ 🄴 𝗩𝗜𝗦𝗔 🅹🅲🅱. ⛟ rest
Meals see rest **Vermeer** below – **Café Barbizon** (open until 11 p.m.) *Lunch 50* - a la carte
63/92 – ☕ 35 – **265 rm** 415/570, 3 suites. LV d

Gd H. Krasnapolsky, Dam 9, ⊠ 1012 JS, ℘ (0 20) 554 91 11, « 19C winter garden »,
🏋, 🚗 – 🛗 ✗, ▤ rm, 🅣🅥 ☎ 🚘 – 🚣 25-700. 🆀🅴 ⓪ 🄴 𝗩𝗜𝗦𝗔 🅹🅲🅱. ⛟ LX k
Meals see rest **Edo and Kyo** below – **Brasserie Reflet** (dinner only until 11 p.m.) 63 –
☕ 35 – **422 rm** 400/660, 7 suites.

Radisson SAS Ⓜ ⮑, Rusland 17, ⊠ 1012 CK, ℘ (0 20) 623 12 31, *Fax (0 20)*
520 82 00, « Patio with 18C presbytery », 🏋, ⇌s, ⚓ – 🛗 ✗ ▤ 🅣🅥 ☎ ♿ 🚘 – 🚣 25-
300. 🆀🅴 ⓪ 🄴 𝗩𝗜𝗦𝗔 🅹🅲🅱. ⛟ rest LX h
Meals **Laxen Oxen** (dinner only) 58/68 – **Brasserie De Palmboom** (lunch only) *Lunch 48*
- a la carte 68/84 – ☕ 41 – **242 rm** 475/640, 1 suite.

Crowne Plaza City Centre, N.Z. Voorburgwal 5, ⊠ 1012 RC, ℘ (0 20) 620 05 00 and
420 22 24 (rest), *Fax (0 20) 620 11 73 and 420 04 65 (rest),* 🏋, ⇌s, 🏊 – 🛗 ✗ ▤ 🅣🅥
☎ 🚘 – 🚣 25-260. 🆀🅴 ⓪ 🄴 𝗩𝗜𝗦𝗔 🅹🅲🅱 LV g
Meals : **Dorrius** (partly Dutch regional cooking, dinner only until 11 p.m.) a la carte 45/93
– ☕ 35 – **268 rm** 425/675, 2 suites.

Pulitzer ⮑, Prinsengracht 323, ⊠ 1016 GZ, ℘ (0 20) 523 52 35, *Fax (0 20) 627 67 53,*
🏖, « 24 terraced canalside houses from 17 and 18C », 🚗, ⚓ – 🛗 ✗ ▤ 🅣🅥 ☎ 🚘
– 🚣 25-150. 🆀🅴 ⓪ 🄴 𝗩𝗜𝗦𝗔 🅹🅲🅱. ⛟ rest KX m
Meals (opening planned May 1999) – ☕ 41 – **224 rm** 525/585, 2 suites.

Victoria, Damrak 1, ⊠ 1012 LG, ℘ (0 20) 623 42 55, *Fax (0 20) 625 29 97,* 🏋, ⇌s,
🏊 – 🛗 ✗ ▤ 🅣🅥 ☎ ♿ – 🚣 30-150. 🆀🅴 ⓪ 🄴 𝗩𝗜𝗦𝗔 🅹🅲🅱 LX j
Meals – a la carte 63/85 – ☕ 33 – **295 rm** 475/560, 10 suites.

Renaissance, Kattengat 1, ⊠ 1012 SZ, ℘ (0 20) 621 22 23, *Fax (0 20) 627 52 45,*
« Contemporary art collection », 🏋, ⇌s, ⚓ – 🛗 ✗ ▤ 🅣🅥 ☎ ♿ 🚘 – 🚣 25-400. 🆀🅴
⓪ 🄴 𝗩𝗜𝗦𝗔 🅹🅲🅱 LV e
Meals (dinner only) (closed Sunday) a la carte 66/88 – ☕ 38 – **370 rm** 375/525, 6 suites.

Jolly Carlton, Vijzelstraat 4, ⊠ 1017 HK, ℘ (0 20) 622 22 66 and 623 83 20 (rest),
Fax (0 20) 626 61 83 – 🛗 ✗ ▤ 🅣🅥 ☎ ♿ 🚘 – 🚣 25-180. 🆀🅴 ⓪ 🄴 𝗩𝗜𝗦𝗔 🅹🅲🅱. ⛟LY n
Meals **Caruso** (Italian cuisine, dinner only until 11 p.m.) (closed Monday) 110 – **219 rm**
☕ 525/690.

American, Leidsekade 97, ⊠ 1017 PN, ℘ (0 20) 624 53 22, *Fax (0 20) 625 32 36,* 🏖,
🏋, ⇌s, ⚓ – 🛗 ✗, ▤ rm, 🅣🅥 ☎ – 🚣 40-160. 🆀🅴 ⓪ 🄴 𝗩𝗜𝗦𝗔 🅹🅲🅱. ⛟ KY q
Meals (Art Deco style pub rest, open until midnight) *Lunch 40* – a la carte 72/90 – ☕ 37
– **186 rm** 295/550, 2 suites.

Swissôtel, Damrak 95, ⊠ 1012 LP, ℘ (0 20) 626 00 66, *Fax (0 20) 627 09 82* – 🛗 ✗
▤ 🅣🅥 ☎ ♿ – 🚣 25-60. 🆀🅴 ⓪ 🄴 𝗩𝗜𝗦𝗔 🅹🅲🅱. ⛟ LX s
Meals (Swiss cuisine) *Lunch 37* – a la carte approx. 60 – ☕ 30 – **109 rm** 310/600.

Sofitel without rest, N.Z. Voorburgwal 67, ⊠ 1012 RE, ℘ (0 20) 627 59 00, *Fax (0 20)*
623 89 32, 🏋, ⇌s – 🛗 ✗ ▤ 🅣🅥 ☎ ♿ – 🚣 25-80. 🆀🅴 ⓪ 🄴 𝗩𝗜𝗦𝗔. ⛟ LX q
☕ 33 – **148 rm** 450/475.

Canal Crown without rest, Herengracht 519, ⊠ 1017 BV, ℘ (0 20) 420 00 55,
Fax (0 20) 420 09 93 – 🛗 🅣🅥 ☎. 🆀🅴 ⓪ 🄴 𝗩𝗜𝗦𝗔 LY d
☕ 25 – **57 rm** 225/420.

Ambassade without rest, Herengracht 341, ⊠ 1016 AZ, ℘ (0 20) 626 23 33, *Fax (0 20)*
624 53 21, ≤, « Typical 17C terraced houses » – 🛗 🅣🅥 ☎. 🆀🅴 ⓪ 🄴 𝗩𝗜𝗦𝗔 KX x
☕ 23 – **46 rm** 335, 6 suites.

Schiller, Rembrandtsplein 26, ⊠ 1017 CV, ℘ (0 20) 554 07 00, *Fax (0 20) 624 00 98,*
🏖, 🏋 – 🛗 ✗ 🅣🅥 ☎. 🆀🅴 ⓪ 🄴 𝗩𝗜𝗦𝗔 🅹🅲🅱. ⛟ LY x
Meals a la carte approx. 55 – ☕ 33 – **90 rm** 345/420, 2 suites.

NETHERLANDS

Inntel M without rest, Nieuwezijdskolk 19, ⊠ 1012 PV, ℘ (0 20) 530 18 18, *Fax (0 20)*
422 19 19 – |$| ✵ ▤ TV ☎ &. AE ① E *VISA* JCB   LV a
☲ 30 – **236 rm** 350/500.

Tulip Inn, Spuistraat 288, ⊠ 1012 VX, ℘ (0 20) 420 45 45, *Fax (0 20) 420 43 00,* ▥
– |$| ✵ ▤ TV ☎ &. ⌂. AE ① E *VISA* JCB   KX c
Meals (Pub rest, partly Italian cuisine, open until midnight) a la carte approx. 45 – ☲ 2:
– **208 rm** 270/290.

Eden, Amstel 144, ⊠ 1017 AE, ℘ (0 20) 530 78 88, *Fax (0 20) 623 32 67,* ▥ – |$| ✵
TV ☎ &. AE ① E *VISA* JCB. ✵   LY
Meals (open until midnight) *Lunch 15* – a la carte approx. 45 – **336 rm** ☲ 225/300.

Mercure Arthur Frommer without rest, Noorderstraat 46, ⊠ 1017 TV, ℘ (0 20)
622 03 28, *Fax (0 20) 620 32 08* – |$| ✵ ▤ TV ☎ ⌂ ℗. AE ① E *VISA*   LYZ
☲ 25 – **90 rm** 190/285.

Cok City M without rest, N.Z. Voorburgwal 50, ⊠ 1012 SC, ℘ (0 20) 422 00 11
Fax (0 20) 420 03 57 – |$| ✵ TV ☎. AE ① E *VISA* JCB. ✵   LV
106 rm ☲ 240/280.

Estheréa without rest, Singel 305, ⊠ 1012 WJ, ℘ (0 20) 624 51 46, *Fax (0 20)*
623 90 01 – |$| TV ☎. AE ① E *VISA* JCB. ✵   KX y
☲ 26 – **70 rm** 355/425.

Canal House ⌂ without rest, Keizersgracht 148, ⊠ 1015 CX, ℘ (0 20) 622 51 82
Fax (0 20) 624 13 17, « Antique furniture » – |$| ☎. AE ① E *VISA* JCB. ✵   KV k
26 rm ☲ 225/290.

Die Port van Cleve, N.Z. Voorburgwal 178, ⊠ 1012 SJ, ℘ (0 20) 624 48 60, *Fax (0 20)*
622 02 40 – |$| TV ☎ – ⚖ 25-50. AE ① E *VISA* JCB. ✵   KX w
Meals (Brasserie) *Lunch 43* – a la carte 55/84 – **117 rm** ☲ 215/415.

Amsterdam, Damrak 93, ⊠ 1012 LP, ℘ (0 20) 555 06 66, *Fax (0 20) 620 47 16* – |$
✵ ▤ TV ☎. AE ① E *VISA* JCB. ✵ rm   LX s
Meals *De Roode Leeuw* (Dutch regional cooking) 53/60 – ☲ 20 – **80 rm** 255/295.

Dikker en Thijs Fenice, Prinsengracht 444, ⊠ 1017 KE, ℘ (0 20) 626 77 21
Fax (0 20) 625 89 86, ▥ – |$| TV ☎ – ⚖ 25. AE ① E *VISA* JCB   KY v
Meals *De Prinsenkelder* (dinner only) a la carte 66/85 – **26 rm** ☲ 280/450.

Caransa without rest, Rembrandtsplein 19, ⊠ 1017 CT, ℘ (0 20) 554 08 00, *Fax (0 20)*
622 27 73 – |$| ▤ TV ☎. AE ① E *VISA* JCB. ✵   LY v
☲ 33 – **66 rm** 420/530.

Wiechmann without rest, Prinsengracht 328, ⊠ 1016 HX, ℘ (0 20) 626 33 21
Fax (0 20) 626 89 62 – TV ☎. ✵   KX c
37 rm ☲ 200/250.

Asterisk without rest, Den Texstraat 16, ⊠ 1017 ZA, ℘ (0 20) 626 23 96, *Fax (0 20)*
638 27 90 – |$| TV ☎. E *VISA*   LZ c
29 rm ☲ 149/195.

Amstel Botel without rest, Oosterdokskade 2, ⊠ 1011 AE, ℘ (0 20) 626 42 47
Fax (0 20) 639 19 52, « Berthed boat » – |$| TV ☎. AE ① E *VISA* JCB. ✵   MX x
☲ 12 – **176 rm** 129/157.

La Rive - (at Amstel H.), Prof. Tulpplein 1, ⊠ 1018 GX, ℘ (0 20) 622 60 60, *Fax (0 20)*
622 58 08, ≼, ⛲, « Amstel-side setting », ▥ – ▤ ℗. AE ① E *VISA* JCB. ✵   MZ a
closed Saturday lunch, Sunday and 9 to 23 January – **Meals** *Lunch 60* – 135/165, – a la carte
167/190
Spec. Beignets de homard aux asperges meunière, amandes et vinaigre de Porto (April
August). Grillade de St-Pierre à l'anguille fumée au jus d'anchois frais. Pigeonneau à la
crémonaise et réduction de Banyuls.

Vermeer - (at Barbizon Palace H.), Prins Hendrikkade 59, ⊠ 1012 AD, ℘ (0 20)
556 48 85, *Fax (0 20) 624 33 53* – ▤ ℗. AE ① E *VISA* JCB. ✵   LV c
closed Saturday lunch, Sunday, 11 July-15 August and 26 December-9 January – **Meals**
Lunch 65 – 95/130, – a la carte 113/150
Spec. Terrine de jambon Jabugo et foie d'oie en gelée de queue de bœuf. Turbot et truffe
enrobés de spaghettis de pommes de terre. Quatre-quarts d'amandes et de chocolat.

Excelsior - (at Europe H.), Nieuwe Doelenstraat 2, ⊠ 1012 CP, ℘ (0 20) 531 17 77
Fax (0 20) 531 17 78, ≼, ⛲, Open until 11 p.m., ▥ – ▤ ℗. AE ① E *VISA* JCB   LY c
closed Saturday lunch – **Meals** *Lunch 70* – a la carte 112/149.

Christophe (Royer), Leliegracht 46, ⊠ 1015 DH, ℘ (0 20) 625 08 07, *Fax (0 20)*
638 91 32 – ▤. AE ① E *VISA*   KVX c
closed Sunday, Monday and early January – **Meals** (dinner only) 85/110, – a la carte
112/130
Spec. Galette d'aubergine aux anchois frais. Homard rôti à l'ail doux et aux pommes de
terre. Agneau rôti au thym et ravioli de ratatouille.

NETHERLANDS

XXX **D'Vijff Vlieghen,** Spuistraat 294, ✉ 1012 VX, ☎ (0 20) 624 83 69, *Fax (0 20) 623 64 04*, « Typical 17C houses », 🔱 – AE ⓪ E VISA JCB
KX p
closed 24 to 30 December – **Meals** (dinner only) 63.

XXX **'t Swarte Schaep** 1st floor, Korte Leidsedwarsstraat 24, ✉ 1017 RC, ☎ (0 20) 622 30 21, *Fax (0 20) 624 82 68*, Open until 11 p.m., « 17C Dutch interior » – 🖥. AE ⓪ E VISA JCB
KY n
closed 30 April, 25, 26 and 31 December and 1 January – **Meals** Lunch 38 – a la carte 83/105.

XXX **Dynasty,** Reguliersdwarsstraat 30, ✉ 1017 BM, ☎ (0 20) 626 84 00, *Fax (0 20) 622 30 38*, ☂, Oriental cuisine, « Terrace » – 🖥. AE ⓪ E VISA JCB. ⊗
KY q
closed Tuesday and January – **Meals** (dinner only) 70.

XX **Het Tuynhuys,** Reguliersdwarsstraat 28, ✉ 1017 BM, ☎ (0 20) 627 66 03, *Fax (0 20) 423 59 99*, ☂, « Terrace » – 🖥. AE ⓪ E VISA JCB
KY q
closed 31 December and 1 January – **Meals** Lunch 55 – a la carte 78/94.

XX **Café Roux** (at The Grand H.), O.Z. Voorburgwal 197, ✉ 1012 EX, ☎ (0 20) 555 31 11, *Fax (0 20) 555 32 22*, ☂, Open until 11 p.m. – 🖥. ℗. AE ⓪ E VISA JCB. ⊗
LY b
Meals Lunch 50 – 55.

XX **Les Quatre Canetons,** Prinsengracht 1111, ✉ 1017 JJ, ☎ (0 20) 624 63 07, *Fax (0 20) 638 45 99*, ☂ – AE ⓪ E VISA JCB
LY m
closed Saturday lunch and Sunday – **Meals** Lunch 65 – a la carte 95/125.

XX **Tout Court,** Runstraat 13, ✉ 1016 GJ, ☎ (0 20) 625 86 37, *Fax (0 20) 625 44 11* – AE ⓪ E VISA
KX s
closed 28 December-10 January – Meals (dinner only until 11.30 p.m.) 58/115.

XX **Sancerre,** Reestraat 28, ✉ 1016 DN, ☎ (0 20) 627 87 94, *Fax (0 20) 623 87 49* – AE ⓪ E VISA JCB
KX a
closed 24 and 31 December and 1 January – **Meals** (dinner only) a la carte 71/92.

XX **Sichuan Food,** Reguliersdwarsstraat 35, ✉ 1017 BK, ☎ (0 20) 626 93 27, *Fax (0 20) 627 72 81*, Chinese cuisine – 🖥. AE ⓪ E VISA. ⊗
KY u
❀
closed 31 December – **Meals** (dinner only until 11 p.m., booking essential) 58/83, – a la carte 58/78
Spec. Dim Sum. Canard laqué à la pékinoise. Huîtres sautées maison.

XX **Long Pura,** Rozengracht 46, ✉ 1016 ND, ☎ (0 20) 623 89 50, *Fax (0 20) 623 46 54*, Indonesian cuisine, « Exotic decor » – 🖥. AE ⓪ E VISA. ⊗
JX d
Meals (dinner only until 11 p.m.) 60/95.

XX **Le Pêcheur,** Reguliersdwarsstraat 32, ✉ 1017 BM, ☎ (0 20) 624 31 21, *Fax (0 20) 624 31 21*, ☂, Seafood, open until midnight – AE ⓪ E VISA JCB. ⊗
KY w
closed Sunday – **Meals** Lunch 54 – 70.

XX **d'theeboom,** Singel 210, ✉ 1016 AB, ☎ (0 20) 623 84 20, *Fax (0 20) 421 25 12*, ☂ – 🖥. AE ⓪ E VISA JCB
KX b
closed Saturday lunch, Sunday and 4 to 20 January – **Meals** – 50.

XX **Van Vlaanderen,** Weteringschans 175, ✉ 1017 XD, ☎ (0 20) 622 82 92, ☂ – AE E VISA
KZ k
closed Sunday, Monday, last 3 weeks July and first week January – Meals (dinner only) 58/68.

XX **Indrapura,** Rembrandtsplein 42, ✉ 1017 CV, ☎ (0 20) 623 73 29, *Fax (0 20) 624 90 78*, Indonesian cuisine – 🖥. AE ⓪ E VISA JCB
LY h
closed 31 December – **Meals** (dinner only) a la carte approx. 65.

XX **Manchurian,** Leidseplein 10a, ✉ 1017 PT, ☎ (0 20) 623 13 30, *Fax (0 20) 626 21 05*, Oriental cuisine – 🖥. AE ⓪ E VISA. ⊗
KY x
closed 31 December – **Meals** 60/90.

XX **Hosokawa,** Max Euweplein 22, ✉ 1017 MB, ☎ (0 20) 638 80 86, *Fax (0 20) 638 22 19*, Japanese cuisine with Teppan-Yaki – AE ⓪ E VISA JCB. ⊗
KY a
closed last week July-first 2 weeks August – **Meals** (dinner only) a la carte 97/133.

XX **De Oesterbar,** Leidseplein 10, ✉ 1017 PT, ☎ (0 20) 626 34 63, *Fax (0 20) 623 21 99*, Seafood, open until midnight – 🖥. AE E VISA. ⊗
KY x
closed 25, 26 and 31 December – **Meals** Lunch 58 – a la carte 81/106.

XX **Sea Palace,** Oosterdokskade 8, ✉ 1011 AE, ☎ (0 20) 626 47 77, Asian cuisine, open until 11 p.m., « Floating restaurant with ≤ town » – 🖥. AE ⓪ E VISA JCB. ⊗
MX b
Meals 45.

X **Bordewijk,** Noordermarkt 7, ✉ 1015 MV, ☎ (0 20) 624 38 99, *Fax (0 20) 420 66 03*, ☂, « Trendy Amsterdam atmosphere » – AE E VISA
KV a
closed Monday, late July-early August and 27 December-4 January – **Meals** (dinner only until 11.30 p.m.)) a la carte approx. 90.

X **De Gouden Reael,** Zandhoek 14, ✉ 1013 KT, ☎ (0 20) 623 38 83, ☂, « 17C house on old harbour site », 🔱 – AE ⓪ E VISA. ⊗
closed Sunday and last week December – **Meals** 55/95.

NETHERLANDS

X **Haesje Claes,** Spuistraat 275, ⊠ 1012 VR, ℘ (0 20) 624 99 98, Fax (0 20) 627 48 17
« Amsterdam atmosphere » – AE ⓞ E VISA JCB. ⚡ KX
Meals Lunch 30 – 45.

X **Tom Yam,** Staalstraat 22, ⊠ 1011 JM, ℘ (0 20) 622 95 33, Fax (0 20) 624 90 62, Tha
cuisine – ▤. AE ⓞ E VISA. ⚡ LY
closed Monday – **Meals** (dinner only) a la carte 86/107.

X **Edo and Kyo** - (at Gd H. Krasnapolsky H.), Dam 9, ⊠ 1012 JS, ℘ (0 20) 554 60 96
Fax (0 20) 639 31 46, Japanese cuisine – AE ⓞ E VISA JCB. ⚡ LX
Meals Lunch 30 – 45/100.

Rijksmuseum (Vondelpark)

🏨 **Marriott,** Stadhouderskade 12, ⊠ 1054 ES, ℘ (0 20) 607 55 55, Fax (0 20) 607 55 11
[], ⊜s – |≢| ⊁ ▤ TV ☎ ₺ ⊸ – ⚙ 25-500. AE ⓞ E VISA. ⚡ JY
Meals Port O'Amsterdam (open until 11.30 p.m.) (closed dinner Sunday and Monday) 4!
– ☕ 34 – **387 rm** 545, 5 suites.

🏨 **Barbizon Centre** Ⓜ, Stadhouderskade 7, ⊠ 1054 ES, ℘ (0 20) 685 13 51
Fax (0 20) 685 16 11, [], ⊜s – |≢| ⊁ ▤ TV ☎ ₺ – ⚙ 25-280. AE ⓞ E VISA JCB
⚡ rest JY
Meals Lunch 48 – a la carte 58/76 – ☕ 33 – **234 rm** 375/540, 2 suites.

🏨 **Memphis** without rest, De Lairessestraat 87, ⊠ 1071 NX, ℘ (0 20) 673 31 41
Telex 12450, Fax (0 20) 673 73 12 – |≢| ⊁ TV ☎ – ⚙ 25-60. AE ⓞ E VISA JCB
⚡
☕ 34 – **74 rm** 380/470.

🏨 **Toro** ⤵ without rest, Koningslaan 64, ⊠ 1075 AG, ℘ (0 20) 673 72 23, Fax (0 20
675 00 31, « Waterside terrace, overlooking the park » – |≢| TV ☎. AE ⓞ E VIS
JCB
22 rm ☕ 200/250.

🏨 **Vondel** (with annex) without rest, Vondelstraat 28, ⊠ 1054 GE, ℘ (0 20) 612 01 2C
Fax (0 20) 685 43 21, « Opulent interior », ⊜s, 🚗 – |≢| TV ☎ – ⚙ 25. AE ⓞ E VIS
JCB JY
☕ 34 – **72 rm** 280/345.

🏨 **Lairesse** without rest, De Lairessestraat 7, ⊠ 1071 NR, ℘ (0 20) 671 95 96, Fax (0 2C
671 17 56 – |≢| TV ☎. AE ⓞ E VISA JCB
☕ 23 – **34 rm** 270/310.

🏨 **Cok Hotels** without rest, Koninginneweg 34, ⊠ 1075 CZ, ℘ (0 20) 664 61 11, Fax (0 2C
664 53 04 – |≢| TV ☎ – ⚙ 25-80. AE ⓞ E VISA JCB. ⚡
110 rm ☕ 210/275.

🏨 **Villa Borgmann** ⤵ without rest, Koningslaan 48, ⊠ 1075 AE, ℘ (0 20) 673 52 52
Fax (0 20) 676 25 80 – |≢| TV ☎. AE ⓞ E VISA JCB
15 rm ☕ 125/255.

🏨 **Fita** without rest, Jan Luykenstraat 37, ⊠ 1071 CL, ℘ (0 20) 679 09 76, Fax (0 2C
664 39 69 – |≢| TV ☎. AE ⓞ E VISA. ⚡ JZ
closed 13 December-3 January – **16 rm** ☕ 155/250.

XXX **Radèn Mas,** Stadhouderskade 6, ⊠ 1054 ES, ℘ (0 20) 685 40 41, Fax (0 20) 685 39 8!
Indonesian cuisine, open until 11 p.m. – ▤. AE ⓞ E VISA JCB. ⚡ JY
Meals Lunch 33 – 55/99.

XX **Le Garage,** Ruysdaelstraat 54, ⊠ 1071 XE, ℘ (0 20) 679 71 76, Fax (0 20) 662 22 49
Open until 11 p.m., « Artistic atmosphere in a contemporary and cosmopolitan brasserie »
– AE ⓞ E VISA JCB
Meals – 75.

XX **Aujourd'hui,** C. Krusemanstraat 15, ⊠ 1075 NB, ℘ (0 20) 679 08 77, Fax (0 2C
676 76 27, 🌿 – AE ⓞ E VISA JCB
closed Saturday, Sunday and last week July-first 2 weeks August – **Meals** Lunch 55 – a l
carte approx. 90.

XX **Beddington's,** Roelof Hartstraat 6, ⊠ 1071 VH, ℘ (0 20) 676 52 01, Fax (0 2C
671 74 29 – AE ⓞ E VISA. ⚡
closed lunch Saturday and Monday, Sunday, 18 July-9 August and 22 December-5 Januar
– **Meals** Lunch 55 – a la carte approx. 90.

XX **Keyzer,** Van Baerlestraat 96, ⊠ 1071 BB, ℘ (0 20) 671 14 41, Fax (0 20) 673 73 53
Pub rest, open until 11.30 p.m., « Amsterdam atmosphere » – AE ⓞ E VISA JCB
⚡
Meals 70.

X **Brasserie van Baerle,** Van Baerlestraat 158, ⊠ 1071 BG, ℘ (0 20) 679 15 32
Fax (0 20) 671 71 96, 🌿, Pub rest – AE ⓞ E VISA. ⚡
closed Saturday and 25 December-1 January – **Meals** Lunch 55 – 58/70.

South and West Quarters

Okura Ⓜ, Ferdinand Bolstraat 333, ⊠ 1072 LH, ℘ (0 20) 678 71 11, *Fax (0 20) 671 23 44*, ≤, ⅙, ≋s, ☒, ⚓ – ⫴ ⤬ ▤ Ⅳ ☎ ⇆ Ⓟ – ⚎ 25-650. Æ Ⓓ E *VISA* JCB.
Meals see rest *Ciel Bleu* and *Yamazato* below – *Sazanka* *(closed lunch Saturday and Sunday)* *(Japanese cuisine with Teppan-Yaki) Lunch 38* - 90/150 – *Brasserie Le Camelia* a la carte 64/83 – ⊑ 42 – **358 rm** 555/605, 12 suites.

Le Meridien Apollo, Apollolaan 2, ⊠ 1077 BA, ℘ (0 20) 673 59 22, *Fax (0 20) 570 57 44*, ⸙, « Terrace with ≤ canal », ⚓ – ⫴ ⤬, ▤ rm, Ⅳ ☎ Ⓟ – ⚎ 25-200. Æ Ⓓ E *VISA* JCB. ⌿ rest
Meals *(open until 11 p.m.) Lunch 48* – a la carte 62/91 – ⊑ 38 – **217 rm** 395/600, 2 suites.

Garden, Dijsselhofplantsoen 7, ⊠ 1077 BJ, ℘ (0 20) 664 21 21, *Fax (0 20) 679 93 56* – ⫴ ⤬ ⅣℲ ☎ – ⚎ 25-150. Æ Ⓓ E *VISA* JCB
Meals see rest *Mangerie De Kersentuin* below – ⊑ 38 – **122 rm** 225/455, 2 suites.

Hilton, Apollolaan 138, ⊠ 1077 BG, ℘ (0 20) 710 60 00, *Telex 11025, Fax (0 20) 710 90 00*, ⸙, « Canalside garden and terraces », ⅙, ≋s, ☒ – ⫴ ⤬ ▤ Ⅳ ☎ ⅋ Ⓟ – ⚎ 25-350. Æ Ⓓ E *VISA* JCB. ⌿ rest
Meals *Roberto's* (Italian cuisine) 53/60 – ⊑ 37 – **268 rm** 585/615, 3 suites.

Mercure a/d Amstel, Joan Muyskenweg 10, ⊠ 1096 CJ, ℘ (0 20) 665 81 81, *Fax (0 20) 694 87 35*, ⅙, ≋s – ⫴ ⤬, ▤ rm, Ⅳ ☎ Ⓟ – ⚎ 25-450. Æ Ⓓ E *VISA*.
Meals a la carte approx. 70 – ⊑ 31 – **178 rm** 380/405.

Ciel Bleu - (at Okura H.), 23th floor, Ferdinand Bolstraat 333, ⊠ 1072 LH, ℘ (0 20) 678 71 11, *Fax (0 20) 671 23 44*, ≤ town, ☒ – ⫴ ▤ Ⓟ. Æ Ⓓ E *VISA* JCB. ⌿
Meals *(dinner only)* 85/128.

Mangerie De Kersentuin - (at Garden H.), Dijsselhofplantsoen 7, ⊠ 1077 BJ, ℘ (0 20) 664 21 21, *Fax (0 20) 679 93 56*, ⸙, Open until 11 p.m. – ▤. Æ Ⓓ E *VISA* JCB. ⌿
closed Saturday lunch, Sunday, 31 December and 1 January – **Meals** *Lunch 48* – 58/78.

Yamazato - (at Okura H.), Ferdinand Bolstraat 333, ⊠ 1072 LH, ℘ (0 20) 678 71 11, *Fax (0 20) 671 23 44*, Japanese cuisine, ☒ – ▤ Ⓟ. Æ Ⓓ E *VISA* JCB. ⌿
Meals *Lunch 33* – 80/160.

Pakistan, Scheldestraat 100, ⊠ 1078 GP, ℘ (0 20) 675 39 76, *Fax (0 20) 675 39 76*, Indian cuisine – Æ Ⓓ E *VISA*
Meals *(dinner only until 11 p.m.)* 43/65.

Buitenveldert (RAI)

Holiday Inn, De Boelelaan 2, ⊠ 1083 HJ, ℘ (0 20) 646 23 00, *Fax (0 20) 646 47 90* – ⫴ ⤬ ▤ Ⅳ ☎ ⅋ Ⓟ – ⚎ 25-350. Æ Ⓓ E *VISA* JCB. ⌿
Meals *(open until midnight)* a la carte 50/91 – ⊑ 36 – **256 rm** 415/475, 2 suites.

Novotel, Europaboulevard 10, ⊠ 1083 AD, ℘ (0 20) 541 11 23, *Fax (0 20) 646 28 23* – ⫴ ⤬ ▤ Ⅳ ☎ ⅋ Ⓟ – ⚎ 25-225. Æ Ⓓ E *VISA*
Meals *(open until midnight) Lunch 38* – 45 – ⊑ 30 – **600 rm** 295.

Halvemaan, van Leyenberghlaan 320 (Gijsbrecht van Aemstelpark), ⊠ 1082 DD, ℘ (0 20) 644 03 48, *Fax (0 20) 644 17 77*, ⸙, « Terrace with ≤ private lake » – Ⓟ. Æ Ⓓ E *VISA*. ⌿
closed Saturday, Sunday and 24 December-mid January – **Meals** *Lunch 65* – 105/125.

North

Galaxy, Distelkade 21, ⊠ 1031 XP, ℘ (0 20) 634 43 66, *Telex 18607, Fax (0 20) 636 03 45* – ⫴, ▤ rest, Ⅳ ☎ Ⓟ – ⚎ 25-200. Æ Ⓓ E *VISA* JCB
Meals *(closed lunch Saturday and Sunday) Lunch 33* – a la carte 45/63 – **281 rm** ⊑ 255/290.

Suburbs

by motorway The Hague (A 4) :

Mercure Airport, Oude Haagseweg 20 (exit ①), ⊠ 1066 BW, ℘ (0 20) 617 90 05, *Fax (0 20) 615 90 27* – ⫴ ⤬ ▤ Ⅳ ☎ Ⓟ – ⚎ 25-300. Æ Ⓓ E *VISA*. ⌿ rest
Meals *Lunch 35* – 45 – ⊑ 31 – **151 rm** 260/365.

Environs

at Amstelveen *S : 11 km – pop. 76 822.*

🛈 Thomas Cookstraat 1, ⊠ 1181 ZS, ℘ (0 20) 441 55 45, *Fax (0 20) 647 19 66*

Grand Hotel Ⓜ, Bovenkerkerweg 81 (S : 2,5 km direction Uithoorn), ⊠ 1187 XC, ℘ (0 20) 645 55 58, *Fax (0 20) 641 21 21* – ⫴ ⤬ Ⅳ ☎ ⅋ Ⓟ. Æ Ⓓ E *VISA*. ⌿
Meals see rest *Résidence Fontaine Royale* below, shuttle service – ⊑ 28 – **81 rm** 290/330, 10 suites.

NETHERLANDS (side tab)

XXX **De Jonge Dikkert**, Amsterdamseweg 104a, ⊠ 1182 HG, ℰ (0 20) 641 13 78, *Fax (0 20) 645 91 62*, 🌱, « *17C windmill* » – 🅿. 🆎 ⓪ Ⓔ *VISA*
closed 31 December – **Meals** – 58/93.

XXX **Résidence Fontaine Royale** - (at Grand Hotel), Dr Willem Dreesweg 1 (S : 2 km direction Uithoorn), ⊠ 1185 VA, ℰ (0 20) 640 15 01, *Fax (0 20) 640 16 61*, 🌱 – 🖿 🅿 – 🔔 25-225. 🆎 ⓪ Ⓔ *VISA* JCB. ✻
closed Sunday – **Meals** *Lunch 53* – a la carte 62/104.

XX **Le Pescadou**, Amsterdamseweg 448, ⊠ 1181 BW, ℰ (0 20) 647 04 43, Seafood – 🖿 🆎 ⓪ Ⓔ *VISA* JCB
closed lunch Saturday and Sunday, 1 to 23 July and 20 December-3 January – **Meals** *Lunch 50* – a la carte 67/87.

at Badhoevedorp *SW : 15 km* Ⓒ *Haarlemmermeer pop. 108 224* :

🏨 **Dorint**, Sloterweg 299, ⊠ 1171 VB, ℰ (0 20) 658 81 11, *Fax (0 20) 658 81 00*, ⊆s, 🖾 – 🛗 ✻ 🖿 rm, 📺 ☎ & 🅿 – 🔔 25-150. 🆎 ⓪ Ⓔ *VISA* JCB
Meals (open until 11 p.m.) *Lunch 40* – a la carte 45/70 – ☕ 30 – **216 rm** 375/440.

XX **De Herbergh** with rm, Sloterweg 259, ⊠ 1171 CP, ℰ (0 20) 659 26 00, *Fax (0 20) 659 83 90*, 🌱 – 🖿 rest, 📺 ☎ 🅿. 🆎 Ⓔ *VISA*. ✻ rm
Meals *Lunch 40* – a la carte 52/71 – ☕ 19 – **15 rm** 170/185.

at Ouderkerk aan de Amstel *S : 10 km* Ⓒ *Amstelveen pop. 76 822* :

XXX **Paardenburg**, Amstelzijde 55, ⊠ 1184 TZ, ℰ (0 20) 496 12 10, *Fax (0 20) 496 40 17*, 🌱, « *19C murals, riverside terrace* » – 🅿. 🆎 ⓪ Ⓔ *VISA* JCB. ✻
closed Saturday lunch, Sunday and 26 December-10 January – **Meals** *Lunch 65* – 83/128.

XX **'t Jagershuis** with rm, Amstelzijde 2, ⊠ 1184 VA, ℰ (0 20) 496 20 20, *Fax (0 20) 496 45 41*, ≤, 🌱, « *Inn with Amstel-side terrace* », 🛉 – 🖿 rest, 📺 ☎ 🅿 – 🔔 30. 🆎 ⓪ Ⓔ *VISA* JCB. ✻ rm
closed 29 December-2 January – **Meals** *Lunch 60* – 63/85 – ☕ 25 – **12 rm** 215/265.

XX **Klein Paardenburg**, Amstelzijde 59, ⊠ 1184 TZ, ℰ (0 20) 496 13 35, *Fax (0 20) 496 16 90*, 🌱, « *Waterside terrace* » – 🆎 ⓪ Ⓔ *VISA* JCB
closed Saturday lunch, Sunday, Bank Holidays and 25 December-4 January – **Meals** *Lunch 68* – 115.

XX **Het Kampje**, Kerkstraat 56, ⊠ 1191 JE, ℰ (0 20) 496 19 43, *Fax (0 20) 496 57 01*, 🌱 – 🆎 Ⓔ *VISA* JCB
closed Saturday, Sunday, 27 April-14 May and 20 December-2 January – **Meals** *Lunch 4* – 53/63.

at Schiphol *(international airport) SW : 15 km* Ⓒ *Haarlemmermeer pop. 108 224* - *Casino, Schiphol airport - Central Terminal* ℰ (0 23) 574 05 74, *Fax (0 23) 574 05 77* :

🏨 **Sheraton Airport** Ⓜ, Schiphol bd 101, ⊠ 1118 BG, ℰ (0 20) 316 43 00, *Fax (0 20) 316 43 99*, 🏋, ⊆s, 🖾 – 🛗 ✻ 🖿 📺 ☎ & 🚗 – 🔔 25-500. 🆎 ⓪ Ⓔ *VISA*
Meals *Voyager* (open until 11 p.m.) a la carte approx. 70 – *Run-Way Café* *Lunch 20* - la carte approx. 50 – ☕ 43 – **399 rm** 610/690, 9 suites.

🏨 **Hilton Schiphol**, Herbergierstraat 1, ⊠ 1118 CA, ℰ (0 20) 603 45 67, *Fax (0 20) 648 09 17*, ⊆s – 🛗 ✻ 🖿 📺 ☎ & 🅿 – 🔔 25-110. 🆎 ⓪ Ⓔ *VISA* JCB
Meals *Greenhouse* (buffets, open until 11.30 p.m.) 55/68 – ☕ 40 – **265 rm** 475/650, 1 suite.

Blokzijl *Overijssel* Ⓒ *Brederwiede pop. 12 235* **210** *Ü 6 and* **908** *İ3* – 102 km.

🏨 **Kaatje bij de Sluis** 🍴, Brouwerstraat 20, ⊠ 8356 DV, ℰ (0 527) 29 18 33, *Fax (0 527) 29 18 36*, ≤, 🌱, « *Terrace and garden along an intersection of canals* », ✻ 🛉 – 🖿 📺 ☎ 🅿. 🆎 ⓪ Ⓔ *VISA*
closed Monday, Tuesday, Saturday lunch, February and late December-early January **Meals** (open until 11 p.m.) 110/180, – a la carte 110/150 – ☕ 38 – **8 rm** 220/285
Spec. Feuillantine au saumon cru et caviar osciètre. Huîtres creuses à la ciboulette et au échalotes. Gratin d'anguille aux fines herbes (June-September).

Haarlem *Noord-Holland* **210** *M 8,* **211** *M 8 and* **908** *È 4* – pop. 147 437 – 24 km.

at Overveen *W : 4 km* Ⓒ *Bloemendaal pop. 16 845* :

XXX **De Bokkedoorns**, Zeeweg 53 (W : 2 km), ⊠ 2051 EB, ℰ (0 23) 526 36 00, *Fax (0 23) 527 31 43*, 🌱, « *Terrace, ≤ lake surrounded by wooded dunes* » – 🖿 🅿. 🆎 ⓪ Ⓔ *VISA* ✻
closed Monday, Saturday lunch, 30 April lunch, 5 and 24 December and 28 December- January – **Meals** *Lunch 80* – 110/155, – a la carte approx. 155
Spec. Roulade de jambon de cerf au homard (November-February). Tartare de St-Jacque et mulet au poivre noir. Filet d'agneau poché à l'huile d'olive, sauce au thym citron (April September).

Hoorn *Noord-Holland* 210 *P* 7 and 908 *G* 4 – pop. 62 313 – 43 km.

XX **De Oude Rosmolen** (Fonk), Duinsteeg 1, ⊠ 1621 ER, ℘ *(0 229) 21 47 52, Fax (0 229) 21 49 38* – . AE ⓪ E VISA
ॐ ॐ
closed Thursday, 2 weeks February, 8 August-1 September and 27 December-5 January – **Meals** (dinner only, booking essential) 75/165 b.i., – a la carte 102/120
Spec. Profiteroles à la mousse de foie gras. Biscuit de brochet et queues de langoustines aux macaronis longs. Pâtisseries maison.

The HAGUE (Den HAAG or 's-GRAVENHAGE) *Zuid-Holland* 211 *K* 10 - ① ② and 908 *D* 5 – pop. 442 159.

See : *Binnenhof★ : The Knight's Room★ (Ridderzaal)* JY – *Court pool (Hofvijver)* ≤★ HJY – *Lange Voorhout★* HJX – *Madurodam★★* – *Scheveningen★★*.
Museums : Mauritshuis★★★ JY – *Prince William V art gallery★ (Schilderijengalerij Prins Willem V)* HY M² – *Panorama Mesdag★* HX – *Mesdag★* – *Municipal★★ (Gemeentemuseum)* – *Bredius★* JY.

ग़ at Rijswijk SE : 5 km, Delftweg 58, ⊠ 2289 AL, ℘ *(0 70) 319 24 24, Fax (0 70) 319 50 40* - ग़ at Wassenaar NE : 11 km, Groot Haesebroekseweg 22, ⊠ 2243 EC, ℘ *(0 70) 517 96 07, Fax (0 70) 514 01 71* and ग़ Hoge Klei 1, ⊠ 2243 XZ, ℘ *(0 70) 511 78 46, Fax (0 70) 511 93 02*.

✈ *Amsterdam-Schiphol NE : 37 km* ℘ *(0 20) 601 91 11* – *Rotterdam-Zestienhoven SE : 17 km* ℘ *(0 10) 446 34 44*.

🛈 *Kon. Julianaplein 30, ⊠ 2595 AA, ℘ 0 900-340 35 05, Fax (0 70) 347 21 02.*
Amsterdam 55 – Brussels 182 – Rotterdam 24 – Delft 13.

Plan on next page

Centre

Des Indes, Lange Voorhout 54, ⊠ 2514 EG, ℘ *(0 70) 363 29 32, Fax (0 70) 345 17 21,* « Late 19C residence » – ⊡ TV ☎ ℗ – ⌁ 25-75. AE ⓪ E VISA JCB. ⁒ rest JX s
Meals : *Le Restaurant* Lunch 55 - 75/113 – ⌂ 38 – **71 rm** 295/540, 5 suites.

Crowne Plaza Promenade, van Stolkweg 1, ⊠ 2585 JL, ℘ *(0 70) 352 51 61, Fax (0 70) 354 10 46,* ≤, 🌿, « Collection of modern Dutch paintings », ⊜ – ⊡ ✻ ▤ TV ☎ ℗ – ⌁ 25-400. AE ⓪ E VISA JCB
Meals : *The Gallery* a la carte 60/80 – *Trattoria del'Arte* (Italian cuisine, open until midnight) *(closed lunch Saturday and Sunday)* Lunch 43 - a la carte 70/86 – ⌂ 38 – **91 rm** 435/455, 4 suites.

Dorint ⓜ, Johan de Wittlaan 42, ⊠ 2517 JR, ℘ *(0 70) 416 91 11, Fax (0 70) 416 91 00,* 🛦, ⊜ – ⊡ ✻, ▤ rm, TV ☎ ⅛ ⇌ – ⌁ 25-2000. AE ⓪ E VISA JCB. ⁒ rest
Meals (open until 11 p.m.) a la carte approx. 70 – ⌂ 30 – **214 rm** 325/385, 2 suites.

Carlton Ambassador ⓜ ঌ, Sophialaan 2, ⊠ 2514 JP, ℘ *(0 70) 363 03 63, Fax (0 70) 360 05 35,* 🌿, « Dutch and English style interior » – ⊡ ✻ ▤ TV ☎ ℗ – ⌁ 25-150. AE ⓪ E VISA JCB. ⁒ HX c
Meals : *Henricus* 53/73 – ⌂ 40 – **71 rm** 405/475, 8 suites.

Sofitel, Koningin Julianaplein 35, ⊠ 2595 AA, ℘ *(0 70) 381 49 01, Fax (0 70) 382 59 27* – ⊡ ✻ ▤ TV ☎ ⅛ ℗ – ⌁ 25-150. AE ⓪ E VISA JCB
Meals Lunch 50 - 85 – ⌂ 33 – **143 rm** 315/375.

Bel Air, Johan de Wittlaan 30, ⊠ 2517 JR, ℘ *(0 70) 352 53 54, Fax (0 70) 353 53 53,* ⊠ – ⊡ ✻, ▤ rm, TV ☎ ℗ – ⌁ 25-250. AE ⓪ E VISA JCB
Meals Lunch 35 – 65/75 – ⌂ 28 – **350 rm** 265/280.

Mercure Central without rest, Spui 180, ⊠ 2511 BW, ℘ *(0 70) 363 67 00, Fax (0 70) 363 93 98* – ⊡ ✻ ▤ TV ☎ ⅛ ℗ – ⌁ 25-130. AE ⓪ E VISA JCB JZ v
⌂ 25 – **156 rm** 210/225, 3 suites.

Corona, Buitenhof 42, ⊠ 2513 AH, ℘ *(0 70) 363 79 30, Fax (0 70) 361 57 85,* 🌿 – ⊡, ▤ rest, TV ☎ ⇌ – ⌁ 30-100. AE ⓪ E VISA JCB HY v
Meals : *Brasserie Buitenhof* Lunch 50 - 55/63 – ⌂ 25 – **26 rm** 180/320.

Parkhotel without rest, Molenstraat 53, ⊠ 2513 BJ, ℘ *(0 70) 362 43 71, Fax (0 70) 361 45 25* – ⊡ TV ☎ – ⌁ 25-100. AE ⓪ E VISA JCB HY a
114 rm ⌂ 190/390.

Novotel, Hofweg 5, ⊠ 2511 AA, ℘ *(0 70) 364 88 46, Fax (0 70) 356 28 89,* 🌿 – ⊡ ✻, ▤ rest, TV ☎ ⇌ – ⌁ 25-100. AE ⓪ E VISA JCB. ⁒ rest HJY e
Meals (open until 11 p.m.) a la carte 45/59 – ⌂ 24 – **106 rm** 235.

Paleis without rest, Molenstraat 26, ⊠ 2513 BL, ℘ *(0 70) 362 46 21, Fax (0 70) 361 45 33,* ⊜ – ⊡ TV ☎. AE ⓪ E VISA JCB HY r
⌂ 23 – **20 rm** 155/219.

NETHERLANDS
The HAGUE
DEN HAAG
0   200 m
Plein 1813
Sophia
PANORAMA MESDAG
Zeestraat
Hogewal
Noordeinde
PALEISTUIN
Paleis Noordeinde
Prinse
Toren
Breedstr.
Geest str.
Vleerstr.
West
einde
Grote Kerk
Groenmarkt
POL.
Prinse gracht
laan
Alexanderstr.
Park
Oranjestr.
straat
Maurits
Willemstr.
Kazernestr.
Klooster Kerk
De Plaats
Hoogstr.
J. Hendrikstr.
Nieuwstr.
Venestr.
Boekhorststr.
Buitenhof
Grote
Tunnelbouw
Paviljoensgracht
Boekhorststr.
Prinse
Dunne
Huygenspark
kade
Denneweg
LANGE VOORHOUT
MUSEUM BREDIUS
HOFVIJVER
MAURITSHUIS
BINNENHOF
Plein
Hof
weg
Lange Poten
Lange
Kalvermarkt
Markt
Wagen
str.
in
K. Voorhout
KONINLIJKE SCHOUWBURG
Lange Houtstr.
Herengracht
Muzenstr.
uitvoering
Prins Bernhard Vladuct
Hout Markt
Spui
Bierkade
Zieken
Konings
kade
MALIEVELD
KOEKAMP
Tunnelbouw in uitvoering
Paleis
100
118
108
105

XXX **De Hoogwerf,** Zijdelaan 20, ✉ 2594 BV, ✆ (0 70) 347 55 14, *Fax (0 70) 381 95 96*, 🏞, « 17C farmhouse, garden » – AE ⓓ E VISA JCB. ⚹
closed Sunday and Bank Holidays except Christmas – **Meals** *Lunch 55* – a la carte 73/102.

XXX **Da Roberto,** Noordeinde 196, ✉ 2514 GS, ✆ (0 70) 346 49 77, *Fax (0 70) 362 52 86*, Italian cuisine – ▤ Ⓟ. AE ⓓ E VISA HX k
closed Sunday – **Meals** *Lunch 58* – a la carte 88/103.

XX ✿ **'t Ganzenest** (Visbeen), Groenewegje 115 (relocation planned Delftweg 58 at Rijswijk), ✉ 2515 LP, ✆ (0 70) 414 06 42, *Fax (0 70) 414 07 05* – AE ⓓ E VISA. ⚹ JZ r
closed Saturday lunch, Sunday, Monday, Easter, Whitsun, late July-early August and first week January – **Meals** 55/75, – a la carte 80/100
Spec. Paupiette de thon mariné et gambas poêlées. Aubergine marinée et chèvre frais, vinaigrette de tomates. Waterzooï d'agneau au ravioli de ses ris et truffes (May-August).

XX **It Rains Fishes,** Noordeinde 123, ✉ 2514 GG, ✆ (0 70) 365 25 98, *Fax (0 70) 365 25 22*, Partly Asian cuisine – ▤. AE ⓓ E VISA HX k
closed lunch Saturday and Sunday and Monday – **Meals** *Lunch 50* – a la carte 80/122.

XX **Rousseau,** Van Boetzelaerlaan 134, ✉ 2581 AX, ✆ (0 70) 355 47 43, 🏞 – AE ⓓ E VISA
closed lunch Saturday and Sunday, Monday, 22 February-1 March and 2 to 16 August – **Meals** *Lunch 45* – 55/98.

XX **Julien,** Vos in Tuinstraat 2a, ✉ 2514 BX, ✆ (0 70) 365 86 02, *Fax (0 70) 365 31 47*, « Art Deco interior » – AE ⓓ E VISA JX s
closed Sunday – **Meals** *Lunch 45* – 50/88.

XX **The Raffles,** Javastraat 63, ✉ 2585 AG, ✆ (0 70) 345 85 87, Indonesian cuisine – ▤. AE ⓓ E VISA JCB
closed Sunday and late July-early August – **Meals** (dinner only) 55/78.

XX **Shirasagi,** Spui 170, ✉ 2511 BW, ✆ (0 70) 346 47 00, *Fax (0 70) 346 26 01*, Japanese cuisine with Teppan-Yaki – ▤. AE ⓓ E VISA JCB. ⚹ JZ v
closed lunch Saturday, Sunday and Monday and 31 December-2 January – **Meals** *Lunch 35* – 65/135.

at Scheveningen 🄲 *'s-Gravenhage – Seaside resort★★ – Casino, Kurhausweg 1, ✉ 2587 RT, ✆ (0 70) 306 77 77, Fax (0 70) 306 78 88.*
ℹ *Gevers Deijnootweg 1134, ✉ 2586 BX, ✆ 0-900-340 35 05, Fax (0 70) 352 04 26*

🏨 **Kurhaus,** Gevers Deijnootplein 30, ✉ 2586 CK, ✆ (0 70) 416 26 36, *Fax (0 70) 416 26 46*, ≤, 🏞, « Former late 19C concert hall », Fā – |‡| ⇆ TV ☎ ♿ Ⓟ – 🏛 35-480. AE ⓓ E VISA JCB
Meals see rest ***Kandinsky*** below – ***Kurzaal*** (buffets) 45/68 – ☕ 45 – **247 rm** 400/560, 8 suites.

🏨 **Europa,** Zwolsestraat 2, ✉ 2587 VJ, ✆ (0 70) 416 95 95, *Fax (0 70) 461 95 55*, 🏞, Fā, ≘s, 🏊 – |‡| ⇆ TV ☎ 🚗 – 🏛 25-460. AE ⓓ E VISA JCB. ⚹
Meals (open until 11 p.m.) *Lunch 38* – 60/70 – ☕ 30 – **173 rm** 300, 1 suite.

🏨 **Carlton Beach,** Gevers Deijnootweg 201, ✉ 2586 HZ, ✆ (0 70) 354 14 14, *Fax (0 70) 352 00 20*, ≤, Fā, ≘s, 🏊 – |‡| ⇆ TV ☎ Ⓟ – 🏛 25-250. AE ⓓ E VISA JCB
Meals (open until midnight) *Lunch 33* – a la carte approx. 65 – ☕ 28 – **183 rm** 270/395.

🏨 **Badhotel,** Gevers Deijnootweg 15, ✉ 2586 BB, ✆ (0 70) 351 22 21, *Fax (0 70) 355 58 70* – |‡| ⇆ TV ☎ Ⓟ – 🏛 25-150. AE ⓓ E VISA JCB. ⚹ rest
Meals (dinner only) 45/90 – ☕ 20 – **90 rm** 180/210.

XXXX **Kandinsky** - (at Kurhaus H.), Gevers Deijnootplein 30, ✉ 2586 CK, ✆ (0 70) 416 26 34, *Fax (0 70) 416 26 46*, ≤, 🏞 – ▤ Ⓟ. AE ⓓ E VISA JCB. ⚹
closed Saturday lunch and Sunday – **Meals** (dinner only July-August) *Lunch 63* – 93/108.

XXX **Seinpost,** Zeekant 60, ✉ 2586 AD, ✆ (0 70) 355 52 50, *Fax (0 70) 355 50 93*, ≤, Seafood – ▤. AE ⓓ E VISA
closed Saturday lunch, Sunday and Bank Holidays – **Meals** *Lunch 63* – a la carte approx. 100.

XXX **Radèn Mas,** Gevers Deijnootplein 125, ✉ 2586 CR, ✆ (0 70) 354 54 32, *Fax (0 70) 350 60 42*, Partly Indonesian cuisine – ▤. ⚹
Meals *Lunch 30* – 50/95.

XX **Rederserf,** Schokkerweg 37, ✉ 2583 BH, ✆ (0 70) 350 50 23, *Fax (0 70) 350 84 54*, ≤, 🏞 – ▤. AE ⓓ E VISA JCB. ⚹
closed 27 December-1 January – **Meals** *Lunch 60* – a la carte 80/112.

XX **China Delight,** Dr Lelykade 116, ✉ 2583 CN, ✆ (0 70) 355 54 50, *Fax (0 70) 354 66 52*, Chinese cuisine – ⓓ E VISA JCB
Meals *Lunch 25* – a la carte 50/83.

NETHERLANDS

XX **Ginza,** Dr Lelykade 28b, ⊠ 2583 CM, ℘ (0 70) 358 96 63, *Fax (0 70) 358 55 48, Japanese cuisine with Teppan-Yaki, open until midnight –* ▤. 𝗔𝗘 ⓞ 𝗘 𝗩𝗜𝗦𝗔 𝗝𝗖𝗕. ⚘
Meals a la carte approx. 60.

XX **Bali** with rm, Badhuisweg 1, ⊠ 2587 CA, ℘ (0 70) 350 24 34, *Fax (0 70) 354 03 63,* 🏠 *Indonesian cuisine –* ▣ ☎ Ⓟ. 𝗔𝗘 ⓞ 𝗘 𝗩𝗜𝗦𝗔. ⚘
closed 31 December – **Meals** (dinner only) 53/70 – **18 rm** � 125/160.

Environs

at Leidschendam *E : 6 km – pop. 34 547*

🏨 **Green Park,** Weigelia 22, ⊠ 2262 AB, ℘ (0 70) 320 92 80, *Fax (0 70) 327 49 07,* ◄
🛁 – 🛗 ⌦ ▣ ☎ Ⓟ – 🔥 25-250. 𝗔𝗘 ⓞ 𝗘 𝗩𝗜𝗦𝗔 𝗝𝗖𝗕
Meals *The Greenery* *Lunch 48 -* a la carte 68/83 – **92 rm** ⊑ 300/325, 3 suites.

XXX **Villa Rozenrust,** Veursestraatweg 104, ⊠ 2265 CG, ℘ (0 70) 327 74 60, *Fax (0 70*
🌸 327 50 62, 🏠, « *Terrace* » – Ⓟ. 𝗔𝗘 ⓞ 𝗘 𝗩𝗜𝗦𝗔
closed Sunday, 25 and 31 December and 1 January – **Meals** *Lunch 60* – 98/120, – a la carte approx. 115
Spec. Emincé de homard chaud, sauce aux pistaches. Fricassée de lapin aux escargots et grenouilles. Enveloppe de langoustines, St-Jacques et huîtres au Porto blanc.

at Voorburg *E : 5 km – pop. 39 357*

🏨 **Mövenpick** Ⓜ, Stationsplein 8, ⊠ 2275 AZ, ℘ (0 70) 337 37 37, *Fax (0 70) 337 37 00*
🏠 – 🛗 ⌦ ▤ ▣ ☎ ♿ 🚗 – 🔥 25-160. 𝗔𝗘 ⓞ 𝗘 𝗩𝗜𝗦𝗔 𝗝𝗖𝗕
Meals (buffets) *Lunch 30* – 45 – ⊑ 20 – **125 rm** 220.

XXX **Savelberg** ⚘ with rm, Oosteinde 14, ⊠ 2271 EH, ℘ (0 70) 387 20 81, *Fax (0 70*
🌸 387 77 15, ◄, 🏠, « *17C residence with terrace in public park* » – 🛗 ⌦ ▣ ☎ Ⓟ – 🔥 35
𝗔𝗘 ⓞ 𝗘 𝗩𝗜𝗦𝗔 𝗝𝗖𝗕
closed 27 December-4 January – **Meals** *(closed Sunday and Monday) Lunch 62* – 85/95, – a la carte approx. 135 – ⊑ 33 – **14 rm** 250
Spec. Salade de homard Savelberg. Turbot grillé, sauce aux pommes de terre et à la truffe. Pigeon de Bresse à la sauge.

XX **Villa la Ruche,** Prinses Mariannelaan 71, ⊠ 2275 BB, ℘ (0 70) 386 01 10, *Fax (0 70*
386 50 64 – ▤. 𝗔𝗘 ⓞ 𝗘 𝗩𝗜𝗦𝗔
closed Sunday, Bank Holidays and 24 December-8 January – **Meals** *Lunch 53* – a la carte 80/116.

XX **De Barbaars,** Kerkstraat 52, ⊠ 2271 CT, ℘ (0 70) 386 29 00, *Fax (0 70) 386 29 00*
🏠, *Open until 11 p.m.,* « *19C listed houses* » – ▤. 𝗔𝗘 ⓞ 𝗘 𝗩𝗜𝗦𝗔
closed 31 December – **Meals** 50/88.

X **Papermoon,** Herenstraat 175, ⊠ 2271 CE, ℘ (0 70) 387 31 61, *Fax (0 70) 386 80 36*
🏠 – ▤. 𝗩𝗜𝗦𝗔. ⚘
closed Monday – **Meals** (dinner only) 45/60.

at Wassenaar *NE : 11 km – pop. 26 195*

🏨 **Aub. de Kieviet** ⚘, Stoeplaan 27, ⊠ 2243 CX, ℘ (0 70) 511 92 32, *Fax (0 70*
511 09 69, 🏠, « *Floral terrace* » – 🛗 ▤ ▣ ☎ ♿ Ⓟ – 🔥 25-90. 𝗔𝗘 ⓞ 𝗘 𝗩𝗜𝗦𝗔
Meals *Lunch 50* – a la carte 84/110 – ⊑ 33 – **23 rm** 185/385, 1 suite.

ROTTERDAM *Zuid-Holland* 🄯 *L* 11 - ㊴ ㊵ *and* 🄯 *È* 6 – ㉕ *N – pop. 589 987 – Casino JY Weena 624* ⊠ *3012 CN,* ℘ *(0 10) 414 77 99, Fax (0 10) 414 92 33.*

See : *Lijnbaan★* JK – *St. Laurence Church (Grote- of St-Laurenskerk) : interior★* KY – *Euromast★ (Tower)* ✳★★, ◄★ JZ – *The harbour★★* KZ – *Willemsbrug★★ Erasmusbrug★★* KZ – *Delftse Poort (building)★* JY C – *World Trade Center★* KY Y – *The Netherlands architectural institute★* JZ W – *Boompjes★* KZ – *Willemswerf (building)★* KY

Museums : History Museum Het Schielandshuis★ KY M² – *Boijmans-van Beuningen★★★* JZ – *History "De Dubbelde Palmboom"★.*

Envir : SE : 7 km, Kinderdijk Windmils★★.

🏌 *at Capelle aan den IJssel E : 8 km, 's Gravenweg 311,* ⊠ *2905 LB,* ℘ *(0 10) 442 21 09 Fax (0 10) 442 24 85 -* 🏌 *at Rhoon SW : 11 km, Veerweg 2a,* ⊠ *3161 EX,* ℘ *(0 10) 501 80 58 -* 🏌 *Kralingseweg 200,* ⊠ *3062 CG,* ℘ *(0 10) 452 22 83.*

✈ *Zestienhoven* ℘ *(0 10) 446 34 44.*

🚢 *Europoort to Hull : P and O North Sea Ferries Ltd* ℘ *(0 181) 25 55 00 (information and (0 181) 25 55 55 (reservations), Fax (0 181) 25 52 15.*

🄑 *Coolsingel 67,* ⊠ *3012 AC,* ℘ *0 900-403 40 65, Fax (0 10) 413 01 24 and – Central Station, Stationsplein 1,* ⊠ *3013 AJ,* ℘ *0-900-403 40 65.*

Amsterdam 76 – The Hague 24 – Antwerp 103 – Brussels 148 – Utrecht 57.

ROTTERDAM

NETHERLANDS

NETHERLANDS

Centre

Parkhotel M, Westersingel 70, ⌧ 3015 LB, ℘ (0 10) 436 36 11, *Fax (0 10) 436 42 12*, 🍃, ⅃₅, ≘ₛ – 🛗 ⁕ ▤ TV ☎ ℗ – 🔬 25-60. AE ① E VISA JCB. ⁒ rest   JZ
Meals *Lunch 48* – a la carte approx. 80 – ☕ 39 – **187 rm** 205/355, 2 suites.

Hilton, Weena 10, ⌧ 3012 CM, ℘ (0 10) 414 40 44, *Fax (0 10) 213 42 63* – 🛗 ⁕ ▤ TV ☎ ⅋ ℗ – 🔬 25-365. AE ① E VISA JCB. ⁒   YY
Meals (dinner only until midnight) a la carte approx. 50 – ☕ 37 – **246 rm** 220/325, 8 suite

Golden Tulip, Aert van Nesstraat 4, ⌧ 3012 CA, ℘ (0 10) 411 04 20, *Fax (0 10* 413 53 20 – 🛗 ⁕ TV ☎ ⅋ ⅌ – 🔬 25-325. AE ① E VISA JCB. ⁒   JY
Meals *Sakura* (Japanese cuisine, open until 11 p.m.) *(closed lunch Saturday and Sunda)*
Lunch 39 - 45/150 – ☕ 29 – **215 rm** 260/335.

Holiday Inn City Centre, Schouwburgplein 1, ⌧ 3012 CK, ℘ (0 10) 433 38 0(
Fax (0 10) 206 25 60 – 🛗 ⁕ TV ☎ ⅌ – 🔬 25-300. AE ① E VISA JCB. ⁒   JY
Meals (dinner only) a la carte 60/83 – ☕ 34 – **100 rm** 325/460.

New York, Koninginnehoofd 1, ⌧ 3072 AD, ℘ (0 10) 439 05 00, *Fax (0 10) 484 27 0(*
≤, 🍃, « Former head office of the Holland-America Line maritime company » – 🛗 ▤
☎ ℗ – 🔬 25-120. AE ① E VISA. ⁒ rm   KZ r
Meals (open until 11 p.m.) 45 – ☕ 20 – **71 rm** 160/275.

Inntel, Leuvehaven 80, ⌧ 3011 EA, ℘ (0 10) 413 41 39, *Fax (0 10) 413 32 22*, ≤, 🍃
≘ₛ, 🏊 – 🛗 ⁕ ▤ rest TV ☎ ℗ – 🔬 25-250. AE ① E VISA. ⁒   KZ
Meals 45 – ☕ 30 – **149 rm** 295/330.

Tulip Inn, Willemsplein 1, ⌧ 3016 DN, ℘ (0 10) 413 47 90, *Fax (0 10) 412 78 90*, ≤
🛗 ⁕ TV ☎ – 🔬 25-60. AE ① E VISA JCB. ⁒ rest   KZ
closed 24 December-4 January – **Meals** (dinner only) 45 – **102 rm** ☕ 160/240.

Van Walsum, Mathenesserlaan 199, ⌧ 3014 HC, ℘ (0 10) 436 32 75, *Fax (0 10* 436 44 10 – 🛗 TV ☎ ℗. AE ① E VISA JCB. ⁒ rest
Meals (dinner residents only) – **25 rm** ☕ 130/170.

Pax without rest, Schiekade 658, ⌧ 3032 AK, ℘ (0 10) 466 33 44, *Fax (0 10) 467 52 7(*
– 🛗 TV ☎ ℗. AE ① E VISA JCB. ⁒
45 rm ☕ 145/275.

Parkheuvel (Helder), Heuvellaan 21, ⌧ 3016 GL, ℘ (0 10) 436 07 66, *Fax (0 1(* 436 71 40, 🍃, « Terrace and ≤ maritime trade » – ℗. AE ① E VISA JCB   JZ
closed Saturday lunch, Sunday and 27 December-3 January – **Meals** *Lunch 73* – 98/158,
a la carte approx. 125
Spec. Ris de veau braisé aux blinis de pommes de terre, salsifis et truffes. Turbot à l
mousseline d'anchois, ragoût de champignons et jus de veau. Râble de lièvre et sa côtelett
farcie à la pomme caramélisée.

Old Dutch, Rochussenstraat 20, ⌧ 3015 EK, ℘ (0 10) 436 03 44, *Fax (0 10) 436 78 2(*
🍃 – ▤ ℗. AE ① E VISA. ⁒   JZ
closed Saturday mid June-mid September, Sunday and Bank Holidays – **Meals** *Lunch 53* –
a la carte 75/103.

Radèn Mas 1st floor, Kruiskade 72, ⌧ 3012 EH, ℘ (0 10) 411 72 44, *Fax (0 1(* 411 97 11, Indonesian cuisine – ▤. AE ① E VISA JCB. ⁒   JY
Meals *Lunch 33* – a la carte approx. 80.

Brasserie La Vilette, Westblaak 160, ⌧ 3012 KM, ℘ (0 10) 414 86 92, *Fax (0 1(* 414 33 91 – ▤. AE ① E VISA. ⁒   JY
closed Saturday lunch, Sunday, 19 July-8 August and 24 December-2 January – **Meal** 55/70.

de Castellane, Eendrachtsweg 22, ⌧ 3012 LB, ℘ (0 10) 414 11 59, *Fax (0 1(* 214 08 97, 🍃, « Terrace » – AE ① E VISA   JZ
closed Sunday, Bank Holidays, first 3 weeks August and 25 December-10 January – **Meal**
Lunch 53 – a la carte approx. 90.

World Trade Center 23rd floor, Beursplein 37, ⌧ 3011 AA, ℘ (0 10) 405 44 65
Fax (0 10) 405 51 20, ✳ city – 🛗 ▤ ℗. AE ① E VISA. ⁒   KY
closed Saturday June-August and Sunday – **Meals** *Lunch 55* – 75.

Brancatelli, Boompjes 264, ⌧ 3011 XD, ℘ (0 10) 411 41 51, *Fax (0 10) 404 57 34*
Italian cuisine, open until 11 p.m. – ▤. AE ① E VISA JCB   KZ
closed 31 December – **Meals** *Lunch 63* – a la carte 77/127.

Chalet Suisse, Kievitslaan 31, ⌧ 3016 CG, ℘ (0 10) 436 50 62, *Fax (0 10) 436 54 62*
≤, 🍃, « Terrace in public park » – ▤. AE ① E VISA   JZ
closed Sunday – **Meals** *Lunch 50* – 63/75.

de Engel (den Blijker), Eendrachtsweg 19, ⌧ 3012 LB, ℘ (0 10) 413 82 56, *Fax (0 1(* 412 51 96 – AE ① E VISA JCB   JZ
closed 24, 25, 26 and 31 December – **Meals** (dinner only) 70/98, – a la carte 85/115
Spec. Velouté de truffes au ris de veau croquant. Carré d'agneau au jus moutardé d
dattes et basilic (April-July). Dos de turbot rôti, sauce dijonnaise (October-January).

X **Brasserie Boompjes,** Boompjes 701, ⊠ 3011 XZ, ☎ (0 10) 413 60 70, *Fax (0 10) 413 70 87*, ≤ Nieuwe Maas (Meuse), 🌿 – 🖻. � ⓞ 🇪 *VISA*. 🛪
closed after 8 p.m. – **Meals** *Lunch* 53 – a la carte 68/109.

KZ e

X **Engels,** Stationsplein 45, ⊠ 3013 AK, ☎ (0 10) 411 95 50, *Fax (0 10) 413 94 21*, Multinational cuisines, open until 11 p.m. – 🅿 – 🔬 25-800. � ⓞ 🇪 *VISA*
Meals – 45.

JY v

X **Anak Mas,** Meent 72a, ⊠ 3011 JN, ☎ (0 10) 414 84 87, *Fax (0 10) 412 44 74*, Indonesian cuisine – 🖻. � ⓞ 🇪 *VISA* ᴊᴄʙ
closed Sunday – **Meals** (dinner only) a la carte approx. 50.

KY s

Suburbs

Airport *N : 2,5 km :*

🏨 **Airport,** Vliegveldweg 59, ⊠ 3043 NT, ☎ (0 10) 462 55 66, *Fax (0 10) 462 22 66*, 🌿 – 🛗 ✉ 📺 ☎ ⚐ 🅿 – 🔬 25-425. � ⓞ 🇪 *VISA* ᴊᴄʙ
Meals *Lunch* 38 – a la carte approx. 75 – ☕ 25 – **97 rm** 148/230, 1 suite.

at Hillegersberg *NE : 10 km* Ⓒ *Rotterdam :*

X **Mangerie Lommerrijk,** Straatweg 99, ⊠ 3054 AB, ☎ (0 10) 422 00 11, *Fax (0 10) 422 64 96*, ≤, 🌿, ⚓ – 🅿 – 🔬 25-250. � ⓞ 🇪 *VISA*
closed Monday and 24 December – **Meals** – a la carte approx. 60.

at Kralingen *E : 2 km* Ⓒ *Rotterdam :*

🏨 **Novotel Brainpark,** K.P. van der Mandelelaan 150 (near A 16), ⊠ 3062 MB, ☎ (0 10) 453 07 77, *Fax (0 10) 453 15 03*, 🌿 – 🛗 ✉ 🖻 📺 ☎ ⚐ 🅿 – 🔬 25-400. � ⓞ 🇪 *VISA*
Meals (open until midnight) *Lunch* 39 – a la carte 45/75 – ☕ 24 – **196 rm** 195.

XXX **In den Rustwat,** Honingerdijk 96, ⊠ 3062 NX, ☎ (0 10) 413 41 10, *Fax (0 10) 404 85 40*, 🌿, « 16C residence in floral garden » – 🖻 🅿. � ⓞ 🇪 *VISA* ᴊᴄʙ. 🛪
closed Sunday and 27 December-3 January – **Meals** *Lunch* 63 – 83/110.

Europoort zone *W : 25 km :*

🏨 **De Beer Europoort,** Europaweg 210 (N 15), ⊠ 3198 LD, ☎ (0 181) 26 23 77, *Fax (0 181) 26 29 23*, ≤, 🌿, 🏊, ✕ – 🛗 📺 ☎ 🅿 – 🔬 25-180. � ⓞ 🇪 *VISA*
Meals *Lunch* 45 – a la carte 63/83 – **78 rm** ☕ 150/190.

Environs

at Capelle aan den IJssel *E : 8 km – pop. 62 366*

🏨 **Barbizon** Ⓜ, Barbizonlaan 2 (near A 20), ⊠ 2908 MA, ☎ (0 10) 456 44 55, *Fax (0 10) 456 78 58*, ≤, 🌿 – 🛗 ✉ 📺 ☎ 🅿 – 🔬 30-250. � ⓞ 🇪 *VISA*
Meals *Lunch* 55 – 68 – ☕ 33 – **100 rm** 160/450, 1 suite.

at Rhoon *S : 10 km* Ⓒ *Albrandswaard pop. 15 249 :*

XXX **Het Kasteel van Rhoon,** Dorpsdijk 63, ⊠ 3161 KD, ☎ (0 10) 501 88 96, *Fax (0 10) 506 72 59*, ≤, 🌿, « Situated in the outbuildings of the mansion » – 🅿. � ⓞ 🇪 *VISA*.
🛪
Meals *Lunch* 78 – 68/98.

at Schiedam *W : 6 km – pop. 74 889.*

🄴 *Buitenhavenweg 9,* ⊠ 3113 BC, ☎ (0 10) 473 30 00, *Fax (0 10) 473 66 95*

🏨 **Novotel,** Hargalaan 2 (near A 20), ⊠ 3118 JA, ☎ (0 10) 471 33 22, *Fax (0 10) 470 06 56*, 🌿, 🏊, 🎾 – 🛗 ✉ 🖻 📺 ☎ ⚐ 🅿 – 🔬 25-200. � ⓞ 🇪 *VISA*
Meals (open until midnight) *Lunch* 28 – 45 – ☕ 24 – **134 rm** 189.

XXX **La Duchesse,** Maasboulevard 9, ⊠ 3114 HB, ☎ (0 10) 426 46 26, *Fax (0 10) 473 25 01*, ≤ Nieuwe Maas (Meuse), 🌿 – 🅿. � ⓞ 🇪 *VISA* ᴊᴄʙ
closed Saturday lunch and Sunday – **Meals** *Lunch* 63 – 75/105.

X **Bistrot Hosman Frères,** Korte Dam 10, ⊠ 3111 BG, ☎ (0 10) 426 40 96, *Fax (0 10) 426 90 41*, Open until 11 p.m. – 🖻. � ⓞ 🇪 *VISA*
closed lunch Saturday and Sunday and 31 December – **Meals** – 50.

X **Orangerie Duchesse,** Maasboulevard 9, ⊠ 3114 HB, ☎ (0 10) 426 46 26, *Fax (0 10) 473 25 01*, ≤ Nieuwe Maas (Meuse), 🌿 – 🅿. � ⓞ 🇪 *VISA* ᴊᴄʙ
closed Sunday and 31 December – **Meals** (dinner only) 55.

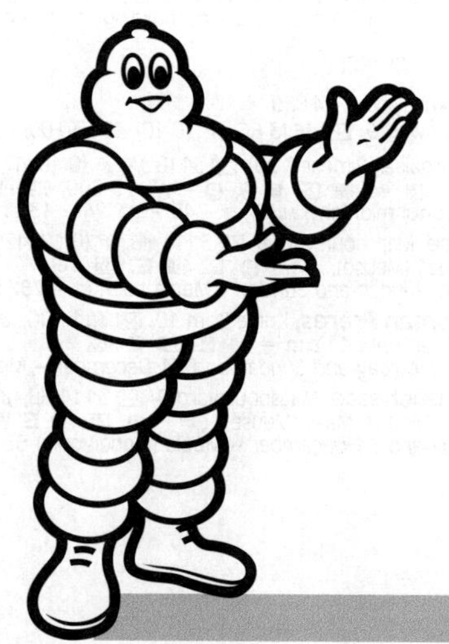

Czech Republic

Česká Republika

PRAGUE

PRACTICAL INFORMATION

LOCAL CURRENCY

Crown : *100 CRT = 2,84 euros (€)*

National Holiday in the Czech Republic : *28 October.*

PRICES

Prices may change if goods and service costs in the Czech Republic are revised and it is therefore always advisable to confirm rates with the hotelier when making a reservation.

FOREIGN EXCHANGE

It is strongly advised against changing money other than in banks, exchange offices or authorised offices such as large hotels, tourist offices, etc... Banks are usually open on weekdays from 9am to 5pm. Some exchange offices in the old city are open 24 hours a day.

HOTEL RESERVATIONS

In case of difficulties in finding a room through our hotel selection, it is always possible to apply to AVE Wilsonova 8, Prague 2, ℰ (02) 24 22 35 21. CEDOK Na příkopě 18, Prague 1 ℰ (02) 24 19 76 15.

POSTAL SERVICES

Post offices are open from 8am to 6pm on weekdays and 12 noon on Saturdays. The **General Post Office** *is open 24 hours a day : Jindřišska 14, Prague 1, ℰ (02) 24 22 85 88.*

SHOPPING IN PRAGUE

In the index of street names, those printed in red are where the principal shops are found. Typical goods to be bought include embroidery, puppets, Bohemian glass, porcelain, ceramics, wooden toys... Shops are generally open from 9am to 7pm.

TIPPING

Hotel, restaurant and café bills include service in the total charge but it is up to you to tip the staff.

CAR HIRE

The international car hire companies have branches in Prague. Your hotel porter should be able to give details and help you with your arrangements.

BREAKDOWN SERVICE

A 24 hour breakdown service is operated by YELLOW ANGELS, Limuzská 12, Prague 10, ℰ (02) 77 34 55, and Accident road service ℰ (02) 12 31 54.

SPEED LIMITS - SEAT BELTS - MOTORWAYS TAX

The maximum permitted speed on motorways is 130 km/h - 80 mph, 90 km/h - 56 mph on other roads and 50 km/h - 31 mph in built up areas except where a lower speed limit is indicated.
The wearing of seat belts is compulsory for drivers and all passengers.
Driving on motorways is subject to the purchase of a single rate annual road tax obtainable from border posts and tourist offices.
In the Czech Republic, drivers must not drink alcoholic beverages at all.

PRAGUE

(PRAHA) *Česká Republika* 9 7 6 F 3 – *Pop. 1 203 230*

Berlin 344 – Dresden 152 – Munich 384 – Nurnberg 287 – Wroclaw 272 – Vienna 291.

Prague İnformation Service : Na Přikope 20 (main office), Staroměstsk a radnice, and Main Railway Station ℰ *187*
CEDOK : Na přikopě 18, Prague 1 ℰ *(02) 24 19 71 11, Fax (02) 232 16 56.*

Golf Club Praha, Motol-Praha 5, ℰ *(02) 651 24 64*
Ruzyně (Prague Airport) NW 20 km, by road n° 7 ℰ *(02) 36 77 60.*
Bus to airport : ČSA Bus at airlines Terminal V. Celnici 5 ℰ *(02) 20 11 42 96.*
CZECH AIRLINES (ČESKÉ AEROLINIE) V. Celnici 5, PRAGUE 1 ℰ *(02) 20 10 41 11.*

See: *Castle District*★★★ *(Hradčany)* ABY *: Prague Castle*★★★ *(Pražský Hrad)* BY*, St Vitus' Cathedral*★★★ *(Katedrála sv. Víta)* BY*, Royal Palace*★★ *(Královský palác)* BY*, St George's Basilica and Convent*★★ *(National Gallery's Collection of Old Czech Art*★★★ *) (Bazilika sv. Jiří/Jiřský Klašter)* BY*, Hradčany Square*★ *(Hradčanské náměsti)* AY **37***, Schwarzenberg Palace*★ *(Schwarzenberský Palác)* ABY **P⁴***, Loretto*★★ *(Loreta)* AY*, Strahov Monastery*★★ *(Strahovský Kláster)* AY *– Lesser Town*★★★ *(Malá Strana)* BY *: Charles Bridge*★★★ *(Karlův Most)* BCY*, Lesser Town Square*★★ *(Malostranské náměstí)* BY*, St Nicholas Church*★★★ *(Sv. Mikuláš)* BY*, Nerudova Street*★★ *(Nerudova)* BY*, Wallenstein Palace*★★ *(Valdštejnský Palác)* BY *– Old Town*★★★ *(Staré Město)* CY *: Old Town Square*★★★ *(Staroměstské náměsti)* CY*, Astronomical Clock*★★ *(Orloj)* CY **B***, Old Town Hall – Extensive view*★★★ *(Staroměstská radnice)* CY **B***, St Nicolas'*★ *(Sv. Mikuláš)* CY*, Týn Church*★ *(Týnský chrám)* CY*, Jewish Quarter*★★★ *(Josefov)* CY*, Old-New Synagogue*★★ *(Staronová Synagóga)* CY*, Old Jewish Cemetery*★★ *(Starý židovský hřbitov)* CY **V***, St Agnes Convent*★★ *(National Gallery's Collection of 19 C Czech Painting and Sculpture) (Anežský kláster)* CY*, Celetná Street*★★ *(Celetná)* CDY*, Powder Tower*★ *(Prašná Brána)* DY*, House of the black Madonna*★ *(Dům u černe Matky boží)* CDY **E***, Municipal House*★★ *(Obecní Dům)* DY **F** *– New Town*★★★ *(Nové Město)* CDZ *: Wenceslas Square*★★★ *(Václavské náměstí)* CDYZ.

Museums: *National Gallery*★★★ *(Národní Galérie)* AY*, National Museum*★ *(Národní muzeum)* DZ*, National Theatre*★★ *(Národní divadlo)* CZ*, Decorative Arts Museum*★ *(Umělecko průmyslové muzeum)* CY **M¹***, City Museum*★ *(Prague model*★★ *) (Muzeum hlavního města Prahy)* DY **M²***, Vila America*★ *(Dvořák Museum)* DZ.

Outskirts: *Karlštejn Castle SW : 30 km* ET *– Konopiště Castle SW : 40 km* FT.

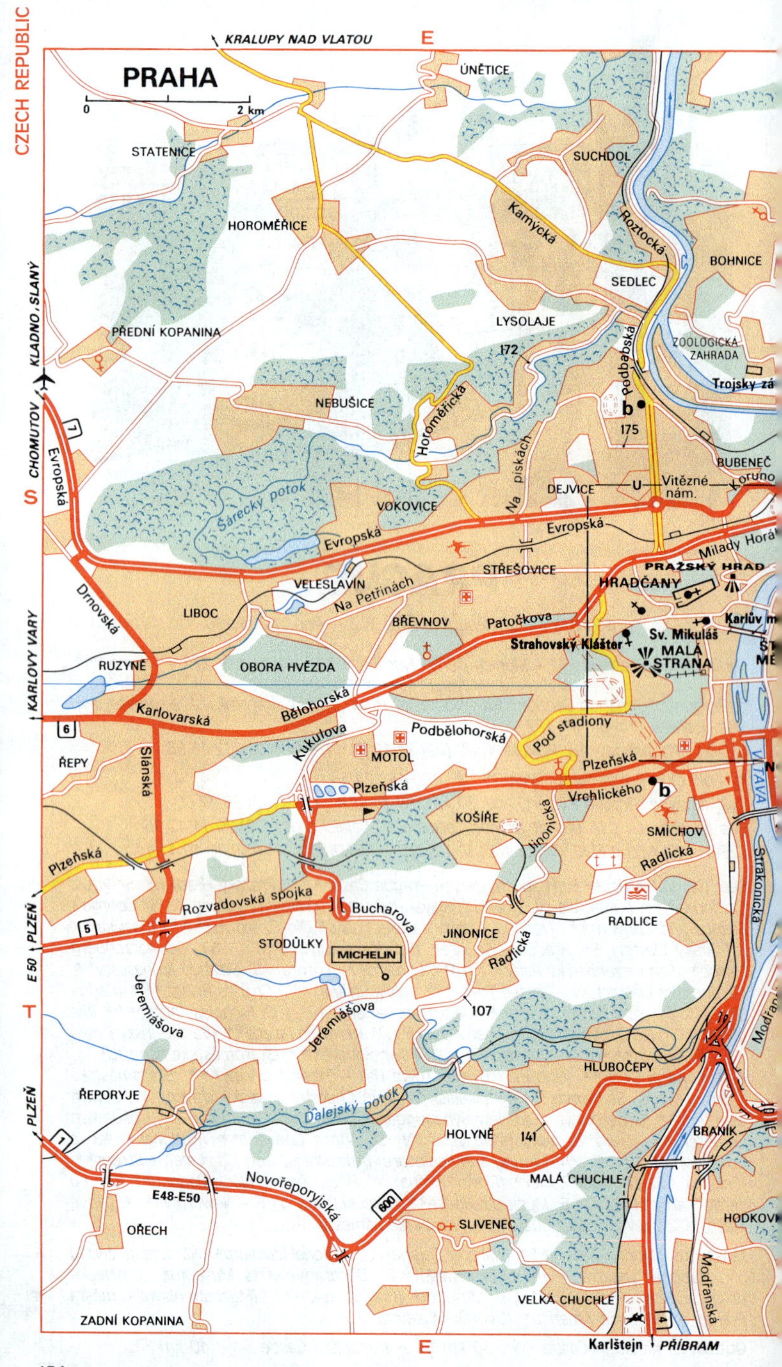

CZECH REPUBLIC
KRALUPY NAD VLATOU
PRAHA
0   2 km
ÚNĚTICE
STATENICE
SUCHDOL
Kamýcká
Roztocká
HOROMĚŘICE
BOHNICE
SEDLEC
PŘEDNÍ KOPANINA
LYSOLAJE
Podbabská
172
ZOOLOGICKÁ ZAHRADA
Trojsky zá
NEBUŠICE
175
b
Horoměřická
Na piskách
BUBENEČ
CHOMUTOV
KLADNO, SLANÝ
Evropská
Šárecký potok
VOKOVICE
DEJVICE
U
Vitězné nám.
Coruno
7
S
Evropská
Evropská
Milady Horá
STŘEŠOVICE
PRAŽSKÝ HRAD
VELESLAVÍN
HRADČANY
Drnovská
Na Petřinách
LIBOC
BŘEVNOV
Patočkova
Karlův m
Strahovský Klášter
Sv. Mikuláš
S
ME
RUZYNĚ
OBORA HVĚZDA
MALÁ STRANA
KARLOVY VARY
Karlovarská
Bělohorská
Pod stadiony
6
Kukulova
Podbělohorská
Plzeňská
ŘEPY
Slánská
MOTOL
Vrchlického
b
VITAVA
Plzeňská
KOŠÍŘE
Jinonická
SMÍCHOV
Radlická
Strakonická
Plzeňská
Rozvadovská spojka
Bucharova
N
RADLICE
PLZEŇ
5
STODŮLKY
MICHELIN
JINONICE
Radlická
E 50
Jeremiášova
Radlická
107
Jeremiášova
Modřan
T
HLUBOČEPY
PLZEŇ
ŘEPORYJE
Dalejský potok
BRANÍK
1
HOLYNĚ
141
Novořeporyjská
MALÁ CHUCHLE
E48-E50
600
Modřanská
OŘECH
SLIVENEC
HODKOV
ZADNÍ KOPANINA
VELKÁ CHUCHLE
E
Karlštejn
PŘÍBRAM
4

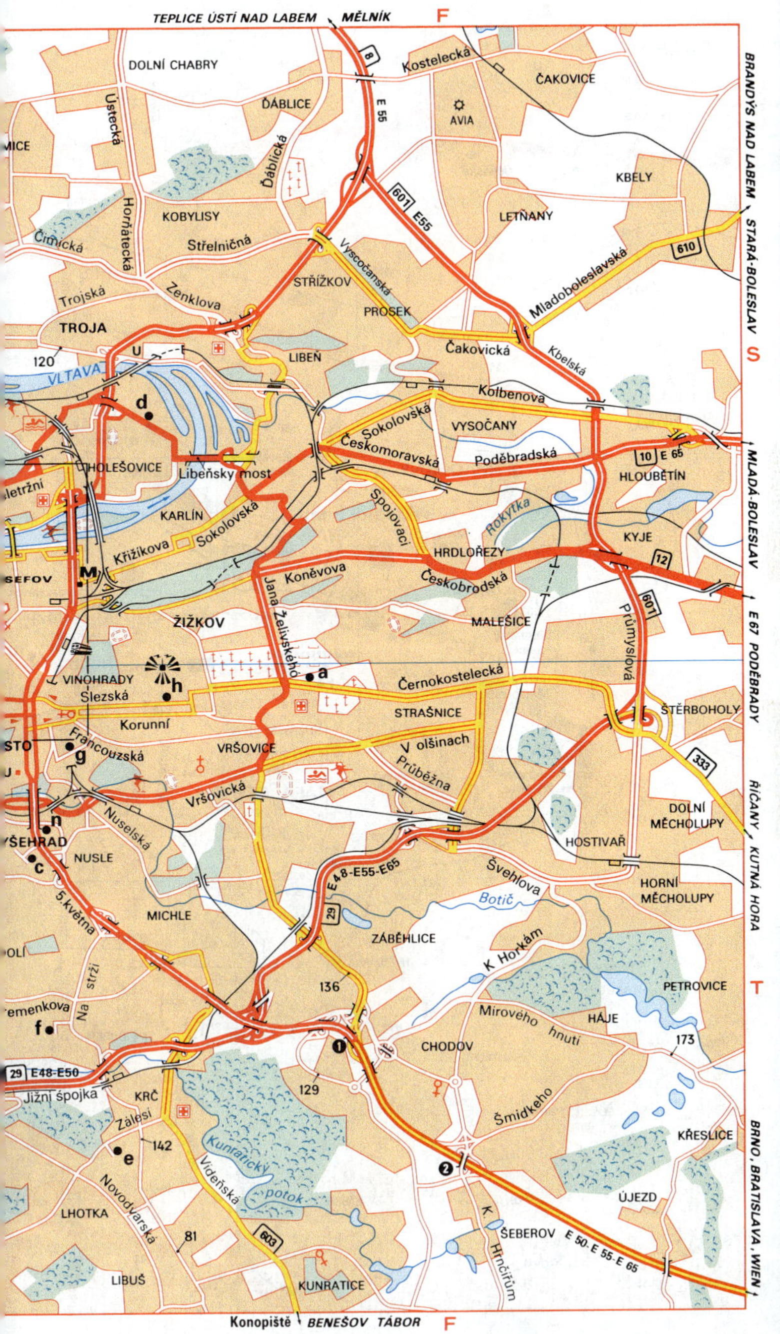

TEPLICE ÚSTÍ NAD LABEM
MĚLNÍK
F
BRANDÝS NAD LABEM
STARÁ-BOLESLAV
S
DOLNÍ CHABRY
Kostelecká
ČAKOVICE
ÚSTECKÁ
ĎÁBLICE
AVIA
ĎÁBLICKÁ
KBELY
E 55
8
MICE
Horňátecká
KOBYLISY
Střelničná
607
E55
LETŇANY
Mladoboleslavská
610
Čimická
Trojská
Zenklova
STŘÍŽKOV
Vysočanská
TROJA
PROSEK
Čakovická
Kbelská
120
U
LIBEŇ
Kolbenova
MLADÁ-BOLESLAV
VLTAVA
d
Sokolovská
VYSOČANY
E 67
Českomoravská
Poděbradská
HLOUBĚTÍN
10
E 65
HOLEŠOVICE
Libeňský most
Spojovací
Rokytka
KYJE
letržní
KARLÍN
HRDLOŘEZY
12
Křižíkova
Sokolovská
Českobrodská
601
SEFOV
M
Koněvova
Jana Želivského
MALEŠICE
Průmyslová
PODĚBRADY
ŽIŽKOV
Černokostelecká
ŠTĚRBOHOLY
VINOHRADY
Slezská
h
a
STRAŠNICE
ŘÍČANY, KUTNÁ HORA
Korunní
333
STO
Francouzská
VRŠOVICE
V olšinach
DOLNÍ MĚCHOLUPY
J
g
Průběžna
Vršovická
HOSTIVAŘ
n
Nuselská
Švehlova
HORNÍ MĚCHOLUPY
VYŠEHRAD
NUSLE
Botič
c
E 48-E 55-E 65
5. května
29
MICHLE
ZÁBĚHLICE
K Horkám
PETROVICE
136
Na stráži
Mírového hnutí
HÁJE
173
emenkova
f
1
CHODOV
Šmídkeho
29
E 48-E 50
Jižní spojka
KRČ
129
KŘESLICE
POLÍ
Záleší
2
BRNO, BRATISLAVA, WIEN
e
142
Kunratický
ÚJEZD
Novodvarská
Vídeňská
potok
LHOTKA
81
ŠEBEROV
E 50, E 55, E 65
603
K Hrnčířům
LIBUŠ
KUNRATICE
Konopiště
BENEŠOV TÁBOR
F
T

CZECH REPUBLIC

PRAHA
0   200 m

A   B   X   Y   Z

U   U   U
Šolínova   50
Zikova
DEJVICE
Evropská
Verdunská
Bubenečská
Pod haštany
110
Vítězné náměstí
b
Dejvická
Československé
armády
Bubenečská
110
25
Generála   Píky
Svatovítská
Devivická
P
Slunná
OŘECHOVKA
165
DEJVICE
Hradčanská
Badeniho
P
Dělostřelecká
Pevnostní   Pod   hradbami
Milady
Horákové
Na   valech
P
Slunná
Cukrovarnická
U Prašného mostu
Mariánské
hradby
Jelení
Královská
zahrada
BELVEDÉR   43
138
Patočkova
Brusnice
HRADČANY
Jízdárna
SV. JIŘÍ
Zlatá Ulička
LEDEBURSKÁ
ZAHRADA
S
63
Keplerova
Nový   Svět
NÁRODNÍ
GALERIE
53
PRAŽSKÝ HRAD
SV. VÍTA
Malostran
Myslbekov
13
LORETA
152
37
KRÁLOVSKÝ
PALÁC
168   80
169
VALDŠTEJNSK
PALÁC
83
P 4
146
154
Černínský
Palác
n
MALOSTRANSKÉ
NÁM.
SV. TOMÁŠ
VOJANOVY
SADY
a
Loretánská
NERUDOVA
SV. MIKULÁŠ
80   h
m
Parléřova
Úvoz
SV. KAREL
BOROMEJSKÝ
r
SV. JOSEF
97
10
Dlabačov
P   P   P
Plohořelec
e
99   f
18
Vlašská   Tržiště
122
P. MARIÁ
POD
ŘETĚZEM
k
SV. ROCH
Vrtbovský palác
171
KARL
Vaníčkova
Strahovská
STRAHOVSKÝ
KLÁŠTER
LOBKOVICKÁ
ZAHRADA
SCHÖNBORNSKÁ
ZAHRADA
P. MARIÁ
VÍTĚZNÁ
Karmelitská
P   d
KAMPA
HLADOVÁ ZED'
Rozhledna
BLUDIŠTĚ
MALÁ   STRANA
Petřín
Na Kampě
Čertovka
RŮŽOVÝ
SAD
SEMINÁŘSKÁ
ZAHRADA
Újezd
M
STŘELEC
OSTROV
mc
P
SV. VAVŘINEC
Vítězná
STADION
STRAHOV
HVĚZDÁRNA
PETŘÍNSKÉ
SADY
HLADOVÁ ZED'
Újezd
Janáčkovo
DĚTSKÝ
OSTROV
Atletická
Šermířská
KINSKÉHO ZAHRADA
nám.
Kinských
Petřínská
174
Z
117   148
Na   Hřebenkách
SV. MICHAL
a
Štefánikova
3   174
158
Hřebenkách
Švédská
SV. GABRIEL
M
Drtinova
Holečkova
158
158
Jiřás
Na
Zapova
Holečkova
93   93
Mošnova
Kartouzská
SV. VÁCLAV
102   P   174
náběžní

CZECH REPUBLIC
C
D
BUBNY
Královskou
oborou
Chechova
Strojnická
Dukelských
Veletržní
Bubenská
HOLEŠOVICE
Zátorce
Korunovační
Nad
Letenské
nám.
Milady
34
Horákové
34
Vltavská
STADIÓN
SPARTA
Veletržní
Kamenická
hrdinů
X
Horákové
101
Letenský
Kostelní
LETNÁ
M
Praha-Expo 58
OSTROV
ŠTVANICE
LETENSKÉ SADY
nábř. kpt. Jaroše
Hlávkův most
navský
vilón
Edvarda
Beneše
Švermův most
Těšnovský
tunel
V
nábřeží
VLTAVA
Na
Františku
nábř. Ludvíka
Svobody
ANEŽSKÝ
KLÁŠTER
128
66
61
20
180
Kozí
66
113
U
STARONOVÁ
SYNAGÓGA
Bilkova
f
v
113
t
143
JOSEFOV
27
e
Rybná
Revoluční
Soukenická
Truhlářská
Na
poříčí
176
M
RUDOLFINUM
M
Kozí
Dlouhá
AIRLINES
TERMINAL
r
31
Na Florenci
Florenc
V
180
103
U
SV. JAKUB
m
F
Náměstí
Republiky
MASARYKOVO
NÁDRAŽÍ
nesův
ost
71
SV.
MIKULÁŠ
TÝNSKÝ
CHRÁM
X
k
161
38
Staroměstská
55
B
STAROMĚSTSKÉ
NÁM.
E
PRAŠNÁ
BRÁNA
Hybernská
Y
FRANTIŠEK
ASSISI
115
88
H
CELETNÁ
příkopě
15
Klementinum
86
178
108
104
71
40
KAROLINUM
T
Na
106
131
Karlova
STARÉ
MĚSTO
Panská
SV. JINDŘICH
Opletalova
Betlémská
a kaple
40
Rytířská
29
ZEC
46
HLAVNÍ
NÁDRAŽÍ
WILSONOVO
156
28. října
Z
105
M
8
111
132
h
Růžová
Národní
46
Wilsonova
Můstek
P. MARIA
SNĚŽNÁ
d
119
f
Národní
Národní
třída
VÁCLAVSKÉ
e
Opletalova
119
Španělská
Italská
90
T
Ostrovní
LUCERNA
NÁMĚSTÍ
SV. VÁCLAV
RODNI
VADLO
140
a
Muzeum
VINOHRADY
VANSKÝ
STROV
75
NOVÉ
MĚSTO
NÁRODNÍ
MUZEUM
78
Vinohradská
Myslíkova
NOVOMĚSTSKÁ
RADNICE
Žitná
95
Z
ŠITKOVSKÁ VĚŽ
náměstí
Ve Smečkách
Žitná
Italská
T
133
90
140
135
Anglická
SV. CYRIL A
METODĚJ
U
Ječná
SV. ŠTĚPÁN
Ječná
78
5
49
SV. LUDMILA
ost
47
f
126
SV. IGNÁC
Lípová
I. P. Pavlova
49
Náměstí
Míru
69
124
Karlovo
náměstí
Ke Karlovu
58
78
ackého
ost
e
U nemocnice
135
VILA AMERIKA
Rumunská
22
Na
Moráni
SV. KATEŘINA
58
h
5
C
D
137

STREET INDEX TO PRAHA TOWN PLAN

Inter-Continental, Nám. Curieových 43-45, ✉ 110 00, ℰ (02) 2488 1111, Fax (02) 2481 1216, ≤, ₺, ⇌s, ▨ – ⊠, ✹ rm ▤ ▣ ☎ ℒ ఉ ⟺ – ✍ 400. ᴁ ⓪ ᴇ VISA JCB. ✹ rest **CY**
Primator : Meals 900 and a la carte (see also **Zlatá** below) – **340 rm** ☕ 9750/10500, 24 suites.

Savoy, Keplerova Ul. 6, ✉ 118 00, ℰ (02) 2430 2430, Fax (02) 2430 2128, « Elegant installation », ⇌s – ⊠, ✹ rm ▤ ▣ ☎ ℒ ఉ ⟺ – ✍ 35. ᴁ ⓪ ᴇ VISA JCB **AY**
Meals (see **Hradčany** below) – **60 rm** ☕ 8190, 1 suite.

Palace, Panská 12, ✉ 111 21, ℰ (02) 2409 3111, Fax (02) 2422 1240, ⇌s – ⊠, ✹ rm ▤ ▣ ☎ ℒ ఉ ⟺ – ✍ 80. ᴁ ⓪ ᴇ VISA JCB **DY**
Meals 350/1100 and a la carte – **Club Restaurant** : Meals (dinner only) 850/4000 and a la carte – **114 rm** ☕ 8190/9260, 10 suites.

Radisson SAS Ⓜ, Štěpanska 40, ✉ 110 00, ℰ (02) 2282 0000, Fax (02) 2282 0100, « Art Deco style », ₺, ⇌s – ⊠ ✹ ▤ ▣ ☎ ఉ ⟺ – ✍ 250. ᴁ ⓪ ᴇ VISA JCB **DZ**
La Rotonde : Meals 590/2000 and a la carte – ☕ 590 – **201 rm** 8815/9525, 10 suites.

Renaissance, V Celnici 7, ✉ 111 21, ℰ (02) 2182 2100, Fax (02) 2182 2200, ₺, ⇌s, ▨ – ⊠, ✹ rm ▤ ▣ ☎ ℒ ఉ ⟺ – ✍ 240. ᴁ ⓪ ᴇ VISA JCB. ✹ rest **DY**
Potomac (ℰ (02) 2182 2431) : Meals (closed Sunday) (dinner only) 1030/1475 – **Pavillion** (ℰ (02) 2182 2431) : Meals (buffet lunch only) 550/595 – **U Korbele** (ℰ (02) 2182 2433) : Meals 800/1500 and a la carte – ☕ 515 – **313 rm** 7580/10755, 11 suites.

Prague Hilton Atrium, Pobřežní 1, ✉ 186 00, ℰ (02) 2484 1111, Fax (02) 2484 2378, ≤, ✹, ₺, ⇌s, ▨, ✹indoor – ⊠, ✹ rm ▤ ▣ ☎ ℒ ఉ ⟺ – ✍ 1350. ᴁ ⓪ ᴇ VISA JCB. ✹ rest **DX**
We Like To Cook : Meals 750/850 and a la carte – **Atrium** : Meals (buffet only) 795/850 – ☕ 530 – **765 rm** 8100/9000, 23 suites.

Mövenpick Ⓜ, Mozartova 261/1, ✉ 151 33, ℰ (02) 5715 1111, Fax (02) 5715 3131, ✹, park – ⊠ ✹ ▤ ▣ ☎ ఉ ⟺ – ✍ 250. ᴁ ⓪ ᴇ VISA JCB **ET**
Meals (buffet lunch) 490 and a la carte 400/580 – **Il Giardino** : Meals 450/1400 and a la carte – **404 rm** ☕ 5160/6055, 31 suites.

Grand Hotel Bohemia, Králodvorská 4, ✉ 110 00, ℰ (02) 2480 4111, Fax (02) 232 9545, « Ballroom » – ⊠, ✹ rm ▤ ▣ ☎ ℒ ఉ. ᴁ ⓪ ᴇ VISA JCB **DY**
Meals a la carte 480/890 – **75 rm** ☕ 6825/9435, 3 suites.

Don Giovanni Ⓜ, Vinohradská 157a, ✉ 130 20, ℰ (02) 6703 1111, Fax (02) 6703 6717, ≤, ⇌s – ⊠, ✹ rm ▤ ▣ ☎ ℒ ఉ ⟺ – ✍ 200. ᴁ ⓪ ᴇ VISA JCB. ✹ **FT**
Meals (buffet lunch) 630/730 and dinner a la carte – **356 rm** ☕ 5340/6855, 42 suites.

Holiday Inn, Koulova 15, ✉ 160 45, ℰ (02) 2439 3111, Fax (02) 2431 0616, ✹, ₺, ⇌s, ✹ – ⊠, ✹ rm, ▤ rest ▣ ☎ ℒ ఉ ⟺ Ⓟ – ✍ 380. ᴁ ⓪ ᴇ VISA JCB **ES**
Meals 320/390 and a la carte – **237 rm** ☕ 5650/5900, 6 suites.

Diplomat, Evropská 15, ⊠ 160 41, ℘ (02) 2439 4111, *Fax (02) 2439 4215,* ⇖s – |‡|, ⇖ rm ▤ 📺 ☎ 📞 🚗 – 👥 250. AE ① E *VISA* JCB
Meals 420/880 – **364 rm** ⊊ 5500/6600, 18 suites.
AX b

Hoffmeister, Pod Bruskou 7, ⊠ 118 00, ℘ (02) 5731 0942, *Fax (02) 5732 0906,*
« Collection of Adolf Hoffmeister's artwork » – |‡|, ▤ rm 📺 ☎ 🚗. AE ① E *VISA* JCB.
Meals 500/1600 and a la carte – ⊊ 330 – **34 rm** 6100/8175, 4 suites.
BXY s

Corinthia Towers, Kongresová 1, ⊠ 140 69, ℘ (02) 6119 1111, *Fax (02) 421 669,* ≤,
↟, ⇖s, ⊠, squash – |‡|, ⇖ rm ▤ 📺 ☎ 🚿 🚗 – 👥 290. ① E *VISA* JCB. ⊗
Meals 400/800 and a la carte – **Ceska** : Meals *(closed 16 February-14 April)* (buffet only) 680/750 – **531 rm** ⊊ 5850.
FT n

Maximilian ⊗ without rest., Haštalská 14, ⊠ 110 00, ℘ (02) 2180 6111, *Fax (02) 2180 6110* – |‡| ⇖ ▤ 📺 ☎ 📞 🚿 🚗 – 👥 50. AE ① E *VISA* JCB
72 rm ⊊ 5325/6340.
CY e

Kinsky Garden, Holečkova 7, ⊠ 150 00, ℘ (02) 5731 1173, *Fax (02) 5731 1184* – |‡|,
⇖ rm ▤ 📺 ☎ 🚿 – 👥 30. AE ① E *VISA* JCB. ⊗
Meals *(closed Sunday)* (dinner only) 520/770 and a la carte – **60 rm** ⊊ 4800/6200.
BZ a

Villa Voyta ⊗ (with guesthouse), K Novému Dvoru 124-54, ⊠ 142 00, ℘ (02) 472 2711, *Fax (02) 472 2918,* ⊹, 🚙 – |‡|, ⇖ rm, ▤ rm 📺 ☎ 🅿 – 👥 25. AE ① E
VISA JCB
closed 24 December – **Meals** 820/1400 and a la carte – **18 rm** ⊊ 4700/5300, 2 suites.
FT e

Esplanade, Washingtonova 19, ⊠ 110 00, ℘ (02) 2421 1715, *Fax (02) 2422 9306,*
« Art Nouveau building » – |‡|, ▤ rm 📺 ☎ 🅿 – 👥 40. AE ① E *VISA* JCB
Meals 700/1500 and a la carte – **68 rm** ⊊ 6600/8400, 6 suites.
DZ f

Paříž, U Obecního Domu 1, ⊠ 110 00, ℘ (02) 2219 5111, *Fax (02) 2422 5475,*
« Neo-Gothic and Art Nouveau architecture » – |‡|, ⇖ rm ▤ 📺 ☎ 🚗 – 👥 55. AE
① E *VISA* JCB
Meals (buffet lunch) 350/1500 and a la carte – **91 rm** ⊊ 7200/7800, 2 suites.
DY m

U Krále Karla, Úvoz 4, ⊠ 118 00, ℘ (02) 538 805, *Fax (02) 538 811,* « 17C baroque house, antique furniture » – |‡| 📺 ☎. AE ① E *VISA*
Meals 340/2500 and a la carte – **19 rm** ⊊ 5600/6100.
AY n

Vyšehrad, Marie Cibulkové 29, ⊠ 140 00, ℘ (02) 436 002, *Fax (02) 6122 5591* – |‡|
▤ 📺 ☎ 🚗. AE ① E *VISA*. ⊗
Meals 230/620 and a la carte – **26 rm** ⊊ 4200/4725, 1 suite.
FT c

Adria, Václavské Nám. 26, ⊠ 120 00, ℘ (02) 2108 1111, *Fax (02) 2108 1300* – |‡|,
⇖ rm, ▤ rest 📺 ☎ 🚗 – 👥 70. AE ① E *VISA* JCB. ⊗
Meals 300/1000 and a la carte – **61 rm** ⊊ 5165/6055, 5 suites.
CZ d

City H. Moran, Na Moráni 15, ⊠ 120 00, ℘ (02) 2491 5208, *Fax (02) 297 533* – |‡|,
▤ rm 📺 ☎ 🚗. AE ① E *VISA*
Meals 500/1000 and a la carte – **57 rm** ⊊ 5005/5910.
CZ e

Jalta, Václavské Nám. 45, ⊠ 110 00, ℘ (02) 2282 2111, *Fax (02) 2421 3866* – |‡| ▤
📺 ☎ – 👥 130. AE ① E *VISA* JCB. ⊗ rest
Meals 450/1900 and a la carte - also Japanese (Teppan-Yaki) - 550/2200 and a la carte – **84 rm** ⊊ 6270/7320, 5 suites.
DZ e

Alta, Ortenovo Nám. 22, ⊠ 170 00, ℘ (02) 800 252, *Fax (02) 6671 2011* – |‡|, ⇖ rm,
▤ rest 📺 ☎ 🚗 – 👥 30. AE ① E *VISA* JCB. ⊗ rest
Meals 300/500 and a la carte – **82 rm** ⊊ 2800/3700, 5 suites.
FS d

Ametyst, Jana Masaryka 11, ⊠ 120 00, ℘ (02) 2425 4185, *Fax (02) 2425 1315,* ⇖s
– |‡|, ⇖ rm, ▤ rest 📺 ☎ 🚿 🚗. AE ① E *VISA* JCB
Meals 250/550 and a la carte – **84 rm** ⊊ 3700/5600.
FT g

Sax, Jánský Vršek 328/3 Praha 1, ⊠ 118 00, ℘ (02) 538 422, *Fax (02) 538 498* – |‡|,
⇖ rm ▤ 📺 ☎ 🚿. AE ① E *VISA* JCB
Meals 170/600 and a la carte – **19 rm** ⊊ 3600/4300, 3 suites.
BY r

Casa Marcello ⊗, Rásnovka 783, ⊠ 110 00, ℘ (02) 231 1230, *Fax (02) 231 3323,*
⊹ – 📺 ☎. AE ① E *VISA* JCB
Meals - Italian - 350/900 and a la carte – **7 rm** ⊊ 6900, 4 suites.
CY v

U Páva, U Lužického Semináře 32, ⊠ 118 00, ℘ (02) 5731 5867, *Fax (02) 533 379* –
▤ rm 📺 ☎. AE ① E *VISA*
Meals 220/600 and a la carte – **6 rm** ⊊ 5200/5700, 5 suites.
BY m

Vladař, Na Dvorcích 144-149, ⊠ 140 00, ℘ (02) 6126 1521, *Fax (02) 6126 4324* – 📺
☎. AE E *VISA*
Meals 230/800 and a la carte – ⊊ 220 – **16 rm** 2400/2800.
FT f

Sieber, Slezská 55, ⊠ 130 00, ℘ (02) 2425 0025, *Fax (02) 2425 0027* – |‡| ▤ 📺 ☎.
AE ① E *VISA* JCB
Meals (dinner only) 400/600 and a la carte – **12 rm** ⊊ 4480/4780.
FT h

CZECH REPUBLIC

Bílá Labuťv, Biskupská 1347-9, ✉ 110 00, ✆ (02) 232 4524, *Fax (02) 232 2905 –*
📺 ☎ ♿. 🅰🅴 ⓪ 🅴 *VISA*. 🍽 rest — DY
Meals 285/445 – **54 rm** ☕ 4540/5075.

Zlatá (at Inter-Continental H.), Nám. Curieových 43-45, ✉ 110 00, ✆ (02) 2488 9914
Fax (02) 2481 1216, ≼ Prague – 🖃. 🅰🅴 ⓪ 🅴 *VISA* 🆓🅲🅱. 🍽 — CY
Meals (dinner only) 1500 and a la carte.

Hradčany (at Savoy H.), Keplerova Ul. 6, ✉ 118 00, ✆ (02) 2430 2430
Fax (02) 2430 2128 – 🖃. 🅰🅴 ⓪ 🅴 *VISA* 🆓🅲🅱 — AY
Meals 590/1200 and a la carte.

La Perle de Prague, (7th floor), Rašínovo Nábřeží 80, ✉ 120 00, ✆ (02) 2198 4160
Fax (02) 2198 4179, ≼, 🛖 – 📶 🖃. 🅰🅴 ⓪ 🅴 *VISA* 🆓🅲🅱 — CZ
closed Monday lunch and Sunday – **Meals** 490/1500 and a la carte.

Flambée, Betlém Palais, Husova 5, ✉ 110 00, ✆ (02) 2424 8512, *Fax (02) 2424 8513*
« 14C vaulted cellar » – 🅿. 🅰🅴 🅴 *VISA* — CY
Meals (dinner booking essential) 1200/3000 and a la carte.

Vinárna V Zatisi, Liliová 1, Betlémské Nám., ✉ 110 00, ✆ (02) 2422 8977
Fax (02) 2422 1187 – 🅰🅴 🅴 *VISA* — CY
closed 24 December – **Meals** (dinner booking essential) 675/1075 and a la carte.

Circle Line, Malostranske Nám. 12, ✉ 118 00, ✆ (02) 530 308, *Fax (02) 530 276,* Vaul
ted cellar – 🅰🅴 🅴 *VISA* — BY
closed Sunday and 24 December – **Meals** (dinner only) 890/1590 and a la carte.

Bellevue, Smetanovo Nábřeží 18, ✉ 110 00, ✆ (02) 2422 1387, *Fax (02) 2422 893.*
– 🅰🅴 🅴 *VISA* — CY
closed 24 December – **Meals** 790/1490 and a la carte.

Francouzská, Náměstí Republiky 5, ✉ 110 00, ✆ (02) 2200 2777, *Fax (02) 2200 2778*
« Restored 1912 Art Nouveau building » – 🅰🅴 🅴 *VISA* 🆓🅲🅱 — DY
Meals 600/1500 and a la carte – **Plzeňská :** **Meals** 600/1500 and a la carte.

Kampa Park, Na Kampě 8b, ✉ 110 00, ✆ (02) 5731 3493, *Fax (02) 5731 3495,* 🛖
« Vltava riverside setting, ≼ Charles Bridge » – 🅰🅴 ⓪ 🅴 *VISA* — BY
closed Christmas – **Meals** (dinner booking essential) 1000/1400 and a la carte.

Bistrot de Marlène, Plavecká 4, ✉ 120 00, ✆ (02) 291 077, *Fax (02) 298 709 –* 🅰🅴
🅴 *VISA* — ET
closed Saturday lunch, Sunday and 22 December-4 January – **Meals** (booking essential) 350
(lunch) and a la carte 720/1030.

U Patrona, Dražického Nám. 4, ✉ 118 00, ✆ (02) 531 512, *Fax (02) 2422 8932 –* 🅰🅴
🅴 *VISA* — BY
closed Sunday – **Meals** (dinner only) 790/1590 and a la carte 870/1470.

La Provence, Štupartská 9, ✉ 110 00, ✆ (02) 232 4801, *Fax (02) 232 4801,* « Vaulted
cellar » – 🅰🅴 🅴 *VISA* — CY
Meals - Mediterranean Bistro - (booking essential) 425/825 and a la carte.

LOCAL ATMOSPHERE AND CZECH CUISINE

U Vladaře, Maltézské Nám. 10, ✉ 110 00, ✆ (02) 538 128, *Fax (02) 530 842,* 🛖
🅰🅴 ⓪ 🅴 *VISA* 🆓🅲🅱 — BY
Meals 350/800 and a la carte.

U Modre Kachnicky, Nebovidská 6, ✉ 118 00, ✆ (02) 5732 0308
Fax (02) 5732 0308, « 14C house with modern murals » – 🅰🅴 — BY
Meals (dinner booking essential) 400/1200 and a la carte.

U Červeného Kola, Anežská 2, ✉ 110 00, ✆ (02) 2481 1118, *Fax (02) 2481 1118*
« Courtyard terrace » – 🅰🅴 ⓪ 🅴 *VISA* 🆓🅲🅱. 🍽 — CY
Meals 500/1200 and a la carte.

Hostinec U Kalicha, Na Bojišti 12, ✉ 120 00, ✆ (02) 291 945, *Fax (02) 290 701*
Typical Prague beerhouse – 🅰🅴 ⓪ *VISA* 🆓🅲🅱 — DZ
Meals 350/1000 and a la carte.

Denmark

Danmark

PRACTICAL INFORMATION

LOCAL CURRENCY

Danish Kroner: *100 DKK = 13,40 euros (€)*

TOURIST INFORMATION

The telephone number and address of the Tourist Information office is given in the text under 🛈.

National Holiday in Denmark: *5 June.*

FOREIGN EXCHANGE

Banks are open between 9.30am and 4.00pm (6.00pm on Thursdays) on weekdays except Saturdays. The main banks in the centre of Copenhagen, the Central Station and the Airport have exchange facilities outside these hours.

AIRLINES

SAS: *Hamerichsgade 1,* ☏ *31 54 17 01*
AIR FRANCE: *Ved Versterpot 6,* ☏ *33 12 76 76*
BRITISH AIRWAYS: *Rådhuspladsen 16,* ☏ *33 14 60 00*
LUFTHANSA: *V. Farimagsgade 7,* ☏ *33 37 73 33*
UNITED AIRLINES: *V. Farimagsgade 1,* ☏ *33 13 47 47*

MEALS

At lunchtime, follow the custom of the country and try the typical buffets of Danish specialities (smørrebrød).
At dinner, the a la carte and set menus will offer you more conventional cooking.

SHOPPING IN COPENHAGEN

Strøget (Department stores, exclusive shops, boutiques).
Kompagnistræde (Antiques). Shops are generally open from 10am to 7pm (Saturday 9am to 4pm).
See also in the index of street names, those printed in red are where the principal shops are found.

THEATRE BOOKINGS

Your hotel porter will be able to make your arrangements or direct you to Theatre Booking Agents.

CAR HIRE

The international car hire companies have branches in Copenhagen. Your hotel porter should be able to give details and help you with your arrangements.

TIPPING

In Denmark, all hotels and restaurants include a service charge. As for the taxis, there is no extra charge to the amount shown on the meter.

SPEED LIMITS

The maximum permitted speed in cities is 50 km/h - 31 mph, outside cities 80 km/h - 50 mph and 110 km/h - 68 mph on motorways. Cars towing caravans 70 km/h – 44 mph and buses 80 km/h – 50 mph also on motorways.
Local signs may indicate lower or permit higher limits. On the whole, speed should always be adjusted to prevailing circumstances. In case of even minor speed limit offences, drivers will be liable to heavy fines to be paid on the spot. If payment cannot be made, the car may be impounded.

SEAT BELTS

The wearing of seat belts is compulsory for drivers and all passengers except children under the age of 3 and taxi passengers.

COPENHAGEN

(KØBENHAVN) *Danmark* 985 *Q 9 – pop. 622 000, Greater Copenhagen 1 354 000.*

Berlin 385 – Hamburg 305 – Oslo 583 – Stockholm 630.

Copenhagen Tourist Information, Bernstorffsgade 1, ✉ *1577 V* ✆ *33 11 13 25, Fax 33 93 49 69.*

Dansk Golf Union 56 ✆ *43 45 55 55.*

Copenhagen/Kastrup SE : 10 km ✆ *31 54 17 01 – Air Terminal : main railway station.*

Motorail for Southern Europe : ✆ *33 14 17 01.*

Further information from the D S B, main railway station or tourist information centre (see above).

See : *Rosenborg Castle*★★★ *(Rosenborg Slot)* CX *– Amalienborg Palace*★★ *(Amalienborg)* DY *– Nyhavn*★★ *(canal)* DY *– Tivoli*★★ *: May to mid September* BZ *– Christiansborg Palace*★ *(Christiansborg)* CZ *– Citadel*★ *(Kastellet)* DX *– Gråbrødretorv*★ CY **28** *– Little Mermaid*★★ *(Den Lille Havfrue)* DX *– Marble Bridge*★ *(Marmorbroen)* CZ **50** *– Marble Church*★ *(Marmorkirke)* DY *– Kongens Nytorv*★ DX *– Round Tower*★ *(Rundetårn)* CY **E** *– Stock Exchange*★ *(Børsen)* CDZ *– Strøget*★ BCYZ *– Town Hall (Rådhuset)* BZ **H** *: Jens Olsen's astronomical clock*★ BZ **H**.

Museums : *National Museum*★★★ *(Nationalmuseet)* CZ *– Ny Carlsberg Glyptotek*★★★ *: art collection* BZ *– National Fine Arts Museum*★★ *(Statens Museum for Kunst)* CX *– Thorvaldsen Museum*★★ *(Thorvaldsens Museum)* CZ **M¹**.

Outskirts : *Ordrupgård*★★ *: art collection (Ordrupgårdsamlingen) N : 10 km* CX *– Louisiana Museum of Modern Art*★★ *(Museum for Moderne Kunst) N : 35 km* CX *– Dragør*★ *SW : 13 km* CZ *– Rungstedlund*★ *: Karen Blixen Museum N : 25 km* CX *– Open-Air Museum*★ *(Frilandsmuseet) NW : 12 km* AX.

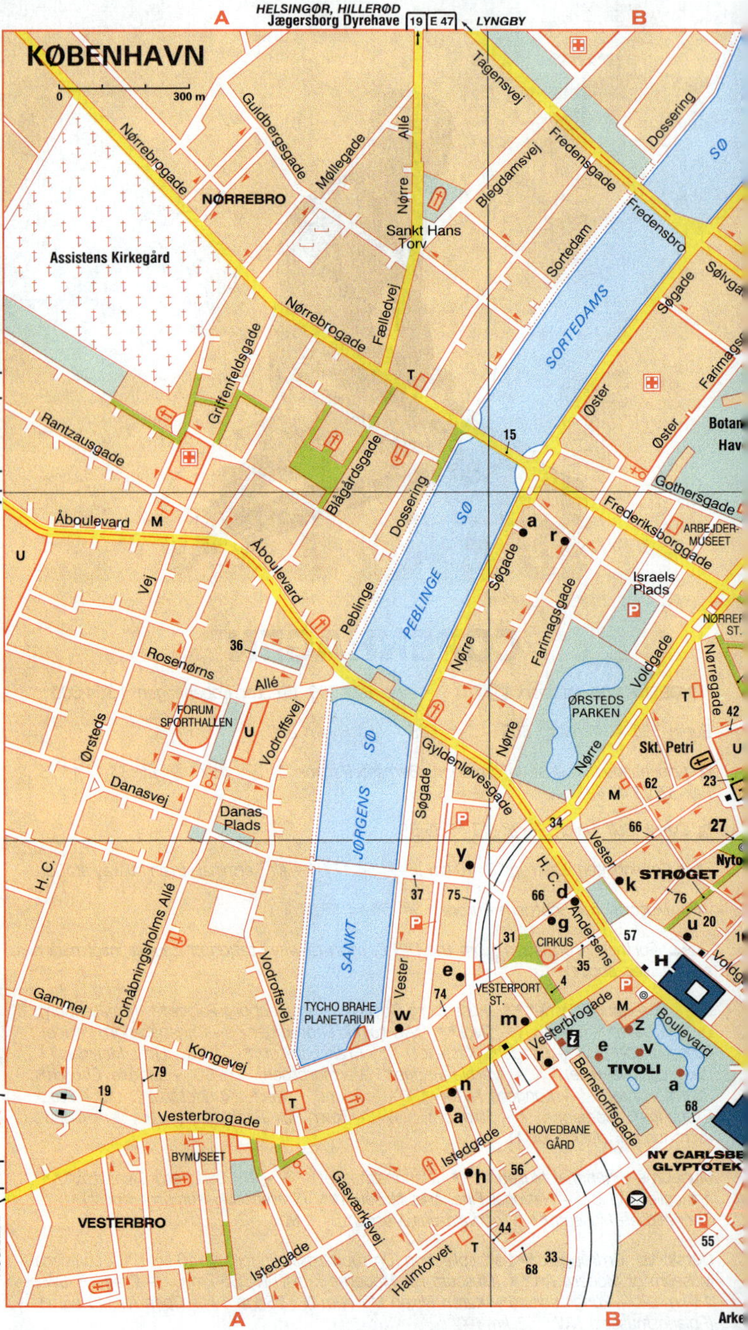

DENMARK

KØBENHAVN

HELSINGØR, HILLERØD
Jægersborg Dyrehave
19 E 47 LYNGBY

0 300 m

Tagensvej

Nørrebrogade

Guldbergsgade

Møllegade

Nørre Allé

Nørre

Bleadamsvej

Fredensgade

Dossering

SØ

NØRREBRO

Sankt Hans Torv

Sortedam

Fredensbro

Fredensbro

X

Assistens Kirkegård

Nørrebrogade

Fælledvej

SORTEDAMS

Øster

Søgade

Sølvga

Farimags

FREDERIKSSUND 211

Rantzausgade

Griffenfeldsgade

Blågårdsgade

Dossering

T

15

Øster

Botan
Hav

HILLERØD 16

Gothersgade

BALLERUP, FARUM

Åboulevard

M

Åboulevard

Peblinge

Dossering

SØ

a r

Frederiksborggade

ARBEJDER-
MUSEET

U

Vej

Peblinge

PEBLINGE
SØ

Nørre

Søgade

Israels
Plads

P

NØRREF
ST.

36

Rosenørns

Allé

Nørre

Farimagsgade

Nørregade

42

Y

Øratads

FORUM
SPORTHALLEN

U

Vodroffsvej

ØRSTEDS
PARKEN

Nørre

T

Skt. Petri

U

23

Danasvej

JØRGENS

SØ

Søgade

Gyldenløvesgade

Nørre

M

62

34

66

27

Danas
Plads

SANKT

SØ

Søgade

y

Vester

STRØGET

Nyto

H. C.

37

75

66

d

Andersens

76

k

u

20

FREDERIKSBERG

Forhåbningsholms Allé

31

CIRKUS

g

57

1

H

Vodroffsvej

Vester

35

VESTERPORT
ST.

4

Voldg

Gammel

e

74

m

Vesterbrogade

P

M

Z

Boulevard

Kongevej

TYCHO BRAHE
PLANETARIUM

W

r

z

e

v

TIVOLI

a

79

19

n

a

Bernstorffsgade

68

N

Vesterbrogade

ROSKILDE 156

BYMUSEET

Istedgade

56

NY CARLSBE
GLYPTOTEK

h

HOVEDBANE
GÅRD

VESTERBRO

Gasværksvej

44

P

55

Istedgade

Halmtorvet

T

68 33

144

Arke

C 152
HELSINGØR by Strandvejen
Ordrupgård
NORDHAVNEN
152
D
LANGELINIE
ŚWINOUJŚCIE
Søgade
Farimagsgade
13
Kristianiagade
Østbanegade
02
Bernadottes Allé
DEN LILLE HAVFRUE
Østergade
Stockholmsgade
ØSTERPORT ST.
Oslo Plads
Folke
Grønningen
KASTELLET
OSLO
X
Øster
Den Hirschsprungske Samling
Skt. Albans
RØNNE
Øster - Voldgade
ØSTRE ANLÆG
Churchill Parken
M
b
Sølvgade
STATENS MUSEUM FOR KUNST
Esplanaden
a
Det Danske Kunstindustrimuseum
OLOGISK USEUM
Sølvgade
c
M
Voldgade
ROSENBORG SLOT
Store Kongensgade
MEDICINSK HISTORISK MUSEUM
Amaliegade
Toldbodgade
MALMÖ
Kronprinsessegade
Borgergade
02
Amaliegade
Kongens Have
Dronningens Tværgade
MARMORKIRKE
g
3
AMALIENBORG
f
Davids Samling
Bredgade
P
Y
r
P
b
60
torvet
Landemærket
P
e
Gothersgade
z
02
x
M
E
8
s
b
a
Z
Købmagergade
b
24
k
Toldbodgade
T
41
c
KONGENS NYTORV
a
49
54
t
POSTKONTOR
d
NYHAVN
28
M
Østergade
FONDSBØRS
77
STRØGET
P
n
q
Kgl. Teater
M
Amagertorv
32
V
M
5
46
a
a
26
e
72
T
39
Holmens Kanal
51
INDERHAVNEN
T
NATIONAL BANKEN
Havnegade
52
78
9
b
Vandet
BØRSEN
Strandgade
ORLOGSMUSEET
7
CHRISTIANS-BORG
38
Torvegade
CHRISTIANSHAVN
NATIONAL-MUSEET
50
TØJHUSMUSEET
Brygge
KGL. BIBLIOTEK
neden Vandet
oven
Vor Frelsers Kirke
21
Christians
B.W. MUSEUM
Overgaden neden Vandet
Prinsessegade
Z
Vester Voldgade
Andersens Boulevard
c
INDERHAVNEN
Overgaden
45
Langebrogade
M
lvebod Brygge
SYDHAVNEN
STADSGRAVEN
12
Vermlandsgade
1 E 47 KØGE, RØDBY HALSSKOV
5 E 20
C
KASTRUP, DRAGØR
D
Øresund Udstilling
KASTRUP

145

STREET INDEX TO KØBENHAVN TOWN PLAN

Angleterre, Kongens Nytorv 34, ⊠ 1021 K, ℰ 33 12 00 95, *Fax 33 12 11 18*, « Elegar 18C hotel overlooking the New Royal Square », ⌧, ⊜s, ⊠ – ⊞ TV ☎ ℰ – ⚒ 400. A Ⓓ E *VISA* JCB. ⫻   —   CDY
D'Angleterre : Meals 295/395 and a la carte – *Wiinblad* : Meals 295 and a la carte ⊃ 125 – **110 rm** 1970/3100, 20 suites.

Scandic ⓜ, Vester Søgade 6, ⊠ 1601 V, ℰ 33 14 35 35, *Fax 33 32 12 23*, ⪕ Coper hagen, ⊜s – ⊞, ⊁ rm ▤ TV ☎ ℰ – ⚒ 1200. AE Ⓓ E *VISA*. ⫻ rest   AZ Meals (buffet lunch) 175/345 and a la carte – **470 rm** ⊃ 995/2045, 2 suites.

Radisson SAS Scandinavia ⓜ, Amager Boulevard 70, ⊠ 2300 S, ℰ 33 96 50 00 *Fax 33 96 55 00*, ⪕ Copenhagen, ⌧, ⊜s, ⊠, *squash* – ⊞, ⊁ rm TV ☎ ℰ ⫠ ℗ ⚒ 1200. AE Ⓓ E *VISA* JCB. ⫻ rest   CZ Meals (closed 21 to 27 December and 1 January) (dinner only) 230/390 and a la cart – **Top of Town** (26th floor) : Meals (closed Sunday, Monday and Bank Holidays) (dinne only) 385 – **Mama's & Papa's** : Meals (buffet lunch) 195 and a la carte 200/400 – **Blu Elephant** (ℰ 33 96 59 70) : Meals - Thai - (closed lunch Saturday, Sunday and Jul) 195/495 and a la carte – **542 rm** ⊃ 1595/1795.

Radisson SAS Royal, Hammerichsgade 1, ⊠ 1611 V, ℰ 33 42 60 00, *Fax 33 42 61 00* ⪕, « Panoramic restaurant on 20th floor », ⌧, ⊜s – ⊞, ⊁ rm ▤ TV ☎ ⫷ ℗ ⚒ 220. AE Ⓓ E *VISA* JCB. ⫻ rest   BZ r *Summit* : Meals (closed Monday dinner and Sunday) 395/625 and a la carte – *Café Roya* Meals 265/300 and a la carte – **263 rm** ⊃ 1950/2250, 2 suites.

Kong Frederik, Vester Voldgade 25, ⊠ 1021 V, ℰ 33 12 59 02, *Fax 33 93 59 0* « Late 19C facade, English-style interior » – ⊞, TV ☎ ℰ – ⚒ 80. AE Ⓓ E *VISA* JCB. ⫻ Meals 295 and a la carte – ⊃ 105 – **98 rm** 1420/1735, 12 suites.   BZ

Phoenix, Bredgade 37, ⊠ 1260 K, ℰ 33 95 95 00, *Fax 33 33 98 33* – ⊞, ⊁ rm E ☎ ℰ ⫠ – ⚒ 100. AE Ⓓ E *VISA* JCB. ⫻ rest   DY Meals (buffet lunch) 200/265 and a la carte – ⊃ 110 – **209 rm** 1190/2390, 3 suite

Plaza, Bernstorffsgade 4, ⊠ 1577 V, ℰ 33 14 92 62, *Fax 33 93 93 62*, « Library bar an Tsars style restaurant » – ⊞, ⊁ rm TV ☎. AE Ⓓ E *VISA* JCB. ⫻   BZ Meals a la carte 335/495 – **93 rm** ⊃ 1650/2050.

Kong Arthur ⑤, Nørre Søgade 11, ☒ 1370 K, ☎ 33 11 12 12, Fax 33 32 61 30, ☷, ⇌ – |♦|, �️ rm TV ☎ 📞 Ⓟ – 🏛 50. AE ⓞ E VISA JCB. ⚠   BY a
Brochner (☎ 33 93 58 05) : **Meals** (closed Sunday and Bank Holidays) (dinner only) 255 and a la carte – **Sticks 'n' Sushi** (☎ 33 11 14 07) : **Meals** - Japanese - (closed Bank Holidays) (dinner only) 180 and a la carte – **107 rm** ☕ 1025/1340.

Radisson SAS Falconer M, Falkoner Allé 9, ☒ 2000 Frederiksberg C, via Gammel Kongevej ☎ 38 15 80 01, Fax 38 15 80 02, ≤ Copenhagen, 🏋, ⇌ – |♦|, ✍ rm, ▤ rm TV ☎ 👍 ⇔ – 🏛 2000. AE ⓞ E VISA JCB. ⚠
Meals (buffet lunch) 185/350 and a la carte – **166 rm** ☕ 1240/2180.

Imperial M, Vester Farimagsgade 9, ☒ 1606 V, ☎ 33 12 80 00, Fax 33 93 80 31 – |♦|, ✍ rm TV ☎ 📞 👍 – 🏛 150. AE ⓞ E VISA JCB. ⚠ rest   AZ e
closed 20 December-2 January – **Imperial Garden** : **Meals** (dinner only) 380/410 and a la carte – **Imperial Brasserie** : **Meals** (buffet lunch) 225 and a la carte 235/310 – **163 rm** ☕ 1280/2545.

Palace, Rådhuspladsen 57, ☒ 1550 V, ☎ 33 14 40 50, Fax 33 14 52 79, ⇌ – |♦|, ✍ rm TV ☎ – 🏛 70. AE ⓞ E VISA JCB. ⚠ rest   BZ u
Meals (buffet lunch) 200/350 and dinner a la carte – **162 rm** ☕ 1525/2025.

Neptun, Sankt Annae Plads 14-20, ☒ 1250 K, ☎ 33 96 20 02, Fax 33 96 20 97 – |♦|, ✍ rm, ▤ rm TV ☎ 📞 – 🏛 40. AE ⓞ E VISA JCB. ⚠
closed 19 December-3 January – **Gendarmen** : **Meals** (closed Sunday, July and Bank Holidays) 220/345 and a la carte – **118 rm** ☕ 1320/1775, 15 suites.   DY a

71 Nyhavn, Nyhavn 71, ☒ 1051 K, ☎ 33 11 85 85, Fax 33 93 15 85, ≤, « Charming former warehouse » – |♦|, ✍ rm TV ☎. AE ⓞ E VISA. ⚠   DY z
Meals (closed Sunday, 23 to 30 December and Bank Holidays) (dinner only) 340/380 – **81 rm** ☕ 1180/1750, 3 suites.

Webers without rest., Vesterbrogade 11B, ☒ 1620 K, ☎ 33 31 14 32, Fax 33 31 14 41, 🏋, ⇌ – |♦|, ✍ rm TV ☎ 📞 – 🏛 30. AE ⓞ E VISA JCB. ⚠   AZ n
closed 23 December-3 January – **156 rm** ☕ 1195/1695, 4 suites.

Sophie Amalie, Sankt Annae Plads 21, ☒ 1021 K, ☎ 33 13 34 00, Fax 33 11 77 07, ≤, ⇌ – |♦|, ▤ rest TV ☎ 📞 – 🏛 50. AE ⓞ E VISA JCB. ⚠   DY x
Sophie : **Meals** 330 and a la carte – ☕ 95 – **134 rm** 880/1135.

Richmond, Vester Farimagsgade 33, ☒ 1780 V, ☎ 33 12 33 66, Fax 33 12 97 17 – |♦|, ✍ rm TV ☎ 📞 – 🏛 120. AE ⓞ E VISA JCB. ⚠   AZ y
Meals (closed Sunday and Monday) (dinner only) a la carte 220/300 – **117 rm** ☕ 1150/1450, 10 suites.

Ascot without rest., Studiestraede 61, ☒ 1554 V, ☎ 33 12 60 00, Fax 33 14 60 40, « Former public baths, vaulted main hall with bathing reliefs », 🏋 – |♦| TV ☎ 📞 Ⓟ – 🏛 90. AE ⓞ E VISA JCB   BZ g
143 rm ☕ 895/1350, 13 suites.

City without rest., Peder Skrams Gade 24, ☒ 1054 K, ☎ 33 13 06 66, Fax 33 13 06 67 – |♦| ✍ TV ☎ 📞. AE ⓞ E VISA JCB. ⚠   DZ a
81 rm ☕ 860/1235.

Mayfair without rest., Helgolandsgade 3, ☒ 1653 K, ☎ 31 31 48 01, Fax 33 31 96 86 – |♦|, ✍ rm TV ☎ 📞. AE ⓞ E VISA JCB. ⚠   AZ a
closed 23 to 30 December – **102 rm** ☕ 925/1125, 4 suites.

Christian IV without rest., Dronningens Tvaergade 45, ☒ 1302 K, ☎ 33 32 10 44, Fax 33 32 07 06 – |♦| TV ☎ 👍. AE ⓞ E VISA JCB   CY f
42 rm ☕ 935/1135.

Ibsen without rest., Vendersgade 23, ☒ 1363 K, ☎ 33 13 19 13, Fax 33 13 19 16 – |♦|, ✍ rm TV ☎. AE ⓞ E VISA JCB. ⚠   BY r
103 rm ☕ 745/1050.

Alexandra without rest., H.C. Andersens Boulevard 8, ☒ 1553 K, ☎ 33 74 44 44, Fax 33 74 44 88 – |♦|, ✍ rm TV ☎ 📞. AE ⓞ E VISA JCB   BZ d
closed 24 to 27 December – **61 rm** ☕ 975/1325.

Absalon without rest., Helgolandsgade 15, ☒ 1653 V, ☎ 33 24 22 11, Fax 33 24 34 11 – |♦| TV ☎. AE ⓞ E VISA JCB. ⚠   AZ h
closed 19 December-3 January – **185 rm** ☕ 790/1200, 1 suite.

Esplanaden M without rest., Bredgade 78, ☒ 1260 K, ☎ 33 96 20 02, Fax 33 96 20 97 – |♦| TV ☎. AE ⓞ E VISA JCB. ⚠   DX a
closed 19 December-3 January – **112 rm** ☕ 750/1080.

Danmark without rest., Vester Voldgade 89, ☒ 1552 V, ☎ 33 11 48 06, Fax 33 14 36 30 – |♦| ✍ TV ☎ 📞 ⇔. AE ⓞ E VISA JCB   BZ t
closed 19 December-3 January – **49 rm** ☕ 850/1050, 2 suites.

XXX **Kong Hans Kaelder,** Vingårdsstraede 6, ⊠ 1070 K, ℘ 33 11 68 68, *Fax 33 32 67 68*
❀ « Vaulted Gothic cellar » – AE ⓪ E VISA JCB   CY
closed Sunday and Monday June-August, 2 weeks late July and 23 December-3 January
– **Meals** (booking essential) (dinner only) 600/850 and a la carte 625/815
Spec. Foie gras prepared three ways with Jurançon. Provence style lobster with artichoke
and tomato. Variations on Valhrona chocolate.

XX **Kommandanten,** Ny Adelgade 7, ⊠ 1104 K, ℘ 33 12 09 90, *Fax 33 93 12 23,* « 17C
❀❀ town house, contemporary furnishings » – AE ⓪ E VISA JCB   CY
closed Saturday lunch, Sunday, 23 December-5 January and Bank Holidays – **Meals** (booking
essential) 350/610 and a la carte 470/650
Spec. Oysters with salmon trout, blinis and caviar. Selection of chocolate desserts.

XX **Restaurationen** (Jacobsen), Møntergade 19, ⊠ 1116 K, ℘ 33 14 94 95 – AE ⓪ E
❀ VISA   CY
closed Sunday, Monday, July, 22 December-5 January and Bank Holidays – **Meals** (booking
essential) (dinner only except December) (set menu only) 505
Spec. Cassoulet of lobster, vegetables and truffles. Fillet of venison with red wine sauce
foie gras butter and pickled mushrooms. Rhubarb tart with vanilla ice cream.

XX **Pierre André** (Houdet), Ny Østergade 21, ⊠ 1101 K, ℘ 33 16 17 19, *Fax 33 16 17 72*
❀ – AE ⓪ E VISA   CY
*closed Saturday lunch, Sunday, Easter, 5 to 25 July, 24 to 26 and 31 December and Bank
Holidays* – **Meals** (booking essential) 250/585 and a la carte 355/530
Spec. Foie gras 'Emilia Romagna'. Noisettes de chevreuil aux épices. Gâteau chaud au cho
colat, glace Gianduja.

XX **Nouvelle,** Gammel Strand 34 (1st floor), ⊠ 1202 K, ℘ 33 13 50 18, *Fax 33 32 07 92*
– AE ⓪ E VISA JCB   CZ
closed Sunday, 23 to 30 December, 1 to 3 January and Bank Holidays – **Meals** (booking
essential) 275/485 and a la carte 315/645.

XX **Era Ora** (Milleri), Torvegade 62, ⊠ 1400 K, ℘ 32 54 06 93, *Fax 32 64 11 39* – ▤ ⓪
❀ E VISA JCB   DZ
closed Sunday and 24 to 27 December – **Meals** - Italian - (booking essential) (dinner only)
435/585
Spec. Marinated turbot with spring onions. Tenderloin of veal with pine nuts, raisins and
sundried tomatoes. Rhubarb cake with apple ice cream.

XX **Krogs,** Gammel Strand 38, ⊠ 1202 K, ℘ 33 15 89 15, *Fax 33 15 83 19,* ✿, 18C house
– AE ⓪ E VISA JCB   CZ
closed Sunday and Christmas – **Meals** - Seafood - (booking essential) 200/825 and a la
carte.

XX **Gammel Mont,** Gammel Mont 41, ⊠ 1117 K, ℘ 33 15 10 60, *Fax 33 15 10 60,* « Half
timbered house from 1732 » – AE ⓪ E VISA   CY
closed Sunday, July and 23 December-3 January – **Meals** 525 and a la carte.

XX **Capo,** Pilestraede 19, ⊠ 1112 K, ℘ 33 32 30 30, *Fax 33 32 30 95,* Modern bistro with
cigar bar – ▤ AE ⓪ E VISA JCB   CY
closed Sunday, July, 25 December and Bank Holidays – **Meals** (booking essential) (dinner
only) a la carte 330/445.

XX **St. Gertruds Kloster,** Hauser Plads 32, ⊠ 1127 K, ℘ 33 14 66 30, *Fax 33 93 93 65*
« Part 14C monastic cellars » – ▤ AE ⓪ E VISA JCB   CY
closed 24 December-1 January – **Meals** (dinner only) 400/1600 and a la carte.

X **Godt,** Gothersgade 38, ⊠ 1123 K, ℘ 33 15 21 22 – ⓪ E VISA JCB   CY
closed Sunday, Monday, 1 to 5 April, 4 to 26 July, 24 December-4 January and Bank Holiday
– **Meals** (booking essential) (dinner only) (set menu only) 305.

X **M/S Amerika,** Dampfaergevej 8 (Pakhus 12, Amerikakaj), ⊠ 2100 K, *via Folke Berna*
dettes Allée ℘ 35 26 90 30, *Fax 35 26 91 30,* ✿, « 19C former warehouse » – AE ⓪
E VISA JCB
closed Sunday and 24 to 26 December – **Meals** 160/275 and a la carte 295/405.

X **Le Sommelier,** Bredgade 63, ⊠ 1260 K, ℘ 33 11 45 15, *Fax 33 11 59 79* – ⓪ E VISA
JCB   DX
closed Saturday lunch, Sunday and 24 December-4 January – **Meals** 165/245 and a la carte
215/355.

X **Lumskebugten,** Esplanaden 21, ⊠ 1263 K, ℘ 33 15 60 29, *Fax 33 32 87 18,* ✿
« Mid 19C café-pavilion » – AE ⓪ E VISA JCB   DX
closed Saturday lunch, Sunday, 1, 2, 5 and 30 April, 13 and 27 May and 24 December-3
January – **Meals** 275/465 and a la carte.

X **Kanalen,** Christianshavn-Wilders Plads 2, ⊠ 1403 K, ℘ 32 95 13 30, *Fax 32 95 13 38*
≼, ✿, « Canalside house » – Ⓟ, AE ⓪ E VISA JCB   DZ
closed Sunday, 29 March-4 April and 24 to 26 December – **Meals** (booking essential)
160/285 and a la carte 315/395.

Den Gyldne Fortun, Ved Stranden 18, ⊠ 1061 K, ℘ 33 12 20 11, Fax 33 93 35 11, 🌳, « Late 16C former inn » – AE ① E VISA JCB   CZ e
closed Saturday and Sunday lunch, 28 March, 31 March-5 April, 13 and 22 to 24 May and 24 December-2 February – **Meals** - Seafood - a la carte 365/800.

Den Sorte Ravn, Nyhavn 14, ⊠ 1051 K, ℘ 33 13 12 33, Fax 33 13 24 72 – ▤. AE ① E VISA JCB   DY q
closed Easter, 24 to 26 December, 1 January and Bank Holidays – **Meals** 300/525 and a la carte.

Els, Store Strandstraede 3, ⊠ 1255 K, ℘ 33 14 13 41, Fax 33 91 07 00, « 19C murals » – AE ① E VISA JCB   DY k
closed Sunday lunch, July and 22 to 27 December – **Meals** 240/380 and a la carte.

Thorvaldsen, Gammel Strand 34 (ground floor), ⊠ 1202 K, ℘ 33 32 04 00, Fax 33 32 07 97, 🌳 – AE ① E VISA JCB   CZ a
closed 24 to 26 December and 1 January – **Meals** (booking essential) 165/195 and a la carte.

in Tivoli : *Vesterbrogade 3* ⊠ *1620 V (Entrance fee payable)*

Divan 2, , ℘ 33 12 51 51, Fax 33 91 08 82, ≤, 🌳, « Floral decoration and terrace » – AE ① E VISA JCB   BZ a
23 April-26 September – **Meals** 295/650 and a la carte.

La Crevette, Bernstorffsgade 5, ⊠ 1577 V, ℘ 33 14 68 47, Fax 33 14 60 06, ≤, 🌳, « Terrace overlooking flowered garden » – AE ① E VISA JCB   BZ e
23 April-26 September – **Meals** - Seafood - 300/425 and a la carte.

Divan 1, ℘ 33 11 42 42, Fax 33 11 74 07, ≤, 🌳, « 19C pavilion » – AE ① E VISA JCB   BZ v
closed 27 September-18 November and 24 December-17 April – **Meals** 195/425 and a la carte.

Bagatellen, , ℘ 33 15 03 89, Fax 33 15 03 76, 🌳, « Modern-style brasserie in mid 19C pavilion » – AE ① E VISA JCB. 🍴   BZ z
Meals a la carte approx. 310.

SMØRREBRØD

The following list of simpler restaurants and cafés/bars specialize in Danish open sandwiches and are generally open from 10.00am to 4.00pm.

Ida Davidsen, St. Kongensgade 70, ⊠ 1264 K, ℘ 33 91 36 55, Fax 33 11 36 55 – AE ① E VISA   DY g
closed Saturday, Sunday, July, Christmas-New Year and Bank Holidays – **Meals** (buffet lunch only) a la carte 170/385.

Slotskaelderen-Hos Gitte Kik, Fortunstraede 4, ⊠ 1065 K, ℘ 33 11 15 37, Fax 33 11 15 37 – AE ① E VISA JCB   CYZ v
closed Sunday, Monday, 27 June-19 July and Bank Holidays – **Meals** (buffet lunch only) a la carte 35/70.

Sankt Annae, Sankt Annae Plads 12, ⊠ 1250 K, ℘ 33 12 54 97 – ① E VISA JCB DY a
closed Sunday – **Meals** (buffet lunch only) a la carte 130/170.

Kanal Caféen, Frederiksholms Kanal 18, ⊠ 1220 K, ℘ 33 11 57 70, Fax 33 13 79 62, 🌳 – AE ① E VISA JCB   CZ r
closed Saturday, Sunday and Bank Holidays – **Meals** (lunch only) a la carte 35/70.

at Hellerup *North : 7 ½ km by Østbanegade* DX *and Road 2* – ⊠ *2900 Hellerup :*

Hellerup Parkhotel, Strandvejen 203, ℘ 39 62 40 44, Fax 39 62 56 57, 🛋, ⌗s – 🛗, 💥 rm TV ☎ 📞 P – 🕍 150. AE ① E VISA. 🍴 rest
Saison : **Meals** *(closed Sunday)* 145/345 and a la carte – **70 rm** ⊡ 995/1450, 1 suite.

at Søllerød *North : 20 km by Tagensvej* BX *and Road 19* – ⊠ *2840 Holte :*

Søllerød Kro, Søllerødvej 35, ⊠ 2840 K, ℘ 45 80 37 72, Fax 45 80 22 70, 🌳, « 17C thatched inn, terrace » – P. AE ① E VISA JCB
closed 24 December and 1 January – **Meals** 170/345 and a la carte 375/540.

at Kastrup Airport *Southeast : 10 km by Amager Boulevard* CZ – ⊠ *2300 S :*

First H. Dan Ⓜ, Kastruplundgade 15, Kastrup, ⊠ 2770, *North : 2 ½ km by coastal rd* ℘ 32 51 14 00, Fax 32 51 37 01, 🌳, ⌗s – 🛗, 💥 rm, ▤ rest TV ☎ 🚻 P – 🕍 120. AE ① E VISA JCB. 🍴
Meals (buffet lunch) 175/215 and a la carte – **218 rm** ⊡ 1095/1395, 10 suites.

Radisson SAS Globetrotter Ⓜ, Engvej 171, ⊠ 2300, *Northwest : 3 km by coastal rd* ℘ 32 87 02 02, Fax 32 87 02 20, 🛋, ⌗s, ▨ – 🛗, 💥 rm TV ☎ 📞 P – 🕍 360. AE ① E VISA JCB. 🍴 rest
Meals (buffet lunch) 190/350 and a la carte – **197 rm** ⊡ 1290/1695.

Finland

Suomi

HELSINKI

PRACTICAL INFORMATION

LOCAL CURRENCY

Finnish Mark: *100 FIM = 16,82 euros (€)*

TOURIST INFORMATION

The Tourist Office is situated near the Market Square, Pohjoisesplanadi 19 ℱ (09) 169 3757. Open from 2 May to 30 September, Monday to Friday 9am - 7pm, Saturday and Sunday 9am - 3pm, and from 1 October to 30 April, Monday to Friday 9am - 5pm and Saturday from 9am to 3pm. Hotel bookings are possible from a reservation board situated in the airport arrival lounge and in the main railway station; information is also available free.

National Holiday in Finland: *6 December.*

FOREIGN EXCHANGE

Banks are open between 9.15am and 4.15pm on weekdays only. Exchange office at Helsinki-Vantaa airport and Helsinki harbour open daily between 6.30am and 11pm.

MEALS

At lunchtime, follow the custom of the country and try the typical buffets of Scandinavian specialities.

At dinner, the a la carte and set menus will offer you more conventional cooking. Booking is essential.

Many city centre restaurants are closed for a few days over the Midsummer Day period.

SHOPPING IN HELSINKI

Furs, jewelry, china, glass and ceramics, Finnish handicraft and wood.

In the index of street names, those printed in red are where the principal shops are found. Your hotel porter will be able to help you with information.

THEATRE BOOKINGS

A ticket service - Lippupalvelu, Mannerheimintie 5, sells tickets for cinema, concert and theatre performances - Telephone (09) 613 86 246, open Mon-Fri 9am to 6pm, Sat. 9am to 2pm. Tickets can also be purchased from the Tourist Office.

CAR HIRE

The international car hire companies have branches in Helsinki and at Vantaa airport. Your hotel porter should be able to help you with your arrangements.

TIPPING

Service is normally included in hotel and restaurant bills. Doormen, baggage porters etc. are generally given a gratuity; taxi drivers are not usually tipped.

SPEED LIMITS

The maximum permitted speed on motorways is 120 km/h - 74 mph (in winter 100 km/h - 62 mph), 80 km/h - 50 mph on other roads and 50 km/h - 31 mph in built-up areas.

SEAT BELTS

The wearing of seat belts in Finland is compulsory for drivers and all passengers.

HELSINKI

Finland 985 *L 21 – Pop. 491 777.*

Lahti 103 – Tampere 176 – Turku 165.

ⓘ *City Tourist Office Pohjoisesplanadi 19 ☎ (09) 169 37 57, Fax (09) 169 38 39 – Automobile and Touring Club of Finland: Autoliitto ☎ (09) 694 00 22, Fax (09) 693 25 78.*

ⓘ₈ *Tali Manor ☎ (09) 550 235.*

✈ *Helsinki-Vantaa N : 19 km ☎ (09) 81 88 00 – Finnair Head Office, Tietotie 11 A – 01053 ☎ (09) 818 8114, Fax (09) 818 40 92 – Air Terminal : Hotel Intercontinental, Mannerheimintie 46 – Finnair City Terminal : Asema – Aukio 3, ☎ (09) 818 77 50, Fax (09) 818 77 65.*

⛴ *To Sweden, Estonia, Poland and boat excursions : contact the City Tourist Office (see above) – Car Ferry: Silja Line – Finnjet Line ☎ (09) 180 41.*

See: *Senate Square*★★★ *(Senaatintori)* DY **53** *– Market Square*★★ *(Kauppatori* DY **26** *– Esplanadi*★★ CDY **8/43** *– Railway Station*★★ *(Rautatiesema)* CX *– Finlandia Hall*★★ *(Finlandia-talo)* BX *– National Opera House*★★ *(Kansallisoopera)* BX *– Church in the Rock*★★ *(Temppeliaukion kirkko)* BX *– Ateneum Art Museum*★★ *(Ateneum, Suomen Taiteen Museo)* CY **M¹** *– National Museum*★★ *(Kansallismuseo)* BX **M²** *– Lutheran Cathedral*★ *(Tuomiokirkko)* DY *– Parliament House*★ *(Eduskuntatalo)* BX *– Amos Anderson Collection*★ *(Amos Andersinin taidemuseo)* BY **M⁴** *– Uspensky Cathedral*★ *(Uspenskin katedraali)* DY *– Cygnaeus home and collection*★ *(Cynaeuksen galleria)* DZ **B** *– Mannerheim home and collection*★ *(Mannerheim-museo)* DZ **M⁵** *– Olympic Stadium*★ *(Olympiastadion)* ✳★★ BX **21** *– Museum of Applied Arts*★ *(Taideteollisuusmuseo)* CZ **M⁶** *– Sibelius Monument*★ *(Sibelius-monumentti)* AX **S** *– Ice-breaker fleet*★ DX.

Outskirts: *Fortress of Suomenlinna*★★ *by boat* DZ *– Seurasaari Open-Air Museum*★★ BX *– Urho Kekkonen Museum*★ *(Urho Kekkosen museo)* BX.

FINLAND
A
TURKU / ÅBO.
1 E 3
HÄMEENLINNA
3 E 79
21
B
SUOMEN
KANSALLISOOPPERA
FINLANDS
NATIONALOPERA
S
SIBELIUKSEN PUISTO
SIBELIUS-PARKEN
64
65
a
c
Töölö
Töölöviken
Taivallahti
Edesviken
67
Runebergsgatan
Mannerheimvägen
Mechelininkatu
40
40
9
65
FINLANDIA - TALO
FINLANDIA - HUSE
X
40
9
Runeberginkatu
Museokatu
4
Museigatan
M²
M
Runeberginkatu
TEMPPELIAUKION KIRKKO
TEMPELPLATSENS KYRKA
P
M
Hietaniemenkatu /
Sanduddsgatan
Arkadiankatu /
Arkadiagatan
EDUSKUNTATALO
RIKSDAGSHUSET
M
Runebersgatan
Fredrikinkatu /
41
S
Y
Lapinlahti
Lappviken
Mechelingatan
12
M
Kamppi Kampen
Kampintori /
Kamptorget
r
41
35
Annankatu /
b
HANKO / HANGÖ
32
32
e
h
51
Länsiväylä
Kalevagatan
Västerleden
50
a
e
Fredriksgatan
Lönnrotsgatan
Länsimäylä
Porkkalankatu /
Porkalagatan
S
Albertinkatu /
T
70
Itämerenkatu /
Östersjögatan
Kalevankatu /
Bulevardi
M
Albersgatan
e
Lönnrotinkatu
22
P
34
Ruoholahti
Gräsviken
Hietalahti
Sandviken
22
46
Z
47
LÄNSISATAMA
VÄSTRA HAMNEN
61
Tehtaankatu /
HELSINKI
HELSINGFORS
EIRA
Merikatu /
0   300 m
LÄNSITERMINAALI
VÄSTRA TERMINALEN
A
B
TALLINN

154

FINLAND
C
D
PORVOO/BORGÅ 7 E3
LAHTI 4 E4
VANTAA/VANDA
45
170 PORVOO/BORGÅ
15
60
6
Hämeentie/
Tavastvägen
Elaintarhanlahti
Djurgårdsviken
Hakaniemi Hagnäs
55
19
16
e
17
Korkeasaari
Högholmen
Sörnäisten satama
Sörnäs hamn
X
Kaisaniemenlahti
Kajsaniemiviken
56
44
KASVITIETEELLINEN PUUTARHA
68
M
BOTANISKA TRÄDGÅRDEN
Liisankatu/
Elisabetsgatan
TERVASAARI
TJÄRHOLMEN
24
58
Mariankatu
AIR TERMINAL
T
Fabianinkatu
68
V
44
Pohjoissatama
Norra Hamnen
24
28
28
Rautatientori
Järnvägstorget
TUOMIOKIRKKO
DOMKYRKAN
Mariegatan
e
25
P
M¹
20
U
53
27
37
a
2
M
31
29
r
H
43
s
k
USPENSKIN-KATEDRAALI
USPENSKIKATEDRALEN
Mannerheimintie
2
Y
43
z
d
26
52
33
KATAJANOKKA
SKATUDDEN
72
Kanavakatu
Kanalgatan
Bulevården
T
b
8
13
KANAVATERMINAALI
KANALTERMINALEN
Korkeavuorenkatu
t
P
c
Korkeasaari
Högholmen
Suomenlinna
Sveaborg
k
Fabiansgatan
c
P
Annegatan
70
P
68
KATAJANOKANTERMINAALI
SKATUDDENSTERMINAL
n
M⁶
M
MAKASIINITERMINAALI
MAGASINSTERMINALEN
Eteläsatama
Södra hamnen
49
Laivurinkatu
Kasarmikatu
30
P
VALKOSAARI
BLEKHOLMEN
TÄHTITORNI
OBSERVATORIET
OLYMPIATERMINAALI
OLYMPIATERMINALEN
Högbergsgatan
Kaserngatan
M
30
Ehrenströmsvägen
Fabriksgatan
Iso Puistotie/
Stora Allén
LUOTO
KLIPPAN
Puistokatu/Parkgatan
B
M⁵
Skepparegatan
38
M
N
KAIVOPUISTO
BRUNNSPARKEN
Havsgatan
P
Ehrenströmintie/
C
D
TUKHOLMA
TRAVEMÜNDE
STOCKHOLM
GDANSK
155

STREET INDEX TO HELSINKI/HELSINGFORS TOWN PLAN

Strand Inter-Continental M, John Stenbergin Ranta 4, ✉ 00530, ℘ (09) 39 351, *Fax (09) 393 5255*, ≤, « Contemporary Finnish architecture and decor », ≦s, ⊠ – |♯|, ✳ rm ▤ TV ☎ ⅙ ⇔ – ⚔ 300. AE ⑪ E VISA JCB ❀ rest
closed Good Friday to Easter Monday and 24 to 26 December – **Atrium Plaza** : Meals (buffet lunch) 235/245 and a la carte – **Pamir** : Meals (closed Saturday, Sunday and 25 June-mid August) (dinner only) a la carte 260/470 – ☕ 55 – **192 rm** 1450/1650, 8 suites.

DX e

Inter-Continental, Mannerheimintie 46, ✉ 00260, ℘ (09) 40 551, *Fax (09) 405 53255*, ≤, ☂, ⅙, ≦s, ⊠ – |♯|, ✳ rm ▤ TV ☎ ⇔ ℗ – ⚔ 700. AE ⑪ E VISA JCB. ❀ rest
Olivo : Meals 135/270 and a la carte – ☕ 80 – **500 rm** 1200/2000, 12 suites.

BX c

Radisson SAS Royal M, Runeberginkatu 2, ✉ 00100, ℘ (09) 69 580, *Fax (09) 695 87100*, ⅙, ≦s – |♯|, ✳ rm ▤ TV ☎ ⅙ ⇔ – ⚔ 250. AE ⑪ E VISA JCB ❀
Johan Ludvig : Meals (closed Saturday lunch and Sunday) (grill rest.) 150/350 and a la carte – **Ströget** : Meals (buffet lunch) 130/220 and a la carte – ☕ 75 – **254 rm** 1200, 8 suites.

BY b

Radisson SAS Hesperia, Mannerheimintie 50, ✉ 00260, ℘ (09) 43 101, *Fax (09) 431 0995*, ⅙, ≦s, ⊠ – |♯|, ✳ rm ▤ TV ☎ ⇔ ℗ – ⚔ 400. AE ⑪ E VISA ❀ rest
Fransmanni : Meals a la carte 115/205 – **383 rm** ☕ 1200/1490, 4 suites.

BX a

Palace, Eteläranta 10, ✉ 00130, ℘ (09) 134 561, *Fax (09) 654 786*, ≤, ≦s – |♯|, ✳ rm ▤ TV ☎ ⇔ – ⚔ 40. AE ⑪ E VISA. ❀
closed Christmas – **La Vista** : Meals - Italian - 120/300 and a la carte (see also **Palace** below) – **42 rm** ☕ 1100/1450, 2 suites.

DZ c

Marski, Mannerheimintie 10, ✉ 00100, ℘ (09) 68 061, *Fax (09) 642 377*, ≦s – |♯|, ✳ rm ▤ TV ☎ ⅙ ⇔ – ⚔ 400. AE ⑪ E VISA JCB. ❀
Marskin Kellari : Meals (dinner only Saturday, Sunday and Bank Holidays) 140/210 and a la carte – **230 rm** ☕ 1100/1400, 6 suites.

CY d

Klaus Kurki, Bulevardi 2, ✉ 00120, ℘ (09) 618 911, *Fax (09) 618 91234*, ≦s – |♯|, ✳ rm TV ☎. AE ⑪ E VISA JCB. ❀
Bulevardi Kaksi : Meals (closed Sunday and Bank Holidays) (dinner only) 180/235 and a la carte – **132 rm** ☕ 915/1130, 2 suites.

CY t

Lord ⬥, Lönnrotinkatu 29, ✉ 00180, ℰ (09) 615 815, *Fax (09) 680 1315*, « Part Jugendstil (Art Nouveau) building, fireplaces », ⇌s – |⋕|, ↳ rm 🖥 📺 ☎ ⅋ 🚗 – 🛱 200. 𝔸𝔼 ⓞ 🄴 𝕍𝕀𝕊𝔸. 🗱 rest
                                                                                                          BZ s
closed 23 to 27 December – **Meals** *(closed Sunday and Bank Holidays)* 170/300 and a la carte – **47 rm** ☕ 680/850, 1 suite.

Vaakuna, Asema-aukio 2, ✉ 00100, ℰ (09) 131 181, *Fax (09) 131 18234*, 🍵, ⇌s – |⋕|, ↳ rm 📺 ☎ ⅋. 𝔸𝔼 ⓞ 🄴 𝕍𝕀𝕊𝔸 𝙹𝙲𝙱
                                                                                                          BY n
closed 23 to 27 December – **10th Floor Dining :** Meals *(dinner only)* 170/300 and a la carte – **Brasserie :** Meals *(closed Sunday and Bank Holidays)* 120/215 and a la carte – **266 rm** ☕ 875/1040, 11 suites.

Seaside, Ruoholahdenranta 3, ✉ 00180, ℰ (09) 69 360, *Fax (09) 69 32123*, ⇌s – |⋕|, ↳ rm 🖥 📺 ☎ ⅋ 🚗 – 🛱 60. 𝔸𝔼 ⓞ 🄴 𝕍𝕀𝕊𝔸. 🗱 rest
                                                                                                          ABZ e
Swing Boat : Meals a la carte 135/270 – **289 rm** ☕ 750/900.

Ramada Presidentti, Eteläinen Rautatiekatu 4, ✉ 00100, ℰ (09) 6911, *Fax (09) 694 7886*, ⇌s, ⬚ – |⋕| ↳ rm 🖥 📺 ☎ ⅋ 🚗 – 🛱 400. 𝔸𝔼 ⓞ 🄴 𝕍𝕀𝕊𝔸 𝙹𝙲𝙱. 🗱 rest
                                                                                                          BY s
Brasserie President : Meals a la carte 170/250 – **485 rm** ☕ 1050/1230, 5 suites.

Torni, Yrjönkatu 26, ✉ 00100, ℰ (09) 131 131, *Fax (09) 131 1361*, ⇌s – |⋕|, ↳ rm 📺 ☎ – 🛱 35. 𝔸𝔼 ⓞ 🄴 𝕍𝕀𝕊𝔸 𝙹𝙲𝙱. 🗱 rest
                                                                                                          BY r
closed 23 to 28 December – **Meals** *(see **Torni** below)* – **154 rm** ☕ 1140/1260.

Rivoli Jardin ⬥ without rest., Kasarmikatu 40, ✉ 00130, ℰ (09) 177 880, *Fax (09) 656 988*, ⇌s – |⋕| ↳ 📺 ☎ 📞 ⅋. 𝔸𝔼 ⓞ 🄴 𝕍𝕀𝕊𝔸
                                                                                                          CYZ k
55 rm ☕ 890/1020.

Pasila, Maistraatinportti 3, ✉ 00240, *North : 3 km by Mannerheimintie* ℰ (09) 148 841, *Fax (09) 143 771*, ⇌s, *squash* – |⋕| ↳ 🖥 📺 ☎ ⅋ 🚗 🅿 – 🛱 100. 𝔸𝔼 ⓞ 🄴 𝕍𝕀𝕊𝔸 𝙹𝙲𝙱. 🗱 rest
closed 23 to 27 December – **Sevilla :** Meals *(buffet lunch)* 125/300 and a la carte – **246 rm** ☕ 730/910, 2 suites.

Seurahuone, Kaivokatu 12, ✉ 00100, ℰ (09) 69 141, *Fax (09) 691 4010*, ⇌s – |⋕|, ↳ rm 📺 ☎ – 🛱 60. 𝔸𝔼 ⓞ 🄴 𝕍𝕀𝕊𝔸. 🗱 rest
                                                                                                          CY e
Meals a la carte 125/210 – **118 rm** ☕ 850/1450.

Savoy, Eteläesplanadi 14 (8th floor), ✉ 00130, ℰ (09) 176 571, *Fax (09) 628 715*, ≼, 🍵, « Typical Finnish design dating from 1937 » – |⋕|. 𝔸𝔼 ⓞ 🄴 𝕍𝕀𝕊𝔸
                                                                                                          CY b
closed Saturday, Sunday, 24 December-1 January and Bank Holidays – **Meals** a la carte 200/455.

G.W.Sundmans, Eteläranta 16 (1st floor), ✉ 00130, ℰ (09) 622 6410, *Fax (09) 661 331*, ≼, « 19C Empire style house » – 🖥 – 🛱 60. 𝔸𝔼 ⓞ 🄴 𝕍𝕀𝕊𝔸. 🗱
                                                                                                          DY c
closed Sunday, 2 to 5 April, 25 to 27 June and 24 to 26 December – **Meals** 150/350 and a la carte.

Palace (at Palace H.), Eteläranta 10 (10th floor), ✉ 00130, ℰ (09) 134 561, *Fax (09) 654 786*, ≼ *harbour and city* – |⋕| 🖥. 𝔸𝔼 ⓞ 🄴 𝕍𝕀𝕊𝔸
                                                                                                          DZ c
closed Saturday, Sunday, 1 week Christmas and Bank Holidays – **Meals** *(dinner only July)* 200/450 and dinner a la carte.

Alexander Nevski, Pohjoisesplanadi 17, ✉ 00170, ℰ (09) 639 610, *Fax (09) 631 435* – 🖥. 𝔸𝔼 ⓞ 🄴 𝕍𝕀𝕊𝔸. 🗱
                                                                                                          DY r
closed Sunday lunch and 24 to 26 December – **Meals** - Russian - 150/350 and a la carte.

Sipuli, Kanavaranta 3 (2nd floor), ✉ 00160, ℰ (09) 179 900, *Fax (09) 630 662*, « Picture window ≼ Uspensky Cathedral (orthodox) » – 𝔸𝔼 ⓞ 🄴 𝕍𝕀𝕊𝔸 𝙹𝙲𝙱
                                                                                                          DY s
closed Saturday, Sunday, Easter, 25 June-8 August and 24 December-9 January – **Meals** *(booking essential)* 190/375 and a la carte.

Havis Amanda, Unioninkatu 23, ✉ 00170, ℰ (09) 666 882, *Fax (09) 631 435* – 🖥. 𝔸𝔼 ⓞ 🄴 𝕍𝕀𝕊𝔸. 🗱
                                                                                                          DY r
closed Sunday, Easter, midsummer and 3 days Christmas – **Meals** - Seafood - *(booking essential)* 130/340 and a la carte.

Bellevue, Rahapajankatu 3, ✉ 00160, ℰ (09) 179 560, *Fax (09) 636 985* – 🖥. 𝔸𝔼 ⓞ 🄴 𝕍𝕀𝕊𝔸
                                                                                                          DY z
closed lunch Saturday and Sunday – **Meals** - Russian - 110/350 and a la carte.

Torni (at Torni H.), Kalevankatu 5, ✉ 00100, ℰ (09) 131 131, *Fax (09) 131 1361* – 𝔸𝔼 ⓞ 🄴 𝕍𝕀𝕊𝔸 𝙹𝙲𝙱. 🗱
                                                                                                          BY r
closed Sunday and 23 to 28 December – **Meals** 160 and a la carte 150/260.

George, Kalevankatu 17, ✉ 00100, ℰ (09) 647 662, *Fax (09) 647 110* – 🖥. 𝔸𝔼 ⓞ 🄴 𝕍𝕀𝕊𝔸
                                                                                                          BY e
closed Saturday lunch, Monday dinner, Sunday, 25 December and Bank Holidays – **Meals** 120/350 and a la carte 190/325.

XX **Rivoli,** Albertinkatu 38, ⊠ 00180, ℘ (09) 643 455, Fax (09) 647 780 – ▤. AE ⓪ E VISA *closed Saturday lunch, Saturday June-July, Sunday, Easter, midsummer, Christmas and Bank Holidays* – **Meals** 180 (dinner) and a la carte 175/250. BZ a

XX **Toulà,** Ratakatu 9, ⊠ 00120, ℘ (09) 61 26 01 50, Fax (09) 61 26 01 55 – ▤. AE ⓪ E VISA. ⍟ CZ n
Meals - Italian - a la carte 140/225.

XX **Kanavaranta,** Kanavaranta 3E-F, ⊠ 00160, ℘ (09) 6222 633, Fax (09) 6222 616, « Mid 19C harbour warehouse with nautical tavern » – ▤. AE ⓪ E VISA DY k *closed Monday and Saturday lunch, Sunday and 23 December-6 January* – Meals (booking essential) (dinner only 25 June-11 August) 140/330 and a la carte 175/255.

XX **Amadeus,** Sofiankatu 4, ⊠ 00170, ℘ (09) 626 676, Fax (09) 636 064 – AE ⓪ E VISA *closed Saturday lunch, Sunday, Christmas and Bank Holidays* – **Meals** - Brasserie - 150/375 and dinner a la carte. DY a

X **Safka,** Vironkatu 8, ⊠ 00170, ℘ (09) 135 7287, Fax (09) 135 7287 – AE ⓪ E VISA DX v *closed Monday dinner, Sunday and 1 to 30 July* – Meals (booking essential) (dinner only in summer) 150/180 and a la carte 150/190.

X **Lappi,** Annankatu 22, ⊠ 00100, ℘ (09) 645 550, Fax (09) 645 551, « Typical Finnish atmosphere » – AE ⓪ E VISA JCB BY h *closed Easter* – **Meals** - Finnish - (booking essential) (dinner only in summer) 265 and a la carte.

at Vantaa *North : 19 km by A 137* DX :

🏨 **Vantaa** M, Hertaksentie 2 (near Tikkurila Railway Station), ⊠ 01300, ℘ (09) 857 851, Fax (09) 857 85555, 🍴, ⌇s, ⌇8 – 📳, ⍟ rm ▤ TV ☎ ও ⇔ Ⓟ – 🕿 95. AE ⓪ E VISA. ⍟ rest
closed Christmas – **Sevilla :** Meals a la carte approx. 200 – **150 rm** ⌄ 750/900, 8 suites.

🏨 **Holiday Inn Garden Court Helsinki Airport** ⌇, Rälssitie 2, ⊠ 01510, *(near the airport)* ℘ (09) 870 900, Fax (09) 870 90101, ⌇s – 📳, ⍟ rm TV ☎ ও Ⓟ – 🕿 30. AE ⓪ E VISA JCB. ⍟ rest
Meals - Bistro - *(closed Saturday and Sunday lunch)* 130 (dinner) and a la carte 135/225 – **287 rm** ⌄ 880/980.

🏨 **Cumulus Airport,** Robert Huberin Tie 4, ⊠ 01510, *(near the airport)* ℘ (09) 415 77100, Fax (09) 415 77101, ⌇s, ⬚ – 📳, ⍟ rm TV ☎ ও Ⓟ – 🕿 250. AE ⓪ E VISA. ⍟ rest
Meals *(closed Saturday and Sunday lunch)* (buffet lunch) 115 and dinner a la carte 170/210 – **272 rm** ⌄ 720/860, 4 suites.

France

PARIS AND ENVIRONS – BORDEAUX
CANNES – LILLE – LYONS
MARSEILLES – PRINCIPALITY OF MONACO
NICE – STRASBOURG
VALLEY OF THE LOIRE

PRACTICAL INFORMATION

LOCAL CURRENCY

French Franc: *100 FRF = 15,24 euros (€)*

TOURIST INFORMATION IN PARIS

Paris "Welcome" Office *(Office du Tourisme et des Congrès de Paris - Accueil de France): 127 Champs-Élysées, 8th, ☏ 01 49 52 53 54, Fax 01 49 52 53 00*
American Express *11 Rue Scribe, 9th, ☏ 01 47 14 50 00, Fax 01 42 68 17 17*
National Holiday in France: *14 July*

AIRLINES

AMERICAN AIRLINES: *109, rue Fg-St-Honoré, 8th, ☏ 01 69 32 73 07, Fax 01 42 99 99 95*
UNITED AIRLINES: *34 av. de l'Opéra, 2ᵈ, ☏ 08 01 72 72 72*
T.W.A.: *6, rue Christophe-Colomb, 8th, ☏ 01 49 19 20 00, Fax 01 49 19 20 09*
DELTA AIRLINES: *4, rue Scribe, 9th, ☏ 01 47 68 92 92, Fax 01 47 68 52 82*
BRITISH AIRWAYS: *13 boulevard de la Madeleine, 1st, ☏ 01 47 78 14 14, Fax 01 78 53 34 43*
AIR FRANCE: *119 Champs-Élysées, 8th, ☏ 08 02 80 28 02, Fax 01 42 99 21 99*

FOREIGN EXCHANGE OFFICES

Banks: *close at 5pm and at weekends*
Orly Airport: *daily 6.30am to 11.30pm*
Roissy-Charles de Gaulle Airport: *daily 7am to 11.30pm*

TRANSPORT IN PARIS

Taxis: *may be hailed in the street when showing the illuminated sign-available day and night at taxi ranks or called by telephone*
Bus-Métro (subway): *for full details see the Michelin Plan de Paris n° 11. The metro is quicker but the bus is good for sightseeing and practical for short distances.*

POSTAL SERVICES

Local post offices: *open Mondays to Fridays 8am to 7pm; Saturdays 8am to noon*
General Post Office: *52 rue du Louvre, 1st: open 24 hours*

SHOPPING IN PARIS

Department stores: *Boulevard Haussmann, Rue de Rivoli and Rue de Sèvres*
Exclusive shops and boutiques: *Faubourg St-Honoré, Rue de la Paix and Rue Royale, Avenue Montaigne.*
Antiques and second-hand goods: *Swiss Village (Avenue de la Motte Picquet), Louvre des Antiquaires (Place du Palais Royal), Flea Market (Porte Clignancourt).*

TIPPING

Service is generally included in hotel and restaurants bills but you may choose to leave more than the expected tip to the staff. Taxi-drivers, porters, barbers and theatre or cinema attendants also expect a small gratuity.

BREAKDOWN SERVICE

Certain garages in central and outer Paris operate a 24 hour breakdown service. If you breakdown the police are usually able to help by indicating the nearest one.

SPEED LIMITS

The maximum permitted speed in built up areas is 50 km/h - 31 mph; on motorways the speed limit is 130 km/h - 80 mph and 110 km/h - 68 mph on dual carriageways. On all other roads 90 km/h - 56 mph.

SEAT BELTS

The wearing of seat belts is compulsory for drivers and all passengers.

PARIS AND ENVIRONS

Maps: **10, 11, 12** G. Paris.

Population: *Paris 2 152 333 ; Ile-de-France region : 10 651 000.*

Altitude: *Observatory : 60 m ; Place Concorde : 34 m*

Air Terminals – To Orly: *Esplanade des Invalides, 7th, ☎ 01 43 17 21 65*
To Charles de Gaulle *(Roissy): Palais des Congrès, Porte Maillot, 17th, ☎ 01 44 09 51 52 and Montparnasse r. du Cdt-Mouchotte (near SNCF railways station) 14th, ☎ 01 48 64 14 24*

Paris'Airports: *see Orly and Charles de Gaulle (Roissy)*

Railways, motorail: *information ☎ 01 36 35 35 35.*

ARRONDISSEMENTS

AND DISTRICTS

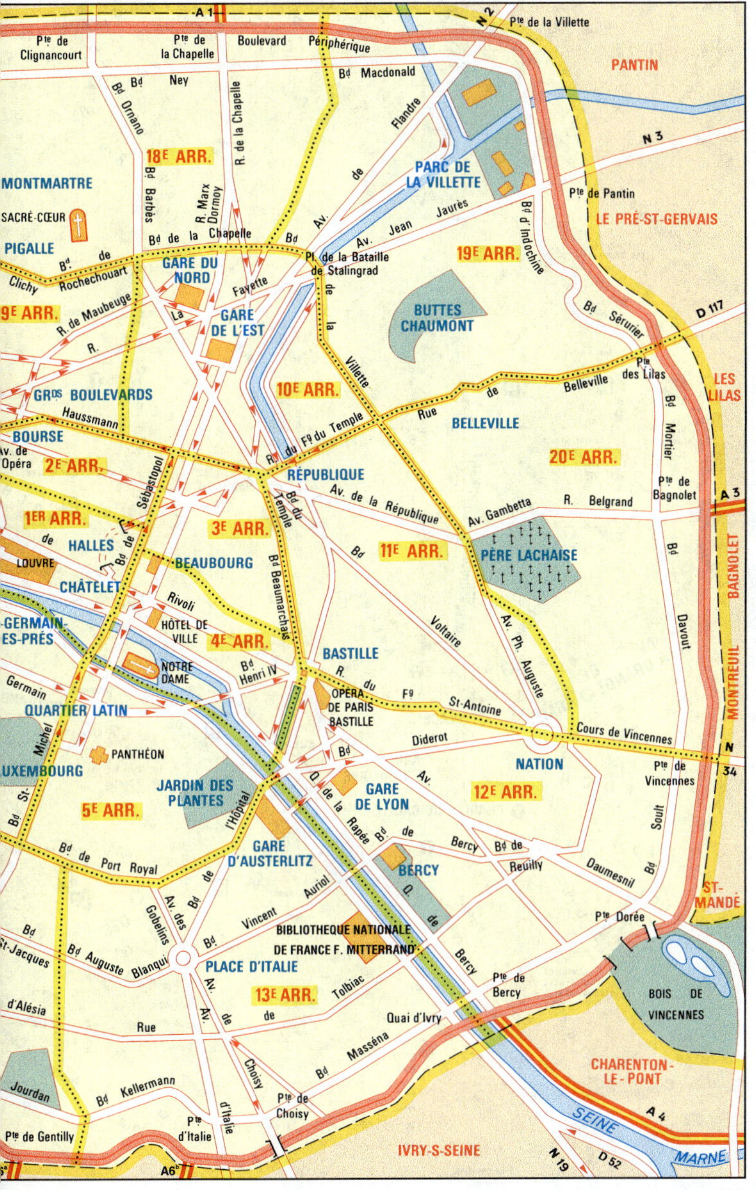

FRANCE
4
0   200 m
BD BERTHIER
LYCÉE STE URSULE LOUISE DE BETTIGNIES
R. A Samain
R. Le Châtelier
R. de Courcelles
AV. GOURGAUD
R. G. Doré
R. Ch. Gerhardt
R. A. de Neuville
R. Puvis de Chavannes
Sqte de l'Amérique Latine
Pl. de la Porte de Champerret
Pl. Stuart Merrill
Square J. Bellat
PORTE DE CHAMPERRET
AVENUE
Pl. du Mal
Rue
Pl. d'Israël
R. Brémontier
R. Ct Debussy
R. Berthier
R. d'Héliopolis
Imp. des Descombes
Imp des Deux Cousins
Tell
PÉREIRE-LEVALLOIS (R.E.R.)
DE R. de VILLIERS
Pl J. Renard
R. Vernier
Rue
R. Guillaume
PÉREIRE
Juin
PÉREIRE
Demours
PRONY
Pl. du Brésil
WAGRAM AV.
R. Galvani
Laugier
R. J.B. Dumas
R. Mline Edwards
Aublet
R. Bainy d'Avricourt
Pierre
V. Monceau
Gounod
AVENUE DE
R. Meissonier
D 7
D 8
Aumont Thieville
R. E. Allez
R. Roger Bacon
Bayen
Faraday
R. de St Senoch
R. du Serol
Lauger
Rue
Rue
R. Th.
de
R. G. Flaubert
R. L. Cognot
R. Barye
BOULEVARD
Demours
Pl A Maillart
V. Niel
Pt Roux
R. G. Flaubert
Banville
Rennequin
P.R.
MARCHÉ DES TERNES
Torricelli
P.
Bayen
Fourcroy
des
Lauger
Renaudes
Renaudes
Théodule Ribot
Marguerite
Courcelles
L.P. HÔ
SVENSKA KYRKAN
Guersant
Rue
Lebon
R. Marcel Renault
Saussier
Leroy
pge Poncelet
Léon
Josl
CLIN. DU PARC MONCEAU
AV.
Pl. Tristan Bernard
R. Villebois Mareuil
Rue
Pt Boudnos
Poncelet
WAGRAM
R. Saint Ferdinand
DES
P.
TERNES
E 8
Pl. des Ternes
BOULEVARD
Daru
Rue
COURCE
ST FERDINAND STE THÉRÈSE DE L'ENFANT JÉSUS
Cité Ferembach
CENTRE MÉDICAL MARMOTTAN
Rue
Acacias
pge des Acacias
de
TERNES
R. de la Néva
R. Pierre le Grand
LYCÉE ACT BILINGUE
E 7
R. des Colonels Renard
AVENUE
R. de l'Arc de Triomphe
ESPACE WAGRAM
Montenotte
272 Rue
du
CATHÉDRALE ST ALEXANDRE NEWSKY
Beaucourt
Sqte de Joyeuse
R. Villaret de Joyeuse
Villa Guyot
d'Armaillé
des
Rue
de
l'Étoile
Villa Wagram St Honoré
Sqte du Roule
SALLE PLEYEL
Av.
HOCH
du Colonel Moll
AVENUE
R. de l'Arc de Triomphe
Brey
V. Nouvelle
N.D. DE L'ANNONCIATION
Villa de la Gde Armée
CARNOT
P.
Troyon
ST JOSEPH
Fg
St Honoré
ARGENTINE
AV. DE LA GRANDE ARMÉE
MAC
MAHON
Rue
de
AVENUE
Houssaye
Balzar
Berryer
FRIEDLAND
Rue d'Argentine
R. de Saigon
Rude
Rue
CH. DE GAULLE ÉTOILE (R.E.R.)
PLACE
Beaujon
Pl. G. Guillaumin
Rue Chalgrin
AV. FOCH
P.
ARC DE TRIOMPHE (R.E.R.)
AVENUE DE
Tilsit
Av. Bertie Albrecht
CORPUS CHRISTI
CHAMBRE DE COMMERCE ET D'INDUSTRIE DE PARIS
Lamennais
de Chateaubriand
Washir
R. Arsene
F 8
FREDERIKSKIRKEN
Rue
Lord
Byron
Cité Odiot
CHARLES DE GAULLE
Presbourg
AVENUE
LIDO
Galerie Berri-Washington
F 7
HUGO
Lauriston
de
Rue
OFFICE DU TOURISME
AIR FRANCE
Rue
Arcade
AV. VICTOR
Rue du Dome
KLÉBER
La Pérouse
d'Urville
AIR FRANCE
P.
GEORGE V
DES
Guise des Champs
CLIN. V. HUGO
Av. des Portugais
R. Newton
Galilée
Euler
Bassano
AVENUE
Gal. Carré d'Or
Vernet
Paul
CENTRE DE CONFÉRENCES INTERNATIONALES
Dumont
Vacquerie
ST GEORGES
de
Rue
R. C.
Magellan
Bauchart
Lincoln
Rue
RÉSERVOIRS DE PASSY
Valéry
Rue
Auguste
Pl. de l'Uruguay
Jean
Kepler
Colomb
Pl.H. Dunant
Pierre Cha
R.
Copernic
Galilée
D'IÉNA
Giraudoux
Quentin
Rue
Imp. Kléber
R. de Belloy
Rue
Maillot
Pl. de Beyrouth
SERBIE
Marbeuf
R. Cimarosa
Rue
Place des
Sqte de Ch
R. de Cerisoles

5
FRANCE
STE-MARIE DES BATIGNOLLES
ASCENSION
Legendre
D 11
D 10
D 9
LYCÉE CARNOT
BOULEVARD
ÉCOLE NORMALE DE MUSIQUE
SALLE CORTOT
UNIVERSITÉ PARIS IV SORBONNE (Centre Malesherbes)
Pl. du Nicaragua
MALESHERBES
MUSÉE HENNER
Pl. du G.al Catroux
ST CHARLES DE MONCEAU
Tocqueville
VILLIERS
DE
MALESHERBES
VILLIERS
Pl. P. Goubaux
LYCÉE CHAPTAL
THÉÂTRE DES ARTS-HEBERTOT
Prony
COURCELLES
LA PLAINE MONCEAU
ROME
Pl. de la République Dominicaine
MONCEAU
Rue
Monceau
DE
MUSÉE CERNUSCHI
PARC DE MONCEAU
MUSÉE NISSIM DE CAMONDO
BOULEVARD
LYCÉE STE MARIE FENELON
TH TRISTAN BERNARD
E 9
E 10
E 11
Rue
de
Lisbonne
MALESHERBES
Pl. de Rio de Janeiro
MARCHE EUROPE
MAIRIE DU 8.e ARR.
Bienfaisance
DIRECTION E.D.F.
Pl. de Narvik
ST AUGUSTIN
Pl. H. Bergson
MESSINE
Miromesnil
MUSÉE JACQUEMART-ANDRÉ
BOULEVARD
HAUSSMANN
BOULEVARD
Pl. St Augustin
La Baume
La Boétie
BOULEVARD
Faubourg
Courcelles
Rue
ST PHILIPPE DU ROULE
La Boétie
SALLE GAVEAU
MIROMESNIL
de
Penthièvre
ST ESPRIT
F 9
F 10
F 11
ST PHILIPPE DU ROULE
MIN. DE L'INTÉRIEUR
La Boétie
CLIN. DU RD PT DES CHAMPS ELYSÉES
Honoré
Pl. Beauvau
Pl. des Saussaies
ARCHEVÊCHÉ DE PAR
Galerie Élysées La Boétie
PALAIS DE L'ÉLYSÉE
ST MICHAEL'S ENGLISH CHURCH
TH. DE LA MADELEINE
Galerie Elysées 26
Galerie Elysée Rond Point
PRÉSIDENCE DE LA RÉPUBLIQUE
Faubourg
ÉLYSÉES
Rond-Point des Champs-Élysées
FRANKLIN D. ROOSEVELT
TH. MARIGNY
Marcel Dassault
AVENUE
THÉÂTRE
165

D 11
D 12
D 1
E 11
E 12
E 1
F 11
F 12
F 1
MAIRIE DU 17e ARR.
INSTITUT UNIVERSITAIRE DE FORMATION DES MAITRES
DESCENTE DU ST-ESPRIT ET ÉGLISE REFORMÉE DES BATIGNOLLES
ROME
GRANDE LOGE
ESPACE EUROPEEN
CLINIQUE VINTIMILLE
PL. DE CLICHY
PL. A. Max
BATIGNOLLES
LYCÉE J. FERRY
STE RITA
BLANCHE
PL. Blanche
BAL DU MOULIN ROUGE
THÉÂTRE DES 2 ÂNES
COMÉDIE DE PARIS
DE
ST ANDRE DE L'EUROPE
PL. Lili Boulanger
MUSÉE DE LA VIE ROMANTIQUE
TH. FONTAINE
PL. de Dublin
TH. DE L'ŒUVRE
LYCÉE ST LOUIS
FEDERATION PROTESTANTE DE FRANCE
CLIN. HENNER
CLIN. TURIN
LIÈGE
DEUTSCHE EVANGELISCHE CHRISTUSKIRCHE
ECOLE NATle SUPRe DES ARTS ET TECHN. DU THÉÂTRE
TH. LA BRUYERE
PL. de l'Europe
EUROPE
TH. DE PARIS
CLIN. MILAN
d'Athenes
CASINO DE PARIS
MUSÉE GUSTAVE MOREAU
PL. de Budapest
STE TRINITÉ
Cour d'Amsterdam
GARE ST LAZARE
DIRECTION GENERALE S.N.C.F.
Londres
LYCÉE RACINE
TRINITÉ
PL. d'Estienne d'Orves
R. Interieure
Cour du Havre
Cour de Rome
ST LAZARE
Laborde
PL. du Havre
Lazare
TH. MOGADOR
PL. G. Péri
(Eole :mi-1999)
R. de la Pépinière
LYCÉE CONDORCET
PL. G. Berry
ST LOUIS D'ANTIN
ST AUGUSTIN
HAUSSMANN
MAGASINS DU PRINTEMPS
GALERIES LAFAYETTE
CHAUSSÉE D'ANTIN
Sqte Louis XVI CHAPELLE EXPIATOIRE
TH. MICHEL
TH. DES MATHURINS
HAVRE-CAUMARTIN
Mathurins
PL. Diaghilev
PARISTORIC
Marché de la Madeleine
AUBER
OPÉRA GARNIER
ARCHEVÊCHÉ DE PARIS
COMÉDIE CAUMARTIN
TH. ATHÉNÉE L. JOUVET
MUSÉE DE LA PARFUMERIE
PL. Ch. Garnier
Sqte de l'Opéra Jouvet
TH. ÉDOUARD VII S. GUITRY
PL. Édouard VII
PL. de
l'Evêque
Marché de la Madeleine
KIOSQUE-THÉÂTRE
PL. de la Madeleine
OLYMPIA
CAPUCINES
l'Opéra
STE MARIE MADELEINE
OPÉRA
QUATRE SEPTEMBRE
BD DE LA MADELEINE
Madeleine
GALERIE DES TROIS QUARTIERS
TH. DE LA MICHODIERE
MICHELIN
TH. DES BOUFFES PARISIENS
Honoré
Le Village Royal
Galle de la Madeleine
CREDIT FONCIER DE FRANCE
TH. DAUNOU
TH. LA PÉPINIÈRE-OPÉRA
MINISTERE DE LA JUSTICE

7
FRANCE
167
BASILIQUE DU SACRÉ CŒUR
ST PIERRE DE MONTMARTRE
MUSÉE D'ART NAIF MAX FOURNY
HALLE ST PIERRE
LARIBOISIÈRE
BARBÈS ROCHECHOUART
D 14
D 15
ANVERS
PIGALLE
CLICHY
BOULEVARD
LYCÉE J. DECOUR
THEATRE LE DIVAN DU MONDE
ELYSÉE MONTMARTRE
ROCHECHOUART
BOULEVARD BARBÈS
BD DE MAGENTA
POISSONNIÈRE
AVENUE TRUDAINE
CLINIQUE MARIE-LOUISE
LYCÉE E. QUINET
Condorcet
Maubeuge
ST VINCENT DE PAUL
LYCÉE TECHN. JULES SIEGFRIED
LYCÉE ROCROI ST LÉON
LYCÉE LAMARTINE
E 14
E 15
ST GEORGES
ST CONSTANTIN STE HELENE
Pl. Franz Liszt
Pl. du 8 Nov. 1942
FAYETTE
POISSONNIÈRE
MUSÉE DES CRISTALLERIES DE BACCARAT
N.D. DE LORETTE
Châteaudun
CADET
LA
Montholon
Sqre de Montholon
MUSÉE DU GRAND ORIENT DE FRANCE
ÉGLISE ADVENTISTE DU 7e JOUR
Cité Paradis
Paradis
LE PELETIER
FAYETTE
Provence
Rue des Petites Écuries
FOLIES BERGERE
Richer
CONSERVATOIRE
HÔTEL DES VENTES DROUOT-RICHELIEU
REDEMPTION
CONSERVATOIRE NAT SUP D'ART DRAMATIQUE
F 14
F 15
STE-CÉCILE
ST-EUGÈNE
HAUSSMANN
MAIRIE DU 9e ARR.
Musée Grévin
d'Enghien
l'Échiquier
ITALIENS
DROUOT
RICHELIEU
MONTMARTRE
GRANDS BOULEVARDS
POISSONNIÈRE
TH. DES NOUVEAUTÉS
OPERA COMIQUE
TH. DES VARIÉTÉS
LYCÉE EDGAR POE
TH DU GYMNASE MARIE BELL
STRASBOURG ST DENIS
BONNE NOUVELLE
Richelieu
LYCÉE J.B. LULLI
BONNE NOUVELLE
Place de la Victoires
LA BOURSE
BOURSE
Septembre
PHONOTHEQUE NATE

G 7
G 8
Place des États Unis
Pl. Amiral de Grasse
Pl. de Beyrouth
SERBIE
MARCEAU
AMERICAN CATHEDRAL IN PARIS
Cimarosa
Rue
Rue
de l'Amiral d'Estaing
Hamelin
LYCÉE ASSOMPTION
CLIN BIZET
ST PIERRE DE CHAILLOT
Sqte de Chaillot
Chaillot
Tremoille
Marbe
Franc
R. Léo Delibes
BOISSIÈRE
Lübeck
MUSÉE GUIMET
D'IÉNA
Place Rochambeau
PIERRE 1ER
ST ÉTIENNE
R. Goethe
Bizet
Pl. P. Brisson
GEORGE
Renaissance
Boccador
Boissière
MUSÉE GUIMET
AVENUE
R. Léonce Reynaud
TH DES CHAMPS ÉLYSÉES DROUOT MONTAIGNE
R. de Longchamp
Pl. d'Iéna
PALAIS GALLIERA
Sqte Brignole Galliera
Galliera
Freycinet
CRAZY HORSE
ALMA MARCEAU
AVENUE
Rue
PRÉSIDENT
Pl. de Tokyo
WILSON
Pl. de l'Alma
IÉNA
DU
R. de la Manutention
Rue Gaston
Freres Peréin
Rue Debrousse
UNION DE L'EUROPE OCCIDENTALE
CONSEIL ÉCONOMIQUE ET SOCIAL
Fresnel
PALAIS DE TOKYO
MUSÉE D'ART MODERNE
Rue de St Paul
AVENUE
Av. Albert de Mun
Rue
Rue Foucault
NEW YORK
Debilly
Pl. Maria Callas
Pont de l'Alma
Port
Port
PALAIS DE CHAILLOT
AV.
de
Mun
Passerelle Debilly
Bourdonnais
PT. DE L'ALMA (R.E.R.)
QUAI
JARDINS
Nations Unies
BRANLY
Pl. de la Résistance
R. Cognacq
H 7
DU
Av. Gustave V de Suède
Port
de
La
H 8
RAPP
l'Universi
Av. Albert 1er de Monaco
Pl. de Varsovie
ESPACE EIFFEL-BRANLY
de
Cité de l'Alma
AVENUE
Villa Bosquet
TROCADÉRO
Av. Franco Russe
LYCÉE ALMA
ST JEAN
Av. des
Pont d'Iéna
Port
QUAI
R.
AVENUE
de
Monttessuy
R. E. Valentin
Landrieu
AVENUE
Suffren
Rue
de
Sacy
R. du Gal Camou
Rue Dupont des Loges
BOSQUET
TOUR EIFFEL
LP G EIFFEL
Sqte Rapp
R. de l'Exposition du Gros Caillou
Av. Élisée Reclus
Mtal
Av. E. Pouvillon
Pl. du Général Gouraud
CHAMP DE MARS TOUR EIFFEL (R.E.R.)
BRANLY
AVENUE
R. de Buenos-Aires
Av. Gustave Eiffel
PARC
Avenue
Maurice
Allée
Gal Ferrie
Bouvard
La
Av. Barbey d'Aurevilly
Augereau
R.
Port
Av. Octave Gréard
DÂTAR
DU
Pl. Jacques Rueff
J 8
R. de Belgrade
STADE ÉMILE-ANTOINE
J 7
Avenue
R. du Gal Lambert
Allée
Av. du
Marguerite
Adrienne
Bourdonna
Rey
Anatole
CHAMP
DESCHANEL
R. Jean
R. du Cap. Scott
Dr Brouardel
Avenue
Pierre
Thomy
Av. du Gal
Avenue Charles Risler
Lecouvreur
Av. Fr. Le Play
Rue
Pl. des Martyrs Juifs du Vélodrome d'Hiver
T.E.P.
Desaix
Charles
DE
Joffre
BIR HAKEIM
Saint Saens
R. Alexis
Carrel
R. Champlicault
MARS
France
LA
BOULEVARD
DIRECTION JOURNAUX OFFICIELS
Pl. A. Sauvy
de
la
Carrel
Av. du Gal Detrie
Floquet
Thierry
ST LOUIS
ÉCOLE SUPRE DE GUERRE
Square Desaix
Cité Morieux
R. G. Dumézil
Imp. de Prestes
Fédération
R. Jean Carriès
Av. E. Acollas
Place
Rue
Charles
R. George Bernard Shaw
Allée M. Yourcenar
Faure Prestes
pge du Guezclin
Dupleix
SUFFREN
K 8
P
ÉCOLE SUPRE D'INTENDANCE
DE
R. Clodion
Allée du Gal Denain
R. Leroi Gourhan
Pl. M. Fourcade
Dupleix
R. Alasseur
VILLAGE SUISSE
Av. de Champaubert
R. Gal Baratier
Docteur Finlay
Daniel Stern
Place Dupleix
ST LÉON
Sqte G de Guingand
AV.
Viala
R. Humblot
R. Auguste Berthold
Card Amette
R. du Général de Larminat
SUISSE
DUPLEIX
GRENELLE
Duplex
R. du
Soudan
Av. P. Déroulède
R. de l'Abbé Roger Derry
K 7
R. B. Dussane
Juge

MONTAGNE
AVENUE
FRANKLIN D. ROOSEVELT
CHAMPS ÉLYSÉES
CLEMENCEAU
AVE DES CHAMPS
Bourdin
CLIN. ELYSÉE-MONTAIGNE
CHURCH OF SCOTLAND
THEATRE DU ROND POINT
Av. de Selves
Eisenhower
Pl. Clemenceau
ESPACE PIERRE CARDIN
Proust
Gabriel
Rue
Av. du Gal
Sq!e J
Perrin
GRAND PALAIS
Av. Ch Girault
Carré Champs Elysées
Marcel
Allée
Avenue
24
G 10
G 11
Imp. d'Antin
Goujon
Rue
Av. W. Churchill
Av. Edward Tuck
ÉLYSÉES
G 9
Jean
Pl. François 1er
PALAIS DE LA DÉCOUVERTE
PETIT PALAIS
DE OBÉ
François 1er
UNIVERSITÉ PARIS IV
Av. Ch Girault
Bayard
N D DE CONSOLATION
ÉGLISE ARMÉNIENNE
Albert 1er
Pl. du Canada
Cours
la
Reine
CONC
Conférence
la
Port des Champs
Elysées
Port de la
Concorde
Gros
Caillou
Port des Invalides
Pont Alexandre III
Port
des
Invalides
Pont de la Concorde
Pl. de Finlande
QUAI
D'ORSAY
QUAI
HE AMERICAN CHURCH IN PARIS
D'ORSAY
R. Desgenettes
Fabert
GALLIENI
(R.E.R.)
MIN. DES AFFAIRES ETRANGÈRES
ASSEMBLÉE NATIONALE
H 11
S.E.I.T.A.
AÉROGARE DES INVALIDES
MIN. DES AFFAIRES EUROPEENNES
PALAIS BOURBON
ASSEMBLÉE NATIONALE
R du Colonel
Moisan
Av. Henri
R. Paul et Jean Lerollé
H 10
R. Robert Esnault Pelterie
Rue
Combes
Schuman S.E.I.T.A. MUSÉE
INVALIDES
Av. R.
CLIN. ALMA
de
l'Université
Pl. du Palais Bourbon
MINISTÈRE DE LA DEFENSE
H 9
Rue
Commun
ESPLANADE
MAISON DE LA CHIMIE
PIERRE DU S CAILLOU
Nicot
Surcouf
DES INVALIDES
Rue
Saint
Malar
Saint
Dominique
DU
R. de Talleyrand
Bourgogne
Rue
BASILIQUE STE CLOTILDE
LYCÉE LA ROCHEFOUCAULT
pge Jean Nicot
AV.
Pl. des Invalides
INSTITUT GÉOGRAPHIQUE NATIONAL
de Champagny
Cité du Gal Negrier
Amélie
la Comète
R. de la
Grenelle
R. de
LYCÉE P. CLAUDEL
MIN. L'ÉDUCA NATION
ST JEAN
La Tour Maubourg
Pl. Santiago du Chili
Square d'Ajaccio
Rue
de
MAIRIE DU 7e ARR
LATOUR MAUBOURG
Sq!e Santiago du Chili
Cité Martignac
R. Valadon
Sq!e Denys Buther
MUSÉE DE L'ARMÉE
MIN. DE L'EMPLOI ET DE LA SOLIDARITÉ
Psichari
PICQUET
HÔTEL DES INVALIDES
VARENNE
MIN. DE L'AGRICULTURE ET DE LA PÊCHE
J 11
Mars
Duvivier
Chevert
ST LOUIS
J 10
Rue
MIN. DES RELATIONS AVEC LE PARLEMENT
Bosquet
Cler
R. Bougainville
MUSÉE DE L'ORDRE DE LA LIBÉRATION
MUSÉE RODIN
MIN. DE LA FONCTION PUBLIQUE
J 9
pge de la Vierge
DE
R. L. Codet
Cité Vaneau
C Vaneau
HÔTEL MATIGNON
MOTTE
ÉCOLE MILITAIRE
R. J. Granier
Jardin de l'Intendant
ÉGLISE DU DÔME
de Jouy
Vaneau
Pl. de École Militaire
Avenue
DES
de
Rue
Pl. D. Cochin
de
Pl. VAUBAN
Tourville
R. de Chanaleilles
AVENUE
LOWENDAL
SÉGUR
R. Bixio
AV. DE VILLARS
BOULEVARD
Barbet
CLIN. ST FRANÇOIS XAVIER
Esplanade du Souvenir Français
LYCÉE VICTOR DURUY
ST DOMINIQUE
COLE LITAIRE
DUQUESNE
DE BRETEUIL
d'Estrées
Rue
PRÉFECTURE D'ILE DE FRANCE
SECRT D'ÉTAT A LA SANTÉ
Pl. André Tardieu
Monsieur
Rue
Jardin Catherine Labouré
de Fontenoy
DE
Rue
MIN. DE L'AMÉNAGEMENT DU TERRITOIRE ET DE L'ENVIRONNEMENT
ST FRANÇOIS XAVIER
AV. de Ségur
ST FRANÇOIS XAVIER
CLIN DES SŒURS AUGUSTINES DE MEAUX
Imp. Oudinot
K 11
SECRT D'ÉTAT AU LOGEMENT
Pl. El Salvador
Mithouard
SECRT D'ÉTAT A LA COOPÉRATION ET À LA FRANCOPHONIE
LT ALBERT DEMUN
K 9
MICHELIN
K 10
Oudinot
N.E.S.C.O.

FRANCE
10
G 11
G 12
G 1
H 11
H 12
H 1
J 11
J 12
J 13
K 11
K 12
PLACE
CONCORDE
DE LA
CONCORDE
OBELISQUE
Place
Vendôme
Saint
RIVOLI
MINISTÈRE DE LA JUSTICE
COUR DES COMPTES
MUSÉE BOUILHET CHRISTOFLE
MUSÉE DES LUNETTES ET LORGNETTES
N D DE L'ASSOMPTION
Pl. M. Barres
Galerie Royale
HÔTEL CRILLON
HÔTEL DE LA MARINE
Castiglione
ST ROCH
PYRAMIDES
DE L'OPÉRA
OPÉRA
PARISIENS
R. Danielle Casanova
Imp Gomboust
Honoré
COMÉDIE FRANÇAISE RICHELIEU
MUSÉE DE LA MODE ET DU TEXTILE
MUSÉE DES ARTS DÉCORATIFS
Pl des Pyramides
GALERIE NATIONALE DU JEU DE PAUME
Terrasse
JARDIN
DES
TUILERIES
TUILERIES
Feuillants
MUSÉE DE L'ORANGERIE
Terrasse
QUAI
Port
Port
des
du
Bord
DES
de
l'Eau
Passerelle Solferino
ouverture : automne 1999
SEINE
(R. E. R.)
MUSÉE D'ORSAY
JARDIN DU CARROUSEL
ARC DE TRIOMPHE DU CARROUSEL
Pl. du CARROUSEL
Av. du Gal Lemonnier
Terrasse des Tuileries
PALAIS ROYAL
MUSÉE DU LOU
PYRA
Nap
ANATOLE
FRANCE
Solferino
Solferino
Pl. H- de Montherlant
GRANDE CHANCELLERIE LÉGION D'HONNEUR
MUSÉE D'ORSAY
R. de la Légion d'Honneur
Bellechasse
CAISSE DES DÉPÔTS ET CONSIGNATIONS
LA DOCUMENTATION FRANÇAISE
Pont Royal
Port
QUAI VOLTAIRE
Pont du Carrousel
Port
QUAI
du
des
Saints
Pères
QUAI MALAQUAIS
Pl. J. Bainville
SOLFERINO
Dominique
Las Cases
de
Villersexel
SAINT
de Poitiers
Rue
Beaune
INSTITUT DES LANGUES ET CIVILISATIONS ORIENTALES
Lille
Verneuil
l'Université
ÉCOLE NAT LE SUP RE DES BEAUX ARTS
Bonaparte
MIN. DE L'ÉDUCATION NATIONALE
SECR! D'ÉTAT AUX ANCIENS COMBATTANTS
PENTEMONT
MIN. DE L'ÉQUIPEMENT, DES TRANSPORTS ET DU LOGEMENT
SECR! D'ÉTAT POUR L'EMPLOI
E.N.A.
R. Montalembert
R. S. Bonin
Grenelle
RUE DU BAC
ST THOMAS D'AQUIN
Pl. St Thomas d'Aquin
R! St Thomas d'Aquin
Saints
Rue
ACADÉMIE NAT LE DE MÉDECINE
Visconti
Jacob
Rue de Furstemb
MUSÉE DELACROIX
de l'Abbaye
MUSÉE MAILLOL
FONTAINE DES QUATRE SAISONS
BOULEVARD
GERMAIN
LYCÉE ST THOMAS D'AQUIN
FOND NAT DES SCIENCES POLITIQUES
UNIVERSITÉ PARIS V
R. Perronet
ST VLADIMIR LE GRD
Sqe Taras Chevtchenko
R. Guillaume Apollinaire
ST GERMAIN DES PRÉS
ST GERMAIN DES PRÉS
Pl. du Québec
B. Palissy
MABI
Varenne
de
LYCÉE D'HULST
C. de Varenne
R. de Narbonne
La Rochefoucauld
R. de Commaille
R. Chomel
Square Chaise Récamier
R. de la Chaise
Grenelle
des
Rue du Dragon
Pl. J. Copeau
Pl. d'Acadie
Rennes
Four
MARCHE ST GERMAIN
R. Princesse
R. Guisarde
SÉMIN. DES MISSIONS ÉTRANGÈRES
Sqe des Missions Étrangères
Babylone
R. de Sèvres
Carref. de la Croix Rouge
TH. DU VIEUX COLOMBIER
Madame
Bonaparte
R. des Canettes
N.D. DE LA MÉDAILLE MIRACULEUSE
BON MARCHÉ
Square Boucicaut
SÈVRES BABYLONE
Pl. Le Corbusier
Cherche Midi
ST SULPICE
Vieux Colombier
Palatine
LAENNEC
R. de Sèvres
ST IGNACE
Pl. A. Deville
MAIRIE DU 6E ARR.
St Sulpice
ST SULPICE
R. de Mézières
Canivet
170

11
FRANCE
PHONOTHÈQUE NAT^{le}
R. Colbert
BIBLIOTHÈQUE NATIONALE
MAIRIE DU 2e ARR
Rue Vivienne
BASILIQUE N D DES VICTOIRES
HÔTEL COLBERT
JARDIN DU PALAIS ROYAL
BANQUE DE FRANCE
CAISSE D'ÉPARGNE DE PARIS
HÔTEL DES POSTES
ST EUSTACHE
BOURSE DU COMMERCE
Place R. Cassin
LES HALLES
PAVILLON DES ARTS
MAISON DE LA POÉSIE
FORUM
ST EUSTACHE
G 14
G 15
SENTIER
RÉAUMUR
RÉAUMUR SEBASTOPOL
Rue Étienne Marcel
ÉTIENNE MARCEL
TURBIGO
Denis
Marcel
TOUR DE JEAN SANS PEUR
TH. MOLIÈRE
Quincampoix
H 14
H 15
Honoré
CHÂTELET LES HALLES (R.E.R.)
CENTRE NAT^l D'ART ET DE CULTURE G. POMPIDOU
Pl. Georges Pompidou
Pl. E. Michelet
IRCAM
LOUVRE RIVOLI
MAIRIE DU 1er ARR
ST GERMAIN L'AUXERROIS
CHÂTELET
LE LOUVRE DES ANTIQUAIRES
Jardin de l'Oratoire
ORATOIRE DU LOUVRE
RIVOLI
COUR CARRÉE
SAMARITAINE
ST MERRI
Rue du Renard
Berger
LOUVRE DU LOUVRE
Pl. de l'École PONT-NEUF
BOULEVARD DE CHÂTELET
TOUR ST JACQUES
Sq^{re} de la Tour St Jacques
CHÂTELET
RIVOLI
HÔTEL DE VILLE
Malaquais
Sq^{re} du Vert Galant
BATEAUX POMPES
QUAI
Voie
Georges
Pl. du Châtelet
TH. DE LA VILLE
VICTORIA
HÔTEL DE VILLE
MAIRIE DE PARIS
HÔTEL DES MONNAIES
Pl. Dauphine
L'HORLOGE
ASSISTANCE PUBLIQUE
Pompidou
J 14
J 15
CONCIERGERIE
PALAIS DE JUSTICE
TRIBUNAL DE COMMERCE
Pl. L. Lépine
HÔTEL DIEU
STE CHAPELLE
CITÉ
PRÉFECTURE DE POLICE
ÎLE DE LA CITÉ
Pont St Louis
CAZAR
Carref. de Buci
ST MICHEL N. DAME (R.E.R.)
ST MICHEL
QUAI ST MICHEL
Place du Parvis Notre Dame
NOTRE DAME
Square Jean XXIII
ODÉON
UNIVERSITÉ SAINT
Square de l'Île de France
MÉMORIAL DE LA DÉPORTATION
CLUNY LA SORBONNE
MUSÉE N^l DU MOYEN-AGE THERMES ET HÔTEL DE CLUNY
MUSÉE DE L'ASSISTANCE PUBLIQUE
UNIVERSITÉ PARIS VI (CORDELIERS)
13
K 14
K 15
Pl. Maubert
ÉCOLE SPÉCIALE DES TRAVAUX PUBLICS DU BÂTIMENT ET DE L'INDUSTRIE
GERMAIN
ST JACQUES
MONTEBELLO

SIGHTS

How to make the most of a trip to Paris – some ideas :

A BIRD'S-EYE VIEW OF PARIS

★★★ *Eiffel Tower* J 7 – ★★★ *Montparnasse Tower* LM 11 – ★★★ *Notre-Dame Towers* K 15 – ★★★ *Sacré Cœur Dome* D 14 – ★★★ *Arc de Triomphe platform* F 8.

FAMOUS PARISIAN VISTAS

★★★ *Arc de Triomphe – Champs-Élysées – Place de la Concorde :* ≼ *from the Rond Point on the Champs-Élysées* G 10.

★★ *The Madeleine – Place de la Concorde – Palais Bourbon (National Assembly) :* ≼ *from the Obelisk in the middle of Place de la Concorde* G 11.

★★★ *The Trocadéro – Eiffel Tower – Ecole Militaire :* ≼ *from the terrace of the Palais de Chaillot* H 7.

★★ *The Invalides – Grand and Petit Palais :* ≼ *from Pont Alexandre III* H 10.

MAIN MONUMENTS

The Louvre★★★ *(Cour Carrée, Perrault's Colonnade, Pyramid)* H 13 – *Eiffel Tower*★★★ J 7 – *Notre-Dame Cathedral*★★★ K 15 – *Sainte-Chapelle*★★★ J 14 – *Arc de Triomphe*★★★ F 8 – *The Invalides*★★★ *(Napoleon's Tomb)* J 10 – *Palais-Royal*★★ H 13 – *The Opéra*★★ F 12 – *The Conciergerie*★★ J 14 – *The Panthéon*★★ L 14 – *Luxembourg*★★ *(Palace and Gardens)* KL 13.

Churches : *The Madeleine*★★ G 11 – *Sacré Cœur*★★ D 14 – *St-Germain-des-Prés*★★ J 13 – *St-Etienne-du-Mont*★★ – *St-Germain-l'Auxerrois*★★ H 14.

In the Marais : *Place des Vosges*★★ – *Hôtel Lamoignon*★★ – *Hôtel Guénégaud*★★ *(Museum of the Chase and of Nature)* – *Hôtel de Soubise*★★ *(Historical Museum of France)* by HJ 15.

MAIN MUSEUMS

The Louvre★★★ H 13 – *Musée d'Orsay*★★★ *(mid-19C to early 20C)* H 12 – *National Museum of Modern Art*★★★ *(Centre Georges-Pompidou)* H 15 – *Army Museum*★★★ *(Invalides)* J 10 – *Museum of Decorative Arts*★★ *(107 rue de Rivoli)* H 13 – *Hôtel de Cluny*★★ *(Museum of the Middle Ages and Roman Baths)* K 14 – *Rodin*★★ *(Hôtel de Biron)* J 10 – *Carnavalet*★★ *(History of Paris)* J 17 – *Picasso*★★ H 17 – *Cité de la Science et de l'Industrie*★★★ *(La Villette)* – *Marmottan*★★ *(Impressionist artists)* – *Orangerie*★★ *(from the Impressionists until 1930)* H 11.

MODERN MONUMENTS

La Défense★★ *(CNIT, Grande Arche)* – *Centre Georges-Pompidou*★★ H 15 – *Forum des Halles* H 14 – *Institut du Monde Arabe*★ – *Opéra Paris-Bastille*★ – *Bercy (Palais Omnisports, Ministry of Finance)* – *Bibliothèque Nationale de France*.

PRETTY AREAS

Montmartre★★★ D 14 – *Ile St-Louis*★★ J 14 J 15 – *the Quays*★★ *(between Pont des Arts and Pont de Sully)* J 14 J 15 – *St Séverin district*★★ K 14.

K 14, G 10 : *Reference letters and numbers on the town plans.*

Use MICHELIN Green Guide Paris *for a well-informed visit.*

Alphabetical list (Hotels and restaurants)

F

G

H - I

HOTELS, RESTAURANTS

Listed by districts and arrondissements

(List of Hotels and Restaurants in alphabetical order, see pp 13 to 21)

G 12: These reference letters and numbers correspond to the squares on the Michelin **Map of Paris** no **10**. **Paris Atlas** no **11**. **Map with street index** no **12** and **Paris Atlas by arrondissements** no **16**.

Consult any of the above publications when looking for a car park nearest to a listed establishment.

Opéra, Palais-Royal, Halles, Bourse.

1st and 2nd arrondissements.
1st: ✉ 75001
2nd: ✉ 75002

Ritz, 15 pl. Vendôme (1st) ℰ 01 43 16 30 30, *Fax 01 43 16 31 78*, 🌳, « Attractive pool and luxurious fitness centre » – ⧉ ▤ TV ☎ – 🏛 30 - 80. AE ⓞ GB JCB
G 12
see **Espadon** below - **Bar Vendôme** : Meals a la carte 410/590 – ☕ 190 – **187 rm** 3300/4400, 45 suites.

Meurice, 228 r. Rivoli (1st) ℰ 01 44 58 10 10, *Fax 01 44 58 10 15* – ⧉, ▤ rm, TV ☎ AE ⓞ GB JCB. ☖ rest
G 12
Meals see **Le Meurice** below – ☕ 170 – **48 rm** 2950/3500, 46 suites.

Inter - Continental, 3 r. Castiglione (1st) ℰ 01 44 77 11 11, *Fax 01 44 77 14 60*, 🌳 – ⧉, ☖ rm, ▤ TV ☎ & – 🏛 400. AE ⓞ GB JCB
G 12
Brasserie 234 Rivoli ℰ 01 44 77 10 40 **Meals** 195 and a la carte 250/370 – **Terrasse Fleurie** ℰ 01 44 77 11 11 (*15 May-15 September and closed Saturday and Sunday*) Meals 295 ☖ – ☕ 145 – **443 rm** 3150/3350, 75 suites.

Costes, 239 r. St-Honoré (1st) ℰ 01 42 44 50 00, *Fax 01 42 44 50 01*, 🌳, « Elegant mansion tastefully decorated », ⮝, ▦ – ⧉ ▤ TV ☎ & – 🏛 30. AE ⓞ GB JCB
G 12
Meals a la carte 260/430 ☖ – ☕ 130 – **83 rm** 1750/3250.

Vendôme M, 1 pl. Vendôme (1st) ℰ 01 55 04 55 00, *Fax 01 49 27 97 89*, « 18C mansion » – ⧉ ▤ TV ☎ & – 🏛 40. AE ⓞ GB JCB. ☖ rm
G 12
Café de Vendôme : Meals 190/350 ☖ – ☕ 165 – **23 rm** 2300/3200, 7 suites.

Westminster, 13 r. Paix (2nd) ℰ 01 42 61 57 46, *Fax 01 42 60 30 66* – ⧉, ☖ rm, ▤ rm, TV ☎ & – 🏛 50. AE ⓞ GB JCB
G 12
Meals see **Céladon** below – ☕ 110 – **84 rm** 2400/2950, 18 suites.

Louvre, pl. A. Malraux (1st) ℰ 01 44 58 38 38, *Fax 01 44 58 38 01*, 🌳 – ⧉ ▤ TV ☎ & – 🏛 15 - 80. AE ⓞ GB JCB
H 13
Brasserie Le Louvre : Meals 130/180 and a la carte 210/340 ☖ – ☕ 125 – **196 rm** 2500/3500.

Castille M, 37 r. Cambon (1st) ℰ 01 44 58 44 58, *Fax 01 44 58 44 00* – ⧉, ☖ rm, ▤ TV ☎ & – 🏛 30. AE ⓞ GB JCB. ☖ rm
G 12
see **Il Cortile** below – ☕ 150 – **86 rm** 2160/4000, 7 suites, 14 duplex.

Lotti, 7 r. Castiglione (1st) ℰ 01 42 60 37 34, *Fax 01 40 15 93 56* – ⧉, ☖ rm, ▤ TV ☎. AE ⓞ GB JCB
G 12
Meals 160/220 and a la carte 260/430 ☖ – ☕ 120 – **128 rm** 2450/3350.

Édouard VII without rest, 39 av. Opéra (2nd) ☎ 01 42 61 56 90, *Fax 01 42 61 47 73* – 📶 🔲 📺 ☎ – 🛗 15 - 25. 🅰🅴 ⓪ 🆖   **G 13**
☕ 110 – **65 rm** 1500/1750, 4 suites.

Royal St-Honoré Ⓜ without rest, 221 r. St-Honoré (1st) ☎ 01 42 60 32 79, *Fax 01 42 60 47 44* – 📶, ⛔ rm, 🔲 📺 ☎ ⚹. 🅰🅴 ⓪ 🆖 🅹🅲🅱. ⚗   **G 12**
☕ 105 – **67 rm** 1600/2100, 5 suites.

Normandy, 7 r. Échelle (1st) ☎ 01 42 60 30 21, *Fax 01 42 60 45 81* – 📶, ⛔ rm, 📺 ☎ – 🛗 30. 🅰🅴 ⓪ 🆖 🅹🅲🅱   **H 13**
L'Échelle (closed Saturday and Sunday) **Meals** 150 – ☕ 80 – **111 rm** 1155/1730, 4 suites.

Régina, 2 pl. Pyramides (1st) ☎ 01 42 60 31 10, *Fax 01 40 15 95 16*, 🌿, « "Art Nouveau" lobby » – 📶, ⛔ rm, 🔲 📺 ☎ – 🛗 30. 🅰🅴 ⓪ 🆖 🅹🅲🅱. ⚗ rest   **H 13**
Meals (closed August, Saturday, Sunday and Bank Holidays) 170/270 b.i. ♀ – ☕ 95 – **116 rm** 1690/2300, 14 suites.

Golden Tulip Opéra Richepanse Ⓜ without rest, 14 r. Richepanse (1st) ☎ 01 42 60 36 00, *Fax 01 42 60 13 03* – 📶 🔲 📺 ☎. 🅰🅴 ⓪ 🆖 🅹🅲🅱   **G 12**
☕ 70 – **35 rm** 1320/1540, 3 suites.

Golden Tulip Washington Opéra Ⓜ without rest, 50 r. Richelieu (1st) ☎ 01 42 96 68 06, *Fax 01 40 15 01 12*, « Marquise de Pompadours mansion house, terrace ≤ Palais Royal » – 📶 🔲 📺 ☎ ⚹. 🅰🅴 ⓪ 🆖 🅹🅲🅱. ⚗   **G 13**
☕ 80 – **36 rm** 1080/1400.

Stendhal without rest, 22 r. D. Casanova (2nd) ☎ 01 44 58 52 52, *Fax 01 44 58 52 00* – 📶 🔲 📺 ☎. 🅰🅴 ⓪ 🆖 🅹🅲🅱   **G 12**
☕ 100 – **20 rm** 1440/2000.

Cambon Ⓜ without rest, 3 r. Cambon (1st) ☎ 01 44 58 93 93, *Fax 01 42 60 30 59* – 📶 🔲 📺 ☎. 🅰🅴 ⓪ 🆖 🅹🅲🅱   **G 12**
☕ 80 – **40 rm** 1380/1680.

Mansart without rest, 5 r. Capucines (1st) ☎ 01 42 61 50 28, *Fax 01 49 27 97 44* – 📶 📺 ☎. 🅰🅴 ⓪ 🆖 🅹🅲🅱. ⚗   **G 12**
☕ 60 – **57 rm** 750/1600.

Novotel Les Halles Ⓜ, 8 pl. M.-de-Navarre (1st) ☎ 01 42 21 31 31, *Fax 01 40 26 05 79*, 🌿 – 📶, ⛔ rm, 🔲 📺 ☎ ⚹ – 🛗 15 - 90. 🅰🅴 ⓪ 🆖 🅹🅲🅱   **H 14**
Meals a la carte approx. 180 ♀ – ☕ 75 – **271 rm** 1160/1500.

L'Horset Opéra Ⓜ without rest, 18 r. d'Antin (2nd) ☎ 01 44 71 87 00, *Fax 01 42 66 55 54* – 📶, ⛔ rm, 🔲 📺 ☎. 🅰🅴 ⓪ 🆖 🅹🅲🅱   **G 13**
☕ 80 – **54 rm** 990/1420.

Noailles Ⓜ without rest, 9 r. Michodière (2nd) ☎ 01 47 42 92 90, *Fax 01 49 24 92 71*, contemporary decor – 📶 📺 ☎. 🅰🅴 ⓪ 🆖 🅹🅲🅱   **G 13**
☕ 50 – **58 rm** 880/960, 6 suites.

États-Unis Opéra without rest, 16 r. d'Antin (2nd) ☎ 01 42 65 05 05, *Fax 01 42 65 93 70* – 📶 🔲 📺 ☎ – 🛗 25. 🅰🅴 ⓪ 🆖 🅹🅲🅱. ⚗   **G 13**
☕ 60 – **45 rm** 660/1020.

Violet Ⓜ without rest, 7 r. J. Lantier (1st) ☎ 01 42 33 45 38, *Fax 01 40 28 03 56* – 📶 📺 ☎ ⚹. 🅰🅴 ⓪ 🆖 🅹🅲🅱. ⚗   **J 14**
☕ 55 – **30 rm** 600/800.

Favart without rest, 5 r. Marivaux (2nd) ☎ 01 42 97 59 83, *Fax 01 40 15 95 58* – 📶 📺 ☎. 🅰🅴 ⓪ 🆖 🅹🅲🅱   **F 13**
☕ 20 – **37 rm** 498/602.

Place du Louvre without rest, 21 r. Prêtres-St-Germain-L'Auxerrois (1st) ☎ 01 42 33 78 68, *Fax 01 42 33 09 95* – 📶 📺 ☎. 🅰🅴 ⓪ 🆖 🅹🅲🅱   **H 14**
☕ 50 – **20 rm** 525/850.

Grand Hôtel de Besançon Ⓜ without rest, 56 r. Montorgueil (2nd) ☎ 01 42 36 41 08, *Fax 01 45 08 08 79* – 📺 ☎. 🅰🅴 ⓪ 🆖 🅹🅲🅱. ⚗   **G 14**
☕ 60 – **20 rm** 680/790.

Baudelaire Opéra without rest, 61 r. Ste Anne (2nd) ☎ 01 42 97 50 62, *Fax 01 42 86 85 85* – 📶 📺 ☎. 🅰🅴 ⓪ 🆖 🅹🅲🅱   **G 13**
☕ 42 – **24 rm** 500/700, 5 duplex.

Vivienne without rest, 40 r. Vivienne (2nd) ☎ 01 42 33 13 26, *Fax 01 40 41 98 19* – 📶 📺 ☎. 🆖   **F 14**
☕ 40 – **44 rm** 370/520.

Opéra Richelieu without rest, 20 r. Molière (1st) ☎ 01 42 60 31 20, *Fax 01 42 60 32 06* – 📶 🔲 📺 ☎ ⚹. 🅰🅴 ⓪ 🆖 🅹🅲🅱   **G 13**
☕ 60 – **30 rm** 780.

FRANCE

XXXXX ✿✿ **L'Espadon** - Hôtel Ritz, 15 pl. Vendôme (1st) ✆ 01 43 16 30 80, *Fax 01 43 16 33 75,*
– 📧. 🆎 ⓓ GB JCB. 🚫
G
Meals 390 (lunch)/800 and a la carte 490/850
Spec. Tranche de foie gras au pacherenc, compotée de fruits secs, gaufre aux épices. Fil
de bar en légère tapenade de truffes et asperges sablées au parmesan. Poulette de Bres
poêlée, purée battue persillée aux truffes.

XXXX ✿✿ **Grand Vefour,** 17 r. Beaujolais (1st) ✆ 01 42 96 56 27, *Fax 01 42 86 80 7*
« Pre-Revolutionary (late 18C) café style » – 📧. 🆎 ⓓ GB JCB. 🚫
G
closed August, Saturday and Sunday – **Meals** 345 (lunch)and a la carte 620/880
Spec. Ravioles de foie gras à l'émulsion de crème truffée. Triple côte d'agneau à l'org
perlé et raisins, jus café-chocolat. Blinis au chocolat et glace pistache.

XXXX ✿ **Le Meurice** - Hôtel Meurice, 228 r. Rivoli (1st) ✆ 01 44 58 10 50, *Fax 01 44 58 10*
– 📧. 🆎 ⓓ GB JCB. 🚫
G
Meals (closed 15 March-27 September for renovation) 290 (lunch)/480 b.i. and a la car
380/550
Spec. Médaillons de homard aux légumes de saison, sauce coraillée. Noisettes d'agneau
citron confit et coriandre. Soufflé de saison et sa quenelle de sorbet.

XXXX ✿✿ **Carré des Feuillants** (Dutournier), 14 r. Castiglione (1st) ✆ 01 42 86 82 8
Fax 01 42 86 07 71 – 📧. 🆎 ⓓ GB JCB
G
closed August, Saturday lunch and Sunday – **Meals** 295 and a la carte 490/700
Spec. Velouté de châtaignes à la truffe blanche (October-November). Langoustine
pimentées à la nougatine d'ail doux. Bœuf de Chalosse grillé, jus d'huîtres à la moelle

XXXX ✿ **Drouant,** pl. Gaillon (2nd) ✆ 01 42 65 15 16, *Fax 01 49 24 02 15,* « Home of the Ac
demie Goncourt since 1914 » see also **Café Drouant** – 📧. 🆎 ⓓ G
JCB
G 1
closed August – **Meals** 290/650 and a la carte 470/690 ♀
Spec. Arlequin de tourteau à la fleur de sel safranée. Blanc de barbue rôti aux truffes
noix fraîches (season). Poularde de Bresse, gâteau de foie blond, girolles et ravioles de céle
et raifort.

XXXX ✿✿ **Gérard Besson,** 5 r. Coq Héron (1st) ✆ 01 42 33 14 74, *Fax 01 42 33 85 71* – 📧.
ⓓ GB JCB
H 1
closed Saturday except dinner from September-June and Sunday – **Meals** 290 (lunch
460/580 and a la carte 460/630 ♀
Spec. Homard breton. Truffes (15 December-15 March). Gibier (season).

XXXX ✿ **Goumard,** 9 r. Duphot (1st) ✆ 01 42 60 36 07, *Fax 01 42 60 04 54* – 📶 📧. 🆎 ⓓ G
JCB
G 1
closed 8 to 23 August, Sunday and Monday – **Meals** - Seafood - (dinner a la carte onl
390 b.i. (lunch)/790 (dinner)and a la carte 430/730
Spec. Rémoulade de tourteau, vinaigrette de crustacés. Bar de ligne poêlé aux spaghet
à l'encre de seiche. Homard de Bretagne rôti.

XXX ✿ **Céladon** - Hôtel Westminster, 15 r. Daunou (2nd) ✆ 01 42 61 57 46, *Fax 01 42 60 30 6*
– 📧. 🆎 ⓓ GB JCB
G 1
closed August, Saturday, Sunday and Bank Holidays – **Meals** 260 (lunch)/290 and a la cart
360/570
Spec. Carpaccio de langoustines à la crème de caviar. Turbot rôti en cocotte, céleri rav
au parfum de truffe. Ananas "Victoria".

XXX **Macéo,** 15 r. Petits-Champs (1st) ✆ 01 42 96 98 89, *Fax 01 47 03 36 93* – 🆎 GB
🚫
G 1
closed Sunday – **Meals** 180 (lunch)/220 ♀.

XXX ✿ **Il Cortile** - Hôtel de Castille, 37 r. Cambon (1st) ✆ 01 44 58 45 67, *Fax 01 40 15 97 6*
🌿 – 🆎 ⓓ GB JCB
G 1
closed Saturday and Sunday – **Meals** - Italian rest. - a la carte 280/350
Spec. Cannelloni au homard, fine crème de fenouil (15 July 15 September). Piccata de vea
à la sauge. Palet "or" moelleux aux noisettes du Piémont.

XXX **Pierre " A la Fontaine Gaillon ",** pl. Gaillon (2nd) ✆ 01 47 42 63 22
Fax 01 47 42 82 84, 🌿 – 📧. 🆎 ⓓ GB JCB
G 1
closed August, Saturday lunch and Sunday – **Meals** 175 and a la carte 250/440.

XX ✿ **Pierre Au Palais Royal,** 10 r. Richelieu (1st) ✆ 01 42 96 09 17, *Fax 01 42 96 09 6*
– 📧. 🆎 ⓓ GB JCB
H 1
closed 24 December-2 January and Sunday – **Meals** a la carte 230/320 ♀
Spec. Quenelle de brochet à la lyonnaise. Escalope de foie gras de canard poêlée. Bœu
ficelle à la ménagère.

XX **Palais Royal,** 110 Galerie de Valois - Jardin du Palais Royal (1st) ✆ 01 40 20 00 2
Fax 01 40 20 00 82, 🌿, « Terrace in Palais Royal garden » – 🆎 ⓓ GB
JCB
G 1
closed 20 December-5 January, Saturday lunch and Sunday from October-April – **Mea**
a la carte 220/350 ♀.

XX **Chez Pauline,** 5 r. Villédo (1st) ✆ 01 42 96 20 70, Fax 01 49 27 99 89 – AE ① GB JCB
G 13
closed Saturday except dinner from October-April and Sunday – **Meals** 220 and a la carte 300/490 ⏣.

XX **Café Drouant,** pl. Galion (2nd) ✆ 01 42 65 15 16, Fax 01 49 24 02 15 – AE ① GB JCB
G 13
Meals 200 and a la carte 230/390 ⏣.

XX **Pays de Cocagne,** -Espace Tarn- 111 r. Réaumur (2nd) ✆ 01 40 13 81 81, Fax 01 40 13 87 70 – AE ① GB JCB
G 14
closed 1 to 22 August, Saturday lunch, Sunday and Bank Holidays – Meals 160 and a la carte 260/360 ⏣.

XX **Aristippe,** 8 r. J. J. Rousseau (1st) ✆ 01 42 60 08 80, Fax 01 43 60 11 13 – ▤. AE GB
closed 9 to 22 August, Saturday lunch and Sunday – **Meals** - Seafood - 170 (lunch)/220 and a la carte 190/300.

XX **Rôtisserie Monsigny,** 1 r. Monsigny (2nd) ✆ 01 42 96 16 61, Fax 01 42 97 40 97 – ▤. AE GB JCB
G 13
closed 10 to 20 August, lunch Saturday and Sunday – **Meals** 160 and a la carte 200/370 ⏣.

XX **Kinugawa,** 9 r. Mont-Thabor (1st) ✆ 01 42 60 65 07, Fax 01 42 60 45 21 – ▤. AE ① GB JCB. ✼
G 12
closed Christmas Holidays and Sunday – **Meals** - Japanese rest. - a la carte 190/400 ⏣.

XX **Au Pied de Cochon** (24 hr service), 6 r. Coquillière (1st) ✆ 01 40 13 77 00, Fax 01 40 13 77 09, 🌿, brasserie – 🍴 ▤. AE ① GB
H 14
Meals 178 b.i. and a la carte 170/370.

XX **Gallopin,** 40 r. N.-D.-des Victoires (2nd) ✆ 01 42 36 45 38, Fax 01 42 36 10 32, « Late 19C brasserie » – ▤. AE ① GB
G 14
closed Saturday lunch and Sunday – **Meals** 149 and a la carte 170/310 ⏣.

XX **Vaudeville,** 29 r. Vivienne (2nd) ✆ 01 40 20 04 62, Fax 01 49 27 08 78, brasserie – AE ① GB
G 14
Meals 132 b.i./179 b.i. and a la carte 180/250.

XX **Grand Colbert,** 2 r. Vivienne (2nd) ✆ 01 42 86 87 88, Fax 01 42 86 82 65, brasserie – AE ① GB JCB
G 13
Meals 155 and a la carte 200/290 ⚬.

XX **Gandhi,** 66 r. Ste-Anne (2nd) ✆ 01 47 03 41 00, Fax 01 49 10 03 73 – ▤. AE ① GB JCB
G 13
Meals - Indian rest. - 75 (lunch), 149/179 and a la carte 140/230 ⏣.

XX **Poquelin,** 17 r. Molière (1st) ✆ 01 42 96 22 19, Fax 01 42 96 05 72 – AE ① GB JCB
G 13
closed 1 to 20 August, Saturday lunch and Sunday – **Meals** 189 and a la carte 240/350 ⏣.

XX **Boutillier,** 46 R. Croix des Petits Champs (1st) ✆ 01 40 20 04 54, Fax 01 40 20 09 81 – ▤. AE GB
G 14
closed 1 to 29 August and Sunday – Meals 165 and a la carte 240/320 ⏣.

XX **Bonne Fourchette,** 320 r. St-Honoré, in the backyard (1st) ✆ 01 42 60 45 27 – ▤. ① GB. ✼
G 12
closed August, February Holidays, Sunday lunch and Saturday – **Meals** 130/170 and a la carte 200/320 ⏣.

XX **Saudade,** 34 r. Bourdonnais (1st) ✆ 01 42 36 30 71, Fax 01 42 36 27 77 – ▤. AE GB JCB. ✼
H 14
closed Sunday – **Meals** - Portuguese rest. - 129 (lunch)and a la carte 170/270.

X **A la Grille St-Honoré,** 15 pl. Marché St-Honoré (1st) ✆ 01 42 61 00 93, Fax 01 47 03 31 64, 🌿 – ▤. AE ① GB
G 12
closed 1 to 26 August, Sunday and Monday – **Meals** 180/250.

X **Bistrot St-Honoré,** 10 r. Gomboust (1st) ✆ 01 42 61 77 78, Fax 01 42 61 77 78 – AE GB JCB
G 13
closed 25 December-5 January, Saturday dinner and Sunday – **Meals** 130 and a la carte 190/350 ⏣.

X **Chez Georges,** 1 r. Mail (2nd) ✆ 01 42 60 07 11, bistro – AE GB
G 14
closed 1 to 23 August and Sunday – **Meals** a la carte 210/340.

X **Café Marly,** 93 r. Rivoli - Cour Napoléon (1st) ✆ 01 49 26 06 60, Fax 01 49 26 07 06, 🌿, « Original decor at the Louvre museum, terrace » – ▤. AE ① GB
H 13
Meals a la carte 210/260 ⏣.

X **L'Ardoise,** 28 r. Mont-Thabor (2nd) ✆ 01 42 96 28 18 – GB
AX 7
closed 17 to 24 May, 9 to 31 August, Christmas-New Year and Monday – Meals 165 ⏣.

✗ **Café Runtz,** 16 r. Favart (2nd) ☏ 01 42 96 69 86, *Fax 01 40 20 92 95*, bistro – AE ◑
GB
F 1
closed 8 to 16 May, 1 to 21 August, Saturday lunch and Sunday from April-September and Bank Holidays – **Meals** Alsatian rest. a la carte 160/260 ☼.

✗ **Willi's Wine Bar,** 13 r. Petits-Champs (1st) ☏ 01 42 61 05 09, *Fax 01 47 03 36 93*
GB
G 1
closed Sunday – **Meals** 148 (lunch)/185 ☼.

✗ **Ragueneau,** 202 r. St-Honoré (1st)-(1st floor) ☏ 01 42 61 29 76, *Fax 01 42 61 29 8*
– ▤. AE ◑ GB JCB
H 1
closed 1 to 30 August and Sunday – **Meals** 115/154 ☼.

✗ **Poule au Pot,** 9 r. Vauvilliers (1st) ☏ 01 42 36 32 96, *Fax 01 40 91 90 64*, bistro – GB
✀
H 1
closed Monday – **Meals** (dinner only) 160 and a la carte 200/300.

✗ **Relais Chablisien,** 4 r. B. Poirée (1st) ☏ 01 45 08 53 73, « 17C house » – ▤
GB
J 1
closed 1 to 22 August, Saturday and Sunday – **Meals** a la carte 170/240 ☼.

✗ **Chez la Vieille "Adrienne",** 1 r. Bailleul (1st) ☏ 01 42 60 15 78, *Fax 01 42 33 85 7*
– AE GB
H 1
closed August, Saturday, Sunday and dinner except Thursday – **Meals** (booking essentia 150 and a la carte approx. 300.

✗ **Souletin,** 6 r. Vrillière (1st) ☏ 01 42 61 43 78, *Fax 01 42 61 43 78*, bistro – GB   G 1
closed Saturday lunch, Sunday and Bank Holidays – **Meals** a la carte 160/240 ☼.

✗ **Lescure,** 7 r. Mondovi (1st) ☏ 01 42 60 18 91, bistro – GB   G 1
closed August, 23 December-1 January, Saturday and Sunday – **Meals** 100 b.i. and a carte 120/200 ☼.

✗ **Entre Ciel et Terre,** 5 r. Hérold (1st) ☏ 01 45 08 49 84, no smoking rest. – AE ◑
GB JCB
G 1
closed 24 July-22 August, Saturday and Sunday – **Meals** - Vegetarian rest. - 87 and a carte approx. 130.

Bastille,
République,
Hôtel de Ville.

3rd, 4th and 11th arrondissements.
3rd: ✉ *75003*
4th: ✉ *75004*
11th: ✉ *75011*

🏨 **Pavillon de la Reine** ⚘ without rest, 28 pl. Vosges (3rd) ☏ 01 40 29 19 19
Fax 01 40 29 19 20, « Fine decor » – ⧫ ▤ TV ☎ ⟷. AE ◑ GB JCB   J 1
⧖ 110 – **31 rm** 1850/2300, 14 suites, 10 duplex.

🏨 **Holiday Inn** M, 10 pl. République (11th) ☏ 01 43 55 44 34, *Fax 01 47 00 32 34* – ⧫
⟷ rm, ▤ TV ☎ &. – ⚒ 200. AE ◑ GB JCB   G 1
Belle Époque : **Meals** a la carte 170/300 – ⧖ 125 – **314 rm** 1995/2995
4 suites.

🏨 **Jeu de Paume** ⚘ without rest, 54 r. St-Louis-en-l'Île (4th) ☏ 01 43 26 14 18
Fax 01 40 46 02 76, « 17C tennis court » – ⧫ TV ☎ – ⚒ 30. AE ◑ GB JCB   K 1
⧖ 80 – **30 rm** 905/1525.

🏨 **Villa Beaumarchais** ⚘, 5 r. Arquebusiers (3rd) ☏ 01 40 29 14 00, *Fax 01 40 29 14 0*
– ⧫, ▤ rm, TV ☎ & – ⚒ 30. AE ◑ GB JCB   H 1
Meals *(closed August, Saturday and Sunday)* 145/185 ☼ – ⧖ 105 – **50 rm** 1600/2100

🏨 **Bretonnerie** without rest, 22 r. Ste-Croix-de-la-Bretonnerie (4th) ☏ 01 48 87 77 63
Fax 01 42 77 26 78 – ⧫ TV ☎. GB. ✀   J 1
closed 30 July-26 August – ⧖ 60 – **27 rm** 650/800, 3 suites.

🏨 **Caron de Beaumarchais** M without rest, 12 r. Vieille-du-Temple (4th
☏ 01 42 72 34 12, *Fax 01 42 72 34 63* – ⧫ ▤ TV ☎. AE ◑ GB JCB. ✀   J 1
⧖ 54 – **19 rm** 730/810.

🏨 **Beaubourg** without rest, 11 r. S. Le Franc (4th) ☏ 01 42 74 34 24, *Fax 01 42 78 68 1*
– ⧫ TV ☎. AE ◑ GB JCB. ✀   H 1
⧖ 40 – **28 rm** 490/690.

Verlain without rest, 97 r. St-Maur (11th) ✆ 01 43 57 44 88, Fax 01 43 57 32 06 – 📶
▦ 📺 ☎. AE ① GB JCB
🍽 45 – 38 rm 520/580.
G 19

Lutèce without rest, 65 r. St-Louis-en-l'Ile (4th) ✆ 01 43 26 23 52, Fax 01 43 29 60 25
– 📶 ▦ 📺 ☎. AE GB. ✺
🍽 53 – 23 rm 860/880.
K 16

Bel Air Ⓜ without rest, 5/7 r. Rampon (11th) ✆ 01 47 00 41 57, Fax 01 47 00 21 56
– 📶 📺 ☎. AE ① GB JCB. ✺
🍽 45 – 48 rm 550/620.
G 17

Rivoli Notre Dame without rest, 19 r. Bourg Tibourg (4th) ✆ 01 42 78 47 39,
Fax 01 40 29 07 00 – 📶 📺 ☎. AE ① GB JCB. ✺
🍽 45 – 31 rm 540/740.
J 16

Grand Prieuré without rest, 20 r. Grand Prieuré (11th) ✆ 01 47 00 74 14,
Fax 01 49 23 06 64 – 📺 ☎. AE ① GB JCB. ✺
🍽 30 – 32 rm 330/370.
G 17

Croix de Malte Ⓜ without rest, 5 r. Malte (11th) ✆ 01 48 05 09 36, Fax 01 43 57 02 54
– 📶, ✺ rm, 📺 ☎. AE ① GB JCB
🍽 45 – 29 rm 540/600.
H 17

Nice without rest, 42 bis r. Rivoli (4th) ✆ 01 42 78 55 29, Fax 01 42 78 36 07 – 📶 📺
☎. GB. ✺
🍽 35 – 23 rm 380/500.
J 16

Beauséjour Ⓜ without rest, 71 av. Parmentier (11th) ✆ 01 47 00 38 16,
Fax 01 43 55 47 89 – 📶 📺 ☎. AE ① GB JCB
🍽 30 – 31 rm 300/380.
H 18

L'Ambroisie (Pacaud), 9 pl. des Vosges (4th) ✆ 01 42 78 51 45 – ▦. AE GB.
✺
J 17
closed 1 to 23 August, February Holidays, Sunday and Monday – **Meals** a la carte 750/1 200
Spec. Feuillantine de langoustines au curry. Agneau en nougatine, ragoût de cocos à la
sauge. Dacquoise au praliné.

Miravile, 72 quai Hôtel de Ville (4th) ✆ 01 42 74 72 22, Fax 01 42 74 67 55 – ▦. AE
GB
J 15
closed 5 to 25 August, Saturday lunch and Sunday – **Meals** 250/450 b.i. and a la carte
330/430.

Ambassade d'Auvergne, 22 r. Grenier St-Lazare (3rd) ✆ 01 42 72 31 22,
Fax 01 42 78 85 47 – ▦. AE GB JCB
H 15
closed Sunday in July-August – **Meals** 160 and a la carte 190/300 ♀.

Benoît, 20 r. St-Martin (4th) ✆ 01 42 72 25 76, Fax 01 42 72 45 68, bistro – ▦.
AE
J 15
closed August – **Meals** 200 (lunch)and a la carte 330/440 ♀
Spec. Ballottine de canard au foie gras.Saint-Jacques au naturel (October-April). Cassoulet
maison.

Bofinger, 5 r. Bastille (4th) ✆ 01 42 72 87 82, Fax 01 42 72 97 68, brasserie, « Belle
Epoque decor » – ▦. AE ① GB JCB
J 17
Meals 119 b.i. (lunch)/178 b.i. and a la carte 180/250.

L'Aiguière, 37bis r. Montreuil (11th) ✆ 01 43 72 42 32, Fax 01 43 72 96 36 – AE ① GB
JCB
K 20
closed Saturday lunch, Sunday and Bank Holidays – **Meals** 138 b.i./280 b.i. (except dinner
Fri. and Sat.)and a la carte 250/340.

A Sousceyrac, 35 r. Faidherbe (11th) ✆ 01 43 71 65 30, Fax 01 40 09 79 75 – ▦. ①
GB
J 19
closed August, Saturday lunch and Sunday – **Meals** 185 and a la carte 220/340 ♀.

L'Excuse, 14 r. Charles V (4th) ✆ 01 42 77 98 97, Fax 01 42 77 88 55 – AE GB
JCB
J 16
closed 2 to 22 August and Sunday – **Meals** 120 b.i. (lunch)/185 and a la carte 270/360
♀.

Vin et Marée, 276 bd Voltaire (11th) ✆ 01 43 72 31 23, Fax 01 40 09 05 24 – ▦. AE
GB
K 21
Meals - Seafood - a la carte 170/250 ♀.

Blue Elephant, 43 r. Roquette (11th) ✆ 01 47 00 42 00, Fax 01 47 00 45 44, « Typical
decor » – ▦. AE ① GB
J 18
closed Saturday lunch – **Meals** - Thai rest. - 150 (lunch), 275/300 and a la carte 180/270
♀.

L'Alisier, 26 r. Montmorency (3rd) ✆ 01 42 72 31 04, Fax 01 42 72 74 83 – AE GB.
✺
H 16
closed August, Saturday and Sunday – **Meals** 145 (lunch)/195.

XX **Péché Mignon,** 5 r. Guillaume Bertrand (11th) ☎ 01 43 57 68 68 – **GB**   H 1
closed August, Sunday dinner and Monday – **Meals** 149.

XX **Les Amognes,** 243 r. Fg St-Antoine (11th) ☎ 01 43 72 73 05, Fax 01 43 28 77 23
GB   K 2
closed 1 to 23 August, Monday lunch, Saturday lunch and Sunday – **Meals** 200 ♀.

XX **Repaire de Cartouche,** 99 r. Amelot (11th) ☎ 01 47 00 25 86 – ▣. **GB**   H 1
closed 15 July-15 August, Sunday and Monday – **Meals** a la carte 150/240 ♀.

X **Bistrot du Dôme,** 2 r. Bastille (4th) ☎ 01 48 04 88 44, Fax 01 48 04 00 59 – ▣. ▣
GB   J 1
Meals - Seafood - a la carte 180/280 ♀.

X **Petit Bofinger,** 6 r. Bastille (4th) ☎ 01 42 72 05 23, Fax 01 42 72 04 94 – ▣. **AE** ◐
GB   J 1
Meals 95 b.i. (lunch)/138 b.i. and a la carte 120/180.

X **Chardenoux,** 1 r. J. Vallès (11th) ☎ 01 43 71 49 52, bistrot, « Early 20C decor » – ▣
◐ **GB**   K 2
closed August, Saturday lunch and Sunday – **Meals** a la carte 160/340 ♀.

X **Mansouria,** 11 r. Faidherbe (11th) ☎ 01 43 71 00 16, Fax 01 40 24 21 97 – ▣. ◐ **GB**
⊗   K 1
closed Monday lunch and Sunday – **Meals** Moroccan rest. 182 and a la carte 180/250

X **Au Bascou,** 38 r. Réaumur (3rd) ☎ 01 42 72 69 25, bistro – **AE** **GB**   G 1
closed in August, Christmas-New Year, Saturday lunch and Sunday – **Meals** a la cart
180/220 ♀.

X **Grizzli,** 7 r. St-Martin (4th) ☎ 01 48 87 77 56, ⌂, bistro – **AE** **GB** **JCB**   J 1
closed Sunday – **Meals** 120 (lunch)/160 and a la carte 170/310 ♀.

X **Astier,** 44 r. J.-P. Timbaud (11th) ☎ 01 43 57 16 35, bistro – **GB**   G 1
closed spring Holidays, 22 July-25 August, Christmas-New Year, Saturday and Sunday
Meals (booking essential) 115 (lunch)/140.

X **Monde des Chimères,** 69 r. St-Louis-en-l'Ile (4th) ☎ 01 43 54 45 27
Fax 01 43 29 84 88 – **GB**   K 1
closed Sunday and Monday – **Meals** 89 (lunch)/160 and a la carte 270/390.

X **Clos du Vert Bois,** 13 r. Vert Bois (3rd) ☎ 01 42 77 14 85 – **GB**   G 1
closed 1 to 25 August, Saturday lunch and Monday dinner – **Meals** 81 (lunch), 127/17
b.i. and a la carte 210/350 ♀.

X **Anjou-Normandie,** 13 r. Folie-Méricourt (11th) ☎ 01 47 00 30 59, Fax 01 47 00 30 5
– **GB**. ⊗   H 1
closed Saturday and Sunday – **Meals** (lunch only) 150 and a la carte 150/250 ♀.

X **Les Fernandises,** 19 r. Fontaine au Roi (11th) ☎ 01 48 06 16 96, bistro – **GB**   G 1
closed 2 to 23 August, Sunday and Monday – **Meals** 100 (lunch)/130 and a la cart
150/270 ♀.

Quartier Latin, Luxembourg, Jardin des Plantes.

5th and 6th arrondissements.
5th: ✉ 75005
6th: ✉ 75006

🏨 **Lutétia,** 45 bd Raspail (6th) ☎ 01 49 54 46 46, Fax 01 49 54 46 00 – ▯, ⇔ rm, ▣ ⓣ
☎ – 🔔 300. **AE** ◐ **GB** **JCB**   K 1
see *Paris* below - *Brasserie Lutétia* ☎ 01 49 54 46 76 **Meals** 195/205 ♀ – ☕ 135
220 rm 1800/2300, 30 suites.

🏨 **Relais Christine** **M** ⊗ without rest, 3 r. Christine (6th) ☎ 01 40 51 60 80
Fax 01 40 51 60 81, « Elegant decor » – ▯, ⇔ rm, ▣ ⓣ ☎ ⇔. **AE** ◐ **GB**
JCB   J 14
☕ 110 – **35 rm** 1850/2300, 16 duplex.

🏨🏨🏨 **Relais St-Germain** M without rest, 9 carrefour de l'Odéon (6th) ℰ 01 44 27 07 97, *Fax 01 46 33 45 30*, « Attractive interior » – |≩| kitchenette ▤ TV ☎. AE ⓪ GB
JCB K 13
22 rm ⌷ 1290/2050.

🏨🏨🏨 **Relais Médicis** M without rest, 23 r. Racine (6th) ℰ 01 43 26 00 60, *Fax 01 40 46 83 39* – |≩| ▤ TV ☎. AE ⓪ GB JCB. ※ K 13
16 rm ⌷ 1290/1595.

🏨🏨🏨 **Aubusson** without rest, 33 r. Dauphine (6e) ℰ 01 43 29 43 43, *Fax 01 43 29 12 62* – |≩|, ⇔ rm, ▤ TV ☎ ৬. AE GB BX 9
⌷ 95 – 50 rm 1350/2000.

🏨🏨🏨 **L'Abbaye** ॐ without rest, 10 r. Cassette (6th) ℰ 01 45 44 38 11, *Fax 01 45 48 07 86* – |≩| ▤ TV ☎. AE GB. ※ K 12
42 rm ⌷ 1100/1650, 4 duplex.

🏨🏨🏨 **Left Bank St-Germain** without rest, 9 r. Ancienne Comédie (6th) ℰ 01 43 54 01 70, *Fax 01 43 26 17 14* – |≩| ▤ TV ☎ ৬. AE ⓪ GB JCB. ※ K 13
31 rm ⌷ 980/1200.

🏨🏨🏨 **Victoria Palace** without rest, 6 r. Blaise-Desgoffe (6th) ℰ 01 45 49 70 00, *Fax 01 45 49 23 75* – |≩|, ⇔ rm, TV ☎ ৬ ⇔ – 🛃 30. AE ⓪ GB JCB L 11
⌷ 95 – 79 rm 1300/2200.

🏨🏨🏨 **Madison** M without rest, 143 bd St-Germain (6th) ℰ 01 40 51 60 00, *Fax 01 40 51 60 01*, « Fine furniture » – |≩| ▤ TV ☎. AE ⓪ GB JCB J 13
54 rm ⌷ 800/1600.

🏨🏨🏨 **Holiday Inn Saint-Germain-des-Prés** M without rest, 92 r. Vaugirard (6th) ℰ 01 42 22 00 56, *Fax 01 42 22 05 39* – |≩|, ⇔ rm, ▤ TV ☎ ৬ ⇔ – 🛃 50. AE ⓪
GB JCB L 12
⌷ 80 – 134 rm 1095/1275.

🏨🏨🏨 **Angleterre** without rest, 44 r. Jacob (6th) ℰ 01 42 60 34 72, *Fax 01 42 60 16 93* – |≩|
TV ☎. AE ⓪ GB JCB. ※ J 13
⌷ 60 – 23 rm 750/1200, 4 suites.

🏨🏨🏨 **Ste-Beuve** M without rest, 9 r. Ste-Beuve (6th) ℰ 01 45 48 20 07, *Fax 01 45 48 67 52* – |≩| TV ☎. AE GB JCB. ※ L 12
⌷ 90 – 22 rm 760/1810.

🏨🏨🏨 **Littré** without rest, 9 r. Littré (6th) ℰ 01 45 44 38 68, *Fax 01 45 44 88 13* – |≩| TV ☎ – 🛃 25. AE ⓪ GB JCB. ※ L 11
⌷ 70 – 88 rm 1100/1650, 3 suites.

🏨🏨🏨 **St-Grégoire** M without rest, 43 r. Abbé Grégoire (6th) ℰ 01 45 48 23 23, *Fax 01 45 48 33 95* – |≩| ▤ TV ☎. AE ⓪ GB JCB. ※ L 12
⌷ 60 – 20 rm 1090/1490.

🏨🏨🏨 **Villa** M without rest, 29 r. Jacob (6th) ℰ 01 43 26 60 00, *Fax 01 46 34 63 63*, « Contemporary decor » – |≩|, ⇔ rm, ▤ TV ☎. AE ⓪ GB JCB. ※ J 13
⌷ 80 – 28 rm 900/2000, 4 suites.

🏨🏨🏨 **Alliance St-Germain-des-Prés** M without rest, 7-11 r. St-Benoit (6th) ℰ 01 42 61 53 53, *Fax 01 49 27 09 33* – |≩| ▤ TV ☎ ৬. AE ⓪ GB JCB J 13
⌷ 75 – 117 rm 1750/1850.

🏨🏨 **St-Germain-des-Prés** without rest, 36 r. Bonaparte (6th) ℰ 01 43 26 00 19, *Fax 01 40 46 83 63* – |≩| ▤ TV ☎. AE GB J 13
⌷ 50 – 30 rm 750/1350.

🏨🏨 **Rives de Notre-Dame** M without rest, 15 quai St-Michel (5th) ℰ 01 43 54 81 16, *Fax 01 43 26 27 09*, ⋖, « 16C house, Provencal decor » – |≩|, ⇔ rm, ▤ TV ☎. AE ⓪
GB JCB J 14
⌷ 65 – 10 rm 1100/2500.

🏨🏨 **Ferrandi** without rest, 92 r. Cherche-Midi (6th) ℰ 01 42 22 97 40, *Fax 01 45 44 89 97* – |≩| ▤ TV ☎. AE ⓪ GB JCB L 11
⌷ 65 – 42 rm 580/1280.

🏨🏨 **Villa des Artistes** M ॐ without rest, 9 r. Grande Chaumière (6th) ℰ 01 43 26 60 86, *Fax 01 43 54 73 70* – |≩| TV ☎. AE ⓪ GB JCB. ※ L 12
⌷ 50 – 59 rm 1200.

🏨🏨 **Régent** M without rest, 61 r. Dauphine (6th) ℰ 01 46 34 59 80, *Fax 01 40 51 05 07* – |≩| ▤ TV ☎. AE ⓪ GB JCB. ※ J 13
⌷ 60 – 25 rm 750/1100.

🏨🏨 **Buci** M without rest, 6 r. Buci (6th) ℰ 01 55 42 74 74, *Fax 01 55 42 74 44* – |≩| TV ☎ ৬. AE ⓪ GB JCB. ※ J 13
⌷ 90 – 24 rm 1250/1850.

Relais St-Jacques without rest, 3 r. Abbé de l'Épée (5th) ℘ 01 53 73 26 00
Fax 01 43 26 17 81 – 🛗 🖥 📺 ☎. AE ① GB JCB. ⚡
🍵 70 – **23 rm** 1135/1365.   L 1

Résidence Henri IV Ⓜ without rest, 50 r. Bernardins (5th) ℘ 01 44 41 31 81
Fax 01 46 33 93 22 – 🛗 kitchenette 📺 ☎. AE ① GB   K 1
🍵 40 – **8 rm** 700/900, 5 suites.

Odéon Hôtel Ⓜ without rest, 3 r. Odéon (6th) ℘ 01 43 25 90 67, Fax 01 43 25 55 9
– 🛗 🖥 📺 ☎. AE ① GB JCB. ⚡   K 1
🍵 60 – **33 rm** 756/1412.

Fleurie without rest, 32 r. Grégoire de Tours (6th) ℘ 01 53 73 70 00, Fax 01 53 73 70 2
– 🛗 🖥 📺 ☎. AE ① GB. ⚡   K 1
🍵 50 – **29 rm** 700/1200.

Grand Hôtel St-Michel without rest, 19 r. Cujas (5th) ℘ 01 46 33 33 02
Fax 01 40 46 96 33 – 🛗 🖥 📺 ☎. AE ① GB JCB. ⚡   K 1
🍵 55 – **38 rm** 690/890, 7 suites.

Saints-Pères without rest, 65 r. Sts-Pères (6th) ℘ 01 45 44 50 00, Fax 01 45 44 90 8
– 🛗 📺 ☎. AE GB. ⚡   J 1
🍵 60 – **36 rm** 650/1250, 3 suites.

Select Ⓜ without rest, 1 pl. Sorbonne (5th) ℘ 01 46 34 14 80, Fax 01 46 34 51 79
🛗 📺 ☎. AE ① GB JCB   K 1
🍵 40 – **68 rm** 670/920.

Panthéon without rest, 19 pl. Panthéon (5th) ℘ 01 43 54 32 95, Fax 01 43 26 64 6
– 🛗 🖥 📺 ☎. AE ① GB JCB. ⚡   L 1
🍵 50 – **34 rm** 800/1000.

Grands Hommes without rest, 17 pl. Panthéon (5th) ℘ 01 46 34 19 60
Fax 01 43 26 67 32, ← – 🛗 🖥 📺 ☎. AE ① GB JCB   L 1
🍵 50 – **32 rm** 700/900.

Sully St-Germain Ⓜ without rest, 31 r. Écoles (5th) ℘ 01 43 26 56 02
Fax 01 43 29 74 42, ⚑ – 🛗, ⚡ rm, 🖥 📺 ☎. AE ① GB JCB. ⚡   K 1
🍵 50 – **58 rm** 750/1200.

Relais St-Sulpice Ⓜ ⚘ without rest, 3 r. Garancière (6th) ℘ 01 46 33 99 00
Fax 01 46 33 00 10 – 🛗, ⚡ rm, 🖥 📺 ☎ &. AE ① GB JCB. ⚡   K 1
🍵 50 – **26 rm** 930/1130.

Royal St-Michel Ⓜ without rest, 3 bd St-Michel (5th) ℘ 01 44 07 06 06
Fax 01 44 07 36 25 – 🛗 🖥 📺 ☎. AE ① GB JCB   K 1
🍵 60 – **39 rm** 990/1160.

Belloy St-Germain Ⓜ without rest, 2 r. Racine (6th) ℘ 01 46 34 26 50
Fax 01 46 34 66 18 – 🛗 📺 ☎. AE GB JCB   K 1
🍵 50 – **50 rm** 690/910.

Jardins du Luxembourg Ⓜ ⚘ without rest, 5 imp. Royer-Collard (5th
℘ 01 40 46 08 88, Fax 01 40 46 02 28 – 🛗, ⚡ rm, 🖥 📺 ☎ &. AE ① GB JCB
⚡   L 1
🍵 50 – **26 rm** 795/840.

Au Manoir St-Germain-des-Prés without rest, 153 bd St-Germain (6th
℘ 01 42 22 21 65, Fax 01 45 48 22 25 – 🛗 🖥 📺 ☎. AE ① GB JCB. ⚡   J 1
32 rm 🍵 850/1300.

de l'Odéon without rest, 13 r. St-Sulpice (6th) ℘ 01 43 25 70 11, Fax 01 43 29 97 34
« 16C house » – 🛗 🖥 📺 ☎. AE ① GB JCB   K 1
🍵 58 – **29 rm** 700/1050.

Jardin de l'Odéon Ⓜ without rest, 7 r. Casimir Delavigne (6th) ℘ 01 46 34 23 90
Fax 01 43 25 28 12 – 🛗 📺 ☎ &. AE GB   K 1
🍵 55 – **41 rm** 665/1050.

Clos Médicis Ⓜ without rest, 56 r. Monsieur Le Prince (6th) ℘ 01 43 29 10 80
Fax 01 43 54 26 90 – 🛗 🖥 📺 ☎ &. AE ① GB JCB   K 1
🍵 60 – **38 rm** 1200.

Parc St-Séverin without rest, 22 r. Parcheminerie (5th) ℘ 01 43 54 32 17
Fax 01 43 54 70 71 – 🛗 📺 ☎. AE ① GB JCB. ⚡   K 1
🍵 50 – **27 rm** 510/1540.

St-Christophe without rest, 17 r. Lacépède (5th) ℘ 01 43 31 81 54
Fax 01 43 31 12 54 – 🛗 📺 ☎. AE ① GB   L 1
🍵 50 – **31 rm** 550/600.

Notre Dame without rest, 1 quai St-Michel (5th) ℘ 01 43 54 20 43, Fax 01 43 26 61 75
← – 🛗 📺 ☎. AE ① GB JCB   K 1
🍵 40 – **23 rm** 630/830, 3 duplex.

Jardin de Cluny without rest, 9 r. Sommerard (5th) ☏ 01 43 54 22 66, Fax 01 40 51 03 36 – 📶 📺 ☎. 🆑 ⓞ 🆖 🇯🇨🇧. 🛇
☕ 50 – **40 rm** 710/1300. — **K 14**

Millésime Hôtel without rest, 15 r. Jacob (6th) ☏ 01 44 07 97 97, Fax 01 46 34 55 97 – 📶 🖿 📺 ☎ &. 🆑 🆖. 🛇
☕ 60 – **21 rm** 850/1100. — **J 13**

Marronniers ⟨S⟩ without rest, 21 r. Jacob (6th) ☏ 01 43 25 30 60, Fax 01 40 46 83 56 – 📶 🖿 📺 ☎. 🆖. 🛇
☕ 55 – **37 rm** 755/985. — **J 13**

St-Jacques without rest, 35 r. Écoles (5th) ☏ 01 44 07 45 45, Fax 01 43 25 65 50 – 📶 📺 ☎. 🆑 ⓞ 🆖 🇯🇨🇧. 🛇
☕ 35 – **35 rm** 365/580. — **K 15**

California without rest, 32 r. Écoles (5th) ☏ 01 46 34 12 90, Fax 01 46 34 75 52 – 📶 📺 ☎. 🆑 ⓞ 🆖. 🛇
☕ 50 – **44 rm** 700/1200. — **K 14-15**

Sèvres Azur without rest, 22 r. Abbé-Grégoire (6th) ☏ 01 45 48 84 07, Fax 01 42 84 01 55 – 📶 📺 ☎. 🆑 ⓞ 🆖 🇯🇨🇧
☕ 38 – **31 rm** 445/530. — **K 11-12**

Familia without rest, 11 r. Écoles (5th) ☏ 01 43 54 55 27, Fax 01 43 29 61 77 – 📶 📺 ☎. 🆑 ⓞ 🆖. 🛇
☕ 38 – **30 rm** 390/550. — **K-L 15**

Albe without rest, 1 r. Harpe (5th) ☏ 01 46 34 09 70, Fax 01 40 46 85 70 – 📶, 🛇 rm, 📺 ☎. 🆑 ⓞ 🆖 🇯🇨🇧. 🛇
☕ 50 – **45 rm** 580/850. — **K 14**

Pierre Nicole without rest, 39 r. Pierre Nicole (5th) ☏ 01 43 54 76 86, Fax 01 43 54 22 45 – 📶 ☎. 🆑 ⓞ 🆖 🇯🇨🇧. 🛇
☕ 35 – **33 rm** 350/450. — **M 13**

Sorbonne without rest, 6 r. Victor Cousin (5th) ☏ 01 43 54 58 08, Fax 01 40 51 05 18 – 📶 📺 ☎. 🆑 🆖 🇯🇨🇧
☕ 35 – **37 rm** 430/510. — **K 14**

Tour d'Argent (Terrail), 15 quai Tournelle (5th) ☏ 01 43 54 23 31, Fax 01 44 07 12 04, ≤ Notre-Dame, « Small museum showing the development of eating utensils. In the cellar : an illustrated history of wine » – 🖿. 🆑 ⓞ 🆖 🇯🇨🇧 — **K 16**
closed Monday – **Meals** 350 (lunch)and a la carte 740/990
Spec. Quenelles de brochet "André Terrail". Caneton "Tour d'Argent". Crêpes "Belle Époque".

Jacques Cagna, 14 r. Grands Augustins (6th) ☏ 01 43 26 49 39, Fax 01 43 54 54 48, « Old Parisian house » – 🖿. 🆑 ⓞ 🆖 🇯🇨🇧 — **J 14**
closed 1 to 24 August, 20 to 27 December, Saturday lunch, Monday lunch and Sunday – **Meals** 270 (lunch)/490 and a la carte 420/640
Spec. Langoustines rôties, piperade de légumes aux aromates, sauce mousseuse au homard et thym citron. Coquilles St-Jacques (season). Côte de veau de lait au gingembre et citron vert.

Paris - Hôtel Lutétia, 45 bd Raspail (6th) ☏ 01 49 54 46 90, Fax 01 49 54 46 00, « "Art Deco" decor » – 🖿. 🆑 ⓞ 🆖 🇯🇨🇧 — **K 12**
closed 30 July-30 August, Saturday, Sunday and Bank Holidays – **Meals** 290 (lunch), 390/580 and a la carte 410/580
Spec. Cannelloni de foie gras de canard à la truffe noire. Turbot cuit dans le sel de Guérande et algues. "Tout chocolat".

Relais Louis XIII (Martinez), 8 r. Grands Augustins (6th) ☏ 01 43 26 75 96, Fax 01 44 07 07 80, « Historical house, 16C cellar » – 🖿. 🆑 🆖 🇯🇨🇧 — **J 14**
closed 2 to 23 August, Monday lunch and Sunday – **Meals** 195 (lunch)/280 and a la carte 330/450 ♀
Spec. Soufflé de poularde au ris de veau et écrevisses (September-December). Double côte de veau de lait à l'estragon. Millefeuille tiède à la vanille.

Closerie des Lilas, 171 bd Montparnasse (6th) ☏ 01 40 51 34 50, Fax 01 43 29 99 94, 🌳, « Former literary café » – 🆑 ⓞ 🆖 🇯🇨🇧 — **M 13**
Meals 250 b.i. (lunch), 350/450 and a la carte 320/460 ♀ - **Brasserie :** Meals 180 b.i./300 b.i. and a la carte 200/280.

Procope, 13 r. Ancienne Comédie (6th) ☏ 01 40 46 79 00, Fax 01 40 46 79 09, « Former 18C literary café » – 🖿. 🆑 ⓞ 🆖 — **K 13**
Meals 109 (lunch)/178 and a la carte 210/360.

Yugaraj, 14 r. Dauphine (6th) ☏ 01 43 26 44 91, Fax 01 46 33 50 77 – 🖿. 🆑 ⓞ 🆖 🇯🇨🇧. 🛇 — **J 14**
closed Monday lunch – **Meals** - Indian rest. - 130 (lunch), 180/220 and a la carte 220/270.

XX **Mavrommatis,** 42 r. Daubenton (5th) ℰ 01 43 31 17 17, Fax 01 43 36 13 08 – 🗏. GB
🐟
M 1
closed Monday – **Meals** - Greek rest. - 120 (lunch)/160 and a la carte 180/270.

XX **Chez Maître Paul,** 12 r. Monsieur-le-Prince (6th) ℰ 01 43 54 74 59, Fax 01 46 34 58 3
– 🗏. AE ① GB
K 1
closed Monday lunch and Sunday in July-August – Meals 165 and a la carte 220/330

XX **Truffière,** 4 r. Blainville (5th) ℰ 01 46 33 29 82, Fax 01 46 33 64 74, « 17C house »
🗏. AE ① GB JCB. 🐟
L 1
closed Monday – **Meals** 110 (lunch)and a la carte 220/280.

XX **Chat Grippé,** 87 r. Assas (6th) ℰ 01 43 54 70 00, Fax 01 43 26 42 05 – 🗏. AE GB
🐟
LM 1
closed August, Saturday lunch, Sunday lunch and Monday – **Meals** 140 (lunch), 200/28
and a la carte 240/310.

XX **Alcazar,** 62 r.Mazarine (6th) ℰ 01 53 10 19 99, Fax 01 53 10 23 23, « Original conten
porary decor » – 🗏. AE ① GB JCB
J 1
Meals a la carte 200/410 ♀.

XX **Marty,** 20 av. Gobelins (5th) ℰ 01 43 31 39 51, Fax 01 43 37 63 70, brasserie, « 193
decor » – AE ① GB JCB
M 1
Meals 139/198 and a la carte 140/210 ♀.

XX **Inagiku,** 14 r. Pontoise (5th) ℰ 01 43 54 70 07, Fax 01 40 51 74 44 – 🗏
GB
K 1
closed 10 to 20 August and Sunday – **Meals** - Japanese rest. - 88 (lunch), 148/348 ar
a la carte 240/300.

XX **Bastide Odéon,** 7 r. Corneille (6th) ℰ 01 43 26 03 65, Fax 01 44 07 28 93 – AE GB. 🐟
closed 1 to 23 August, Christmas-New Year, Sunday and Monday – **Meals** 190 ♀.   K 1

XX **Rond de Serviette,** 97 r. Cherche-Midi (6th) ℰ 01 45 44 01 02, Fax 01 42 22 50
– 🗏. AE ① GB JCB
L 1
closed 29 July-24 August, Saturday lunch and Sunday – **Meals** 138 b.i. (lunch), 178/27
b.i. ♀.

XX **Catalogne,** 6 cour du Commerce (6th) ℰ 01 55 42 16 19, Fax 01 55 42 16 33 – AE ①
GB
K 1
Meals Catalan rest. 180/200 ♀.

XX **Chez Toutoune,** 5 r. Pontoise (5th) ℰ 01 43 26 56 81, Fax 01 40 46 80 34 – AE GB K 1
closed Monday lunch – **Meals** 188/198 ♀.

XX **Atelier Maître Albert,** 1 r. Maître Albert (5th) ℰ 01 46 33 13 78, Fax 01 44 07 01 8
– 🗏. AE GB
K 1
closed Monday lunch, Sunday and Bank Holidays – **Meals** 190/250 b.i..

XX **Les Brézolles,** 5 r. Mabillon (6th) ℰ 01 53 10 16 10, Fax 01 56 24 98 59 – GB
closed August, Monday lunch, Sunday and Bank Holidays – **Meals** 195 ♀.

X **Campagne et Provence,** 25 quai Tournelle (5th) ℰ 01 43 54 05 1
Fax 01 43 29 74 93 – 🗏. GB
K 1
closed Sunday and lunch Saturday and Monday – **Meals** 220.

X **Bouillon Racine,** 3 r. Racine (6th) ℰ 01 44 32 15 60, Fax 01 44 32 15 61, brasseri
« "Art Nouveau" decor » – 🗏. AE GB
K 1
Meals 107 (lunch)/169 and a la carte 180/270 ♀.

X **Les Bouchons de François Clerc,** 12 r. Hôtel Colbert (5th) ℰ 01 43 54 15 3
Fax 01 46 34 68 07, « Old Parisian house » – 🗏. AE GB
K 1
closed Saturday lunch and Sunday – **Meals** 227.

X **Les Bookinistes,** 53 quai Grands Augustins (6th) ℰ 01 43 25 45 9
Fax 01 43 25 23 07 – 🗏. AE ① GB JCB
J 1
closed lunch Saturday and Sunday – **Meals** 160 (lunch)and a la carte 210/280 ♀.

X **Dominique,** 19 r. Bréa (6th) ℰ 01 43 27 08 80, Fax 01 43 26 88 35 – 🗏. AE ① G
JCB
L 1
closed 18 July-18 August and Sunday – **Meals** - Russian rest. - (dinner only) 175 and a
carte 240/290 ♀.

X **L'O à la Bouche,** 157 bd Montparnasse (6th) ℰ 01 43 26 26 53, Fax 01 43 26 43 4
– GB
M 1
closed 10 to 17 April, 1 to 22 August, 1 to 8 January, Sunday and Monday – **Meals** 13
(lunch), 190/255 ♀.

X **Rotonde,** 105 bd Montparnasse (6th) ℰ 01 43 26 48 26, Fax 01 46 34 52 40, brasser
– 🗏. AE GB JCB
L 1
Meals 180/300 and a la carte 280/350 ♀.

X **Rôtisserie d'en Face,** 2 r. Christine (6th) ℰ 01 43 26 40 98, Fax 01 43 54 54 48 – 🗏
AE ① GB JCB
J 1
closed Saturday lunch and Sunday – **Meals** 159 (lunch)/210 ♀.

X **Rôtisserie du Beaujolais,** 19 quai Tournelle (5th) ✆ 01 43 54 17 47, Fax 01 44 07 12 04 – 🖭. **GB**
K 15
closed Monday – **Meals** a la carte 160/230.

X **Bistrot d'Alex,** 2 r. Clément (6th) ✆ 01 43 54 09 53, Fax 01 43 25 77 66 – 🖭. **AE GB** JCB
K 13
closed 8 to 16 August, 24 December-2 January, Saturday lunch and Sunday – **Meals** 140/170 and a la carte 160/240.

X **Joséphine "Chez Dumonet",** 117 r. Cherche Midi (6th) ✆ 01 45 48 52 40, Fax 01 42 84 06 83, bistro – **AE GB**
L 11
closed August, Saturday and Sunday – a la carte 210/350 - **Charroi** ✆ 01 42 22 81 19 (closed July, Sunday from 03-09, Tuesday from 10-03 and Monday) **Meals** a la carte approx. 160.

X **L'Épi Dupin,** 11 r. Dupin (6th) ✆ 01 42 22 64 56, Fax 01 42 22 30 42 – **AE GB**
K 12
closed Saturday and Sunday – **Meals** (booking essential) 165 ♀.

X **Bauta,** 129 bd Montparnasse (6th) ✆ 01 43 22 52 35, Fax 01 43 22 10 99 – 🖭. **GB**. ⊗
M 12
closed Saturday lunch and Sunday – **Meals** - Italian rest. - 149 b.i. (lunch), 250 b.i./300 b.i. and a la carte 230/320.

X **Cafetière,** 21 r. Mazarine (6th) ✆ 01 46 33 76 90, Fax 01 43 25 76 90 – **GB** J 13
closed 9 to 30 August, 24 December-5 January, Sunday and Monday – **Meals** - Italian rest. - a la carte 200/300 ♀.

X **Allard,** 41 r. St-André-des-Arts (6th) ✆ 01 43 26 48 23, Fax 01 46 33 04 02, bistro – 🖭. **AE ① GB** JCB
K 14
closed 1 to 23 August and Sunday – **Meals** 200 and a la carte 260/390.

X **L'Espadon Bleu,** 25 r. Grands Augustins (6th) ✆ 01 46 33 00 85 – 🖭. **AE GB** JCB J 14
closed Saturday lunch, Sunday lunch and Monday – **Meals** - Seafood - 165 (lunch)/195 and a la carte 220/480 ♀.

X **Au Moulin à Vent "Chez Henri",** 20 r. Fossés-St-Bernard (5th) ✆ 01 43 54 99 37, bistrot – **GB** JCB. ⊗
K 15
closed August, Sunday and Monday – **Meals** a la carte 240/320.

X **Balzar,** 49 r. Écoles (5th) ✆ 01 43 54 13 67, Fax 01 44 07 14 91, brasserie – 🖭. **AE GB**
K 14
Meals a la carte 150/250 ♀.

X **Moissonnier,** 28 r. Fossés-St-Bernard (5th) ✆ 01 43 29 87 65, bistro – **GB** K 15
closed 1 to 23 August, Sunday dinner and Monday – **Meals** 150 and a la carte 190/290.

X **Reminet,** 3 r. Grands Degrés (5th) ✆ 01 44 07 04 24, Fax 01 44 07 17 37 – **AE GB** K 15
closed 16 to 31 August, 4 to 24 January, Tuesday lunch and Monday – **Meals** 85 (lunch)/110 ♀.

X **Palanquin,** 12 r. Princesse (6th) ✆ 01 43 29 77 66 – **GB**
K 13
closed Sunday – **Meals** - Vietnamese rest. - 70 (lunch), 110/148 and a la carte 140/220 ♀.

Faubourg-St-Germain, Invalides, École Militaire.

7th arrondissement.
7th: ✉ *75007*

🏠 **Montalembert** Ⓜ, 3 r. Montalembert ✆ 01 45 49 68 68, Fax 01 45 49 69 49, ☂
« Original decor » – |‡| 🖭 📺 ☎ – 🕰 25. **AE ① GB**
J 12
Meals a la carte 240/360 – ☕ 100 – **50 rm** 1750/2300, 6 suites.

🏠 **Duc de Saint-Simon** ⊗ without rest, 14 r. St-Simon ✆ 01 44 39 20 20, Fax 01 45 48 68 25 – |‡| 📺 ☎. **AE GB**. ⊗
J 11
☕ 70 – **29 rm** 1350/1475, 5 suites.

🏠 **Golden Tulip Cayré** Ⓜ without rest, 4 bd Raspail ✆ 01 45 44 38 88, Fax 01 45 44 98 13 – |‡|, ⊱ rm, 🖭 📺 ☎ ⅙. **AE ① GB** JCB
J 12
☕ 80 – **119 rm** 1400.

FRANCE

Bellechasse M without rest, 8 r. Bellechasse ℰ 01 45 50 22 31, Fax 01 45 51 52 3
– ⌷, ⇥ rm, TV ☎ ♿. AE ⓸ GB JCB H 1
☕ 75 – **41 rm** 955/1025.

Verneuil without rest, 8 r. Verneuil ℰ 01 42 60 82 14, Fax 01 42 61 40 38, « Fin
decor » – ⌷ TV ☎. AE ⓸ GB. ✗ J 1
☕ 50 – **26 rm** 670/980.

Tourville M without rest, 16 av. Tourville ℰ 01 47 05 62 62, Fax 01 47 05 43 90 – ⌷
🗏 TV ☎. AE ⓸ GB JCB J
☕ 60 – **30 rm** 790/1990.

Lenox Saint-Germain without rest, 9 r. Université ℰ 01 42 96 10 95
Fax 01 42 61 52 83 – ⌷ TV ☎. AE ⓸ GB JCB J 1
☕ 45 – **34 rm** 680/1500.

Splendid M without rest, 29 av. Tourville ℰ 01 45 51 29 29, Fax 01 44 18 94 60 – ⌷
TV ☎ ♿. AE ⓸ GB J
☕ 50 – **48 rm** 640/1090.

Bourgogne et Montana without rest, 3 r. Bourgogne ℰ 01 45 51 20 22
Fax 01 45 56 11 98 – ⌷ TV ☎. AE ⓸ GB JCB H 1
☕ 70 – **29 rm** 690/1200, 4 suites.

Eiffel Park Hôtel M without rest, 17 bis r. Amélie ℰ 01 45 55 10 01
Fax 01 47 05 28 68 – ⌷ 🗏 TV ☎ – 🔬 25. AE ⓸ GB JCB. ✗ J
☕ 55 – **36 rm** 650/750.

Les Jardins d'Eiffel M without rest, 8 r. Amélie ℰ 01 47 05 46 21, Fax 01 45 55 28 0
– ⌷, ⇥ rm, 🗏 TV ☎ ♿ 🚗. AE ⓸ GB JCB H
☕ 60 – **80 rm** 710/970.

La Bourdonnais without rest, 111 av. La Bourdonnais ℰ 01 47 05 45 42
Fax 01 45 55 75 54 – ⌷ 🗏 TV ☎. AE ⓸ GB JCB J
☕ 45 – **57 rm** 580/780, 3 suites.

Muguet M without rest, 11 r. Chevert ℰ 01 47 05 05 93, Fax 01 45 50 25 37 – ⌷ 🗏
TV ☎. AE GB J
☕ 45 – **45 rm** 500/580.

Cadran M without rest, 10 r. Champ-de-Mars ℰ 01 40 62 67 00, Fax 01 40 62 67 1
– ⌷, ⇥ rm, 🗏 TV ☎. AE ⓸ GB. ✗ J
☕ 55 – **42 rm** 850/950.

Relais Bosquet without rest, 19 r. Champ-de-Mars ℰ 01 47 05 25 45
Fax 01 45 55 08 24 – ⌷ TV ☎. AE ⓸ GB JCB J
☕ 57 – **40 rm** 850/900.

Timhôtel Invalides without rest, 35 bd La Tour Maubourg ℰ 01 45 56 10 78
Fax 01 45 05 65 08 – ⌷ TV ☎. AE ⓸ GB JCB H 1
☕ 60 – **30 rm** 680/895.

Sèvres Vaneau without rest, 86 r. Vaneau ℰ 01 45 48 73 11, Fax 01 45 49 27 74
⌷, ⇥ rm, TV ☎. AE ⓸ GB JCB K 1
☕ 75 – **39 rm** 865/935.

St-Germain without rest, 88 r. Bac ℰ 01 49 54 70 00, Fax 01 45 48 26 89 – ⌷ TV ☎
AE GB. ✗ J 1
☕ 55 – **29 rm** 500/850.

Varenne ⌕ without rest, 44 r. Bourgogne ℰ 01 45 51 45 55, Fax 01 45 51 86 63
⌷ TV ☎. AE GB J 1
☕ 50 – **24 rm** 610/740.

Londres Eiffel without rest, 1 r. Augereau ℰ 01 45 51 63 02, Fax 01 47 05 28 96
⌷ TV ☎. AE ⓸ GB JCB J
☕ 40 – **30 rm** 495/595.

Beaugency without rest, 21 r. Duvivier ℰ 01 47 05 01 63, Fax 01 45 51 04 96 – ⌷ TV
☎. AE ⓸ GB J
☕ 45 – **30 rm** 500/700.

Champ-de-Mars without rest, 7 r. Champ-de-Mars ℰ 01 45 51 52 30
Fax 01 45 51 64 36 – ⌷ TV ☎. AE ⓸ GB JCB. ✗ J
☕ 35 – **25 rm** 365/430.

Bersoly's without rest, 28 r. Lille ℰ 01 42 60 73 79, Fax 01 49 27 05 55 – ⌷ 🗏 TV ☎
AE GB J 1
closed 12 to 31 August – ☕ 50 – **16 rm** 700/750.

L'Empereur without rest, 2 r. Chevert ℰ 01 45 55 88 02, Fax 01 45 51 88 54, ≤ – ⌷
TV ☎. AE GB J
☕ 37 – **38 rm** 430/500.

France without rest, 102 bd La Tour Maubourg ✆ 01 47 05 40 49, *Fax 01 45 56 96 78* – |≡| TV ☎. AE ◑ GB JCB
J 9
☕ 35 – **60 rm** 395/500.

Lévêque without rest, 29 r. Clerc ✆ 01 47 05 49 15, *Fax 01 45 50 49 36* – |≡| TV ☎. AE GB. ✗
J 9
☕ 35 – **50 rm** 270/450.

Turenne without rest, 20 av. Tourville ✆ 01 47 05 99 92, *Fax 01 45 56 06 04* – |≡| ≡ TV ☎. AE ◑ GB
J 9
☕ 38 – **34 rm** 350/570.

Arpège (Passard), 84 r. Varenne ✆ 01 45 51 47 33, *Fax 01 44 18 98 39* – ≡. AE ◑ GB JCB
J 10
closed Saturday and Sunday – **Meals** 390 (lunch)/960 and a la carte 620/880 ♈
Spec. Consommé de crustacés et ravioles d'oignons blancs au citron. Dragée de pigeonneau vendéen à l'hydromel. Tomate confite farcie aux douze saveurs (dessert).

Jules Verne, Eiffel Tower : 2nd platform, lift in south leg ✆ 01 45 55 61 44, *Fax 01 47 05 29 41,* ≤ Paris – ≡. AE ◑ GB JCB. ✗
J 7
Meals 290 (lunch)/680 and a la carte 510/690 ♈
Spec. Grosses langoustines à la vapeur, tomates grappe au basilic. Sauté de poulet de Bresse aux légumes confits et champignons. Chutney aux mangues et fruits secs, madeleine tiède.

Le Divellec, 107 r. Université ✆ 01 45 51 91 96, *Fax 01 45 51 31 75* – ≡. AE ◑ GB JCB. ✗
H 10
closed Christmas-New Year and Sunday – **Meals** - Seafood - 290/390 (lunch)and a la carte 500/840
Spec. Tartelette de pommes "ratte" à l'anguille fumée. Poêlée d'ormeaux et casserons, riz à l'encre de seiche. Homard à la presse avec son corail.

Paul Minchelli, 54 bd La Tour Maubourg ✆ 01 47 05 89 86, *Fax 01 45 56 03 84* – ≡. GB. ✗
J 9
closed August, Christmas Holidays, Sunday and Monday – **Meals** - Seafood - a la carte 470/670 ♈
Spec. Poissons crus. Homard au miel et aux épices. Pâtes et St-Jacques au citron (October-May).

Violon d'Ingres (Constant), 135 r. St-Dominique ✆ 01 45 55 15 05, *Fax 01 45 55 48 42* – ≡. AE GB
J 8
closed Sunday and Monday – **Meals** 240 (lunch)/400 and a la carte 290/400 ♈
Spec. Salade de Saint-Jacques aux truffes, copeaux de parmesan. Suprême de bar croustillant aux amandes, jus acidulé aux câpres. Tatin de pied de porc caramélisé, moelleux de pommes "ratte".

Cantine des Gourmets, 113 av. La Bourdonnais ✆ 01 47 05 47 96, *Fax 01 45 51 09 29* – ≡. AE GB
J 9
Meals 240 (lunch), 320/480 and a la carte 380/510
Spec. Salade de langoustines et tourteau (Winter). Fricassée de grillons de ris de veau en escabèche. Farçons à l'oseille et blettes, fricassée de cèpes (Autumn).

Boule d'Or, 13 bd La Tour Maubourg ✆ 01 47 05 50 18, *Fax 01 47 05 91 21* – ≡. AE ◑ GB
H 10
closed Saturday lunch – **Meals** 175/210 and a la carte 180/250 ♈

Petit Laurent, 38 r. Varenne ✆ 01 45 48 79 64, *Fax 01 45 44 15 95* – AE ◑ GB JCB
J 11
closed August, Saturday lunch and Sunday – **Meals** 190/250 and a la carte 270/410 ♈

Bellecour (Goutagny), 22 r. Surcouf ✆ 01 45 51 46 93, *Fax 01 45 50 30 11* – ≡. AE ◑ GB
H 9
closed 30 July-30 August, Saturday lunch and Sunday – **Meals** 220
Spec. Quenelles de brochet. Truffière de Saint-Jacques (15 December-15 April). Lièvre à la cuillère de "douze heures" (15 October-15 January).

Récamier (Cantegrit), 4 r. Récamier ✆ 01 45 48 86 58, *Fax 01 42 22 84 76,* 🌿 – ≡. AE ◑ GB JCB
K 12
closed Sunday – **Meals** a la carte 300/450 ♈
Spec. Oeufs en meurette. Mousse de brochet sauce Nantua. Boeuf bourguignon.

Maison de l'Amérique Latine, 217 bd St-Germain ✆ 01 45 49 33 23, *Fax 01 40 49 03 94,* 🌿, « *18C mansion, terrace opening onto the garden* » – AE ◑ GB. ✗
J 11
closed 1 to 22 August, 24 December-2 January, dinner from October-May, Saturday, Sunday and Bank Holidays – **Meals** 230 (lunch) and a la carte approx. 350.

Beato, 8 r. Malar ✆ 01 47 05 94 27, *Fax 01 45 55 64 41* – ≡. AE GB
H 9
closed 24 December-2 January and Monday – **Meals** - Italian rest. - 145 and a la carte 230/350 ♈

XX **Ferme St-Simon,** 6 r. St-Simon ✆ 01 45 48 35 74, Fax 01 40 49 07 31 – 🗐. AE ⓘ
GB   J 1
closed 6 to 16 August, Saturday lunch and Sunday – **Meals** 178 (lunch)/195 and a la cart
250/380.

XX **6 Bosquet,** 6 av. Bosquet ✆ 01 45 56 97 26, Fax 01 45 56 98 44 – 🗐. AE ⓘ G
JCB   H
closed 7 to 24 August, 24 December-4 January, Saturday and Sunday – **Meals** 175 ar
a la carte 190/250 ♀.

XX **Télégraphe,** 41 r. de Lille ✆ 01 42 92 03 04, Fax 01 42 92 02 77 – 🗐. AE ⓘ
GB   H 1
closed Saturday lunch – **Meals** 135 (lunch), 200/300 b.i. and a la carte 240/390 ♀.

XX **Vin sur Vin,** 20 r. Monttessuy ✆ 01 47 05 14 20 – 🗐. GB   H
closed 1 to 15 August, 23 December-2 January, Monday lunch, Saturday lunch and Sunda
– **Meals** a la carte 270/400 ♀.

XX **Les Glénan,** 54 r. Bourgogne ✆ 01 47 05 96 65, Fax 01 45 51 27 34 – 🗐. AE G
JCB   J 1
closed August, February Holidays, Saturday and Sunday – **Meals** - Seafood - 210 b.i. ar
a la carte 290/350.

XX **Bamboche,** 15 r. Babylone ✆ 01 45 49 14 40, Fax 01 45 49 14 44 – 🗐. AE GB   K 1
closed Saturday and Sunday – **Meals** 190 and a la carte 340/410 ♀.

XX **New Jawad,** 12 av. Rapp ✆ 01 47 05 91 37, Fax 01 45 50 31 27 – 🗐. AE ⓘ GB
🍽   H
Meals Indian and Pakistani rest. 99/140 and a la carte 150/220.

XX **Gildo,** 153 r. Grenelle ✆ 01 45 51 54 12, Fax 01 45 51 54 12 – 🗐. AE G
JCB   J
closed 25 July-25 August, Christmas-New Year, Monday lunch and Sunday – **Meals** - Itali
rest. - a la carte 230/360.

XX **D'Chez Eux,** 2 av. Lowendal ✆ 01 47 05 52 55, Fax 01 45 55 60 74 – 🗐. AE ⓘ
GB   J
closed 1 to 23 August and Sunday – **Meals** 270 b.i. (lunch)/570 b.i. and a la carte 250/42

XX **Bar au Sel,** 43 quai d'Orsay ✆ 01 45 51 58 58, Fax 01 40 62 97 30 – AE ⓘ GB   H
Meals - Seafood - 190 and a la carte 220/320 ♀.

XX **Foc Ly,** 71 av. Suffren ✆ 01 47 83 27 12, Fax 01 46 24 48 46 – 🗐. AE GB   K
closed Monday in August – **Meals** - Chinese and Thai rest. - 130 b.i. (lunch), 150 b.i./2C
b.i. and a la carte 150/240.

XX **Tan Dinh,** 60 r. Verneuil ✆ 01 45 44 04 84, Fax 01 45 44 36 93   J 1
closed August and Sunday – **Meals** - Vietnamese rest. - a la carte 260/310.

X **Gaya Rive Gauche,** 44 r. Bac ✆ 01 45 44 73 73, Fax 01 45 44 73 73 – AE GB   J 1
closed August and Sunday – **Meals** - Seafood - a la carte 280/490.

XX **Chez Françoise,** Invalides airport station ✆ 01 47 05 49 03, Fax 01 45 51 96 20, 🍽
– AE ⓘ GB JCB   H 1
Meals 179 and a la carte 200/330 ♀.

XX **Champ de Mars,** 17 av. La Motte-Picquet ✆ 01 47 05 57 99, Fax 01 44 18 94 69 – [
ⓘ GB JCB   J
closed 18 July-18 August and Monday – **Meals** 118/155 b.i. and a la carte 170/300.

X **Les Olivades,** 41 av. Ségur ✆ 01 47 83 70 09, Fax 01 42 73 04 75 – AE GB JCB   K
closed 2 to 23 August, Monday lunch, Saturday lunch and Sunday – **Meals** 130 (lunch
179/230 and a la carte 250/310 ♀.

X **Bistrot de Paris,** 33 r. Lille ✆ 01 42 61 15 84, Fax 01 49 27 06 09, 1900 bistro – [
GB   J 1
Meals 155/195 ♀.

X **P'tit Troquet,** 28 r. Exposition ✆ 01 47 05 80 39, Fax 01 47 05 80 39, bistro
GB   J
closed August, Christmas-New Year, Monday lunch and Sunday – **Meals** (booking essentia
158.

X **Thoumieux** with rm, 79 r. St-Dominique ✆ 01 47 05 49 75, Fax 01 47 05 36 96, bra
serie – 🗐 rest, 📺 ☎. AE GB   H
Meals 82/170 b.i. and a la carte 180/250 – 🍵 35 – **10 rm** 700/800.

X **Maupertu,** 94 bd La Tour Maubourg ✆ 01 45 51 37 96 – GB   J 1
closed 8 to 30 August, Saturday and Sunday – **Meals** 139 and a la carte 240/320 ♀.

X **L'Oeillade,** 10 r. St-Simon ✆ 01 42 22 01 60 – 🗐. GB   J 1
closed 15 August-1 September, Saturday lunch and Sunday – **Meals** 168/220 and a la cart
200/280.

X **Fontaine de Mars,** 129 r. St-Dominique ℘ 01 47 05 46 44, *Fax 01 47 05 11 13,* 🌴,
bistro – ⒶⒺ ⒼⒷ   J 9
Meals a la carte 180/270 ⓨ.

X **Chez Collinot,** 1 r. P. Leroux ℘ 01 45 67 66 42 – ⒼⒷ   K 11
closed August, Saturday except dinner from October-June and Sunday – **Meals** 135.

X **Du Côté 7ᵉᵐᵉ,** 29 r. Surcouf ℘ 01 47 05 81 65, *Fax 01 47 05 80 03,* bistro – ⒶⒺ ⓞ ⒼⒷ
ⒿⒸⒷ   H 9-10
closed 10 to 17 August and Monday – **Meals** 185 b.i..

X **Au Bon Accueil,** 14 r. Monttessuy ℘ 01 47 05 46 11
ⒼⒷ   H 8
closed Saturday and Sunday – **Meals** 135 (lunch)/155 and a la carte 280/340 ⓨ.

X **Florimond,** 19 av. La Motte-Picquet ℘ 01 45 55 40 38, *Fax 01 45 55 40 38* –
ⒼⒷ   H 9
closed 1 to 22 August, Saturday lunch and Sunday – **Meals** 108/164 and a la carte
180/260.

X **Auberge Bressane,** 16 av. La Motte-Picquet ℘ 01 47 05 98 37, *Fax 01 47 05 92 21*
– 🍽. ⒶⒺ ⒼⒷ ⒿⒸⒷ. 🚫   H 9
closed 10 to 20 August and Saturday lunch – **Meals** 129 b.i./149 b.i. (lunch only)and a la
carte 180/260.

X **Calèche,** 8 r. Lille ℘ 01 42 60 24 76, *Fax 01 47 03 31 10* – 🍽. ⒶⒺ ⓞ ⒼⒷ ⒿⒸⒷ   J 12
closed 4 to 30 August, 24 December-2 January, Saturday and Sunday – **Meals** 100/175
and a la carte 180/260 ⓨ.

X **Apollon,** 24 r. J. Nicot ℘ 01 45 55 68 47, *Fax 01 47 05 13 60*   H 9
closed 20 December-10 January and Sunday – **Meals** - Greek rest. - 128/150 b.i. and a la
carte 140/190 ⓨ.

X **Bistrot du 7ᵉ,** 56 bd La Tour-Maubourg ℘ 01 45 51 93 08 – ⒶⒺ ⒼⒷ   J 10
closed lunch Saturday and Sunday – **Meals** 75 (lunch)/95 🍷.

Champps-Élysées, St-Lazare, Madeleine.

8th arrondissement.
8th: ✉ *75008*

🏨 **Plaza Athénée,** 25 av. Montaigne ℘ 01 53 67 66 65, *Fax 01 53 67 66 66,* 🌴, Ⓕ🅖 –
🛗 🖥 📺 ☎ – 🍽 20 - 60. ⒶⒺ ⓞ ⒼⒷ ⒿⒸⒷ. 🚫   G 9
see rest. *Régence* below - *Relais-Plaza* ℘ 01 53 67 64 00 *(closed 1 to 22 August and
February Holidays)* **Meals** 290 and a la carte 250/450 ⓨ – *La Cour Jardin* (terrace)
℘ 01 53 67 66 02 *(May-October)* **Meals** a la carte 370/600 ⓨ – ☕ 160 – **143 rm**
3000/4800, 42 suites.

🏨 **Bristol,** 112 r. Fg St-Honoré ℘ 01 53 43 43 00, *Fax 01 53 43 43 01,* « Attractive cour-
tyard with French-style garden », Ⓕ🅖, 🏊, 🚗 – 🛗, 🖥 rm, 📺 ☎ 🚗 – 🍽 30 - 60. ⒶⒺ
ⓞ ⒼⒷ ⒿⒸⒷ. 🚫   F 10
Meals see *Bristol* below – ☕ 175 – **156 rm** 2950/3950, 26 suites.

🏨 **Crillon,** ℘ 01 44 71 15 00, *Fax 01 44 71 15 02,* Ⓕ🅖 – 🛗, 🚭 rm, 🖥 📺 ☎ – 🍽 30 -
60. ⒶⒺ ⓞ ⒼⒷ ⒿⒸⒷ   G 11
see *Les Ambassadeurs* and *L'Obélisque* below – ☕ 240 – **120 rm** 2950/4300, 43 suites.

🏨 **Prince de Galles,** 33 av. George-V ℘ 01 53 23 77 77, *Fax 01 53 23 78 78,* 🌴, Ⓕ🅖 –
🛗, 🚭 rm, 🖥 📺 ☎ – 🍽 25 - 100. ⒶⒺ ⓞ ⒼⒷ ⒿⒸⒷ. 🚫   G 8
Jardin des Cygnes ℘ 01 53 23 78 50 **Meals** 280(lunch)/350 and a la carte 460/640 –
☕ 160 – **138 rm** 2150/3350, 30 suites.

🏨 **Royal Monceau,** 37 av. Hoche ℘ 01 42 99 88 00, *Fax 01 42 99 89 90,* 🌴, « Pool and
fitness centre » – 🛗 🖥 📺 ☎ 🚗 – 🍽 25 - 100. ⒶⒺ ⓞ ⒼⒷ ⒿⒸⒷ. 🚫   E 8
see *Le Jardin* below - *Carpaccio* ℘ 01 42 99 98 90, Fax 01 42 99 89 94, Italian rest.
(closed 17 July-23 August) **Meals** 280 and a la carte 340/4500 – ☕ 210 – **142 rm**
3150/3750, 38 suites.

Lancaster, 7 r. Berri ℰ 01 40 76 40 76, *Fax 01 40 76 40 00*, 🏖, « Tasteful decor »
↥ – 🛗, ⌖ rm, 🍽 rm, 🆃🆅 ☎ – 🔥 16. 🆃🅴 ⓪ 🅶🅱 🎴
F
Meals (residents only) a la carte approx. 300 �]– ⎯ 120 – **50 rm** 1950/2750
10 suites.

Vernet, 25 r. Vernet ℰ 01 44 31 98 00, *Fax 01 44 31 85 69* – 🛗 🍽 🆃🆅 ☎. 🆃🅴 ⓪ 🅶🅱
🎴. ⌖
F
see *Les Élysées* below – ⎯ 130 – **54 rm** 2200/2600, 3 suites.

de Vigny Ⓜ without rest, 9 r. Balzac ℰ 01 42 99 80 80, *Fax 01 42 99 80 40*, « Tasteful
decor » – 🛗, ⌖ rm, 🍽 🆃🆅 ☎ 🚗. 🆃🅴 ⓪ 🅶🅱 🎴
F
⎯ 100 – **26 rm** 2000/2500, 11 suites.

San Régis, 12 r. J. Goujon ℰ 01 44 95 16 16, *Fax 01 45 61 05 48*, « Tasteful decor
– 🛗 🍽 🆃🆅 ☎. 🆃🅴 ⓪ 🅶🅱 🎴. ⌖
G
Meals *(closed August)* 200/250 (lunch) and a la carte 270/360 �]– ⎯ 110 – **33 rr**
1700/2950, 11 suites.

Sofitel Arc de Triomphe, 14 r. Beaujon ℰ 01 53 89 50 50, *Fax 01 53 89 50 51*
🛗, ⌖ rm, 🍽 🆃🆅 ☎ 🔥 – 🔥 40. 🆃🅴 ⓪ 🅶🅱
F
see *Clovis* below – ⎯ 140 – **135 rm** 2400/4500.

Hyatt Regency Ⓜ, 24 bd Malhesherbes ℰ 01 55 27 12 34, *Fax 01 55 27 12 35,*
– 🛗, ⌖ rm, 🍽 🆃🆅 ☎ 🔥 – 🔥 20. 🆃🅴 ⓪ 🅶🅱 🎴
F 1
Café M ℰ 01 55 27 12 57 *closed lunch Saturday and Sunday* **Meals** 185 (dinner)/230
– ⎯ 130 – **86 rm** 2700/3100.

Astor Ⓜ 🕊, 11 r. d'Astorg ℰ 01 53 05 05 05, *Fax 01 53 05 05 30*, ↥ – 🛗, ⌖ rm
🍽 rm, 🆃🆅 ☎ 🔥. 🆃🅴 ⓪ 🅶🅱 🎴
F 1
Meals see *L'Astor* below – ⎯ 140 – **129 rm** 2070/3150, 5 suites.

Marriott Ⓜ, 70 av. Champs-Élysées ℰ 01 53 93 55 00, *Fax 01 53 93 55 01*, 🏖, ↥
🛗, ⌖ rm, 🍽 🆃🆅 ☎ 🔥 🚗 – 🔥 150. 🆃🅴 ⓪ 🅶🅱 🎴. ⌖
F
Pavillon ℰ 01 53 93 55 44 **Meals** 260/280 – ⎯ 175 – **174 rm** 3600/5100, 18 suite

California, 16 r. Berri ℰ 01 43 59 93 00, *Fax 01 45 61 03 62*, 🏖, « Important co
lection of paintings » – 🛗, ⌖ rm, 🍽 🆃🆅 ☎ – 🔥 20 - 100. 🆃🅴 ⓪ 🅶🅱 🎴
⌖
F
Meals *(closed August, Saturday and Sunday)* (lunch only) 180 �]– ⎯ 130 – **161 rr**
2200/2500, 13 duplex.

Balzac Ⓜ, 6 r. Balzac ℰ 01 44 35 18 00, *Fax 01 44 35 18 05* – 🛗, 🍽 rm, 🆃🆅 ☎. 🆃🅴 ⓪
🅶🅱 🎴
F
see *Pierre Gagnaire* below – ⎯ 100 – **56 rm** 1800/2000, 14 suites.

Warwick Ⓜ, 5 r. Berri ℰ 01 45 63 14 11, *Fax 01 45 63 75 81* – 🛗, ⌖ rm, 🍽 🆃🆅
– 🔥 30 - 110. 🆃🅴 ⓪ 🅶🅱 🎴
F
Couronne ℰ 01 45 61 82 08 *(closed August, Saturday lunch, Sunday and Bank Holidays*
Meals 260 – ⎯ 110 – **142 rm** 2600/2800, 5 suites.

Concorde St-Lazare, 108 r. St-Lazare ℰ 01 40 08 44 44, *Fax 01 42 93 01 20*, « Lat
19 C lobby, superb billiards room » – 🛗, ⌖ rm, 🍽 🆃🆅 ☎ – 🔥 25 - 150. 🆃🅴 ⓪ 🅶🅱
🎴
E 1
Café Terminus : **Meals** 152/200 bi – ⎯ 120 – **269 rm** 1800/3500, 11 suites.

Trémoille, 14 r. La Trémoille ℰ 01 47 23 34 20, *Fax 01 40 70 01 08* – 🛗 🍽 🆃🆅 ☎
🔥 25. 🆃🅴 ⓪ 🅶🅱 🎴
G
Louis d'Or *(closed August, Saturday, Sunday and Bank Holidays)* **Meals** 250 �]– ⎯ 12
– **107 rm** 2290/3370.

Napoléon without rest, 40 av. Friedland ℰ 01 47 66 02 02, *Fax 01 47 66 82 33* – 🛗
🆃🆅 ☎ – 🔥 30 - 60. 🆃🅴 ⓪ 🅶🅱 🎴
F
⎯ 110 – **102 rm** 1300/2100.

Château Frontenac without rest, 54 r. P. Charron ℰ 01 53 23 13 13
Fax 01 53 23 13 01 – 🛗 🆃🆅 ☎ – 🔥 25. 🆃🅴 ⓪ 🅶🅱. ⌖
G
⎯ 90 – **100 rm** 1000/1500, 4 suites.

Bedford, 17 r. de l'Arcade ℰ 01 44 94 77 77, *Fax 01 44 94 77 97* – 🛗 🍽 🆃🆅 ☎ – 🔥 50
🆃🅴 🅶🅱. ⌖ rest
F 1
Meals *(closed 2 to 29 August, Saturday and Sunday)* (lunch only) 180 – ⎯ 75 – **135 rr**
860/1050, 11 suites.

Queen Elizabeth, 41 av. Pierre-1er-de-Serbie ℰ 01 53 57 25 25, *Fax 01 53 57 25 2*
– 🛗, ⌖ rm, 🍽 🆃🆅 ☎ – 🔥 30. 🆃🅴 ⓪ 🅶🅱 🎴
G
Meals *(closed August, Saturday and Sunday)* (lunch only) 175/230 b.i. – ⎯ 100 – **53 rr**
1350/2000, 12 suites.

Montaigne Ⓜ without rest, 6 av. Montaigne ℰ 01 47 20 30 50, *Fax 01 47 20 94*
– 🛗 🍽 🆃🆅 ☎ 🔥. 🆃🅴 ⓪ 🅶🅱 🎴
G
⎯ 95 – **29 rm** 1350/1950.

Élysées Star Ⓜ without rest, 19 r. Vernet ✆ 01 47 20 41 73, *Fax 01 47 23 32 15* – |♣|, ⇔ rm, 🖿 📺 ☎ – 🔺 30. 🆎 ⓪ 🅶🅱 🗌🅲🅱 F 8
☕ 90 – **42 rm** 1700/3500.

Royal Hôtel Ⓜ without rest, 33 av. Friedland ✆ 01 43 59 08 14, *Fax 01 45 63 69 92*
– |♣| 🖿 📺 ☎. 🆎 ⓪ 🅶🅱 🗌🅲🅱 F 8
☕ 105 – **58 rm** 1350/2150.

Élysées-Ponthieu and Résidence without rest, 24 r. Ponthieu ✆ 01 53 89 58 58,
Fax 01 53 89 59 59 – |♣| kitchenette, ⇔ rm, 📺 ☎ &. 🆎 ⓪ 🅶🅱 🗌🅲🅱 F 9
☕ 75 – **92 rm** 920/1780, 6 suites.

Powers without rest, 52 r. François 1er ✆ 01 47 23 91 05, *Fax 01 49 52 04 63* – |♣| 🖿
📺 ☎. 🆎 ⓪ 🅶🅱 🗌🅲🅱 G 9
☕ 65 – **55 rm** 912/1462.

Sofitel Champs-Élysées Ⓜ, 8 r. J. Goujon ✆ 01 40 74 64 64, *Fax 01 40 74 64 99*,
🚁 – |♣|, ⇔ rm, 🖿 📺 ☎ &. 🚗 – 🔺 15 - 150. 🆎 ⓪ 🅶🅱 🗌🅲🅱 G 9
Les Saveurs ✆ 01 40 74 64 94 *(closed August, Saturday, Sunday and Bank Holidays)*
Meals 185/350 – ☕ 125 – **40 rm** 2000/2625.

Résidence du Roy Ⓜ without rest, 8 r. François 1er ✆ 01 42 89 59 59,
Fax 01 40 74 07 92 – |♣| kitchenette 🖿 📺 ☎ &. 🚗 – 🔺 25. 🆎 ⓪ 🅶🅱 🗌🅲🅱 G 9
☕ 105, 28 suites1400/3500, 4 studios, 3 duplex.

Concortel without rest, 19 r. Pasquier ✆ 01 42 65 45 44, *Fax 01 42 65 18 33* – |♣| 🖿
📺 ☎. 🆎 ⓪ 🅶🅱 🗌🅲🅱 F 11
☕ 50 – **46 rm** 610/900.

Résidence Monceau without rest, 85 r. Rocher ✆ 01 45 22 75 11, *Fax 01 45 22 30 88*
– |♣| 📺 ☎ &. 🆎 ⓪ 🅶🅱 🗌🅲🅱. 🕸 E 11
☕ 50 – **51 rm** 740.

Chateaubriand without rest, 6 r. Chateaubriand ✆ 01 40 76 00 50,
Fax 01 40 76 09 22 – |♣| 🖿 📺 ☎. 🆎 ⓪ 🅶🅱 🗌🅲🅱 F 9
☕ 80 – **28 rm** 1800/1900.

New Hôtel Roblin, 6 r. Chauveau-Lagarde ✆ 01 44 71 20 80, *Fax 01 42 65 19 49* –
|♣|, ⇔ rm, 🖿 📺 ☎. 🆎 ⓪ 🅶🅱 🗌🅲🅱 F 11
Mazagran *(closed Saturday, Sunday and Bank Holidays)* **Meals** 92/155 – ☕ 75 – **77 rm**
776/962.

Beau Manoir without rest, 6 r. de l'Arcade ✆ 01 42 66 03 07, *Fax 01 42 68 03 00*,
« Attractive interior » – |♣| 🖿 📺 ☎ &. 🆎 ⓪ 🅶🅱 🗌🅲🅱 F 11
29 rm ☕ 1100/1300, 3 suites.

L'Arcade Ⓜ without rest, 9 r. de l'Arcade ✆ 01 53 30 60 00, *Fax 01 40 07 03 07* – |♣|
🖿 📺 ☎ & – 🔺 25. 🆎 🅶🅱 🗌🅲🅱 F 11
☕ 55 – **37 rm** 800/1000, 4 duplex.

Élysées Mermoz Ⓜ without rest, 30 r. J. Mermoz ✆ 01 42 25 75 30,
Fax 01 45 62 87 10 – |♣| 🖿 📺 ☎ &. 🆎 ⓪ 🅶🅱 🗌🅲🅱 F 10
☕ 50 – **26 rm** 750/920, 5 suites.

Franklin Roosevelt without rest, 18 r. Clément-Marot ✆ 01 53 57 49 50,
Fax 01 47 20 44 30 – |♣| ☎ &. 🆎 🅶🅱. 🕸 G 9
☕ 110 – **45 rm** 1000/1800.

Queen Mary Ⓜ without rest, 9 r. Greffulhe ✆ 01 42 66 40 50, *Fax 01 42 66 94 92* –
|♣| 🖿 📺 ☎. 🆎 ⓪ 🅶🅱 🗌🅲🅱. 🕸 F 12
☕ 85 – **35 rm** 755/975.

Lido Ⓜ without rest, 4 passage Madeleine ✆ 01 42 66 27 37, *Fax 01 42 66 61 23* – |♣|
🖿 📺 ☎. 🆎 ⓪ 🅶🅱 🗌🅲🅱 F 11
32 rm ☕ 980/1100.

Étoile Friedland without rest, 177 r. Fg St-Honoré ✆ 01 45 63 64 65,
Fax 01 45 63 88 96 – |♣| 🖿 📺 ☎ &. 🆎 ⓪ 🅶🅱 🗌🅲🅱. 🕸 F 9
☕ 80 – **40 rm** 1300/1700.

Élysées Céramic without rest, 34 av. Wagram ✆ 01 42 27 20 30, *Fax 01 46 22 95 83*,
« "Art Nouveau" façade » – |♣| 🖿 📺 ☎. 🆎 ⓪ 🅶🅱
☕ 45 – **57 rm** 850/1000.

Relais Mercure Opéra Garnier Ⓜ without rest, 4 r. de l'Isly ✆ 01 43 87 35 50,
Fax 01 43 87 03 29 – |♣|, ⇔ rm, 🖿 📺 ☎ &. 🆎 ⓪ 🅶🅱 F 12
☕ 69 – **139 rm** 1050/1390.

Atlantic Hôtel without rest, 44 r. Londres ✆ 01 43 87 45 40, *Fax 01 42 93 06 26* –
|♣| 📺 ☎. 🆎 🅶🅱 🗌🅲🅱. 🕸 E 12
☕ 55 – **85 rm** 550/950.

Flèche d'Or Ⓜ without rest, 29 r. Amsterdam ✆ 01 48 74 06 86, *Fax 01 48 74 06 04*
– |♣| 🖿 📺 ☎. 🆎 ⓪ 🅶🅱 E 12
☕ 40 – **61 rm** 550/850.

Mayflower without rest, 3 r. Chateaubriand ⚘ 01 45 62 57 46, *Fax 01 42 56 32 38*
|≑| [TV] ☎. [AE] [GB] F
⌣ 60 – **24 rm** 690/970.

West-End without rest, 7 r. Clément-Marot ⚘ 01 47 20 30 78, *Fax 01 47 20 34 42*
|≑| [≣] [TV] ☎. [AE] [①] [GB] [JCB] G
⌣ 65 – **50 rm** 850/1350.

l'Élysée without rest, 12 r. Saussaies ⚘ 01 42 65 29 25, *Fax 01 42 65 64 28* – |≑| [≣] [
☎. [AE] [①] [GB] [JCB]. ⌦ F 1
⌣ 65 – **32 rm** 780/1280.

Cordélia without rest, 11 r. Greffulhe ⚘ 01 42 65 42 40, *Fax 01 42 65 11 81* – |≑| [
☎. [AE] [①] [GB]. ⌦ F 1
⌣ 55 – **30 rm** 740/850.

Fortuny without rest, 35 r. de l'Arcade ⚘ 01 42 66 42 08, *Fax 01 42 66 00 32* – |≑| [
[TV] ☎. [AE] [①] [GB] [JCB] F 1
⌣ 50 – **30 rm** 750/850.

Pavillon Montaigne [M] without rest, 34 r. J. Mermoz ⚘ 01 53 89 95 00
Fax 01 42 89 33 00 – |≑| [≣] [TV] ☎. [AE] [①] [GB] [JCB] F 1
⌣ 45 – **17 rm** 695/950.

Alison without rest, 21 r. de Surène ⚘ 01 42 65 54 00, *Fax 01 42 65 08 17* – |≑| [TV] ☎
[AE] [①] [GB] [JCB]. ⌦
⌣ 45 – **35 rm** 480/780.

Newton Opéra without rest, 11 bis r. de l'Arcade ⚘ 01 42 65 32 13
Fax 01 42 65 30 90 – |≑| [≣] [TV] ☎. [AE] [①] [GB] [JCB]. ⌦ F 1
⌣ 50 – **31 rm** 850.

Les Ambassadeurs - Hôtel Crillon, 10 pl. Concorde ⚘ 01 44 71 16 16
Fax 01 44 71 15 02, « 18C decor » – [≣]. [AE] [①] [GB] [JCB]. ⌦ G 1
Meals 360 (lunch)/650 and a la carte 520/800
Spec. Confit de foie gras d'oie, gelée de griottes et brioche truffée. Médaillon de homar
à la civette, rattes et fleurette au caviar. Truffe glacée à la fleur de thym, ganache a
chocolat Guanaja.

Taillevent (Vrinat), 15 r. Lamennais ⚘ 01 44 95 15 01, *Fax 01 42 25 95 18* – [≣]. [AE] [①
[GB] [JCB]. ⌦ F
closed 24 July-24 August, Saturday, Sunday and Bank Holidays – **Meals** (booking essentia
a la carte 540/880
Spec. Boudin de homard à la nage. Ballottine d'agneau à la périgourdine. Sablé aux épice
et aux fruits.

Lasserre, 17 av. F.-D.-Roosevelt ⚘ 01 43 59 53 43, *Fax 01 45 63 72 23*, « Retractab
roof » – [≣]. [AE] [①] [GB] [JCB]. ⌦ G 1
closed August, Monday lunch and Sunday – **Meals** a la carte 560/800
Spec. Homard et langoustines en mousseline, jus de crustacés. Filet de veau de lait rôt
gâteau de navets et jus au beurre de fèves. Succés aux griottines, semoule d'amande
douces.

Lucas Carton (Senderens), 9 pl. Madeleine ⚘ 01 42 65 22 90, *Fax 01 42 65 06 2.*
« Authentic 1900 decor » – [≣]. [AE] [①] [GB] [JCB]. ⌦ G 1
closed 1 to 22 August, Monday lunch, Saturday lunch and Sunday – **Meals** 395 (lunch)an
a la carte 680/1 430
Spec. Quenelle de brochet, asperges vertes de Villelaure, marinière de coquillages. Carr
d'agneau de Sisteron rôti aux trois aubergines. Glace à la réglisse et sa meringue à la menth
poivrée.

Ledoyen, carré Champs-Élysées (1st floor) ⚘ 01 53 05 10 01, *Fax 01 47 42 55 01*, - se
also rest. *Le Cercle* – [≣] [P.] [AE] [①] [GB] [JCB]. ⌦ G 1
closed August, Saturday and Sunday – **Meals** 310 (lunch), 530/620 and a la cart
560/920
Spec. Grosses langoustines bretonnes, émulsion d'agrumes à l'huile d'olive. Cochon de la
parfumé d'épices de tandoori, barigoule d'artichauts. Mousse légère à la rose, citron ve
poêlé au miel.

Laurent, 41 av. Gabriel ⚘ 01 42 25 00 39, *Fax 01 45 62 45 21*, ⌂, « Pleasant summe
terrace » – [AE] [①] [GB]. ⌦ G 1
closed Sunday except dinner from June-October and Saturday lunch – **Meals** 390/680 an
a la carte 560/950
Spec. Homard entier en salade. Carré d'agneau persillé, pommes de terre confites au ju
Variation sur le chocolat.

Bristol - Hôtel Bristol, 112 r. Fg St-Honoré ⚘ 01 53 43 43 40, *Fax 01 53 43 43 01*, ⌂
– [≣]. [AE] [①] [GB] [JCB]. ⌦ F 1
Meals 360/680 and a la carte 650/780
Spec. Galette "sans pâte" de peau de courgettes (June-mid-September). Pavé de lou
piqué à l'anchois cuit sur la peau. Fruits de la passion soufflés servis dans leur coque.

XX **Le Pichet,** 68 r. P. Charron ✆ 01 43 59 50 34, *Fax 01 42 89 68 91* – ▤. AE ⓓ GB GF 9
closed Saturday except dinner from September-April and Sunday – **Meals** a la carte 280/510.

XX **Bistro de l'Olivier,** 13 r. Quentin Bauchart ✆ 01 47 20 17 00, *Fax 01 47 20 17 04* – ▤. AE GB G 8
closed Saturday lunch and Sunday – **Meals** (booking essential) 190 ♀.

XX **L'Alsace** (24 hr service), 39 av. Champs-Élysées ✆ 01 53 93 97 00, *Fax 01 53 93 97 09,* 🏞, brasserie – ▤. AE ⓓ GB F 9
Meals 178 and a la carte 170/360 ♀.

XX **Kok Ping,** 4 r. Balzac ✆ 01 42 25 28 85, *Fax 01 53 75 11 49* – ▤. AE ⓓ GB. ✻ F 8
closed Saturday lunch – **Meals** - Chinese and Thai rest - 92 (lunch), 120/200 and a la carte 180/260 ♀.

XX **Les Persiennes,** 28 r. Marbeuf ✆ 01 56 69 26 90, *Fax 01 53 75 39 89* – ▤. AE GB G 9
closed 10 to 25 August, Saturday lunch and Sunday – **Meals** a la carte 180/310 ♀.

X **Cap Vernet,** 82 av. Marceau ✆ 01 47 20 20 40, *Fax 01 47 20 95 36,* 🏞 – ▤. AE ⓓ GB JCB F 8
Meals - Seafood - a la carte 210/280 ♀.

X **L'Appart',** 9 r. Colisée ✆ 01 53 75 16 34, *Fax 01 53 76 15 39* – ▤. AE GB JCB F 9
Meals 175 and a la carte 220/270.

X **Saveurs et Salon,** 3 r. Castellane ✆ 01 40 06 97 97, *Fax 01 40 06 98 06* – ▤. GB F 12
closed August, Saturday and Sunday – **Meals** 185 and a la carte 200/300.

X **Ferme des Mathurins,** 17 r. Vignon ✆ 01 42 66 46 39, *Fax 01 42 66 00 27* – ⓓ GB JCB F 12
closed August, Sunday and Bank Holidays – **Meals** 160/210 and a la carte 180/310 ♀.

X **Boucoléon,** 10 r. Constantinople ✆ 01 42 93 73 33, *Fax 01 42 93 17 44* – GB E 11
closed 31 July-22 August, 25 December-2 January, Saturday and Sunday – **Meals** (booking essential) a la carte 140/160 ♀.

X **Rocher Gourmand,** 89 r. Rocher ✆ 01 40 08 00 36, *Fax 01 40 08 05 29* – GB E 10
closed August, Saturday lunch and Sunday – **Meals** 175/220.

Opéra, Gare du Nord, Gare de l'Est, Grands Boulevards.

9th and 10th arrondissements.
9th: ✉ 75009
10th: ✉ 75010

Grand Hôtel Inter-Continental, 2 r. Scribe (9th) ✆ 01 40 07 32 32, *Fax 01 42 66 12 51,* ₺ – ⫼, ⇹ rm, ▤ TV ☎ ♿ 🚗 – 🏛 300. AE ⓓ GB JCB. ✻ rest F 12
see ***Rest. Opéra*** and ***Brasserie Café de la Paix*** below - ***La Verrière*** ✆ 01 40 07 31 00 *(closed dinner and Saturday)* **Meals** 200/275 ♀ – ☕ 140 – **488 rm** 1850/3700, 22 suites.

Scribe Ⓜ, 1 r. Scribe (9th) ✆ 01 44 71 24 24, *Fax 01 42 65 59 97* – ⫼, ⇹ rm, ▤ TV ☎ ♿ – 🏛 50. AE ⓓ GB JCB F 12
see ***Les Muses*** below - ***Jardin des Muses :*** **Meals** 170 ♀ – ☕ 130 – **206 rm** 2015/3250, 11 suites.

Ambassador, 16 bd Haussmann (9th) ✆ 01 44 83 40 40, *Fax 01 42 46 20 83* – ⫼, ▤ rm, TV ☎ – 🏛 110. AE ⓓ GB JCB F 13
see ***16 Haussmann*** below – ☕ 120 – **288 rm** 1650/2200.

Millennium Commodore, 12 bd Haussmann (9th) ✆ 01 49 49 16 00, *Fax 01 49 49 17 00* – ⫼, ⇹ rm, TV ☎ – 🏛 25. AE ⓓ GB JCB. ✻ rest F 13
Brasserie Haussmann ✆ 01 49 49 16 09 **Meals** 185 (dinner) and a la carte 200/290 ♀ – ☕ 145 – **163 rm** 2700/2900, 10 suites.

Terminus Nord M without rest, 12 bd Denain (10th) ☎ 01 42 80 20 00
Fax 01 42 80 63 89 – 🛗, ⇔ rm, TV ☎ & – 🕍 80. AE ① GB JCB   E 1
☞ 75 – **236 rm** 1035/1105.

Lafayette M without rest, 49 r. Lafayette (9th) ☎ 01 42 85 05 44, Fax 01 49 95 06 6
– 🛗, ⇔ rm, TV ☎ &. AE ① GB JCB   F 1
☞ 80 – **96 rm** 955/1125, 7 suites.

St-Pétersbourg, 33 r. Caumartin (9th) ☎ 01 42 66 60 38, Fax 01 42 66 53 54 – 🛗
TV ☎ – 🕍 25. AE ① GB JCB. ⚠ rest   F 1
Relais (closed August, Saturday and Sunday) **Meals** 148 ♀ – ☞ 70 – **100 rm** 995/110(

Brébant, 32 bd Poissonnière (9th) ☎ 01 47 70 25 55, Fax 01 42 46 65 70 – 🛗, ⇔ rm
▤ rest, TV ☎ – 🕍 25 - 100. AE ① GB JCB   F 1
Vieux Pressoir : **Meals** 98/198 ♀ – ☞ 48 – **122 rm** 790/930.

Holiday Inn Paris Opéra, 38 r. Échiquier (10th) ☎ 01 42 46 92 75, Fax 01 42 47 03 9
– 🛗, ⇔ rm, ▤ TV ☎. AE ① GB JCB. ⚠ rm   F 1
Meals *(closed Saturday lunch and Sunday)* 90/220 ⚘ – ☞ 90 – **92 rm** 1090/1550.

Richmond Opéra without rest, 11 r. Helder (9th) ☎ 01 47 70 53 20
Fax 01 48 00 02 10 – 🛗 ▤ TV ☎. AE ① GB JCB. ⚠   F 1
☞ 40 – **59 rm** 840/980.

Bergère Opéra without rest, 34 r. Bergère (9th) ☎ 01 47 70 34 34, Fax 01 47 70 36 3
– 🛗 ▤ TV ☎ – 🕍 40. AE ① GB JCB. ⚠   F 1
☞ 80 – **134 rm** 890/1090.

Franklin without rest, 19 r. Buffault (9th) ☎ 01 42 80 27 27, Fax 01 48 78 13 04 – 🛗
⇔ rm, TV ☎ &. AE ① GB JCB   E 1
☞ 75 – **68 rm** 865/990.

Blanche Fontaine ⚘ without rest, 34 r. Fontaine (9th) ☎ 01 44 63 54 9!
Fax 01 42 81 05 52 – 🛗, ⇔ rm, ▤ TV ☎ 🚗. AE ① GB JCB. ⚠   D 1
☞ 50 – **49 rm** 1390, 4 suites.

Carlton's Hôtel without rest, 55 bd Rochechouart (9th) ☎ 01 42 81 91 00
Fax 01 42 81 97 04, « Rooftop panoramic terrace, ≤ Paris » – 🛗 TV ☎. AE ① GB JC
☞ 50 – **103 rm** 800/850.

Anjou-Lafayette without rest, 4 r. Riboutté (9th) ☎ 01 42 46 83 44
Fax 01 48 00 08 97 – 🛗 TV ☎. AE ① GB JCB   E 1
☞ 50 – **39 rm** 510/690.

Frantour Paris-Est M, 4 r. 8 Mai 1945 (cour d'Honneur gare de l'Est)(10th
☎ 01 44 89 27 00, Fax 01 44 89 27 49 – 🛗, ▤ rm, TV ☎ – 🕍 250. AE GB
Meals 130 ♀ – ☞ 55 – **45 rm** 545/1070.

Albert 1er M without rest, 162 r. Lafayette (10th) ☎ 01 40 36 82 40
Fax 01 40 35 72 52 – 🛗 ▤ TV ☎. AE ① GB JCB. ⚠   E 1
☞ 45 – **57 rm** 650/750.

Opéra Cadet M without rest, 24 r. Cadet (9th) ☎ 01 53 34 50 50, Fax 01 53 34 50 6
– 🛗 ▤ TV ☎ & 🚗. AE ① GB JCB   F 1
☞ 70 – **82 rm** 880/1030, 3 suites.

Touraine Opéra without rest, 73 r. Taitbout (9th) ☎ 01 48 74 50 49
Fax 01 42 81 26 09 – 🛗, ⇔ rm, TV ☎. AE ① GB JCB   E 1
☞ 75 – **39 rm** 865/990.

Paix République without rest, 2 bis bd St-Martin (10th) ☎ 01 42 08 96 9!
Fax 01 42 06 36 30 – 🛗, ⇔ rm, TV ☎. AE ① GB JCB. ⚠   G 1
☞ 45 – **45 rm** 650/1200.

Mercure Monty without rest, 5 r. Montyon (9th) ☎ 01 47 70 26 10
Fax 01 42 46 55 10 – 🛗, ⇔ rm, TV ☎ – 🕍 50. AE ① GB   F 1
☞ 60 – **71 rm** 760/810.

Corona ⚘ without rest, 8 cité Bergère (9th) ☎ 01 47 70 52 96, Fax 01 42 46 83 4
– 🛗 TV ☎ &. AE ① GB JCB. ⚠   F 1
☞ 45 – **56 rm** 750/1150, 4 suites.

Capucines without rest, 6 r. Godot de Mauroy (9th) ☎ 01 47 42 25 0!
Fax 01 42 68 05 05 – 🛗 TV ☎. AE ① GB JCB   F 1
☞ 38 – **45 rm** 520/600.

Amiral Duperré without rest, 32 r. Duperré (9th) ☎ 01 42 81 55 3:
Fax 01 44 63 04 73 – 🛗, ⇔ rm, TV ☎. AE ① GB JCB   D 1
☞ 45 – **52 rm** 540/750.

Suède without rest, 106 bd Magenta (10th) ☎ 01 40 36 10 12, Fax 01 40 36 11 98
🛗, ⇔ rm, TV ☎. AE ① GB JCB   E 15-1
☞ 45 – **52 rm** 540/600.

Ibis Gare de l'Est without rest, 197 r. Lafayette (10th) ℰ 01 44 65 70 00, Fax 01 44 65 70 07 – |≜|, ⅍ rm, ▤ ▯ ☎ ₰ ⇔. ᴁ ◑ ᴳᴮ   E 17
☕ 40 – **165 rm** 430/480.

Modern'Est without rest, 91 bd Strasbourg (10th) ℰ 01 40 37 77 20, Fax 01 40 37 17 55 – |≜| ▤ ▯ ☎. ᴳᴮ   E 16
☕ 35 – **30 rm** 390/470.

Alba ⅍ without rest, 34 ter r. La Tour d'Auvergne (9th) ℰ 01 48 78 80 22, Fax 01 42 85 23 13 – |≜| kitchenette, ⅍ rm, ▯ ☎. ᴁ ◑ ᴳᴮ ᴶᶜᴮ. ⅍   E 14
☕ 40 – **24 rm** 500/1400.

Trois Poussins without rest, 15 r. Clauzel (9th) ℰ 01 53 32 81 81, Fax 01 53 32 81 82 – |≜|, ⅍ rm, ▯ ☎ ₰. ᴁ ᴳᴮ. ⅍   E 13
☕ 45 – **40 rm** 480/830.

Rest. Opéra - Grand Hôtel Inter-Continental, pl. Opéra (9th) ℰ 01 40 07 30 10, Fax 01 40 07 33 86, « Second Empire decor » – ▤. ᴁ ◑ ᴳᴮ ᴶᶜᴮ. ⅍   F 12
closed 17 July-30 August, 18 December-2 January, 20 to 28 February, Saturday and Sunday – **Meals** 240 (lunch), 345/585 and a la carte 460/630 ♀
Spec. Huîtres de Marennes, nage crémée à la parisienne aux grains de caviar. Noix de ris de veau aux pistaches, jus de rôti au citron confit et bois de réglisse. Petits babas bouchons caramélisés au miel, crème fouettée à la vanille.

Les Muses - Hôtel Scribe, 1 r. Scribe (9th) ℰ 01 44 71 24 26, Fax 01 44 71 24 64 – ▤. ᴁ ◑ ᴳᴮ ᴶᶜᴮ   F 12
closed August, Saturday, Sunday and Bank Holidays – **Meals** 260/330 and a la carte 330/370
Spec. Parmentier fumé de foie gras de canard. Noix de Saint-Jacques croustillantes, risotto aux cèpes (September-May). Macaron moelleux aux fruits de la passion et son caviar de mangues.

Table d'Anvers (Conticini), 2 pl. Anvers (9th) ℰ 01 48 78 35 21, Fax 01 45 26 66 67 – ▤. ᴁ ᴳᴮ ᴶᶜᴮ   D 14
closed Saturday lunch and Sunday – **Meals** 190 (lunch), 250/450 and a la carte 490/690 ♀
Spec. Brochette de thon au gingembre et rouleaux de printemps grillés. Ruffian de foie gras, aubergines et mousserons, caramel au beurre salé. Les croquettes au chocolat de Philippe.

Charlot "Roi des Coquillages", 12 pl. Clichy (9th) ℰ 01 53 20 48 00, Fax 01 53 20 48 09 – ▤. ᴁ ◑ ᴳᴮ   D 12
Meals - Seafood - 178 and a la carte 240/410.

Au Chateaubriant, 23 r. Chabrol (10th) ℰ 01 48 24 58 94, Fax 01 42 47 09 75, Collection of paintings – ▤. ᴁ ᴳᴮ ᴶᶜᴮ   E 15
closed August, Sunday and Monday – **Meals** - Italian rest. - 165 and a la carte 240/420 ♀.

Brasserie Café de la Paix - Grand Hôtel Inter-Continental, 12 bd Capucines (9th) ℰ 01 40 07 30 20, Fax 01 40 07 33 86 – ▤. ᴁ ◑ ᴳᴮ ᴶᶜᴮ. ⅍   F 12
Meals 176 and a la carte 260/380 ♀.

Julien, 16 r. Fg St-Denis (10th) ℰ 01 47 70 12 06, Fax 01 42 47 00 65, « Belle Epoque brasserie » – ▤. ᴁ ◑ ᴳᴮ   F 15
Meals 132 b.i./189 b.i. and a la carte 180/250.

Grand Café Capucines (24 hr service), 4 bd Capucines (9th) ℰ 01 43 12 19 00, Fax 01 43 12 19 09, brasserie, « Belle Epoque decor » – ▤. ᴁ ◑ ᴳᴮ   F 13
Meals 178 and a la carte 190/370 ♀.

Grange Batelière, 16 r. Grange Batelière (9th) ℰ 01 47 70 85 15, Fax 01 47 70 85 15 – ▤. ᴁ ᴳᴮ   G 10
closed 1 to 21 August, Saturday lunch, Sunday and Bank Holidays – **Meals** 190/300 and a la carte 250/360 ♀.

Quercy, 36 r. Condorcet (9th) ℰ 01 48 78 30 61, Fax 01 48 78 16 29 – ᴁ ◑ ᴳᴮ ᴶᶜᴮ   E 14
closed August, Sunday and Bank Holidays – **Meals** 152 and a la carte 170/320.

Bistrot Papillon, 6 r. Papillon (9th) ℰ 01 47 70 90 03, Fax 01 48 24 05 59 – ▤. ᴁ ◑ ᴳᴮ   E 15
closed 3 to 11 April, 7 to 29 August, Saturday lunch and Sunday – **Meals** 150 and a la carte 200/320.

Au Petit Riche, 25 r. Le Peletier (9th) ℰ 01 47 70 68 68, Fax 01 48 24 10 79, bistro, « Late 19C decor » – ▤. ᴁ ◑ ᴳᴮ ᴶᶜᴮ   F 13
closed Sunday – **Meals** 140 (dinner), 165/180 and a la carte 180/340.

Brasserie Flo, 7 cour Petites-Écuries (10th) ℰ 01 47 70 13 59, Fax 01 42 47 00 80, « 1900 decor » – ▤. ᴁ ◑ ᴳᴮ   F 15
Meals 132 b.i./179 b.i. and a la carte 180/250.

Terminus Nord, 23 r. Dunkerque (10th) ✆ 01 42 85 05 15, *Fax 01 40 16 13 98,* bras
serie – 🗐. **AE ⓪ GB**   E 1
Meals 132 b.i./179 b.i. and a la carte 180/250.

16 Haussmann - Hôtel Ambassador, 16 bd Haussmann ✆ 01 48 00 06 38
Fax 01 48 00 06 38 – 🗐
closed Saturday and Sunday – **Meals** 180 ℈.

Paprika, 28 av. Trudaine (9th) ✆ 01 44 63 02 91, *Fax 01 44 63 09 62* – 🗐. **GB**   E 1
closed August and Sunday – **Meals** - Hungarian rest. - 75 (lunch), 120/180 and a la cart
190/330 ℈.

Saintongeais, 62 r. Fg Montmartre (9th) ✆ 01 42 80 39 92, *Fax 01 42 80 39 92* – **A**
⓪ GB   E 1
closed 15 to 25 August, Saturday and Sunday – **Meals** 135/168 and a la carte 170/280

Wally Le Saharien, 36 r. Rodier (9th) ✆ 01 42 85 51 90, *Fax 01 45 86 08 35* – 🗐. **GB**
🛇   E 1
closed Monday lunch and Sunday – **Meals** - North African rest. - 155 (lunch), 240/290 an
a la carte 150/240 ℈.

Pré Cadet, 10 r. Saulnier (9th) ✆ 01 48 24 99 64 – 🗐. **AE ⓪ GB**   F 1
closed 1 to 8 May, 1 to 22 August, Christmas-New Year, Saturday lunch and Sunday – **Meal**
(booking essential) 150 and a la carte 200/290 ℈.

Paludier, 5 r. Clichy (9th) ✆ 01 48 74 32 13, *Fax 01 48 74 32 13* – 🗐. **A**
GB   E 1
closed Saturday and Sunday – **Meals** 158/250 b.i. and a la carte 170/210.

L'Oenothèque, 20 r. St-Lazare (9th) ✆ 01 48 78 08 76, *Fax 01 40 16 10 27* – 🗐. **A**
⓪ GB   E 1
closed 9 to 22 August, Saturday and Sunday – **Meals** 180 and a la carte 200/350 ℈.

Chez Jean, 8 r. St-Lazare (9th) ✆ 01 48 78 62 73, *Fax 01 48 78 35 30*
GB   E 1
closed 8 to 15 August, Saturday lunch and Sunday – **Meals** 175 ℈.

Bistro de Gala, 45 r. Fg Montmarte (9th) ✆ 01 40 22 90 50, *Fax 01 40 22 90 50* – 🗐
AE GB   F 1
closed Sunday – **Meals** 165 ℈.

I Golosi, 6 r. Grange Batelière (9th) ✆ 01 48 24 18 63, *Fax 01 45 23 18 96,* « Venetia
decor » – 🗐. **GB**   F 1
closed August, Saturday dinner and Sunday – **Meals** - Italian rest - a la carte 150/25
℈.

Aux Deux Canards, 8 r. Fg Poissonnière (10th) ✆ 01 47 70 03 23 – **AE ⓪ GB**   F 1
closed 20 July-20 August, Saturday lunch and Sunday – **Meals** a la carte 160/280.

Bistro des Deux Théâtres, 18 r. Blanche (9th) ✆ 01 45 26 41 43, *Fax 01 48 74 08 9*
– 🗐. **AE GB**   E 1
Meals 169 b.i..

Chez Michel, 10 r. Belzunce (10th) ✆ 01 44 53 06 20, *Fax 01 44 53 61 31* – **GB**   F 1
closed August, Christmas-New Year, Sunday and Monday – **Meals** 180 ℈.

Casa Olympe, 48 r. St-Georges (9th) ✆ 01 42 85 26 01, *Fax 01 45 26 49 33* – 🗐. **⓪**
🛇   E 1
closed August and 24 December-2 January – **Meals** 190.

Petite Sirène de Copenhague, 47 r. N.-D. de Lorette (9th) ✆ 01 45 26 66 66
GB   E 1
closed 27 July-16 August, 25 to 31 January, Sunday and Monday – **Meals** - Danish res
- (booking essential) 120 and a la carte 180/270 ℈.

Relais Beaujolais, 3 r. Milton (9th) ✆ 01 48 78 77 91, bistro – **GB**   E 1
closed August, Saturday and Sunday – **Meals** 150/300 and a la carte 150/220 ℈.

Petit Batailley, 26 r. Bergère (9th) ✆ 01 47 70 85 81 – **AE ⓪ GB JCB**   F 1
closed 24 July-25 August, 23 December-3 January, Saturday lunch, Sunday and Bank Hol
days – **Meals** 150 and a la carte 180/270.

L'Alsaco Winstub, 10 r. Condorcet (9th) ✆ 01 45 26 44 31 – **AE GB**   E 1
closed August, Saturday lunch and Sunday – **Meals** 87 (lunch), 95/190 b.i. ℈.

Chez Catherine, 65 r. Provence (9th) ✆ 01 45 26 72 88, *Fax 01 42 80 96 88,* bistr
– **GB**   F 1
closed August, 1 to 10 January, Saturday, Sunday and Bank Holidays – **Meals** a la cart
170/270 ℈.

L'Excuse Mogador, 21 r. Joubert (9th) ✆ 01 42 81 98 19 – **GB**   F 1
closed August, 24 to 31 December, Monday dinner, Friday dinner, Saturday and Sunda
– **Meals** 80 (lunch), 98/100 and a la carte 100/200 ℈.

Bastille, Gare de Lyon, Place d'Italie, Bois de Vincennes.

12th and 13th arrondissements.
12th: ⊠ *75012*
13th: ⊠ *75013*

Holiday Inn Bastille Ⓜ without rest, 11 r. Lyon (12th) ✆ 01 53 02 20 00, *Fax 01 53 02 20 01* – |≴|, ⇔ rm, 🔲 TV ☎ – ⚓ 80. AE ⓞ GB JCB   L 18
⊇ 80 – **125 rm** 890/1130.

Novotel Bercy Ⓜ, 86 r. Bercy (12th) ✆ 01 43 42 30 00, *Fax 01 43 45 30 60*, 🌴 –
|≴|, ⇔ rm, 🔲 TV ☎ & 🚗 – ⚓ 80. AE ⓞ GB   M 19
Meals a la carte approx. 160 – ⊇ 72 – **129 rm** 860/910.

Holiday Inn Tolbiac Ⓜ without rest, 21 r. Tolbiac (13th) ✆ 01 45 84 61 61, *Fax 01 45 84 43 38* – |≴|, ⇔ rm, 🔲 TV ☎ & – ⚓ 25. AE ⓞ GB JCB   P 18
⊇ 70 – **71 rm** 970.

Mercure Pont de Bercy Ⓜ without rest, 6 bd Vincent Auriol (13th) ✆ 01 45 82 48 00, *Fax 01 45 82 19 16* – |≴| 🔲 TV ☎ & – ⚓ 60. AE ⓞ GB JCB
⊇ 65 – **90 rm** 990.   M 18

Mercure Blanqui Ⓜ without rest, 25 bd Blanqui (13th) ✆ 01 45 80 82 23, *Fax 01 45 81 45 84* – |≴|, ⇔ rm, 🔲 TV ☎ &. AE ⓞ GB JCB   P 15
⊇ 60 – **50 rm** 950.

Pavillon Bastille Ⓜ without rest, 65 r. Lyon (12th) ✆ 01 43 43 65 65, *Fax 01 43 43 96 52*, « Elegant contemporary decor » – |≴|, ⇔ rm, 🔲 TV ☎ &. AE ⓞ
GB JCB   K 18
⊇ 70 – **24 rm** 815/955.

Paris Bastille Ⓜ without rest, 67 r. Lyon (12th) ✆ 01 40 01 07 17, *Fax 01 40 01 07 27* – |≴| 🔲 TV ☎ & – ⚓ 25. AE ⓞ GB JCB   K 18
⊇ 75 – **37 rm** 800/1000.

Nation Ⓜ without rest, 33 av. Dr A. Netter (12th) ✆ 01 40 04 90 90, *Fax 01 40 04 99 20* – |≴|, ⇔ rm, 🔲 TV ☎ 🚗. AE ⓞ GB   M 12
⊇ 75 – **49 rm** 905.

Ibis Gare de Lyon Ⓜ without rest, 43 av. Ledru-Rollin (12th) ✆ 01 53 02 30 30, *Fax 01 53 02 30 31* – |≴|, ⇔ rm, TV ☎ & 🚗 – ⚓ 25. AE ⓞ
GB   K 18
⊇ 39 – **119 rm** 450/460.

Manufacture Ⓜ without rest, 8 r. Philippe de Champagne (13th) ✆ 01 45 35 45 25, *Fax 01 45 35 45 40* – |≴| 🔲 TV ☎. GB   N 16
⊇ 42 – **57 rm** 420/750.

Ibis Place d'Italie Ⓜ without rest, 25 av. Stephen Pichon (13th) ✆ 01 44 24 94 85, *Fax 01 44 24 20 70* – |≴|, ⇔ rm, TV ☎ &. AE ⓞ GB   N 16
⊇ 40 – **58 rm** 420/460.

Ibis Italie Tolbiac Ⓜ without rest, 177 r. Tolbiac (13th) ✆ 01 45 80 16 60, *Fax 01 45 80 95 80* – |≴|, ⇔ rm, TV ☎ &. AE ⓞ GB   P 15
⊇ 39 – **60 rm** 390/430.

Touring H. Magendie Ⓜ without rest, 2 r. Magendie (13th) ✆ 01 43 36 13 61, *Fax 01 43 36 47 48* – |≴| TV ☎ & 🚗 – ⚓ 30. GB   N 14
⊇ 26 – **112 rm** 340/390.

Nouvel H. without rest, 24 av. Bel Air (12th) ✆ 01 43 43 01 81, *Fax 01 43 44 64 13* –
TV ☎. AE ⓞ GB   L 21
⊇ 42 – **28 rm** 370/570.

Viator without rest, 1 r. Parrot (12th) ✆ 01 43 43 11 00, *Fax 01 43 43 10 89* – |≴| TV ☎. AE GB. ✖   L 18
⊇ 35 – **45 rm** 330/380.

XXX **Au Pressoir** (Seguin), 257 av. Daumesnil (12th) ℘ 01 43 44 38 21, *Fax 01 43 43 81 7*
ⓈⓈ – 🖻. 🄰🄴 🄶🄱 🄹🄲🄱 M 2
closed August, Saturday and Sunday – **Meals** a la carte 390/510
Spec. Millefeuille de champignons aux truffes. Filets de rougets rôtis, aubergines et citro
Lièvre à la royale (October-November).

XXX **Train Bleu,** Gare de Lyon (12th) ℘ 01 43 43 09 06, *Fax 01 43 43 97 96*, brasseri
« Murals depicting the journey from Paris to the Mediterranean » – 🄰🄴 🄓 🄶
🄹🄲🄱 L 1
Meals (1st floor) 250 b.i. and a la carte 220/460.

XXX **L'Oulette,** 15 pl. Lachambeaudie (12th) ℘ 01 40 02 02 12, *Fax 01 40 02 04 77*,
🄰🄴 🄓 🄶🄱 N 2
closed Saturday lunch and Sunday – **Meals** 165/250 b.i. and a la carte 290/340 ♀.

XX **Au Trou Gascon,** 40 r. Taine (12th) ℘ 01 43 44 34 26, *Fax 01 43 07 80 55* – 🖻.
ⓈⓈ 🄓 🄶🄱 🄹🄲🄱 M 2
closed August, Christmas-New Year, Saturday lunch and Sunday – **Meals** (booking essentia
200 (lunch)/320 b.i. and a la carte 290/380
Spec. Chipirons sautés "façon pibale" (June-September). Petit pâté chaud de cèpes au ju
de persil (season). Volaille de Chalosse rôtie, jus clair.

XX **Frégate,** 30 av. Ledru-Rollin (12th) ℘ 01 43 43 90 32 – 🖻. 🄶🄱 L 1
closed August, Saturday and Sunday – **Meals** - Seafood - 160/320 and a la carte 290/40
♀.

XX **Gourmandise,** 271 av. Daumesnil (12th) ℘ 01 43 43 94 41, *Fax 01 43 43 94 41* – 🄓
🄶🄱 🄹🄲🄱 M 2
closed 2 to 10 May, 1 to 23 August, Monday dinner and Sunday – **Meals** 170/199 b.i. an
a la carte 260/380.

XX **Petit Marguery,** 9 bd Port-Royal (13th) ℘ 01 43 31 58 59, bistro – 🄰🄴 🄓 🄶🄱 M 1
closed August, 24 December-3 January, Sunday and Monday – **Meals** 165 (lunch)/215

XX **Traversière,** 40 r. Traversière (12th) ℘ 01 43 44 02 10, *Fax 01 43 44 64 20* – 🄰🄴 🄓
🄶🄱 🄹🄲🄱 K 1
closed August, Sunday dinner and Monday – **Meals** 120 (lunch)/170 and a la cart
260/340 ♀.

XX **Les Marronniers,** 53 bis bd Arago (13th) ℘ 01 47 07 58 57 – 🖻. 🄶🄱 N 1
closed August, Sunday dinner and Monday – **Meals** 155 and a la carte 180/350 ♀.

XX **Sologne,** 164 av. Daumesnil (12th) ℘ 01 43 07 68 97, *Fax 01 43 44 66 23* – 🖻.
🄶🄱 M 2
closed Saturday lunch and Sunday – **Meals** 165 and a la carte 200/370.

X **Bistrot de la Porte Dorée,** 5 bd Soult (12th) ℘ 01 43 43 80 07, *Fax 01 43 42 32 6*
– 🖻. 🄶🄱 N 2
Meals 185.

X **Jean-Pierre Frelet,** 25 r. Montgallet (12th) ℘ 01 43 43 76 65 – 🖻. 🄶🄱 L 2
closed August, Saturday lunch and Sunday – **Meals** 140 (dinner only)and a la cart
170/250.

X **Quincy,** 28 av. Ledru-Rollin (12th) ℘ 01 46 28 46 76, *Fax 01 46 28 46 76*, bistro
🖻 L 1
closed 15 August-15 September, 15 to 28 February, Saturday, Sunday and Monday – **Mea
a la carte 220/420.

X **L'Escapade en Touraine,** 24 r. Traversière (12th) ℘ 01 43 43 14 96 – 🄶🄱 L 1
closed August, Saturday, Sunday and Bank Holidays – **Meals** 110/140 and a la car
150/300.

X **Anacréon,** 53 bd St-Marcel (13th) ℘ 01 43 31 71 18, *Fax 01 43 31 94 94* – 🖻. 🄰🄴 🄓
🄶🄱 🄹🄲🄱 M 1
closed August, 8 to 14 March, Sunday and Monday – **Meals** 120 (lunch)/180.

X **Chez Jacky,** 109 r. du Dessous-des-Berges (13th) ℘ 01 45 83 71 55
Fax 01 45 86 57 73 – 🖻. 🄶🄱 P 1
closed August, Saturday and Sunday – **Meals** 188 and a la carte 220/360 ♀.

X **Temps des Cerises,** 216 r. Fg St-Antoine (12th) ℘ 01 43 67 52 08, *Fax 01 43 67 60 9*
– 🖻. 🄰🄴 🄓 🄶🄱 🄹🄲🄱 K 2
closed 9 to 16 August and Monday – **Meals** 100/230 and a la carte 210/330 🌡.

X **L'Avant Goût,** 26 r. Bobillot (13th) ℘ 01 53 80 24 00, bistro – 🄶🄱 P 1
closed 1 to 23 August, 2 to 10 January, Sunday and Monday – **Meals** (booking essentia
135/180 ♀.

X **A la Biche au Bois,** 45 av. Ledru-Rollin (12th) ℘ 01 43 43 34 38 – 🄰🄴 🄓 🄶🄱 K 1
closed mid-July-mid-August, Christmas-New Year, Saturday and Sunday – **Meals** 110/12
and a la carte 120/220 ♀.

※ **St-Amarante,** 4 r. Biscornet (12th) ✆ 01 43 43 00 08, *Fax 01 45 35 57 48,* bistro –
GB   K 18
closed 24 July-24 August, Sunday and Monday – **Meals** (booking essential) a la carte
150/220 ♈.

※ **Chez Françoise,** 12 r. Butte aux Cailles (13th) ✆ 01 45 80 12 02, *Fax 01 45 65 13 67,*
bistro – **AE ① GB JCB.** ⊗   P 15
closed 5 August-1 September, 25 December-2 January and Sunday – **Meals** 69/146 and
a la carte 120/300 ♈.

※ **Rhône,** 40 bd Arago (13th) ✆ 01 47 07 33 57, ⌸ – **GB**   N 14
closed August, Saturday, Sunday and Bank Holidays – **Meals** 75/115 and a la carte
140/240.

※ **Chez Paul,** 22 r. Butte aux Cailles (13th) ✆ 01 45 89 22 11, bistro – **GB.** ⊗   P 15
Meals a la carte 170/250.

※ **Michel,** 20 r. Providence (13th) ✆ 01 45 89 99 27, *Fax 01 45 89 99 27* – **GB**   P 15
closed 8 to 29 August and Sunday – **Meals** 120/195 and a la carte 230/360 ♈.

※ **Les Zygomates,** 7 r. Capri (12th) ✆ 01 40 19 93 04, *Fax 01 44 73 46 63,* bistro – **GB.**
⊗   N 21
closed August, Saturday lunch and Sunday – **Meals** 80 (lunch)/130 and a la carte 160/230.

Vaugirard, Gare Montparnasse, Grenelle, Denfert-Rochereau.

14th and 15th arrondissements.
14th: ✉ *75014*
15th: ✉ *75015*

🏨 **Hilton,** 18 av. Suffren (15th) ✆ 01 44 38 56 00, *Fax 01 44 38 56 10,* ⌸ – ▮, ⟵⟶ rm,
▤ TV ☎ ৬ ⇔ – ⚇ 400. **AE ① GB JCB**   J 7
Pacific Eiffel : **Meals** 170 and a la carte 190/350 ♈ – ⊑ 140 – **453 rm** 2000/2650, 9
suites.

🏨 **Nikko** M, 61 quai Grenelle (15th) ✆ 01 40 58 20 00, *Fax 01 40 58 24 44,* ≤, ⸦ᵬ, 🏊 –
▮, ⟵⟶ rm, ▤ TV ☎ ৬ ⇔ – ⚇ 600. **AE ① GB JCB**   K 6
see *Les Célébrités* below - *Brasserie Pont Mirabeau* : Meals 180 ♈ – *Benkay* Japanese
rest. **Meals** 145(lunch) and a la carte 230/420 – ⊑ 110 – **755 rm** 1900/2700, 9 suites.

🏨 **Sofitel Forum Rive Gauche** M, 17 bd St-Jacques (14th) ✆ 01 40 78 79 80,
Fax 01 45 88 43 93, Convention centre, ⸦ᵬ – ▮, ⟵⟶ rm, ▤ TV ☎ ৬ ⇔ – ⚇ 25 - 1
200. **AE ① GB JCB**   N 13-14
Café Français (lunch only) *(closed 24 July-22 August, Saturday and Sunday)* **Meals** 169
and a la carte 180/260 ♈ – *La Table et la Forme* (low-calorie menu) *(closed 17 July-15
August)* **Meals** a la carte 160/210 ৬ – *Patio* (lunch only) **Meals** 135 ♈ – ⊑ 115 – **772 rm**
1300/1550, 13 suites.

🏨 **Sofitel Porte de Sèvres** M, 8 r. L. Armand (15th) ✆ 01 40 60 30 30,
Fax 01 45 57 04 22, ≤, ⸦ᵬ, 🏊 – ▮, ⟵⟶ rm, ▤ TV ☎ ৬ ⇔ – ⚇ 450. **AE ① GB**
JCB   N 5
see *Relais de Sèvres* below - *Brasserie* : **Meals** 140 ♈ – ⊑ 100 – **524 rm** 1600/2200,
14 suites.

🏨 **Méridien Montparnasse,** 19 r. Cdt Mouchotte (14th) ✆ 01 44 36 44 36,
Fax 01 44 36 49 00, ≤, ⌸ – ▮, ⟵⟶ rm, ▤ TV ☎ ৬ – ⚇ 25. **AE ① GB JCB**   M 11
see *Montparnasse 25* below - *Justine* ✆ 01 44 36 44 00, fax 01 44 36 49 03 **Meals**
160/340 ♈ – ⊑ 120 – **916 rm** 2400/2600, 37 suites.

🏨 **Novotel Porte d'Orléans** M, 15-19 bd R. Rolland (14th) ✆ 01 41 17 26 00,
Fax 01 41 17 26 26 – ▮, ⟵⟶ rm, ▤ TV ☎ ৬ ⇔ – ⚇ 100. **AE ① GB**   S 12
Meals 134 ♈ – ⊑ 70 – **150 rm** 780/1200.

🏨 **Novotel Vaugirard** M, 253 r. Vaugirard (15th) ✆ 01 40 45 10 00, *Fax 01 40 45 10 10,*
⌸, ⸦ᵬ – ▮, ⟵⟶ rm, ▤ TV ☎ ৬ ⇔ – ⚇ 300. **AE ① GB JCB**   M 9
Transatlantique : **Meals** 175 ♈ – ⊑ 75 – **184 rm** 1025/1100, 3 suites.

FRANCE

Mercure Montparnasse M, 20 r. Gaîté (14th) ℘ 01 43 35 28 28, *Fax 01 43 27 98 6*
– |≜|, ✦ rm, ▤ rest, 📺 ☎ & ⇔ – 🏊 50. 🆎 ⓪ 🆖 JCB   M 1
Bistrot de la Gaîté : Meals 135/180 ♀ – ⊑ 78 – **181 rm** 1120, 4 suites.

L'Aiglon without rest, 232 bd Raspail (14th) ℘ 01 43 20 82 42, *Fax 01 43 20 98 72*
|≜| 📺 ☎. 🆎 ⓪ 🆖 JCB   M 1
⊑ 40 – **38 rm** 610/780, 9 suites.

Mercure Porte de Versailles M, 69 bd Victor (15th) ℘ 01 44 19 03 03
Fax 01 48 28 22 11 – |≜|, ✦ rm, ▤ 📺 ☎ & ⇔ – 🏊 250. 🆎 ⓪ 🆖   N
Meals 115/170 ♀ – ⊑ 80 – **91 rm** 1500/1600.

Mercure Tour Eiffel M without rest, 64 bd Grenelle (15th) ℘ 01 45 78 90 90
Fax 01 45 78 95 55 – |≜|, ✦ rm, 📺 ☎ & ⇔ – 🏊 25. 🆎 ⓪ 🆖 JCB   K
⊑ 72 – **76 rm** 990.

Raspail Montparnasse without rest, 203 bd Raspail (14th) ℘ 01 43 20 62 86
Fax 01 43 20 50 79 – |≜| ▤ 📺 ☎. 🆎 ⓪ 🆖 JCB. ✄   M 1
⊑ 50 – **38 rm** 520/890.

Lenox Montparnasse without rest, 15 r. Delambre (14th) ℘ 01 43 35 34 50
Fax 01 43 20 46 64 – |≜| 📺 ☎. 🆎 ⓪ 🆖 JCB   M 1
⊑ 50 – **46 rm** 560/690, 6 suites.

Delambre M without rest, 35 r. Delambre (14th) ℘ 01 43 20 66 31, *Fax 01 45 38 91 7*
– |≜| 📺 ☎ &. 🆎 🆖   M 1
⊑ 45 – **30 rm** 460/550.

Apollinaire without rest, 39 r. Delambre (14th) ℘ 01 43 35 18 40, *Fax 01 43 35 30 7*
– |≜| 📺 ☎. 🆎 ⓪ 🆖   M 1
⊑ 45 – **36 rm** 585/680.

Tour Eiffel Dupleix M without rest, 11 r. Juge (15th) ℘ 01 45 78 29 29
Fax 01 45 78 60 00 – |≜|, ✦ rm, 📺 ☎. 🆎 ⓪ 🆖 JCB   K
⊑ 43 – **40 rm** 490/690.

Mercure Paris XV M without rest, 6 r. St-Lambert (15th) ℘ 01 45 58 61 00
Fax 01 45 54 10 43 – |≜|, ✦ rm, 📺 ☎ & ⇔ – 🏊 30. 🆎 ⓪ 🆖   M
⊑ 60 – **56 rm** 695/730.

Daguerre M without rest, 94 r. Daguerre (14th) ℘ 01 43 22 43 54, *Fax 01 43 20 66 8*
– |≜| 📺 ☎ &. 🆎 ⓪ 🆖 JCB. ✄   N 1
⊑ 42 – **30 rm** 420/650.

Lilas Blanc M without rest, 5 r. Avre (15th) ℘ 01 45 75 30 07, *Fax 01 45 78 66 65*
|≜|, ✦ rm, 📺 ☎. 🆎 ⓪ 🆖   K
⊑ 35 – **32 rm** 380/455.

Ibis Brancion M without rest, 105 r. Brancion (15th) ℘ 01 42 50 86 00
Fax 01 42 50 99 63 – |≜|, ✦ rm, 📺 ☎ &. 🆎 ⓪ 🆖   P 8-
⊑ 39 – **71 rm** 410/450.

Istria without rest, 29 r. Campagne Première (14th) ℘ 01 43 20 91 82
Fax 01 43 22 48 45 – |≜| 📺 ☎. 🆎 ⓪ 🆖 JCB. ✄   M 1
⊑ 40 – **26 rm** 500/600.

Apollon Montparnasse without rest, 91 r. Ouest (14th) ℘ 01 43 95 62 00
Fax 01 43 95 62 10 – |≜| 📺 ☎. 🆎 ⓪ 🆖 JCB   N 10-1
⊑ 35 – **33 rm** 395/470.

Ariane Montparnasse without rest, 35 r. Sablière (14th) ℘ 01 45 45 67 13
Fax 01 45 45 39 49 – |≜|, ✦ rm, 📺 ☎. 🆎 ⓪ 🆖 JCB   N 1
⊑ 38 – **30 rm** 395/460.

Carladez Cambronne without rest, 3 pl. Gén. Beuret (15th) ℘ 01 47 34 07 12
Fax 01 40 65 95 68 – |≜| 📺 ☎. 🆎 ⓪ 🆖 JCB   M
⊑ 38 – **26 rm** 395/445.

Les Célébrités - Hôtel Nikko, 61 quai Grenelle (15th) ℘ 01 40 58 20 00
Fax 01 40 58 24 44, ≼ – ▤. 🆎 ⓪ 🆖 JCB   K
closed August – **Meals** 290/420 and a la carte 340/630
Spec. Galantine de volaille de Bresse au foie gras. Tronçon de turbot de St-Guénolé rôt
Epaule d'agneau de Lozère confite.

Montparnasse 25 - Hôtel Méridien Montparnasse, 19 r. Cdt Mouchott
(14th) ℘ 01 44 36 44 25, *Fax 01 44 36 49 03* – ▤ 🅟. 🆎 ⓪ 🆖 JCB
✄   M 1
closed August, 20 to 30 December, Saturday, Sunday and Bank Holidays – **Meals** 24
(lunch), 300/390 and a la carte 350/500 ♀
Spec. Lapin du Poitou et foie gras en fine gelée. Blanc de Saint-Pierre doré au
épices, marinière de petits coquillages. Noix de ris de veau rôti au parfum d'ara
bica.

XXXX **Relais de Sèvres** - Hôtel Sofitel Porte de Sèvres, 8 r. L. Armand (15th)
✓ *01 40 60 30 30, Fax 01 40 57 04 22* – AE ① GB JCB. ✓✓   N 5
closed 24 July-22 August, 24 December-2 January, Saturday, Sunday and Bank Holidays
– **Meals** 250/385 b.i. and a la carte 310/400
Spec. Galette croustillante de champignons et rillons. Fricassée de filets de sole à la ventrèche, jus de poulet et son risotto. Gros macaron au pralin, sorbet cacao.

XXX **Morot Gaudry,** 6 r. Cavalerie (15th) (8th floor) *01 45 67 06 85, Fax 01 45 67 55 72,*
≤, 🍽 – 🛗 ▤. AE ① GB   K 8
closed 8 to 22 August, Saturday and Sunday – **Meals** 180/340 and a la carte
350/460 ⚓.

XXX **Le Duc,** 243 bd Raspail (14th) *01 43 20 96 30, Fax 01 43 20 46 73* – ▤. AE ① GB
JCB   M 12
closed Saturday lunch, Sunday and Monday – **Meals** - Seafood - 260 and a la carte 300/470
Spec. Poissons crus. Soupe tiède de homard (October-May). Langoustines rôties au gingembre.

XXX **Pavillon Montsouris,** 20 r. Gazan (14th) *01 45 88 38 52, Fax 01 45 88 63 40,* ≤,
🍽, « 1900 pavilion beside the park » – P. GB. ✓✓   R 14
Meals 198.

XXX **Dôme,** 108 bd Montparnasse (14th) *01 43 35 25 81, Fax 01 42 79 01 19,* brasserie
– ▤. AE ① GB JCB   LM 12
Meals - Seafood - a la carte 280/420.

XXX **Chen-Soleil d'Est,** 15 r. Théâtre (15th) *01 45 79 34 34, Fax 01 45 79 07 53* – ▤.
AE GB JCB   K 6
closed Sunday – **Meals** - Chinese rest. - 190 b.i. (lunch), 250/450 and a la carte 370/420
Spec. Dégustation de ravioli à la vapeur. Demi-canard pékinois en 3 services. Boules de neige parfumées à la noix de coco.

XXX **Moniage Guillaume,** 88 r. Tombe-Issoire (14th) *01 43 22 96 15, Fax 01 43 27 11 79*
– AE ① GB JCB   P 12
closed Sunday – **Meals** - Seafood - 245 and a la carte 280/430 ⚓.

XX **Lous Landès,** 157 av. Maine (14th) *01 45 43 08 04, Fax 01 45 45 91 35* – ▤. AE ①
GB JCB   N 11
closed August, Saturday lunch and Sunday – **Meals** 195 and a la carte 270/390.

XX **Lal Qila,** 88 av. É. Zola (15th) *01 45 75 68 40, Fax 01 45 79 68 61,* « Original decor »
– ▤. AE GB JCB   L 7
Meals - Indian rest. - 59 (lunch), 129/250 and a la carte 170/230.

XX **Yves Quintard,** 99 r. Blomet (15th) *01 42 50 22 27, Fax 01 42 50 22 27* – ▤. GB
JCB   M 8
closed 15 to 30 August, Saturday lunch and Sunday – **Meals** 135 (lunch), 185/250.

XX **La Dînée,** 85 r. Leblanc (15th) *01 45 54 20 49, Fax 01 40 60 73 76* – AE GB   M 5
closed 8 to 23 August, Saturday lunch and Sunday – **Meals** 210/450 b.i. ⚓.

XX **Coupole,** 102 bd Montparnasse (14th) *01 43 20 14 20, Fax 01 43 35 46 14,* « 1920
Parisian brasserie » – ▤. AE ① GB   L 12
Meals 98 b.i. (lunch), 132/179 and a la carte 180/250.

XX **Aux Senteurs de Provence,** 295 r. Lecourbe (15th) *01 45 57 11 98,*
Fax 01 45 58 66 84 – AE ① GB JCB   M 6
closed 8 to 22 August, Saturday lunch and Sunday – **Meals** - Seafood - 148 and a la carte
190/340.

XX **Philippe Detourbe,** 8 r. Nicolas Charlet (15th) *01 42 19 08 59, Fax 01 45 67 09 13*
– ▤. GB   L 10
closed August, Saturday lunch and Sunday – **Meals** 180 (lunch)/220.

XX **Mille Colonnes,** 20 bis r. Gaîté (14th) *01 40 47 08 34, Fax 01 40 64 37 49,* 🍽 – ▤.
AE ① GB JCB   M 11
closed 24 July-22 August, Saturday lunch and Sunday – **Meals** 165 ⚓.

XX **Erawan,** 76 r. Fédération (15th) *01 47 83 55 67, Fax 01 47 34 85 98* – ▤. AE GB.
✓✓   K 8
closed August and Sunday – **Meals** Thaï rest. 116/175 and a la carte 150/270.

XX **Caroubier,** 122 av. Maine (14th) *01 43 20 41 49* – ▤. GB   N 11
closed 21 July-30 August – **Meals** - North African rest. - 140/198 b.i. and a la carte
150/190 ⚓.

XX **Gauloise,** 59 av. La Motte-Picquet (15 th) *01 47 34 11 64, Fax 01 40 61 09 70,* 🍽
– AE GB JCB   K 8
Meals 155/350 b.i. and a la carte 190/420 ⚓.

XX **L'Etape,** 89 r. Convention (15th) *01 45 54 73 49, Fax 01 45 58 20 91* – ▤. AE
GB   M 6
closed 8 to 22 August, Sunday except lunch in winter and Saturday lunch – **Meals** 130/170 ⚓.

Fontana Rosa, 28 bd Garibaldi (15th) ℘ 01 45 66 97 84 – AE GB   L
Meals - Italian rest. - 120 and a la carte 240/330 ♀.

L'Épopée, 89 av. É. Zola (15th) ℘ 01 45 77 71 37 – AE GB JCB   L
closed August, Saturday lunch and Sunday – **Meals** 185 ♀.

Les Cévennes, 55 r. Cévennes (15th) ℘ 01 45 54 33 76, *Fax 01 44 26 46 95* – ▤. GB   L
⌁
closed 1 to 20 August, Saturday lunch and Sunday – **Meals** 175/300 and a la carte appro: 350.

Gastroquet, 10 r. Desnouettes (15th) ℘ 01 48 28 60 91, *Fax 01 45 33 23 70* – AE GB   N
closed August, Saturday and Sunday – **Meals** 155.

Père Claude, 51 av. La Motte-Picquet (15th) ℘ 01 47 34 03 05, *Fax 01 40 56 97 84*   K
▤. AE ① GB
Meals 110 (lunch)/165 and a la carte 230/330.

de la Tour, 6 r. Desaix (15th) ℘ 01 43 06 04 24, *Fax 01 43 56 03 32* – AE GB   J
closed August, Saturday lunch and Sunday – **Meals** 125 (lunch)/190 and a la carte 240/300

Bistrot du Dôme, 1 r. Delambre (14th) ℘ 01 43 35 32 00, *Fax 01 48 04 00 59* – ▤   M 1
AE GB
Meals - Seafood - a la carte 190/280 ♀.

Petit Plat, 49 av. É. Zola (15th) ℘ 01 45 78 24 20, *Fax 01 45 78 23 13* – ▤. GB   L
closed 1 to 17 August, Sunday and Monday – **Meals** 135 and a la carte 190/240 ♀.

A la Bonne Table, 42 r. Friant (14th) ℘ 01 45 39 74 91, *Fax 01 45 43 66 92* – AE GB
closed 14 July-15 August, Saturday lunch and Sunday – **Meals** 146 ♀.

Contre-Allée, 83 av. Denfert-Rochereau (14th) ℘ 01 43 54 99 86, *Fax 01 43 25 05 2*
– AE GB   N 1
closed Sunday – **Meals** 150/190.

L'Armoise, 67 r. Entrepreneurs (15th) ℘ 01 45 79 03 31, *Fax 01 45 79 44 69* – ▤   L
GB
closed 1 to 21 August, Saturday lunch and Sunday – **Meals** 148 ⌕.

Quercy, 5 r. Mouton-Duvernet (14th) ℘ 01 45 39 39 61, *Fax 01 45 39 39 61*   N 1
GB
closed August, Sunday dinner and Monday – **Meals** 99 (lunch), 119/179 and a la cart 180/270 ♀.

Troquet, 21 r. F. Bonvin (15th) ℘ 01 45 66 89 00, *Fax 01 45 66 89 83*   L
GB
closed August, Sunday and Monday – Meals 130 (lunch), 160/175 ♀.

Les P'tits Bouchons de François Clerc, 32 bd Montparnasse (15th
℘ 01 45 48 52 03, *Fax 01 45 48 52 17,* bistrot – AE GB   L 1
closed Saturday lunch and Sunday – **Meals** 174.

Murier, 42 r. Olivier de Serres (15th) ℘ 01 45 32 81 82   N
GB
Meals 125 ♀.

Bistro d'Hubert, 41 bd Pasteur (15th) ℘ 01 47 34 15 50, *Fax 01 45 67 03 09* –   L 1
GB
Meals 195.

L'Os à Moelle, 3 r. Vasco de Gama (15th) ℘ 01 45 57 27 27, *Fax 01 45 57 27 27,* bistr   M
– GB
closed August, Sunday and Monday – **Meals** 155 (lunch)/190.

Château Poivre, 145 r. Château (14th) ℘ 01 43 22 03 68 – AE GB JCB   N 1
closed 8 to 21 August, 24 December-3 January and Sunday – **Meals** 89 and a la cart 150/270 ♀.

Régalade, 49 av. J. Moulin (14th) ℘ 01 45 45 68 58, *Fax 01 45 40 96 74,* bistro – ▤   R 1
GB. ⌁
closed August, Saturday lunch, Sunday and Monday – Meals (booking essential) 170.

Les Gourmands, 101 r. Ouest (14th) ℘ 01 45 41 40 70, *Fax 01 45 41 17 66* –   N 1
GB
closed August, Sunday and Monday – **Meals** 145/185.

St-Vincent, 26 r. Croix-Nivert (15th) ℘ 01 47 34 14 94, *Fax 01 45 66 02 80,* bistro   L
▤. AE GB
closed 10 to 20 August, Saturday lunch and Sunday – **Meals** a la carte 180/260 ♀.

Petit Mâchon, 123 r. Convention (15th) ℘ 01 45 54 08 62, bistro – GB   N
closed August, February Holidays and Sunday – **Meals** 95 (lunch), 145/230 and a la cart 180/300 ♀.

✗ **L'Agape,** 281 r. Lecourbe (15th) ☎ 01 45 58 19 29
GB   M 7
closed August, Saturday lunch and Sunday – **Meals** 120 ℣.

✗ **L'Amuse Bouche,** 186 r. Château (14th) ☎ 01 43 35 31 61, *Fax 01 45 38 96 60* –
GB   N 11
closed August, Monday lunch and Sunday – **Meals** (booking essential) 178 ℣.

✗ **Les Coteaux,** 26 bd Garibaldi (15th) ☎ 01 47 34 83 48, bistro – **GB**   L 9
closed August, Monday dinner, Saturday and Sunday – **Meals** 130.

Passy, Auteuil, Bois de Boulogne, Chaillot, Porte Maillot.

16th arrondissement.
16th: ✉ *75016 or 75116*

Raphaël, 17 av. Kléber ✉ 75116 ☎ 01 44 28 00 28, *Fax 01 45 01 21 50,* 🎋, « Elegant period decor and panoramic terrace with ≤ Paris » – 📶, ✼ rm, 🔲 📺 ☎ – 🔧 50. **AE**
① **GB** **JCB**   F 7
Salle à Manger ☎ 01 44 00 00 17 *(closed August, Saturday, Sunday and Bank Holidays)*
Meals 300 b.i.(lunch) and a la carte 340/410 – ☐ 175 – **62 rm** 2340/2820, 25 suites.

Parc Ⓜ ⊗, 55 av. R. Poincaré ✉ 75116 ☎ 01 44 05 66 66, *Fax 01 44 05 66 00,* 🎋,
« Fine English furniture » – 📶, ✼ rm, 🔲 📺 ☎ ♿ – 🔧 30 - 250. **AE** **①** **GB**
JCB   G 6
see **Alain Ducasse** below - **Relais du Parc** ☎ 01 44 05 66 10 **Meals** a la carte 230/370
– ☐ 140 – **116 rm** 2100/3100, 3 duplex.

St-James Paris ⊗, 43 av. Bugeaud ✉ 75116 ☎ 01 44 05 81 81, *Fax 01 44 05 81 82,*
🎋, « Attractive 19C mansion », ⅃, 🛋 – 📶 🔲 📺 ☎ Ⓟ – 🔧 25. **AE** **①** **GB**
JCB   F 5
Meals *(closed weekends and Bank Holidays)* (residents only) 250 and a la carte 290/450
– ☐ 110 – **20 rm** 1850/2500, 20 suites, 8 duplex.

Baltimore Ⓜ, 88bis av. Kléber ✉ 75116 ☎ 01 44 34 54 54, *Fax 01 44 34 54 44,*
« Attractive decor » – 📶, ✼ rm, 🔲 📺 ☎ – 🔧 80. **AE** **①** **GB** **JCB**   G 7
Bertie's ☎ 01 44 34 54 34 - British rest. *(closed Saturday and Sunday)* **Meals** 220 and a
la carte 230/340 – ☐ 140 – **105 rm** 2170/3500.

K. Palace Ⓜ without rest, 81 av. Kléber ✉ 75116 ☎ 01 44 05 75 75,
Fax 01 44 05 74 74, « Contemporary decor », ⅃ – 📶, ✼ rm, 🔲 📺 ☎ ♿ 🚗. **AE** **①**
GB **JCB**   G 7
☐ 130 – **82 rm** 1990/2890.

Trocadero Dokhan's without rest, 117 r. Lauriston ✉ 75116 ☎ 01 53 65 66 99,
Fax 01 53 65 66 88, « Elegant decor and fine furniture » – 📶, ✼ rm, 🔲 📺 ☎. **AE** **①**
GB **JCB**. ✼   G 6
☐ 120 – **41 rm** 2300, 4 suites.

Square Ⓜ without rest, 3 r. Boulainvilliers ✉ 75016 ☎ 01 44 14 91 90,
Fax 01 44 14 91 99, « Contemporary decor » – 📶 🔲 📺 ☎ ♿ 🚗. **AE** **①** **GB** **JCB**.
✼   K 5
see **Zébra Square** below – ☐ 90 – **22 rm** 1400/2600.

Pergolèse Ⓜ without rest, 3 r. Pergolèse ✉ 75116 ☎ 01 53 64 04 04,
Fax 01 53 64 04 40, « Contemporary decor » – 📶, ✼ rm, 🔲 📺 ☎. **AE** **①** **GB**
JCB   E 6
☐ 80 – **40 rm** 1000/1800.

Élysées Régencia Ⓜ without rest, 41 av. Marceau ✉ 75116 ☎ 01 47 20 42 65,
Fax 01 49 52 03 42, « Attractive decor » – 📶, ✼ rm, 🔲 📺 ☎. **AE** **①** **GB** **JCB**.
✼   G 8
☐ 115 – **41 rm** 1560/2000.

Villa Maillot Ⓜ without rest, 143 av. Malakoff ✉ 75116 ☎ 01 53 64 52 52,
Fax 01 45 00 60 61 – 📶 🔲 📺 ☎ ♿ – 🔧 25. **AE** **①** **GB** **JCB**   F 6
☐ 110 – **39 rm** 1580/1800, 3 suites.

Garden Élysée Ⓜ ⊗ without rest, 12 r. St-Didier ✉ 75116 ☎ 01 47 55 01 11,
Fax 01 47 27 79 24 – 📶, ✼ rm, 🔲 📺 ☎ ♿. **AE** **①** **GB** **JCB**. ✼   G 7
☐ 100 – **48 rm** 1200/1800.

Majestic without rest, 29 r. Dumont d'Urville ✉ 75116 ℰ 01 45 00 83 7(
Fax 01 45 00 29 48 – |≜|, ✳ rm, 🖵 📺 ☎. ΑΕ ⓪ GB JCB   F
☕ 70 – **27 rm** 1300/1900, 3 suites.

Libertel Auteuil Ⓜ without rest, 8 r. F. David ✉ 75016 ℰ 01 40 50 57 5‹
Fax 01 40 50 57 50 – |≜|, ✳ rm, 🖵 📺 ☎ �&. 🚗 – ᙛ 35. ΑΕ ⓪ GB   K
☕ 75 – **94 rm** 1025/1400.

Argentine Ⓜ without rest, 1 r. Argentine ✉ 75116 ℰ 01 45 02 76 7‹
Fax 01 45 02 76 00 – |≜|, ✳ rm, 📺 ☎ �&. ΑΕ ⓪ GB JCB   E
☕ 75 – **40 rm** 1300/1620.

Élysées Sablons Ⓜ without rest, 32 r. Greuze ✉ 75116 ℰ 01 47 27 10 0(
Fax 01 47 27 47 10 – |≜|, ✳ rm, 📺 ☎ �&. ΑΕ ⓪ GB JCB. ✵   G
☕ 75 – **41 rm** 1025/1350.

Élysées Bassano without rest, 24 r. Bassano ✉ 75116 ℰ 01 47 20 49 0‹
Fax 01 47 23 06 72 – |≜|, ✳ rm, 📺 ☎. ΑΕ ⓪ GB JCB   G
☕ 75 – **40 rm** 950/1290.

Alexander without rest, 102 av. V. Hugo ✉ 75116 ℰ 01 45 53 64 6‹
Fax 01 45 53 12 51 – |≜| 📺 ☎. ΑΕ ⓪ GB JCB. ✵   G
☕ 95 – **62 rm** 990/1690.

Frémiet without rest, 6 av. Frémiet ✉ 75016 ℰ 01 45 24 52 06, *Fax 01 42 88 77 4*
– |≜| 📺 ☎. ΑΕ ⓪ GB JCB   J
☕ 60 – **36 rm** 600/1200.

Élysées Union without rest, 44 r. Hamelin ✉ 75116 ℰ 01 45 53 14 9‹
Fax 01 47 55 94 79 – |≜| kitchenette 📺 ☎. ΑΕ ⓪ GB JCB   G
☕ 45 – **28 rm** 820/940, 13 suites.

Résidence Impériale Ⓜ without rest, 155 av. Malakoff ✉ 75116 ℰ 01 45 00 23 4‹
Fax 01 45 01 88 82 – |≜|, ✳ rm, 🖵 📺 ☎. ΑΕ ⓪ GB   E
☕ 55 – **37 rm** 790/890.

Kléber without rest, 7 r. Belloy ✉ 75116 ℰ 01 47 23 80 22, *Fax 01 49 52 07 20* – |≜
✳ rm, 🖵 📺 ☎. ΑΕ ⓪ GB JCB   G
☕ 65 – **23 rm** 950/1290.

Floride Étoile without rest, 14 r. St-Didier ✉ 75116 ℰ 01 47 27 23 3‹
Fax 01 47 27 82 87 – |≜| 📺 ☎ – ᙛ 30. ΑΕ ⓪ GB JCB. ✵   G
☕ 60 – **60 rm** 850/980.

Jardins du Trocadéro Ⓜ without rest, 35 r. Franklin ✉ 75116 ℰ 01 53 70 17 7(
Fax 01 53 70 17 80 – |≜|, ✳ rm, 🖵 📺 ☎. ΑΕ ⓪ GB. ✵   H
☕ 75 – **18 rm** 790/1450.

Passy Eiffel without rest, 10 r. Passy ✉ 75016 ℰ 01 45 25 55 66, *Fax 01 42 88 89 8*
– |≜| 📺 ☎. ΑΕ ⓪ GB JCB   J
☕ 50 – **48 rm** 580/900.

Sévigné without rest, 6 r. Belloy ✉ 75116 ℰ 01 47 20 88 90, *Fax 01 40 70 98 73*
|≜| 📺 ☎. ΑΕ ⓪ GB JCB   G
☕ 50 – **30 rm** 650/770.

Victor Hugo without rest, 19 r. Copernic ✉ 75116 ℰ 01 45 53 76 0‹
Fax 01 45 53 69 93 – |≜| 🖵 📺 ☎. ΑΕ ⓪ GB JCB. ✵   G
☕ 65 – **75 rm** 690/860.

Chambellan Morgane without rest, 6 r. Keppler ✉ 75116 ℰ 01 47 20 35 7‹
Fax 01 47 20 95 69 – |≜| 📺 ☎. ΑΕ ⓪ GB JCB   GF
☕ 55 – **20 rm** 700/900.

Étoile Maillot without rest, 10 r. Bois de Boulogne (angle r. Duret) ✉ 7511
ℰ 01 45 00 42 60, *Fax 01 45 00 55 89* – |≜| 📺 ☎. ΑΕ ⓪ GB JCB   F
☕ 45 – **28 rm** 570/850.

Royal Élysées without rest, 6 av. V. Hugo ✉ 75116 ℰ 01 45 00 05 5‹
Fax 01 45 00 13 88 – |≜| 🖵 📺 ☎. ΑΕ ⓪ GB JCB   F
☕ 50 – **35 rm** 1107/1214.

Hameau de Passy Ⓜ ᙏ without rest, 48 r. Passy ✉ 75016 ℰ 01 42 88 47 5‹
Fax 01 42 30 83 72 – 📺 ☎. ΑΕ ⓪ GB JCB   J 5‹
☕ 30 – **32 rm** 530/570.

Eiffel Kennedy without rest, 12 r. Boulainvilliers ✉ 75016 ℰ 01 45 24 45 7‹
Fax 01 42 30 83 32 – |≜|, ✳ rm, 🖵 📺 ☎. ΑΕ ⓪ GB JCB   K
☕ 50 – **30 rm** 700/800.

Gavarni without rest, 5 r. Gavarni ✉ 75116 ℰ 01 45 24 52 82, *Fax 01 40 50 16 95*
|≜| 📺 ☎. ΑΕ ⓪ GB JCB. ✵   J
☕ 35 – **30 rm** 395/530.

Queen's Hôtel without rest, 4 r. Bastien Lepage ✉ 75016 ℰ 01 42 88 89 85, *Fax 01 40 50 67 52* – |♯|, ✺ rm, TV ☎. AE ① GB JCB. ✖
K 4
☕ 40 – **22 rm** 390/590.

Nicolo without rest, 3 r. Nicolo ✉ 75116 ℰ 01 42 88 83 40, *Fax 01 42 24 45 41* – |♯|
TV ☎. AE GB JCB
J 6
☕ 40 – **28 rm** 415/460.

Longchamp without rest, 68 r. Longchamp ✉ 75116 ℰ 01 47 27 13 48, *Fax 01 47 55 68 26* – |♯| TV ☎. AE ① GB JCB
G 6
☕ 50 – **23 rm** 680/750.

Palais de Chaillot without rest, 35 av. R. Poincaré ✉ 75116 ℰ 01 53 70 09 09, *Fax 01 53 70 09 08* – |♯| TV ☎. AE ① GB JCB. ✖
G 6
☕ 42 – **28 rm** 470/620.

Boileau without rest, 81 r. Boileau ✉ 75016 ℰ 01 42 88 83 74, *Fax 01 45 27 62 98* –
TV ☎ – 🛁 15. AE ① GB JCB
M 3
☕ 40 – **30 rm** 390/480.

XXXX ✿✿✿ **Alain Ducasse,** 59 av. R. Poincaré ✉ 75116 ℰ 01 47 27 12 27, *Fax 01 47 27 31 22,* « Elegant mansion with Art Nouveau decor » – ▤. AE ① GB JCB. ✖
G 6
closed 16 July-17 August, 24 December-4 January, Saturday and Sunday – **Meals** 950/1520 and a la carte 770/1 040
Spec. Pâtes mi-séchées, crémées et truffées aux ris de veau, crêtes et rognons de coqs. Pièce de bœuf Rossini, pommes soufflées. Coupe glacée selon saison.

XXXX ✿✿ **Faugeron,** 52 r. Longchamp ✉ 75116 ℰ 01 47 04 24 53, *Fax 01 47 55 62 90,* « Attractive decor » – ▤. AE GB JCB. ✖
G 7
closed August, 23 December-3 January, Saturday except dinner from October-April and Sunday – **Meals** 320 (lunch), 470/550 and a la carte 490/720 ♀
Spec. Œufs coque à la purée de truffe. Truffes (January-March). Gibier (15 October-10 January).

XXXX ✿ **Maison Prunier,** 16 av. V. Hugo ✉ 75116 ℰ 01 44 17 35 85, *Fax 01 44 17 90 10,* « Art Deco decor » – ▤. AE ① GB JCB
FG 8
closed 18 July-16 August, Monday lunch and Sunday – **Meals** - Seafood - a la carte 400/660 ♀
Spec. Soupe crémeuse de homard aux haricots blancs et chorizo. Gros filets de sole cuits au beurre demi-sel et aux herbes fraîches. Petits pots de crème Emile Prunier.

XXXX ✿✿ **Vivarois** (Peyrot), 192 av. V. Hugo ✉ 75116 ℰ 01 45 04 04 31, *Fax 01 45 03 09 84* –
▤. AE ① GB JCB
G 5
closed August, Saturday and Sunday – **Meals** 355 (lunch) and a la carte 430/650 ♀
Spec. Salade de légumes à la coriandre. Bar au caviar d'aubergine. Ris de veau braisé aux champignons des bois.

XXX ✿✿ **Jamin** (Guichard), 32 r. Longchamp ✉ 75116 ℰ 01 45 53 00 07, *Fax 01 45 53 00 15* –
▤. AE ① GB
G 7
closed 1 to 25 August, Saturday and Sunday – **Meals** 300 (lunch)/410 and a la carte 390/550
Spec. Velouté aux langoustines de petite pêche (April-October). Filet de bar aux pistaches, crème légère de langoustines et coques. Carré d'agneau grillé aux herbes potagères, petits légumes glacés à l'huile d'olive.

XXX ✿✿ **Relais d'Auteuil** (Pignol), 31 bd Murat ✉ 75016 ℰ 01 46 51 09 54, *Fax 01 40 71 05 03* – ▤. AE ① GB JCB
L 3
closed 1 to 21 August, Saturday lunch and Sunday – **Meals** 260 (lunch), 490/590 and a la carte 420/600
Spec. Amandine de foie gras. Dos de bar à la croûte poivrée. Madeleines au miel de bruyère, glace miel et noix.

XXX ✿ **Pergolèse** (Corre), 40 r. Pergolèse ✉ 75116 ℰ 01 45 00 21 40, *Fax 01 45 00 81 31* –
▤. AE GB
F 6
closed August, Saturday and Sunday – **Meals** 235/390 and a la carte 310/480
Spec. Saint-Jacques en robe des champs (October-February). Côte de veau de lait en casserole aux champignons. Moelleux au chocolat, glace vanille.

XXX **Tsé-Yang,** 25 av. Pierre 1er de Serbie ✉ 75016 ℰ 01 47 20 70 22, *Fax 01 49 52 03 68,* « Tasteful decor » – ▤. AE ① GB JCB. ✖
G 8
Meals - Chinese rest. - 180 (lunch), 200/300 and a la carte 250/310.

XXX ✿ **Port Alma** (Canal), 10 av. New-York ✉ 75116 ℰ 01 47 23 75 11, *Fax 01 47 20 42 92* – ▤. AE ① GB
H 8
closed August and Sunday – **Meals** - Seafood - 200 and a la carte 300/440
Spec. Gaspacho de homard (May-September). Bar en croûte de sel de Guérande. Soufflé au chocolat.

XXX **Pavillon Noura,** 21 av. Marceau ✉ 75116 ℰ 01 47 20 33 33, *Fax 01 47 20 60 31* –
▤. AE ① GB. ✖
G 8
Meals - Lebanese rest. - 168 (lunch), 280/350 and a la carte 160/220.

XX **Zébra Square,** 3 pl. Clément Ader ⊠ 75016 ℘ 01 44 14 91 91, Fax 01 45 20 46 4
« Original contemporary decor » – AE ⓪ GB JCB   K
Meals a la carte 180/330 ♀.

XX **Marius,** 82 bd Murat ⊠ 75016 ℘ 01 46 51 67 80, Fax 01 47 43 10 24, 🌳 – A
GB   M
closed 1 to 22 August, Saturday lunch and Sunday – **Meals** a la carte 200/290 ♀.

XX **Giulio Rebellato,** 136 r. Pompe ⊠ 75116 ℘ 01 47 27 50 26 – ▤. AE GB. ✊   G
closed 20 July-20 August – **Meals** - Italian rest. - 190 (lunch)and a la carte 280/380.

XX **Al Mounia,** 16 r. Magdebourg ⊠ 75116 ℘ 01 47 27 57 28, « Moorish decor » – ▤
AE GB. ✊   G
closed 14 July-31 August and Sunday – **Meals** - Moroccan rest. - (dinner booking essentia
a la carte 200/260.

XX **San Francisco,** 1 r. Mirabeau ⊠ 75016 ℘ 01 46 47 75 44, Fax 01 46 47 84 89 – ▤
⓪ GB
closed Sunday – **Meals** - Italian rest. - a la carte 240/310 ♀.

XX **Bellini,** 28 r. Lesueur ⊠ 75116 ℘ 01 45 00 54 20, Fax 01 45 00 11 74 – ▤. A
GB   F
closed Saturday lunch and Sunday – **Meals** - Italian rest. - 180 (lunch)/185 and a la cart
210/340 ♀.

XX **Paul Chêne,** 123 r. Lauriston ⊠ 75116 ℘ 01 47 27 63 17, Fax 01 47 27 53 18 – ▤
AE ⓪ GB   G
closed 7 to 29 August, 24 December-1 January, Saturday lunch and Sunday – **Mea
200/250 and a la carte 200/400.

XX **Conti,** 72 r. Lauriston ⊠ 75116 ℘ 01 47 27 74 67, Fax 01 47 27 37 66 – ▤. AE ⓪
❀ GB   G
closed 2 to 21 August, 24 December-3 January, Saturday, Sunday and Bank Holidays
Meals - Italian rest. - 198 (lunch)and a la carte 310/420
Spec. Tortellini au crabe (April-October). Agneau de lait au romarin et anchois truffé
(February-May). Figues rôties farcies aux amaretti (September and October).

XX **Vinci,** 23 r. P. Valéry ⊠ 75116 ℘ 01 45 01 68 18, Fax 01 45 01 60 37 – ▤. GB   F
closed 1 to 21 August, Saturday, Sunday and Bank Holidays – **Meals** - Italian rest. - 165 ♀.

XX **Tang,** 125 r. de la Tour ⊠ 75116 ℘ 01 45 04 35 35, Fax 01 45 04 58 19 – AE G
✊   H
closed 26 July-25 August and Monday – **Meals** - Chinese and Thai rest. - 200 (lunch)/25
and a la carte 250/360.

XX **Chez Géraud,** 31 r. Vital ⊠ 75016 ℘ 01 45 20 33 00, Fax 01 45 20 46 60, « Longw
porcelain mural » – AE GB   H
closed August, Sunday dinner and Saturday – **Meals** 180 and a la carte 220/340 ♀.

XX **Fontaine d'Auteuil,** 35bis r. La Fontaine ⊠ 75016 ℘ 01 42 88 04 4
Fax 01 42 88 95 12 – ▤. AE ⓪ GB   K
closed 1 to 23 August, Saturday lunch and Sunday – **Meals** 175 ♀.

XX **Petite Tour,** 11 r. de la Tour ⊠ 75116 ℘ 01 45 20 09 31 – AE ⓪ GB JCB   H
closed 1 to 24 August and Sunday – **Meals** a la carte 260/480.

XX **Detourbe Duret,** 23 r. Duret ⊠ 75116 ℘ 01 45 00 10 26, Fax 01 45 00 10 16 – ▤
AE GB   F
closed 24 July-24 August, Saturday lunch and Sunday – **Meals** 160 (lunch)/220 and a
carte 180/300 ♀.

X **A et M Le Bistrot,** 136 bd Murat ⊠ 75016 ℘ 01 45 27 39 60, Fax 01 45 27 69 7
🌳 – AE GB   M
closed 7 to 23 August, Saturday lunch and Sunday – **Meals** a la carte 170/210.

X **Vin et Marée,** 2 r. Daumier ⊠ 75016 ℘ 01 46 47 91 39, Fax 01 46 47 69 07 – AE G
Meals - Seafood - a la carte 170/270 ♀.

X **Butte Chaillot,** 110 bis av. Kléber ⊠ 75116 ℘ 01 47 27 88 88, Fax 01 47 04 85 7
– ▤. AE ⓪ GB JCB   G
Meals 150/195 and a la carte 220/310 ♀.

X **Cuisinier François,** 19 r. Le Marois ⊠ 75016 ℘ 01 45 27 83 74, Fax 01 45 27 83 7
– AE GB JCB   M
closed August, February Holidays, Sunday and Monday – **Meals** 160 and a la cart
270/430 ♀.

X **Les Ormes,** 8 r. Chapu ⊠ 75016 ℘ 01 46 47 83 98, Fax 01 46 47 83 98 – GB   M
closed 1 to 23 August, Monday lunch, Sunday and Bank Holidays – **Meals** 190 (dinner)/20
b.i. (lunch) ♀.

X **Gare,** 19 chaussée de la Muette ⊠ 75016 ℘ 01 42 15 15 31, Fax 01 42 15 15 23, 🌳
« Original decor in converted 1854 railway station » – AE GB   J
Meals a la carte 150/270 ♀.

✃ **Bistrot de l'Étoile Lauriston,** 19 r. Lauriston ✉ 75016 ☎ 01 40 67 11 16,
Fax 01 45 00 99 87 – 🔲. **AE** ⓪ **GB** **JCB**   F 7
closed Saturday lunch and Sunday – **Meals** 165 and a la carte 200/260 ♈.

✃ **Rosimar,** 26 r. Poussin ✉ 75016 ☎ 01 45 27 74 91, *Fax 01 45 27 34 10* – 🔲. **AE GB**
JCB   K 3
closed August, 24 to 30 December, Saturday lunch, Sunday and Bank Holidays – **Meals**
- Spanish rest- 175 and a la carte 180/310 🍶.

✃ **Scheffer,** 22 r. Scheffer ✉ 75116 ☎ 01 47 27 81 11, bistro – **AE GB**   H 6
closed 24 December-1 January, Sunday and Bank Holidays – **Meals** a la carte 140/210 ♈.

✃ **Mathusalem,** 5 bis bd Exelmans ✉ 75016 ☎ 01 42 88 10 73, *Fax 01 42 88 42 43,*
bistro – **GB**   M 4
closed Saturday, Sunday and Bank Holidays – **Meals** 133 ♈.

✃ **Brasserie de la Poste,** 54 r. Longchamp ✉ 75116 ☎ 01 47 55 01 31 – **AE**
GB   G 7
Meals 125/185 and a la carte 160/300 ♈.

✃ **Victor,** 101 bis r. Lauriston ✉ 75116 ☎ 01 47 27 72 21, bistro – 🔲. **AE GB**   G 7
closed 1 to 23 August, Saturday lunch, Sunday and Bank Holidays – **Meals** a la carte
200/270 ♈.

n the Bois de Boulogne :

✃✃✃✃ **Pré Catelan,** rte Suresnes ✉ 75016 ☎ 01 44 14 41 14, *Fax 01 45 24 43 25,* 🌯,
❀❀ « Napoleon III pavillon », 🍴 – 🔲 **P. AE** ⓪ **GB JCB**   H 2
closed February Holidays, Sunday dinner and Monday – **Meals** 295 (lunch), 550/690 and
a la carte 430/800
Spec. Feuilles sèches de poireau, poulette d'escargots de Champagne aux champignons
poêlés (April-October). Saint-Pierre poêlé, pétales de brocoli, bouillon aux câpres. Etuvée
de petites bananes, bugnes au sucre, crème glacée rhum-raisin.

✃✃✃✃ **Grande Cascade,** allée de Longchamp (opposite the hippodrome) ✉ 75016
❀ ☎ 01 45 27 33 51, *Fax 01 42 88 99 06,* 🌯, « Second Empire pavilion » – **P. AE** ⓪ **GB**
JCB
closed 20 December-20 January – **Meals** 295/600 and a la carte 460/720
Spec. Pâté en croûte. Macaroni aux truffes noires, foie gras et céleri. Caneton de Challans
rôti aux épices, navets et échalotes confits.

Clichy, Ternes,
Wagram.

17th arrondissement.
17th: ✉ 75017

🏨 **Meridien Étoile** Ⓜ, 81 bd Gouvion St-Cyr ☎ 01 40 68 34 34, *Fax 01 40 68 31 31* – 🛗,
✓ rm, 🔲 **TV** ☎ ♿ – 🛎 50 - 1 500. **AE** ⓪ **GB JCB**   E 6
Café Arlequin ☎ 01 40 68 30 85 **Meals** 169 – **Yamato** ☎ 01 40 68 30 41, Japanese
rest. *(closed August, 1 to 7 January, Saturday lunch, Sunday and Monday)* **Meals** 175 and
a la carte approx. 230 – 🍵 115 – **1 005 rm** 2400/2900, 20 suites.

🏨 **Concorde La Fayette** Ⓜ, 3 pl. Gén. Koenig ☎ 01 40 68 50 68, *Fax 01 40 68 50 43,*
« Panoramic bar on 33rd floor with ⩽ Paris » – 🛗, ✓ rm, 🔲 **TV** ☎ – 🛎 40 - 2 000.
AE ⓪ **GB JCB**   E 6
see *L'Étoile d'Or* below - *L'Arc-en-Ciel* (buffet) ☎ 01 40 68 51 25 *(closed July, August
and February Holidays)* **Meals** 168/278 ♈ – *Les Saisons* (rest.-tea room) ☎ 01 40 68 51 19
Meals 159 ♈ – 🍵 135 – **943 rm** 1850/2400, 27 suites.

🏨 **Splendid Étoile** without rest, 1bis av. Carnot ☎ 01 45 72 72 00, *Fax 01 45 72 72 01*
– 🛗 **TV** ☎. **AE** ⓪ **GB**. ⛌   F 7
🍵 90 – **53 rm** 1000/1300, 4 suites.

🏨 **Balmoral** without rest, 6 r. Gén. Lanrezac ☎ 01 43 80 30 50, *Fax 01 43 80 51 56* – 🛗,
✓ rm, 🔲 **TV** ☎. **AE** ⓪ **GB**   E 7
🍵 45 – **57 rm** 600/895.

🏨 **Regent's Garden** without rest, 6 r. P. Demours ☎ 01 45 74 07 30, *Fax 01 40 55 01 42,*
« Garden » – 🛗 **TV** ☎. **AE** ⓪ **GB JCB**. ⛌   E 7
🍵 50 – **39 rm** 710/1030.

Banville without rest, 166 bd Berthier ℰ 01 42 67 70 16, *Fax 01 44 40 42 77*, « Elegan atmosphere » – 🛗 ▤ ▣ ☎. AE ① GB JCB   D
☕ 65 – **38 rm** 760/1050.

Villa Alessandra Ⓜ 🦢 without rest, 9 pl. Boulnois ℰ 01 56 33 24 24 *Fax 01 56 33 24 30* – 🛗, ↹ rm, ▤ ▣ ☎ & 🚗. AE ① GB JCB. 🛇   E
☕ 80 – **49 rm** 890/1210.

Magellan 🦢 without rest, 17 r. J.B.-Dumas ℰ 01 45 72 44 51, *Fax 01 40 68 90 36,* 🦢 – 🛗 ▣ ☎. AE ① GB. 🛇   D
☕ 40 – **75 rm** 610/650.

Champerret Elysées without rest, 129 av. Villiers ℰ 01 47 64 44 00 *Fax 01 47 63 10 58* – 🛗, ↹ rm, ▤ ▣ ☎. AE ① GB JCB   D
☕ 60 – **45 rm** 585/675.

de Neuville without rest, 3 r. Verniquet ℰ 01 43 80 26 30, *Fax 01 43 80 38 55* – ▣ ☎. AE ① GB JCB   C
☕ 55 – **28 rm** 750.

Cheverny without rest, 7 villa Berthier ℰ 01 42 12 44 00, *Fax 01 47 63 26 62* – 🛗 ▣ ☎ – 🔼 40. AE ① GB JCB. 🛇   D
☕ 60 – **48 rm** 610/810.

Mercure Étoile Ⓜ without rest, 27 av. Ternes ℰ 01 47 66 49 18, *Fax 01 47 63 77 9* – 🛗, ↹ rm, ▤ ▣ ☎. AE ① GB JCB   E
☕ 72 – **56 rm** 900.

Quality Inn Pierre Ⓜ without rest, 25 r. Th.-de-Banville ℰ 01 47 63 76 6 *Fax 01 43 80 63 96* – 🛗, ↹ rm, ▣ ☎ & – 🔼 30. AE ① GB JCB   D
☕ 75 – **50 rm** 850/1500.

Ternes Arc de Triomphe Ⓜ without rest, 97 av. Ternes ℰ 01 53 81 94 94 *Fax 01 53 81 94 95* – 🛗, ↹ rm, ▤ ▣ ☎ &. AE ① GB JCB   E
☕ 70 – **39 rm** 690/1150.

Neva Ⓜ without rest, 14 r. Brey ℰ 01 43 80 28 26, *Fax 01 47 63 00 22* – 🛗 ▤ ▣ &. AE ① GB JCB. 🛇   E
☕ 45 – **31 rm** 685/780.

Étoile St-Ferdinand without rest, 36 r. St-Ferdinand ℰ 01 45 72 66 66 *Fax 01 45 74 12 92* – 🛗 ▣ ☎. AE ① GB JCB. 🛇   E 6
☕ 60 – **42 rm** 950/1300.

Étoile Park Hôtel without rest, 10 av. Mac Mahon ℰ 01 42 67 69 63 *Fax 01 43 80 18 99* – 🛗 ▣ ☎. AE ① GB JCB   E
closed 24 December-2 January – ☕ 52 – **28 rm** 490/710.

Astrid without rest, 27 av. Carnot ℰ 01 44 09 26 00, *Fax 01 44 09 26 01* – 🛗 ▣ ☎ AE ① GB JCB   E
☕ 50 – **40 rm** 495/795.

Comfort Hôtel Villiers Étoile Ⓜ without rest, 6 r. Lebouteux ℰ 01 40 53 05 0 *Fax 01 40 53 05 06* – 🛗, ↹ rm, ▣ ☎ &. AE ① GB JCB   D
☕ 60 – **55 rm** 600/800.

Flaubert without rest, 19 r. Rennequin ℰ 01 46 22 44 35, *Fax 01 43 80 32 34* – 🛗 ▣ ☎ &. AE ① GB   D
☕ 40 – **37 rm** 480/650.

Campanile, 4 bd Berthier ℰ 01 46 27 10 00, *Fax 01 46 27 00 57*, 🌳 – 🛗, ↹ rm, ▣ ☎ & 🚗 – 🔼 15 - 40. AE ① GB   B
Meals 94/109 ♟ – ☕ 39 – **246 rm** 550.

Guy Savoy, 18 r. Troyon ℰ 01 43 80 40 61, *Fax 01 46 22 43 09* – ▤. AE ① GB JCB   E
closed Saturday lunch and Sunday – **Meals** 880 and a la carte 630/850 ♟
Spec. Crème légère de lentilles et langoustines. Côte de Veau rôtie, purée de pommes d terre à la truffe. Menu autour de la truffe (10 January-15 March).

L'Étoile d'Or - Hôtel Concorde La Fayette, 3 pl. Gén. Koenig (1st floor) ℰ 01 40 68 51 2 *Fax 01 40 68 50 43* – ▤. AE ① GB JCB   E
closed 31 July-30 August, 20 February-7 March, Saturday, Sunday and Bank Holidays **Meals** 270 and a la carte 310/580 ♟
Spec. Foie gras frais de canard aux quatre épices, compotée de fruits secs. Joue de bœu en ravigote. Soufflé chaud au chocolat.

Michel Rostang, 20 r. Rennequin ℰ 01 47 63 40 77, *Fax 01 47 63 82 75*, « Elegan decor » – ▤. AE ① GB JCB   D
closed 1 to 15 August, Saturday lunch, Monday lunch and Sunday – **Meals** 350 (lunch 650/870 and a la carte 590/970 ♟
Spec. Brochettes de langoustines au romarin, grappes de tomates farcies. Canette au sar en deux services. Carte des truffes (15 December-15 March).

FRANCE

XXX **Apicius** (Vigato), 122 av. Villiers *01 43 80 19 66, Fax 01 44 40 09 57* – ☰. **AE ①** **GB** **JCB**
D 8
closed August, Saturday and Sunday – **Meals** 620 and a la carte 370/590
Spec. Foie gras de canard poêlé en aigre-doux aux radis noirs confits. Tronçon de homard bleu au four. Grand dessert tout chocolat.

XXX **Faucher,** 123 av. Wagram *01 42 27 61 50, Fax 01 46 22 25 72,* 🌳 – **AE GB**
D 8
closed Saturday lunch and Sunday – **Meals** a la carte 280/510 ♀
Spec. Œuf au plat, foie gras chaud et coppa grillée. Ris de veau croustillant, pommes "Nikko". Moelleux de chocolat tiède, glace à la menthe.

XXX **Sormani** (Fayet), 4 r. Gén. Lanrezac *01 43 80 13 91, Fax 01 40 55 07 37* – ☰.
GB
E 7
closed 1 to 22 August, Saturday, Sunday and Bank Holidays – **Meals** - Italian rest. - 250 (lunch)and a la carte 320/430 ♀
Spec. Risotto "Primavera" (1 April-30 June). Salade de cèpes crus, parmesan et truffes blanches (1 September-15 November). Fritto Misto de légumes et de fruits de mer.

XXX **Pétrus,** 12 pl. Mar. Juin *01 43 80 15 95, Fax 01 43 80 06 96* – ☰. **AE ① GB**
D 8
closed 1 to 15 August – **Meals** - Seafood - 250 and a la carte 350/510 ♀.

XXX **Amphyclès** (Groult), 78 av. Ternes *01 40 68 01 01, Fax 01 40 68 91 88* – ☰. **AE ①**
GB JCB
E 7
closed Saturday lunch and Sunday – **Meals** 280 (lunch), 580/680 b.i. and a la carte 410/590 ♀
Spec. Omble chevalier et anguille fumée en brochette. Araignée de mer, tourteau et homard. Poularde de Bresse "vapeur" en risotto aux herbes.

XXX **Manoir Detourbe,** 6 r. P. Demours *01 45 72 25 25, Fax 01 45 74 80 98* – ☰. **AE**
① GB
E 7
closed Sunday – **Meals** (set dinner menu only) 180 (lunch)/220 ♀.

XXX **Augusta,** 98 r. Tocqueville *01 47 63 39 97, Fax 01 47 63 39 97* – ☰. **GB**
C 9
closed 2 to 23 August, Saturday except dinner from October-April and Sunday – **Meals** - Seafood - a la carte 320/550.

XXX **Timgad,** 21 r. Brunel *01 45 74 23 70, Fax 01 40 68 76 46,* « Moorish decor » – ☰.
AE ① GB. 🐾
E 7
Meals - Moroccan rest. - a la carte 230/380
Spec. Couscous. Tagine. Pastilla.

XX **Petit Colombier** (Fournier), 42 r. Acacias *01 43 80 28 54, Fax 01 44 40 04 29* – ☰.
AE GB
E 7
closed 1 to 18 August, Sunday except dinner from 15 September-1 May and Saturday – **Meals** 190 (lunch)/360 and a la carte 280/460 ♀
Spec. Œufs rôtis à la broche aux truffes fraîches (15 December-15 March). Grand pot-au-feu à l'ancienne (November-March). Pigeonneau fermier et sa farce fine à la croque au sel, sauce Périgueux.

XX **Les Béatilles** (Bochaton), 11 bis r. Villebois-Mareuil *01 45 74 43 80, Fax 01 45 74 43 81* – ☰. **AE GB**
E 7
closed 2 to 22 August, 24 December-3 January, Saturday and Sunday – **Meals** 180/310 and a la carte 260/360 ♀
Spec. Filets de maquereaux, champignons et bigorneaux. Croustillant de pied de porc, jus de persil et mesclun. Tarte tiède de noix et chocolat, crème glacée à la vanille.

XX **Braisière** (Vaxelaire), 54 r. Cardinet *01 47 63 40 37, Fax 01 47 63 04 76* – **AE**
GB
D 9
closed 8 to 16 May, August, Saturday and Sunday – **Meals** 185 and a la carte 280/370
Spec. Saint-Jacques aux pommes de terre et fleur de sel de Ré (October-April). Foie gras poêlé aux aubergines confites. Ris de veau entier au jus de veau et pommes de terre au foie gras.

XX **Dessirier,** 9 pl. Mar. Juin *01 42 27 82 14, Fax 01 47 66 82 07* – ☰. **AE ① GB**
D 8
Meals - Seafood - 208 and a la carte 290/490.

XX **Graindorge,** 15 r. Arc de Triomphe *01 47 54 00 28, Fax 01 47 54 00 28* – **AE GB**
JCB
E 7
closed 9 to 22 August, Saturday lunch and Sunday – **Meals** 168 (lunch), 188/250 and a la carte 220/330.

XX **L'Atelier Gourmand,** 20 r. Tocqueville *01 42 27 03 71, Fax 01 42 27 03 71* – **AE**
GB
D 10
closed 2 to 23 August, Saturday except dinner from 1 September-14 June and Sunday – **Meals** 175 ♀.

FRANCE

XX **Paolo Petrini,** 6 r. Débarcadère ✆ 01 45 74 25 95, *Fax 01 45 74 12 95* – 国. AE GB
JCB. ✗
E 6
closed 2 to 23 August and Saturday lunch – **Meals** - Italian rest. - 130 (lunch)/190 and a
la carte 200/360 ♀.

XX **Truite Vagabonde,** 17 r. Batignolles ✆ 01 43 87 77 80, *Fax 01 43 87 31 50,* ☂ – AE
GB
D 11
closed Sunday dinner – **Meals** 179 ♀.

XX **Ballon des Ternes,** 103 av. Ternes ✆ 01 45 74 17 98, *Fax 01 45 72 18 84,* brasserie
– AE GB JCB
E 6
closed 26 July-26 August – **Meals** a la carte 180/310 ♀.

XX **Auberge des Dolomites,** 38 r. Poncelet ✆ 01 42 27 94 56, *Fax 01 47 66 38 54* – AE
GB
E 8
closed 30 July-30 August, Saturday lunch and Sunday – **Meals** 138/188 and a la carte
200/356 ♀.

XX **Taïra,** 10 r. Acacias ✆ 01 47 66 74 14, *Fax 01 47 66 74 14* – 国. AE ①
GB
E 7
closed 15 to 25 August, February Holidays, Saturday lunch and Sunday – **Meals** - Seafood
- 180/330 and a la carte approx. 320.

XX **Beudant,** 97 r. des Dames ✆ 01 43 87 11 20, *Fax 01 43 87 27 35* – 国. AE ① GB
JCB
D 11
closed 8 to 26 August, Saturday lunch and Sunday – **Meals** 165/300 and a la carte
210/340 ♀.

XX **Chez Léon,** 32 r. Legendre ✆ 01 42 27 06 82, *Fax 01 46 22 63 67,* bistro – ①
GB
D 10
closed August, Saturday and Sunday – **Meals** (booking essential) 120/185 and a la carte
160/290 ♀.

XX **Les Blés Coupés,** 4 r. P. Demours ✆ 01 45 74 42 41, *Fax 01 45 74 80 98* – 国. AE ①
GB
E 7
Meals 175.

X **Rôtisserie d'Armaillé,** 6 r. Armaillé ✆ 01 42 27 19 20, *Fax 01 40 55 00 93* – 国. AE
① GB JCB
E 7
closed 1 to 15 August, Saturday lunch and Sunday – **Meals** 218.

X **Bistrot de l'Étoile Niel,** 75 av. Niel ✆ 01 42 27 88 44, *Fax 01 42 27 32 12* – 国. AE
① GB JCB
D 8
Meals 160/200 (lunch)and a la carte 200/300 ♀.

X **Soupière,** 154 av. Wagram ✆ 01 42 27 00 73 – 国. AE GB
D 9
closed 7 to 22 August, Saturday lunch and Sunday – **Meals** 138/295 and a la carte 190/240.

X **Petite Auberge,** 38 r. Laugier ✆ 01 47 63 85 51, *Fax 01 47 63 85 81* – AE
GB
D 7-8
closed August, Monday lunch and Sunday – **Meals** (booking essential) 170.

X **Caves Petrissans,** 30 bis av. Niel ✆ 01 42 27 52 03, *Fax 01 40 54 87 56,* ☂, bistro
– AE GB
D 8
closed 2 to 22 August, Saturday, Sunday and Bank Holidays – **Meals** 170 and a la carte
210/280 ♀.

X **L'Impatient,** 14 passage Geffroy Didelot ✆ 01 43 87 28 10 – GB   D 10-11
closed 1 to 15 August, 28 February-5 March, Monday dinner, Saturday and Sunday – **Meals**
102 (lunch), 120/285 and a la carte 240/320 ♀.

X **Troyon,** 4 r. Troyon ✆ 01 40 68 99 40, *Fax 01 40 68 99 57* – AE GB   E 8
closed 10 to 31 August, Saturday lunch and Sunday – **Meals** (booking essential) 198 ♀.

X **Café d'Angel,** 16 r. Brey ✆ 01 47 54 03 33, *Fax 01 47 54 03 33,* bistro –
GB
E 8
closed 1 to 21 August, 24 December-5 January, Saturday and Sunday – **Meals** 95 (lunch),
145/180 ♀.

X **L'Ampère,** 1 r. Ampère ✆ 01 47 63 72 05, *Fax 01 47 63 37 33,* bistro – AE GB   D 9
closed Saturday lunch and Sunday – **Meals** a la carte 160/220 ♀.

X **Chez Ballot,** 14 r. Thann ✆ 01 42 27 25 43 – GB   D 10
closed August, Saturday, Sunday and Bank Holidays – **Meals** 148 and a la carte
150/250.

X **Bistrot de l'Étoile Troyon,** 13 r. Troyon ✆ 01 42 67 25 95, *Fax 01 46 22 43 09* –
国. AE ① GB JCB
E 8
closed 25 July-25 August, Saturday lunch and Sunday – **Meals** (booking essential) 175 and
a la carte 210/280 ♀.

X **Bistro du 17ᵉ,** 108 av. Villiers ✆ 01 47 63 32 77, *Fax 01 42 27 67 66* – 国. AE GB   D 8
Meals 169 b.i..

✗ **Petit Gervex,** 2 r. Gervex ✆ 01 43 80 53 63, Fax 01 40 53 93 53, 🌤 – **GB**   C 8
closed 1 to 23 August, Sunday dinner and Saturday – **Meals** 150 and a la carte 150/210.

✗ **Petite Provence,** 69 rue des Dames ✆ 01 45 22 03 03 – **GB**   D 11
closed 5 August-1 September, Saturday lunch and Monday – **Meals** - Provence specialities and fish - (booking essential) 135 and a la carte 210/310 ♀.

✗ **L'Huîtrier,** 16 r. Saussier-Leroy ✆ 01 40 54 83 44, Fax 01 40 54 83 86 – **AE GB**   E 8
closed August, Sunday dinner and Monday – **Meals** - Seafood - a la carte 180/380 ♀.

Montmartre, La Villette, Belleville.

18th, 19th and 20th arrondissements.
18th: ✉ *75018*
19th: ✉ *75019*
20th: ✉ *75020*

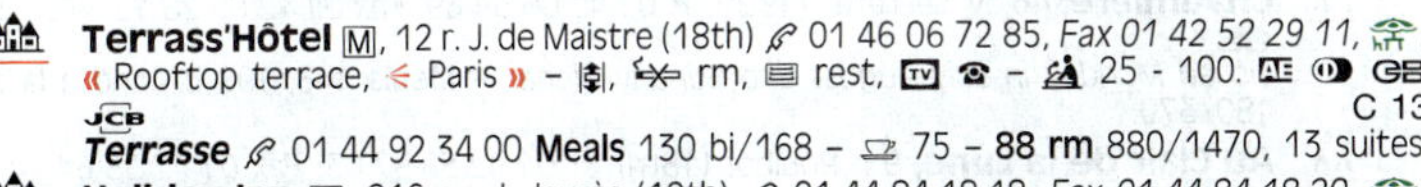

🏨 **Terrass'Hôtel** Ⓜ, 12 r. J. de Maistre (18th) ✆ 01 46 06 72 85, Fax 01 42 52 29 11, 🌤 « Rooftop terrace, ≤ Paris » – |♦|, ⊁ rm, ▤ rest, 📺 ☎ – 🛉 25 - 100. **AE ① GB JCB**   C 13
Terrasse ✆ 01 44 92 34 00 **Meals** 130 bi/168 – ⊡ 75 – **88 rm** 880/1470, 13 suites.

🏨 **Holiday Inn** Ⓜ, 216 av. J. Jaurès (19th) ✆ 01 44 84 18 18, Fax 01 44 84 18 20, 🌤 ♨ – |♦|, ⊁ rm, ▤ 📺 ☎ & 🅿 – 🛉 15 - 140. **AE ① GB JCB**. ⅍ rest   C 21
Meals 120/150 and a la carte 150/240 – ⊡ 75 – **176 rm** 1550/1750, 6 suites.

🏨 **Mercure Montmartre** without rest, 1 r. Caulaincourt (18th) ✆ 01 44 69 70 70, Fax 01 44 69 70 71 – |♦|, ⊁ rm, ▤ 📺 ☎ & – 🛉 20 - 70. **AE ① GB**   D 12
⊡ 70 – **308 rm** 920/1110.

🏨 **Holiday Inn Garden Court** Ⓜ without rest, 23 r. Damrémont (18th) ✆ 01 44 92 33 40, Fax 01 44 92 09 30 – |♦|, ⊁ rm, ▤ 📺 ☎ & – 🛉 20. **AE ① GB JCB**   C 13
⊡ 95 – **54 rm** 1250.

🏨 **Parc des Buttes Chaumont** without rest, 1 pl. Armand Carrel (19th) ✆ 01 42 08 08 37, Fax 01 42 45 66 91 – |♦| ▤ 📺 ☎. **AE ① GB**   D 19
⊡ 55 – **45 rm** 450/700.

🏨 **Clarine** Ⓜ, 147 av. Flandres (19th) ✆ 01 44 72 46 46, Fax 01 44 72 46 47 – |♦|, ⊁ rm, ▤ rest, 📺 ☎ & 🚗 – 🛉 70. **AE ① GB JCB**   B 19
Meals 65/75 and a la carte 100/170 ⅃ – ⊡ 38 – **207 rm** 380.

🏨 **Roma Sacré Cœur** without rest, 101 r. Caulaincourt (18th) ✆ 01 42 62 02 02, Fax 01 42 54 34 92 – |♦| 📺 ☎. **AE ① GB JCB**   C 14
⊡ 37 – **57 rm** 400/570.

🏨 **Palma** without rest, 77 av. Gambetta (20th) ✆ 01 46 36 13 65, Fax 01 46 36 03 27 – |♦| 📺 ☎. **AE ① GB JCB**   G 21
⊡ 35 – **32 rm** 340/390.

🏨 **Crimée** without rest, 188 r. Crimée (19th) ✆ 01 40 36 75 29, Fax 01 40 36 29 57 – |♦| ▤ 📺 ☎. **AE GB JCB**   C 18
⊡ 35 – **31 rm** 280/350.

🏨 **Laumière** without rest, 4 r. Petit (19th) ✆ 01 42 06 10 77, Fax 01 42 06 72 50 – |♦| 📺 ☎. **GB**   D 19
⊡ 36 – **54 rm** 290/390.

🏨 **Super Hôtel** without rest, 208 r. Pyrénées (20th) ✆ 01 46 36 97 48, Fax 01 46 36 26 10 – |♦| 📺 ☎. **AE GB JCB**   G 21
closed August – ⊡ 35 – **32 rm** 250/520.

🏨 **Abricôtel** without rest, 15 r. Lally Tollendal (19th) ✆ 01 42 08 34 49, Fax 01 42 40 83 95 – |♦| 📺 ☎ &. **AE ① GB**. ⅍   D 18
⊡ 33 – **39 rm** 300/400.

Eden Hôtel without rest, 90 r. Ordener (18th) ☎ 01 42 64 61 63, Fax 01 42 64 11 4
– |$| 📺 ☎. AE ① GB JCB   B 1·
☷ 35 – **35 rm** 395/440.

Damrémont without rest, 110 r. Damrémont (18th) ☎ 01 42 64 25 75
Fax 01 46 06 74 64 – |$|, ⇅ rm, 📺 ☎. AE ① GB JCB   B 1:
☷ 40 – **35 rm** 440/490.

Beauvilliers (Carlier), 52 r. Lamarck (18th) ☎ 01 42 54 54 42, Fax 01 42 62 70 3(
« 1900 decor, terrace » – ▤. AE ① GB JCB. ⇗   C 1·
closed Monday lunch and Sunday – **Meals** 185 (lunch)/400 b.i. and a la cart(
410/580
Spec. Papillotes de langoustines au basilic. Rognonnade de veau au jus de truffes. Ent
remets aux chocolats, croustillant-praliné.

Pavillon Puebla, Parc Buttes-Chaumont, entrance : av. Bolivar, r. Botzaris (19th
☎ 01 42 08 92 62, Fax 01 42 39 83 16, ⇞, « Pleasant setting in the park » – P. A
GB   E 1!
closed 8 to 23 August, Sunday and Monday – **Meals** 190/260 and a la cart(
330/500.

Cottage Marcadet, 151 bis r. Marcadet (18th) ☎ 01 42 57 71 22 – ▤. GB
⇗   C 1:
Meals 160 (lunch)/215 b.i. and a la carte 250/350.

Les Allobroges, 71 r. Grands-Champs (20th) ☎ 01 43 73 40 00 – AE GB   K 2:
closed 27 May-3 June, August, Sunday, Monday and Bank Holidays – **Meals** 97/174 an(
a la carte 210/380.

Relais des Buttes, 86 r. Compans (19th) ☎ 01 42 08 24 70, Fax 01 42 03 20 44, ⇞
– GB   E 2(
closed 8 to 29 August, Saturday lunch and Sunday – **Meals** 178 and a la carte 210/34(
♀.

Chaumière, 46 av. Secrétan (19th) ☎ 01 42 06 54 69, Fax 01 42 06 28 12 – ▤. AE ①
GB   E 18
closed Monday in July-August and Sunday dinner – **Meals** 143/198 b.i. and a la cart(
180/370.

Au Clair de la Lune, 9 r. Poulbot (18th) ☎ 01 42 58 97 03, Fax 01 42 55 64 74 – A
GB JCB   D 1·
closed 22 March-8 April, 23 August-13 September, Monday lunch and Sunday – **Meals** 16!
and a la carte 210/350.

Eric Frechon, 10 r. Gén. Brunet (19th) ☎ 01 40 40 03 30, Fax 01 40 40 03 30 – ▤
GB   E 2(
closed August, Sunday and Monday – **Meals** 210 ♀.

Poulbot Gourmet, 39 r. Lamarck (18th) ☎ 01 46 06 86 00, Fax 01 46 06 86 00 –
GB   C 1·
closed Sunday except lunch from October-May – **Meals** 180 and a la carte 210/330.

L'Oriental, 76 r. Martyrs (18th) ☎ 01 42 64 39 80, Fax 01 42 64 39 80 – AE GB
⇗   D 13-1·
closed 24 July-20 August and Sunday – **Meals** North-African rest. 85/210 and a la cart(
140/220 ♀.

Marie-Louise, 52 r. Championnet (18th) ☎ 01 46 06 86 55, bistro – GB   B 1!
closed 1 to 23 August, Monday dinner and Sunday – **Meals** 130 and a la carte 250/30(

Bouclard, 1 r. Cavallotti (18th) ☎ 01 45 22 60 01, Fax 01 45 22 00 48, bistro – A
GB   D 1:
closed Monday lunch, Saturday lunch and Sunday – **Meals** 120 (lunch)and a la cart(
210/350.

Village Kabyle, 4 r. Aimé Lavy (18th) ☎ 01 42 55 03 34, Fax 01 42 86 08 35 – GB
⇗   B 1·
closed Monday lunch and Sunday – **Meals** North-African rest. 200/250 and a la cart(
150/190 ♀.

Aucune Idée ? 2 pl. St-Blaise (20th) ☎ 01 40 09 70 67, Fax 01 43 56 12 34 – AE GB
JCB   H 2:
closed 1 to 7 March, 2 to 16 August, Sunday dinner and Monday – **Meals** 135 (lunch)
165/175 and a la carte 160/290 ♀.

L'Étrier, 154 r. Lamarck (18th) ☎ 01 42 29 14 01, bistro – ▤. GB   C 1:
closed 2 to 23 August, Sunday and Monday – **Meals** (booking essential) 82 (lunch), 160/25(
and a la carte approx. 250 ♀.

Rughetta, 41 r. Lepic (18e) ☎ 01 42 23 41 70, Fax 01 42 23 41 70, bistro – GB
⇗   D 1:
closed August, Christmas-New Year, February Holidays and Monday – **Meals** - Italian rest
- (booking essential) 110 and a la carte 150/220 ♨.

ENVIRONS

The outskirts of Paris up to 25Km

11: These reference letters and numbers correspond to the squares on the **Michelin plans of Parisian suburbs** nos 18, 20, 22, 24, 25.

La Défense 92 Hauts-de-Seine 101 ⑭, 18 – ⊠ 92400 Courbevoie.

See : Quarter★★ : perspective★ from the parvis.

Paris 8,5.

Sofitel CNIT M ⅀, 2 pl. Défense ⊠ 92053 ℘ 01 46 92 10 10, Fax 01 46 92 10 50 – 🛗, ⅄ rm, ▤ rm, TV ☎ ᴋ – 🏊 20 - 100. AE ◑ GB JCB   AV-AW40
closed 31 July-23 August - see **Les Communautés** below – ⌸ 130 – **141 rm** 1800/2100, 6 suites.

Renaissance M, 60 Jardin de Valmy, by ring road, exit La Défense 7 ⊠ 92918 Puteaux ℘ 01 41 97 50 50, Fax 01 41 97 51 51, 🛦 – 🛗, ⅄ rm, ▤ TV ☎ ᴋ 🚗 – 🏊 220. AE ◑ GB JCB. ⅀   AW 40
Meals 170 ⅄ – ⌸ 100 – **314 rm** 1400/1700, 20 suites.

Sofitel La Défense M ⅀, 34 cours Michelet by ring road, exit La Défense 4 ⊠ 92060 Puteaux ℘ 01 47 76 44 43, Fax 01 47 76 72 10 – 🛗, ⅄ rm, ▤ TV ☎ ᴋ 🚗 – 🏊 100. AE ◑ GB   AW 41
Les 2 Arcs (closed Friday dinner, Sunday lunch and Saturday) Meals 310 – **Botanic** (closed dinner except Friday and Saturday) Meals 195 – ⌸ 95 – **151 rm** 1750/2150.

Novotel La Défense M, 2 bd Neuilly ℘ 01 41 45 23 23, Fax 01 41 45 23 24, ≼ – 🛗, ⅄ rm, ▤ TV ☎ ᴋ – 🏊 130. AE ◑ GB JCB   AW 42
Meals a la carte approx. 180 ⅄ – ⌸ 70 – **280 rm** 950/980.

Ibis La Défense M, 4 bd Neuilly ℘ 01 41 97 40 40, Fax 01 41 97 40 50, 🌳 – 🛗, ⅄ rm, ▤ TV ☎ ᴋ – 🏊 40. AE ◑ GB JCB   AW 42
Meals a la carte approx. 130 ⅄ – ⌸ 39 – **284 rm** 560.

Les Communautés - Hôtel Sofitel CNIT, 2 pl. Défense, 5th floor ℘ 01 46 92 10 30, Fax 01 46 92 10 50 – ▤. AE ◑ GB JCB   AV-AW40
closed 31 July-23 August, Saturday and Sunday – **Meals** a la carte 300/350.

Marne-la-Vallée 77206 S.-et-M. 101 ⑲.

🏌 of Bussy-St-Georges (private) ℘ 01 64 66 00 00 ; 🏌 🏌 of Disneyland Paris ℘ 01 60 45 68 04.

🛈 Tourist Office - Disney Village ℘ 01 60 43 33 33, Fax 01 60 43 36 91.

Paris 28.

at Collégien - pop. 2 331 alt. 105 – ⊠ 77080 :

Novotel, at Motorway junction Lagny A 4 ℘ 01 64 80 53 53, Fax 01 64 80 48 37, 🌳, 🏊, 🎾 – 🛗, ⅄ rm, ▤ TV ☎ ᴋ 🅿 – 🏊 250. AE ◑ GB
Meals 118 ⅄ – ⌸ 70 – **197 rm** 520/590.

at Disneyland Paris access by Highway A 4 and Disneyland exit.

See : Disneyland Paris★★★

Disneyland Hôtel M, ℘ 01 60 45 65 00, Fax 01 60 45 65 33, ≼, « Victorian style architecture, at the entrance to the Disneyland Resort », 🛦, 🏊, 🎾 – 🛗, ⅄ rm, ▤ TV ☎ ᴋ 🅿 – 🏊 25 - 50. AE ◑ GB JCB. ⅀
California Grill - (dinner only) Meals 195 ⅄ – **Inventions** self-service Meals 180 (lunch)/250 ⅄ – **478 rm** ⌸ 2390/3640, 18 suites.

New-York M, ℘ 01 60 45 73 00, Fax 01 60 45 73 33, ≼, 🌳, « Evokes the architecture of Manhattan », 🛦, 🏊, 🏊 – 🛗, ⅄ rm, ▤ TV ☎ ᴋ 🅿 – 🏊 1 500. AE ◑ GB JCB. ⅀
Manhattan Restaurant (dinner only) Meals 195 ⅄ – **Parkside Diner** : Meals 115/150 ⅄ – **536 rm** ⌸ 1490/1690, 27 suites.

Newport Bay Club M, ℘ 01 60 45 55 00, Fax 01 60 45 55 33, ≼, 🌳, Convention centre, « In the style of a New England seaside resort », 🛦, 🏊, 🏊 – 🛗, ⅄ rm, ▤ TV ☎ ᴋ 🅿 – 🏊 5 000. AE ◑ GB JCB. ⅀
Cape Cod : Meals 115(lunch)/150 ⅄ – **Yacht Club** (dinner only) Meals 150/230 ⅄ – **1 082 rm** ⌸ 1250/1650, 11 suites.

FRANCE

Séquoia Lodge M, 𝄢 01 60 45 51 00, *Fax 01 60 45 51 33*, « The atmosphere of an American mountain lodge », – rm, TV ☎ ⅁ P – 35
AE ① GB JCB
Hunter's Grill (dinner only) **Meals** (set menu only)150 ♀ – **Beaver Creek Tavern** (dinner only) **Meals** 150 ♀ – **1 001 rm** ⌴ 1120/1320, 10 suites.

Cheyenne, 𝄢 01 60 45 62 00, *Fax 01 60 45 62 33*, « Resembles a frontier town of the American Wild West » – rm, rest, TV ☎ ⅁ P. AE ① GB JCB
Chuck Wagon Café : **Meals** a la carte approx. 130 ♂ – **1 000 rm** ⌴ 980.

Santa Fé, 𝄢 01 60 45 78 00, *Fax 01 60 45 78 33*, « Evokes a New Mexican pueblo »
– , rm, rest, TV ☎ ⅁ P. AE ① GB JCB
La Cantina : **Meals** a la carte approx. 130 – **1 000 rm** ⌴ 830.

Orly (Paris Airports) 94396 Val-de-Marne 101 ㉖, 24 – pop. 21 646.
𝄢 01 49 75 15 15.
Paris 15.

Hilton Orly M, near airport station ✉ 94544 𝄢 01 45 12 45 12, *Fax 01 45 12 45 00*
– , rm, TV ☎ ⅁ P – 300. AE ① GB JCB   BR 51
Meals 198 ♂ – ⌴ 115 – **356 rm** 990/1570.

Mercure M, N 7, Z.I. Nord, Orlytech ✉ 94547 𝄢 01 46 87 23 37, *Fax 01 46 87 71 92*
– , rm, TV ☎ ⅁ P – 40. AE ① GB
Meals 135/145 – ⌴ 68 – **190 rm** 650/750.

Orly Airport West :
XXX **Maxim's**, 2nd floor ✉ 94547 𝄢 01 49 75 16 78, *Fax 01 46 87 05 39* – . AE ① GB
❀ *closed 31 July-31 August, 25 December-2 January, Saturday, Sunday and Bank Holidays*
– **Meals** 230/480 and a la carte 300/400 ♀
Spec. Terrine de canard "Alex Humbert". Sole braisée au vermouth. Filet de boeuf aux pommes Maxim's.

See also *Rungis*

Roissy-en-France (Paris Airports) 95700 Val-d'Oise 101 ⑧ – pop. 2 054 alt. 85.
𝄢 01 48 62 22 80.
Paris 26.

at Roissy-Town :
Copthorne M, allée Verger 𝄢 01 34 29 33 33, *Fax 01 34 29 03 05*, , –
rm, TV ☎ ⅁ – 150. AE ① GB JCB
Meals 169/300 ♀ – ⌴ 85 – **237 rm** 1500/1700.

Mercure, allée Verger 𝄢 01 34 29 40 00, *Fax 01 34 29 00 18*, – , rm, TV
☎ ⅁ P – 90. AE ① GB
Meals 142 b.i. (lunch)/155 b.i. – ⌴ 70 – **202 rm** 1205, 4 suites.

Bleu Marine M, Z.A. parc de Roissy 𝄢 01 34 29 00 00, *Fax 01 34 29 00 11*, –
rm, TV ☎ ⅁ P – 80. AE ① GB JCB
Meals 145 ♀ – ⌴ 60 – **153 rm** 750.

Ibis M, av. Raperie 𝄢 01 34 29 34 34, *Fax 01 34 29 34 19* – , rm, TV ☎ ⅁
P – 70. AE ① GB. rest
Meals 95/125 ♂ – ⌴ 42 – **300 rm** 395/995.

in Airport terminal nr 2 :
Sheraton M, Aérogare n° 2 𝄢 01 49 19 70 70, *Fax 01 49 19 70 71*, , « Original contemporary architecture », – , rm, TV ☎ ⅁ – 80. AE ① GB JCB
Les Étoiles (*closed 15 July-31 August, Saturday and Sunday*) **Meals** 305(lunch)/340 – **Les Saisons** : **Meals** 195(lunch), 250 – ⌴ 135 – **242 rm** 1850/2500, 14 suites.

at Roissypole :
Hilton M, 𝄢 01 49 19 77 77, *Fax 01 49 19 77 78*, , – , rm, TV ☎
⅁ – 500. AE ① GB JCB. rest
Gourmet (*closed 14 July-31 August, Saturday and Sunday*) **Meals** 200/400 ♀ – **Aviateurs** - brasserie **Meals** 85 b.i. – **Oyster bar** - Seafood (*closed 14 July-31 August, Sunday and Monday*) **Meals** a la carte approx. 240 – ⌴ 110 – **378 rm** 1350/1800, 4 suites.

Sofitel M, Zone centrale Ouest 𝄢 01 49 19 29 29, *Fax 01 49 19 29 00*, , –
rm, TV ☎ ⅁ P – 150. AE ① GB JCB
Meals brasserie 115 b.i. – ⌴ 90 – **344 rm** 1100/1850, 8 suites.

Novotel M, 𝄢 01 49 19 27 27, *Fax 01 49 19 27 99* – , rm, TV ☎ ⅁ P – 60
AE ① GB JCB
Meals a la carte approx. 160 ♀ – ⌴ 70 – **201 rm** 820.

Z.I. Paris Nord II – ⊠ 95912 :

Hyatt Regency Ⓜ ⤜, 351 av. Bois de la Pie ☎ 01 48 17 12 34, *Fax 01 48 17 17 17*, ♨, « Original contemporary decor », ⛴, ⬛, ✕ – ⬛, ✳ rm, ▤ Ⓣ ☎ ⅋ 🅿 – ⬛ 300. 🄰🄴 ⓓ 🄶🄱 🄹🄲🄱
Meals 185 (lunch)/220 ♀ – ☕ 95 – **383 rm** 1400/2000, 5 suites.

Rungis 94150 Val-de-Marne 🆒🆒🆒 ㉖, 🆓 – *pop. 2 939 alt. 80.*
Paris 14.

at Pondorly : *Access : from Paris, Highway A 6 and take Orly Airport exit ; from outside of Paris, A 6 and Rungis exit :*

Grand Hôtel Mercure Orly Ⓜ, 20 av. Ch. Lindbergh ⊠ 94656 ☎ 01 46 87 36 36, *Fax 01 46 87 08 48*, ⬛ – ⬛, ✳ rm, ▤ Ⓣ ☎ 🚗 🅿 – ⬛ 180. 🄰🄴 ⓓ 🄶🄱 BM 50
Rungisserie (closed lunch Saturday and Sunday) Meals a la carte approx. 190 ♀ – ☕ 68 – **190 rm** 690/890.

Holiday Inn Ⓜ, 4 av. Ch. Lindbergh ⊠ 94656 ☎ 01 46 87 26 66, *Fax 01 45 60 91 25* – ⬛, ✳ rm, ▤ Ⓣ ☎ ⅋ 🅿 – ⬛ 150. 🄰🄴 ⓓ 🄶🄱 BM 50
Meals 165 ♀ – ☕ 80 – **168 rm** 880/980.

Novotel Ⓜ, Zone du Delta, 1 r. Pont des Halles ☎ 01 45 12 44 12, *Fax 01 45 12 44 13*, ♨, ⬛ – ⬛, ✳ rm, ▤ Ⓣ ☎ ⅋ 🅿 – ⬛ 150. 🄰🄴 ⓓ 🄶🄱 🄹🄲🄱 BM 50
Meals a la carte approx. 180 ♀ – ☕ 68 – **181 rm** 710/1050.

Ibis, 1 r. Mondétour ⊠ 94656 ☎ 01 46 87 22 45, *Fax 01 46 87 84 72*, ♨ – ⬛, ✳ rm, Ⓣ ☎ ⅋ 🅿 – ⬛ 60. 🄰🄴 ⓓ 🄶🄱 BM 50
Meals 95 ♀ – ☕ 39 – **119 rm** 360.

Versailles 78000 Yvelines 🆒🆒🆒 ㉒, 🆓 – *pop. 87 789 alt. 130.*
See : Palace★★★ Y – Gardens★★★ (fountain display★★★ (grandes eaux) and illuminated night performances★★★ (fêtes de nuit) in summer) – Ecuries Royales★ Y – The Trianons★★ – Lambinet Museum★ Y M.
⛳ of la Boulie (private) ☎ 01 39 50 59 41 by ③ : 2,5 km.
🄱 Tourist Office 7 r. Réservoirs ☎ 01 39 50 36 22, *Fax 01 39 50 68 07.*
Paris 20 ①

Plan on next page

Trianon Palace Ⓜ ⤜, 1 bd Reine ☎ 01 30 84 38 00, *Fax 01 39 49 00 77*, ≤, park, « Tasteful early 20C decor », ⛴, ⬛, ✕ – ⬛ Ⓣ ☎ 🚗 🅿 – ⬛ 30. 🄰🄴 ⓓ 🄶🄱 🄹🄲🄱. ✳ rest
see **Les Trois Marches** below - **Café Trianon** : Meals 140 /280 and a la carte 210/280
♀ – ☕ 160 – **190 rm** 2200/2900, 25 suites.
X r

Sofitel Château de Versailles Ⓜ, 2 av. Paris ☎ 01 39 07 46 46, *Fax 01 39 07 46 47*, ♨ – ⬛, ✳ rm, ▤ Ⓣ ☎ ⅋ 🚗 – ⬛ 150. 🄰🄴 ⓓ 🄶🄱 🄹🄲🄱
Meals 195 and a la carte 280/370 ♀ – ☕ 110 – **146 rm** 1290, 6 suites.
Y a

Versailles Ⓜ ⤜ without rest, 7 r. Ste-Anne (Petite place) ☎ 01 39 50 64 65, *Fax 01 39 02 37 85* – ⬛, ✳ rm, Ⓣ ☎ ⅋ 🅿. 🄰🄴 ⓓ 🄶🄱 🄹🄲🄱
☕ 57 – **46 rm** 480/580.
Y p

Résidence du Berry Ⓜ without rest, 14 r. Anjou ☎ 01 39 49 07 07, *Fax 01 39 50 59 40* – ⬛, ✳ rm, Ⓣ ☎. 🄰🄴 ⓓ 🄶🄱 🄹🄲🄱
☕ 50 – **38 rm** 450/600.
Z s

Relais Mercure Ⓜ without rest, 19 r. Ph. de Dangeau ☎ 01 39 50 44 10, *Fax 01 39 50 65 11* – ⬛ Ⓣ ☎ ⅋ – ⬛ 35. 🄰🄴 ⓓ 🄶🄱 🄹🄲🄱
☕ 45 – **60 rm** 440.
Y n

Ibis without rest, 4 av. Gén. de Gaulle ☎ 01 39 53 03 30, *Fax 01 39 50 06 31* – ⬛, ✳ rm, Ⓣ ☎ ⅋ 🚗. 🄰🄴 ⓓ 🄶🄱
☕ 39 – **85 rm** 395.
Y u

Les Trois Marches, 1 bd Reine ☎ 01 39 50 13 21, *Fax 01 30 21 01 25*, ≤, ♨ – ▤ 🅿. 🄰🄴 ⓓ 🄶🄱 🄹🄲🄱
X r
❀❀ *closed 31 July-2 September* – Meals 295 (lunch)/625 and a la carte 570/860 ♀
Spec. Foie gras poêlé au pamplemousse. Pain perdu aux truffes. Fruits rouges en coque de crème glacée.

Rescatore, 27 av. St-Cloud ☎ 01 39 25 06 34, *Fax 01 39 51 68 11* – 🄰🄴 🄶🄱
Y s
closed August, Saturday lunch and Sunday – **Meals** - Seafood - 180/250 and a la carte 300/370.

Valmont, 20 r. au Pain ☎ 01 39 51 39 00, *Fax 01 30 83 90 99* – ▤. 🄰🄴 ⓓ 🄶🄱
Y v
closed Sunday dinner and Monday – Meals 160 and a la carte 230/310.

Potager du Roy, 1 r. Mar.-Joffre ☎ 01 39 50 35 34, *Fax 01 30 21 69 30* – ▤. 🄰🄴 🄶🄱
Z r
closed Sunday dinner and Monday – **Meals** 175 ♀.

FRANCE

Carnot (R.) . . . . Y
Chancellerie (R. de la) . Y 3
Clemenceau
(R. Georges) . . . . Y 7
Cotte (R. Robert-de) . . . Y 10
États-Généraux (R. des). Z

Europe (Av. de l') . . . . . Y 14
Foch (R. du Mar.) . . . . XY
Gambetta (Pl.) . . . . Y 17
Gaulle (Av. Gén.-de) . . . YZ 19
Hoche (R.) . . . . Y
Indép. Américaine (R.) . . Y 20
Leclerc (R. du Gén.) . . . Z 24
Marché N.D. (Pl. du) . . . Y 25
Mermoz (R. Jean) . . . . . Z 27

Nolhac
(R. Pierre-de) . . . . Y 30
Orangerie (R. de l') . . . . YZ
Paroisse (R. de la) . . . . . Y
Porte de Buc (R. de la) . . Z 34
Rockefeller (Av.) . . . . Y
Royale (R.) . . . . Z
Satory (R. de) . . . . YZ 42
Vieux-Versailles (R. du) . YZ 47

D 186 ST-GERMAIN-EN-L.
RUEIL, LA DÉFENSE
N 321 LA CELLE-ST-CLOUD
7
8
ROUEN
MANTES A 13
LE HAMEAU
TRIANONS
GRAND CANAL
ST-CYR-L'ÉCOLE
RAMBOUILLET, DREUX
N 286 ST-QUENTIN-EN-Y.
Boulevard
Saint-
Antoine
Rue
de
l'Ermitage
PARC DE
SÉMALLÉ
Place de la Loi
R. de Versailles
ST-ANTOINE
DE PADOUE
LE CHESNAY
A
Av. Debasseux
R. du Maréchal de Lattre de T.
R. A. Lange
Clagny
Parc
de
Av. Mal Leclerc
R. du Cer de Bange
Roi
NOTRE-DAME
Rue des Missionnaires
Foch
Square
J. Houdon
Rue Rémilly
R. Berthier
R. d'Angiviller
Maréchal
STE-JEANNE-D'ARC
R. Albert
Joly
Porte de
la Reine
Boulevard
de
la
Reine
VERSAILLES R.D.
S.N.C.F.
Bin de Neptune
JARDINS
PARTERRES
DU NORD
Rue
de
la
Notre-Dame
RICHAUD
R. de Provence
Reservoirs
Rue des
Rue
Hoche
Paroisse
25
t
s
Saint-Cloud
PARTERRES
DU MIDI
CHÂTEAU
Pl.
d'Armes
Carnot
Avenue
Grandes
Écuries
Avenue
R. de
Place
Alexandre 1er
Louis Barthou
CENTRE
ADMINISTRATIF
RÉSERVOIRS
A 13 PARIS
PARIS (Pte de St-Cloud)
BOULOGNE-BILLANCOURT
ÉLE SUPRE
DU GÉNIE
MILITAIRE
PALAIS DES
CONGRÈS
Bibliothèque
Petites
Écuries
HÔTEL
DU DÉPT
BIBLIOTHÈQUE
NATIONALE
POL.
Montbauron
6
D 10
Rue de l'Orangerie
Avenue
de
Paris
VERSAILLES R.G.
CHÂTEAU DE
VERSAILLES
R.E.R.
MAISON
D'ARRÊT
Noailles
R. des États-Généraux
D 10
ORLY-CRÉTEIL A 86
JOUY-EN-JOSAS D 446
ÉCOLE NATLE SUPRE
D'HORTICULTURE
ST-LOUIS
POTAGER
DU ROI
Parc
Balbi
Joffre
Maréchal
Rue
du
Royale
Sceaux
d'Anjou
Carrés
St-Louis
RÉSERVOIR
VERSAILLES
CHANTIERS
R.E.R.
STE-ÉLISABETH
R. de Vergennes
27
Chantiers
N 186
ST-LOUIS
R. Mgr Gibier
R. H. de Régnier
Saint
Louis
Charton
Rue
34
D 939
LES GONARDS
5
4
D 938, TOUSSUS-LE-N.
ST-RÉMY-LES-CH.
0   200 m
1
2
3

VERSAILLES

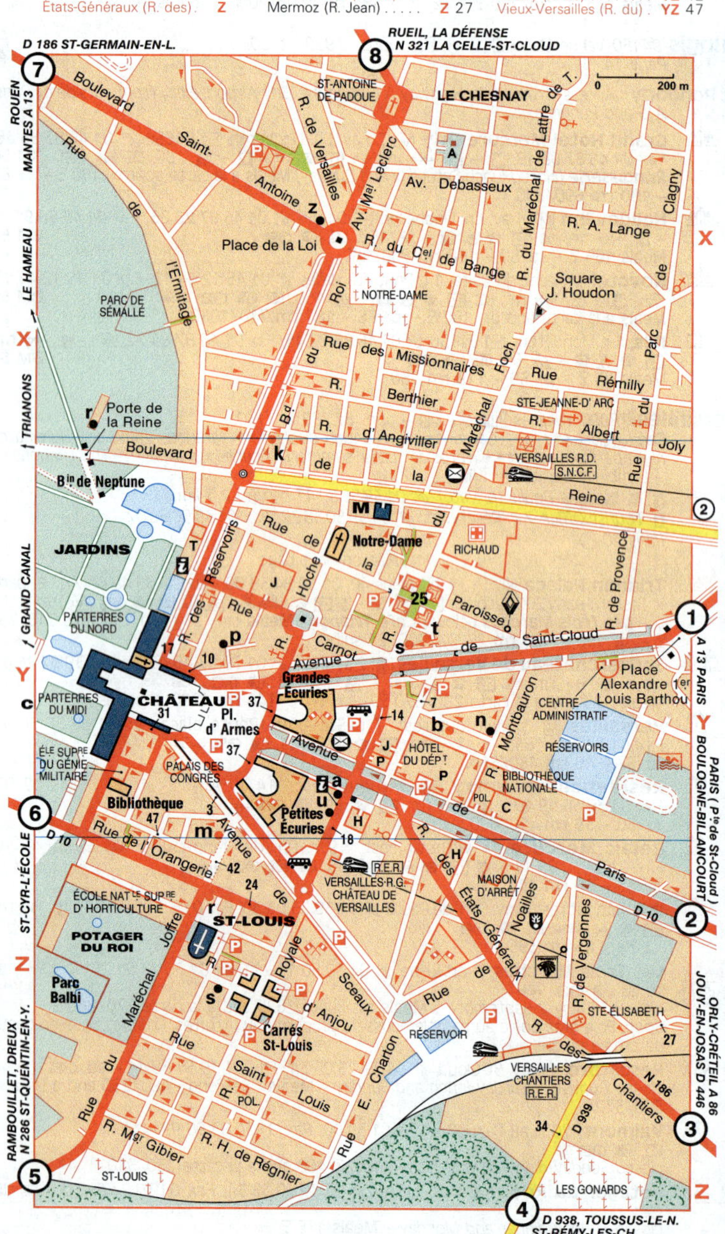

FRANCE

XX **Marée de Versailles,** 22 r. au Pain ℘ 01 30 21 73 73, Fax 01 39 50 55 87 – ▣. AE GB Y t
closed 3 to 18 August, February Holidays, Sunday and Monday – **Meals** - Seafood - 290 and a la carte 210/300 ⚜.

X **Cuisine Bourgeoise,** 10 bd Roi ℘ 01 39 53 11 38, Fax 01 39 53 25 26 – AE GB
closed 7 to 30 August, February Holidays, Saturday lunch and Sunday – **Meals** 175 (lunch)/250 and a la carte 250/350 ⚜. XY k

X **Chevalet,** 6 r. Ph. de Dangeau ℘ 01 39 02 03 13, Fax 01 39 50 81 41 – GB JCB
closed 9 to 23 August, Monday dinner and Sunday – **Meals** 118/145 and a la carte 160/230 ⚜. Y b

X **Le Falher,** 22 r. Satory ℘ 01 39 50 57 43, Fax 01 39 49 04 66 – AE GB. ✍ Y m
closed 10 to 26 August, Saturday lunch and Sunday – **Meals** 132/185 and a la carte 220/290 ⚜.

at Le Chesnay – *pop. 29 542 alt. 120* – ✉ *78150* :

Novotel M, 4 bd St-Antoine ℘ 01 39 54 96 96, Fax 01 39 54 94 40 – |≴|, ✲ rm, ▣ TV ☎ & ⇔ – 🛋 25 - 150. AE ⓞ GB X z
Meals 120 and a la carte approx. 180 ⚜ – ☕ 65 – **105 rm** 580/630.

Mercure M without rest, r. Marly-le-Roi, in front of Commercial Centre Parly II
℘ 01 39 55 11 41, Fax 01 39 55 06 22 – |≴|, ✲ rm, TV ☎ & P. AE ⓞ GB JCB
☕ 60 – **80 rm** 650.

Ibis without rest, av. Dutartre, Commercial Centre Parly II ℘ 01 39 63 37 93, Fax 01 39 55 18 66 – |≴|, ✲ rm, TV ☎ &. AE ⓞ GB
☕ 40 – **72 rm** 390.

XX **Au Comptoir Nordique,** 6 av. Rocquencourt ℘ 01 39 55 13 31, Fax 01 39 55 40 57, ⛱ – P. AE GB
closed 1 to 24 August, 24 to 30 December and Sunday – **Meals** 145 and a la carte 170/260 ⚜ - *Brasserie* : Meals 95/145 and a la carte 170/260 ⚜.

XX **Connemara,** 41 rte Rueil ℘ 01 39 55 63 07, Fax 01 39 55 63 07 – AE GB
closed 1 to 23 August, Sunday dinner and Monday – **Meals** 170 and a la carte 230/300.

AND BEYOND...

Joigny *89300 Yonne* 65 ④ – *pop. 9 697 alt. 79.*

See : *Vierge au Sourire*★ *in St-Thibault's Church – Côte St-Jacques* ≤★ *1,5 km by D 20*

ſ18 *of Roncemay* ✆ *03 86 73 68 87.*

🛈 *Tourist Office 4 quai H.-Ragobert* ✆ *03 86 62 11 05, Fax 03 86 91 76 38.*

Paris 147 – Auxerre 27 – Gien 75 – Montargis 59 – Sens 30 – Troyes 76.

Côte St-Jacques (Lorain) Ⓜ ☜, 14 fg Paris ✆ *03 86 62 09 70, Fax 03 86 91 49 70*
≤, « Tasteful decor », ▨, 🚣 – 🛗, 🍽 rest, TV ☎ 🚗 P. – 🏊 30. A
◑ GB
closed 3 to 27 January – **Meals** *(Sunday booking essential)* 350 b.i. *(lunch)*/750 *and a la carte*
650/920 – ☕ 120 – **25 rm** 750/1790, 4 suites
Spec. Huîtres de marennes en petite terrine océane. Noix de Saint-Jacques, endives e
chanterelles, jus de champignons monté en capuccino (October-April). Côte de veau d
lait, crème de petits pois au lard et côtes de blettes truffées. **Wines** Bourgogn
Irancy.

Pontoise *95300 Val d'Oise* 106 ⑤ – *pop. 27 150 alt. 48.*

Paris 36 – Beauvais 50 – Dieppe 135 – Mantes-la-Jolie 39 – Rouen 91.

at Cormeilles-en-Vexin *NW – alt. 111 –* ✉ *95830 :*

Relais Ste-Jeanne (Cagna), *on D 915* ✆ *01 34 66 61 56, Fax 01 34 66 40 31*
« Garden » – P. AE ◑ GB
*closed 1 to 25 August, 19 to 27 December, Sunday (except lunch from Easter-1 Nov. an
Bank Holidays) and Monday –* **Meals** 230/620 b.i. *and a la carte* 480/620
Spec. Douceur de homard breton aux aromates et huile d'olive. Croustade de langoustine
au jus de truffe. Aiguillettes de pigeon en mille-feuille de navets, jus au porto.

Rheims *51100 Marne* 56 ⑥ ⑯ – *pop. 180 620 alt. 85.*

See : *Cathedral*★★★ *– St-Remi Basilica*★★ *: interior*★★★ *– Palais du Tau*★★ *– Champagn
cellars*★ *– Place Royale*★ *– Porte Mars*★ *– Hôtel de la Salle*★ *– Foujita Chapel*★ *– Librar
of Ancien Collège des Jésuites – St-Remi Museum*★★ *– Hôtel le Vergeur Museum*★ *– Fin
Arts Museum*★ *– French Automobile Heritage Centre*★*.*

Envir. : *Fort de la Pompelle : German helmets*★ *9 km to the SE by N 44.*

ſ18 *Rheims-Champagne* ✆ *03 26 05 46 10 at Gueux ; to the NW by N 31-E 46 : 9,5 km.*

✈ *Rheims-Champagne* ✆ *03 26 07 15 15 : 6 km.*

🚗 ✆ *08 36 35 35 35.*

🛈 *Tourist Office 2 r. Guillaume-de-Machault* ✆ *03 26 77 45 25, Fax 03 26 77 45 27 – A.C
de Champagne 7 bd Lundy* ✆ *03 26 47 34 76, Fax 03 26 88 52 24.*

Paris 144 – Brussels 214 – Châlons-sur-Marne 48 – Lille 199 – Luxembourg 232.

Boyer "Les Crayères" Ⓜ ☜, 64 bd Vasnier ✆ *03 26 82 80 80, Fax 03 26 82 65 52*
≤, 🌳, « Elegant mansion in park », ✕ – 🛗 ▤ TV ☎ P. AE ◑ GB JCB
closed 23 December-12 January – **Meals** *(closed Tuesday lunch and Monday) (bookin
essential)* 910/1070 *and a la carte* 540/670 � – ☕ 125 – **16 rm** 1350/2100
3 suites
Spec. Escalope de foie gras de canard poêlée servie dans un bouillon. Filet de bar de lign
cuit au four, légumes étuvés croquants. Noisettes d'agneau en crépinette à la purée d
dattes et foie gras. **Wines** Champagne.

Saulieu *21210 Côte-d'Or* 65 ⑰ – *pop. 2 917 alt. 535.*

See : *St-Andoche Basilica*★ *: capitals*★★*.*

🛈 *Tourist Office 24 r. d'Argentine* ✆ *03 80 64 00 21, Fax 03 80 64 21 96.*

Paris 249 – Autun 41 – Avallon 38 – Beaune 64 – Clamecy 76 – Dijon 73.

Côte d'Or (Loiseau) Ⓜ ☜, 2 r. Argentine ✆ *03 80 90 53 53, Fax 03 80 64 08 92*
« Tasteful inn with flowered garden » – TV ☎ 🚗 – 🏊 30. AE ◑ GB JCB
Meals 420/920 *and a la carte* 740/910 ♔ – ☕ 150 – **27 rm** 560/2100, 7 suites, 3 duple
Spec. Jambonnettes de grenouilles à la purée d'ail et jus de persil. Sandre à la fondu
d'échalotes et sauce au vin rouge. Blanc de volaille au foie gras chaud et purée truffée
Wines Bourgogne.

BORDEAUX 33000 Gironde **71** ⑨ – pop. 210 336 alt. 4 Greater Bordeaux 696 364 h.

See : 18C Bordeaux : façades along the quayside★★ EX, Esplanade des Quinconces DX, Grand Théâtre★★ DX, Notre-Dame Church★ DX, Allées de Tourny DX, – Cours Clemenceau DX, Place Gambetta DX, Cours de l'Intendance DX – Old Bordeaux★★ : Place de la Bourse★★ EX, Place du Parlement★ EX **109**, St-Michel Basilica★ EY, Great Bell★ (Grosse Cloche) EY D – Pey-Berland district : St-André Cathedral★ DY (Pey-Berland Tower★ : ≤★★ E) – Mériadeck district CY – Battle-Cruiser Colbert★★ – Museums : Fine Arts★ (Beaux-Arts) CDY M³, Decorative Arts★ DY M², Aquitaine★★ DY M⁴ – Entrepôt Laîné★★ : Museum of Contemporary Art★.

⌐₁₈ Golf Bordelais ℘ 05 56 28 56 04 by av. d'Eysines : 4 km ; ⌐₁₈ ⌐₁₈ de Bordeaux Lac ℘ 05 56 50 92 72, to the N by D 209 : 10 km ; ⌐₁₈ ⌐₁₈ of Medoc at Louens ℘ 05 56 70 21 10 to the NW by D 6 : 6 km ; ⌐₉ ⌐₉ ⌐₉ Internat. of Bordeaux-Pessac ℘ 05 56 36 03 33 by N 250 ; ⌐₁₈ Bordeaux-Cameyrac ℘ 05 56 72 96 79 by N 89 : 18 km.

✈ of Bordeaux-Mérignac : ℘ 05 56 34 50 50 to the W : 11 km.

🚗 ℘ 08 36 35 35 35.

🛈 Tourist Office 12 cours 30-Juillet ℘ 05 56 00 66 00, Fax 05 56 00 66 01 – Automobile-Club du Sud-Ouest 8 espl. des Quinconces ℘ 05 56 44 22 9 2, Fax 05 56 48 57 47 – Bordeaux wine Exhibition (Maison du vin de Bordeaux) 1 cours 30-juil. (closed weekend from mid Oct.-mid May) ℘ 05 56 00 22 66, Fax 05 56 00 22 77 DX .

Paris 579 – Lyons 531 – Nantes 324 – Strasbourg 919 – Toulouse 245.

Plans on following pages

Burdigala M, 115 r. G. Bonnac ℘ 05 56 90 16 16, Fax 05 56 93 15 06, « Tasteful decor » – 100. CX r
Meals 200/300 – ☕ 90 – **68 rm** 930/1500, 8 suites, 7 duplex.

Mercure Château Chartrons M, 81 cours St-Louis ⊠ 33300 ℘ 05 56 43 15 00, Fax 05 56 69 15 21, – 150.
Meals 85/115 ♀ – ☕ 59 – **144 rm** 550/760.

Claret M, Cité Mondiale du Vin, 18 parvis des Chartrons ℘ 05 56 01 79 79, Fax 05 56 01 79 00, – 800.
Le 20 (closed 14 July-15 August, Christmas Holidays, Saturday and Sunday) **Meals** 130bi/160bi – ☕ 65 – **92 rm** 590/670, 4 suites.

Mercure Mériadeck M, 5 r.-Lateulade ℘ 05 56 56 43 43, Fax 05 56 96 50 59 – rm, – 150. CY v
Festival (closed Saturday and Sunday) **Meals** 98/170 ♀ – ☕ 60 – **194 rm** 520/650.

Holiday Inn Garden Court, 30 r. de Tauzia ⊠ 33800 ℘ 05 56 92 21 21, Fax 05 56 91 08 06, – rm, – 70. FZ v
Meals (closed Saturday lunch and Sunday lunch) 89 ♀ – ☕ 60 – **89 rm** 570/720.

Novotel Bordeaux-Centre M, 45 cours Mar. Juin ℘ 05 56 51 46 46, Fax 05 56 98 25 56, – rm, P – 80. CY m
Meals 97 ♀ – ☕ 60 – **138 rm** 510/550.

Ste-Catherine M without rest, 27 r. Parlement Ste-Catherine ℘ 05 56 81 95 12, Fax 05 56 44 50 51 – rm, – 40. DX m
☕ 70 – **84 rm** 530/1200.

Normandie without rest, 7 cours 30-Juillet ℘ 05 56 52 16 80, Fax 05 56 51 68 91 – – 30. DX z
☕ 55 – **100 rm** 320/720.

Majestic without rest, 2 r. Condé ℘ 05 56 52 60 44, Fax 05 56 79 26 70 – DX a
☕ 50 – **49 rm** 390/600.

Grand Hôtel Français without rest, 12 r. Temple ℘ 05 56 48 10 35, Fax 05 56 81 76 18 – DX v
☕ 60 – **35 rm** 390/660.

Bayonne Etche-Ona M without rest, 4 r. Martignac ℘ 05 56 48 00 88, Fax 05 56 48 41 60 – DX f
☕ 60 – **36 rm** 400/800.
Annexe M without rest, 11 r. Mautrec – – 25.
☕ 60 – **28 rm** 400/800.

Presse M without rest, 6 r. Porte Dijeaux ℘ 05 56 48 53 88, Fax 05 56 01 05 82 – DX k
☕ 45 – **29 rm** 285/465.

Continental without rest, 10 r. Montesquieu ℘ 05 56 52 66 00, Fax 05 56 52 77 97 – DX b
☕ 40 – **50 rm** 310/570.

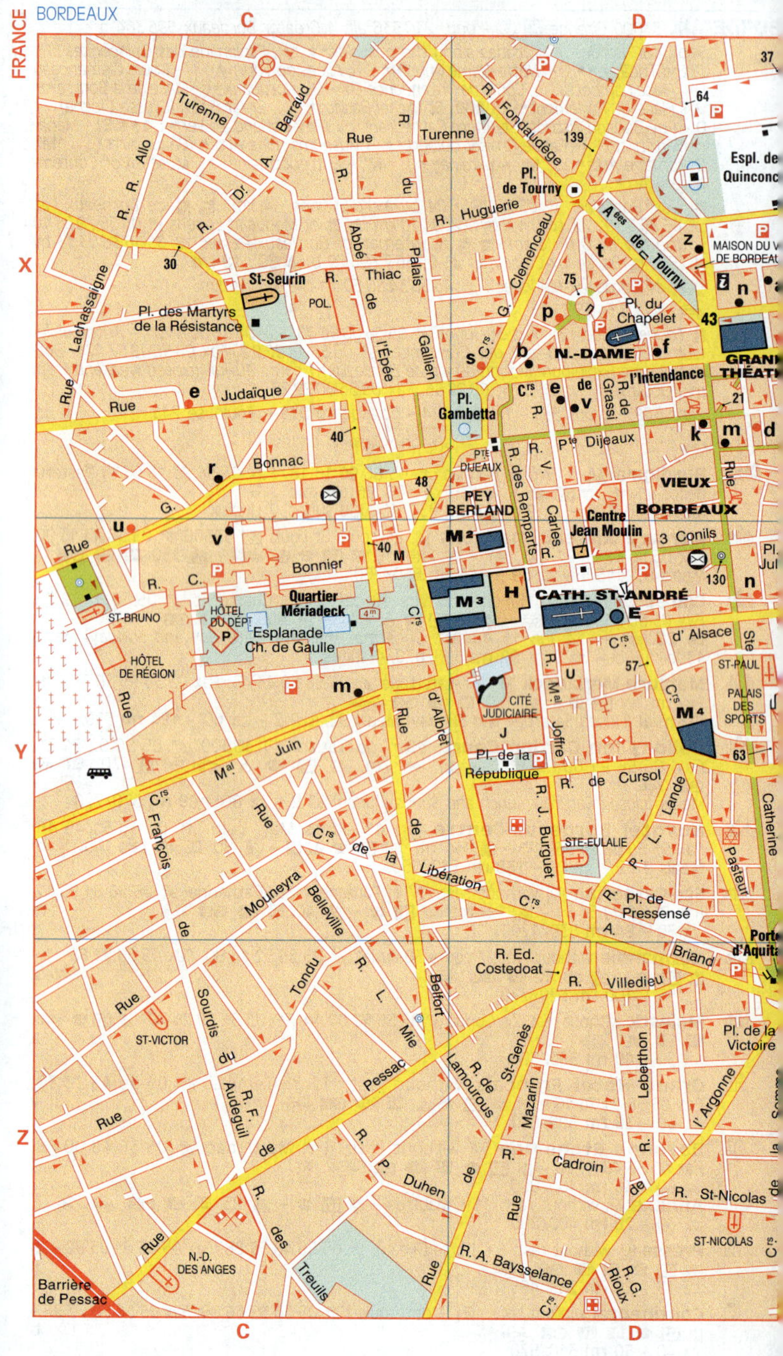
C
D
37
64
139
Espl. de
Quinconc
Turenne
R. R. Allo
R. A. Barraud
Rue
R. du Palais
Turenne
R. Fondaudège
Pl. de Tourny
A. ées de Tourny
MAISON DU V
DE BORDEAt
z
X
Dr.
R.
30
R. Abbé de l'Épée
Rue Huguerie
Clemenceau
75
t
n
p
Pl. du
Chapelet
43
n
St-Seurin
R.
Thiac
G.
GRANI
THÉATI
Pl. des Martyrs
de la Résistance
POL.
Gallien
s
C rs
b
N.-DAME
f
e
Rue
Judaïque
C rs
de R.
e
de l'Intendance
21
R. de Grassi
V
Rue
Lachassaigne
Rue
Pl.
Gambetta
R.
R. V.
P te Dijeaux
k
m
d
r
Bonnac
40
P te
DIJEAUX
R. des Remparts
R.
Carles
VIEUX
BORDEAUX
G.
48
PEY
BERLAND
Centre
Jean Moulin
3 Conils
u
v
Rue
Bonnier
40
M
R.
130
n
Pl.
Jul
C.
M 2
R.
CATH. ST-ANDRÉ
ST-BRUNO
HÔTEL
DU DÉPT
Quartier
Mériadeck
4 m
C rs
M 3
H
E
P
Esplanade
Ch. de Gaulle
d'Alsace
HÔTEL
DE RÉGION
Ste
57
ST-PAUL
Rue
P
m
CITÉ
JUDICIAIRE
R. Mié
U
M 4
PALAIS
DES
SPORTS
Y
M al
Juin
Rue
d'Albret
J
Pl. de la
République
Joffre
63
Catherine
C rs
François
C rs
de
R. de Cursol
Lande
de
la
Libération
R. J. Burguet
STE-EULALIE
C rs
P. L.
Pasteur
Mouneyra
Belleville
C rs
A.
R. Pl. de
Pressensé
R. Ed.
Costedoat
R. Villedieu
Briand
Porte
d'Aquita
Rue
Tondu
R. L.
Mle
Belfort
St-Genès
R. de Lamourous
Mazarin
Leberthon
Pl. de la
Victoire
ST-VICTOR
Sourdis
du
Pessac
l' Argonne
Rue
R. F. Audeguil
de
R. P.
Duhen
R. de
R.
Cadroin
de
R. St-Nicolas
Z
Rue
des
Treuils
Rue
R. A. Baysselance
R. G.
Rioux
ST-NICOLAS
C
Barrière
de Pessac
N.-D.
DES ANGES
C
D

BORDEAUX
FRANCE
BORDEAUX
E
F
X
Y
Z
U
LA BASTIDE
Rue Reignier
0 300 m
Nuyens
Carde
G.
R.
R.
Serr
R.
Queyries
Quai des
STE-CROIX
Thiers
Camelle
Av. R. P.
R.
de la
Bénauge
Q. Louis XVIII
u
Pl. J. Jaurès
P
PL. DE LA BOURSE
Musée des Douanes
ST-PIERRE
52
09
110
129
Pte Cailhau
Pl. du Palais
4
7
t
r
Lorraine
126
122
Pl. de Bir-Hakeim
Pte des Salinières
ST-ÉLOI
Neuve
R.
Lafargue
Victor
Hugo
Leyteire
R.
Mirail
R. des Faures
65
St-François
102
ST-MICHEL
Pl. Duburg
Pl. Canteloup
R.
C.
118
Sauvageau
33
a
Pl. de Stalingrad
Pont Pierre de
4m2
GARONNE
Deschamps
Quai
R.
Q. de la Monnaie
Q. Ste-Croix
Pont St-Jean
U
U
Rue
Pl. des Capucins
R.
du
Hamel
R. des Douves
P
P
de
la
Marne
Pl. A. Meunier
THÉÂTRE PORT DE LA LUNE
CENTRE ANDRÉ MALRAUX
Ste-Croix
120
R.
Peyronnet
v
de
Tauzia
Q. de Paludate
P
P
49
u
Kléber
Crs
de l'Yser
Rue
de
Bègles
Lafontaine
R. J. Steeg
Crs
Barbey
Malbec
R. Eug. le Roy
P
P
142
i
ST-JEAN
231

STREET INDEX TO BORDEAUX TOWN PLAN

Abbé de l'Epée (R.) CX
Albret (Crs d') . . . . . . CY
Allo (R. R.) CX
Alsace-Lorraine (Crs d') . . . . DEZ
Argentiers (R. des) . . . . . . EY 4
Argonne (Crs de l') . . . . . . DZ
Audegil (R.F.) . . . . CZ
Ausone (R.) . . . . EY 7
Barbey (Crs) . . . . EFZ
Baysselance (R. A.) . . . . . . DZ
Bègles (R. de) . . . . EZ
Belfort (R. de) . . . . CYZ
Belleville (R.) . . . . CY
Bénauge (R. de la) . . . . . . FX
Bir-Hakeim (Pl. de) . . . . . . EY
Bonnac (R. G.) . . . . CXY
Bonnier (R. C.) . . . . CY
Bordelaises (Galeries) . . . . DX 21
Bourse (Pl. de la) . . . . EX
Briand (Crs A.) . . . . DYZ
Burguet (R. J.) . . . . DY
Cadroin (R.) . . . . DZ
Camelle (R.P.) . . . . FX
Canteloup (Pl.) . . . . EY
Capdeville (R.) . . . . CX 30
Carde . . . . EZ
Carde (R. G.) . . . . FX
Carles (R. V.) . . . . DXY
Carpenteyre (R.) . . . . EFY 33
Chapeau-Rouge (Crs) . . . . EX 36
Chapelet (Pl. du) . . . . DX
Chartres (Allées de) . . . . . . DX 37
Château-d'Eau (R. du) . . . . CXY 40
Clemenceau (Crs G.) . . . . . DX
Comédie (Pl. de la) . . . . . . DX 43
Costedoat (R. Ed.) . . . . DZ
Croix de Seguey (R.) . . . . . CX 45
Cursol (R. de) . . . . DY
Deschamps (Quai) . . . . FY
Dr. Barraud (R. A.) CX
Dr. Nancel-Pénard (R.) . . . . CX 48
Domercq (R. C.) . . . . FZ 49
Douane (Quai de la) . . . . . EX 52
Douves (R. des) . . . . EZ
Duburg (Pl.) . . . . EY
Duffour-Dubergier (R.) . . . . DY 57
Duhen (R.P.) . . . . CDZ
Duplessy (R.) . . . . DX 58
Esprit des Lois (R. de l') . . EX 62
Faures (R. des) . . . . EY
Ferme de Richemont (Pl. de la) . . . . DY 63
Foch (R. Mar.) . . . . DX 64
Fondaudège (R.) . . . . DX
Fusterie (R. de la) . . . . EY 65
Gambetta (Pl.) . . . . DX
Gaulle (Espl. Ch. de) . . . . . CY
Grands Hommes (Pl. des) . . . . DX 75
Grassi (R. de) . . . . DX
Hamel (R. du) . . . . EZ
Huguerie (R.) . . . . DX
Intendance (Crs de l') . . . . DX
Jaurès (Pl. J.) . . . . EX
Joffre (Crs Mar.) . . . . DY
Judaïque (R.) CX
Juin (Crs Mar.) . . . . CY
Jullian (Pl. C.) . . . . DY
Kléber (R.) . . . . EZ
Lachassaigne (R.) CX
Lafargue (Pl.) . . . . EY
Lafontaine (R.) . . . . EZ
Lamourous (R. de) . . . . . . CDZ
Lande (R. P. L.) . . . . DY
Leberthon (R.) . . . . DZ
Leyteire (R.) . . . . EYZ
Libération (Crs de la) . . . . CDY
Louis XVIII (Quai) . . . . EX
Malbec (R.) . . . . FZ
Marne (Crs de la) . . . . EZ
Martyrs de la Résistance (Pl. des) CX
Mazarin (R.) . . . . DZ
Meuniers (Pl. A.) . . . . FZ
Meynard (Pl.) . . . . EY 102
Mie (R. L.) . . . . CZ
Mirail (R. du) . . . . EY
Monnaie (Quai de la) . . . . . FY
Mouneyra (R.) . . . . CYZ
Neuve (R.) . . . . EY
Notre-Dame (R.) . . . . EX 105
Nuyens (R.) . . . . FX
Orléans (Allées d') . . . . EX 106
Palais (Pl. du) . . . . EY
Palais Gallien (R. du) CX
Paludate (Quai de) . . . . FZ
Parlement (Pl. du) . . . . EX 109
Parlement St-Pierre (R. du) . . . . EX 110
Pas-St-Georges (R. du) . . . . EXY 112
Pasteur (R. de) . . . . DY
Pessac (Barrière de) . . . . . CZ
Pessac (R. de) . . . . CZ
Peyronnet (R.) . . . . FZ
Philippart (R. F.) . . . . EX 11
Pierre (Pont de) . . . . EFY
Porte de la Monnaie (R.) . . FY 11
Porte-Dijeaux (R. de la) . . . DX
Pressensé (Pl. de) . . . . DZ
Queyries (Quai des) . . . . . . EFX
Quinconces (Espl. des) . . . DX
Reignier (R.) . . . . FX
Remparts (R. des) . . . . DXY
Renaudel (Pl. P.) . . . . FZ
République (Pl. de la) . . . . DY
Richelieu (Quai) . . . . EY
Rioux (R. G.) . . . . DZ
Rousselle (R. de la) . . . . . . EY 12
Roy (R. Eug. le) . . . . FZ
St-François (R.) . . . . EY
St-Genès (R. de) . . . . DZ
St-James (R.) . . . . EY
St-Jean (Pont) . . . . FY
St-Nicolas (R.) . . . . DZ
St-Pierre (Pl.) . . . . EX 12
St-Projet (Pl.) . . . . DY 13
St-Rémi (R.) . . . . EX 13
Ste-Catherine (R.) . . . . DXY
Ste-Croix (Quai) . . . . FY
Sauvageau (R. C.) . . . . EFY
Serr (R.) . . . . FX
Somme (Crs de la) . . . . DZ
Sourdis (R. F. de) . . . . CYZ
Stalingrad (Pl. de) . . . . FX
Steeg (R. J.) . . . . EZ
Tauzia (R. des) . . . . FZ
Thiac (R.) CX
Thiers (Av.) . . . . EX
Tondu (R. du) . . . . CZ
Tourny (Allées de) . . . . DX
Tourny (Pl. de) . . . . DX
Treuils (R. des) . . . . CZ
Turenne (R.) . . . . CDX
Verdun (Crs de) . . . . DX 13
Victoire (Pl. de la) . . . . DZ
Victor-Hugo (Crs) . . . . EY
Vilaris (R.) . . . . EZ 14
Villedieu (R.) . . . . DZ
Yser (Crs de l') . . . . EZ
Zola (R. E.) . . . . CX 14
3 Conils (R. des) . . . . DY

Royal St-Jean without rest, 15 r. Ch. Domercq ✉ 33800 ✆ 05 56 91 72 16, *Fax 05 56 94 08 32* – ▮ TV ☎ ♿. AE ⓓ GB JCB FZ
☐ 45 – **37 rm** 330/440.

Opéra without rest, 35 r. Esprit des Lois ✆ 05 56 81 41 27, *Fax 05 56 51 78 80* – TV
☎. GB – *closed 24 December-2 January* – ☐ 35 – **27 rm** 200/310. DX

XXXX ✿ **Chapon Fin** (Garcia), 5 r. Montesquieu ✆ 05 56 79 10 10, *Fax 05 56 79 09 10*
« Authentic 1900 rocaille decor » – ▤. AE ⓓ GB JCB DX
closed 16 to 23 August, Sunday and Monday – **Meals** 170 (lunch), 275/440 and a la carte 390/470 ♀
Spec. Foie gras de canard aigre doux. Lamproie bordelaise (March-December). Bœuf à la moelle bordelaise. **Wines** Côtes de Blaye.

XXX **Dubern,** 44 allées de Tourny ✆ 05 56 79 07 70, *Fax 05 56 51 60 38* – ▤. AE ⓓ GB
closed Sunday – **Meals** 180/280 and a la carte 230/300 - ***Petit Dubern*** brasserie **Meals** 100/160 ♀. DX

XXX ✿ **Pavillon des Boulevards** (Franc), 120 r. Croix de Seguey ✆ 05 56 81 51 02
Fax 05 56 51 14 58, 🏡 – ▤. AE ⓓ GB
closed 9 to 23 August, 1 to 8 January, Saturday lunch and Sunday – **Meals** 220 (lunch), 290/450 and a la carte 320/430
Spec. Liégeois de caviar, homard à la crème de châtaignes. Bar aux aromates en cocotte lutée. Saveur des îles en chaud-froid. **Wines** Médoc, Saint-Emilion.

XXX ✿ **Plaisirs d'Ausone** (Gauffre), 10 r. Ausone ✆ 05 56 79 30 30, *Fax 05 56 51 38 16* – AE
ⓓ GB EY
closed 14 to 24 August, 4 to 10 January, Monday lunch, Saturday lunch and Sunday – **Meals** 170/350 and a la carte 290/440
Spec. Foie gras de canard aux 3 façons. Alose "sans arêtes" façon gribiche (February-May). Fricassée de sole et Saint-Jacques aux cèpes (15 November-15 April). **Wines** Graves blanc, Saint-Estèphe.

XXX · **Jean Ramet,** 7 pl. J. Jaurès ℘ 05 56 44 12 51, *Fax 05 56 52 19 80* – 🔲. 🅰🅴 **GB**
EX u
closed 7 to 29 August, Saturday lunch and Sunday – **Meals** 160 (lunch), 260/320 and a la carte 280/440 ♀
Spec. Taboulé de Saint-Jacques, sauce à l'anis étoilé (November-March). Duo de Saint-Pierre et rouget, poivre de Séchouan, gingembre confit (April-October). Souris d'agneau cuite 7 heures, jus aux truffes. **Wines** Pessac Léognan, Graves.

XXX · **Vieux Bordeaux** (Bordage), 27 r. Buhan ℘ 05 56 52 94 36, *Fax 05 56 44 25 11*, 🌳 – 🔲. 🅰🅴 ⑩ **GB**
EY a
closed 1 to 21 August, 1 to 15 February, Saturday lunch, Sunday and Bank Holidays – **Meals** 110 (lunch), 170/280 and a la carte 260/400
Spec. Salade de homard à l'huile d'orange, guacamole de mangues et avocats. Pièce de charolais aux truffes. Fleurette battue à la vanille, craquelin glacé au praliné. **Wines** Pessac Léognan, Côtes de Bourg.

XXX **L'Alhambra,** 111 bis r. Judaïque ℘ 05 56 96 06 91, *Fax 05 56 98 00 52* – 🔲. **GB**
CX e
closed 25 July-15 August, Saturday lunch and Sunday – **Meals** 110 (lunch), 160/220 and a la carte 250/390 ♨.

XX **Didier Gélineau,** 26 r. Pas St-Georges ℘ 05 56 52 84 25, *Fax 05 56 51 93 25* – 🔲. 🅰🅴 ⑩ **GB** 🇯🇨🇧
EX n
closed 10 to 24 August, Saturday lunch and Sunday – **Meals** (booking essential) 120/290 ♀.

XX **Chamade,** 20 r. Piliers de Tutelle ℘ 05 56 48 13 74, *Fax 05 56 79 29 67* – 🔲. 🅰🅴 ⑩ **GB** 🇯🇨🇧
DX d
closed 19 July-9 August, 4 to 10 January, and Saturday lunch – **Meals** 120/350.

XX **Rose des Vents,** 23 r. Ausonne ℘ 05 56 48 55 85, *Fax 05 56 48 55 85*, « 16C wine cellar » – 🔲. 🅰🅴 **GB**
EY r
closed 1 to 24 August, Monday lunch, Saturday lunch, Sunday and Bank Holidays – **Meals** 100/250 ♀.

XX **Buhan,** 28 r. Buhan ℘ 05 56 52 80 86, *Fax 05 56 52 80 86* – 🅰🅴 ⑩ **GB**
EY a
closed 1 to 16 August, February Holidays, Sunday dinner and Monday – **Meals** 135/250 ♀.

XX **Café Régent,** 46 pl. Gambetta ℘ 05 56 44 16 20, *Fax 05 56 51 36 81*, 🌳 – 🔲. 🅰🅴 ⑩ **GB**
DX s
Meals brasserie 125/150 ♀.

X **Croc-Loup,** 35 r. Loup ℘ 05 56 44 21 19 – **GB**
DY n
closed 26 July-24 August, Sunday and Monday – **Meals** 79 (lunch), 135/165 ♀.

X **Oiseau Bleu,** 65 cours Verdun ℘ 05 56 81 09 39, *Fax 05 56 81 09 39* – 🔲. 🅰🅴 **GB**
closed 2 to 8 August, 24 to 29 December, Saturday lunch and Sunday – **Meals** 109 (lunch), 170/195 ♀.

X **Bistro du Sommelier,** 163 r. G. Bonnac ℘ 05 56 96 71 78, *Fax 05 56 24 52 36*, 🌳 – **GB**
CY u
closed 9 to 15 August, Saturday lunch and Sunday – **Meals** 130 ♀.

at Parc des Expositions *North of the town* – ✉ 33300 Bordeaux :

🏨 **Sofitel Aquitania** Ⓜ, ℘ 05 56 69 66 66, *Fax 05 56 69 66 00*, 🌳, ⌇ – 🛗, ✵ rm, 🔲 📺 ☎ 🅿 – 🔔 25 - 400. 🅰🅴 ⑩ **GB** 🇯🇨🇧
Le Flore : Meals 175 – ☕ 95 – **183 rm** 795/905.

🏨 **Novotel-Bordeaux Lac** Ⓜ, ℘ 05 56 50 99 70, *Fax 05 56 43 00 66*, 🌳, ⌇, 🐎 – 🛗, ✵ rm, 🔲 📺 ☎ ♿ 🅿 – 🔔 200. 🅰🅴 ⑩ **GB**
Meals 179 ♀ – ☕ 57 – **176 rm** 475/525.

🏨 **Mercure Pont d'Aquitaine,** ℘ 05 56 43 36 72, *Fax 05 56 50 23 95*, 🌳, ⌇, 🐎, ✗ – 🛗, ✵ rm, 🔲 📺 ☎ ♿ 🅿 – 🔔 80. 🅰🅴 ⑩ **GB**
Meals 120/150 ♀ – ☕ 60 – **100 rm** 475/530.

at Bouliac *SE : 8 km – alt. 74 –* ✉ 33270 :

🏨 **St-James** (Amat) Ⓜ 🍴, pl. C. Hostein, near church ℘ 05 57 97 06 00, *Fax 05 56 20 92 58*, ≤ Bordeaux, 🌳, « Original contemporary decor », ⌇, 🐎 – 🛗, 🔲 rm, 📺 ☎ ♿ 🅿 – 🔔 25 - 40. 🅰🅴 ⑩ **GB**. 🍴
Meals 255/400 and a la carte 320/450 ♀ - *Le Bistroy* ℘ 05 57 97 06 06 **Meals** a la carte 150/230 ♀ – ☕ 80 – **18 rm** 800/1550
Spec. Fleurs de courgettes farcies, tomates au basilic (Summer). Chipirons farcis grillés, risotto à l'encre. Pigeon grillé aux épices et sa pastilla. **Wines** Saint-Emilion.

to the W :

at the airport of Mérignac *11 km by A 630 : from the North, exit n° 11ᵇ, from the South exit n°11 –* ✉ *33700 Mérignac :*

Mercure Aéroport Ⓜ, 1 av. Ch. Lindbergh ℘ 05 56 34 74 74, Fax 05 56 34 30 84, ☆
⊥ – ⒔, ⤢ rm, ▤ rest, TV ☎ ⑂ P – ▲ 110. AE ⑩ GB
Meals 120 ♀ – ☕ 57 – **148 rm** 750/800.

Novotel Aéroport, av. J. F. Kennedy ℘ 05 56 34 10 25, Fax 05 56 55 99 64, ☆, ⊥
≋ – ⒔, ⤢ rm, ▤ TV ☎ ⑂ P – ▲ 70. AE ⑩ GB JCB
Meals 98 ♀ – ☕ 57 – **137 rm** 520/550.

Eugénie-les-Bains

Eugénie-les-Bains 40320 Landes 🔟 ① – *pop. 467 alt. 65 – Spa Spa (Feb.-Nov.).*
⛳ *Golf du Tursan* ℘ 05 58 51 11 63 by D 11 and D 62 : 2 km.
🛈 *Tourist Office 147 r. René Vielle (Feb.-Nov.)* ℘ 05 58 51 13 16, Fax 05 58 51 12 02.
Bordeaux 151.

Les Prés d'Eugénie (Guérard) Ⓜ ⊛, ℘ 05 58 05 06 07, Fax 05 58 51 10 10, ≤, ☆
« **Elegantly decorated 19C mansion, park** », ⅙, ⊥, ※ – ⒔ TV ☎ P – ▲ 80. AE ⑩
GB. ⤪
closed 1 to 17 December and 3 January-6 February – (low-calorie menu for residents only
- rest. Michel Guérard (booking essential) *(closed Thursday lunch and Wednesday from
1/9-9/7 except Bank Holidays)* **Meals** 600/780 and a la carte 570/740 – ☕ 130 – **23 rm**
1350/1750, 12 suites
Spec. Friture légère de langoustines. Pigeonneau à la diable rôti à l'âtre. Clafoutis baba aux
cerises noires. **Wines** Tursan blanc.
Couvent des Herbes Ⓜ ⊛, ≤, park, « **18C convent** » – TV ☎ P, AE ⑩ GB. ⤪ rest
Meals see **Les Prés d'Eugénie** and **Michel Guérard** – ☕ 130 – **5 rm** 1550/1900
3 suites.

Maison Rose Ⓜ ⊛ (see also rest. Michel Guérard), ℘ 05 58 05 06 07
Fax 05 58 51 10 10, « **Guesthouse ambience** », ⊥, ≋ – kitchenette TV ☎ ⑂ P, AE ⑩
GB. ⤪
closed 1 to 17 December, 3 January-6 February – **Meals** (residents only) – ☕ 70 – **32 rm**
500/600.

✗ **Ferme aux Grives** Ⓜ ⊛ with rm, ℘ 05 58 05 05 06, Fax 05 58 51 10 10, ☆, « **Old
country inn** », ≋ – TV ☎ P, GB
closed 3 January-6 February, Monday dinner and Tuesday from 1 to 15 December – **Meals**
(closed Monday dinner and Tuesday from 1 September-7 July except Bank Holidays) 195
♀ – ☕ 90 – **4 rm** 1700/1900.

CANNES

CANNES 06400 Alpes-Mar. 🔠 ⑨, 🔢 ㉟ ㊳ – *pop. 68 676 alt. 2 – Casinos Carlton Casino* BYZ,
Croisette BZ.
See : *Site★★ – Seafront★★ : Boulevard★★* BCDZ *and Pointe de la Croisette★* X *– ≤★ from
the Mont Chevalier Tower* AZ V *– The Castre Museum★ (Musée de la Castre)* AZ *– Tour
into the Hills★ (Chemin des Collines) NE : 4 km* V *– The Croix des Gardes* X E *≤★ W : 2
km then 15 mn.*
⛳ *of Cannes-Mougins* ℘ 04 93 75 79 13 by ⑤ : 9 km ; ⛳ ⛳ *of Cannes-Mandelieu*
℘ 04 93 49 55 39 by ② : 6.5 km ; ⛳ *Royal Mougins Golf Club at Mougins* ℘ 04 92 92 49 69
by ④ : 10 km ; ⛳ *Riviera Golf Club at Mandelieu* ℘ 04 93 97 67 67 by ② : 8 km.
🛈 *Tourist Office "SEM", Palais des Festivals* ℘ 04 93 39 24 53, Fax 04 93 39 37 06 *and railway station, first floor* ℘ 04 93 99 19 77, Fax 04 93 39 40 19 *– A.C. 12bis r. L.-Blanc*
℘ 04 93 39 38 94, Fax 04 93 38 30 65.
Paris 903 ⑤ *– Aix-en-Provence 146* ⑤ *– Grenoble 312* ⑤ *– Marseilles 159* ⑤ *– Nice 32*
⑤ *– Toulon 121* ⑤

Plans on following pages

Carlton Inter-Continental, 58 bd Croisette ℘ 04 93 06 40 06, Fax 04 93 06 40 25,
≤, ☆, ⅙, ⛱ – ⒔, ⤢ rm, ▤ TV ☎ ⑂ ⇔ – ▲ 25 - 250. AE ⑩ GB JCB CZ e
see **Belle Otéro** below - *La Côte* ℘ 04 93 06 40 23 (15 June-15 September and closed
Sunday and Monday)(dinner only) Meals 620 ♀ – **Brasserie Carlton** ℘ 04 93 06 40 21
Meals 240(lunch), 350/450 ♀ – ☕ 165 – **310 rm** 2170/3995, 28 suites.

Majestic, 14 bd Croisette ℘ 04 92 98 77 00, Fax 04 93 38 97 90, ≤, ⊥, ⛱ – ⒔ ▤
TV ☎ ⇔ – ▲ 400. AE ⑩ GB JCB   BZ n
see **Villa des Lys** below – ☕ 120 – **280 rm** 2110/4430, 24 suites.

Martinez, 73 bd Croisette ℘ 04 92 98 73 00, Fax 04 93 39 67 82, ≤, ☆, ⊥, ⛱, ※
– ⒔ ▤ TV ☎ – ▲ 600. AE ⑩ GB   DZ n
see **Palme d'Or** below - *Relais Martinez* ℘ 04 92 98 74 12 Meals 195 ♀ – ☕ 130 –
380 rm 2800/4800, 24 suites.

Noga Hilton Ⓜ, 50 bd Croisette ℰ 04 92 99 70 00, *Fax 04 92 99 70 11,* 🌳, « Rooftop swimming pool and terrace ≤ Cannes », ₤₅, 🏖, – 🛗, 🍴 rm, 🖥 TV ☎ ♿ 🚗 – 🅰 800.
AE ⓞ GB JCB
CZ b
Scala : ℰ 04 92 99 70 93 (dinner only in July-August) **Meals** 220 ♀ – ☕ 115 – **196 rm** 1690/3790, 33 suites.

Sofitel Méditerranée Ⓜ, 2 bd J. Hibert ℰ 04 92 99 73 00, *Fax 04 92 99 73 29,* 🌳, « Rooftop swimming pool and restaurant ≤ bay of Cannes » – 🛗, 🍴 rm, 🖥 TV ☎ ♿ 🚗 – 🅰 100. AE ⓞ GB
AZ n
Méditerranée (7th floor) ℰ 04 92 99 73 02 *(closed 20/11-15/12, Sun. dinner and Mon. from 01-03 and lunch in summer)* **Meals** 180(lunch)/340 ♀ – **Chez Panisse** ℰ 04 92 99 73 10 - Provencal decor **Meals** 150/180 ♀ – ☕ 105 – **141 rm** 1185/2095, 8 suites.

Savoy Ⓜ, 5 r. F. Einesy ℰ 04 92 99 72 00, *Fax 04 93 68 25 59,* 👁, « Rooftop swimming pool and terrace », 🏖 – 🛗, 🍴 rm, 🖥 TV ☎ ♿ 🚗 – 🅰 90. AE ⓞ GB
CZ u
Roseraie ℰ 04 92 99 72 09 **Meals** 160 ♀ – ☕ 100 – **101 rm** 880/1520, 5 suites.

Gray d'Albion Ⓜ, 38 r. Serbes ℰ 04 92 99 79 79, *Fax 04 93 99 26 10,* 👁, 🏖 – 🛗, 🍴 rm, 🖥 ☎ ♿ – 🅰 150. AE ⓞ GB JCB
BZ d
Royal Gray ℰ 04 92 99 79 60 **Meals** 220/350 – ☕ 97 – **172 rm** 1200/1900, 14 suites.

Croisette Beach Hôtel Ⓜ without rest, 13 r. Canada ℰ 04 92 18 88 00, *Fax 04 93 68 35 38* – 🛗, 🍴 rm, 🖥 TV ☎ ♿ 🚗. AE ⓞ GB
DZ y
closed 20 November-25 December – ☕ 95 – **94 rm** 1190/1290.

Belle Plage Ⓜ without rest, 6 r. J. Dollfus ℰ 04 93 06 25 50, *Fax 04 93 99 61 06,* ≤, « Rooftop terrace, ≤ sea » – 🛗 🖥 TV ☎ ♿ 🚗. AE ⓞ GB JCB
AZ u
closed 15 November-25 January – ☕ 85 – **48 rm** 1060/1660.

Amarante Ⓜ, 78 bd Carnot ℰ 04 93 39 22 23, *Fax 04 93 39 40 22,* 🌳, 🎿 – 🛗, 🍴 rm, 🖥 TV ☎ ♿ 🚗 – 🅰 25. AE ⓞ GB JCB
V e
closed December – **Meals** 130/170 b.i. 🍷 – ☕ 70 – **70 rm** 790/990.

Sun Riviera Ⓜ without rest, 138 r. d'Antibes ℰ 04 93 06 77 77, *Fax 04 93 38 31 10,* 🎿, 🚤 – 🛗, 🍴 rm, 🖥 TV ☎ ♿ 🚗. AE ⓞ GB JCB
CZ h
☕ 85 – **42 rm** 890/1800.

Splendid without rest, 4 r. F. Faure ℰ 04 93 99 53 11, *Fax 04 93 99 55 02,* ≤ harbour – 🛗 kitchenette 🖥 TV ☎. AE ⓞ GB
BZ a
closed 15 November-25 December – ☕ 60 – **64 rm** 590/960.

Cristal Ⓜ, 15 rd-pt Duboys d'Angers ℰ 04 93 39 45 45, *Fax 04 93 38 64 66,* 🌳 – 🛗, 🍴 rm, 🖥 TV ☎ 🚗. AE ⓞ GB JCB
CZ s
closed 15 November-28 December – **Meals** *(closed Sunday dinner from 1 November-15 February and Monday lunch)* 145/350 ♀ – ☕ 82 – **51 rm** 910/2045.

Victoria without rest, rd-pt Duboys d'Angers ℰ 04 92 59 40 00, *Fax 04 93 38 03 91* – 🛗 🖥 TV ☎ 🚗. AE ⓞ GB
CZ x
closed 19 November-27 December – ☕ 70 – **25 rm** 750/1150.

Fouquet's without rest, 2 rd-pt Duboys d'Angers ℰ 04 92 59 25 00, *Fax 04 92 98 03 39* – 🖥 TV ☎ 🚗. AE ⓞ GB
CZ y
1 April-30 October – ☕ 60 – **10 rm** 820/1300.

Paris without rest, 34, bd Alsace ℰ 04 93 38 30 89, *Fax 04 93 39 04 61,* 🎿, 🚤 – 🛗 🖥 TV ☎ 🚗 – 🅰 25. AE ⓞ GB JCB
CY a
closed 20 November to 25 December – ☕ 65 – **47 rm** 650/720, 3 suites.

America Ⓜ without rest, 13 r. St-Honoré ℰ 04 93 06 75 75, *Fax 04 93 68 04 58* – 🛗 🖥 TV ☎. AE ⓞ GB JCB. 🚭
BZ r
closed 27 November-27 December – ☕ 60 – **28 rm** 595/795.

Mondial without rest, 1 r. Tesseire ℰ 04 93 68 70 00, *Fax 04 93 99 39 11* – 🛗, 🍴 rm, 🖥 TV ☎ ♿. AE ⓞ GB
CY e
☕ 65 – **58 rm** 670/800.

Embassy, 6 r. Bône ℰ 04 93 38 79 02, *Fax 04 93 99 07 98* – 🛗, 🖥 rm, TV ☎ 🚗. AE ⓞ GB JCB
DY j
Meals 125 ♀ – ☕ 40 – **60 rm** 610/950.

Villa de l'Olivier without rest, 5 r. Tambourinaires ℰ 04 93 39 53 28, *Fax 04 93 39 55 85,* 🎿 – 🖥 TV ☎ Ⓟ. AE ⓞ GB. 🚭
AZ e
☕ 52 – **24 rm** 550/740.

Renoir without rest, 7 r. Edith Cavell ℰ 04 92 99 62 62, *Fax 04 92 99 62 82* – 🛗 kitchenette 🖥 ☎. AE ⓞ GB JCB
BY x
☕ 65 – **17 rm** 525/665, 10 suites.

Beau Séjour, 5 r. Fauvettes ℰ 04 93 39 63 00, *Fax 04 92 98 64 66,* 🌳, 🎿, 🚤 – 🛗, 🖥 rm, TV ☎ 🚗. AE ⓞ GB JCB
AZ d
Meals 75/110 🍷 – ☕ 60 – **45 rm** 650/750.

CANNES

Albert-Édouard (Jetée)	**BZ**	
Alexandre-III (Bd)	**X**	2
Alsace (Bd)	**BDY**	
Anc. Combattants d'Afrique du Nord (Av.)	**AYZ**	4
André (R. du Cdt)	**CZ**	
Antibes (R. d')	**BCY**	
Bachaga Saïd Boualam (Av.)	**AY**	5
Beauséjour (Av.)	**DYZ**	
Beau-Soleil (Bd)	**X**	10
Belges (R. des)	**BZ**	12
Blanc (R. Louis)	**AYZ**	
Broussailles (Av. des)	**V**	16
Buttura (R.)	**BZ**	17
Canada (R. du)	**DZ**	
Carnot (Bd)	**X**	
Carnot (Square)	**V**	20
Castre (Pl. de la)	**AZ**	21
Chabaud (R.)	**CY**	22
Clemenceau (R. G.)	**AZ**	
Coteaux (Av. des)	**V**	
Croisette (Bd de la)	**BDZ**	
Croix-des-Gardes (Bd)	**VX**	29
Delaup (Bd)	**AY**	30
Dr-Pierre Gazagnaire (R.)	**AZ**	32
Dr-R. Picaud (Av.)	**X**	
Dollfus (R. Jean)	**AZ**	33
Etats-Unis (R. des)	**CZ**	35
Faure (R. Félix)	**ABZ**	
Favorite (Av. de la)	**X**	38
Félix-Faure (R.)	**ABZ**	
Ferrage (Bd de la)	**ABY**	40
Fiesole (Av.)	**X**	43
Foch (R. du Mar.)	**BY**	44
Gallieni (R. du Mar.)	**BY**	48
Gaulle (Pl. Gén.-de)	**BZ**	51
Gazagnaire (Bd Eugène)	**X**	
Grasse (Av. de)	**VX**	53
Guynemer (Bd)	**AY**	
Hespérides (Av. des)	**X**	55
Hibert (Bd Jean)	**AZ**	
Hibert (R.)	**AZ**	

Isola-Bella (Av. d')	**X**	
Jaurès (R. Jean)	**BCY**	
Joffre (R. du Mar.)	**BY**	60
Juin (Av. Mar.)	**DZ**	
Koenig (Av. Gén.)	**DY**	
Lacour (Bd Alexandre)	**X**	62
Latour-Maubourg (R.)	**DZ**	
Lattre-de-T. (Av. de)	**AY**	63
Laubeuf (Quai Max)	**AZ**	
Leader (Bd)	**VX**	64
Lérins (Av. de)	**X**	65
Lorraine (Bd. de)	**CDY**	
Macé (R.)	**CZ**	66
Madrid (Av. de)	**DZ**	
Meynadier (R.)	**ABY**	
Midi (Bd du)	**X**	
Mimont (R. de)	**BY**	
Mont-Chevalier (R. du)	**AZ**	72
Montfleury (Bd)	**CDY**	74
Monti (R. Marius)	**AY**	75
Noailles (Av. J.-de)	**X**	
Observatoire (Bd de l')	**X**	84
Oxford (Bd d')	**V**	87
Pantiero (la)	**ABZ**	
Paradis-Terrestre (Corniches du)	**V**	88
Pasteur (R.)	**DZ**	
Pastour (R. Louis)	**AY**	90
Perier (Bd du)	**V**	92
Perrissol (R. Louis)	**AZ**	93
Petit-Juas (Av. du)	**VX**	
Pins (Bd des)	**X**	95
Pompidou (Espl. G.)	**BZ**	
Prince-de-Galles (Av. du)	**X**	97
République (Bd de la)	**X**	
Riou (Bd du)	**VX**	
Riouffe (R. Jean de)	**BY**	98
Roi-Albert 1er (Av.)	**X**	
Rouguière (R.)	**BY**	100
St-Antoine (R.)	**AZ**	102
St-Nicolas (Av.)	**BY**	105
St-Pierre (Quai)	**AZ**	
Sardou (R. Léandre)	**X**	108
Serbes (R. des)	**BZ**	110
Source (Bd de la)	**X**	112
Stanislas (Pl.)	**AY**	
Strasbourg (Bd de)	**CDY**	
Teisseire (R.)	**CY**	114

Tuby (Bd Victor)	**AYZ**	115
Vallauris (Av. de)	**VX**	116
Vallombrosa (Bd)	**AY**	118
Vautrin (Bd Gén.)	**DZ**	
Vidal (R. du Cdt)	**CY**	120
Wemyss (Av. Amiral Wester)	**X**	122

LE CANNET

Aubarède (Ch. de l')	**V**	8
Bellevue (Pl.)	**V**	13
Bréguières (Ch. de)	**V**	14
Cannes (R. des)	**V**	19
Carnot (Bd de)	**V**	
Cheval (Av. Maurice)	**V**	23
Collines (Ch. des)	**V**	
Doumer (Bd Paul)	**V**	
Écoles (R. des)	**V**	34
Four-à-Chaux (Bd du)	**V**	45
Gambetta (Bd)	**V**	50
Gaulle (Av. Gén.-de)	**V**	
Jeanpierre (Av. Maurice)	**V**	58
Mermoz (Av. Jean)	**V**	67
Monod (Bd Jacques)	**V**	68
Mont-Joli (Av. du)	**V**	73
N.-D.-des-Anges (Av.)	**V**	79
Olivet (Ch. de l')	**V**	85
Olivetum (Av. d')	**V**	86
Paris (R. de)	**V**	89
Pinède (Av. de la)	**V**	94
Pompidou (Av. Georges)	**V**	96
République (Bd de la)	**V**	
Roosevelt (Av. Franklin)	**V**	99
St-Sauveur (R.)	**V**	106
Victor-Hugo (R.)	**V**	115
Victoria (Av.)	**V**	

VALLAURIS

Cannes (Av. de)	**V**	18
Clemenceau (Av. G.)	**V**	25
Fournas (Av. du)	**V**	46
Golfe (Av. du)	**V**	52
Isnard (Pl. Paul)	**V**	56
Rouvier (Bd Maurice)	**V**	102
Tapis-Vert (Av. du)	**V**	113

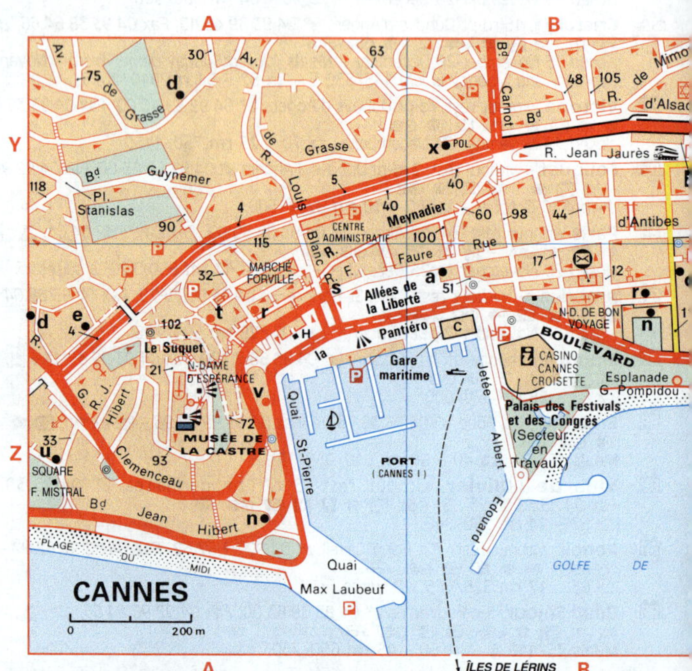

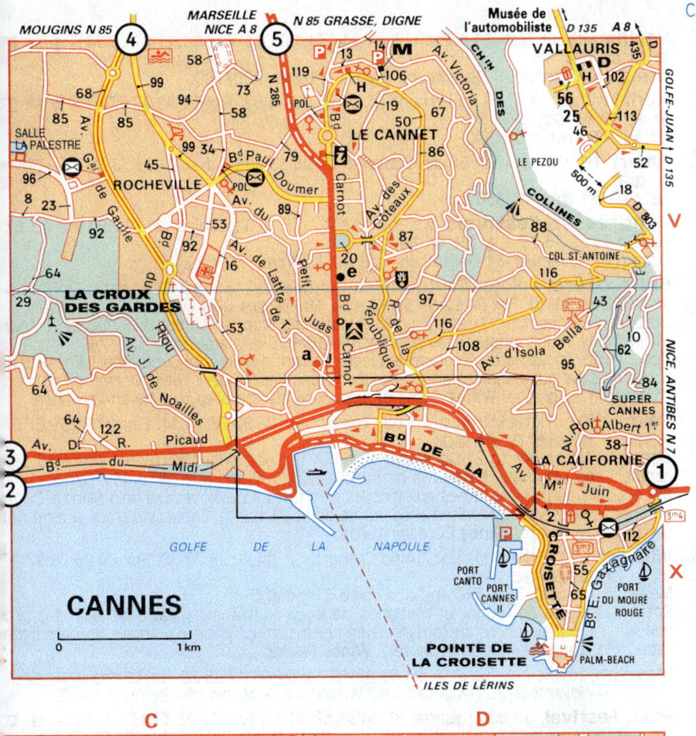

MOUGINS N 85
MARSEILLE NICE A 8
N 85 GRASSE, DIGNE
Musée de l'automobiliste
D 135
A 8
VALLAURIS
GOLFE-JUAN D 135
4
5
P
M
P
H
D
H
435
102
56
25
46
113
POL
52
58
99
68
73
94
58
119
106
14
13
19
50
67
86
18
D 803
V
85
85
Av. Gal de Gaulle
45
99 34
79
Bd Paul Doumer
POL
Av. du
89
LE CANNET
Av. des Côteaux
87
LE PEZOU
COLLINES
88
COL ST-ANTOINE
116
ROCHEVILLE
96
8
23
92
Bd du Riou
92
16
53
LA CROIX
DES GARDES
20
e
Bd de la République
Bd Carnot
97
116
43
Bella
95
10
62
84
SUPER
CANNES
64
29
53
Av. de Lattre de T.
Petit Juas
108
Av. d'Isola
64
a
j
Roi Albert 1er
38
64
122
Av. Dr R. Picaud
Av. J. de Noailles
Bd DE
LA
Av.
LA CALIFORNIE
3
Bd
du
Midi
Mal Juin
1
2
2
112
GOLFE
DE
LA
NAPOULE
P
CROISETTE
Bd E. Gazagnaire
55
65
X
CANNES
PORT
CANTO
PORT
CANNES
II
PORT
DU MOURÉ
ROUGE
0
1 km
POINTE DE
LA CROISETTE
PALM-BEACH
ÎLES DE LÉRINS

C
D
CHAPELLE 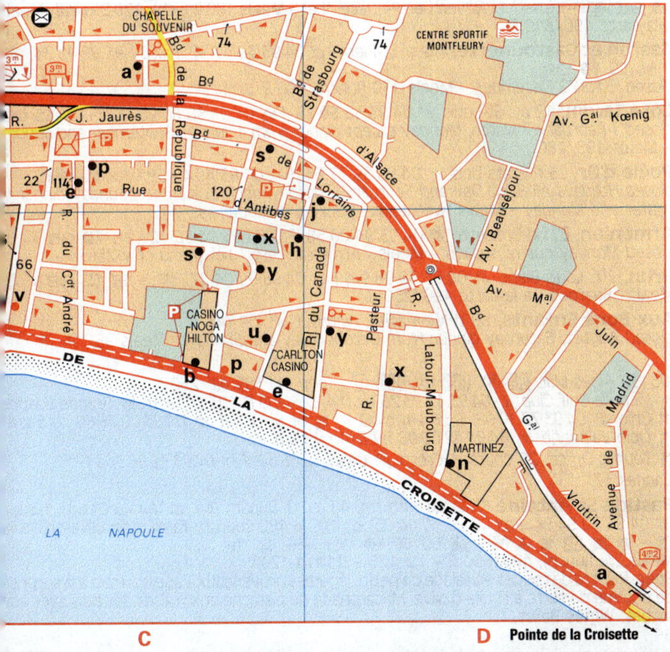
DU SOUVENIR
74
74
CENTRE SPORTIF
MONTFLEURY
Bd de la République
a
Bd
Bd de Strasbourg
Av. Gal Kœnig
Y
R.
J. Jaurès
3m
3m
P
Bd
d'Alsace
s de
p
22
114
e
Rue
120
d'Antibes
Lorraine
j
R. du Cdt André
s
x
h
y
Av. Beauséjour
R. du Canada
v
66
Av. Mal
CASINO
NOGA
HILTON
u
Pasteur
y
Juin
b
p
CARLTON
CASINO
x
Bd
Madrid
Z
e
DE
LA
R.
Latour-Maubourg
Gal
de
Avenue
MARTINEZ
n
Vautrin
CROISETTE
LA
NAPOULE
a
4m2
C
D
Pointe de la Croisette

Régina without rest, 31 r. Pasteur ℘ 04 93 94 05 43, *Fax 04 93 43 20 54* – ⊡ ⊟ TV
☎ P. AE GB. ✀   DZ
closed late October-26 December – ☕ 60 – **18 rm** 680/780.

Abrial without rest, 24 bd Lorraine ℘ 04 93 38 78 82, *Fax 04 92 98 67 41* – ⊡ ⊟ TV
☎ P. AE ⓘ GB JCB   CY
☕ 55 – **50 rm** 730/1300.

Albert 1er without rest, 68 av. Grasse ℘ 04 93 39 24 04, *Fax 04 93 38 83 75* – TV ☎
P. GB   AY
☕ 35 – **11 rm** 310/350.

Congrès et Festivals without rest, 12 r. Teisseire ℘ 04 93 39 13 81
Fax 04 93 39 56 28 – ⊡ TV ☎. AE GB   CY
closed 15 November-31 December – ☕ 40 – **20 rm** 350/680.

Belle Otéro - Hôtel Carlton Inter-Continental, 58 bd Croisette, 7th floor
℘ 04 92 99 51 10, *Fax 04 92 99 51 13* – ⊟. AE ⓘ GB JCB – *closed 6 June-6 July, 3*
October-16 November, Tuesday lunch, Sunday and Monday except July-August – Meals
(*dinner only in July-August*) 290 b.i. (lunch), 410/620 and a la carte 520/740   CZ
Spec. Petite fricassée de crustacés en léger parfum d'aïoli (April-September). Rougets de
roche du pays aux banettes en jus de coco (June-September). "Belle Otéro" en douceur
chocolatée au praliné. **Wines** Côtes de Provence blanc, Coteaux d'Aix-en-Provence.

Palme d'Or - Hôtel Martinez, 73 bd Croisette ℘ 04 92 98 74 14, *Fax 04 93 39 67 82*
≤, ⌇ – ⊡ ⊟ P. AE ⓘ GB   DZ
closed 14 November to 21 December, Tuesday (except dinner from 15 June to 15 Sep-
tember) and Monday – Meals 295 b.i. (lunch), 350/580 and a la carte 430/670 ♀
Spec. Œufs au plat retournés aux lentilles et truffes (late-November-mid-March). Dégustation de poissons de Méditerranée au jus de bouillabaisse. Capuccino glacé praliné noisette, sabayon café. **Wines** Coteaux Varois.

Villa des Lys - Hôtel Majestic, 14 bd Croisette ℘ 04 92 98 77 00, *Fax 04 93 38 97 90*
⌇ – ⊟. AE ⓘ GB JCB
Meals 260 (lunch), 350/540 and a la carte 430/630 ♀
Spec. Cassolette de rouget et matignon de légumes (summer). Râble de lapin à la pro-
vençale, ragoût de cocos au romarin (summer-autumn). Gratin d'oranges, sorbet citron
capuccino d'agrumes (autumn-winter). **Wines** Palette.

Mesclun, 16 r. St-Antoine ℘ 04 93 99 45 19, *Fax 04 93 47 68 29* – ⊟. AE GB JCB AZ
closed 20 November-20 December and Wednesday – Meals (*dinner only*) 185 ♀

Rest. Festival, 52 bd Croisette ℘ 04 93 38 04 81, *Fax 04 93 38 13 82*, ⌇ – ⊟. AE
ⓘ GB JCB – *closed 17 November-24 December* – Meals 180 (lunch)/220 ♀ - *Grill* : Meals
a la carte 190/310 ♀   CZ

Gaston et Gastounette, 7 quai St-Pierre ℘ 04 93 39 47 92, *Fax 04 93 99 45 34*, ⌇
– ⊟. AE ⓘ GB   AZ
closed 1 to 20 December – Meals 130 (lunch)/200 ♀

Côté Jardin, 12 av. St-Louis ℘ 04 93 38 60 28, *Fax 04 93 38 60 28*, ⌇ – ⊟. AE GB
closed 1 February-7 March, Monday except dinner from 1 July-15 September and Sunday
– Meals 195/280.   X

Poêle d'Or, 23 r. États-Unis ℘ 04 93 39 77 65, *Fax 04 93 40 45 59* – ⊟. AE GB CZ
closed Holidays All Saint Day and February, Tuesday lunch in summer, Sunday dinner in
winter and Monday – Meals (*weekends : booking essential*) 135/245.

Arménien, 82 bd Croisette ℘ 04 93 94 00 58, *Fax 04 93 94 56 12* – ⊟. ⓘ GB DZ
closed Monday out of season – Meals - Armenian rest. - set menu only 250.

Brun, 2 r. Louis-Blanc ℘ 04 93 39 98 94, *Fax 04 93 39 74 27*, ⌇ – ⊟. AE GB AZ
Meals - Seafood - a la carte 190/250 ♀

Aux Bons Enfants, 80 r. Meynadier, (without ℘) – ✀   AZ
closed August, Saturday dinner from October-May and Sunday – Meals 95.

Grasse 06130 Alpes-Mar. 84 ⑧, 114 ⑬, 115 ㉔ – *pop. 41 388 alt. 250.*
ᚦ *Victoria Golf Club* ℘ 04 93 12 23 26 *by D 4, D 3 and D 103 : 13 km ;* ᚦ *Grande Bastide*
at Opio ℘ 04 93 77 70 08, *E : 6 km by D 7 ;* ᚦ *of St-Donat* ℘ 04 93 09 76 60 : 5,5 km
ᚦ *Opio-Valbonne* ℘ 04 93 42 00 08 *by D 4 : 11 km.*
🛈 *Tourist Office, 22 cours H. Cresp* ℘ 04 93 36 66 66, *Fax 04 93 36 86 36.*
Cannes 17.

Bastide St-Antoine (Chibois) with rm, 48 av. H. Dunant (by bd Mar. Leclerc) : 1,5 km
℘ 04 93 70 94 94, *Fax 04 93 70 94 95*, ≤, ⌇, « *18C country farm in an olive-grove* »
⌇ – ⊡ ⊟ TV ☎ & P. – ⌇ 60. AE ⓘ GB JCB. ✀ rm
Meals 240 (lunch), 490/650 ♀ – ☕ 125 – **11 rm** 1200
Spec. Palette de rouget en salade de petits légumes provençaux. Lapereau rôti à la surprise
de pomme de terre à l'huile d'olive. Macaronade de pistache aux fraises des bois avec son
sorbet. **Wines** Bellet.

Juan-les-Pins 06160 *Alpes-Mar.* 84 ⑨, 115 ㉟ ㊴

🛈 *Tourist Office 51 bd Ch.-Guillaumont ℘ 04 92 90 53 05.*

Cannes 8,5.

Juana ⓢ, *la Pinède, av. G. Gallice ℘ 04 93 61 08 70, Fax 04 93 61 76 60,* ≤, 🏯, ⤵ – 🛗, 🔲 rm, 📺 ☎ 🅿 – 🔺 25. 🆎 ⒼⒷ
1 April-10 October – **Terrasse** *(closed Wednesday except dinner in 7/8, Monday lunch except Bank Holidays)* **Meals** 280/650 ⓨ – 🍽 100 – **45 rm** 1150/2450, 5 suites
Spec. Cannelloni de supions et palourdes à l'encre de seiche. Selle d'agneau de Pauillac cuite en terre d'argile de Vallauris. Fruits rouges aux saveurs d'huile de vanille et vieux balsamique. **Wines** Bellet, Côtes de Provence.

La Napoule 06210 *Alpes-Mar.* 84 ⑧, 115 ㉞.

🏌₉ 🏌₁₈ *of Mandelieu ℘ 04 93 49 55 39 ;* 🏌₁₈ *Riviera Golf Club ℘ 04 92 97 67 67.*

🛈 *Tourist Office av. Cannes at Mandelieu ℘ 04 92 97 86 46, Fax 04 92 97 67 79.*

Cannes 9,5.

L'Oasis, *r. J. H. Carle ℘ 04 93 49 95 52, Fax 04 93 49 64 13,* 🏯, « Shaded and flowered patio » – 🔲. 🆎 ⓞ ⒼⒷ
Meals 230 (lunch), 320/680 and a la carte 510/650 ⓨ
Spec. Huîtres spéciales marinées au raifort, granité d'eau de mer. Foie gras de canard chaud en verdure de blettes. Pêche locale rôtie en tian aux senteurs de Provence. **Wines** Côtes de Provence, Bandol.

LILLE 59000 *Nord* 51 ⑯, 111 ㉒ – *pop. 172 142 alt. 10.*

See : *Old Lille★★ : Old Stock Exchange★★ (Vieille Bourse)* EY, *Place du Général-de-Gaulle★* EY **66,** *Hospice Comtesse★ (panelled timber vault★★)* EY, – *Rue de la Monnaie★* EY **120** – *Vauban's Citadel★* BV – *St-Sauveur district : Paris Gate★* EFZ, ≤★ *from the top of the belfry of the Hôtel de Ville* FZ – *Fine Arts Museum★★★ (Musée des Beaux-Arts)* EZ – *Général de Gaulle's Birthplace (Maison natale)* EY.

🏌₉ *of Flandres (private) ℘ 03 20 72 20 74 : 4,5 km ;* 🏌₁₈ *of Sart (private) ℘ 03 20 72 02 51 : 7 km ;* 🏌₁₈ *of Brigode at Villeneuve d'Ascq ℘ 03 20 91 17 86 : 9 km ;* 🏌₁₈ 🏌₁₈ *of Bondues ℘ 03 20 23 20 62 : 9,5 km.*

✈ *of Lille-Lesquin : ℘ 03 20 49 68 68 : 8 km.*

🚗 *℘ 08 36 35 35 35.*

🛈 *Tourist Office Palais Rihour ℘ 03 20 21 94 21, Fax 03 20 21 94 20 – Automobile Club du Nord 8 r. Quennette ℘ 03 20 55 21 41.*

Paris 221 ④ – Brussels 116 ② – Ghent 71 ② – Luxembourg 312 ④ – Strasbourg 525 ④

Plans on following pages

Alliance M ⓢ, *17 quai du Wault* ✉ 59800 *℘ 03 20 30 62 62, Fax 03 20 42 94 25,* « 17C former convent » – 🛗, ⤢ rm, 📺 ☎ ♿ 🅿 – 🔺 35 - 80. 🆎 ⓞ ⒼⒷ 🅹🅲🅱.
❀ rest   BV **d**
Meals 95/180 b.i. ⓨ – 🍽 80 – **80 rm** 770/1000, 3 suites.

Carlton *without rest, 3 r. Paris* ✉ 59800 *℘ 03 20 13 33 13, Fax 03 20 51 48 17* – 🛗, ⤢ rm, 📺 ☎ ♿ 🅿 – 🔺 25 - 100. 🆎 ⓞ ⒼⒷ 🅹🅲🅱   EY **u**
🍽 80 – **57 rm** 840/1100, 3 suites.

Novotel Centre M, *116 r. Hôpital Militaire* ✉ 59800 *℘ 03 28 38 53 53, Fax 03 28 38 53 54* – 🛗, ⤢ rm, 🔲 📺 ☎ ♿ – 🔺 30 - 50. 🆎 ⓞ ⒼⒷ   EY **s**
Meals a la carte approx. 180 – 🍽 59 – **102 rm** 570/595.

Mercure Royal M *without rest, 2 bd Carnot* ✉ 59800 *℘ 03 20 14 71 47, Fax 03 20 14 71 48* – 🛗, ⤢ rm, 📺 ☎ – 🔺 25. 🆎 ⓞ ⒼⒷ   EY **h**
🍽 60 – **102 rm** 450/580.

Holiday Inn Express M, *75 bis r. Gambetta ℘ 03 20 42 90 90, Fax 03 20 57 14 24* – 🛗, ⤢ rm, 📺 ☎ ♿ 🚗 – 🔺 25 - 100. 🆎 ⓞ ⒼⒷ 🅹🅲🅱   EZ **e**
Meals *(closed Sunday lunch and Saturday)* 105/125 ⓨ – **97 rm** 🍽 600.

Paix *without rest, 46 bis r. Paris* ✉ 59800 *℘ 03 20 54 63 93, Fax 03 20 63 98 97* – 🛗 📺 ☎. 🆎 ⓞ ⒼⒷ   EY **r**
🍽 40 – **35 rm** 360/450.

Treille M *without rest, 7 pl. L. de Bettignies* ✉ 59800 *℘ 03 20 55 45 46, Fax 03 20 51 51 69* – 🛗 📺 ☎ – 🔺 25. 🆎 ⓞ ⒼⒷ   EY **d**
🍽 50 – **40 rm** 380/410.

Lille Europe M *without rest, av. Le Corbusier ℘ 03 20 21 41 51, Fax 03 20 21 41 59* – 🛗 📺 ☎ ♿. 🆎 ⓞ ⒼⒷ   FY **m**
🍽 40 – **97 rm** 360.

FRANCE
LILLE
A 25 ARMENTIÈRES
IEPER (YPRES)
ST-GÉRARD
LE CANON D' OR
P.T.T.
Avenue
Becquart
G. DELFOSSE
de
Lille
Bois
du
D 357
A. MAX
114
54 104
St-An
LAMBERSART
H
R. Auguste
Bonte
de
Av. H. Delecaux
Av.
l' Hippodrome
GRIMONPREZ JORRIS
109
N.-D. DE FATIMA
CANTELEU
LE CHAMP DE COURSES
CITADELLE
CHAMP DE MARS
S
D 933
St-SÉPULCRE
G. LEFORT
168
Av.
Canteleu
Av. du Colisée
33
54
42
P
Ste-Cather
ZOO
LOMME ARMENTIÈRES
R. du Marais
Dunkerque
Deûle
BOIS DE BOULOGNE
Jouhaux
Vauban
Bd
R. de Hégel
H.te
Av. de
Bois Blancs
111
Av. Léon
JARDIN VAUBAN
SACRÉ CŒUR
Rue de
N.-D. DE CONSOLATION
R. de Toul
ST-CHARLES
Dunkerque
Bd. de la Lorraine
VAUBAN-
H
Colbert
R. du Port
Boulevard
118
PONT DE DUNKERQUE
Roland
R.
Rue Nationale
Solferino
BOIS BLANCS
Rue de
ESQUERMES
R.
R.
145
Port de Lille
R. de Turenne
Colbert L.
Gambetta
PORT
Pl. du Ma Leclerc
145
Bd. de la Moselle
145
Gambe
18
P
la Bassée
Cormontaigne
ST-PIERRE ST-PAUL
R. Jules
H
Wazemmes
R. de
d' Isly
Bd
ST-MARTIN
WAZEMMES
Guesde
Montebello
5
Rue
Rue d' Esquermes
Montebello
85
A 25
ST-BEN LABR
DUNKERQUE BÉTHUNE
Bd. de la Moselle
Pl. B. Dorez
N.-D. DES VICTOIRES
12
Bd
de
Metz
Bd.
H
ST- CURÉ D' ARS
Porte des Postes
Bd de Strasbo
THIRIEZ
R. du Fg de Béthune
Fg DE BÉTHUNE
88
4
3
D 941 HAUBOURDIN
CENTRE HOSPITALIER

LILLE
FRANCE
OOSTENDE
A 22 GENT, ROUBAIX, TOURCOING
C
D
LA MADELEINE
Schuman
Av. W. Churchill
67
67
140
R. de Gand
Bd P. de Coubertin
N.-D. DE LOURDES
R. de la République
Av. de la
R. É. Zola
R. du Busson
PARC MONCEAU
R. de la Louvière
N.-D. DE PELLEVOISIN
ST-MAURICE PELLEVOISIN
U
A 22 GENT, ROUBAIX, TOURCOING
Pte de Gand
Carref. Pasteur
CIMETIÈRE DE L'EST
HÔTEL DE LA COMMUNAUTÉ URBAINE
R. de la Madeleine
R. de la
St-Maurice Pellevoisin
Roubaix
5
HOSPICE COMTESSE
VIEUX LILLE
Carnot
Bd
Opéra
GARE T.G.V. LILLE-EUROPE
TOUR DU CRÉDIT LYONNAIS
Gare Lille-Europe
Gare Lille Flandres
CENTRE EURALILLE
Rue
du
D 14
Fg de
ST-MAURICE DES CHAMPS
R. St-Gabriel
N 356
VIEILLE BOURSE
Nationale
Rihour
ST-MAURICE
LILLE-FLANDRES
HÔTEL DE RÉGION
CITÉ ADMTIVE
HÔTEL DE DÉPARTEMENT
PARC DES DONDAINES
Printemps 1999
Eugène Jacquet
Caulier
N.-D. DE FIVES
FIVES
Fives
4
CENTRE
Mairie de Lille
ST-SAUVEUR
ZÉNITH LILLE GRAND PALAIS
PONT DES FLANDRES
13
D 941
de
P
République
la
Liberté
PALAIS DES BEAUX-ARTS
H
POL
Lille Grand Palais
R. P. Legrand
du Long
BALLET
U
U
R.
E.N.S.A.M.
93
R. C. Guérin
GARE ST-SAUVEUR
N 351
ouv. prévue Printemps 1999
ST-LOUIS
Solferino
R. de Cambrai
Rue
112
R.
156
159
Av. D. Cordonnier
Pot
R. Matteoti
163
Hugo
d'Arras
d'Artois
60
de Trévise
Porte de Valenciennes
PONT DE TOURNAI
X
VILLENEUVE D'ASCQ
Victor-
7
d'Artois
MOULINS
R. de Douai
ST-VINCENT DE PAUL
R.
Belfort
Bd de
Av. J. Perrin
SEITA
LILLE
56
Rue
37
U
25
Porte de Douai
1
21
0   300 m
Porte d'Arras
Bd
2
d'Alsace
J. BOIN
JARDIN DES PLANTES
Fg DE DOUAI
A 1
D 549 SECLIN
C
D
PARIS
A 23 VALENCIENNES

R. Princesse
Mon natale du Gal de Gaulle
R. St-André
R. Voltaire
R. Négrier
R. de la Halle
Ste-Marie Madeleine
Pont-Neuf
Gand
Porte de Gand
Bd Pierre de Coubertin
Av. de la République
Av. Louise
Ballon
CIMETIÈRE DE L'EST
HÔTEL DE LA COMMUNAUTÉ URBAINE
Pl. du Concert
VIEUX
Carref. Pasteur
R. de Thionville
Peuple Belge
R. de Courtrai
R. des Urbanistes
Parc H. Matisse
Gare Lille Europe
Rue d'Angleterre
HOSPICE COMTESSE
Rue St-Jacques
R. des Carnot
Porte de Roubaix
GARE T.G.V. LILLE-EUROPE
Pl. F. Mitterrand
Pl. de Valladolid
N.-D. de la Treille
Pl. du Lion d'Or
Royale
Ste-Catherine
Esquermoise
Basse
LILLE
R.
R. des Arts
138
Cannoniers
Gare Lille Flandres
TOUR DU CRÉDIT LYONNAIS
Corbusier
TOUR LILLEUROPE WTC
CENTRE EURALILLE
Pl. de l'Arsenal
Thiers
102
C
Opéra
h
R. Faidherbe
64
Gare Lille Flandres
LILLE-FLANDRES
AÉRONEF
PONT DES FLANDRES
Printemps 1999
NOUVEAU SIÈCLE
66
150
VIEILLE BOURSE
Av. Willy Brandt
148
Av. Foch
135
133
Rihour
St-MAURICE
R. de Tournai
ZÉNITH
LILLE-GRAND PALAIS
Nationale
Palais Rihour
162
144
139
Molinel
HÔTEL DE RÉGION
R. Javary
ST-ETIENNE (MILITAIRE)
R. de Béthune
147
141
FORUM
Delory
CITÉ ADMTIVE
Bd
Peur
Sans
Jean
du
de
R.
45
CENTRE
Kennedy
HÔTEL DU DÉPARTEMENT
Pl. Richebé
R. Plat
Av.
du
Prés!
Mairie de Lille
43
ST-SAUVEUR
100
République
Pl. de la République
Pl. Jacquart
la
Valmy
Paris
Liberté
R. St-Sauveur
Lille Grand Palais
Bd Dubuisson
R. L. Gambetta
R. d'Inkermann
R. N. Leblanc
PALAIS DES BEAUX-ARTS
(ANNEXE)
Liberté
PORTE DE PARIS
132
46
POL
Lille Grand Palais
51
Pl. Sébastopol
Postes
Pl. Ph. le-Bon
de
U
ÉCOLE NATLE SUPRE DES ARTS ET MÉTIERS
XIV
Mal Vaillant
Prés! Hoover
Bd Louis
ST-MICHEL
Brûle-
Maison
Solférino
Jeanne d'Arc
Jean Bart
R. C. Guérin
LILLE
Pl. J. d'Arc
R. Gosselet
93
0   300 m

🏨 **Ibis Centre,** av. Ch. St-Venant ✉ 59800 ℘ 03 20 55 44 44, *Fax 03 20 31 06 25,* 🌳
– 🛗, ⚡ rm, 📺 ☎ 🕭 🚗 – 🔬 25 - 60. AE Ⓞ GB   FYZ a
Meals 95 ♈ – ☕ 35 – **151 rm** 370.

🏨 **Clarine,** 46 r. Fg d'Arras ℘ 03 20 53 53 40, *Fax 03 20 53 20 95* – 🛗 📺 ☎ 🚗 – 🔬 40.
AE Ⓞ GB
Meals 78/130 ♈ – ☕ 35 – **80 rm** 290.

🍴🍴🍴🍴 **A L'Huîtrière,** 3 r. Chats Bossus ✉ 59800 ℘ 03 20 55 43 41, *Fax 03 20 55 23 10,*
❀   « Original decoration with ceramics in the fish shop » – 🍽. AE Ⓞ GB JCB   EY g
closed 22 July-31 August, dinner Sunday and Bank Holidays – **Meals** 260 (lunch), 450/600
and a la carte 330/540 ♈
Spec. Huîtres et produits de la mer. Baluchons de Saint-Jacques au chou vert et à la truffe
(1 October-15 May). Turbot rôti aux échalotes grises et vinaigre de bière.

🍴🍴🍴 **Sébastopol,** 1 pl. Sébastopol ℘ 03 20 57 05 05, *Fax 03 20 40 11 31* –
AE GB   EZ a
closed 9 to 19 August, Sunday in July-August and Saturday lunch – **Meals** 165/265 and
a la carte 300/410.

🍴🍴🍴 **Laiterie,** 138 av. Hippodrome at Lambersart NW : 2 km ✉ 59130 *Lambersart*
℘ 03 20 92 79 73, *Fax 03 20 22 16 19,* 🌳, 🍽 – 🅿. AE GB   AV s
closed 15 to 31 August, February Holidays, Monday, dinner Wednesday and Sunday – **Meals**
160/275 and a la carte 300/440.

🍴🍴 **Baan Thaï,** 22 bd J.-B. Lebas ℘ 03 20 86 06 01, *Fax 03 20 86 03 23* – 🍽. AE Ⓞ GB
closed 24 July-22 August, Sunday dinner and Monday lunch – **Meals** - Thai rest. - 148
(lunch)/220 ♈.   EZ s

🍴🍴 **Clément Marot,** 16 r. Pas ✉ 59800 ℘ 03 20 57 01 10, *Fax 03 20 57 39 69* – 🍽. AE
Ⓞ GB JCB   EY n
closed August, Christmas-New Year, Monday dinner and Sunday – **Meals** 185/250 ♈.

🍴🍴 **Champlain,** 13 r. N. Leblanc ℘ 03 20 54 01 38, *Fax 03 20 40 07 28,* 🌳 – AE Ⓞ GB.
🚫   EZ u
closed 1 to 15 August, Saturday lunch and Sunday dinner – **Meals** 150 b.i. (lunch), 170/360
b.i.

🍴🍴 **Cour des Grands,** 61 r. Monnaie ✉ 59800 ℘ 03 20 06 83 61, *Fax 03 20 14 03 75* –
AE GB   EY v
*closed 20 July-17 August, February Holidays, Saturday lunch, Monday lunch, Sunday and
Bank Holidays* – **Meals** (booking essential) 185/295.

🍴🍴 **Cardinal,** 84 façade Esplanade ✉ 59800 ℘ 03 20 06 58 58, *Fax 03 20 51 42 59* – AE
GB   BV x
closed 9 to 15 August and Sunday – **Meals** 160/320 b.i.

🍴🍴 **Varbet,** 2 r. Pas ✉ 59800 ℘ 03 20 54 81 40, *Fax 03 20 57 55 18* – AE Ⓞ GB
closed 14 July-15 August, Christmas-New Year, Sunday, Monday and Bank Holidays – **Meals**
170 (lunch), 250/400.   EY t

🍴🍴 **Bistrot Tourangeau,** 61 bd Louis XIV ✉ 59800 ℘ 03 20 52 74 64,
Fax 03 20 85 06 39 – 🍽. AE GB JCB   FZ t
closed Sunday – **Meals** 159 ♈.

🍴🍴 **L'Écume des Mers,** 10 r. Pas ✉ 59800 ℘ 03 20 54 95 40, *Fax 03 20 54 96 66* – 🍽.
AE GB JCB   EY n
closed 2 to 22 August and Sunday dinner – **Meals** 130 (dinner) and a la carte 170/300 ♈.

🍴 **Coquille,** 60 r. St-Étienne ✉ 59800 ℘ 03 20 54 29 82, *Fax 03 20 54 29 82* – GB
closed 2 to 22 August, Saturday lunch and Sunday – **Meals** 160/239 ♈.   EY e

at Marcq-en-Barœul – *pop. 36 601 alt. 15* – ✉ 59700 :

🏨🏨 **Sofitel** Ⓜ, av. Marne, by N 350 : 5 km ℘ 03 20 72 17 30, *Fax 03 20 89 92 34* – 🛗, ⚡ rm,
🍽 📺 ☎ 🕭 🅿 – 🔬 30 - 200. AE Ⓞ GB
Europe (*closed Saturday lunch*) Meals 120/250 ♈ – ☕ 95 – **124 rm** 800/900.

🍴🍴🍴 **Septentrion,** parc du Château Vert Bois, by N 17 : 9 km ℘ 03 20 46 26 98,
Fax 03 20 46 38 33, 🌳, « In a park with a lake » – 🅿. AE GB
closed 1 to 25 August, 25 to 30 December, dinner Sunday and Monday – **Meals** 120 (lunch),
145/350 and a la carte 200/280 ♈.

🍴🍴🍴 **Épicurien,** 18 av. Flandre by N 350 : 4 km ℘ 03 20 45 82 15, *Fax 03 20 72 21 45,* 🌳
– 🅿. AE GB JCB
closed Sunday dinner – **Meals** 150/290 and a la carte 150/250.

🍴🍴 **Auberge de la Garenne,** 17 chemin de Ghesles ℘ 03 20 46 20 20,
Fax 03 20 46 32 33, 🌳, 🍽 – 🅿. AE GB
*closed 1 to 27 August, Tuesday dinner, Wednesday dinner in Winter, Sunday dinner and
Monday* – **Meals** 135/410 ♈.

at Lille-Lesquin airport *by A 1 : 8 km* – ✉ *59810 Lesquin* :

🏨 **Mercure Aéroport** Ⓜ ✈, ✆ *03 20 87 46 46, Fax 03 20 87 46 47,* ✖ – |☰| ✺ rm,
📖 TV ☎ ⅋ 🅿 – ⚑ 25 - 700. 🄰🄴 ⓪ 🄶🄱 🄹🄲🄱
Grill La Flamme : Meals 190/225 – **Poêlon** : Meals a la carte 60/90 – ☕ 58 – **212 rm**
515/550.

🏨 **Novotel Aéroport,** ✆ *03 20 62 53 53, Fax 03 20 97 36 12,* 🌿, ⚓, 🛶 – ✺ rm, 📖
TV ☎ ⅋ 🅿 – ⚑ 25 - 120. 🄰🄴 ⓪ 🄶🄱
Meals 95/165 b.i. ♀ – ☕ 57 – **92 rm** 490/505.

🏠 **Agena** *without rest,* ✉ *59155 Faches-Thumesnil* ✆ *03 20 60 13 14, Fax 03 20 97 31 7*
– TV ☎ ⅋ 🅿. 🄰🄴 ⓪ 🄶🄱 🄹🄲🄱
☕ 50 – **40 rm** 350/380.

✖✖ **Septième Ciel,** *niveau supérieur de l'aérogare* ✆ *03 20 49 67 77, Fax 03 20 49 67 75*
≼ – 📖. 🄰🄴 ⓪ 🄶🄱 🄹🄲🄱
closed Sunday dinner – Meals 165/230 ♀ - **Zingue** : brasserie Meals 95/120 ♀.

at Englos *by A 25 : 10 km (exit Lomme)* – *alt. 46* – ✉ *59320* :

🏨 **Novotel Englos,** ✆ *03 20 10 58 58, Fax 03 20 10 58 59,* 🌿, ⚓, 🛶 – ✺ rm, TV
⅋ 🅿 – ⚑ 30 - 120. 🄰🄴 ⓪ 🄶🄱 🄹🄲🄱
Meals a la carte approx. 160 ♀ – ☕ 55 – **124 rm** 440/490.

Béthune *62400 P.-de-C.* 🔢 ⑭ – *pop. 24 556 alt. 34.*
🛈 *Tourist Office 69 pl. Senis* ✆ *03 21 57 25 47, Fax 03 21 68 26 29.*
Lille 39.

✖✖✖ **Meurin** *with rm, 15 pl. République* ✆ *03 21 68 88 88, Fax 03 21 68 88 89* – 📖 rest,
❀❀ ☎. 🄰🄴 ⓪ 🄶🄱 🄹🄲🄱
closed 2 to 23 August, 3 to 9 January, Sunday dinner (except hotel) and Monday – Meal
180 (lunch), 260/380 and a la carte 320/500 ♀ – ☕ 50 – **6 rm** 550/650
Spec. Anguille de la Somme au vert sur toast. Noix de Saint-Jacques caramélisées à l'endive
Coeur de ris de veau à l'oignon brûlé.

LYONS *69000 Rhône* 🔟 ⑪ ⑫ – *pop. 415 487 alt. 175.*
See : Site★★★ (panorama★★ from Fourvière) – Fourvière hill : Notre-Dame Basilica EX
Museum of Gallo-Roman Civilization★★ (Claudian tablet★★★) EY M³, Roman ruins EY – Ol
Lyons★★★ : Rue St-Jean★ FX, St-Jean Cathedral★ FY, Hôtel de Gadagne★ (Lyons Historica
Museum★ and International Marionette Museum★) EX M¹ – Guignol de Lyon FX N – Centra
Lyons (Peninsula) : to the North, Place Bellecour FY, Hospital Museum (pharmacy★) FY M
Museum of Printing and Banking★★ FX M⁶, – Place des Terreaux FX, Hôtel de Ville FX, Pala
St-Pierre, Fine Arts Museum (Beaux-Arts)★★ FX M⁴ – to the South, St-Martin-d'Ainay Bas
lica (capitals★) FY, Weaving and Textile Museum★★★ FY M², Decorative Arts Museum★★
FY M⁵ – La Croix-Rousse : Silkweavers' House FV M¹¹, Trois Gaules Amphitheatre FV E
Tête d'Or Park★ GHV – Guimet Museum of Natural History★★ GV M⁷ – Historical Infor
mation Centre on the Resistance and the Deportation★ FZ M⁹.
Envir. : Rochetaillée : Henri Malartre Car Museum★★, 12 km to the North.
🏌 Verger-Lyon at St-Symphorien-d'Ozon ✆ 04 78 02 84 20, S : 14 km ; 🏌 🏌 Lyon-Chassie
at Chassieu ✆ 04 78 90 84 77, E : 12 km by D 29 ; 🏌 Salvagny (private) at the Tour c
Salvagny ✆ 04 78 48 83 60 ; junction Lyon-Ouest : 8 km ; 🏌 🏌 Golf Club of Lyon at Villette
d'Anthon ✆ 04 78 31 11 33.
✈ of Lyon-Satolas ✆ 04 72 22 72 21 to the E : 27 km.
🚗 ✆ 08 36 35 35 35.
🛈 Tourist Office pl. Bellecour ✆ 04 72 77 69 69, Fax 04 78 42 04 32 – A.C. du Rhône 7
Grolée ✆ 04 78 42 51 01, Fax 04 78 37 73 74.
Paris 462 – Geneva 151 – Grenoble 105 – Marseilles 313 – St-Étienne 60 – Turin 300

Plans on following pages
Hotels

Town Centre (Bellecour-Terreaux) :

🏨 **Sofitel** Ⓜ, 20 quai Gailleton ✉ 69002 ✆ 04 72 41 20 20, Fax 04 72 40 05 50, ≼ – |☰
✺ rm, 📖 TV ☎ ⅋ 🚗 – ⚑ 200. 🄰🄴 ⓪ 🄶🄱 🄹🄲🄱   FY
Les Trois Dômes (8th floor) ✆ 04 72 41 20 97 Meals 185350 ♀ – **Sofi Shop** (ground floor
✆ 04 72 41 20 80 Meals 97132 – ☕ 95 – **138 rm** 1050/1800, 29 suites.

🏨 **Grand Hôtel Concorde,** 11 r. Grolée ✉ 69002 ✆ 04 72 40 45 45, Fax 04 78 37 52 5
– |☰|, ✺ rm, 📖 TV ☎ ⅋ – ⚑ 60. 🄰🄴 ⓪ 🄶🄱 🄹🄲🄱. ✻ rest   FX
Fiorelle : ✆ 04 78 42 99 84 (closed 7 to 23 August, Sunday lunch and Saturday) Mea
98(lunch)/130 – ☕ 80 – **143 rm** 740/1180.

🏨 **Royal,** 20 pl. Bellecour ✉ 69002 ✆ 04 78 37 57 31, Fax 04 78 37 01 36 – |☰| ✺ rm
📖 TV ☎. 🄰🄴 ⓪ 🄶🄱 🄹🄲🄱   FY
closed August and Saturday – Meals 96 (lunch), 135/150 – ☕ 74 – **80 rm** 710/1700

STREET INDEX TO LYON TOWN PLAN

Carlton without rest, 4 r. Jussieu ⊠ 69002 ℘ 04 78 42 56 51, *Fax 04 78 42 10 71* – ⬜ ⬜ TV ☎. AE ⓪ GB JCB   **FX** b
☕ 60 – **83 rm** 450/830.

Plaza République M without rest, 5 r. Stella ⊠ 69002 ℘ 04 78 37 50 50, *Fax 04 78 42 33 34* – ⬜, ⥅ rm, ⬜ TV ☎ ⓺ – 🛆 35. AE ⓪ GB JCB   **FY** k
☕ 60 – **78 rm** 515/790.

Beaux-Arts without rest, 75 r. Prés. E. Herriot ⊠ 69002 ℘ 04 78 38 09 50, *Fax 04 78 42 19 19* – ⬜, ⥅ rm, ⬜ TV ☎. AE ⓪ GB JCB   **FX** t
☕ 60 – **75 rm** 460/680.

Globe et Cécil without rest, 21 r. Gasparin ⊠ 69002 ℘ 04 78 42 58 95, *Fax 04 72 41 99 06* – ⬜ TV ☎. AE ⓪ GB JCB   **FY** b
60 rm ☕ 455/690.

Résidence without rest, 18 r. V. Hugo ⊠ 69002 ℘ 04 78 42 63 28, *Fax 04 78 42 85 76* – ⬜ TV ☎. AE ⓪ GB   **FY** s
☕ 36 – **66 rm** 310/340.

Perrache :

Château Perrache, 12 cours Verdun ⊠ 69002 ℘ 04 72 77 15 00, *Fax 04 78 37 06 56*, « Art Nouveau decor » – ⬜, ⥅ rm, ⬜ TV ☎ ⓺ ⊂⊃ – 🛆 250. AE ⓪ GB   **EY** a
Les Belles Saisons : Meals 145/185 ⓨ – ☕ 72 – **117 rm** 690/1300.

Charlemagne M, 23 cours Charlemagne ⊠ 69002 ℘ 04 72 77 70 00, *Fax 04 78 42 94 84*, ⵣ – ⬜, ⬜ rest, TV ☎ – 🛆 120. AE ⓪ GB   **EZ** t
Meals 90 ⓨ – ☕ 53 – **116 rm** 405/560.

Berlioz without rest, 12 cours Charlemagne ⊠ 69002 ℘ 04 78 42 30 31, *Fax 04 72 40 97 58* – ⬜ TV ☎. AE ⓪ GB   **EZ** z
☕ 35 – **38 rm** 278/396.

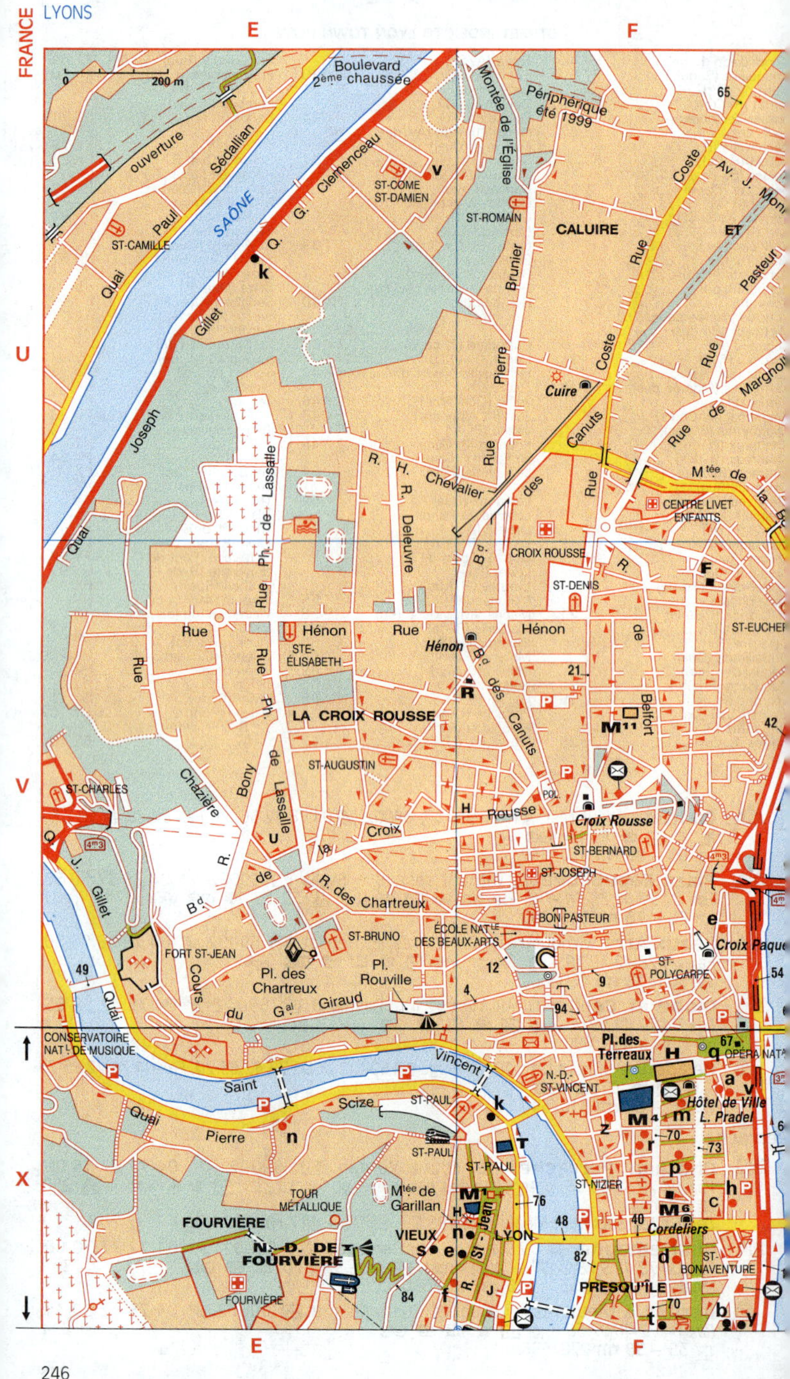
E
F
0   200 m
Boulevard 2ème chaussée
Montée de l'Église
Périphérique été 1999
65
Coste
Av. J. Mon
ET
Pasteur
SAÔNE
ouverture
Sédallian
Q. G. Clemenceau
ST-CÔME ST-DAMIEN
v
ST-ROMAIN
CALUIRE
Paul
Quai
Gillet
ST-CAMILLE
Q.
k
Brunier
Pierre
Coste
Rue
Rue
de
Margnol
U
Joseph
Quai
Cuire
des
Canuts
Rue
Mtée de la
Ph. de Lassalle
Rue
R. H. Chevalier
R. Deleuvre
Bd des Canuts
Rue
CENTRE LIVET ENFANTS
CROIX ROUSSE
ST-DENIS
F
ST-EUCHER
Rue
Rue
Héron
Rue
STE-ÉLISABETH
Héron
Héron
de
21
R.
Rue
Ph.
LA CROIX ROUSSE
R
Belfort
M 11
42
V
ST-CHARLES
Chazière
Bony
de Lassalle
ST-AUGUSTIN
P
POL
H
Rousse
Croix Rousse
ST-BERNARD
4m3
4m
Q.
J. J. Gillet
4m3
R.
U
Croix
de
R. des Chartreux
ST-JOSEPH
BON PASTEUR
e
Croix Paque
49
Bd
FORT ST-JEAN
ST-BRUNO
ÉCOLE NATle DES BEAUX-ARTS
12
ST-POLYCARPE
54
Cours
Pl. des Chartreux
Pl. Rouville
9
du
Gal Giraud
4
94
CONSERVATOIRE NATl DE MUSIQUE
Pl. des Terreaux
H
67
OPÉRA NATl
Vincent
Saint
P
N.-D. ST-VINCENT
a
v
Quai
Scize
ST-PAUL
k
Hôtel de Ville L. Pradel
Pierre
n
z
M 4
m
ST-PAUL
T
r
70
73
TOUR MÉTALLIQUE
Mtée de Garillan
ST-NIZIER
p
h
P
X
FOURVIÈRE
M 1
H
c
76
M 6
VIEUX LYON
48
40
Cordeliers
N.-D. DE FOURVIÈRE
n
St-Jean
s
e
d
ST-BONAVENTURE
FOURVIÈRE
R.
84
f
J
82
PRESQU'ÎLE
70
t
b
v

LYONS
FRANCE
G
H
U
V
X
Pasteur
FORT DE MONTESSUY
PARC J. CORBEL
STE-BERNADETTE ouv. 2ème chaussée été 1999
TUNNEL DE CALUIRE
CUIRE
de Margnolles
Av.
rue ET CUIRE A PEAGE
Vignal
Ch^in de Boutary
St-Clair
91
R^te de Strasbourg
Pte DE ST-CLAIR
PEAGE
PEAGE
PEAGE
Grande
ST-CLAIR
S
RHÔNE
Briand
Aristide
Charles
Quai
Gaulle
de
CITÉ INTERNATIONALE
PALAIS DES CONGRÈS
MUSÉE D'ART CONTEMPORAIN
GRANDE ROSÉRAIE
INTERPOL
VÉLODROME
Pont R. Poincaré
PARC DE LA FEYSSINE
B^d L. Bonnevay
UNIVERSITÉ CLAUDE BERNARD LYON I
P
Île du Souvenir
PARC
DE LA
Pl. du Gal Leclerc
18
Quai
Stalingrad
de
B^d du 11 Novembre 1918
R. du Tonkin
Av. Galline
80
JARDIN ZOOLOGIQUE
TÊTE D'OR
Bataille
la
de
Av. de Grande-Bretagne
Boulevard
Rue
des
Av. M^al
M^7
Duquesne
Rue
Verguin
Av.
SERRES
Cours
de
VILLEURBANNE
A. Philip
STE-MADELEINE
Rue
Foch
de
Rue
Sully
RÉDEMPTION
ST-JOSEPH
Sully
Rue
R.
de
Berges
34
CHARPENNES
B^d
4^m1
R. G. Péri
24
4^m
Cours É. Zola
Rue
Foch
d
e
Roosevelt
la
F.
Masséna
z Cours
Vitton
Cours
Charpennes Charles Hernu
Charmettes
Pl. du M^al
Cours
Lyautey
Av.
Créqui
LES BROTTEAUX
Garibaldi
Tête
H
Bugeaud
des
Brotteaux
n v
Brotteaux
31
ST-NICOLAS
CHARMETTES
R. de la Viabert
N.-D. DE BELLECOMBE
des
ST-POTHIN
Duguesclin
R.
ST-NOM-DE-JÉSUS
Vauban
d'Or
30
4^m1
Thiers
87
a
Rue
Lafayette
Cours
b
Cours
M^al
Rue Bonnel
de
s
Rue
TOUR CRÉDIT LYONNAIS
3^m8
Lafayette
Cours
R. d'Aubigny
2^m6
HÔTEL DU DÉPT
POL
t
J
h
u
Part Dieu
a
LA PART DIEU
3^m6

CONSERVATOIRE NAT. DE MUSIQUE
Saint
Scize
Quai
Pierre
FOURVIÈRE
TOUR MÉTALLIQUE
N.-D. DE FOURVIÈRE
FOURVIÈRE
Mtée de Garillan
VIEUX LYON
ST-PAUL
ST-PAUL
Vincent
N.-D. ST-VINCENT
Pl. des Terreaux
OPÉRA NAT.
Hôtel de Ville L. Pradel
ST-NIZIER
Cordeliers
ST-BONAVENTURE
PRESQU'ÎLE
Aqueducs Romains
R. Radisson
THÉÂTRES ROMAINS
L'ANTIQUAILLE
MINIMES
ST-GEORGES
ST-JEAN
Vieux Lyon Cath. St-Jean
Pl. de Trion
POL.
ST-JUST
Trion
ST-JUST
ST-IRÉNÉE
Chemin
Choulan
Av. Debrousse
des Étroits
DEBROUSSE
Bellecour
Pl. Bellecour
HÔTEL DIEU
Tilsitt
St-François
St-Martin d'Ainay
Ampère V. Hugo
STE-CROIX
Condé
Gailleton
Bernard
GARE AUTO-TRAIN
PERRACHE
Perrache
Pl. Carnot
PRISONS
POL.
OBJETS TROUVES
Suchet
STE-BLANDINE
PERRACHE
Charlemagne
Quai Perrache
Rambaud
Rousseau
Jean-Jacques
Quai
SAÔNE
RHÔNE
MARCHÉ DE GROS
DOUANES
Quai
Cours
Leclerc
Av. Leclerc
Boulevard
N.-D. DES ANGES
R. G. Nadaud
Rue Lorte
Farge
Yves
R. Crépet
Avenue
ST-LUC
J. MOULIN LYON III
LUMIÈRE LYON III
ST-JOSEPH
Avenue
Docteur
St-François
Renault
39
39
6
104
60
5
28
7
46
55
37
96
41
84
76
82
48
40
70
73
70
73
67
69
99

G
H
Lyautey
Cours
LES BROTTEAUX
H
Garibaldi
Tête
Bugeaud
n
V
ST-NICOLAS
CHARMETTES
31
Brotteaux
Av.
Créqui
R.
Duguesclin
ST-NOM-DE-JÉSUS
30
R. de la Viabert
N.-D. DE BELLECOMBE
ST-POTHIN
POL.
Vauban
Brotteaux
Thiers
X
87
a
d'Or
Lafayette
Cours
Lafayette
Rue
Cours
Cours
Cours
b
Bonnel
Mal.
de
Rue
TOUR CRÉDIT LYONNAIS
Part Dieu
Rue
R. d'Aubigny
s
u
a
Rue
de
t
J
h
LA PART DIEU
HÔTEL DU DEPT
POL.
H
Servient
CITÉ ADMVE D'ÉTAT
POL.
M.
100
IMMACULÉE CONCEPTION
de
Liberté
R.
n
R.
Pl. Guichard
PART DIEU
Av.
G.
Pompidou
ST-SACREMENT
k
58
Bert
A.
Rue
Duguesclin
Paul
Av. Lacassagne
Flandin
Liberté
Cours
Créqui
Garibaldi
Guillotière
Saxe
ST-JACQUES
Faure
58
Y
Marseille
Saxe Gambetta
Secteur en travaux
F. Faure
Grande
Av.
Félix
ST-ANDRÉ
Jaurès
Rue
Garibaldi
M
Gambetta
PRISON MONTLUC
97
de
N.-D. ST-LOUIS
Faure
e
la
M
Sans Souci
u
R.
Pl. de Stalingrad
LA GUILLOTIÈRE
STE-MARIE DE LA GUILLOTIÈRE
Cours
U
A.
Chevreul
L'ANNONCIATION
Garibaldi
Guillotière
J. MOULIN LYON III
Thomas
EL
Av.
M.
Bloch
Villon
POL.
Pl. J. Macé
Av. des
Frères
J. Macé
71
Lumière
Berthelot
Rue
Route
25
POL.
Rue
Z
102
de
25
M.
Gerland
Avenue
Villon
Berliet
CIMETIÈRE ISRAÉLITE
B.d des Tchécoslovaques
Rue
Berthelot
Vienne
B.d des États-Unis
Barret
Rue
Musée urbain Tony-Garnier
Rue
Croix
ST-VINCENT DE PAUL
G
H

FRANCE

at Vaise :

🏨 **Holiday Inn Lyon Fourvière** Ⓜ, 18 r. L. Loucheur ✉ 69009 𝒫 04 78 83 48 75
Fax 04 78 83 30 81 – |☆|, ⇞ rm, 🖩 📺 ☎ ⅙ 🚗 – 🕴 50. 🄰🄴 ⑩ 🄶🄱 🄹🄲🄱. ⚒ res
Meals 98/132 ♨ – ☕ 50 – **111 rm** 550/750.

Vieux-Lyon :

🏰 **Villa Florentine** Ⓜ ⤳, 25 montée St-Barthélémy ✉ 69005 𝒫 04 72 56 56 56
❀ Fax 04 72 40 90 56, ≼ Lyon, 🌳, 🏊 – |☆| 🖩 📺 ☎ ⅙ 🚗 🄿 🄰🄴 ⑩
🄶🄱 🄹🄲🄱 EFX
Les Terrasses de Lyon : Meals 280(lunch), 310/420 and a la carte 440/640 – ☕ 10
– **16 rm** 1300/2100, 3 suites
Spec. Homard du Maine rôti, royale de foie gras de canard tiède. Canette de Challan
étouffée, poêlée aux sarments de vigne. Galette de pommes, sirop de citron aux pisti
de safran.

🏰 **Cour des Loges** Ⓜ ⤳, 6 r. Boeuf ✉ 69005 𝒫 04 72 77 44 44, Fax 04 72 40 93 6
« Contemporary decor in houses of Old Lyons », 🛌 – |☆|, ⇞ rm, 🖩 📺 ☎ ⅙ 🚗 – 🕴 40
🄰🄴 ⑩ 🄶🄱 🄹🄲🄱. ⚒ rest FX
Meals a la carte 220/380 ♀ – ☕ 110 – **53 rm** 1200/1900, 10 suites.

🏰 **Tour Rose** (Chavent) Ⓜ ⤳, 22 r. Bœuf ✉ 69005 𝒫 04 78 37 25 9C
❀ Fax 04 78 42 26 02, « 17C house, tasteful silk themed decor » – |☆| 🖩 📺 ☎ 🚗 – 🕴 35
🄰🄴 ⑩ 🄶🄱 🄹🄲🄱 EFX
Meals (closed Sunday) 295/595 and a la carte 440/600 ♀ – ☕ 105 – **6 rm** 1200/1650
6 suites1650/2800, 4 duplex
Spec. Saumon mi-cuit au fumoir servi tiède au naturel. Foie chaud de canard, filets d
rougets barbets poêlés aux lentilles confites à l'ail. Ris de veau rôti au pain d'épice, fève
et morilles au beurre. **Wines** Brouilly, Viognier.

🏨 **Phénix Hôtel** Ⓜ without rest, 7 quai Bondy ✉ 69005 𝒫 04 78 28 24 24
Fax 04 78 28 62 86 – |☆| 🖩 📺 ☎ ⅙ 🚗 – 🕴 35. 🄰🄴 ⑩ 🄶🄱 🄹🄲🄱 FX
☕ 60 – **36 rm** 640/1080.

La Croix-Rousse (bank of the River Saône) :

🏨 **Lyon Métropole** Ⓜ, 85 quai J. Gillet ✉ 69004 𝒫 04 72 10 44 44, Fax 04 78 39 99 2C
🌂, 🏊, 🎾 – |☆| 🖩 📺 ☎ ⅙ 🚗 🄿 – 🕴 350. 🄰🄴 ⑩ 🄶🄱 🄹🄲🄱 EU
Les Eaux Vives 𝒫 04 72 10 44 30 (closed 28 July-18 August, 20 December-6 January
Sunday dinner and Monday) Meals 150(lunch), 175/300 – **Grill** 𝒫 04 72 10 44 44 Meal
59 (lunch)/130 – ☕ 80 – **118 rm** 590/980.

Les Brotteaux :

🏨 **Holiday Inn Garden Court** Ⓜ without rest, 114 bd Belges ✉ 6900
𝒫 04 78 24 44 68, Fax 04 78 24 82 36 – |☆|, ⇞ rm, 🖩 📺 ☎. 🄰🄴 ⑩ 🄶🄱 HX
☕ 52 – **55 rm** 570.

🏨 **Olympique** without rest, 62 r. Garibaldi ✉ 69006 𝒫 04 78 89 48 04
Fax 04 78 89 49 97 – |☆|, ⇞ rm, 📺 ☎. 🄶🄱 GV
☕ 35 – **23 rm** 249/299.

La Part-Dieu :

🏰 **Saxe-Lafayette**, 29 r. Bonnel ✉ 69003 𝒫 04 72 61 90 90, Fax 04 72 61 17 54, ⅃
– |☆|, ⇞ rm, 🖩 📺 ☎ ⅙ 🚗 – 🕴 120. 🄰🄴 ⑩ 🄶🄱 🄹🄲🄱 GX
Meals 99/195 ♨ – ☕ 90 – **149 rm** 940/1090, 7 suites.

🏨 **Méridien** Ⓜ ⤳, 129 r. Servient (32nd floor) ✉ 69003 𝒫 04 78 63 55 0C
Fax 04 78 63 55 20, ≼ Lyons and Rhône Valley – |☆|, ⇞ rm, 🖩 📺 ☎ 🚗 – 🕴 170
🄰🄴 ⑩ 🄶🄱 🄹🄲🄱 GX
L'Arc-en-Ciel (closed 15 July-22 August and Saturday lunch) Meals 170/210 ♀ – **Bistro
de la Tour** (ground floor) (closed Friday dinner, Saturday dinner and Sunday) Meals 11
♀ – ☕ 80 – **245 rm** 895/1250.

🏨 **Novotel La Part-Dieu** Ⓜ, 47 bd Vivier-Merle ✉ 69003 𝒫 04 72 13 51 51
Fax 04 72 13 51 99 – |☆|, ⇞ rm, 🖩 📺 ☎ ⅙ 🚗 – 🕴 80. 🄰🄴 ⑩
🄶🄱 🄹🄲🄱 HX
Meals a la carte approx. 170 – ☕ 63 – **124 rm** 650/680.

🏨 **Créqui** Ⓜ, 158 r. Créqui ✉ 69003 𝒫 04 78 60 20 47, Fax 04 78 62 21 12, 🌂 – |☆
⇞ rm, 📺 ☎. 🄰🄴 ⑩ 🄶🄱 GX
Meals (closed August, 24 December-2 January, Saturday and Sunday) 89/99 ♀ – ☕ 4
– **28 rm** 434/459.

🏨 **Ibis La Part-Dieu Gare**, pl. Renaudel ✉ 69003 𝒫 04 78 95 42 11, Fax 04 78 60 42 85
🌂 – |☆|, ⇞ rm, 🖩 📺 ☎ ⅙ 🚗 – 🕴 40. 🄰🄴 ⑩ 🄶🄱 HY
Meals 95/130 – ☕ 35 – **144 rm** 380.

La Guillotière :

Wilson Ⓜ without rest, 6 r. Mazenod ⊠ 69003 ℘ 04 78 60 94 94, *Fax 04 78 62 72 01*
– |♯|, ⇔ rm, ▤ ⧉ ☎ ⅋ ☞. 🄰🄴 ① ⅁🄱
⬡ 65 – **54 rm** 510/560.

Ibis Université without rest, 51 r. Université ⊠ 69007 ℘ 04 78 72 78 42,
Fax 04 78 69 24 36 – |♯|, ⇔ rm, ▤ ⧉ ☎ ☞. 🄰🄴 ① ⅁🄱   GY u
⬡ 36 – **53 rm** 355.

Gerland :

Mercure Gerland Ⓜ, 70 av. Leclerc ⊠ 69007 ℘ 04 72 71 11 11, *Fax 04 72 71 11 00,*
🎋, ⊼ – |♯|, ⇔ rm, ▤ ⧉ ☎ ⅋ ☞ – 🕴 200. 🄰🄴 ① ⅁🄱 🄹🄲🄱
Meals 105 ♈ – ⬡ 60 – **187 rm** 575/830.

Montchat-Monplaisir :

Mercure Lumière Ⓜ, 69 cours A. Thomas ℘ 04 78 53 76 76, *Fax 04 72 36 97 65* –
|♯|, ⇔ rm, ▤ ⧉ ☎ ⅋ ☞ – 🕴 30. 🄰🄴 ① ⅁🄱 🄹🄲🄱
Meals *(closed 1 to 15 August and Saturday)* 105/140 ♈ – ⬡ 58 – **78 rm** 395/600.

at Bron – *pop. 39 683 alt. 204* – ⊠ *69500 :*

Novotel Bron Ⓜ, av. J. Monnet ℘ 04 72 15 65 65, *Fax 04 72 15 09 09,* 🎋, ⊼, ⚿
– |♯|, ⇔ rm, ▤ ⧉ ☎ ⅋ 🄿 – 🕴 25 - 800. 🄰🄴 ① ⅁🄱
Meals 110/150 ♈ – ⬡ 60 – **189 rm** 570/600.

Restaurants

Paul Bocuse, bridge of Collonges N : 12 km by the banks of River Saône (D 433, D 51
⊠ 69660 *Collonges-au-Mont-d'Or* ℘ 04 72 42 90 90, *Fax 04 72 27 85 87,* « Fresco
depicting great chefs » – ▤ 🄿. 🄰🄴 ① ⅁🄱 🄹🄲🄱
Meals 480 (lunch), 540/780 and a la carte 510/810
Spec. Soupe aux truffes. Rouget barbet en écailles de pommes de terre. Volaille de Bresse
rôtie à la broche. **Wines** Saint-Véran, Brouilly.

Léon de Lyon (Lacombe), 1 r. Pleney ⊠ 69001 ℘ 04 72 10 11 12, *Fax 04 72 10 11 13*
– ▤. 🄰🄴 ⅁🄱 🄹🄲🄱   FX r
closed 1 to 23 August, Sunday and Monday – **Meals** 290 (lunch), 560/720 and a la carte
460/620
Spec. Cochon fermier, foie gras, oignons confits en "terrine rustique". Quenelles de brochet de la Dombes, queues d'écrevisses "pattes rouges", sauce Nantua. Six petits desserts
sur le thème de la praline de Saint-Genix. **Wines** Saint-Véran, Chiroubles.

Pierre Orsi, 3 pl. Kléber ⊠ 69006 ℘ 04 78 89 57 68, *Fax 04 72 44 93 34,* 🎋, « Elegant
decor » – ▤. 🄰🄴 ⅁🄱 🄹🄲🄱   GV e
closed Saturday in August and Sunday except Bank Holidays – **Meals** 200 (lunch), 300/600
and a la carte 420/600 ♈
Spec. Ravioles de foie gras, jus de porto et truffes. Homard en carapace. Pigeonneau en
cocotte aux gousses d'ail confites en chemise. **Wines** Mâcon Clessé, Saint-Joseph.

Christian Têtedoie, 54 quai Pierre Scize ⊠ 69005 ℘ 04 78 29 40 10,
Fax 04 72 07 05 65 – ▤ ☞. 🄰🄴 ⅁🄱   EX n
closed 5 to 22 August, Saturday lunch and Sunday except Bank Holidays – **Meals** 170/340
and a la carte 250/340 ♈.

L'Auberge de Fond Rose, 23 quai G. Clemenceau ⊠ 69300 *Caluire-et-Cuire*
℘ 04 78 29 34 61, *Fax 04 72 00 28 67,* « Shaded and flowered garden, terrace » – ▤
🄿. 🄰🄴 ⅁🄱   EU v
closed Sunday dinner and Monday except Bank Holidays – **Meals** 120 (lunch), 180/400 ♈.

Mère Brazier, 12 r. Royale ⊠ 69001 ℘ 04 78 28 15 49, *Fax 04 78 28 63 63,*
« Lyonnaise atmosphere » – 🄰🄴 ① ⅁🄱 🄹🄲🄱   FV e
*closed 26 July-29 August, Saturday except dinner from September-mid-June, Sunday and
Bank Holidays* – **Meals** 185 (lunch), 270/325 and a la carte 240/380
Spec. Fond d'artichaut au foie gras. Quenelle au gratin. Volaille de Bresse "demi-deuil".
Wines Crozes-Hermitage, Saint-Joseph.

St-Alban, 2 quai J. Moulin ⊠ 69001 ℘ 04 78 30 14 89, *Fax 04 72 00 88 82* – ▤. 🄰🄴
① ⅁🄱   FX v
closed 20 July-20 August, February Holidays, Saturday lunch and Sunday – **Meals** 155/320
and a la carte 260/350.

L'Alexandrin (Alexanian), 83 r. Moncey ⊠ 69003 ℘ 04 72 61 15 69,
Fax 04 78 62 75 57 – ▤. 🄰🄴 ⅁🄱   GX h
*closed 13-17 May, 11-14 July, 1-22 August, 11-15 November, 24 December-2 January,
Sunday, Monday and Bank Holidays* – **Meals** 160/360
Spec. Blinis au caviar, sauce saumon fumé. Grouse à la feuille de vigne et cuisse en crépi-
nette de cèpes et foie gras (untumn). Feuillantine et sorbet "pur cacao".

XX **Passage,** 8 r. Plâtre ⊠ 69001 ✆ 04 78 28 11 16, *Fax 04 72 00 84 34* – ▤. AE ⓞ GB
JCB   FX
closed Saturday lunch, Sunday and Bank Holidays – **Meals** 95 (lunch), 125/
290 ☒.

XX **Auberge de l'Île** (Ansanay-Alex), sur l'Île Barbe ⊠ 69009 ✆ 04 78 83 99 49
✿ *Fax 04 78 47 80 46* – ℙ. AE GB JCB. ✗
closed 9 to 23 August, February Holidays, Sunday and Monday – **Meals** 190/390 and à
la carte 370/490
Spec. Gnocchi d'escargots au pistou (15 June-15 September). Volaille au torchon, rizotto
au parmesan et truffe (15 December-15 March). Glace réglisse, lait d'amande et pain
d'épice. **Wines** Condrieu, Morgon.

XX **Le Nord,** 18 r. Neuve ⊠ 69002 ✆ 04 72 10 69 69, *Fax 04 72 10 69 68,* 🌳 – ▤. AE
⊚ ⓞ GB JCB   FX
Meals brasserie 115/158 ☒.

XX **Vivarais,** 1 pl. Gailleton ⊠ 69002 ✆ 04 78 37 85 15, *Fax 04 78 37 59 49* – ▤. AE ⓞ
⊚ GB JCB   FY
closed 26 July-22 August, 24 December-1 January and Sunday – **Meals** 115 (lunch)
140/170 ⌀.

XX **Gourmet de Sèze,** 129 r. Sèze ⊠ 69006 ✆ 04 78 24 23 42, *Fax 04 78 24 66 81* –
▤. AE GB   HV
closed 15 July-15 August, Sunday and Monday – **Meals** (booking essential) 180/
300 ☒.

XX **Chez Jean-François,** 2 pl. Célestins ⊠ 69002 ✆ 04 78 42 08 26, *Fax 04 72 40 04 51*
⊚ – ▤. AE GB JCB   FY
closed 24 July-23 August, Sunday and Bank Holidays – **Meals** (booking essential) 100/
180 ☒.

XX **Fleur de Sel,** 3 r. Remparts d'Ainay ⊠ 69002 ✆ 04 78 37 40 37, *Fax 04 78 37 26 37*
– GB   FY
closed August, Saturday and Sunday – **Meals** 200 ☒.

XX **Mère Vittet,** 26 cours de Verdun ⊠ 69002 ✆ 04 78 37 20 17, *Fax 04 78 42 40 70*
open 24 hours – ▤. AE ⓞ GB   FY
Meals 110/195 ☒.

XX **Tassée,** 20 r. Charité ⊠ 69002 ✆ 04 72 77 79 00, *Fax 04 72 40 05 91* – ▤. AE ⓞ GB
JCB   FY
closed Saturday in July-August and Sunday – **Meals** 135/270.

XX **Brasserie Georges,** 30 cours Verdun ⊠ 69002 ✆ 04 72 56 54 54
Fax 04 78 42 51 65, « 1925 Brasserie » – AE ⓞ GB JCB   FZ
Meals 99/148 ☒.

XX **Grenier des Lyres,** 21 r. Creuzet ⊠ 69007 ✆ 04 78 72 81 77, *Fax 04 78 72 01 75*
– ▤. AE GB JCB   GY
closed 8 to 23 August and Sunday – **Meals** 110 b.i. (lunch), 128/398 ⌀.

XX **Boeuf d'Argent,** 29 r. Boeuf ⊠ 69005 ✆ 04 78 42 21 12, *Fax 04 72 40 24 65,* 🌳
⊚ – AE GB   EFX
closed 15 to 30 August, 1 to 20 February, Saturday lunch and Sunday – **Meals** 78 b.i. (lunch)
92/225 ⌀.

XX **La Voûte - Chez Léa,** 11 pl. A. Gourju ⊠ 69002 ✆ 04 78 42 01 33, *Fax 04 78 37 36 41*
– ▤. AE ⓞ GB   FY
closed Sunday – **Meals** 115 b.i. (lunch), 138/183 ☒.

XX **Philippe B.,** 42 r. P. Corneille ✆ 04 78 52 19 13, *Fax 04 72 74 99 14* – ▤. AE
ⓞ GB   GX
closed 2 to 22 August, Saturday lunch and Sunday – **Meals** 135/225.

X **L'Est,** Gare des Brotteaux, 14 pl. J. Ferry ⊠ 69006 ✆ 04 37 24 25 26
Fax 04 37 24 25 25, 🌳 , « Brasserie in an old railway station, travel related decor » – ▤
⊚ AE ⓞ GB JCB   HX
Meals brasserie 115/158 ☒.

X **Assiette et Marée,** 49 r. Bourse ⊠ 69002 ✆ 04 78 37 36 58, *Fax 04 78 37 98 52*
🌳 – ▤. AE GB   FX
closed Sunday – **Meals** - Seafood - 118 and à la carte 160/210 ☒.

X **Le Sud,** 11 pl. Antonin Poncet ⊠ 69002 ✆ 04 72 77 80 00, *Fax 04 72 77 80 01,* 🌳
⊚ – ▤. AE ⓞ GB JCB   FY
Meals (booking essential) 115/158 ☒.

X **Francotte,** 8 pl. Célestins ⊠ 69002 ✆ 04 78 37 38 64, *Fax 04 78 38 20 35* – ▤. AE
GB   FY
closed Sunday – **Meals** à la carte 160/230 ☒.

✗ **Les Muses de l'Opéra,** pl. Comédie, 7th floor of the Opera ✉ 69001 ℰ 04 72 00 45 58, Fax 04 78 29 34 01, ≼ Fourvière, 🌿, « Contemporary decor » – 🗐.
Ⓐ Ⓖ⬛   FX q
closed Sunday – **Meals** 105 (lunch)/169 ℒ.

✗ **Assiette et Marée,** 26 r. Servient ✉ 69003 ℰ 04 78 62 89 94, Fax 04 78 38 20 35
– 🗐. Ⓐ Ⓖ⬛   GY n
closed Sunday – **Meals** - Seafood - 118 and a la carte 160/210 ℒ.

✗ **Terrasse St-Clair,** 2 Grande r. St-Clair ✉ 69300 *Caluire-et-Cuire* ℰ 04 72 27 37 37,
Fax 04 72 27 37 38, 🌿 – Ⓐ Ⓖ⬛   GU s
closed 2 to 22 January and Sunday – **Meals** 120 ℒ.

✗ **Daniel et Denise,** 156 r. Créqui ✉ 69003 ℰ 04 78 60 66 53, *Fax 04 78 60 66 53,*
😊 bistro – 🗐. Ⓖ⬛   GX s
closed August, Saturday and Sunday – Meals a la carte 120/220 ℒ.

BOUCHONS : *Regional specialities and wine tasting in a Lyonnaise atmosphere*

✗ **Chez Hugon,** 12 rue Pizay ✉ 69001 ℰ 04 78 28 10 94 – Ⓖ⬛   FX m
closed August, Saturday and Sunday – **Meals** (booking essential) 120/145 ℒ.

✗ **Au Petit Bouchon "Chez Georges",** 8 r. Garet ✉ 69001 ℰ 04 78 28 30 46 – Ⓖ⬛
closed 1 to 22 August, Saturday and Sunday – **Meals** 88/118 (lunch only) and a la carte
140/190.   FX a

✗ **Jura,** 25 r. Tupin ✉ 69002 ℰ 04 78 42 20 57 – Ⓖ⬛   FX d
*closed August, Monday lunch from September-April, Saturday from May-August and Sun-
day* – **Meals** (booking essential) 99 ℒ.

✗ **Café des Fédérations,** 8 r. Major Martin ✉ 69001 ℰ 04 78 28 26 00,
Fax 04 78 07 74 52 – Ⓖ⬛ Ⓙ⬛   FX z
closed August, Saturday and Sunday – **Meals** (booking essential) 118 (lunch)/145 ℒ.

✗ **Garet,** 7 r. Garet ✉ 69001 ℰ 04 78 28 16 94, *Fax 04 72 00 06 84* – 🗐. Ⓐ Ⓖ⬛ FX a
closed 23 July-23 August, Saturday and Sunday – **Meals** (booking essential) 98 (lunch)/125
ℒ.

✗ **Meunière,** 11 r. Neuve ✉ 69001 ℰ 04 78 28 62 91 – Ⓐ Ⓞ Ⓖ⬛   FX p
closed 14 July-17 August, Sunday and Monday – **Meals** (booking essential) 95 (lunch),
110/150 ⓑ.

Environs

to the NE :

at Rillieux-la-Pape : *7 km by N 83 and N 84 – pop. 30 791 alt. 269 –* ✉ *69140 :*

✗✗✗ **Larivoire** (Constantin), chemin des Iles ℰ 04 78 88 50 92, Fax 04 78 88 35 22, 🌿 – Ⓟ.
❀ Ⓖ⬛
closed 16 to 25 August, Monday lunch and Tuesday – **Meals** 180/440 and a la carte
320/480
Spec. Quenelles de sandre aux moules, nage de légumes au basilic. Filet de féra, crème
de haricots tarbais à l'épeautre. Fricassée de volaille de Bresse au vinaigre. **Wines** Chardonnay du Bugey, Coteaux du Lyonnais.

to the E :

at the Satolas airport : *27 km by A 43 –* ✉ *69125 Lyon Satolas Airport :*

🏨 **Sofitel Lyon Aéroport** Ⓜ without rest, 3rd floor ℰ 04 72 23 38 00,
Fax 04 72 23 98 00, ≼ – 🛗, ⇟ rm, 🗐 �📺 ☎ 🛗, Ⓐ Ⓞ Ⓖ⬛ Ⓙ⬛
⚏ 90 – **120 rm** 890/950.

✗✗✗ **Grande Corbeille,** 1st floor ℰ 04 72 22 71 76, Fax 04 72 22 71 72, ≼ – 🗐. Ⓐ Ⓞ Ⓖ⬛
closed August, 23 December-3 January, Saturday, Sunday and dinner – **Meals** 140/190
and a la carte 190/320.

✗ **Bouchon,** 1st floor ℰ 04 72 22 72 31, Fax 04 72 22 71 72 – 🗐. Ⓐ Ⓞ Ⓖ⬛
Meals brasserie 125 b.i. ⓑ.

to the NW :

Porte de Lyon - *motorway junction A 6 N 6 Exit road signposted Limonest N : 10 km –* ✉ *69570*
Dardilly :

🏨 **Novotel Lyon Nord** Ⓜ, ℰ 04 72 17 29 29, Fax 04 78 35 08 45, 🌿, 🏊, 🎾 – 🛗,
⇟ rm, 🗐 📺 ☎ Ⓟ – 🔔 80. Ⓐ Ⓞ Ⓖ⬛
Meals 125 ℒ – ⚏ 60 – **107 rm** 485/550.

🏠 **Ibis Lyon Nord,** ℰ 04 78 66 02 20, Fax 04 78 47 47 93, 🌿, 🏊, 🎾 – ⇟ rm, 📺 ☎
🛗 Ⓟ. Ⓐ Ⓞ Ⓖ⬛
Meals 95/150 ℒ – ⚏ 39 – **68 rm** 355.

Annecy 74000 H.-Savoie **74** ⑥ – pop. 49 644 alt. 448.

    See : Old Annecy★★ : Descent from the Cross★ in church of St-Maurice, Palais de l'Isle★
rue Ste-Claire★, bridge over the Thiou ⩥★ – Château★ – Jardins de l'Europe★.

    Envir. : Tour of the lake★★★ 39 km (or 1 hour 30 min by boat).

    🏌 of the lac d'Annecy ℘ 04 50 60 12 89 : 10 km ; 🏌 of Giez ℘ 04 50 44 48 41 ; o
Belvédère at St-Martin-Bellevue ℘ 04 50 60 31 78.

    ✈ of Annecy-Meythet ℘ 04 50 27 30 06 by N 508 and D 14 : 4 km.

    🛈 Tourist Office Clos Bonlieu 1 r. J. Jaurès ℘ 04 50 45 00 33, Fax 04 50 51 87 20 – A.C
15 r. Préfecture ℘ 04 50 45 09 12, Fax 04 50 51 40 11.

    Lyons 140.

at Veyrier-du-Lac E : 5,5 km – pop. 1 967 alt. 504 – ⊠ 74290

    Auberge de l'Éridan (Veyrat) Ⓜ 🍴 with rm, 13 Vieille rte des Pensières
℘ 04 50 60 24 00, Fax 04 50 60 23 63, ⩽ lake, 🏠, 🌳 – 📶 🖥 📺 ☎ 🚿 🚗 🅿 🅰 🅞
🆖 🆃🆑🅱 – closed December and January – **Meals** (closed Monday) 385 (lunch), 685/99
and a la carte 870/1 100 – ⊡ 235 – **11 rm** 1550/3250
Spec. Ravioli de légumes aux senteurs de sous-bois et prairie. Omble chevalier au petit lai
d'armoise. Cinq crèmes brûlées à la flore du tour du lac. **Wines** Chignin-Bergeron, Mondeuse.

Le Bourget-du-Lac 73370 Savoie **74** ⑮ – pop. 2 886 alt. 240.

    Lyons 105.

    Bateau Ivre - Hôtel Ombremont (Jacob), Nord : 2 km par N 504 ℘ 04 79 25 00 23
Fax 04 79 25 25 77, 🌿 – 🅿 🅰 🅞 🆖
early May-early November and closed Tuesday except from June-August and Wednesda
lunch in September-October – **Meals** 195/560 and a la carte 450/520
Spec. Poêlée de filets de perche en salade de pommes de terre (June-October). Cuisse
de grenouilles rôties, fidès croquants et œuf mollet. Lavaret doré à l'huile de poivron
rouges aux aromates. **Wines** Roussette, Mondeuse.

Chagny 71150 S.-et-L. **69** ⑨ – pop. 5 346 alt. 215.

    🛈 Tourist Office 2 r. des Halles ℘ 03 85 87 25 95, Fax 03 85 87 14 44.

    Lyons 145.

    Lameloise Ⓜ, pl. d'Armes ℘ 03 85 87 65 65, Fax 03 85 87 03 57, « Old Burgundia
house, tasteful decor » – 📶 🖥 📺 ☎ 🚗. 🅰 🆖 🆃🆑🅱
closed 22 December-27 January, Thursday lunch and Wednesday – **Meals** (booking essen
tial) 400/600 and a la carte 400/590 – ⊡ 100 – **16 rm** 750/1500
Spec. Ravioli d'escargots de Bourgogne dans leur bouillon d'ail doux. Pigeonneau rôti
l'émietté de truffes. Griottines au chocolat noir sur une marmelade d'orange. **Wines** Rull
blanc, Chassagne-Montrachet.

Fleurie 69820 Rhône **74** ① – pop. 1 105 alt. 320.

    Lyons 59.

    Auberge du Cep, pl. Église ℘ 04 74 04 10 77, Fax 04 74 04 10 28 – 🖥. 🅰 🆖
closed early December-mid January, Sunday and Monday except Bank Holidays – **Meal**
(booking essential) 200/575 and a la carte 360/530 ⾕
Spec. Cuisses de grenouilles rôties aux fines herbes. Volaille mijotée façon coq au vin. Cassi
du terroir en sorbet. **Wines** Beaujolais blanc, Fleurie.

Mionnay 01390 Ain **74** ② – pop. 1 103 alt. 276.

    Lyons 23.

    Alain Chapel with rm, ℘ 04 78 91 82 02, Fax 04 78 91 82 37, 🌿, « Flowere
garden » – 📺 ☎ 🚗 🅿 🅰 🅞 🆖
closed January, Tuesday lunch and Monday except Bank Holidays – **Meals** 380 b.i. (lunch
595/800 and a la carte 530/660 ⾕ – ⊡ 92 – **13 rm** 625/850
Spec. Pâtissons en nage tiède à l'orange et poivre noir, de grosses écrevisses "patte
rouges"(Summer). Jeunes poireaux à l'étuvée et turbot cuit sur l'arête au safran du Gâtinai
(Summer). Poulette en vessie. **Wines** Morgon, Roussette du bugey.

Montrond-les-Bains 42210 Loire **73** ⑱ – pop. 3 627 alt. 356 – Spa (April-November) – Casin

    🏌 Forez ℘ 04 77 30 86 85 at Craintilleux, S : 12 km by N 82 and D 16.

    🛈 Syndicat d'Initiative 1 r. des Ecoles ℘ 04 77 94 64 74.

    Lyons 62.

    Hostellerie La Poularde (Etéocle), ℘ 04 77 54 40 06, Fax 04 77 54 53 14, 🏊 – 🖥
📺 ☎ 🚗 – 🕍 30. 🅰 🅞 🆖 🆃🆑🅱
closed 2 to 15 January, Sunday dinner, Tuesday lunch and Monday except Bank Holiday.
– **Meals** (Sunday : booking essential) 240/600 and a la carte 580/760 – ⊡ 90 – **10 rm**
480/580, 5 suites, 3 duplex
Spec. Lobe de foie gras poché à la lie de vin. Sandre de Loire rôti aux échalotes. Pigeonnea
du Forez amandine entre chair et peau. **Wines** Condrieu, Saint-Joseph.

Roanne 42300 Loire 🗚 ⑦ – pop. 41 756 alt. 265.

🛐 of Champlong at Villerest ℰ 04 77 69 70 60.

✈ Roanne-Renaison ℰ 04 77 66 85 77 by D 9.

🛈 Tourist Office 1 cours République ℰ 04 77 71 51 77, Fax 04 77 70 96 62 – A.C. 24/26 r. Rabelais ℰ 04 77 71 31 67, Fax 04 77 71 27 00.

Lyons 87.

Troisgros M, pl. Gare ℰ 04 77 71 66 97, Fax 04 77 70 39 77, « Tasteful contemporary decor », 🚿 – 🛗 📺 ☎ 🚗. AE ① GB JCB

closed 3 to 18 August, February Holidays, Tuesday except lunch from May-October and Wednesday – **Meals** (booking essential) 340 (lunch), 650/790 and a la carte 500/880 ⌸ – 🍽 120 – **15 rm** 800/1500, 4 suites

Spec. Fritot de tomate aux escargots. Pavé de colin, fenouil et langues d'oursin. Tourte au chocolat et sésame blanc. **Wines** Condrieu, Bourgogne rouge.

St-Bonnet-le-Froid 43290 H.-Loire 🗚 ⑨ – pop. 180 alt. 1 126.

Lyons 101.

Auberge des Cimes (Marcon) M 🍴 with rm, ℰ 04 71 59 93 72, Fax 04 71 59 93 40, ⩽, 🚿 – 🛏 rm, ▤ rest, 📺 ☎ ⚫ 🅿. AE GB

Easter-15 November and closed Monday dinner and Tuesday – **Meals** 180/580 and a la carte 320/530 ⌸ – 🍽 90 – **12 rm** 670/850

Spec. Croustillant de foie gras aux amandes. Agneau noir du Velay en croûte de foin. Menu "champignons" (season). **Wines** Saint-Pourçain, Crozes-Hermitage.

Valence 26000 Drôme 🗚 ⑫ – pop. 63 437 alt. 126.

See : House of the Heads (Maison des Têtes)★ – Interior★ of the cathedral – Champ de Mars ⩽★ – Red chalk sketches by Hubert Robert★★ in the museum.

🛐 of Chanalets ℰ 04 75 55 16 23 ; 🛐 of St-Didier ℰ 04 75 59 67 01, E : 14 km by D 119 ; 🛐 of Bourget ℰ 04 75 59 48 18 at Montmeyran.

✈ of Valence-Chabeuil ℰ 04 75 85 26 26.

🛈 Tourist Office Parvis de la Gare ℰ 04 75 44 90 44, Fax 04 75 44 90 41 – A.C. 33 bis av. F. Faure ℰ 04 75 43 61 07, Fax 04 75 42 27 03.

Lyons 101.

Pic M, 285 av. V. Hugo, Motorway exit signposted Valence-Sud ℰ 04 75 44 15 32, Fax 04 75 40 96 03, ⛱, 🏊, 🚿 – 🛗 ▤ 📺 ☎ ⚫ 🚗 🅿 – 🔔 50. AE ①
GB JCB

Meals (closed 9 to 25 August and Sunday dinner) (Sunday : booking essential) 340 b.i. (lunch)/660 and a la carte 540/730 ⌸ – 🍽 90 – **12 rm** 900/1350, 3 suites

Spec. Petit homard et artichauts mêlés, foie gras et noix caramélisées à la gelée de coings. Filet de loup au caviar "Jacques Pic". Aile de pigeon de la Drôme en croustillant de pomme de terre. **Wines** Crozes-Hermitage, Saint-Joseph.

at Pont-de-l'Isère to the N by N 7 : 9 km – alt. 120 – ✉ 26600 :

Michel Chabran with rm, N 7 ℰ 04 75 84 60 09, Fax 04 75 84 59 65, ⛱ – ▤ 📺 ☎ 🅿. AE GB

closed Sunday dinner in winter except school holidays – **Meals** 225 b.i. (lunch), 350/695 and a la carte 430/650 – 🍽 80 – **12 rm** 400/690

Spec. Salade de pommes de terre "rattes" aux truffes fraîches (December-March). Turbot de ligne poêlé aux champignons. Pintade de la Drôme, son aile farcie au foie gras, sa cuisse en salmis. **Wines** Crozes Hermitage, Hermitage.

Vienne 38200 Isère 🗚 ⑪ ⑫ – pop. 29 449 alt. 160.

See : Site★ – St-Maurice cathedral★★ – Temple of Augustus and Livia★★ – Roman Theatre★ – Church★ and cloisters★ of St-André-le-Bas – Mont Pipet Esplanade ⩽★ – Old church of St-Pierre★ : lapidary museum★ – Gallo-roman city★ of St-Romain-en-Gal – Sculpture group★ in the church of Ste-Colombe.

🛈 Tourist Office 3 cours Brillier ℰ 04 74 85 12 62, Fax 04 74 31 75 98.

Lyons 31.

Pyramide (Henriroux) M, 14 bd F. Point ℰ 04 74 53 01 96, Fax 04 74 85 69 73, ⛱, 🚿 – 🛗, 🛏 rm, ▤ 📺 ☎ ⚫ 🚗 🅿 – 🔔 25. AE ① GB JCB

Meals (closed Tuesday and Wednesday from October-April) 290 b.i. (lunch), 460/680 and a la carte 590/750 ⌸ – 🍽 90 – **20 rm** 780/990, 4 suites

Spec. Crème soufflée de dormeur au caviar osciètre blond. Minestrone de Saint-Pierre au pistou d'aromates. "Piano en ut" praliné, amandes et noisettes, sauce café grillé. **Wines** Côtes-du-Rhône.

Vonnas 01540 Ain **74** ② – pop. 2 381 alt. 200.
Lyons 63.

Georges Blanc Ⓜ ⌂, ℘ 04 74 50 90 90, Fax 04 74 50 08 80, « Elegant inn on the banks of the Veyle, flowered garden », ⌿, ✕ – 🛗 🖥 📺 ☎ 🚗 – ⚓ 80. AE ① GB closed 3 January-13 February – **Meals** (closed Tuesday except dinner from 15 June-15 September and Monday) (booking essential) 490/900 and a la carte 500/700 – ☕ 115 – **32 rm** 900/1800, 6 suites

Spec. Crêpe parmentière au saumon et caviar. Poulet de Bresse aux gousses d'ail et foie gras. Panouille bressane glacée à la confiture de lait. **Wines** Mâcon-Azé, Chiroubles.

MARSEILLES 13000 B.-du-R. **84** ⑬ – pop. 800 550.

See : Site★★★ – N.-D.-de-la-Garde Basilica ⚡★★★ – Old Port★★ : Fish market (quai des Belges ET 5) – Palais Longchamp★ GS : Fine Arts Museum★, Natural History Museum★ – St-Victor Basilica★ : crypt★★ DU – Old Major Cathedral★ DS N – Pharo Park ≼★ DU – Hôtel du département et Dôme-Nouvel Alcazar★ – Vieille Charité★★ (Mediterranean archeology) DS R – Museums : Grobet-Labadié★★ GS M⁷, Cantini★ FU M⁵, Vieux Marseille★★ DT M², History of Marseilles★ ET M¹.

Envir. : Corniche road★★ of Callelongue S : 13 km along the sea front.

Exc. : – Château d'If★★ (⚡★★★) 1 h 30.

🏌 of Marseilles-Aix ℘ 04 42 24 20 41 to the N : 22 km ; 🏌 of Allauch-Fonvieille (private) ℘ 04 91 07 28 22 ; junction Marseilles-East : 15 km, by D 2 and D 4=A ; 🏌 Country Club of la Salette ℘ 04 91 27 12 16 by A 50.

✈ Marseilles-Provence : ℘ 04 42 78 21 00 to the N : 28 km.

🚗 ℘ 08 36 35 35 35.

🛈 Tourist Office 4 Canebière, 13001 ℘ 04 91 13 89 00, Fax 04 91 13 89 20 and St-Charles railway station ℘ 04 91 50 59 18 – A.C. of Provence 149 bd Rabatau, 13010 ℘ 04 91 78 83 00, Fax 04 91 25 74 38.

Paris 772 – Lyons 312 – Nice 188 – Turin 407 – Toulon 64 – Toulouse 401.

Plans on following pages

Sofitel Vieux Port Ⓜ, 36 bd Ch. Livon ⊠ 13007 ℘ 04 91 15 59 00, Fax 04 91 15 59 50, ≼, « Panoramic restaurant ≼ old port », ⌿ – 🛗, ❀ rm, 🖥 📺 ☎ 🚗 – ⚓ 130. AE ① GB JCB
DU r
Les Trois Forts ℘ 04 91 15 59 56 **Meals** 255 – ☕ 100 – **127 rm** 890/1400, 3 suites

Petit Nice (Passédat) Ⓜ ⌂, anse de Maldormé (turn off when level with no 160 Corniche Kennedy) ⊠ 13007 ℘ 04 91 59 25 92, Fax 04 91 59 28 08, ☀, « Villas overlooking the sea, elegant decor, ≼ », ⌿ – 🛗 🖥 📺 ☎ 🅿. AE ① GB JCB
closed 1 to 15 November and February Holidays – **Meals** (closed Sunday Monday except Bank Holidays from mid-Oct.-mid-April Monday lunch from mid-April-mid-Oct.) 400 b.i. (lunch), 680/890 and a la carte 570/950 – ☕ 120 – **15 rm** 1200/2600
Spec. Tronçon de loup "Lucie Passedat". Denti de palangre en barigoule d'artichauts violets (March-September). Rougets de roche à l'huile de pistache (May-September). **Wines** Cassis.

Holiday Inn Ⓜ, 103 av. Prado ⊠ 13008 ℘ 04 91 83 10 10, Fax 04 91 79 84 12 – 🛗 ❀ rm, 🖥 📺 ☎ 🚗 – ⚓ 150. AE ① GB JCB
Meals 90/135 ♀ – ☕ 60 – **115 rm** 650/750, 4 suites.

Mercure Beauvau Vieux Port without rest, 4 r. Beauvau ⊠ 13001 ℘ 04 91 54 91 00, Fax 04 91 54 15 76, ≼, « Antique furniture » – 🛗, ❀ rm, 🖥 📺 ☎ AE ① GB JCB
☕ 65 – **72 rm** 550/780.

Mercure Euro-Centre Ⓜ, r. Neuve St-Martin ⊠ 13001 ℘ 04 91 39 20 00, Fax 04 91 56 24 57, ≼, ☀ – 🛗, ❀ rm, 🖥 📺 ☎ 🚗 – ⚓ 200. AE ① GB JCB
EST g
L'Oursinade : (closed 14 July-9 September, Sunday lunch and Saturday) **Meals** 150/250 – **L'Oliveraie** grill (lunch only) (closed Sunday) **Meals** 88 ♀ – ☕ 65 – **200 rm** 490/600

Frantour Tonic Hôtel Ⓜ without rest, 43 quai des Belges ⊠ 13001 ℘ 04 91 55 67 46, Fax 04 91 55 67 56, ≼ – 🛗 🖥 📺 ☎ AE ① GB JCB
☕ 49 – **56 rm** 340/590.

Novotel Vieux Port Ⓜ, 36 bd Ch. Livon ⊠ 13007 ℘ 04 91 59 22 22, Fax 04 91 31 15 48, ☀, ⌿ – 🛗, ❀ rm, 🖥 📺 ☎ 🚗 – ⚓ 250. AE ① GB DU r
Meals 140/160 and a la carte approx. 170 ♀ – ☕ 65 – **90 rm** 580/680.

New Hôtel Bompard ⌂ without rest, 2 r. Flots Bleus ⊠ 13007 ℘ 04 91 52 10 93, Fax 04 91 31 02 14, ⌿, ⚘ – 🛗 kitchenette 🖥 📺 ☎ 🅿 – ⚓ 25. AE ① GB JCB
☕ 55 – **46 rm** 420/470.

St-Ferréol's [M] without rest, 19 r. Pisançon ⊠ 13001 ℰ 04 91 33 12 21, *Fax 04 91 54 29 97* – 🛗 ▤ TV ☎. AE ① GB JCB   FU h
⊡ 42 – **19 rm** 340/580.

Résidence du Vieux Port without rest, 18 quai du Port ⊠ 13002 ℰ 04 91 91 91 22, *Fax 04 91 56 60 88*, ≤ – 🛗, ⇥ rm, ▤ TV ☎ ᷤ – 🕍 30. AE ① GB JCB
⊡ 59 – **38 rm** 490/1250.

Mascotte [M] without rest, 5 La Canebière ⊠ 13001 ℰ 04 91 90 61 61, *Fax 04 91 90 95 61* – 🛗, ⇥ rm, ▤ TV ☎ – 🕍 30. AE ① GB   ET s
⊡ 45 – **45 rm** 370/530.

New Hôtel Vieux Port without rest, 3 bis r. Reine Élisabeth ⊠ 13001 ℰ 04 91 90 51 42, *Fax 04 91 90 76 24* – 🛗 ▤ TV ☎ – 🕍 25. AE ①
GB JCB   ET u
⊡ 48 – **47 rm** 400/440.

New Hôtel Sélect without rest, 4 allées Gambetta ⊠ 13001 ℰ 04 91 50 65 50, *Fax 04 91 50 45 56* – 🛗 ▤ TV ☎ – 🕍 40. AE ① GB JCB   FS k
⊡ 48 – **60 rm** 330/360.

Alizé without rest, 35 quai Belges ⊠ 13001 ℰ 04 91 33 66 97, *Fax 04 91 54 80 06*, ≤
– 🛗 ▤ TV ☎. AE ① GB JCB   ETU b
⊡ 35 – **37 rm** 305/455.

Clarine without rest, 31 r. Rouet ⊠ 13006 ℰ 04 91 79 56 66, *Fax 04 91 78 33 85* –
🛗, ⇥ rm, ▤ TV ☎. AE ① GB
⊡ 38 – **53 rm** 280/330.

XXX **Miramar** (Minguella), 12 quai Port ⊠ 13002 ℰ 04 91 91 10 40, *Fax 04 91 56 64 31*, 🌿
❀ – ▤. AE ① GB JCB   ET v
closed 1 to 22 August, 3 to 17 January and Sunday – **Meals** - Seafood - a la carte 330/
500 ♈
Spec. Bouillabaisse. Poisson du jour au beurre de pisala. Daurade rôtie à la "Raimu", poivrons croquants à la crème de brebis. **Wines** Cassis, Côtes de Provence.

XXX **Ferme**, 23 r. Sainte ⊠ 13001 ℰ 04 91 33 21 12, *Fax 04 91 33 81 21* – ▤. AE ① GB
JCB   EU m
closed August, Saturday lunch and Sunday – **Meals** 215 and a la carte 260/
320.

XX **Michel-Brasserie des Catalans**, 6 r. Catalans ⊠ 13007 ℰ 04 91 52 30 63,
❀ *Fax 04 91 59 23 05* – ▤. AE GB
Meals - Seafood - a la carte 220/330
Spec. Bouillabaisse, Bourride. La pêche du jour.

XX **Les Échevins**, 44 r. Sainte ⊠ 13001 ℰ 04 91 33 08 08, *Fax 04 91 54 08 21* – ▤. AE
① GB JCB   EU x
closed 19 July-9 August, Saturday lunch and Sunday – **Meals** 120/300 ♈

XX **Les Arcenaulx**, 25 cours d'Estienne d'Orves ⊠ 13001 ℰ 04 91 59 80 30,
Fax 04 91 54 76 33, 🌿, « Bookshop and restaurant in original decor » – ▤. AE ① GB
JCB   EU s
closed Monday in July-August and Sunday – **Meals** 135/280 ♈

XX **Les Mets de Provence "Chez Maurice Brun"**, 18 quai de Rive Neuve (2nd floor)
⊠ 13007 ℰ 04 91 33 35 38, *Fax 04 91 33 05 69*, « Provençal ambience » –
▤. GB   EU d
closed Monday lunch and Sunday – **Meals** 200 b.i. (lunch)/290.

XX **L'Ambassade des Vignobles**, 42 pl. aux Huiles ⊠ 13001 ℰ 04 91 33 00 25,
Fax 04 91 54 25 60 – ▤. AE GB JCB   EU h
closed August, Saturday lunch and Sunday – **Meals** 120/300 b.i. ♈

XX **René Alloin**, 9 pl. Amiral Muselier (by prom. G. Pompidou) ⊠ 13008 ℰ 04 91 77 88 25,
Fax 04 91 71 82 46, 🌿 – ▤. GB
closed Saturday lunch and Sunday dinner – **Meals** 135 (lunch), 195/270.

Aix-en-Provence 13100 B.-du-R. **84** ③ – pop. *123 842 alt. 206*.
🛈 *Tourist Office 2 pl. Gén.-de-Gaulle* ℰ *04 42 16 11 61, Fax 04 42 16 11 62 – Automobile-Club 7 bd J.-Jaurès* ℰ *04 42 23 33 73, Fax 04 42 23 13 77.*
Marseilles 31.

XXX **Clos de la Violette** (Banzo), 10 av. Violette ℰ 04 42 23 30 71, *Fax 04 42 21 93 03*,
❀❀ 🌿 – ▤. AE GB. ✍
closed All Saints Holidays, February Holidays, Monday except dinner from April-October and Sunday – **Meals** (booking essential) 250/550 and a la carte 430/550
Spec. Truffe sous toutes les formes (December-April). Petits farcis de légumes provençaux (June-October). Biscuit sablé de brousse fraîche à la vanille. **Wines** Coteaux d'Aix-en-Provence.

0   200 m

BASSIN DE LA GRANDE JOLIETTE

DIGUE DU LARGE

TUNISIE, ALGÉRIE

CALANQUES, CHÂTEAU D'IF

GARE MARITIME INTERNATIONALE

S.N.C.M.

Quai de la Joliette

Joliette

Pl. Marceau — ST-LAZARE

R. V. Leblanc — Fauchier

Av. C. Pelletan

R. de la Joliette

Dames — J. Guesde

HÔTEL DE LA RÉGION

CITÉ DE LA MUSIQUE

LES CARMES — 57

Colbert — H. de la Région — 54 — 18

l'Évêché — R. Rue des

Cath. de la Major

Quartier du Panier

R. du Panier — Hôtel-Dieu

ST-CANNAT

Accoules — 33

Pl. de Lenche — R. Caisserie

République

CENTRE BOURSE

Espl. de la Tourette

ST-LAURENT — Av. St-Jean

FORT ST-JEAN

St-Ferréol

Vieux Port Hôtel de Ville

Quai du Port

Ferry Boat

TUNNEL ST-LAURENT

CHÂTEAU

Parc du Pharo

VIEUX PORT

OPÉRA

Théâtre de la Criée

Quartier de l'Arsenal — 62

Quai de Rive Neuve

R. Fort N.-Dame — ST-CHARLES

FORT ST-NICOLAS

Bd C. Livon — Av. Pasteur

Neuve Ste-Catherine

Rue Sainte

BASILIQUE ST-VICTOR

Bd de la Corderie

Puget — Breteuil

Bd de la Corse

Av. de la Corse

22

R. d'Endoume

R. du Chin du Roucas Blanc

TUNNEL

Notre-Dame

N.-D. DE LOURDES ST-PHILIPPE

R. Dragon — PRADO — Dame

Tellene

NOTRE-DAME DE LA GARDE — 29

ST-FRANÇOIS D'ASSISE

MARSEILLE

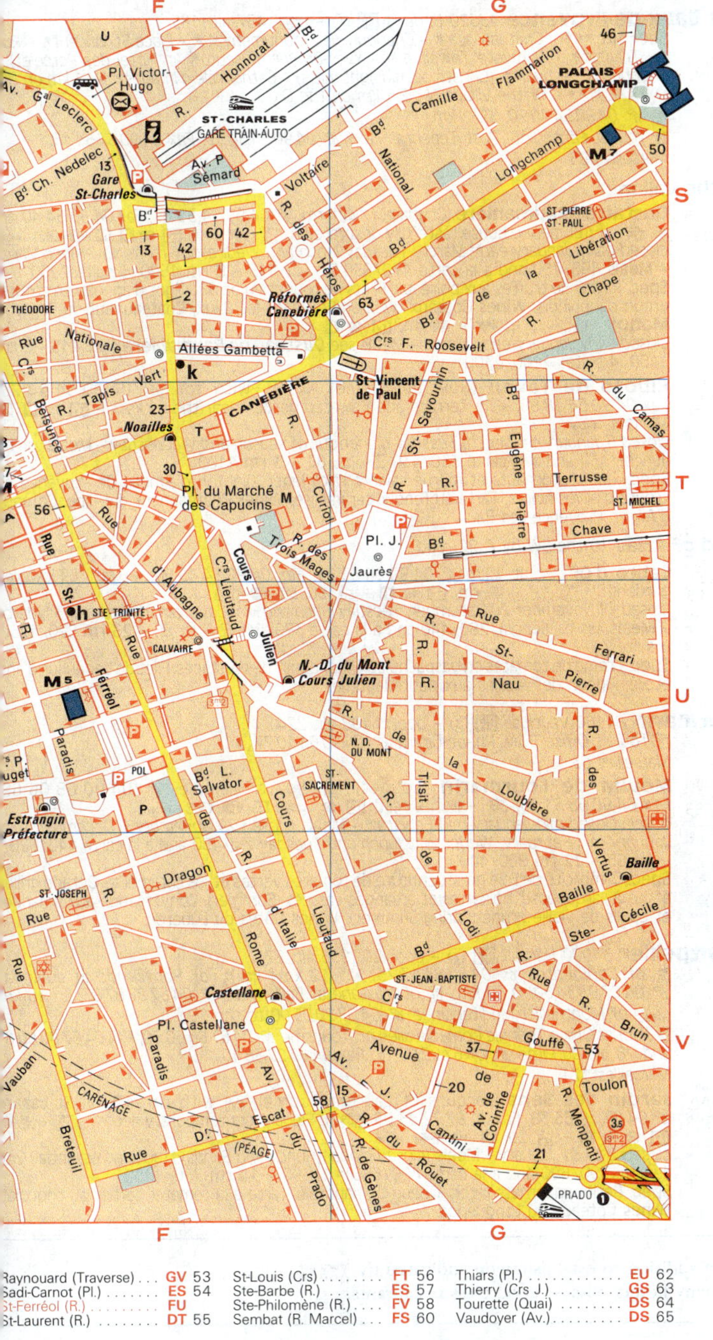
U
Pl. Victor-Hugo
Honnorat
R.
Camille
Flammarion
PALAIS LONGCHAMP
46
Av. Gal Leclerc
ST-CHARLES
GARE TRAIN-AUTO
Av. P. Sémard
Longchamp
M
50
S
Bd Ch. Nedelec
13
Voltaire
R. des Héros
Bd
ST-PIERRE
ST-PAUL
Gare St-Charles
Bd
60 42
42
National
Libération
13
42
la
Chape
2
Réformés
Canebière
63
Bd
de
R.
ST-THÉODORE
Rue
Nationale
Allées Gambetta
Crs F. Roosevelt
R.
du
Crs
Bersunce
R. Tapis
Vert
k
St-Vincent de Paul
Bd Savournin
Camas
CANEBIÈRE
23
Noailles
T
R.
R.
Bd Eugène Pierre
Terrusse
ST-MICHEL
T
30
Pl. du Marché des Capucins
M
Curiol
R.
R.
Chave
56
Rue
R. des Trois Mages
P
Pl. J. Jaurès
Bd
M
di Aubagne
Crs Lieutaud
St-
h
STE-TRINITÉ
Rue
Julien
Rue
Ferrari
CALVAIRE
N.-D. du Mont
Cours Julien
R.
Nau
St-Pierre
U
M 5
Ferréol
R.
de
R.
Paradis
N.D. DU MONT
la
Loubière
des
Estrangin Préfecture
POL
Bd L. Salvator
ST-SACREMENT
R.
Tilsit
Vertus
Baille
P
Cours
de
Dragon
R.
d'Italie
Lodi
Baille
Cécile
ST-JOSEPH
Rome
Lieutaud
Bd
R.
Ste-
Rue
Vauban
Crs
ST-JEAN-BAPTISTE
Rue
Brun
Castellane
Pl. Castellane
Av.
Avenue
37
Gouffé
53
V
Paradis
Av.
J.
20
de Corinthe
Toulon
R. Menpenti
CARÉNAGE
58
15
Cantini
21
Breteuil
Rue
Escat
D.
(PÉAGE)
du Prado
R. de Gênes
R. du Rouet
PRADO
F
G

Les Baux-de-Provence 13520 B.-du-R. 84 ① – *pop. 457 alt. 185.*
See : Site★★★ – Château ❋★★ – Charloun Rieu monument ≤★ – Place St-Vincent★ – Ru
du Trencat★ – Paravelle Tower ≤★ – Yves-Brayer museum★ (in Hôtel des Porcelet)
Shepherds' Festival★★ (Christmas midnight mass) – Cathédrale d'Images★ N : 1 km on th
D 27 – ❋★★★ of the village N : 2,5 km on the D 27.
⌐₉ ℘ 04 90 54 40 20, S : 2 km.
🛈 *Tourist Office Ilôt "Post Tenebras Lux"* ℘ 04 90 54 34 39, Fax 04 90 54 51 15.
Marseilles 83.

in the Vallon :

XXXXX **Oustaù de Baumanière** (Charial) 🦢 with rm, ℘ 04 90 54 33 07, Fax 04 90 54 40 46
❀❀ ≤, 🌿, « *16C period house tastefully decorated* », 🏊, 🎾 – ▦ TV ☎ P. AE ① GB JCB
closed early January-early March, Tuesday lunch and Wednesday from November-Marc
– **Meals** 495/750 and a la carte 470/830 ♀ – ☲ 115 – **8 rm** 1500, 5 suites2200
Spec. Ravioli de truffes aux poireaux. Filets de rouget au basilic. Gigot d'agneau en croûte
gratin dauphinois. **Wines** Coteaux d'Aix-en-Provence-les Baux, Châteauneuf-du-Pape.
Manoir 🏛 🦢, ≤, 🎾 – ▦ rm, TV ☎ P
closed early January-early March – **Meals** see **Ousteau de Baumanière** – ☲ 115 – **5 rm**
1450, 4 suites 2100/2300.

XXXX **Riboto de Taven** (Novi et Theme) M 🦢 with rm, ℘ 04 90 54 34 23
❀ Fax 04 90 54 38 88, ≤, « *Terrace and flowered garden near the rocks* » – TV ☎ P. A
① GB JCB
closed 5 January-11 March, Tuesday dinner out of season and Wednesday – **Meals** 230 b.
(lunch)/330 and a la carte 330/430 ♀ – ☲ 80 – **3 rm** 1100
Spec. Tian d'artichauts et morue salée à l'aïoli léger. Gigoton d'agneau de Provence e
croûte d'olives noires. Tarte au fenouil caramelisé. **Wines** Châteauneuf-du-Pape, Coteau
d'Aix-en-Provence-Les Baux.

road of Arles *to the SW by D 27 road :*

🏛 **Cabro d'Or** 🦢, at 1 km ℘ 04 90 54 33 21, Fax 04 90 54 45 98, ≤, 🌿, « *Flowere*
❀ gardens », 🏊, 🎾 – ▦ rm, TV ☎ P – 🎱 60. AE ① GB JCB
closed 11 November-20 December, Tuesday lunch and Monday from 15 October-31 Marc
– **Meals** 195 b.i. (lunch), 280/440 and a la carte 390/510 ♀ – ☲ 80 – **23 rm** 820/1200
8 suites
Spec. Crème de tomates en gaspacho aux "bonbons" de crustacés. Filet de bar au jus d'ani
étoilé. Pigeon des Alpilles aux petits légumes.

Lourmarin 84160 Vaucluse 84 ③ – *pop. 1 108 alt. 224.*
🛈 *Tourist Office 8 av. Ph.-de-Girard* ℘ 04 90 68 10 77.
Marseilles 63.

🏛 **Moulin de Lourmarin** (Loubet) M 🦢, r. Temple ℘ 04 90 68 06 69
❀❀ Fax 04 90 68 31 76, 🌿 – 🛗, ▦ rest, TV ☎ 🚗. AE ① GB JCB
hôtel : closed mid-January-mid-February – **Meals** (*closed 29 November-8 December, mi*
January-mid-February, Wednesday lunch and Tuesday 200/450 and a la carte 440/620
– ☲ 85 – **22 rm** 900/1400
Spec. Complicité de foie gras, confiture de tomates vertes et jus caramélisé. Dorade grillé
et jus à l'arquebuse, noisettes et amandes cassées (Summer). Conversation aux amande
et coulis de vieille prune (Spring-Summer). **Wines** Côtes du Lubéron.

Montpellier 34000 Hérault 83 ⑦ – *pop. 207 996 alt. 27.*
⌐₁₈ *of Coulondres* ℘ 04 67 84 13 75, N : 12 km ; ⌐₁₈ ⌐₉ *of Fontcaude at Juvigna*
℘ 04 67 03 34 30, O : 9 km ; ⌐₁₈ *of Massane at Baillargues* ℘ 04 67 87 87 87, E : 13 km
✈ *of Montpellier-Méditerranée* ℘ 04 67 20 85 00 te the SE :.
🛈 *Tourist Office Triangle Comédie allée du Tourisme* ℘ 04 67 60 60 60, Fax 04 67 60 60 6
and 78 av. du Pirée ℘ 04 67 22 06 16, Fax 04 67 22 38 10.
Marseilles 171.

XXXX **Jardin des Sens** (Jacques et Laurent Pourcel) M with rm, 11 av. St-Lazar
❀❀❀ ℘ 04 67 79 63 38, Fax 04 67 72 13 05, 🌿, « *Elegant contemporary decor* », 🏊 – 🛗 ▦
TV ☎ 🚹 P – 🎱 20. AE ① GB JCB
closed 2 to 31 January – **Meals** (*closed Monday lunch and Sunday*) (booking essential) 240
(lunch), 390/600 and a la carte 480/650 – ☲ 90 – **14 rm** 750/1300
Spec. Petits encornets farcis. Queue de baudroie, tarte à la tomate. Cornet au chocolat
Wines Coteaux du Languedoc.

In addition to establishments indicated by XXXXX ... X,
many hotels possess good class restaurants.

MONACO (Principality of) 84 ⑩, 115 ㉗ ㉘ – *pop. 29 972 alt. 65 – Casino.*

Monaco *Capital of the Principality –* ✉ *98000.*

See : *Tropical Garden★★ (Jardin exotique) : ≤★ – Observatory Caves★ (Grotte de l'Observatoire) – St-Martin Gardens★ – Early paintings of the Nice School★★ in Cathedral – Recumbent Christ★ in the Misericord Chapel – Place du Palais★ – Prince's Palace★ – Museums : oceanographic★★★ (aquarium★★, ≤★★ from the terrace), Prehistoric Anthropology★, Napoleon and Monaco History★, Royal collection of vintage cars★.*
Urban racing circuit – A.C.M. 23 bd Albert-1ᵉʳ ℘ (00-377) 93 15 26 00, Fax (00-377) 93 25 80 08.
Paris 956 – Nice 21 – San Remo 44.

Monte-Carlo *Fashionable resort of the Principality – Casinos Grand Casino, Monte-Carlo Sporting Club, Sun Casino.*

See : *Terrace★★ of the Grand Casino – Museum of Dolls and Automata★.*
🏌18 *Monte-Carlo ℘ 93 41 09 11 to the S by N 7 : 11 km.*
🛈 *Tourist Office 2A bd Moulins ℘ (00-377) 92 16 61 66, Fax (00-377) 9 2 16 60 00.*

Paris, pl. Casino ℘ (00-377) 92 16 30 00, Fax (00-377) 92 16 38 50, ≤, 🌉, health centre, ₆, ⊠ – 🛗, ✻ rm, 🖩 TV ☎ ⇔ – 👥 70. AE ⓓ GB JCB. ✻ rest
see **Louis XV** and **Grill** below - **Côté Jardin** ℘ (00-377) 92 16 68 44 (lunch only) *(closed 3 July-29 August)* **Meals** 320 and a la carte 340/420 – **Salle Empire** ℘ (00-377) 92 16 29 52 *(3 July-29 August)* **Meals** a la carte 450/690 ♀ – ☕ 170 – **160 rm** 2300/3400, 40 suites.

Hermitage, square Beaumarchais ℘ (00-377) 92 16 40 00, Fax (00-377) 92 16 38 52, ≤, 🌉, health centre, « Dining room in baroque style », ₆, ⊠ – 🛗 🖩 TV ☎ ⇔ – 👥 80. AE ⓓ GB JCB. ✻ rest
Meals 340/450 – ☕ 150 – **215 rm** 1950/2950, 15 suites.

Monte-Carlo Grand Hôtel Ⓜ, 12 av. Spélugues ℘ (00-377) 93 50 65 00, Fax (00-377) 93 30 01 57, ≤, 🌉, Casino and cabaret, ₆, ⊠ – 🛗 🖩 TV ☎ ₆ ⇔ – 👥 450. AE ⓓ GB JCB. ✻ rest
Truffe (dinner only) **Meals** a la carte approx. 400 – **L'Argentin** (dinner only) *(closed 15 June-15 September)* **Meals** 380 – **Pistou** *(open 15 June-16 September)* **Meals** à la carte 260/350 – **Café de la Mer** (lunch only) *(closed 15 June-15 September)* **Meals** a la carte 220/320 – ☕ 125 – **580 rm** 1950/2350, 20 suites.

Méridien Beach Plaza Ⓜ, av. Princesse Grace, à la Plage du Larvotto ℘ (00-377) 93 30 98 80, Fax (00-377) 93 50 23 14, ≤, 🌉, « Extensive swimming complex and luxurious conference centre », ₆, ⊠, ⊠, ⛺ – 🛗, ✻ rm, 🖩 TV ☎ ₆ ⇔ – 👥 340. AE ⓓ GB JCB
Les Pergolas : **Meals** 190/245 ♀ – ☕ 150 – **301 rm** 2200/3200, 7 suites.

Métropole Palace Ⓜ, 4 av. Madone ℘ (00-377) 93 15 15 15, Fax (00-377) 93 25 24 44, 🌉, ⊠ – 🛗 🖩 TV ☎ ₆ ⇔ – 👥 220. AE ⓓ GB JCB
Jardin : **Meals** 225, (lunch) 300/350 – ☕ 150 – **138 rm** 1450/2000, 12 suites.

Mirabeau Ⓜ, 1 av. Princesse Grace ℘ (00-377) 92 16 65 65, Fax (00-377) 93 50 84 85, ≤, 🌉, ⊠ – 🛗, ✻ rm, 🖩 TV ☎ ⇔ – 👥 80. AE ⓓ GB JCB. ✻ rest
see **La Coupole** below - **Café Mirabeau** at the swimming pool (lunch only) *(June-September)* **Meals** a la carte 230/340 – ☕ 140 – **83 rm** 1500/2450, 10 suites.

Alexandra without rest, 35 bd Princesse Charlotte ℘ (00-377) 93 50 63 13, Fax (00-377) 92 16 06 48 – 🛗 🖩 TV ☎. AE ⓓ GB JCB. ✻
☕ 70 – **56 rm** 700/850.

Balmoral, 12 av. Costa ℘ (00-377) 93 50 62 37, Fax (00-377) 93 15 08 69, ≤ – 🛗 TV ☎. AE ⓓ GB JCB. ✻
Meals coffee shop *(closed November, Sunday dinner and Monday)* 160 – ☕ 85 – **64 rm** 470/1050, 6 suites.

Louis XV - Hôtel de Paris, pl. Casino ℘ (00-377) 92 16 30 01, Fax (00-377) 92 16 69 21 – 🖩 🅿. AE ⓓ GB JCB. ✻
closed 30 November-27 December, 15 February-3 March, Wednesday except dinner from 16 June-25 August and Tuesday – **Meals** 500 b.i. (lunch), 840/950 and a la carte 360/920
Spec. Légumes de Provence mijotés à la truffe noire rapée. Poitrine de pigeonneau, foie gras de canard et pommes de terre. Le "Louis XV" au croustillant de pralin. **Wines** Côtes de Provence.

Grill de l'Hôtel de Paris, pl. Casino ℘ (00-377) 92 16 29 66, Fax (00-377) 92 16 38 40, « Rooftop restaurant with sliding roof and ≤ the Principality » – 🛗 🖩 🅿. AE ⓓ GB JCB. ✻
closed 3 January-3 February – **Meals** a la carte 540/880 ♀
Spec. Ravioli de gambari et courgettes trompettes au jus de ratatouille (spring-summer). Assortiment de poissons et légumes grillés, coulis de tomates à l'origan. Carré d'agneau de Sisteron rôti aux herbes, tartelette de légumes frais. **Wines** Côtes de Provence.

MONACO (Principality of)

XXXX
❀
La Coupole - Hôtel Mirabeau, 1 av. Princesse Grace ✆ (00-377) 92 16 65 65, *Fax (00-377) 93 50 84 85* – ▮, ⌂. **AE** Ⓞ **GB** **JCB**. ✍
closed lunch in July-August – **Meals** 310/450 and a la carte 400/530
Spec. Carpaccio de tomates "grappe" à la grillade de thon (1 July-30 September). Filet de petits rougets cuits à l'unilatérale, huile de basilic. Cône de chocolat "manjani", crème aux fruits de la passion (1 August-31 October). **Wines** Côtes de Provence.

XXX
Saint Benoit, 10 ter av. Costa ✆ (00-377) 93 25 02 34, *Fax (00-377) 93 30 52 64*
≼ port and Monaco, ☂ – ▮. **AE** Ⓞ **GB** **JCB**
closed 20 December-5 January and Monday except dinner in July-August – **Meals** 168/23 and a la carte 240/440.

XX
Café de Paris, pl. Casino ✆ (00-377) 92 16 20 20, *Fax (00-377) 92 16 38 58,* ☂, « 190 brasserie decor » – ▮. **AE** Ⓞ **GB** **JCB**. ✍
Meals 180 (lunch), 200/450.

X
Polpetta, 2 r. Paradis ✆ (00-377) 93 50 67 84 – ▮. **AE** **GB**
closed 15 to 30 October, 10 to 29 February, Saturday lunch and Tuesday – **Meals** - Italia rest. - 150.

at Monte-Carlo-Beach *(06 Alpes-Mar.) at 2,5 km* – ✉ *06190 Roquebrune-Cap-Martin* :

Monte-Carlo Beach Hôtel Ⓜ ⊶, av. Princesse Grace ✆ 04 93 28 66 66
Fax 04 93 78 14 18, ≼ sea and Monaco, ☂, « Extensive swimming complex », ⚲, ⛵
– ▯, ▮ rm, **TV** ☎ ☕ **P** – ⚑ 40. **AE** Ⓞ **GB** **JCB**. ✍ rest
closed 29 November-31 January – **Salle à Manger** (dinner only) (residents only) Meal a la carte 300/470 – **Potinière** (lunch only) (3 June-13 September) **Meals** a la cart 320/430 – **Rivage** (lunch only) (1 April-4 October) **Meals** a la carte 210/340 – **Vigi** -buffet- (25 June-6 September) **Meals** 280/300 – ⊿ 150 – **45 rm** 2400/2700.

NICE 06000 *Alpes-Mar.* **84** ⑨ ⑩, **115** ㉖ ㉗ – *pop. 342 439 alt. 6 – Casino Ruhl* FZ.

See : *Site*★★ – *Promenade des Anglais*★★ EFZ – *Old Nice*★ : *Château* ≼★★ JZ, *Interior of church of St-Martin-St-Augustin* HY D – *Balustraded staircase*★ *of the Palais Lascar* HZ K, *Interior*★ *of Ste-Réparate Cathedral* – HZ L, *St-Jacques Church*★ HZ N, *Decoration of St-Giaume's Chapel* HZ R – *Mosaic*★ *by Chagall in Law Faculty* DZ U – *Palais des Arts* HJY – *Miséricorde Chapel*★ HZ S – *Cimiez : Monastery*★ *(Masterpieces*★★ *of the early Nic School in the church)* HV Q, *Roman Ruins*★ HV – *Museums : Marc Chagall*★★ GX, *Matisse*★★ HV M², *Fine Arts Museum*★★ DZ M, *Masséna*★ FZ M¹ – *Modern and Contemporary Art*★★ HY – *Parc Phoenix*★ – *Carnival*★★★ *(before Shrove Tuesday)*.

Envir. : *St-Michel Plateau* ≼★★ *9,5 km.*

✈ *of Nice-Côte d'Azur* ✆ *04 93 21 30 12 : 7 km.*

☎ ✆ *08 36 35 35 35.*

🛈 *Tourist Office 5 prom. des Anglais* ✆ *04 92 14 48 00, SNCF Station* ✆ *04 93 87 07 07 Fax 04 93 16 85 16, Nice-Ferber (Near the Airport)* ✆ *04 93 83 32 64, Fax 04 93 72 08 27 and Airport, Terminal 1* ✆ *04 93 21 44 11, Fax 04 93 21 44 50 – Automobile-Club, 9 Massenet* ✆ *04 93 87 18 17, Fax 04 93 88 90 00.*

Paris 932 – Cannes 32 – Genova 194 – Lyons 472 – Marseilles 188 – Turin 220.

Plans on following pages

Négresco, 37 promenade des Anglais ✆ 04 93 16 64 00, *Fax 04 93 88 35 68,* ≼, ☂
« 17C, 18C, Empire and Napoléon III furnishings » – ▯ ▮ **TV** ☎ ⌂ – ⚑ 50 - 200. **A**
Ⓞ **GB** **JCB**   FZ
see **Chantecler** below - **Rotonde :** Meals 165, Sunday a la carte ♀ – ⊿ 130 – **122 rm** 1700/2550, 18 suites.

Palais Maeterlinck Ⓜ ⊶, 6 km by Inferior Corniche ✉ 06300 ✆ 04 92 00 72 00
Fax 04 92 04 18 10, ≼, ☂, « Swimming pool, garden and terraces overlooking sea », ⛵ ⚲ – ▯ kitchenette ▮ **TV** ☎ ☕ ⌂ **P** – ⚑ 25. **AE** Ⓞ **GB**. ✍ rm
closed 11 January-12 March – **Mélisande** ✆ 04 92 00 72 01 Meals 200(déj.), 240/550 – ⊿ 160 – **18 rm** 2000/2900, 11 suites 3500/10000, 11 duplex.

Radisson SAS Ⓜ, 223 promenade des Anglais ✉ 06200 ✆ 04 93 37 17 17
Fax 04 93 71 21 71, ☂, « Rooftop swimming pool ≼ bay », ⛵ – ▯, ✑ rm, ▮ **TV** ☎
– ⚑ 30 - 180. **AE** Ⓞ **GB** **JCB**
Les Mosaïques : Meals 175 – **La Terrasse-Les Jardins** grill Meals 175/195 – ⊿ 110 – **316 rm** 1100/1675, 12 suites.

Méridien, 1 promenade des Anglais ✆ 04 93 82 25 25, *Fax 04 93 16 08 90,* ☂
« Rooftop swimming pool, ≼ bay » – ▯, ✑ rm, ▮ **TV** ☎ – ⚑ 25 - 200. **AE** Ⓞ **GE**
JCB. ✍ rm   FZ
Colonial Café : Meals a la carte 190/280 – **La Terrasse** ✆ 04 93 82 69 23 (oper 1 May-20 September) Meals a la carte 180/280 – ⊿ 95 – **314 rm** 1450 8 suites.

Élysée Palace Ⓜ, 2. Sauvan ℰ 04 93 86 06 06, *Fax 04 93 44 50 40*, ☂, « Rooftop swimming pool ≤ Nice » – ⧉ ▤ ⓉⓋ ☎ ⅋ ⇌ – ⚏ 45. ᴀᴇ ⓸ ɢʙ ᴊᴄʙ
Meals 110/250 ⓨ – ☕ 100 – **143 rm** 1150/1850.   EZ d

Plaza Concorde, 12 av. Verdun ℰ 04 93 16 75 75, *Fax 04 93 88 61 11*, ≤, ☂, « Rooftop terrace » – ⧉ ▤ ⓉⓋ ☎ – ⚏ 260. ᴀᴇ ⓸ ɢʙ ᴊᴄʙ
Meals 180/280 ⓨ – ☕ 90 – **173 rm** 1100/1700, 10 suites.   GZ f

Sofitel Ⓜ, 2-4 parvis de l'Europe ⊠ 06300 ℰ 04 92 00 80 00, *Fax 04 93 26 27 00*, ☂, « Panoramic rooftop swimming pool », ⌧ – ⧉, ⇤ rm, ▤ ⓉⓋ ☎ ⅋ ⇌ – ⚏ 30. ᴀᴇ ⓸ ɢʙ ᴊᴄʙ
Meals 120 ⓨ – ☕ 98 – **152 rm** 990/1350.   JX t

New Hotel Beau Rivage Ⓜ, 24 r. St-François-de-Paule ⊠ 06300 ℰ 04 93 80 80 70, *Fax 04 93 80 55 77*, ☂ – ⧉, ⇤ rm, ▤ ⓉⓋ ☎ ⅋ – ⚏ 35. ᴀᴇ ⓸ ɢʙ ᴊᴄʙ   GZ y
Bistrot du Rivage (closed Sunday dinner) **Meals** a la carte 180/290 – **Plage** ℰ 04 93 80 75 06 **Meals** a la carte approx. 200 – ☕ 95 – **118 rm** 900/1900.

Splendid, 50 bd V. Hugo ℰ 04 93 16 41 00, *Fax 04 93 16 42 70*, ☂, « Rooftop swimming pool ≤ Nice » – ⧉, ⇤ rm, ▤ ⓉⓋ ☎ ⇌ – ⚏ 30 - 100. ᴀᴇ ⓸ ɢʙ ᴊᴄʙ. ❊ rest
Meals 120 (lunch)/160 ⓨ – ☕ 85 – **114 rm** 990/1350, 14 suites.   FYZ g

West End, 31 promenade des Anglais ℰ 04 92 14 44 00, *Fax 04 93 88 85 07*, ≤, ☂ – ⧉, ⇤ rm, ▤ ⓉⓋ ☎ – ⚏ 120. ᴀᴇ ⓸ ɢʙ ᴊᴄʙ   FZ p
Meals 130/250 ⓨ – ☕ 70 – **126 rm** 850/1450, 4 suites.

Westminster Concorde, 27 promenade des Anglais ℰ 04 92 14 86 86, *Fax 04 93 82 45 35*, ☂ – ⧉, ▤ rm, ⓉⓋ ☎ – ⚏ 150. ᴀᴇ ⓸ ɢʙ ᴊᴄʙ. ❊   FZ m
Le Farniente (closed 15 November-15 December and Sunday from October-April) **Meals** 180 – ☕ 100 – **102 rm** 750/1500.

La Pérouse ⌂, 11 quai Rauba-Capéu ⊠ 06300 ℰ 04 93 62 34 63, *Fax 04 93 62 59 41*, ☂, « ≤ Nice and Baie des Anges », ⌧ – ⧉, ▤ rm, ⓉⓋ ☎. ᴀᴇ ⓸ ɢʙ ᴊᴄʙ. ❊ rest   HZ k
Meals grill (15 May-16 September) a la carte 250/350 ⓨ – ☕ 90 – **64 rm** 570/1490.

Mercure Centre Notre Dame Ⓜ without rest, 28 av. Notre-Dame ℰ 04 93 13 36 36, *Fax 04 93 62 61 69*, ≤, « Hanging garden on 2nd floor, ⌧ on 8th floor » – ⧉, ⇤ rm, ▤ ⓉⓋ ☎ ⅋ – ⚏ 25 - 120. ᴀᴇ ⓸ ɢʙ ᴊᴄʙ   FXY q
☕ 75 – **200 rm** 650/825.

Holiday Inn Ⓜ, 20 bd V. Hugo ℰ 04 97 03 22 22, *Fax 04 97 03 22 23*, ☂ – ⧉, ⇤ rm, ▤ ⓉⓋ ☎ ⅋ – ⚏ 90. ᴀᴇ ⓸ ɢʙ ᴊᴄʙ   FY a
Meals 155 (lunch), 178/240 ⓨ – ☕ 75 – **131 rm** 800/1250.

Atlantic, 12 bd V. Hugo ℰ 04 93 88 40 15, *Fax 04 93 88 68 60*, ☂ – ⧉, ⇤ rm, ▤ ⓉⓋ ☎ – ⚏ 50. ᴀᴇ ⓸ ɢʙ ᴊᴄʙ   FY d
Meals 120/130 ⓨ – ☕ 85 – **123 rm** 650/950.

Novotel, 8-10 Parvis de l'Europe ⊠ 06300 ℰ 04 93 13 30 93, *Fax 04 93 13 09 04*, ☂, « Panoramic rooftop swimming pool », ⌧ – ⧉, ⇤ rm, ▤ ⓉⓋ ☎ ⅋ ⇌ – ⚏ 80. ᴀᴇ ⓸ ɢʙ   JX v
Meals 115/150 ⓨ – ☕ 58 – **173 rm** 560/660.

Mercure Promenade des Anglais Ⓜ without rest, 2 r. Halévy ℰ 04 93 82 30 88, *Fax 04 93 82 18 20* – ⧉, ⇤ rm, ▤ ⓉⓋ ☎ – ⚏ 25. ᴀᴇ ⓸ ɢʙ   FZ v
☕ 85 – **122 rm** 690/975.

Frantour Napoléon without rest, 6 r. Grimaldi ℰ 04 93 87 70 07, *Fax 04 93 16 17 80* – ⧉ ▤ ⓉⓋ ☎. ᴀᴇ ⓸ ɢʙ ᴊᴄʙ   FZ r
☕ 65 – **83 rm** 655/980.

Mercure Masséna Ⓜ without rest, 58 r. Gioffredo ℰ 04 93 85 49 25, *Fax 04 93 62 43 27* – ⧉, ⇤ rm, ▤ ⓉⓋ ☎ ⇌. ᴀᴇ ⓸ ɢʙ ᴊᴄʙ   GZ k
☕ 75 – **106 rm** 610/890.

Petit Palais ⌂ without rest, 10 av. E. Bieckert ℰ 04 93 62 19 11, *Fax 04 93 62 53 60*, ≤ Nice and sea – ⧉ ▤ ⓉⓋ ☎. ᴀᴇ ⓸ ɢʙ ᴊᴄʙ   HX p
☕ 65 – **25 rm** 530/780.

Apogia Ⓜ without rest, 26 r. Smolett ⊠ 06300 ℰ 04 93 89 18 88, *Fax 04 93 89 16 06* – ⧉, ⇤ rm, ▤ ⓉⓋ ☎ ⅋ ⇌. ᴀᴇ ⓸ ɢʙ ᴊᴄʙ   JY e
☕ 55 – **101 rm** 580.

Grimaldi without rest, 15 r. Grimaldi ℰ 04 93 16 00 24, *Fax 04 93 87 00 24* – ⧉ ▤ ⓉⓋ ☎. ᴀᴇ ɢʙ   FY s
closed 19 to 26 December – ☕ 65 – **24 rm** 430/690.

Windsor, 11 r. Dalpozzo ℰ 04 93 88 59 35, *Fax 04 93 88 94 57*, ☂, ⌧, ⌧, ❃ – ⧉ ⓉⓋ ☎. ᴀᴇ ⓸ ɢʙ. ❊ rest   FZ f
Meals (coffee shop) (closed Saturday lunch and Sunday) a la carte approx. 200 – ☕ 40 – **57 rm** 525/700.

NICE

E
F
ST-MAURICE
St-BARTHÉLEMY
63
Bounin
St-Barthélemy
Av. de Brancola
Sqre R. Boyer
Av. Cyrille Besset
Av. de Valrose
Av. de Cyrnos
Boulevard
R. Michelet
Ste-Jeanne d'Arc
Bd de Gorbella
Av. de
Borriglione
Lambert
Caravadossi
Raynaud
Cessole
V
D
X
Rte de St-Pierre de Féric
Av. de
Pessicart
ST PAUL
Bd Joseph Garnier
R. A. Binet
Pl. Ch. de Gaulle
P.T.T.
Av. Comboul
C.F.P.
ST-ÉTIENNE Vernier
R. Malaussèna
R. Marcea
Av. Primerose
Arène
Parc Impérial
CATH. RUSSE ST-NICOLAS
ST-ÉTIENNE
Rue Trachel
NICE-VILLE
44
q
GARE TRAIN-AUTO
Bd du Tzarewitch
Thiers
N.-DAME
Av.
Gounod
Auber
Durante
Grosso
ST-PHILIPPE
d'Orves
P.T.T.
G.
Clemenceau
Y
d'Estienne
de Châteauneuf
Av. Rossini
ST-PHILIPPE
LA BUFFA
n A
a
d
57
12
g
Victor Hugo
s
Z
Av. des Fleurs
3
Joffre
François
Gambetta
k
r
LES BAUMETTES
65 n
SACRÉ-CŒUR
f
France
U
45
Dante
MUSÉE DES BEAUX ARTS
Av. des Baumettes
Bd
R.
France
ST-PIERRE D'ARÈNE
M4
P
V
CASINO RUHL
d
84
d
k p m
ANGLAIS
de
PROMENADE DES
F
BAIE
DES
ÎLE STE-MARGUERITE
D
E
F

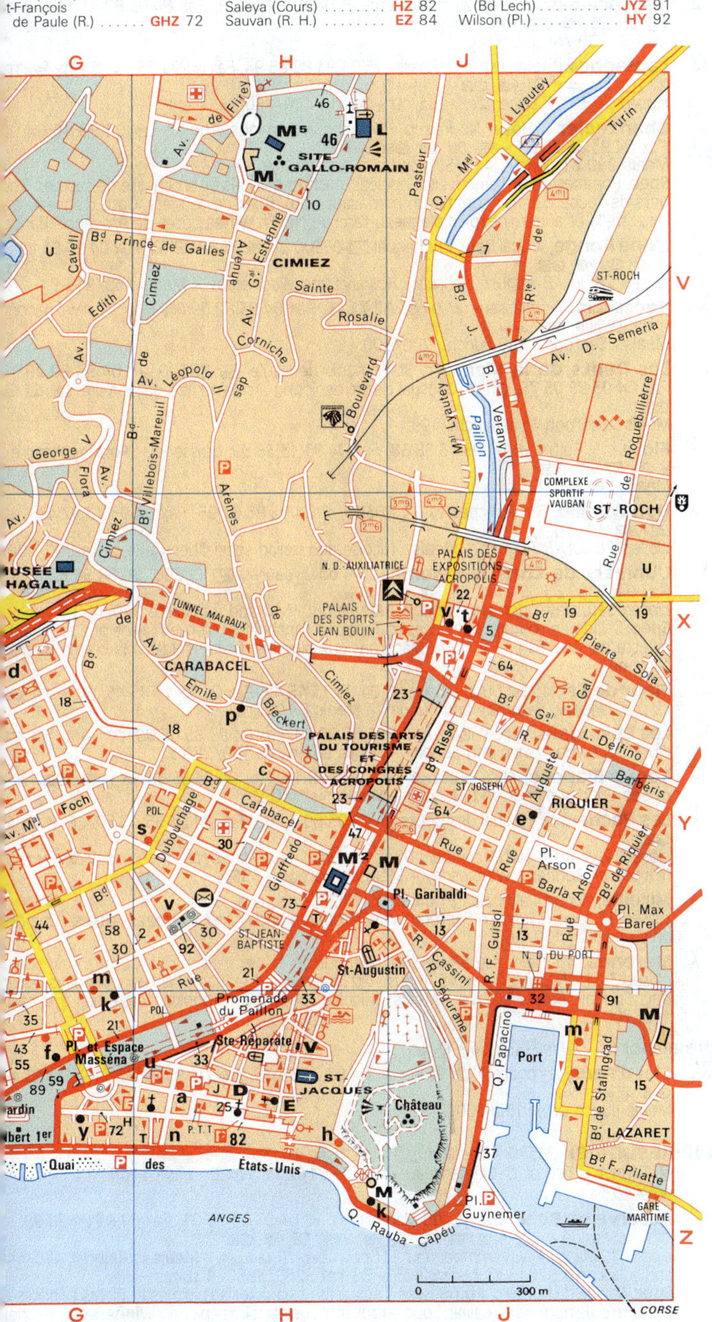
épublique (Av. de la) . JXY 64
ivoli (R. de) . . . . FZ 65
t-François
de Paule (R.) . . . . . GHZ 72
St-Jean Baptiste
(Av.) . . . . HY 73
Saleya (Cours) . . . . . . HZ 82
Sauvan (R. H.) . . . . EZ 84
Verdun (Av.de) . . . . . . FGZ 89
Walesa
(Bd Lech) . . . . JYZ 91
Wilson (Pl.) . . . . HY 92

G
H
J

de Flirey
46
M 5
46
L
SITE
GALLO-ROMAIN
M
10
Pasteur
Q.
Mal.
Lyautey
Turin
4 m1
Rte. de
ST-ROCH
V
Bd. Prince de Galles
U
Cavell
Edith
CIMIEZ
Sainte
Av.
Av. G. Estienne
Avenue
Rosalie
Bd. J.
Av. D. Semeria
George
Flora
Av.
Av. Léopold II
Corniche
des
Boulevard
Mal Lyautey
B. Verany
Paillon
COMPLEXE
SPORTIF
VAUBAN
ST-ROCH
Roquebillière
de
Cimiez
Bd. Villebois-Mareuil
Arènes
P
4 m2
3 m9
4 m2
2 m6
N. D. AUXILIATRICE
PALAIS DES
EXPOSITIONS
ACROPOLIS
4 m
Rue
Turin
U
MUSÉE
CHAGALL
TUNNEL MALRAUX
de
PALAIS
DES SPORTS
JEAN BOUIN
P
V
t
22
5
Bd. 19
19
19
Pierre
Sola
X
d
18
18
CARABACEL
Emile
Bleckert
Cimiez
p
64
Bd.
Gal.
Gal
L. Delfino
PALAIS DES ARTS
DU TOURISME
ET
DES CONGRÈS
ACROPOLIS
23
23
Bd. Risso
ST JOSEPH
R.
Auguste
Barbéris
RIQUIER
Foch
Av. Mal.
Dubouchage
POL.
Carabacel
Bd.
30
P
47
64
Rue
Pl.
Arson
Bd. de Riquier
Y
s
Bd.
Giofredo
M 2
M
e
Barla
Rue Arson
Pl. Max
Barel
V
73
30
92
St-Jean
Baptiste
T
Pl. Garibaldi
13
R. F. Guisol
13
N. D. DU PORT
44
58
2
St-Augustin
R. Cassini
R. Ségurane
m
Rue
21
Promenade
du Paillon
33
35
k
POL.
32
91
m
M
21
Pl. et Espace
Masséna
Ste-Réparate
Papacino
Q.
Port
43
f
u
33
V
55
89
59
ST
JACQUES
V
15
jardin
y
72
H
T
n
P. T. T.
82
Château
h
Bd. de Stalingrad
Bd. F. Pilatte
LAZARET
bert 1er
a
J
D
25
E
t
37
Quai
P
des
États-Unis
M
k
Pl.
Guynemer
P
GARE
MARITIME
ANGES
Q. Rauba - Capéu
Z

0
300 m
CORSE

G
H
J

Régence without rest, 21 r. Masséna ℘ 04 93 87 75 08, Fax 04 93 82 41 31 – 🛗 🖪
📺 ☎. AE ① GB JCB
☕ 35 – **39 rm** 335/380.
FZ

Lausanne without rest, 36 r. Rossini ℘ 04 93 88 85 94, Fax 04 93 88 15 88 – 🛗, ⤬ rm
🖪 📺 ☎ 🚗. AE ① GB
FY
closed 20 to 27 December – ☕ 40 – **36 rm** 400/450.

XXXX **Chantecler** - Hôtel Négresco, 37 promenade des Anglais ℘ 04 93 16 64 00
❀❀ Fax 04 93 88 35 68 – 🖪. AE ① GB JCB
FZ
Meals 290 b.i. (lunch), 415/590 and a la carte 430/650
Spec. Pommes de terre nouvelles poêlées, anchois marinés et brochette de supions. Rou-
gets de roche cuisinés comme un nem, sauce aux foies de rougets. Côte d'agneau à
mozzarella et aubergine, pied d'agneau farci de cèpes. **Wines** Côtes-de-Provence, Bando

XXX **L'Ane Rouge,** 7 quai Deux-Emmanuel ✉ 06300 ℘ 04 93 89 49 63, Fax 04 93 89 49 6
– 🖪. AE ① GB
JZ r
closed 28 July-8 August, February Holidays and Wednesday – **Meals** 158/258 ♀.

XX **Boccaccio,** 7 r. Masséna ℘ 04 93 87 71 76, Fax 04 93 82 09 06, 🌞, « Carvel decor
– 🖪. AE ① GB JCB
GZ
Meals - Seafood - 145 (lunch), 200/300.

XX **Les Dents de la Mer,** 2 r. St-François-de-Paule ✉ 06300 ℘ 04 93 80 99 1
Fax 04 93 85 05 78, 🌞, « Unusual decor depicting a submerged galleon » – 🖪. AE ①
GB
HZ
Meals - Seafood - 148 (lunch)/199.

XX **Flo,** 4 r. S. Guitry ℘ 04 93 13 38 38, Fax 04 93 13 38 39, brasserie, « Former theatre
– 🖪. AE ① GB
GYZ r
Meals 119 b.i./159 b.i..

XX **Don Camillo,** 5 r. Ponchettes ✉ 06300 ℘ 04 93 85 67 95, Fax 04 93 13 97 43 – 🖪
AE GB
HZ
closed 26 July-8 August, – **Meals** - Niçoise and Italian specialities - a la carte 200/300.

XX **L'Univers de Christian Plumail,** 54 bd J. Jaurès ✉ 06300 ℘ 04 93 62 32 22
❀ Fax 04 93 62 55 69 – 🖪. AE ① GB JCB
HZ
closed Saturday lunch and Sunday – **Meals** 180/310 and a la carte 220/400 ♀
Spec. Salade de rougets de roches et fenouil à l'anchoïade. Morue fraîche aux artichauts
galette de stockfish à l'ail doux. Macarons aux pignons, fruits rouges à la crème de mas
carpone.

XX **Fleur de Sel,** 10 bd Dubouchage ℘ 04 93 13 45 45, Fax 04 93 13 45 45, 🌞 – 🖪. GB
closed January, Saturday and Sunday – **Meals** 83/150 ♀.
HY

XX **Les Épicuriens,** 6 pl. Wilson ℘ 04 93 80 85 00, Fax 04 93 85 65 00, 🌞 – 🖪. ① GB
closed Saturday lunch and Sunday – **Meals** a la carte 190/270 ♀.
HY

XX **Toque Blanche,** 40 r. Buffa ℘ 04 93 88 38 18, Fax 04 93 88 38 18 – 🖪. GB FZ
closed Sunday dinner and Monday – **Meals** 145/160 ♀.

X **Les Pêcheurs,** 18 quai des Docks ℘ 04 93 89 59 61, Fax 04 93 55 47 50, 🌞 – 🖪. A
GB
JZ
closed November-mid December, Thursday lunch from May-October, Tuesday dinner fron
November-April and Wednesday – **Meals** - Seafood - 155.

X **Mireille,** 19 bd Raimbaldi ℘ 04 93 85 27 23 – 🖪. GB
GX
closed 13 June-6 July, 26 September-5 October, Monday and Tuesday – **Meals** - One dis
only : paella - 150/160.

X **Merenda,** 4 r. Terrasse ✉ 06300, (without ℘) – 🖪
HZ
closed 3 to 19 April, 24 July-15 August, 20 December-4 January, February Holidays, Satur
day, Sunday, Bank Holidays – **Meals** - Niçoise specialities - (booking essential) a la cart
160/200 ♀.

at the airport : 7 km – ✉ 06200 Nice :

XXX **Ciel d'Azur,** aérogare 1, 2e étage ℘ 04 93 21 36 36, Fax 04 93 21 35 31 – 🖪. AE
GB JCB
Meals (lunch only) 130/300 ♀.

Beaulieu-sur-Mer 06310 Alpes-Mar. **84** ⑩ – pop. 4 013.
🛈 Tourist Office pl. G.-Clémenceau ℘ 04 93 01 02 21, Fax 04 93 01 44 04.
Nice 10.

🏰 **Réserve de Beaulieu** ⟡, bd Mar. Leclerc ℘ 04 93 01 00 01, Fax 04 93 01 28 99, ⟨
❀❀ 🌞, « Seaside », 🏊 – 🛗, 🖪 rm, 📺 ☎ 🚗. AE ① GB
closed 12 March-7 Novermber and 23 December-10 January – **Meals** 280 (lunch), 420/640
and a la carte 520/680 ♀ – ☕ 125 – **33 rm** 3250/3850, 4 suites
Spec. Salade de homard aux pousses d'épinards et panisses au parmesan. Pistes à l'encre e
petit farçi de pomme au caviar. Loup au bellet rouge et poires épicées. **Wines** Bellet, Bandol

St-Martin-du-Var 06670 Alpes-Mar. 84 ⑨, 115 ⑯ – *pop. 1869 alt. 110.*
Nice 26.

XXXX ❀❀ **Jean-François Issautier,** on Nice road (N 202) 3 km ℘ 04 93 08 10 65, *Fax 04 93 29 19 73* – ▤ P. AE Ⓞ GB
closed 11 to 20 October, 3 January-2 February, Sunday except lunch from 15 September-21 June and Monday – **Meals** *270 b.i./540 and a la carte 420/590*
Spec. Grosses crevettes en robe de pommes de terre sur une salade de chou frisé. Petit "capoun" et pied de cochon en persillade à la truffe écrasée (December-April). "Tournedos" de lapin fermier en barigoule d'artichauts violets. **Wines** Côtes de Provence, Bellet.

Vence 06140 Alpes-Mar. 84 ⑨, 115 ㉕ – *pop. 15 330 alt. 325.*
🛈 *Tourist Office, pl. Grand-Jardin* ℘ 04 93 58 06 38, *Fax 04 93 58 91 81.*
Nice 23.

XXX ❀❀ **Jacques Maximin,** 689 chemin de La Gaude, by road of Cagnes : 3 km ℘ 04 93 58 90 75, *Fax 04 93 58 22 86,* 🌳, 🚗 – P. AE GB
closed 8 November-9 December, Monday except Bank Holidays and Sunday dinner – **Meals** *(booking essential) 240 (lunch), 350/550 and a la carte 460/710*
Spec. Salade de pigeonneau du Lauragais au riz paëlla et chorizo Jabugo. "Fritto-misto" de homard, "chips légumiers", coulis tomaté et orangé. Poissons du pays rôtis à la niçoise.
Wines Bellet.

STRASBOURG 67000 B.-Rhin 62 ⑩ – *pop. 252 338 alt. 143.*
See : Cathedral★★★ : Astronomical clock★ – La Petite France★★ : rue du Bains-aux-Plantes★★ HJZ – Barrage Vauban ☀★★ – Ponts couverts★ – Place de la Cathédrale★ KZ 26 : Maison Kammerzell★ KZ **e** – Mausoleum★★ in St-Thomas Church JZ – Place Kléber★ – Hôtel de Ville★ KY **H** – Orangery★ – Palais de l'Europe★ – Museum of Oeuvre N.-Dame★★ KZ **M'** – Boat trips on the Ill river and the canals★ KZ – Museums★★ (decorative Arts, Fine Arts, Archeology) in the Palais Rohan★ KZ – Alsatian Museum★★ KZ **M²** – Historical Museum★ KZ **M³** – Museum of Modern Art★ KZ – Guided tours of the Port★ by boat.

🚩 🚩 🚩 at Illkirch-Graffenstaden (private) ℘ 03 88 66 17 22 ; 🏴 of the Wantzenau at Wantzenau (private) ℘ 03 88 96 37 73 ; N by D 468 : 12 km ; 🏴 of Kempferhof at Plobsheim ℘ 03 88 98 72 72, S by D 468 : 15 km.
✈ of Strasbourg International : ℘ 03 88 64 67 67 by D 392 : 12 km FR.
🚗 ℘ 08 36 35 35 35.
🛈 Tourist Office 17 pl. de la Cathédrale ℘ 03 88 52 28 28, Fax 03 88 52 28 29, pl. gare ℘ 03 88 32 51 49, Pont de l'Europe ℘ 03 88 61 39 23 – Automobile Club, 5 av. Paix ℘ 03 88 36 04 34, Fax 03 88 36 00 63.
Paris 490 – Basle 145 – Bonn 360 – Bordeaux 915 – Frankfurt 218 – Karlsruhe 81 – Lille 545 – Luxembourg 223 – Lyons 485 – Stuttgart 157.

Plans on following pages

🏨 **Régent Petite France** M 🐟, 5 r. Moulins ℘ 03 88 76 43 43, *Fax 03 88 76 43 76,* ⋘, 🌳, « Former ice factory on the banks of River Ill - contemporary decor », 🏋 – 🛗, ✳ rm, ▤ TV ☎ 🖑 🚗 – 🔔 30. AE ⓄD GB JCB   JZ **z**
Meals *(closed Monday from June-September and week ends from October-May) 160/300* ♀ – ☲ 90 – **63 rm** 1150/1550, 5 suites, 4 duplex.

🏨 **Hilton,** av. Herrenschmidt ℘ 03 88 37 10 10, *Fax 03 88 36 83 27,* 🌳 – 🛗, ✳ rm, ▤ TV ☎ 🖑 P – 🔔 25 - 300. AE ⓄD GB JCB
Jardin ℘ 03 88 35 72 61 **Meals** *159 (lunch), /182* ♀ – ☲ 95 – **241 rm** 1200/1600, 6 suites.

🏨 **Sofitel** M, pl. St-Pierre-le-Jeune ℘ 03 88 15 49 00, *Fax 03 88 15 49 99,* 🌳, patio – 🛗, ✳ rm, ▤ TV ☎ 🚗 – 🔔 120. AE ⓄD GB JCB   JY **s**
L'Alsace Gourmande ℘ 03 88 15 49 10 **Meals** *155/230* ♀ – ☲ 105 – **153 rm** 1350/1550.

🏛 **Régent Contades** M without rest, 8 av. Liberté ℘ 03 88 15 05 05, *Fax 03 88 15 05 15,* « 19C mansion » – 🛗, ✳ rm, TV ☎. AE ⓄD GB JCB   LY **f**
☲ 90 – **45 rm** 1150/1590.

🏛 **Beaucour** M without rest, 5 r. Bouchers ℘ 03 88 76 72 00, *Fax 03 88 76 72 60,* « Old Alsatian houses elegantly decorated » – 🛗 ▤ TV ☎ 🖑 – 🔔 30. AE ⓄD GB   KZ **k**
☲ 65 – **49 rm** 550/950.

🏛 **Holiday Inn,** 20 pl. Bordeaux ℘ 03 88 37 80 00, *Fax 03 88 37 07 04,* 🏋, ⊠ – 🛗, ✳ rm, ▤ TV ☎ 🖑 P – 🔔 450. AE ⓄD GB JCB
Meals *150* ♀ – ☲ 85 – **170 rm** 980/1250.

🏛 **Maison Rouge** without rest, 4 r. Francs-Bourgeois ℘ 03 88 32 08 60, *Fax 03 88 22 43 73,* « Tasteful decor » – 🛗 TV ☎ 🖑 – 🔔 50. AE ⓄD GB   JZ **g**
☲ 65 – **142 rm** 560/600.

STRASBOURG

Abreuvoir (R. de l') .... **LZ** 3
Arc-en-Ciel (R. de l') ... **KLY** 7
Austerlitz (R. d') ..... **KZ** 10
Auvergne (Pont d') .... **LY** 12
Bateliers (R. des) ...... **LZ** 14
Bonnes-Gens (R. des) ... **JY** 19
Boudier (R. du) .... **JZ** 20
Castelnau (R. Gén. de) .. **KY** 25
Cathédrale (Pl. de la) ... **KZ** 26
Chaudron (R. du) ...... **KY** 28
Cheveux (R. des) ...... **JZ** 29
Corbeau (Pl. du) ...... **KZ** 31

Cordiers (R. des) .... **KZ** 32
Courtine (R. de la) ...... **LY** 34
Dentelles (R. des) ...... **JZ** 36
Division-Leclerc (R.) ..... **JKZ**
Écarlate (R. de l') ...... **JZ** 43
Escarpée (R.) .... **JZ** 45
Étudiants (R. et Pl. des)... **KY** 46
Faisan (Pont du) .... **JZ** 47
Fossé-des-Tanneurs
  (Rue du) .... **JZ** 57
Fossé-des-Treize (R. du) .. **KY** 58
Francs-Bourgeois
  (R. des) .... **JZ** 60
Frey (Q. Charles) .... **JZ** 63
Gdes-Arcades (R. des) ... **JKY**

Grande-Boucherie
  (Pl. de la) .... **KZ** 76
Gutenberg (R.) .... **JKZ** 78
Haute-Montée (R.) ..... **JY** 82
Homme-de-Fer (Pl. de l') . **JY** 90
Hôpital-Militaire (R. de l') . **LZ** 91
Humann (R.) .... **HZ** 94
Ill (Quai de l') .... **HZ** 95
Kellermann (Quai) ..... **JY** 10
Kléber (Place) .... **JY**
Krutenau (Rue de la) .... **LZ** 10
Kuss (Pont) .... **HY** 10
Lamey (R. Auguste) .... **LY** 10
Lezay-Marnésia (Quai) ... **LY** 11
Luther (R. Martin) ...... **JZ** 11

For maximum information from town plans: consult the conventional signs key.

Monopole-Métropole without rest, 16 r. Kuhn ℰ 03 88 14 39 14
Fax 03 88 32 82 55, « Alsatian and contemporary decor » – |‡|, ⊱ rm, TV ☎ ⇌. A
ⓞ GB JCB
HY
⊆ 65 – **90 rm** 450/770.

Europe without rest, 38 r. Fossé des Tanneurs ℰ 03 88 32 17 88, *Fax 03 88 75 65 4*
« Half timbered Alsatian house, beautiful 1/50th copy of the Cathedral » – |‡|, ⊱ rn
TV ☎ ⇌ – 🛦 30. AE ⓞ GB JCB
JZ
closed 23 to 29 December – ⊆ 49 – **61 rm** 410/630.

France without rest, 20 r. Jeu des Enfants ℰ 03 88 32 37 12, *Fax 03 88 22 48 08* – |‡|
⊱ rm, TV ☎ ⇌ – 🛦 30. AE ⓞ GB
JY
⊆ 65 – **66 rm** 490/720.

Novotel Centre Halles M, 4 quai Kléber ℰ 03 88 21 50 50, *Fax 03 88 21 50 51* – |‡|
⊱ rm, 🗏 TV ☎ ⅙ – 🛦 80. AE ⓞ GB
JY
Meals a la carte approx. 190 – ⊆ 59 – **98 rm** 695.

Mercure Centre M without rest, 25 r. Thomann ℰ 03 88 75 77 88
Fax 03 88 32 08 66 – |‡|, ⊱ rm, 🗏 TV ☎ ⅙ ⇌. AE ⓞ GB JCB
JY
⊆ 59 – **98 rm** 595/690.

Grand Hôtel without rest, 12 pl. Gare ℰ 03 88 52 84 84, *Fax 03 88 52 84 00* – |‡| 🗏
☎. AE ⓞ GB
HY r
⊆ 65 – **85 rm** 395/660.

Cathédrale M without rest, 12 pl. Cathédrale ℰ 03 88 22 12 12, *Fax 03 88 23 28 00*
« In front of the Cathedral » – |‡| 🗏 TV ☎. AE ⓞ GB JCB
KZ
⊆ 55 – **47 rm** 450/790, 3 duplex.

des Rohan without rest, 17 r. Maroquin ℰ 03 88 32 85 11, *Fax 03 88 75 65 37* – |‡|
⊱ rm, TV ☎. AE ⓞ GB JCB
KZ
⊆ 52 – **36 rm** 410/795.

Dragon M without rest, 2 r. Ecarlate ℰ 03 88 35 79 80, *Fax 03 88 25 78 95* – |‡|, ⊱ rn
TV ☎. AE ⓞ GB JCB. ⌇
JZ
closed 23 to 27 December – ⊆ 62 – **32 rm** 430/705.

Dauphine without rest, 30 r. 1e Armée ℰ 03 88 36 26 61, *Fax 03 88 35 50 07* – |‡| 🗏
☎ ⇌. AE ⓞ GB JCB
closed 23 December-3 January – ⊆ 45 – **45 rm** 390/580.

Couvent du Franciscain without rest, 18 r. Fg de Pierre ℰ 03 88 32 93 93
Fax 03 88 75 68 46 – |‡| TV ☎ ⅙ P. AE ⓞ GB
JY
closed 24 December-9 January – ⊆ 46 – **43 rm** 290/340.

Pax, 24 r. Fg National ℰ 03 88 32 14 54, *Fax 03 88 32 01 16*, 🌿 – |‡|, ⊱ rm, TV
⅙ ⇌ – 🛦 25. AE ⓞ GB JCB – *closed 24 December-3 January* – **Meals** *(closed Sunda*
from November-February) 90/130 ♀ – ⊆ 40 – **106 rm** 370/410.
HYZ

Continental without rest, 14 r. Maire Kuss ℰ 03 88 22 28 07, *Fax 03 88 32 22 25*
|‡| TV ☎. AE ⓞ GB. ⌇
HY
closed 1 to 7 January – ⊆ 36 – **48 rm** 310/340.

XXXX
❀❀❀ **Au Crocodile** (Jung), 10 r. Outre ℰ 03 88 32 13 02, *Fax 03 88 75 72 01*, « Elegar
decor » – 🗏. AE ⓞ GB. ⌇
KY
closed 12 July-2 August, 24 to 30 December, 1 to 6 January, Sunday and Monday – Mea
295 (lunch), 430/660 and a la carte 450/650 ♀
Spec. Sandre et queues d'écrevisses aux quenelles de carpe. Lobe de foie de canard truff
cuit tel un baeckeoffe. Pampre au muscat d'Alsace en sorbet, crème aux noix. Wine
Riesling, Tokay-Pinot gris.

XXXX
❀❀❀ **Buerehiesel** (Westermann), set in the Orangery Park ℰ 03 88 45 56 65
Fax 03 88 61 32 00, ≤, « Reconstructed authentic Alsatian farmhouse with conservatory
– 🗏 P. AE ⓞ GB – *closed 3 to 18 August, 24 December-6 January, 21 February-2 March*
Tuesday and Wednesday – **Meals** 300 (lunch), 530/750 and a la carte 560/720 ♀
Spec. Hors d'œuvres choisis. Schniederspaetle et cuisses de grenouille poêlées au cerfeu
Canard braisé et caramélisé aux épices, semoule de blé dur, légumes au bouillon. Wine
Riesling, Pinot gris.

XXX
Maison Kammerzell and H. Baumann M with rm, 16 pl. Cathédral
ℰ 03 88 32 42 14, *Fax 03 88 23 03 92*, « Attractive 16C Alsatian house » – |‡|, 🗏 rn
TV ☎ – 🛦 80. AE ⓞ GB
KZ
accommodation : closed in February – **Meals** 177/295 and a la carte 190/370 ♀ – ⊆ 5
– **9 rm** 420/630.

XXX
❀ **Vieille Enseigne** (Langs), 9 r. Tonneliers ℰ 03 88 32 58 50, *Fax 03 88 75 63 80* – 🗏
AE ⓞ GB JCB
KZ
closed Saturday lunch and Sunday – **Meals** 185 (lunch), 275/395 and a la carte 340/460 ♀
Spec. Langoustines royales rôties en gaufrettes de pomme de terre. Filets de rouget
grillés et fleur de courgette en beignet. Croustillant de caille désossée façon "pastilla"
Wines Tokay-Pinot gris, Pinot blanc.

XXX **Zimmer,** 8 r. Temple Neuf ℘ 03 88 32 35 01, *Fax 03 88 32 42 28* – ▤. 𝖠𝖤 ⓓ
GB   KY y
closed 4 to 18 August, 24 December-3 January and Sunday – **Meals** 180/280 ♀.

XXX **Maison des Tanneurs dite "Gerwerstub",** 42 r. Bain aux Plantes
℘ 03 88 32 79 70, *Fax 03 88 22 17 26,* « Old Alsatian house on the banks of the River
Ill » – 𝖠𝖤 ⓓ GB   JZ t
closed 19 July-9 August, 30 December-20 January, Sunday and Monday – **Meals** a la carte
260/350.

XXX **Estaminet Schloegel,** 19 r. Krütenau ℘ 03 88 36 21 98, *Fax 03 88 36 21 98* – ▤.
𝖠𝖤 GB   LZ q
closed 1 to 22 August, Saturday lunch and Sunday – **Meals** 130 (lunch), 180/300 and a
la carte 200/220 ♀.

XX **Julien,** 22 quai Bateliers ℘ 03 88 36 01 54, *Fax 03 88 35 40 14* – ▤. 𝖠𝖤 GB   KZ x
❀ *closed Sunday and Monday* – **Meals** 195 (lunch)/425 and a la carte 310/430 ♀
Spec. Escalopes de foie gras poêlées aux coings et chasselas. Croustillants de filets de
perche aux navets salés et foie gras poêlé. Noisettes de chevreuil d'Alsace au poivre girofle.
Wines Riesling, Pinot noir.

XX **Au Boeuf Mode,** 2 pl. St-Thomas ℘ 03 88 32 39 03, *Fax 03 88 21 90 80,* 🍽 – 𝖠𝖤 GB
closed Sunday – **Meals** 150/200 ♀.   JZ k

XX **Pont des Vosges,** 15 quai Koch ℘ 03 88 36 47 75, *Fax 03 88 25 16 85,* 🍽 – 𝖠𝖤
GB   LY h
closed Saturday lunch, Sunday and Bank Holidays – **Meals** a la carte 180/300 ♀.

XX **Buffet de la Gare,** pl. Gare ℘ 03 88 32 68 28, *Fax 03 88 32 88 34* – 𝖠𝖤 ⓓ GB HY r
Meals 68/150 ♨.

X **Ami Schutz,** 1 r. Ponts Couverts ℘ 03 88 32 76 98, *Fax 03 88 32 38 40,* 🍽 – 𝖠𝖤 ⓓ
GB   HZ r
Meals 185 b.i./210 b.i..

X **Au Rocher du Sapin,** 6 r. Noyer ℘ 03 88 32 39 65, *Fax 03 88 75 60 99,* 🍽, brasserie
– GB   JY f
closed Sunday except December – **Meals** 90/125 ♀.

VINSTUBS : *Regional specialities and wine tasting in a typical Alsatian atmosphere :*

X **S'Burjerstuewel (Chez Yvonne),** 10 r. Sanglier ℘ 03 88 32 84 15,
Fax 03 88 23 00 18 – 𝖠𝖤 GB   KYZ r
closed 15 July-15 August, 20 December-2 January, Monday lunch and Sunday – **Meals**
(booking essential) a la carte 130/260 ♨.

X **Le Clou,** 3 r. Chaudron ℘ 03 88 32 11 67, *Fax 03 88 75 72 83* – ▤. 𝖠𝖤 GB   KY n
closed Wednesday lunch, Sunday and Bank Holidays – **Meals** a la carte 170/300 ♀.

X **S'Muensterstuewel,** 8 pl. Marché aux Cochons de Lait ℘ 03 88 32 17 63,
Fax 03 88 21 96 02, 🍽 – 𝖠𝖤 ⓓ GB   KZ y
closed 1 to 21 August, February Holidays, Sunday and Monday – **Meals** 128 b.i. (lunch)/198
b.i. ♀.

X **Zum Strissel,** 5 pl. Gde Boucherie ℘ 03 88 32 14 73, *Fax 03 88 32 70 24,* rustic decor
– ▤. GB   KZ a
closed 2 to 29 July, February Holidays, Sunday and Monday – **Meals** 64/135 ♀.

X **Au Pont du Corbeau,** 21 quai St-Nicolas ℘ 03 88 35 60 68, *Fax 03 88 25 72 45* – ▤.
GB   KZ b
closed August, February Holidays, Sunday lunch and Saturday – **Meals** a la carte approx.
180 ♀.

X **Fink'Stuebel,** 26 r. Finkwiller ℘ 03 88 25 07 57, *Fax 03 88 22 11 05* – GB   JZ x
closed 9 to 29 August, 31 January-13 February, Sunday dinner and Monday – **Meals**
118/158 ♀.

X **Petite Mairie,** 8 r. Brûlée ℘ 03 88 32 83 06, *Fax 03 88 32 83 06* – GB   KY d
closed 1 to 24 August, February Holidays, Saturday dinner and Sunday – **Meals** 90 (lunch),
110/165 ♀.

Environs

t La Wantzenau *NE by D 468 : 12 km – pop. 4 394 alt. 130 –* ✉ 67610 :

🏨 **Hôtel Au Moulin** 🌜, S : 1,5 km by D 468 ℘ 03 88 59 22 22, *Fax 03 88 59 22 00,* ≼,
« Old watermill on a branch of the River Ill », 🌿 – ⎹§⎸ 📺 ☎ 🅿. 𝖠𝖤 GB
closed 24 December-2 January – **Meals** see rest. *Au Moulin* below – ⌸ 58 – **20 rm**
360/475.

🏠 **Roseraie** without rest, 32 r. Gare ℘ 03 88 96 63 44, *Fax 03 88 96 64 95* – 📺 ☎ 🅿. GB
closed 23 December-3 January – ⌸ 38 – **15 rm** 260/300.

XXX **Relais de la Poste** M with rm, 21 r. Gén. de Gaulle ℘ 03 88 59 24 80, Fax 03 88 59 24 89, 🐀, « Attractive Alsatian decor » – 🛗, 🍽 rest, 📺 ☎ ⚕ 🅿 🆎 ⓘ GB
closed 26 July-8 August, 2 to 22 January, Saturday lunch, Sunday dinner and Monday except Bank Holidays – **Meals** 175 (lunch), 235/420 and a la carte 290/490 ♀ – ☷ 50 – **19 rm** 350/650.

XXX **A la Barrière** (Sutter), 3 rte Strasbourg ℘ 03 88 96 20 23, Fax 03 88 96 25 59, 🐀 🅿 🆎 ⓘ GB JCB
🕸 closed 10 to 31 August, February Holidays, Tuesday dinner and Wednesday – **Meals** (Sunday : booking essential) 150 (lunch)/260 and a la carte 290/440 ♀
Spec. Streusel croustillant d'escargots au poireau. Escalope de foie d'oie chaud et poire confite au gewztraminer. Lièvre à la royale (November-January). **Wines** Riesling.

XXX **Zimmer,** 23 r. Héros ℘ 03 88 96 62 08, Fax 03 88 96 37 40, 🐀 – 🆎 ⓘ GB
closed 18 July-3 August, 17 January-5 February, Sunday dinner and Monday – Meals 140/330 and a la carte 200/350 ♀.

XX **Rest. Au Moulin** - Hôtel Au Moulin, S : 1,5 km by D 468 ℘ 03 88 96 20 01, Fax 03 88 68 07 97, 🐀, « Floral garden » – 🍽 🅿 🆎 ⓘ GB JCB
closed 5 to 26 July, 31 December-17 January, Sunday dinner and dinner Bank Holidays – **Meals** 140/395 ♀.

XX **Les Semailles,** 10 r. Petit-Magmod ℘ 03 88 96 38 38, Fax 03 88 96 38 38, 🐀 – GB
closed 10 to 23 August, Sunday dinner and Monday – **Meals** 110/245 ♀.

Baerenthal 57 Moselle 57 ⑱ – pop. 723 alt. 220 – ✉ 57230 Bitche.
Strasbourg 64.

at Untermuhthal SE : 4 km by D 87 – ✉ 57230 Baerenthal :

XXX **L'Arnsbourg** (Klein), ℘ 03 87 06 50 85, Fax 03 87 06 57 67, 🚗 – 🍽 🅿 🆎 ⓘ GB
🕸🕸 closed 30 August-16 September, January, Tuesday and Wednesday – **Meals** (weekend booking essential) 210/455 and a la carte 370/490
Spec. Grenouilles aux herbes et coriandre. Carré de porcelet au foin (June-September). Filet de chevreuil (November-January). **Wines** Sylvaner, Muscat.

Illhaeusern 68970 H.-Rhin 62 ⑲ – pop. 578 alt. 173.
Strasbourg 60.

🏨 **Clairière** M 🛏 without rest, rte Guémar ℘ 03 89 71 80 80, Fax 03 89 71 86 22, 🛁 – 🛗, 🚭 rm, 📺 ☎ 🅿 GB
closed January and February – ☷ 80 – **25 rm** 460/1150.

XXXXX **Auberge de l'Ill** (Haeberlin), ℘ 03 89 71 89 00, Fax 03 89 71 82 83, « Elegant installation, on the banks of the River Ill, ≤ floral gardens » – 🍽 🅿 🆎 ⓘ GB
🕸🕸🕸 closed 1 February-7 March, Monday and Tuesday – **Meals** (booking essential) 520 (lunch) 630/750 and a la carte 500/670 ♀
Spec. Salade de tripes aux fèves et foie d'oie. Timbale de sole et de homard "Edouard Weber". Volaille de Bresse rôtie à la broche et petit ""baeckaoffa" aux truffes. **Wines** Sylvaner, Pinot blanc.
Hôtel des Berges M 🛏, ℘ 03 89 71 87 87, Fax 03 89 71 87 88, ≤, « Resembling tobacco shed in the Ried country », 🚗 – 🛗, 🚭 rm, 📺 ☎ ⚕ 🚗 🆎 ⓘ GB
closed February, Monday and Tuesday – **Meals** see **Aub. de l'Ill** – ☷ 130 – **11 rm** 1500/1750.

Lembach 67510 B.-Rhin 57 ⑲ – pop. 1 710 alt. 190.
🛈 Tourist Office 23 rte Bitche ℘ 03 88 94 43 16, Fax 03 88 94 20 04.
Strasbourg 55.

XXXX **Auberge du Cheval Blanc** (Mischler), 4 rte Wissembourg ℘ 03 88 94 41 86, 🕸🕸 Fax 03 88 94 20 74, « Old coaching inn », 🚗 – 🍽 🅿 🆎 ⓘ GB
closed 5 to 23 July, 31 January-25 February, Monday and Tuesday – **Meals** 185/450 and a la carte 290/450 ♀
Spec. Soupière feuilletée d'escargots au pied de veau et orge perlée. Farandole de quatre foies d'oie chauds. Médaillons de dos de chevreuil à la moutarde de fruits rouges (15 May-late February). **Wines** Riesling, Pinot blanc.

Marlenheim 67520 B.-Rhin 62 ⑨ – pop. 2 956 alt. 195.
Strasbourg 20.

🏨 **Cerf** (Husser), ℘ 03 88 87 73 73, Fax 03 88 87 68 08, 🐀, « Flowered inn » – 🍽 rest, 🕸🕸 📺 ☎ 🅿 🆎 ⓘ GB
closed Tuesday and Wednesday – **Meals** 250 b.i. (lunch), 295/600 and a la carte 350/460 ♀ – ☷ 65 – **17 rm** 285/850
Spec. Presskopf de tête de veau poêlée en croustille. Choucroute au cochon de lait et foie gras fumé. Aumônière aux griottines et glace au fromage blanc. **Wines** Riesling, Pinot noir.

Plans on following pages

Tours *37000 I.-et-L.* **64** ⑮ *– pop. 129 509 alt. 60.*

See : *Cathedral quarter★★ : Cathedral★★ CDY, Fine Arts Museum★★ CDY, Historial de Touraine★ (Château) CY M³, The Psalette★ CY, – Place Grégoire de Tours★ DY 46 – Old Tours★★ : Place Plumereau★ ABY, Hôtel Gouin★ BY, rue Briçonnet★ AY 12 – St-Julien quarter★ : Craft Guilds Museum★★ (Musée du Compagnonnage) BY, Beaune-Semblançay Garden★ BY B – St-Cosme Priory★ W : 3 km V – Museum of military transport and trains★ V M⁶ – Meslay Tithe Barn★ (Grange de Meslay) NE : 10 km par ②.*

ſ₁₈ *of Touraine* ℰ *02 47 53 20 28, domaine de la Touche at Ballan-Miré : 14 km ;* ſ₁₈ *of Ardrée* ℰ *02 47 56 77 38 : 14 km.*

✈ *of Tours-St-Symphorien* ℰ *02 47 49 37 00, NE : 7 km.*

🛈 *Tourist Office 78 r. Bernard Palissy* ℰ *02 47 70 37 37, Fax 02 47 61 14 22 – A.C. 4 pl. J. Jaurès* ℰ *02 47 05 50 19, Fax 02 47 05 47 61.*

Paris 234 – Angers 109 – Bordeaux 346 – Chartres 140 – Clermont-Ferrand 335 – Limoges 220 – Le Mans 80 – Orléans 115 – Rennes 219 – St-Étienne 474.

Jean Bardet Ⓜ ⤳, *57 r. Groison* ⊠ *37100* ℰ *02 47 41 41 11, Fax 02 47 51 68 72,* ≤, « Flowered park, attractive kitchen garden », ⣇ – ▤ ⊺⊽ ☎ Ⓟ – ⚒ *30.* ⒶⒺ ⓄⒹ ⒼⒷ ⒿⒸⒷ
Meals *(closed Monday except dinner from April-October and Sunday dinner from November-March) 250/750 and a la carte 450/730* ♀ – ⌑ *120 –* **16 rm** *750/1400, 5 suites*
Spec. Pannequet de jeunes légumes primeurs, fleurette d'herbes truffées. Fricassée de petites anguilles, pommes de terre rattes écrasées à l'ail, jus au vinaigre de bourgueil. Dessert fascination. **Wines** Vouvray, Bourgueil.

Univers, *5 bd Heurteloup* ℰ *02 47 05 37 12, Fax 02 47 61 51 80,* « Murals depicting famous past visitors » – |≣|, ⟵ *rm,* ▤ ⊺⊽ ☎ ⴺ ⌂ – ⚒ *20 - 120.* ⒶⒺ ⓄⒹ ⒼⒷ ⒿⒸⒷ
Touraine : **Meals** *140/180* ♀ – ⌑ *70 –* **77 rm** *710/860, 8 suites.*   CZ u

Holiday Inn Ⓜ, *15 r. Ed. Vaillant* ℰ *02 47 31 12 12, Fax 02 47 38 53 35,* ⴺ₅ – |≣|, ⟵ *rm,* ▤ ⊺⊽ ☎ ⴺ ⌂ – ⚒ *50.* ⒶⒺ ⓄⒹ ⒼⒷ ⒿⒸⒷ   DZ m
Meals *90 b.i./110 –* ⌑ *60 –* **105 rm** *550.*

Harmonie ⤳ *without rest, 15 r. F. Joliot-Curie* ℰ *02 47 66 01 48, Fax 02 47 61 66 38* – |≣| kitchenette ⊺⊽ ☎ ⴺ ⌂ – ⚒ *40.* ⒶⒺ ⓄⒹ ⒼⒷ ⒿⒸⒷ   DZ b
closed 20 December-5 January, Friday, Saturday and Sunday from November-March – ⌑ *55 –* **54 rm** *475/550.*

Quality Turone Ⓜ, *4 pl. Thiers* ℰ *02 47 05 50 05, Fax 02 47 20 22 07* – |≣|, ⟵ *rm,* ▤ ⊺⊽ ☎ ⴺ ⌂ – ⚒ *70.* ⒶⒺ ⓄⒹ ⒼⒷ
Meals *78 (lunch), 98/160 b.i. –* ⌑ *57 –* **120 rm** *430/550.*

Royal Clarine *without rest, 65 av. Grammont* ℰ *02 47 64 71 78, Fax 02 47 05 84 62* – |≣| ⊺⊽ ☎ ⴺ ⌂ – ⚒ *35.* ⒶⒺ ⓄⒹ ⒼⒷ
closed 27 December-4 January – ⌑ *39 –* **50 rm** *298/355.*

Manoir *without rest, 2 r. Traversière* ℰ *02 47 05 37 37, Fax 02 47 05 16 00* – |≣| ⊺⊽ ☎ Ⓟ. ⒶⒺ ⓄⒹ ⒼⒷ   CZ h
⌑ *30 –* **20 rm** *240/320.*

Mirabeau *without rest, 89 bis bd Heurteloup* ℰ *02 47 05 24 60, Fax 02 47 05 31 09* – |≣| ⊺⊽ ☎ ⌂. ⒶⒺ ⒼⒷ ⒿⒸⒷ   DZ e
⌑ *35 –* **25 rm** *220/310.*

Holiday Inn Express Ⓜ, *247 r. Giraudeau* ℰ *02 47 37 00 36, Fax 02 47 38 50 91* – |≣|, ⟵ *rm,* ⊺⊽ ☎ ⴺ Ⓟ – ⚒ *40.* ⒶⒺ ⓄⒹ ⒼⒷ ⒿⒸⒷ
Meals *75 b.i./99* ♀ – ⌑ *30 –* **48 rm** *370.*

Charles Barrier, *101 av. Tranchée* ⊠ *37100* ℰ *02 47 54 20 39, Fax 02 47 41 80 95,* 🌿 – ▤ Ⓟ. ⒶⒺ ⓄⒹ ⒼⒷ
closed Sunday dinner – **Meals** *150/470 and a la carte 350/500* ♀
Spec. Pied de cochon farci aux ris d'agneau et aux truffes. Suprême de géline de Touraine en papillote. Matelote d'anguille au chinon et aux pruneaux. **Wines** Montlouis, Bourgueil.

La Roche Le Roy *(Couturier), 55 rte St-Avertin* ⊠ *37200* ℰ *02 47 27 22 00, Fax 02 47 28 08 39,* 🌿 – Ⓟ. ⒶⒺ ⓄⒹ ⒼⒷ
closed 31 July-23 August, 2 to 11 January, February Holidays, Saturday lunch, Sunday dinner and Monday – **Meals** *160 (lunch), 220/350 and a la carte 270/420* ♀
Spec. Fricassée de homard à l'escargot. Dos de sandre rôti sur peau, beurre blanc et pain d'épice. Ris de veau braisé aux morilles. **Wines** Vouvray, Chinon.

Ruche, *105 r. Colbert* ℰ *02 47 66 69 83, Fax 02 47 20 41 76* – ▤. ⒼⒷ   CY a
closed Christmas Holidays, Sunday dinner and Monday – **Meals** *90/150* ⸙.

L'Arc-en-Ciel, *2 pl. Aumônes* ℰ *02 47 05 48 88, Fax 02 47 66 94 05* – ⒶⒺ ⓄⒹ ⒼⒷ   CZ v
closed Sunday dinner and Monday – **Meals** *88/230* ♀.

Rif, *12 av. Maginot* ⊠ *37100* ℰ *02 47 51 12 44* – ⒶⒺ ⒼⒷ
closed August, Sunday dinner and Monday – **Meals** *North-African rest. a la carte 140/170.*

TOURS

EUROPE on a single sheet Michelin Map no **970**.

LOIRE
Av. André Malraux
Pont Mirabeau
A. Blanqui
Château
Pl. des Turones
R. des Maures
R. des A. Thomas
SAINT-PIERRE VILLE
Pl. Foire-le-Roi
LA PSALETTE
CATHÉDRALE ST-GATIEN
ARCHIVES DÉPARTEMENTALES
Colbert
Pl. de la Cathédrale
Rue
Rue
Lobin
R. des Cordeliers
R. de la Barre
MUSÉE DES BEAUX-ARTS
Avisseau
F. Clouet
Voltaire
GRAND THÉÂTRE
Scellerie
Pl. Fr. Sicard
Rue des
St-Michel
Ursulines
Rue
R. Mirabeau
R. Gutenberg
la Zola
Préfecture
Rue
PARC MIRABEAU
Pl. de la Préfecture
HÔTEL DU DÉPARTEMENT
R. du Petit-
Mirabeau
de la
de
Rue
Traversière
Heurteloup
Pl. Loiseau d'Entraigues
Minimes
Centre International de Congrès Vinci
Palissy
Simon
Pré
Rempart
R. J.-J. Noirmant
des
Buffon
JARDIN DE LA PRÉFECTURE
H
B
JARDIN DU VINCI
Rue
du
Place Dublineau
Bordeaux
Pl. du Gén. Leclerc
Rue
M. Tribut
J.
Gille
Nantes
Rue
CENTRE ADMINISTRATIF
R. du Dr.
Ch.
Pl. des Aumones
V
m
Édouard
R. du Dr. Desnoyelle
Av. de Grammont
Michelet
Comte
Pl. F. Truffaut
Blaise
Pascal
Herpin
Vaillant
ST-ÉTIENNE
R. J.-B. Jacquemin
C. Desmoulins

FRANCE

at Rochecorbon *NE : 6 km by N 152 – alt. 58 –* ✉ *37210 :*

Les Hautes Roches Ⓜ, 86 quai Loire ℰ 02 47 52 88 88, Fax 02 47 52 81 30, ≤, 🌸
« Former troglodyte dwelling », 🌊, 🚤 – 🛗 ⅣV ☎ 🅿 – 🔒 15. 🅰🅴 ⓞ ⒼⒷ
closed late January-mid-March – **Meals** *(closed Monday except dinner in season (excep*
Bank Holidays) and Sunday dinner out of season) 215/280 *and a la carte* 320/410 ♀
☕ 85 – **15 rm** 650/1350
Spec. Foie gras frais de canard en terrine au vin du côteau. Dos de sandre grillé au beurr
blanc nantais (September-April). Tarte fine aux pommes caramélisées, rafraîchie au la
d'amande. **Wines** Vouvray, Saint-Nicolas-de-Bourgueil.

Onzain *41150 L.-et-Ch.* 🔢 ⑯ *– pop. 3 080 alt. 69.*
🏌 *Golf de la Carte at Chouzy-sur-Cisse* ℰ *02 54 33 42 43.*
Tours 47.

Domaine des Hauts de Loire Ⓜ 🐎, NW : 3 km by D 1 and private lan
ℰ 02 54 20 72 57, Fax 02 54 20 77 32, 🌸, « Elegant hunting lodge in a park », 🌊, 🏊
– ⅣV ☎ 🅖 🅿 – 🔒 70. 🅰🅴 ⓞ ⒼⒷ. 🚫
March-November – **Meals** *(closed Tuesday lunch and Monday in November)* (booking esser
tial) 315/650 *and a la carte* 370/670 ♀ – ☕ 95 – **25 rm** 950/1500, 10 suites
Spec. Salade d'anguille croustillante à la vinaigrette d'échalotes. Pigeonneau rôti, jus c
presse aux noisettes torréfiées. Soufflé au citron vert. **Wines** Touraine Mesland.

Romorantin-Lanthenay *41200 L.-et-Ch.* 🔢 ⑱ *– pop. 17 865 alt. 93.*
🏢 *Tourist Office 32 pl. Paix* ℰ *02 54 76 43 89, Fax 02 54 76 96 24.*
Tours 91.

Grand Hôtel du Lion d'Or Ⓜ, 69 r. Clemenceau ℰ 02 54 94 15 1∫
Fax 02 54 88 24 87, 🌸, « Tasteful decor, flowered patio » – 🛗 ▤ ⅣV ☎ 🅖 🚗 – 🔒 5
🅰🅴 ⓞ ⒼⒷ
closed mid February-mid March – **Meals** (booking essential) 420/630 *and a la cart*
510/670 ♀ – ☕ 110 – **13 rm** 700/1900, 3 suites
Spec. Cuisses de grenouilles à la rocambole. Langoustines bretonnes rôties à la graine c
paradis. Fraises "Mara" des bois confites au lait glacé (June-October). **Wines** Pouilly Fum
Bourgueil.

Germany
Deutschland

PRACTICAL INFORMATION

LOCAL CURRENCY

Deutsche Mark: *100 DEM = 51,13 euros (€)*

TOURIST INFORMATION

Deutsche Zentrale für Tourismus (DZT):
Beethovenstr. 69, 60325 Frankfurt, ☎ (069) 97 46 40, Fax (069) 75 19 03

Hotel booking service:
Allgemeine Deutsche Zimmerreservierung (ADZ)
Corneliusstr. 34, 60325 Frankfurt, ☎ (069) 74 07 67
Fax (069) 75 10 56

National Holiday in Germany: *3 Octobre.*

AIRLINES

DEUTSCHE LUFTHANSA AG: *☎ (01803) 803803, Fax (0561) 9933115*
AIR CANADA: *☎ (069) 27 11 51 11, Fax (069) 27 11 51 12*
AIR FRANCE: *☎ (0180) 5 36 03 70, Fax (069) 23 05 81*
AMERICAN AIRLINES: *☎ (01803) 242 324, Fax (069) 230 461*
BRITISH AIRWAYS: *☎ (0180) 340 340, Fax (0421) 55 75189*
JAPAN AIRLINES: *☎ (0180) 22 28 700, Fax (069) 29 57 84*
AUSTRIAN SWISSAIR SABENA: *☎ (0180) 52 58 520, Fax (0180) 52 21 591*

FOREIGN EXCHANGE

In banks, savings banks and at exchange offices.
Hours of opening from Monday to Friday 8.30am to 12.30pm and 2.30pm to 4pm except Thursday 2.30pm to 6pm.

SHOPPING

In the index of street names, those printed in red are where the principal shops are found.

BREAKDOWN SERVICE

ADAC: *for the addresses see text of the towns mentioned*
AvD: *Lyoner Str. 16, 60528 Frankfurt-Niederrad, ☎ (069) 6 60 60, Fax (069) 660 67 89*
In Germany the ADAC (emergency number (01802) 22 22 22), and the AvD (emergency number (0130) 99 09), make a special point of assisting foreign motorists. They have motor patrols covering main roads.

TIPPING

In Germany, prices include service and taxes. You may choose to leave a tip if you wish but there is no obligation to do so.

SPEED LIMITS

The speed limit, generally, in built up areas is 50 km/h - 31 mph and on all other roads it is 100 km/h - 62mph. On motorways and dual carriageways, the recommended speed limit is 130 km/h - 80 mph.

SEAT BELTS

The wearing of seat belts is compulsory for drivers and all passengers.

BERLIN

L Berlin 416 418, I 23, 24 – 3 500 000 Ew – Höhe 40 m.

Frankfurt/Oder 105 – Hamburg 289 – Hannover 288 – Leipzig 183 – Rostock 222.

🛈 Berlin Tourismus Marketing GmbH – Information at Europa-Center (Budapester Straße), ✉ 10787 ✆ (030) 25 00 25, Fax (030) 25 00 24 24, and information in Brandenburer Tar (side-wing).

ADAC, Berlin-Wilmersdorf, ✉ 10717, Bundesallee 29-30, ✆ (030) 8 68 60, Fax (030) 86 16 025.

🏌 Berlin-Wannsee, Golfweg 22, ✆ (030) 8 06 70 60 – Berlin-Gatow, Kladower Damm 182, ✆ (030) 3 65 76 60 – Gross Kienitz (S : 23 km), ✆ (033708) 53 70 – Kallin (NW : 32 km), an der B273, ✆ (033230) 89 40 – Mahlow (S : 20 km), Kiefernweg, ✆ (033379) 37 05 95 – Potsdam (W : 38 km), Tremmener Landstraße, ✆ (033233) 8 02 44 – Seddiner See (SW : 37 km), Zum Weicher 44, ✆ (033205) 73 20 – Stolper Heide (N : 20 km), Frohnauer Weg 3, ✆ (03303) 54 90.

✈ Berlin-Tegel EX, ✆ (030) 4 10 11
✈ Berlin-Schönefeld (S : 25 km), ✆ (030) 6 09 10
✈ Berlin-Tempelhof GZ, ✆ (030) 69 51 29 88
Deutsche Lufthansa City Center, Kurfürstendamm 220, ✆ (030) 88 75 38 00, Fax (030) 88 75 38 01

🚗 Berlin-Wannsee, Nibelungenstraße.
Exhibition Centre (Messegelände am Funkturm) BU, ✆ (030) 3 03 80, Fax (030) 30 38 23 25.

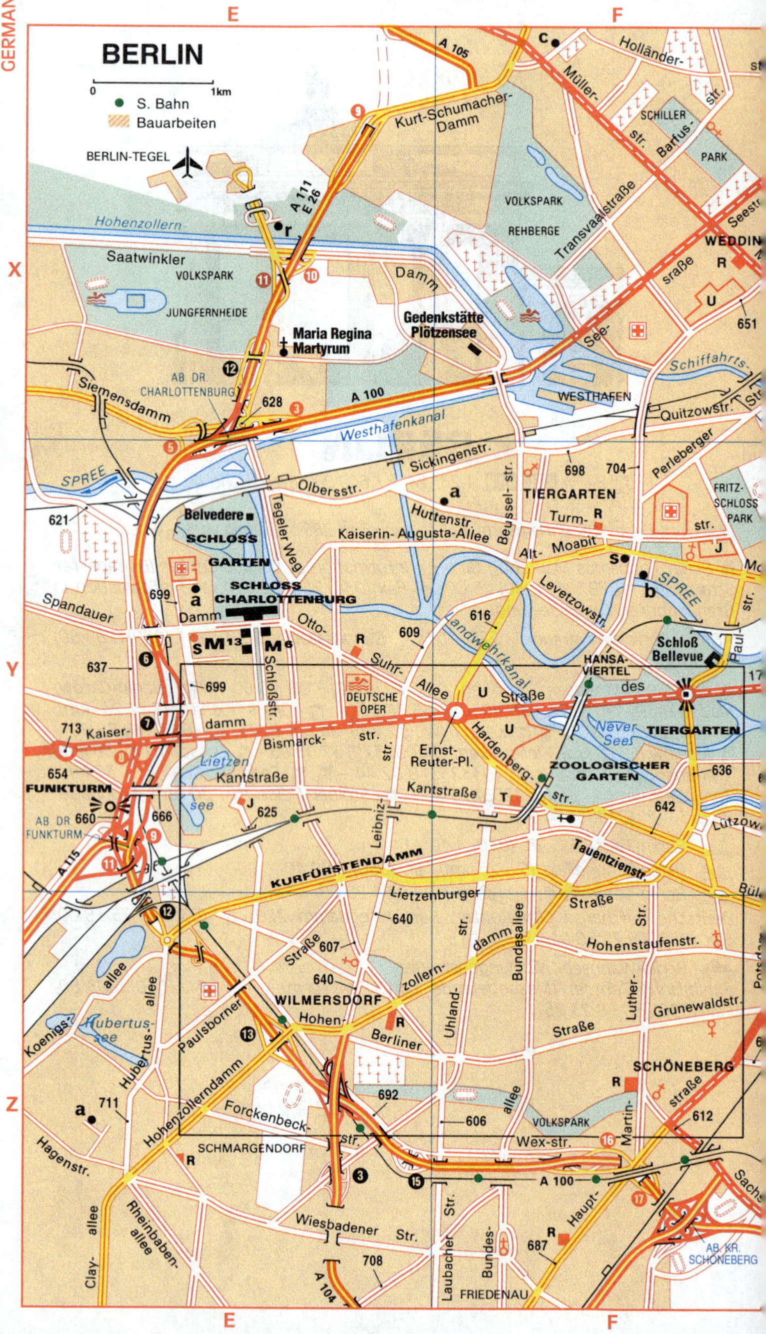

BERLIN
0 1km
S. Bahn
Bauarbeiten
BERLIN-TEGEL
A 105
Holländer-
Müller-
Kurt-Schumacher-Damm
SCHILLER
Barfus-
str.
PARK
str.
A 111
E 26
Hohenzollern-
Saatwinkler
VOLKSPARK
Damm
VOLKSPARK
REHBERGE
Transvaalstraße
Seestr.
WEDDIN
straße
R
JUNGFERNHEIDE
U
651
Maria Regina
Martyrum
Gedenkstätte
Plötzensee
Schiffahrts-
AB. DR.
CHARLOTTENBURG
A 100
WESTHAFEN
Siemensdamm
628
Westhafenkanal
Quitzowstr.
SPREE
Sickingenstr.
698
704
Perleberger
Olbersstr.
a
Beussel-str.
TIERGARTEN
FRITZ-
SCHLOSS
PARK
621
Huttenstr.
Turm-
R
Belvedere
Kaiserin-Augusta-Allee
Alt- Moabit
J
SCHLOSS
Tegeler Weg
S
GARTEN
SPREE
699
a
b
SCHLOSS
CHARLOTTENBURG
616
Schloß
Bellevue
Spandauer
Damm
Otto-
609
Landwehrkanal
Paul-
17
637
S M 13 M 6
Suhr-
R
HANSA-
VIERTEL
des
Schloßstr.
Allee
U Straße
TIERGARTEN
699
DEUTSCHE
OPER
Hardenberg-
Never
Sees
713 Kaiser-
damm
Bismarck-
str.
Ernst-
Reuter-Pl.
U
654
str.
ZOOLOGISCHER
GARTEN
636
FUNKTURM
Lietzen-
Kantstraße
Kantstraße
str.
642
AB. DR.
FUNKTURM
660
666
see
J 625
Leibniz-
T
Lützow-
A 115
KURFÜRSTENDAMM
Tauentzienstr.
Bül-
Lietzenburger
Straße
Str.
allee
640
Hohenstaufenstr.
allee
Straße
607
damm
Bundesallee
Luther-
Grunewaldstr.
Koenigs
Hubertus-
see
640
WILMERSDORF
Hohen-
R
zollern-
Uhland-
Straße
SCHÖNEBERG
Paulsborner
Berliner
str.
R
711
a
Hohenzollerndamm
Forckenbeck-
692
VOLKSPARK
straße
612
SCHMARGENDORF
606
Wex-str.
16
Martin-
Hagenstr.
R
str.
A 100
17
AB. KR.
SCHÖNEBERG
Clay-
allee
Rheinbaben-
allee
Wiesbadener
Str.
Laubacher
Str.
Bundes-
R
687
Haupt-
Sachs
708
FRIEDENAU
A 104

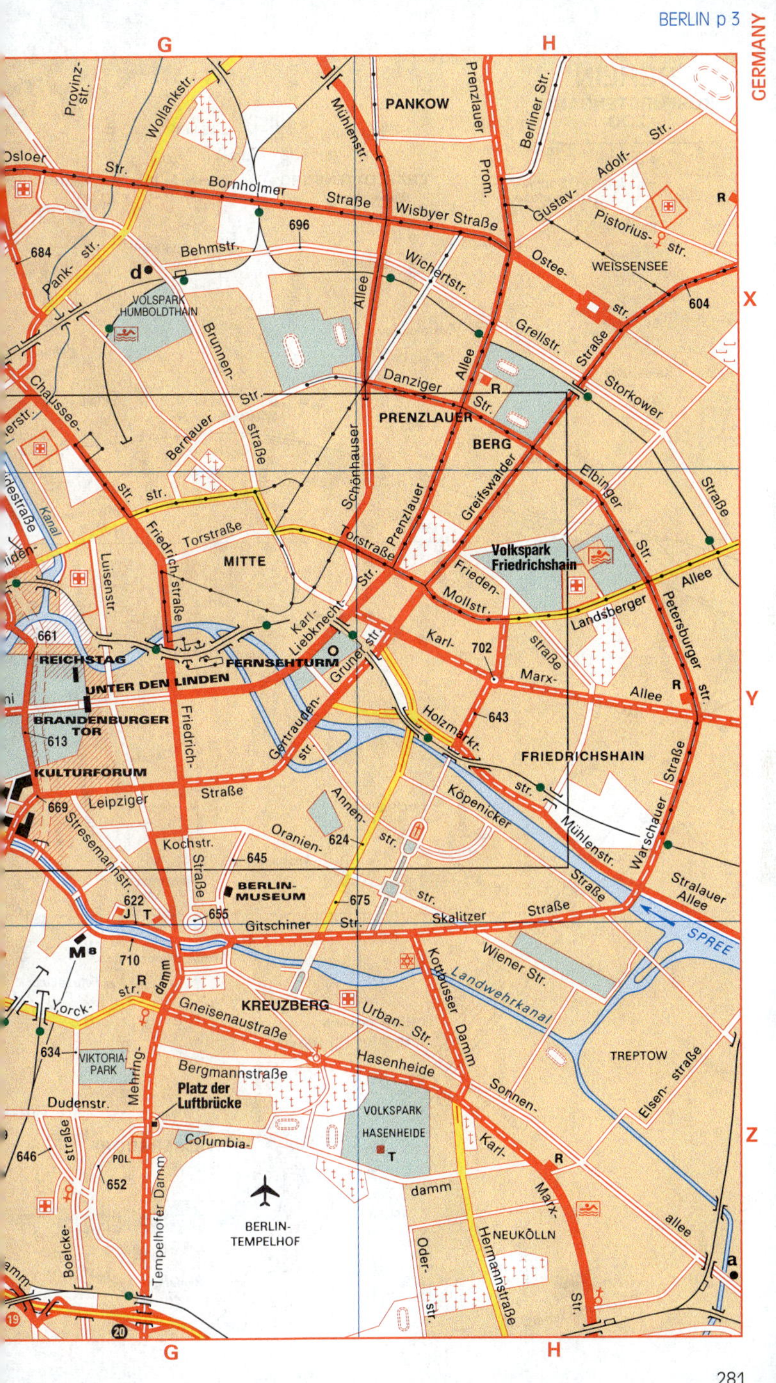

BERLIN p 3
GERMANY
G
H
PANKOW
Provinz-str.
Wollankstr.
Mühlenstr.
Prenzlauer Prom.
Berliner Str.
Adolf-
Str.
Osloer
Str.
Bornholmer
Straße
Wisbyer Straße
Gustav-
Pistorius-str.
R
WEISSENSEE
696
Pank-str.
Behmstr.
Wichertstr.
Ostee-
str.
604
X
684
VOLSPARK
HUMBOLDTHAIN
Brunnen-
Allee
Grellstr.
Straße
Storkower
Chaussee-
Bernauer
straße
Danziger
Str.
R
Schönhauser
PRENZLAUER
Greifswalder
Elbinger
Straße
str.
str.
Torstraße
BERG
Prenzlauer
Str.
Landsberger
Allee
Friedrichstraße
MITTE
Torstraße
Frieden-
Volkspark
Friedrichshain
Luisenstr.
Karl-
Liebknecht-
Mollstr.
Karl-
702
straße
Petersburger str.
661
Gruner-str.
Marx-
Allee
R
Y
REICHSTAG
FERNSEHTURM
Holzmarkt-
643
UNTER DEN LINDEN
Friedrich-
FRIEDRICHSHAIN
BRANDENBURGER
TOR
613
Gertrauden-
str.
Köpenicker
str.
Warschauer Straße
KULTURFORUM
Straße
Annen-
Mühlenstr.
Stralauer
Allee
669
Leipziger
Stresemannstr.
Oranien-
624
str.
SPREE
Kochstr.
645
BERLIN-
MUSEUM
675
str.
Skalitzer
Straße
622
J T
655
Gitschiner
Str.
Wiener Str.
710
str. R damm
KREUZBERG
Urban-Str.
Landwehrkanal
Kottbusser Damm
M 8
Yorck-
Gneisenaustraße
Hasenheide
Sonnen-
TREPTOW
634
VIKTORIA-
PARK
Bergmannstraße
Elsen-straße
Dudenstr.
Mehringdamm
Platz der
Luftbrücke
VOLKSPARK
HASENHEIDE
T
Karl-
646
straße
Columbia-
R
POL
652
damm
Marx-
allee
Tempelhofer Damm
BERLIN-
TEMPELHOF
NEUKÖLLN
Hermannstraße
Oder-
a
Boelcke-
damm
Str.
19
20
G
H

GERMANY
BERLIN
KURFÜRSTENDAMM
ZOO
0   400 m
S.Bahn
J
K
X
Y
Z
CHARLOTTENBURG
Zillestraße
a
DEUTSCHE OPER
Deutsche Oper
Otto-
Fraunho
609
T
A
Zillestraße
Leibnizstr.
Suhr-
Bismarckstr.
Kaiser-
R-Wagner-
R-
SCHILLER-
THEATER
Bismarck-
str.
Bismarckstraß
Sophie-
Charlotte-
Pl.
Schloßstr
Schillerstr.
Wilmersdorfer
Schillerstr.
Schlüterstr.
Kaiserdamm
Bismarck-
Sophie-Ch.-Pl.
Friedrich-
Wundt-
J
Pestalozzistr.
Krumme
Pestalozzis
LIETZENSEE PARK
Lietzen
Suarezstr.
Windscheidstraße
S
Kantstraße
Kantstraße
Kantstraße
Neue   Kantstraße
r
see
Amtsgerichts-
platz
Straße
e
Wilmersdorfer Str
SAVIGNYP
J
Leonhardtstr.
705
CHARLOTTENBURG
Straße
Mommsenstr.
Leibnizstr.
Mommsen
Suarezstr.
625
Rönne-
straße
Gervinusstr.
Dahlmannstr.
Drysenstr.
Lewishamstr.
Holtzendorff-
platz
Heilbronner Str.
Damaschke-
Adenauerpl.
Adenauerpl.
n
Schlüterstr.
e
g
Lietzenbu
Georg-Wilhelm-
Straße
Straße
str.
Xantener   Str.
Straße
KURFÜRSTENDAMM
Friedrich-
T
600
667
Brandenburgische
Düsseldorfer
Pariser   St
Straße
Straße
d
HALENSEE
Westfälische
Nestorstraße
Str.
Straße
Würtembergische
Sächsische
Emser
12
Joachim-
Hochmeister-
platz
Straße
Eisenzahnstraße
Konstanzer
Str.
PREUSSEN
PARK
BAB
Paulsborner
Grieser
Pl.
Stadtring
Seesener Straße
Konstanzer
Straße
Fehrbelliner Platz
Hohenzollernd
Straße
Fehrbelliner
Pl.
Brandenburgische S
Sigmaringer
Straße
Paulsborner
Straße
Cunostr.
HOHENZOLLERNDAMM
damm
Hohenzollerndamm
R
str.
Bar-
Blisses
13
Hohenzollern-
Rudolstädter
BAB Abzweig
Berliner
WILMERSDORF
Straße
Viktoria-
A 100
Str.
Bar-
VOLKSPARK
Mecklenburgische Straße
Auguste-
EISSTADION
STADION
Steglitz
Heidelbgr.
Pl.
Cunostraße
AB. KR.
WILMERSDORF
Forckenbeckstraße
HEIDELBERGER PL.

GERMANY
TECHNISCHE UNIVERSITÄT
Einsteinufer
CHARLOTTENBURGER TOR
Bach- str.
TIERGARTEN
TIERGARTEN
Altonaer Straße
Spreeweg
Siegessäule
st-Reuter-
Straße
des
17. Juni
Straße
17.
Juni
des
Großer Stern
Hofjägerallee
Straße
des
TIERGARTEN
t-Reuter
TECHNISCHE UNIVERSITÄT
Fasanenstr.
U
Landwehrkanal
Klingelhöferstr.
Tiergarten- str.
X
Hardenberg-
straße
U
ZOOLOGISCHER GARTEN
Stüler-str.
Stein- pl.
T
b
J
Zoolog. Gtn.
Aquarium
a
Budapester
Str.
M
e
P
gnypl.
Uhlandstr.
THEATER DES WESTENS
Kaiser-Wilhelm-Gedächtniskirche
k
Kurfürsten-
r
Lützowplatz
Kantstraße
s
c
Europa Center
t
693
s
b
Grolman-str.
e
m
Fasanenstr.
DAMM
707
z
d
Einemstraße
Uhlandstr.
n
630
Augsburger
Str.
d
603
str.
KURFÜRSTEN-
s
657
d
Joachimstaler Str.
676
Augsburger Str.
d
707
Wittenbergpl.
t
M
Lietzenburger
T
M
9
e
n
Nürnberger Str.
r
Lietzenburger Str.
Kleiststraße
str.
Schaper-
str.
Passauer Str.
Fugger-
s
str.
Nollendorfpf
Maaßenstr.
648
T
BUNDESHAUS
Spichernstraße
Motzstraße
Straße
wigkirch-platz
Meierottostr.
Ansbacher Str.
Geisbergstraße
Hohenstaufenstr.
Pariser Str.
Fasanen-
Spichernstr.
b
717
straße
Straße
Winterfeldt-platz
Uhland-
Hohenzollerndamm
Viktoria-Luise-Pl.
Hohenstaufenstr.
Münchener Str.
Bundesallee
Nachodstr.
Motzstr.
Landshuter Str.
Goltzstraße
Hohenzollernpl.
673
Aschaffenburger Str.
Bamberger Str.
Barbarossa-
straße
Eisenacher
Str.
Güntzelstr.
t
Prinzregentenstraße
Straße
Bayerischer Platz
Grunewaldstraße
Güntzel-
ADAC
straße
Luther-
Eisenacher Str.
Nassauische
Straße
Bayerischer Pl.
SCHÖNEBERG
Akazienstr.
Berliner Str.
Innsbrucker
Salzburger Str.
Belziger
Straße
Berliner
Badensche
Meraner
Straße
Kufsteiner
R
J
633
VOLKSPARK
Rathaus Schöneberg
Albertstr.
Am
Freiherr-vom-Stein-Str.
Martin
Hauptstraße
Dominicusstr.
Ebersstraße
Volkspark
WILMERSDORF
Fritz-Elsas-Str.
Str.
Heylstr.
L
M
N

BERLIN
UNTER DEN LINDEN

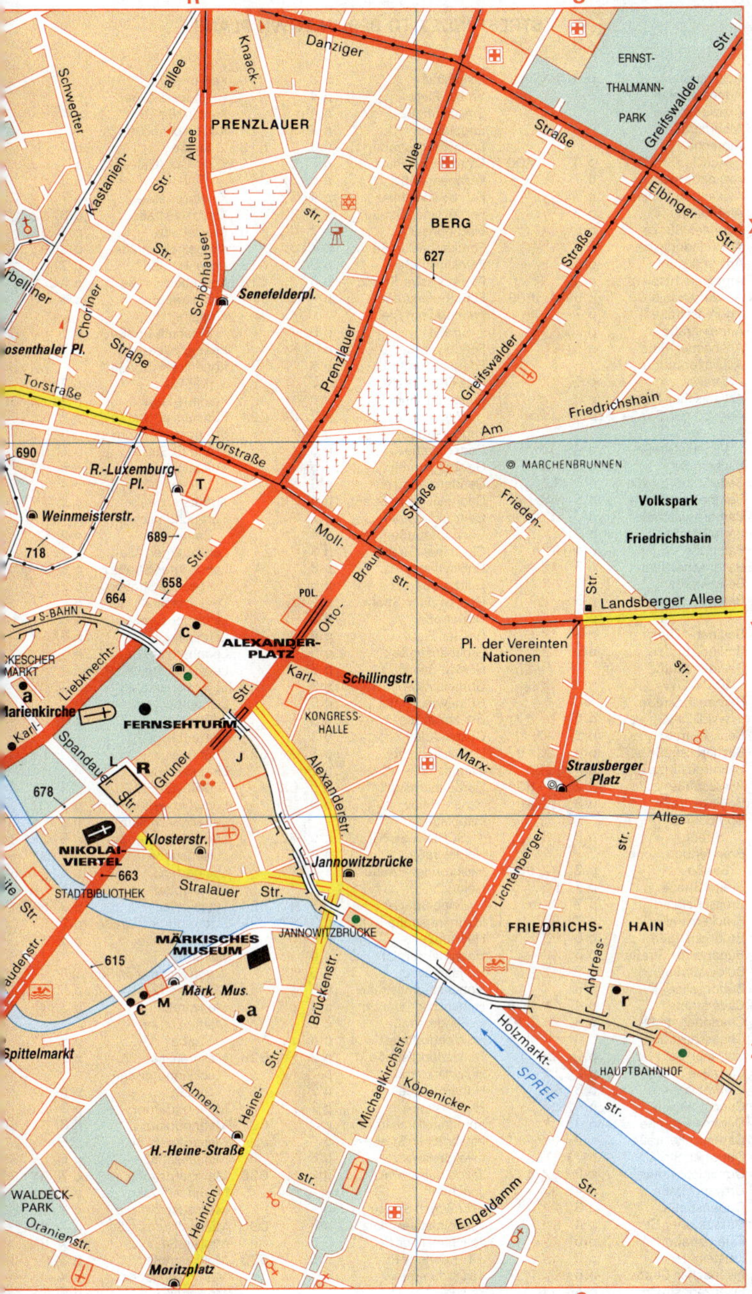

GERMANY
R
S
X
Y
Z
Schwedter
Kastanien-
Str.
Allee
Schönhauser
allee
Knaack-
Danziger
PRENZLAUER
ERNST-
THALMANN-
PARK
Greifswalder
Str.
Straße
Elbinger
Str.
BERG
627
Senefelderpl.
Straße
Choriner
fbelliner
osenthaler Pl.
Straße
Prenzlauer
Greifswalder
Str.
Straße
Straße
Torstraße
Am
Friedrichshain
Torstraße
MÄRCHENBRUNNEN
Volkspark
Friedrichshain
690
R.-Luxemburg-Pl.
T
Weinmeisterstr.
718
689
Moll-
Frieden-
Str.
658
664
Braun-
str.
Landsberger Allee
S-Bahn
POL.
Otto-
C
ALEXANDER-
PLATZ
Karl-
Schillingstr.
Pl. der Vereinten
Nationen
str.
ckescher
MARKT
a
Marienkirche
Str.
KONGRESS-
HALLE
Marx-
Karl-
FERNSEHTURM
Spandauer
Gruner
L
R
str.
J
Alexanderstr.
Strausberger
Platz
678
Klosterstr.
Allee
NIKOLAI-
VIERTEL
663
Stralauer
Str.
Jannowitzbrücke
Lichtenberger
str.
STADTBIBLIOTHEK
MÄRKISCHES
MUSEUM
Jannowitzbrücke
FRIEDRICHS-
HAIN
615
Andreas-
r
e Str.
Märk. Mus.
c M
a
Brückenstr.
Holzmarkt-
SPREE
str.
Spittelmarkt
HAUPTBAHNHOF
Annen-
Köpenicker
Str.
Heine-
Str.
Michaelkirchstr.
H.-Heine-Straße
Heinrich-
WALDECK-
PARK
str.
Engeldamm
Str.
Oranienstr.
Moritzplatz
R
S
285

STREET INDEX TO BERLIN TOWN PLANS

STREET INDEX TO BERLIN TOWN PLANS (Concluded)

SIGHTS

MUSEUMS, GALLERIES, COLLECTIONS

Museum Island (Museumsinsel)★★★ PY; *Pergamon-Museum; Collection of Antiquities (Antikensammlung)*★★★, *Altar of Pergamon (Pergamon-Altar)*★★★, *Gate to the Milet market (Markttor von Milet)*★★ – *Middle East Museum (Vorderasiatisches Museum)*★ – *Processional way and Gate of Ishtar (Prozessionsstraße und Ischtartor)*★★ – *National Gallery (Alte Nationalgalerie)*★★ **M¹** – *Bodemuseum* **M²**, *Egyptian Museum (Ägyptisches Museum)*★★, *Gallery of Paintings (Gemälde-galerie)*★ – *Old Museum (Altes Museum)*★★ **M³** — *Forum of Culture (Kulturforum)*★★★ NZ – *Museum of Decorative Arts (Kunstgewerbe-museum)*★★ NZ **M⁴**, *Guelph Treasure (Welfenschatz)*★★★, *Lüneburg Treasure (Lüneburger Ratssilber)*★★★ – *New National Gallery (Neue Nationalgalerie)*★★ NZ **M⁵** – *German Historiy Museum (Deutsches Historisches Museum; Zeughaus)* PY – *Friedrichswerdersche Church* PZ *(Schinkel-Museum)*★ – *Prussian State Library (Staatsbliothek preußischer Kulturbesitz)*★ NZ – *Dahlem Museums (Museumszentrum Dahlem)*★★★ *by Clayalle* EZ – *Gallery of Paintings (Germäldegalerie)*★★★, *Museum of Ethnography (Museum für Völkerkunde)*★★★ – *Museum of Moslem Art (Museum für islamische Kunst)*★★, *Museum of Indian Art (Museum für indische Kunst)*★★ – *Sculpture Gallery (Skulpturengalerie)*★★ – *Museum for German Folklore (Museum für Deutsche Volkskunde)*★ – *Scholß Charlottenburg*★★ EY: *Historical Rooms (Historische Räume)*★★ *Porcelain Room (Porzellan-Kabinett)*★★, *The Kronprinz's Silver (Kronprinzsilber)*★★ – *Knobelsdorff-wing (Knobelsdorff-Flügel)*★★ *Golden Gallery (Goldene Galerie)*★★, *Winter-kammer*★, *Gallery of Romanticism (Gallerie der Romantik)*★★ – *Museum of Pre- and Proto-History (Museum für Vor-und Frühgeschichte)*★ – *Collection Berggruen (Sammlung Berggruen)*★★ EY **M¹³** – *Bröhan Museum*★ EY **M¹³** – *Egyptian Museum (Ägyptisches Museum)*★★★ EY **M⁶** – *Schloßgarten*★★ *(Schinkel-Pavillon*★, *Belvedere*★, *Mausoleum*★*)* – *Museum of Contemporary Art (Museum für Gegenwart-Berlin)*★★ NX – *Museum of Natural History (Museum für Naturkunde)*★ NX – *German Museum of Technic (Deutsches Technik Museum)*★★ GZ **M⁸** – *Käthe-Kollwitz Museum*★ LXY **M⁹** – *Brücke Museum*★ BY **M³⁶** – *Brandenburg March Museum (Märkisches Museum)*★ RZ

PARKS, GARDENS, LAKES

Tiergarten★★ MX – *Zoological Park (Zoologischer Garten)*★★★ MX – *Wannsee*★★ *by Clay-Allee* EZ *(Volkspark Klein Glienicke*★★*)* – *Havel*★★ – *Peacook Island (Pfaueninsel)*★★ *by Clay-Allee* EZ – *Tegeler See*★★ *by Müllerstraße* FX – *Großer Müggelsee*★★ *by Stralauer Allee* HYZ – *Grunewald*★★ *by Clay-Allee* EZ *(Jagdschloß Grunewald*★ **M²⁸** – *Botanical Gardens (Botanischer Garten Dahlem)*★★ *by Rheinbabenallee* EZ

HISTORIC BUILDINGS, STREETS, SQUARES

Philharmonie★★★ NZ **T¹** – *Martin-Gropius-Building*★★ NZ – *Brandenburg Gate (Brandenburger Tor)*★★ NZ – *Reichstag*★ NY – *Unter den Linden*★★ NPZ – *Gendarmenmarkt*★★ PZ *German National Theatre (Schauspielhaus)*★★, *German Cathedral (Deutscher Dom)*★, *French Cathedral (Französischer Dom)*★ – *Arsenal (Zeughaus)*★★ PY – *Berliner Dom*★ PY – *Alexandersquare (Alexanderplatz)*★ RY – *St-Nicholas District (Nikolaiviertel)*★ RZ – *Friedrichstraße*★ PYZ – *Oranienburger Straße*★ PY – *Kunfürstendamm*★★ LXY *(Kaiser-Wilhlem-Gedächtniskirche*★*)* – *Olympic Stadium*★ *by Kaiserdamm* EY

GERMANY

Town Centre : Charlottenburg, Mitte, Schöneberg, Tiergarten, Wilmersdorf

Adlon, Unter den Linden 77, ⊠ 10177, ℘ (030) 2 26 10, Fax (030) 22612222, 👭, Massage ⒻⓈ, ⬅s, ⬛ – 🛗, ✳ rm, 🖳 TV 📞 & ⬥ – ⚓ 250. AE ⓞ Ⓔ VISA JCB. ✵ rest
NZ s
Meals à la carte 73/115 – **337 rm** ☕ 479/738 – 37 suites.

Grand Hyatt, Marlene-Dietrich-Platz 2, ⊠ 10785, ℘ (030) 25 53 12 34, Fax (030) 25531235, Massage, ⒻⓈ, ⬅s, ⬛ – 🛗, ✳ rm, 🖳 TV 📞 ⬥ – ⚓ 440. AE ⓞ Ⓔ VISA JCB. ✵
NZ a
Meals 89 and à la carte 58/98 – **340 rm** ☕ 465/690 – 15 suites.

Four Seasons, Charlottenstr. 49/at Gendarmenmarkt, ⊠ 10177, ℘ (030) 2 03 38, Fax (030) 20336166, Massage, ⬅s – 🛗, ✳ rm, 🖳 TV 📞 ⬥ – ⚓ 75. AE ⓞ Ⓔ VISA JCB. ✵ rest
PZ n
Seasons : Meals à la carte 55/90 – ☕ 446/717 – 42 suites.

Kempinski Hotel Bristol Berlin ⬧, Kurfürstendamm 27, ⊠ 10719, ℘ (030) 88 43 40, Fax (030) 8836075, 👭, Massage, ⬅s, ⬛ – 🛗, ✳ rm, 🖳 TV 📞 ⬥ – ⚓ 250. AE ⓞ Ⓔ VISA JCB. ✵ rest
LX n
Kempinski Grill (closed Monday and 4 weeks July - August) **Meals** à la carte 83/122 – **Kempinski-Eck** : Meals à la carte 41/63 – **301 rm** ☕ 399/628 – 29 suites.

Grand Hotel Esplanade, Lützowufer 15, ⊠ 10785, ℘ (030) 25 47 80, Fax (030) 2651171, (conference boat with own landing stage), « Modern hotel featuring contemporary art », Massage, ⒻⓈ, ⬅s, ⬛ – 🛗, ✳ rm, 🖳 TV 📞 ⬥ – ⚓ 260. AE ⓞ Ⓔ VISA JCB. ✵ rest
MX e
see also **Harlekin** below – **Eckkneipe** : Meals à la carte 37/59 – **402 rm** ☕ 446/682 – 33 suites.

The Westin Grand, Friedrichstr. 158, ⊠ 10117, ℘ (030) 2 02 70, Fax (030) 20273362, Massage ⒻⓈ, ⬅s, ⬛ – 🛗, ✳ rm, TV & ⬥ – ⚓ 100. AE ⓞ Ⓔ VISA JCB
PZ a
Meals à la carte 35/45 – **Forellenquintett** (mainly seafood) **Meals** à la carte 58/61 – **358 rm** ☕ 414/493 – 20 suites.

Palace, Budapester Str. 42 (Europa-Centre), ⊠ 10789, ℘ (030) 2 50 20, Fax (030) 2626577, free entrance to the thermal recreation centre – 🛗, ✳ rm, TV – ⚓ 260. AE ⓞ Ⓔ VISA. ✵ rest
MX k
see also **First Floor** below – **Alt Nürnberg** : Meals à la carte 37/60 – **321 rm** ☕ 361/642 – 18 suites.

Inter-Continental, Budapester Str. 2, ⊠ 10787, ℘ (030) 2 60 20, Fax (030) 26022600, Massage, ⬅s, ⬛ – 🛗, ✳ rm, 🖳 TV 📞 & ⬥ Ⓟ – ⚓ 800. AE ⓞ Ⓔ VISA JCB
MX a
see also **Zum Hugenotten** below – **L.A. Café** : Meals à la carte 50/65 – **511 rm** ☕ 388/611 – 40 suites

Radisson SAS-Hotel, Karl-Liebknecht-Str. 5, ⊠ 10178, ℘ (030) 2 38 28, Fax (030) 23827590, 👭, Massage, ⒻⓈ, ⬅s – 🛗, ✳ rm, TV ⬥ Ⓟ – ⚓ 360. AE ⓞ Ⓔ VISA JCB. ✵ rest
RY s
Meals à la carte 43/65 – **540 rm** ☕ 337/454 – 17 suites.

Berlin, Lützowplatz 17, ⊠ 10785, ℘ (030) 2 60 50, Fax (030) 26052716, 👭, ⬅s – 🛗, ✳ rm, 🖳 TV ⬥ Ⓟ – ⚓ 400. AE ⓞ Ⓔ VISA JCB
MX b
Meals 32 (buffet lunch) à la carte 51/80 – **701 rm** ☕ 250/410 – 7 suites.

Hilton ⬧ (with 🏰 Kroneflügel), Mohrenstr. 30, ⊠ 10117, ℘ (030) 2 02 30, Fax (030) 20234269, ⒻⓈ, ⬅s – 🛗, ✳ rm, 🖳 TV & ⬥ – ⚓ 300. AE ⓞ Ⓔ VISA JCB
PZ r
Fellini (Italian rest.) (dinner only) **Meals** à la carte 56/76 – **Mark Brandenburg** (vegetarian menu available) (dinner only) **Meals** à la carte 45/72 – **493 rm** ☕ 248/621 – 12 suites.

Steigenberger Berlin, Los-Angeles-Platz 1, ⊠ 10789, ℘ (030) 2 12 70, Fax (030) 212117, 👭, Massage, ⬅s, ⬛ – 🛗, ✳ rm, 🖳 TV 📞 & ⬥ – ⚓ 300. AE ⓞ Ⓔ VISA JCB. ✵ rest
MY d
Parkrestaurant (dinner only, closed Sunday - Monday and 18 July - 16 August) **Meals** à la carte 54/81 – **Berliner Stube** : Meals à la carte 33/50 – **397 rm** ☕ 341/532 – 11 suites.

Holiday Inn Crowne Plaza Ⓜ ⬧, Nürnberger Str. 65, ⊠ 10787, ℘ (030) 21 00 70, Fax (030) 2132009, Massage, ⬅s, ⬛ – 🛗, ✳ rm, 🖳 TV 📞 & ⬥ Ⓟ – ⚓ 120. AE ⓞ Ⓔ VISA JCB. ✵ rest
MX t
Meals (closed Sunday dinner)/35 (lunchbuffet) and à la carte 52/75 – **425 rm** ☕ 320/590 – 10 suites.

Brandenburger Hof Ⓜ, Eislebener Str. 14, ⊠ 10789, ℘ (030) 21 40 50, Fax (030) 21405100, « Modernized Wilhelminian mansion with Bauhaus furniture » – 🛗, TV 📞 ⬥ – ⚓ 30. AE ⓞ Ⓔ VISA JCB. ✵ rest
LY n
see also **Die Quadriga** below – **Der Wintergarten** : Meals à la carte 52/85 – **80 rm** ☕ 275/455.

GERMANY

Maritim Pro Arte Ⓜ, Friedrichstr. 151, ✉ 10117, ℰ (030) 2 03 35
Fax (030) 20334209, 🛖, Ⅰ₅, ⊜s, 🖼 – 🛗, ✻ rm, 🖥 📺 ☎ &. ⇔ – 🏄 720. AE ⓞ
E VISA JCB
PY
Galerie : Meals 49 (buffet lunch only) – **Atelier** (dinner only) Meals à la carte 52/80
403 rm ☕ 294/558 – 28 suites.

Savoy, Fasanenstr. 9, ✉ 10623, ℰ (030) 31 10 30, Fax (030) 31103333, Ⅰ₅, ⊜s – 🛗
✻ rm, 📺 ☎ – 🏄 40. AE ⓞ E VISA JCB
LX
Meals à la carte 48/70 – **125 rm** ☕ 277/455 – 18 suites.

Mondial ⬧, Kurfürstendamm 47, ✉ 10707, ℰ (030) 88 41 10, Fax (030) 8841115O
🛖, Massage, 🖼 – 🛗 📺 ☎ &. ⇔ – 🏄 50. AE ⓞ E VISA
KY
Meals à la carte 47/69 – **75 rm** ☕ 180/480.

President, An der Urania 16, ✉ 10787, ℰ (030) 21 90 30, Fax (030) 2141200, Ⅰ₅, ⊜
– 🛗, ✻ rm, 🖥 📺 ☎ ⇔ Ⓟ – 🏄 80. AE ⓞ E VISA. ✻ rest
MY
Meals (closed Sunday) à la carte 42/67 – **188 rm** ☕ 242/337.

Sorat Hotel Spree-Bogen Ⓜ ⬧, Alt Moabit 99, ✉ 10559, ℰ (030) 39 92 0O
Fax (030) 39920999, 🛖, ⊜s – 🛗, ✻ rm, 🖥 📺 ☎ &. ⇔ – 🏄 150. AE ⓞ
VISA JCB
FY
Meals (closed Sunday dinner) à la carte 47/66 – **221 rm** ☕ 230/450.

Alexander Plaza Ⓜ, Rosenstr. 1, ✉ 10178, ℰ (030) 24 00 10, Fax (030)240017?
Ⅰ₅, ⊜s – 🛗, ✻ rm, 🖥 📺 ☎ ⇔ – 🏄 80. AE ⓞ E VISA JCB
RY
Meals à la carte 34/53 – **92 rm** ☕ 225/385.

Großer Kurfürst Ⓜ without rest, Neue Roßstr. 11, ✉ 10179, ℰ (030) 24 60 0O
Fax (030) 24600300, Ⅰ₅, ⊜s – 🛗, ✻ rm, 🖥 📺 ☎ &. – 🏄 30. AE ⓞ E VISA JCB
RZ
144 rm ☕ 195/295 – 7 suites.

Seehof Ⓜ ⬧, Lietzensee-Ufer 11, ✉ 14057, ℰ (030) 32 00 20, Fax (030) 32002251, ⇆
« Garden terrace », ⊜s, 🖼 – 🛗 🖥 📺 ⇔ – 🏄 40. AE ⓞ E VISA. ✻ rest
JX
Meals 43 à la carte 58/81 – **77 rm** ☕ 235/475.

Alsterhof, Augsburger Str. 5, ✉ 10789, ℰ (030) 21 24 20, Fax (030) 2183949, beer ga
den, Massage, ⊜s, 🖼 – 🛗, ✻ rm, 📺 ☎ ⇔ – 🏄 45. AE ⓞ E VISA JCB
MY
Alsterstuben (closed Sunday dinner) Meals à la carte 44/64 – **Zum Lit-Fass** (Monda
to Thursday dinner only) Meals à la carte 32/53 – **200 rm** ☕ 265/450.

art'otel Ermelerhaus Ⓜ, Wallstr. 70, ✉ 10179, ℰ (030) 24 06 2O
Fax (030) 25062222, « Reconstructed nobleman's house with modern hotel wing », ⊜
– 🛗, ✻ rm, 🖥 📺 ☎ &. ⇔ – 🏄 45. AE ⓞ E VISA
RZ
Im Ermelerhaus (dinner only) (closed Sunday - Monday and mid July - end August) Mea
à la carte 60/80 – **Raabe - Diele** : Meals à la carte 35/56 – **95 rm** ☕ 235/375.

Luisenhof without rest, Köpenicker Str. 92, ✉ 10179, ℰ (030) 2 41 59 0€
Fax (030) 2792983, « Elegant installation » – 🛗 📺 ☎ ☎ – 🏄 30. AE ⓞ E VISA JC
✻ rest
RZ
Meals à la carte 29/61 – **27 rm** ☕ 210/390.

Forum-Hotel, Alexanderplatz, ✉ 10178, ℰ (030) 2 38 90, Fax (030) 23894305, Ⅰ₅
⊜s – 🛗, ✻ rm, 📺 ☎ ☎ &. ⇔ – 🏄 240. AE ⓞ E VISA JCB
RY
Meals à la carte 29/56 – **1006 rm** ☕ 235/345.

Ambassador, Bayreuther Str. 42, ✉ 10787, ℰ (030) 21 90 20, Fax (030) 21902380, Ma
sage, ⊜s, 🖼 – 🛗, ✻ rm, 🖥 📺 ☎ ⇔ Ⓟ – 🏄 70. AE ⓞ E VISA JCB
MX
Meals à la carte 32/58 – **199 rm** ☕ 200/290.

Berlin Excelsior Hotel, Hardenbergstr. 14, ✉ 10623, ℰ (030) 3 15 5O
Fax (030) 31551002, 🛖 – 🛗, ✻ rm, 🖥 rest, 📺 ☎ ⇔ Ⓟ – 🏄 60. AE ⓞ E VISA JCB
LX
Meals (closed Sunday - Monday) à la carte 44/70 – **317 rm** ☕ 250/395.

Hamburg, Landgrafenstr. 4, ✉ 10787, ℰ (030) 26 47 70, Fax (030) 2629394 – 🛗
✻ rm, 📺 ☎ ☎ ⇔ Ⓟ – 🏄 60. AE ⓞ E VISA JCB. ✻ rest
MX
Meals à la carte 44/72 – **240 rm** ☕ 199/320.

Residenz, Meinekestr. 9, ✉ 10719, ℰ (030) 88 44 30, Fax (030) 8824726 – 🛗 📺 ☎
AE ⓞ E VISA. ✻ rest
LY
Meals à la carte 58/78 – **88 rm** ☕ 220/360.

Bleibtreu-Hotel, Bleibtreustr. 31, ✉ 10707, ℰ (030) 88 47 40, Fax (030) 8847444
« Modern interior », Massage, ⊜s – 🛗, ✻ rm, 📺 ☎ ☎ &. AE ⓞ E VISA JCB KY
Meals à la carte 46/81 – **60 rm** ☕ 275/441.

Park Consul without rest, Alt-Moabit 86a, ✉ 10555, ℰ (030) 39 07 8O
Fax (030) 39078900 – 🛗 ✻ 📺 ☎ ☎ ⇔. AE ⓞ E VISA
FY
52 rm ☕ 217/327.

Sorat Art'otel, Joachimstalerstr. 28, ✉ 10719, ℰ (030) 88 44 7O
Fax (030) 88447700, 🛖, « Modern hotel with exhibition of contemporary art » – 🛗
✻ rm, 🖥 📺 ☎ ☎ &. ⇔ – 🏄 65. AE ⓞ E VISA JCB
LY
Meals (closed Sunday) à la carte 34/69 – **133 rm** ☕ 180/415.

GERMANY

Sylter Hof, Kurfürstenstr. 114, ✉ 10787, ℰ (030) 2 12 00, Fax (030) 2142826 – |≝|
📺 ☎ 🅿 – 🏊 90. AE ⓪ E VISA
MX d
Meals (closed Sunday) à la carte 26/41 – **160 rm** ☕ 228/338 – 18 suites.

Hecker's Hotel, Grolmanstr. 35, ✉ 10623, ℰ (030) 8 89 00, Fax (030) 8890260 – |≝|,
↔ rm, 📺 ☎ 🍴 🚗 🅿. AE ⓪ E VISA JCB
LX e
Cassambalis : Meals 30 (buffet) and à la carte 57/72 – **72 rm** ☕ 280/350.

Queens Hotel without rest, Güntzelstr. 14, ✉ 10717, ℰ (030) 8 73 02 41,
Fax (030) 8619326 – |≝| ↔ 📺 ☎ 🍴 🚗 🅿 – 🏊 m0. AE ⓪ E VISA
LZ t
108 rm ☕ 199/295.

Kanthotel without rest, Kantstr. 111, ✉ 10627, ℰ (030) 32 30 20, Fax (030) 3240952
– |≝| 📺 ☎ 🅿. AE ⓪ E VISA JCB
JX e
55 rm ☕ 150/350.

Concept Hotel, Grolmanstr. 41, ✉ 10623, ℰ (030) 88 42 60, Fax (030) 88426820, 🌴,
Massage, ⌂ – |≝|, ↔ rm, 📺 ☎ ♿ 🚗 – 🏊 85. AE ⓪ E VISA JCB
LX m
Meals à la carte 34/59 – **106 rm** ☕ 220/350 – 5 suites.

Holiday Inn Garden Court without rest, Bleibtreustr. 25, ✉ 10707, ℰ (030)
88 09 30, Fax (030) 88093939 – |≝| ↔ 📺 ☎ 🍴 – 🏊 15. AE ⓪ E VISA JCB
KY g
73 rm ☕ 245/370.

Albrechtshof, Albrechtstr. 8, ✉ 10117, ℰ (030) 30 88 60, Fax (030) 30886100, 🌴
– |≝|, ↔ rm, 📺 ☎ 🍴 ♿ 🅿 – 🏊 50. AE ⓪ E VISA JCB. ⌾ rest
NY a
Meals à la carte 35/67 – **99 rm** ☕ 208/365.

Hackescher Markt, Große Präsidentenstr. 8, ✉ 10178, ℰ (030) 28 00 30,
Fax (030) 28003111 – |≝|, ↔ rm, 📺 ☎ 🍴 🚗. AE ⓪ E VISA. ⌾
PY c
Meals (closed Monday, Tuesday to Friday dinner only) à la carte 52/68 – **31 rm**
☕ 160/320.

Kronprinz without rest, Kronprinzendamm 1, ✉ 10711, ℰ (030) 89 60 30,
Fax (030) 8931215, (restored 1894 house) – |≝| ↔ 📺 ☎ – 🏊 25. AE ⓪ E
VISA JCB
JY d
61 rm ☕ 195/295.

Schloßparkhotel 🏌, Heubnerweg 2a, ✉ 14059, ℰ (030) 3 26 90 30,
Fax (030) 3258861, ◳, 🚗 – |≝| 📺 ☎ 🅿 – 🏊 50. AE ⓪ E VISA JCB
EY a
Meals à la carte 32/63 – **39 rm** ☕ 189/244.

Boulevard without rest, Kurfürstendamm 12, ✉ 10719, ℰ (030) 88 42 50,
Fax (030) 88425450 – |≝| ↔ 📺 ☎ 🍴 – 🏊 25. AE ⓪ E VISA
LX c
57 rm ☕ 185/368.

Kurfürstendamm am Adenauerplatz without rest, Kurfürstendamm 68,
✉ 10707, ℰ (030) 88 46 30, Fax (030) 8825528 – |≝| 📺 ☎ 🍴 🅿 – 🏊 30. AE ⓪ E
VISA
JY n
34 rm ☕ 180/270 – 4 suites.

Scandotel Castor without rest, Fuggerstr. 8, ✉ 10777, ℰ (030) 21 30 30,
Fax (030) 21303160 – |≝| ↔ 📺 ☎ 🍴. AE ⓪ E VISA. ⌾
MY s
78 rm ☕ 210/265.

XXX **Zum Hugenotten** - Hotel Inter-Continental, Budapester Str. 2, ✉ 10787, ℰ (030)
26 02 12 63, Fax (030) 26022600 – 📧. AE ⓪ E VISA JCB. ⌾
MX a
closed Sunday – **Meals** (dinner only) (outstanding wine list) 115/160 and à la carte 87/102.

XXX **First Floor** - Hotel Palace, Budapester Str. 42, ✉ 10789, ℰ (030) 25 02 10 20,
❀ Fax (030) 25021197 – AE ⓪ E VISA. ⌾
MX k
closed Saturday lunch, 28 March - 11 April and 25 July - 22 August – **Meals** à la carte
94/146
Spec. Lauwarm marinierter Kalbskopf mit Langustinen-Croustillant. Bretonischer Hummer
mit eingelegten grünen Tomaten und Vanillesauce. Marbre von U.S. Rinderfilet mit Gänseleber und Trüffel.

XXX **Harlekin** - Grand Hotel Esplanade, Lützowufer 15, ✉ 10785, ℰ (030) 25 47 88 58,
❀ Fax (030) 2651171 – 📧. AE ⓪ E VISA JCB. ⌾
MX e
closed Sunday - Monday, 1 to 4 January and 18 July - 16 August – **Meals** (dinner only)
à la carte 106/140
Spec. Gänselebervariation mit Weinbeerensauce und Apfel-Selleriesalat. Zander und Krebse
mit Leipziger Allerlei und Morchelravioli. Lammfilet im Crepinette gebraten mit Pistousauce
und Zucchiniblüte.

XXX **Die Quadriga** - Hotel Brandenburger Hof, Eislebener Str. 14, ✉ 10789, ℰ (030)
❀ 21 40 50, Fax (030) 21405100 – AE ⓪ E VISA JCB. ⌾
LY n
closed Saturday - Sunday. 1 to 10 January and 19 July - 21 August – **Meals** (dinner only)
à la carte 74/119
Spec. Taube mit Lauch-Kartoffelsalat. Seezungen-Langustinengalantine mit geschmortem
Fenchel. Lammrückenfilet im Kartoffelnetz mit Estragonsauce.

XXX ✿ **Bamberger Reiter**, Regensburger Str. 7, ⊠ 10777, ℰ (030) 2 18 42 8
Fax (030) 2142348, 🌳 – AE ⓘ E VISA. ✸
closed Sunday - Monday, 2 weeks January and August – **Meals** (dinner only, booking esse
tial) 165/195 and à la carte 99/117 – **Bistro** : Meals à la carte 51/80
Spec. Gänsemastleberterrine mit Sauternegelee und gebackenem Sellerie. Gebundene R
barbensuppe mit Jakobsmuscheln. Bresse Taube auf Trüffelrisotto.

XX ✿ **VAU**, Jägerstr. 54, ⊠ 10117, ℰ (030) 2 02 97 30, Fax (030) 20297311,
« Bistro-restaurant with modern interior » – AE ⓘ E VISA JCB. ✸
closed Sunday – **Meals** 54 (lunch) and à la carte 92/117
Spec. Geräucherter Stör mit Imperial Kaviar und jungen Erbsen. Ente aus der Röhre
Pfifferlingen und Frühlingsgemüse (June). Topfensoufflé.

XX ✿ **Alt Luxemburg**, Windscheidtstr. 31, ⊠ 10627, ℰ (030) 3 23 87 30, Fax (030) 32740
– 🖿. AE ⓘ E VISA
closed Sunday – **Meals** (dinner only, booking essential) 105/135 à la carte 95/135
Spec. Gebratene Gänsetopfleber mit asiatischem Gemüse. Hummercremesuppe. Lam
rücken mit Rosmarinkartoffel und Artischocken-Tomatengemüse.

XX **Ponte Vecchio**, Spielhagenstr. 3, ⊠ 10585, ℰ (030) 3 42 19 99, Fax (030) 33247
– ⓘ
closed Tuesday and 4 weeks July - August – **Meals** (dinner only, booking essential, Ital
rest.) à la carte 58/90.

XX **Ana e Bruno**, Sophie-Charlotten-Str. 101, ⊠ 14059, ℰ (030) 3 25 71
Fax (030) 3226895 – AE. ✸
closed Sunday and Monday, 1 week January and 3 weeks June - July – **Meals** (dinner or
Italian rest., outstanding Italian wine list) à la carte 80/100.

XX **Il Sorriso**, Kurfürstenstr. 76, ⊠ 10787, ℰ (030) 2 62 13 13, Fax (030) 2650277,
– AE ⓘ E VISA. ✸
closed Sunday and 22 December - 5 January – **Meals** (booking essential for dinner, Ital
rest.) à la carte 56/80.

XX **Borchardt**, Französische Str. 47, ⊠ 10117, ℰ (030) 20 38 71 10, Fax (030) 203871
« Courtyard-terrace » – AE VISA
Meals à la carte 54/79.

X **Maxwell**, Bergstr. 22 (Entrance in courtyard), ⊠ 10115, ℰ (030) 2 80 71
Fax (030) 2807121, « Art nouveau facade ; courtyard-terrace » – AE ⓘ E VISA
Meals (booking essential) 29/35 (lunch) and à la carte 67/88.

X 🐌 **Am Karlsbad**, Am Karlsbad 11, ⊠ 10785, ℰ (030) 2 64 53 49, Fax (030) 2644240,
(modern restaurant in bistro style) ℗. E VISA
closed Saturday lunch and Sunday – **Meals** 24 (lunch) and à la carte 50/83.

at Berlin-Britz by Karl-Marx-Straße HZ :

🏨 **Park Hotel Blub**, Buschkrugallee 60, ⊠ 12359, ℰ (030) 60 00 36
Fax (030) 60003777 – 📳, ✸ rm, TV ☎ 🐾 🖔 🚗 ℗ – 🛎 50. AE ⓘ E VISA
Meals (dinner only) à la carte 31/48 – **120 rm** ☕ 185/240.

🏠 **Buschkrugpark** without rest, Buschkrugallee 107, ⊠ 12359, ℰ (030) 6 00 99
Fax (030) 60099020 – 📳 TV ☎. AE ⓘ E VISA
closed 23 December - 1 January – **25 rm** ☕ 197/259.

at Berlin-Friedrichshain

🏨 **Inn Side Residence-Hotel** Ⓜ, Lange Str. 31, ⊠ 10243, ℰ (030) 29 30
Fax (030) 29303199, ⊆s – 📳, ✸ rm, TV 🐾 🖔 🚗 – 🛎 40. AE ⓘ E VISA JCB. ✸
Meals à la carte 50/65 – **133 rm** ☕ 195/395.

at Berlin-Grunewald

🏨 **Ritz-Carlton Schlosshotel**, Brahmsstr. 10, ⊠ 14193, ℰ (030) 89 58
Fax (030) 89584800, 🌳, « Former Wilhelminian mansion », Massage, 🏋, ⊆s, 🏊 –
✸ rm, 🖿 TV 🐾 🚗 ℗ – 🛎 40. AE ⓘ E VISA JCB. ✸ rest
Vivaldi (dinner only) (closed Monday, Tuesday, 1 to 19 January and 14 July - 3 Augu
Meals à la carte 111/140 – **Le Jardin** (in winter Wednesday - Sunday lunch only) Me
à la carte 69/88 – **52 rm** ☕ 581/871 – 12 suites.

XXXX **Grand Slam**, Gottfried-von-Cramm-Weg 47, ⊠ 14193, ℰ (030) 8 25 38
Fax (030) 8266300, 🌳 – AE ⓘ E VISA. ✸
closed Sunday - Monday and 2 weeks July - August – **Meals** (dinner only) (booking essent
135/175 à la carte 104/116.

at Berlin-Kreuzberg :

🏨 **Stuttgarter Hof**, Anhalter Str. 9, ⊠ 10963, ℰ (030) 26 48 30, Fax (030) 264839
⊆s – 📳, ✸ rm, TV ☎ 🚗 – 🛎 25. AE ⓘ E VISA JCB. ✸ rest
Meals (closed Sunday) à la carte 33/59 – **110 rm** ☕ 200/390.

Berlin-Lichtenberg *by Karl-Marx-Allee* HY :

Abacus Tierpark Hotel M, Franz-Mett-Str. 3, ⊠ 10319, ℰ (030) 5 16 20, *Fax (030) 5162400* – |♯|, ⇔ rm, 🆃🆅 ☎ 📞 ⅙ 🅿 – 🕰 300. 🆎 ⓪ 🅴 *VISA* Meals 32 (buffet only) – **278 rm** ⌲ 190/280.

Berlin-Lichterfelde *by Boelcke Straße* GZ :

Villa Toscana without rest, Bahnhofstr. 19, ⊠ 12207, ℰ (030) 7 68 92 70, *Fax (030) 7734488*, « Villa with elegant installation » – |♯| 🆃🆅 ☎. 🆎 ⓪ 🅴 *VISA* JCB. ⅙ **16 rm** ⌲ 160/220.

Berlin-Mariendorf *by Tempelhofer Damm* GZ :

Landhaus Alpinia, Säntisstr. 32, ⊠ 12107, ℰ (030) 76 17 70 (hotel) 7 41 99 98 (rest.), *Fax (030) 7419835*, « Garden-terrace », ⇔s – |♯|, ⇔ rm, 🆃🆅 📞 🚗 – 🕰 20. 🅴 *VISA* JCB **Villa Rossini** (weekdays dinner only) **Meals** à la carte 34/69 – **58 rm** ⌲ 175/350.

Berlin-Neukölln :

Estrel M, Sonnenallee 225, ⊠ 12057, ℰ (030) 6 83 10, *Fax (030) 68312345*, beer garden, Massage, ♣, ⇔s – |♯|, ⇔ rm, 🆃🆅 📞 ⅙ 🏃 🚗 – 🕰 700. 🆎 ⓪ 🅴 *VISA* JCB   HZ   a **Portofino** (Italian rest.) **Meals** à la carte 36/52 – **Sans Souci** (dinner only) (closed mid July - end August) **Meals** à la carte 37/66 – **Sun Thai** (Thai. rest.) **Meals** à la carte 34/59 – **1125 rm** ⌲ 190/315 – 80 suites.

Berlin-Reinickendorf *by Sellerstr.* GX :

Rheinsberg am See, Finsterwalder Str. 64, ⊠ 13435, ℰ (030) 4 02 10 02, *Fax (030) 4035057*, « Lakeside garden terrace », Massage, ♣, ⇔s, ☒ , ☒ , ⇝ – |♯|, ⇔ rm, 🆃🆅 ☎ 📞 🅿 – 🕰 50. 🅴 *VISA* Meals à la carte 36/62 – **81 rm** ⌲ 195/245.

Dorint Budget Hotel Airport Tegel, Gotthardstr. 96, ⊠ 13403, ℰ (030) 49 88 40, *Fax (030) 49884555* – |♯|, ⇔ rm, 🆃🆅 ☎ 📞 ⅙ 🚗 🅿 – 🕰 70. 🆎 ⓪ 🅴 *VISA* JCB. ⅙ rest Meals à la carte 32/53 – **303 rm** ⌲ 196/312.   FX   c

Berlin-Rudow :

Sorat Hotel u. Office without rest, Rudower Str. 90, ⊠ 12351, ℰ (030) 60 00 80, *Fax (030) 60008666* – |♯| ⇔ 🖳 🆃🆅 ☎ 📞 🚗 – 🕰 60. 🆎 ⓪ 🅴 *VISA* JCB **96 rm** ⌲ 185/290.   by Karl-Marx-Straße   HZ

Berlin-Siemensstadt *by Siemensdamm* EX :

Holiday Inn Berlin Esplanade M, Rohrdamm 80, ⊠ 13629, ℰ (030) 38 38 90, *Fax (030) 38389900*, ⇔, ⇔s, ☒ – |♯|, ⇔ rm, 🖳 🆃🆅 📞 ⅙ 🚗 – 🕰 170. 🆎 ⓪ 🅴 *VISA* JCB. ⅙ rest **Il Faggio** (closed Saturday and Sunday dinner) **Meals** à la carte 42/65 – **336 rm** ⌲ 269/418 – 4 suites.

Novotel, Ohmstr. 4, ⊠ 13629, ℰ (030) 3 80 30, *Fax (030) 3819403*, ☒ – |♯|, ⇔ rm, 🆃🆅 ☎ 📞 ⅙ – 🕰 200. 🆎 ⓪ 🅴 *VISA* JCB Meals à la carte 33/58 – **119 rm** ⌲ 219/285.

Berlin-Steglitz *by Hauptstr.* FZ :

Steglitz International, Albrechtstr. 2 (corner of Schloßstraße), ⊠ 12165, ℰ (030) 79 00 50, *Fax (030) 79005550* – |♯|, ⇔ rm, 🖳 🆃🆅 ⅙ – 🕰 300. 🆎 ⓪ 🅴 *VISA*. ⅙ rest Meals à la carte 43/68 – **200 rm** ⌲ 210/360 – 3 suites.

Berlin-Tegel :

Sorat-Hotel Humboldt-Mühle M, An der Mühle 5, ⊠ 13507, ℰ (030) 43 90 40, *Fax (030) 43904444*, ⇔, ♣, ⇔s – |♯|, ⇔ rm, 🖳 🆃🆅 ☎ 📞 ⅙ 🚗 – 🕰 50. 🆎 ⓪ 🅴 *VISA* JCB   by Müllerstraße   FX Meals (closed Saturday - Sunday) à la carte 35/67 – **120 rm** ⌲ 205/395.

Novotel Berlin Airport, Kurt-Schumacher-Damm 202 (by airport approach), ⊠ 13405, ℰ (030) 4 10 60, *Fax (030) 4106700*, ⇔, ⇔s, ☒ (heated) – |♯|, ⇔ rm, 🆃🆅 ☎ 📞 ⅙ 🅿 – 🕰 150. 🆎 ⓪ 🅴 *VISA*   EX   r Meals à la carte 44/64 – **184 rm** ⌲ 219/271.

Berlin-Waidmannslust *by Sellerstr.* GX :

XXX **Rockendorf's Restaurant**, Düsterhauptstr. 1, ⊠ 13469, ℰ (030) 4 02 30 99, ⛴ *Fax (030) 4022742* – 🅿. 🆎 ⓪ 🅴 *VISA* closed Sunday - Monday and 15 - 30 July – **Meals** (booking essential) 75/145 (lunch) 145/198 (dinner) **Spec.** Tarte von geräuchertem Havelaal. Bresse Poularde auf Steinplilz-Rissotto. Soufflé von Ziegenkäse mit süßem Gemüse.

COLOGNE (KÖLN) *Nordrhein-Westfalen* 💶17 *N 4,* 💶87 ㉕ ㉖ – *pop. 1 005 000 – alt. 65 n*

See : *Cathedral (Dom)*★★ *(Magi's Shrine*★★★*, Gothic stained glass windows*★ *Cross of G (Gerokreuz)*★*, South chapel (Marienkapelle) : altarpiece*★★★*, stalls*★*, treasury*★ GY
Roman-Germanic Museum (Römisch-Germanisches Museum)★★ *(Dionysos Mosaic*★*, Ron glassware collection*★★*)* GY *M¹ – Wallraf-Richartz-Museum and Museum Ludwig*★★★ *(P to-Historama Agfa*★*)* Gy *M² – Diocesan Museum (Diözesean Museum)*★ GY M³
Schnütgen-Museum★★ GZ *M⁴ – Museum of East-Asian Art (Museum für Ostasiatisc Kunst)*★★ *by Hahnenstraßeand Richard Wagner Straße* EV *– Museum for Applied Art (Mu um für Angewandte Kunst)*★ GYZ *M⁶ – St. Maria Lyskirchen (frescoes*★★*)* FX *– St. Seve (interior*★*)* FX *– St. Pantaleon (rood screen*★*)* EX *– St. Kunibert (chancel : stained gl windows*★*)* FU *– St. Mary the Queen (St. Maria Königin) : wall of glass*★ *by Bonnerstr̄a FX *– St. Aposteln (apse*★*)* EV K *– St. Ursula (treasury*★*)* FU *– St. Mary of the Capitol Maria im Kapitol) (romanesque wooden church door*★*, trefoil chancel*★*)* GZ
Imhoff-Stollwerrk-Museum★ FX *– Old Town Hall (Altes Rathaus)*★ GZ *– Botanical gard Flora*★ *by Konrad-Adenauer-Ufer* FU.

🏌 *Köln-Marienburg, Schillingsrotter Weg,* ✆ *(0261) 38 40 33 ;* 🏌 *Köln-Rogendorf, Pa lelweg 1* ① *: 16km), (0221) 78 40 18 ;* 🏌 *Bergisch-Gladbach-Refrath, Golfplatz 2* ③ *(km), (02204) 6 31 14 ;* 🏌 *Pulheim Gut Lärchenhof* ② *: 19 km über Stomme (022389 92 39 00.*

✈ *Köln-Bonn at Wahn (South-East : 17 km)* ✆ *(02203) 4 01.*

🚗 *Köln-Deutz, Barmer Straße by Deutzer Brücke* FV.

Exhibition Centre (Messegelände) by Deutzer Brücke (FV), ✆ *(0221) 82 11, Telex (02 8212574.*

🛈 *Tourist office (Verkehrsamt), Am Dom* ✉ *50667,* ✆ *(0221) 2 21 33 45, Fax (02 2213320.*

ADAC, *Luxemburger Str. 169,* ✉*50963,* ✆ *(0221) 472747, Fax (0221) 4727452. Düsseldorf 40 – Aachen 69 – Bonn 28 – Essen 68.*

Plans on following pages

Excelsior Hotel Ernst, Domplatz, ✉ 50667, ✆ (0221) 27 01, *Fax (0221) 13515* 🛗, ✬ rm, 🖳 TV – ☖ 80. AE ⓸ E VISA　　　　　　　　　　　　　　　　GY
see also ***Hanse-Stube*** below – **161 rm** ☕ 350/765 – 8 suites.

Maritim M, Heumarkt 20, ✉ 50667, ✆ (0221) 2 02 70, *Fax (0221) 20278* Massage ⻌, ⊆s, 🛋 – 🛗, ✬ rm, 🖳 TV 📞 ♿ ➾ – ☖ 1300. AE ⓸
VISA JCB　　　　　　　　　　　　　　　　　　　　　　　　　　GZ
Bellevue « Terrace with ≤ Cologne » **Meals** à la carte 65/96 – ***La Galerie*** (dinner c closed Sunday - Monday and July - mid August) **Meals** à la carte 56/83 – **454** ☕ 405/531 – 28 suites.

Hotel im Wasserturm ⟆, Kaygasse 2, ✉ 50676, ✆ (0221) 2 00 Fax (0221) 2008888, 🌳, roof garden terrace with ≤ Cologne, (former 19C water tow elegant modern installation), ⊆s – 🛗, ✬ rm, 🖳 rest, TV ➾ – ☖ 25. AE ⓸ E JCB. ✗ rest　　　　　　　　　　　　　　　　　　　　　　　　　FX
Meals à la carte 72/105 – **90 rm** ☕ 449/648 – 42 suites.

Dom-Hotel ⟆, Domkloster 2a, ✉ 50667, ✆ (0221) 2 02 40, *Fax (0221)20244* « Terrace with ≤ » – 🛗 TV – ☖ 60. AE ⓸ E VISA JCB　　　　　　　GY
Meals à la carte 65/98 – **125 rm** ☕ 385/795.

Dorint Kongress-Hotel, Helenenstr. 14, ✉ 50667, ✆ (0221) 27 Fax (0221) 2751301, Massage, ⊆s, 🛋 – 🛗, ✬ rm, 🖳 TV 📞 ♿ ➾ – ☖ 500. AE E VISA JCB. ✗ rest　　　　　　　　　　　　　　　　　　　　EV
Meals à la carte 66/95 – ***Kabuki*** (Japanese rest.) (closed Monday lunch) **Meals** à la ca 42/64 – **285 rm** ☕ 299/417 – 15 suites.

Renaissance Köln Hotel, Magnusstr. 20, ✉ 50672, ✆ (0221) 2 03 Fax (0221) 2034777, 🌳, Massage, ⊆s, 🛋 – 🛗, ✬ rm, 🖳 TV ♿ ➾ – ☖ 220. ⓸ E VISA JCB. ✗ rest　　　　　　　　　　　　　　　　　　　　　EV
Meals à la carte 48/72 – **236 rm** ☕ 268/378.

Crowne Plaza, Habsburger Ring 9, ✉ 50674, ✆ (0221) 22 80, *Fax (0221) 2512* Massage, ⊆s, 🛋 – 🛗, ✬ rm, 🖳 TV 📞 ♿ ➾ – ☖ 230. AE ⓸ E VISA J ✗ rest
Meals à la carte 47/75 – ***Die Auster*** (dinner only) **Meals** à la carte 52/83 – **301** ☕ 334/658.　　　　　　　　　　　　　　　　　　　　　　　by Hahnenstraße EV

Savoy without rest, Turiner Str. 9, ✉ 50668, ✆ (0221) 1 62 30, *Fax (0221) 16232* ⊆s – 🛗 ✬ TV 📞 ➾ Ⓟ – ☖ 70. AE ⓸ E VISA　　　　　　　　　FU
closed 24 December - 2 January – **Meals** à la carte 40/56 – **103 rm** ☕ 175/550.

Mondial am Dom, Kurt-Hackenberg-Platz 1, ✉ 50667, ✆ (0221) 2 06 Fax (0221) 2063522, 🌳 – 🛗, ✬ rm, TV ♿ ➾ – ☖ 180. AE ⓸ E VISA J ✗ rest　　　　　　　　　　　　　　　　　　　　　　　　　　GY
Meals à la carte 43/75 – **205 rm** ☕ 268/464.

Haus Lyskirchen, Filzengraben 32, ⊠ 50676, ℰ (0221) 2 09 70, *Fax (0221) 2097718*, ⇌, ▨ – 🛗, ⇥ rm, 🍴 rest, 📺 ☎ 📞 ⬅ – 🛎 60. 🆎 ⓪ Ⅽ 𝗩𝗜𝗦𝗔 𝗝𝗖𝗕. ✗   FX u
Meals *(closed Saturday lunch, Sunday and Bank Holidays)* à la carte 42/64 – **94 rm** ⊑ 185/380.

Euro Plaza Cologne, Breslauer Platz 2, ⊠ 50668, ℰ (0221) 1 65 10, *Fax (0221) 1651333* – 🛗, ⇥ rm, 🍴 📺 ☎ – 🛎 20. 🆎 ⓪ Ⅽ 𝗩𝗜𝗦𝗔   GY c
Meals à la carte 40/55 – **118 rm** ⊑ 198/260 – 6 suites.

Ascot without rest, Hohenzollernring 95, ⊠ 50672, ℰ (0221) 9 52 96 50, *Fax (0221) 952965100*, ⸤, ⇌ – 🛗 ⇥ 📺 ☎ 📞. 🆎 ⓪ Ⅽ 𝗩𝗜𝗦𝗔   EV a
closed 23 December - 2 January – **46 rm** ⊑ 194/418.

Flandrischer Hof, Flandrische Str. 3, ⊠ 50674, ℰ (0221) 25 20 95, *Fax (0221) 251052* – 🛗, ⇥ rm, 📺 ☎ 🅿 – 🛎 20. 🆎 ⓪ Ⅽ 𝗩𝗜𝗦𝗔   by HahnenStraße EV
Meals à la carte 44/68 – **143 rm** ⊑ 125/380.

Senats Hotel, Unter Goldschmied 9, ⊠ 50667, ℰ (0221) 2 06 20, *Fax (0221) 2062200* – 🛗, ⇥ rm, 📺 ☎ – 🛎 200. 🆎 Ⅽ 𝗩𝗜𝗦𝗔 𝗝𝗖𝗕   GZ b
closed 23 December - 3 January – **Falstaff** *(closed Saturday lunch and Sunday)* **Meals** à la carte 41/66 – **59 rm** ⊑ 170/440.

Dorint, Friesenstr. 44, ⊠ 50670, ℰ (0221) 1 61 40, *Fax (0221) 1614100*, ⛲ – 🛗, ⇥ rm, 📺 ☎ ♿ ⬅ – 🛎 100. 🆎 ⓪ Ⅽ 𝗩𝗜𝗦𝗔 𝗝𝗖𝗕   EV n
Meals *(closed Saturday and Sunday dinner)* à la carte 38/54 – **103 rm** ⊑ 225/445.

Viktoria without rest, Worringer Str. 23, ⊠ 50668, ℰ (0221) 9 73 17 20, *Fax (0221) 727067* – 🛗 ⇥ 📺 ☎ 📞 🅿. 🆎 ⓪ Ⅽ 𝗩𝗜𝗦𝗔 𝗝𝗖𝗕. ✗   FU t
closed 24 December - 1 January – **47 rm** ⊑ 175/485.

Mercure Severinshof, Severinstr. 199, ⊠ 50676, ℰ (0221) 2 01 30, *Fax (0221) 2013666*, ⛲, ⸤, ⇌ – 🛗, ⇥ rm, 📺 ☎ 📞 ⬅ – 🛎 120. 🆎 ⓪ Ⅽ 𝗩𝗜𝗦𝗔 𝗝𝗖𝗕. ✗ rest   FX a
Meals à la carte 37/66 – **252 rm** ⊑ 222/450 – 11 suites.

Coellner Hof, Hansaring 100, ⊠ 50670, ℰ (0221) 1 66 60, *Fax (0221) 1666166* – 🛗, ⇥ rm, 🍴 rest, 📺 ☎ ⬅ – 🛎 30. 🆎 ⓪ Ⅽ 𝗩𝗜𝗦𝗔. ✗ rest   FU k
Meals *(closed Friday and Sunday) (dinner only)* à la carte 28/65 – **70 rm** ⊑ 140/360.

Hopper Ⓜ, Brüsseler Str. 26, ⊠ 50674, ℰ (0221) 92 44 00, *Fax (0221) 924406*, ⛲, « Modern hotel in a former monastery », ⇌ – 🛗, ⇥ rm, 📺 ☎ 📞 ♿ ⬅ – 🛎 10. 🆎 ⓪ Ⅽ 𝗩𝗜𝗦𝗔   by Hahnenstr. S j
Meals *(closed Saturday lunch)* à la carte 46/61 – **49 rm** ⊑ 158/237.

Cristall without rest, Ursulaplatz 9, ⊠ 50668, ℰ (0221) 1 63 00, *Fax (0221) 1630333*, « Modern interior » – 🛗 ⇥ 🍴 📺 ☎. 🆎 ⓪ Ⅽ 𝗩𝗜𝗦𝗔 𝗝𝗖𝗕. ✗   FU r
84 rm ⊑ 190/250.

Euro Garden Cologne without rest, Domstr. 10, ⊠ 50668, ℰ (0221) 1 64 90, *Fax (0221) 1649333*, ⇌ – 🛗 ⇥ 📺 ☎ ⬅ – 🛎 50. 🆎 ⓪ Ⅽ 𝗩𝗜𝗦𝗔   FU a
85 rm ⊑ 198/260.

Königshof without rest, Richartzstr. 14, ⊠ 50667, ℰ (0221) 2 57 87 71, *Fax (0221) 2578762* – 🛗 ⇥ 📺 ☎ 📞. 🆎 ⓪ Ⅽ 𝗩𝗜𝗦𝗔   GY n
82 rm ⊑ 155/395.

Kommerzhotel without rest, Breslauer Platz, ⊠ 50668, ℰ (0221) 1 61 00, *Fax (0221) 1610122*, ⇌ – 🛗 ⇥ 📺 ☎. 🆎 ⓪ Ⅽ 𝗩𝗜𝗦𝗔 𝗝𝗖𝗕   GY r
77 rm ⊑ 190/366.

Antik Hotel Bristol without rest, Kaiser-Wilhelm-Ring 48, ⊠ 50672, ℰ (0221) 12 01 95, *Fax (0221) 131495*, *(antique furniture)* – 🛗 ⇥ 📺 ☎ 📞 ♿. 🆎 ⓪ Ⅽ 𝗩𝗜𝗦𝗔 𝗝𝗖𝗕   EU m
closed 24 December - 2 January – **44 rm** ⊑ 165/220.

Esplanade without rest, Hohenstaufenring 56, ⊠ 50674, ℰ (0221) 9 21 55 70, *Fax (0221) 216822* – 🛗 📺 ☎. 🆎 ⓪ Ⅽ 𝗩𝗜𝗦𝗔   EX a
closed 24 December - 2 January – **33 rm** ⊑ 185/235.

Astor und Aparthotel Concorde without rest, Friesenwall 68, ⊠ 50672, ℰ (0221) 25 31 01, *Fax (0221) 253106* – 🛗 ⇥ 📺 ☎ 🅿. 🆎 ⓪ Ⅽ 𝗩𝗜𝗦𝗔. ✗   EV y
closed 24 December - 1 January – **50 rm** ⊑ 185/360.

Leonet without rest, Rubensstr. 33, ⊠ 50676, ℰ (0221) 23 60 16, *Fax (0221) 210893*, ⇌ – 🛗 ⇥ 📺 ☎ 📞 🅿 – 🛎 20. 🆎 Ⅽ 𝗩𝗜𝗦𝗔   EX s
78 rm ⊑ 148/195.

Conti without rest, Brüsseler Str. 40, ⊠ 50674, ℰ (0221) 9 25 92 80, *Fax (0221) 252107* – 🛗 ⇥ ☎ ⬅. 🆎 ⓪ Ⅽ 𝗩𝗜𝗦𝗔   by Hahnenstraße EV
43 rm ⊑ 168/386.

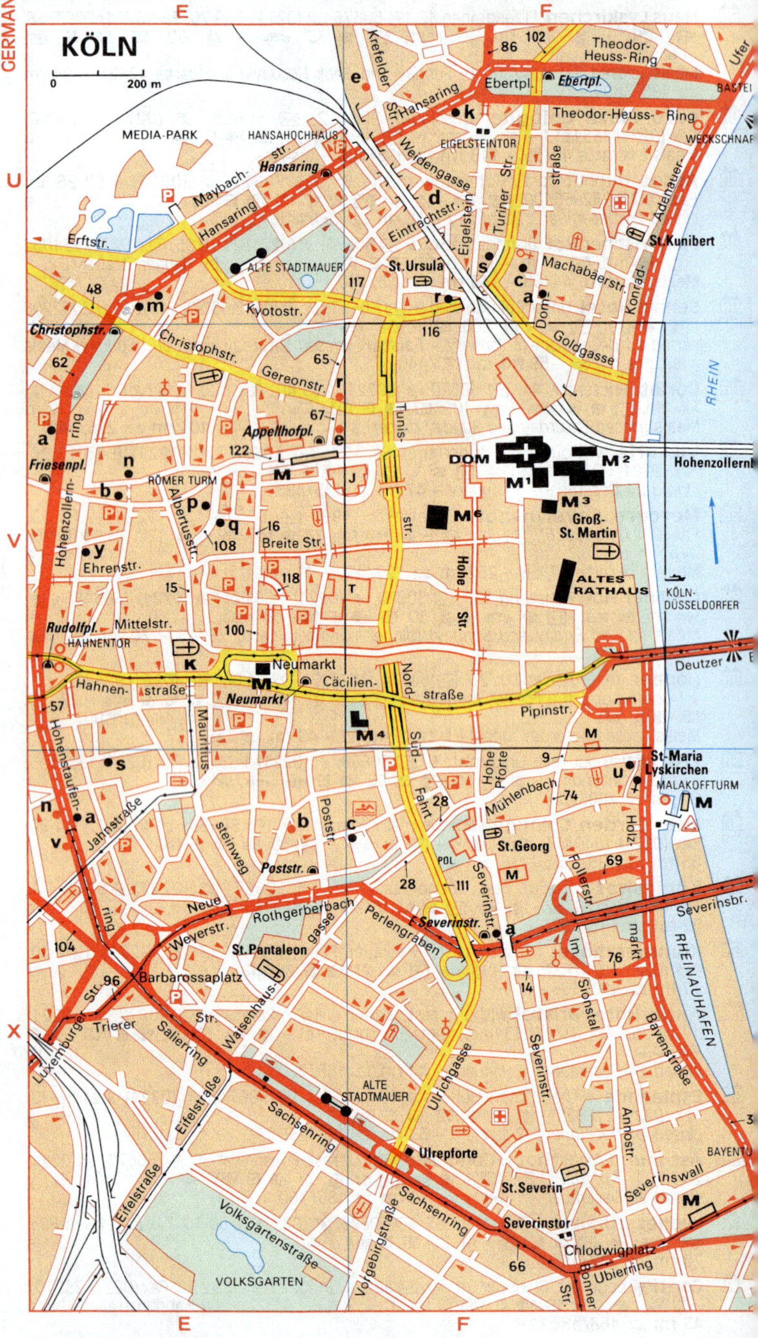

KÖLN
0   200 m
MEDIA-PARK
HANSAHOCHHAUS
Maybach-
Hansaring
Hansaring
str.
Erftstr.
48
Christophstr.
Christophstr.
Gereonstr.
ring
Hohenzollern-
62
a
Friesenpl.
b
n
RÖMER TURM
Albertusstr.
p
q
y
16
108
Ehrenstr.
Breite Str.
15
118
100
Rudolfpl.
Mittelstr.
HAHNENTOR
K
Hahnen-
straße
57
Neumarkt
Neumarkt
Cäcilien-
Mauritius-
steinweg
s
Jahnstraße
n
a
v
Neue
Rothgerberbach
gasse
Weverstr.
Poststr.
b
c
Poststr.
104
St. Pantaleon
Perlengraben
Barbarossaplatz
96
Str.
Waisenhaus-
Luxemburger
Trier
Salierring
Str.
ALTE
STADTMAUER
Eifelstraße
Sachsenring
Eifelstraße
Vorgebirgstraße
Volksgartenstraße
VOLKSGARTEN
Krefelder
Str. Hansaring
e
Weidengasse
Eintrachtstr.
Eigelstein
St. Ursula
117
116
65
67
Appellhofpl.
122
L
M
e
J
Tunis-
str.
T
Hohe
Str.
Nord-
Süd-
Fahrt
straße
L 4
M 4
Hohe
Pforte
Mühlenbach
28
POL
28
111
E Severinstr.
Severinstr.
Ulrichgasse
Ulrepforte
Sachsenring
St. Severin
Severinstor
Severinstraße
Chlodwigplatz
66
Bonner Str.
Ubierring
86   102
Theodor-
Heuss-Ring
Ebertpl.   Ebertpl.
k
Theodor-Heuss-Ring
EIGELSTEINTOR
Turiner Str.
straße
d
s
c
a
r
St. Kunibert
Machabaerstr.
Adenauer-
Konrad-
Dom-
Goldgasse
RHEIN
Hohenzollernbr.
DOM
M 2
M 1
M 3
M 6
Groß-
St. Martin
ALTES
RATHAUS
KÖLN-
DÜSSELDORFER
Deutzer Br.
Pipinstr.
M
9
St-Maria
Lyskirchen
u
MALAKOFFTURM
M
74
Holz-
markt
St. Georg
M
Follerstr.
69
a
76
14
Siegburger
Severinstr.
Bayenstraße
Severinsbr.
RHEINAUHAFEN
Annostr.
BAYENTURM
Severinswall
M
BASTEI
WECKSCHNAPP
Uferstraße
EBERTPLATZ

KÖLN

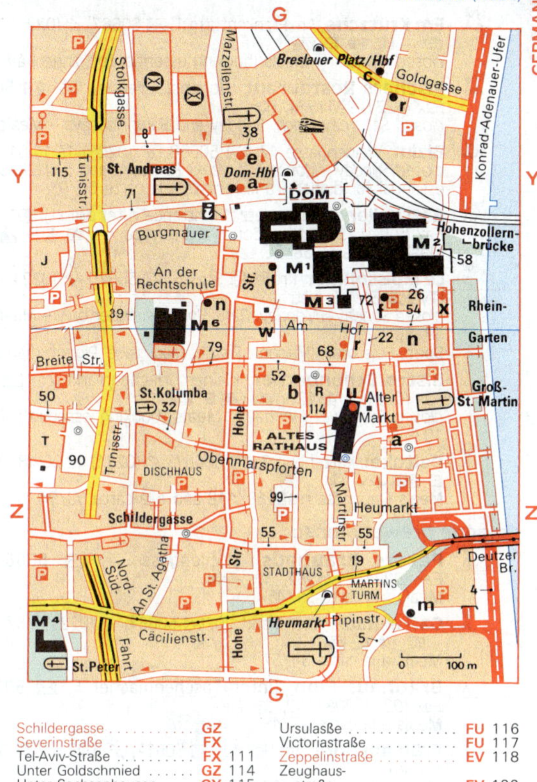

Merian-Hotel without rest, Allerheiligenstr. 1, ✉ 50668, ✆ (0221) 1 66 50, *Fax (0221) 1665200* – 🛗 TV ☎ 🚗. AE ◑ E VISA **FU** c
31 rm ☕ 120/375.

Metropol without rest, Hansaring 14, ✉ 50670, ✆ (0221) 13 33 77, *Fax (0221) 138307* – 🛗 TV ☎. AE ◑ E VISA **EU** m
closed 22 December - 2 January – **26 rm** ☕ 145/320.

Altstadt Hotel without rest, Salzgasse 7, ✉ 50667, ✆ (0221) 2 57 78 51, *Fax (0221) 2577853,* 🔊 – 🛗 TV ☎. AE ◑ E VISA **GZ** p
closed 20 December - 4 January – **28 rm** ☕ 110/180.

Hanse Stube - Excelsior Hotel Ernst, Dompropst-Ketzer-Str. 2, ✉ 50667, ✆ (0221) 2 70 34 02, *Fax (0221) 135150* – 🍽. AE ◑ E VISA **GY** e
Meals 55 (lunch) and à la carte 88/120.

Ambiance am Dom - Excelsior Hotel Ernst, Trankgasse 1, ✉ 50667, ✆ (0221) 1 39 19 12 – AE ◑ E VISA. 🚫 **GY** a
closed Saturday - Sunday, Bank Holidays and 3 weeks July - August – **Meals** à la carte 81/104.

Börsen-Restaurant Maître, Unter Sachsenhausen 10, ✉ 50667, ✆ (0221) 13 30 21, *Fax (0221) 133040,* 🌿 – 🍽. AE ◑ E VISA. 🚫 **EV** r
closed Saturday lunch, Sunday, Bank Holidays and 5 July - 1 August – **Meals** à la carte 73/90
– *Börsenstube (closed Saturday dinner, Sunday and Bank Holidays)* **Meals** à la carte 50/75.

Grande Milano, Hohenstaufenring 37, ✉ 50674, ✆ (0221) 24 21 21, *Fax (0221) 244846,* 🌿 – 🍽. AE ◑ E VISA **EX** v
closed Saturday lunch, Sunday and 2 weeks July - August – **Meals** (Italian rest.) à la carte 64/100 – *Pinot di Pinot :* **Meals** à la carte 38/59.

XX **Em Krützche**, Am Frankenturm 1, ⊠ 50667, ℰ (0221) 2 58 08 39, Fax (0221) 2534… GY
🌳 – AE ⓘ E VISA
closed Monday – **Meals** (booking essential for dinner) à la carte 52/85.

XX **Fischers Restaurant**, Hohenstaufenring 53, ⊠ 50674, ℰ (0221) 9 23 15 2… EX
Fax (0221) 9231524, 🌳
closed Saturday lunch, Sunday and Bank Holidays – **Meals** à la carte 52/80.

XX **Bizim**, Weidengasse 47, ⊠ 50668, ℰ (0221) 13 15 81 – AE ⓘ E. ✗ FU
closed Sunday - Monday, 2 weeks February and 3 weeks July - August – **Meals** (booki…
essential for dinner, Turkish rest.) à la carte 66/93.

XX **Ratskeller**, Rathausplatz 1 (entrance Alter Markt), ⊠ 50667, ℰ (0221) 2 57 69 2… GZ
Fax (0221) 2576946, « Courtyard-terrace » – 🍽 🅰 – 🍴 80. AE ⓘ E VISA
Meals à la carte 38/75.

X **Le Moissonnier**, Krefelder Str. 25, ⊠ 50670, ℰ (0221) 72 94 79, Fax (0221) 73254… FU
❀ (Typical French bistro)
closed Sunday - Monday, Bank Holidays dinner only – **Meals** (booking essential) à la ca…
58/86
Spec. Foie gras "Maison". Ris de veau glacé. Pigeon mariné.

X **Bistro Schönberner**, Kleiner Griechenmarkt 23, ⊠ 50676, ℰ (0221) 21 45 … EX
Fax (0221) 214512 – 🍽. ⓘ E VISA
closed Sunday - Monday – **Meals** (booking essential) 45 (lunch) and à la carte 5…
107.

X **Daitokai**, Kattenbug 2, ⊠ 50667, ℰ (0221) 12 00 48, Fax (0221) 137503 – 🍽. AE EV
E VISA JCB. ✗
Meals (Japanese rest.) 68/118 and à la carte 58/84.

Cologne brewery inns :

X **Peters Brauhaus**, Mühlengasse 1, ⊠ 50667, ℰ (0221) 2 57 39 5… GZ
Fax (0221) 2573962, 🌳 – ✗
Meals à la carte 31/45.

X **Gaffel-Haus**, Alter Markt 20, ⊠ 50667, ℰ (0221) 2 57 76 92, Fax (0221) 253879, … GZ
– AE ⓘ E VISA
Meals à la carte 34/57.

X **Brauhaus Sion**, Unter Taschenmacher 5, ⊠ 50667, ℰ (0221) 2 57 85 … GZ
Fax (0221) 2081750, 🌳
Meals à la carte 27/48.

X **Früh am Dom**, Am Hof 12, ⊠ 50667, ℰ (0221) 2 58 03 97, Fax (0221) 256326, b… GY
garden
Meals à la carte 28/57.

at Cologne-Braunsfeld *by Rudolfplatz* EV *and Aachener Str. :*

🏨 **Regent** without rest, Melatengürtel 15, ⊠ 50933, ℰ (0221) 5 49 …
Fax (0221) 5499998, ⓢ – 🛗 ⚡ TV 📞 🅿 – 🍴 80. AE ⓘ E VISA
closed 21 December - 4 January – **148 rm** 😊 228/492 – 5 suites.

at Cologne-Deutz *by Deutzer Brücke* FV :

🏨 **Hyatt Regency**, Kennedy-Ufer 2a, ⊠ 50679, ℰ (0221) 8 28 12 …
Fax (0221) 8281370, ≤, beer garden, Massage, 🗴, ⓢ, 🏊 – 🛗, ⚡ rm, 🍽 TV 📞
🚗 🅿 – 🍴 330. AE ⓘ E VISA JCB. ✗ rest
Graugans *(closed Saturday and Sunday lunch)* **Meals** à la carte 77/106 – **Glashaus** (Ita…
rest.) **Meals** à la carte 65/80 – **305 rm** 😊 343/703 – 17 suites.

XX **Der Messeturm**, Kennedy-Ufer (18th floor, 🛗), ⊠ 50679, ℰ (0221) 88 10 …
Fax (0221) 818575, ≤ Cologne – 🍽 – 🍴 30. AE ⓘ E VISA. ✗
closed Saturday lunch – **Meals** à la carte 58/87.

at Cologne-Ehrenfeld *by Rudolfplatz* EV *and Aachener Str. :*

🏨 **Imperial**, Barthelstr. 93, ⊠ 50823, ℰ (0221) 51 70 57, Fax (0221) 520993, ⓢ
⚡ rm, 🍽 rest, TV 📞 📞 🅰 🚗. AE ⓘ E VISA. ✗ rest
Meals *(closed Saturday - Sunday)* *(dinner only)* à la carte 39/65 – **36 rm** 😊 19…
360.

at Cologne-Junkersdorf *by Rudolfplatz* EV *and Aachener Str. :*

🏨 **Brenner'scher Hof** ⤢, Wilhelm-von-Capitaine-Str. 15, ⊠ 50858, ℰ (02…
9 48 60 00 (hotel) 9 48 34 00 (rest.), Fax (0221) 94860010, 🌳, « Installation in cour…
house style » – 🛗 TV 📞 🚗 – 🍴 50. AE ⓘ E VISA. ✗ rm
Meals *(closed Monday)* à la carte 65/78 – **48 rm** 😊 255/580 – 6 suites.

Cologne-Lindenthal *by Rudolfplatz* EV *and B 264* :

Queens Hotel, Dürener Str. 287, ⊠ 50935, ℰ (0221) 4 67 60, Fax (0221) 433765, « Garden terrace » – ▯, ⇔ rm, ▤ rest, 🆃🆅 占 ⇔ 🅿 – 🖴 350. 🅰🅴 ⓪ 🄴 𝘝𝘐𝘚𝘈
Meals à la carte 52/79 – **147 rm** ⊂ 266/430.

Cologne-Marienburg *by Bonner Straße* FX :

Marienburger Bonotel, Bonner Str. 478, ⊠ 50968, ℰ (0221) 3 70 20, Fax (0221) 3702132, ⇔ – ▯, ⇔ rm, 🆃🆅 ☎ ⇔ 🅿 – 🖴 40. 🅰🅴 ⓪ 🄴 𝘝𝘐𝘚𝘈
Meals *(dinner only)* à la carte 44/61 – **93 rm** ⊂ 195/235 – 4 suites.

Cologne-Marsdorf *by Rudolfplatz* EV *and B 264* :

Novotel Köln-West, Horbeller Str. 1, ⊠ 50858, ℰ (02234) 51 40, Fax (02234) 514106, 🌳, beer garden, ⇔, ⊴ (heated), 🔲 – ▯, ⇔ rm, ▤ rest, 🆃🆅 ☎ 📞 占 🅿 – 🖴 120. 🅰🅴 ⓪ 🄴 𝘝𝘐𝘚𝘈 🄹🄲🄱
Meals à la carte 43/76 – **199 rm** ⊂ 199/324.

Cologne-Müngersdorf *by Rudolfplatz* EV *and B 55* :

XXX **Landhaus Kuckuck**, Olympiaweg 2, ⊠ 50933, ℰ (0221) 4 91 23 23, Fax (0221) 4972847, 🌳 – 🖴 100. 🅰🅴 ⓪ 🄴 𝘝𝘐𝘚𝘈 – *closed Sunday dinner - Monday and 8 - 17 February* – **Meals** *(booking essential)* 45 *(lunch)* and à la carte 65/85.

Cologne-Porz-Grengel *South-East : 15 km by A 59* :

Holiday Inn, Waldstr. 255, ⊠ 51147, ℰ (02203) 56 10, Fax (02203) 5619, 🌳 – ▯, ⇔ rm, ▤ 🆃🆅 占 🅿 – 🖴 90. 🅰🅴 ⓪ 🄴 𝘝𝘐𝘚𝘈 🄹🄲🄱
Meals à la carte 52/80 – **177 rm** ⊂ 288/550.

ᴇRGISCH GLADBACH *Nordrhein-Westfalen* 𝟰𝟭𝟳 *N 5,* 𝟵𝟴𝟳 ㉖ – *pop. 104 000 – alt. 86 m.*
Köln 17.

XXX **Restaurant Dieter Müller** - Schloßhotel Lerbach, Lerbacher Weg, ⊠ 51465,
⁕⁕ ℰ (02202) 20 40, Fax (02202) 204940 – 🅿. 🅰🅴 ⓪ 🄴 𝘝𝘐𝘚𝘈 🄹🄲🄱. ⇔
closed Sunday - Monday, 1 to 15 January and 3 weeks July - August – **Meals** *(booking essential)* 158/198 and à la carte 121/155
Spec. Triologie von der Gänsestopfleber mit Trauben in Verjus du Périgord. Gebratener Loup de mer mit marinierten Gemüsen und Bouillabaisse-Sauce. Crépinette von der Taube mit Blutwurstscheibe und Trüffelsauce.

asphe, Bad *Nordrhein-Westfalen* 𝟰𝟭𝟳 *N 9 – pop. 16 000 – alt. 335 m.*
Köln 144.

Bad Laasphe-Hesselbach *South-West : 10 km* :

XXX **L'école**, Hesselbacher Str. 23, ⊠ 57334, ℰ (02752) 53 42, Fax (02752) 6900, 🌳,
⁕⁕ « Elegant installation » – 🅿. 🅰🅴 🄴
closed Monday - Tuesday, 2 weeks January and September – **Meals** *(dinner only)* *(booking essential)* 98/145 and à la carte 80/112
Spec. Gebratene Gänseleber mit glacierten Apfelspalten. Wittgensteiner Rehrücken mit schwarzer Pfeffersauce. Sorbetteller mit gefüllter Babyananas.

ᴇuenahr-Ahrweiler, Bad *Rheinland-Pfalz* 𝟰𝟭𝟳 *O 5 – pop. 28 000 – alt. 92 m.*
Köln 63.

Bad Neuenahr-Ahrweiler-Heppingen : *East : 5 km* :

XXX **Steinheuers Restaurant Zur Alten Post** with rm, Landskroner Str. 110 (entrance
⁕⁕ Konsumgasse), ⊠ 53474, ℰ (02641) 70 11, Fax (02641) 7013, 🌳 – 🆃🆅 ☎ 🅿. 🅰🅴 ⓪
🅴 𝘝𝘐𝘚𝘈. ⇔ rm   BY e
Meals *(closed Tuesday - Wednesday lunch and 3 weeks July - August)* 135/165 and à la carte 90/118 – **Landgasthof Poststuben** *(closed Tuesday - Wednesday lunch)* Meals à la carte 45/70 – **6 rm** ⊂ 160/260
Spec. Kaninchen-Gänselebertorte mit Schalottenkruste und Trüffel-Rahmspinat. Eifeler Reh. Variation Valrhona-Orange.

ttlich *Rheinland - Pfalz* 𝟰𝟭𝟳 *Q 4 – pop. 17 300 – alt. 155 m.*
Köln 130.

Dreis *South-West : 8 km* :

XXX **Waldhotel Sonnora** ⇔ with rm, Auf dem Eichelfeld, ⊠ 54518, ℰ (06578) 9 82 20,
⁕⁕ Fax (06578) 1402, ≤, « Garden » – 🆃🆅 ☎ 🅿. 🅰🅴 ⓪ 🄴 𝘝𝘐𝘚𝘈. ⇔
closed January – **Meals** *(closed Monday - Tuesday)* *(booking essential)* 149/185 and à la carte 100/129 – **20 rm** ⊂ 100/300
Spec. Felsenrotbarbe und gebackener Kaisergranat mit marinierten Kräutern. Törtchen vom Rinderfilet-Tatar mit persischem Kaviar und Kartoffelrösti. Blutente mit Gewürzhaut und Limonenjus.

DRESDEN Ⓛ *Sachsen* 4̲1̲8̲ *M 25,* 9̲8̲7̲ ⑲ – *pop. 480 000 – alt. 105 m.*

See : *Zwinger*★★★ *(Wall Pavilion*★★*, Nymphs' Bath*★★*, Porcelain Collection*★★*, Mathe*-
tical-Physical Salon★★*, Armoury*★★*)* AY – *Semper Opera*★★ AY – *Former court church*
(Hofkirche) BY – *Palace (Schloß) : royal houses*★ *(Fürstenzug-Mosaik), Long Passage*★ *(L*-
ger Gang) BY – *Albertinum : Picture Gallery Old Masters*★★★ *(Gemäldegalerie Alte Meist*-
Picture Gallery New Masters★★★ *(Gemäldegalerie Neue Meister), Green Vault*★★★ *(Grü*-
Gewölbe) BY – *Prager Straße*★ ABZ – *Museum of History of Dresden*★ *(Museum*
Geschichte der Stadt Dresden) BY L – *Church of the Cross*★ *(Kreuzkirche)* BY – *Japan*-
Palace★ *(Japanisches Palais)(garden* ≤★*)* ABX – *Museum of Folk Art*★ *(Museum für Vo*-
kunst) BX M² – *Great Garden*★ *(Großer Garten)* CDZ – *Russian-Orthodox Church*★ *(R*-
sisch-orthodoxe Kirche) (by Leningrader Str. BZ *) – Brühl's Terrace* ≤★ *(Brühlsche Terras*-
BY – *Equestrian statue of Augustus the Strong* ★ *(Reiterstandbild Augusts des Stark*-
BX E – *Pfunds dairy (Pfunds Molkerei) (interior*★*) Bautzener Straße 97* CX.

Envir. : *Schloß (palace) Moritzburg*★ *(North-West : 14 km by Hansastr.* BX*) – Schloß (pala*-
Pillnitz★ *(South-East : 15 km by Bautzener Str.* CX*) – Saxon Swiss*★★★ *(Sächsische Schwe*-
Bastei★★★*, Festung (fortress) Königstein*★★ ≤★★*, Großsedlitz : Baroque Garden*★.

🖈 *Possendorf (South : 13 km)* ℰ *(035206) 24 30 ;* 🖈 *Herzogswaldeb (South-West : 19 k*
ℰ *(0172) 3 53 09 10 ;* 🖈 *Ullersdorf (East : 8 km)* ℰ *(03528) 44 73 48.*

✈ *Dresden-Klotzsche (North : 13 km),* ℰ *(0351) 8 81 33 60 City Office, Rampsche*
2, ✉ *01067* ℰ *(0351) 4 99 88.*

🛈 *Tourist-Information, Prager Str. 10,* ✉ *01069,* ℰ *(0351) 49 19 20.*

🛈 *Tourist-Information, Neustädter Narkt,* ✉ *01097,* ℰ *(0351) 49 19 20.*

ADAC, *Schandauer Str. 46,* ✉ *01277,* ℰ *(0351) 44 78 80, Fax (0351) 4478850.*

Berlin 198 – Chemnitz 70 – Görlitz 98 – Leipzig 111 – Praha 152.

Plans on following pages

Kempinski Hotel Taschenbergpalais Ⓜ, Taschenberg 3, ✉ 01067, ℰ (03
4 91 20, Fax (0351) 4912812, 🌐, « Modern hotel in 18C baroque palace », Massage,
⊆s, ▨ – |⧎|, ↦ rm, ▤ 📺 ☎ & 🚗 – 🔺 320. 🆎 ⓞ E 𝗩𝗜𝗦𝗔 𝗝𝗖𝗕　　　　BY
Meals à la carte 59/80 – **213 rm** ⊇ 432/644 – 19 suites.

Radisson SAS Gewandhaushotel Ⓜ, Ringstr. 1, ✉ 01067, ℰ (0351) 4 94
Fax (0351) 4949490, 🏋, ⊆s, ▨ – |⧎|, ↦ rm, ▤ 📺 ☎ & 🅿 – 🔺 60. 🆎
E 𝗩𝗜𝗦𝗔　　　　BY
Meals à la carte 60/81 – **97 rm** ⊇ 324/513.

The Westin Bellevue, Große Meißner Str. 15, ✉ 01097, ℰ (0351) 80
Fax (0351) 8051609, ≤, « Courtyard terraces », 🏋, ⊆s, ▨ – |⧎|, ↦ rm, ▤ 📺 ☎
🚗 🅿 – 🔺 260. 🆎 ⓞ E 𝗩𝗜𝗦𝗔 𝗝𝗖𝗕　　　　BX
Meals à la carte 45/91 – **339 rm** ⊇ 240/440 – 16 suites.

Dresden Hilton, An der Frauenkirche 5, ✉ 01067, ℰ (0351) 8 64
Fax (0351) 8642725, 🏋, ⊆s, ▨ – |⧎|, ↦ rm, ▤ 📺 ☎ & 🚗 🅿 – 🔺 350. 🆎
E 𝗩𝗜𝗦𝗔 𝗝𝗖𝗕　　　　BY
Rossini (Italian rest.) **Meals** à la carte 52/88 – ***Wettiner Keller*** (closed Sunday - Mond
(dinner only) **Meals** à la carte 40/66 – **333 rm** ⊇ 436/539 – 4 suites.

Dorint Hotel Ⓜ, Grunauer Str. 14, ✉ 01069, ℰ (0351) 4 91 50, Fax (0351) 49151
⊆s, ▨ – |⧎|, ↦ rm, 📺 ☎ & 🚗 – 🔺 160. 🆎 ⓞ E 𝗩𝗜𝗦𝗔 𝗝𝗖𝗕　　　　CYZ
Meals à la carte 40/68 – **244 rm** ⊇ 245/295.

Bülow Residenz, Rähnitzgasse 19, ✉ 01097, ℰ (0351) 8 00 30, Fax (0351) 8003
« Courtyard terrace » – |⧎| 📺 ☎ & 🅿 – 🔺 25. 🆎 ⓞ E 𝗩𝗜𝗦𝗔. ⋇ rest　　BX
Meals (dinner only) (booking essential) à la carte 76/94 – **30 rm** ⊇ 315/650.
Spec. Gebratene Seezungenstreifen mit Tomatenconfit. Perlhuhnessenz mit Gänseleb
ravioli. Lammrücken in der Zucchiniblüte gebacken mit provenzialischem Gemüse.

Bayerischer Hof, Antonstr. 35, ✉ 01097, ℰ (0351) 82 93 70, Fax (0351) 80148
🌐 – |⧎|, ↦ rm, 📺 🚗 🅿 – 🔺 40. 🆎 ⓞ E 𝗩𝗜𝗦𝗔 𝗝𝗖𝗕. ⋇ rest　　BX
closed 20 December - 3 January – **Meals** (closed Saturday - Sunday) (dinner only) à la ca
31/52 – **50 rm** ⊇ 165/220 – 5 suites.

Park Inn Ⓜ, Königsbrückerstr. 121a, ✉ 01099, ℰ (0351) 8 06 30, Fax (0351) 8063
berr garden, « 19 C dance hall », ⊆s – |⧎|, ↦ rm, 📺 ☎ 🚗 – 🔺 330. 🆎 ⓞ E
⋇ rest　　U
Meals à la carte 26/44 – **148 rm** ⊇ 180/315.

art'otel, Ostra-Allee 33, ✉ 01067, ℰ (0351) 4 92 20, Fax (0351) 4922777, « Moo
interior », 🏋, ⊆s – |⧎|, ↦ rm, ▤ 📺 ☎ & 🚗 – 🔺 280. 🆎 ⓞ E 𝗩𝗜𝗦𝗔　　AY
Meals à la carte 45/62 – **174 rm** ⊇ 225/450.

Holiday Inn Ⓜ, Stauffenbergallee 25a, ✉ 01099, ℰ (0351) 8 15
Fax (0351) 8151333, 🏋, ⊆s – |⧎|, ↦ rm, ▤ rest, 📺 ☎ ☎ & 🚗 🅿 – 🔺 120,
ⓞ E 𝗩𝗜𝗦𝗔 𝗝𝗖𝗕　　　　by Königsbrücker Straße　　X
Meals à la carte 35/67 – **119 rm** ⊇ 145/240.

Elbflorenz Ⓜ without rest, Rosenstr. 36, ✉ 01067, ℘ (0351) 8 64 00, Fax (0351) 8640100, 🖾s – 📶 ⤧ 📺 ☎ 📞 🚗 – 🏛 150. 🆎 ⓪ ⓔ 𝘝𝘐𝘚𝘈 AZ v
209 rm ☕ 185/240.

Am Terrassenufer, Terrassenufer 12, ✉ 01069, ℘ (0351) 4 40 95 00, Fax (0351) 4409600, 🍃 – 📶, ⤧ rm, 📺 ☎ 📞 – 🏛 20. 🆎 ⓪ ⓔ 𝘝𝘐𝘚𝘈 𝐉𝐂𝐁 CY a
Meals à la carte 27/49 – **196 rm** ☕ 240/370 – 6 suites.

Astron Ⓜ, Hansastr. 37, ✉ 01097, ℘ (0351) 8 42 40, Fax (0351) 8424200, 🛋, 🖾s – 📶, ⤧ rm, 🖃 📺 ☎ 📞 ♿ 🚗 – 🏛 220. 🆎 ⓪ ⓔ 𝘝𝘐𝘚𝘈 𝐉𝐂𝐁
Meals *(dinner only)* à la carte 36/55 – **269 rm** ☕ 210/290.   by Hansastraße BX

Ramada Ⓜ without rest, Melanchthonstr. 2, ✉ 01099, ℘ (0351) 8 06 10, Fax (0351) 8061444 – 📶 ⤧, 🖃 rm, 📺 ☎ 📞 ♿ 🚗 – 🏛 25. 🆎 ⓪ ⓔ
𝘝𝘐𝘚𝘈 𝐉𝐂𝐁 CX a
132 rm ☕ 169/213 – 6 suites.

Verde Ⓜ, Buchenstr. 10, ✉ 01097, ℘ (0351) 8 11 10, Fax (0351) 8111333, 🖾s – 📶, ⤧ rm, 📺 ☎ 📞 ♿ 🚗 – 🏛 15. 🆎 ⓪ ⓔ 𝘝𝘐𝘚𝘈 𝐉𝐂𝐁. ⌘ rest   by Königsbrücker Str. BX
Meals *(closed Sunday dinner)* à la carte 27/46 – **77 rm** ☕ 180/230 – 9 suites.

Transmar Leonardo Ⓜ, Bamberger Str. 12, ✉ 01187, ℘ (0351) 4 66 00, Fax (0351) 4660100, 🍃 – 📶, ⤧ rm, 🖃 📺 ☎ 📞 ♿ 🚗 – 🏛 35. 🆎 ⓪ ⓔ
𝘝𝘐𝘚𝘈 𝐉𝐂𝐁 V v
Meals *(closed Saturday lunch)* à la carte 30/60 – **92 rm** ☕ 150/235.

Mercure Newa, St Petersburger Str. 34, ✉ 01069, ℘ (0351) 4 81 41 09, Fax (0351) 4955137, 🍃, 🖾s – 📶, ⤧ rm, 🖃 📺 ☎ 🚗 – 🏛 180. 🆎 ⓪ ⓔ 𝘝𝘐𝘚𝘈.
⌘ rest BZ n
Meals à la carte 39/61 – **315 rm** ☕ 165/252.

Windsor, Roßmäßlerstr. 13, ✉ 01139, ℘ (0351) 8 49 01 41, Fax (0351) 8490144 – 📶
📺 ☎. 🆎 ⓪ ⓔ 𝘝𝘐𝘚𝘈   by Leipziger Straße AX
Meals à la carte 27/42 – **25 rm** ☕ 160/250.

Martha Hospiz without rest, Nieritzstr. 11, ✉ 01097, ℘ (0351) 8 17 60, Fax (0351) 8176222 – 📶 📺 ☎ 📞 ♿. 🆎 ⓔ 𝘝𝘐𝘚𝘈. ⌘ BX s
closed 23 to 27 December – **50 rm** ☕ 90/230.

Tulip Inn, Fritz-Reuter-Str. 21, ✉ 01097, ℘ (0351) 8 09 50, Fax (0351) 8095555, 🖾s – 📶, ⤧ rm, 📺 ☎ 📞 Ⓟ – 🏛 15. 🆎 ⓪ ⓔ 𝘝𝘐𝘚𝘈. ⌘ rest   by Hansastr. BX
Meals *(closed Sunday)* à la carte 33/53 – **75 rm** ☕ 140/230.

Novalis Ⓜ, Bärnsdorfer Str. 185, ✉ 01127, ℘ (0351) 8 21 30, Fax (0351) 8213180, 🖾s – 📶, ⤧ rm, 📺 ☎ 📞 Ⓟ – 🏛 40. 🆎 ⓪ ⓔ 𝘝𝘐𝘚𝘈   by Hansastraße BX
Meals (dinner for residents only) – **84 rm** ☕ 145/170.

Achat Ⓜ without rest, Budapester Str. 34, ✉ 01069, ℘ (0351) 47 38 00, Fax (0351) 47380999 – 📶 ⤧ 📺 ☎ 📞 🚗 – 🏛 20. 🆎 ⓔ 𝘝𝘐𝘚𝘈 AZ e
160 rm ☕ 139/179.

Wenotel without rest, Schlachthofring 24, ✉ 01067, ℘ (0351) 4 97 60, Fax (0351) 4976100 – 📶 ⤧ 📺 ☎ Ⓟ – 🏛 20. 🆎 ⓪ ⓔ 𝘝𝘐𝘚𝘈   by Pieschener Allee AX
82 rm ☕ 114/140.

Italienisches Dörfchen, Theaterplatz 3, ✉ 01067, ℘ (0351) 49 81 60, Fax (0351) 4981688, beer garden, « Terrace with ≤ » – 🆎 ⓪ ⓔ 𝘝𝘐𝘚𝘈 𝐉𝐂𝐁 BY n
Weinzimmer : Meals à la carte 43/60 – *Kurfürstenzimmer :* Meals à la carte 35/50.

Opernrestaurant, Theatherplatz 2 (1st floor), ✉ 01067, ℘ (0351) 4 91 15 21, Fax (0351) 4956097 – 🆎 ⓪ ⓔ 𝘝𝘐𝘚𝘈 𝐉𝐂𝐁 AY r
closed Monday and 20 July - 30 August – **Meals** *(weekdays dinner only)* à la carte 40/70.

Ars Vivendi, Bürgerstr. 14, ✉ 01127, ℘ (0351) 8 40 09 69, Fax (0351) 8400969, 🍃 – 🆎 ⓔ 𝘝𝘐𝘚𝘈   by Leipziger Str. AX
Meals *(dinner only)* (booking essential) 49/92 and à la carte.

Fischgalerie, Maxstr. 2, ✉ 01067, ℘ (0351) 4 90 35 06, Fax (0351) 4903508, 🍃 – 🆎 ⓔ 𝘝𝘐𝘚𝘈 𝐉𝐂𝐁 AY s
closed Saturday lunch, Sunday dinner - Monday lunch and Bank Holidays – **Meals** (only fish dishes), (booking essential) à la carte 49/84.

König Albert, Königstr. 26, ✉ 01097, ℘ (0351) 8 04 48 83, Fax (0351) 8042958, 🍃 – 🆎 ⓔ 𝘝𝘐𝘚𝘈 𝐉𝐂𝐁. ⌘ BX e
closed Sunday – **Meals** (dinner only) à la carte 42/68.

Dresden-Blasewitz :

Am Blauen Wunder, Loschwitzer Str. 48, ✉ 01309, ℘ (0351) 3 36 60, Fax (0351) 3366299, 🍃 – 📶 📺 ☎ 🚗 – 🏛 25. 🆎 ⓔ 𝘝𝘐𝘚𝘈   by Blasewitzer Straße DY
closed 23 to 30 December – **Meals** *(closed Sunday - Monday lunch and 2 to 23 August)* (Italian rest.) à la carte 44/72 – **38 rm** ☕ 190/260.

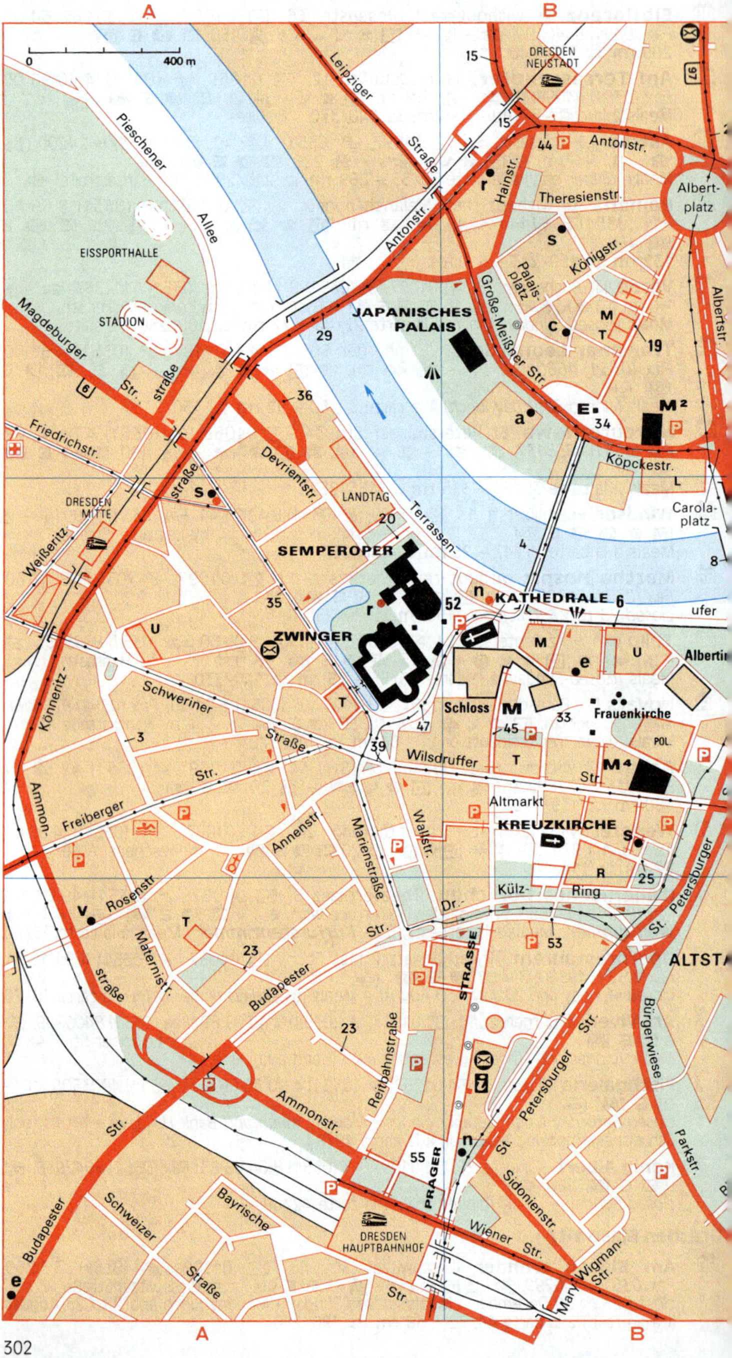

0   400 m

Pieschener Allee
Leipziger Straße
DRESDEN NEUSTADT
15
15
44
Antonstr.
Albert-platz
Hainstr.
Theresienstr.
EISSPORTHALLE
Magdeburger Str. straße
STADION
Antonstr.
Palais-platz
Königstr.
S
C
M
T
19
29
JAPANISCHES PALAIS
Große-Meißner Str
a
E
34
M 2
Köpckestr.
L
36
Friedrichstr.
Devrientstr.
LANDTAG
Terrassen-
Carola-platz
8
DRESDEN MITTE
S
Weißeritz
straße
20
4
ufer
SEMPEROPER
35
r
n
KATHEDRALE
6
52
U
ZWINGER
M
e
U
Albertin
Könneritz-
Schloss
M
33
Frauenkirche
T
45
POL.
Schweriner
47
39
Wilsdruffer
T
M 4
3
Straße
Str.
Ammon-
Str.
Freiberger
Annenstr.
Marienstraße
Wallstr.
Altmarkt
KREUZKIRCHE
S
R
25
Maternistr.
Rosenstr.
V
Külz- Ring
Dr.
St. Petersburger
T
23
Str.
53
ALTSTA
Budapester
Reitbahnstraße
STRASSE
Petersburger Str.
Bürgerwiese
Parkstr.
Ammonstr.
23
55
n
PRAGER
St.
Schweizer
Bayrische
Sidonienstr
DRESDEN HAUPTBAHNHOF
Wiener Str.
Mary Wigman-Str.
e
Straße
Str.

DRESDEN
GERMANY

NEUSTADT
ELBE
GROSSER
GARTEN
ZOOLOGISCHER-GARTEN
BOTANISCHER GARTEN
AUSSTELLUNGS-HALLE
PALAIS
Palaisteich
Neuer Teich

Louisenstr.
Radeberger Str.
Straße
Hoyerswerdaer Str.
Glacisstraße
Rosa-Luxemburg-Platz
Terrassenufer
Florian-Geyer-Str.
Sachsenplatz
Käthe-Kollwitz-Str.
Ufer
Rietschel-str.
Ziegelstr.
Pillnitzer Str.
Mathildenstr.
Güntzstraße
Marschnerstr.
Grunaer Str.
Straßburger Platz
Stübel-allee
Comeniusstraße
Dinglingerstr.
Striesener Straße
Holbeinstraße
Dürerstr.
Dürerstr.
Gerokstraße
Blasewitzer Straße
Thomaestr.
Wallot-straße
Fetscher-allee
Stübelallee
Blüherstr.
Lennéstr.
Hauptallee
Herkulesallee
Südallee

at Dresden-Cotta :

🏠 **Cotta-Hotel** Ⓜ, Mobschatzer Str. 17, ✉ 01157, ☎ (0351) 4 28 6
Fax (0351) 4286333, ≋ – 🛗, ⇥ rm, 📺 ☎ 🚹 🚗 – 🛐 45. 🆎 ⓸ ⅇ ᵛⁱˢᵃ J
🍽 rest   by Freiberger Straße and Emerich-Ambros-Ufer   AY
Meals à la carte 27/47 – **44 rm** ☕ 170/255.

🏠 **Residenz Alt Dresden**, Mobschatzerstr. 29, ✉ 01157, ☎ (0351) 4 28 ⁱ
Fax (0351) 4281988, ≋, 🛌, ⊜ – 🛗, ⇥ rm, 📺 ☎ 🚹 🚗 🅿 – 🛐 100. 🆎 ⓸
ᵛⁱˢᵃ Jᴄᴮ   by Freiberger Straße an Emerich-Ambros-Ufer   AY
Meals à la carte 46/61 – **124 rm** ☕ 168/198.

🏠 **Mercure Elbpromenade** Ⓜ, Hamburger Str. 64, ✉ 01157, ☎ (0351) 4 25 ⁱ
Fax (0351) 4252420 – 🛗, ⇥ rm, 📺 ☎ 🚗 🅿 – 🛐 50. 🆎 ⓸ ⓵
ᵛⁱˢᵃ   by Magdeburger Straße   AX
Meals à la carte 32/51 – **103 rm** ☕ 159/234.

In Dresden-Kemnitz :

🏰 **Romantik-Hotel Pattis** Ⓜ, Merbitzer Str. 53, ✉ 01157, ☎ (0351) 4 25 ⁱ
👩 Fax (0351) 4255255, ≋, « Health, fitness and beauty centre ; small park
Massage, ⊜, 🏊 – 🛗, ⇥ rm, 🍽 rest, 📺 ☎ 🚹 🚗 🅿 – 🛐 35. 🆎 ⓸
ᵛⁱˢᵃ   by Magdeburger Straße   AX
Gourment-Restaurant (closed Sunday) (dinner only) **Meals** à la carte 71/97 – **Erholur**
Meals à la carte 36/62 – **46 rm** ☕ 210/360 – 3 suites.

at Dresden-Klotzsche :

🏠 **Airport Hotel** Ⓜ, Karl-Marx-Str. 25, ✉ 01109, ☎ (0351) 8 83 30, Fax (0351) 88333
≋, ⊜ – 🛗, ⇥ rm, 🍽 rest, 📺 ☎ 📞 🚹 🚗 🅿 – 🛐 45. 🆎 ⓸ ⅇ
Jᴄᴮ   by Königsbrücker Straße   BX
Meals à la carte 31/60 – **100 rm** ☕ 240/310 – 7 suites.

at Dresden-Laubegast *East : 9 km by Striesener Straße DY* :

🏠 **Treff Resident Hotel** Ⓜ, Brünner Str. 11, ✉ 01279, ☎ (0351) 2 56 ⁱ
Fax (0351) 2562800 – 🛗, ⇥ rm, 📺 ☎ 📞 🚗 🅿 – 🛐 45. 🆎 ⓸ ⅇ ᵛⁱˢᵃ Jᴄᴮ
Meals (dinner only) à la carte 31/52 – **124 rm** ☕ 116/235.

at Dresden-Leubnitz-Neuostra *by Parkstr. BCZ and Teplitzer Str.* :

🏠 **Treff Hotel Dresden** Ⓜ, Wilhelm-Franke-Str. 90, ✉ 01219, ☎ (0351) 4 78
Fax (0351) 4782550, ≋, 🛌, ⊜ – 🛗, ⇥ rm, 📺 ☎ 🚹 🚗 🅿 – 🛐 370. 🆎 ⓸
ᵛⁱˢᵃ Jᴄᴮ
Meals à la carte 37/55 – ☕ 165/230.

In Dresden-Loschwitz :

🏰 **Schloß Eckberg** (with separate hotel wing), Bautzner Str. 134, ✉ 01099, ☎ (03
8 09 90, Fax (0351) 8099199, ≤ Dresden and Elbe, ≋, « Neo Gothic mansion ; extens
parkland », Massage, ⊜, 🏊 – 🛗, ⇥ rm, 📺 ☎ 📞 🅿 – 🛐 70. 🆎 ⓸ ⅇ ᵛⁱˢᵃ ⱼ
🍽 rest   U
Meals 39 (lunch) and à la carte 60/85 – **84 rm** ☕ 170/430.

at Dresden-Niedersedlitz *South-East : 10 km by Parkstraße BZ* :

🏠 **Ambiente** 🦢 without rest, Meusegaster Str. 23, ✉ 01259, ☎ (0351) 20 78
Fax (0351) 2078836 – 🛗 📺 ☎ 📞 🅿. ⅇ ᵛⁱˢᵃ
20 rm ☕ 158/265.

at Dresden-Reick *by Parkstraße (B 172) BCZ* :

🏠 **Coventry** without rest, Hülßestr. 1, ✉ 01237, ☎ (0351) 2 82 60, Fax (0351) 2816.
– 🛗 ⇥ 📺 ☎ 📞 🚹 🚗 🅿 – 🛐 25. 🆎 ⓸ ⅇ ᵛⁱˢᵃ
53 rm ☕ 165/210.

at Dresden-Strehlen *by Parkstraße and Gerhart-Hauptmann-Straße CZ* :

🏠 **Königshof** Ⓜ without rest, Kreischaer Str. 2, ✉ 012119, ☎ (0351) 8 73
Fax (0351) 8731499 – 🛗, ⇥ rm, 📺 ☎ 📞 🚹 – 🛐 60. 🆎 ⓸ ⅇ ᵛⁱˢᵃ Jᴄᴮ
94 rm ☕ 165/290 – 10 suites.

at Dresden-Weißer Hirsch *by Bautzner Straße CDX* :

🏠 **Villa Emma** Ⓜ 🦢, Stechgrundstr. 2, ✉ 01324, ☎ (0351) 26 48
Fax (0351) 2648118, ≋, « Modernized Art Deco villa », ⊜ – ⇥ rm, 📺 ☎ 🅿. 🆎
ⅇ ᵛⁱˢᵃ
closed 23 December - 3 January – **Meals** (dinner only) (booking essential) à la carte 49,
– **21 rm** ☕ 240/380.

Radebeul *North-West : 7 km by Leipziger Straße* AX :

🏨 **Steigenberger Parkhotel** Ⓜ ⚲, Nizzastr. 55, ✉ 01445, ℰ (0351) 8 32 10, Fax (0351) 8321445, 🌳, Massage, ↧, ⇌s, ☒ – 🛗 ⇌ 📺 ☎ 🚗 – 🏛 170. 𝔸𝔼 ⓪ 🅔 𝓥𝓘𝓢𝓐 𝗝𝗖𝗕
Lössnitz : Meals à la carte 40/65 – *Bistro :* Meals à la carte 37/63 – **200 rm** ☕ 245/300 – 11 suites.

JSSELDORF Ⓛ *Nordrhein-Westfalen* **417** *M 4,* **987** ㉕ ㉖ – *pop. 540 000 – alt. 40 m.*
See : *Königsallee★ EZ – Hofgarten★ DEY und Schloß Jägerhof (Goethemuseum★ EY* M¹)
– Hetjensmuseum★ DZ M⁴ *– Land Economic Museum (Landesmuseum Volk u. Wirtschaft)★*
DY M⁵ *– Museum of Art (Kunstmuseum)★ DY* M² *– Collection of Art (Kunstsammlung*
NRW)★ DY M³ *– Löbbecke-Museum und Aquazoo★ by Kaiserswerther Str. AU.*
Envir. : *Chateau of Benrath (Schloß Benrath) (Park★) South : 10 km by Siegburger Str. CX.*
🏌 *Düsseldorf-Grafebberg, Rennbahnstr. 24,* ℰ *(0211) 96 49 50 ;* 🏌 *Gut Rommeljans,*
North-East : 12 km, ℰ *(02102) 8 10 92 ;* 🏌 *Düsseldorf-Hubbelrath, East : 12 km,* ℰ *(02104)*
7 70 60 ; 🏌 *Düsseldorf-Hafen, Auf der Lausward,* ℰ *(0211) 39 66 17.*
✈ *Düsseldorf-Lohausen (North : 8 km),* ℰ *(0211) 42 10.*
🚃 *Hauptbahnhof.*
Exhibition Centre (Messegelände), ℰ *(0211) 4 56 01, Fax (0211) 4560668.*
🛈 *Tourist office, Immermannstr. 65b,* ✉ *40210,* ℰ *(0211) 17 20 20, Fax (0211) 161071.*
ADAC, *Himmelgeister Str. 63,* ✉ *40225,* ℰ *(0221) 47 27 47, Fax (0211) 332633.*
Berlin 552 – Amsterdam 225 – Essen 31 – Köln 40 – Rotterdam 237.

Plans on following pages

🏨 **Breidenbacher Hof,** Heinrich-Heine-Allee 36, ✉ 40213, ℰ (0211) 1 30 30, Fax (0211) 1303830, 🌳 – 🛗, ⇌ rm, ▤ 📺 ☎ 🚗 – 🏛 60. 𝔸𝔼 ⓪ 🅔 𝓥𝓘𝓢𝓐 𝗝𝗖𝗕. ⚘   EY a
Grill Royal (closed Saturday lunch and Sunday lunch) Meals à la carte 83/139 – *Breidenbacher Eck :* Meals à la carte 52/77 – *Trader Vic's (dinner only)* Meals à la carte 50/83 – **129 rm** ☕ 510/850 – 7 suites.

🏨 **Steigenberger Parkhotel,** Corneliusplatz 1, ✉ 40213, ℰ (0211) 1 38 10, Fax (0211) 131679, 🌳 – 🛗, ⇌ rm, ▤ rest, 📺 ☎ Ⓟ – 🏛 120. 𝔸𝔼 ⓪ 🅔 𝓥𝓘𝓢𝓐 𝗝𝗖𝗕. ⚘ rest   EY p
Meals à la carte 64/97 – **135 rm** ☕ 345/620 – 9 suites.

🏨 **Nikko,** Immermannstr. 41, ✉ 40210, ℰ (0211) 83 40, Fax (0211) 161216, ⇌s, ☒ – 🛗, ⇌ rm, ▤ 📺 ☎ ♿ – 🏛 300. 𝔸𝔼 ⓪ 🅔 𝓥𝓘𝓢𝓐 𝗝𝗖𝗕. ⚘ rest   BV g
Benkay (Japanese rest.) Meals à la carte 65/90 – *Brasserie Nikkolette :* Meals à la carte 37/60 – **301 rm** ☕ 380/650 – 5 suites.

🏨 **Queens Hotel** Ⓜ, Ludwig-Erhard-Allee 3, ✉ 40227, ℰ (0211) 7 77 10, Fax (0211) 7771777, ⇌s – 🛗, ⇌ rm, ▤ 📺 ☎ ♿ 🚗 – 🏛 50. 𝔸𝔼 ⓪ 🅔 𝓥𝓘𝓢𝓐. ⚘ rest   BV s
Meals à la carte 47/65 – **120 rm** ☕ 310/640 – 5 suites

🏨 **Holiday Inn,** Graf-Adolf-Platz 10, ✉ 40213, ℰ (0211) 3 84 80, Fax (0211) 3848390, ⇌s, ☒ – 🛗, ⇌ rm, ▤ rm, 📺 ☎ 🚗 – 🏛 50. 𝔸𝔼 ⓪ 🅔 𝓥𝓘𝓢𝓐 𝗝𝗖𝗕   EZ t
Meals à la carte 55/82 – **177 rm** ☕ 388/720.

🏨 **Majestic,** Cantadorstr. 4, ✉ 40211, ℰ (0211) 36 70 30, Fax (0211) 3670399, ⇌s – 🛗, ⇌ rm, 📺 ☎ ☎ – 🏛 30. 𝔸𝔼 ⓪ 🅔 𝓥𝓘𝓢𝓐 𝗝𝗖𝗕. ⚘   BV a
closed 21 December - 5 January – Il Casale (Italian rest.) (closed Saturday lunch and Sunday) Meals à la carte 46/70 – **52 rm** ☕ 265/460.

🏨 **Günnewig Hotel Esplanade** without rest, Fürstenplatz 17, ✉ 40215, ℰ (0211) 38 68 50, Fax (0211) 374032, ⇌s, ☒ – 🛗 ⇌ 📺 ☎ ☎ 🚗 – 🏛 m0. 𝔸𝔼 ⓪ 🅔 𝓥𝓘𝓢𝓐 𝗝𝗖𝗕   BX s
81 rm ☕ 179/498.

🏨 **Madison I** without rest, Graf-Adolf-Str. 94, ✉ 40210, ℰ (0211) 1 68 50, Fax (0211) 1685328, ⇌s, ☒ – 🛗 ⇌ 📺 ☎ 🚗 – 🏛 40. 𝔸𝔼 ⓪ 🅔 𝓥𝓘𝓢𝓐 𝗝𝗖𝗕 BV n
100 rm ☕ 190/339.

🏨 **Eden,** Adersstr. 29, ✉ 40215, ℰ (0211) 3 89 70, Fax (0211) 3897777 – 🛗, ⇌ rm, 📺 ☎ ☎ 🚗 – 🏛 80. 𝔸𝔼 ⓪ 🅔 𝓥𝓘𝓢𝓐 𝗝𝗖𝗕   EZ m
Meals *(closed Saturday lunch and Sunday except exhibitions)* à la carte 39/71 – **120 rm** ☕ 173/336

🏨 **Dorint Hotel,** Stresemannplatz 1, ✉ 40210, ℰ (0211) 3 55 40, Fax (0211) 354120 – 🛗, ⇌ rm, 📺 ☎ 🚗 – 🏛 50. 𝔸𝔼 ⓪ 🅔 𝓥𝓘𝓢𝓐 𝗝𝗖𝗕. ⚘ rest   EZ j
Meals à la carte 42/60 – **162 rm** ☕ 224/448 – 3 suites.

🏨 **Hotel An der Kö** without rest, Talstr. 9, ✉ 40217, ℰ (0211) 37 10 48, Fax (0211) 370835 – 🛗 📺 ☎ Ⓟ. 𝔸𝔼 ⓪ 🅔 𝓥𝓘𝓢𝓐 𝗝𝗖𝗕   EZ n
45 rm ☕ 160/230.

DÜSSELDORF

Kaiserswerther Str.
Reeser Pl.
s
GOLZHEIM
16
Johannstr.
Heinrich-Ehrhardt Str.
77
e
Th.-Heuss-Brücke
Uerdinger Str.
r
Roßstr.
Ulmen-
Rather
Straße
Grashofstr.
Münsterstr.
Brehmstr.
ADAC
Cecilien-
Kaiserswerther
Kennedydamm
c
DERENDORF
str.
Collenbachstr.
DERENDORF
h
U
q
Gruner-
str.
THEODOR-HEUSS-BRÜCKE
Golzheimer
Platz
KÖLN-
DÜSSELDORFER
RHEIN-
PARK
46
Straße
Kennedydamm
Klever Straße
Roßstr.
Nordstr.
n
52
Münsterstr.
52
S-BAHN
E STA
24
Kaiser-
Friedrich-
Ring
allee
J
Klever
Str.
c
f
Duisburger
Prinz-
Georg-
Str.
Moltkestr.
Bagelstr.
D.-ZOO
Rethelstr.
9
J
105
Str.
93
RHEIN
OBERKASSEL
Joseph-Beuys-Uler
M
Kaiserstr.
Schinkel-
strs.
Rethelstr.
Luegallee
Luegplatz
M
94
Schumann-
Grafenber
OBERKASSELER BRÜCKE
HOF-
GARTEN
Jägerhofstr.
Adlerstr.
c
Kaiser-Wilhelm-Ring
Stromstr.
M
70
HOF-
GARTEN
104
84
M
3
D.-WEHRHAHN
V
Schlossturm
ALTSTADT
M
51
P
a
Kölner
3
d
z
Str.
Königsallee
Allee
r
k
115
RHEINKNIEBRÜCKE
Rheinufertunnel
M
g
56
str.
Worlinger
59
s
Handelszent
Berliner
Karl-
i
u
Str.
LANDTAG
RHEINTURM
33
Graf-
Adolf-
n
Hauptbahnhof
Stahlwerkstr.
Eisenstr.
a
HAFEN
Hüttenstr.
92
71
40
80
d
e
POL.
Reichsstr.
54
t
Fürstenwall
Ellerstr.
Oberbilker
Markt
64
Kronprinzen-
Elisabethstr.
Fürstenwall
30
Lessingplatz
t
Kruppstraße
99
31
b
s
D.-VOLKLINGER
STR.
Bilker
D.-FRIEDRICHSTADT
Oberbilker
Alle
86
c
Str.
5
Bachstr.
Allee
D.-VOLKSGARTEN
S-BAHN
S-BAH
D.-BILK
S-Bahn
Völklinger
Straße
Aachener
Merowingerstr.
12
43
22
VOLKSGARTEN
12
Mecum-
Hennekamp
Südring
Südring
60
60
Auf'm
114
ADAC
a
Stofleler Kapellen

STREET INDEX

DÜSSELDORF

D
E
0 200 m
Victoriapl.
Ufer
Beuys-
Joseph-
M²
M⁵
EHRENHOF
Oederallee
TONHALLE
Inselstr.
Nordstr.
Kaiserstr.
Nordstr.
Duisburger
Sternstr.
Straße
Prinz-Georg-Str.
104
105
v
s
r
27
Heine-
Denkmal
Y
Oberkasseler Brücke
P
45 Tonhalle
HOFGARTEN
Gartenstr.
Jägerhofstr.
Jacobistr.
HOFGARTEN
Fritz- Roeber- Str.
RATINGER TOR
70
88
M³
42
SCHAUSPIEL HAUS
T
J
32
KUNSTHALLE
OPERNHAUS
T
51
91
101
Schlossturm
STADTHAUS
c
z
21 p
90
RHEIN
Burgpl. 73
R
8
95
H.-Heine-Allee
Altstadt
42
91
Immermannstr.
68
28
a
ALTER
HAFEN
W-MARX-HAUS
v 7
69
Rheinufertunnel
M
M⁴
96
f
Karlplatz
Steinstr./
Königsallee
c
Ostr.
Bismarckstr.
13
n
M
Str.
r
Benrather
Str.
Steinstr.
d
Mannesmannufer
Berger-Allee
Bilker
Poststr.
Bastion-
Kasernen-
Breite
straße
Straße
straße
KÖNIGSALLEE
P
Stresemannstr.
Ostr.
L
L
97
Graf-Adolf-
Platz
Berliner
Allee
f
Haroldstr.
Kavalleriestr.
Elisabethstr.
Friedrichstr.
Graf-
t
Adolf-
Str.
23
Hubertusstr.
Luisenstr.
m
n
Luisenstr.
15
Z

Astoria without rest, Jahnstr. 72, ✉ 40215, ℘ (0211) 38 51 30, Fax (0211) 372089 –
|‡| ⠀ TV ☎ ℘. AE ① E VISA JCB. ✍⠀⠀⠀⠀⠀⠀⠀⠀⠀⠀⠀⠀⠀⠀⠀⠀⠀⠀⠀⠀⠀⠀⠀⠀⠀⠀⠀BX b
closed 22 December - 8 January – **26 rm** ☞ 152/380 – 4 suites.

Rema-Hotel Concorde without rest, Graf-Adolf-Str. 60, ✉ 40210, ℘ (0211)
36 98 25, Fax (0211) 354604 – |‡| ⠀ TV ☎ ℘. AE ① E VISA JCB⠀⠀⠀⠀⠀⠀⠀⠀⠀⠀⠀⠀EZ f
84 rm ☞ 170/390.

Carat Hotel without rest, Benrather Str. 7a, ✉ 40213, ℘ (0211) 1 30 50,
Fax (0211) 322214, ⠀ – |‡| ⠀ TV ☎ – ⠀ 20. AE ① E VISA⠀⠀⠀⠀⠀⠀⠀⠀⠀⠀⠀⠀⠀⠀⠀⠀DZ r
73 rm ☞ 160/420.

Rema-Hotel Monopol without rest, Oststr. 135, ✉ 40210, ℘ (0211) 8 42 08,
Fax (0211) 328843 – |‡| ⠀ TV ☎. AE ① E VISA JCB⠀⠀⠀⠀⠀⠀⠀⠀⠀⠀⠀⠀⠀⠀⠀⠀⠀⠀⠀⠀EZ d
51 rm ☞ 170/390.

Günnewig Hotel Uebachs without rest, Leopoldstr. 5, ✉ 40211, ℘ (0211) 17 37 10,
Fax (0211) 358064 – |‡| ⠀ TV ☎ ℘ ⇔ – ⠀ 30. AE ① E VISA JCB⠀⠀⠀⠀⠀⠀⠀⠀⠀⠀BV r
82 rm ☞ 179/390.

Amber Hotel Cornelius without rest, Corneliusstr. 82, ✉ 40215, ℘ (0211) 38 65 60,
Fax (0211) 382050, ⠀ – |‡| TV ☎ ℘ Ⓟ – ⠀ 30. AE ① E VISA⠀⠀⠀⠀⠀⠀⠀⠀⠀⠀⠀⠀⠀BX s
closed 20 December - 7 January – **52 rm** ☞ 120/240.

Orangerie ⠀ without rest, Bäckergasse 1, ✉ 40213, ℘ (0211) 86 68 00,
Fax (0211) 8668099 – |‡| TV ☎ – ⠀ 30. AE ① E VISA. ✍⠀⠀⠀⠀⠀⠀⠀⠀⠀⠀⠀⠀⠀⠀⠀DZ n
27 rm ☞ 195/295.

Residenz without rest, Worringer Str. 88, ✉ 40211, ℘ (0211) 36 08 54,
Fax (0211) 364676 – |‡| ⠀ TV ☎. AE ① E VISA JCB⠀⠀⠀⠀⠀⠀⠀⠀⠀⠀⠀⠀⠀⠀⠀⠀⠀⠀BV z
40 rm ☞ 128/350.

Ibis Hauptbahnhof without rest, Konrad-Adenauer-Platz 14, ✉ 40210, ℘ (0211)
1 67 20, Fax (0211) 1672101 – |‡| ⠀ TV ☎ ♿ – ⠀ 30. AE ① E VISA
JCB⠀⠀BV u
166 rm ☞ 148/213.

Schumacher without rest, Worringer Str. 55, ✉ 40211, ℘ (211) 36 78 50,
Fax (0211) 3678570, ⠀ – |‡| TV ☎ ℘ ⇔. AE ① E VISA JCB⠀⠀⠀⠀⠀⠀⠀⠀⠀⠀⠀⠀⠀BV d
29 rm ☞ 150/300.

Victorian, Königstr. 3a (1st floor), ✉ 40212, ℘ (0211) 8 65 50 22, Fax (0211) 8655013
– ▤. AE ① E VISA. ✍⠀⠀⠀⠀⠀⠀⠀⠀⠀⠀⠀⠀⠀⠀⠀⠀⠀⠀⠀⠀⠀⠀⠀⠀⠀⠀⠀⠀⠀⠀⠀⠀⠀⠀⠀⠀EZ c
closed Sunday and Bank Holidays – **Meals** (booking essential, outstanding wine list) 55
(lunch) and à la carte 88/122 – **Bistro im Victorian** *(closed Sunday July - August)* **Meals**
à la carte 39/72.
Spec. Gänseleberterrine mit marinierten weißen Feigen. Seezungenspitzen und Hummer
in Aromaten. Rehbockmedaillons mit Sauerkirsch-Pfeffersauce (season).

Weinhaus Tante Anna, Andreassstr. 2, ✉ 40213, ℘ (0211) 13 11 63,
Fax (0211) 132974, (former 16C private chapel), « Antique pictures and furniture » – AE
① E VISA JCB⠀⠀⠀⠀⠀⠀⠀⠀⠀⠀⠀⠀⠀⠀⠀⠀⠀⠀⠀⠀⠀⠀⠀⠀⠀⠀⠀⠀⠀⠀⠀⠀⠀⠀⠀⠀⠀⠀⠀DY c
closed Sunday except exhibitions – **Meals** (dinner only, booking essential, outstanding wine
list) à la carte 58/85.

La Terrazza, Königsallee 30 (Kö-Centre, 2nd floor, |‡|), ✉ 40212, ℘ (0211) 32 75 40,
Fax (0211) 320975 – ▤. AE ① E VISA JCB⠀⠀⠀⠀⠀⠀⠀⠀⠀⠀⠀⠀⠀⠀⠀⠀⠀⠀⠀⠀⠀⠀⠀EZ v
closed Sunday and Bank Holidays except exhibitions – **Meals** (booking essential, Italian rest.)
à la carte 69/95.

Nippon Kan, Immermannstr. 35, ✉ 40210, ℘ (0211) 17 34 70, Fax (0211) 3613625
– AE ① E VISA⠀⠀⠀⠀⠀⠀⠀⠀⠀⠀⠀⠀⠀⠀⠀⠀⠀⠀⠀⠀⠀⠀⠀⠀⠀⠀⠀⠀⠀⠀⠀⠀⠀⠀⠀⠀⠀⠀BV g
closed Easter and Christmas – **Meals** (booking essential, Japanese rest.) à la carte 43/
124.

Daitokai, Mutter-Ey-Str. 1, ✉ 40213, ℘ (0211) 32 50 54, Fax (0211) 325056 – AE ①
E VISA JCB. ✍⠀⠀⠀⠀⠀⠀⠀⠀⠀⠀⠀⠀⠀⠀⠀⠀⠀⠀⠀⠀⠀⠀⠀⠀⠀⠀⠀⠀⠀⠀⠀⠀⠀⠀⠀⠀⠀DY z
closed Monday April - October except exhibitions – **Meals** (Japanese rest.) à la carte 60/80.

Brewery-inns :

Zum Schiffchen, Hafenstr. 5, ✉ 40213, ℘ (0211) 13 24 21, Fax (0211) 134596, ⛱
– AE ① E VISA⠀⠀⠀⠀⠀⠀⠀⠀⠀⠀⠀⠀⠀⠀⠀⠀⠀⠀⠀⠀⠀⠀⠀⠀⠀⠀⠀⠀⠀⠀⠀⠀⠀⠀⠀⠀⠀DZ f
closed Christmas - New Year, Sunday and Bank Holidays except exhibitions – **Meals** à la
carte 40/68.

at Düsseldorf-Angermund North : 15 km by Danziger Straße AU :

Haus Litzbrück, Bahnhofstr. 33, ✉ 40489, ℘ (0203) 99 79 60, Fax (0203) 9979653,
« Garden terrace », ⠀, ⠀, ⠀ – TV ☎ ⇔ Ⓟ – ⠀ 30. AE ① E VISA
Meals à la carte 44/77 – **21 rm** ☞ 145/295.

at Düsseldorf-Bilk :

Grand Hotel without rest, Varnhagenstr. 37, ⌧ 40225, ℘ (0211) 31 08 00, *Fax (0211) 316667,* ⊜s – ⊟ 📺 ☎ & ⇔ – ⚑ 30. AE ⓞ E VISA JCB
70 rm ⌑ 298/388.
BX a

Aida without rest, Ubierstr. 36, ⌧ 40223, ℘ (0211) 1 59 90, *Fax (0211) 1599103,* ⊜s
– ⊟ 📺 ☎ & Ⓟ – ⚑ 30. AE ⓞ E VISA JCB
93 rm ⌑ 158/295.
by Aachener Str. AX

at Düsseldorf-Derendorf *by Prinz-Georg-Str.* BU :

Villa Viktoria without rest, Blumenthalstr. 12, ⌧ 40476, ℘ (0211) 46 90 00, *Fax (0211) 46900601,* « Elegant modern installation », ⊜s, 🌿 – ⊟ ⊱ 📺 ⇔. AE ⓞ
E VISA JCB
closed 24 December - 1 January – **40 suites** ⌑ 377/955.

Lindner Hotel Rhein Residence Ⓜ, Kaiserswerther Str. 20, ⌧ 40477, ℘ (0211)
4 99 90, *Fax (0211) 4999499,* 🌿, Massage ⒑, ⊜s – ⊟, ⊱ rm, 📺 ☏ – ⚑ 18. AE ⓞ
E VISA JCB
ABU f
Meals à la carte 43/64 – **126 rm** ⌑ 233/531.

Gildors Hotel without rest (with guest house), Collenbachstr. 51, ⌧ 40476, ℘ (0211)
48 80 05, *Fax (0211) 444844* – ⊟ 📺 ☎ ⇔. AE ⓞ E VISA
BU n
50 rm ⌑ 175/350.

Cascade without rest, Kaiserswerther Str. 59, ⌧ 40477, ℘ (0211) 49 22 00,
Fax (0211) 4922022 – ⊟ 📺 ☎ ⇔. AE ⓞ E VISA. ⊁
AU c
29 rm ⌑ 155/320.

at Düsseldorf-Düsseltal :

Haus am Zoo ⊗ without rest, Sybelstr. 21, ⌧ 40239, ℘ (0211) 6 16 96 10,
Fax (0211) 61696169, « Garden », ⊜s, 🌊 (heated) – ⊟ 📺 ☎ ⇔. AE E VISA BU h
23 rm ⌑ 180/350.

at Düsseldorf-Golzheim :

Radisson SAS Hotel, Karl-Arnold-Platz 5, ⌧ 40474, ℘ (0211) 4 55 30,
Fax (0211) 4553110, 🌿, Massage, ⊜s, 🌊 – ⊟, ⊱ rm, 🗏 📺 ☏ & ⇔ Ⓟ – ⚑ 400.
AE ⓞ E VISA JCB. ⊁ rest
AU q
Meals à la carte 48/76 – **309 rm** ⌑ 385/755 – 15 suites.

Hilton, Georg-Glock-Str. 20, ⌧ 40474, ℘ (0211) 4 37 70, *Fax (0211) 4377650,* 🌿, Massage, ⊜s, 🌊, 🌿 – ⊟, ⊱ rm, 🗏 📺 ☏ & ⇔ Ⓟ – ⚑ 900. AE ⓞ E VISA JCB.
⊁ rest
AU r
Meals à la carte 56/77 – **372 rm** ⌑ 362/763 – 9 suites.

Rosati, Felix-Klein-Str. 1, ⌧ 40474, ℘ (0211) 4 36 05 03, *Fax (0211) 452963,* 🌿 – Ⓟ.
AE ⓞ E VISA JCB. ⊁
AU s
closed Saturday lunch and Sunday except exhibitions – **Meals** (booking essential, Italian rest.) à la carte 63/92.

at Düsseldorf-Kaiserswerth *by Kaiserswerther Str.* AU :

Im Schiffchen, Kaiserswerther Markt 9 (1st floor), ⌧ 40489, ℘ (0211) 40 10 50,
Fax (0211) 403667 – AE ⓞ E VISA. ⊁
closed Sunday - Monday – **Meals** (dinner only, booking essential) 179/198 and à la carte
111/151
Spec. Aufgeschäumter Sainte-Maure-Frischkäse mit Ossetra-Kaviar. Gebratene Brust vom Bresse-Perlhuhn mit Mokka-Duft. Depeche aus Ceylon.

Aalschokker, Kaiserswerther Markt 9 (ground floor), ⌧ 40489, ℘ (0211) 40 39 48,
Fax (0211) 403667 – AE ⓞ E VISA. ⊁
closed Sunday - Monday – **Meals** (dinner only, booking essential) à la carte 80/100
Spec. Geräuchertes Saiblingsfilet nach "Heinrich Heine". Düsseldorfer Senfbraten. Westfälischer Bettelmann auf Zitronenschaum.

at Düsseldorf-Lörick *by Luegallee* AV :

Fischerhaus ⊗, Bonifatiusstr. 35, ⌧ 40547, ℘ (0211) 59 79 79, *Fax (0211) 5979759*
– 📺 ☎ ☏ Ⓟ. AE ⓞ E VISA
Meals see also *Hummerstübchen* below – **40 rm** ⌑ 182/375.

Hummerstübchen - Hotel Fischerhaus, Bonifatiusstr. 35, ⌧ 40547, ℘ (0211)
59 44 02, *Fax (0211) 5979759* – Ⓟ. AE ⓞ E VISA
closed Sunday, Monday and 1 to 10 January – **Meals** (dinner only, booking essential)
135/175 and à la carte 111/139
Spec. Hummer-Menu. Hummersuppe mit Champagner. Lammrücken mit Olivenkruste und Kartoffelratatouille.

at Düsseldorf-Lohausen *by Danziger Str.* AU :

ArabellaSheraton Airport Hotel, at airport, ⊠ 40474, ℘ (0211) 4 17 30,
Fax (0211) 4173707 – |≴|, ⇥ rm, TV க் – ♨ 180. AE ⓞ E VISA JCB
Meals à la carte 48/68 – **200 rm** �ⁱ 306/372.

at Düsseldorf-Mörsenbroich *by Rethelstr.* DV :

Renaissance Hotel, Nördlicher Zubringer 6, ⊠ 40470, ℘ (0211) 6 21 60,
Fax (0211) 6216666, ☂, Massage, ≦s, ℥ – |≴|, ⇥ rm, ▤ TV ☏ க் ⇋ – ♨ 260. AE
ⓞ E VISA JCB
Meals à la carte 56/82 – **245 rm** ⊆ 320/700 – 3 suites.   BU e

at Düsseldorf-Oberkassel *by Luegallee* AV :

Lindner Hotel Rheinstern, Emanuel-Leutze-Str. 17, ⊠ 40547, ℘ (0211) 5 99 70,
Fax (0211) 5997339, ≦s, ℥ – |≴|, ⇥ rm, ▤ TV ☏ ⇋ ℗ – ♨ 240. AE ⓞ E VISA
JCB. ⅍ rest
Meals 40 buffet lunch and à la carte 48/93 – **254 rm** ⊆ 313/441.

Courtyard by Mariott, Am Seestern 16, ⊠ 40547, ℘ (0211) 59 59 59,
Fax (0211) 593569, ≦s, ℥ – |≴|, ⇥ rm, ▤ TV ℗ – ♨ 120. AE ⓞ E VISA JCB. ⅍ rest
Meals à la carte 45/72 – **222 rm** ⊆ 186/252.

Hanseat without rest, Belsenstr. 6, ⊠ 40545, ℘ (0211) 57 50 69, *Fax (0211) 589662*,
« Elegant installation » – TV ☎. AE ⓞ E VISA
closed Christmas - New Year – **37 rm** ⊆ 180/350.

De'Medici, Amboßstr. 3, ⊠ 40547, ℘ (0211) 59 41 51, *Fax (0211) 592612* – AE ⓞ E VISA
closed Saturday lunch, Sunday and Bank Holidays except exhibitions – **Meals** (booking
essential, Italian rest.) à la carte 48/82.

Edo, Am Seestern 5, ⊠ 40547, ℘ (0211) 59 10 82, *Fax (0211) 591394*, « Japanese
garden, terrace » – ▤ rest, ℗. AE ⓞ E VISA JCB. ⅍
closed Saturday lunch, Sunday and Bank Holidays except exhibitions – **Meals** (Japanese
rest.) 90/160 and à la carte 46/93.

at Düsseldorf-Unterbilk :

Sorat M, Volmerswerther Str. 35, ⊠ 40221, ℘ (0211) 3 02 20, *Fax (0211) 3022555*,
≦s – |≴|, ⇥ rm, ▤ TV ☎ ⇋ – ♨ 160. AE ⓞ E VISA JCB   AX c
Meals à la carte 44/62 – **160 rm** ⊆ 215/480.

Savini, Stromstr. 47, ⊠ 40221, ℘ (0211) 39 39 31, *Fax (0211) 391719*, ☂ – E   AX e
closed Saturday lunch and Sunday except exhibitions – **Meals** (booking essential) (outstanding wine list) à la carte 62/93.

An'ne Bell, Kaistr. 16, ⊠ 40221, ℘ (0211) 3 00 67 50, *Fax (0211) 30067515*, ☂ – AE E
closed Saturday lunch, Sunday and 1 to 7 January – **Meals** à la carte 79/127   AX d
Spec. Blumenkohlragout mit Kartoffeln und Persischem Kaviar. Gebratener Zander mit
Kohlrabi und Trüffeljus. Crème brûlée mit Lavendelduft.

Rheinturm Top 180, Stromstr. 20, ⊠ 40221, ℘ (0211) 8 48 58, *Fax (0211) 325619*,
❋ Düsseldorf and Rhein, (revolving restaurant at 172 m) (|≴|, charge) – ▤ – ♨ 40. AE
ⓞ E VISA JCB. ⅍   AV a
Meals à la carte 54/87.

Schorn with rm, Martinstr. 46a, ⊠ 40223, ℘ (0211) 3 98 19 72, *Fax (0211) 3981972*
– ⅍ rm   AX s
Meals (closed Sunday - Monday, Easter and 4 weeks July - August) (dinner only, booking
essential, outstanding wine list) à la carte 56/82 – **3 rm** ⊆ 200/400.

at Düsseldorf-Unterrath *by Ulmenstraße* BU :

Lindner Hotel Airport M, Unterrather Str. 108, ⊠ 40468, ℘ (0211) 9 51 60,
Fax (0211) 9516516, ₤ᛃ, ≦s – |≴|, ⇥ rm, TV ☎ ☏ ⇋ ℗ – ♨ 140. AE ⓞ E VISA JCB.
⅍ rest
Meals à la carte 43/61 – **201 rm** ⊆ 298/606.

at Meerbusch-Büderich *by Luegallee* AV :

Landsknecht with rm, Poststr. 70, ⊠ 40667, ℘ (02132) 9 33 90, *Fax (02132) 10978*,
☂ – ⇥ rm, TV ☎ ℗. AE E VISA
Meals (closed Saturday lunch and Monday) (outstanding wine list) à la carte 59/81 – **9 rm**
⊆ 165/240.

Landhaus Mönchenwerth, Niederlöricker Str. 56 (at the boat landing stage),
⊠ 40667, ℘ (02132) 7 79 31, *Fax (02132) 71899*, ≤, « Garden terrace » – ℗. AE E VISA
closed Saturday lunch and Monday – **Meals** (outstanding wine list) à la carte 49/80.

Lindenhof, Dorfstr. 48, ⊠ 40667, ℘ (02132) 26 64, *Fax (02132) 10196*, ☂
AE VISA
closed Monday – **Meals** (booking essential) à la carte 42/72.

In Meerbusch - Langst-Kirst *North-West : 14 km by Luegallee* AV *and Neusser Straße :*

🏨 **Rheinhotel Vier Jahreszeiten** 🅼 🐾, Zur Rheinfähre 14, ✉ 40668, ✆ (02150) 91 40, Fax (02150) 914900, 🌳, beer garden, ⮂ – 🛗, ⚟ rm, ▤ 📺 ✆ 🅿 – 🏛 120. 🆎 ⓞ Ⓔ 𝗩𝗜𝗦𝗔
Bellevue *(dinner only)* **Meals** à la carte 62/90 – **Orangerie** *(lunch only)* **Meals** à la carte 34/59 – **78 rm** � 198/378 – 3 suites.

Dortmund *Nordrhein-Westfalen* 𝟰𝟭𝟳 *L 6 – pop. 610 000 – alt. 87 m.*
Düsseldorf 78.

at Dortmund-Syburg *South-West : 13 km :*

XXXX   **La Table**, Hohensyburgstr. 200 (at the casino), ✉ 44265, ✆ (0231) 9 77 70 37,
✿✿   Fax (0231) 9777077, 🌳 – 🅿 – 🏛 30. 🆎 ⓞ Ⓔ 𝗩𝗜𝗦𝗔 𝗝𝗖𝗕. ⚟
closed Monday and 4 weeks June - July – **Meals** *(dinner only, outstanding wine list)* 99/158 and à la carte 98/120
Spec. Zweierlei von geräuchertem Lachs mit Sevruga Kaviar. Jakobsmuscheln und Hummer im Lauchmantel mit Tomatenconfit. Charlotte von der Taubenbrust mit Kartoffeln und Périgord Trüffeln.

Essen *Nordrhein-Westfalen* 𝟰𝟭𝟳 *L 5,* 𝟵𝟴𝟳 ⑭ *– pop. 604 000 – alt. 120 m.*
Düsseldorf 31.

at Essen-Kettwig *South : 11 km :*

XXXX   **Résidence** 🐾 with rm, Auf der Forst 1, ✉ 45219, ✆ (02054) 9 55 90,
✿✿   Fax (02054) 82501, 🌳 – 📺 ☎ 🚗 🅿. 🆎 ⓞ Ⓔ 𝗩𝗜𝗦𝗔
closed 1 to 8 January and 3 weeks July - August – **Meals** *(closed Sunday - Monday)* *(dinner only, booking essential)* *(outstanding wine list)* 135/178 and à la carte 91/136 – **Benedikt** *(Euro-Asian rest.)* **Meals** 149/189 – **18 rm** � 188/337
Spec. Getrüffeltes Kartoffel-Gänselebertörtchen mit Wachtelcrêpinette. Atlantik Hummer mit Dicken Bohnen. Schokoladenauflauf mit Curry-Caramel.

Grevenbroich *Nordrhein-Westfalen* 𝟰𝟭𝟳 *M 3,* 𝟵𝟴𝟳 ㉕ *– pop. 62 000 – alt. 60 m.*
Düsseldorf 28.

XXXXX   **Zur Traube** with rm, Bahnstr. 47, ✉ 41515, ✆ (02181) 6 87 67, Fax (02181) 61122
✿✿   – 📺 🅿. ⓞ Ⓔ 𝗩𝗜𝗦𝗔 ⚟ rm
closed 28 March - 5 April, 15 July - 5 August and 24 December - 16 January – **Meals** *(closed Sunday and Monday)* *(booking essential, outstanding wine list)* 78 *(lunch)* and à la carte 97/132 – **6 rm** ⊃ 230/360.
Spec. Lauwarmer Wildlachs mit Kaviarschaum. Taubenbrüstchen und Gänseleber im Spitzkohlblatt. Vanillesoufflé mit marinierten Waldbeeren und weißem Schokoladeneis.

*If you would like a more complete selection of hotels
and restaurants, consult the MICHELIN Red Guides
for the following countries :*

*Benelux, Deutschland, España Portugal, France,
Great Britain and Ireland, Italia, Suisse*

all in annual editions.

FRANKFURT ON MAIN *Hessen* 𝟰𝟭𝟳 *P 10,* 𝟵𝟴𝟳 ㉗ *– pop. 60 000 – alt. 91 m.*
See : *Zoo*★★★ FX *– Goethe's House (Goethehaus)*★ GZ *– Cathedral (Dom)*★ *(Gothic Tower*★★*, Choir-stalls*★*, Museum*★*)* HZ *– Tropical Garden (Palmengarten)*★ CV *– Senckenberg-Museum*★ *(Palaeontology department*★★*)* CV M⁹ *– Städel Museum (Städelsches Museum and Städtische Galerie)* ★★ GZ *– Museum of Applied Arts (Museum für Kunsthandwerk)*★ HZ *– German Cinema Museum*★ GZ M⁷ *– Henninger Turm* ☀★ FX *– Museum of Modern Art (Museum für moderne Kunst)*★ HY M¹⁰.
🛫 *Frankfurt-Niederrad, by Kennedy-Allee* CDX, ✆ (069) 6 66 23 18 ; 🛬 *Frankfurt-Niederrad, By Kennedy-Allee* CDX, ✆ (069) 96 74 13 53.
✈ *Rhein-Main (South-West : 12 km),* ✆ (069) 6 90 25 95.
🚗 *at Neu-Isenburg (South : 7 km).*
Exhibition Centre (Messegelände) (CX), ✆ (069) 7 57 50, Fax (069) 75756433.
🛈 *Tourist Information, im Römer,* ✉ 60311, ✆ (069) 21 23 87 08.
ADAC, *Schumannstr. 4,* ✉ 60325, ✆ (069) 74 38 00, Fax (069) 749254.
ADAC, *Schillerstr. 12,* ✉ 60313, ✆ (069) 74 38 03 35, Fax (069) 283597.
Berlin 537 – Wiesbaden 41 – Bonn 178 – Nürnberg 226 – Stuttgart 204.

Steigenberger Frankfurter Hof, Bethmannstr. 33, ✉ 60311, ☏ (069) 2 15 02, Fax (069) 215900, 🌰, Massage – |彙|, ⇔ rm, 🖥 TV ☏ – 🛎 120. AE Ⓞ E VISA JCB. ※ rest
Restaurant Français (booking essential) (closed Saturday lunch, Sunday, Monday, Bank Holidays and 3 weeks July - August) **Meals** à la carte 84/132 – *Oscar's* (closed 4 weeks July - August) **Meals** à la carte 44/75 – **332 rm** 🍵 431/722 – 20 suites.

Hessischer Hof, Friedrich-Ebert-Anlage 40, ✉ 60325, ☏ (069) 7 54 00, Fax (069) 7540924, « Rest. with collection of Sèvres porcelain » – |彙|, ⇔ rm, 🖥 TV ☏ ⇔ P – 🛎 120. AE Ⓞ E VISA JCB. ※ rest   CX p
Meals 49 (lunch) and à la carte 67/102 – **117 rm** 🍵 395/672 – 11 suites.

ArabellaSheraton Grand Hotel, Konrad-Adenauer-Str. 7, ✉ 60313, ☏ (069) 2 98 10, Fax (069) 2981810, Massage, ₤, ⇔s, ▨ – |彙|, ⇔ rm, 🖥 TV ☏ ⇔ – 🛎 300. AE Ⓞ E VISA JCB. ※ rest   HY c
Premiere (closed Saturday lunch, Sunday, 11 July - 8 August and 25 to 30 December) **Meals** 48 (lunch) and à la carte 67/102 – *Brasserie* (lunch only) **Meals** à la carte 47/89 – **378 rm** 🍵 468/611 – 11 suites.

Martim Hotel Frankfurt Ⓜ, Theodor-Heuss-Allee 3, ✉ 60486, ☏ (069) 7 57 80, Fax (069) 75781000, Massage, ₤, ⇔s, ▨ – |彙|, ⇔ rm, 🖥 TV ☏ & ⇔ – 🛎 1900. AE Ⓞ E VISA JCB. ※ rest   CVX c
Classico (closed Saturday and Sunday lunch) **Meals** à la carte 56/90 – *Ambiente :* **Meals** 50 (buffet lunch only) – **543 rm** 🍵 365/740 – 24 suites.

Intercontinental Frankfurt, Wilhelm-Leuschner-Str. 43, ✉ 60329, ☏ (069) 2 60 50, Fax (069) 252467, ₤, ⇔s, ▨ – |彙|, ⇔ rm, 🖥 TV ☏ & – 🛎 500. AE Ⓞ E VISA JCB   GZ a
Meals à la carte 56/89 – **65 rm** 🍵 412/693 – 35 suites.

Frankfurt Marriott Hotel, Hamburger Allee 2, ✉ 60486, ☏ (069) 7 95 50, Fax (069) 79552432, ≤ Frankfurt, Massage, ₤, ⇔s – |彙|, ⇔ rm, 🖥 TV ☏ ⇔ – 🛎 600. AE Ⓞ E VISA. ※ rest   CV a
Meals à la carte 46/81 – **588 rm** 🍵 330/565 – 17 suites.

Le Meridien Parkhotel, Wiesenhüttenplatz 28, ✉ 60329, ☏ (069) 2 69 70, Fax (069) 2697884, ₤, ⇔s – |彙|, ⇔ rm, 🖥 TV ☏ ⇔ P – 🛎 160. AE Ⓞ E VISA JCB
Meals à la carte 49/82 – **296 rm** 🍵 375/605 – 11 suites.

Alexander am Zoo Ⓜ without rest, Waldschmidtstr. 59, ✉ 60316, ☏ (069) 94 96 00, Fax (069) 94960720, ⇔s – |彙| ⇔ TV ☏ ⇔ – 🛎 30. AE Ⓞ E VISA JCB. ※   FV c
9 rm 🍵 215/390 – 9 suites.

Palmenhof, Bockenheimer Landstr. 89, ✉ 60325, ☏ (069) 7 53 00 60, Fax (069) 75300666 – |彙| TV ☏ ⇔. AE Ⓞ E VISA JCB   CV m
closed 23 December - 2 January – **Meals** (closed Saturday, Sunday and Bank Holidays) à la carte 66/84 – **46 rm** 🍵 195/350.

An der Messe without rest, Westendstr. 104, ✉ 60325, ☏ (069) 74 79 79, Fax (069) 748349 – |彙| TV ⇔. AE Ⓞ E VISA JCB   CV e
46 rm 🍵 230/480.

Sofitel, Savignystr. 14, ✉ 60325, ☏ (069) 7 53 30, Fax (069) 7533175 – |彙|, ⇔ rm, TV – 🛎 80. AE Ⓞ E VISA JCB. ※ rest   CX f
Meals à la carte 53/87 – **155 rm** 🍵 390/480.

Forum Hotel Ⓜ without rest, Wilhelm-Leuschner-Str. 34, ✉ 60329, ☏ (069) 2 60 60, Fax (069) 260602925, ₤, ⇔s, ▨ – |彙| ⇔ 🖥 TV ☏ – 🛎 500. AE Ⓞ E VISA JCB   CZ z
301 rm 🍵 331/593.

Mercure, Voltastr. 29, ✉ 60486, ☏ (069) 7 92 60, Fax (069) 79261606, 🌰, ⇔s – |彙|, ⇔ rm, TV ☎ ☏ ⇔ – 🛎 80. AE Ⓞ E VISA JCB   by Th.-Heuss-Allee CV
Meals à la carte 38/80 – **346 rm** 🍵 206/433 – 12 suites.

Savoy, Wiesenhüttenstr. 42, ✉ 60329, ☏ (069) 27 39 60, Fax (069) 27396795, Massage, ⇔s, ▨ – |彙| ⇔ rm, 🖥 rest, TV ☎ – 🛎 100. AE Ⓞ E VISA JCB   CX s
Meals à la carte 46/67 – **144 rm** 🍵 260/335.

Imperial, Sophienstr. 40, ✉ 60487, ☏ (069) 7 93 00 30, Fax (069) 79300388 – |彙|, ⇔ rm, 🖥 TV ☎ ⇔ P. AE Ⓞ E VISA JCB   CV t
Meals (closed Sunday) (dinner only) à la carte 44/66 – **60 rm** 🍵 190/480.

Victoria Hotel without rest, Elbestr. 24, ✉ 60329, ☏ (069) 27 30 60, Fax (069) 27306100 – |彙| ⇔ TV ☎ ☏. AE Ⓞ E VISA JCB   CDX t
75 rm 🍵 160/390.

Domicil without rest, Karlstr. 14, ✉ 60329, ☏ (069) 27 11 10, Fax (069) 253266 – |彙| ⇔ TV ☎. AE Ⓞ E VISA JCB   CX d
closed Christmas - New Year – **70 rm** 🍵 169/309.

Atlantic Ⓜ without rest, Düsseldorfer Str. 20, ✉ 60329, ☏ (069) 27 21 20, Fax (069) 27212100 – |彙| ⇔ TV ☎ ☏ ⇔. ※   CX b
60 rm 🍵 210/310.

GERMANY

A 66
EUROPATURM
21
Frauenlobstr.
Franz-
Rücker-
Allee
Sophienstr.
Miquelallee
n
BOCKENHEIM
Leipziger Str.
Schloß.
Bockenheimer Warte
Adalbertstr.
Gräfstr.
Sophienstr.
t
U
U
U
U
U
M 9
U
h
Hamburger Allee
r
x
ADAC
Th.-Heuss-Allee
Senckenberganlage
a
e
Westendstr.
d
Friedrich-Ebert-Anlage
p
P
Lc
MESSETURM
FESTHALLE
MESSEGELÄNDE
Hemmerichsweg
S-BAHN
7
Frankenallee
Mainzer
Frankenallee
Mainzer Landstr.
GALLUSWARTE
Tunnel im Bau
Gutleutstr.
Gutleutstr.
WESTHAFEN
MAIN
Botanischer Garten
GRÜNEBURG-PARK
EHEM. I.-G.-FARBEN VERWALTUNGSGEBÄUDE
PALMENGARTEN
Grüneburgweg
Siesmayerstr.
Fürstenberger Str.
P
Bockenheimer
m
Beethoven-
Westend
o
b
s
z
Liebigstr.
k
v
Grüneburgweg
Grüneburgweg
Holzhausenstr.
12
Str.
ROTHSCHILD PARK
Landstr.
Bockenheimer Anlag
Hochstr.
Neue Mainzer
Taunus Anlage
Goetheplatz
Guiollettstr.
S. BAHN
Westendstr.
Landstr.
Mainzer
n
f
o
d
Taunusstr.
33
r
b
d
P
POL
Platz der Republik
14
e
HAUPT-BAHNHOF
c
a
Hafenstr.
Landstr.
a
s
k
P
Baseler Str.
Untermainkai
v
t
M
M
Schaumainkai-(Museumsufer)
STÄDELSCHES MUSEUM
M
M
Friedensbr.
Stresemann-
allee
Gartenstr.
Kennedy-
43·44
STRESEMANNALLEE
WESTBAHNHOF
straße
Miquelallee
Miquel-Adickesallee
e
Eschersheimer Landstr.
Eysseneckstr.
Miquelallee
0   500 m

FRANKFURT AM MAIN

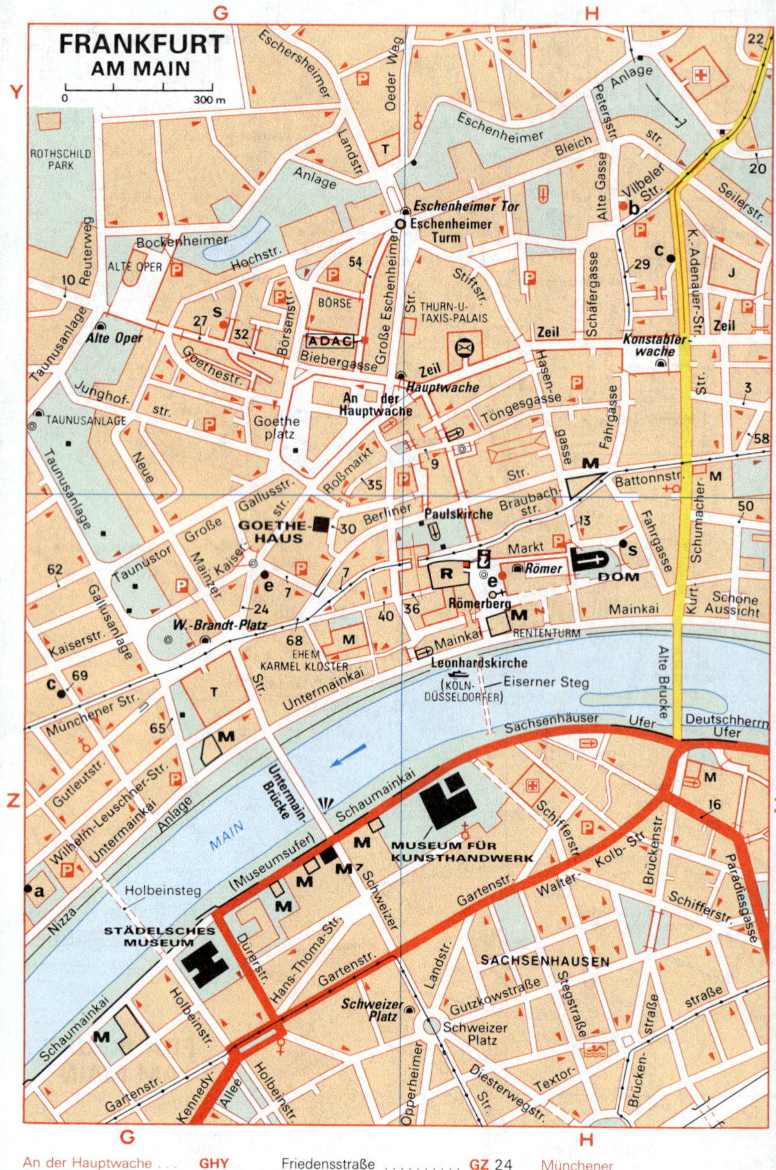

FRANKFURT
AM MAIN
0   300 m
G
H
Y
Z
ROTHSCHILD PARK
Eschersheimer
Oeder Weg
Eschenheimer
Landstr.
Anlage
Bockenheimer
Hochstr.
ALTE OPER
Reuterweg
Taunusanlage
Alte Oper
Junghof.
str.
TAUNUSANLAGE
Taunusanlage
Neue
Taunustor
Gallusanlage
Kaiserstr.
Münchener Str.
Gutleutstr.
Wilhelm-Leuschner-Str.
Untermainkai
Anlage
MAIN
Nizza
Holbeinsteg
a
STÄDELSCHES MUSEUM
Schaumainkai
Gartenstr.
Kennedy-Allee
Holbeinstr.
Dürerstr.
Hans-Thoma-Str.
Gartenstr.
Untermain-Brücke
(Museumsufer)
Schaumainkai
MUSEUM FÜR KUNSTHANDWERK
Schweizer
Gartenstr.
Schweizer Platz
Gutzkowstraße
Opperheimer
Diesterwegstr.
Str.
SACHSENHAUSEN
Walter-Kolb-Str.
Stegstraße
Textor-straße
Brücken-straße
Schifferstr.
Brückenstr.
Paradiesgasse
Anlage
Petersstr.
Alte Gasse
Bleich
str.
Vilbeler Str.
b
29
C
J
K.-Adenauer-Str.
Zeil
Eschenheimer Tor
Eschenheimer Turm
54
BÖRSE
S
27
32
Börsenstr.
ADAC
Biebergasse
Goethestr.
Goethe platz
Stiftstr.
Str.
THURN-U.-TAXIS-PALAIS
Zeil
Hauptwache
An der Hauptwache
Töngesgasse
Hasen-gasse
Fahrgasse
Konstablerwache
3
58
Roßmarkt
Gallusstr.
Große
Kaiser
Mainzer
str.
62
Taunustor
e
7
W.-Brandt-Platz
24
68
EHEM KARMEL KLOSTER
Untermainkai
T
65
M
c
69
Berliner
35
Kleiner Hirschgraben
Str.
30
GOETHE-HAUS
Paulskirche
Braubach-str.
Battonnstr.
13
9
M
Schumacher Str.
50
Markt
R
Römer
Römerberg
40
36
Mainkai
RENTENTURM
Leonhardskirche
(KÖLN-DÜSSELDORFER)
Eiserner Steg
DOM
S
Schöne Aussicht
Alte Brücke
Sachsenhäuser Ufer
Deutschherrn Ufer
M
16
20
22
Seilerstr.
Zeil

Rema-Hotel Bristol without rest, Ludwigstr. 13, ⊠ 60327, 𝄞 (069) 24 23 90, *Fax (069) 251539* – ▯ ⊁ TV ☎ – ♨ 25. AE ⓘ E VISA JCB
45 rm ⌣ 170/390.
CX a

InterCityHotel, Poststr. 8, ⊠ 60329, 𝄞 (069) 27 39 10, *Fax (069) 27391999* – ▯, ⊁ rm, TV ☎ 📞 – ♨ 80. AE ⓘ E VISA JCB. ⚹ rest
Meals *(closed Saturday - Sunday lunch)* à la carte 38/61 – **384 rm** ⌣ 234/398.
CX e

Novotel Frankfurt City West, Lise-Meitner-Str. 2, ⊠ 60486, 𝄞 (069) 79 30 30, *Fax (069) 79303930*, ☲, ≋ – ▯, ⊁ rm, 🖥 TV ☎ ♿ 🚗 🅿 – ♨ 140. AE ⓘ E VISA
Meals à la carte 41/59 – **235 rm** ⌣ 210/331.
CV r

Die Villa without rest, Emil-Sulzbach-Str. 14, ⊠ 60486, 𝄞 (069) 9 79 90 70, *Fax (069) 97990711* – TV ☎ 🅿. AE ⓘ E VISA JCB
closed 20 December - 2 January – **22 rm** ⌣ 273/496.
CV x

Atrium without rest, Beethovenstr. 30, ⊠ 60325, 𝄞 (069) 97 56 70, *Fax (069) 97567100* – ▯ TV ☎. AE E VISA JCB. ⚹
closed 22 December - 2 January and Easter – **45 rm** ⌣ 195/455.
CV d

Manhattan without rest, Düsseldorfer Str. 10, ⊠ 60329, 𝄞 (069) 23 47 48, *Fax (069) 234532* – ▯ TV ☎. AE ⓘ E VISA JCB
60 rm ⌣ 160/390.
CX r

Liebig-Hotel without rest, Liebigstr. 45, ⊠ 60323, 𝄞 (069) 72 75 51, *Fax (069) 727555* – ⊁ TV ☎. AE ⓘ E VISA JCB
19 rm ⌣ 205/360.
CV z

Cosmos M without rest, Weserstr. 17, ⊠ 60329, 𝄞 (069) 31 08 10, *Fax (069) 31081555* – ▯ ⊁ TV ☎ 📞. AE ⓘ E VISA JCB
52 rm ⌣ 160/198.
GZ c

Columbus M without rest, Moselstr. 23, ⊠ 60329, 𝄞 (069) 27 28 00, *Fax (069) 27280555* – ▯ ⊁ TV ☎ 📞. AE ⓘ E VISA JCB
45 rm ⌣ 160/198.
CX x

Am Dom without rest, Kannengießergasse 3, ⊠ 60311, 𝄞 (069) 1 38 10 30, *Fax (069) 283237* – ▯ TV ☎. AE VISA
30 rm ⌣ 155/300.
HZ s

Cristall without rest, Ottostr. 3, ⊠ 60329, 𝄞 (069) 23 03 51, *Fax (069) 253368* – ▯ TV ☎. AE ⓘ E VISA JCB. ⚹
30 rm ⌣ 110/310.
CX c

XXX **Humperdinck**, Grüneburgweg 95, ⊠ 60323, 𝄞 (069) 72 21 22, *Fax (069) 97203155*, ☲ – AE ⓘ VISA
❀ *closed Saturday lunch, Sunday and Bank Holidays, 3 weeks July - August and Christmas - early January* – **Meals** 49 (lunch) and à la carte 85/137
CV v
Spec. Hummercarpaccio mit gefülltem Hühnerflügel. Gänsestopfleber mit Pfirsich, Bohnen und Lavendel (June-September). Zwiebeltarte mit Kalbsbries und Alba-Trüffel (October-December).

XXX **Union Club Restaurant**, Am Leonhardsbrunnen 12, ⊠ 60487, 𝄞 (069) 70 30 33, *Fax (069) 7073820*, ☲ – AE ⓘ E VISA JCB
closed Sunday dinner, Saturday and 25 December - 5 January – **Meals** (booking essential) à la carte 75/98.
CV n

XX **Tigerpalast-Restaurant**, Heiligkreuzgasse 20, ⊠ 60313, 𝄞 (069) 92 00 22 25, *Fax (069) 92002217*, (with variety-theatre) – 🖥. AE ⓘ E VISA. ⚹
❀ *closed Monday and mid July - end August* – **Meals** (dinner only) à la carte 92/120
FV s
Spec. Kanadischer Hummer mit Kräutersalat und ofengetrockneten Tomaten. Crêpinette und Ragout vom Neuseeländischen Milchkalb mit Zuckerschoten. Crème brûlée mit marinierten Aprikosen.

XX **Aubergine**, Alte Gasse 14, ⊠ 60313, 𝄞 (069) 9 20 07 80, *Fax (069) 9200786* – AE ⓘ E VISA
closed Saturday lunch, Sunday except exhibitions and 3 weeks July - August – **Meals** (booking essential) (outstanding wine list) à la carte 70/89.
HY b

XX **Tse-Yang**, Kaiserstr. 67, ⊠ 60329, 𝄞 (069) 23 25 41, *Fax (069) 237825* – AE ⓘ E VISA JCB
Meals (Chinese rest.) à la carte 44/80.
CX v

XX **Gallo Nero**, Kaiserhofstr. 7, ⊠ 60313, 𝄞 (069) 28 48 40, *Fax (069) 291645*, ☲ – AE ⓘ E VISA JCB
closed Sunday except exhibitions – **Meals** (Italian rest.) à la carte 63/94.
GY s

XX **La Trattoria**, Fürstenberger Str. 179, ⊠ 60322, 𝄞 (069) 55 21 30, *Fax (069) 552130* – AE ⓘ E VISA JCB
closed Saturday lunch, Sunday except exhibitions, 24 December - 3 January – **Meals** (Italian rest.) à la carte 78/85.
DV s

X **Gargantua**, Liebigstr. 47, ⊠ 60323, ℘ (069) 72 07 18, *Fax (069) 720717*, � – AE ⓪
E VISA
CV s
closed Saturday lunch, Sunday and late December - early January – **Meals** (booking essential) 49 (lunch) and à la carte 82/108.

X **Ernos Bistro**, Liebigstr. 15, ⊠ 60323, ℘ (069) 72 19 97, *Fax (069) 173838*, � – AE
E VISA
CV k
*closed Saturday - Sunday except exhibitions, 24 July - 15 August and 23 December -
9 January* – **Meals** (booking essential) (French rest.) 50 (lunch) und à la carte 91/115
Spec. Gänseleberpastete "à la cuillère". Zander auf elsäßischem Sauerkraut mit Blutwurstsauce. Lammfilet in eigener Jus mit getrockneten Tomaten.

X **Tao**, Friedberger Anlage 14, ⊠ 60316, ℘ (069) 44 98 44, *Fax (069) 432596*, � – AE
⓪ E VISA
FV a
closed Monday and Saturday lunch – **Meals** (Vietnamese rest.) à la carte 33/57.

Frankfurter Äppelwoilokale *(mainly light meals only)* :

X **Zum Rad**, Leonhardsgasse 2 (Seckbach), ⊠ 60389, ℘ (069) 47 91 28, *Fax (069) 472942*,
�   by Im Prüfling and Seckbacher Landstraße   FV
closed Tuesday, November - March Monday and Tuesday – **Meals** (weekdays open from
5.00 pm, Sunday and Bank Holidays from 3.00 pm) à la carte 25/47.

X **Römerbembel**, Römerberg 22, ⊠ 60311, ℘ (069) 28 83 83, *Fax (069) 557644*, �
– AE ⓪ E VISA
HZ e
Meals à la carte 25/37.

X **Klaane Sachsehäuser**, Neuer Wall 11 (Sachsenhausen), ⊠ 60594, ℘ (069) 61 59 83,
Fax (069) 622141, �
FX n
closed Sunday – **Meals** (open from 4 pm) à la carte 21/42.

X **Zum gemalten Haus**, Schweizer Str. 67 (Sachsenhausen), ⊠ 60594, ℘ (069) 614559,
Fax (069) 6031457, �
EX c
closed Monday - Tuesday, late December - early January and late July - mid August – **Meals**
à la carte 20/27.

at Frankfurt-Bergen-Enkheim *by Wittelsbacherallee* FV ✪ *06109* :

Amadeus, Röntgenstr. 5, ⊠ 60338, ℘ (06109) 37 00, *Fax (06109) 370720* – ⫴, ⊱⊰ rm,
▤ TV ☎ 📞 👤 ⇔ Ⓟ – 🔬 80. AE ⓪ E VISA. ⊁ rest
Meals à la carte 43/66 – **160 rm** ⊑ 199/345.

at Frankfurt-Griesheim *by Th.-Heuss-Allee* CV :

Courtyard by Marriott, Oeserstr. 180, ⊠ 65933, ℘ (069) 3 90 50,
Fax (069) 3808218, ⇌s, ⊠ – ⫴, ⊱⊰ rm, ▤ rest, TV Ⓟ – 🔬 220. AE ⓪ E VISA JCB
Meals à la carte 36/59 – **236 rm** ⊑ 180/240.

at Frankfurt-Höchst *West : 10 km by Mainzer Landstraße* CX :

Lindner Congress Hotel Ⓜ, Bolongarostr. 100, ⊠ 65929, ℘ (069) 3 30 02 00,
Fax (069) 33002999, ⫙, ⇌s – ⫴, ⊱⊰ rm, ▤ TV ☎ 📞 👤 ⇔ – 🔬 160. AE ⓪ E VISA
JCB. ⊁ rest
Meals à la carte 48/87 – **85 rm** ⊑ 289/538.

at Frankfurt-Nieder-Erlenbach *by Friedberger Lamdstr.* FV *and Homburger Landstr. North :
14 Km* :

XX **Erlenbach 33**, Alt Erlenbach 33, ⊠ 60437, ℘ (06101) 4 80 98, *Fax (06101) 48783* –
AE ⓪ E VISA
closed Tuesday and 3 weeks July - August – **Meals** (weekdays dinner only) à la carte 46/69.

at Frankfurt-Niederrad *by Kennedy-Allee* CDX :

Queens Hotel, Isenburger Schneise 40, ⊠ 60528, ℘ (069) 6 78 40, *Fax (069) 6784190*,
� – ⫴, ⊱⊰ rm, ▤ rest, TV 📞 Ⓟ – 🔬 250. AE ⓪ E VISA JCB
Meals à la carte 58/74 – **295 rm** ⊑ 321/593.

Arabella Sheraton Congress Hotel, Lyoner Str. 44, ⊠ 60528, ℘ (069) 6 63 30,
Fax (069) 6633666, ⇌s, ⊠ – ⫴, ⊱⊰ rm, ▤ TV 📞 ⇔ Ⓟ – 🔬 290. AE ⓪ E VISA JCB
Meals (closed Saturday - Sunday) à la carte 47/72 – **396 rm** ⊑ 251/365 – 4 suites.

Dorint Ⓜ, Hahnstr. 9, ⊠ 60528, ℘ (069) 66 30 60, *Fax (069) 66306600*, ⇌s, ⊠ – ⫴,
⊱⊰ rm, ▤ TV ☎ 📞 👤 Ⓟ – 🔬 180. AE ⓪ E VISA JCB
Meals à la carte 42/66 – **191 rm** ⊑ 306/552.

XX **Weidemann**, Kelsterbacher Str. 66, ⊠ 60528, ℘ (069) 67 59 96, *Fax (069) 673928*,
� – Ⓟ. AE ⓪ E VISA
by Gartenstraße   CX
closed Saturday lunch, Sunday and Bank Holidays – **Meals** (booking essential) 53 (lunch)
and à la carte 77/115.

at Frankfurt-Nordweststadt *by Miquelallee* CV :

Courtyard by Marriott Nordwest Zentrum [M] without rest, Walter-Möller-Platz, ✉ 60439, ℰ (069) 58 09 30, Fax (069) 582447 – 📶 ⊁ [TV] ☎ 📞 ♿ 🚗 – 🛥 20. AE ⓓ E VISA JCB. ⊁
93 rm ☕ 198/236.

at Frankfurt-Rödelheim *North-West : 6 km by Theodor-Heuss-Allee* CV *and Ludwig-Landmann-Str :*

Osteria Enoteca, Arnoldshainer Str. 2 (corner Lorscher Str.), ✉ 60489, ℰ (069) 7 89 22 16, 🌿 – AE E VISA. ⊁
closed Saturday lunch, Sunday and late December - early January – **Meals** (booking essential) (Italian rest.) 115/105 and à la carte 87/95
Spec. Presskopf vom Octopus mit Sauerampfer-Kerbelvinaigrette. Kräutersuppe mit gebratenen Gamberoni. Chateaubriand con Ratatouille di Parmigiano di Melanzane e Cipolle.

at Frankfurt-Sachsenhausen :

Crowne Plaza [M], Mailänder Str. 1, ✉ 60598, ℰ (069) 6 80 20, Fax (069) 6802333, 👟, ⊆s – 📶, ⊁ rm, 🖥 [TV] ♿ 🚗 P – 🛥 220. AE ⓓ E VISA JCB. ⊁ rest
Meals à la carte 40/75 – **404 rm** ☕ 302/493.   *by Darmstädter Landstr.* (B 3)   FX

Bistrot 77, Ziegelhüttenweg 1, ✉ 60598, ℰ (069) 61 40 40, Fax (069) 615998, 🌿 – AE E VISA
EX a
closed Saturday lunch, Sunday and Christmas - early January – **Meals** (outstanding wine list) 38 (lunch) and à la carte 75/114.

at Eschborn *North-West : 12 km by A66 :*

Novotel, Philipp-Helfmann-Str. 10, ✉ 65760, ℰ (06196) 90 10, Fax (06196) 482114, 🌿, ☇ (heated), 🎾 – 📶, ⊁ rm, 🖥 [TV] ☎ ♿ P – 🛥 200. AE ⓓ E VISA JCB
by A 66   CV
Meals à la carte 37/65 – **224 rm** ☕ 200/285.

at Neu-Isenburg - Gravenbruch *South-East : 11 km by Darmstädter Landstr.* FX *and B 459 :*

Kempinski Hotel Gravenbruch Frankfurt, ✉ 63263, ℰ (06102) 50 50, Fax (06102) 505900, 🌿, « Park », Massage, ⊆s, ☇ (heated), 🏊, 🎾, ⊁ – 📶, ⊁ rm, 🖥 [TV] 📞 🚗 P – 🛥 350. AE ⓓ E VISA JCB. ⊁ rest
Meals 50 (lunch) and à la carte 58/103 – **285 rm** ☕ 289/604 – 21 suites.

near Rhein-Main airport *South-West : 12 km by Kennedy-Allee* CX :

Sheraton [M], Hugo-Eckener-Ring (Terminal 1), ✉ 60549 *Frankfurt*, ℰ (069) 6 97 70, Fax (069) 69772209, Massage, ⊆s, 🏊 – 📶, ⊁ rm, 🖥 [TV] 📞 ♿ P – 🛥 700. AE ⓓ E VISA JCB. ⊁ rest
Papillon (dinner only, outstanding wine list) *(closed Sunday, Bank Holidays and 3 weeks July - August)* **Meals** à la carte 85/127 – **Maxwell's Bistro :** Meals à la carte 50/84 – **Taverne** *(closed Saturday - Sunday lunch)* Meals à la carte 54/82 – **1050 rm** ☕ 465/745 – 30 suites.

Steigenberger Airport Hotel, Unterschweinstiege 16, ✉ 60549, ℰ (069) 6 97 50, Fax (069) 69752505, Massage, ⊆s, 🏊 – 📶, ⊁ rm, 🖥 [TV] 📞 🚗 P – 🛥 300. AE ⓓ E VISA
Meals 49 lunch buffet only – **420 rm** ☕ 327/714 – 10 suites.   AU n

Eltville *Hessen* 🔟🖽 *P 8 – pop. 16 500 – alt. 90 m.*
Frankfurt on Main 55.

at Eltville-Erbach *West : 2 km :*

Marcobrunn - Hotel Schloß Reinhartshausen, Hauptstr. 43, ✉ 65346, ℰ (06123) 67 64 32, Fax (06123) 676400, « Terrace in park » – 🖥 P. AE ⓓ E VISA. ⊁
closed Monday-Tuesday, January and 3 weeks July-August, Monday-Friday dinner only –
Menu 105/195 and à la carte 90/136
Spec. Kalbsfuß mit Trüffeln und Kartoffeln gefüllt auf Wirsinggemüse. Steinbutt mit geschmolzener Gänseleber und Petersilienpüree. Bresse Taube mit Oliven in der Artischocke geschmort und Rosmarinjus.

Maintal *Hessen* 🔟🖽 *P 10 – pop. 40 000 – alt. 95 m.*
Frankfurt on Main 13.

at Maintal-Dörnigheim :

Hessler with rm, Am Bootshafen 4, ✉ 63477, ℰ (06181) 4 30 30, Fax (06181) 430333 – [TV] ☎ P. AE E VISA
closed 3 weeks July – **Meals** *(closed Monday - Tuesday)* (booking essential, outstanding wine list) 108/175 and à la carte 88/105 – **Kathis Bistro** *(closed Monday - Tuesday)* **Meals** 49 and à la carte 54/66 – **7 rm** ☕ 180/295
Spec. Marinierter Seeteufel mit schwarzem Kokosreis und Erdnußbuttersauce. Gefüllte Taube im Strudelteig mit Trüffeljus. Rehrücken mit Walnußkruste und Kirsch-Holundersauce.

Mannheim *Baden-Württemberg* 417 419 *R 9,* 987 ㉗ *– pop. 330 000 – alt. 95 m.*
Frankfurt am Main 79.

XXX   **Da Gianni**, R 7, 34, ✉ 68161, ℰ (0621) 2 03 26 – 📧. 𝔸𝔼 ⊑. ⌗
❀❀   *closed Monday, Bank Holidays and 3 weeks July - August –* **Meals** (booking essential) (Italian
      rest.) 149 and à la carte 91/115
      Spec. Variation von Kaninchen und Gänseleber. Canelloni von Meeresfrüchten. Steinbutt
      im Vongolesud.

Stromberg Kreis Kreuznach *Rheinland-Pfalz* 417 *Q 7,* 987 ㉖ *– pop. 3 000 – alt. 235 m.*
Frankfurt am Main 82.

XXXX **Le Val d'Or in Johann Lafer's Stromburg** 🐾 with rm, Schloßberg 1, ✉ 55442,
❀❀   ℰ (06724) 9 31 00, Fax (06724) 931090, ≼, 🌳, beer garden – 📺 ☎ 🅿 – 🔥 100. 𝔸𝔼
      ⓓ ⊑ 𝘝𝘐𝘚𝘈
      Meals *(Tuesday - Friday dinner only, closed Monday)* 169/198 and à la carte 106/130 –
      Turmstube : Meals à la carte 55/78 – **14 rm** ⌑ 209/428
      Spec. Weißer Tomatenschaum mit gegrillten Scampis und Estragon. Asiatische Fischva-
      riation mit Singapurnudeln und Thaisud. Mohrenkopp mit eingelegten Gewürzorangen und
      Grand Marniereis.

Wertheim *Baden-Württemberg* 417 419 *Q 12,* 987 ㉗ *– pop. 21 700 – alt. 142 m.*
Frankfurt am Main 87.

at Wertheim-Bettingen *East : 10 km :*

🏛   **Schweizer Stuben** 🐾, Geiselbrunnweg 11, ✉ 97877, ℰ (09342) 30 70,
❀❀ Fax (09342) 307155, 🌳, « Hotel in a park », Massage, ⊆s, ⌇ (heated), ⌇, 🚣,
     ⌗ (indoor) – 📺 🅿 – 🔥 30. 𝔸𝔼 ⓓ ⊑ 𝘝𝘐𝘚𝘈
     Meals *(closed Tuesday and January)* (weekdays dinner only) (booking essential) 145/210
     and à la carte 87/157 – **33 rm** ⌑ 240/520 – 3 suites
     Spec. Entenstopfleberterrine mit Gelee von Muscat de Beaumes-de-Venise. Rotbarbe mit
     Sauce à la bourride und barbouillade de nice. Sisteron-Lamm mit Artischocken à la barigoule.

HAMBURG Ⓛ *Stadtstaat Hamburg* 415 416 *F 14,* 987 ⑤ *– pop. 1 650 000 – alt. 10 m.*
See : *Jungfernstieg★ GY – Außenalster★★★ (trip by boat★★★) GHXY – Hagenbeck Zoo*
(Tierpark Hagenbeck)★★ by Schröderstiftstr. EX – Television Tower (Fernsehturm)★ (✳★★)
EX – Fine Arts Museum (Kunsthalle)★★ HY M[1] *– St. Michael's church (St. Michaelis)★ (tower*
✳★) EFZ – Stintfang (≼★) EZ – Port (Hafen)★★ EZ – Decorative Arts and Crafts Museum
(Museum für Kunst und Gewerbe)★ HY M[2] *– Historical Museum (Museum für Hamburgische*
Geschichte)★ EYZ M[3] *– Post-Museum★ FY* M[4] *– Planten un Blomen Park★ EFX – Museum of*
Ethnography (Hamburgisches Museum für Völkerkunde)★ by Rothenbaumchaussee FX.

Envir. : *Altona : Northern Germany Museum (Norddeutsches Landesmuseum)★★ by Ree-*
perbahn EZ – Altona Balcony (Altonaer Balkon) ≼★ by Reeperbahn EZ – Elbchaussee★ by
Reeperbahn EZ.

🏌 *Hamburg-Blankenese, In de Bargen 59 (West : 17 km),* ℰ *(040) 81 21 77 ;* 🏌 *Hamburg-*
Lehmsahl (North : 16 km), Lemsahler Landstr.45, ℰ *(040) 608 22 500 ;* 🏌 *Hamburg-*
Wendlohe (North : 14 km), ℰ *(040) 5 50 50 14 ;* 🏌 *Wentorf, Golfstr. 2 (South-East : 20 km),*
ℰ *(040) 72 97 80 66.*

✈ *Hamburg-Fuhlsbüttel (North : 15 km),* ℰ *(040) 50 80.*

🚗 *Hamburg-Altona, Sternschanze.*

Exhibition Centre (Messegelände) (EFX), ℰ *(040) 3 56 91, Fax (040)35692181.*
Berlin 284 – Bremen 120 – Hannover 151.

Plans on following pages

Town centre :

🏰   **Vier Jahreszeiten**, Neuer Jungfernstieg 9, ✉ 20354, ℰ (040) 3 49 40,
     Fax (040) 3494602, « ≼ Binnenalster-side setting » – 📶, ⇥ rm, 📺 📞 🚗 – 🔥 80.
     𝔸𝔼 ⓓ ⊑ 𝘝𝘐𝘚𝘈 𝙅𝘾𝘉. ⌗   GY v
     see also **Rest. Haerlin** below – **Jahreszeiten Grill** : Meals à la carte 57/103 – **Doc**
     Cheng's : Meals à la carte 52/82 – **Condi** (lunch only, closed Sunday) Meals à la carte
     45/60 – **158 rm** ⌑ 433/700 – 12 suites.

🏰   **Kempinski Hotel Atlantic Hamburg** 🐾, An der Alster 72, ✉ 20099, ℰ (040)
     2 88 80, Fax (040) 247129, 🌳, « ≼ Außenalster-side setting », Massage, ⊆s, ⌇ – 📶,
     ⇥ rm, 📺 📞 🚗 – 🔥 300. 𝔸𝔼 ⓓ ⊑ 𝘝𝘐𝘚𝘈 𝙅𝘾𝘉. ⌗ rest   HY a
     Meals 49 (lunch) and à la carte 74/118 – **Atlantic-Mühle** (dinner only) Meals à la carte
     45/70 – **254 rm** ⌑ 404/553 – 13 suites.

🏰   **Park Hyatt Hamburg**, Bugenhagenstr. 8, ✉ 20095, ℰ (040) 33 32 12 34,
     Fax (040) 33321235, 🌳, Massage, 🏋, ⊆s, ⌇ – 📶, ⇥ rm, 📧 📺 📞 ♿ 🚗 – 🔥 200.
     𝔸𝔼 ⓓ ⊑ 𝘝𝘐𝘚𝘈 𝙅𝘾𝘉   HYZ t
     Apples : Meals à la carte 43/73 – **252 rm** ⌑ 384/563 – 34 suites.

Steigenberger Hamburg [M], Heiligengeistbrücke 4, ⊠ 20459, ℰ (040) 36 80 60, Fax (040) 36806777 – 📶, 🔆 rm, 📺 ☎ & 🚗 – 🕍 180. 🅰🅴 ① 🄴 🆅🅸🆂🅰 🄹🄲🄱 ❌ rest   FZ s
Calla (dinner only, closed Sunday - Monday and July - August) Meals à la carte 65/96 –
Bistro am Fleet : Meals à la carte 44/62 – **234 rm** ☕ 324/588 – 4 suites.

Marriott Hotel [M], ABC-Str. 52, ⊠ 20354, ℰ (040) 3 50 50, Fax (040) 35051777, 🌳, Massage, 🏋, 😓, 🏊 – 📶, 🔆 rm, 📺 ☎ & 🚗 – 🕍 160. 🅰🅴 ① 🄴 🆅🅸🆂🅰 🄹🄲🄱   FY b
Meals 28 (buffet lunch) à la carte 51/79 – **277 rm** ☕ 304/555 – 4 suites.

Renaissance Hotel, Große Bleichen, ⊠ 20354, ℰ (040) 34 91 80, Fax (040) 34918919, Massage, 😓 – 📶, 🔆 rm, 📺 ☎ Ⓟ – 🕍 100. 🅰🅴 ① 🄴 🆅🅸🆂🅰 🄹🄲🄱 ❌ rest   FY e
Meals à la carte 49/82 – **205 rm** ☕ 297/356 – 3 suites.

Radisson SAS Hotel, Marseiller Str. 2, ⊠ 20355, ℰ (040) 3 50 20, Fax (040) 35023530, ≼ Hamburg, 🏋, 😓, 🏊 – 📶, 🔆 rm, 📺 ☎ & 🚗 – 🕍 320. 🅰🅴 ① 🄴 🆅🅸🆂🅰 🄹🄲🄱. ❌ rest   FX a
Vierländer Stuben : Meals à la carte 43/71 – **Trader Vic's** (dinner only, closed 15 July - 16 August) Meals à la carte 46/80 – **560 rm** ☕ 309/528 – 26 suites.

Crowne Plaza [M], Graumannsweg 10, ⊠ 22087, ℰ (040) 22 80 60, Fax (040) 2208704, Massage, 😓, 🏊 – 📶, 🔆 rm, 📺 ☎ & 🚗 – 🕍 120. 🅰🅴 ① 🄴 🆅🅸🆂🅰 🄹🄲🄱. ❌ rest   by Lange Reihe HX
Lord Nelson : Meals à la carte 50/70 – **King George Pub** : Meals à la carte 34/51 – **285 rm** ☕ 308/456.

Europäischer Hof [M], Kirchenallee 45, ⊠ 20099, ℰ (040) 24 82 48, Fax (040) 24824799, 🌳, Massage, 🏋, 😓, 🏊 Squash – 📶, 🔆 rm, 📺 rest, 📺 🚗 – 🕍 150. 🅰🅴 ① 🄴 🆅🅸🆂🅰   HY e
Meals à la carte 43/70 – **320 rm** ☕ 190/440.

Maritim Hotel Reichshof, Kirchenallee 34, ⊠ 20099, ℰ (040) 24 83 30, Fax (040) 24833588, 😓, 🏊 – 📶 🔆 📺 🚗 – 🕍 150. 🅰🅴 ① 🄴 🆅🅸🆂🅰 🄹🄲🄱. ❌ rest   HY d
Meals à la carte 57/75 – **303 rm** ☕ 219/376 – 6 suites.

Prem, An der Alster 9, ⊠ 20099, ℰ (040) 24 17 26, Fax (040) 2803851, « Antique furnishings ; garden terrace », 😓 – 📶 📺 Ⓟ. 🅰🅴 ① 🄴 🆅🅸🆂🅰 🄹🄲🄱   HX c
La mer (closed Saturday and Sunday lunch) Meals à la carte 72/107 – **53 rm** ☕ 290/455 – 3 suites.

Residenz Hafen Hamburg [M], Seewartenstr. 7, ⊠ 20459, ℰ (040) 31 11 90, Fax (040) 314505, ≼ – 📶 🔆 📺 🚗 Ⓟ – 🕍 60. 🅰🅴 ① 🄴 🆅🅸🆂🅰   EZ y
Meals see **Hotel Hafen Hamburg** – **125 rm** ☕ 220/300.

Berlin [M], Borgfelder Str. 1, ⊠ 20537, ℰ (040) 25 16 40, Fax (040) 25164413, 🌳 – 📶, 🔆 rm, 📺 rest, 📺 ☎ 🚗 Ⓟ – 🕍 30. 🅰🅴 ① 🄴 🆅🅸🆂🅰. ❌ rest
Meals à la carte 41/67 – **93 rm** ☕ 180/225.   by Kurt-Schumacher-Allee HY

Senator, Lange Reihe 18, ⊠ 20099, ℰ (040) 24 12 03, Fax (040) 2803717 – 📶, 🔆 rm, 📺 ☎ 🚗 – 🕍 30. 🅰🅴 ① 🄴 🆅🅸🆂🅰 🄹🄲🄱. ❌ rest   HY u
Meals (dinner only) (residents only) – **56 rm** ☕ 185/320.

Novotel City Süd, Amsinckstr. 53, ⊠ 20097, ℰ (040) 23 63 80, Fax (040) 234230, 😓 – 📶 🔆 📺 ☎ & 🚗 Ⓟ – 🕍 50   by Amsinckstraße HZ
185 rm /320 m.

Hafen Hamburg, Seewartenstr. 9, ⊠ 20459, ℰ (040) 31 11 30, Fax (040) 31113755, ≼, 🌳 – 📶 📺 ☎ 🚗 Ⓟ – 🕍 70. 🅰🅴 ① 🄴 🆅🅸🆂🅰. ❌ rest   EZ y
Meals à la carte 46/80 – **239 rm** ☕ 183/241.

Bellevue, An der Alster 14, ⊠ 20099, ℰ (040) 28 44 40, Fax (040) 28444222 – 📶, 🔆 rm, 📺 ☎ 🚗 Ⓟ – 🕍 40. 🅰🅴 ① 🄴 🆅🅸🆂🅰   HX d
Meals à la carte 48/63 – **93 rm** ☕ 196/330.

St. Raphael, Adenauerallee 41, ⊠ 20097, ℰ (040) 24 82 00, Fax (040) 24820333, 😓 – 📶, 🔆 rm, 📺 ☎ Ⓟ – 🕍 40. 🅰🅴 ① 🄴 🆅🅸🆂🅰 🄹🄲🄱. ❌ rest by Adenauerallee HY
Meals (closed Saturday lunch and Sunday) à la carte 33/50 – **130 rm** ☕ 198/308.

Baseler Hof, Esplanade 11, ⊠ 20354, ℰ (040) 35 90 60, Fax (040) 35906918 – 📶 📺 ☎ – 🕍 30. 🅰🅴 ① 🄴 🆅🅸🆂🅰 🄹🄲🄱. ❌ rm   GY x
Meals (closed Saturday and Sunday lunch, 19 July - 16 August) 25 (lunch) and à la carte 49/71 – **153 rm** ☕ 150/225.

Alster-Hof without rest, Esplanade 12, ⊠ 20354, ℰ (040) 35 00 70, Fax (040) 35007514 – 📶 📺 ☎. 🅰🅴 ① 🄴 🆅🅸🆂🅰   GY x
closed 24 December - 2 January – **118 rm** ☕ 145/220 – 3 suites.

Aussen-Alster-Hotel, Schmilinskystr. 11, ⊠ 20099, ℰ (040) 24 15 57, Fax (040) 2803231, 🌳, 😓 – 📶 📺 ☎. 🅰🅴 ① 🄴 🆅🅸🆂🅰   HX e
closed 24 to 27 December – **Meals** (closed Saturday lunch and Sunday) (Italian rest.) à la carte 48/65 – **27 rm** ☕ 180/310.

E
F
STERNSCHANZENPARK
Schröderstiftstr.
Rentzelstr.
Grindelallee
Johns-
alle
b
U
An der
Verbindungsbahn
n
Bundesstr.
72
Sternschanze
Tiergartenstr.
Moorweidenstr.
Sternschanze
Edmund-Siemers-Allee
X
FERNSEHTURM
CONGRESS CENTRUM
HAMBURG
U
Lagerstr.
Karolinenstr.
Junglusstr.
PARK „ PLANTEN UN BLOMEN "
a
Th-Heuss
Platz
S. Bahn
DAMMTOR
MESSEGELÄNDE
Marseiller Str.
ALTER
BOTANISCHER GARTEN
23
Bei den
Kirchhöfen
Junglusstr.
U
Stephanspl.
Marktstraße
Messehallen
U
Wall
M4
46
KLEINE
WALLANLAGEN
Gorch-
Fock-
STAATSOPER
Dammtor str.
Colonnade
Feldstr.
Neuer Kamp Feldstraße
a
J
J
Dammtorwall
Gänsemarkt
Gänse-
markt
Feldstr.
Sievekingplatz
MUSIKHALLE
Valentinskamp
ST-PAULI
J
b
Str.
WILHELM-KOCH-
STADION
Kaiser-Wilhelm-Str.
A B C
Post-
c
29
HEILIGENGEISTFELD
GROSSE
WALLANLAGEN
Pilatuspool
Poolstr.
Hohe Bleichen
e
33
Glacischaussee
Holstenwall
HUMMEL
DENKMAL
33
Budapester
Straße
M3
Hütten
Thielbek
Wexstraße
77
Bleichen-
fleet
Neuer
Alster-
Wall
St. Pauli
T
Neuer Steinweg
Alter Steinweg
S. BAHN STADTHAUSBR.
31
Alter Wall
70
63
Ludwig-
Erhard-
Str.
35
BISMARCK-
DENKMAL
ST. MICHAELIS
54
Rödingsmarkt
43
16
NEUSTADT
Ost-
West-
St
Seewartenstr.
Schaarmarkt
fleet
graben-
Z
y
Stintfang
Deichstr.
a
Landungsbr.
Ditmar-Koel-Str.
Herren-
c
Kajen
21
10
Johannisbollwerk
9
Hafenrundfahrt
M
Vorsetzen
Hohe Brücke
ELBE
BINNENHAFEN
HAFEN
NIEDER-
HAFEN
Baumwall
E
F

HAMBURG

Adenauerallee . . . . . . HY 2
Alsterarkaden . . . . . . GY 3
Bei dem Neuen Krahn FZ 9
Bei den St.-Pauli-
Landungsbrücken . . EZ 10
Bergstraße . . . . GY
Böhmkenstraße . . . . . EZ 16
Börsenbrücke . . . . . GZ 18
Colonnaden . . . . FY
Cremon . . . . FZ 21
Dammtordamm . . . . FX 23
Dammtorstraße . . . . . FY

Gerhofstraße . . . . FY 29
Graskeller . . . . FZ 31
Große Bleichen . . . . . FY 33
Große
  Johannisstraße . . . GZ 34
Großer Burstah . . . . . FZ 35
Große
  Reichenstraße . . . . GZ 37
Hachmannplatz . . . . . . HY 39
Helgoländer Allee . . . . EZ 43
Holstenglacis . . . . . . EY 46
Jungfernstieg . . . . . . GY
Kleine Reichenstraße . GZ 50
Klingberg . . . . GZ 51
Krayenkamp . . . . . . FZ 54

G

H

X

Y

MOORWEIDE

ROTHERBAUM

Fontenay

Heimhuder Str.

Mittelweg

Mittelweg

Alsterufer

Warburgstraße

Alsterufer

AUSSENALSTER

0   200 m

c

d

e

b

An der Alster

Koppel

Lange Reihe

ST. GEORG

Alsterglacis

Esplanade

x

v

Kennedybrücke

Lombardsbrücke

Neuer Jungfernstieg

BINNENALSTER

a

Holzdamm

u

Glockengießerwall

M¹

Hauptbf. Nord

39

d

e

r

T

Hansa-
platz

Kirchenallee

Steindamm

Kreuz-
weg

2

ALTERRUNDFAHRT
ANLEGESTELLE

ALSTERPAVILLON

JUNGFERNSTIEG

Jungfernstieg

Ballindamm

Ferdinandstr.

Hermannstr.

Bergstr.

3

fleet

75

71

T

Spitalerstr.

str.

Hauptbf. Süd

80

79

M²

Kurt-Schumacher-

Allee

Rathaus-
markt

R

BÖRSE

Mönckebergstr.

t

Steintorwall

Mönckeberg-

St. Jakobi

Steinstr.

Speersort

Burchard-
platz

Altmann-
brücke

MP

HAMMERBROOK

N

34

a

18

v

Domstr.

b

69

76

Neß

37

50

51

68

Steinstr.

a

Meßberg

NIKOLAI
KIRCHTURM

88

e

Speicherstadt

St. Katharinen

STADT

bei den Mühren

Zollkanal

Ost-   West-   Str.

Dovenfleet

Deichtorplatz

Amsinckstr.

Högerdamm

G

H

Millerntordamm . . . . EZ 63
Mönckebergstraße . GHY
Neuer Wall . . . . FYZ 2
Poststraße . . . . FY
Pumpen . . . . HZ 68
Rathausstraße . . . . . GZ 69
Reeperbahn . . . . . . EZ 70
Reesendamm . . . . . GY 71

Rothenbaumchaussee . FX 72
Schleusenbrücke . . . . . GY 75
Schmiedestraße . . . . . GZ 76
Spitalerstraße . . . . . GHY
Stadthausbrücke . . . . FY 77
Steintordamm . . . . . HY 79
Steintorplatz . . . . . HY 80
Zippelhaus . . . . GZ 88

Eden without rest, Ellmenreichstr. 20, ✉ 20099, ℘ (040) 24 84 80, *Fax (040) 241521* – |$| TV ☎. AE ⓓ E VISA HY r
63 rm ☕ 140/225.

Wedina without rest, Gurlittstr. 23, ✉ 20099, ℘ (040) 24 30 11, *Fax (040) 2803894* – TV ☎ P. AE ⓓ E VISA HY b
28 rm ☕ 155/240.

XXXXX **Haerlin** - Hotel Vier Jahreszeiten, Neuer Jungfernstieg 9, ✉ 20354, ℘ (040) 3 49 46 41, *Fax (40) 3494602*, < Binnenalster – AE ⓓ E VISA. ✈ GY v
closed Sunday - Monday, Saturday lunch and 2 January - 2 February – **Meals** 62 (lunch) and à la carte 95/135.

XXX ✿ **Cölln's Austernstuben**, Brodschrangen 1, ✉ 20457, ℘ (040) 32 60 59, *Fax (040) 326059*, « Private dining rooms » – AE ⓓ E GZ v
closed Saturday lunch, Sunday and Bank Holidays – **Meals** (booking essential) (mainly seafood) 89/147 à la carte 74/100
Spec. Ravioli von Austern mit Tomaten-Fondue und Nüssen. Seeteufel mit Kartoffel-Olivenpüree und Ochsenschwanzsauce. Holsteiner Auflauf mit Zwergorangen.

XX **il Ristorante**, Große Bleichen 16 (1st floor), ✉ 20354, ℘ (040) 34 33 35, *Fax (040) 345748* – AE ⓓ E FY c
Meals (Italian rest.) à la carte 56/83.

XX **Zippelhaus**, Zippelhaus 3, ✉ 20457, ℘ (040) 30 38 02 80, *Fax (040) 321777* – AE E VISA GZ e
closed Saturday lunch, Sunday and 20 July - 10 August – **Meals** à la carte 39/56 (lunch) 59/79 (dinner).

XX **Peter Lembcke**, Holzdamm 49, ✉ 20099, ℘ (040) 24 32 90, *Fax (040) 2804123* – AE ⓓ E VISA HY t
closed Saturday lunch, Sunday and Bank Holidays, October - April Sunday and Bank Holidays dinner only – **Meals** (booking essential) à la carte 61/110.

XX **Deichgraf**, Deichstr. 23, ✉ 20459, ℘ (040) 36 42 08, *Fax (040) 364268* – AE ⓓ E VISA FZ a
closed Sunday – **Meals** (booking essential) à la carte 55/86.

XX **Ratsweinkeller**, Große Johannisstr. 2, ✉ 20457, ℘ (040) 36 41 53, *Fax (040) 372201*, « 1896 Hanseatic rest. » – 🏛 280. AE ⓓ E VISA JCB GZ R
closed Sunday dinner and Bank Holidays – **Meals** à la carte 36/75.

XX **al Pincio**, Schauenburger Str. 59 (1st floor, |$|), ✉ 20095, ℘ (040) 36 52 55, *Fax (040) 362244* – AE ⓓ E VISA. ✈ GZ a
closed Saturday, Sunday Bank Holidays and 4 weeks July - August – **Meals** (booking essential) (Italian rest.) à la carte 54/80.

X **Vero**, Domstr. 17, ✉ 20095, ℘ (040) 33 90 51, *Fax (040) 339052* – AE ⓓ E VISA GZ b
closed Sunday - Monday – **Meals** (Italian rest.) à la carte 60/68.

X **Le Plat du Jour**, Dornbusch 4, ✉ 20095, ℘ (040) 32 14 14, *Fax (040) 4105857* – AE ⓓ E VISA JCB GZ v
closed Sunday, July - August also Saturday – **Meals** (booking essential) à la carte 43/62.

X **Jena Paradies**, Klosterwall 23, ✉ 20095, ℘ (040) 32 70 08, *Fax (040) 327598* HZ a
Meals (booking essential) à la carte 43/62.

at Hamburg-Alsterdorf *by Grindelallee* FX :

Alsterkrug-Hotel, Alsterkrugchaussee 277, ✉ 22297, ℘ (040) 51 30 30, *Fax (040) 51303403*, 🏋, ≘s – |$|, ⇔ rm, TV ☎ 🚗 P – 🏛 50. AE ⓓ E VISA JCB. ✈
Meals à la carte 48/66 – **105 rm** ☕ 215/297.

at Hamburg-Altona *by Reeperbahn* EZ :

Rema-Hotel Domicil without rest, Stresemannstr. 62, ✉ 22769, ℘ (040) 4 31 60 26, *Fax (040) 4397579* – |$| ⇔ TV ☎ 🚗. AE ⓓ E VISA JCB
75 rm ☕ 200/390. by Budapester Straße EY

InterCityHotel, Paul-Nevermann-Platz 17, ✉ 22765, ℘ (040) 38 03 40, *Fax (040) 38034999* – |$|, ⇔ rm, TV ☎ ☎ ♿ – 🏛 70. AE ⓓ E VISA
Meals *(closed Sunday)* à la carte 31/56 – **133 rm** ☕ 193/272.

XXXX ✿ **Landhaus Scherrer**, Elbchaussee 130, ✉ 22763, ℘ (040) 8 80 13 25, *Fax (040) 8806260* – P. AE ⓓ E VISA
closed Sunday and Bank Holidays – **Meals** (outstanding wine list) 159/186 and à la carte 81/138 – ***Bistro-Restaurant*** *(lunch only)* **Meals** à la carte 68/94
Spec. Steinbutt an der Gräte gebraten. Hamburger Pfannfisch mit Senfsauce. Krosse Vierländer Ente im Ganzen gebraten (2 Pers.).

GERMANY

Le Canard, Elbchaussee 139, ✉ 22763, ℘ (040) 8 80 50 57, Fax (040) 88913259, ≤, ⇔ – ℗. AE ⓸ E VISA. ✗
closed Sunday and 2 weeks early January – **Meals** (booking essential) (outstanding wine list) 60 (lunch) and à la carte 100/129
Spec. Hummer in der Schale gebraten. Steinbutt "Bordelaise". Topfensoufflé mit Rotweineis.

Fischereihafen-Restaurant Hamburg, Große Elbstr. 143, ✉ 22767, ℘ (040) 38 18 16, Fax (040) 3893021, ≤ – ℗. AE ⓸ E VISA
Meals (seafood only) (booking essential) 35 (lunch) and à la carte 49/88.

Rive Bistro, Van-der-Smissen-Str. 1 (Kreuzfahrt-Center), ✉ 22767, ℘ (040) 3 80 59 19, Fax (040) 3894775, ≤, ⇔ – AE
Meals (booking essential) à la carte 47/79.

at Hamburg-Bahrenfeld *by Budapester Str.* EY :

Novotel Hamburg West Ⓜ, Albert-Einstein-Ring 2, ✉ 22761, ℘ (040) 89 95 20, Fax (040) 89952333, ⇔s – ⧮, ⇔ rm, ▤ TV ☎ ℡ & ⇔ ℗ – ▵ 50. AE ⓸ E VISA
Meals à la carte 36/67 – **137 rm** ⊑ 194/283 – 4 suites.

Tafelhaus, Holstenkamp 71, ✉ 22525, ℘ (040) 89 27 60, Fax (040) 8993324, ⇔ – ℗
closed Saturday lunch, Sunday - Monday, 3 weeks January and late July - mid August –
Meals (booking essential) 63 (lunch) and à la carte 79/85
Spec. Gänseleberravioli mit karamelisierter Mango. Steinbutt in der Folie (2 pers.). Holunderblüten auf dreierlei Art (Season).

at Hamburg-Barmbek *by An der Alster* HX :

Rema-Hotel Meridian without rest, Holsteinischer Kamp 59, ✉ 22081, ℘ (040) 2 91 80 40, Fax (040) 2983336, ⇔s, ▨ – ⧮ ⇔ TV ☎ & ℗ – ▵ 30. AE ⓸ E VISA JCB
68 rm ⊑ 290/390.

at Hamburg-Billbrook *by Amsinckstr.* HZ *and Billstr.* :

Böttcherhof, Wöhlerstr. 2, ✉ 22113, ℘ (040) 73 18 70, Fax (040) 73187899, �, ⇔s – ⧮, ⇔ rm, TV ℡ & ⇔ ℗ – ▵ 140. AE E VISA. ✗ rest
Meals à la carte 49/69 – **155 rm** ⊑ 217/334.

at Hamburg-Billstedt *by Kurt Schumacher-Allee and B 5* HY :

Panorama without rest, Billstedter Hauptstr. 44, ✉ 22111, ℘ (040) 73 35 90, Fax (040) 73359950, ▨ – ⧮ ⇔ TV ☎ ℡ ⇔ ℗ – ▵ 150. AE ⓸ E VISA JCB
closed 23 to 27 December – **111 rm** ⊑ 180/275 – 7 suites.

at Hamburg-City Nord *by Grindelallee* FX :

Queens Hotel Ⓜ, Mexikoring 1, ✉ 22297, ℘ (040) 63 29 40, Fax (040) 6322472, ⇔, ⇔s – ⧮ ⇔ TV ⇔ ℗ – ▵ 120. AE ⓸ E VISA. ✗ rest
Meals (closed Sunday dinner) à la carte 41/65 – **182 rm** ⊑ 259/350.

at Hamburg-Duvenstedt *by Grindelallee* FX :

Le Relais de France, Poppenbütteler Chaussee 3, ✉ 22397, ℘ (040) 6 07 07 50, Fax (040) 6072673, ⇔ – ℗. ✗
closed Sunday - Monday, 2 weeks February and September – **Meals** (dinner only) (booking essential) à la carte 59/75 – **Bistro** (also lunch) **Meals** à la carte 50/65.

at Hamburg-Eimsbüttel *by Schröderstiftstraße* EX :

Norge, Schäferkampsallee 49, ✉ 20357, ℘ (040) 44 11 50, Fax (040) 44115577 – ⧮, ⇔ rm, ▤ rest, TV ☎ ℗ – ▵ 80. AE ⓸ E VISA
Meals à la carte 43/67 – **130 rm** ⊑ 199/328.

at Hamburg-Eppendorf *by Grindelallee* FX :

Sellmer, Ludolfstr. 50, ✉ 20249, ℘ (040) 47 30 57, Fax (040) 4601569 – ℗. AE ⓸ E VISA
Meals (mainly seafood) à la carte 52/109.

at Hamburg-Flottbek *by Budapester Straße* EY :

Landhaus Flottbek, Baron-Voght-Str. 179, ✉ 22607, ℘ (040) 8 22 74 10, Fax (040) 82274151, ⇔, « Hotel in former farmhouses ; elegant rustic installation », ⇔ – TV ☎ ℡ ℗ – ▵ 30. AE ⓸ E VISA JCB
Meals (closed Sunday) 49 and à la carte 55/80 – **25 rm** ⊑ 175/295.

at Hamburg-Fuhlsbüttel *by Grindelallee* FX :

Airport Hotel [M], Flughafenstr. 47, ⊠ 22415, ℰ (040) 53 10 20, *Fax (040) 53102222*, ⊆s, ⊠ – |‡|, ⇥ rm, ▤ rest, [TV] ℰ ⇐ ℗ – ⚐ 140. ℀ ⑪ ⒠ *VISA*
Meals à la carte 51/82 – **159 rm** ⊔ 274/423 – 10 suites.

XX **top air**, Flughafenstr. 1 (at the airport, terminal 4, level 3), ⊠ 22335, ℰ (040) 50 75 33 24, *Fax (040) 50751842* – ℀ ⑪ ⒠ *VISA*
closed Saturday – **Meals** à la carte 61/96.

at Hamburg-Hamm *by Kurt-Schumacher-Allee* HY :

Hamburg International, Hammer Landstr. 200, ⊠ 20537, ℰ (040) 21 14 01, *Fax (040) 211409* – |‡| [TV] ☏ ⇐ ℗ – ⚐ 20. ℀ ⒠ *VISA*. ⇥ rest
Meals *(dinner only, closed Sunday)* à la carte 60/94 – **112 rm** ⊔ 130/290.

at Hamburg-Harburg *2100 S : 15 km by Amsinckstr.* HZ :

Lindtner [M] ⤸, Heimfelder Str. 123, ⊠ 21075, ℰ (040) 79 00 90, *Fax (040) 79009482*, ⇗, « Elegant modern installation ; collection of contemporary art » – |‡|, ⇥ rm, [TV] ℰ ⅙ ℗ – ⚐ 450. ℀ ⑪ ⒠ *VISA*. ⇥ rest
Lilium : Meals à la carte 60/81 – **Hofgarten :** Meals à la carte 53/85 – **115 rm** ⊔ 245/355 – 7 suites.

Panorama, Harburger Ring 8, ⊠ 21073, ℰ (040) 76 69 50, *Fax (040) 76695183* – |‡|, ⇥ rm, [TV] ☏ ⇐ – ⚐ 110. ℀ ⑪ ⒠ *VISA*
Meals *(closed Sunday dinner)* à la carte 38/65 – **99 rm** ⊔ 180/210.

XX **Marinas**, Schellerdamm 26, ⊠ 21079, ℰ (040) 7 65 38 28, *Fax (040) 7651491*, ⇗ – ℀ ⑪ ⒠ *VISA*
closed Saturday lunch and Sunday – **Meals** *(booking essential for dinner)* 44 (lunch) and à la carte 57/99
Spec. Bouillabaisse von Nordseefischen. Angeldorsch mit Pommery-Senfsauce. Gratiniertes Hamburger Rote Grützeparfait.

at Hamburg-Harvestehude :

Inter-Continental, Fontenay 10, ⊠ 20354, ℰ (040) 41 41 50, *Fax (040) 41415186*, ⇐ Hamburg and Alster, ⇗, Massage, ⊆s, ⊠ – |‡|, ⇥ rm, ▤ [TV] ℰ ⇐ ℗ – ⚐ 350. ℀ ⑪ ⒠ *VISA* *JCB*. ⇥ rest
GX r
Fontenay-Grill *(dinner only)* Meals à la carte 65/117 – **Orangerie :** Meals 45/55 (lunch buffet) and à la carte – **286 rm** ⊔ 324/454 – 12 suites.

Garden Hotels [M] ⤸ without rest, Magdalenenstr. 60, ⊠ 20148, ℰ (040) 41 40 40, *Fax (040) 4140420*, « Elegant modern installation » – |‡| ⇥ [TV] ℰ ⇐. ℀ ⑪ ⒠ *VISA* *JCB*
by Mittelweg GX
60 rm ⊔ 205/430.

Abtei, Abteistr. 14, ⊠ 20149, ℰ (040) 44 29 05, *Fax (040) 449820*, ⇗, ⅋ – ▤ rest, [TV] ☏ ⇐. ℀ ⑪ ⒠ *VISA*. ⇥ rest
by Rothenbaumchaussee FX
Meals *(dinner only, closed Sunday - Monday, 1 week January and July) (booking essential)* 120/180 – **11 rm** ⊔ 260/450
Spec. Wachtel und Gänsestopflebermousse in Morchelgelee (April-May). Zander und Jacobsmuscheln auf Gemüsesugo. Ragout vom Deichlammrücken mit Balsamicosauce.

Smolka, Isestr. 98, ⊠ 20149, ℰ (040) 48 09 80, *Fax (040) 4809811* – |‡|, ⇥ rm, [TV] ☏. ℀ ⑪ ⒠ *VISA* *JCB*. ⇥ rest
by Rothenbaumchaussee FX
Meals *(dinner only, closed Sunday and Bank Holidays)* à la carte 48/70 – **40 rm** ⊔ 171/322.

XXX **Wollenberg**, Alsterufer 35, ⊠ 20354, ℰ (040) 4 50 18 50, *Fax (040) 45018511*, « Villa with Alsters-side setting and modern elegant interior » – ⚐ 40. ℀ ⑪ ⒠ *VISA*. ⇥
GX c
closed Saturday lunch – **Meals** 48 (lunch) and à la carte 70/95.

at Hamburg-Langenhorn *North : 8 km by B 433* :

Dorint-Hotel-Airport [M], Langenhorner Chaussee 183, ⊠ 22415, ℰ (040) 53 20 90, *Fax (040) 53209600*, ⇗, ⊆s, ⊠ – |‡|, ⇥ rm, [TV] ⅙ ⇐ – ⚐ 80. ℀ ⑪ ⒠ *VISA* *JCB*. ⇥ rest
Meals à la carte 41/68 – **146 rm** ⊔ 245/408.

XX **Zum Wattkorn**, Tangstedter Landstr. 230, ⊠ 22417, ℰ (040) 5 20 37 97, *Fax (040) 5209044*, ⇗ – ℗
closed Monday – **Meals** à la carte 61/81.

at Hamburg-Lemsahl-Mellingstedt *by An der Alster North-East : 16 km* :

Marriott Hotel Treudelberg [M] ⤸, Lemsahler Landstr. 45, ⊠ 22397, ℰ (040) 60 82 20, *Fax (040) 60822444*, ⇐, ⇗, Massage, ⛳, ⊆s, ⊠, ✕, ⌖ – |‡|, ⇥ rm, [TV] ℰ ℗ – ⚐ 150. ℀ ⑪ ⒠ *VISA* *JCB*. ⇥ rest
Meals à la carte 56/86 – **135 rm** ⊔ 245/500.

XXX **Dante**, An der Alsterschleife 3, ⊠ 22399, ℘ (040) 6 02 00 43, Fax (040) 6022826, 🌿 – 🅿. AE E VISA
closed Monday, Tuesday to Friday dinner only – **Meals** (Italian rest.) (booking essential) à la carte 50/85.

at Hamburg-Nienstedten *West : 13 km by Reeperbahn* EZ :

Louis C. Jacob M, Elbchaussee 401, ⊠ 22609, ℘ (040) 82 25 50, Fax (040) 82255444, ≼ Habour and Elbe, « Elbe-side setting ; lime-tree terrace », ⊜ – |🛗|, ✸ rm, 🖥 TV 📞 🚗 – 🔏 120. AE ① E VISA JCB. ✸ rest
Meals à la carte 72/116 – ***Weinwirtschaft Kleines Jacob*** *(weekdays dinner only, closed Sunday dinner - Monday)* **Meals** à la carte 38/48 – **86 rm** ⊇ 319/608 – 8 suites
Spec. Kalbskopf mit Flußkrebsen und Schnittlauchvinaigrette. Seeteufel mit Ratatouille und Kartoffel-Olivenpüree. Tarte Tatin mit Karameleis und Vanilleschaum.

at Hamburg-Rothenburgsort *by Amsinkstr.* HZ :

Forum Hotel, Billwerder Neuer Deich 14, ⊠ 20539, ℘ (040) 78 84 00, Fax (040) 78841000, ≼, 🌿, ⌐�, ⊜, 🏊 – |🛗| ✸ TV 📞 ᕧ 🚗 🅿 – 🔏 90. AE ① E VISA JCB. ✸
Meals à la carte 46/67 – **385 rm** ⊇ 250/320 – 12 suites.

at Hamburg-Rotherbaum :

Elysee 🐬, Rothenbaumchaussee 10, ⊠ 20148, ℘ (040) 41 41 20, Fax (040) 41412733, 🌿, Massage, ⊜, 🏊 – |🛗|, ✸ rm, 🖥 TV ᕧ 🚗 – 🔏 350. AE ① E VISA JCB   FX m
Piazza Romana (Italian rest.) **Meals** à la carte 51/71 – ***Brasserie :*** **Meals** à la carte 39/60 – **305 rm** ⊇ 276/492 – 4 suites.

Vorbach without rest, Johnsallee 63, ⊠ 20146, ℘ (040) 44 18 20, Fax (040) 44182888 – |🛗| ✸ TV ☎ 🚗 – 🔏 20. AE E VISA   FX b
115 rm ⊇ 170/280.

at Hamburg-St. Pauli :

Astron Suite-Hotel without rest, Feldstr. 53, ⊠ 20357, ℘ (040) 43 23 20, Fax (040) 43232300, ⊜ – |🛗| ✸ TV ☎ 📞 ᕧ 🚗 – 🔏 15. AE ① E VISA JCB   EY a
119 rm ⊇ 253/370.

at Hamburg-Stellingen *by Grindelallee* FX :

Helgoland, Kieler Str. 177, ⊠ 22525, ℘ (040) 85 70 01, Fax (040) 8511445 – |🛗|, ✸ rm, TV ☎ 🚗 🅿 – 🔏 150. AE ① E VISA JCB. ✸
Meals *(dinner only, closed Sunday)* à la carte 35/52 – **110 rm** ⊇ 160/230.

Holiday Inn, Kieler Str. 333, ⊠ 22525, ℘ (040) 54 74 00, Fax (040) 54740100, ⊜ – |🛗|, ✸ rm, TV ☎ 📞 🚗 🅿 – 🔏 25. AE ① E VISA JCB
Meals à la carte 32/51 – **105 rm** ⊇ 231/254.

at Hamburg-Stillhorn *by Amsinckstr.* HZ :

Le Méridien, Stillhorner Weg 40, ⊠ 21109, ℘ (040) 75 01 50, Fax (040) 75015444, ⌐�, ⊜, 🏊 – |🛗|, ✸ rm, 🖥 rest, TV 📞 ᕧ 🅿 – 🔏 160. AE ① E VISA. ✸ rest
Meals à la carte 55/80 – **146 rm** ⊇ 205/355.

at Hamburg-Uhlenhorst *by An der Alster* HX :

Nippon, Hofweg 75, ⊠ 22085, ℘ (040) 2 27 11 40, Fax (040) 22711490, (Japanese installation and rest.) – |🛗| TV ☎ 🚗 – 🔏 20. AE ① E VISA. ✸
Meals *(dinner only, closed Monday)* à la carte 46/69 – **42 rm** ⊇ 200/314.

HANOVER (HANNOVER) L *Niedersachsen* 415 416 417 418 *I 13,* 987 ⑯ – *pop. 510 000 – alt. 55 m.*

See : *Herrenhausen Gardens (Herrenhäuser Gärten)★★ (Großer Garten★★, Berggarten★)* CV – *Kestner-Museum★* DY M1 – *Market Church (Marktkirche) (Altarpiece★★)* DY – *Museum of Lower Saxony (Niedersächsisches Landesmuseum) (Prehistorical department★)* EZ M2 – *Museum of Arts (Kunstmuseum) (Collection Sprengel★)* EZ.

🐴8 *Garbsen, Am Blauen See (West : 14 km), ℘ (05137) 7 30 68 ; 2g Isernhagen, Gut Lohne, ℘ (05139) 89 31 85 ;* 🐴8 *Langenhagen, Hainhaus 22 (North : 12 km), ℘ (0511) 73 93 00.*
✈ *Hanover-Langenhagen (North : 11 km), ℘ (0511) 9 77 12 23.*
🚗 *Raschplatz* (EX).
Exhibition Centre (Messegelände) (by Bischofsholer Damm FY *and Messe Schnellweg), ℘ (0511) 8 90, Fax (0511) 8931216.*
🎫 *Hannover Tourist-Information, Ernst-August-Platz 2, ⊠ 30159, ℘ (0511) 3 01 40, Fax (0511) 301414.*
ADAC, *Nordmann Passage 4, ⊠ 30159, ℘ (0511) 1 24 05 60, Fax (0511) 8500333.*
Berlin 289 – Bremen 123 – Hamburg 151.

HANOVER (HANNOVER)

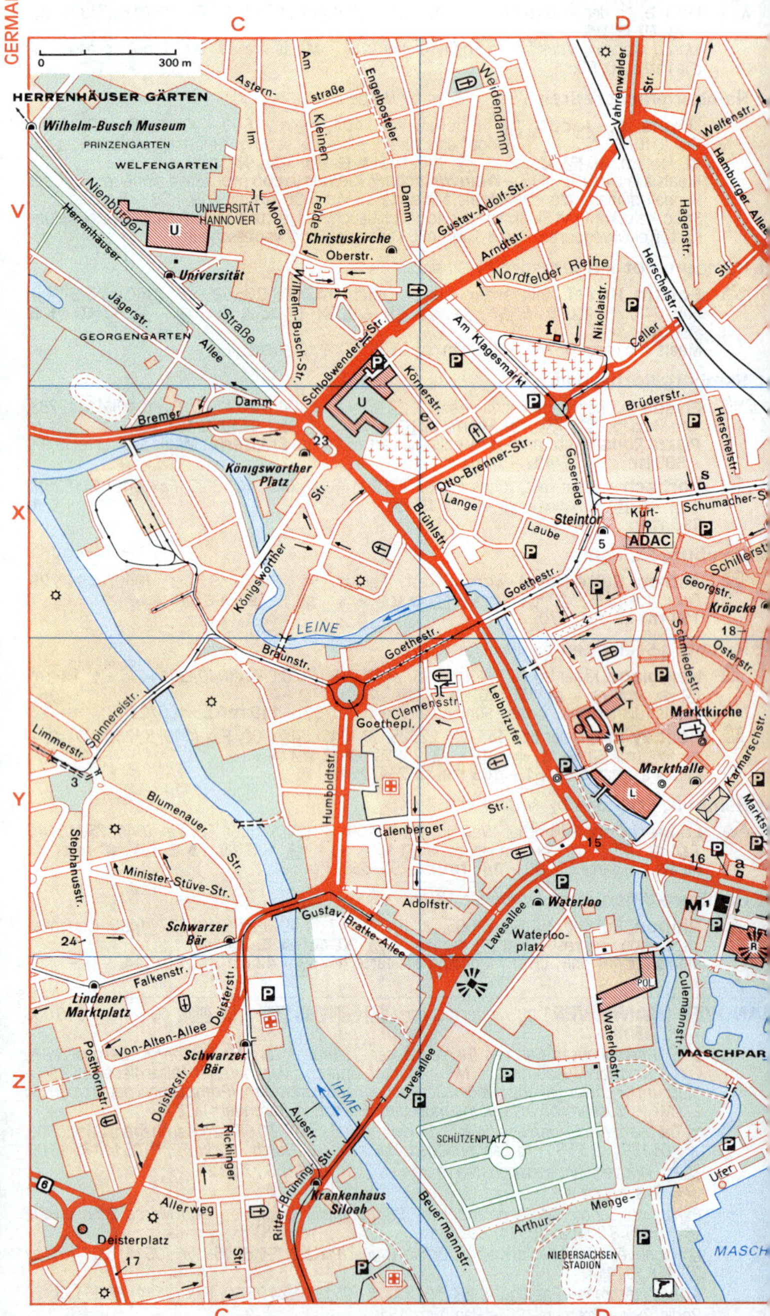

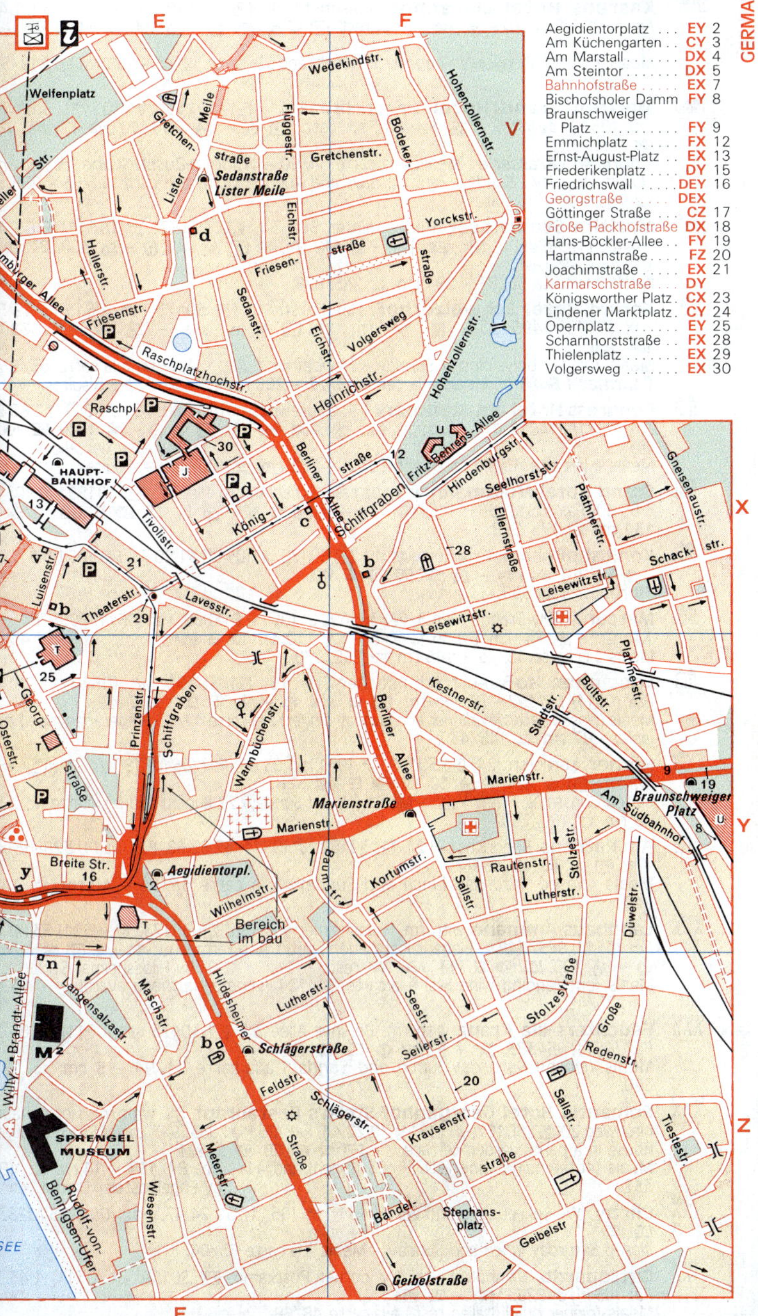

HANNOVER
GERMANY

Aegidientorplatz . . . EY 2
Am Küchengarten . . CY 3
Am Marstall . . . . DX 4
Am Steintor . . . . . . DX 5
Bahnhofstraße . . . . . EX 7
Bischofsholer Damm FY 8
Braunschweiger
  Platz . . . . FY 9
Emmichplatz . . . . . . FX 12
Ernst-August-Platz . . EX 13
Friederikenplatz . . . . DY 15
Friedrichswall . . . . DEY 16
Georgstraße . . . . . . DEX
Göttinger Straße . . . CZ 17
Große Packhofstraße DX 18
Hans-Böckler-Allee . . FY 19
Hartmannstraße . . . . FZ 20
Joachimstraße . . . . . EX 21
Karmarschstraße . . . DY
Königsworther Platz . CX 23
Lindener Marktplatz . CY 24
Opernplatz . . . . EY 25
Scharnhorststraße . . FX 28
Thielenplatz . . . . . . EX 29
Volgersweg . . . . . . EX 30

Welfenplatz
Wedekindstr.
Hohenzollernstr.
V
Gretchen-
Meile
Flüggestr.
Gretchenstr.
Bödeker-
straße
Str.
Lister
Sedanstraße
Lister Meile
Eichstr.
Yorckstr.
straße
d
straße
Hallerstr.
Friesen-
Friesenstr.
Sedanstr.
Eichstr.
Volgersweg
Raschplatzhochstr.
Heinrichstr.
Hohenzollernstr.
Raschpl.
P
P
Berliner
30
straße
12
Fritz-Behrens-Allee
HAUPT-
BAHNHOF
J
König-
Schiffgraben
Hindenburgstr.
Seelhorststr.
Gneseaustr.
X
13
d
c
Plathnerstr.
Schack-
str.
Tivolistr.
Luisenstr.
21
Ellernstraße
Leisewitzstr.
v
b
b
28
Theaterstr.
Lavesstr.
Leisewitzstr.
Leisewitzstr.
29
Berliner Allee
Plathnerstr.
Georg-
Osterstr.
25
Prinzenstr.
Schiffgraben
Warmbüchenstr.
Kestnerstr.
Stadtstr.
Bultstr.
straße
T
9
19
Marienstr.
Am
Braunschweiger
Platz
Marienstraße
Berliner Allee
Marienstr.
U
Y
8
Breite Str.
16
Aegidientorpl.
Wilhelmstr.
Baumstr.
Kortumstr.
Sallstr.
Rautenstr.
Stolzestr.
Lutherstr.
Düwelstr.
2
T
Bereich
im bau
n
Willy-
Brandt-Allee
Langensalzastr.
Maschstr.
Hildesheimer
Lutherstr.
Seestr.
Stolzestraße
Große
Redenstr.
M
b
Schlägerstraße
Seilerstr.
Sallstr.
SEE
Rudolf-von-
Bennigsen-Ufer
SPRENGEL
MUSEUM
Meterstr.
Wiesenstr.
Feldstr.
Schlägerstr.
Straße
Krausenstr.
straße
Tiestestr.
N
Bandel-
Stephans-
platz
Geibelstr.
Geibelstraße

GERMANY

Kastens Hotel Luisenhof, Luisenstr. 1, ✉ 30159, ℰ (0511) 3 04 4
Fax (0511) 3044807 – |♯|, ⇥ rm, ▤ rest, TV ☏ 👤 ⇦ Ⓟ – ♨ 100. 𝖠𝖤 Ⓞ 𝖤 𝖵𝖨𝖲𝖠 ⌛
⇥
EX
Meals (closed Sunday July - August) 36 (lunch) and à la carte 59/83 – **158 rm** ⌑ 219/59
– 5 suites.

Maritim Grand Hotel, Friedrichswall 11, ✉ 30159, ℰ (0511) 3 67 7
Fax (0511) 325195 – |♯|, ⇥ rm, ▤ rest, TV ⇦ – ♨ 250. 𝖠𝖤 Ⓞ 𝖤 𝖵𝖨𝖲𝖠 𝖩𝖢
⇥ rest
DY
L'Adresse - Brasserie : Meals à la carte 54/90 – **Wilhelm-Busch-Stube** (dinner on
closed Saturday - Sunday, Bank Holidays and August) **Meals** à la carte 36/53 – **285 r**
⌑ 255/598 – 15 suites.

Maritim Stadthotel, Hildesheimer Str. 34, ✉ 30169, ℰ (0511) 9 89 4
Fax (0511) 9894900, 🌤, ⇔s, 🏊 – |♯|, ⇥ rm, ▤ TV ⇦ ⇦ Ⓟ – ♨ 380. 𝖠𝖤 Ⓞ
𝖵𝖨𝖲𝖠 𝖩𝖢𝖡 ⇥ rest
EZ
Meals à la carte 56/83 – **291 rm** ⌑ 245/678.

Forum Hotel Schweizerhof, Hinüberstr. 6, ✉ 30175, ℰ (0511) 3 49 5
Fax (0511) 3495123 – |♯|, ⇥ rm, ▤ TV ☏ ⇦ ⇦ – ♨ 280. 𝖠𝖤 Ⓞ
𝖵𝖨𝖲𝖠 𝖩𝖢𝖡
EX
Meals (dinner only, closed Sunday - Monday and July - August) à la carte 55/86
Gourmet's Buffet : Meals à la carte 48/77 – **200 rm** ⌑ 330/521 – 3 suites.

Congress-Hotel am Stadtpark Ⓜ, Clausewitzstr. 6, ✉ 30175, ℰ (0511) 2 80 5
Fax (0511) 814652, 🌤, Massage, ⇔s, 🏊 – |♯|, ⇥ rm, TV ☏ Ⓟ – ♨ 1300. 𝖠𝖤 Ⓞ
𝖵𝖨𝖲𝖠
by Hans-Böckler Allee **FY**
Meals à la carte 43/70 (also diet menu) – **252 rm** ⌑ 190/498 – 4 suites.

Grand Hotel Mussmann without rest, Ernst-August-Platz 7, ✉ 30159, ℰ (051
3 65 60, Fax (0511) 3656145, ⇔s – |♯| ⇥ TV ☏ 👤 – ♨ 50. 𝖠𝖤 Ⓞ 𝖤 𝖵𝖨𝖲𝖠 **EX**
134 rm ⌑ 178/598.

Königshof without rest, Königstr. 12, ✉ 30175, ℰ (0511) 31 20 71, Fax (0511) 3120.
– |♯| ⇥ TV ☏ ⇦ – ♨ 30. 𝖠𝖤 Ⓞ 𝖤 𝖵𝖨𝖲𝖠
EX
79 rm ⌑ 158/398 – 3 suites.

Mercure, Willy-Brandt-Allee 3, ✉ 30169, ℰ (0511) 8 00 80, Fax (0511) 8093704, 🌤
ⅉ, ⇔s – |♯|, ⇥ rm, TV ☏ 👤 ⇦ – ♨ 110. 𝖠𝖤 Ⓞ 𝖤 𝖵𝖨𝖲𝖠
EZ
Meals à la carte 38/73 – **145 rm** ⌑ 239/279.

Loccumer Hof, Kurt-Schumacher-Str. 16, ✉ 30159, ℰ (0511) 1 26 4
Fax (0511) 131192 – |♯|, ⇥ rm, TV ☏ ⇦ Ⓟ – ♨ 35. 𝖠𝖤 Ⓞ 𝖤 𝖵𝖨𝖲𝖠
DX
Meals (closed Saturday dinner and Sunday dinner) à la carte 42/83 (vegetarian menu av
lable) – **87 rm** ⌑ 145/430.

Körner, Körnerstr. 24, ✉ 30159, ℰ (0511) 1 63 60, Fax (0511) 18048, 🌤, 🏊 – |
⇥ rm, TV ☏ ⇦ – ♨ 50. 𝖠𝖤 Ⓞ 𝖤 𝖵𝖨𝖲𝖠 𝖩𝖢𝖡
DX
closed Christmas - New Year – **Meals** (closed Sunday) 22 (lunch) and à la carte 43/63
75 rm ⌑ 160/250.

Am Rathaus, Friedrichswall 21, ✉ 30159, ℰ (0511) 32 62 68, Fax (0511) 328868, ⇔
– |♯| TV ☏ 𝖠𝖤 Ⓞ 𝖤 𝖵𝖨𝖲𝖠
EY
Meals (closed Saturday lunch and Sunday) à la carte 33/66 – **40 rm** ⌑ 14
240.

XXX **Landhaus Ammann** with rm, Hildesheimer Str. 185, ✉ 30173, ℰ (0511) 83 08 1
Fax (0511) 8437749, « Elegant installation ; patio with terrace », 🍽 – |♯| TV ☏ ⇦
Ⓟ – ♨ 100. 𝖠𝖤 Ⓞ 𝖤 𝖵𝖨𝖲𝖠 𝖩𝖢𝖡. ⇥ rest
by Hildesheimer Str. **EFZ**
Meals (outstanding wine list) à la carte 84/124 (vegetarian menu available) – **15 r**
⌑ 275/450.

XXX **Feuchters lila Kranz** with rm, Berliner Allee 33, ✉ 30175, ℰ (0511) 85 89 2
Fax (0511) 854383, 🌤 – TV ☏ Ⓟ. 𝖠𝖤 Ⓞ 𝖵𝖨𝖲𝖠
FX
Meals (closed Saturday lunch and Sunday) à la carte 71/94 – **5 rm** ⌑ 180
320.

XXX **Romantik Hotel Georgenhof-Stern's Restaurant** 🦢 with rm, Herrenhäus
Kirchweg 20, ✉ 30167, ℰ (0511) 70 22 44, Fax (0511) 708559, « Lower Saxony count
house in a park ; garden terrace » – TV ☏ Ⓟ. 𝖠𝖤 Ⓞ 𝖤 𝖵𝖨𝖲𝖠
Meals (outstanding wine list) 36/63 (lunch) and à la carte 87/137 – **14 rm** ⌑ 19
332.
by Engelbosteler Damm **CV**

XX **Clichy**, Weißekreuzstr. 31, ✉ 30161, ℰ (0511) 31 24 47, Fax (0511) 318283
𝖠𝖤 𝖵𝖨𝖲𝖠
EV
closed Saturday lunch and Sunday – **Meals** à la carte 63/96.

XX **Gattopardo**, Hainhölzer Str. 1 / corner Postkamp, ✉ 30159, ℰ (0511) 1 43 7
Fax (0511) 318283, 🌤 – 𝖠𝖤 𝖵𝖨𝖲𝖠
DV
Meals (dinner only) (Italian rest.) à la carte 48/68.

Hannover-Bemerode *by Bischofsholer Damm* FY :

Treff Hotel Europa, Bergstr. 2, ⌗ 30539, ✆ (0511) 9 52 80, *Fax (0511) 9528488*, 😊, ≘s – 🛗, ⇥ rm, 📺 📞 ⏃ 🅿 – 🕮 300. 🆎 ⑩ ⋿ 𝘝𝘐𝘚𝘈. 🛇 rest
Meals à la carte 40/72 – **183 rm** ⌂ 195/600.

Hanover-Buchholz *by Bödekerstr.* FV :

Pannonia Atrium Hotel Ⓜ, Karl-Wiechert-Allee 68, ⌗ 30625, ✆ (0511) 5 40 70, *Fax (0511) 5407826*, 😊, 🏋, ≘s – 🛗, ⇥ rm, 📺 ⏃ 🚗 🅿 – 🕮 140. 🆎 ⑩ ⋿ 𝘝𝘐𝘚𝘈
Meals à la carte 40/77 – **222 rm** ⌂ 220/600 – 6 suites.

Gallo Nero, Groß Buchholzer Kirchweg 72 b, ⌗ 30655, ✆ (0511) 5 46 34 34, *Fax (0511) 548283*, 😊, « 18C farmhouse with contemporary interior design » – 🅿. 🆎 ⋿ 𝘝𝘐𝘚𝘈
closed Sunday, 1 week January and 3 weeks July - August – **Meals** (outstanding Italian wine and grappa list) (Italian rest.) à la carte 64/91.

Hanover-Döhren :

Wichmann, Hildesheimer Str. 230, ⌗ 30519, ✆ (0511) 83 16 71, *Fax (0511) 8379811*, « Courtyard »   *by Hildesheimer Str.* EFZ
Meals à la carte 71/102.

Die Insel, Rudolf-von-Bennigsen-Ufer 81, ⌗ 30519, ✆ (0511) 83 12 14, *Fax (0511) 831322*, ≤, 😊 – 🅿. 🆎 𝘝𝘐𝘚𝘈   *by Rudolf-von Benningsen-Ufer*   EZ
closed Monday, except lunch during exhibitions – **Meals** (booking essential) à la carte 53/99.

Hanover-Flughafen (Airport) *by Vahrenwalder Str* DV : *11 km* :

Maritim Airport Hotel Ⓜ, Flughafenstr. 5, ⌗ 30669, ✆ (0511) 9 73 70, *Fax (0511) 9737590*, ≘s, 🏊 – 🛗, ⇥ rm, 📺 📞 ⏃ 🚗 – 🕮 850. 🆎 ⑩ ⋿ 𝘝𝘐𝘚𝘈 ᴶᶜᴮ. 🛇 rest
Meals 47/52 (buffet only) – **Bistro Bottaccio** *(closed Sunday - Monday)* Meals à la carte 46/85 – **527 rm** ⌂ 270/620 – 30 suites.

Holiday Inn Crowne Plaza Ⓜ, Petzelstr. 60, ⌗ 30855 *Langenhagen*, ✆ (0511) 7 70 70, *Fax (0511) 737781*, 😊, ≘s, 🏊 a – 🛗, ⇥ rm, 🖳 📺 📞 ⏃ 🅿 – 🕮 150. 🆎 ⑩ ⋿ 𝘝𝘐𝘚𝘈 ᴶᶜᴮ
Meals 37 (buffet lunch) and à la carte 58/83 – **210 rm** ⌂ 239/626.

Hanover-Kirchrode *by Hans-Böckler Allee* FY :

Queens Hotel 🍃, Tiergartenstr. 117, ⌗ 30559, ✆ (0511) 5 10 30, *Fax (0511) 526924*, 🏋, ≘s – 🛗, ⇥ rm, 📺 📞 ⏃ 🚗 🅿 – 🕮 160. 🆎 ⑩ ⋿ 𝘝𝘐𝘚𝘈 ᴶᶜᴮ. 🛇 rest
Meals à la carte 42/75 – **178 rm** ⌂ 236/520 – 3 suites.

Hanover-Kleefeld *by Hans-Böckler Allee* FY :

Kleefelder Hof without rest, Kleestr. 3a, ⌗ 30625, ✆ (0511) 5 30 80, *Fax (0511) 5308333* – 🛗 ⇥ 📺 ☎ 📞 ⏃ 🚗 🅿 – 🕮 20. 🆎 ⑩ ⋿ 𝘝𝘐𝘚𝘈 ᴶᶜᴮ
86 rm ⌂ 165/250.

Hanover-Lahe *by Hohenzollernstraße* FV :

Holiday Inn, Oldenburger Allee 1, ⌗ 30659, ✆ (0511) 6 15 50, *Fax (0511) 6155555*, 😊 – 🛗, ⇥ rm, 📺 ☎ 📞 ⏃ 🚗 🅿 – 🕮 280. 🆎 ⑩ ⋿ 𝘝𝘐𝘚𝘈 ᴶᶜᴮ
Meals à la carte 36/66 – **150 rm** ⌂ 217/267.

Hannover-List *by Hohenzollernstr.* FV :

Arabella Sheraton Pelikan Ⓜ, Podbielskistr. 145, ⌗ 30177, ✆ (0511) 9 09 30, *Fax (0511) 9093555*, 😊, « Hotel with modern interior in a former factory », 🏋, ≘s – 🛗, ⇥ rm, 📺 📞 ⏃ 🚗 🅿 – 🕮 140. 🆎 ⑩ ⋿ 𝘝𝘐𝘚𝘈 ᴶᶜᴮ. 🛇 rest
closed 2 weeks December – **Signatur :** Meals à la carte 44/83 – **Edo** (Japanese rest.) *(dinner only, closed Sunday and 3 weeks July - August)* Meals 68/150 – **138 rm** ⌂ 263/612 – 8 suites.

Dorint Ⓜ, Podbielskistr. 21, ⌗ 30163, ✆ (0511) 3 90 40, *Fax (0511) 3904100*, ≘s – 🛗, ⇥ rm, 📺 ☎ 📞 ⏃ 🚗 – 🕮 250. 🆎 ⑩ ⋿ 𝘝𝘐𝘚𝘈 ᴶᶜᴮ
Meals à la carte 39/79 – **206 rm** ⌂ 229/642.

Hanover-Messe (near Exhibition Centre) *by Hans-Böckler Allee* FY :

Parkhotel Kronsberg, Laatzener Str. 18 (at Exhibition Centre), ⌗ 30539, ✆ (0511) 8 74 00, *Fax (0511) 867112*, 😊, 🏋, ≘s, 🏊, 🚵 – 🛗, ⇥ rm, 🖳 rest, 📺 🚗 🅿 – 🕮 150. 🆎 ⑩ ⋿ 𝘝𝘐𝘚𝘈
Meals *(closed 27 December - 4 January)* à la carte 46/71 – **169 rm** ⌂ 190/480.

at Hanover-Roderbruch by Hans-Böckler Allee FY East : 7 km :

Novotel, Feodor-Lynen-Str. 1, ⊠ 30625, ℘ (0511) 9 56 60, Fax (0511) 9566333,
⊆s, ⊼ (heated) – |≉|, ↦ rm, TV ☎ ✆ & P – 🕭 100. AE ① E VISA
Meals à la carte 47/72 – **112 rm** � 187/350.

Ibis, Feodor-Lynen-Str. 1, ⊠ 30625, ℘ (0511) 9 56 70, Fax (0511) 576128 – |≉|, ↦ r
TV ☎ ✆ & P – 🕭 30. AE ① E VISA
Meals (dinner only) 26 – **96 rm** ⊔ 136/210.

at Hanover-Vahrenwald by Vahrenwalder Str. DV North : 4km :

Fora, Großer Kolonnenweg 19, ⊠ 30163, ℘ (0511) 6 70 60, Fax (0511) 6706111,
⊆s – |≉|, ↦ rm, ▤ rest, TV ☎ ✆ & ⇔ – 🕭 100. AE ① E VISA JCB
Meals à la carte 37/56 – **142 rm** ⊔ 195/285.

at Laatzen by Hildesheimer Str. EFZ South : 9 km :

Copthorne M, Würzburger Str. 21, ⊠ 30880, ℘ (0511) 9 83 60, Fax (0511) 983666
🐾, ⅙, ⊆s, ⊼ – |≉|, ↦ rm, TV ✆ & ⇔ P – 🕭 280. AE ① E VISA JCB
Meals à la carte 45/69 – **222 rm** ⊔ 275/534.

Europa-Congress-Hotel M, Karlsruher Str. 8 a, ⊠ 30880, ℘ (0511) 87 57 3
Fax (0511) 87573555 – |≉|, ↦ rm, ▤ TV ☎ ✆ & P – 🕭 100. AE ① E VISA. ⅍ re
Meals à la carte 48/66 – **120 rm** ⊔ 189/476.

Treff-Hotel Britannia Hannover, Karlsruher Str. 26, ⊠ 30880, ℘ (0511) 8 78 2
Fax (0511) 863466, 🐾, ⊆s, ✕ (indoor) golf simulator – |≉|, ↦ rm, TV ☎ & P – 🕭 1
AE ① E VISA. ⅍ rest
Meals à la carte 40/72 – **100 rm** ⊔ 195/600.

at Ronnenberg-Benthe by Bornumer Str. CZ and B 65, South-West : 10 km :

Benther Berg ⌂, Vogelsangstr. 18, ⊠ 30952, ℘ (05108) 6 40 6
Fax (05108) 640650, 🐾, ⊆s, ⊼, 🐎 – |≉|, ▤ rest, TV P – 🕭 60. AE ① E VISA
Meals à la carte 65/98 – **70 rm** ⊔ 145/240.

Nenndorf, Bad Niedersachsen 415 417 I 12 – pop. 10 000 – alt. 70 m – Heilbad.
Hannover 33.

at Bad Nenndorf-Riepen North-West : 4,5 km by B 65 :

XXX **La Forge** (in Schmiedegasthaus Gehrke), Riepener Str. 21, ⊠ 31542, ℘ (05725) 50 5
⊛ Fax (05725) 7282 – P. AE ① VISA. ⅍ – closed Monday - Tuesday, January, and 2 wee
July - August – **Meals** (dinner only)(booking essential) 105/150
Spec. Boddermelksanballerße mit in Piment gebeizter Lachsforelle. Seezungenröllchen u
Langustinenravioli mit Portwein-Ingwersauce. Malzkaffeemousse mit eingeweckten Birn
und Karamelparfait.

LEIPZIG Sachsen 418 L 21, 987 ⑰ – pop. 480 000 – alt. 118 m.
See : Old Town Hall★ (Altes Rathaus) BY – Old Stock Exchange★ (Naschmarkt) BY
Museum of Fine Arts★ (Museum der Bildenden Künste) BZ – Thomaskirche★ BZ – Egypt
Museum★ (Ägyptisches Museum) BZ.
ⓕ₉ Noitzsch (North-East : 29 Km by B2), ℘ (034242) 5 03 02.
✈ Leipzig-Halle (North-West : 13 km by Gerberstr. und Eutritzscher Str.BY), ℘ (03∆
22 40.
Exhibition Grounds (Neue Messe), Messe Allee1 (by Eutritzscher Str BY), ⊠ 043∆
℘ (0341) 67 80, Fax (0341) 6788762.
🛈 Tourist-Information, Richard-Wagner Str.1, ⊠ 04109, ℘ (0341) 7 10 40, Fax (03∆
7104271.
ADAC, Augustusplatz 6, ⊠ 04109, ℘ (0351) 44 78 80, Fax (0341) 2110540.
Berlin 180 – Dresden 109 – Erfurt 126.

Plans on following pages

Kempinski Hotel Fürstenhof M, Tröndlinring 8, ⊠ 04105, ℘ (0341) 14 0
Fax (0341) 1403700, 🐾, « 1770 Patrician palace ; fitness and beauty centre », Massa
⅙, ⊆s, ⊼ – |≉|, ↦ rm, ▤ TV ✆ & ⇔ – 🕭 60. AE ① E VISA JCB   BY
Meals 40 (lunch) and à la carte 53/80 – **92 rm** ⊔ 340/510 – 4 suites.

Marriott M, Am Hallischen Tor 1, ⊠ 04109, ℘ (0341) 9 65 30, Fax (0341) 96539
⅙, ⊆s, ⊼ – |≉|, ↦ rm, ▤ TV ✆ & ⇔ – 🕭 220. AE ① E VISA JCB   BY
Meals (weekdays dinner only) à la carte 40/56 – **231 rm** ⊔ 175/325 – 11 suites.

Inter-Continental, Gerberstr. 15, ⊠ 04105, ℘ (0341) 98 80, Fax (0341) 9881229, be
garden, Massage, ⊆s, ⊼ – |≉|, ↦ rm, ▤ TV ✆ & P – 🕭 400. AE ① E VISA JCB. ⅍ res
Meals à la carte 52/77 – **Yamato** (Japanese rest.) Meals 30/50 and à la carte – **447**
⊔ 298/408 – 21 suites.   BY

Renaissance M, Querstr. 12, ⊠ 04103, ℘ (0341) 1 29 20, Fax (0341) 1292800, ⅃₅, ≘s, ☒ – ⌷, ⇔ rm, ▤ ⊤⊽ ☎ ⅊ ⇔ – ⚓ 350. ᴀᴇ ⓪ ᴇ ᴠɪsᴀ ᴊᴄʙ   DY a
Meals à la carte 40/58 – **356 rm** ⌛ 160/206.

Dorint M, Stephanstr. 6, ⊠ 04103, ℘ (0341) 9 77 90, Fax (0341) 9779100, beer garden, ≘s – ⌷, ⇔ rm, ⊤⊽ ☎ ⅊ ⇔ – ⚓ 150. ᴀᴇ ⓪ ᴇ ᴠɪsᴀ ᴊᴄʙ   DZ n
Meals à la carte 46/72 – **177 rm** ⌛ 193/283.

Seaside Park Hotel M, Richard-Wagner-Str. 7, ⊠ 04109, ℘ (0341) 9 85 20, Fax (0341) 9852750, Massage, ≘s – ⌷ ⇔, ▤ rest, ⊤⊽ ☎ ⅊ ⇔ – ⚓ 80. ᴀᴇ ⓪ ᴇ ᴠɪsᴀ ᴊᴄʙ. ⅍ rest   CY s
Meals (closed Sunday and July - mid August) (dinner only) à la carte 36/60 – **288 rm** ⌛ 195/268 – 9 suites.

Michaelis M, Paul-Gruner-Str. 44, ⊠ 04107, ℘ (0341) 2 67 80, Fax (0341) 2678100, ⇪ – ⌷, ⇔ rm, ⊤⊽ ☎ ☎ ⅊ ⇔ – ⚓ 45. ᴀᴇ ⓪ ᴇ ᴠɪsᴀ by Peterssteinweg BZ
Meals (closed Saturday lunch and Sunday) à la carte 42/66 – **59 rm** ⌛ 160/195.

Ramada Hotel M without rest, Gutenbergplatz 1, ⊠ 04103, ℘ (0341) 1 29 30, Fax (0341) 1293444 – ⌷ ⇔ ▤ ⊤⊽ ☎ ☎ ⅊ – ⚓ 20. ᴀᴇ ⓪ ᴇ ᴠɪsᴀ ᴊᴄʙ   DZ s
122 rm ⌛ 136/209.

Novotel M, Goethestr. 11, ⊠ 04109, ℘ (0341) 9 95 80, Fax (0341) 9958200, ⇪, ≘s – ⌷, ⇔ rm, ▤ ⊤⊽ ☎ ⅊ ⇔ – ⚓ 100. ᴀᴇ ⓪ ᴇ ᴠɪsᴀ   CY n
Meals à la carte 34/65 – **200 rm** ⌛ 193/225.

Holiday Inn Garden Court, Rudolf-Breitscheid-Str. 3, ⊠ 04105, ℘ (0341) 1 25 10, Fax (0341) 1251100, ≘s – ⌷, ⇔ rm, ▤ ⊤⊽ ☎ ⅊ – ⚓ 25. ᴀᴇ ⓪ ᴇ ᴠɪsᴀ ᴊᴄʙ. ⅍ rest   CY g
Meals à la carte 28/51 – **121 rm** ⌛ 190/250 – 6 suites.

Rema-Hotel Vier Jahreszeiten M without rest, Rudolf Breitscheidstr. 23, ⊠ 04105, ℘ (0341) 9 85 10, Fax (0341) 985122 – ⌷ ⇔ ⊤⊽ ☎ ⅊. ᴀᴇ ⓪ ᴇ ᴠɪsᴀ ᴊᴄʙ   CY b
67 rm ⌛ 150/330.

Leipziger Hof M, Hedwigstr. 1, ⊠ 04315, ℘ (0341) 6 97 40, Fax (0341) 6974150, beer garden, « Permanent exhibition of paintings », ≘s – ⌷, ⇔ rm, ⊤⊽ ☎ ⅊ ⅊ – ⚓ 50. ᴀᴇ ⓪ ᴇ ᴠɪsᴀ   by Eisenbahnstraße DY
Meals (closed Saturday - Sunday) (dinner only) à la carte 33/50 – **73 rm** ⌛ 99/250.

Markgraf without rest, Körnerstr. 36, ⊠ 04107, ℘ (0341) 30 30 30, Fax (0341) 3030399 – ⌷ ⇔ ⊤⊽ ☎ ☎ ⇔. ᴀᴇ ⓪ ᴇ ᴠɪsᴀ by Peterssteinweg BZ
54 rm ⌛ 77/139.

Mercure, Augustusplatz 5, ⊠ 04109, ℘ (0341) 2 14 60, Fax (0341) 9604916 – ⌷, ⇔ rm, ▤ rest, ⊤⊽ ☎ ⅊ – ⚓ 120. ᴀᴇ ⓪ ᴇ ᴠɪsᴀ ᴊᴄʙ   CZ f
Meals à la carte 35/60 – **283 rm** ⌛ 140/200.

Am Bayrischen Platz without rest, Paul-List-Str. 5, ⊠ 04103, ℘ (0341) 14 08 60, Fax (0341) 1408648 – ⌷ ⇔ ⊤⊽ ☎ ⅊. ᴀᴇ ⓪ ᴇ ᴠɪsᴀ by Windmühlenstraße CZ
32 rm ⌛ 108/148.

Ibis without rest, Brühl 69, ⊠ 04109, ℘ (0341) 2 18 60, Fax (0341) 2186222 – ⌷ ⇔ ⊤⊽ ☎ ☎ ⇔. ᴀᴇ ⓪ ᴇ ᴠɪsᴀ ᴊᴄʙ   CY a
126 rm ⌛ 125.

XX **Kaiser Maximilian**, Neumarkt 9, ⊠ 04105, ℘ (0341) 9 98 69 00, Fax (0341) 9986901, ⇪ – ᴀᴇ ᴇ   BZ a
Meals à la carte 47/69.

XX **Auerbachs Keller**, Grimmaische Str. 2 (Mädler-Passage), ⊠ 04109, ℘ (0341) 21 61 00, Fax (0341) 2161011, « 16C historical wine tavern » – ᴀᴇ ⓪ ᴇ ᴠɪsᴀ   BYZ
Historische Weinstuben (dinner only) (closed Sunday) Meals à la carte 59/75 – **Großer Keller** : Meals à la carte 36/63.

XX **Medici**, Nikolaikirchhof 5, ⊠ m4109, ℘ (0341) 2 11 38 78, Fax (0341) 9262200 – ᴀᴇ ⓪ ᴇ ᴠɪsᴀ ᴊᴄʙ   CY c
closed Sunday and 22 December - 3 January – **Meals** (Italian rest.) à la carte 52/67.

XX **Coffe Baum**, Kleine Fleischergasse 4, ⊠ 04109, ℘ (0341) 9 61 00 61, Fax (0341) 9610030, ⇪, « Historic inn from 1645 ; museum of coffee » – ⅊ ᴇ ᴠɪsᴀ AY b
Lusatia : (first floor) (booking essential for dinner) Meals à la carte 38/58 – **Lehmannsche Stube and Schuhmannzimmer** : Meals à la carte 32/48.

XX **Classico**, Nikolaistr. 16, ⊠ 04109, ℘ (0341) 2 11 13 55, Fax (0341) 2111355, ⇪   CY
closed Sunday – **Meals** (Italian rest.) à la carte 50/88.

XX **Stadtpfeiffer**, Augustusplatz 8 (Neues Gewandhaus), ⊠ 04109, ℘ (0341) 9 60 51 86, Fax (0341) 2113594, ⇪ – ᴀᴇ ᴇ ᴠɪsᴀ   CZ
closed Sunday – **Meals** à la carte 42/70.

XX **Apels Garten**, Kolonnadenstr. 2, ⊠ 04109, ℘ (0341) 9 60 77 77, Fax (0341) 9607777, ⇪ – ⚓ 30. ᴀᴇ ᴇ ᴠɪsᴀ   AZ q
closed dinner Sunday and Bank Holidays – **Meals** à la carte 27/45.

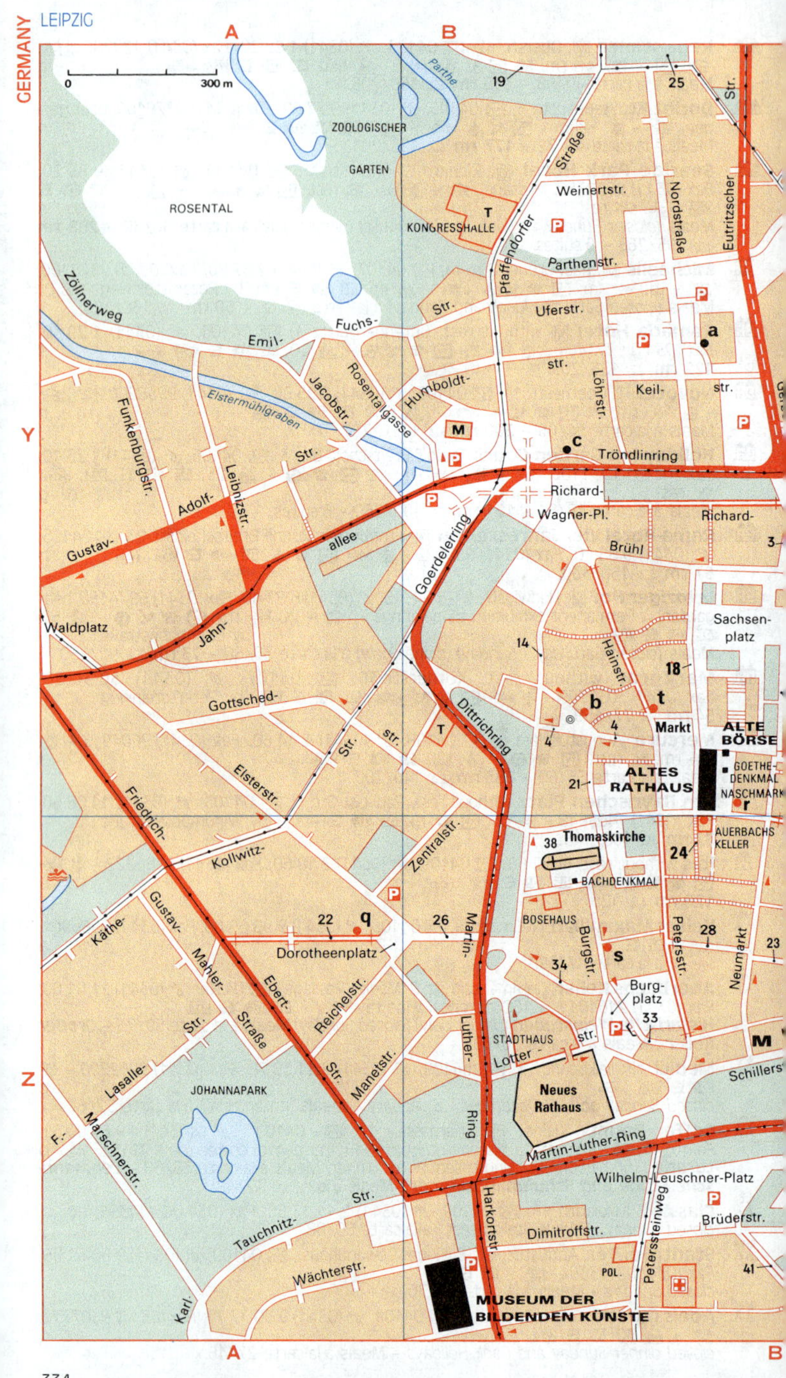
GERMANY
LEIPZIG
0   300 m
Parthe
ZOOLOGISCHER
GARTEN
ROSENTAL
KONGRESSHALLE
Zöllnerweg
Elstermühlgraben
Funkenburgstr.
Jacobstr.
Rosentalgasse
Humboldt-
Emil-
Fuchs-
Str.
Straße
Weinertstr.
Nordstraße
Eutritzscher
Pfaffendorfer
Parthenstr.
Uferstr.
str.
Löhrstr.
Keil-
str.
a
Leibnizstr.
Adolf-
Gustav-
Jahn-
allee
Waldplatz
M
P
P
Goerdelerring
Tröndlinring
c
Richard-
Wagner-Pl.
Brühl
Richard-
3
Sachsen-
platz
14
Hainstr.
18
b
t
4
4
Markt
ALTE
BÖRSE
GOETHE-
DENKMAL
NASCHMARKT
r
ALTES
RATHAUS
21
Gottsched-
Elsterstr.
Str.
str.
T
Dittrichring
Zentralstr.
Kollwitz-
Friedrich-
Käthe-
Gustav-
Mahler-
Ebert-
Reichelstr.
Str.
Manetstr.
Str.
Lasalle-
Marschnerstr.
Karl-
JOHANNAPARK
Dorotheenplatz
22
q
26
Martin-
Luther-
Ring
P
38
Thomaskirche
BACHDENKMAL
BOSEHAUS
Burgstr.
s
34
Burg-
platz
33
str.
Peterstr.
28
Neumarkt
23
AUERBACHS
KELLER
24
M
Schillers-
STADTHAUS
Lotter-
Neues
Rathaus
Martin-Luther-Ring
Wilhelm-Leuschner-Platz
Harkortstr.
Dimitroffstr.
Petersteinweg
Brüderstr.
P
POL.
41
Str.
Wächterstr.
Tauchnitz-
P
MUSEUM DER
BILDENDEN KÜNSTE
19
25

LEIPZIG
GERMANY

Althner Straße — DY 2
Am Hallischen Tor — BY 3
Barfußgäßchen — BY 4
Dörrienstraße — DY 8
Grimmaischer Steinweg — CZ 12
Grimmaische Str. — BCYZ 13
Große Fleischergasse — BY 14
Katharinenstraße — BY 18
Kickerlingsberg — BY 19
Klostergasse — BY 21
Kolonnadenstr. — AZ 22
Kupfergasse — BZ 23
Mädlerpassage — BZ 24
Nordplatz — BY 25
Otto-Schill-Str. — BZ 26
Preußergäßchen — BZ 28
Reichsstraße — BY 29
Reudnitzer Str. — DY 32
Schloßgasse — BZ 33
Schulstraße — BZ 34
Schützenstraße — DY 37
Thomaskirchhof — BYZ 38
Universitätsstr. — CZ 39
Windmühlenstr. — BCZ 41
Wintergartenstr. — CY 42

C
D
Y
N

Berliner Str.
heid-Str.
S. Bahn
Willy-Brandt-Platz
Brühl
Str.
Schwanen-teich
Goethestr.
Georgi-ring
Ritterstr.
Ritterstr.
Gellertstr.
Opernhaus
Augustus-
platz
Neues Gewandhaus
LEIBNIZ-DENKMAL
platz
SPORTHALLE
Seeburg-str.
Nürnberger Str.
Brüder-str.
Talstr.
Talstr.
Stephanstr.
Goldschmidtstr.
Johannis-platz
ADAC
Prager Str.
Gutenbergplatz
Gerichts-str.
Eilenburger Str.
Oststr.
Johannisallee
Johannisstraße
Täubchenweg
weg
Brandenburger Str.
Eisenbahnstr.
Fr.-List-Platz
Hofmeisterstr.
Rosa-Luxemburg-Str.
Kohlgartenstr.
Chopinstr.
straße
Inselstr.
Str.
straße
Kreuzstr.
Lange
Grenz-
Salomon-
Inselstr.
Querstr.
Dresdner Str.
Querstr.
Waldstr.
M
U
Str.
Goldschmidtstr.
2
32
37
42
8
12

✗ **Weinstock**, Marktplatz 7, ✉ 04109, ✆ (0341) 14 06 06 06, Fax (0341) 14060607, 🌳
« 16C former bank » – AE ⓘ E VISA   BY
Meals à la carte 38/70.

✗ **Thüringer Hof**, Burgstr. 19, ✉ 04109, ✆ (0341) 9 94 49 99, Fax (0341) 9944933, 🌳
« Restored 15C tavern » – AE E VISA   BZ
Meals à la carte 26/55.

✗ **Mövenpick**, Am Naschmarkt 1, ✉ 04109, ✆ (0341) 2 11 77 22, Fax (0341) 211481
🌳 – ⇥. AE ⓘ E VISA   BY
Meals à la carte 31/58.

at Lindenthal-Breitenfeld *North-West : 8 km, by Euritzscher Str.* BX :

Breitenfelder Hof M 🦢, Lindenallee 8, ✉ 04466, ✆ (0341) 4 65 1
Fax (0341) 4651133, 🌳, (Park) – ⇥ rm, TV ☎ ✆ P. AE ⓘ E VISA
Meals à la carte 28/45 – **72 rm** ☕ 180/225.

at Leipzig-Eutritzsch : *by Eutritzscher Str.* BY :

Vivaldi M without rest, Wittenberger Str. 87, ✉ 04129, ✆ (0341) 9 03 6
Fax (0341) 9036234 – 🛗 ⇥ TV ☎ 🚗 – 🛋 40. AE ⓘ E VISA   U
107 rm ☕ 120.

at Leipzig-Gohlis *by Pfaffendorfer Str.* BY :

De Saxe, Gohliser Str. 25, ✉ 01455, ✆ (0341) 5 93 80, Fax (0341) 5938299 – 🛗
☎ P. AE ⓘ E VISA
Meals à la carte 31/49 – **33 rm** ☕ 130/170.

at Leipzig-Grosszschocher *by Käthe-Kollwitz-Str.* AZ *and Erich-Zeigner-Allee :*

Windorf, Gerhard-Ellrodt-Str. 21, ✉ 04249, ✆ (0341) 4 27 70, Fax (0341) 4277222, 🌳
– 🛗, ⇥ rm, TV ☎ ✆ P – 🛋 50. AE ⓘ E VISA
Meals à la carte 31/50 – **97 rm** ☕ 145/185.

at Leipzig-Leutzsch *by Friedrich-Ebert-Str.* AY :

Lindner Business Aktiv Hotel M, Hans-Driesch-Str. 27, ✉ 04179, ✆ (034
4 47 80, Fax (0341) 4478478, 🌳, ≘s, 🏊 – 🛗, ⇥ rm, TV ✆ 🚻 🚗 – 🛋 110. AE ⓘ
E VISA JCB
Meals à la carte 36/68 – **200 rm** ☕ 160/260 – 15 suites.

at Leipzig-Lindenau *by Jahn-Allee* AY :

Lindenau, Georg-Schwarz-Str. 33, ✉ 04177, ✆ (0341) 4 48 03 10, Fax (0341) 44803C
≘s – 🛗, ⇥ rm, TV ☎ P – 🛋 25. AE E VISA
Meals à la carte 28/47 – **52 rm** ☕ 110/150.

at Leipzig-Möckern *by Eutritzscher Str.* BY :

Silencium without rest, Georg-Schumann-Str. 268 (B 6), ✉ 04159, ✆ (034
9 01 29 90, Fax (0341) 9012991 – 🛗 ⇥ TV ☎ ✆ 🚗 – 🛋 40. AE E VISA
closed 24 December - 6 January – **35 rm** ☕ 99/169.

at Leipzig-Paunsdorf *by Eisenbahnstraße* DY :

Treff Hotel Leipzig M, Schongauer Str. 39, ✉ 04329, ✆ (0341) 25 4
Fax (0341) 2541550, 🌳, Massage, ≘s – 🛗, ⇥ rm, 🖥 TV ✆ 🚻 P – 🛋 600. AE
E VISA JCB
Meals à la carte 36/73 – **91 rm** ☕ 149/299.

at Leipzig-Portitz *by Berliner Str.* CY :

Accento, Tauchaer Str. 260, ✉ 04349, ✆ (0341) 9 26 20, Fax (0341) 9262100, 🌳
≘s – 🛗, ⇥ rm, 🖥 rest, TV ☎ ✆ 🚗 P – 🛋 60. AE ⓘ E VISA JCB
closed 20 December - 4 January – **Meals** (closed Saturday and Sunday) (dinner only) à
carte 25/48 – **15 rm** ☕ 179/249.

at Leipzig-Reudnitz *by Dresdner Str.* DZ *and Breite Str. :*

Berlin without rest, Riebeckstr. 30, ✉ 04317, ✆ (0341) 2 67 30 00, Fax (0341) 267328
– 🛗 ⇥ TV ☎ – 🛋 10. AE ⓘ E VISA
51 rm ☕ 129/149.

at Leipzig-Stötteritz *by Prager Str.* DZ :

Balance Hotel M, Wasserturmstr. 33, ✉ 04299, ✆ (0341) 8 67 9
Fax (0341) 8679444, 🌳, ≘s – 🛗, ⇥ rm, 🖥 rest, TV ☎ ✆ 🚻 🚗 – 🛋 35. AE ⓘ
E VISA JCB. 🚭 rest
Meals à la carte 30/53 – **126 rm** ☕ 165/195 – 9 suites.

t Leipzig-Wiederitzsch *North : 7 km, by Eutritzscher Straße* BY *and Delitzscher Straße*

Astron Hotel M, Fuggerstr. 2, ⌂ 04448, ℰ (0341) 5 25 10, Fax (0341) 5251300, ╔═,
⌂ – 📶, ⋞ rm, 🖼 TV ☏ ⴺ 🚗 – 🖿 230. AE ⓞ E VISA
Meals à la carte 30/60 – **308 rm** ⌂ 203/226.

t Wachau *South-East : 8 km, by Prager Straße* DZ :

Atlanta Park Inn M, Südring 21, ⌂ 04445, ℰ (034297) 8 40, Fax (034297) 84999,
⌂ – 📶, ⋞ rm, 🖼 TV ☏ ⴺ 🅿 – 🖿 220. AE ⓞ E VISA
Meals à la carte 39/58 – **197 rm** ⌂ 130/185 – 6 suites.

For the quickest route, use Michelin maps at a scale of 1:1 000 000.

MUNICH (MÜNCHEN) L *Bayern* 419 420 *V 18,* 987 ⓺ *– pop. 1 300 000 – alt. 520 m.*
See : *Marienplatz*★ KZ *– Church of Our Lady (Frauenkirche)*★ *(tower ☀★)* KZ *– Old Pin-
akothek (Alte Pinakothek)*★★★ KY *– German Museum (Deutsches Museum)*★★★ LZ *– The
Palace (Residenz)*★ *(Treasury*★★ *Palace Theatre*★*)* KY *– Church of Asam Brothers
(Asamkirche)*★ KZ *– Nymphenburg*★★ *(Castle*★*, Park*★*, Amalienburg*★★*, Botanical Garden
(Botanischer Garten)*★★*, Carriage Museum (Marstallmuseum) and China-Collection
(Porzellansammlung*★*) by Arnulfstr.* EV *– New Pinakothek (Neue Pinakothek)*★ KY *– City
Historical Museum (Münchener Stadtmuseum)*★ *(Moorish Dancers*★★*)* KZ M[7] *– Villa Len-
bach Collections (Städt. Galerie im Lenbachhaus) (Portraits by Lenbach*★*)* JY M[4] *– Antique
Collections (Staatliche Antikensammlungen)*★ JY M[3] *– Glyptothek*★ JY M[2] *– German Hun-
ting Museum (Deutsches Jagdmuseum)*★ KZ M[1] *– Olympic Park (Olympia-Park) (Olympic
Tower ☀★★★) by Schleißheimer Str.* FU *– Hellabrunn Zoo (Tierpark Hellabrunn)*★ *by Lindwurmstr. (B 11)* EX *– English Garden (Englischer Garten)*★ *(view from Monopteros Temple*★*)* LY.

⌂ *Straßlach, Tölzer Straße (South : 17 km), ℰ (08170) 4 50 ;* ⌂ *München-Thalkirchen,
Zentralländstr. 40, ℰ (089) 7 23 13 04 ;* ⌂ ⌂ *Eichenried (North-East : 24 km), Kurfür-
stenweg 10, ℰ (08131) 8 72 38.*

✈ *Flughafen München (North-East : 29 km) by Ungererstraße* HU*, ℰ (089) 9 75 00, Fax
(089) 97557906, City Air Terminal, Arnulfstraße (Main Station).*

🚂 *Ostbahnhof, Friedenstraße(*HX*).*

Exhibition Centre (Messegelände) (by ③*), ⌂ 81823, ℰ (089) 9 49 01, Fax (089) 94909.*
🛈 *Tourist-office, airport "Franz-Josef-Strauß", ℰ (089) 97 59 28 15, Fax (089) 975292813.*
ADAC, *Sendlinger-Tor-Platz 9, ⌂ 80336, ℰ (089) 5 40 19 44 56, Fax(089) 5504449.*
Berlin 586 – Innsbruck 162 – Nürnberg 165 – Salzburg 140 – Stuttgart 222.

Plans on following pages

Bayerischer Hof, Promenadeplatz 2, ⌂ 80333, ℰ (089) 2 12 00, Fax (089) 2120906,
╔═, Massage, ⋞s, ⊠ – 📶, ⋞ rm, TV ☏ ⴺ 🚗 – 🖿 600. AE ⓞ E
VISA JCB
KY y
Garden-Restaurant *(booking essential)* **Meals** à la carte 72/116 – ***Trader Vic's*** *(Poly-
nesian rest.) (dinner only)* **Meals** à la carte 50/87 – ***Palais Keller*** (Bavarian pub) **Meals** à
la carte 31/54 – **396 rm** ⌂ 377/612 – 45 suites.

Rafael, Neuturmstr. 1, ⌂ 80331, ℰ (089) 29 09 80, Fax (089) 222539, « Roof garden
with terrace and ⊠ » – 📶, ⋞ rm, 🖼 TV ☏ 🚗 – 🖿 35. AE ⓞ E VISA JCB.
⋞ rest
KZ s
Meals 48 (lunch) and à la carte 70/90 – **73 rm** ⌂ 508/825 – 7 suites.

Kempinski Hotel Vier Jahreszeiten, Maximilianstr. 17, ⌂ 80539, ℰ (089) 2 12 50,
Fax (089) 21252000, Massage, ⋞s, ⊠ – 📶, ⋞ rm, 🖼 TV ☏ 🚗 – 🖿 450. AE ⓞ E
VISA JCB
LZ a
Meals *(closed August)* à la carte 65/106 – ***Bistro-Eck :*** **Meals** à la carte 46/81 – **316 rm**
⌂ 383/866 – 50 suites.

Königshof, Karlsplatz 25, ⌂ 80335, ℰ (089) 55 13 60, Fax (089) 55136113 – 📶,
⋞ rm, 🖼 TV ☏ 🚗 – 🖿 80. AE ⓞ E VISA JCB. ⋞ rest
JY s
Meals *(booking essential) (outstanding wine list)* à la carte 83/126 – **90 rm** ⌂ 382/619
– 9 suites.

Excelsior, Schützenstr. 11, ⌂ 80335, ℰ (089) 55 13 70, Fax (089) 55137121 – 📶,
⋞ rm, TV – 🖿 25. AE ⓞ E VISA JCB
JY z
Vinothek : **Meals** à la carte 45/57 – **113 rm** ⌂ 252/429.

Park Hilton, Am Tucherpark 7, ⌂ 80538, ℰ (089) 3 84 50, Fax (089) 38452555, beer
garden, Massage, ⋞s, ⊠ – 📶, ⋞ rm, 🖼 TV ☏ ⴺ 🚗 – 🖿 750. AE ⓞ E VISA JCB.
⋞ rest
HU n
Hilton Grill *(closed Saturday lunch, 2-16 January, Holy Week and late July-mid August)*
Meals à la carte 77/109 – ***Tse Yang*** *(Chinese rest.) (closed Monday)* **Meals** à la carte 47/88
– ***Isar Terrassen :*** **Meals** à la carte 51/79 – **477 rm** ⌂ 337/592 – 23 suites.

Continued on following pages

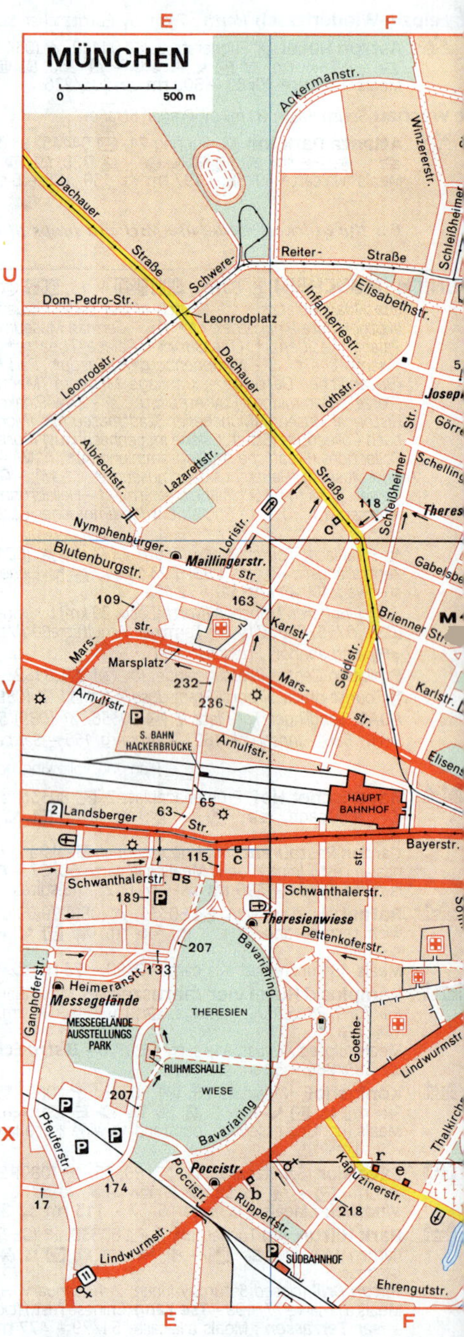

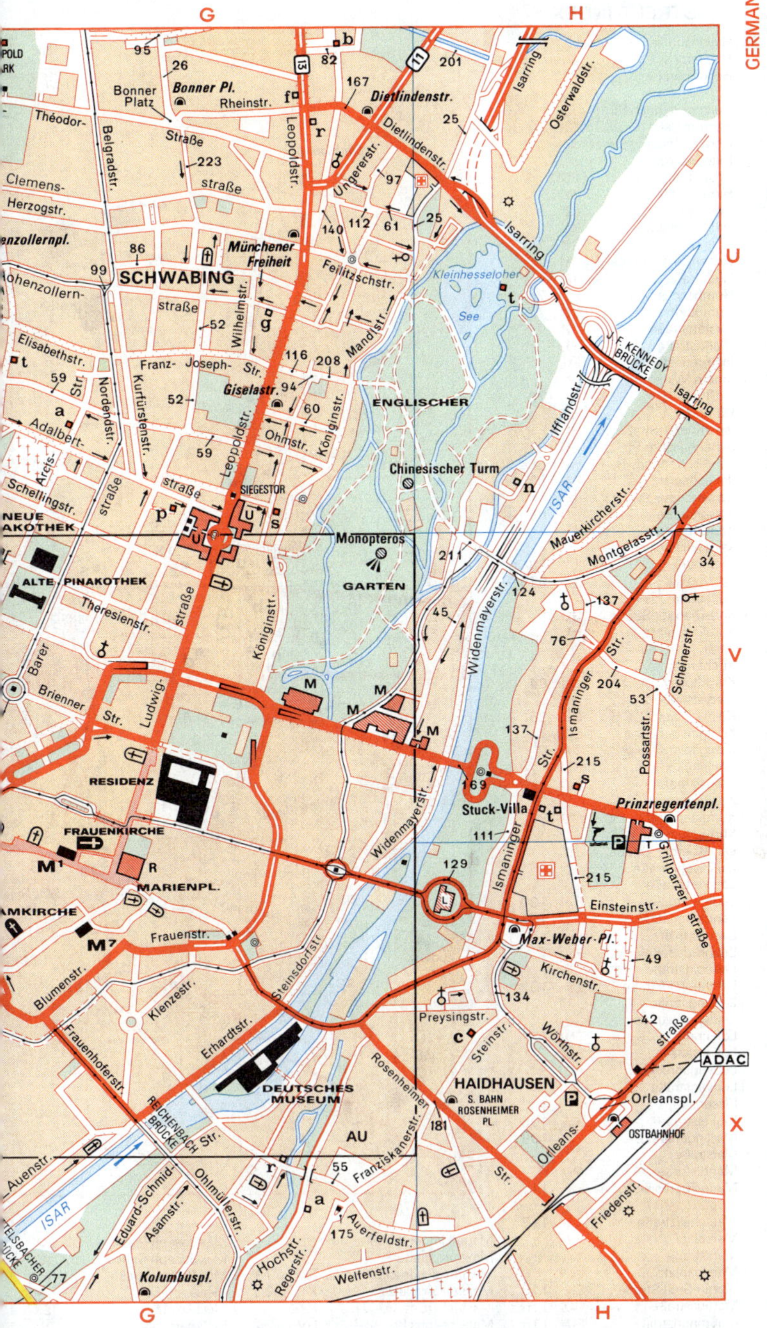
G
H
U
V
X
95
b
82
26
167
201
Bonner Pl.
Bonner Platz
Rheinstr.
f
Dietlindenstr.
r
25
Dietlindenstr.
Straße
223
Ungererstr.
Osterwaldstr.
Isarring
Théodor-
Leopoldstr.
Belgradstr.
straße
97
Clemens-
Herzogstr.
140
112
61
25
Isarring
enzollernpl.
86
Münchener Freiheit
Feilitzschstr.
99
SCHWABING
Kleinhesseloher
Hohenzollern-
52
g
See
t
straße
Elisabethstr.
116
208
Mandlstr.
J. F. KENNEDY BRÜCKE
59
Franz- Joseph- Str.
ENGLISCHER
t
Str.
Giselastr. 94
Isarring
a
52
60
Ifflandstr.
Adalbert-
59
Ohmstr.
Königinstr.
Nordendstr.
Kurfürstenstr.
Chinesischer Turm
n
Aeis
ISAR
Schellingstr.
straße
SIEGESTOR
Mauerkircherstr.
71
NEUE
p
U
s
Montgelasstr.
34
AKOTHEK
U
Monopteros
211
137
ALTE PINAKOTHEK
Königinstr.
GARTEN
124
Theresienstr.
45
76
Str.
Ismaninger
204
Scheinerstr.
Barer
Ludwig-
Widenmayerstr.
53
Possartstr.
Brienner
M
137
V
Str.
M
215
Str.
M
s
RESIDENZ
M
169
Prinzregentenpl.
FRAUENKIRCHE
Stuck-Villa
t
P
T
Grillparzerstr.
M
R
111
MARIENPL.
129
215
AMKIRCHE
Einsteinstr.
M
Frauenstr.
Max-Weber-Pl.
straße
Steinsdorfstr.
49
Blumenstr.
Kirchenstr.
Klenzestr.
134
Frauhoferstr.
Erhardtstr.
Preysingstr.
42
Rosenheimer
Steinstr.
Wörthstr.
straße
c
ADAC
Auenstr.
DEUTSCHES MUSEUM
HAIDHAUSEN
Orleanspl.
REICHENBACH BRÜCKE
S. Bahn
P
ROSENHEIMER PL
Ostbahnhof
X
AU
Orleans-
ELSBACHER
r
55
Franziskanerstr.
Str.
BRÜCKE
181
Friedenstr.
a
ISAR
Eduard-Schmid-Str.
175
Auerfeldstr.
Asamstr.
Ohlmüllerstr.
77
Kolumbuspl.
Hochstr.
Regerstr.
Welfenstr.
G
H

STREET INDEX

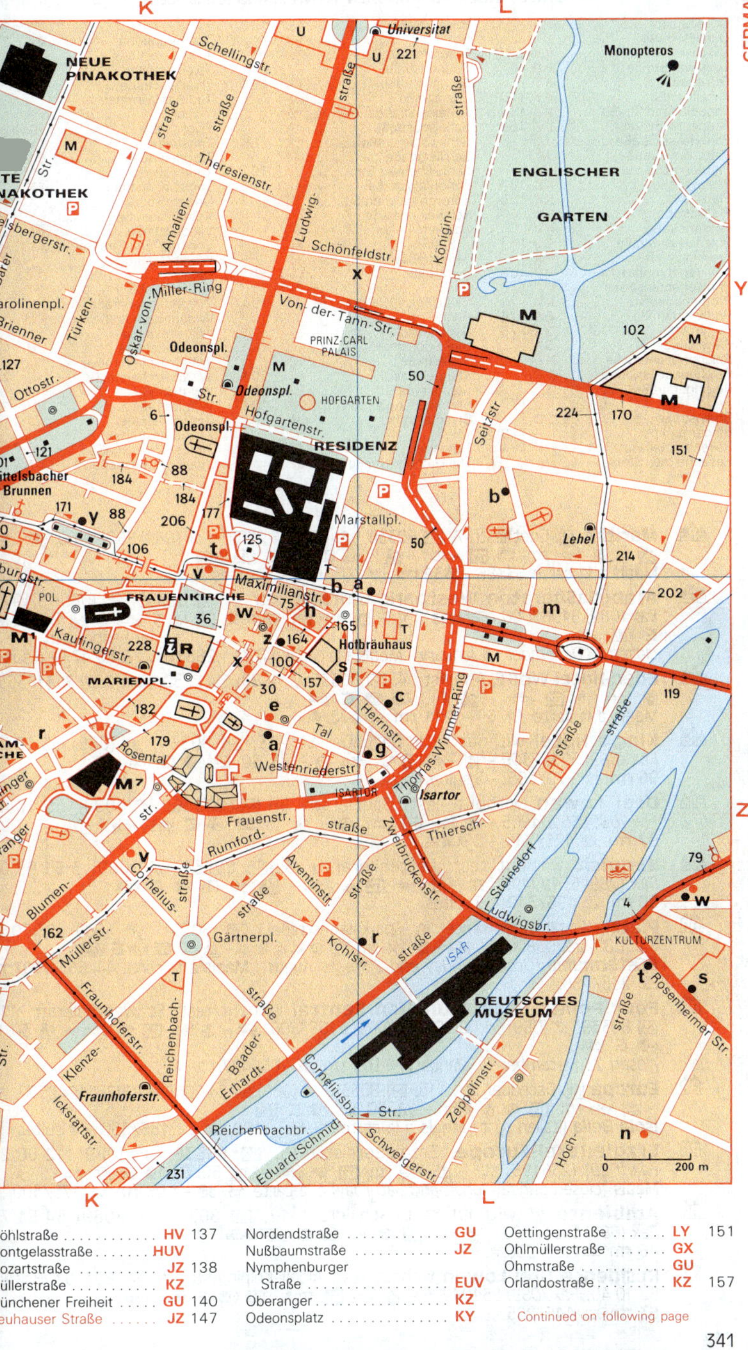

Continued on following page

GERMANY

STREET INDEX TO MÜNCHEN TOWN PLANS (Concluded)

Maritim Ⓜ, Goethestr. 7, ⊠ 80336, ℰ (089) 55 23 50, *Fax (089) 55235900*, 🌳, 🌊 – 🛗, 🔄 rm, 🍽 📺 🚗 – 🏛 250. 🆎 ⓪ Ⓔ *VISA* JCB — JZ
Meals à la carte 53/86 – **339 rm** ☕ 303/610 – 5 suites.

ArabellaSheraton Westpark, Garmischer Str. 2, ⊠ 80339, ℰ (089) 5 19 6
Fax (089) 51963000, 🌳, ⓢ, 🌊 – 🛗, 🔄 rm, 🍽 rest, 📺 🕻 ⅙ 🚗 – 🏛 80. 🆎 Ⓒ
Ⓔ *VISA* JCB
by Leopoldstr. GU
closed 18 December - 6 January – **Meals** à la carte 44/71 – **258 rm** ☕ 245/471 – 6 suites

Eden-Hotel-Wolff, Arnulfstr. 4, ⊠ 80335, ℰ (089) 55 11 50, *Fax (089) 55115555*
🛗, 🔄 rm, 📺 🚗 – 🏛 140. 🆎 ⓪ Ⓔ *VISA* JCB — JY
Meals à la carte 34/65 – **211 rm** ☕ 220/460.

King's Hotel without rest, Dachauer Str. 13, ⊠ 80335, ℰ (089) 55 18 7
Fax (089) 55187300 – 🛗 🔄 📺 🕻 🚗 ℗ – 🏛 30. 🆎 ⓪ Ⓔ *VISA* JCB — JY
96 rm ☕ 220/305 – 5 suites.

Drei Löwen without rest, Schillerstr. 8, ⊠ 80336, ℰ (089) 55 10 4
Fax (089) 55104905 – 🛗 🔄 📺 🚗 ℗ – 🏛 15. 🆎 ⓪ Ⓔ *VISA* JCB — JZ
97 rm ☕ 175/245 – 3 suites.

Exquisit without rest, Pettenkoferstr. 3, ⊠ 80336, ℰ (089) 5 51 99 0
Fax (089) 55199499, ⓢ – 🛗 🔄 📺 ⅙ 🚗 – 🏛 30. 🆎 ⓪ Ⓔ *VISA* — JZ
50 rm ☕ 195/340 – 5 suites.

Platzl, Platzl 1 (entrance in Sparkassenstraße), ⊠ 80331, ℰ (089) 23 70 3
Fax (089) 23703800, 🏋, ⓢ – 🛗, 🔄 rm, 📺 ☎ 🕻 ⅙ 🚗 – 🏛 60. 🆎 ⓪ Ⓔ *VISA* — KZ
Pfistermühle (*closed Sunday and 2 weeks August*) **Meals** à la carte 44/66 – **167 rm**
☕ 235/430.

Four Points Hotel München Central without rest, Schwanthalerstr. 11
⊠ 80339, ℰ (089) 51 08 30, *Fax (089) 51083800*, ⓢ – 🛗 🔄 📺 ☎ 🚗 – 🏛 30.
⓪ Ⓔ *VISA* — EX
closed 23 December - 6 January – **102 rm** ☕ 205/427.

Europa Ⓜ, Dachauer Str. 115, ⊠ 80335, ℰ (089) 54 24 20, *Fax (089) 54242500*,
– 🛗 🔄 rm, 📺 ☎ ⅙ 🚗 – 🏛 60. 🆎 ⓪ Ⓔ *VISA* — FU
Isola Bella (Italian rest.) **Meals** à la carte 30/56 – **180 rm** ☕ 155/350 – 7 suites.

Erzgießerei-Europe, Erzgießereistr. 15, ⊠ 80335, ℰ (089) 12 68 2
Fax (089) 1236198, 🌳 – 🛗, 🔄 rm, 📺 ☎ 🚗 – 🏛 50. 🆎 ⓪ Ⓔ *VISA* — JY
Meals (*closed Sunday lunch and Saturday*) à la carte 33/58 – **106 rm** ☕ 175/300.

Ambiente Ⓜ without rest, Schillerstr. 12, ⊠ 80336, ℰ (089) 54 51 7
Fax (089) 54517200 – 🛗 🔄 📺 ☎. 🆎 ⓪ Ⓔ *VISA* JCB — JZ
46 rm ☕ 182/250.

Residence Drei Löwen without rest, Aldolf-Kolping-Str. 11, ⊠ 80336, ℰ (08
55 10 40, *Fax (089) 55104905* – 🛗 🔄 📺 ☎ 🕻. 🆎 ⓪ Ⓔ *VISA* JCB — JZ
63 rm ☕ 145/205.

Astron Hotel Deutscher Kaiser Ⓜ without rest, Arnulfstr. 2, ✉ 80335, ℘ (089) 5 45 30, *Fax (089) 54532255* – 🛗 ⇤ TV ☎ – 🔺 80. AE ⓪ E *VISA* JCB   JY r
174 rm ⊑ 256/390.

InterCityHotel, Bayerstr. 10, ✉ 80335, ℘ (089) 54 55 60, *Fax (089) 54556610* – 🛗, ⇤ rm, TV ☎ – 🔺 100. AE ⓪ E *VISA* JCB   JY u
Meals *(closed Sunday)* à la carte 41/67 – **200 rm** ⊑ 203/430 – 4 suites.

Mercure City Ⓜ without rest, Senefelder Str. 9, ✉ 80336, ℘ (089) 55 13 20, *Fax (089) 596444* – 🛗 ⇤ TV ☎ ✆ & ⇌ – 🔺 50. AE ⓪ E *VISA* JCB   JZ v
167 rm ⊑ 205/285.

Admiral without rest, Kohlstr. 9, ✉ 80469, ℘ (089) 21 63 50, *Fax (089) 293674* – 🛗 ⇤ TV ☎ ⇌. AE ⓪ E *VISA* JCB   LZ r
33 rm ⊑ 215/315.

Torbräu without rest, Tal 41, ✉ 80331, ℘ (089) 22 50 16, *Fax (089) 225019* – 🛗 ⇤ TV ☎ ✆ ⇌ Ⓟ – 🔺 15. AE E *VISA* JCB   LZ g
86 rm ⊑ 265/410 – 3 suites.

Sol Inn Hotel Ⓜ, Paul-Heyse-Str. 24, ✉ 80336, ℘ (089) 51 49 00, *Fax (089) 51490701* – 🛗, ⇤ rm, TV ☎ ✆ & ⇌ – 🔺 35. AE ⓪ E *VISA* JCB   JZ c
Meals *(closed Saturday and Sunday lunch)* à la carte 38/52 – **207 rm** ⊑ 189/219.

Domus without rest, St.-Anna-Str. 31, ✉ 80538, ℘ (089) 22 17 04, *Fax (089) 2285359* – 🛗 ⇤ TV ☎ ⇌. AE ⓪ E *VISA*   LY b
closed 23 to 28 December – **45 rm** ⊑ 198/290.

Carathotel Ⓜ without rest, Lindwurmstr. 13, ✉ 80337, ℘ (089) 23 03 80, *Fax (089) 23038199* – 🛗 ⇤ TV ☎ ⇌. AE ⓪ E *VISA*   JZ f
70 rm ⊑ 205/320.

Kraft without rest, Schillerstr. 49, ✉ 80336, ℘ (089) 59 48 23, *Fax (089) 5503856* – 🛗 TV ☎. AE ⓪ E *VISA*   JZ y
closed 23 to 26 December – **35 rm** ⊑ 140/260.

Concorde without rest, Herrnstr. 38, ✉ 80539, ℘ (089) 22 45 15, *Fax (089) 2283282* – 🛗 TV ☎ ✆ ⇌. AE ⓪ E *VISA*   LZ c
closed Christmas - early January – **71 rm** ⊑ 180/300.

Cristal Ⓜ without rest, Schwanthalerstr. 36, ✉ 80336, ℘ (089) 55 11 10, *Fax (089) 55111992* – 🛗 TV ☎ ⇌ – 🔺 75. AE ⓪ E *VISA*   JZ h
100 rm ⊑ 215/370.

Schlicker without rest, Tal 8, ✉ 80331, ℘ (089) 22 79 41, *Fax (089) 296059* – 🛗 TV ☎ Ⓟ. AE ⓪ E *VISA*   KZ a
closed 20 December - 7 January – **69 rm** ⊑ 130/390.

Brack without rest, Lindwurmstr. 153, ✉ 80337, ℘ (089) 7 47 25 50, *Fax (089) 74725599* – 🛗 TV ☎ ✆ ⇌. AE ⓪ E *VISA* JCB   EX b
50 rm ⊑ 150/298.

Europäischer Hof without rest, Bayerstr. 31, ✉ 80335, ℘ (089) 55 15 10, *Fax (089) 55151222* – 🛗 ⇤ TV ☎ ✆ ⇌ Ⓟ – 🔺 20. AE ⓪ E *VISA* JCB   JZ b
148 rm ⊑ 199/441.

Astor without rest, Schillerstr. 24, ✉ 80336, ℘ (089) 54 83 70, *Fax (089) 54837666* – ☎ ⇌. AE ⓪ E *VISA* JCB   JZ e
46 rm ⊑ 120/280.

Olympic without rest, Hans-Sachs-Str. 4, ✉ 80469, ℘ (089) 23 18 90, *Fax (089) 23189199* – TV ☎ ⇌. AE ⓪ E *VISA*   KZ c
32 rm ⊑ 175/280.

XXX ❀ **Am Marstall**, Maximilianstr. 16, ✉ 80539, ℘ (089) 29 16 55 11, *Fax (089) 29165512* – AE ⓪ E *VISA* JCB. ⊗   KZ b
closed Sunday - Monday – **Meals** 59 (lunch) and à la carte 83/122
Spec. Pochiertes Kalbsfilet mit Bohnen. Rochenflügel gebraten mit Muscheln. Schokoladenvariation.

XX ❀ **Gasthaus Glockenbach**, Kapuzinerstr. 29, ✉ 80337, ℘ (089) 53 40 43, *Fax (089) 534043,* (former old Bavarian pub) – AE E *VISA*   FX e
closed Sunday - Monday, Bank Holidays and 2 weeks August – **Meals** (booking essential) 45 (lunch) and à la carte 73/108
Spec. Rote Beete-Sülze mit marinierten Fischen. Geschmorte Kutteln mit Octopus. Fasanenbrust mit ihrer Farce im Netz gebraten (season).

XX **Boettner's**, Pfisterstr. 9, ✉ 80331, ℘ (089) 22 12 10, *Fax (089) 29162024* – AE ⓪ E *VISA*   KZ h
closed Sunday and Bank Holidays – **Meals** (booking essential) à la carte 68/120.

GERMANY

XX **Halali**, Schönfeldstr. 22, ✉ 80539, 𝓟 (089) 28 59 09, *Fax (089) 282786* – AE E VISA JC
closed Saturday lunch, Sunday, Bank Holidays and 2 weeks August – **Meals** (booking esser
tial) 35 (lunch) and à la carte 52/74.   LY

XX **Nymphenburger Hof**, Nymphenburger Straße 24, ✉ 80335, 𝓟 (089) 1 23 38 3C
Fax (089) 1233852, 🌳 – AE E VISA. 🛇   EV
closed Saturday lunch, Sunday and Bank Holidays – **Meals** à la carte 53/89.

XX **Weinhaus Neuner**, Herzogspitalstr. 8, ✉ 80331, 𝓟 (089) 2 60 39 54
Fax (089) 266933, (16C wine-restaurant) – AE E VISA JCB   JZ
closed Sunday and Bank Holidays – **Meals** à la carte 44/67.

XX **Galleria**, Ledererstr. 2 (corner of Sparkassenstr.), ✉ 80331, 𝓟 (089) 29 79 95
Fax (089) 2913653 – AE ① E VISA JCB   KZ
closed Sunday and 10 to 24 July – **Meals** (booking essential) (Italian rest.) à la carte 62/8C

XX **Austernkeller**, Stollbergstr. 11, ✉ 80539, 𝓟 (089) 29 87 87, *Fax (089) 22316C
« Vaulted cellar with collection of china dishes »* – AE ① E VISA JCB   LZ
closed 23 to 26 December – **Meals** (dinner only) (booking essential) à la carte 53/81.

XX **Lenbach**, Ottostr. 6, ✉ 80333, 𝓟 (089) 5 49 13 00, *Fax (089) 54913075*, 🌳
« Mansion with modern interior »* – AE ① E VISA   JY
Menu à la carte 54/87.

X **Straubinger Hof**, Blumenstr. 5, ✉ 80331, 𝓟 (089) 2 60 84 44, *Fax (089) 260891*,
(Bavarian inn) beer garden – AE E VISA JCB   KZ
closed Saturday dinner, Sunday and Bank Holidays – **Meals** à la carte 24/55.

Brewery - inns :

X **Spatenhaus-Bräustuben**, Residenzstr. 12, ✉ 80333, 𝓟 (089) 2 90 70 6C
Fax (089) 2913054, 🌳, « Furnished in traditional Alpine style »* – AE E VISA   KY
Meals à la carte 42/74.

X **Weisses Bräuhaus**, Tal 7, ✉ 80331, 𝓟 (089) 29 98 75, *Fax (089) 29013815*, 🌳
🪑 30. AE   KZ
Meals à la carte 27/48.

X **Augustiner Gaststätten**, Neuhauser Str. 27, ✉ 80331, 𝓟 (089) 23 18 32 57
Fax (089) 2605379, « Beer garden »* – AE ① E VISA   JZ V
Meals à la carte 29/59.

X **Altes Hackerhaus**, Sendlinger Str. 14, ✉ 80331, 𝓟 (089) 2 60 50 26
Fax (089) 2605027, 🌳 – AE ① E VISA JCB   KZ
Meals à la carte 30/67.

X **Franziskaner Fuchsenstuben**, Perusastr. 5, ✉ 80333, 𝓟 (089) 2 31 81 2C
Fax (089) 23181244, 🌳 – AE ① E VISA JCB   KY
Meals à la carte 33/66.

X **Paulaner Bräuhaus**, Kapuzinerplatz 5, ✉ 80337, 𝓟 (089) 5 44 61 1C
Fax (089) 54461118, beer garden – E VISA   FX
Meals à la carte 36/62.

at Munich-Allach *by Arnulfstr.* EV :

🏨 **Lutter** *without rest*, Eversbuschstr. 109, ✉ 80999, 𝓟 (089) 8 92 67 8C
Fax (089) 89267810 – TV ☎ ℗. E VISA. 🛇
closed 20 December - 9 January – **22 rm** 🍵 110/200.

at Munich-Bogenhausen :

🏨 **Palace** Ⓜ, Trogerstr. 21, ✉ 81675, 𝓟 (089) 41 97 10, *Fax (089) 41971819*, « Elegan
installation with period furniture »*, 🛗, ≋s, 🌳 – 🛗 ⊁ rm, TV 📞 ↔ – 🪑 40. AE ①
E VISA JCB. 🛇 rest   HV
Meals à la carte 49/74 – **71 rm** 🍵 272/573 – 7 suites.

🏨 **Prinzregent** *without rest*, Ismaninger Str. 42, ✉ 81675, 𝓟 (089) 41 60 5C
Fax (089) 41605466, ≋s – 🛗 ⊁ TV 📞 ↔ – 🪑 35. AE ① E VISA JCB   HV
23 December - 7 January – **64 rm** 🍵 295/405.

🏨 **Rothof** *without rest*, Denniger Str. 114, ✉ 81925, 𝓟 (089) 9 10 09 5C
Fax (089) 915066, 🌳 – 🛗 ⊁ TV ↔. AE ① E VISA   by Einsteinstr. HX
closed 19 December - 10 January – **37 rm** 🍵 198/390.

🏨 **Queens Hotel**, Effnerstr. 99, ✉ 81925, 𝓟 (089) 92 79 80, *Fax (089) 983813*, 🛗, ≋
– 🛗, ⊁ rm, TV ☎ 📞 ↔ ℗ – 🪑 200. AE ① E VISA. 🛇 rest
Meals à la carte 31/69 – **152 rm** 🍵 265/340.   by Ismaninger Str. HV

XXX **Bogenhauser Hof**, Ismaninger Str. 85, ✉ 81675, 𝓟 (089) 98 55 86, *Fax (089) 981022*
(1825 former hunting lodge), « Garden terrace »* – AE ① VISA   HV
closed Sunday, Bank Holidays and Christmas - 12 January – **Meals** (booking essential) à l
carte 69/106.

XX **Acquarello**, Mühlbaurstr. 36, ✉ 81677, ℘ (089) 4 70 48 48, *Fax (089) 476464*, 🌳 –
ÆE E. 🚫   by Mühlbaurstr   HV
closed Saturday and Sunday lunch – **Meals** (Italian rest.) à la carte 68/87.

XX **Käfer Schänke**, Prinzregentenstr. 73, ✉ 81675, ℘ (089) 4 16 82 47,
Fax (089) 4168623, 🌳, « Several rooms with elegant rustic installation » – ÆE ① E VISA
closed Sunday and Bank Holidays – **Meals** (booking essential) 48 (lunch) and à la carte
58/111.   HV s

t Munich-Denning *by Denninger Str.* HV :

XXX **Casale**, Ostpreußenstr. 42, ✉ 81927, ℘ (089) 93 62 68, *Fax (089) 9306722*, 🌳 – Ⓟ.
ÆE ① E VISA
Meals (Italian rest.) à la carte 56/76.

t Munich-Haidhausen :

🏨 **City Hilton** Ⓜ, Rosenheimer Str. 15, ✉ 81667, ℘ (089) 4 80 40, *Fax (089) 48044804*,
🌳 – 🛗, ⇆ rm, 📺 🖥 📞 ♿ 🚗 – 🔥 180. ÆE ① E VISA JCB   LZ s
Meals à la carte 54/78 – **479 rm** ⇌ 493/616 – 4 suites.

🏨 **Preysing**, Preysingstr. 1, ✉ 81667, ℘ (089) 45 84 50, *Fax (089) 45845444*, ⊆s, 🏊
– 🛗 🖥 📺 🚗 – 🔥 40. ÆE ① E VISA   LZ w
closed 23 December - 6 January – **Meals** see **Preysing-Keller** below – **76 rm** ⇌ 169/298
– 5 suites.

🏨 **Forum Hotel**, Hochstr. 3, ✉ 81669, ℘ (089) 4 80 30, *Fax (089) 4488277*, ⊆s, 🏊 –
🛗, ⇆ rm, 📺 📺 📞 – 🔥 350. ÆE ① E VISA JCB   LZ t
Meals à la carte 51/83 – **582 rm** ⇌ 265/505 – 12 suites.

XXX **Preysing-Keller** - Hotel Preysing, Innere-Wiener-Str. 6, ✉ 81667, ℘ (089) 45 84 52 60,
❀ *Fax (089) 45845444* – 🖥. ÆE ① E VISA   LZ w
closed Sunday, Bank Holidays and 23 December - 6 January – **Meals** (dinner only) (outstanding wine list) 89/125 and à la carte 69/103
Spec. Rotbarbe mit Artischocken-Lauchsalat. Taubenbrust mit Portweinsauce und Kar-
toffel-Mohnravioli. Mille-feuille mit Haselnusscreme und Karameleis.

XX **Massimiliano**, Rablstr. 10, ✉ 81699, ℘ (089) 4 48 44 77, *Fax (089) 4484405*, 🌳 –
❀ Ⓟ. ① E VISA JCB   LZ n
closed Saturday lunch – **Meals** 39 (lunch) and à la carte 70/110
Spec. Artischockenvariation mit Trüffelvinaigrette. Gefüllte Lammkeule mit Thymian-
Salzkruste. Pusterthaler Apfelcrêpe.

X **Vinaiolo**, Steinstr. 42, ✉ 81667, ℘ (089) 48 95 03 56, « Interior from a former
pharmacy » – E   HX c
Meals (booking essential for dinner) à la carte 57/68.

t Munich-Laim *by Landsberger Str. (B 2)* EV :

🏨 **Park Hotel Laim** without rest, Zschokkestr. 55, ✉ 80686, ℘ (089) 57 93 60,
Fax (089) 57936100, ⊆s – 🛗 ⇆ 📺 ☎ 🚗 – 🔥 30. ÆE ① E VISA
68 rm ⇌ 180/340.

t Munich-Neu Perlach *by Rosenheimer Str.* HX :

🏨 **Mercure**, Karl-Marx-Ring 87, ✉ 81735, ℘ (089) 6 32 70, *Fax (089) 6327407*, 🌳, ↕,
⊆s, 🏊 – 🛗, ⇆ rm, 📺 rest, 📺 🚗 Ⓟ – 🔥 100. ÆE ① E VISA
Meals à la carte 37/68 – **184 rm** ⇌ 205/350 – 3 suites.

🏨 **Villa Waldperlach** Ⓜ without rest, Putzbrunner Str. 250(Waldperlach), ✉ 81739,
℘ (089) 6 60 03 00, *Fax (089) 66003066* – 🛗 ⇆ 📺 ☎ 📞 🚗. ÆE ① E VISA
21 rm ⇌ 150/250.

t Munich-Pasing *by Landsberger Straße* EV :

XX **Zur Goldenen Gans**, Planegger Str.31, ✉ 81241, ℘ (089) 83 70 33,
😊 *Fax (089) 8204680*, 🌳, « Atmospheric Bavarian inn » – Ⓟ. E VISA
closed Sunday and Bank Holidays – **Meals** 25 (lunch) and à la carte 47/71.

t Munich-Schwabing :

🏨 **Marriott-Hotel** Ⓜ, Berliner Str. 93, ✉ 80805, ℘ (089) 36 00 20, *Fax (089) 36002200*,
Massage, ↕, ⊆s, 🏊 – 🛗, ⇆ rm, 📺 📺 📞 ♿ – 🔥 320. ÆE ① E VISA JCB. 🚫 rest
Meals à la carte 47/62 – **348 rm** ⇌ 454/533 – 16 suites.   by Ungererstr. (B 11) HU

🏨 **Crowne Plaza**, Leopoldstr. 194, ✉ 80804, ℘ (089) 38 17 90, *Fax (089) 38179888*, 🌳,
Massage, ⊆s, 🏊 – 🛗, ⇆ rm, 📺 📞 🚗 – 🔥 320. ÆE ① E VISA JCB
Meals à la carte 55/87 – **365 rm** ⇌ 330/619.   by Leopoldstr. GU

🏨 **Renaissance Hotel**, Theodor-Dombart-Str. 4 (corner of Berliner Straße), ✉ 80805,
℘ (089) 36 09 90, *Fax (089) 36099684*, 🌳, ⊆s – 🛗, ⇆ rm, 📺 📞 🚗 – 🔥 40. ÆE
① E VISA JCB   by Ungererstr. (B 11) HU
Meals à la carte 36/66 – **260 rm** ⇌ 290/320 – 80 suites.

MUNICH (MÜNCHEN)

Four Points Hotel München Olympiapark, Helene-Mayer-Ring 12, ✉ 8080⁹
℘ (089) 35 75 10, *Fax (089) 35751800* – |‡|, ≒ rm, TV ☎ ℘ – ⌂ 30. AE ⑩ Ɛ VISA
closed 20 December - 6 January – **Meals** *(closed Sunday and Saturday lunch)* à la cart
34/62 – **105 rm** ⬭ 201/427. by Schleißheimer Str. FU

Cosmopolitan M without rest, Hohenzollernstr. 5, ✉ 80801, ℘ (089) 38 38 1(
Fax (089) 38381111 – |‡| ≒ TV ☎ ℘ ⇔. AE ⑩ Ɛ VISA JCB GU
71 rm ⬭ 160/220.

Mercure without rest, Leopoldstr. 120, ✉ 80802, ℘ (089) 39 05 50, *Fax (089) 34934*
– |‡| ≒ TV ☎ ⇔. AE ⑩ Ɛ VISA GU
65 rm ⬭ 172/294.

Leopold, Leopoldstr. 119, ✉ 80804, ℘ (089) 36 04 30, *Fax (089) 36043150*, ☲ – |
TV ☎ ℘ ⇔ ℗. AE ⑩ Ɛ VISA JCB. ⋇ rest GU
closed 23 to 30 December – **Meals** à la carte 31/63 – **75 rm** ⬭ 165/295.

Tantris, Johann-Fichte-Str. 7, ✉ 80805, ℘ (089) 3 61 95 90, *Fax (089) 3618469*, ☲
– ◼ ℗. AE ⑩ Ɛ VISA. ⋇ GU
closed Sunday - Monday, Bank Holidays and 1 week January – **Meals** *(booking essentia*
198/225 and à la carte 89/145
Spec. Gefüllte Ofenkartoffel mit Wildlachs und Imperial-Caviar. Rehrückenmedaillon m
Steinpilz-Radicchio-Nudeln. Gelierte Champagner-Suppe mit Waldbeeren und Sauerrahme

Savoy, Tengstr. 20, ✉ 80798, ℘ (089) 2 71 14 45 – AE Ɛ GU
closed Sunday – **Meals** *(booking essential for dinner)* (Italian rest.) à la carte 47/73.

Spago, Neureutherstr. 15, ✉ 80799, ℘ (089) 2 71 24 06, *Fax (089) 2780442*, ☲ – A
⑩ Ɛ VISA GU
closed Saturday and Sunday lunch – **Meals** (Italian rest.) à la carte 50/74.

Seehaus, Kleinhesselohe 3, ✉ 80802, ℘ (089) 3 81 61 30, *Fax (089) 341803*,
« Lakeside setting terrace » – ℗. AE Ɛ VISA HU
Meals à la carte 39/73.

Bistro Terrine, Amalienstr. 89 (Amalien-Passage), ✉ 80799, ℘ (089) 28 17 8(
Fax (089) 2809316, ☲ – AE Ɛ VISA GU
closed Saturday and Monday lunch, Sunday and Bank Holidays – **Meals** *(booking essenti*
for dinner) 43 (lunch) and à la carte 48/73
Spec. Rochen mit Artischocken und Tomaten-Basilikum. Lammcarré mit Kräutern und Bo
nen. Crème brûlée.

Bamberger Haus, Brunnenstr. 2 (at Luitpoldpark), ✉ 80804, ℘ (089) 3 08 89 6(
Fax (089) 3003304, « 18C palace ; terrace » – ℗. AE ⑩ Ɛ VISA GU
Meals à la carte 31/55.

at Munich-Sendling *by Lindwurmstr. (B 11)* EX :

Holiday Inn München - Süd, Kistlerhofstr. 142, ✉ 81379, ℘ (089) 78 00 2(
Fax (089) 78002672, beer garden, Massage, ≋s, ⊠ – |‡|, ≒ rm, ◼ TV & ⇔ – ⌂ 9
AE ⑩ Ɛ VISA JCB
Meals à la carte 43/64 – **320 rm** ⬭ 284/440 – 7 suites.

Ambassador Parkhotel, Plinganserstr. 102, ✉ 81369, ℘ (089) 72 48 9(
Fax (089) 72489100, beer garden – |‡|, ≒ rm, TV ☎ ⇔. AE ⑩ Ɛ VISA
closed 24 December - 6 January – **Meals** *(closed Saturday)* (Italian rest.) à la carte 38/6
– **42 rm** ⬭ 175/425.

K+K Hotel am Harras without rest, Albert-Rosshaupter-Str. 4, ✉ 81369, ℘ (08⁹
74 64 00, *Fax (089) 7212820* – |‡| ≒ TV ☎ ℘ ⇔. AE ⑩ Ɛ VISA JCB
120 rm ⬭ 205/390.

at Munich-Untermenzing *by Arnulfstr.* EV :

Romantik-Hotel Insel Mühle, Von-Kahr-Str. 87, ✉ 80999, ℘ (089) 8 10 1(
Fax (089) 8120571, ☲, beer garden, « Converted 16C riverside mill », ☲ – TV & ⇔
℗ – ⌂ 40. ⑩ Ɛ VISA
Meals *(closed Sunday and Bank Holidays)* à la carte 56/77 – **37 rm** ⬭ 185/380.

at Unterhaching *by Kapuzinerstr.* GX :

Schrenkhof without rest, Leonhardsweg 6, ✉ 82008, ℘ (089) 6 10 09 1(
Fax (089) 61009150, « Bavarian farmhouse furniture », ≋s – |‡| TV ⇔ ℗ – ⌂ 40.
⑩ Ɛ VISA
closed Christmas - early January and Easter – **25 rm** ⬭ 185/240.

Holiday Inn Garden Court M, Inselkammer Str. 7, ✉ 82008, ℘ (089) 66 69 1
Fax (089) 66691600, beer garden, ⨐, ≋s – |‡|, ≒ rm, TV & & ⇔ ℗ – ⌂ 230.
⑩ Ɛ VISA JCB
Meals à la carte 36/85 – **282 rm** ⬭ 234/420 – 6 suites.

at Aschheim *North-East : 13 km by Riem :*

Schreiberhof Ⓜ, Erdinger Str. 2, ✉ 85609, ✆ (089) 90 00 60, *Fax (089) 90006459,* 瑞, Massage, ⌂, ⌂ – ⟨♦⟩, ⌿ rm, 📺 ✆ ⌂ ⊂ ⓟ – ⚿ 90. 🄰🄴 ⓞ Ⓔ 𝗩𝗜𝗦𝗔 *closed Christmas - early January –* **Alte Gaststube :** Menu à la carte 49/84 – **87 rm** ⌷ 235/385.

at Grünwald *South : 13 km by Wittelsbacher Brücke* GX – ⊛ *089 :*

Tannenhof without rest, Marktplatz 3, ✉ 82031, ✆ (089) 6 41 89 60, *Fax (089) 6415608,* « Period house with elegant interior » – ⌿ 📺 ☎ ⓟ. 🄰🄴 ⓞ Ⓔ 𝗩𝗜𝗦𝗔 ⌿ *closed 20 December - 6 January –* **21 rm** ⌷ 150/210.

at airport Franz-Josef-Strauß *North-East : 37 km by A 9 and A 92 :*

Kempinski Airport München Ⓜ, Terminalstraße/Mitte 20, ✉ 85356 *München,* ✆ (089) 9 78 20, *Fax (089) 97822610,* ⌂, ⌂, ⬚ – ⟨♦⟩, ⌿ rm, ▤ 📺 ✆ ⌂ ⊂ ⓟ – ⚿ 280. 🄰🄴 ⓞ Ⓔ 𝗩𝗜𝗦𝗔 𝗝𝗖𝗕. ⌿ rest **Meals** à la carte 48/84 – **389 rm** ⌷ 413/556 – 17 suites.

Il Mondo, Area B - level 07, ✉ 85356 *München,* ✆ (089) 97 59 32 22, *Fax (089) 97593222,* ≼ – ⓟ. 🄰🄴 ⓞ Ⓔ 𝗩𝗜𝗦𝗔 **Meals** (Italian rest.) à la carte 49/71.

Aschau im Chiemgau *Bayern* 🄸🄻🄾 *W 20 – pop. 5 200 – alt. 615 m.*

München 82.

Restaurant Heinz Winkler - in Hotel Residenz Heinz Winkler, Kirchplatz 1, ✉ 83229, ✆ (08052) 1 79 90, *Fax (08052) 179966,* 瑞 – ⓟ. 🄰🄴 ⓞ Ⓔ 𝗩𝗜𝗦𝗔 𝗝𝗖𝗕. ⌿ rest *closed Monday lunch –* **Meals** 175/215 and à la carte 85/145 **Spec.** Salat von der Bresse Taubenbrust mit Artischocken in Balsamico. Gebratener Steinbutt mit Spinat und Madeirasauce. Chârtreuse vom Lamm mit Paprika und Kräuterglace.

STUTTGART Ⓛ *Baden-Württemberg* 🄸🄸🄹 *T 11,* 🄰🄰🄷 ㊳ *– pop. 565 000 – alt. 245 m.*

See : *Linden Museum* ★★ KY M[1] *– Park Wilhelma* ★ HT *and Killesberg-Park* ★ GT *– Television Tower (Fernsehturm)* ✳★ HX *– Stuttgart Gallery (Otto-Dix-Collection* ★ *)* LY M[4] *– Swabian Brewery Museum (Schwäb. Brauereimuseum)* ★ *by Böblinger Straße* FX *– Old Castle (Altes Schloß) (Renaissance courtyard* ★ *) – Württemberg Regional Museum* ★ *(Sacred Statuary* ★★ *)* LY M[3] *– State Gallery* ★ *(Old Masters Collection* ★★ *)* LY M[2] *– Collegiate church (Stiftskirche) (Commemorative monuments of dukes* ★ *)* KY A *– State Museum of Natural History (Staatl. Museum für Naturkunde)* ★ HT M[5] *– Daimler-Benz Museum* ★ JV M[6] *– Porsche Museum* ★ *by Heilbronner Straße* GT *– Schloß Solitude* ★ *by Rotenwaldstraße* FX.

Envir. : *Bad Cannstatt Spa Park (Kurpark)* ★ *East : 4 km* JT.

🄸🄸 *Kornwestheim, Aldinger Str. (North : 11 km),* ✆ *(07141) 87 13 19 ;* 🄸🄸 *Mönsheim (North-West : 30 km by A 8),* ✆ *(07044) 69 09.*

✈ *Stuttgart-Echterdingen, by Obere Weinsteige (B 27)* GX, ✆ *(0711) 94 80, City Air Terminal, Stuttgart, Lautenschlagerstr. 14* (LY)*,* ✆ *(0711) 20 12 68.*

Exhibition Centre (Messegelände Killesberg) (GT)*,* ✆ *(0711) 2 58 90, Fax (0711) 2589440.*

🄱 *Tourist-Info, Königstr. 1a,* ✉ *70173,* ✆ *(0711) 2 22 82 40, Fax (0711) 2228253.*

ADAC, *Am Neckartor 2,* ✉ *70190,* ✆ *(0711) 2 80 00, Fax (0711) 2800167.*

Berlin 630 – Frankfurt on Main 204 – Karlsruhe 88 – München 222 – Strasbourg 156.

Plans on following pages

Steigenberger Graf Zeppelin Ⓜ, Arnulf-Klett-Platz 7, ✉ 70173, ✆ (0711) 2 04 80, *Fax (0711) 2048542,* Massage, ⌂, ⬚ – ⟨♦⟩, ⌿ rm, ▤ 📺 ✆ ⌂ ⊂ – ⚿ 300. 🄰🄴 ⓞ Ⓔ 𝗩𝗜𝗦𝗔 𝗝𝗖𝗕. ⌿ rest LY v *Graf Zeppelin* (dinner only, closed Sunday - Monday, 1 to 11 January and August) **Meals** à la carte 76/104 – **Zeppelin Stüble :** **Meals** à la carte 41/67 – **195 rm** ⌷ 375/505.

Maritim Ⓜ, Forststr. 2, ✉ 70174, ✆ (0711) 94 20, *Fax (0711) 9421000,* Massage, ⌂, ⌂, ⬚ – ⟨♦⟩, ⌿ rm, ▤ 📺 ✆ ⌂ ⊂ – ⚿ 800. 🄰🄴 ⓞ Ⓔ 𝗩𝗜𝗦𝗔 𝗝𝗖𝗕. ⌿ rest FV r **Meals** à la carte 58/80 – **555 rm** ⌷ 303/472 – 46 suites.

Inter-Continental, Willy-Brandt-Str. 30, ✉ 70173, ✆ (0711) 2 02 00, *Fax (0711) 202012,* Massage, ⌂, ⌂, ⬚ – ⟨♦⟩, ⌿ rm, ▤ 📺 ✆ ⌂ ⊂ – ⚿ 300. 🄰🄴 ⓞ Ⓔ 𝗩𝗜𝗦𝗔 𝗝𝗖𝗕 HV t **Meals** à la carte 48/70 (Vegetarian menu available) – **276 rm** ⌷ 329/508 – 28 suites.

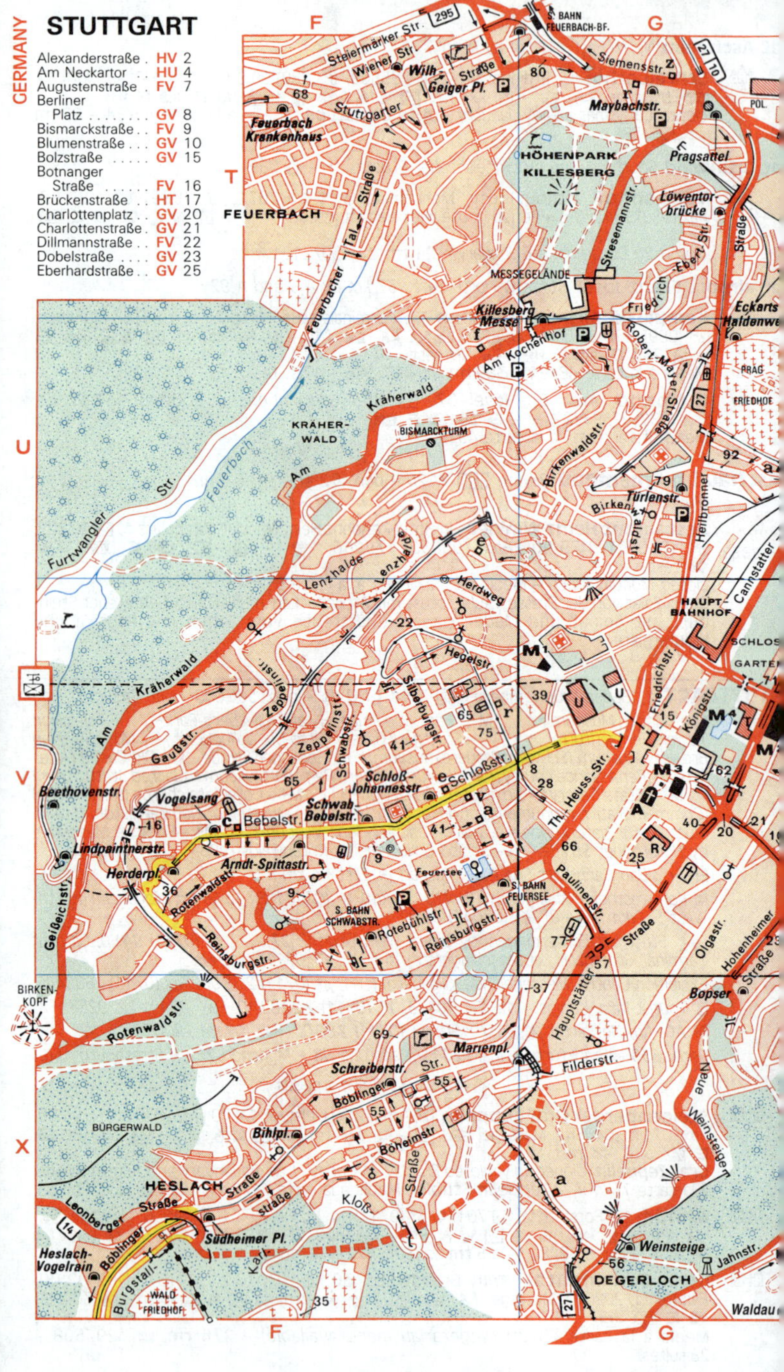

GERMANY
STUTTGART

Alexanderstraße . HV 2
Am Neckartor . . HU 4
Augustenstraße . FV 7
Berliner
  Platz . . . . GV 8
Bismarckstraße . FV 9
Blumenstraße . . . GV 10
Bolzstraße . . . . GV 15
Botnanger
  Straße . . . . . . FV 16
Brückenstraße . . HT 17
Charlottenplatz . GV 20
Charlottenstraße . GV 21
Dillmannstraße . FV 22
Dobelstraße . . . . GV 23
Eberhardstraße . . GV 25

F
G
T
U
V
X

Steiermärker Str.
Wiener Str.
Wilh.-Geiger Pl.
Stuttgarter Straße
Feuerbach
Krankenhaus
FEUERBACH
Siemensstr.
Maybachstr.
HÖHENPARK
KILLESBERG
Pragsattel
Löwentor
brücke
MESSEGELÄNDE
Stresemannstr.
Friedrich-Ebert-Str.
Eckarts
Haldenwe
Killesberg
Messe
Am Kochenhof
Robert-Mayer-Straße
PRAG
FRIEDHOF
Kräherwald
KRÄHER-
WALD
BISMARCKTURM
Birkenwaldstr.
Türlenstr.
Birkenwaldstr.
Heilbronner Straße
Furtwangler Str.
Feuerbacher Str.
Am Kräherwald
Lenzhalde
Herdweg
Lenzhalde
HAUPT-
BAHNHOF
Cannstatter
SCHLOSS
GARTEN
Kräherwald
Hegelstr.
Silberburgstr.
M
Friedrichstr.
Königstr.
Am Kräherwald
Gaußstr.
Zeppelinstr.
Zeppelinstr.
Schwabstr.
Schloß-
Johannesstr.
Schloßstr.
Th.-Heuss-Str.
Beethovenstr.
Vogelsang
Bebelstr.
Schwab-
Bebelstr.
Lindpaintnerstr.
Herderpl.
Arndt-Spittastr.
Rotenwaldstr.
Reinsburgstr.
S. Bahn
SCHWABSTR.
Rotebühlstr.
Reinsburgstr.
Paulinenstr.
S. Bahn
FEUERSEE
Feuersee
Olgastr.
Hohenheimer
Straße
Hauptstätter Straße
Geißeichstr.
BIRKEN-
KOPF
Rotenwaldstr.
Bopser
BÜRGERWALD
Marienpl.
Filderstr.
Schreiberstr. Str.
Böblinger Str.
Bihlpl.
Böhmstr.
Neue Weinsteige
HESLACH
Straße
Straße
Kloß
Leonberger Straße
Böblinger
Südheimer Pl.
Heslach-
Vogelrain
WALD
FRIEDHOF
Burgstall-
Weinsteige
Jahnstr.
DEGERLOCH
Waldau

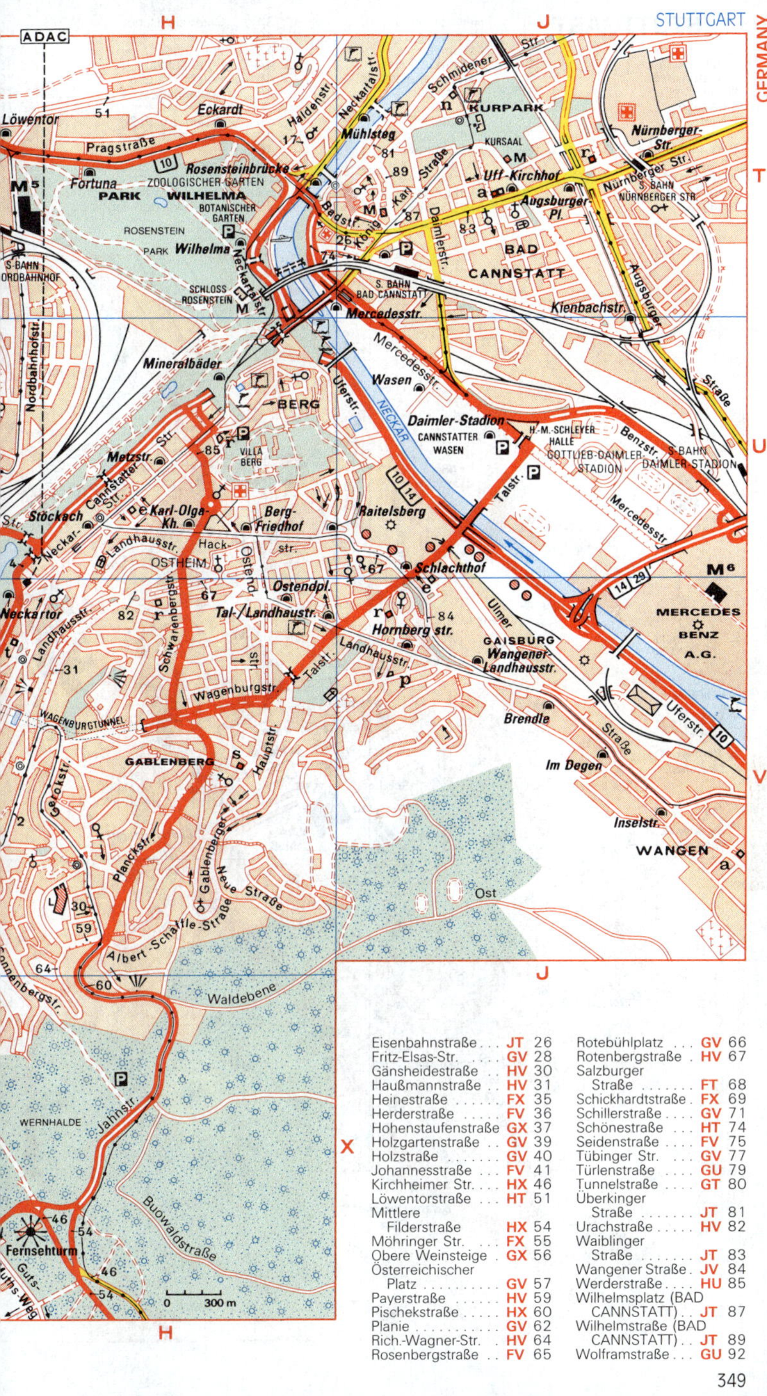

ADAC
STUTTGART
GERMANY
H
J
T
U
V
X
Löwentor
51
Eckardt
Haldenstr.
Neckartalstr.
Schmidener Str.
KURPARK
Nürnberger-Str.
Pragstraße
10
Mühlsteg
81
KURSAAL
Nürnberger Str.
Rosensteinbrücke
89
Uff-Kirchhof
Fortuna
ZOOLOGISCHER GARTEN
Augsburger-Pl.
Nürnberger Str.
PARK
WILHELMA
BOTANISCHER GARTEN
87
83
ROSENSTEIN
PARK Wilhelma
26
74
BAD
CANNSTATT
S-Bahn
NORDBAHNHOF
SCHLOSS
ROSENSTEIN
S. Bahn
BAD CANNSTATT
Kienbachstr.
Mercedesstr.
Augsburger
Nordbahnhofstr.
Mineralbäder
Mercedesstr.
Straße
BERG
Wasen
NECKAR
Daimler-Stadion
H.-M. SCHLEYER HALLE
Benzstr.
S. Bahn
DAIMLER-STADION
Metzstr.
85
VILLA BERG
CANNSTATTER WASEN
GOTTLIEB-DAIMLER-STADION
Mercedesstr.
Cannstatter Str.
10 14
Talstr.
Stöckach
Karl-Olga-Kh.
Berg-Friedhof
Raitelsberg
Neckar
Landhausstr.
Hackstr.
Ostendstr.
OSTHEIM
str.
67
Schlachthof
14 29
MERCEDES BENZ A.G.
Neckartor
82
Ostendpl.
67
Landhausstr.
Tal-/Landhaustr.
84
Ulmer Str.
Hornberg str.
GAISBURG
31
str.
Talstr.
Wangener-Landhausstr.
Wagenburgstr.
Brendle
Straße
Uferstr.
10
WAGENBURGTUNNEL
Im Degen
GABLENBERG
Planckstr.
Hauptstr.
Gablenberger
Neue Straße
Inselstr.
WANGEN
30
59
Ost
Albert-Schäffle-Straße
64
60
Waldebene
WERNHALDE
Jahnstr.
Buowaldstraße
46
54
Fernsehturm
46
46
54
Guts-Muths-Weg
0   300 m
349

STUTTGART

K
L
Seestr.
Panoramastr.
MITTLERER
SCHLOSS-
GARTEN
PLANETARIUM
Jäger-
straße
Cannstatter
Str.
Herdweg
Kriegsbergstraße
Keplerstraße
Staatsgalerie
Willy- Brandt- Str.
M1
Hegelstr.
32
S. BAHN
Schiller-
straße
Friedrichstraße
Lautenschlagerstr.
STADT-
GARTEN
OBERER
SCHLOSS-
GARTEN
Y
Holzgartenstr.
Keplerstr.
König-
M4
M2
T
KONGRESS-
CENTRUM
Schloßstr.
Urbanstr.
LIEDERHALLE
M
Neues
Schloß
LANDTAG
Ulrich-
Berliner Pl.
Liederhalle
Buchsen-
straße
Planie
Schloßpl.
47
U
str.
Lange
Schiller-
platz
M3
AKADEMIE
GARTEN
LANDES
BIBLIOTHEK
J
Fritz-
ADAC
Berliner Pl.
Hohe Str.
Elsas-
Altes
Schloß
Charlottenplatz
M
Olgastr.
S. BAHN
STADTMITTE
Str.
König-
straße
Charlotten-straße
Olgaeck
ROTEBÜHLBAU
Hirsch-
straße
R
Rathaus
Katharinenstr.
Alexander-
Rotebühlplatz
Paulinen-
straße
TURMHAUS
Tübinger Straße
Gerberstr.
Olgastr.
Dobelstr.
N
Reinsburgstr.
Marien-
straße
Österreichischer
Platz
Hohenheimer
Danneckerstraße
Tübinger Str.
Weißenburgstr.
Heusteig-
straße
Alexanderstr.
Bopser
0   200 m

Am Schloßgarten, Schillerstr. 23, ✉ 70173, ℰ (0711) 2 02 60, *Fax (0711) 2026888,* « Terrace with ≼ » – |₿|, ⇖ rm, TV 🚗 – 🛳 100. AE ⓪ E *VISA*. ⇖ rest LY u
Meals à la carte 64/96 – **118 rm** ☕ 258/475.

Royal, Sophienstr. 35, ✉ 70178, ℰ (0711) 62 50 50, *Fax (0711) 628809* – |₿|, ⇖ rm, ▤ TV ☎ 🚗 Ⓟ – 🛳 70. AE ⓪ E *VISA* JCB KZ b
closed Christmas – **Meals** *(closed Sunday and Bank Holidays)* à la carte 43/84 – **100 rm** ☕ 185/490 – 3 suites.

Parkhotel, Villastr. 21, ✉ 70190, ℰ (0711) 2 80 10, *Fax (0711) 2864353,* 🌳 – |₿|, ⇖ rm, TV ☎ 📞 🚗 Ⓟ – 🛳 80. AE ⓪ E *VISA* JCB. ⇖ HU r
Meals à la carte 53/73 – **72 rm** ☕ 195/290.

Rega Hotel, Ludwigstr. 18, ✉ 70176, ℰ (089) 61 93 40, *Fax (089) 6193477* – |₿| TV ☎ 📞 🚗 – 🛳 20. AE ⓪ E *VISA* FV a
Meals *(closed Sunday dinner)* à la carte 29/55 – **60 rm** ☕ 175/235.

Kronen-Hotel without rest, Kronenstr. 48, ✉ 70174, ℰ (0711) 2 25 10, *Fax (0711) 2251404,* ⇘s – |₿| ⇖ TV ☎ 🚗 – 🛳 20. AE ⓪ E *VISA* JCB KY m
closed 22 December - 7 January – **84 rm** ☕ 162/330.

Rema-Hotel-Ruff, Friedhofstr. 21, ✉ 70191, ℰ (0711) 2 58 70, *Fax (0711) 2587404,* ⇘s, 🏊 – |₿|, ⇖ rm, TV ☎ 🚗 Ⓟ. AE ⓪ E *VISA* JCB GU a
Meals *(dinner only, closed Saturday - Sunday)* à la carte 43/60 – **90 rm** ☕ 170/390.

InterCityHotel Ⓜ without rest, Arnulf-Klett-Platz 2, ✉ 70173, ℰ (0711) 2 25 00, *Fax (0711) 2250499* – |₿| ⇖ TV ☎ 📞 – 🛳 25. AE ⓪ E *VISA* LY p
112 rm ☕ 205/255.

Unger without rest, Kronenstr. 17, ✉ 70173, ℰ (0711) 2 09 90, *Fax (0711) 2099100* – |₿| ⇖ TV ☎ 📞 – 🛳 20. AE ⓪ E *VISA* LY a
97 rm ☕ 189/349.

Bergmeister without rest (with guest-house), Rotenbergstr. 16, ✉ 70190, ℰ (0711) 28 33 63, *Fax (0711) 283719,* ⇘s – |₿| ⇖ TV ☎ 🚗. AE ⓪ E *VISA* JCB HV r
46 rm ☕ 132/210.

Azenberg 🐾, Seestr. 114, ✉ 70174, ℰ (0711) 2 25 50 40, *Fax (0711) 22550499,* ⇘s, 🏊, 🚲 – |₿|, ⇖ rm, TV ☎ 🚗 Ⓟ – 🛳 20. AE ⓪ E *VISA* JCB FU e
Meals *(dinner only) (residents only)* – **54 rm** ☕ 150/260.

Wörtz zur Weinsteige, Hohenheimer Str. 30, ✉ 70184, ℰ (0711) 2 36 70 00, *Fax (0711) 2367007* – ⇖ rm, TV ☎ Ⓟ. AE ⓪ E *VISA* JCB LZ p
Meals *(closed Sunday - Monday, Bank Holidays, January and 3 weeks August)* (outstanding wine list) à la carte 30/89 – **25 rm** ☕ 140/280.

Wartburg, Lange Str. 49, ✉ 70174, ℰ (0711) 2 04 50, *Fax (0711) 2045450* – |₿|, ⇖ rm, ▤ rest, TV ☎ Ⓟ – 🛳 60. AE ⓪ E *VISA* JCB. ⇖ rest KY g
closed Easter and 22 December - 2 January – **Meals** *(lunch only, closed Saturday - Sunday and Bank Holidays)* à la carte 36/55 – **80 rm** ☕ 165/265.

Rema-Hotel Astoria without rest, Hospitalstr. 29, ✉ 70174, ℰ (0711) 29 93 01, *Fax (0711) 299307* – |₿| ⇖ TV ☎ Ⓟ – 🛳 20. AE ⓪ E *VISA* JCB KY r
57 rm ☕ 170/390.

Ambassador without rest, Tübinger Str. 17b, ✉ 70173, ℰ (0711) 6 01 74 10, *Fax (0711) 60174160* – |₿| ⇖ TV ☎ 📞. AE ⓪ E *VISA* KZ n
27 rm ☕ 125/165.

Rieker without rest, Friedrichstr. 3, ✉ 70174, ℰ (0711) 22 13 11, *Fax (0711) 293894* – |₿| ⇖ TV ☎ 🚗. AE ⓪ E *VISA* JCB LY d
66 rm ☕ 178/258.

City-Hotel without rest, Uhlandstr. 18, ✉ 70182, ℰ (0711) 21 08 10, *Fax (0711) 2369772* – TV ☎ Ⓟ. AE ⓪ E *VISA* JCB. ⇖ LZ a
31 rm ☕ 150/220.

Bellevue, Schurwaldstr. 45, ✉ 70186, ℰ (0711) 48 07 60, *Fax (0711) 4807631* – TV ☎ 🚗 Ⓟ. AE ⓪ E *VISA* JV p
Meals *(closed Tuesday - Wednesday)* 24 and à la carte 34/60 – **12 rm** ☕ 90/150.

Délice, Hauptstätter Str. 61, ✉ 70178, ℰ (0711) 6 40 32 22, « Vaulted cellar with contemporary art » KZ a
closed Saturday - Sunday and Bank Holidays – **Meals** *(dinner only)* (booking essential, outstanding wine list) 130 and à la carte 74/102
Spec. Nudeln mit Kaviar. Taubenbrust im Strudelteig auf Taubenlebersauce. Topfenknödel mit Pflaumenröster.

GERMANY

XX **La Fenice**, Rotebühlplatz 29, ✉ 70178, ℰ (0711) 6 15 11 44, *Fax (0711) 6151146*, ⇱
– AE E VISA   KZ
closed Monday – **Meals** (Italian rest.) à la carte 56/74.

XX **Gaisburger Pastetchen**, Hornbergstr. 24, ✉ 70188, ℰ (0711) 48 48 55
Fax (0711) 487565   JV
closed Sunday and Bank Holidays – **Meals** *(dinner only)* à la carte 68/86.

XX **La nuova Trattoria da Franco**, Calwer Str. 32, ✉ 70173, ℰ (0711) 29 47 44
Fax (0711) 294549, ⇱ – AE ⓪ E VISA   KYZ
Meals (Italian rest.) à la carte 43/67.

XX **La Scala**, Friedrichstr. 41 (1st floor, ⟦⟧), ✉ 70174, ℰ (0711) 29 06 07
Fax (0711) 2991640 – ▣. AE ⓪ E VISA   KY
closed Sunday and 3 weeks August - September – **Meals** (Italian rest.) à la carte 44/65

X **Der Zauberlehrling**, Rosenstr. 38, ✉ 70182, ℰ (0711) 2 37 77 70
Fax (0711) 2377775 – ⨯   LZ
closed Saturday lunch, January to October also Sunday and Bank Holidays – **Meals** à la carte
68/85.

X **Rösch**, Scheffelstr. 23, ✉ 70193, ℰ (0711) 65 47 47, *Fax (0711) 654767*, Beer garden
– E   FV
closed Tuesday – **Meals** à la carte 41/64.

Swabian wine taverns (Weinstuben) *(mainly light meals only)* :

X **Kachelofen**, Eberhardstr. 10 (entrance in Töpferstraße), ✉ 70173, ℰ (0711) 24 23 78
⇱   KZ
closed Sunday – **Meals** (open from 5pm) à la carte 47/65.

X **Weinstube Schellenturm**, Weberstr. 72, ✉ 70182, ℰ (0711) 2 36 48 88
Fax (0711) 2262699, ⇱ – AE. ⨯   LZ
closed Sunday and Bank Holidays – **Meals** *(dinner only)* à la carte 36/65.

X **Weinstube Klink**, Epplestr. 1 (Degerloch), ✉ 70597, ℰ (0711) 7 65 32 05
Fax (0711) 760307, ⇱   by Obere Weinsteige GX
closed Saturday, Sunday and Bank Holidays – **Meals** *(open from 5 pm)* (booking essential)
à la carte 37/74.

X **Weinstube Träuble**, Gablenberger Hauptstr. 66 (entrance in Bussenstraße), ✉ 70186
ℰ (0711) 46 54 28, ⇱ – ⨯   HV
closed Sunday, Bank Holidays and late August - mid September – **Meals** *(open from 5pm*
only cold and warm light meals.

X **Weinhaus Stetter**, Rosenstr. 32, ✉ 70182, ℰ (0711) 24 01 63, *Fax (0711) 240193*
⇱   LZ
open Monday to Friday from 3 pm, Saturday 10 am to 3 pm, closed Sunday, Bank Holidays
and 24 December - 8 January – **Meals** (outstanding wine list) only cold and warm light meals

at Stuttgart-Büsnau *by Rotenwaldstraße* FX :

🏨 **Relexa Waldhotel Schatten**, Magstadter Straße (Solitudering), ✉ 70569, ℰ (0711)
6 86 70, *Fax (0711) 6867999*, ⇱, ☑, ⇌ – ⟦⟧, ↭ rm, TV & ⊶ ℗ – ⚐ 80. AE ⓪
E VISA JCB. ⨯ rest
La Fenêtre *(closed Sunday - Monday and Bank Holidays)* **Meals** à la carte 57/80 – **Kamin**
restaurant : **Meals** à la carte 45/75 – **136 rm** ⊇ 210/390 – 7 suites.

at Stuttgart-Bad Cannstatt :

🏨 **Pannonia Hotel** M, Teinacher Str. 20, ✉ 70372, ℰ (0711) 9 54 00
Fax (0711) 9540630, ⇱, ⇌ – ⟦⟧, ↭ rm, ▤ rest, TV ☎ & ⊶ – ⚐ 120. AE ⓪ E
VISA JCB   JT
Meals à la carte 54/78 – **156 rm** ⊇ 187/298 – 5 suites.

XX **Krehl's Linde** with rm, Obere Waiblinger Str. 113, ✉ 70374, ℰ (0711) 52 75 67
Fax (0711) 5286370, ⇱ – TV ☎ ⊶. AE E   JT
closed 3 weeks July - August – **Meals** *(closed Sunday - Monday)* à la carte 43/74 – **18 rm**
100/220.

at Stuttgart-Degerloch :

🏨 **Waldhotel Degerloch** ⌖, Guts-Muths-Weg 18, ✉ 70597, ℰ (0711) 76 50 17
Fax (0711) 7653762, ⇱, ⇌, ⨯v – ⟦⟧ TV ☎ & ℗ – ⚐ 100. AE ⓪ E VISA JCB
Meals à la carte 45/75 – **50 rm** ⊇ 180/265.   by Guts-Muths-Weg HX

XXXX **Wielandshöhe**, Alte Weinsteige 71, ✉ 70597, ℰ (0711) 6 40 88 48
Fax (0711) 6409408, ⇱, « Beautiful situation ≤ Stuttgart » – AE ⓪ E VISA   GX
closed Sunday - Monday – **Meals** (booking essential) 128/188 and à la carte 88/132
Spec. Gratinierter Hummer mit Basilikum-Kartoffelsalat. Fränkischer Bauernhahn mi
Nudeln. Quarksoufflé mit Rhabarberkompott.

XXX **Skyline-Restaurant**, Jahnstr. 120, ⊠ 70597, ℰ (0711) 24 61 04, Fax (0711) 2360633, ✳ Stuttgart and surroundings, (in TV-tower at 144 m, 🛗) – 🅿. AE ① E VISA
closed Thursday lunch and Monday – **Meals** (booking essential for dinner) à la carte 65/97

XX **Das Fässle**, Löwenstr. 51, ⊠ 70597, ℰ (0711) 76 01 00, Fax (0711) 764432, 🍃 – AE ① E VISA
by Jahnstraße GX
closed Sunday – **Meals** (booking essential) à la carte 48/77.

at Stuttgart-Fasanenhof *by Obere Weinsteige (B 27)* GX :

🏨 **Mercure** M, Eichwiesenring 1, ⊠ 70567, ℰ (0711) 7 26 60, Fax (0711) 7266444, 🍃, ㄥ, ⊆s – 🛗, ⇥ rm, ▤ TV ☎ 🖐 ☞ 🅿 – 🕿 120. AE ① E VISA
Meals à la carte 45/68 – **128 rm** ☕ 215/298.

🏨 **Fora Hotel** M, Vor dem Lauch 20 (Businesspark), ⊠ 70567, ℰ (0711) 7 25 50, Fax (0711) 7255666, 🍃, ⊆s – 🛗, ⇥ rm, TV ☎ 🖐 ☞ – 🕿 55. AE ① E VISA JCB
Meals *(closed Sunday dinner)* à la carte 38/60 – **101 rm** ☕ 198/238.

at Stuttgart-Feuerbach :

🏨 **Messehotel Europe** M, Siemensstr. 33, ⊠ 70469, ℰ (0711) 81 00 40 (hotel) 8 10 04 24 55 (rest.), Fax (0711) 810042555 – 🛗, ⇥ rm, ▤ TV 🖐 ☞. AE ①
E VISA
GT r
Landhausstuben *(dinner only, closed Sunday - Monday)* – **114 rm** ☕ 192/310.

🏨 **Kongresshotel Europe**, Siemensstr. 26, ⊠ 70469, ℰ (0711) 81 00 40, Fax (0711) 810041444, ⊆s – 🛗 ⇥ ▤ TV 🖐 ☞ – 🕿 120. AE ① E VISA
GT z
Meals *(closed Saturday and Sunday lunch)* à la carte 43/72 – **145 rm** ☕ 135/325.

at Stuttgart-Flughafen (Airport) *South : 15 km by Obere Weinsteige (B 27)* GX :

🏨 **Mövenpick-Hotel** M, Randstr. 7, ⊠ 70629, ℰ (0711) 7 90 70, Fax (0711) 793585, 🍃, ⊆s – 🛗, ⇥ rm, ▤ TV 🖐 ㄥ 🅿 – 🕿 45. AE ① E VISA JCB
Meals *(closed 1 to 10 January)* à la carte 37/68 – **229 rm** ☕ 294/534.

XXX **top air**, at the airport (terminal 1, level 4), ⊠ 70629, ℰ (0711) 9 48 21 37, Fax (0711) 7979210 – ▤ 🅿 – 🕿 40. AE ① E VISA
✿
closed Saturday lunch, 1 week January and 3 weeks August – **Meals** 82/150 and à la carte 74/118
Spec. St. Petersfisch und Hummer im Sepiacrêpesmantel mit Blattspinat. Ballotine vom Perlhuhn mit Lauchgemüse und Perigord-Trüffelsauce. Karamelisierte Ananastarte mit Zitronengraseis und Pistazienschaum.

at Stuttgart-Hoheheim *by Mittlere Filderstraße* HX :

XXXX **Speisemeisterei**, Am Schloß Hohenheim, ⊠ 70599, ℰ (0711) 4 56 00 37, Fax (0711) 4560038, 🍃 – 🅿
✿✿
closed Sunday dinner - Monday, 1 to 12 January and 26 July - 18 August – **Meals** (weekdays dinner only, booking essential) 135/158 and à la carte 84/122
Spec. Feuilleté von Hummer und Imperial Kaviar. Torte und Kotelett vom Salzwiesenlamm mit gefüllten Gemüsen. Rehnüsschen mit Gänseleber und Karamel-Blutsauce.

at Stuttgart-Möhringen *South-West : 7 km by Obere Weinsteige* GX :

🏨 **Copthorne Hotel Stuttgart International** M (with 🏨 SI), Plienienger Str. 100, ⊠ 70567, ℰ (0711) 7 21 10 50, Fax (0711) 7212931, 🍃, beer garden, (direct entrance to the recreation centre Schwaben Quelle) – 🛗, ⇥ rm, ▤ TV 🖐 ㄥ ☞ – 🕿 500. AE ① E VISA JCB
Meals (19 different restaurants, bars and cafes) à la carte 31/72 – **454 rm** ☕ 287/528.

🏨 **Fora Hotel** without rest, Filderbahnstr. 43, ⊠ 70567, ℰ (0711) 71 60 80, Fax (0711) 7160850 – 🛗 ⇥ TV ☎ ☞. AE ① E VISA JCB
closed late December - early January – **41 rm** ☕ 178/208.

at Stuttgart-Obertürkheim *by Augsburger Straße* JU :

🏨 **Brita Hotel**, Augsburger Str. 671, ⊠ 70329, ℰ (0711) 32 02 30, Fax (0711) 324440 – 🛗, ⇥ rm, TV ☎ 🖐 ☞ – 🕿 80. AE ① E VISA
closed 24 December - 1 January – **Meals** *(closed Saturday - Sunday)* à la carte 32/53 – **70 rm** ☕ 128/232.

at Stuttgart-Stammheim *by Heilbronner Straße* GT :

🏨 **Novotel-Nord**, Korntaler Str. 207, ⊠ 70439, ℰ (0711) 98 06 20, Fax (0711) 803673, 🍃, ⊆s, ⬙ (heated) – 🛗, ⇥ rm, ▤ TV ☎ ㄥ 🅿 – 🕿 200. AE ① E VISA
Meals à la carte 35/60 – **113 rm** ☕ 175/229.

at Stuttgart-Vaihingen *by Böblinger Str.* FX :

Dorint-Hotel Fontana Ⓜ, Vollmöllerstr. 5, ✉ 70563, ☏ (0711) 73 00
Fax (0711) 7302525, Massage, ♨, ⅃ঌ, ≘s, ⅃, 🐎 – ៕, ⅍ rm, ▤ ᵀⱽ ⚏ ⅍ ☁ – ⏫ 250
ᴁ ⓪ Ⅎ ᵛᴵˢᴬ ᴊᴄʙ ⅍ rest
Meals à la carte 39/82 – **252 rm** ⌸ 289/455 – 5 suites.

at Stuttgart-Weilimdorf *by B 295* FT :

Holiday Inn Ⓜ, Mittlerer Pfad 27, ✉ 70499, ☏ (0711) 98 88 80, *Fax (0711) 988889*
🌿, beer garden, ≘s – ៕, ⅍ rm, ᵀⱽ ☏ ⚏ ⅍ ☁ – ⏫ 150. ᴁ ⓪ Ⅎ
ᵛᴵˢᴬ ᴊᴄʙ
Meals à la carte 29/58 – **325 rm** ⌸ 246/410 – 6 suites.

at Stuttgart-Zuffenhausen *by Heilbronner Straße* GT :

Fora Hotel Residence, Schützenbühlstr. 16, ✉ 70435, ☏ (0711) 8 20 01 00
Fax (0711) 8200101, 🌿 – ៕, ⅍ rm, ᵀⱽ ☏ ⚏ ⅍ ☁ – ⏫ 90. ᴁ ⓪
Ⅎ ᵛᴵˢᴬ
Meals *(dinner only, closed Saturday)* à la carte 33/58 – **119 rm** ⌸ 195/
265.

Achat Ⓜ without rest, Wollinstr. 6, ✉ 70439, ☏ (0711) 82 00 80, *Fax (0711) 8200899*
– ៕ ⅍ ᵀⱽ ☏ ⚏ ☁. ᴁ Ⅎ ᵛᴵˢᴬ   CP
104 rm ⌸ 129/189.

at Fellbach *North-East : 8 km by Nürnberger Straße (B 14)* JT – ✆ 0711 :

Classic Congress Hotel, Tainer Str. 7, ✉ 70734, ☏ (0711) 5 85 90
Fax (0711) 5859304, « Changing exhibition of paintings », ⅃ঌ, ≘s – ៕, ⅍ rm, ᵀⱽ ☏
☁ Ⓟ – ⏫ 55. ᴁ ⓪ Ⅎ ᵛᴵˢᴬ ᴊᴄʙ
closed 23 December - 6 January – see **Alt Württemberg** *below* – **148 rm** ⌸ 195/
260.

✕✕ Alt Württemberg, Tainer Str. 7 (Schwabenlandhalle), ✉ 70734, ☏ (0711) 5 85 94 11
Fax (0711) 5859427, 🌿 – ▤. ᴁ ⓪ Ⅎ ᵛᴵˢᴬ ᴊᴄʙ
Meals à la carte 48/84.

✕✕ Zum Hirschen with rm, Hirschstr. 1, ✉ 70734, ☏ (0711) 9 57 93 70
Fax (0711) 95793710, 🌿, « Modernised 16C timbered house » – ᵀⱽ
☏   ER
Meals *(closed Saturday lunch, Sunday and Monday)* (booking essential) à la carte 66/86 –
9 rm ⌸ 120/180.

✕ Aldinger's Weinstube Germania with rm, Schmerstr. 6, ✉ 70734, ☏ (0711
58 20 37, *Fax (0711) 582077,* 🌿 – ᵀⱽ ☏. ⅍
closed 2 weeks February - March and 3 weeks July - August – **Meals** *(closed Sunday
Monday and Bank Holidays)* (booking essential) à la carte 42/70 – **7 rm** ⌸ 80/
140.

at Gerlingen *West : 10 km by Rotenwaldstraße* FX – ✆ 07156 :

Krone, Hauptstr. 28, ✉ 70839, ☏ (07156) 4 31 10, *Fax (07156) 4311100,* 🌿, ≘s
៕, ⅍ rm, ᵀⱽ ☏ ☁ Ⓟ – ⏫ 110. ᴁ ⓪ Ⅎ ᵛᴵˢᴬ
Meals *(closed Sunday - Monday, Bank Holidays, Easter and Christmas)* (booking essentia
à la carte 41/82 – **56 rm** ⌸ 142/249.

Ramada, Dieselstr. 2, ✉ 70839, ☏ (07156) 43 13 00, *Fax (07156) 431343,* ≘s – ៕
⅍ rm, ᵀⱽ ☏ ⅍ ☁ Ⓟ – ⏫ 100. ᴁ ⓪ Ⅎ ᵛᴵˢᴬ ᴊᴄʙ
Meals à la carte 32/58 – **96 rm** ⌸ 143/186.

at Korntal-Münchingen *North-West : 9 km, by Heilbronner Str.* GT :

Mercure, Siemensstr. 50, ✉ 70825, ☏ (07150) 1 30, *Fax (07150) 13266,* 🌿, bee
garden, ≘s, ⅃ – ៕, ⅍ rm, ▤ ᵀⱽ ⅍ Ⓟ – ⏫ 180. ᴁ ⓪ Ⅎ ᵛᴵˢᴬ
Meals à la carte 45/68 – **200 rm** ⌸ 165/227.

at Leinfelden-Echterdingen *South : 11 km by Obere Weinsteige (B 27)* GX :

Hotel am Park Ⓜ, Lessingstr. 4 (Leinfelden), ✉ 70771, ☏ (0711) 90 31 00
Fax (0711) 9031099, Beer garden – ៕ ᵀⱽ ☏ ⚏ Ⓟ – ⏫ 20. ᴁ ⓪ Ⅎ
ᵛᴵˢᴬ
closed 24 December - 6 January – **Meals** *(closed Saturday - Sunday)* à la carte 42/70 –
42 rm ⌸ 136/187.

Filderland without rest, Tübinger Str. 16 (Echterdingen), ✉ 70771, ☏ (0711) 9 49 46
Fax (0711) 9494888 – ៕ ⅍ ᵀⱽ ☏ ⚏ ☁ – ⏫ 15. ᴁ ⓪ Ⅎ
ᵛᴵˢᴬ
closed 22 December - 9 January – **48 rm** ⌸ 135/180.

Baiersbronn *Baden-Württemberg* 419 *U 9,* 987 ㉜ *– pop. 16 000 – alt. 550 m.*
Stuttgart 100.

XXXX **Schwarzwaldstube** - Hotel Traube Tonbach, Tonbachstr. 237, ✉ 72270, ✆ (07442)
❀❀❀ 49 26 65, *Fax (0742) 492692,* ≤ – 🍴 🅿. 🆎 ⓞ ⓔ 𝗩𝗜𝗦𝗔
closed Monday - Tuesday, 11 January - 2 February and 2 to 26 August – **Meals** (booking
essential) 168/210 and à la carte 99/146
Spec. Salat von Meeresfrüchten mit jungen Algenspitzen und Zitronengrasmarinade. Stein-
buttschnitte mit schwarzem Pfeffer an der Gräte gebraten. Gegrillte Taube mit Stein-
pilzrisotto und geschmortem Knoblauch, Trüffeljus.

XXXX **Restaurant Bareiss** -Hotel Bareiss, Gärtenbühlweg 14, ✉ 72270, ✆ (07224) 4 70,
❀❀ *Fax (07224) 47320,* ≤ – 🍴 🅿. 🆎 ⓞ ⓔ 𝗩𝗜𝗦𝗔
closed Monday - Tuesday, 7 June - 9 July and 22 November - 24 December – **Meals** (booking
essential) (outstanding wine list) 158/189 and à la carte 103/128 – ***Kaminstube :*** **Meals**
à la carte 52/79
Spec. Gratinierte Rosette von Jakobsmuscheln mit Imperial-Kaviar (season). Bretonischer
Steinbutt mit Pinienkernen gratiniert und Kräuternudeln. Variation vom Bresse Täubchen
mit Trüffelglace.

Haigerloch *Baden-Württemberg* 419 *U 10,* 987 ㉜ *– pop. 11 000 – alt. 425 m.*
Stuttgart 70.

XXX **Schwanen** with rm and guest house, Marktplatz 5 (Unterstadt), ✉ 72401, ✆ (07474)
❀❀ 9 54 60, *Fax (07474) 954610,* 🌳, « Restored 17C baroque house » – 📺 ☎ 📞 🚗 –
🛎 18. 🚫
Meals *(closed Monday - Tuesday and 2 weeks October - November)* 92/172 and à la carte
89/126 – **23 rm** 🍴 135/330
Spec. Pot-au-feu von Krustentieren und St. Jakobsmuscheln. Lammrücken in der Arti-
schockenkruste. Schokoladensoufflé mit eingelegten Kumquats.

Greece

Elláda

ATHENS

PRACTICAL INFORMATION

LOCAL CURRENCY

Greek Drachma: *100 GRD = 0,28 euros (€)*

TOURIST INFORMATION

National Tourist Organisation (EOT): *2, Amerikis, ☎ (01) 331 05 61. Hotel reservation: Hellenic Chamber of Hotels, 24 Stadiou, ☎ (01) 323 71 93. Fax (01) 322 54 49, also at East Airport ☎ (01) 961 27 22 - Tourist Police: 4 Stadiou ☎ 171.*

National Holidays in Greece: *25 March and 28 October.*

FOREIGN EXCHANGE

Banks are usually open on weekdays from 8am to 2pm. A branch of the National Bank of Greece is open daily from 8am to 2pm (from 9am to 1pm at weekends) at 2 Karageorgi Servias (Sindagma). East Airport offices operate a 24-hour service.

AIRLINES

OLYMPIC AIRWAYS: *96 Singrou 117 41 Athens, ☎ (01) 926 73 33/926 91 11-3, 2 Kotopouli (Omonia), ☎ (01) 926 72 16-9, reservations only ☎ (01) 966 66 66. All following Companies are located in Sindagma area:*

AIR FRANCE: *18 Vouliagmenis, Glyfada 166 75 Athens, ☎ (01) 960 11 00.*

BRITISH AIRWAYS: *10 Othonos 105 57 Athens, ☎ (01) 325 06 01-9.*

JAPAN AIRLINES: *22 Voulis 105 63 Athens, ☎ (01) 324 82 11-2.*

LUFTHANSA: *11 Vas. Sofias 106 71 Athens, ☎ (01) 369 2200.*

SABENA: *41 c, Vouliagmenis, Glyfada ☎ (01) 960 00 71-4.*

SWISSAIR: *4 Othonos, (lst floor) 105 57 Athens, ☎ (01) 323 5811-7.*

TRANSPORT IN ATHENS

Taxis: *may be hailed in the street even when already engaged; it is always advisable to pay by the meter (double fare after midnight).*

Bus: *good for sightseeing and practical for short distances: 100 GRD.*

Metro: *one single line crossing the city from North (Kifissia) to South (Pireas) : 80 GRD.*

POSTAL SERVICES

General Post Office: *100 Eolou (Omonia) with poste restante, and also at Sindagma.*

Telephone (OTE): *15 Stadiou 322-1002 and 85 Patission (all services).*

SHOPPING IN ATHENS

In summer, shops are usually open from 8am to 1.30pm, and 5.30 to 8.30pm. They close on Sunday, and at 2.30pm on Monday, Wednesday and Saturday. In winter they open from 9am to 5pm on Monday and Wednesday, from 10am to 7pm on Tuesday, Thursday and Friday, from 8.30am to 3.30pm on Saturday. Department Stores in Patission and Eolou are open fron 8.30 am to 8 pm on weekdays and 3 pm on Saturdays. The main shopping streets are to be found in Sindagma, Kolonaki, Monastiraki and Omonia areas. Flea Market (generally open on Sunday) and Greek Handicraft in Plaka and Monastiraki.

TIPPING

Service is generally included in the bills but it is usual to tip employees.

SPEED LIMITS

The speed limit in built up areas is 50 km/h (31 mph); on motorways the maximum permitted speed is 100 km/h (62 mph) and 80 km/h (50 mph) on others roads.

SEAT BELTS

The wearing of seat belts is compulsory for drivers and front seat passengers.

BREAKDOWN SERVICE

The ELPA (Automobile and Touring Club of Greece, ☎ (01) 74 88 800) operate a 24 hour breakdown service: phone 174 for tourist information, 104 for emergency road service.

ATHENS

(ATHÍNA) *Atikí* 980 ⑨ – *Pop. 3 076 786 (Athens and Piraeus area).*

Igoumenítsa 581 – Pátra 215 – Thessaloníki 479.

🛈 *Tourist Information (EOT), 2 Amerikis* 🕾 *(01) 331 05 61, Information center* 🕾 *(01) 322 25 45 and East Airport* 🕾 *(01) 961 27 22.*
ELPA (Automobile and Touring Club of Greece), 2 Messogion 🕾 *(01) 748 88 00.*
🏌 *Glifáda (near airport)* 🕾 *(01) 894 68 20, Fax (01) 894 37 21.*
✈ *S : 15 km, East Airport* 🕾 *(01) 969 41 11 (International Airport – All companies except Olympic Airways), West Airport* 🕾 *(01) 966 66 66 (Elinikó Airport – Olympic Airways only).*
🚗 *1 Karolou* 🕾 *(01) 524 06 01.*

SIGHTS

Views of Athens: Lycabettos (Likavitós) ☀★★★ DX *– Philopappos Hill (Lófos Filopá-pou)* ≤★★★ AY.

ANCIENT ATHENS

Acropolis★★★ (Akrópoli) ABY *– Theseion★★ (Thissío)* AY *and Agora★ (Arhéa Agorá)* AY *– Theatre of Dionysos★★ (Théatro Dioníssou)* BY *and Odeon of Herod Atticus★ (Odío Iródou Atikoú)* AY *– Olympieion★★ (Naós Olimbíou Diós)* BY *and Hadrian's Arch★ (Píli Adrianoú)* BY *– Tower of the Winds★* BY **A** *in the Roman Forum (Romaïkí Agorá).*

OLD ATHENS AND THE TURKISH PERIOD

Pláka★★ : Old Metropolitan★★ BY **P¹** *– Monastiráki★ (Old Bazaar) : Kapnikaréa (Church)* BY **K**, *Odós Pandróssou★* BY **29**, *Monastiráki Square★* BY.

MODERN ATHENS

Sindagma Square★ CY *: Greek guard on sentry duty – Academy, University and Library Buildings★ (Akadimía* CX, *Panepistímio* CX, *Ethnikí Vivliothíki* BX*) – National Garden★ (Ethnikós Kípos)* CY.

MUSEUMS

National Archaelogical Museum★★★ (Ethnikó Arheologikó Moussío) BX *– Acropolis Museum★★★* BY **M⁵** *– Museum of Cycladic and Ancient Greek Art★★* DY **M¹⁰** *– Byzantine Museum★★ (Vizandinó Moussío)* DY *– Benaki Museum★★ (Moussío Benáki, private collection of antiquities and traditional art)* CDY *– Museum of Traditional Greek Art★* BY **M⁷** *– National Historical Museum★* BY **M²** *– Jewish Museum of Greece★* BY **M³** *– National Gallery and Soutzos Museum★ (painting and sculpture)* DY **M¹**.

EXCURSIONS

Cape Sounion★★★ (Soúnio) SE : 71 km BY *– Kessariani Monastery★★ , E : 9 km* DY *– Daphne Monastery★★ (Dafní) NW : 10 km* AX *– Aigina Island★ (Égina) : Temple of Aphaia★★ , 3 hours return.*

A
ΛΑΡΙΣΑ
LARISSA
AHARNÉS
B
THESALONÍKI
LAMÍA
PÁRNITHA
Ioulianou
28 ΟΚΤΩΒΡΙΟΥ
33
ΜΕΤΣΟΒΟΥ
ΙΩΑΝΝΙΝΩΝ
ΝΕΟΦ. ΜΕΤΑΞΑ
Neof. Metaxa
ΗΠΕΙΡΟΥ
ΑΧΑΡΝΩΝ
ΣΕΠΤΕΜΒΡΙΟΥ
ΕΤΗΝΙΚΟ
ARHEOLOGIKO
MOUSSÍO
ΠΕΤΡΑΣ
ΛΙΟΣΙΩΝ
Γ.
Liossion
t
H
ΜΑΡΝΗ
Marni
Γ
ΛΕΝΟΡΜΑΝ
ΠΕΛΟΠΟΝΝΗΣΟΣ
PELOPONISSOS
ΨΑΡΩΝ
ΣΤΟΥΡΝΑΡΑ
Deligiani
ΦΑΒΙΕΡΟΥ
3 Septemvriou (Patission)
ΠΛΑΤ.
ΒΑΘΗΣ
Pl. Vathis
ΠΟΛΙΤΕΗΝΙΟΥ
X
ΔΕΛΗΓΙΑΝΝΗ
ΚΑΡΟΛΟΥ
ΜΑΡΝΗ
Marni
ΠΛΑΤ. ΚΑΝΙΓΓΟΣ
Pl. Kaningos
ΧΙΟΥ
ΠΛΑΤ.
ΚΑΡΑΙΣΚΑΚΗ
Pl. Karaïskaki
Karolou
28 Οκτωβρίου
ΘΕΜΙΣΤΟΚΛΕΟΥΣ
ΑΧΙΛΛΕΩΣ
ΑΓ. ΚΩΝΣΤΑΝΤΙΝΟΥ
T
ΑΚΑΔΗΜΙΑΣ
Dafní KÓRINTHOS
Ahileos
Ag. Konstandinou
OMONOIA
OMONOIA
Omónia
ΑΛΕΞΑΝΔΡΟΥ
ΔΕΛΗΓΙΩΡΓΗ
Omónia
c
DEUTSCH.
ARCH. INSTITU
ΜΕΓ.
ΘΕΡΜΟΠΥΛΩΝ
ΜΥΛΛΕΡΟΥ
ΚΟΛΟΚΥΝΘΟΥΣ
ΜΕΤΑΧΟΥΡΓΙΟ
ΜΕΝΑΝΔΡΟΥ
ΑΙΟΛΟΥ
ΣΤΑΔΙΟΥ
ΠΑΝΕΠΙΣΤΗΜΙΟΥ
ΕΤΗΝΙΚΙ
VIVLIOTHÍKÍ
ΚΕΡΑΜΕΙΚΟΥ
ΠΑΝΑΓΗ
ΤΣΑΛΔΑΡΗ
Tsaldari
ΠΛΑΤ.
ΚΟΤΖΙΑ
Pl. Kodzia
ΣΟΦΟΚΛΕΟΥΣ
Sofokleous
ΠΛΑΤ.
ΕΛΕΥΘΕΡΙΑΣΧ
Panagi
Pl. Eleftherias
ΑΡΙΣΤΟΦΑΝΟΥΣ
KENDRIKÍ AGORÁ
Eolou
ΠΑΝΕΠΙΣΤΙΜΙΟΥ
(ΠΕΙΡΑΙΩΣ)
(Pireos)
ΚΡΙΕΖΗ
ΣΑΡΡΗ
ΕΥΡΙΠΙΔΟΥ
ΠΛΑΤ.
ΚΛΑΥΘΜΩΝΟΣ
Pl. Klafthmonos
P
Stadiou
KERAMIKÓS
M
S
PSÍRI
ΑΘΗΝΑΣ
Athinas
ΑΙΟΛΟΥ
ΚΟΛΟΚΟΤΡΩΝΗ
M
M²
PIREAS
ΕΡΜΟΥ
ΠΛΑΤ.
ΜΟΝΑΣΤΗΡΑΚΙΟΥ
V
MONASTIRÁKI
ΜΟΝΑΣΤΗΡΑΚΙ
MONASTIRAKI
13
b
ΘΗΣΕΙΟ
Thissio
ΜΟΝΑΣΤΗΡΑΚΙ
Monastiráki
a
Ermou
K
THISSIO
Apostolou
Mitropoleos
e
Y
Αποστόλου
i
29
P1
ΜΗΤΡΟΠΟΛΕΩΣ
ARHÉA AGORÁ
A
PLÁKA
ΑΔΡΙΑΝΟΥ
ΝΑΥΑΡΧΟΥ
ΝΙΚΟΔΗΜΟ
h
ÁRIOS
PÁGOS
Pavlou
M
ANAFIOTIKA
M
16
LÓFOS NIMFÓN
(Nympheíon)
Παύλου
M⁷
AKRÓPOLI
M³
PNÍKA
(Pnyx)
ODÍO IRÓDOU
ATIKOÚ
M¹
n
PÍLI
ADRIANOU
Ag. Dimitrios
ΔΙΟΝΥΣΙΟΥ
THÉATRO DIONÍSSOU
Dionissiou
ΑΡΕΟΠΑΓΙΤΟΥ
NAÓS
OLIMBÍOU
DIOS
LÓFOS
FILOPÁPOU
(Mouseíon)
Dionyssis
Aeropagítou
ΡΟΒ. ΓΚΑΛΙ
r
30
M
L
ΜΑΚΡΗ
ΔΙΑΚΟΥ
P
a
14
p
21
Singrou Diakou
36
ΧΑΤΖΗΧΡΗΣΤΟΥ
T
r
f
MAKRIGIÁNI
ΚΑΒΑΛΛΟΤΙ
ΣΥΓΓΡΟΥ
n
A
B
PIREÁS
ELINIKÓ WEST
Soúnio
ELINIKÓ EAST

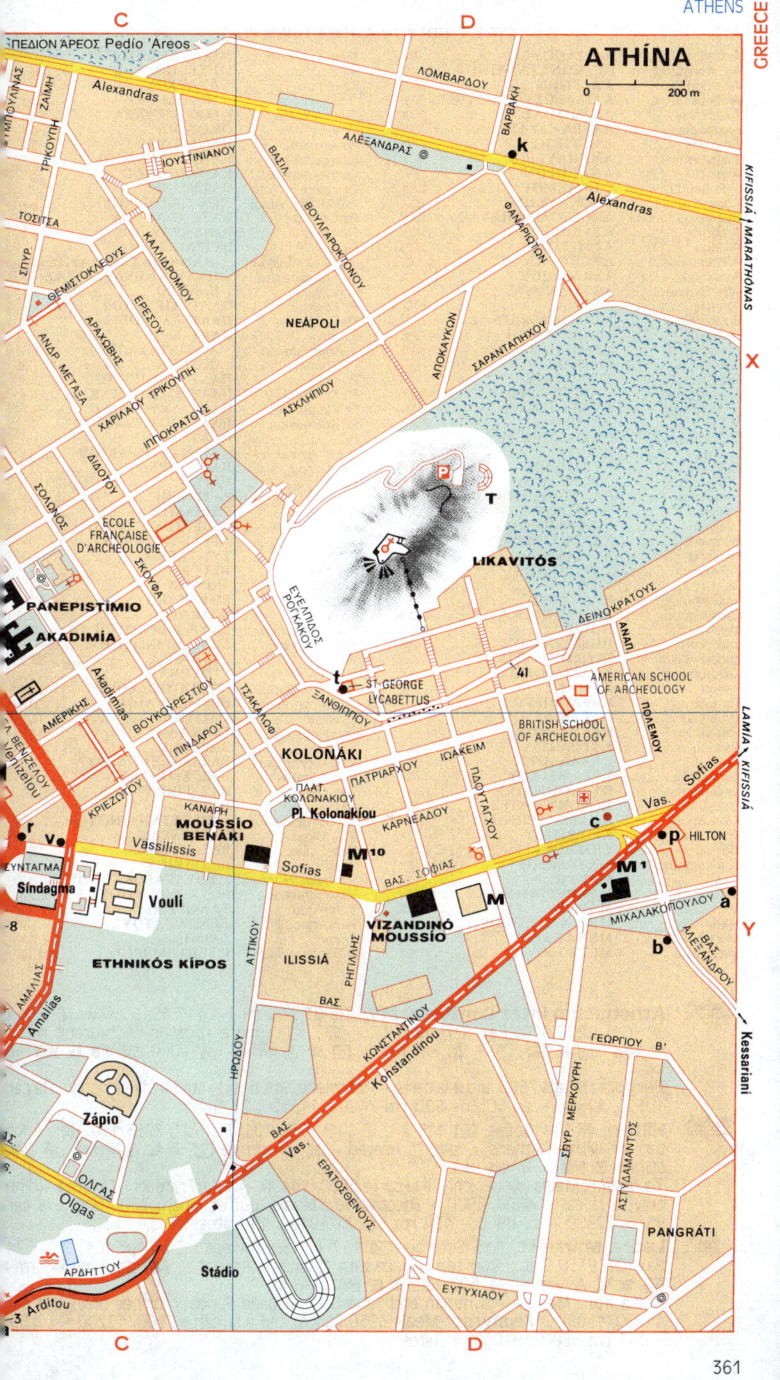
ATHENS
GREECE
ATHÍNA
0 200 m
ΣΠΕΔΙΟΝ ΑΡΕΟΣ Pedío 'Areos
ΛΟΜΒΑΡΔΟΥ
Alexandras
ΜΠΟΥΛΓΑΡΟΚΤΟΝΟΥ
ΖΑΙΜΗ
ΤΡΙΚΟΥΠΗ
ΙΟΥΣΤΙΝΙΑΝΟΥ
ΒΑΣΙΛ.
ΑΛΕΞΑΝΔΡΑΣ
ΒΑΡΒΑΚΗ
k
Alexandras
KIFISSIÁ / MARATHÓNAS
ΤΟΣΙΤΣΑ
ΣΠΥΡ.
ΚΑΛΛΙΔΡΟΜΙΟΥ
ΒΟΥΛΓΑΡΟΚΤΟΝΟΥ
ΦΑΝΑΡΙΩΤΩΝ
ΑΝΔΡ. ΜΕΤΑΞΑ
ΘΕΜΙΣΤΟΚΛΕΟΥΣ
ΑΡΑΧΩΒΗΣ
ΕΡΕΣΟΥ
ΝΕΑΡΟLI
ΑΠΟΚΑΥΚΩΝ
ΣΑΡΑΝΤΑΠΗΧΟΥ
X
ΧΑΡΙΛΑΟΥ ΤΡΙΚΟΥΠΗ
ΙΠΠΟΚΡΑΤΟΥΣ
ΑΣΚΛΗΠΙΟΥ
ΔΙΔΟΤΟΥ
ΣΟΛΩΝΟΣ
ECOLE FRANÇAISE D'ARCHÉOLOGIE
ΣΚΟΥΦΑ
P
T
ΕΥΕΛΠΙΔΟΣ
ΡΟΓΚΑΚΟΥ
LIKAVITÓS
PANEPISTÍMIO
AKADIMÍA
Akadimías
ΒΟΥΚΟΥΡΕΣΤΙΟΥ
ΤΣΑΚΑΛΩΦ
ΞΑΝΘΙΠΠΟΥ
ΔΕΙΝΟΚΡΑΤΟΥΣ
ΑΝΑΠ.
t
41
ST-GEORGE LYCABETTUS
AMERICAN SCHOOL OF ARCHEOLOGY
ΑΜΕΡΙΚΗΣ
ΠΙΝΔΑΡΟΥ
BRITISH SCHOOL OF ARCHEOLOGY
ΠΟΛΕΜΟΥ
Α. ΒΕΝΙΖΕΛΟΥ
Venizelou
ΚΡΙΕΖΩΤΟΥ
KOLONÁKI
ΠΑΤΡΙΑΡΧΟΥ
ΙΩΑΚΕΙΜ
ΠΛ. ΦΥΤΑΓΧΟΥ
Sofias
ΚΑΝΑΡΗ
ΠΛΑΤ. ΚΟΛΩΝΑΚΙΟΥ
Pl. Kolonakíou
ΚΑΡΝΕΑΔΟΥ
Vas.
r
v
MOUSSÍO BENÁKI
Vassilissis
Sofias
M 10
ΒΑΣ. ΣΟΦΙΑΣ
c
p HILTON
ΣΥΝΤΑΓΜΑ
Síndagma
Vouli
ΒΑΣ. ΣΟΦΙΑΣ
M 1
M
ΜΙΧΑΛΑΚΟΠΟΥΛΟΥ
a
VIZANDINÓ MOUSSÍO
LAMÍA / KIFISSIÁ
ΕΘΝΙΚΟΣ ΚΙΡΟΣ
ΑΤΤΙΚΟΥ
ILISSIÁ
ΡΗΓΙΛΗΣ
ΒΑΣ.
b
ΒΑΣ. ΑΛΕΞΑΝΔΡΟΥ
Y
ΑΜΑΛΙΑΣ
Amalías
ΗΡΩΔΟΥ
ΚΩΝΣΤΑΝΤΙΝΟΥ
Konstandinou
ΓΕΩΡΓΙΟΥ Β'
Kessariani
Zápio
ΒΑΣ.
Vas.
ΕΡΑΤΟΣΘΕΝΟΥΣ
ΣΠΥΡ. ΜΕΡΚΟΥΡΗ
ΑΣΤΥΔΑΜΑΝΤΟΣ
ΟΛΓΑΣ
Olgas
ΑΡΔΗΤΤΟΥ
Stádio
Arditou
PANGRÁTI
ΕΥΤΥΧΙΑΟΥ

STREET INDEX TO ATHÍNA TOWN PLAN

Athenaeum Inter-Continental M, 89-93 Singrou, ✉ 117 45, *Southwest* : 2 ¾ k ☎ (01) 9206 000, *Fax (01) 9243 000*, « Première rooftop restaurant with Athens », ⅃ゟ, ≦s, ⌿ – 🛗, ✻ rm 🔲 TV ☎ ♿ 🚗 – 🏛 2000. AE ⓪ E VISA JC

Pergola : Meals 7500 and a la carte – **Première** (9th floor) : Meals (dinner only) a la car 10300/12800 – ☕ 6050 – **520 rm** 74800/115500, 23 suites.

Hilton, 46 Vas. Sofias, ✉ 115 28, ☎ (01) 7250 201, *Fax (01) 7253 110*, 🏞, « Roo terrace with ≺ Athens », ≦s, ⌿ heated – 🛗, ✻ rm 🔲 TV ☎ ♿ 🚗 – 🏛 240 AE ⓪ E VISA JCB. ✻ rest DY
Ta Nissia : Meals (dinner only) a la carte 5600/14400 – **Kellari** : Meals - Taverna - (dinn only) a la carte 4800/6900 – **Byzantine** : Meals (buffet lunch) 7200 and a la car 9100/12800 – ☕ 4900 – **434 rm** 65200/89100, 19 suites.

Ledra Marriott, 115 Singrou, ✉ 117 45, *Southwest* : 3 km ☎ (01) 9347 71 *Fax (01) 9358 603*, « Rooftop terrace with ⌿ and ✻ Athens », ⅃ゟ, ≦s – 🛗, ✻ rm TV ☎ ♿ 🚗 – 🏛 500. AE ⓪ E VISA JCB. ✻
Kona Kai : Meals - Polynesian and Japanese - (closed Sunday) (dinner only) a la car 11400/15050 – **Zephyros** : Meals 3950 (lunch) and a la carte 7900/12200 – ☕ 590 – **255 rm** 55000/92000, 4 suites.

Grande Bretagne, 1 Vas. Georgiou A, Sindagma Sq., ⊠ 105 63, ℘ (01) 3330 000, Fax (01) 3328 064 – 📶, ⇔ rm 📺 ☎ 📞 – 🕍 500. AE ① E VISA JCB. ⛝   CY v
G B Corner : Meals (buffet lunch) 8600/11500 and a la carte – ☕ 5000 – **341 rm** 93400/113500, 23 suites.

NJV Athens Plaza M, 2 Vas. Georgiou A, Sindagma Sq., ⊠ 105 64, ℘ (01) 325 5301, Fax (01) 323 5856 – 📶, ⇔ rm 📺 ☎ 📞 – 🕍 250. AE ① E VISA JCB. ⛝ rest   CY r
The Parliament : Meals a la carte 11100/16800 – ☕ 4200 – **152 rm** 70000/195000, 30 suites.

Divani Palace Acropolis, 19-25 Parthenonos, ⊠ 117 42, ℘ (01) 9222 945, Fax (01) 9214 993, « Ancient ruins of Themistocles wall in basement », 🏊 – 📶 📺 ☎ 📞 – 🕍 300. AE ① E VISA JCB. ⛝   BY r
Aspassia : Meals 6500 and a la carte – *Roof Garden* : Meals (closed Tuesday and November-April) (live music) (buffet dinner only) 6500 – ☕ 5000 – **253 rm** 58000/68000, 7 suites.

St. George Lycabettus, 2 Kleomenous, ⊠ 106 75, ℘ (01) 7290 712, Fax (01) 7290 439, 🌿, « < Athens from rooftop restaurant », 🏊 – 📶 📺 ☎ 📞 🚗 – 🕍 150. AE ① E VISA JCB. ⛝ rest   DX t
Le Grand Balcon : Meals (closed Sunday and Monday) (dinner only) 8000/10000 and a la carte – *Mediterraneo* : Meals (buffet lunch) 5800 and a la carte 6000/9500 – ☕ 4800 – **162 rm** 45300/90800, 5 suites.

Divani Caravel, 2 Vas. Alexandrou, ⊠ 116 10, ℘ (01) 7253 725, Fax (01) 7253 770, « Rooftop 🏊 with < Athens » – 📶, ⇔ rm 📺 ☎ 📞 🚗 – 🕍 800. AE ① E VISA JCB. ⛝   DY b
Amalia : Meals (buffet lunch) 6000/6500 and a la carte – ☕ 4500 – **423 rm** 65000/78000, 48 suites.

Holiday Inn, 50 Mihalakopoulou, ⊠ 115 28, ℘ (01) 7248 322, Fax (01) 7248 187, <, « Rooftop terrace with 🏊 », 🚲, ⊜s – 📶, ⇔ rm 📺 ☎ 📞 🚗 – 🕍 650. AE ① E VISA JCB. ⛝   DY a
Meals 6000/6500 and a la carte – ☕ 4000 – **188 rm** 64000/75000, 3 suites.

Zafolia, 87-89 Alexandras, ⊠ 114 74, ℘ (01) 6449 002, Fax (01) 6442 042, « Rooftop terrace with 🏊 and < Athens » – 📶 📺 ☎ 🚗 – 🕍 200. AE ① E VISA JCB. ⛝   DX k
Meals 3500/4500 – **183 rm** ☕ 23200/28600, 7 suites.

Andromeda Athens M, 22 Timoleontos Vassou St., ⊠ 115 21, via Vas Sofias behind U.S. Embassy ℘ (01) 6437 302, Fax (01) 6466 361, « Contemporary interior design » – 📶, ⇔ rm 📺 ☎ 📞 – 🕍 100. AE ① E VISA JCB. ⛝
Meals a la carte 10000/17500 – ☕ 6000 – **24 rm** 90000/105000, 17 suites.

Herodion, 4 Rovertou Galli, ⊠ 117 42, ℘ (01) 9236 832, Fax (01) 9235 851, « Roof garden with < Acropolis » – 📶 📺 ☎ – 🕍 50. AE ① E VISA JCB. ⛝   BY p
Meals 5500 and a la carte – **90 rm** ☕ 33800/44500.

Novotel, 4-6 Mihail Voda, ⊠ 104 39, ℘ (01) 8250 422, Fax (01) 8837 816, « Roof terrace with 🏊 and ☀ Athens » – 📶 📺 ☎ 🚗 – 🕍 600. AE ① E VISA JCB   AX t
Meals a la carte 5400/7700 – ☕ 3800 – **190 rm** 36000/40000, 5 suites.

Electra Palace, 18 Nikodimou, ⊠ 105 57, ℘ (01) 3370 000, Fax (01) 3241 875, « Terrace with 🏊 and < Athens » – 📶, ⇔ rm 📺 ☎ 📞 🚗 – 🕍 200. AE ① E VISA JCB. ⛝   BY h
Meals 5200/5500 and a la carte – **101 rm** ☕ 36800/44800, 5 suites.

Electra, 5 Ermou, ⊠ 105 63, ℘ (01) 3223 222, Fax (01) 3220 310 – 📶, ⇔ rm 📺 ☎. AE ① E VISA JCB. ⛝   BY e
Meals 4900 and a la carte – **110 rm** ☕ 36800/44800.

Philippos without rest., 3 Mitseon, ⊠ 117 42, ℘ (01) 9223 611, Fax (01) 9223 615 – 📶 📺 ☎. AE ① E VISA JCB. ⛝   BY f
48 rm ☕ 24500/31000.

Jason Inn without rest., 12 Assomaton St. Thission, ⊠ 105 53, ℘ (01) 3251 106, Fax (01) 3243 132 – 📶 📺 ☎. AE E VISA. ⛝   AY s
57 rm ☕ 17200/23000.

Pil-Poul, 51 Apostolou Pavlou, ⊠ 118 51, ℘ (01) 3423 665, Fax (01) 3413 046, « Former mansion with < Acropolis and Athens from rooftop terrace » – AE ① E VISA JCB   AY b
closed Sunday and 1 week Easter – **Meals** (dinner only) a la carte 16500/22100.

Boschetto, Evangelismou, off Vas. Sofias, ⊠ 106 76, ℘ (01) 7210 893, Fax (01) 7223 598, 🌿, « Summerhouse in small park » – 🔲. AE VISA   DY c
closed Saturday lunch, Sunday, Easter, 1 to 20 August, 25 December and 1 January – **Meals** - Italian - (dinner only except Easter-September) a la carte 11500/19600.

XXX **Bajazzo,** 1 Tyrteou & corner of Anapavseos, ⊠ 116 36, ℘ (01) 9213 01
Fax (01) 9213 013, 🏠 – 🔲. AE ⓪ E *VISA*. ✖   CY
Meals (booking essential) (dinner only) 25000/35000 and a la carte.

XXX **Symbosio,** 46 Erehthiou, ⊠ 117 42, ℘ (01) 9225 321, *Fax (01) 9232 780,* « Attractiv
conservatory in winter, terrace in summer » – AE ⓪ E *VISA*. ✖   AY
closed Sunday, 2 weeks Easter and 2 weeks August – **Meals** (booking essential) (dinn
only) a la carte 12600/27900.

XX **Mezzo Mezzo,** 58 Singrou, ⊠ 117 42, ℘ (01) 9242 444, *Fax (01) 9242 71*
« Warehouse style conversion, modern art » – 🔲 **P**. AE ⓪ E *VISA* JCB. ✖   AY
closed Sunday and June-September – **Meals** (dinner only) a la carte 11800/16000.

XX **7 Anemous,** 121 Ermou (17 Astingos), Monastiraki, ⊠ 105 55, ℘ (01) 3240 386 – E
AE ⓪ E *VISA*. ✖   AY
closed August – **Meals** a la carte 7150/12050.

XX **Daphne's,** 4 Lysikratous, Plaka, ⊠ 105 58, ℘ (01) 3227 971, *Fax (01) 3227 971,* 🏠
« Frescoes depicting ancient Greek myths ; attractive inner courtyard » – 🔲. AE ⓪
VISA   BY
Meals (booking essential) (dinner only) a la carte 11400/16400.

XX **Ideal,** 46 Panepistimiou, (El. Venizelou), ⊠ 106 78, ℘ (01) 3303 000, *Fax (01) 3303 00*
– 🔲. AE ⓪ E *VISA* JCB. ✖   BX
closed Sunday, Easter Monday, 15 August and 25-26 December – **Meals** a la cart
6200/8600.

X **Taverna Strofi,** 25 Rovertou Galli, ⊠ 117 42, ℘ (01) 9214 130, 🏠, « ← Acropo
from rooftop terrace » – 🔲. ⓪ E *VISA*   AY
closed Sunday, 4 days Easter and 1 week Christmas – **Meals** (dinner only) a la cart
5000/6500.

X **Taverna Sigalas,** 2 Monastiraki Sq., ⊠ 105 55, ℘ (01) 3213 036, *Fax (01) 3252 44*
« Traditional Greek atmosphere », Live music – AE E *VISA*. ✖   BY
Meals 2000/6000 and a la carte.

Environs

at Kifissia *Northeast : 15 km by Vas. Sofias* DY :

🏨 **Pentelikon** 🦅, 66 Diligianni, Kefalari, ⊠ 145 62, *off Harilaou Trikoupi, follow signs t*
Politia ℘ (01) 6230 650, *Fax (01) 8010 314,* 🏊, 🌿 – 📶 🔲 📺 ☎ **P** – 🎪 150. AE ⓪
E *VISA*. ✖
Meals - (see *Vardis* and *La Terrasse* below) – 🍽 4100 – **33 rm** 82000/120000, 6 suite

XXXX **Vardis** (at Pentelikon H.), 66 Diligianni, Kefalari, ⊠ 145 62, *off Harilaou Trikoupi, follo*
❀ *signs to Politia* ℘ (01) 6230 650, *Fax (01) 8010 314,* 🏠 – 🔲. AE ⓪ E *VISA*. ✖
Meals - French - (dinner only) 12500/18500 and a la carte 12200/18800
Spec. Terrine de foie gras et de lapereau à la crème de cèpes. Roulades de volaille au
morilles et petits légumes. Gâteau chaud au chocolat.

XX **La Terrasse** (at Pentelikon H.), 66 Diligianni, Kefalari, ⊠ 145 62, *off Harilaou Trikoup*
follow signs to Politia ℘ (01) 6230 650, *Fax (01) 8010 314,* 🏠 – 🔲. AE ⓪ E *VISA*. ✖
Meals a la carte 8800/12700.

at Pireas *Southwest : 10 km by Singrou* BY :

XX **Varoulko,** 14 Deligiorgi, off Omiridou Skilitsi, ⊠ 185 33, ℘ (01) 4112 043
☺ *Fax (01) 4221 283 –* 🔲. AE ⓪ E *VISA* JCB. ✖
closed Sunday, August and Christmas – **Meals** - Seafood - (booking essential) (dinner onl
(set menu only) 8400/10700.

Hungary

Magyarország

BUDAPEST

PRACTICAL INFORMATION

LOCAL CURRENCY

Forint: *100 HUF = 0,39 euro (€)*
National Holidays in Hungary: *15 March, 20 August, and 23 October.*

PRICES

Prices may change if goods and service costs in Hungary are revised and it is therefore always advisable to confirm rates with the hotelier when making a reservation.

FOREIGN EXCHANGE

It is strongly advised against changing money other than in banks, exchange offices or authorised offices such as large hotels, tourist offices, etc... Banks are usually open on weekdays from 8.30am to 4pm.

HOTEL RESERVATIONS

In case of difficulties in finding a room through our hotel selection, it is always possible to apply to IBUSZ Hotel Service, Apáczai ut. 1, Budapest 5th ☏ (01) 318 57 76, Fax (01) 317 90 99. This office offers a 24-hour assistance to the visitor.

POSTAL SERVICES

Main Post offices are open from 8am to 7pm on weekdays and 8am to 3pm on Saturdays.
General Post Office: *Városház ut. 18, Budapest 5th, ☏ (01) 318 48 11.*

SHOPPING IN BUDAPEST

In the index of street names, those printed in red are where the principal shops are found. Typical goods to be bought include embroidery, lace, china, leather goods, paprika, salami, Tokay (Tokaij), palinka, foie-gras... Shops are generally open from 10am to 6pm on weekdays (7pm on Thursday) and 9am to 1pm on Saturday.

TIPPING

Hotel, restaurant and café bills often do not include service in the total charge. In these cases it is usual to leave the staff a gratuity which will vary depending upon the service given.

CAR HIRE

The international car hire companies have branches in Budapest. Your hotel porter should be able to give details and help you with your arrangements.

BREAKDOWN SERVICE

A breakdown service is operated by SARGA ANGYAL (Yellow Angel), ☏ (01) 252 80 00.

SPEED LIMIT

On motorways, the maximum permitted speed is 120 km/h – 74 mph, 100 km/h – 62 mph on main roads, 80 km/h – 50 mph on others roads and 50 km/h – 31 mph in built up areas.

SEAT BELTS

In Hungary, the wearing of seat belts is compulsory for drivers and front seat passengers. On motorways : all passengers.

TRANSPORT

The three metro lines (yellow, red and blue) and the trams and buses make up an extensive public transport network. Tickets must be purchased in advance. Daily, weekly and monthly passes are available.
Airport busses : apply to your hotel porter.

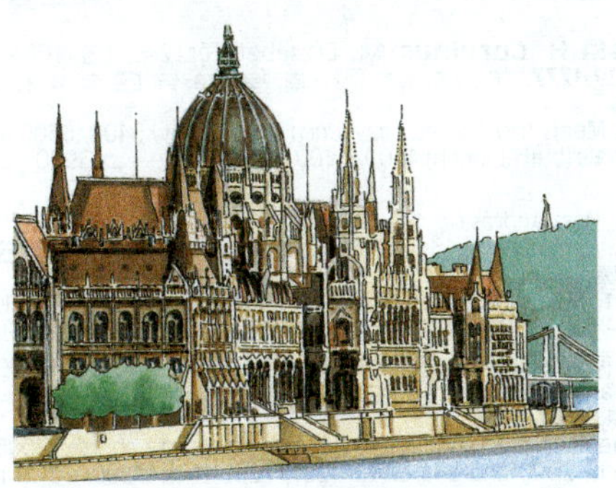

BUDAPEST

Hungary **970** *N 6 – Pop. 1 909 000.*

Munich 678 – Prague 533 – Venice 740 – Vienna 243 – Zagreb 350

🛈 *Tourinform, Sütő u. 2,* ✉ *H 1052* ☏ *(01) 317 98 00, Fax (01) 317 96 56 – IBUSZ Head Office, Ferenciek tér 5, Budapest 5th* ☏ *(01) 318 68 66.*

✈ *Ferihegy SE : 16 km by Üllol* FX, ☏ *(01) 296 96 96 (information), Bus to airport : from International Bus station, Erzsébet tér, Station 6 Budapest 5th and Airport Minibus Service LRI – MALEV, Roosevelt tér 2, Budapest 5th* ☏ *(01) 267 29 11*

Views of Budapest

St. Gellert Monument and Citadel (Szt. Gellért-szobor, Citadella) ⩽★★★ EX *– Fishermen's Bastion (Halászbástya)* ⩽★★ DU.

BUDA

Matthias Church★★ (Mátyás-templom) DU *– Attractive Streets★★ (Tancsics Mihaly utca – Fortuna utca – Uri utca)* CDU *– Royal Palace★★ (Budavári palota)* DV *– Hungarian National Gallery★★ (Magyar Nemzeti Galéria)* DV **M¹** *– Budapest Historical Museum★ (Budapesti Történeti Múzeum)* DV **M¹** *– Vienna Gate★ (Bécsi kapu)* CU *– War History Museum★ (Hadtörténety Múzeum)* CU.

PEST

Parliament Building★★★ (Országház) EU *– Museum of Fine Arts★★★ (Szepmüveszeti Múzeum)* BY **M³** *– Hungarian National Museum★★ (Magyar Nemzeti Múzeum)* FVX *– Museum of Applied Arts★★ (Iparmüvészeti Múzeum)* BZ **M⁵** *– Szechenyi Thermal Baths★★ (Széchenyi Gyógyés Strandfürdö)* BY **F²** *– Hungarian State Opera House★ (Magyar Állami Operaház)* FU *– Liszt Conservatory : foyer★ (Liszt Ferenc Zenemüvészeti Föiskola)* FU *– Chinese Art Museum★ (Kína Muzéum)* BYZ **M⁶** *– St. Stephen's Basilica★ (Szt. István-bazilika)* EU *– City Parish Church★ (Belvárosi plébániatemplom)* EV *– University Church★ (Egyetemi Templom)* FX *– Franciscan Church★ (Ferences templom)* FV *– Municipal Concert Hall★ (Vigadó)* EV *– Town Hall★ (Fövárosi Tanács)* EFV *– Paris Arcade★ (Párizsi udvar)* EV *– Vaci Street★ (Váci utca)* EV *– Hungaria Restaurant★ (Hungaria Ettermek)* BZ **N** *– Budapest West Station★ (Nyugati pályaudvar)* AY *– Millenary Monument★ (Millenniumi emlékmu)* BY **D** *– City Park★ (Városliget)* BYZ *– Vajdahunyad Castle★ (Vajdahunyad vára)* BY **B** *– Hungarian Transport Museum★ (Magyar Közlekedesi Múzeum)* BY **M⁷**.

ADDITIONAL SIGHTS

Chain Bridge★★ (Széchenyi Lánchíd) DEV *– Margaret Island★ (Margitsziget)* AY *– Aquincum Museum★ (Aquincumi Muzéum) N : 12 km by Szentendrei út* AY *– Gellert Thermal Baths★ (Gellért gyógyfürdö)* EX *– St. Ann's Church★ (Szent Anna templom)* DU.

Envir.: *Szentendre★ N : 20 km – Visegrad N : 42 km : Citadel, view★★*

Kempinski H. Corvinus M, Erzsébet tér 7-8, ⊠ 1051, ℘ (01) 429 3777, Fax (01) 429 4777, 💧, ⅙, ≘s, ⊠ – 📲, ↯ rm, 🖩 TV ☎ 📞 ♿ 🚗 – 🛎 450. AE ①
E VISA JCB. 💥
EV
Corvinus : Meals *(closed Saturday lunch and Sunday)* 5400/6600 and a la carte – **Bistro**
Jardin : Meals (buffet lunch) 4600/5100 and a la carte – ☕ 3900 – **345 rm** 62300/71800,
22 suites.

Hilton ⤱, Hess András tér 1-3, ⊠ 1014, ℘ (01) 214 3000, Fax (01) 356 0285, ≼ Danube
and Buda, « Remains of a 13C Dominican church » – 📲, ↯ rm, 🖩 TV ☎ & 🚗 – 🛎 600.
AE ① E VISA JCB. 💥 rest
DU
Dominican : Meals 6000 and a la carte – **Kalocsa** : Meals (buffet lunch) 3900/4800 and
a la carte – ☕ 3900 – **295 rm** 46700/52700, 27 suites.

Marriott M, Apáczai Csere János útca 4, ⊠ 1016, ℘ (01) 266 7000, Fax (01) 266 5000,
≼ Danube and Buda, 💧, ⅙, ≘s – 📲, ↯ rm, 🖩 TV ☎ 📞 🚗 – 🛎 650. AE ① E
VISA JCB. 💥 rest
EV
Csarda : Meals *(closed Sunday)* (dinner only) a la carte approx. 8000 – **Duna Grill** : Meals
(buffet lunch) 2900 and a la carte 4200/7200 – ☕ 3500 – **349 rm** 47800/53800, 1
suites.

Atrium Hyatt M, Roosevelt tér 2, ⊠ 1051, ℘ (01) 266 1234, Fax (01) 266 9101, ≼, ⅙,
≘s, ⊠ – 📲, ↯ rm, 🖩 TV ☎ 📞 ♿ 🚗 – 🛎 350. AE ① E VISA JCB. 💥 rest
EV
Atrium Terrace : Meals 4200/9600 and a la carte – ☕ 3500 – **355 rm** 46700/
52700.

Inter-Continental, Apáczai Csere János útca 12-14, ⊠ 1052, ℘ (01) 327 6333,
Fax (01) 327 6357, ≼ Danube and Buda, ⅙, ≘s, ⊠ – 📲, ↯ rm, 🖩 TV ☎ & 🚗 –
🛎 280. AE ① E VISA JCB. 💥
EV
Silhouette : Meals *(closed Saturday lunch)* 5000/10000 and a la carte – **Grill** : Meals
(closed Sunday lunch) 4000/9000 and a la carte – ☕ 3500 – **383 rm** 50300/65900, 1
suites.

Aquincum Corinthia M ⤱, Árpád Fejedelem útja 94, ⊠ 1036, ℘ (01) 436 4100,
Fax (01) 436 4156, ≼, Therapy centre, ⅙, ≘s, ⊠ – 📲, ↯ rm, 🖩 TV ☎ & 🚗 –
– 🛎 280. ① E VISA JCB. 💥 rest
AY
Ambrosia : Meals 3400/3600 and a la carte – **Apicius** : Meals 3400/3600 and a la carte
– **304 rm** ☕ 35800/44200, 8 suites.

Radisson SAS Béke, Teréz körút 43, ⊠ 1067, ℘ (01) 301 1600, Fax (01) 301 1615,
≘s, ⊠ – 📲, ↯ rm, 🖩 TV ☎ 🚗 – 🛎 200. AE ① E VISA JCB
FU
Shakespeare : Meals (lunch only) 3600/5400 and a la carte – **Szondi** : Meals (dinner only)
3600/6000 and a la carte – ☕ 3000 – **239 rm** 37100, 8 suites.

Danubius Grand H. ⤱, Margitsziget, ⊠ 1138, ℘ (01) 329 2300, Fax (01) 329 3923,
≼, 💧, Direct entrance to Thermal Hotel, ≘s, ⊠ – 📲, ↯ rm, TV ☎ & 🚗 – 🛎 85.
AE ① E VISA JCB. 💥 rest
AY
Meals 2400/9600 and a la carte – **154 rm** ☕ 32400/38300, 10 suites.

Thermal H. Helia M, Kárpát útca 62-64, ⊠ 1133, ℘ (01) 452 5800, Fax (01) 452 5801,
≼, Therapy centre, ⅙, ≘s, ⊠, ✗ – 📲, ↯ rm, 🖩 TV ☎ ♿ P – 🛎 400. AE ① E
VISA JCB. 💥 rest
AY
Meals (buffet lunch) 3500/7200 and a la carte – **254 rm** ☕ 26400/32400, 8 suites.

Gellert, Gellért tér 1, ⊠ 1111, ℘ (01) 385 2200, Fax (01) 466 6631, « Art Nouveau
decor », Direct entrance to the Therapeutic baths, ≘s, ⊠ heated, ⊠ – 📲, ↯ rm, 🖩
TV ☎ 🚗 – 🛎 300. AE ① E VISA JCB
EX
Meals 3500/5400 and a la carte – **220 rm** ☕ 26400/45000, 13 suites.

K + K Hotel Opera M ⤱, Révay útca 24, ⊠ 1065, ℘ (01) 269 0222,
Fax (01) 269 0230, « Stylish modern interior design », ⅙, ≘s – 📲, ↯ rm, 🖩 TV ☎
– 🛎 60. AE ① E VISA. 💥 rest
FU
Meals 3600/4800 and a la carte 3300/5100 – **203 rm** ☕ 27600/32400, 2 suites.

Mercure Buda M, Krisztina körút 41-43, ⊠ 1013, ℘ (01) 356 6333, Fax (01) 356 6964,
≘s, ⊠ – 📲, ↯ rm, 🖩 TV ☎ & 🚗 P – 🛎 120. AE ① E VISA JCB. 💥 rest
CV
closed 2 weeks late July and 23 to 26 December – Meals 4200 (dinner) and a la carte
4200/7200 – **388 rm** ☕ 22800/27600, 6 suites.

Mercure Korona M, Kecskeméti útca 14, ⊠ 1053, ℘ (01) 317 4111,
Fax (01) 318 3867, ≘s, ⊠ – 📲, ↯ rm 🖩 TV ☎ & 🚗 – 🛎 100. AE ① E VISA JCB.
💥 rest
FX
Meals (buffet lunch) 3000 and a la carte – **423 rm** ☕ 27600/32400, 10 suites.

Astoria, Kossuth Lajos útca 19-21, ⊠ 1053, ℘ (01) 317 3411, Fax (01) 318 6798, « Art
Nouveau decor » – ↯ rm, TV ☎ – 🛎 80. AE ① E VISA JCB. 💥 rest
FV
Meals 2000/6000 and a la carte – **124 rm** ☕ 21600/30000, 5 suites.

Park H. Flamenco, Tas Vezér útca 7, ⊠ 1113, ℘ (01) 372 2000, Fax (01) 365 8007, 💧,
≘s, ⊠ – 📲, ↯ rm, 🖩 TV ☎ 🚗 P – 🛎 160. AE ① E VISA JCB. 💥 rest
AZ
Meals 2500/5000 and a la carte – **348 rm** ☕ 26400/32400.

BUDAPEST

HUNGARY

HUNGARY
BUDAPEST
C
D
69
Moszkva
Csalogány
Széna Tér
22
5
Tér
Moszkva Tér
24
Donáti
Toldy
5
Bem
Batthyány Tér
SZENT ANNA TEMPLOM
Várfok
BÉCSI KAPU
63
42
Lovas út
71
17
U
Városmajor
HADTÖRTÉNETY MÚZEUM
15
M
Ferenc
Körút
Attila
ÚRI
50
M
HALÁSZBÁSTYA
17
VÁRHEGY
U. c
t
a
Corvin Tér
Déli pu
M
MÁTYÁS-TEMPLOM
17
d
Rakpart
Lovas út
Szenth Tér
Tárnok
DUNA
Krisztina
út
Hunyadi János út
DÉLI PU
70
Dísz Tér
P
SZÉCHEN LÁNCHÍ
f
Palota
T
a
Alkotás
Clark Ádám Tér
28
46
Körút
út
P
37
Alagút
Attila
BUDAVÁRI PALOTA
39
Krisztina Tér
48
M¹
V
Márvány
Mi
Győri
Liszinyai
út
U
Krisztina
M
Avar
Mészáros
Naphegy Tér
Fém
48
Körút
Tigris
Deszõ u.
Kereszt
Derék
Csörsz
u.
Hegyalja
h
Aladár
TABÁN
Hegyalja
út
Sánc
X
Mihály
Szirtes
Somlói
Kelenhegyi
Szirtes
út
Hegyalja
Budaörsi
út
Villányi út
Ménesi
út
BUDAPEST
0   300 m
C
D
GELLÉRTHEGY

370

E
F
BUDAPEST
HUNGARY
SZÁGHÁZ
M
Honvéd
Alkotmány
u.
Bajcsy
Szondi u.
Csengery
a
Kossuth
Lajos
Tér
29
Podmaniczky
Jókai u.
Teréz
Aradi
Vörösmarty
u.
T
Báthory
Lovag
Nagymező
Dessewffy
Jenő
Jókai
Tér
Hunyadi
Tér
Kossuth
Tér
Vadász
Hold
Mozsár
Oktogon
U
Zoltán
Szabadság
Tér
Bank
Hajós
T
T
Liszt Ferenc
Zeneművészeti
Főiskola
Akadémia
Nádor
Alpári
Gyula
Zichy
T
T
Operaház
P
Kertész
Széchenyi
u.
Arany
János u.
Lázár
T
f
Liszt
Ferenc
Tér
Krt.
Arany
János
Október 6.
Sas
Révay
Opera
Ede
Király
Csányi
Dob
u.
Zrínyi
Szent
István
Tér
BAZILIKA
Andrássy
Székely M. u.
Kis Diófa u.
Klauzál
Tér
Klauzál
M
Roosevelt
Tér
József
Attila
Bajcsy-Zs. út
Kazinczy
Nagy
Diófa
u.
Belgrád
Dorottya
József
Nádor
Tér
Erzsébet
Tér
P
Paulay
Király
60
u.
u.
Vörösmarty Tér
c
Bécsi
a
POL
Deák
Ferenc
Tér
Deák
Tér
T
P
Dob
Wesselényi
u.
út
VIGADÓ
Vörösmarty
Tér
s
8
Z
b
Károly
ZSINAGÓGORA
Dohány
T
V
VÁCI
T
FŐVÁROSI
TANÁCS
Körút
M
k
Rákóczi
Szentkirályi
8
P
19
PEST
MEGYEI
TANÁCS
r
58
h
55
53
73
Astoria
Puskin
U
21
Kossuth L. u.
q
Múzeum
Petőfi
Tér
T
f
Párizsi
udvar
FERENCES
TEMPLOM
Bródy
Sándor
20
12
a
57
44
M
MAGYAR
NEMZETI
MÚZEUM
BELVÁROSI
PLÉBÁNIATEMPLOM
P
Ferenciek Tere
33
Körút
Erzsébet Híd
Belgrád
c
26
EGYETEMI
TEMPLOM
U
Veres
r
Múzeum
s
Molnár
Váci
66
t
35
Kálvin
Kálvin Tér
SZT.
ELLÉRT
Palné
e
Tér
Baross
n
Ráday
Üllői
X
CITADELLA
DUNA
Rakpart
Körút
Lónyai
út
adella Sétány
SZABADSÁG
Vámház
Csarnok
Tér
Erkel
M
BILEUMI
PARK
VÁSÁRCSARNOK
U
P
Szabadság Híd
Mátyás
GYÓGYFÜRDŐ
GELLÉRT
n
Szent
Gellért
Tér
Kinizsi
Kelenhegyi
út
U
E
F

Novotel, Alkotás útca 63-67, ✉ 1123, ℰ (01) 209 1990, Fax (01) 466 5636, –
rm, TV ☎ P – 1200. AE Ⓞ E VISA JCB
Meals 2500/4000 and a la carte – 2400 – **321 rm** 21600, 3 suites.
CX

Grand H. Hungaria, Rákóczí útca 90, ✉ 1074, ℰ (01) 322 9050, Fax (01) 351 067
– TV ☎ – 350. AE Ⓞ E VISA JCB
Meals 1000/6000 and a la carte – **479 rm** 26400/32400, 20 suites.
BZ

Taverna, Váci útca 20, ✉ 1052, ℰ (01) 338 4999, Fax (01) 318 7188, – , r
TV ☎ – 120. AE Ⓞ E VISA JCB
Meals (dinner only) 3500/4500 and a la carte – **224 rm** 25200/33000.
EV

Relais Mercure Duna Ⓜ without rest., Soroksári útca 12, ✉ 1095, ℰ (01) 455 830
Fax (01) 455 8385 – , rm, TV P – 50. AE Ⓞ E VISA JCB
124 rm 18000/20400, 6 suites.
BZ

Victoria Ⓜ without rest., Bem Rakpart 11, ✉ 1011, ℰ (01) 457 808
Fax (01) 457 8088, , – TV ☎ P. AE Ⓞ E VISA JCB
27 rm 17300/23900.
DU

Liget Ⓜ without rest., Dózsa György útca 106, ✉ 1068, ℰ (01) 269 530
Fax (01) 269 5329, – TV ☎ P. AE Ⓞ E VISA JCB
139 rm 20400/26400.
BY

Ibis Centrum Ⓜ without rest., Raday útca 6, ✉ 1092, ℰ (01) 215 858
Fax (01) 215 8787 – TV ☎ . AE Ⓞ E VISA
126 rm 15600/19200.
FX

Queen Mary , Béla Király útca 47, ✉ 1121, Zugliget, West : 9 km by Szilágyi Erzsébetf
sor ℰ (01) 274 4000, Fax (01) 395 8377, , , – rest, TV ☎ P. AE E VISA
Meals (dinner only) 2100/3000 and a la carte – **22 rm** 8400/14200.

Alba without rest., Apor Péter útca 3, ✉ 1011, ℰ (01) 375 9244, Fax (01) 375 98
– TV ☎ – 30. AE Ⓞ E VISA
95 rm 20400/30000.
DV

Art, Királyi Pál útca 12, ✉ 1053, ℰ (01) 266 2166, Fax (01) 266 2170, , –
☎ . AE Ⓞ E VISA JCB. rest
Meals 3000/5000 and a la carte – **29 rm** 18000/22200, 3 suites.
FX

City Panzió Mátyás Ⓜ, Március 15 tér, No. 8, ✉ 1056, ℰ (01) 338 471
Fax (01) 317 9086 – TV ☎ . AE Ⓞ E VISA .
Meals (see **Mátyás Pince** below) – **52 rm** 15600/19200, 2 suites.
EX

Gundel, Állatkertí útca 2, ✉ 1146, ℰ (01) 321 3550, Fax (01) 342 2917, « Summ
terrace », Gypsy and classical music at dinner – P. AE Ⓞ E VISA JCB
closed 24 December – **Meals** (booking essential) 2800/3100 (lunch) and a la cart
4400/7000.
BY

Vadrózsa, Pentelei Molnár útca 15, ✉ 1025, via Rómer Flóris útca ℰ (01) 326 581
Fax (01) 326 5809, « Summer terrace » – AE Ⓞ E VISA JCB
closed last 2 weeks July and 23 to 26 December – **Meals** a la carte 6700/12200.
AY

Garvics, Urömí Köz 2, ✉ 1023, ℰ (01) 326 3878, Fax (01) 326 3876, « Converte
vaulted chapel » – . AE Ⓞ E VISA
closed Saturday, Sunday, 24 December and Bank Holidays – **Meals** (booking essential)
la carte 2500/5900.
AY

Alabárdos, Országház útca 2, ✉ 1014, ℰ (01) 356 0851, Fax (01) 214 3814,
« Vaulted Gothic interior, covered courtyard » – . AE Ⓞ E VISA JCB
closed Sunday and 24 December – **Meals** (booking essential) 3000/9000 and a la cart
CU

Fortuna, Hess András tér 4, ✉ 1014, ℰ (01) 375 6857, Fax (01) 375 6857, –
AE E VISA
Meals 3000/10000 and a la carte.
CDU

Légrádi Antique, Bárczy István útca 3-5 (first floor), ✉ 1052, ℰ (01) 266 499
« Elegant decor, antiques », Gypsy music at dinner – AE Ⓞ E VISA
closed Saturday lunch and Sunday – **Meals** (booking essential) 3500/8500 and a la cart
EV

Légrádí & Tsa, Magyar útca 23, ✉ 1053, ℰ (01) 318 6804, Vaulted cellar, Gypsy mus
at dinner – . AE E VISA
closed Sunday and 15 June-5 July – **Meals** (booking essential) (dinner only) a la cart
3000/5000.
FX

Marco Polo, Vigadó tér 3, ✉ 1051, ℰ (01) 338 3354, Fax (01) 266 2727 – . E VI
Meals - Italian - a la carte 7000/14100.
EV

Bagolyvár, Allatkertí útca 2, ✉ 1146, ℰ (01) 343 0217, Fax (01) 342 2917, , Mus
at dinner – AE Ⓞ E VISA JCB
closed 24 December – **Meals** 2400 (lunch) and a la carte 2200/3800.
BY

Oroszlános Kîthoz, Vörösmarty tér 7 (in Gerbeaud House), ✉ 1051, ℰ (01) 429 900
Fax (01) 429 9029 – Ⓞ E VISA
closed Sunday dinner - **Meals** a la carte 3300/4500.
EV

XX **Fausto's,** Dohány útca 5, ⊠ 1072, ℰ (01) 269 6806, *Fax (01) 269 6806* – ▣. AE E VISA
closed Sunday, 24 December, 1 week January and 3 weeks July – **Meals** - Italian - FV k
7000/12000 and a la carte.

XX **Robinson,** Városligeti tó, ⊠ 1146, ℰ (01) 343 3776, *Fax (01) 343 0955*, 🌣, « Lakeside
setting » – ▣. AE ① E VISA JCB   BY a
Meals 3100/7200 and a la carte.

XX **Belcanto,** Dalszínház útca 8, ⊠ 1061, ℰ (01) 269 2786, *Fax (01) 311 9547*, « Classical
and operatic recitals » – AE ① E VISA JCB   FU f
closed 24 December – **Meals** (booking essential) 3500/15000 and a la carte.

XX **Kárpátia,** Ferencíek tere 7-8, ⊠ 1053, ℰ (01) 317 3596, *Fax (01) 318 0591*, « Part of
former Franciscan monastery », Gypsy music at dinner – AE ① E VISA   FV a
Meals 2400/15600 and a la carte.

XX **Mátyás Pince,** Március 15 tér, No. 7, ⊠ 1056, ℰ (01) 318 1693, *Fax (01) 318 1650*,
« Vaulted cellar, murals », Gypsy music – ▣. AE ① E VISA JCB   EX c
closed 24 December – **Meals** 3000/6500 and a la carte.

OCAL ATMOSPHERE

X **Aranymókus,** Istenhegyi útca 25, ⊠ 1126, *via Nagyenyed Îtca* ℰ (01) 355 9594,
Fax (01) 355 6728, 🌣 – AE ① E VISA JCB
closed 24 December – **Meals** (dinner only) a la carte 1500/4000.

X **Náncsi Néni,** Órdögárok útca 80, Pesthidegkút, ⊠ 1029, *Northwest : 12 km by Szilágyi
Erzsébetfasor* ℰ (01) 397 2742, *Fax (01) 397 2742*, 🌣, Accordion music at dinner except
Saturday – AE E VISA JCB
Meals a la carte 1700/4000.

X **Kisbuda Gyöngye,** Kenyeres útca 34, ⊠ 1034, ℰ (01) 368 6402, *Fax (01) 368 9227*,
Music at dinner – ▣. AE ① E VISA   AY f
closed Sunday – **Meals** (booking essential) a la carte 3500/5500.

X **Apostolok,** Kígyó útca 4, ⊠ 1052, ℰ (01) 318 3559, *Fax (01) 318 3559*, « Old chapel
decor, wood carvings » – ▣. AE ① E VISA JCB   EV f
Meals 2000/3800 and a la carte.

X **Fatâl,** Váci útca 67, ⊠ 1056, *entrance on Pintér útca* ℰ (01) 266 2607, Vaulted basement   FX e
Meals a la carte 990/3290.

t the Motorway *M 1/M 7, South 12 km* BZ – ⊠ Budapest :

🏨 **AFI H. Budapest** M, Agip útca 2, ⊠ 2040, ℰ (023) 415 500, *Fax (023) 415 505*, 🌣,
⇕s – ▮, ✕ rm, ▣ TV ☎ ⅙ ⌕ ⑫ – ⚐ 250. AE ① E VISA JCB
Meals 1700/2900 and a la carte – **160 rm** ⊐ 19100/22700, 3 suites.

Republic of Ireland

Eire

PRACTICAL INFORMATION

LOCAL CURRENCY

Punt (Irish Pound): *1 IEP = 1,27 euro (€)*

TOURIST INFORMATION

The telephone number and address of the Tourist Information office is given in the text under **🛈**.

National Holiday in the Republic of Ireland: *17 March.*

FOREIGN EXCHANGE

Banks are open between 10am and 4pm on weekdays only.
Banks in Dublin stay open to 5pm on Thursdays and banks at Dublin and Shannon airports are open on Saturdays and Sundays.

SHOPPING IN DUBLIN

In the index of street names, those printed in red are where the principal shops are found.

CAR HIRE

The international car hire companies have branches in each major city. Your hotel porter should be able to give details and help you with your arrangements.

TIPPING

Many hotels and restaurants include a service charge but where this is not the case an amount equivalent to between 10 and 15 per cent of the bill is customary. Additionally doormen, baggage porters and cloakroom attendants are generally given a gratuity.
Taxi drivers are tipped between 10 and 15 per cent of the amount shown on the meter in addition to the fare.

SPEED LIMITS

The maximum permitted speed in the Republic is 60 mph (97 km/h) except where a lower speed limit is indicated.

SEAT BELTS

The wearing of seat belts is compulsory if fitted for drivers and front seat passengers. Additionally, children under 12 are not allowed in front seats unless in a suitable safety restraint.

ANIMALS

It is forbidden to bring domestic animals (dogs, cats...) into the Republic of Ireland.

DUBLIN

(Baile Átha Cliath) *Dublin* 923 N 7 – *pop. 481 854.*

Belfast 103 – Cork 154 – Londonderry 146.

🛈 *Baggot Street Bridge, D2,* ✆ *(01) 602 4000 – Arrivals Hall, Dublin Airport – Taltaght, D24.*

🛈 *Elm Park, G & S.C., Nutley House, Donnybrook* ✆ *(01) 269 3438 –* 🛈 *Milltown, Lower Churchtown Rd,* ✆ *(01) 497 6090,* EV *–* 🛈 *Royal Dublin, North Bull Island, Dollymont,* ✆ *(01) 833 6346 NE : by R 105 –* 🛈 *Forrest Little, Cloghran* ✆ *(01) 840 1183 –* 🛈 *Lucan, Celbridge Rd, Lucan* ✆ *(01) 628 0246.*

🛬 *Dublin Airport* ✆ *(01) 844 4900, N : 5 ½ m. by N 1 – Terminal : Busaras (Central Bus Station) Store St.*

🛳 *to Holyhead (Irish Ferries) 2 daily (3 h 15 mn) – to Holyhead (Stena Line) daily (4 h) – to the Isle of Man (Douglas) (Isle of Man Steam Packet Co Ltd.) (4 h 30 mn).*

See: *City★★★ – Trinity College★★★ (Library★★★)* JY *– Chester Beatty Library★★★* FV *– Phoenix Park★★★ – Dublin Castle★★* HY *– Christ Church Cathedral★★* HY *– St. Patrick's Cathedral★★* HZ *– Marsh's Library★★* HZ *– National Museum★★ (Treasury★★),* KZ *– National Gallery★★* KZ *– Merrion Square★★* KZ *– Rotunda Hospital Chapel★★* JX *– Kilmainham Hospital★★ – Kilmainham Gaol Museum★★ – National Botanic Gardens★★ – Nº 29★* KZ D *– Liffey Bridge★* JY *– Taylors' Hall★* HY *– City Hall★* HY *– St. Audoen's Gate★* HY B *– St. Stephen's Green★* JZ *– Grafton Street★* JZ *– Powerscourt Centre★* JY *– Civic Museum★* JY M1 *– Bank of Ireland★* JYZ *– O'Connell Street★ (Anna Livia Fountain★),* JX *– St. Michan's Church★* HY E *– Hush Lane Municipal Gallery of Modern Art★* JX M4 *– Pro-Cathedral★* JX *– Garden of Remembrance★* JX *– Custom House★* KX *– Bluecoat School★ – Guinness Museum★ – Marino Casino★ – Zoological Gardens★ – Newman House★* JZ.

Envir.: *Powerscourt★★ (Waterfall★★★), S : 14 m by N 11 and R 117* EV *– Russborough House★★★, SW : 22 m by N 81 – Rathfarnham Castle★, S : 3 m by N 81 and R 115 8 T.*

DUBLIN
SOUTH EAST
BUILT UP AREA

Ailesbury Road .... FV 4
Baggot Street Upper ..... EU 7
Beech Hill Avenue ...... FV 10
Beechwood Road .... EV 12
Belgrave Road .... DV 13

Bloomfield Avenue ...... DU 18
Brighton Road .... DV 22
Camden Street .... DU 28
Castlewood Avenue ..... DV 31
Charlemont Street ...... DU 34
Charlotte Street .... DU 36
Chelmsford Road .... EV 37
Church Avenue .... FU 39
Clyde Road .... EFU 43
Eastmoreland Place ..... EU 61

Elgin Road .... EFU 6
Harrington Street ...... DU 7
Herbert Place .... EU 7
Irishtown Road .... FU 8
Lansdowne Road ...... FU 9
Lea Road .... GU 9
Leeson Street Lower .... EU 9
Leinster Road West .... DV 9
Londonbridge Road ..... FU 9
Maxwell Road .... DV 1

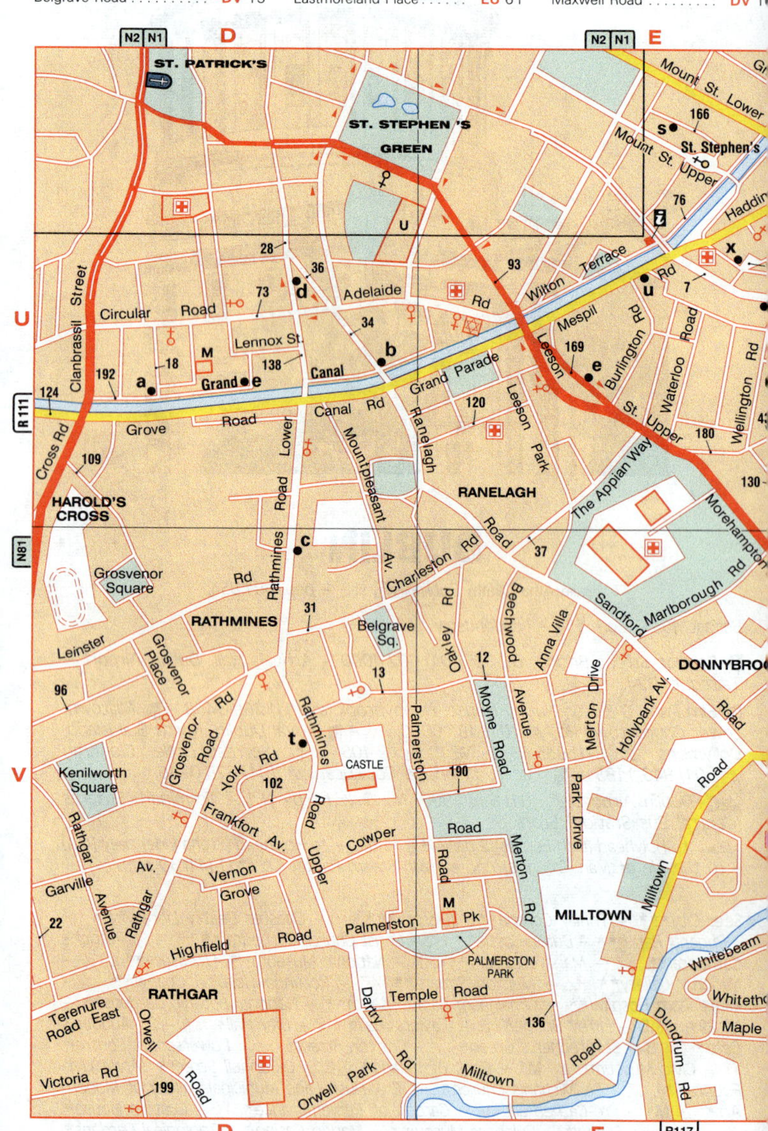

Your recommendation is self-evident if you always walk into a hotel Guide in hand.

CAR FERRY TERMINAL
IRISHTOWN
Bath St.
SEAN MOORE PARK
500 m
500 yards
Bath Avenue
Shelbourne Road
Tritonville Road
Herbert Rd
Sandymount Road
Beach Road
Claremont Rd
DUBLIN BAY
SANDYMOUNT
Gifford Rd
Gifford Av.
Gifford Pk
BALLSBRIDGE
Merrion
Anglesea
Road
Park
Strand Road
HERBERT PARK
Sandymount
Road
Pembroke Road
MARTELLO TOWER
R 131
CHESTER BEATTY LIBRARY
Shrewsbury Rd
Merrion
Road
Avenue
Parade
Strand Road
Av.
Road
Ailesbury
onnybrook Road
DODDER
Stillorgan Road
Seaview Terrace
Beaver Row
Beech Hill Rd
Greenfield Park
RTE
Nutley
Nutley Rd
Nutley Avenue
Nutley Lane
Nutley Park
Merrion Road
CLONSKEAGH
MERRION
Woodbine Road
Woodbine Av.
Trimbleston Road
R 118
N11

DUBLIN
CENTRE

Anne Street South	JYZ	6
Brunswick Street North	HX	24
Buckingham Street	KX	25
Bull Alley	HZ	27
Chancery Street	HY	33
Clanbrassil Street	HZ	40
College Green	JY	45
College Street	JY	46
Cornmarket	HY	49
Dawson Street	JYZ	
D'Olier Street	JY	51
Duke Street	JY	58
Earlsfort Terrace	JZ	60
Essex Quay	HY	66
Fishamble Street	HY	67
George's Quay	KY	69
Golden Lane	HZ	70
Grafton Street	JYZ	
Henrietta Street	HX	75
Henry Street	JX	
High Street	HY	78
Ilac Centre	HJX	
Irish Life Mall Centre	JKX	
Jervis Centre	HJX	
Kevin Street Upper	HZ	85
Kildare Street	JKZ	87
King Street South	JZ	88
Marlborough Street	JX	100
Merchants Quay	HY	103
Merrion Street	KZ	104
Montague Street	JZ	106
Mount Street Upper	KZ	112
Nicholas Street	HY	118
O'Connell Street	JX	
Parnell Square East	JX	126
Parnell Square North	JX	127
Parnell Square West	HJX	129
St Mary's Abbey Street	HY	148
St Patrick Close	HZ	150
Stephens Green	JZ	
Stephen Street	HJY	165
Tara Street	KY	171
Wellington Quay	HJY	181
Werburgh Street	HY	183
Westland Row	KY	186
Westmoreland Street	JY	187
Wexford Street	HZ	189
Winetavern Street	HY	193
Wood Quay	HY	196

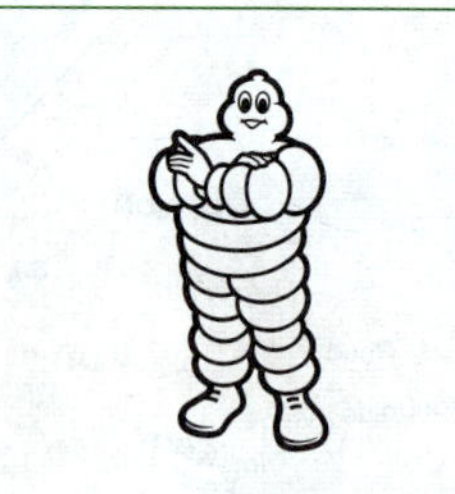

Town plans: roads most used by traffic and those on which guide-listed hotels and restaurants stand are fully drawn; the beginning only of lesser roads is indicated.

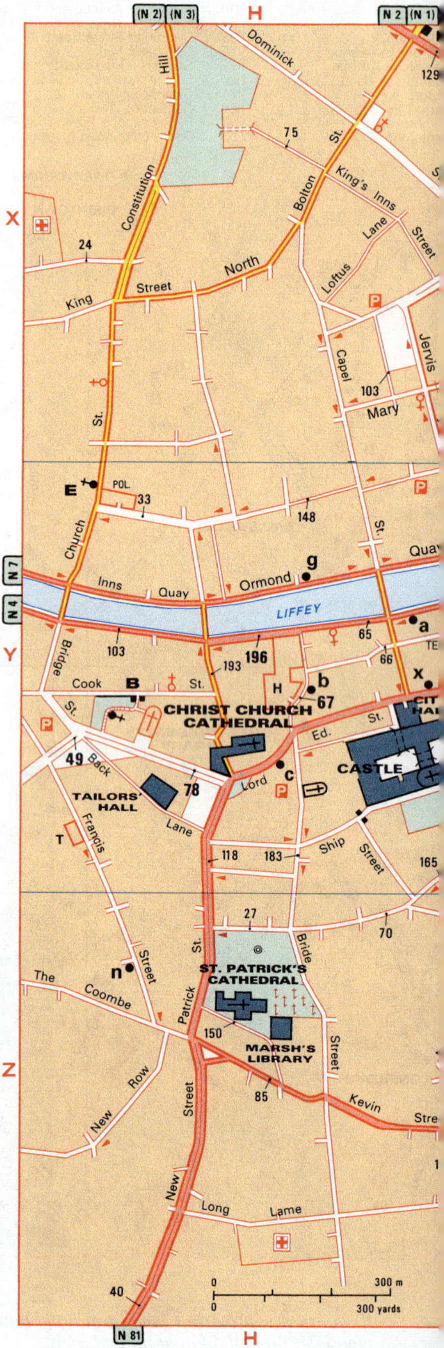

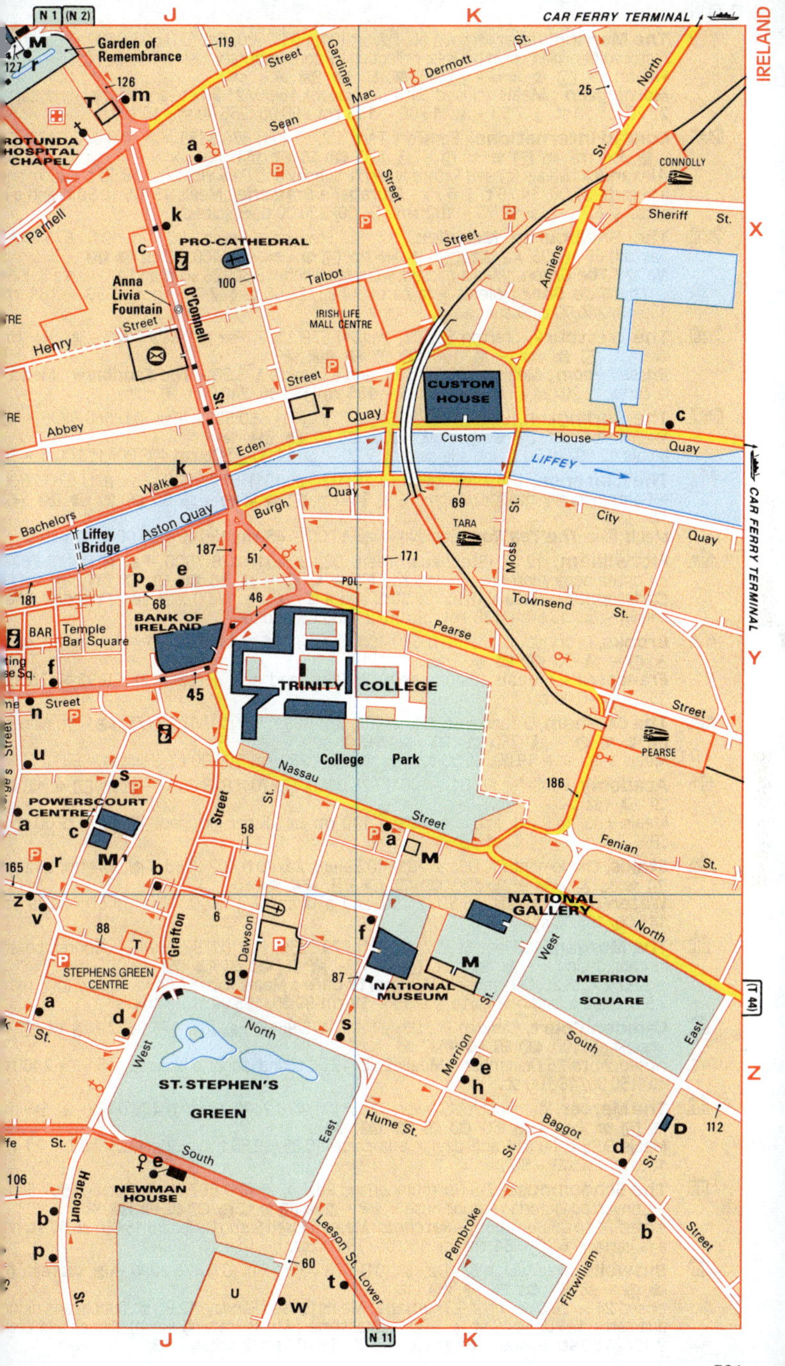

IRELAND
N 1 (N 2)
J
K
CAR FERRY TERMINAL
Garden of Remembrance
119
Street
Gardiner
Mac
Dermott
St.
M
127
126
25
North
St.
m
T
a
Sean
Street
Amiens
CONNOLLY
Sheriff
St.
X
ROTUNDA
HOSPITAL
CHAPEL
k
c
PRO-CATHEDRAL
Street
Street
Talbot
Anna
Livia
Fountain
100
O'Connell
IRISH LIFE
MALL CENTRE
c
Henry
Street
CUSTOM
HOUSE
Quay
Abbey
T
Quay
Custom
House
Quay
Eden
LIFFEY
CAR FERRY TERMINAL
k
Walk
Quay
69
TARA
St.
City
Quay
Bachelors
Aston Quay
Burgh
Moss
Liffey
Bridge
187
51
171
Townsend
St.
181
p
e
POL.
68
46
BANK OF
IRELAND
Pearse
BAR
Temple
Bar Square
f
45
TRINITY   COLLEGE
PEARSE
n
College   Park
Street
186
u
Nassau
Street
s
POWERSCOURT
CENTRE
Street
St.
Street
a
c
58
a
M
Fenian
St.
M1
r
165
b
NATIONAL
GALLERY
z
6
Dawson
North
v
West
88
T
Grafton
f
MERRION
SQUARE
STEPHENS GREEN
CENTRE
g
87
NATIONAL
MUSEUM
M
East
a
d
North
S
Merrion
West
South
e
ST. STEPHEN'S
GREEN
h
Baggot
Z
d
D
112
Hume St.
106
South
e
Pembroke
St.
b
NEWMAN
HOUSE
Leeson St. Lower
Fitzwilliam
b
p
60
t
Harcourt
U
W
J
K
N 11
(T 44)
Y

The Merrion, Upper Merrion St., D2, ℘ (01) 603 0600, *Fax (01) 603 0700*, « Carefull restored Georgian town houses, collection of contemporary Irish art », ₤, ☒, ☞ –
⇜ rm, ▤ TV ☎ ☞ – 45. ⦿ AE ⓓ VISA JCB. ※

KZ

Mornington : Meals *(closed Saturday lunch)* 16.00/23.00 **st.** and dinner a la carte 22.20/35.50 **st.** 7.50 – ☕ 13.00 – **135 rm** 190.00/255.00 **st.,** 10 suites.

Conrad International, Earlsfort Terr., D2, ℘ (01) 676 5555, *Fax (01) 676 5424,*
– |彡|, ⇜ rm, ▤ TV ☎ ☏ ℗ – 370. ⦿ AE ⓓ VISA JCB. ※

JZ

Alexandra : Meals *(closed Saturday lunch, Sunday and Bank Holidays)* 18.50 **t.** (lunch) an a la carte 27.00/34.75 **t.** 6.75 – *Plurabelle Brasserie* : Meals 15.50/18.50 **t.** and a l carte 6.75 – ☕ 12.50 – **182 rm** 195.00/220.00 **t.,** 9 suites.

The Shelbourne Meridien, 27 St. Stephen's Green, D2, ℘ (01) 676 647
Fax (01) 661 6006, ₤, ☞s, ☒ – |彡|, ⇜ rm, TV ☎ ☞ – 400. ⦿ AE ⓓ VISA

JZ

No. 27 The Green : Meals *(closed Saturday lunch)* 18.50/28.50 **t.** and a la carte 8.5
– *The Side Door* : Meals a la carte 14.95/25.00 **t.** 7.00 – ☕ 13.50 – **181 rm** 180.00/240.00 **t.,** 9 suites.

The Westbury, Grafton St., D2, ℘ (01) 679 1122, *Fax (01) 679 7078* – |彡|, ⇜ rm
▤ rest, TV ☎ ☞ – 150. ⦿ AE ⓓ VISA. ※

JY

Russell Room : Meals 15.00/27.50 **t.** and a la carte 5.90 – *The Sandbank* : Meals la carte 12.20/23.25 **t.** – ☕ 10.95 – **195 rm** 195.00/240.00 **t.,** 8 suites.

The Burlington, Upper Leeson St., D4, ℘ (01) 660 5222, *Fax (01) 660 8496* – |彡|
⇜ rm, ▤ rest, TV ☎ ℗ – 1200. ⦿ AE ⓓ VISA. ※

EU

Meals 12.00/19.50 **t.** and a la carte 7.00 – ☕ 11.00 – **506 rm** 108.00/133.00 **t.** – SB

The Clarence, 6-8 Wellington Quay, D2, ℘ (01) 670 9000, *Fax (01) 670 7800*
« Contemporary interior design » – |彡|, ⇜ rm, TV ☎ ☏ ℗ – 60. ⦿ AE ⓓ VISA JCB
※

HY

Meals (see *The Tea Room* below) – ☕ 14.00 – **45 rm** 180.00/195.00 **t.,** 4 suites.

Fitzwilliam, 12 St. Stephens Green, D2, ℘ (01) 478 7000, *Fax (01) 478 7878*
« Contemporary interior » – ⇜ rm, TV ☎ ☏ ℗ – 80. ⦿ AE ⓓ VISA. ※ JZ

Christopher's : Meals 18.95/22.50 **t.** and a la carte 11.00 (see also *Peacock Alle* below) – ☕ 13.50 – **128 rm** 190.00/210.00 **t.,** 2 suites.

Brooks, Drury St., D2, ℘ (01) 670 4000, *Fax (01) 670 4455* – |彡|, ⇜ rm, ▤ TV ☎
☞ ℗ – 70. ⦿ AE VISA. ※

JY

Francesca's : Meals (dinner only) 21.95 **t.** and a la carte – ☕ 10.95 – **75 rm** 135.00/210.00 **t.**

The Gresham, O'Connell St., D1, ℘ (01) 874 6881, *Fax (01) 878 7175*, ₤ – |彡|, ▤ rest
TV ☎ ☏ ℗ – 250. ⦿ AE ⓓ VISA. ※

JX

Meals a la carte 19.00/35.00 **t.** – ☕ 15.00 – **282 rm** 200.00 **t.,** 6 suites – SB.

Academy, Findlater Pl., D1, ℘ (01) 878 0666, *Fax (01) 878 0600* – |彡| ▤ TV ☎ ☏ ⦿
AE ⓓ VISA JCB

JX

Meals 9.95/14.95 **st.** and a la carte – **100 rm** ☕ (dinner included) 109.00/129.00 **st.** SB.

Stakis, Charlemont Pl., D2, ℘ (01) 402 9988, *Fax (01) 402 9966* – |彡|, ⇜ rm, ▤ rest
TV ☎ ☏ ☞ – 300. ⦿ AE ⓓ VISA JCB. ※

DU

Waterfront : Meals 15.50/21.50 and a la carte 5.50 – ☕ 11.50 – **189 rm** 145.00/185.00 **st.**

The Morgan, 10 Fleet St., D2, ℘ (01) 679 3939, *Fax (01) 679 3946*, « Contemporar
interior design » – |彡|, ▤ rest, TV ☎ ☏ – 30. ⦿ AE ⓓ VISA. ※ JY

closed 24 to 26 December – *All Sports Cafe* : Meals *(closed Good Friday)* (grill rest 7.95/10.00 **t.** and a la carte 7.95 – **59 rm** 99.00/155.00 **st.,** 2 suites.

Camden Court, Camden St., D2, ℘ (01) 475 9666, *Fax (01) 475 9677* – |彡| ▤ TV
☞ – 100. ⦿ AE ⓓ VISA. ※

DU

closed 24 to 26 December – Meals 9.50/12.00 **t.** and dinner a la carte 5.50 – **246 rm** ☕ 150.00/180.00 **st.**

The Mercer, Mercer Street Lower, D2, ℘ (01) 478 2179, *Fax (01) 478 0328* – |彡|, ⇜ rm
▤ TV ☎ ☞ – 50. ⦿ AE ⓓ VISA. ※

JZ

Meals 9.95 **t.** (lunch) and dinner a la carte 10.85/19.85 **t.** 5.95 – ☕ 7.00 – **21 rm** 100.00/132.00 – SB.

The Schoolhouse, 2-8 Northumberland Rd, D4, ℘ (01) 667 5014, *Fax (01) 667 501*
« Converted Victorian schoolhouse », ☞ – |彡| ▤ TV ☎ ☏ ℗. ⦿ AE ⓓ VISA. ※ EU

closed 24 to 26 December – *Satchels* : Meals *(closed Saturday lunch)* 15.00/26.00 **st.** an a la carte 6.00 – **31 rm** ☕ 150.00/180.00 **st.**

Buswells, Molesworth St., D2, ℘ (01) 676 4013, *Fax (01) 676 2090* – |彡|, ▤ rest, T
☎ ℗ – 80. ⦿ AE ⓓ VISA. ※

KZ

closed 24 to 26 December – *Trumans* : Meals *(closed Sunday)* 12.95 **st.** (lunch) and dinne a la carte 18.20/34.40 **st.** 6.00 – *Brasserie* : Meals (carving lunch)/dinner a la cart 9.40/24.50 **st.** 6.00 – **67 rm** ☕ 99.00/160.00 **st.,** 2 suites – SB.

Ormond, 7-11 Upper Ormond Quay, D7, ✆ (01) 872 1811, *Fax (01) 872 1362* – |♯| TV ☎ 📞. M◎ AE VISA. ⇗
HY g
closed 23 to 27 December – **Meals** 12.50/16.50 **t.** and a la carte ⁑ 6.95 – **60 rm** ⌷ 70.00/150.00 **st.** – SB.

Cassidys, Cavendish Row, Upper O'Connell St., D1, ✆ (01) 878 0555, *Fax (01) 878 0687* – |♯|, ⇥ rm, TV ☎ 📞 – ⚘ 80. M◎ AE ◍ VISA. ⇗
JX m
closed 24 to 27 December – **Meals** 13.95 **st.** (dinner) and a la carte 10.75/22.40 **st.** ⁑ 4.95 – **73 rm** ⌷ 75.00/105.00 **st.**, 1 suite.

Jurys Custom House Inn, Custom House Quay, D1, ✆ (01) 607 5000, *Fax (01) 829 0400*, ⌧ – |♯|, ⇥ rm, TV ☎ 📞 ⅙ – ⚘ 100. M◎ AE ◍ VISA. ⇗
KX c
closed 24 to 26 December – **Meals** (bar lunch)/dinner 14.50 **st.** and a la carte – ⌷ 6.00 – **239 rm** 62.00 **t.**

Holiday Inn Dublin, 99-107 Pearse St., D2, ✆ (01) 670 3666, *Fax (01) 670 3636*, ⌧, ⇌s – |♯|, ⇥ rm, 🗐 rest, TV ☎ ⅙ 🚗 – ⚘ 40. M◎ AE ◍ VISA. ⇗
Meals 10.50/15.95 **t.** and a la carte – ⌷ 8.95 – **90 rm** 119.00/139.00 **st.** – SB.

Russell Court, 21-25 Harcourt St., D2, ✆ (01) 478 4066, *Fax (01) 478 1576* – |♯| TV ☎ Ⓟ – ⚘ 150. M◎ AE ◍ VISA. ⇗
JZ p
closed 23 to 26 December – **Meals** 11.95/19.00 **st.** and dinner a la carte ⁑ 6.00 – ⌷ 6.95 – **41 rm** 70.00/95.00 **t.**, 6 suites – SB.

George Frederic Handel, 16-18 Fishamble St., Christchurch, D2, ✆ (01) 670 9400, *Fax (01) 670 9410* – |♯|, 🗐 rest TV ☎. M◎ AE ◍ VISA. ⇗
HY b
closed 24 to 27 December – **Meals** a la carte approx. 16.95 **st.** ⁑ 7.00 – **40 rm** ⌷ 90.00/130.00 **st.**

Adams Trinity, 28 Dame St., D2, ✆ (01) 670 7100, *Fax (01) 670 7101* – |♯| TV ☎ 📞. M◎ AE ◍ VISA. ⇗
JY n
closed 24 to 26 December – **Meals** 10.95 **t.** (dinner) and a la carte 14.50/15.50 **t.** ⁑ 5.50 – **28 rm** ⌷ 75.00/120.00 **st.** – SB.

Central, 1-5 Exchequer St., D2, ✆ (01) 679 7302, *Fax (01) 679 7303* – |♯|, 🗐 rest, TV ☎ 📞 – ⚘ 80. M◎ AE ◍ VISA JCB. ⇗
JY u
closed 23 to 26 December – **Meals** (bar lunch)/dinner a la carte 14.50/23.00 **t.** ⁑ 4.95 – **68 rm** ⌷ 99.00/142.00 **st.**, 2 suites – SB.

Stephen's Hall, Earlsfort Centre, 14-17 Lower Leeson St., D2, ✆ (01) 638 1111, *Fax (01) 638 1122* – |♯| ⇥ TV ☎ 📞 🚗. M◎ AE ◍ VISA. ⇗
JZ t
restricted service 24 to 30 December – **Meals** (see **Morels at Stephen's Hall** below) – ⌷ 8.00 – **3 rm** 130.00/160.00 **st.**, **34 suites** 160.00 **st.**

Bewley's Principal, 19-20 Fleet St., D2, ✆ (01) 670 8122, *Fax (01) 670 8103* – |♯|, ⇥ rm TV ☎. M◎ AE ◍ VISA. ⇗
JY d
closed 24 to 26 December – **Meals** (dinner only) 15.00 **st.** – ⌷ 6.00 – **70 rm** 78.00/98.00 **st.** – SB.

Temple Bar, Fleet St., D2, ✆ (01) 677 3333, *Fax (01) 677 3088* – |♯| TV ☎ Ⓟ – ⚘ 75. M◎ AE ◍ VISA. ⇗
JY e
closed 24 to 26 December – **Meals** 10.50/17.00 **st.** and a la carte – **126 rm** ⌷ 100.00/130.00 **st.**, 1 suite – SB.

Grafton Plaza, Johnsons Pl., Lower Stephens St., D2, ✆ (01) 475 0888, *Fax (01) 475 0908* – |♯| TV ☎. M◎ AE ◍ VISA. ⇗
JZ v
closed 23 to 26 December – **Meals** (grill rest.) (dinner only) a la carte 14.25/23.00 **st.** – ⌷ 8.50 – **75 rm** 105.00/120.00 **st.**

Mespil, 50-60 Mespil Rd, D4, ✆ (01) 667 1222, *Fax (01) 667 1244* – |♯|, ⇥ rm, TV ☎ 📞 Ⓟ – ⚘ 50. M◎ AE ◍ VISA. ⇗
EU u
closed 24 to 26 December – **Meals** (bar lunch)/dinner a la carte 16.85/24.45 **st.** ⁑ 7.50 – ⌷ 8.50 – **153 rm** 85.00 **st.** – SB.

Drury Court, 28-30 Lower Stephens St., D2, ✆ (01) 475 1988, *Fax (01) 478 5730* – |♯|, ⇥ rm TV ☎. M◎ AE ◍ VISA. ⇗
JYZ z
closed 24 to 26 December – **Meals** (bar lunch)/dinner a la carte 15.20/21.35 **t.** ⁑ 5.00 – **32 rm** ⌷ 90.00/150.00 **t.** – SB.

Jurys Christchurch Inn, Christchurch Pl., D8, ✆ (01) 454 0000, *Fax (01) 454 0012* – |♯|, ⇥ rm, 🗐 rest, TV ☎ ⅙ Ⓟ. M◎ AE ◍ VISA. ⇗
HY c
closed 24 to 26 December – **Meals** (bar lunch)/dinner 15.50 **st.** and a la carte – ⌷ 6.50 – **182 rm** 62.00 **st.**

Arlington, 23-25 Bachelors Walk, D1, ✆ (01) 804 9100, *Fax (01) 804 9112* – |♯| TV ☎ – ⚘ 35. M◎ AE VISA. ⇗
JY k
Meals (bar lunch)/dinner a la carte 12.95/21.40 **t.** – **115 rm** ⌷ 90.00/120.00 **st.**

Trinity Arch, 46-49 Dame St., D2, ✆ (01) 679 4455, *Fax (01) 679 4511* – |♯| TV ☎. M◎ VISA. ⇗
JY f
Meals (bar lunch)/dinner a la carte 12.85/20.65 **t.** ⁑ 6.00 – **29 rm** ⌷ 75.00/110.00 **st.**

XXXX
✿✿ **Patrick Guilbaud,** 21 Upper Merrion St., D2, ℘ (01) 676 4192, Fax (01) 661 0052, 🌿
« Contemporary Irish Art collection » – 🍽. **MC** **AE** **①** **VISA**   KZ
closed Sunday, Monday, 17 March, Good Friday and 1 week January – **Meals** 20.00 st
(lunch) and a la carte 42.00/64.00 **st.** 🍸 15.00
Spec. Poached Connemara lobster with apple and lemon jus. Roast new seaso
Wicklow lamb with oriental spices. Croustillant of spiced pineapple with a ginge
sorbet.

XXX **The Commons,** Newman House, 85-86 St. Stephen's Green, D2, ℘ (01) 478 0530
Fax (01) 478 0551, « Contemporary collection of James Joyce inspired Irish Art » – **M**
AE **①** **VISA**   JZ
closed Saturday lunch, Sunday, 1 week Christmas and Bank Holidays – **Meal**
20.00/35.00 **st.** and a la carte 🍸 9.00.

XXX **Thornton's,** 1 Portobello Rd, D8, ℘ (01) 454 9067, Fax (01) 453 2947 – 🍽. **MC** **AE** **①**
✿ **VISA**   DU
closed Sunday, Monday and 2 weeks Christmas-New Year – **Meals** (booking essential) (din
ner only and lunch Thursday-Friday) 22.00 **t.** (lunch) and a la carte 37.45/45.45 t
🍸 10.00
Spec. Sautéed foie gras with scallops, celeriac and cep jus. Suckling pig with trotter, Maxin
potatoes and poitin jus. Nougat pyramid with glazed fruit and orange sauce.

XXX **Peacock Alley** (Gallagher) (at Fitzwilliam H.), St. Stephen's Green, D2, ℘ (01) 478 7015
✿ *Fax (01) 478 7025 –* 🍽 **P.** **MC** **AE** **①** **VISA**   JZ
closed Sunday, 25 December and Bank Holidays – **Meals** 18.95 **t.** (lunch) and a la cart
29.85/42.40 **t.** 🍸 12.00
Spec. Roast scallops, grilled aubergine and coconut cream. Terrine of foie gras with pai
d'épices, salad of truffles and apricots. Loin of lamb wrapped in leeks, ratatouille, polent
and thyme jus.

XX **The Tea Room** (at The Clarence H.), 6-8 Wellington Quay, D2, ℘ (01) 670 7766
Fax (01) 670 7800 – **MC** **AE** **①** **VISA** **JCB**   HY
closed lunch Saturday, Sunday and Bank Holidays – **Meals** (booking essential) 18.50 st
(lunch) and a la carte 24.50/42.00 **st.** 🍸 12.50.

XX **Chapter One,** The Dublin Writers Museum, 18-19 Parnell Sq., D1, ℘ (01) 873 2266
☺ *Fax (01) 873 2330 –* 🍽 **P.** **MC** **AE** **①** **VISA**   JX
closed Saturday lunch, Monday dinner, Sunday, 24 December-7 January and Bank Holiday
– **Meals** 14.50 **t.** (lunch) and dinner a la carte 23.00/25.50 **t.**

XX **Saagar,** 16 Harcourt St., D2, ℘ (01) 475 5060, Fax (01) 475 5741 – **MC** A
① **VISA**
closed Saturday and Sunday lunch, 25 December and 1 January – **Meals** - Indian
7.70/19.00 **t.** and a la carte 🍸 9.25.   JZ

XX **L'Ecrivain,** 109 Lower Baggot St., D2, ℘ (01) 661 1919, Fax (01) 661 0617, 🌿 – 🍽
☺ **MC** **AE** **①** **VISA**   KZ
closed Saturday lunch, Sunday, 10 days Christmas and Bank Holidays – **Meals** (bookin
essential) 15.50/25.00 **t.** and dinner a la carte approx. 34.50 **t.** 🍸 7.00.

XX **Les Frères Jacques,** 74 Dame St., D2, ℘ (01) 679 4555, Fax (01) 679 4725 – **MC** A
① **VISA**   HY
closed Saturday lunch, Sunday, 24 December-2 January and Bank Holidays – **Meals** - Frenc
- 13.50/21.00 **t.** and dinner a la carte 🍸 5.50.

XX **Morels at Stephen's Hall,** 14-17 Lower Leeson St., D2, ℘ (01) 662 2480
☺ *Fax (01) 662 8595 –* 🍽. **MC** **AE** **①** **VISA**   JZ
closed Saturday lunch, Sunday and 6 days Christmas – **Meals** (booking essentia
13.95/25.00 **t.** and dinner a la carte 18.40/28.65 **t.** 🍸 9.50.

XX **Locks,** 1 Windsor Terr., Portobello, D8, ℘ (01) 4543391, Fax (01) 4538352 – **MC** **AE** **①**
VISA   DU
closed Saturday lunch, Sunday, last week July-first week August, 25 December-5 Januar
and Bank Holidays – **Meals** 15.95/26.50 **t.** and a la carte 🍸 10.95.

XX **Old Dublin,** 90-91 Francis St., D8, ℘ (01) 4542028, Fax (01) 4541406 – **MC** A
① **VISA**   HZ
closed Saturday lunch, Sunday and Bank Holidays – **Meals** - Russian-Scandinavian
12.00/21.50 **t.** and dinner a la carte 🍸 7.80.

XX **La Stampa,** 35 Dawson St., D2, ℘ (01) 677 8611, Fax (01) 677 3336, « 19C forme
ballroom » – 🍽. **MC** **AE** **①** **VISA**   JZ
closed lunch Saturday and Sunday, Good Friday and 25-26 December – **Meals** a la cart
11.10/30.95 **t.** 🍸 8.00.

XX **Eden,** Meeting House Sq., Templebar, D2, ℘ (01) 670 5372, Fax (01) 670 3330, 🌿
🍽. **MC** **AE**   HY
closed 25 December and Bank Holidays – **Meals** 15.00 **t.** (lunch) and dinner a la cart
17.00/26.00 **t.** 🍸 6.00.

✗ **Jacobs Ladder,** 4-5 Nassau St., D2, ℰ (01) 670 3865, *Fax (01) 670 3868* – **MC AE D VISA**
KY a
closed Sunday, Monday, 17 March and 25 December-15 January – **Meals** a la carte 20.75/28.95 **st.** 🍷 9.50.

✗ **Cooke's Café,** 14 South William St., D2, ℰ (01) 679 0536, *Fax (01) 679 0546,* 🌐 – 🔲. **MC AE D VISA**
JY c
Meals 18.00 **st.** (lunch) and a la carte 35.00/50.00 **st.** 🍷 7.00.

✗ **Muscat,** 64 South William St., D2, ℰ (01) 679 7699 – **MC AE VISA**
JY s
closed Sunday, Monday, 10 days Christmas and New Year and 2 weeks in summer – **Meals** a la carte 19.15/28.70 **t.** 🍷 6.50.

✗ **Lloyds Brasserie,** 20 Upper Merrion St., D2, ℰ (01) 662 7240, *Fax (01) 662 7243* – 🔲. **MC AE D VISA**
KZ h
closed 25 December and 1 January – **Meals** 13.50 **t.** (lunch) and a la carte 18.85/30.85 **t.** 🍷 9.50.

✗ **Mermaid Cafe,** 69-70 Dame St., D2, ℰ (01) 670 8236, *Fax (01) 670 8205* – 🔲. **MC VISA**
closed Sunday dinner and Christmas-New Year – **Meals** a la carte 18.95/28.20 🍷 8.50.
HY d

✗ **Rhino Room,** 14a South William St., D2, ℰ (01) 670 5260, *Fax (01) 679 0546* – 🔲. **MC AE D VISA JCB**
JY c
Meals a la carte 20.00/30.00 **st.**

✗ **Dobbin's,** 15 Stephen's Lane, off Lower Mount St., D2, ℰ (01) 676 4679, *Fax (01) 661 3331,* 🌐 – 🔲 **P. MC AE D VISA**
EU s
closed Saturday lunch, Monday dinner, Sunday and Bank Holidays – **Meals** - Bistro - (booking essential) 15.50/30.00 **t.** and a la carte 🍷 6.75.

Ballsbridge

Dublin 4.

🏨 **Berkeley Court,** Lansdowne Rd, D4, ℰ (01) 660 1711, *Fax (01) 661 7238,* ⅃₆ – 🛗, ⇆ rm, 🔲 rest, 📺 ☎ 📞 🚗 **P.** – 🎓 450. **MC AE D VISA**. ✗
FU c
Berkeley Room : **Meals** 17.95/29.95 **t.** and a la carte 🍷 6.75 – ***Conservatory Grill*** : **Meals** a la carte 12.95/24.65 **t.** 🍷 6.90 – ☕ 10.75 – **183 rm** 165.00/185.00 **t.**, 5 suites – SB.

🏨 **The Towers,** Lansdowne Rd, D4, ℰ (01) 667 0033, *Fax (01) 660 5540,* ⅃₆, ⇌s, ⛲ heated – 🛗, ⇆ rm, 🔲 📺 ☎ ⅒ **P.** **MC AE D VISA**. ✗
FU p
☕ 13.40 – **100 rm** 190.00/220.00 **t.**, 4 suites – SB.

🏨 **Jurys** (at The Towers H.), Pembroke Rd, D4, ℰ (01) 660 5000, *Fax (01) 660 5540,* ⅃₆, ⇌s, ⛲ heated – 🛗, ⇆ rm, 🔲 rest, 📺 ☎ ⅒ **P.** – 🎓 850. **MC AE D VISA**. ✗
FU p
Raglans : **Meals** 18.00/25.00 **t.** and a la carte 🍷 6.00 – ☕ 10.75 – **290 rm** 155.00/195.00 **t.**, 3 suites – SB.

🏨 **Herbert Park,** , D4, ℰ (01) 667 2200, *Fax (01) 667 2595,* 🌐, ⅃₆ – 🛗, ⇆ rm, 🔲 📺 ☎ 📞 **P.** – 🎓 180. **MC AE D VISA**. ✗
FU m
The Pavilion : **Meals** 17.50/27.50 **st.** and dinner a la carte 🍷 8.50 – ☕ 11.50 – **150 rm** 150.00/185.00 **t.**, 3 suites.

🏨 **The Hibernian,** Eastmoreland Pl., D4, ℰ (01) 668 7666, *Fax (01) 660 2655* – 🛗, ⇆ rm, 📺 ☎ 📞 **P.** **MC AE D VISA JCB**. ✗
EU x
closed 25 and 26 December – ***Patrick Kavanagh Room*** : **Meals** (*closed Saturday lunch and Sunday dinner to non-residents*) 14.95/29.50 **t.** 🍷 8.50 – **40 rm** ☕ 120.00/185.00 **st.** – SB.

🏨 **Ariel House** without rest., 52 Lansdowne Rd, D4, ℰ (01) 668 5512, *Fax (01) 668 5845,* 🌿 – ⇆ 📺 ☎ **P.** **MC VISA**. ✗
FU n
closed 24 December-12 January – ☕ 8.50 – **28 rm** 70.00/170.00 **t.**

🏠 **Butlers Town House,** 44 Lansdowne Rd, D4, ℰ (01) 667 4022, *Fax (01) 667 3960* – 🔲 📺 ☎ 📞 **P.** **MC AE D VISA**. ✗
FU v
closed 24 to 27 December – **Meals** (room service only) – **19 rm** ☕ 96.00/143.00 **st.**

✗✗✗ **Le Coq Hardi,** 35 Pembroke Rd, D4, ℰ (01) 668 9070, *Fax (01) 668 9887* – **P.** **MC AE D VISA JCB**
EU m
closed Saturday lunch, Sunday, 2 weeks August and 2 weeks Christmas – **Meals** 21.00/35.00 **t.** and a la carte 🍷 8.00.

✗✗ **Fitzers,** RDS, Merrion Rd, D4, ℰ (01) 667 1301, *Fax (01) 667 1303,* « Located in east wing of Royal Dublin Society » – **P.** **MC AE D VISA**
FU a
closed Sunday dinner, 25-26 December and Bank Holidays – **Meals** (booking essential) a la carte 27.50/34.50 **t.** 🍷 8.95.

✗ **Roly's Bistro,** 7 Ballsbridge Terr., D4, ℰ (01) 668 2611, *Fax (01) 660 8535* – 🔲. **MC AE D VISA**
FU r
closed Good Friday and 25 to 27 December – **Meals** (booking essential) 12.50 **t.** (lunch) and dinner a la carte 19.80/25.65 **t.** 🍷 5.25.

IRELAND

Donnybrook
Dublin 4.

XX **Ernie's,** Mulberry Gdns., off Morehampton Rd, D4, ℰ (01) 269 3300, *Fax (01) 269 3266*
« Contemporary Irish Art collection » – ▣. 〇〇 ⒶⒺ 〇 ⱽⁱˢᴬ   FV
closed Sunday, Monday and 1 week Christmas – **Meals** 14.25/25.00 **t.** and a la cart
28.20/38.10 **t.** ⓑ 8.00.

Drumcondra
Dublin 5.

🏨 **Doyle Skylon,** Upper Drumcondra Rd, D9, *North : 2 ½ m. on N 1* ℰ (01) 837 912
Fax (01) 837 2778 – |≑|, ⟳ rm, ▤ rest, ⓉⓋ ☎ ⓖ ⓟ. 〇〇 ⒶⒺ 〇 ⱽⁱˢᴬ. ⌦
Meals 12.00/16.00 **t.** and a la carte ⓑ 5.60 – ⌇ 7.35 – **88 rm** 95.00/115.00 **t.** – SB.

Merrion
Dublin 6.

🏨 **Doyle Tara,** Merrion Rd, D4, *Southeast : 4 m. on R 118* ℰ (01) 269 4666
Fax (01) 269 1027 – |≑|, ▤ rest, ⓉⓋ ☎ ⓖ ⓟ – ⚑ 300. 〇〇 ⒶⒺ 〇 ⱽⁱˢᴬ. ⌦   GV
Meals 17.00 **t.** (dinner) and a la carte 15.45/20.00 ⓑ 6.00 – ⌇ 7.35 – **114 rm**
95.00/115.00 **t.** – SB.

Rathmines
Dublin 6.

🏨 **Rathmines Plaza,** Lower Rathmines Rd, D6, ℰ (01) 496 6966, *Fax (01) 491 0603 –*
ⓉⓋ ☎ ⓖ ⓟ. 〇〇 ⒶⒺ 〇 ⱽⁱˢᴬ. ⌦   DV
closed 24 to 26 December – **Meals** (carving lunch) 8.50/14.50 **st.** and dinner a la cart
– **54 rm** ⌇ 70.00/90.00 **st.** – SB.

XX **Zen,** 89 Upper Rathmines Rd, D6, ℰ (01) 4979428 – ▣. 〇〇 ⒶⒺ 〇 ⱽⁱˢᴬ   DV
closed lunch Monday to Wednesday, Saturday and 25 to 27 December – **Meals** - Chines
(Szechuan) - a la carte 12.00/21.00 **t.** ⓑ 6.00.

Terenure
Dublin 4.

XX **Popjoys,** 4 Rathfarnham Rd, D6, *South : 3 m. on N 81* ℰ (01) 492 934
Fax (01) 492 9293 – ▣. 〇〇 ⒶⒺ 〇 ⱽⁱˢᴬ
closed Saturday lunch, Sunday dinner, Monday, Good Friday and 25-26 December – **Mea**
12.95 **t.** (lunch) and a la carte 16.50/29.50 **t.** ⓑ 6.75.

at Clontarf *Northeast : 3 ½ m. by R 105* KX – ✉ *Dublin*

🏰 **Clontarf Castle,** Castle Av., D3, ℰ (01) 853 2321, *Fax (01) 833 0418,* « Part 18C »
|≑| ⓉⓋ ☎ ⓖ ⓟ – ⚑ 550. 〇〇 ⒶⒺ 〇 ⱽⁱˢᴬ. ⌦
closed 25 December – **Templars Bistro :** **Meals** (bar lunch Saturday) 14.50/23.50 **st.** ar
dinner a la carte ⓑ 6.50 – ⌇ 9.95 – **111 rm** 119.00/145.00 **st.** – SB.

at Blackrock *Southeast : 5 ½ m. by R 118* GV – ✉ *Dublin*

X **Ayumi-Ya,** Newpark Centre, Newtownpark Av., *Southeast : 1 ¼ m. on R 113* ℰ (0
283 1767, *Fax (01) 288 0478* – ▣. 〇〇 ⒶⒺ 〇 ⱽⁱˢᴬ
closed 1 January, Good Friday and 24-25 December – **Meals** - Japanese - (dinner onl
12.95 **t.** and a la carte ⓑ 6.45.

at Tallaght *Southwest : 7 ½ m. by N 81* DV – ✉ *Dublin*

🏨 **Abberley Court,** Belgard Rd, D24, *on R 113* ℰ (01) 459 6000, *Fax (01) 462 1000 –*
⟳ rm, ⓉⓋ ☎ ⓖ ⇔ – ⚑ 200. 〇〇 ⒶⒺ 〇 ⱽⁱˢᴬ. ⌦
closed 25 and 26 December – **Meals** (*closed lunch Saturday and Sunday and Bank Holiday*
12.95/16.95 **st.** ⓑ 6.95 – **40 rm** ⌇ 79.00/98.00 **st.** – SB.

at Saggart *Southwest : 9 ¼ m. off N 7* HY – ✉ *Dublin*

🏰 **Citywest,** ℰ (01) 458 8566, *Fax (01) 458 8565,* ⅃₆, ≋ₛ, ┌₁₈, ↘, ⚑, *park* – |≑|, ▤ res
ⓉⓋ ☎ ⓒ ⓖ ⓟ – ⚑ 600. 〇〇 ⒶⒺ 〇 ⱽⁱˢᴬ. ⌦
Meals 13.95/24.95 **t.** ⓑ 6.50 – **200 rm** ⌇ 99.00/180.00 **st.** – SB.

to the Southeast :

🏰 **Radisson SAS St. Helen's,** Stillorgan Rd, *Southeast : 4 ½ m. on N 11* ℰ (01) 218 600
Fax (01) 260 2295, « Part 18C », ⅃₆, ⚑ – ▤ ⓉⓋ ☎ ⓒ ⓖ ⓟ – ⚑ 350. 〇〇 ⒶⒺ 〇 ⱽⁱˢᴬ ⒿⒸⒷ
Meals a la carte 24.85/33.50 **t.** – ⌇ 11.50 – **151 rm** 175.00/195.00 **st.**

🏰 **Stillorgan Park,** Stillorgan Rd, *Southeast : 5 m. on N 11* ℰ (01) 288 162
Fax (01) 283 1610 – ⟳ rm, ▤ ⓉⓋ ☎ ⓖ ⓟ – ⚑ 180. 〇〇 ⒶⒺ 〇 ⱽⁱˢᴬ. ⌦
Meals 11.95 **t.** (lunch) and dinner a la carte 16.85/24.45 **t.** ⓑ 8.00 – **99 rm**
⌇ 95.00/125.00 **st.** – SB.

 **Doyle Montrose,** Stillorgan Rd, D4, *Southeast : 4 m. by N 11* ☎ (01) 269 3311, *Fax (01) 269 1164* – |▮|, ⇥ rm, TV ☎ ✆ P – ⚓ 70. MC AE O VISA. ⚒   GV y
Meals a la carte 15.00/21.50 **t.** ⚗ 6.50 – ☕ 7.50 – **179 rm** 89.00/119.00 **t.**

to the Southwest :

 **Red Cow Moran's,** Naas Rd, D22, *Southwest : 5 m. on N 7* ☎ (01) 459 3650, *Fax (01) 459 1588* – |▮|, ⇥ rm, ▤ TV ☎ ✆ ♿ P – ⚓ 700. MC AE O VISA. ⚒
Meals 14.50/22.50 **t.** and dinner a la carte ⚗ 8.50 – **120 rm** ☕ 90.00/170.00 **t.,** 3 suites
– SB.

 **Doyle Green Isle,** Naas Rd, D22, *Southwest : 7 ¾ m. off N7 (eastbound carriageway)*
☎ (01) 459 3406, *Fax (01) 464 1532* – |▮|, ⇥ rm, TV ☎ ♿ P – ⚓ 250. MC AE O VISA.
⚒
Meals 14.00/21.00 **st.** and a la carte ⚗ 6.50 – ☕ 7.50 – **90 rm** 95.00 **t.**

 **Bewley's H. at Newlands Cross,** Newlands Cross, D22, *Southwest : 7 m. by N 7 on
R 113* ☎ (01) 464 0140, *Fax (01) 464 0900* – |▮|, ⇥ rm, ▤ rest, TV ☎ ♿ P – ⚓ 30.
MC AE O VISA. ⚒
closed 24 to 26 December – **Meals** (carving lunch) a la carte 13.50/24.50 **st.** ⚗ 7.50 –
☕ 5.50 – **200 rm** 49.00 **st.**

Sheldon Park, Kylemore Rd, D12, *Southwest : 4 ¾ m. by N 7 on R 112* ☎ (01) 460 1055,
Fax (01) 460 1880, ⚖, ≋s – |▮| TV ☎ P – ⚓ 550. MC AE O VISA. ⚒
closed 25 December – **Meals** (carving lunch)/dinner 12.95 **t.** and a la carte ⚗ 4.50 – **72 rm**
☕ 60.00/85.00 **st.** – SB.

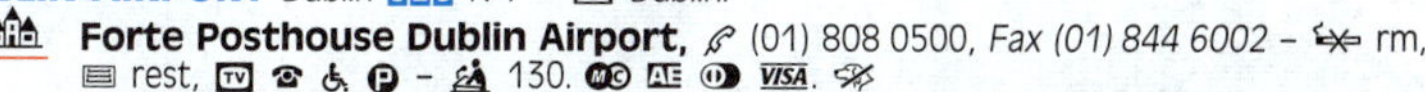 **DUBLIN AIRPORT** *Dublin* 923 *N 7* – ⊠ *Dublin.*

Forte Posthouse Dublin Airport, ☎ (01) 808 0500, *Fax (01) 844 6002* – ⇥ rm,
▤ rest, TV ☎ ♿ P – ⚓ 130. MC AE O VISA. ⚒
closed 24 and 25 December – **Bistro :** **Meals** *(closed Saturday lunch)* 11.50/18.50 **t.** and
a la carte ⚗ 6.50 – **Sampan's :** **Meals** - South East Asian - *(closed Bank Holidays)* (dinner
only) a la carte 14.25/26.95 **t.** ⚗ 6.75 – ☕ 12.00 – **249 rm** 108.00 **t.** – SB.

Great Southern, , ☎ (01) 844 6000, *Fax (01) 844 6001* – |▮|, ⇥ rm TV ☎ ✆ P –
⚓ 350. MC AE O VISA. ⚒
closed 24 and 25 December – **Potters Bistro :** **Meals** (bar lunch Monday to
Saturday)/dinner 18.00 **st.** and a la carte ⚗ 7.00 – ☕ 10.00 – **147 rm** 110.00 **st.**

Italy

Italia

PRACTICAL INFORMATION

LOCAL CURRENCY

Italian Lire: *1000 ITL = 0,52 euro (€)*

TOURIST INFORMATION

Welcome Office *(Ente Provinciale per il Turismo):*
– Via Parigi 11 - 00185 ROMA (closed Sunday), ✆ 06 488991, Fax 06 488 99 250
– Via Marconi 1 - 20123 MILANO, ✆ 02 72 52 43 00, Fax 02 72 52 43 50
See also telephone number and address of other Tourist Information offices in the text of the towns under 🛈.
American Express:
– Piazza di Spagna 38 - 00187 ROMA, ✆ 06 67641, Fax 06 67 64 24 99
– Via Brera 3 - 20121 MILANO, ✆ 02 72 00 36 96, Fax 02 86 10 28

National Holiday in Italy: *25 April.*

AIRLINES

ALITALIA: *Via Bissolati 20 - 00187 ROMA, ✆ 06 65621, Fax 06 656 28 282*
Via Albricci 5 - 20122 MILANO, ✆ 02 24992700, Fax 02 805 67 57
AIR FRANCE: *Via Sardegna 40 - 00187 ROMA, ✆ 06 48791555, Fax 06 483803*
Piazza Cavour 2 - 20121 MILANO, ✆ 02 760731, Fax 02 760 73 333
DELTA AIRLINES: *Viale Liberazione 18 - 20124 MILANO, ✆ 02 67 07 00 47, Fax 02 67 07 31 82*
TWA: *Via Barberini 67 - 00187 ROMA, ✆ 06 47241, Fax 06 474 61 25*
Corso Europa 11 - 20122 MILANO, ✆ 02 77961, Fax 02 76 01 45 83

FOREIGN EXCHANGE

Money can be changed at the Banca d'Italia, other banks and authorised exchange offices (Banks close at 1.30pm and at weekends).

POSTAL SERVICES

Local post offices: *open Monday to Saturday 8.30am to 2.00pm*
General Post Office *(open 24 hours only for telegrams):*
– Viale Europa 190 00144 ROMA – Piazza Cordusio 20123 MILANO

SHOPPING

In the index of street names, those printed in red are where the principal shops are found. In Rome, the main shopping streets are: Via del Babuino, Via Condotti, Via Frattina, Via Vittorio Veneto; in Milan: Via Dante, Via Manzoni, Via Monte Napoleone, Corso Vittorio Emanuele, Via della Spiga.

BREAKDOWN SERVICE

Certain garages in the centre and outskirts of towns operate a 24 hour breakdown service. If you break down the police are usually able to help by indicating the nearest one.
A free car breakdown service (a tax is levied) is operated by the A.C.I. for foreign motorists carrying the fuel card (Carta Carburante). The A.C.I. also offers telephone information in English (24 hours a day) for road and weather conditions and tourist events: 06 4477.

TIPPING

As well as the service charge, it is the custom to tip employees. The amount can vary depending upon the region and the service given.

SPEED LIMITS

On motorways, the maximum permitted speed is 130 km/h - 80 mph. On other roads, the speed limit is 110 km/h - 68 mph.

ROME

(ROMA) *00100* 9|8|8 ㉖ 4|3|0 *Q 19* 3|8 *– Pop. 2 653 245 – alt. 20.*

Distances from Rome are indicated in the text of the other towns listed in this Guide.

🛈 *via Parigi 5* ✉ *00185* ℘ *06 48 89 92 53, Fax 06 481 93 16 ; at Termini Station* ℘ *06 4871270 ; at Fiumicino Airport* ℘ *06 65956074.*

A.C.I. *via Cristoforo Colombo 261* ✉ *00147* ℘ *06 514 971 and via Marsala 8* ✉ *00185* ℘ *06 49981, Fax 06 499 822 34.*

🏌 *Parco de' Medici (closed Tuesday)* ✉ *00148 Roma SW : 4,5 km* ℘ *06 655 34 77 – Fax 06 655 33 44.*

🏌 *(closed Monday) at Acquasanta* ✉ *00178 Roma SE : 12 km.* ℘ *06 78 34 07, Fax 06 78 34 62 19.*

🏌 *and* 🏌 *Marco Simone (closed Tuesday) at Guidonia Montecelio* ✉ *00012 Roma W : 7 km* ℘ *0774 366 469, Fax 0774 366 476.*

🏌 🏌 *Arco di Costantino (closed Monday)* ✉ *00188 Roma N : 15 km* ℘ *06 33 62 44 40, Fax 06 33 61 29 19*

🏌 *and* 🏌 *(closed Monday) at Olgiata* ✉ *00123 Roma NW : 19 km* ℘ *06 308 89 141, Fax 06 308 89 968.*

🏌 *Fioranello (closed Wednesday) at Santa Maria delle Mole* ✉ *00040 Roma SE : 19 km* ℘ *06 713 80 80, Fax 06 713 82 12.*

✈ *Ciampino SW : 15 km* ℘ *794941 and Leonardo da Vinci di Fiumicino SE : 26 km* ℘ *06 65951 – Alitalia, via Bissolati 13* ✉ *00187* ℘ *06 65621 and via della Magliana 886* ✉ *00148* ℘ *06 65643.*

🚗 *Termini* ℘ *06 47 30 60 35.*

SIGHTS

Rome's most famous sights are listed after town plans. For a more complete visit use the Michelin Green Guide to Rome.

ROMA
NORTH CENTRE

Traffic restricted
in the town centre

ITALY

J
K
L
Milizie
V. Damiata
V. Lepanto
Cesare
Lepanto
V. Lepanto
Via
e
d
Magno
Pompeo
Michelangelo
L. A. da Brescia
111
V. Beccaria
73
Pza DEL POPOLO
V. L. di Savoia
166
Giulio
Scipioni
60
Colonna
Rienzo
Pza della Libertà
139
L. in Augusta
U
Germanico
Gracchi
di
141
Via
F. Cesi
m
b
f
L. dei Mellini
TEVERE
dei
Cola
V.
Virgilio
Via
Cicerone
V.
f
Crescenzio
c
Piazza Cavour
48
ARA PACIS AUGUSTAE
Ripetta
Piazza
Adriana
J
Ponte Cavour
c
Pio
Passetto
CASTEL
L. Prati
V. di Ripetta
onciliazione
151
SANT'ANGELO
L. Marzio
V. della Scrofa
108
P
V
Spirito
190
34
Umberto I
Ponte
L.
M
Ponte S. Angelo
L. Tor di Nona
199
g
G
m
7
195
16
Via dei Coronari
43
R
S. LUIGI D. FRANCESI
57
135
r
L.go Tassoni
142
PIAZZA
58
C.o
13
88
CHIESA NUOVA
E
PALAZZO MADAMA
V. Giulia
Vittorio
NAVONA
k
15
88
T
S
Emanuele II
M
A
142
30
J
K
L
Spirito L. in Sassia
V. dei Sangallo
Gianicolense
V. della
P
70

L
M
N
VILLA
VITERBO
Flaminio
Viale
del
Muro
PINCIO
D
Pza DEL POPOLO
166
Torto
55
P
U
in
Augusta
Mellini
TEVERE
k
y
V. di Ripetta
Via
Via
del
Margutta
Babuino
Viale d. Trinità
VILLA MEDICI
Spagna
V. di P.ta Pin
ARA PACIS AUGUSTAE
MAUSOLEO DI AUGUSTO
del
Corso
Monti
PZA DI
SPAGNA
a
TRINITÀ D. MONTI
c
V.
e
Condotti
Ponte
Ripetta
Cavour
Prati
V. di
Via
Tomacelli
Via d.
h
f
Frattina
Via
Sistina
Due
Macelli
Tritone
76
Marzio
V.
108
P
45
a
d
Via
del
g
181
Scrofa
V
PALAZZO DI MONTECITORIO
del
V.
m
u
FONTANA DI TREVI
p
QUIRIN
g
G
174
186
b
n
46
del
m
43
V.
S. LUIGI D. FRANCESI
T
PZA DEL QUIRINÂLE
142
PIAZZA
58
168
156
P
E
PALAZZO MADAMA
L
NAVONA
PANTHEON
Corso
147
v
M
X
k
153
201
r
d
M5
19
201
142
180
P
L
M
N

ITALY

O
P
U
V
X
BORGHESE
Borghese
Museo
d.
Viale
Via
Pincianna
Via Po
Corso
d' Italia
Campania
P^za Fiume
94
27
Co.
d' Italia
PORTA PIA
V. Po
V.
Tevere
Salaria
V.
Nizza
a
d
x
Brasile
zale
V. Vitorio Veneto
n
w
p
a
d
Piemonte
Via
Boncompagni
q
Via
Collina
Plave
Ludovisi
m
t
c
Via
Sallustiana
c
m
Montebello
Vittorio Veneto
V.
L. Bissolati
h
Settembre
20
Via
Barberini
Via
P
S. MARIA D.
VITTORIA
MUSEO NAZIONALE
ROMANO
198
Barberini
Via
f
S. SUSANNA
c
i
P
b
196
N
P
PALAZZO
BARBERINI
Via
delle
Via
P^za della
Repubblica
Piazza dei
Cinquecento
61
Quattro
K
h
Fontane
T
TERMINI
F
138
b
V.
A.
V. del Viminale
y
p
w
POL.
Via
Cavour
r
Nazionale
Depretis
k
Principe
V.
g
c
m
P^za d. Esquilino
S. MARIA
MAGGIORE
s
T
Milano
Via
Panisperna
Cavour
160
Via
z
h
Amadeo
d
0   200 m

ROMA
SOUTH CENTRE

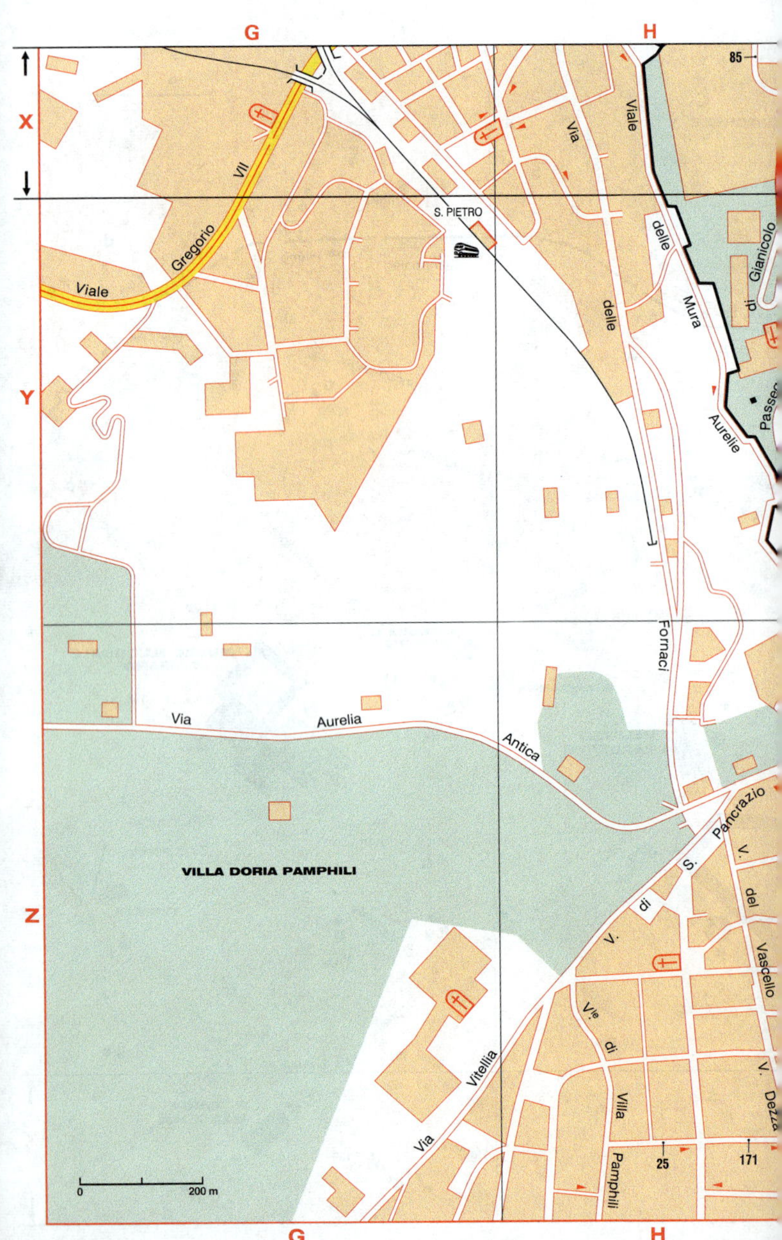

NAVONA
Emanuele II
Giulia
PAL. FARNESE
VILLA FARNESINA
GIANICOLO
PAL. SPADA
TEVERE
Tebaldi
Farnesina
della
dei
P.te Mazzini
Lungara
Gianicolense
V. della
Sangallo
P.te Sisto
Vitt.
V. dei Giubbonari
Arenula
Vallati
ISO
R. Sanzio
Scala
V. d.
S. PIETRO IN MONTORIO
Garibaldi
Medici
V. G.
Via
Rossetti
V. Bassi
Dandolo
V.le Dandolo
Via Glorioso
Viale
Manara
V. L.
Mameli
V. G.
P.za S. Cosimato
V. E. Morosini
V. di S. Francesco
Francesco a Ripa
Trastevere
Via
Via G. Induno
P.za S. Francesco d' Assisi
P.za di P.ta Portese
Porto
P.te Sublicio
TEVERE
TRASTEVERE
P.za S. Sonnino
Lucce
Co
Pass. di Gianicolo
M
A
Q
S
T
b
c
k
m
q
r
t
u
v
15
30
28
103
106
142
88
81
96
21
10
96
114
192
105
202
150
150
129
132
178

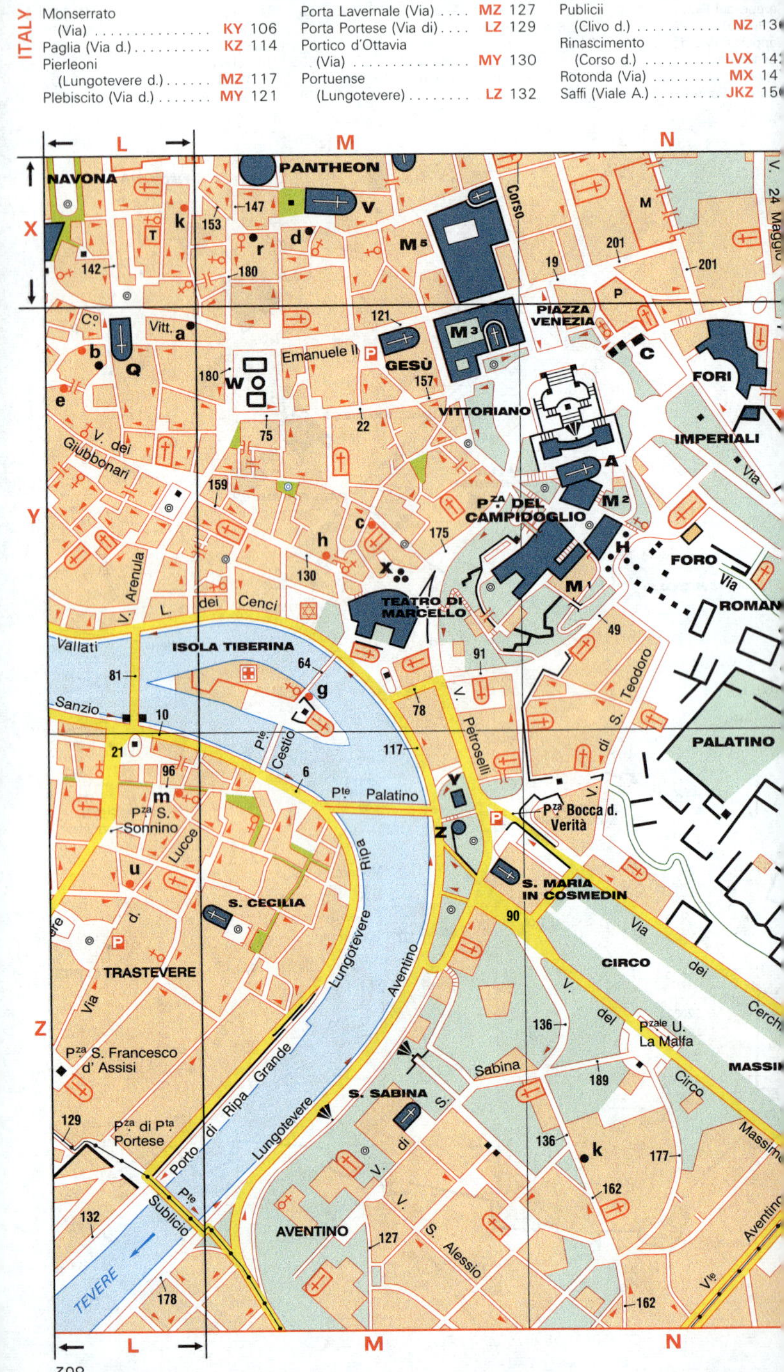

ITALY
Monserrato (Via) .... KY 106
Paglia (Via d.) .... KZ 114
Pierleoni (Lungotevere d.) ..... MZ 117
Plebiscito (Via d.) .... MY 121
Porta Lavernale (Via) .... MZ 127
Porta Portese (Via di) .... LZ 129
Portico d'Ottavia (Via) .... MY 130
Portuense (Lungotevere) .... LZ 132
Publicii (Clivo d.) .... NZ 13
Rinascimento (Corso d.) .... LVX 14
Rotonda (Via) .... MX 14
Saffi (Viale A.) .... JKZ 15

L
M
N
NAVONA
PANTHEON
X
k
T
r
d
V
147
153
142
180
M 5
Corso
M
201
19
201
P
PIAZZA
VENEZIA
C°.
Vitt.
a
b
Q
e
W
180
Emanuele II
GESÙ
121
M 3
157
VITTORIANO
FORI
IMPERIALI
Via
V. dei
Giubbonari
159
75
22
130
h
c
X
175
A
M 2
M
FORO
Via
ROMAN
Y
V. Arenula
L. dei Cenci
TEATRO DI
MARCELLO
H
M
49
91
S. Teodoro
Vallati
ISOLA TIBERINA
64
g
81
78
V. Petroselli
PALATINO
Sanzio
10
117
V. di
21
96
Pte. Cestio
6
m
Pza S. Sonnino
Pte. Palatino
V
Ripa
Z
Pza Bocca d.
Verità
Lucce
u
P
Z
d.
S. CECILIA
90
S. MARIA
IN COSMEDIN
Lungotevere
Aventino
Via dei
CIRCO
Cerch
TRASTEVERE
Via
136
Pzale U.
La Malfa
MASSI
Z
Circo
Pza S. Francesco d' Assisi
Porto di Ripa Grande
Sabina
189
Massim
129
Pza di Pta Portese
S. SABINA
136
k
177
Lungotevere
V. di
162
Pte. Sublicio
132
V.
162
S. Alessio
178
AVENTINO
127
TEVERE
Aventino
Vle.
L
M
N

O
P
X
Y
Z
S. MARIA MAGGIORE
Milano
Panisperna
Cavour
160
Amadeo
Via
Via
Via
Via
Cavour
Via
G.
Lanza
V. d. Statuto
z
h
d
c
a
Cavour
Via
S. PIETRO
IN VINCOLI
T
Mecenate
Merulana
Fori
Imperiali
DOMUS AUREA
Via
COLOSSEO
V. Domus Aurea
V.
R.
Bonghi
Via
V. di S. Giovanni
Via
Labicana
ARCO DI
COSTANTINO
S. CLEMENTE
in
Laterano
Gregorio
V.
e
Claudia
Rotondo
San
P
S. Stefano
di
V. di
V.
Pza di Porta Capena
Navicella
Aradam
Vle
d.
dell'
Amba
d.
Ferratella
Terme
di
V.
Ipponio
Caracalla
Pza di Porta
Metronia
V.
0
200 m
Gallia

SIGHTS

How to make the most of a trip to Rome – some ideas :

Borghese Museum★★★ *– Villa Giulia*★★★ *– Catacombs*★★★ *– Santa Sabina*★★ MZ *– Villa Borghese*★★ NOU *– Baths of Caracalla*★★★ *– St Lawrence Without the Walls*★★ *– St Paul Without the Walls*★★ *– Old Appian Way*★★ *– National Gallery of Modern Art*★ *– Mausoleum of Caius Cestius*★ *– St Paul's Gate*★ *– San'Agnese and Santa Costanza*★ *– Santa Croce in Gerusalemme*★ *– San Saba*★ *– E.U.R.*★ *– Museum of Roman Civilisation*★★.

ANCIENT ROME

Colosseum★★★ OYZ *– Roman Forum*★★★ NOY *– Basilica of Maxentius*★★★ OY **B** *– Imperial Fora*★★★ NY *– Trajan's Column*★★★ NY **C** *– Palatine Hill*★★★ NOYZ *– Pantheon*★★★ MVX *– Largo Argentina Sacred Precinct*★★ MY **W** *– Altar of Augustus*★★ LU *– Temple of Apollo Sosianus*★★ MY **X** *– Theatre of Marcellus*★★ MY *– Tempio della Fortuna Virile*★ MZ **Y** *– Tempio di Vesta*★ MZ **Z** *– Isola Tiberina*★ MY.

CHRISTIAN ROME

Gesù Church★★★ MY *– St Mary Major*★★★ PX *– St John Lateran*★★★ *– Santa Maria d'Aracoeli*★★ NY **A** *– San Luigi dei Francesi*★★ LV *– Sant'Andrea al Quirinale*★★ OV **F** *– St Charles at the Four Fountains*★★ OV **K** *– St Clement's Basilica*★★ PZ *– Sant'Ignazio*★★ MV **L** *– Santa Maria degli Angeli*★★ PV **N** *– Santa Maria della Vittoria*★★ PV *– Santa Susanna*★★ OV *– Santa Maria in Cosmedin*★★ MNZ *– Basilica of St Mary in Trastevere*★★ KZ **S** *– Santa Maria sopra Minerva*★★ MX **V** *– Santa Maria del Popolo*★★ MU **D** *– New Church*★ KX *– Sant'Agostino*★ LV **G** *– St Peter in Chains*★ OY *– Santa Cecilia*★ MZ *– San Pietro in Montorio*★ JZ ⩽★★★ *– Sant'Andrea della Valle*★★ LY **Q** *– Santa Maria della Pace*★ KV **R**.

PALACES AND MUSEUMS

Conservators' Palace★★★ MNY **M¹** *– New Palace*★★★ *(Capitoline Museum*★★*)* NY **M¹** *– Senate House*★★★ NY **H** *– Castel Sant'Angelo*★★★ JKV *– National Roman Museum*★★★ PV *– Chancery Palace*★★ KX **A** *– Palazzo Farnese*★★ KY *– Quirinal Palace*★★ NOV *– Barberini Palace*★★ OV *– Villa Farnesina*★★ KY *– Palazzo Venezia*★ MY **M³** *– Palazzo Braschi*★ KX **M⁴** *– Palazzo Doria Pamphili*★ MX **M⁵** *– Palazzo Spada*★ KY *– Museo Napoleanico*★ KV.

THE VATICAN

St Peter's Square★★★ HV *– St Peter's Basilica*★★★ *(Dome* ⩽★★★*)* GV *– Vatican Museums*★★★ *(Sistine Chapel*★★★*)* GHUV *– Vatican Gardens*★★★ GV.

PRETTY AREAS

Pincian Hill ⩽★★★ MU *– Capitol Square*★★★ MNY *– Spanish Square*★★★ MNU *– Piazza Navona*★★★ LVX *– Fountain of the Rivers*★★★ LV **E** *– Trevi Fountain*★★★ NV *– Victor Emmanuel II Monument (Vittoriano)* ⩽★★ MNY *– Quirinale Square*★★ NV *– Piazza del Popolo*★★ MU *– Gianicolo*★ JY *– Via dei Coronari*★ KV *– Ponte Sant'Angelo*★ JKV *– Piazza Bocca della Verità*★ MNZ *– Piazza Campo dei Fiori*★ KY **28** *– Piazza Colonna*★ MV **46** *– Porta Maggiore*★ *– Piazza Venezia*★ MNY.

Historical Centre corso Vittorio Emanuele, piazza Venezia, Pantheon e Quirinale, piazza di Spagna, piazza Navona :

Hassler Villa Medici, piazza Trinità dei Monti 6 ⊠ 00187 ℘ 06 699340, Fax 06 6789991, ≤ City from roof-garden rest. – |❃| ▤ ⊡ ☎ ℡ – ⏏ 70. 🝣 ⓢ ⓞ ⋿ ₥ 🝩. ⅏
NU c
Meals a la carte 140/225000 – ⵣ 58000 – **85 rm** 540/1080000, 15 suites.

Crowne Plaza Roma Minerva Ⓜ, piazza della Minerva 69 ⊠ 00186 ℘ 06 69941888, Fax 06 6794165, « Terrace roof garden with summer evening rest. service » – |❃|, ⋇ rm, ▤ ⊡ ☎ ℡ ⅊ – ⏏ 120. 🝣 ⓢ ⓞ ⋿ ₥ 🝩. ⅏
MX d
Meals a la carte 85/160000 – ⵣ 45000 – **118 rm** 600/770000, 3 suites.

D'Inghilterra, via Bocca di Leone 14 ⊠ 00187 ℘ 06 69981, Fax 06 69922243, « Former boarding house traditional furnishings » – |❃| ▤ ⊡ ☎. 🝣 ⓢ ⓞ ⋿ ₥. ⅏
Meals a la carte 80/110000 – ⵣ 38000 – **89 cam** 430/660000, 9 suites.   MV f

De la Ville Inter-Continental, via Sistina 69 ⊠ 00187 ℘ 06 67331, Fax 06 6784213, 🛖 – |❃| ▤ ⊡ ☎ ℡ – ⏏ 70. 🝣 ⓢ ⓞ ⋿ ₥ 🝩. ⅏
NU e
Meals a la carte 100/180000 – ⵣ 30000 – **169 rm** 645/790000, 23 suites.

Plaza, via del Corso 126 ⊠ 00186 ℘ 06 69921111, Fax 06 69941575, « Art Nouveau style halls and floral terrace with ≤ » – |❃| ▤ ⊡ ☎ – ⏏ 60. 🝣 ⓢ ⓞ ⋿ ₥ 🝩. ⅏
MV h
Meals *Bar-Bistrot* a la carte 60/95000 – ⵣ 40000 – **207 rm** 410/630000, 10 suites.

Dei Borgognoni without rest., via del Bufalo 126 ⊠ 00187 ℘ 06 69941505, Fax 06 69941501 – |❃| ▤ ⊡ ☎ ⇋. 🝣 ⓢ ⓞ ⋿ ₥ 🝩. ⅏
NV g
ⵣ 20000 – **50 rm** 430/490000.

Valadier, via della Fontanella 15 ⊠ 00187 ℘ 06 3611998 and rest. ℘ 06 3610880, Fax 06 3201558, 🛖 – |❃| ▤ ⊡ ☎ – ⏏ 35. 🝣 ⓢ ⓞ ⋿ ₥ 🝩. ⅏ rest   MU k
Meals *Valentino* Rest. (closed Sunday lunch) a la carte 60/85000 – **49 rm** ⵣ 390/490000, 3 suites.

White Ⓜ without rest., via in Arcione 77 ⊠ 00187 ℘ 06 6991242, Fax 06 6788451 – |❃| ▤ ⊡ ☎ – ⏏ 40. 🝣 ⓢ ⓞ ⋿ ₥
NV p
44 rm ⵣ 340/430000.

Delle Nazioni, via Poli 7 ⊠ 00187 ℘ 06 6792441 and rest. ℘ 06 6795761, Fax 06 6782400 – |❃| ▤ ⊡ ☎ ⇋. 🝣 ⓢ ⓞ ⋿ ₥ 🝩. ⅏
NV m
Meals *Le Grondici* Rest. (closed Sunday) a la carte 55/90000 – ⵣ 25000 – **83 rm** 340/430000.

Santa Chiara without rest., via Santa Chiara 21 ⊠ 00186 ℘ 06 6872979, Fax 06 6873144 – |❃| ▤ ⊡ ☎ – ⏏ 40. 🝣 ⓢ ⓞ ⋿ ₥ 🝩. ⅏
MX r
96 rm ⵣ 270/370000.

Accademia without rest., piazza Accademia di San Luca 75 ⊠ 00187 ℘ 06 69922607, Fax 06 6785897 – ▤ ⊡ ☎. 🝣 ⓢ ⓞ ⋿ ₥
NV u
58 rm ⵣ 280/330000.

Fontanella Borghese without rest., largo Fontanella Borghese 84 ⊠ 00188 ℘ 06 68809504, Fax 06 6861295 – ▤ ⊡ ☎. 🝣 ⓢ ⓞ ⋿ ₥ 🝩. ⅏
MV d
25 rm ⵣ 230/360000.

Teatro di Pompeo without rest., largo del Pallaro 8 ⊠ 00186 ℘ 06 68300170, Fax 06 68805531, « Vaults of Pompeius' theatre » – |❃| ▤ ⊡ ☎. 🝣 ⓢ ⓞ ⋿ ₥ 🝩
13 rm ⵣ 240/310000.   LY b

El Toulà, via della Lupa 29/b ⊠ 00186 ℘ 06 6873498, Fax 06 6871115, Elegant rest. – ▤. 🝣 ⓢ ⓞ ⋿ ₥ 🝩. ⅏
MV a
closed Sunday, Saturday and Monday lunch, August and 24 to 26 December – **Meals** (booking essential) a la carte 90/140000 (15 %).

Enoteca Capranica, piazza Capranica 100 ⊠ 00186 ℘ 06 69940992, Fax 06 69940989 – ▤. 🝣 ⓢ ⓞ ₥ 🝩. ⅏
MV n
closed Saturday lunch, Sunday and August – **Meals** (booking essential for dinner) a la carte 65/100000.

Camponeschi, piazza Farnese 50 ⊠ 00186 ℘ 06 6874927, Fax 06 6865244, « Summer service with ≤ Farnese palace » – ▤. 🝣 ⓢ ⓞ ⋿ ₥
KY c
closed Sunday and 13 to 22 August – **Meals** (dinner only) (booking essential) a la carte 95/155000 (13 %).

Vecchia Roma, via della Tribuna di Campitelli 18 ⊠ 00186 ℘ 06 6864604, 🛖, Elegant rest. – ▤. 🝣 ⓞ. ⅏
MY c
closed Wednesday and 10 to 25 August – **Meals** Roman and seafood rest. a la carte 65/105000 (12 %).

Taverna Giulia, vicolo dell'Oro 23 ⊠ 00186 ℘ 06 6869768, Fax 06 6893720 – ▤. 🝣 ⓢ ⓞ ⋿ ₥ 🝩. ⅏
JV r
closed Sunday and August – **Meals** (booking essential for dinner) Ligurian rest. a la carte 55/70000.

XXX **Il Convivio**, via dei Soldati 28 ✉ 00186 ✆ 06 6869432, *Fax 06 6869432* – 🖹. 📧
🕲 🕕 E 𝑉𝐼𝑆𝐴 𝐽𝐶𝐵. ✕   KV g
closed Sunday, Monday lunch and 9 to 15 August – **Meals** (booking essential) a la cart
95/150000
Spec. Fiori di zucchina ripieni di caprino e guanciale croccante con salsa di melone (June
August). Stracci di pasta con finferli e ragù di quaglia e pesto. Crostacei in crosta con sals
all'aglio dolce e zenzero.

XX **La Rosetta**, via della Rosetta 9 ✉ 00187 ✆ 06 6861002, *Fax 06 6872852* – 🖹. 📧
🕲 🕕 E 𝑉𝐼𝑆𝐴 𝐽𝐶𝐵   MV
closed Saturday lunch, Sunday and 5 to 25 August – **Meals** (booking essential) seafood
a la carte 130/190000.

XX **Quinzi Gabrieli**, via delle Coppelle 6 ✉ 00186 ✆ 06 6879389, *Fax 06 6874940* – 📧
🕲 🕕 E 𝑉𝐼𝑆𝐴. ✕   MV
closed Sunday and August – **Meals** (dinner only) (booking essential) seafood a la cart
100/140000
Spec. Carpaccio di pesce e crostacei. Pappardelle ai frutti di mare e scampi. Scorfan
"all'acqua pazza".

XX **La Fontanella**, largo della Fontanella Borghese 86 ✉ 00186 ✆ 06 6871582
Fax 06 6871092 – 🖹. 📧 🕲 🕕 E 𝑉𝐼𝑆𝐴. ✕   MV
closed Monday and 10 to 24 August – **Meals** (booking essential for dinner) a la cart
70/110000 (12 %).

XX **Il Drappo**, vicolo del Malpasso 9 ✉ 00186 ✆ 06 6877365, 🌳 – 🖹. 📧 🕲 🕕 E 𝑉𝐼𝑆𝐴
closed Sunday and August – **Meals** (booking essential) Sardinian rest. 70000 b.i. KX

XX **Eau Vive**, via Monterone 85 ✉ 00186 ✆ 06 68801095, *Fax 06 68802571*, Catholi
missionaries, « 16C building » – ✕ 🖹. 📧 🕲 🕕 E 𝑉𝐼𝑆𝐴 𝐽𝐶𝐵. ✕   LX
closed Sunday and August – **Meals** (booking essential for dinner) French and exotic cuisin
15/50000 and a la carte 40/75000.

XX **Passetto**, via Zanardelli 14 ✉ 00186 ✆ 06 68803696, *Fax 06 68806569*, 🌳 – 🖹. 📧
🕲 🕕 E 𝑉𝐼𝑆𝐴 𝐽𝐶𝐵. ✕   LV n
Meals a la carte 70/140000.

X **Costanza**, piazza del Paradiso 63/65 ✉ 00186 ✆ 06 6861717, « Pompeius' theatr
ruins – 📧 🕲 🕕 E 𝑉𝐼𝑆𝐴   LY
closed Sunday and August – **Meals** a la carte 45/70000.

X **Da Giggetto**, via del Portico d'Ottavia 21/a ✉ 00186 ✆ 06 6861105, 🌳 – 📧 🕲 🕕
E 𝑉𝐼𝑆𝐴. ✕   MY
closed Monday and 19 to 31 July – **Meals** Typical Roman trattoria a la carte 50/70000

X **La Buca di Ripetta**, via di Ripetta 36 ✉ 00186 ✆ 06 3219391, Habitués trattoria
🖹. 📧 🕲 🕕 E 𝑉𝐼𝑆𝐴. ✕   MU
closed Sunday dinner, Monday and August – **Meals** a la carte 40/60000.

Termini Railway Station via Vittorio Veneto, via Nazionale, Viminale, Santa Mari
Maggiore, Porta Pia :

🏛 **Excelsior**, via Vittorio Veneto 125 ✉ 00187 ✆ 06 47081, *Fax 06 4826205* – 🛗, ✕ rm
🖹 📺 ☎ – 🛠 600. 📧 🕲 🕕 E 𝑉𝐼𝑆𝐴 𝐽𝐶𝐵. ✕   OU
Meals a la carte 90/150000 – ☕ 38500 – **282 rm** 525/850000, 45 suites.

🏛 **Le Grand Hotel**, via Vittorio Emanuele Orlando 3 ✉ 00185 ✆ 06 47091
Fax 06 4747307 – 🛗 🖹 📺 ☎ – 🛠 300. 📧 🕲 🕕 E 𝑉𝐼𝑆𝐴 𝐽𝐶𝐵. ✕   PV
Meals a la carte 100/175000 – ☕ 38500 – **134 rm** 520/805000, 36 suites.

🏛 **Eden**, via Ludovisi 49 ✉ 00187 ✆ 06 478121, *Fax 06 4821584*, ≤, 🏋 – 🛗 🖹 📺
– 🛠 100. 📧 🕲 🕕 E 𝑉𝐼𝑆𝐴 𝐽𝐶𝐵   NU
Meals (see rest. **La Terrazza** below) – ☕ 53000 – **101 rm** 900/1250000, 11 suites.

🏛 **Majestic**, via Vittorio Veneto 50 ✉ 00187 ✆ 06 486841, *Fax 06 4880984* – 🛗 🖹 📺
☎ 🕭 – 🛠 150. 📧 🕲 🕕 E 𝑉𝐼𝑆𝐴 𝐽𝐶𝐵. ✕   OU
Meals a la carte 85/155000 – **76 rm** ☕ 580/790000, 10 suites.

🏛 **Bernini Bristol**, piazza Barberini 23 ✉ 00187 ✆ 06 4883051, *Fax 06 4824266* – 🛗
✕ rm, 🖹 📺 ☎ 🕻 – 🛠 100. 📧 🕲 🕕 E 𝑉𝐼𝑆𝐴 𝐽𝐶𝐵. ✕   OV
Meals a la carte 70/110000 – ☕ 38000 – **110 rm** 465/650000, 15 suites.

🏛 **Regina Baglioni**, via Vittorio Veneto 72 ✉ 00187 ✆ 06 421111, *Fax 06 4201213*
– 🛗, ✕ rm, 🖹 📺 ☎ 🕭 – 🛠 40. 📧 🕲 🕕 E 𝑉𝐼𝑆𝐴. ✕   OU n
Meals *(closed Sunday)* a la carte 90/120000 – **123 rm** ☕ 490/540000, 7 suites.

🏛 **Jolly Hotel Vittorio Veneto**, corso d'Italia 1 ✉ 00198 ✆ 06 8495, *Fax 06 884110*
– 🛗, ✕ rm, 🖹 📺 ☎ 🕻 🕭 🚗 – 🛠 380. 📧 🕲 🕕 E 𝑉𝐼𝑆𝐴. ✕ rest   OU
Meals a la carte 65/105000 – **203 rm** ☕ 380/480000, 2 suites.

🏛 **Grand Hotel Palace**, via Veneto 70 ✉ 00187 ✆ 06 478719, *Fax 06 47871800* – 🛗
🖹 📺 ☎ 🕻 🕭 – 🛠 200. 📧 🕲 🕕 E 𝑉𝐼𝑆𝐴. ✕ rest   OU
Meals a la carte 60/85000 – **85 rm** ☕ 490/600000, 4 suites.

Artemide [M], via Nazionale 22 ⊠ 00184 ℰ 06 489911, *Fax 06 48991700* – ⧉ ▤ ▣ ☎ ♿ – ⚒ 110. AE ⑤ ⑥ E VISA JCB. ⚹
OV b
Meals a la carte 35/65000 – **85 rm** ⊃ 380/540000.

Mecenate Palace Hotel, via Carlo Alberto 3 ⊠ 00185 ℰ 06 44702024, *Fax 06 4461354*, « Roof garden rest. » – ⧉, ⇔ rm, ▤ ▣ ☎ ♦ ♿ – ⚒ 45. AE ⑤ ⑥ E VISA JCB. ⚹
PX h
Meals *(closed Sunday)* a la carte 75/115000 – **59 rm** ⊃ 430/560000, 3 suites.

Quirinale, via Nazionale 7 ⊠ 00184 ℰ 06 4707, *Fax 06 4820099*, « Summer service rest. in the garden » – ⧉ ▤ ▣ ☎ ♿ – ⚒ 250. AE ⑤ ⑥ E VISA JCB. ⚹
PV h
Meals a la carte 65/115000 – **210 rm** ⊃ 350/470000, 4 suites.

Starhotel Metropole, via Principe Amedeo 3 ⊠ 00185 ℰ 06 4774, *Fax 06 4740413* – ⧉ ▤ ▣ ☎ 🚗 – ⚒ 200. AE ⑤ ⑥ E VISA. ⚹
PV p
Meals a la carte 65/95000 – **265 rm** ⊃ 370/495000.

Londra e Cargill, piazza Sallustio 18 ⊠ 00187 ℰ 06 473871, *Fax 06 4746674* – ⧉ ▤ ▣ ☎ ♦ 🚗. AE ⑤ ⑥ E VISA JCB. ⚹
PU q
Meals *(closed Saturday, Sunday lunch and August)* a la carte 70/100000 – **103 rm** ⊃ 350/435000, suite.

Imperiale, via Vittorio Veneto 24 ⊠ 00187 ℰ 06 4826351, *Fax 06 4826351* – ⧉ ▤ ▣ ☎. AE ⑤ ⑥ E VISA. ⚹
OV s
Meals a la carte 55/90000 – **95 rm** ⊃ 380/600000.

Genova without rest., via Cavour 33 ⊠ 00184 ℰ 06 476951, *Fax 06 4827580* – ⧉ ▤ ▣ ☎. AE ⑤ ⑥ E VISA JCB. ⚹
PV r
91 rm ⊃ 310/420000.

Sofitel, via Lombardia 47 ⊠ 00187 ℰ 06 478021 and rest. ℰ 06 4818965, *Fax 06 4821019* – ⧉, ⇔ rm, ▤ ▣ ☎ – ⚒ 70. AE ⑤ ⑥ E VISA. ⚹
NU s
Meals a la carte 45/70000 – **124 rm** ⊃ 400/600000.

Mascagni, via Vittorio Emanuele Orlando 90 ⊠ 00185 ℰ 06 48904040 – ⧉ ▤ ▣ ☎ ♦. AE ⑤ ⑥ E VISA. ⚹ rest
PV b
Meals *(closed Sunday)* (residents only) 50/75000 – **40 rm** ⊃ 450/500000.

Rex without rest., via Torino 149 ⊠ 00184 ℰ 06 4824828, *Fax 06 4882743* – ⧉ ▤ ▣ ☎ ♦ – ⚒ 50. AE ⑤ ⑥ E VISA JCB
PV w
45 rm ⊃ 300/400000, 2 suites.

La Residenza without rest., via Emilia 22 ⊠ 00187 ℰ 06 4880789, *Fax 06 485721* – ⧉ ▤ ▣ ☎. AE ⑤ VISA
OU t
29 rm ⊃ 155/350000.

Britannia without rest., via Napoli 64 ⊠ 00184 ℰ 06 4883153, *Fax 06 4882343* – ⧉ ▤ ▣ ☎ ♦. AE ⑤ ⑥ E VISA JCB
PV y
32 rm ⊃ 285/385000.

Virgilio without rest., via Palermo 30 ⊠ 00184 ℰ 06 4884360, *Fax 06 4884360* – ⧉ ▣ ☎. AE ⑤ ⑥ E VISA JCB. ⚹
OV c
33 rm ⊃ 250/340000.

Ariston without rest., via Turati 16 ⊠ 00185 ℰ 06 4465399, *Fax 06 4465396* – ⧉ ▤ ▣ ☎ – ⚒ 100. AE ⑤ ⑥ E VISA JCB. ⚹
PV g
97 rm ⊃ 250/350000.

Barocco without rest., via della Purificazione 4 angolo piazza Barberini ⊠ 00187 ℰ 06 4872001, *Fax 06 485994* – ⧉ ▤ ▣ ☎. AE ⑤ ⑥ E VISA JCB. ⚹
OV a
28 rm ⊃ 360/460000.

Diana, via Principe Amedeo 4 ⊠ 00185 ℰ 06 4827541, *Fax 06 486998*, « Summer rest. service on terrace roof garden » – ⧉ ▤ ▣ ☎ ♦ – ⚒ 100. AE ⑤ ⑥ E VISA JCB. ⚹
PV d
Meals 40000 – **188 rm** ⊃ 225/320000, 2 suites.

Turner without rest., via Nomentana 29 ⊠ 00161 ℰ 06 44250077, *Fax 06 44250165* – ⧉ ▤ ▣ ☎ ♦. AE ⑤ ⑥ E VISA. ⚹
PU x
45 rm ⊃ 285/360000, suite.

XXXX · **La Terrazza** - Hotel Eden, via Ludovisi 49 ⊠ 00187 ℰ 06 478121, *Fax 06 4821584*, ❀ « Roof garden with ≤ city » – ▤. AE ⑤ ⑥ E VISA JCB. ⚹
NU a
Meals 120000 and a la carte 105/180000
Spec. Fiori di zucchina ripieni di taleggio, ricotta ed olive nere. Tagliolini ai pistilli di zafferano, gamberoni, zucchine e malva. Filetto di rombo al forno con limone e capperi.

XXXX · **Sans Souci,** via Sicilia 20/24 ⊠ 00187 ℰ 06 4821814, *Fax 06 4821771*, Elegant rest., ❀ late night dinners – ▤. AE ⑤ ⑥ E VISA JCB. ⚹
OU a
closed Monday and 13 to 20 August – **Meals** (dinner only) (booking essential) a la carte 105/150000
Spec. Terrina di foie gras con gelatina al Sauternes. Tortelli farciti di tartufo bianco e nero cremolati al parmigiano. Scaloppa di spigola brasata con millefoglie di zucchine e pomodori.

XXX **Asador Cafè Veneto**, via Vittorio Veneto 116 ✉ 00187 ✆ 06 4827107, 🍽, Res
cocktail bar – 🖩. AE S ⑤ ⑩ E VISA JCB. ✸
closed Monday – **Meals** Classical and Argentinian rest. a la carte 70/110000.   OU

XXX **Harry's Bar**, via Vittorio Veneto 150 ✉ 00187 ✆ 06 484643, *Fax 06 4883117*, 🍽
🖩. AE S ⑤ ⑩ E VISA JCB. ✸
closed Sunday, 15 August and Christmas – **Meals** (booking essential) a la carte 70/115000   OU

XX **Al Grappolo d'Oro**, via Palestro 4/10 ✉ 00185 ✆ 06 4941441, *Fax 06 4452350*
🖩. AE S ⑤ ⑩ E VISA JCB
closed Sunday and August – **Meals** a la carte 45/65000.   PU

XX **Agata e Romeo**, via Carlo Alberto 45 ✉ 00185 ✆ 06 4466115, *Fax 06 4465842*
🖩. AE S ⑤ ⑩ E VISA JCB. ✸
closed Sunday, August and 6 to 12 January – **Meals** (booking essential) a la cart
90/140000.   PX

XX **Edoardo**, via Lucullo 2 ✉ 00187 ✆ 06 486428, *Fax 06 486428* – 🖩. AE S ⑤ ⑩ E VIS
closed Sunday and August – **Meals** 45/80000 (lunch) 55/90000 (dinner) and a la cart
60/85000 (15 %).   OU

XX **Giovanni**, via Marche 64 ✉ 00187 ✆ 06 4821834, *Fax 06 4817366*, Habitués rest.
🖩. AE S ⑤ ⑩ E VISA
closed Friday dinner, Saturday and August – **Meals** a la carte 65/115000.   OU

XX **Cicilardone Monte Caruso**, via Farini 12 ✉ 00185 ✆ 06 483549 – AE S ⑤ ⑩ E VISA. ✸
closed Sunday, Monday lunch and August – **Meals** Lucan rest. a la carte 50/95000.   PV

XX **Girarrosto Fiorentino**, via Sicilia 46 ✉ 00187 ✆ 06 42880660, *Fax 06 4201007*
– 🖩. AE S ⑤ ⑩ E VISA   OU
Meals a la carte 65/85000.

XX **Dai Toscani**, via Forlì 41 ✉ 00161 ✆ 06 44231302 – 🖩. AE S ⑤ E VIS
JCB   by via 20 Settembre PU
closed Sunday and August – **Meals** Tuscan rest. a la carte 50/70000.

XX **Mangrovia**, via Milazzo 6/a ✉ 00185 ✆ 06 4452755, *Fax 06 4959204* – 🖩. AE S ⑩
E VISA JCB   by via Volturno PV
Meals seafood a la carte 55/85000.

XX **Girarrosto Toscano**, via Campania 29 ✉ 00187 ✆ 06 4823835, *Fax 06 4821899*
🖩. AE S ⑤ ⑩ E VISA JCB. ✸   OU
closed Wednesday – **Meals** a la carte 60/95000.

XX **Tullio**, via San Nicola da Tolentino 26 ✉ 00187 ✆ 06 4745560, *Fax 06 4818564*, Tusca
trattoria with rotisserie – 🖩. AE S ⑤ ⑩ E VISA JCB. ✸   OV
closed Sunday and August – **Meals** a la carte 70/90000.

XX **Papà Baccus**, via Toscana 36 ✉ 00187 ✆ 06 42742808, *Fax 06 42742808* – ✸ 🖩
AE S ⑤ ⑩ E VISA JCB. ✸   OU
closed Saturday lunch, Sunday, 10 to 20 August and 25 December-6 January – **Mea
(booking essential) Tuscan and seafood specialties a la carte 65/100000.

XX **Peppone**, via Emilia 60 ✉ 00187 ✆ 06 483976, *Fax 06 483976*, Traditional rest. –
S ⑩ E VISA. ✸   OU
closed Saturday and Sunday in August, only Sunday other months – **Meals** a la cart
45/75000 (15 %).

X **Trimani il Wine Bar**, via Cernaia 37/b ✉ 00185 ✆ 06 4469630, *Fax 06 446835*
Wine bar serving quick meals – 🖩. AE S ⑤ ⑩ E VISA JCB   PU
closed Sunday and 10 to 23 August – **Meals** a la carte 45/65000.

X **Colline Emiliane**, via degli Avignonesi 22 ✉ 00187 ✆ 06 4817538 – 🖩. S E VIS
closed Friday and August – **Meals** (booking essential) Emilian rest. a la carte 50
65000.   NV

X **Cantina Cantarini**, piazza Sallustio 12 ✉ 00187 ✆ 06 485528, 🍽, Rustic trattor
– AE S ⑩ E VISA JCB. ✸   PU
closed Sunday, 15 to 30 August and 24 December-6 January – **Meals** (booking essentia
seafood Thursday dinner, Friday and Saturday a la carte 40/60000.

Ancient Rome Colosseo, Fori Imperiali, Aventino, Terme di Caracalla, Porta San Paolo
Monte Testaccio :

🏛 **Forum**, via Tor de' Conti 25 ✉ 00184 ✆ 06 6792446, *Fax 06 6786479*, « Roof garde
rest. with ≤ Imperial Forum » – 🛗 🖩 TV ☎ 📞 🚗 – 🕸 100. AE S ⑤ ⑩ E VISA JCB. ✸
Meals (closed Sunday) a la carte 90/140000 – **73 rm** ☕ 340/490000.   OY

🏨 **Duca d'Alba** without rest., via Leonina 12/14 ✉ 00184 ✆ 06 484471, *Fax 06 488484*
– 🛗 🖩 TV ☎. AE S ⑤ ⑩ E VISA JCB
☕ 15000 – **28 rm** 170/240000, suite.   OY

🏨 **Borromeo** without rest., via Cavour 117 ✉ 00184 ✆ 06 485856, *Fax 06 4882541*
🛗 🖩 TV ☎ 📞 ♿. AE S ⑤ ⑩ E VISA JCB   PX
30 rm ☕ 320/420000, suite.

Domus Aventina ⬧ without rest., via Santa Prisca 11/b ✉ 00153 ✆ 06 5746135,
Fax 06 57300044 – 🖥 📺 ☎. AE ⑤ ⓞ ⋹ VISA. ✗   NZ k
26 rm ☕ 210/320000.

Piccadilly without rest., via Magna Grecia 122 ✉ 00183 ✆ 06 77207017,
Fax 06 70476686 – 🛗 ⇥ 🖥 📺 ☎ ☏. AE ⑤ ⓞ ⋹ VISA. ✗   by via Gallia PZ
55 rm ☕ 175/255000.

Nerva without rest., via Tor de' Conti 3/4/4 a ✉ 00184 ✆ 06 6781835,
Fax 06 69922204 – 🛗 🖥 📺 ☎. AE ⑤ ⓞ VISA   NY h
☕ 18000 – **19 rm** 240/345000.

Sant'Anselmo ⬧ without rest., piazza Sant'Anselmo 2 ✉ 00153 ✆ 06 5748119,
Fax 06 5783604, « Art Nouveau style villa with small garden » – 📺 ☎. AE ⑤ ⓞ ⋹ VISA
JCB. ✗   MZ m
45 rm ☕ 190/290000.

Villa San Pio ⬧ without rest., via di Sant'Anselmo 19 ✉ 00153 ✆ 06 5743547, ⊜
– 🛗 📺 ☎. AE ⑤ ⓞ ⋹ VISA JCB. ✗   MZ m
59 rm ☕ 190/290000.

Solis Invictus Ⓜ without rest., via Cavour 305 00184 ✆ 06 69920587,
Fax 06 69923395 – 🖥 📺 ☎. AE ⑤ ⓞ ⋹ VISA   OY b
10 rm ☕ 195/250000.

Checchino dal 1887, via Monte Testaccio 30 ✉ 00153 ✆ 06 5746318,
Fax 06 5743816, Historical building – AE ⑤ ⓞ ⋹ VISA. ✗
closed August, 24 December-3 January, Sunday dinner and Monday, also Sunday lunch
June-September – **Meals** (booking essential) Roman rest. a la carte 65/
105000   by lungotevere Aventino MZ
Spec. Carciofi alla romana (October-April). Bucatini alla gricia. Cinghiale alle prugne (January-
February).

Maharajah, via dei Serpenti ✉ 00184 ✆ 06 4747144, *Fax 06 4465597* – 🖥. AE ⑤ ⓞ
⋹ VISA JCB   OX s
Meals a la carte 50/65000 (10 %).

Mario's Hostaria, piazza del Grillo 9 ✉ 00184 ✆ 06 6793725, ⛱ – 🖥. AE ⑤ ⓞ ⋹
VISA. ✗   NY b
closed Sunday – **Meals** (booking essential) a la carte 45/90000.

Charly's Sauciere, via di San Giovanni in Laterano 270 ✉ 00184 ✆ 06 70495666,
Fax 06 7077483 – 🖥. AE ⑤ ⓞ ⋹ VISA JCB   PZ e
closed 5 to 20 August, Sunday and lunch Saturday-Monday – **Meals** (booking essential)
French-Swiss rest. a la carte 55/80000.

St. Peter's Basilica (Vatican City) Gianicolo, Monte Mario, Stadio Olimpico :

Cavalieri Hilton Ⓜ, via Cadlolo 101 ✉ 00136 ✆ 06 35091, *Fax 06 35092241,* ⩽ city,
⛱, « Terrace solarium and park with ⊿ », 🏋, ⇆s, ⊠, ✗ – 🛗, ⇥ rm, 🖥 📺 ☎ ☏
♿ ⊜ Ⓟ – 🔺 2100. AE ⑤ ⓞ ⋹ VISA JCB. ✗   by via Trionfale GU
Meals a la carte 105/155000 see also rest. *La Pergola* – ☕ 49000 – **358 rm** 700/875000,
18 suites.

Dei Mellini Ⓜ without rest., via Muzio Clementi 81 ✉ 00193 ✆ 06 324771,
Fax 06 32477801 – 🛗 ⇥ 🖥 📺 ☎ ☏ ♿ ⊜ – 🔺 70. AE ⑤ ⓞ ⋹
VISA. ✗   KU f
67 rm ☕ 380/420000, 13 suites

Visconti Palace without rest., via Federico Cesi 37 ✉ 00193 ✆ 06 36841,
Fax 06 3200551 – 🛗, ⇥ rm, 🖥 📺 ☎ ☏ ♿ ⊜ – 🔺 150. AE ⑤ ⓞ ⋹ VISA JCB. ✗
234 rm ☕ 320/420000, 13 suites.   KU b

Atlante Star, via Vitelleschi 34 ✉ 00193 ✆ 06 6873233, *Fax 06 6872300* – 🛗 🖥 📺
☎ ⊜ – 🔺 50. AE ⑤ ⓞ ⋹ VISA JCB   JV c
Meals (see rest. *Les Etoiles* below) – **70 rm** ☕ 450/650000, 3 suites.

Giulio Cesare without rest., via degli Scipioni 287 ✉ 00192 ✆ 06 3210751,
Fax 06 3211736, ⊜ – 🛗 📺 ☎ ☏ – 🔺 40. AE ⑤ ⓞ ⋹ VISA JCB. ✗   KU d
90 rm ☕ 370/470000.

Farnese without rest., via Alessandro Farnese 30 ✉ 00192 ✆ 06 3212553,
Fax 06 3215129 – 🛗 🖥 📺 ☎ Ⓟ. AE ⑤ ⓞ ⋹ VISA. ✗   KU e
23 rm ☕ 290/460000.

Sant'Anna without rest., borgo Pio 133 ✉ 00193 ✆ 06 68801602, *Fax 06 68308717*
– 🛗 🖥 📺 ☎ ☏. AE ⑤ ⓞ ⋹ VISA JCB   HV m
20 rm ☕ 220/280000.

Arcangelo without rest., via Boezio 15 ✉ 00192 ✆ 06 6874143, *Fax 06 6893050* –
🛗 🖥 📺 ☎. AE ⑤ ⓞ ⋹ VISA. ✗   JU f
33 rm ☕ 220/300000.

La Pergola - Hotel Cavalieri Hilton, via Cadlolo 101 ✉ 00136 ☎ 06 35091, ≤ city, Elegant rest., « Summer service on terrace » – ▤. AE ⓢ ⓞ E VISA JCB. ✈ by via Trionfale GU
closed Sunday, Monday and January – **Meals** *(dinner only)* (booking essential) 120/170000 and a la carte 105/155000
Spec. Panachè di pesce all'olio di basilico. Ravioli di verdure con frutti di mare. Soufflè di ricotta su ragù d'ananas e lychees.

Les Etoiles - Hotel Atlante Star, via dei Bastioni 1 ✉ 00193 ☎ 06 6893434, *Fax 06 6872300*, « Roof garden and summer service on terrace with ≤ St. Peter's Basilica » – ▤. AE ⓢ ⓞ E VISA JCB. ✈ JV
Meals 85/135000 (lunch) 105/190000 (dinner) and a la carte 120/180000.

Il Simposio-di Costantini, piazza Cavour 16 ✉ 00193 ☎ 06 3211502, *Fax 06 3213210*, Wine bar and rest. – ▤. AE ⓢ ⓞ E VISA JCB. ✈ KU
closed Saturday lunch, Sunday and 10 to 25 August – **Meals** (booking essential) a la carte 50/100000.

Taverna Angelica, piazza delle Vaschette 14/a ✉ 00193 ☎ 06 6874514, Post theatre restaurant, open until late – ▤. AE ⓢ E VISA. ✈ JV
closed Sunday, Monday lunch, 10 to 30 August and 23 December-3 January – **Meals** (booking essential) a la carte 55/90000.

Dal Toscano-al Girarrosto, via Germanico 58 ✉ 00192 ☎ 06 39725717, *Fax 06 39730748*, Habitués rest. – ▤. ⓢ ⓞ E VISA. ✈ HU
closed Monday and August – **Meals** Tuscan specialities a la carte 50/80000.

Da Enzo, via Ennio Quirino Visconti 39/41 ✉ 00193 ☎ 06 3215743 – ▤. AE ⓢ ⓞ E VISA JCB. ✈ KU
closed Sunday and August – **Meals** a la carte 50/80000.

Parioli via Flaminia, Villa Borghese, Villa Glori, via Nomentana, via Salaria :

Lord Byron ⛰, via De Notaris 5 ✉ 00197 ☎ 06 3220404, *Fax 06 3220405* – |◆| ▤ TV ☎. AE ⓢ ⓞ E VISA JCB. ✈ by lungotevere A. da Brescia KU
Meals (see rest. ***Relais le Jardin*** below) – **28 rm** ☐ 660/825000, 9 suites.

Aldrovandi Palace Hotel, via Aldrovandi 15 ✉ 00197 ☎ 06 3223993, *Fax 06 3221435*, « Small shaded park with ⛱ », ƒ₆ – |◆| ⇔ ▤ TV ☎ ✆ P – 🏛 350. AE ⓢ ⓞ E VISA JCB. ✈ by via Flaminia LU
Meals (see rest. ***Relais La Piscine*** below) – **127 rm** ☐ 500/650000, 10 suites.

Parco dei Principi, via Gerolamo Frescobaldi 5 ✉ 00198 ☎ 06 854421, *Fax 06 8845104*, ≤, ♣, « Small botanical park with ⛱ » – |◆| ▤ TV ☎ ✆ 🚗 – 🏛 1000. AE ⓢ ⓞ E VISA JCB. ✈ by via Pinciana OU
Meals a la carte 75/100000 – **155 rm** ☐ 400/700000, 15 suites.

Albani, via Adda 45 ✉ 00198 ☎ 06 84991, *Fax 06 8499399* – |◆| ▤ TV ☎ 🚗 – 🏛 40. AE ⓢ ⓞ E VISA JCB. ✈ by via Salaria PU
Meals *(dinner only)* 45/65000 – **127 rm** ☐ 250/400000.

Executive without rest., via Aniene 3 ✉ 00198 ☎ 06 8552030, *Fax 06 8414078* – |◆| ▤ TV ☎ ♿. AE ⓢ ⓞ E VISA JCB. ✈ PU
56 rm ☐ 260/340000.

Villa Glori without rest., via Celentano 11 ✉ 00196 ☎ 06 3227658, *Fax 06 321949* – |◆| ▤ TV ☎ ✆. AE ⓢ ⓞ E VISA JCB. ✈ by lungotevere in Augusta KLU
57 rm ☐ 270/340000.

Fenix, viale Gorizia 5 ✉ 00198 ☎ 06 8540741, *Fax 06 8543632*, ♣ – |◆| ▤ TV ☎ 🚗. AE ⓢ ⓞ E VISA. ✈ by via 20 Settembre PU
Meals *(closed Saturday dinner, Sunday and August)* a la carte 40/60000 – **73 rm** ☐ 200/300000.

Relais le Jardin - Hotel Lord Byron, via De Notaris 5 ✉ 00197 ☎ 06 3220404, *Fax 06 3220405*, Elegant rest. – ▤. AE ⓢ ⓞ E VISA JCB. ✈
closed Sunday – **Meals** (booking essential) 145000 and a la carte 85/170000 by lungotevere A. da Brescia KU
Spec. Carpaccio d'agnello in salmì di finocchietto selvatico con caponatina di verdure (spring-summer). Trofiette in salsa di ricotta forte, pomodori di Pachino, mais e olive nere all'origano fresco (summer). Costata di Chianina all'olio di peperoncino con limoni canditi.

Relais la Piscine - Hotel Aldrovandi Palace, via Mangili 6 ✉ 00197 ☎ 06 3216126, « Outdoor summer service » – ⇔ ▤ P. AE ⓢ ⓞ E VISA JCB. ✈ by lungotevere A. da Brescia KU
Meals 60/90000 (lunch) 80/110000 (dinner) and a la carte 85/115000.

XX **Al Ceppo**, via Panama 2 ⊠ 00198 ℰ 06 8551379, *Fax 06 85301370* – 𝔸𝔼 Ⓢ ⓄⒾ Ⓔ 𝑉𝐼𝑆𝐴.
by via Salaria **PU**
closed Monday and 8 to 24 August – **Meals** (booking essential) a la carte 55/95000.

XX **Da Ezio le Scalette**, via Chiana 89/91 ⊠ 00198 ℰ 06 8411714, *Fax 06 8540467* – 𝔼. 𝔸𝔼 Ⓢ ⓄⒾ Ⓔ 𝑉𝐼𝑆𝐴 𝐽𝐶𝐵
by via Nizza **PU**
closed Saturday lunch and Sunday – **Meals** (booking essential) seafood a la carte 85/175000 (12 %).

XX **Coriolano**, via Ancona 14 ⊠ 00198 ℰ 06 44249863, *Fax 06 44249724*, Elegant trattoria – 𝔼. 𝔸𝔼 Ⓢ ⓄⒾ Ⓔ 𝑉𝐼𝑆𝐴 𝐽𝐶𝐵
PU d
closed 5 to 30 August and Sunday July – **Meals** (booking essential) a la carte 65/95000 (15 %).

XX **Il Caminetto**, viale dei Parioli 89 ⊠ 00197 ℰ 06 8083946, 🍽 – 𝔼. 𝔸𝔼 Ⓢ ⓄⒾ Ⓔ 𝑉𝐼𝑆𝐴.
by lungotevere A. Da Brescia **KU**
Meals a la carte 55/85000.

XX **La Scala**, viale dei Parioli 79/d ⊠ 00197 ℰ 06 8083978, 🍽 – 𝔼. 𝔸𝔼 Ⓢ ⓄⒾ Ⓔ 𝑉𝐼𝑆𝐴.
by lungotevere A. da Brescia **KU**
closed Wednesday and 6 to 21 August – **Meals** a la carte 40/55000.

XX **Le Coppedè**, via Taro 28 a ⊠ 00199 ℰ 06 8411772 – 𝔸𝔼 Ⓢ ⓄⒾ Ⓔ 𝑉𝐼𝑆𝐴 𝐽𝐶𝐵
by via Nizza **PU**
closed Sunday – **Meals** Apulian rest. 45000 and a la carte 40/55000.

X **Franco l'Abruzzese**, via Anerio 23/25 ⊠ 00199 ℰ 06 8600704, Habituès trattoria – 𝔸𝔼 Ⓢ ⓄⒾ Ⓔ 𝑉𝐼𝑆𝐴.
by via Nizza **PU**
closed Sunday and August – **Meals** a la carte 35/60000.

Trastevere area (typical district) :

XXX **Alberto Ciarla**, piazza San Cosimato 40 ⊠ 00153 ℰ 06 5818668, *Fax 06 5884377*, 🍽 – 𝔼. 𝔸𝔼 Ⓢ ⓄⒾ Ⓔ 𝑉𝐼𝑆𝐴 𝐽𝐶𝐵.
KZ k
closed Sunday – **Meals** (dinner only) (booking essential) seafood 75/110000 and a la carte 75/105000.

XX **Corsetti-il Galeone**, piazza San Cosimato 27 ⊠ 00153 ℰ 06 5816311, *Fax 06 5896255*, 🍽, « Typical atmosphere » – 𝔼. 𝔸𝔼 Ⓢ ⓄⒾ Ⓔ 𝑉𝐼𝑆𝐴 𝐽𝐶𝐵.
KZ m
closed Wednesday and 15 to 27 July – **Meals** Roman and seafood rest. a la carte 50/80000.

XX **Sora Lella**, via di Ponte Quattro Capi 16 (Isola Tiberina) ⊠ 00186 ℰ 06 6861601, *Fax 06 6861601* – 𝔼. 𝔸𝔼 Ⓢ ⓄⒾ Ⓔ 𝑉𝐼𝑆𝐴.
MY g
closed Sunday and August – **Meals** Traditional Roman rest. a la carte 60/85000.

XX **Galeassi**, piazza di Santa Maria in Trastevere 3 ⊠ 00153 ℰ 06 5803775, 🍽 – 𝔸𝔼 Ⓢ ⓄⒾ Ⓔ 𝑉𝐼𝑆𝐴 𝐽𝐶𝐵.
KZ q
closed Monday and 20 December-20 January – **Meals** Roman and seafood rest. a la carte 60/100000.

XX **Il Cortile**, via Alberto Mario 26 ⊠ 00152 ℰ 06 5803433 – 𝔸𝔼 Ⓢ ⓄⒾ Ⓔ 𝑉𝐼𝑆𝐴.
closed 8 August-8 September – **Meals** a la carte 45/70000.
by via Carini **JZ**

XX **Paris**, piazza San Callisto 7/a ⊠ 00153 ℰ 06 5815378, 🍽 – 𝔼. 𝔸𝔼 Ⓢ ⓄⒾ Ⓔ 𝑉𝐼𝑆𝐴.
closed Sunday dinner, Monday and August – **Meals** Roman and Jewish rest. a la carte 50/85000.
KZ r

XX **Pastarellaro**, via di San Crisogono 33 ⊠ 00153 ℰ 06 5810871, *Fax 06 5810871*, Rest.-wine bar with live piano music at dinner – 𝔼. 𝔸𝔼 Ⓢ ⓄⒾ Ⓔ 𝑉𝐼𝑆𝐴.
LZ u
closed Wednesday and August – **Meals** Roman and seafood rest. a la carte 55/85000 (12 %).

X **Checco er Carettiere**, via Benedetta 10 ⊠ 00153 ℰ 06 5817018, 🍽 – 𝔼. 𝔸𝔼 Ⓢ ⓄⒾ Ⓔ 𝑉𝐼𝑆𝐴 𝐽𝐶𝐵.
KY t
closed Sunday dinner – **Meals** Roman and seafood rest. a la carte 60/80000.

X **Taverna Trilussa**, via del Politeama 23 ⊠ 00153 ℰ 06 5818918, *Fax 06 5811064*, 🍽 – 𝔼. 𝔸𝔼 Ⓢ ⓄⒾ Ⓔ 𝑉𝐼𝑆𝐴
KY v
closed Sunday dinner, Monday and 30 July-28 August – **Meals** Typical Roman rest. a la carte 40/60000.

North western area via Flaminia, via Cassia, Balduina, Prima Valle, via Aurelia :

🏨 **Jolly Hotel Midas**, via Aurelia 800 (al km 8) ⊠ 00165 ℰ 06 66396, *Fax 06 66418457*, ⏋, 🍽, 🍴 – 📶, ✳ rm, 🍽 📺 ☎ 🅿 – 🛎 650. 𝔸𝔼 Ⓢ ⓄⒾ Ⓔ 𝑉𝐼𝑆𝐴. rest
by via Aurelia **GV**
Meals a la carte 60/90000 – **342 rm** ☕ 250/330000, 5 suites.

🏨 **Afi Hotel**, via Aurelia al km 8 ⊠ 00165 ℰ 06 66411200, *Fax 06 66414437*, 🍽, ⏋, 🍽 – 📶, ✳ rm, 🍽 📺 ☎ 📞 🅿 – 🛎 120. 𝔸𝔼 Ⓢ ⓄⒾ Ⓔ 𝑉𝐼𝑆𝐴 𝐽𝐶𝐵.
Meals a la carte 55/85000 – **213 rm** ☕ 230/270000.
by via Aurelia **GV**

🏨 **Colony Flaminio** 🐾 without rest., via Monterosi 18 ✉ 00191 ✆ 06 36301843, Fax 06 36309495 – 🛗 ▤ TV ☎ P – 🏊 90. AE 🅂 ⓸ E VISA JCB by via Po **OPU**
74 rm ☕ 190/230000, suite.

🍴 **L'Ortica,** via Flaminia Vecchia 573 ✉ 00191 ✆ 06 3338709, Fax 06 3338709, 🌳 – A 🅂 ⓸ E VISA JCB by via Po **OPU**
closed Sunday dinner – **Meals** (dinner only) Napolitan rest. a la carte 65/95000.

North eastern area via Salaria, via Nomentana, via Tiburtina :

🏨 **Eurogarden** without rest., raccordo anulare Salaria-Flaminia uscita n. 7 ✉ 00013 ✆ 06 8852751, Fax 06 88527577, 🏊, 🌳 – ▤ TV ☎ P. AE 🅂 ⓸ E VISA. 🐾
48 rm ☕ 170/200000. by via Salaria **PU**

Southern western area via Aurelia Antica, E.U.R., Città Giardino, via della Magliana, Portuense :

🏰 **Sheraton Roma Hotel** M, viale del Pattinaggio 100/102 ✉ 00144 ✆ 06 5453, Fax 06 5940689, 🏋, 🌊, 🏊, 🎾 – 🛗, 🚭 rm, ▤ TV ☎ 🚪 🚗 P – 🏊 1800. AE ⓸ E VISA JCB. 🐾 by viale Aventino **NZ**
Meals a la carte 70/110000 – **626 rm** ☕ 480/585000, 22 suites.

🏰 **Holiday Inn St. Peter's,** via Aurelia Antica 415 ✉ 00165 ✆ 06 6642, Fax 06 6637190, 🌳, « Garden with 🏊 », 🌊, 🎾 – 🛗, 🚭 rm, ▤ TV ☎ 🖂 🚪 P – 🏊 240. AE 🅂 ⓸ E VISA JCB. 🐾 by via Garibaldi **JZ**
Meals a la carte 65/105000 – ☕ 25000 – **318 rm** 380/500000.

🏰 **Sheraton Golf** 🐾, viale Parco de Medici 167 ✉ 00148 ✆ 06 658588, Fax 06 65858742, 🌳, 🏋, 🌊, 🏊, 🌳, – 🛗, 🚭 rm, ▤ TV ☎ P – 🏊 500. AE 🅂 ⓸ E VISA JCB. 🐾 by viale Trastevere **KZ**
Meals a la carte 80/135000 – **285 rm** ☕ 295/335000, 14 suites.

🏰 **Villa Pamphili** 🐾, via della Nocetta 105 ✉ 00164 ✆ 06 5862, Fax 06 66157747, 🌳 🏋, 🌊, 🏊 (covered in winter), 🌳, 🎾 – 🛗, 🚭 rm, ▤ TV ☎ 🖂 🚪 P – 🏊 500. A 🅂 ⓸ E VISA. 🐾 by via Garibaldi **JZ**
Meals a la carte 60/85000 – **238 rm** ☕ 370/440000, 10 suites.

🏰 **Holiday Inn-Parco dei Medici,** viale Castello della Magliana 65 ✉ 00148 ✆ 06 6558, Fax 06 6557005, 🏊, 🌳, 🎾 – 🛗, 🚭 rm, ▤ TV ☎ 🖂 🚪 P – 🏊 650. AE 🅂 ⓸ E VIS JCB. 🐾 by viale Trastevere **KZ**
Meals a la carte 70/90000 – **317 rm** ☕ 350/450000.

🏰 **Shangri Là-Corsetti,** viale Algeria 141 ✉ 00144 ✆ 06 5916441, Fax 06 5413813, heated, 🌳 – ▤ TV ☎ P – 🏊 80. AE 🅂 ⓸ E VISA. 🐾 by viale Aventino **NZ**
Meals (see rest. *Shangri Là-Corsetti* below) – **52 rm** ☕ 300/360000, 11 suites.

🏨 **Dei Congressi,** viale Shakespeare 29 ✉ 00144 ✆ 06 5926021, Fax 06 5911903, 🌳 – 🛗 ▤ TV ☎ 🖂 – 🏊 250. AE 🅂 ⓸ E VISA. 🐾 by via Dell'Amba Aradam **PZ**
closed August – **Meals** (see rest. *La Glorietta* below) – **105 rm** ☕ 190 260000.

🍴🍴🍴 **Shangri-Là Corsetti,** viale Algeria 141 ✉ 00144 ✆ 06 5918861, Fax 06 5413813, 🌳 – ▤ P. AE 🅂 ⓸ E VISA JCB by viale Aventino **NZ**
closed 9 to 22 August – **Meals** seafood a la carte 50/90000.

🍴🍴 **La Glorietta,** viale Shakesperare 25/33 ✉ 00144 ✆ 06 5926021, Fax 06 5911903, 🌳 – ▤. AE 🅂 ⓸ E VISA. 🐾 by via Dell'Amba Aradam **PZ**
closed Sunday and August – **Meals** a la carte 40/85000.

🍴 **La Maielletta,** via Aurelia Antica 270 ✉ 00165 ✆ 06 39366595, Fax 06 39366595 P. AE 🅂 ⓸ E VISA JCB. 🐾 by via Cipro **GU**
closed Monday – **Meals** Abruzzi rest. 35/45000 b.i..

🍴 **Pietro al Forte,** via dil Capasso 56/64 ✉ 00164 ✆ 06 66158531, Fax 06 6615853 🌳 – AE 🅂 ⓸ E VISA. 🐾 by via Aurelia **GV**
closed Monday and 24 December-7 January – **Meals** Rest. and pizzeria a la carte 40/7000

Outskirts of Rome

on national road 6 - Casilina :

🏨 **Myosotis** 🐾, piazza Pupinia 2, località Torre Gaia ✉ 00133 ✆ 06 205447, Fax 06 2053671, 🏊, 🌳 – ▤ TV ☎ 🖂 P – 🏊 35. AE 🅂 ⓸ E VISA. 🐾
Meals (see rest. *Villa Marsili* below) – **19 rm** ☕ 180/220000. by via Merulana **PY**

🏠 **Città 2000** without rest., via della Tenuta di Torrenova 60/68 ✉ 00133 ✆ 06 202554, Fax 06 2025539 – 🛗 ▤ TV ☎ 🖂 🚗 P – 🏊 30. AE 🅂 ⓸ E VISA. 🐾
85 rm ☕ 100/110000. by via Merulana **PY**

🍴🍴 **Villa Marsili,** via Casilina 1604 ✉ 00133 ✆ 06 2050200, Fax 06 2055176, « Outdoo summer service » – ▤ P. AE 🅂 ⓸ E VISA. 🐾 by via Merulana **PY**
closed 15 to 25 August – **Meals** 30/50000 and a la carte 35/60000.

at Ciampino *SE : 15 km : – ✉ 00043 :*

✗ **Da Giacobbe**, via Appia Nuova 1681 ✆ 06 79340131, *Fax 06 79340859*, 🌇 – ▣ ⓟ.
ᴁ Ⓢ ⓞ ⅇ *VISA*. ⚘   by via Labicana   PZ
closed Sunday dinner, Monday and 10 to 30 August – **Meals** (booking essential) Homely
rest. a la carte 40/60000.

Baschi *05023 Terni* 🆂🆂🆂 ㉕, 🔢 *N 18 – pop. 2 698 alt. 165.*
Roma 118 – Orvieto 10 – Terni 70 – Viterbo 46.

XXXX **Vissani**, *N : 12 km* ✉ 05020 Civitella del Lago ✆ 0744 950396, *Fax 0744 950396* – ✖
❀❀ ▣ ⓟ. ᴁ Ⓢ ⓞ ⅇ *VISA* ᴊᴄʙ. ⚘
closed Sunday dinner, Wednesday and Thursday lunch – **Meals** (booking essential)
180/230000 and a la carte 155/235000 (15 %)
Spec. Aragosta di Gallipoli al rosmarino e cannoncini al tartufo nero. Lasagna di animelle
tostate e tartufo nero, mirepoix di foie gras e gobbi. Anatra a la "presse" con parmigiana
di melanzane e tortino di mele annurche.

FLORENCE *(FIRENZE) 50100* ℗ 🆂🆂🆂 ⑮, 🔢🔢 *K 15 G. Tuscan – pop. 379 687 alt. 49.*
See : *Cathedral*★★★ *(Duomo)* **Y** *: east end*★★★, *dome*★★★ (❊★★) *Campanile*★★★ **YB** :
❊★★ *Baptistry*★★★ **YC** : *doors*★★★, *mosaics*★★★ *Cathedral Museum*★★ **Y** **M¹** *– Piazza della
Signoria*★★ **Z** *– Loggia della Signoria*★★ **Z** **D** : *Perseus*★★★ *by B. Cellini Palazzo Vecchio*★★★
Z **H** *– Uffizi Gallery*★★★ **EU** **M¹⁰** *– Bargello Palace and Museum*★★★ **EU** *– San Lorenzo*★★★
DU **V** *– Church*★★, *Laurentian Library*★★, *Medici Tombs*★★★ *in Medicee Chapels – Medici-
Riccardi Palace*★★ **EU** **W** : *Chapel*★★★, *Luca Giordano Gallery*★★ *– Church of Santa Maria
Novella*★★ **DU** **S** : *frescoes*★★★ *by Ghirlandaio – Ponte Vecchio*★★ **Z** *– Pitti Palace*★★ **DV** :
Palatine Gallery★★★, *Silver Museum*★★, *Works*★★ *by Macchiaioli in Modern Art Gallery*★ *–
Boboli Garden*★ **DV** : ❊★ *from the Citadel Belvedere Porcelain Museum*★ **DV** *Monastery
and Museum of St. Mark*★★ **ET** : *works*★★★ *by Beato Angelico – Academy Gallery*★★ **ET** :
Michelangelo gallery★★★ *Piazza della Santissima Annunziata*★ **ET** **168** : *frescoes*★ *in the
church, portico*★★ *with corners decorated with terracotta Medallions*★★ *in the Foundling
Hospital*★ *– Church of Santa Croce*★★ **EU** : *Pazzi Chapel*★★ *Excursion to the hills*★★ : ❊★★★
from Michelangiolo Square **EFV**, *Church of San Miniato al Monte*★★ **EFV** *– Strozzi Palace*★★
DU **Y** *– Rucellai Palace*★★ **DU** **E** *– Masaccio's frescoes*★★ *in the Chapel Brancacci in Santa
Maria del Carmine* **DUV** *Last Supper of Foligno*★ **DT**, *Last Supper of San Salvi*★ **BS** **G**
Orsanmichele★ **EU** **N** : *tabernacle*★★ *by Orcagna – La Badia* **EU** **X** : *campanile*★, *delicate
relief sculpture in marble*★★, *tombs*★, *Madonna appearing to St. Bernard*★ *by Filippino Lippi
– Sassetti Chapel*★★ *and the Chapel of the Annunciation*★ *in the Holy Trinity Church*
DU **Z** *Church of the Holy Spirit*★ **DUV** *– Last Supper*★ *of Sant'Apollonia* **ET** *All Saints' Church*
DU : *Last Supper*★ *by Ghirlandaio Davanzanti Palace*★ **Z** **M²** *New Market Loggia*★ **Z** **K** *–
Museums : Archaeological*★★ *(Chimera from Arezzo*★★ *Françoise Vase*★★) **ET**, *Science*★
EU **M⁶** *Marino Marini*★ **Z** **M⁷** *Bardini*★ **EV** *La Specola*★ **DV** *Casa BuonArroti*★ **EU** **M³** *Semi-
precious Stone Workshop*★ **ET** **M⁴** *Crucifixion*★ *by Perugino* **EU** **Q**.

Envir. : *Medicee Villas*★ : *villa della Petraia*★, *villa di Castello*★, *villa di Poggio a Caiano*★★
by via P. Toselli **CT** : *17 km Galluzzo Carthusian Monastery*★★ *by via Senese* **CV**.

🏌 *Dell'Ugolino (closed Monday), to Grassina* ✉ 50015 ✆ 055 2301009, *Fax
055 23011411, South : 12 km* **BS**.

✈ *Amerigo Vespucci North-West : 4 km by via P. Toselli* **CT** ✆ 055 373498 *– Alitalia,
lungarno Acciaiuoli 10/12 r,* ✉ 50123 ✆ 055 27881, *Fax 055 2788400.*

🅰 *via Cavour 1 r* ✉ 50129 ✆ 055 290832, *Fax 055 2760383.*

A.C.I. *viale Amendola 36* ✉ 50121 ✆ 055 24861.
Roma 277 – Bologna 105 – Milano 298.

Plans on following pages

Excelsior, piazza Ognissanti 3 ✉ 50123 ✆ 055 264201, *Fax 055 210278* – 🛗 ▤ 📺
☎ ✆ ⅊ – 🎪 150. ᴁ Ⓢ ⓞ ⅇ *VISA* ᴊᴄʙ. ⚘   DU **b**
Meals a la carte 100/185000 – ☕ 66000 – **152 rm** 795/955000,
12 suites.

Grand Hotel, piazza Ognissanti 1 ✉ 50123 ✆ 055 288781, *Fax 055 217400* – 🛗 ▤
📺 ☎ ✆ – 🎪 220. ᴁ Ⓢ ⓞ ⅇ *VISA* ᴊᴄʙ. ⚘   DU **a**
Meals a la carte 105/185000 – ☕ 66000 – **90 rm** 635/955000, 17 suites.

Villa Medici, via Il Prato 42 ✉ 50123 ✆ 055 2381331, *Fax 055 2381336*, 🌇, ⊼, 🌳
– 🛗 ▤ 📺 ☎ ⓟ – 🎪 90. ᴁ Ⓢ ⓞ ⅇ *VISA* ᴊᴄʙ. ⚘   CT **c**
Meals a la carte 75/105000 – ☕ 38500 – **90 rm** 550/785000, 14 suites.

Regency, piazza Massimo D'Azeglio 3 ✉ 50121 ✆ 055 245247, *Fax 055 2346735*, 🌇,
🌳 – 🛗 ▤ 📺 ☎ 🚗. ᴁ Ⓢ ⓞ ⅇ *VISA* ᴊᴄʙ. ⚘   FU **a**
Meals *Relais le Jardin* Rest. (booking essential) a la carte 85/110000 – **35 rm**
☕ 550/680000, 2 suites.

ITALY
FLORENCE
FIRENZE
PORTA AL PRATO
FORTEZZA DA BASSO
PAL. D. CONGRESSI
PAL. D. AFFARI
Cenacolo di Fuligno
P.za d'Indipenden
135
Ognissanti
S. SPIRITO
S. MARIA DEL CARMINE
Piazza del Carmine
Piazza S. Spirito
Piazza dei Pitti
PALAZZO PIT
MUSEO LA SPECOLA
GIARDINO DI BOBOLI
VIOTTOLONE
PIAZZALE D. ISOLOTTO
MUSEO DELL PORCELLAN
Forte de Belvedere
PONTE VECCHIO
Corridoio Vasariano
S. Felici
PORTA ROMANA
PASSEGGIATA AI COL
Machiavelli
P.za Vittorio Veneto
P.za Gaddi
ARNO
Via del Ponte alle Mosse
V. del Ponte alle Mosse
G. Galliano
Marcello
B.
V. d. Porte Nuove
V.le F. Redi
V.le Belfiore
V.le Fratelli Rosselli
V. G. Monaco
F. Strozzi
V. L. Alamanni
V. Valfonda
V. Nazionale
V. Faenza
Guelfa
Viale
il
V. Montebello
Prato
r V. J. da Diacceto
Via della
Scala
Corso Italia
Lungarno Amerigo Vespucci
Palazzuolo
V. de' Fossi
Ponte Vespucci
L. Vespucci
L. Corsini
L. Guicciardini
P.te alla Carraia
Soderini
Borgo S. Frediano
V. Serragli
V. S. Spirito
V. Maggio
Fonderia
L. S. Rosa
Pisana
V. Cavallotti
V. Sanzio
V.le A. Aleardi
V.le Ariosto
V. d. Orto
P.za T. Tasso
Villani
Via di Bellosguardo
V. d. Casone
F. Petrarca
Foscolo
Ugo Foscolo
Via
Via Romana
Viale N.
P.te d. Vittoria
PORTA AL PRATO
93
102
39
34
138
178
193
184
166
181
126
153
66
145
156
84
124
15
300m
410
Traffic restricte

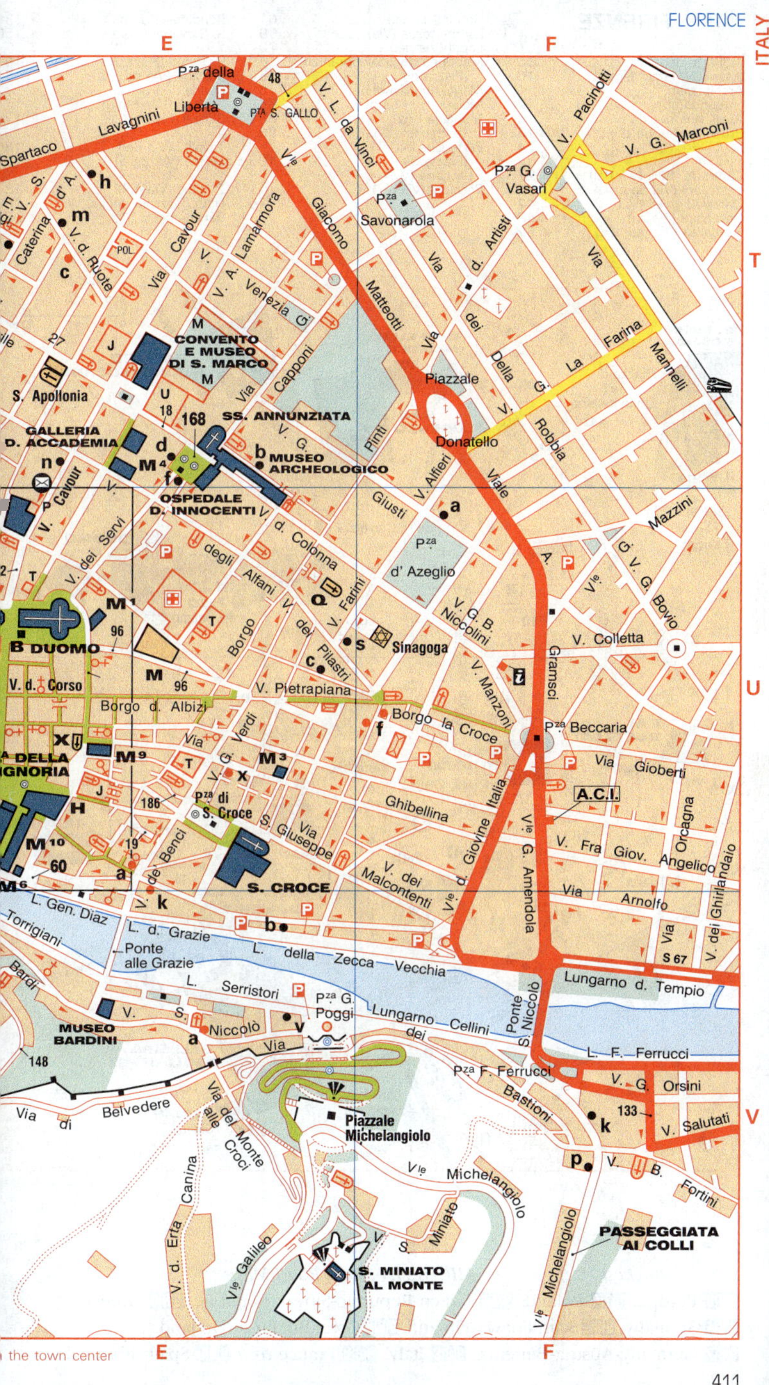

FLORENCE
ITALY
the town center
411
E
F
T
U
V
P za della
Libertà
48
PTA. S. GALLO
V. L. da Vinci
V. Pacinotti
Spartaco
Lavagnini
V. G. Marconi
h
m
c
Caterina
V. d. Ruote
d'A.
E.
V. S.
E. g.
POL
Cavour
V. A. Venezia G.
V. Lamarmora
Giacomo
Matteotti
P za
Savonarola
V. G. Vasari
d. Artisti
V. dei
Della
G.
La Farina
Mannelli
V.
V.
27
J
M
CONVENTO
E MUSEO
DI S. MARCO
M
S. Apollonia
U
18
168
SS. ANNUNZIATA
V. G.
b MUSEO
ARCHEOLOGICO
Piazzale
Donatello
V. Robbia
GALLERIA
D. ACCADEMIA
n
M 4
d
f
Capponi
Pinti
V. Alfieri
Viale
Mazzini
V. Cavour
V. dei Servi
OSPEDALE
D. INNOCENTI
V. d. Colonna
Giusti
a
P za
d' Azeglio
A.
V le
G. V. G. Bovio
2
T
V. d. Alfani
degli
Alfani
V. d. Farini
Q
V. G. B.
Niccolini
V. Colletta
M 1
96
Borgo
V. dei Pilastri
S
Sinagoga
V. Manzoni
Gramsci
B DUOMO
M
96
c
V. Pietrapiana
V. d. Corso
Borgo d. Albizi
f
Borgo la Croce
P za Beccaria
A DELLA
IGNORIA
Via
Verdi
V. G.
M 9
M 3
Gioberti
Orcagna
T
X
V. Fra Giov. Angelico
A.C.I.
H
J
186
P za di
S. Croce
Ghibellina
V. dei Ghirlandaio
M 10
60
a
de Benci
19
S. Giuseppe
Via
S. CROCE
V. dei
Malcontenti
V le G. Amendola
Arnolfo
Via
M 6
k
L. Gen. Diaz
b
V le Giovine Italia
S 67
Torrigiani
L. d. Grazie
L. della Zecca Vecchia
Ponte S. Niccolò
Lungarno d. Tempio
Bardi
Ponte
alle Grazie
L. Serristori
P za G.
Poggi
Lungarno
Cellini
dei
L. F. Ferrucci
MUSEO
BARDINI
V.
S.
Niccolò
v
a
Via
P za F. Ferrucci
V. G. Orsini
148
Bastioni
133
k
V. Salutati
Via
di
Belvedere
V. d. Erta Canina
V le del Monte Croci
Piazzale
Michelangiolo
p
V.
B. Fortini
V le Galileo
V le Michelangiolo
V. S. Miniato
V. S. Miniato
PASSEGGIATA
AI COLLI
S. MINIATO
AL MONTE

FIRENZE

Traffic restricted in the town centre

STREET INDEX TO FIRENZE TOWN PLAN

Discover **ITALY** with the **Michelin** Green Guide

Picturesque scenery, buildings

History and geography

Works of art

Touring programmes

Town plans

Helvetia e Bristol, via dei Pescioni 2 ✉ 50123 ℘ 055 287814, *Fax 055 288353* – 🛗
🖥 📺 ☎. AE 🅢 ⓞ E *VISA*. ⚹
Meals a la carte 70/110000 – ☕ 38000 – **34 rm** 420/640000, 18 suites 805/1650000

Z

Gd H. Minerva Ⓜ, piazza Santa Maria Novella 16 ✉ 50123 ℘ 055 284555
Fax 055 268281, 🏊 – 🛗 🖥 📺 ☎ – 🔬 90. AE 🅢 ⓞ E *VISA* JCB. ⚹ rest
Meals 55/80000 – **89 rm** ☕ 360/500000, 6 suites.

Y

Albani, via Fiume 12 ✉ 50123 ℘ 055 26030, *Fax 055 211045* – 🛗 🖥 📺 ☎ 🅿 – 🔬 100
AE 🅢 ⓞ E *VISA* JCB. ⚹
Meals a la carte 60/90000 – **90 rm** ☕ 350/490000, 4 suites.

DT

Brunelleschi, piazza Santa Elisabetta 3 ✉ 50122 ℘ 055 290311, *Fax 055 219653*,
« Small private museum in a Byzantine tower » – 🛗, ⚹ rm, 🖥 📺 ☎ – 🔬 100. AE 🅢
ⓞ E *VISA* JCB. ⚹
Meals (residents only) a la carte 70/100000 – **88 rm** ☕ 360/480000, 9 suites.

Z

Astoria Palazzo Gaddi, via del Giglio 9 ✉ 50123 ℘ 055 2398095, *Fax 055 214463*
– 🛗 🖥 📺 ☎ ㏂ – 🔬 130. AE 🅢 ⓞ E *VISA* JCB. ⚹
Meals (closed Sunday) a la carte 60/85000 – **100 rm** ☕ 250/360000, suite.

Y

Plaza Hotel Lucchesi, lungarno della Zecca Vecchia 38 ✉ 50122 ℘ 055 26236
Fax 055 2480921, ≤ – 🛗, ⚹ rm, 🖥 📺 ☎ 🚗 – 🔬 160. AE 🅢 ⓞ E *VISA* JCB. ⚹ rest
Meals (closed Sunday) (residents only) a la carte 65/75000 – **87 rm** ☕ 370/550000, 10
suites.

EV

Grand Hotel Baglioni, piazza Unità Italiana 6 ✉ 50123 ℘ 055 23580
Fax 055 2358895, « Roof garden rest. with ≤ city » – 🛗 🖥 📺 ☎ – 🔬 200. AE 🅢 ⓞ
E *VISA* JCB. ⚹
Meals a la carte 80/120000 – **195 rm** ☕ 340/460000, 5 suites.

Y

Sofitel Ⓜ 🐾, via de' Cerretani 10 ✉ 50123 ℘ 055 2381301, *Fax 055 2381312* – 🛗
⚹ rm, 🖥 📺 ☎ ㏂. AE 🅢 ⓞ E *VISA* JCB. ⚹ rest
Meals *Il Patio* Rest. a la carte 65/80000 – **83 rm** ☕ 370/490000.

Y

Lungarno without rest., borgo Sant'Jacopo 14 ✉ 50125 ℘ 055 27261
Fax 055 268437, ≤, « Collection of modern pictures » – 🛗 🖥 📺 ☎ ㏉ – 🔬 30. AE 🅢
ⓞ E *VISA* JCB
57 rm ☕ 530/590000, 9 suites.

Z

Berchielli without rest., piazza del Limbo 6 r ✉ 50123 ℘ 055 264061, *Fax 055 218636*
≤ – 🛗 🖥 📺 ☎ – 🔬 100. AE 🅢 ⓞ E *VISA* JCB. ⚹
76 rm ☕ 430/470000, 3 suites.

Z

Executive without rest., via Curtatone 5 ✉ 50123 ℘ 055 217451, *Fax 055 26834*
– 🛗 🖥 📺 ☎ – 🔬 50. AE 🅢 ⓞ E *VISA* JCB
38 rm ☕ 320/440000.

CU

Londra, via Jacopo da Diacceto 18 ✉ 50123 ℘ 055 2382791, *Fax 055 210682*,
– 🛗 🖥 📺 ☎ 🚗 – 🔬 200. AE 🅢 ⓞ E *VISA* JCB. ⚹ rest
Meals a la carte 55/80000 – **158 rm** ☕ 340/440000.

DT

Pierre without rest., via De' Lamberti 5 ✉ 50123 ℘ 055 216218, *Fax 055 2396573*
🛗 🖥 📺 ☎. AE 🅢 ⓞ E *VISA* JCB
40 rm ☕ 340/460000.

Z

Starhotel Michelangelo, viale Fratelli Rosselli 2 ✉ 50123 ℘ 055 2784
Fax 055 2382232 – 🛗, ⚹ rm, 🖥 📺 ☎ – 🔬 250. AE 🅢 ⓞ E *VISA* JCB. ⚹
Meals a la carte 50/100000 – ☕ 30000 – **128 rm** 410/530000.

CT

Continental without rest., lungarno Acciaiuoli 2 ✉ 50123 ℘ 055 27262
Fax 055 283139, « Floral terrace with ≤ » – 🛗 🖥 📺 ☎ ㏂. AE 🅢 ⓞ E *VISA* JCB
48 rm ☕ 350/470000, suite.

Z

Rivoli without rest., via della Scala 33 ✉ 50123 ℘ 055 282853, *Fax 055 294041*,
– 🛗 🖥 📺 ☎ ㏂ – 🔬 100. AE 🅢 ⓞ E *VISA* JCB. ⚹
65 rm ☕ 330/440000.

DU

De la Ville, piazza Antinori 1 ✉ 50123 ℘ 055 2381805, *Fax 055 2381809* – 🛗 🖥 📺
☎ ㏉ – 🔬 60. AE 🅢 ⓞ E *VISA* JCB. ⚹ rest
Meals (residents only) a la carte 60/80000 – **71 rm** ☕ 400/565000, 4 suites.

Y

J and J without rest., via di Mezzo 20 ✉ 50121 ℘ 055 2345005, *Fax 055 240282*
🖥 📺 ☎. AE 🅢 ⓞ E *VISA* JCB. ⚹
15 rm ☕ 500000, 5 suites.

EU

Montebello Splendid, via Montebello 60 ✉ 50123 ℘ 055 2398051, *Fax 055 211867*
㏋ – 🛗 🖥 📺 ☎ 🅿 – 🔬 100. AE 🅢 ⓞ E *VISA* JCB
Meals a la carte 70/105000 – ☕ 30000 – **54 rm** 335/485000, suite.

CU

Il Guelfo Bianco without rest., via Cavour 29 ✉ 50129 ℘ 055 28833C
Fax 055 295203 – 🛗 🖥 📺 ☎ ㏂. AE 🅢 E *VISA*. ⚹
29 rm ☕ 205/285000.

ET

Botticelli without rest., via Taddea 8 ✉ 50123 ✆ 055 290905, *Fax 055 294322* – 🛗 🖭 📺 ☎ ⟁. AE 🅂 ⓪ E VISA JCB
34 rm ☕ 210/320000.
ET p

Malaspina without rest., piazza dell'Indipendenza 24 ✉ 50129 ✆ 055 489869, *Fax 055 474809* – 🛗 🖭 📺 ☎ ⟁. AE 🅂 ⓪ E VISA. ✘
31 rm ☕ 195/290000.
ET g

Porta Faenza without rest., via Faenza 77 ✉ 50123 ✆ 055 217975, *Fax 055 210101* – 🛗, ✄, 🖭 📺 ☎ ⟁ 🚗 – 🏛 30. AE 🅂 ⓪ E VISA JCB
25 rm ☕ 300/340000.
DT d

Palazzo Benci without rest., piazza Madonna degli Aldobrandini 3 ✉ 50123 ✆ 055 2382821, *Fax 055 288308* – 🛗 🖭 📺 ☎ – 🏛 30. AE 🅂 ⓪ E VISA JCB. ✘
35 rm ☕ 200/300000.
Y y

Select without rest., via Giuseppe Galliano 24 ✉ 50144 ✆ 055 330342, *Fax 055 351506* – 🛗 🖭 📺 ☎ – 🏛 25. AE 🅂 ⓪ E VISA JCB
☕ 10000 – 36 rm 200/260000.
CT t

Grifone without rest., via Pilati 22 ✉ 50136 ✆ 055 661367, *Fax 055 677628* – 🛗 🖭 📺 ☎ Ⓟ. AE 🅂 ⓪ E VISA. ✘
58 rm ☕ 185/250000, 9 suites.
by via Gioberti FU

David without rest., viale Michelangiolo 1 ✉ 50125 ✆ 055 6811695, *Fax 055 680602*, ✍ – 🛗 🖭 📺 ☎ Ⓟ. AE 🅂 ⓪ E VISA JCB. ✘
24 rm ☕ 140/240000.
FV k

Villa Liberty without rest., viale Michelangiolo 40 ✉ 50125 ✆ 055 6810581, *Fax 055 6812595*, ✍ – 🛗 🖭 📺 ☎ Ⓟ. AE 🅂 ⓪ E VISA JCB
15 rm ☕ 230/290000, 2 suites.
FV p

Royal without rest., via delle Ruote 52 ✉ 50129 ✆ 055 483287, *Fax 055 490976*, « Garden » – 🛗 🖭 📺 ☎ Ⓟ. AE 🅂 ⓪ E VISA JCB
39 rm ☕ 180/300000.
ET m

De Rose Palace Hotel without rest., via Solferino 5 ✉ 50123 ✆ 055 2396818, *Fax 055 268249* – 🛗 🖭 📺 ☎. AE 🅂 ⓪ E VISA JCB
18 rm ☕ 230/360000
CU c

Goldoni without rest., via Borgo Ognissanti 8 ✉ 50123 ✆ 055 284080, *Fax 055 282576* – 🛗 🖭 📺 ☎. AE 🅂 E VISA
☕ 10000 – 20 rm 180/280000.
DU w

City without rest., via Sant'Antonino 18 ✉ 50123 ✆ 055 211543, *Fax 055 295451* – 🛗 🖭 📺 ☎. AE 🅂 ⓪ E VISA JCB
20 rm ☕ 230/290000.
Y x

Loggiato dei Serviti without rest., piazza SS. Annunziata 3 ✉ 50122 ✆ 055 289592, *Fax 055 289595*, « 16C building » – 🛗 🖭 📺 ☎. AE 🅂 ⓪ E VISA JCB
25 rm ☕ 220/325000, 4 suites.
ET d

Villa Azalee without rest., viale Fratelli Rosselli 44 ✉ 50123 ✆ 055 214242, *Fax 055 268264*, ✍ – 🖭 📺 ☎. AE 🅂 ⓪ E VISA
24 rm ☕ 250/270000.
CT r

Morandi alla Crocetta without rest., via Laura 50 ✉ 50121 ✆ 055 2344747, *Fax 055 2480954* – 🖭 📺 ☎. AE 🅂 ⓪ E VISA
☕ 20000 – 10 rm 160/250000.
ET b

Pitti Palace without rest., via Barbadori 2 ✉ 50125 ✆ 055 2398711, *Fax 055 2398867* – 🛗 🖭 📺 ☎. AE 🅂 ⓪ E VISA JCB. ✘
☕ 25000 – 72 rm 220/320000, suite.
Z g

Vasari without rest., via Cennini 9/11 ✉ 50123 ✆ 055 212753, *Fax 055 294246* – 🖭 📺 ☎ ⟁ Ⓟ. AE 🅂 ⓪ E VISA JCB
30 rm ☕ 180/230000.
DT c

Silla without rest., via dei Renai 5 ✉ 50125 ✆ 055 2342888, *Fax 055 2341437* – 🛗 🖭 📺 ☎ 🚗. AE 🅂 ⓪ E VISA
36 rm ☕ 200/235000.
EV r

Sanremo without rest., lungarno Serristori 13 ✉ 50125 ✆ 055 2342823, *Fax 055 2342269* – 🛗 🖭 📺 ☎. AE 🅂 ⓪ E VISA
closed 15 January-15 February – 20 rm ☕ 170/230000.
EV v

Residenza Johanna without rest., via Cinque Giornate 12 ✉ 50129 ✆ 055 473377, *Fax 055 473377* – Ⓟ. ✘
6 rm ☕ 140000.
by viale Redi CT

Residenza Hanna e Johanna without rest., via Bonifacio Lupi 14 ✉ 50129 ✆ 055 481896, *Fax 055 482721* – 🛗. ✘
11 rm ☕ 75/120000
ET h

XXXXX 🕸🕸 **Enoteca Pinchiorri,** via Ghibellina 87 ✉ 50122 ✆ 055 242777, Fax 055 24498:
« Summer service in a cool courtyard » – 🈲. AE VISA JCB EU
closed Sunday, Monday-Wednesday lunch, August and 18 to 27 December – **Meals** (boc
king essential) 110000 (lunch) 180000 (dinner) and a la carte 150/250000
Spec. Fagottino croccante alle cipolle candite con timo, punte d'asparagi e scaglie di pecc
rino. Risotto alle erbe e zenzero con ragù di faraona e porcini (autumn). Tagliata di manz
al vino rosso con frittelle di granturco al rosmarino.

XXXX **Sabatini,** via de' Panzani 9/a ✉ 50123 ✆ 055 211559, Fax 055 210293, Elegant tra
ditional decor – 🈲. AE 🛈 ⓪ E VISA JCB. 🦺 Y
closed Monday – **Meals** 50/90000 and a la carte 85/115000 (13 %).

XXX **Don Chisciotte,** via Ridolfi 4 r ✉ 50129 ✆ 055 475430, Fax 055 485305 – 🈲. AE
⓪ E VISA JCB DT
closed Sunday, Monday lunch and August – **Meals** (booking essential) a la carte 65/10500
(10 %).

XXX **Taverna del Bronzino,** via delle Ruote 25/27 r ✉ 50129 ✆ 055 495220 – 🈲. A
🛈 ⓪ E VISA ET
closed Sunday and August – **Meals** (booking essential) a la carte 70/100000.

XX **Osteria n. 1,** via del Moro 20 r ✉ 50123 ✆ 055 284897, Fax 055 294318 – 🈲. A
🛈 ⓪ E VISA JCB Z
closed Sunday, Monday lunch and 3 to 26 August – **Meals** a la carte 55/105000.

XX **Il Barrino,** via Gioberti 71 r ✉ 50121 ✆ 055 660565 – 🈲. AE 🛈 E VISA FU
closed Sunday dinner and Saturday – **Meals** a la carte 50/90000.

XX **Trattoria Vittoria,** via della Fonderia 52 r ✉ 50142 ✆ 055 225657 – 🈲. AE 🛈 ⓪
E VISA JCB CU
closed Wednesday and August – **Meals** seafood a la carte 65/85000.

XX **La Vecchia Cucina,** viale Edmondo De Amicis 1 r ✉ 50137 ✆ 055 66014:
Fax 055 660143 – 🈲. AE 🛈 ⓪ E VISA. 🦺 by via Gioberti FU
closed Saturday lunch and Sunday – **Meals** a la carte 50/75000.

XX **Cantinetta Antinori,** piazza Antinori 3 ✉ 50123 ✆ 055 292234, Rest. and wine ba
– 🈲. AE 🛈 ⓪ E VISA JCB. 🦺 Y
closed Saturday, Sunday, August and Christmas – **Meals** (booking essential for dinne
Tuscan rest. a la carte 70/90000 (10 %).

XX **Enoteca Pane e Vino,** via di San Niccolò 70 a/r ✉ 50125 ✆ 055 247695(
Fax 055 2476956 – AE 🛈 ⓪ E VISA. 🦺 EV
closed Sunday and August – **Meals** (dinner only) 45000 and a la carte 50/75000.

XX **Paoli,** via dei Tavolini 12 r ✉ 50122 ✆ 055 216215, Fax 055 216215, « Decorated i
13C style » – 🈲. AE 🛈 ⓪ E VISA Z
closed Tuesday and August – **Meals** a la carte 50/80000.

XX **Ottorino,** via delle Oche 12/16 r ✉ 50122 ✆ 055 215151, Fax 055 287140 – 🈲. A
🛈 ⓪ E VISA JCB. 🦺 YZ
closed Sunday and 15 to 31 August – **Meals** a la carte 60/90000.

X **Vineria Cibreino,** piazza Ghiberti 35 ✉ 50122 – 🈲. AE 🛈 ⓪ E
VISA JCB FU
closed Sunday, Monday, 26 July-6 September and 31 December-6 January – **Meals** (bookin
essential) a la carte 40/50000.

X **Il Profeta,** borgo Ognissanti 93 r ✉ 50123 ✆ 055 212265 – 🈲. AE 🛈 ⓪
E VISA DU
closed Sunday and 15 to 31 August – **Meals** a la carte 45/70000 (12 %).

X **Fiorenza,** via Reginaldo Giuliani 51 r ✉ 50141 ✆ 055 416903, Fax 055 416903 – 🈲
AE 🛈 ⓪ E VISA by viale Lavagnini ET
closed Sunday and August – **Meals** Thursday, Friday and Saturday only seafood a la cart
45/70000.

X **Pandemonio,** via del Leone 50 r ✉ 50124 ✆ 055 224002 – AE 🛈 ⓪ E VISA JC
🦺 CU
closed Sunday and August – **Meals** a la carte 65/100000 (10 %).

X **Cafaggi,** via Guelfa 35 r ✉ 50129 ✆ 055 294989, Fax 055 294989 – 🈲. AE 🛈 E VIS
closed Sunday and 18 July-15 August – **Meals** a la carte 40/95000. ET

X **Da Carmine-il Pizzaiuolo,** via De' Macci 113 r ✉ 50122 ✆ 055 241171
🈲 FU
closed Sunday – **Meals** (booking essential) Napolitan rest. and pizzeria a la carte 55
70000.

X **Del Carmine,** piazza del Carmine 18 r ✉ 50124 ✆ 055 218601 – AE 🛈 ⓪
E VISA DU
closed Sunday and 7 to 21 August – **Meals** (booking essential) a la carte 35/50000.

✗ **Baldini,** via il Prato 96 r ✉ 50123 ✆ 055 287663, *Fax 055 287663* – ▣. ⒶⒺ ⑤ ⓪ Ⓔ
VISA. ✬   CT h
*closed 1 to 20 August, 24 December-3 January, Saturday and Sunday dinner, June-July
also Sunday lunch* – **Meals** a la carte 40/55000.

✗ **Osteria de' Benci,** via de' Benci 10/13 r ✉ 50122 ✆ 055 2344923, *Fax 055 2344932*
– ▣. ⒶⒺ ⑤ ⓪ Ⓔ *VISA* JCB   EU a
closed Sunday – **Meals** (booking essential) a la carte 45/60000 (10 %).

✗ **Osteria Antica Mescita,** via San Nicolò 60 r ✉ 50125 ✆ 055 2342836, Osteria with
wine bar – ▣   EV a
closed Sunday, August and 1 to 15 January – **Meals** a la carte 30/45000.

✗ **Il Latini,** via dei Palchetti 6 r ✉ 50123 ✆ 055 210916, *Fax 055 289794*, Typical trattoria
– ⒶⒺ ⑤ ⓪ Ⓔ *VISA*. ✬   Z j
closed Monday and 24 December-1 January – Meals a la carte 50/65000.

✗ **La Carabaccia,** via Palazzuolo 190 r ✉ 50123 ✆ 055 214782 – ⒶⒺ ⑤ Ⓔ
VISA JCB   CDU f
closed Sunday, Monday lunch and 13 August-4 September – **Meals** (booking essential) a
la carte 50/70000.

✗ **Del Fagioli,** corso Tintori 47 r ✉ 50122 ✆ 055 244285, Typical Tuscan trattoria – ✬
closed Saturday, Sunday and August – **Meals** a la carte 40/55000.   EV k

✗ **Ruth's,** via Farini 2 ✉ 50121 ✆ 055 2480888 – ▣   EU s
closed Friday dinner and Saturday lunch on Jewish holidays – **Meals** (booking essential)
Jewish rest. a la carte 30/40000.

on the hills *South : 3 km :*

🏨 **Gd H. Villa Cora** ⟡, viale Machiavelli 18 ✉ 50125 ✆ 055 2298451, *Fax 055 229086,*
🌳, Shuttle service to city centre, « 19C house in floral park with ⌁ » – ▮ ▣ �📺 ☎
🅿 – ⚓ 150. ⒶⒺ ⑤ ⓪ Ⓔ *VISA* JCB. ✬ rest   DV b
Meals *Taverna Machiavelli* Rest. a la carte 70/130000 – **33 rm** ⌑ 460/860000, 15
suites 1100/1900000.

🏨 **Torre di Bellosguardo** ⟡ without rest., via Roti Michelozzi 2 ✉ 50124
✆ 055 2298145, *Fax 055 229008,* ✳ town and hills, « Park with botanical garden, aviary
and ⌁ » – ▮ ☎ 🅿. ⒶⒺ ⑤ Ⓔ *VISA*   CV a
⌑ 35000 – **10 rm** 340/450000, 6 suites 550/650000.

🏨 **Villa Belvedere** ⟡ without rest., via Benedetto Castelli 3 ✉ 50124 ✆ 055 222501,
Fax 055 223163, ≤ town and hills, « Garden-park with ⌁ », ✗ – ▮ ▣ 📺 ☎ 🅿. ⒶⒺ ⑤
⓪ Ⓔ *VISA*. ✬   by via Senese CV
March-November – **23 rm** ⌑ 240/330000, 3 suites.

🏨 **Classic** without rest., viale Machiavelli 25 ✉ 50125 ✆ 055 229351, *Fax 055 229353,*
🚃 – ▮ 📺 ☎ 🅿. ⒶⒺ ⑤ Ⓔ *VISA*   DV c
⌑ 12000 – **16 rm** 135/195000, 3 suites.

at Arcetri *South : 5 km –* ✉ **50125** *Firenze :*

✗ **Omero,** via Pian de' Giullari 11 r ✆ 055 220053, *Fax 055 2336183*, Country trattoria with
≤, « Summer service dinner on terrace » – ⒶⒺ ⑤ ⓪ Ⓔ *VISA* JCB. ✬
closed Tuesday and August – **Meals** a la carte 55/60000 (13 %). by viale Machiavelli DV

at Galluzzo *South : 6,5 km –* ✉ **50124** *Firenze :*

✗ **Trattoria Bibe,** via delle Bagnese 15 ✆ 055 2049085, *Fax 055 2047167,* « Outdoor
summer service » – 🅿. ⒶⒺ ⑤ Ⓔ *VISA*   AS c
closed Wednesday, Thursday lunch, 10 to 25 November and 15 to 28 February – **Meals**
a la carte 45/55000.

at Serpiolle *North : 8 km –* ✉ **50141** *Firenze :*

✗✗✗ **Lo Strettoio,** via Serpiolle 7 ✆ 055 4250044, *Fax 055 4250044,* ≤, 🌳, « 17C villa
among the olive trees » – 🅿. ⒶⒺ ⑤ Ⓔ *VISA*. ✬
closed Sunday, Monday and August – **Meals** (booking essential) a la carte 60/85000.

on the motorway at ring-road A1-A11 Florence North *North-West : 10 km :*

🏨 **Afi Hotel,** ✉ 50013 Campi Bisenzio ✆ 055 4205081, *Fax 055 4219015* – ▮, ✲ rm,
▣ 📺 ☎ ♿ 🅿 – ⚓ 200. ⒶⒺ ⑤ ⓪ Ⓔ *VISA*. ✬
Meals *(closed Sunday)* a la carte 50/85000 – **163 rm** ⌑ 190/250000.

close to motorway station A1 Florence South *South-East : 6 km :*

🏨 **Sheraton Firenze Hotel,** via Agnelli 33 ✉ 50126 ✆ 055 64901, *Fax 055 680747,*
⌁, ✗ – ▮, ✲ rm, ▣ 📺 ☎ ♿ 🚗 🅿 – ⚓ 1500. ⒶⒺ ⑤ ⓪ Ⓔ *VISA* JCB. ✬
Meals a la carte 55/95000 *Il Cortile* Rest. a la carte 55/65000 and *Primavera* Rest. a
la carte 55/85000 – **319 rm** ⌑ 330/400000, 3 suites.

San Casciano in Val di Pesa
50026 Firenze 🔢988 ⑭ ⑮, 🔢429, 🔢430 L 15 *G. Toscana* – pop. 16130 alt. 306.
Roma 283 – Firenze 17 – Livorno 84 – Siena 53.

a Cerbaia *North-West : 6 km –* ✉ *50020 :*

XXX **La Tenda Rossa,** piazza del Monumento 9/14 ℘ 055 826132, Fax 055 825210 – 🖃
AE 🅂 ⓪ E *VISA* JCB 🛇
closed Sunday, Monday lunch and August – **Meals** (booking essential) a la carte 95/14500
Spec. Insalata di mazzancolle con olio al rosmarino e sale grosso. Tortelli di triglia salta
con olive nere tritate e foglie di cipolla dolce al balsamico. Carrè d'agnello rosolato nel lard
con vellutata di rosmarino e salvia al profumo d'aglio.

San Vincenzo
57027 Livorno 🔢988 ⑭, 🔢430 M 13 *G. Toscana* – pop. 6940 – High Season
15 June-15 September.
🛈 via Beatrice Alliata 2 ℘ 0565 701533, Fax 0565 701533.
Roma 260 – Firenze 146 – Grosseto 73 – Livorno 60 – Piombino 21 – Siena 109.

XXX **Gambero Rosso,** piazza della Vittoria 13 ℘ 0565 701021, Fax 0565 704542, ≼ – 🖃
🅂 ⓪ E *VISA* 🛇
closed Christmas, Tuesday (except November), and Monday December-April – **Meals** (boo
king essential) 110/130000 (10 %) and a la carte 100/150000 (10 %)
Spec. Passatina di ceci con gamberi. Lasagnette alla marinara con zuppa di finocchi. Maialin
"cinta senese" al mirto.

MILAN
20100 🅿 🔢988 ③, 🔢428 F 9 *G. Italy* – pop. 1302808 alt. 122.
See : *Cathedral*★★★ *(Duomo)* MZ – *Cathedral Museum*★★ MZ M¹ – *Via and Piazz
Mercanti*★ MZ **155** – *La Scala Opera House*★★ MZ *Manzoni House*★ MZ M⁷ – *Brera A*
Gallery★★★ KV – *Castle of the Sforza*★★★ JV – *Ambrosian Library*★★ MZ : *portraits*★★
of Gaffurio and Isabella d'Este, Raphael's cartoons★★★ – *Poldi-Pezzoli Museum*★★ KV M¹
portrait of a woman★★★ *(in profile) by Pollaiolo Palazzo Bagatti Valsecchi*★★ KV L – *Palazz*
Bagatti Valsecchi★★ KV L – *Natural History Museum*★ LV M⁶ – *Leonardo da Vinci Museu*
of Science and Technology★ HX M⁴ – *Church of St. Mary of Grace*★ HX : *Leonardo da Vinci*
Last Supper★★★ – *Basilica of St. Ambrose*★★ HJX : *altar front*★★ – *Church of S*
Eustorgius★ JY : *Portinari Chapel*★★ – *General Hospital*★ KXY – *Church of St. Satiro*★
dome★ MZ – *Church of St. Maurice*★★ JX – *Church of St. Lawrence Major*★ JY.
Envir. : *Chiaravalle Abbey*★ *South-East : 7 km by corso Lodi* LY.
🏌️₁₈, 🏌️₉ *(closed Monday) at Monza Park* ✉ *20052 Monza* ℘ *039 303081, Fax 039 30442*
by North : 20 km;
🏌️₁₈ *Molinetto (closed Monday) at Cernusco sul Naviglio* ✉ *20063* ℘ *02 92105128, Fa*
02 92106635, by North-East : 14 km;
🏌️₁₈ *Barlassina (closed Monday) at Birago di Camnago* ✉ *20030* ℘ *0362 560621, Fa*
0362 560934, by North : 26 km;
🏌️₁₈ *(closed Monday) at Zoate di Tribiano* ✉ *20067* ℘ *02 90632183, Fax 02 9063186*
South-East : 20 km;
🏌️₁₈ *Le Rovedine (closed Monday) at Noverasco di Opera* ✉ *20090* ℘ *02 57606420, Fa*
02 57606405, by via Ripamonti BP.
Motor-Racing circuit *at Monza Park by North : 20 km,* ℘ *039 24821.*
✈ *Forlanini of Linate East : 8 km* ℘ *02 74852200 and Malpensa by North-West : 4*
km ℘ *02 74852200 – Alitalia Sede* ℘ *02 24991, corso Como 15* ✉ *2015*
℘ *02 24992500, Fax 02 24992525 and via Albricci 5* ✉ *20122* ℘ *02 24992700, Fa*
02 8056757.
🛈 *via Marconi 1* ✉ *20123* ℘ *02 72524300, Fax 02 72524350 – Central Station* ✉ *2012*
℘ *02 72524360.*
A.C.I. *corso Venezia 43* ✉ *20121* ℘ *02 77451.*
Roma 572 – Genève 323 – Genova 142 – Torino 140.

Plans on following pages

Historical centre Duomo, Scala, Sforza Castle, corso Magenta, via Torino, corso Vittori
Emanuele, via Manzoni

🏨 **Four Seasons,** via Gesù 8 ✉ 20121 ℘ 02 77088, Fax 02 77085000, 🏋, 🍽 – 🛗 🕩
🖃 📺 ☎ 📞 ☯ 🚗 – 🛎 280. AE 🅂 ⓪ E *VISA* JCB 🛇 rest   KV
Meals *Il Teatro* Rest. *(closed lunch, Sunday and August)* a la carte 80/140000 and *L*
Veranda Rest. a la carte 70/125000 – ☕ 45000 – **82 rm** 965/1215000, 16 suites.

🏨 **Grand Hotel et de Milan,** via Manzoni 29 ✉ 20121 ℘ 02 723141, Fax 02 8646086
– 🛗 🖃 📺 ☎ 📞 ☯ – 🛎 100. AE 🅂 ⓪ E *VISA* JCB   KV
Meals *Caruso* Rest. *(closed dinner)* a la carte 70/100000 see also rest **Don Carlos** belo
– ☕ 35000 – **95 rm** 695/815000, 8 suites.

Jolly Hotel President, largo Augusto 10 ⊠ 20122 ℘ 02 77461, Fax 02 783449 – |≢|, ⇜ rm, ▤ 📺 ☎ 📞 – 🔬 100. 🄰🄴 🛅 ⓪ ⱻ 𝗩𝗜𝗦𝗔 𝗝𝗖𝗕. 🗶 rest   NZ q
Meals a la carte 70/115000 – **206 rm** ☕ 485/575000, 14 suite.

Brunelleschi Ⓜ, via Baracchini 12 ⊠ 20123 ℘ 02 8843, Fax 02 804924 – |≢| ▤ 📺 ☎ 🔬 – 🔬 50. 🄰🄴 🛅 ⓪ ⱻ 𝗩𝗜𝗦𝗔 𝗝𝗖𝗕. 🗶   MZ z
Meals a la carte 60/90000 – **123 rm** ☕ 350/450000, 5 suites.

De la Ville Ⓜ, via Hoepli 6 ⊠ 20121 ℘ 02 867651, Fax 02 866609 – |≢|, ⇜ rm, ▤ 📺 ☎ 🔬 – 🔬 85. 🄰🄴 🛅 ⓪ ⱻ 𝗩𝗜𝗦𝗔. 🗶   NZ h
Meals (see rest. **Canova** below) – **99 rm** ☕ 450/580000, 3 suites.

Carlton Hotel Baglioni, via Senato 5 ⊠ 20121 ℘ 02 77077, Fax 02 783300 – |≢|, ⇜ rm, ▤ 📺 ☎ 📞 🔬 🚗. 🄰🄴 🛅 ⓪ ⱻ 𝗩𝗜𝗦𝗔. 🗶 rest   KV b
Meals a la carte 80/135000 – **60 rm** ☕ 520/770000, 2 suites.

Grand Hotel Duomo, via San Raffaele 1 ⊠ 20121 ℘ 02 8833, Fax 02 86462027, ≼ Duomo, 🌿 – |≢|, ⇜ rm, ▤ 📺 ☎ 🔬 – 🔬 100. 🄰🄴 🛅 ⓪ ⱻ 𝗩𝗜𝗦𝗔 𝗝𝗖𝗕. 🗶   MZ u
Meals a la carte 70/90000 – **137 rm** ☕ 495/695000, 16 suites.

Sir Edward without rest., via Mazzini 4 ⊠ 20123 ℘ 02 877877, Fax 02 877844, ≋s – |≢|, ⇜, ▤ 📺 ☎ 🔬. 🄰🄴 🛅 ⓪ ⱻ 𝗩𝗜𝗦𝗔 𝗝𝗖𝗕. 🗶   MZ h
38 rm ☕ 320/420000, suite.

Spadari al Duomo Ⓜ without rest., via Spadari 11 ⊠ 20123 ℘ 02 72002371, Fax 02 861184, « Collection of modern art » – |≢| ▤ 📺 ☎. 🄰🄴 🛅 ⓪ ⱻ 𝗩𝗜𝗦𝗔 𝗝𝗖𝗕. 🗶
40 rm ☕ 320/450000.   MZ f

Radisson SAS Bonaparte Hotel, via Cusani 13 ⊠ 20121 ℘ 02 85601, Fax 02 8693601 – |≢| ▤ 📺 ☎ 📞 🚗 – 🔬 25. 🄰🄴 🛅 ⓪ ⱻ 𝗩𝗜𝗦𝗔 𝗝𝗖𝗕. 🗶 rest JV a
Meals a la carte 70/105000 – **55 rm** ☕ 440/510000, 10 suites.

Galileo, corso Europa 9 ⊠ 20122 ℘ 02 77431, Fax 02 76020584 – |≢| ▤ 📺 ☎ – 🔬 30. 🄰🄴 🛅 ⓪ ⱻ 𝗩𝗜𝗦𝗔 𝗝𝗖𝗕. 🗶   NZ x
Meals a la carte 60/90000 – **81 rm** ☕ 330/450000, 8 suites.

Cavour, via Fatebenefratelli 21 ⊠ 20121 ℘ 02 6572051, Fax 02 6592263 – |≢| ▤ 📺 ☎ 📞 – 🔬 100. 🄰🄴 🛅 ⓪ ⱻ 𝗩𝗜𝗦𝗔 𝗝𝗖𝗕   KV x
closed 11 to 24 August and 24 December-6 January – **Meals** (see rest. **Conte Camillo** below) – ☕ 25000 – **113 rm** 240/300000.

Starhotel Rosa, via Pattari 5 ⊠ 20122 ℘ 02 8831, Fax 02 8057964 – |≢| ⇜ ▤ 📺 ☎ 🔬 🚗 – 🔬 150. 🄰🄴 🛅 ⓪ ⱻ 𝗩𝗜𝗦𝗔 𝗝𝗖𝗕. 🗶   NZ v
Meals (residents only) – **185 rm** ☕ 445/580000.

Regina without rest., via Cesare Correnti 13 ⊠ 20123 ℘ 02 58106913, Fax 02 58107033, « 18C building » – |≢| ▤ 📺 ☎ 🔬 – 🔬 40. 🄰🄴 🛅 ⓪ ⱻ 𝗩𝗜𝗦𝗔 JY a
closed August and 24 December-7 January – **43 rm** ☕ 290/340000.

Dei Cavalieri, piazza Missori 1 ⊠ 20123 ℘ 02 88571, Fax 02 72021683 – |≢| ▤ 📺 ☎ 📞 – 🔬 60. 🄰🄴 🛅 ⓪ ⱻ 𝗩𝗜𝗦𝗔 𝗝𝗖𝗕. 🗶   MZ m
Meals (closed 2 to 23 August and 23 December-6 January) a la carte 75/125000 – **178 rm** ☕ 325/375000, 7 suites.

Ascot without rest., via Lentasio 3/5 ⊠ 20122 ℘ 02 58303300, Fax 02 58303203 – |≢| ▤ 📺 ☎. 🄰🄴 🛅 ⓪ ⱻ 𝗩𝗜𝗦𝗔. 🗶   KY c
closed August and 23 December-7 January – **63 rm** ☕ 230/320000.

Carrobbio without rest., via Medici 3 ⊠ 20123 ℘ 02 89010740, Fax 02 8053334 – |≢| ▤ 📺 ☎. 🄰🄴 🛅 ⓪ ⱻ 𝗩𝗜𝗦𝗔 𝗝𝗖𝗕   JX d
closed August and 22 December-6 January – **35 rm** ☕ 310/360000.

Manzoni without rest., via Santo Spirito 20 ⊠ 20121 ℘ 02 76005700, Fax 02 784212 – |≢| 📺 ☎ 📞 🚗. 🄰🄴 🛅 ⓪ ⱻ 𝗩𝗜𝗦𝗔 𝗝𝗖𝗕. 🗶   KV s
closed 22 July-August and 24 December-2 January – ☕ 20000 – **49 rm** 195/250000, 3 suites.

Lloyd without rest., corso di Porta Romana 48 ⊠ 20122 ℘ 02 58303332, Fax 02 58303365 – |≢| ▤ 📺 ☎ – 🔬 100. 🄰🄴 🛅 ⓪ ⱻ 𝗩𝗜𝗦𝗔   KY c
closed 8 to 24 August and 22 December-6 January – **56 rm** ☕ 280/380000, suite.

Ambrosiano without rest., via Santa Sofia 9 ⊠ 20122 ℘ 02 58306044, Fax 02 58305067, 🕁 – |≢| ▤ 📺 ☎ – 🔬 35. 🄰🄴 🛅 ⓪ ⱻ 𝗩𝗜𝗦𝗔. 🗶   KY f
closed 23 December-7 January – **78 rm** ☕ 180/265000.

Zurigo without rest., corso Italia 11/a ⊠ 20122 ℘ 02 72022260, Fax 02 72000013 – |≢| ▤ 📺 ☎. 🄰🄴 🛅 ⓪ ⱻ 𝗩𝗜𝗦𝗔 𝗝𝗖𝗕   KY j
closed 24 December-7 January – ☕ 10000 – **41 rm** 190/275000.

Casa Svizzera without rest., via San Raffaele 3 ⊠ 20121 ℘ 02 8692246, Fax 02 72004690 – |≢| ▤ 📺 ☎. 🄰🄴 🛅 ⓪ ⱻ 𝗩𝗜𝗦𝗔   MZ u
closed 28 July-24 August – **45 rm** ☕ 230/290000.

MILANO

Aurispa (V.)	JY	14
Battisti (V. C.)	KLX	20
Bocchetto (V.)	JX	30
Borgogna (V.)	KX	36
Borgonuovo (V.)	KV	38
Calatafimi (V.)	JY	45
Caradosso (V.)	HX	49
Ceresio (V.)	JU	59
Circo (V.)	JX	63
Col di Lana (Via)	JY	65
Col Moschin (V.)	JY	66
Conça del Naviglio (V.)	JY	69
Copernico (V.)	LT	72
Cordusio (Pza)	KX	73
Cune (Vie P.M.)	HV	77
Dugnani (V.)	HY	80
Fatebenefratelli (V.)	KV	92
Gangliano (V.)	KT	98
Generale Fara (V.)	KT	10
Ghislen (V. A.)	HY	10
Giardini (V. dei)	KV	10.

Within the green shaded area, the city is divided into zones wich are signposted all the way round.
Once entered, it is not possible to drive from one zone into another.

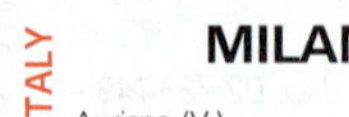

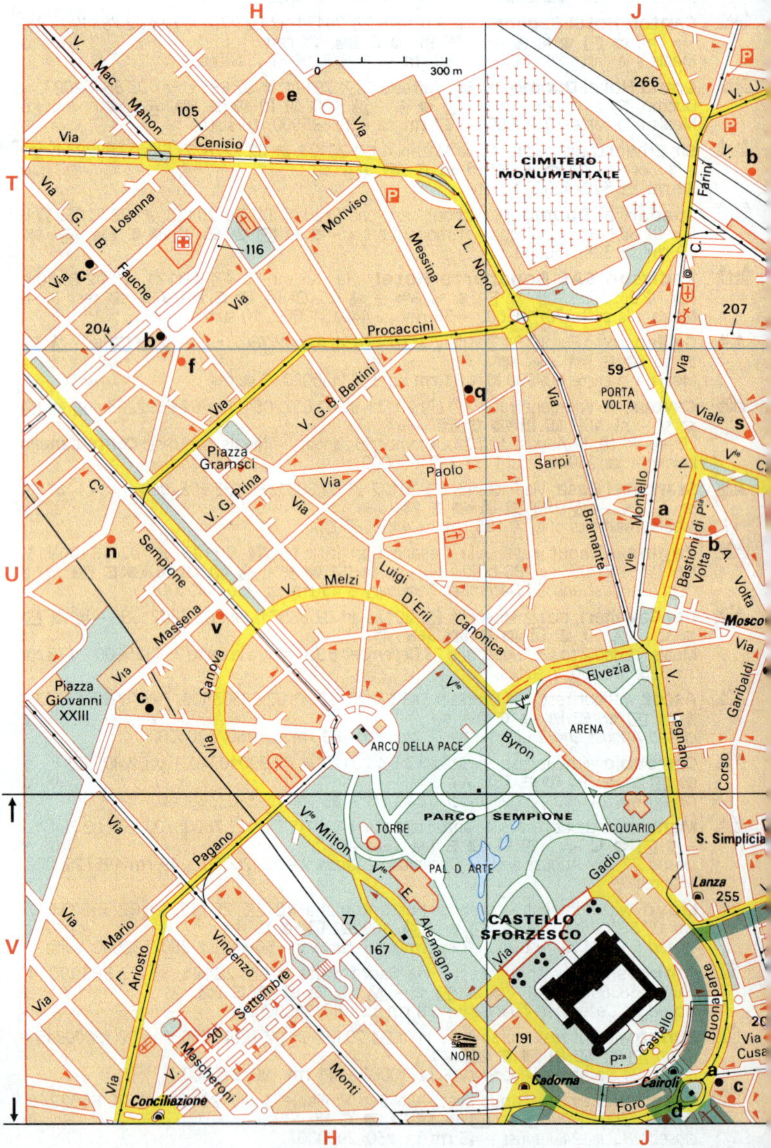

K
L
Bassi
260
198
122
Borsieri
98
Via
Pola
Via
Via
T
195
Pepe
Via
V. Confalonieri
Sassetti
V. G. de Castilla
A.C.I.
Via
214
Melchiorre
Gioia
Sondrio
v
V.
Gioia
j
Tonale
Sammartini
72
G. B.
V. G.
c
Filzi
a
Galvani
CENTRALE
100
PORTA GARIBALDI
Gioia
G. B.
b
f
Pirelli
p
m
s
k
Pisani
u
V.
Vitruvio
Vle
L.
Sturzo
Via
n
281
q
h
C° Como
Via
t
128
Via
d
Vle della
Liberazione
Via
San
n
y
Boscovich
Vle Monte
Grappa
V. Galileí
243
Via C.
258
Tenca
V. L. Settembrini
Subio
Vle Monte
T
Pta NUOVA
V.
d
Lazzaretto
Gregorio
Bastioni di Porta
Nuova
Monte
Santo
a
c
Repubblica
b
r
m
Nuova
Vle
Tunisia
Solferino
Pta
di Pta
della
j
Turati
f
Manin
e
c
Corso Buenos Aires
Statuto
P
h
Moscova
Bastioni di Pta Venezia
GIARDINO
ZOOLOGICO
278
g
Pta Venezia
b
V. San Marco
T
Turati
x
152
m
S. Marco
d
Manin
GIARDINI
PUBBLICI
Venezia
Viale
Viale
Staccio
POL.
92
Turati
Via
h
M6
Palestro
M
Piave
w
e
x
Via
Palestro
c
38
U
M
102
T
Via
Senato
Via
L
f
PINACOTECA
DI BRERA
A.C.I.
Palestro
g
Montenapoleone
S
c
Brera
V. Monte di Pieta
u
L
a
Maino
dell'Orso
M2
Napoleone
Via
Mia
M
Spiga
b
V. San Damiano
Corso
269
K
L

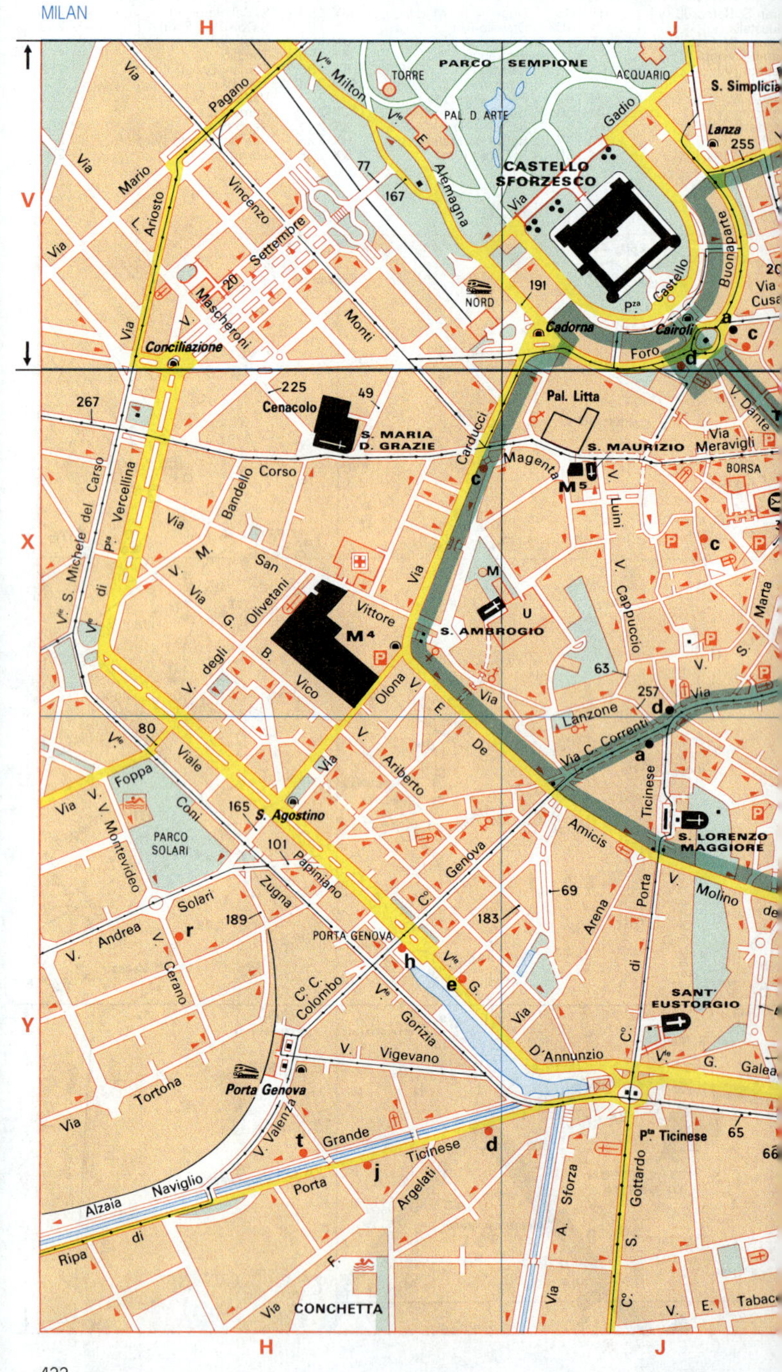
PARCO SEMPIONE
TORRE
PAL. D. ARTE
ACQUARIO
S. Simplici
Lanza
255
CASTELLO
SFORZESCO
Buonaparte
Via
Cusa
20
Via
Castello
pza
NORD
191
Cadorna
Cairoli
a
c
Foro
d
Via Milton
V.le Milton
V.le E
Alemagna
77
167
Via Pagano
Via Mario
T. Arioto
Vincenzo
20 Settembre
Mascheroni
Via
Via
Monti
Conciliazione
267
225
49
Cenacolo
S. MARIA
D. GRAZIE
Pal. Litta
S. MAURIZIO
Via Meravigli
V. Dante
Carducci
Magenta
BORSA
M 5
Vercellina
P.za
V.le di
V.le S. Michele del Carso
Corso
Bandello
Via
V. M.
San
Via
G. Olivetani
V.
degli
B.
Vico
Vittore
M 4
S. AMBROGIO
M
U
V. Luini
V. Cappuccio
Marta
V.
c
P
c
P
Olona V. E.
63
Lanzone
257
d
a
Via
Via C. Correnti
Ticinese
80
V.le
Viale
Foppa
V. V.
Coni
Via
V. V. Montevideo
PARCO
SOLARI
165
S. Agostino
Via
Ariberto
De
Via C. Correnti
a
S. LORENZO
MAGGIORE
Amicis
Porta
V. Molino
de
101
Papiniano
Genova
69
183
Arena
di
Solari
189
r
V. Andrea
V. Cerano
Zugna
PORTA GENOVA
C.o
h
V.le G
e
SANT'
EUSTORGIO
C.o C. Colombo
Gorizia
V.le
Via
D'Annunzio
C.o
V.le
Tortona
Via
Porta Genova
V. Vigevano
G. Galea
P.ta Ticinese
65
66
V. Valenza
t
Grande
Ticinese
d
S. Gottardo
j
Porta
Argelati
A. Sforza
Naviglio
Alzaia
di
Ripa
F.
C.o
V. E. Tabac
CONCHETTA
Via

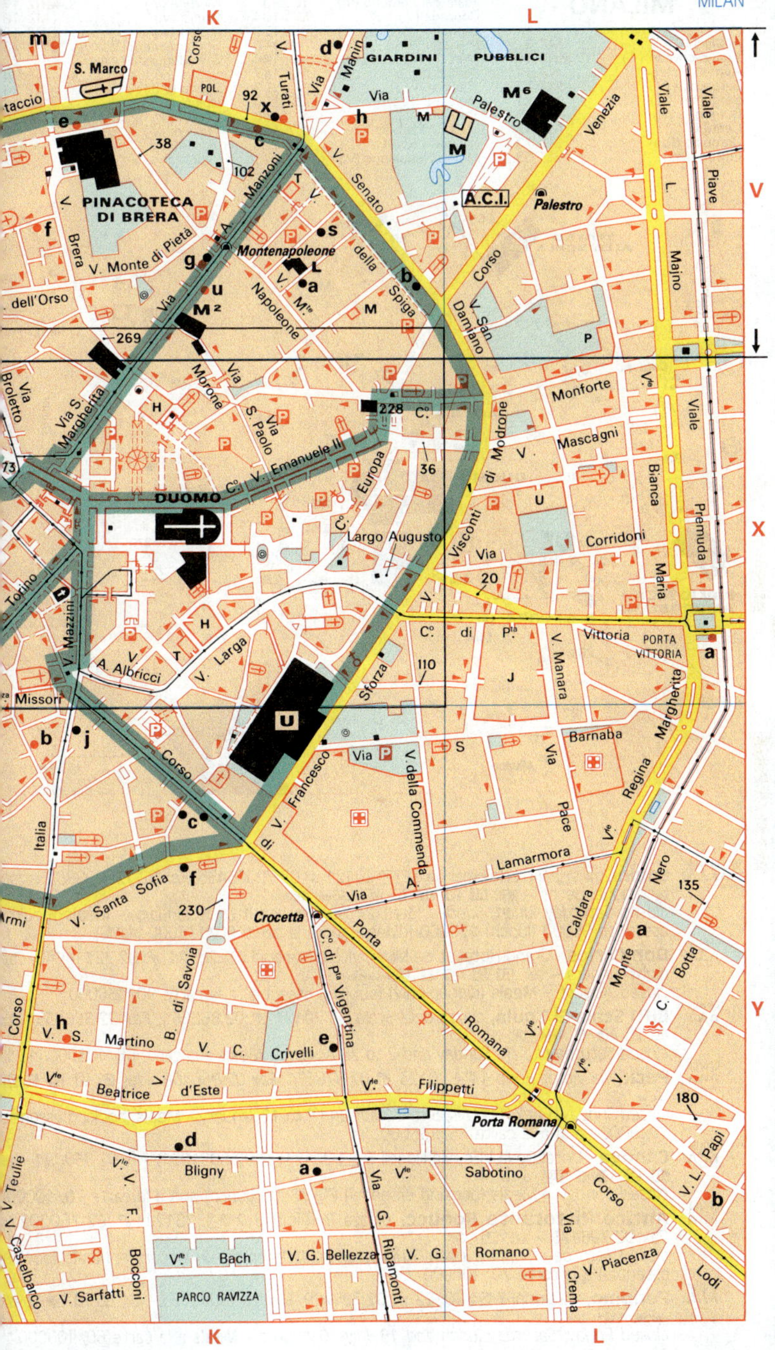
K
L
GIARDINI
PUBBLICI
S. Marco
POL.
92
x
Turati
d
Manin
Via
Via
Senato
h
M⁶
Palestro
M
M
M
38
102
c
Manzoni
V.
T
T
A.C.I.
Palestro
PINACOTECA
DI BRERA
f
Brera
V. Monte di Pietà
g
Montenapoleone
s
L
a
V. M.ᵗᵉ
M
b
Corso
V. San Damiano
dell'Orso
u
M²
Napoleone
M
della
Spiga
Via S. Margherita
Morone
Via
269
V. S. Paolo
Via
C°. V. Emanuele II
Europa
228
C°.
Monforte
V.
Mascagni
Via
Broletto
H
Bianca
73
DUOMO
C°.
C°.
Largo Augusto
36
Visconti di Modrone
Via
U
Corridoni
Maria
V. Mazzini
20
Premuda
V. Torino
Viale
X
D
H
C°. di P.ᵗᵃ
Vittoria
PORTA VITTORIA
a
A. Albricci
V
T
V. Larga
Sforza
110
J
V. Manara
Margherita
Missori
b
j
Corso
Francesco
Via
S
Via
Barnaba
Regina
Italia
c
V. della Commenda
Pace
Nero
135
V. Santa Sofia
f
di
Lamarmora
Caldara
a
230
Crocetta
C°. di P.ᵗᵃ Vigentina
Via
A.
Botta
di
Porta
C.
Savoia
Romana
V.ᵗᵉ
Monte
Corso
h
V. S.
Martino
C.
Crivelli
e
Romana
Y
V.ᵗᵉ
Beatrice
d'Este
V.ᵗᵉ
Filippetti
180
d
Porta Romana
Bligny
a
Via
V.ᵗᵉ
Sabotino
V. L. Papi
V. Teulie
V. V.
F.
V.ᵗᵉ
Bach
V. G. Bellezza
Ripamonti
V. G.
Romano
V. Piacenza
b
Castelbarco
Bocconi
Crema
V. Sarfatti
PARCO RAVIZZA
Lodi
K
L

MILANO

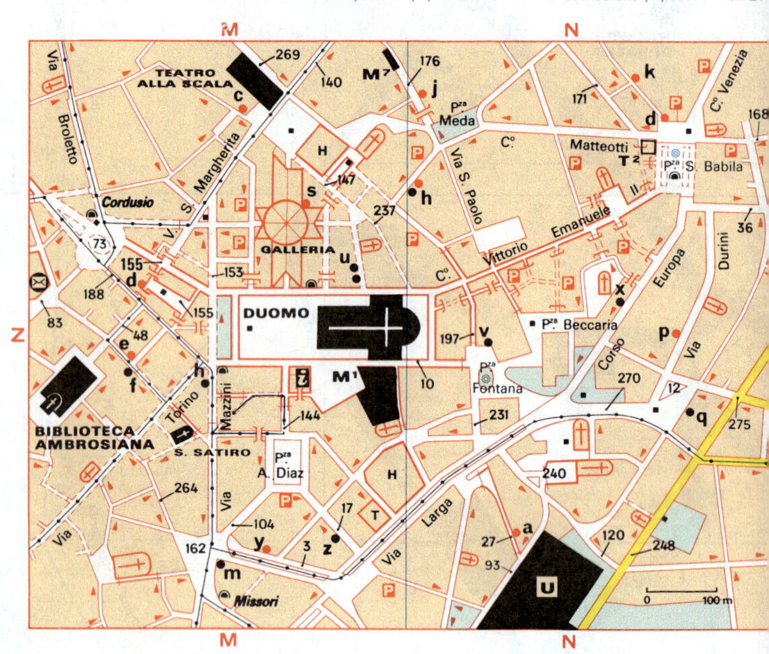

XXXXX **Savini,** galleria Vittorio Emanuele II ✉ 20121 ☎ 02 72003433, Fax 02 72022888, Elegan
traditional decor – ▤. AE ⑤ ⑩ E VISA JCB. ⌘   MZ
closed Saturday lunch, Sunday, 3 to 24 August and 1 to 6 January – **Meals** *(bookin
essential) 95000 (lunch) 120000 (dinner) and a la carte 90/135000 (12 %).*

XXXX **Don Carlos** - Grand Hotel et de Milan, vicolo Manzoni ✉ 20121 ☎ 02 72314640, Lat
night dinners – ▤. AE ⑤ ⑩ E VISA JCB   KV
closed August – **Meals** *(dinner only) (booking essential) a la carte 90/135000.*

XXX **Biffi Scala-El Toulà,** piazza della Scala ✉ 20121 ☎ 02 866651, Fax 02 866653 – ▤
AE ⑤ ⑩ E VISA. ⌘   MZ
closed Saturday lunch, Sunday and 2 to 28 August – **Meals** *a la carte 65/105000 (13 %*

XXX **Peck,** via Victor Hugo 4 ✉ 20123 ☎ 02 876774, Fax 02 860408 – ▤. AE ⑤ ⑩ E VIS
JCB. ⌘   MZ
closed Sunday, Bank Holidays, 5 to 24 July and 1 to 12 January – **Meals** *(booking essentia
70/90000 and a la carte 75/135000.*

XXX **Canova** - Hotel De la Ville, via Hoepli 6 ✉ 20121 ☎ 02 8051231, Fax 02 860094 – ▤
AE ⑤ ⑩ E VISA JCB. ⌘   NZ
closed Sunday – **Meals** *(booking essential) 60/75000 (lunch) and a la carte 70/100000*

XXX **Antico Ristorante Boeucc,** piazza Belgioioso 2 ✉ 20121 ☎ 02 76020224
Fax 02 796173 – ▤. AE. ⌘   NZ
closed Saturday, Sunday lunch, August and 24 December-2 January – **Meals** *(bookin
essential) a la carte 70/100000.*

XXX **Peppino,** via Durini 7 ✉ 20122 ☎ 02 781729, Fax 02 76002591 – ▤. AE ⑤ ⑩ E VIS
JCB. ⌘   NZ
closed Friday, Saturday lunch and 18 July-10 August – **Meals** *a la carte 60/100000.*

XXX **Don Lisander**, via Manzoni 12/a ⊠ 20121 ℘ 02 76020130, *Fax 02 784573*, « Outdoor summer service » – ▤. AE ⑤ ⓪ E *VISA* JCB — KV u
closed Sunday, 12 to 22 August and 24 December-10 January – **Meals** (booking essential) *a la carte 75/110000.*

XXX **Conte Camillo** - Hotel Cavour, via Fatebenefratelli 21 (galleria di Piazza Cavour) ⊠ 20121 ℘ 02 657205 – ▤. AE ⑤ ⓪ E *VISA* JCB — KV x
closed Sunday, 11 to 24 August and 24 December-6 January – **Meals** *65/75000 and a la carte 60/95000.*

XX **La Dolce Vita**, via Bergamini 11 ⊠ 20122 ℘ 02 58303843 – ▤. ⑤ ⓪ E *VISA* — NZ a
closed Saturday lunch, Sunday and August – **Meals** (booking essential for dinner) *20/30000 (lunch only) and a la carte 50/60000 (dinner only).*

XX **Orient Express**, via Fiori Chiari 8 ⊠ 20121 ℘ 02 8056227 – ▤. AE ⑤ ⓪ E *VISA* JCB. ✸ — KV w
closed Sunday and August – **Meals** *a la carte 75/105000.*

XX **La Bitta**, via del Carmine 3 ⊠ 20121 ℘ 02 72003185, *Fax 02 72003185* – ▤. AE ⑤ ⓪ E *VISA* — KV f
closed Saturday lunch, Sunday and 19 January-4 February – **Meals** seafood *a la carte 50/70000.*

XX **4 Mori,** largo Maria Callas 1 (angolo Largo Cairoli) ⊠ 20121 ℘ 02 878483, « Outdoor summer service » – AE ⑤ ⓪ E *VISA* — JV d
closed Saturday lunch, Sunday, 5 to 25 August and 24 December-6 January – **Meals** *a la carte 55/85000.*

XX **Sogo-Brera**, via Fiori Oscuri 3 ⊠ 20121 ℘ 02 86465367, *Fax 02 86465368* – ▤. AE ⑤ ⓪ E *VISA* JCB. ✸ — KV e
closed Sunday, 2 to 27 August and 25-26 December – **Meals** Japanese rest. *25/40000 (lunch only) and a la carte 70/90000 (15 %).*

XX **Al Mercante**, piazza Mercanti 17 ⊠ 20123 ℘ 02 8052198, *Fax 02 86465250*, « Outdoor summer service » – ▤. AE ⑤ ⓪ E *VISA* — MZ d
closed Sunday, 3 to 28 August and 1 to 7 January – **Meals** *a la carte 55/75000.*

XX **Moon Fish,** via Bagutta 2 ⊠ 20121 ℘ 02 76005780, ☂ – ▤. ⑤ ⓪ — NZ d
closed Sunday, 7 to 28 August and 24 December-4 January – **Meals** seafood *35000 (lunch only) and a la carte 60/135000.*

XX **Albric,** via Albricci 3 ⊠ 20122 ℘ 02 72004766, *Fax 02 86461329* – ▤. AE ⑤ ⓪ E *VISA* JCB. ✸ — MZ y
closed Saturday lunch, Sunday, 8 to 30 August and 25 December-6 January – **Meals** *a la carte 70/95000.*

XX **Rovello 18,** via Rovello 18 ⊠ 20121 ℘ 02 864396 – ✸ ▤. AE ⓪ E *VISA*. ✸ — JV c
closed Saturday lunch and Sunday – **Meals** (booking essential) *a la carte 70/95000.*

XX **Alla Collina Pistoiese,** via Amedei 1 ⊠ 20123 ℘ 02 877248, *Fax 02 86452179*, Old Milan atmosphere – ▤. AE ⑤ ⓪ E *VISA* — KY b
closed Friday, Saturday lunch, Easter, 10 to 20 August and 24 December-2 January – **Meals** *a la carte 65/115000.*

XX **Boccondivino,** via Carducci 17 ⊠ 20123 ℘ 02 866040, *Fax 02 867368* – ▤. AE ⑤ ⓪ E *VISA* — HX c
closed Sunday, August and 23 December-2 January – **Meals** (dinner only) (booking essential) specialities salami, cheese and regional wines *40/60000.*

X **Bagutta,** via Bagutta 14 ⊠ 20121 ℘ 02 76002767, *Fax 02 799613*, ☂, Meeting place for artists, « Original paintings and caricatures » – AE ⑤ ⓪ E *VISA*. ✸ — NZ k
closed Sunday and 23 December-5 January – **Meals** *a la carte 75/120000.*

X **Hostaria Borromei,** via Borromei 4 ⊠ 20123 ℘ 02 86453760, *Fax 02 86453760* – AE ⑤ ⓪ E *VISA*. ✸ — JX c
closed Saturday lunch, Sunday, 9 to 29 August and 24 December-4 January – **Meals** (booking essential) *a la carte 50/70000.*

X **La Tavernetta-da Elio,** via Fatebenefratelli 30 ⊠ 20121 ℘ 02 653441 – ▤. AE ⑤ E *VISA* JCB — KV c
closed Saturday lunch, Sunday, Bank Holidays, August and 24 December-2 January – **Meals** Tuscan rest. *a la carte 60/80000.*

Directional centre via della Moscova, via Solferino, via Melchiorre Gioia, viale Zara, via Carlo Farini

🏨 **Executive**, viale Luigi Sturzo 45 ⊠ 20154 ℘ 02 62941, *Fax 02 29010238* – |≑|, ✸ rm, ▤ TV ☎ ✆ – 🔬 800. AE ⑤ ⓪ E *VISA* JCB. ✸ — KTU e
Meals *a la carte 60/95000* – ☕ *25000* – **414 rm** *340/440000,* 6 suites.

🏨 **Carlyle Brera Hotel,** corso Garibaldi 84 ⊠ 20121 ℘ 02 29003888, *Fax 02 29003993* – |≑|, ✸ rm, ▤ TV ☎ ♿ 🚗. AE ⑤ ⓪ E *VISA* JCB. ✸ — JU u
closed August – **Meals** *a la carte 50/85000* – **96 rm** ☕ *385/455000.*

Royal Hotel Mercure, via Cardano 1 ⊠ 20124 ℰ 02 667461, *Fax 02 6703024* – ⊨ ⇥ rm, 🖾 TV 🕿 ✆ – 🕍 180. AE 🖲 ⓪ Ε *VISA* JCB
KT
Meals a la carte 80/115000 – **205 rm** ⬰ 350/480000, 10 suites.

Sunflower without rest., piazzale Lugano 10 ⊠ 20158 ℰ 02 3931407 *Fax 02 39320377* – 🛗 🖾 TV 🕿 & ⬟ – 🕍 100. AE 🖲 ⓪ Ε *VI* JCB. ⨝
by via Mac Mahon HT
closed August and 23 to 27 December – ⬰ 18000 – **55 rm** 200/280000.

Santini, via San Marco 3 20121 ℰ 02 6555587, *Fax 02 6595573* – 🖾. AE 🖲 ⓪ Ε *VI* JCB. ⨝
KV
closed Sunday – **Meals** a la carte 75/120000.

A Riccione, via Taramelli 70 ⊠ 20124 ℰ 02 6686807, *Fax 02 66803616* – 🖾. AE ⓪ Ε *VISA* JCB
by via Melchiorre Gioia KLT
closed Saturday lunch, Monday and August – **Meals** (booking essential) seafood a la carte 85/115000.

Gianni e Dorina, via Pepe 38 ⊠ 20159 ℰ 02 606340, *Fax 02 606340*, ⛩ – 🖾. 🖲 ⓪ Ε *VISA*
JT
closed Saturday lunch, Sunday, 31 July-10 September and Christmas – **Meals** (booking essential) Pontremolesi rest. 50/60000 (lunch) 60/80000 (dinner) and a la carte 75/110000

Al Tronco, via Thaon di Revel 10 ⊠ 20159 ℰ 02 606072, *Fax 02 6686732* – 🖾. 🖲 ⓪ Ε *VISA* JCB. ⨝
by via Melchiorre Gioia KLT
closed Saturday lunch, Sunday, August and 1 to 7 January – **Meals** a la carte 45/85000.

Piccolo Teatro-Fuori Porta, viale Pasubio 8 ⊠ 20154 ℰ 02 6572105 – 🖾. AE ⓪ Ε *VISA*. ⨝
JU
closed Friday – **Meals** (booking essential) a la carte 65/100000.

Serendib, via Pontida 2 ⊠ 20121 ℰ 02 6592139, *Fax 02 6592139* – 🖾. 🖲 *VISA*. ⨝
JU
closed Sunday and 13 to 25 August – **Meals** (dinner only) (booking essential) Sri Lankan and Indian Rest. a la carte 25/30000.

Casa Fontana-23 Risotti, piazza Carbonari 5 ⊠ 20125 ℰ 02 670471 *Fax 02 66800465* – 🖾. AE 🖲 Ε *VISA*. ⨝
by via M. Gioia LT
closed 5 to 27 August, 24 December-11 January, Monday, Saturday lunch and Saturday dinner-Sunday in July – **Meals** (booking essential) risotto specialities a la carte 55/90000.

Alla Cucina delle Langhe, corso Como 6 ⊠ 20154 ℰ 02 6554279 – 🖾. AE 🖲 ⓪ Ε *VISA*. ⨝
KU
closed Sunday and August – **Meals** a la carte 60/95000.

Antica Trattoria della Pesa, viale Pasubio 10 ⊠ 20154 ℰ 02 655574 *Fax 02 29006859*, Typical old Milanese trattoria – 🖾. AE 🖲 ⓪ Ε *VISA*. ⨝
JU
closed Sunday and August – **Meals** Lombardy rest. a la carte 80/115000.

Rigolo, largo Treves ⊠ 20121 ℰ 02 86463220, *Fax 02 86463220*, Habitués rest. – ⇥ 🖾. AE 🖲 ⓪ Ε *VISA*. ⨝
KU
closed Monday and August – **Meals** a la carte 50/60000.

13 Giugno 2, piazza Mirabello 1 ⊠ 20121 ℰ 02 29003300 – 🖾. AE 🖲 ⓪ Ε *VISA*
closed Sunday and 5 to 20 August – **Meals** (booking essential for dinner) crustacean specialities a la carte 70/95000.
KU

Fuji, viale Montello 9 ⊠ 20154 ℰ 02 6552517 – 🖾. AE 🖲 ⓪ Ε *VISA* JCB. ⨝
JU
closed Sunday, Easter, August and 24 December-2 January – **Meals** (dinner only) (booking essential) Japanese rest. a la carte 60/115000.

Central Station corso Buenos Aires, via Vittor Pisani, piazza della Repubblica

Principe di Savoia, piazza della Repubblica 17 ⊠ 20124 ℰ 02 62301 and rest ℰ 02 62302026, *Fax 02 6595838*, ⑤, ⇌, ⬚ – 🛗 ⇥ 🖾 TV 🕿 & ⬟ – 🕍 700. AE 🖲 *VISA* JCB. ⨝
KU
Meals *Galleria* Rest. a la carte 130/185000 – ⬰ 66000 – **252 rm** 830/1040000, 47 suites

Palace, piazza della Repubblica 20 ⊠ 20124 ℰ 02 63361 and rest ℰ 02 2900080 *Fax 02 654485* – 🛗, ⇥ rm, 🖾 TV 🕿 & ⬟ 🅿 – 🕍 170. AE 🖲 ⓪ Ε *VISA* JC ⨝ rest
LU
Meals *Casanova Grill* Rest. (booking essential) a la carte 100/150000 – ⬰ 60000 **201 rm** 650/760000, 15 suites.

Excelsior Gallia, piazza Duca d'Aosta 9 ⊠ 20124 ℰ 02 67851, *Fax 02 66713239* 🛗, ⇥ rm, 🖾 TV 🕿 ✆ – 🕍 700. AE 🖲 ⓪ Ε *VISA* JCB. ⨝
LT
Meals a la carte 65/120000 – ⬰ 42000 – **238 rm** 525/650000, 13 suites.

Duca di Milano, piazza della Repubblica 13 ⊠ 20124 ☎ 02 62841, *Fax 02 6555966* – ⊛ 回 TV ☎ ✆ ⅋ – ⚓ 110. AE ⑤ ⑩ E VISA JCB. ⅋ rest — KU c
closed August – **Meals** 90000 – ☕ 58000 – 99 suites 660/840000.

Michelangelo, via Scarlatti 33 ang. piazza Luigi di Savoia ⊠ 20124 ☎ 02 67551, *Fax 02 6694232* – ⊛, ⅋ rm, 回 TV ☎ ✆ ⅋ ⇔ – ⚓ 500. AE ⑤ ⑩ E VISA JCB — LTU s
closed August – **Meals** a la carte 85/115000 – **300 rm** ☕ 400/500000, 7 suites.

Starhotel Ritz, via Spallanzani 40 ⊠ 20129 ☎ 02 2055, *Fax 02 29518679* – ⊛ ⅋ 回 TV ☎ – ⚓ 180. AE ⑤ ⑩ E VISA JCB. ⅋ — by Corso Buenos Aires — LU
Meals (residents only) – **195 rm** ☕ 400/540000.

Century Tower Hotel, via Fabio Filzi 25/b ⊠ 20124 ☎ 02 67504, *Fax 02 66980602* – ⊛, ⅋ rm, 回 TV ☎ ✆ ⅋ – ⚓ 60. AE ⑤ ⑩ E VISA JCB. ⅋ — LT f
Meals (residents only) (closed August) a la carte 50/70000 – 144 suites ☕ 310/380000.

Milano Hilton, via Galvani 12 ⊠ 20124 ☎ 02 69831, *Fax 02 66710810* – ⊛, ⅋ rm, 回 TV ☎ ⅋ ⇔ – ⚓ 240. AE ⑤ ⑩ E VISA JCB. ⅋ — LT c
Meals a la carte 80/115000 – ☕ 35000 – **317 rm** 520/570000, 2 suites.

Jolly Hotel Touring, via Tarchetti 2 ⊠ 20121 ☎ 02 6335, *Fax 02 6592209* – ⊛, ⅋ rm, 回 TV ☎ ⅋ – ⚓ 120 — KU f
294 rm, 7 suites.

Sheraton Diana Majestic, viale Piave 42 ⊠ 20129 ☎ 02 20581, *Fax 02 20582058*, ⛲, « Shaded garden », ↨ – ⊛, ⅋ rm, 回 TV ☎ ✆ – ⚓ 80. AE ⑤ ⑩ E VISA JCB. ⅋ rest — LV a
closed August – **Meals** *Il Milanese* Rest. a la carte 70/110000 – **99 rm** ☕ 455/610000, suite.

Doria Grand Hotel, viale Andrea Doria 22 ⊠ 20124 ☎ 02 6696696, *Fax 02 6696669* – ⊛, ⅋ rm, 回 TV ☎ ⅋ ⇔ – ⚓ 80. AE ⑤ ⑩ E VISA JCB
Meals *(closed lunch Saturday-Sunday, 27 July-23 August and 24 December-6 January)* a la carte 65/100000 – **118 rm** ☕ 270/310000, 2 suites. — by corso Buenos Aires — LU

Manin, via Manin 7 ⊠ 20121 ☎ 02 6596511, *Fax 02 6552160*, 🛥 – ⊛ 回 TV ☎ – ⚓ 100. AE ⑤ ⑩ E VISA JCB. ⅋ rest — KV d
closed 1 to 23 August – **Meals** *(closed Saturday)* a la carte 70/105000 – ☕ 25000 – **112 rm** 275/360000, 6 suites.

Bristol without rest., via Scarlatti 32 ⊠ 20124 ☎ 02 6694141, *Fax 02 6702942* – ⊛ 回 TV ☎ – ⚓ 50. AE ⑤ ⑩ E VISA — LT m
closed August – **68 rm** ☕ 205/300000.

Atlantic without rest., via Napo Torriani 24 ⊠ 20124 ☎ 02 6691941, *Fax 02 6706533* – ⊛ ⅋ 回 TV ☎ ⇔ – ⚓ 25. AE ⑤ ⑩ E VISA JCB — LU h
62 rm ☕ 230/300000.

Augustus without rest., via Napo Torriani 29 ⊠ 20124 ☎ 02 66988271, *Fax 02 6703096* – ⊛ 回 TV ☎. AE ⑤ ⑩ E VISA JCB — LU q
closed 25 July-22 August and 23 to 29 December – **56 rm** ☕ 155/240000.

Mediolanum without rest., via Mauro Macchi 1 ⊠ 20124 ☎ 02 6705312, *Fax 02 66981921* – ⊛ 回 TV ☎ ✆. AE ⑤ ⑩ E VISA JCB — LU n
52 rm ☕ 200/260000.

Sanpi without rest., via Lazzaro Palazzi 18 ⊠ 20124 ☎ 02 29513341, *Fax 02 29402451* – ⊛ 回 TV ☎ ✆ – ⚓ 60. AE ⑤ ⑩ E VISA JCB. ⅋ — LU e
closed 2 to 23 August and 24 December-5 January – **67 rm** ☕ 310/410000.

Berna without rest., via Napo Torriani 18 ⊠ 20124 ☎ 02 6691441, *Fax 02 6693892* – ⊛ ⅋ 回 TV ☎ – ⚓ 30. AE ⑤ ⑩ E VISA JCB. ⅋ — LU h
115 rm ☕ 240/340000.

Auriga without rest., via Pirelli 7 ⊠ 20124 ☎ 02 66985851, *Fax 02 66980698* – ⊛ 回 TV ☎ – ⚓ 25. AE ⑤ ⑩ E VISA JCB. ⅋ — LTU k
closed 1 to 23 August – **52 rm** ☕ 270/300000.

Madison without rest., via Gasparotto 8 ⊠ 20124 ☎ 02 67074150, *Fax 02 67075059* – ⊛ 回 TV ☎ – ⚓ 100. AE ⑤ ⑩ E VISA — LT j
83 rm ☕ 220/330000.

Galles, piazza Lima ang. corso Buenos Aires ⊠ 20124 ☎ 02 204841, *Fax 02 204822* – ⊛, ⅋ rm, 回 TV ☎ ✆ – ⚓ 100. AE ⑤ ⑩ E VISA JCB. ⅋ rest
Meals *(closed Sunday)* a la carte 70/100000 – **120 rm** ☕ 480/580000, 2 suites. — by corso Buenos Aires — LU

Grand Hotel Puccini without rest., corso Buenos Aires 33, galleria Puccini ⊠ 20124 ☎ 02 29521344, *Fax 02 2047825* – ⅋ rm, 回 TV ☎ ⅋. AE ⑤ ⑩ E VISA
65 rm ☕ 320/450000. — by corso Buenos Aires — LU

Fenice without rest., corso Buenos Aires 2 ✉ 20124 ☎ 02 29525541, *Fax 02 2952394* – 🛗 ▤ TV ☎. AE 🅂 ⓞ E VISA LU
closed 1 to 23 August and 24 December-6 January – **42 rm** ☕ 185/250000.

Albert without rest., via Tonale 2 ang. Sammartini ✉ 20125 ☎ 02 6698544(*Fax 02 66985624* – 🛗 ▤ TV ☎ ♿ – 🏛 40. AE 🅂 ⓞ E VISA. ✂
closed 9 to 23 August and 24 December-8 January – **62 rm** ☕ 170 260000. by via G.B. Sammartini LT

Demidoff without rest., via Plinio 2 ✉ 20129 ☎ 02 29513889, *Fax 02 29405816* – ▤ TV ☎ 📞. AE 🅂 ⓞ E VISA by via Vitruvio LU
closed 2 to 26 August and 24 December-2 January – **40 rm** ☕ 150/210000.

Mini Hotel Aosta without rest., piazza Duca d'Aosta 16 ✉ 20124 ☎ 02 669195 *Fax 02 6696215* – 🛗 ▤ TV ☎. AE 🅂 ⓞ E VISA LT
63 rm ☕ 170/240000.

New York without rest., via Pirelli 5 ✉ 20124 ☎ 02 66985551, *Fax 02 6697267* – ▤ TV ☎. AE 🅂 ⓞ E VISA LTU
closed 1 to 28 August and 24 December-5 January – **69 rm** ☕ 160/250000.

San Carlo without rest., via Napo Torriani 28 ✉ 20124 ☎ 02 6693236, *Fax 02 670311* – 🛗 ▤ TV ☎ – 🏛 30. AE 🅂 ⓞ E VISA JCB LU
75 rm ☕ 185/250000.

Sempione without rest., via Finocchiaro Aprile 11 ✉ 20124 ☎ 02 657032 *Fax 02 6575379* – 🛗 ▤ TV ☎. AE 🅂 E VISA JCB LU
43 rm ☕ 180/240000.

Florida without rest., via Lepetit 33 ✉ 20124 ☎ 02 6705921, *Fax 02 6692867* – 🛗 ▤ TV ☎. AE 🅂 ⓞ E VISA LTU
☕ 23000 – **55 rm** 165/230000.

Club Hotel without rest., via Copernico 18 ✉ 20125 ☎ 02 67072221, *Fax 02 6707205* – 🛗 ▤ TV ☎. AE 🅂 ⓞ E VISA LT
53 rm ☕ 140/210000.

Bolzano without rest., via Boscovich 21 ✉ 20124 ☎ 02 6691451, *Fax 02 6691455*, – 🛗 ▤ TV ☎. AE 🅂 ⓞ E VISA. ✂ LU
☕ 15000 – **35 rm** 150/200000.

La Terrazza di Via Palestro, via Palestro 2 ✉ 20121 ☎ 02 7600218(*Fax 02 76003328*, ≤, « Summer service on terrace » – ▤ – 🏛 200. AE 🅂 ⓞ E VIS JCB KV
closed Sunday, Monday lunch, 8 to 24 August and 24 December-12 January – **Meals** (boc king essential) a la carte 75/90000.

Mediterranea, piazza Cincinnato 4 ✉ 20124 ☎ 02 29522076, *Fax 02 29522076* – ▤ AE 🅂 ⓞ E VISA. ✂ LU
closed Sunday, Monday lunch, 5 to 25 August and 1 to 10 January – **Meals** seafood a carte 65/100000.

Calajunco, via Stoppani 5 ✉ 20129 ☎ 02 2046003 – ▤. 🅂 ⓞ E VISA. ✂
closed Sunday, August and 23 December-4 January – **Meals** (dinner only) (booking esser tial) Aeolian rest. a la carte 100/155000. by corso Buenos Aires LU

Cavallini, via Mauro Macchi 2 ✉ 20124 ☎ 02 6693771, *Fax 02 6693174*, « Summe service under pergola » – AE 🅂 ⓞ E VISA LU
closed Saturday, Sunday, 3 to 23 August and 22 to 26 December – **Meals** 40000 and la carte 55/70000.

Joia, via Panfilo Castaldi 18 ✉ 20124 ☎ 02 29522124, *Fax 02 2049244* – ✈ ▤. A 🅂 ⓞ E VISA JCB LU
✿ *closed Saturday lunch, Sunday, Easter, August and 28 December-11 January* – **Meals** (boc king essential) 55/95000 and a la carte 70/105000
Spec. "Colori gusti e consistenze". "Gli strati dell'asparago" in tre preparazioni (spring). "L legge del caso" con salsa al cocco, scorza d'arancia e pinoli (autumn-winter).

I Malavoglia, via Lecco 4 ✉ 20124 ☎ 02 29531387, *Fax 02 29531387* – ▤. AE ⓞ E VISA. ✂ LU
closed Easter, 1 May, August, 24 December-4 January, lunch (except Sunday and Bar Holidays) and Monday – **Meals** (booking essential) Sicilian and seafood rest. a la cart 60/85000.

13 Giugno, via Goldoni 44 ang. via Uberti ✉ 20129 ☎ 02 719654, *Fax 02 713875*, – ▤. AE 🅂 ⓞ E VISA by via Mascagni LX
closed Sunday – **Meals** (booking essential) Sicilian rest. a la carte 75/120000.

Le 5 Terre, via Appiani 9 ✉ 20121 ☎ 02 6575177, *Fax 02 653034* – ▤. AE 🅂 ⓞ VISA JCB KU
closed Saturday lunch, Sunday and 9 to 22 August – **Meals** seafood a la carte 50/9000(

XX **Al Girarrosto da Cesarina,** corso Venezia 31 ⊠ 20121 ℘ 02 76000481 – 🖪. AE 🖪 ⓪ ⴹ *VISA*
LV c
closed Saturday, Sunday lunch, August, Christmas and 6 January – **Meals** a la carte 65/90000.

XX **Giglio Rosso,** piazza Luigi di Savoia 2 ⊠ 20124 ℘ 02 6696659, *Fax 02 6694174,* 🌳
– 🖪. AE 🖪 ⓪ ⴹ *VISA*
LT p
closed Saturday, Sunday lunch, August and 24 December-6 January – **Meals** 40000 b.i. (lunch only) and a la carte 50/75000 (12 %).

XX **Hana,** via Lecco 15 ⊠ 20124 ℘ 02 29523227, *Fax 02 29522043* – 🖪. AE 🖪 ⴹ *VISA* JCB.
🚫
LU m
closed Saturday lunch, Sunday and 15 to 25 August – **Meals** (booking essential for dinner) Korean rest. 20/60000 (lunch) 40/60000 (dinner) and a la carte 50/70000.

XX **Altopascio,** via Gustavo Fara 17 ⊠ 20124 ℘ 02 6702458 – 🖪. AE 🖪 ⓪
ⴹ *VISA*
KU n
closed Saturday, Sunday lunch and August – **Meals** Tuscan rest. a la carte 50/75000.

XX **Osteria la Risacca 2,** viale Regina Giovanna 14 ⊠ 20129 ℘ 02 29531801 – 🖪. AE
VISA. 🚫
by corso Buenos Aires LU
closed Saturday lunch, Sunday and August – **Meals** seafood a la carte 50/70000.

X **Centro Ittico,** via Ferrante Aporti 35 ⊠ 20125 ℘ 02 26823449, *Fax 02 26143774*
– 🖪. 🖪 ⴹ *VISA*. 🚫
by via Vittor Pisani LU
closed Sunday, Monday, August and 31 December-7 January – **Meals** (booking essential for dinner) seafood a la carte 55/85000.

Romana-Vittoria corso Porta Romana, corso Lodi, corso XXII Marzo, corso Porta Vittoria

XXXX **Giannino,** via Amatore Sciesa 8 ⊠ 20135 ℘ 02 55195582, *Fax 02 55195790,* Historic ⬡ tradition, « Belle epoque atmosphere, winter garden » – 🖪 ❶. AE 🖪 ⓪ ⴹ *VISA*
JCB. 🚫
by corso di Porta Vittoria LX
closed Sunday, Monday lunch and August – **Meals** (booking essential) a la carte 100/190000
Spec. Riso e zafferano alla milanese. Rombo picchettato d'alloro con salsa all'aglio dolce e aneto. Savarin d'albicocche e panna.

XX **Mistral,** viale Monte Nero 34 ⊠ 20135 ℘ 02 55019104 – 🖪. AE 🖪 ⴹ *VISA* LY a
closed Saturday lunch and Sunday – **Meals** (booking essential) Mediterranean and Provençal cuisine a la carte 60/105000.

XX **I Matteoni,** piazzale 5 Giornate 6 - angolo Regina Margherita ⊠ 20129 ℘ 02 5463520, *Fax 02 5511458,* Habitués rest. – 🖪. AE 🖪 ⓪ ⴹ *VISA*
LX a
closed Sunday, 1 to 21 August and 1 to 7 January – **Meals** a la carte 60/90000.

X **Masuelli San Marco,** viale Umbria 80 ⊠ 20135 ℘ 02 55184138, *Fax 02 55184138,* Typical trattoria – 🖪. AE 🖪 ⓪ ⴹ *VISA* JCB
by corso di Porta Vittoria LX
closed Sunday, Monday lunch, 16 August-10 September and 25 December-6 January – **Meals** (booking essential for dinner) Lombardy-Piedmontese rest. a la carte 55/80000.

X **Merluzzo Felice,** via Lazzaro Papi 6 ⊠ 20135 ℘ 02 5454711 – AE 🖪 ⓪
😀 ⴹ *VISA*
LY b
closed Sunday and 7 to 31 August – **Meals** (booking essential) Sicilian rest. a la carte 50/80000.

Navigli via Solari, Ripa di Porta Ticinese, viale Bligny, piazza XXIV Maggio

🏨 **D'Este** without rest., viale Bligny 23 ⊠ 20136 ℘ 02 58321001, *Fax 02 58321136* – 🔼
🖪 TV ☎ – 🛗 80. AE 🖪 ⓪ ⴹ *VISA*. 🚫
KY d
79 rm ⊑ 250/340000.

🏨 **Crivi's** without rest., corso Porta Vigentina 46 ⊠ 20122 ℘ 02 582891, *Fax 02 58318182*
– 🔼 🖪 TV ☎ 📞 🚗 – 🛗 120. AE 🖪 ⓪ ⴹ *VISA* JCB. 🚫
KY e
closed August – 86 rm ⊑ 250/360000, 3 suites.

🏨 **Liberty** without rest., viale Bligny 56 ⊠ 20136 ℘ 02 58318562, *Fax 02 58319061* –
🔼 🖪 TV ☎ 🚗. AE 🖪 ⴹ *VISA*. 🚫
KY a
closed 1 to 24 August – ⊑ 20000 – 52 rm 210/350000.

XXX **Sadler,** via Ettore Troilo 14 angolo via Conchetta ⊠ 20136 ℘ 02 58104451, ⬡ *Fax 02 58112343,* 🌳 – 🖪. 🖪 ⓪ ⴹ *VISA*
by corso S. Gottardo JY
closed Sunday, 8 August-2 September and 1 to 12 January – **Meals** (dinner only) (booking essential) 120/160000 and a la carte 90/135000
Spec. Sformato di ricotta piemontese al tartufo d'Alba (autumn-winter). Ravioli di melanzane e mozzarella ai filetti di pomodoro (summer). Crostacei in padella con passato di fave al peperoncino.

Al Porto, piazzale Generale Cantore ✉ 20123 ✆ 02 89407425, *Fax 02 8321481* – 🖿
AE ⑩ E *VISA*   HY
closed Sunday, Monday lunch, August and 24 December-3 January – **Meals** (booking essential) seafood a la carte 65/95000.

Osteria di Porta Cicca, ripa di Porta Ticinese 51 ✉ 20143 ✆ 02 837276
Fax 02 8372763 – 🖿. AE Ⓢ ⑩ E *VISA*. ⅀   HY
closed Saturday lunch and Sunday – **Meals** (booking essential) a la carte 50/70000.

Il Torchietto, via Ascanio Sforza 47 ✉ 20136 ✆ 02 8372910, *Fax 02 8372000* – 🖿
AE Ⓢ ⑩ E *VISA*. ⅀   by via A. Sforza   JY
closed Monday, August and 26 December-3 January – **Meals** Mantuan rest. a la carte 55/75000.

Le Buone Cose, via San Martino 8 ✉ 20122 ✆ 02 58310589 – 🖿. AE Ⓢ ⑩ E *VIS*
⅀   KY
closed Saturday lunch, Sunday and August – **Meals** (booking essential) seafood 30/4000 (lunch) and a la carte 55/105000.

Al Capriccio, via Washington 106 ✉ 20146 ✆ 02 48950655 – 🖿. AE Ⓢ ⑩ E *VIS*
⅀   by via Foppa   JY
closed Monday and August – **Meals** (booking essential) seafood a la carte 70/90000.

Olivia, viale D'Annunzio 7/9 ✉ 20123 ✆ 02 89406052 – 🖿. AE Ⓢ ⑩
VISA   HY
closed Saturday lunch, Sunday, 10 to 25 August and 23 December-7 January – **Meals**
la carte 45/60000.

Il Navigante, via Magolfa 14 ✉ 20143 ✆ 02 89406320, *Fax 02 89420897* – 🖿
AE Ⓢ ⑩ E *VISA*   JY
closed Sunday lunch, Monday and August – **Meals** a la carte 60/110000.

Trattoria all'Antica, via Montevideo 4 ✉ 20144 ✆ 02 58104860 – 🖿. AE Ⓢ ⑩
VISA. ⅀   HY
closed Saturday lunch, Sunday, August and 26 December-7 January – **Meals** Lombardy rest. 45000 and a la carte 40/75000.

Ponte Rosso, Ripa di Porta Ticinese 23 ✉ 20143 ✆ 02 8373132, Trattoria
bistrot   HY
closed Sunday and August – **Meals** Triestine and Lombardy specialities a la carte 45/65000.

Asso di Fiori-Osteria dei Formaggi, alzaia Naviglio Grande 54 ✉ 2014
✆ 02 89409415 – AE Ⓢ ⑩ *VISA*. ⅀   HY
closed Sunday, 10 to 25 August and 25 December-2 January – **Meals** (booking essential) (dinner only) 50000.

Fiera-Sempione corso Sempione, piazzale Carlo Magno, via Monte Rosa, via Washingto

Hermitage Ⓜ, via Messina 10 ✉ 20154 ✆ 02 33107700, *Fax 02 33107399*, 🛌 – 🖿
↔ rm, 🖿 TV ☎ ♿ 🚗 – 🛄 200. AE Ⓢ ⑩ E *VISA*. ⅀   HU
closed August – **Meals** (see rest. **Il Sambuco** below) – **119 rm** ☕ 300/360000
12 suites.

Milan Marriott Hotel Ⓜ, via Washington 66 ✉ 20146 ✆ 02 48521, *Fax 02 481892*
– 📶, ↔ rm, 🖿 TV ☎ 🚗 – 🛄 1200. AE Ⓢ ⑩ E *VISA* JCB. ⅀
Meals *La Brasserie de Milan* Rest. *(closed Monday)* a la carte 60/85000 – **323 rm**
☕ 340/400000, suite.   by corso Magenta   HX

Radisson SAS Scandinavia Hotel Milano Ⓜ, via Fauchè 15 ✉ 2015
✆ 02 336391, *Fax 02 33104510*, 🏕, 🍴 – 📶 ↔ 🖿 TV ☎ 📞 ♿ 🚗 – 🛄 100. 🖿
Ⓢ ⑩ E *VISA* JCB. ⅀   HT
Meals *Giardino-Sempione* Rest. a la carte 65/90000 – **149 rm** ☕ 440/500000, suite

Regency without rest., via Arimondi 12 ✉ 20155 ✆ 02 39216021, *Fax 02 3921773*
« In a late 19C mansion » – 📶 ↔ 🖿 TV ☎ – 🛄 50. AE Ⓢ ⑩ E *VISA*
⅀   by corso Sempione   HU
closed August and 24 December-5 January – **59 rm** ☕ 270/360000.

Domenichino without rest., via Domenichino 41 ✉ 20149 ✆ 02 48009692
Fax 02 48003953 – 📶 🖿 TV ☎ 🚗 – 🛄 50. AE Ⓢ ⑩ E *VISA*. ⅀
closed 1 to 22 August and 23 December-6 January – **75 rm** ☕ 190/260000
2 suites.   by corso Sempione   HU

Mozart without rest., piazza Gerusalemme 6 ✉ 20154 ✆ 02 3310421
Fax 02 33103231 – 📶 🖿 TV ☎ 🚗 – 🛄 40. AE Ⓢ ⑩ E *VISA* JCB. ⅀   HT
closed August and 24 December-7 January – **116 rm** ☕ 230/330000, 3 suites.

Admiral without rest., via Domodossola 16 ✉ 20145 ✆ 02 3492151, *Fax 02 3310666*
– 📶 🖿 TV ☎ 📞 🚗 🅿 – 🛄 80. AE Ⓢ ⑩ E *VISA*   by via Procaccini HTU
closed 25 July-1 September and 24 December-7 January – **60 rm** ☕ 160/180000.

Metrò without rest., corso Vercelli 61 ⊠ 20144 ℘ 02 468704, Fax 02 48010295 – |≡|
≡ TV ☎ – 🏊 35. AE S Ⓞ E VISA   by via Ariosto HV
37 rm ☕ 180/250000.

Lancaster without rest., via Abbondio Sangiorgio 16 ⊠ 20145 ℘ 02 344705,
Fax 02 344649 – |≡| ≡ TV ☎. AE S Ⓞ E VISA. ⌾   HU c
closed August and Christmas – **30 rm** ☕ 170/260000.

Mini Hotel Tiziano without rest., via Tiziano 6 ⊠ 20145 ℘ 02 4699035,
Fax 02 4812153, « Small park » – |≡| ≡ TV ☎ � 🄿. AE S Ⓞ E
VISA JCB   by Vincenzo Monti HV
54 rm ☕ 170/240000.

Berlino without rest., via Plana 33 ⊠ 20155 ℘ 02 324141, Fax 02 39210611 – |≡| ≡
TV ☎. AE S Ⓞ E VISA   by corso Sempione HU
closed 26 July-25 August and 24 December-3 January – **48 rm** ☕ 175/270000.

XXX **Il Sambuco** - Hotel Hermitage, via Messina 10 ⊠ 20154 ℘ 02 33610333,
Fax 02 33611850 – ≡. AE S Ⓞ E VISA   HU q
closed Saturday lunch, Sunday, 1 to 20 August and 25 December-3 January – **Meals** seafood a la carte 90/120000.

XXX **Alfredo-Gran San Bernardo**, via Borgese 14 ⊠ 20154 ℘ 02 3319000 – ≡. AE S
✿ Ⓞ E VISA   HT e
closed August, 20 December-7 January, Sunday and Saturday June-July – **Meals** (booking
essential for dinner) Milanese rest. a la carte 100/125000
Spec. Risotto al salto o all'onda. Stracotto al Barbaresco. Foiolo alla milanese.

XX **Trattoria del Ruzante**, via Massena 1 angolo corso Sempione ⊠ 20145
℘ 02 316102, Fax 02 316102 – AE S Ⓞ E VISA. ⌾   HU v
closed Saturday lunch, Sunday and 7 to 30 August – **Meals** (booking essential) a la carte
80/100000.

XX **Arrow's**, via Mantegna 17/19 ⊠ 20154 ℘ 02 341533, Fax 02 341533, 🌿 – ≡. AE
S Ⓞ E VISA JCB. ⌾   HU f
closed Sunday and August – **Meals** seafood a la carte 75/90000.

XX **Taverna della Trisa**, via Francesco Ferruccio 1 ⊠ 20145 ℘ 02 341304, « Summer
service in garden » – S E VISA   HU n
closed Monday and August – **Meals** Trentine rest. a la carte 50/80000.

Zone periferiche

North-Western area viale Fulvio Testi, Niguarda, viale Fermi, viale Certosa, San Siro,
via Novara

Grand Hotel Brun 🏖, via Caldera 21 ⊠ 20153 ℘ 02 452711, Fax 02 48204746 –
|≡| ≡ TV ☎ 🚗 🄿 – 🏊 500. AE S Ⓞ E VISA. ⌾   by corso Sempione HU
closed 23 December-7 January – **Meals** (closed Sunday) a la carte 60/75000 – **300 rm**
☕ 300/380000, 24 suites.

Rubens without rest., via Rubens 21 ⊠ 20148 ℘ 02 40302, Fax 02 48193114,
« Rooms with fresco murals » – |≡| ✗ ≡ TV ☎ ☏ 🄿 – 🏊 35. AE S Ⓞ E
VISA   by corso Magenta HX
87 rm ☕ 300/430000.

Accademia, viale Certosa 68 ⊠ 20155 ℘ 02 39211122, Fax 02 33103878, « Rooms
with fresco murals » – |≡| ≡ TV ☎ ☏ 🚗 – 🏊 30. AE S Ⓞ E
VISA. ⌾ rest   by corso Sempione HU
Meals (residents only) 35/45000 – **67 rm** ☕ 320/450000, 2 suites.

Blaise e Francisc, via Butti 9 ⊠ 20158 ℘ 02 66802366, Fax 02 66802909 – |≡|,
✗ rm, ≡ TV ☎ & 🚗 – 🏊 200. AE S Ⓞ E VISA JCB. ⌾ rest
closed August – **Meals** (closed June-August) (residents only) (dinner only) a la carte
50/75000 – ☕ 20000 – **110 rm** 280/320000.   by via Carlo Farini JT

Novotel Milano Nord, viale Suzzani 13 ⊠ 20162 ℘ 02 66101861,
Fax 02 66101961, 🏊 – |≡|, ✗ rm, ≡ TV ☎ & 🚗 – 🏊 500. AE S Ⓞ E VISA.
⌾ rest   by via Valtellina JT
Meals a la carte 50/80000 – **172 rm** ☕ 340/360000.

Valganna without rest., via Varè 32 ⊠ 20158 ℘ 02 39310089, Fax 02 39312566 –
≡ TV ☎ 🚗. AE S Ⓞ E VISA JCB   by via Carlo Farini JT
40 rm ☕ 100/150000.

Mirage without rest., via Casella 61 angolo viale Certosa ⊠ 20156 ℘ 02 39210471,
Fax 02 39210589 – |≡| ≡ TV ☎ – 🏊 60. AE S Ⓞ E VISA
50 rm ☕ 255/355000.   by corso Sempione HU

XX **Innocenti Evasioni**, via privata della Bindellina ⊠ 20155 ℘ 02 33001882,
Fax 02 33001882, 🌿 – AE S Ⓞ VISA. ⌾   by via Carlo Farini JT
closed Sunday, Monday, August and Christmas – **Meals** (booking essential) (dinner only)
55000 and a la carte 50/70000.

XX **La Pobbia 1821,** via Gallarate 92 ⊠ 20151 ℘ 02 38006641, *Fax 02 3800664* Ancient Milanese rest., « Outdoor summer service » – 🏛 40. 🆎 ⑤ ⑩
VISA   by corso Sempione HU
closed Sunday and August – **Meals** a la carte 60/95000.

XX **Ribot,** via Cremosano 41 ⊠ 20148 ℘ 02 33001646, *Fax 02 39267187,* « Summer service in garden » – Ⓟ. 🆎 ⑤ ⑩ Ⓔ VISA   by corso Sempione HU
closed Monday, 10 to 25 August and 24 December-2 January – **Meals** a la cart 60/80000.

X **Il Faraone,** via Masolino da Panicale 13 ⊠ 20155 ℘ 02 33001337, 🏖 – ▤. 🆎 ⑤ ⑩
Ⓔ VISA JCB   by corso Sempione HU
closed Wednesday except August and December – **Meals** Rest. and pizzeria, Arab specialities a la carte 45/65000.

Northern-Eastern area viale Monza, via Padova, via Porpora, viale Romagna, via Argonne, viale Forlanini

🏨 **Starhotel Tourist,** viale Fulvio Testi 300 ⊠ 20126 ℘ 02 6437777, *Fax 02 647251*
🔧 – 🛗, ⇖ rm, ▤ 📺 ☎ 🚗 Ⓟ – 🏛 150. 🆎 ⑤ ⑩ Ⓔ VISA JCB. ❄
Meals a la carte 65/95000 – **140 rm** ⊇ 315/410000. by corso Buenos Aires LU

🏨 **Lombardia,** viale Lombardia 74 ⊠ 20131 ℘ 02 2824938, *Fax 02 2893430* – 🛗, ⇖ rm
▤ 📺 ☎ 🚗 – 🏛 100. 🆎 ⑤ ⑩ Ⓔ VISA JCB. ❄   by corso Buenos Aires LU
closed 9 to 24 August – **Meals** *(closed Saturday and Sunday)* (dinner only) 40000 – **83 rm**
⊇ 190/280000.

XXXX **L'Ami Berton,** via Nullo 14 angolo via Goldoni ⊠ 20129 ℘ 02 713669, Elegant rest.
❀ – ▤. 🆎 ⑤ Ⓔ VISA. ❄   by via Mascagni LX
closed Saturday lunch, Sunday, August and 1 to 10 January – **Meals** (booking essential for dinner) 100000 and a la carte 100/155000
Spec. Gamberi marinati al cipollotto e caviale. Spaghetti ai filetti di sogliola e taccole (spring-summer). Filetto di rombo con asparagi e salsa al ribes (spring-summer).

XX **Osteria Corte Regina,** via Rottole 60 ⊠ 20132 ℘ 02 2593377, *Fax 02 2593377,* 🏖
Elegant rustic rest. – 🆎 ⑤ ⑩ Ⓔ VISA   by corso Buenos Aires LU
closed Saturday lunch, Sunday and 10 to 25 August – **Meals** (booking essential for dinner) a la carte 55/85000.

XX **L'Altra Scaletta,** viale Zara 116 ⊠ 20125 ℘ 02 6888093, *Fax 02 6888093* – ▤. 🆎
⑤ ⑩ Ⓔ VISA. ❄   by corso Buenos Aires LU
closed Saturday lunch, Sunday and August – **Meals** a la carte 50/65000.

XX **Tre Pini,** via Tullo Morgagni 19 ⊠ 20125 ℘ 02 66805413, *Fax 02 66801346,* « Summer service under pergola » – 🆎 ⑤ ⑩ Ⓔ VISA   by corso Buenos Aires LU
closed Saturday, 5 to 31 August and 25 December-4 January – **Meals** (booking essential) char-grilled specialities a la carte 60/90000.

XX **Da Renzo,** piazza Sire Raul 4 ⊠ 20131 ℘ 02 2846261, *Fax 02 2896634,* 🏖 – ▤. 🆎
⑤ ⑩ Ⓔ VISA   by corso Buenos Aires LU
closed Monday dinner, Tuesday, August and 26 December-2 January – **Meals** a la carte 45/70000.

XX **Piero e Pia,** piazza Aspari 2 angolo via Vanvitelli ⊠ 20129 ℘ 02 718541, *Fax 02 71854*
🏖, Trattoria – ▤. 🆎 ⑤ ⑩ Ⓔ VISA JCB   by viale Tunisia LU
closed Sunday and August – **Meals** (booking essential for dinner) Piacentine specialities la carte 50/80000.

XX **Alla Capanna-da Attilio e Maria,** via Donatello 9 ⊠ 20131 ℘ 02 2940088,
Fax 02 29521491 – ▤. 🆎 ⑤ ⑩ Ⓔ VISA JCB   by corso Buenos Aires LU
closed Saturday – **Meals** a la carte 45/60000.

X **Mykonos,** via Tofane 5 ⊠ 20125 ℘ 02 2610209   by corso Buenos Aires LU
closed Tuesday and August – **Meals** (dinner only) (booking essential) Greek rest. a la carte 35/50000.

Southern-Eastern area viale Molise, corso Lodi, via Ripamonti, corso San Gottardo

🏨 **Quark,** via Lampedusa 11/a ⊠ 20141 ℘ 02 84431, *Fax 02 8464190,* 🏖, 🔧, 🏊 – 🛗
⇖ rm, ▤ 📺 ☎ 🚗 Ⓟ – 🏛 1100. 🆎 ⑤ ⑩ Ⓔ VISA. ❄   by corso Italia KY
closed 24 July-22 August – **Meals** a la carte 70/120000 – **193 rm** ⊇ 320/405000, 92 suites.

🏨 **Starhotel Business Palace,** via Gaggia 3 ⊠ 20139 ℘ 02 53545, *Fax 02 5730755*
– 🛗 ▤ 📺 ☎ 🚗 – 🏛 200. 🆎 ⑤ ⑩ Ⓔ VISA JCB. ❄   by corso Italia KY
Meals a la carte 60/90000 – **248 rm** ⊇ 340/480000.

🏨 **Novotel Milano Est Aeroporto,** via Mecenate 121 ⊠ 20138 ℘ 02 58011085,
Fax 02 58011086, 🏊 – 🛗, ⇖ rm, ▤ 📺 ☎ 📞 ♿ Ⓟ – 🏛 350. 🆎 ⑤ ⑩
VISA. ❄ rest   by corso di Porta Vittoria LX
Meals a la carte 50/80000 – **206 rm** ⊇ 340/420000.

XX **Antica Trattoria Monluè,** via Monluè 75 ⊠ 20138 ℘ 02 7610246, *Fax 02 7610246,* Country trattoria with summer service – 🗏 **Ⓟ**. AE Ⓢ Ⓞ Ⓔ VISA
closed Saturday lunch, Sunday and 4 to 20 August – **Meals** a la carte 65/90000.
by corso di Porta Vittoria   LX

XX **La Plancia,** via Cassinis 13 ⊠ 20139 ℘ 02 5390558, *Fax 02 5390558* – 🗏. AE Ⓢ Ⓞ Ⓔ VISA. �><
by corso Lodi   LY
closed Sunday and August – **Meals** seafood and pizzeria a la carte 45/70000.

X **Taverna Calabiana,** via Calabiana 3 ⊠ 20139 ℘ 02 55213075 – 🗏. AE Ⓢ Ⓞ Ⓔ VISA. �><
by corso Lodi   LY
closed Sunday, Monday, 1 to 8 April, August and 24 December-5 January – **Meals** Rest. and pizzeria a la carte 50/70000.

Southern-Western area viale Famagosta, viale Liguria, via Lorenteggio, viale Forze Armate, via Novara

🏨 **Holiday Inn,** via Lorenteggio 278 ⊠ 20152 ℘ 02 410014, *Fax 02 48304729,* ⊡ – |‡|, ✸ rest, 🗏 TV ☎ ৬ ⇔ **Ⓟ** – 🔏 85. AE Ⓢ Ⓞ Ⓔ VISA JCB. ✖ rest
Meals *L'Univers Gourmand* Rest. a la carte 50/90000 – ⊑ 32000 – **119 rm** 360/440000.
by via Foppa   HY

XXX **Aimo e Nadia,** via Montecuccoli 6 ⊠ 20147 ℘ 02 416886, *Fax 02 48302005* – 🗏. AE Ⓢ Ⓞ Ⓔ VISA. ✖
❀❀
by via Foppa   HY
closed Saturday lunch, Sunday, August and 1 to 6 January – **Meals** (booking essential) 65000 (only lunch) 120000 and a la carte 105/155000
Spec. Purea di fagioli con filetti di triglia, scampi, totani e riso selvatico. Quaglia farcita con fiori di zucchina, prosciutto e il suo fegato al Vin Santo (spring-autumn). Composizione di semifreddi e parfait al miele con salsa di pinoli.

on national road 35-Milanofiori by via Francesco Sforza JY : 10 km :

🏨 **Royal Garden Hotel** Ⓜ ✸, via Di Vittorio ⊠ 20090 Assago ℘ 02 457811, *Fax 02 45702901,* ✖ – |‡| 🗏 TV ☎ ৬ ⇔ **Ⓟ** – 🔏 180. AE Ⓢ Ⓞ Ⓔ VISA. ✖
closed 5 to 20 August and 24 December-5 January – **Meals** a la carte 75/120000 – **111 rm** ⊑ 280/350000, 40 suites.

🏨 **Jolly Hotel Milanofiori,** Strada 2 ⊠ 20090 Assago ℘ 02 82221, *Fax 02 89200946,* ✖ – |‡|, ✸ rm, 🗏 TV ☎ **Ⓟ** – 🔏 120. AE Ⓢ Ⓞ Ⓔ VISA. ✖ rest
Meals a la carte 60/85000 – **250 rm** ⊑ 260/295000.

at Forlanini Park (West Wide) by corso di Porta Vittoria LX : 10 km :

XX **Osteria i Valtellina,** via Taverna 34 ⊠ 20134 Milano ℘ 02 7561139, « Summer service under pergola » – **Ⓟ**. AE Ⓢ Ⓞ Ⓔ VISA
closed Monday, 4 to 24 August and 26 December-7 January – **Meals** (booking essential) Valtellina rest. a la carte 60/110000.

on national road West-Assago by via Foppa HY : 11 km :

🏨 **Afi Hotel,** ⊠ 20090 Assago ℘ 02 4880441, *Fax 02 48843958,* ₤₰, ⊡ – |‡| ✸ 🗏 TV ☎ ℰ ৬ **Ⓟ** – 🔏 300. AE Ⓢ Ⓞ VISA JCB. ✖ rest
Meals a la carte 50/75000 – **194 rm** ⊑ 240/260000.

Abbiategrasso 20081 Milano 𝟵𝟴𝟴 ③, 𝟰𝟮𝟴 F 8 – pop. 27454 alt. 120.
Roma 590 – Alessandria 80 – Milano 24 – Novara 29 – Pavia 33.

at Cassinetta di Lugagnano North : 3 km – ⊠ 20081 :

XXXX **Antica Osteria del Ponte,** piazza G. Negri 9 ℘ 02 9420034, *Fax 02 9420610,* 🌳
❀❀
– 🗏 **Ⓟ**. AE Ⓢ Ⓞ Ⓔ VISA. ✖
closed Sunday, Monday, August and 25 December-12 January – **Meals** (booking essential) 80/160000 and a la carte 100/195000
Spec. Uovo in camicia con salsa di foie gras e tartufo bianco (September-December). Carrè d'agnello disossato, arrostito in forno, alla crema d'aglio dolce e patate (April-September). Flan di cioccolato caldo con salsa di cioccolato bianco.

Bergamo 24100 **Ⓟ** 𝟵𝟴𝟴 ③, 𝟰𝟮𝟴 E 11 *G. Italy* – pop. 117619 alt. 249.
🏌 parco dei Colli (closed Monday) ℘ 035 4548811, Fax 035 260444;
🏌, 🏌 and 🏌 L'Albenza (closed Monday) at Almenno San Bartolomeo ⊠ 24030 ℘ 035 640028, Fax 035 643066;
🏌 La Rossera (closed Tuesday) at Chiuduno ⊠ 24060 ℘ 035 838600, Fax 035 4427047.
✈ Orio al Serio ℘ 035 326323, Fax 035 313432 – Alitalia, via Casalino 5 ℘ 035 224044, Fax 035 235127.

[A.C.I.] via Angelo Maj 16 ⊠ 24121 ℘ 035 247621.
Roma 601 – Brescia 52 – Milano 47.

XXX ✝✝

Da Vittorio, viale Papa Giovanni XXIII 21 ✉ 24121 ☎ 035 213266, Fax 035 218060
✝ ☰. AE S O E VISA
closed Wednesday and August – **Meals** (booking essential) 70000 (only lunch) 100/15000
and a la carte 105/150000
Spec. Scampi al vapore con citronette e maionese leggera. Lasagna di cappesante cc
purea di carote e spinaci (spring). Filetto di branzino alla ligure con lumachine di mare
patate.

Canneto sull'Oglio 46013 Mantova 428 429 G 13 – *pop. 4 534 alt. 35.*
Roma 493 – Brescia 51 – Cremona 32 – Mantova 38 – Milano 123 – Parma 44.

towards Carzaghetto *North-West : 3 km :*

XXXX ✝✝✝

Dal Pescatore, ✉ 46013 ☎ 0376 723001, Fax 0376 70304, « Outdoor summer dinne
service » – ☰ P. AE S O E VISA JCB. ✝
closed Monday, Tuesday, 4 August-3 September, Christmas and 1 to 18 January – **Mea**
(booking essential) 170000 and a la carte 120/190000
Spec. Tinca e pesciolini in carpione al profumo d'arancia. Tortelli di pecorino, ricotta
parmigiano. Luccio al vapore con prezzemolo, acciughe, capperi e olio extravergine (Noven
ber-May).

Erbusco 25030 Brescia 428 429 F 11 – *pop. 6 669 alt. 251.*
Roma 578 – Bergamo 35 – Brescia 22 – Milano 69.

XXXX ✝✝

Gualtiero Marchesi, via Vittorio Emanuele 11, località Bellavista North : 1,5 kr
☎ 030 7760562, Fax 030 7760379, ≺ lake and mountains, Elegant installation – ☰ F
AE S O E VISA JCB. ✝
closed Sunday dinner, Monday and 12 January-2 February – **Meals** (booking essentia
180/240000 and a la carte 120/200000
Spec. Stravaganza "Marchesiana". Riso, oro e zafferano. Filetto di vitello alla Rossini.

Soriso 28018 Novara 428 E 7, 219 (16) – *pop. 761 alt. 452.*
Roma 654 – Arona 20 – Milano 78 – Novara 40 – Stresa 35 – Torino 114 – Varese 4

XXXX ✝✝✝

Al Sorriso with rm, via Roma 18 ☎ 0322 983228, Fax 0322 983328 – ☰ rest, TV (
AE S E VISA. ✝
closed 3 to 26 August and 24 December-15 January – **Meals** *(closed Monday and Tuesda
lunch)* (booking essential) a la carte 105/145000 – **8 rm** ⎈ 170/280000
Spec. Sfogliatina di patate con ragoût di animelle e gamberi di fiume (March-October
Cannelloni croccanti alla toma di Bettelmat e tartufo d'Alba (September-January). Faraon
con composta di pesche e purea al prezzemolo.

NAPLES *(NAPOLI) 80100* P 988 ㉗, 431 *E 24 G. Italy – pop. 1035835 – High Season : April-October.*

See : *National Archaeological Museum*★★★*KY – New Castle*★★ *KZ – Port of Santa Lucia*★★ *BU :* ≤★★ *of Vesuvius and bay –* ≤★★★ *at night from via Partenope of the Vomero and Posillipo FX – San Carlo Theatre*★ *KZ T¹ – Piazza del Plebiscito*★ *JKZ – Royal Palace*★ *KZ – Carthusian Monastery of St. Martin*★★ *JZ.*
Spaccanapoli quarter and Decumano Maggiore★★ *KLY – Tomb*★★ *of King Robert the Wise and Cloisters*★ *in Church of Santa Chiara*★ *KY – Sculptures*★ *in Chapel Sansevero KY – Arch*★*, Tomb*★ *of Catherine of Austria, apse*★ *in Church of St. Lawrence Major LY – Capodimonte Palace and National Gallery*★★*.*
Mergellina★ *:* ≤★★ *of the bay – Villa Floridiana*★ *EVX :* ≤★ *– Catacombs of St. Gennaro*★★ *– Church of Santa Maria Donnaregina*★ *LY – Church of St. Giovanni a Carbonara*★ *LY – Capuan Gate*★ *LMY – Como Palace*★ *LY – Sculptures*★ *in the Church of St. Anne of the Lombards KYZ – Posillipo*★ *– Marechiaro*★ *–* ≤★★ *of the Bay from Virgiliano Park (or Rimembranza Park).*

Exc. : *Bay of Naples*★★★ *road to Campi Flegrei*★★*, to Sorrento Penisula Island of Capri*★★★ *Island of Ischia*★★★*.*

☂₉ *(closed Tuesday) at Arco Felice* ✉ *80078* ✆ *081 660772, Fax 081 660566, West : 19 km.*

✈ *Ugo Niutta of Capodichino North-East : 6 km* ✆ *081 7091111 – Alitalia, via Medina 41*

✉ *80133* ✆ *081 5513188, Fax 081 5513709.*

🚢 *to Capri (1 h 15 mn), Ischia (1 h 25 mn) e Procida (1 h), daily – Caremar-Travel and Holidays, molo Beverello* ✉ *80133* ✆ *081 5513882, Fax 081 5522011; to Cagliari 19 June-14 July Thursday and Saturday, 15 July-11 September Thursday and Tuesday (15 h 45 mn) and Palermo daily (11 h) – Tirrenia Navigazione, Stazione Marittima, molo Angioino* ✉ *80133* ✆ *081 2514740, Fax 081 2514767 to Ischia daily (1 h 20 mn) – Linee Lauro, molo Beverello* ✉ *80133* ✆ *081 5522838, Fax 081 5513236; to Aeolian Island Wednesday and Friday, 15 June-15 September Monday, Tuesday, Thursday, Friday, Saturday and Sunday (14 h) – Siremar-Genovese Agency, via De Petris 78* ✉ *80133* ✆ *081 5512112, Fax 081 5512114.*

🚤 *to Capri (45 mn), Ischia (45 mn) and Procida (35 mn), daily – Caremar-Travel and Holidays, molo Beverello* ✉ *80133* ✆ *081 5513882, Fax 081 5522011; to Ischia (30 mn) and Capri (40 mn), daily – Alilauro, via Caracciolo 11* ✉ *80122* ✆ *081 7611004, Fax 081 7614250 and Linee Lauro, molo Beverello* ✉ *80133* ✆ *081 5522838, Fax 081 5513236; to Capri daily (50 mn) – Navigazione Libera del Golfo, molo Beverello* ✉ *80133* ✆ *081 5520763, Fax 081 5525589; to Capri (45 mn), to Aeolian Island June-September (4 h) and Procida-Ischia daily (35 mn) – Aliscafi SNAV, via Caracciolo 10* ✉ *80122* ✆ *081 7612348, Fax 081 7612141.*

🛈 *piazza dei Martiri 58* ✉ *80121* ✆ *081 405311 – piazza del Plebiscito (Royal Palace)* ✉ *80132* ✆ *081 418744, Fax 081 418619 – Central Station* ✉ *80142* ✆ *081 268779 - Capodichino Airport* ✉ *80133* ✆ *081 7805761 – piazza del Gesì Nuovo 7* ✉ *80135* ✆ *081 5523328 - Passaggio Castel dell'Ovo* ✉ *80132* ✆ *081 7645688.*

A.C.I. *piazzale Tecchio 49/d* ✉ *80125* ✆ *081 2394511.*
Roma 219 – Bari 261

Plans on following pages

Grande Albergo Vesuvio, *via Partenope 45* ✉ *80121* ✆ *081 7640044, Fax 081 7644483,* ≤ *gulf and Castel dell'Ovo, ₤₆ – ▮, ⇔ rm, ▦ TV ☎ 🚗 – 🔁 400.* AE ⑤ ⓪ E VISA JCB. ⁂
FX n
Meals (see rest. **Caruso** below) – **165 rm** ⊇ 400/500000, 16 suites.

Excelsior, *via Partenope 48* ✉ *80121* ✆ *081 7640111, Fax 081 7649743,* « *Roof garden, solarium with* ≤ *gulf and Castel dell'Ovo* » *– ▮ ▦ TV ☎ ☏.* AE ⑤ ⓪ E VISA JCB. ⁂ rest
GX w
Meals **La Terrazza** Rest. a la carte 65/110000 – **104 rm** ⊇ 380/480000, 12 suites.

Santa Lucia, *via Partenope 46* ✉ *80121* ✆ *081 7640666, Fax 081 7648580,* ≤ *gulf and Castel dell'Ovo – ▮ ▦ TV ☎ ☏ – 🔁 110.* AE ⑤ ⓪ E VISA. ⁂ *GX* c
Meals (see rest. **Megaris** below) – **105 rm** ⊇ 350/460000, 5 suites.

Grand Hotel Terminus Ⓜ, *piazza Garibaldi 91* ✉ *80142* ✆ *081 7793111, Fax 081 206689, ₤₆, ⇌ₛ – ▮ ▦ TV ☎ 🚗 – 🔁 300.* AE ⑤ ⓪ E VISA. ⁂ rest *MY* a
Meals a la carte 50/75000 – **168 rm** ⊇ 250/360000, 2 suites.

Holiday Inn Ⓜ, *centro direzionale Isola e/6* ✉ *80143* ✆ *081 2250111, Fax 081 5628074, ₤₆, ⇌ₛ – ▮, ⇔ rm, ▦ TV ☎ ☏ ⇔ 🚗 – 🔁 1200.* AE ⑤ ⓪ E VISA JCB. ⁂
by corso Meridionale MY
Meals 35/60000 and **Bistrot Victor** Rest. a la carte 60/90000 – ⊇ 28000 – **330 rm** 305/355000, 31 suites.

Oriente without rest., *via Diaz 44* ✉ *80134* ✆ *081 5512133, Fax 081 5514915 – ▦ TV ☎ ☏ – 🔁 300.* AE ⑤ ⓪ E VISA. ⁂
KZ d
130 rm ⊇ 230/330000, 2 suites.

NAPOLI

ARENELLA
CAMALDOLI
V. Bernardo Cavallino
TANGENZIALE
Via
Via
S. Giacomo dei Capri
Castellino
Pietro
Fontana
V. D. Fontana
Fontana
V. del Sanit
Via Fontanelle
Via B. Caracciolo
Via Matteo Renato Imbriani
Gigante
Via B. Caracciolo
G. Orsi
V. Salvator
Rosa
Via Salvator Rosa
Rosa
Santacroce
75
90
119
98
77
V. Suarez
P V. Salvator
Emanuele
Via
Altamura
S.
Gemito
Via
V.
131
130
153
Via Cilea
153
VOMERO
V. Giotto
Pza Medaglie d'Oro
134
162
140
9
64
12
13
12
40
86
86
86
166
153
156
Via Michelangelo
Viale
G.
Via Tito
Angelini
CASTEL SANT' ELMO
CERTOSA DI S. MARTINO
FUNICOLARE
Vittorio
Corso
Vitto
Cimarosa
Via
Via A.
64
Falcone
Falcone
VILLA FLORIDIANA
M
FUNICOLARE
Via A.
Via
Tasso
Vittorio
Corso
Emanuele
Piazza Amedeo
106
29
Via dei Mille
Via M. Schipa
Via
Via A. d'Isernia
Francesco Crispi
Mirelli
M
147
20
b
Via Chiar
di
Chiaia
Pza dei Martiri
a
133
Riviera
113
VILLA COMUNALE
ACQUARIO
Caracciolo
61
84
Galleria
Vitto
170
5
25
Mergellina
V. G. Bruno
Via
107
107
151
ISCHIA, PROCIDA, CAPRI
E
F

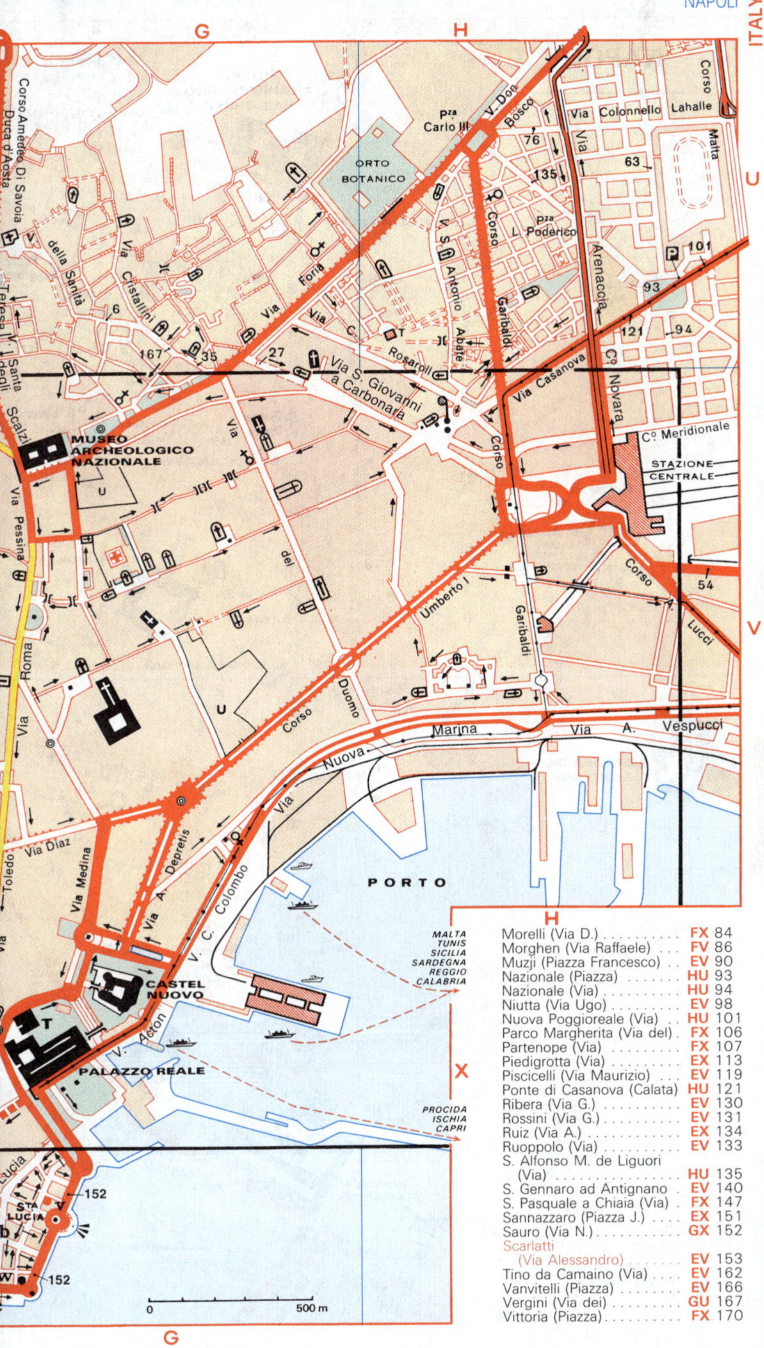

437

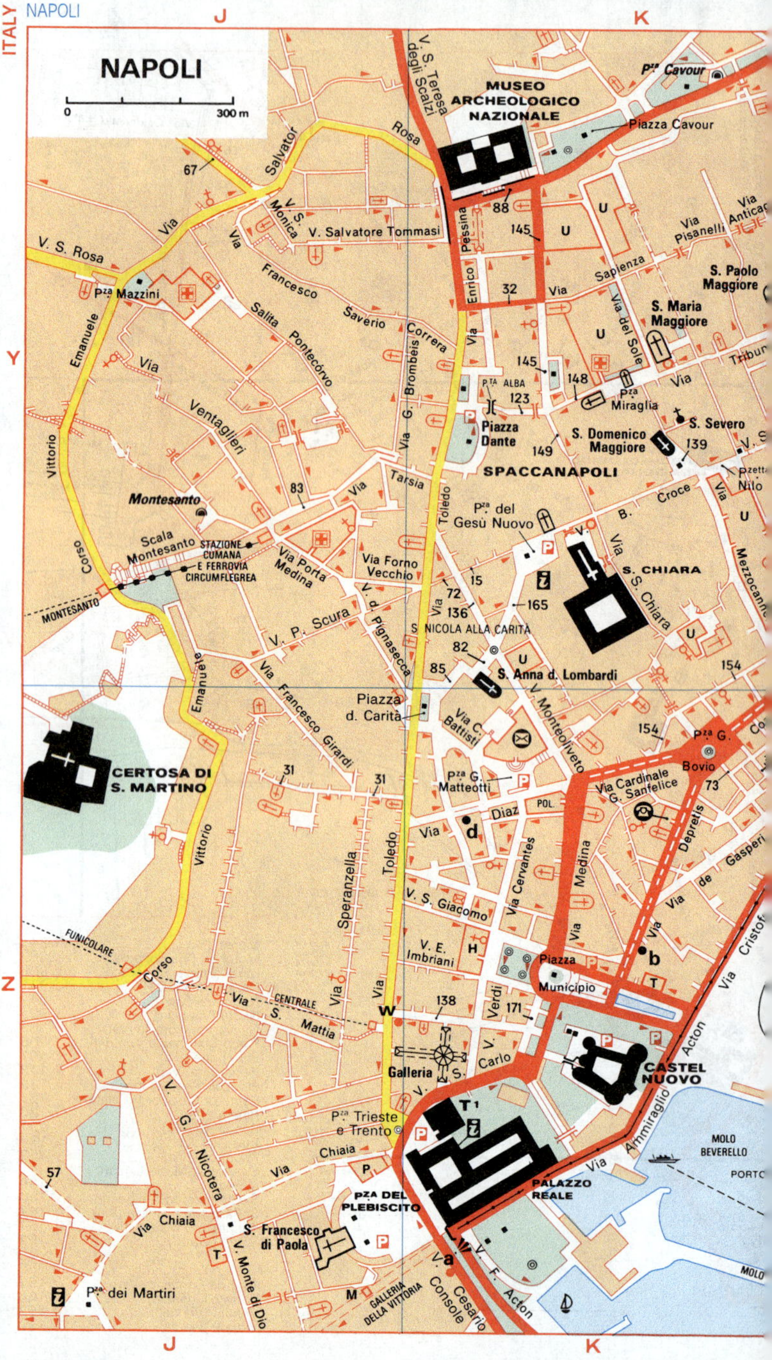

NAPOLI

0   300 m

67

MUSEO
ARCHEOLOGICO
NAZIONALE

P.za Cavour
Piazza Cavour

V. S. Teresa
degli Scalzi

Rosa

88
145

U

Via
Pisanelli

Via
Antica

S. Paolo
Maggiore

V. S. Rosa

Salvator

V. S.
Monica

V. Salvatore Tommasi

Francesco

Saverio

Correra

Via

Enrico
Pessina

32

Via

Saplenza

Via del Sole

S. Maria
Maggiore

Tribur

Via

P.za Mazzini

Salita
Pontecorvo

Via

Ventaglieri

Via G. Brombeis

145

P.TA ALBA

123

148

P.za
Miraglia

S. Severo

148

Emanuele

Vittorio

Piazza
Dante

149

S. Domenico
Maggiore

139

V. S.

P.zetta
Nilo

U

Montesanto

Via

Tarsia

Via

SPACCANAPOLI

Croce

B.

Via

83

P.za del
Gesù Nuovo

V.

Scala
Montesanto

STAZIONE
CUMANA
E FERROVIA
CIRCUMFLEGREA

Via Porta
Medina

Via Forno
Vecchio

Toledo

15

S. S. Chiara

S. CHIARA

Mezzocann

MONTESANTO

Corso

V. d. Pignasecca

V. P. Scura

72
136

S. NICOLA ALLA CARITA

165

82

U

U

85

S. Anna d. Lombardi

154

CERTOSA DI
S. MARTINO

Emanuele

Via Francesco Girardi

31

31

Piazza
d. Carità

Via C.
Battisti

P.za G.
Bovio

154

V. Monteoliveto

73

P.za G.
Matteotti

POL.

Via Cardinale
G. Sanfelice

Depretis

de Gasperi

Vittorio

FUNICOLARE

Corso

Toledo

Speranzella

V. S. Giacomo

Diaz

d

Via

Via Cervantes

Medina

Via

Via

Via

de

Via

b

T

de Cristofe

V. E.
Imbriani

H

Piazza
Municipio

Verdi

Via

CENTRALE

Via

V. S. Mattia

138

W

Via

171

CASTEL
NUOVO

Acton

Galleria

V. S.

V.
Carlo

Ammiraglio

MOLO
BEVERELLO

PORTO

57

V. G.

Nicotera

P.za Trieste
e Trento

T

i

PALAZZO
REALE

Via

P.za dei Martiri

Via Chiaia

Chiaia

S. Francesco
di Paola

V. Monte di Dio

P.ZA DEL
PLEBISCITO

P

a

V. F. Acton

MOLO

M

GALLERIA
DELLA VITTORIA

V. F. Console

Cesario

L
M
NAPOLI
ITALY
S. GIOVANNI A CARBONARA
Via S. Giovanni a Carbonara
pza S. Francesco di Paola
V. Casanova
Corso
Corso
Novara
S. MARIA DONNAREGINA
Largo Donnaregina
V. O. Costa
V. S. Apostoli
PORTA CAPUANA
89
Via Firenze
Co. Meridionale
CENTRALE
Duomo
J
Castel Capuano
f
Pza Principe Umberto
Via del
Via
Tribunali
Colletta
120
71
Pza Garibaldi
Garibaldi
Via delle Zite
V. P. S. Mancini
P
P
a
65
V. Pietro
V. Ranieri
4
50
P
Umberto I
60
169
142
S. LORENZO MAGGIORE
S. Gregorio Armeno
del
Librai
Duomo
Vico del Grande Archivio
137
V. Nolana
Pza Nolana
V. S. Cosmo Fuori Porta Nolana
Co. A. Lucci
Y
PALAZZO COMO
a
117
Via. Mattei
Corso
Via
Giacomo
Savarese
Lavinaio
Giuseppe Garibaldi
VESUVIANA
8
14
Via
del Duomo
Pza Nicola Amore
49
Via del Carmine
Via S. Baldacchini
Pza del Mercato
Pza G. Pepe
81
49
STA. MARIA DEL CARMINE
P
P
Marina
Via Amerigo Vespucci
Umberto I
74
Nuova
Via Marinella
U
Via
Via di Porta di Massa
N
ISOLE EOLIE O LIPARI SARDEGNA
BACINO DEL PILIERO
PORTO
ISOLE EOLIE O LIPARI SARDEGNA SICILIA
ANGIOINO
STAZIONE MARITTIMA
SARDEGNA SICILIA
ISCHIA, PROCIDA, CAPRI
VERELLO
SAN VINCENZO
L
M
439

Villa Capodimonte ⚐, via Moiariello 66 ✉ 80131 ☎ 081 459000
Fax 081 299344, ≤, 🌳, 🌿, ✂ – 📶 ▤ TV ☎ 🚗 P – 🛗 50. AE 🏦 ⓪ E
VISA
                                                  by corso Amedeo di Savoia GU
Meals (dinner only) a la carte 40/85000 – **49 rm** ☕ 180/280000.

Paradiso, via Catullo 11 ✉ 80122 ☎ 081 7614161, *Fax 081 7613449*, ≤ gulf, city an
Vesuvius, 🌳 – 📶 ▤ TV ☎ – 🛗 80. AE 🏦 ⓪ E VISA. ✆ rest
Meals a la carte 50/80000 – **74 rm** ☕ 190/290000.   by Riviera di Chiaia EFX

Mercure Angioino without rest., via Depretis 123 ✉ 80133 ☎ 081 5529500
Fax 081 5529509 – 📶 ▤ TV ☎. AE 🏦 ⓪ E VISA   KZ
85 rm ☕ 200/240000.

San Germano, via Beccadelli 41 ✉ 80125 ☎ 081 5705422, *Fax 081 5701546*, ≈
📶 ▤ TV ☎ 🚗 – 🛗 150. AE 🏦 ⓪ E VISA. ✆ rest   by Riviera di Chiaia EFX
Meals a la carte 45/75000 (10 %) – **105** ☕ 120/180000.

Majestic, largo Vasto a Chiaia 68 ✉ 80121 ☎ 081 416500, *Fax 081 410145* – 📶
TV ☎ 🚗 – 🛗 100. AE 🏦 ⓪ E VISA JCB. ✆   FX
Meals (closed Sunday) a la carte 50/90000 – **106 rm** ☕ 220/290000, 2 suites.

Miramare without rest., via Nazario Sauro 24 ✉ 80132 ☎ 081 764758
Fax 081 7640775, ≤ gulf and Vesuvius, « Roof garden » – 📶 ▤ TV ☎. AE 🏦 ⓪ E VISA JC
31 rm ☕ 220/450000.   GX

Suite Esedra without rest., via Cantani 12 ✉ 80133 ☎ 081 5537087, *Fax 081 553708*
– 📶 ▤ TV ☎ ☏. AE 🏦 ⓪ E VISA JCB. ✆   LY
17 rm ☕ 160/220000, 2 suites.

Montespina Park Hotel, via San Gennaro 2 ✉ 80125 ☎ 081 762968
Fax 081 5702962, « Park » – 📶 ▤ TV ☎ P. AE 🏦 ⓪ E VISA. ✆ rest
Meals a la carte 30/45000 – **22 rm** ☕ 145/190000.   by Riviera di Chiaia EFX

Caruso - Hotel Grande Albergo Vesuvio, via Partenope 45 ✉ 80121 ☎ 081 764052
Fax 081 7644483, « Roof garden with ≤ gulf and Castel dell'Ovo » – 🚗. AE 🏦 ⓪
VISA JCB. ✆   FX
Meals a la carte 80/115000.

La Cantinella, via Cuma 42 ✉ 80132 ☎ 081 7648684, *Fax 081 7648769* – ▤. AE
⓪ E VISA JCB. ✆   GX
❀
closed 11 to 18 August, 24 to 26 December and Sunday (except October-May) – Mea
a la carte 60/100000 (12 %)
Spec. Salmone fresco in crosta di zucchine con ragù di melanzane. Fettuccine con se
pioline, vongole veraci e champignon. Filetto di manzo scaloppato con purea di patat
tartufo nero e olio extravergine.

Megaris - Hotel Santa Lucia, via Santa Luci 175 ✉ 80121 ☎ 081 764051
Fax 081 7648580 – ▤. AE 🏦 ⓪ E VISA. ✆   GX
closed Sunday and 1 to 22 August – **Meals** a la carte 65/110000.

Giuseppone a Mare, via Ferdinando Russo 13-Capo Posillipo ✉ 8012
☎ 081 5756002, ≤ – P. AE 🏦 ⓪ E VISA. ✆   by via Caracciolo FX
closed Sunday dinner, Monday, 24-25 December and New Year – **Meals** a la cart
60/80000.

Ciro a Santa Brigida, via Santa Brigida 73 ✉ 80132 ☎ 081 552407
Fax 081 5528992 – ▤. AE 🏦 ⓪ E VISA JCB   JZ
closed Sunday and 14 to 29 August – **Meals** Rest. and pizzeria a la carte 50
85000.

A' Fenestella, via Marechiaro 23 ✉ 80123 ☎ 081 7690020, *Fax 081 575068*
« Summer service on terrace with ≤ » – P. AE 🏦 E VISA   by via V. G. Bruno EX
closed Sunday dinner, Wednesday lunch and 11 to 18 August – **Meals** a la carte 45/800
(15 %).

Il Posto Accanto, via Nazario Sauro 2 ✉ 80132 ☎ 081 7649873, *Fax 081 764054*
– ▤ – 🛗 70. AE 🏦 ⓪ VISA JCB   GX
closed Sunday dinner – **Meals** Rest. and pizzeria a la carte 35/65000 (15 %).

Da Mimì alla Ferrovia, via Alfonso d'Aragona 21 ✉ 80139 ☎ 081 5538525 – ▤
AE 🏦 ⓪ E VISA   MY
closed Sunday and 10 to 20 August – **Meals** a la carte 45/65000 (10 %).

Don Salvatore, strada Mergellina 4 A ✉ 80122 ☎ 081 681817, *Fax 081 661241*
▤. AE 🏦 ⓪ E VISA   by Riviera di Chiaia EFX
closed Wednesday – **Meals** Rest. and pizzeria a la carte 50/75000.

San Carlo, via Cesario Console 17/19 ✉ 80132 ☎ 081 7649757, *Fax 081 7649757*
▤. AE 🏦 ⓪ E VISA. ✆   KZ
closed Sunday and 10 to 24 August – **Meals** (booking essential) a la carte 50/80000 (10 %

Marino, via Santa Lucia 118/120 ✉ 80132 ☎ 081 7640280 – ▤. AE 🏦 E VISA JC
✆   GX
closed Monday and August – **Meals** Rest. and pizzeria a la carte 30/55000 (15 %)

Island of Capri 80073 Napoli 🎑🎑🎑 ㉗, 🎑🎑🎑 F 24 *G. Italy* – pop. 13 054 alt. – *High Season :
Easter and June-September.*
The limitation of motor-vehicles' access is regulated by legislative rules.

Gd H. Quisisana, via Camerelle 2 ✆ 081 8370788, *Fax 081 8376080,* ≤ sea and Certosa,
« Garden with 🏊 », ℷ६, ≘s, 🎑, ✗ – 🛗 🖭 TV ☎ ✆ – 🛗 550. AE 🚫 ⓞ ⋿ VISA

Easter-October – **Meals** *La Colombaia* Rest. *(closed dinner)* a la carte 90/130000 see also
rest. **Quisi** – **150 rm** ⌑ 370/850000, 13 suites.

Scalinatella 🍃 without rest., via Tragara 8 ✆ 081 8370633, *Fax 081 8378291,* ≤ sea
and Certosa, 🏊 heated – 🛗 🖭 TV ☎. AE 🚫 ⋿ VISA
15 March-5 November – **28 rm** ⌑ 550/850000.

Punta Tragara 🍃, via Tragara 57 ✆ 081 8370844, *Fax 081 8377790,* ≤ Faraglioni and
coast, 🏊, « Panoramic terrace with 🏊 heated » – 🛗 🖭 TV ☎. AE 🚫 ⓞ ⋿ VISA. ✗
Easter-October – **Meals** a la carte 55/80000 (15 %) – **35 rm** ⌑ 560000, 15 suites
⌑ 600/900000.

Casa Morgano 🍃 without rest., via Tragara 6 ✆ 081 8370158, *Fax 081 8370681,* ≤
sea and Certosa, « Floral terraces in pinewood », 🏊 heated – 🛗 🖭 TV ☎. AE 🚫 ⓞ ⋿
VISA
26 March-5 November – **28 rm** ⌑ 350/650000.

Luna 🍃, viale Matteotti 3 ✆ 081 8370433, *Fax 081 8377459,* ≤ sea, Faraglioni and
Certosa, 🏊, « Terraces and garden with 🏊 » – 🛗 🖭 TV ☎ ✆. AE 🚫 ⓞ ⋿ VISA. ✗
Easter-October – **Meals** (residents only) a la carte 65/85000 – **50 rm** ⌑ 400/500000,
4 suites.

Mamela 🍃 without rest., via Campo di Teste 8 ✆ 081 8375255, *Fax 081 8378865,* ≤,
🏊, « Terrace-solarium with 🏊 », ≘s – 🛗 🖭 TV ☎. AE 🚫 ⓞ ⋿ VISA JCB. ✗
March-October – **35 rm** ⌑ 320/390000.

Villa Brunella 🍃, via Tragara 24 ✆ 081 8370122, *Fax 081 8370430,* ≤ sea and coast,
🏊, « Panoramic floral terraces with rest. service », 🏊 heated – 🖭 rm, TV ☎. AE 🚫 ⓞ
⋿ VISA. ✗
19 March-5 November – **Meals** a la carte 50/85000 (12 %) – **20 rm** ⌑ 350/500000.

Syrene, via Camerelle 51 ✆ 081 8370102, *Fax 081 8370957,* ≤, 🏊, « Lemon garden
with 🏊 » – 🛗 🖭 TV ☎. AE 🚫 ⓞ ⋿ VISA JCB. ✗
April-October – **Meals** *(closed Tuesday except June to September)* a la carte 55/70000
– **34 rm** ⌑ 290/440000.

Canasta without rest., via Campo di Teste 6 ✆ 081 8370561, *Fax 081 8376675,* ✗
– 🖭 TV ☎ ✆. AE 🚫 ⓞ ⋿ VISA. ✗
closed 10 January-15 March – **17 rm** ⌑ 160/300000.

Quisi - Gd H. Quisisana, via Camerelle 2 ✆ 081 8370788, *Fax 081 8376080,* 🏊 – 🖭. AE
🚫 ⓞ ⋿ VISA. ✗
Easter-October dinner only – **Meals** (booking essential) a la carte 95/145000.

La Capannina, via Le Botteghe 14 ✆ 081 8370732, *Fax 081 8376990* – 🖭. AE 🚫 ⓞ
⋿ VISA. ✗
27 December-5 January and 10 March-10 November – **Meals** (booking essential for dinner)
a la carte 55/80000 (15 %).

at Anacapri *alt. 275* – ✉ 80071 :

Europa Palace, via Capodimonte 2 ✆ 081 8373800, *Fax 081 8373191,* ≤, 🏊, Rooms
with small private swimming pools « Floral terraces with 🏊 », ℷ६, ≘s, 🎑 – 🛗 🖭 TV
☎ – 🛗 200. AE 🚫 ⓞ ⋿ VISA JCB. ✗
27 March-15 November – **Meals** a la carte 95/145000 – **74 rm** ⌑ 580/680000, 4 suites.

at Marina Piccola – ✉ 80073 Capri :

Canzone del Mare, via Marina Piccola 93 ✆ 081 8370104, *Fax 081 8370541,*
≤ Faraglioni and sea, 🏊, « Bathing establishment with 🏊 » – AE 🚫 ⓞ ⋿ VISA.
✗
Easter-October – **Meals** (lunch only) a la carte 70/115000.

Sant'Agata sui due Golfi 80064 Napoli 🎑🎑🎑 F 25 *G. Italy* – *alt. 391* – *High Season :* April-
September.
Roma 266 – Castellammare di Stabia 28 – Napoli 55 – Salerno 56 – Sorrento 9.

Don Alfonso 1890 with rm, corso Sant'Agata 11 ✆ 081 8780026, *Fax 081 5330226,*
🏊 – 🖭 🅿. AE 🚫 ⓞ ⋿ VISA. ✗
closed 7 January-27 February – **Meals** *(closed Monday June-September and Tuesday October-May)* (booking essential) 110/140000 and a la carte 90/145000 – 3 suites
⌑ 170/270000
Spec. Nastri di pasta con cozze, bottarga di tonno e timo. Casseruola di pesci di scoglio,
crostacei e frutti di mare. Coniglio con peperoni ed olive al profumo di rosmarino (summer).

PALERMO (Sicily) 90100 🅿 **988** ㉟, **432** M 22 *G. Italy* – *pop. 688 396*.

See : *Palace of the Normans★★ : the palatine Chapel★★★, mosaics★★★ AZ – Region. Gallery of Sicily★★ in Abbatellis Palace★ : Death Triumphant fresco★★★ CY – Piazza Bellini BY : Martorana Church★★, Church of St. Cataldo★★ – Church of St. John of the Hermits★★ AZ – Capuchin Catacombs★★ – Piazza Pretoria★ BY : fountain★★ – Archaeological Museum★ : metopes from the temples at Selinus★★, the Ram★★ BY – Chiaramonte Palace★ magnolia fig trees★★ in Garibaldi Gardens CY – Quattro Canti★ BY – Cathedral★ AYZ Mirt Palace★ CY B Villa Bonanno★ AZ Zisa Palace★ – Botanical garden★ CDZ – Internation. Museum of Marionettes★ CY A Sicilian carts★ in Ethnographic Museum M.*

Envir. : *Monreale★★★ AZ by Corso Calatafimi : 8 km – Monte Pellegrino★★ BX by via Crisp. 14 km.*

✈ *Punta Raisi East : 30 km ℰ 091 7020111, Fax 091 7020394 – Alitalia, via Mazzini 5 ☒ 90139 ℰ 091 6019111, Fax 091 6019346.*

⛴ *to Genova daily (20 h) and to Livorno Tuesday, Thursday and Saturday (17 h) – Grand Navi Veloci, calata Marinai d'italia ☒ 90133 ℰ 091 587404, Fax 091 6110088; to Napc. daily (11 h), to Genova Monday, Wednesday and Friday and Sunday 18 June-31 Decembe. (24 h) and Cagliari Saturady (14 h 30 mn) – Tirrenia Navigazione, calata Marinai d'Ital. ☒ 90133 ℰ 091 333300, Fax 091 6021221.*

⛴ *to Aeolian Island June-September daily (1 h 50 mn) – SNAV Barbaro Agency, piazz. Principe di Belmonte 51/55 ☒ 90139 ℰ 091 586533, Fax 091 584830.*

🛈 *piazza Castelnuovo 34 ☒ 90141 ℰ 091 583847, Fax 091 331854 – Punta Raisi Airpor. at Cinisi ℰ 091 591698.*

A.C.I. *via delle Alpi 6 ☒ 90144 ℰ 091 300468.*

Messina 235.

Plans on following pages

Villa Igiea Gd H., salita Belmonte 43 ☒ 90142 ℰ 091 543744, Fax 091 547654, ≤
, « 19C mansion with seafront terrace », ⊼ sea water, ⚲, ✗ – ♦ 🗏 📺 ☎ ₺
– 🏊 400. 🆎 Ⓢ ⓪ E 𝖵𝖨𝖲𝖠. ✗   by via Crispi BX
Meals a la carte 80/130000 – **117 rm** ⊇ 250/390000, 6 suites.

Astoria Palace Hotel, via Montepellegrino 62 ☒ 90142 ℰ 091 6282111
Fax 091 6372178 – ♦ 🗏 📺 ☎ 🅿 – 🏊 800. 🆎 Ⓢ ⓪ E 𝖵𝖨𝖲𝖠. ✗   by via Crispi BX
Meals 45/65000 and *Il Cedro* Rest. a la carte 60/85000 – **326 rm** ⊇ 225/275000
8 suites.

Centrale Palace Hotel Ⓜ, corso Vittorio Emanuele 327 ☒ 90134 ℰ 091 336666
Fax 091 334881, « In a 17C building » – ♦ 🗏 📺 ☎ ₺. 🆎 Ⓢ ⓪ E 𝖵𝖨𝖲𝖠
✗   BY

Meals (residents only) 60000 – ⊇ 20000 – **63 rm** 230/325000, 3 suites.

San Paolo Palace, via Messina Marine 91 ☒ 90123 ℰ 091 6211112, Fax 091 6215300
≤, « Roof garden rest. », 🏋, ≋s, ⊼, ✗ – ♦ 🗏 📺 ☎ ₺ 🚗 🅿 – 🏊 1500. 🆎 E
⓪ E 𝖵𝖨𝖲𝖠. ✗   by via Ponte di Mare DZ
Meals 50000 – **285 rm** ⊇ 170/220000, 10 suites.

Jolly, Foro Italico 22 ☒ 90133 ℰ 091 6165090, Fax 091 6161441, ⚲, ⊼, ⚐ – ♦
🗏 📺 ☎ 🅿 – 🏊 300. 🆎 Ⓢ ⓪ E 𝖵𝖨𝖲𝖠. ✗ rest   DY
Meals a la carte 55/85000 – **213 rm** ⊇ 190/255000.

Afi Hotel Ⓜ, viale della Regione Siciliana 2620 ☒ 90145 ℰ 091 552033
Fax 091 408198 – ♦ 🗏 📺 ☎ 📞 🅿 – 🏊 90. 🆎 Ⓢ ⓪ E 𝖵𝖨𝖲𝖠 𝖩𝖢𝖡. ✗
Meals a la carte 40/65000 – **105 rm** ⊇ 200/240000.   by via della Libertà AX

Villa d'Amato, via Messina Marine 180 ☒ 90123 ℰ 091 6212767, Fax 091 621276
– ♦ 🗏 📺 ☎ 🅿 – 🏊 100. 🆎 Ⓢ ⓪ E 𝖵𝖨𝖲𝖠. ✗   by via Ponte di Mare DZ
Meals (closed Sunday) a la carte 50/60000 – **38 rm** ⊇ 150/180000.

La Scuderia, viale del Fante 9 ☒ 90146 ℰ 091 520323, Fax 091 520467 – 🗏 🅿. 🆎
Ⓢ ⓪ E 𝖵𝖨𝖲𝖠. ✗   by via C.A. Dalla Chiesa AX
closed Sunday – **Meals** 60/80000 (lunch) 70/90000 (dinner) and a la carte 60
105000.

Friend's Bar, via Brunelleschi 138 ☒ 90145 ℰ 091 201401, Fax 091 201066, ⚲
🗏. 🆎 Ⓢ ⓪ E 𝖵𝖨𝖲𝖠. ✗   by via della Libertà AX
closed Monday and 16 to 31 August – **Meals** (booking essential) a la carte 55
75000.

Lo Scudiero, via Turati 7 ☒ 90139 ℰ 091 581628 – 🗏. 🆎 Ⓢ ⓪ E 𝖵𝖨𝖲𝖠 𝖩𝖢
✗   AX
closed Sunday dinner, Monday lunch and 10 to 20 August – **Meals** a la carte 50
80000.

Il Ristorantino, piazza De Gasperi 19 ☒ 90146 ℰ 091 512861, Fax 091 6702999, ⚲
– 🗏. 🆎 Ⓢ ⓪ E 𝖵𝖨𝖲𝖠. ✗   by via C.A. Dalla Chiesa AX
closed Monday and 1 to 20 August – **Meals** a la carte 55/80000.

STREET INDEX TO PALERMO TOWN PLAN

XX **Santandrea,** piazza Sant'Andrea 4 ⊠ 90133 ℘ 091 334999, 🎋 – ▤. 🄰🄴 🛈 🔘 ᴇ 𝘝𝘐𝘚𝘈 𝘑𝘊𝘉   BY d
closed Tuesday and January – **Meals** (booking essential) local dishes a la carte 55/80000.

X **Trattoria Biondo,** via Carducci 15 ⊠ 90141 ℘ 091 583662 – ▤. 🄰🄴 🛈 ᴇ 𝘝𝘐𝘚𝘈. ⚘   AX a
closed Wednesday and 15 July-15 September – **Meals** a la carte 40/50000 (15 %).

X **Il Vespro,** via B. D'Acquisto 9 ⊠ 90141 ℘ 091 589932, *Fax 091 589932* – ▤. 🄰🄴 🛈 🔘 ᴇ 𝘝𝘐𝘚𝘈. ⚘   AX b
Meals Rest. and pizzeria a la carte 35/70000.

t Sferracavallo *North-West : 12 Km –* ⊠ 90148 Palermo :

X **Il Delfino,** via Torretta 80 ℘ 091 530282
▤. 🄰🄴 🛈 🔘 ᴇ 𝘝𝘐𝘚𝘈. ⚘
closed Monday – **Meals** seafood 40000.

illafrati 90030 Palermo 🗺 988 ㊱, 432 N 22 – *pop. 3 442 alt. 450.*
Palermo 36 – Agrigento 87 – Caltanissetta 100.

XX **Mulinazzo,** strada statale 121, località Bolognetta N : 9 Km ℘ 091 8724870, *Fax 091 8724870* – ▤ 🄿. 🄰🄴 🛈 🔘 ᴇ 𝘝𝘐𝘚𝘈
closed Sunday dinner, Monday, 6 to 26 July and 5 to 18 January – **Meals** a la carte 50/75000
Spec. Calamaretti con scorze d'arancia. Timballo di tagliolini con filetti di triglia e finocchietto selvatico. Involtini di mupa con caponata croccante.

A
B
X
Y
Z
Catania
S 113
V.
Via
Via Siracusa
XX
V. Messina
E. Parisi
148
V. Marconi
Nicolò
Villafranca
Via Dante
138
69
150
97
S. Oliva
67
127
102
54
Corso
Goethe
V. N. Turrisi
J
Mercato
di Capo
124
10
133
99
84
Amedeo
Alberto
Papireto
9 V.
24
V. G. Mazzini
La Lumia
V. Puglisi
della Libertà
Settembre
Garzilli
a
b
c
AIR TERMINAL
30
118
GALLERIA
D'ARTE
MODERNA
Pza
Nasce
Piazza
L. Sturzo
V. Ruggero
Settimo
111
Pza
S. Oliva
75
Via
Via Volturno
Pza
Verdi
Teatro
Massimo
43
S. Agostino
S. Agostino
Via
142
Via dei Candelai
120
CATTEDRALE
139
31
Vittorio
Porta
Nuova
Co
94
VILLA
BONANNO
POL
132
Emanuele
SS. Salvatore
QUATTRO CANTI
S. Giuseppe
ai Teatini
36
Scina
Via
Via Emerico
Amari
Principe
di
Belmonte
111 Stabile
Via Onorato
Scordia
Crispi
Crispi
Via
Principe
V.
Mariano
Via Roma
Via R. Pilo
Cavour
153
130
S. Gior
dei Genov
144
S. CITA
149
M¹
N¹
91
82
33
9
Via Ma
N²
M
S. Domenico
126
R²
d
R¹
V. Bandiera
V. Napoli
T
22
Corso
Via Roma
Maqueda
27
PZA
PRETORIA
b
H
PZA
BELLINI
121
MARTORAN
S. CATALDO
13
105
63
Pal.
Marchesi
Chiesa d. Gesù
134 Via
Pal.
Comitini
16
19
37
CAPPELLA
PALATINA
Piazza
Indipendenza
90
Lav.
in
Corso
12
Co Re
Parco
D'Orléans
103
U
145
12
106
PALAZZO
DEI
NORMANNI
151
59
Via
S. GIOVANNI
DEGLI EREMITI
3
Castro
di
Porta
A. Mongitore
Chiesa
d. Carmine
25
Mercato
di Ballarò
108
M
Tukory
S. ANTONINO
123
Ruggero
V. d. Scienze
52
Corso
V. G. Arcoleo
Perni
V. Maggiore
73
49
A
B

PALERMO
ITALY
C
D
PALERMO
X
PALERMO CENTRO
0   300 m
GOLFO
DI
PALERMO
ZIONE
TTIMA
ORTO
Patti
TORRE MASTRA
MOLO
SUD
LA CALA
Cala
della
Porta Felice
Foro
S 3
Via
M 3
Palazzo
Branciforte-Butera
109
nuele
Y
pza Marina
Giardino
Garibaldi
Butera
Italico
PALAZZO
CHIARAMONTE
FRANCESCO
D'ASSISI
85
PAL.
MIRTO
G
147
7
Alloro
La
Gancia
Porta dei Greci
96
Via
141
136
Pza
d. Kalsa
Foro
Pza
d. Magione
34
7
S. Maria
d. Spasimo
Italico
117
Pza
d. Spasimo
Lincoln
Via
VILLA GIULIA
La
Magione
Via
ORTO
BOTANICO
Pza
Gasometro
Corso
Lincoln
V.
Via
GIARDINO
TROPICALE
Via Ponte di Mare
Z
Via
U
AIR TERMINAL
io Cesare
dei
Via G. F. Ingrassia
Architafi
Tiro a segno Nazionale
Oreto
Via
ENTRALE
Cipolla
Mille
Via
Boccone
S.
S 113
C
D

TAORMINA (Sicily) *98039 Messina* 988 ㊲, 432 N 27 *G. Italy – pop. 10 560 alt. 250.*

See : *Site★★★ – Greek Theatre★★ : ≤★★★* B *– Public garden★★* B *– ★★ from the Square 9 Aprile* A **13** *– Corso Umberto★* A *– Belvedere★* B *– Castle★ : ≤★* A.

Exc. : *Etna★★★, SW : for Linguaglossa.*

Picciolo (closed Tuesday) contrada Rovitello ✉ 95012 Castiglione di Sicilia ☎ 0942 986171, Fax 0942 986252, W : 25 km.

piazza Santa Caterina (Corvaja palace) ☎ 0942 23243, Fax 0942 24941 1.

Catania 52 ② – Enna 135 ② – Messina 52 ① – Palermo 255 ② – Siracusa 111 ② – Trapani 359 ②

Grand Hotel Timeo, via Teatro Greco 59 ☎ 0942 23801, *Fax 0942 628501*, ≤ sea, coast and Etna, « Large park and floral terraces » – ☎ P. AE VISA. B
Meals *Il Dito e La Luna* Rest. a la carte 95/140000 – **56 rm** 480/620000, 9 suites.

San Domenico Palace, piazza San Domenico 5 ☎ 0942 23701, *Fax 0942 625506*, « 15C monastery with floral garden, ≤ sea, coast and Etna », heated – ☎ – 400. AE VISA. A
Meals 110000 – **100 rm** 440/750000, 9 suites.

Villa Diodoro, via Bagnoli Croci 75 ☎ 0942 23312, *Fax 0942 23391*, ≤ sea, coast and Etna, « on panoramic terrace », – TV ☎ P – 300. AE VISA. B
Meals a la carte 55/85000 – **102 rm** 250/350000.

Excelsior Palace, via Toselli 8 ☎ 0942 23975, *Fax 0942 23978*, ≤ sea, coast and Etna, « Small park and heated on panoramic terrace » – TV ☎ P – 100. AE VISA JCB. rest A
Meals 50/70000 – **88 rm** 210/320000.

Gd H. Miramare, via Guardiola Vecchia 27 ☎ 0942 23401, *Fax 0942 626223*, ≤ sea and coast, heated, , – TV ☎ P. AE VISA JCB. B
March-October – **Meals** a la carte 65/90000 – **67 rm** 260/320000.

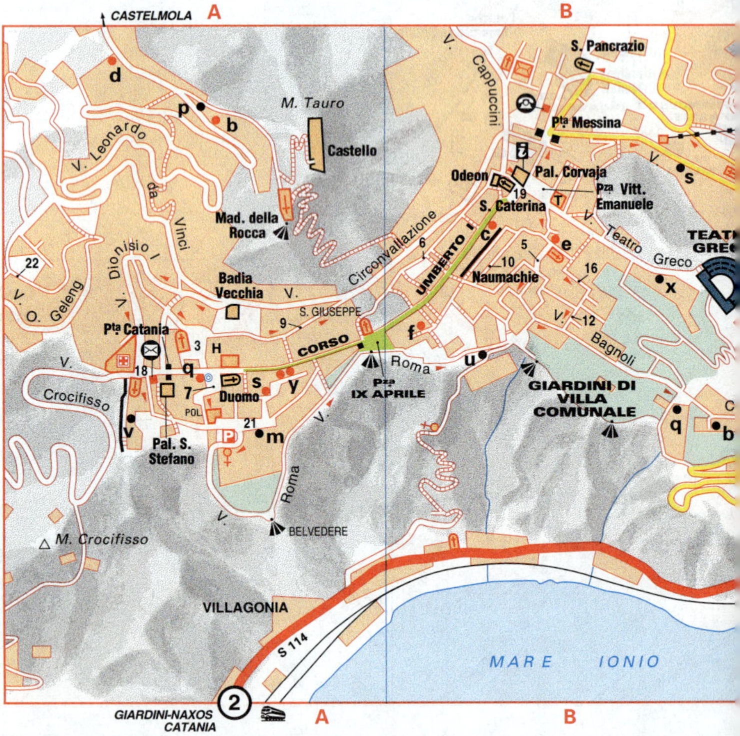

Monte Tauro ⚜, via Madonna delle Grazie 3 ℘ 0942 24402, Fax 0942 24403, ≤ sea and coast, ⤢ – 🛗 ▤ TV ☎ 🅿 – ⛲ 100. AE ⑤ ⓪ E VISA JCB. ⛽ AB u
Meals a la carte 40/60000 – **71 rm** ☕ 210/300000.

Villa Ducale ⚜ without rest., via Leonardo da Vinci 60 ℘ 0942 28153, Fax 0942 28710, ≤ sea, coast and Etna – ▤ TV ☎ 🅿. AE ⑤ ⓪ E VISA JCB. ⛽ A p
closed 15 January-15 February – **12 rm** ☕ 250/380000.

Villa Fiorita without rest., via Pirandello 39 ℘ 0942 24122, Fax 0942 625967, ≤ sea and coast, ⇌s, ⤢, 🚗 – 🛗 ▤ TV ☎ �'. AE ⑤ E VISA – **24 rm** ☕ 185000. B s

Villa Belvedere without rest., via Bagnoli Croci 79 ℘ 0942 23791, Fax 0942 625830, ≤ gardens, sea and Etna, « Garden with ⤢ » – 🛗 ☎ 🅿. ⑤ E VISA B b
closed 12 November-20 December and 13 January-15 March – **47 rm** ☕ 165/255000.

Villa Sirina, contrada Sirina ℘ 0942 51776, Fax 0942 51671, ⤢, 🚗 – ▤ TV ☎ 🅿. AE ⑤ ⓪ E VISA. ⛽　　　　　　　　　　　　　2 km by via Crocifisso　A
closed 10 January-20 March – **Meals** (residents only) (dinner only) – **15 rm** ☕ 220000.

La Giara, vico La Floresta 1 ℘ 0942 23360, Fax 0942 23233, Rest. and piano bar – ▤. AE ⑤ ⓪ E VISA. ⛽ A f
closed November, February, March (except Friday-Saturday) and Monday (except July-September) – **Meals** (dinner only) (booking essential) a la carte 65/95000.

Maffei's, via San Domenico de Guzman 1 ℘ 0942 24055, Fax 0942 24055, 🌳 – AE ⑤ ⓪ E VISA – closed 10 January – 20 February and Tuesday (except Easter to October) – **Meals** (booking essential) a la carte 65/100000. A y

La Griglia, corso Umberto 54 ℘ 0942 23980 – ▤. AE ⑤ ⓪ E VISA. ⛽ A c
closed Tuesday and 20 November-20 December – **Meals** a la carte 40/60000.

Al Duomo, vico Ebrei 11 ℘ 0942 625656, « Summer service on terrace » – ▤. AE ⑤ ⓪ E VISA A q
Meals (booking essential) Sicilian rest. a la carte 50/75000.

TAORMINA

XX **Al Castello**, via Madonna della Rocca 11 ℘ 0942 28158, « Summer service on panoramic terrace with ⩽ sea and coast » – ⒶⒺ Ⓢ ⓄⒹ Ⓔ 𝗩𝗜𝗦𝗔. ⅋   A b
closed 15 January-20 February, Wednesday lunch June-September, all day in other months – **Meals** a la carte 55/75000.

XX **La Piazzetta**, via Paladini 5 ℘ 0942 626317, Fax 0942 626317 – ▤. ⒶⒺ Ⓢ ⓄⒹ Ⓔ
𝗩𝗜𝗦𝗔   A s
closed Monday, 15 to 30 November and 15 to 30 January – **Meals** a la carte 40/70000.

X **Il Baccanale**, piazzetta Filea 1 ℘ 0942 625390, 🍽 – ▤. Ⓢ Ⓔ 𝗩𝗜𝗦𝗔. ⅋   B e
closed Thursday except April-September – **Meals** a la carte 40/65000.

X **La Chioccia d'Oro**, via Leonardo da Vinci ℘ 0942 28066, ⩽   A d
closed Thursday and 15 to 30 November – **Meals** a la carte 30/50000.

at Mazzarò *by ② : 5,5 km –* ⊠ *98030 :*

🏨 **Mazzarò Sea Palace**, via Nazionale 147 ℘ 0942 24004, Fax 0942 626237, ⩽ small bay, 🍽, « Solarium terrace with ⚒ », 🏖 – 🛗 ▤ 📺 ☎ – 🏊 90. ⒶⒺ Ⓢ ⓄⒹ Ⓔ 𝗩𝗜𝗦𝗔. ⅋
April-October – **Meals** a la carte 75/95000 – **88 rm** ⊡ 350/490000, 2 suites.

at Capo Taormina *by ② : 7 Km –* ⊠ *98030 Mazzarò :*

🏨 **Grande Albergo Capotaormina**, via Nazionale 105 ℘ 0942 572111, Fax 0942 625467, ⩽ sea and coast, « Garden terrace on cliffs, lifts to beach », ⚒ sea water, 🏖 – 🛗, ⟲ rm, ▤ 📺 ☎ Ⓟ – 🏊 450. ⒶⒺ Ⓢ ⓄⒹ Ⓔ 𝗩𝗜𝗦𝗔. ⅋ rest
April-October – **Meals** a la carte 60/100000 and **La Scogliera** Rest. *(closed until 15 June, October and dinner Monday and Tuesday) (booking essential for dinner)* a la carte 65/110000 – **203 rm** ⊡ 280/400000.

at Lido di Spisone *by ① : 7 km –* ⊠ *98030 Mazzarò :*

🏨 **Lido Caparena**, via Nazionale 189 ℘ 0942 652033, Fax 0942 36913, ⩽, « Extensive flower garden with outdoor rest. summer service », ⚒, 🏖 – 🛗 ▤ 📺 ☎ ♿ Ⓟ – 🏊 200. ⒶⒺ Ⓢ ⓄⒹ Ⓔ 𝗩𝗜𝗦𝗔. ⅋
Meals a la carte 55/85000 – **88 rm** ⊡ 250/350000.

🏨 **Lido Mediterranée**, ℘ 0942 24422, Fax 0942 24774, ⩽, 🍽, 🏖 – 🛗 ▤ 📺 ☎ Ⓟ – 🏊 100. ⒶⒺ Ⓢ ⓄⒹ Ⓔ 𝗩𝗜𝗦𝗔. ⅋ rest
20 March-October – **Meals** 60000 – **72 rm** ⊡ 300/350000.

🏨 **Bay Palace**, via Nazionale ℘ 0942 626200, Fax 0942 626199, « Solarium terrace with panoramic ⚒ » – 🛗 ▤ ☎. ⒶⒺ Ⓢ ⓄⒹ Ⓔ 𝗩𝗜𝗦𝗔. ⅋ rest
Meals (dinner only) 35/65000 – **47 rm** ⊡ 165/230000.

TURIN (TORINO) *10100* ℗ 𝟵𝟴𝟴 ⑫, 𝟰𝟮𝟴 *G 5 G. Italy – pop. 914818 alt. 239.*

See : *Piazza San Carlo*★★ CXY *– Egyptian Museum*★★, *Sabauda Gallery*★★ *in Academy of Science* CX M¹ *– Cathedral*★ VX : *relic of the Holy Shroud*★★★ *– Mole Antonelliana*★ : ❈★★ DX *– Madama Palace*★ : *museum of Ancient Art*★ CX A *– Royal Palace*★ : *Royal Armoury*★ CDVX *– Risorgimento Museum*★ *in Carignano Palace* CX M² *– Carlo Biscaretti di Ruffia Motor Museum*★ *– Model medieval village*★ *in the Valentino Park* CDZ.

Envir. : *Basilica of Superga*★ : ⩽★★★ *– Tour to the pass, Colle della Maddalena*★ : ⩽★★ *of the city from the route Superga-Pino Torinese,* ⩽★ *of the city from the route Colle Colle della Maddalena-Cavoretto.*

🏌₁₈, 🏌₉ *I Roveri (closed Monday) at La Mandria* ⊠ *10070 Fiano Torinese 011 9235719, Fax 011 9235669, N : 18 km;*

🏌₁₈, 🏌₁₈ *(closed Monday, January and February), at Fiano Torinese* ⊠ *10070 ℘ 011 9235440, Fax 011 9235886, N : 20 km;*

🏌₁₈ *Le Fronde (closed Tuesday, January and February) at Avigliana* ⊠ *10051 ℘ 011 9328053, Fax 011 9320928, W : 24 km;*

🏌₉ *Stupinigi (closed Monday),* ℘ *011 3472640, Fax 011 3978038;*

🏌₉ *Vinovo (closed Monday and 21 December-9 January) at Vinovo* ⊠ *10048 ℘ 011 9653880, Fax 011 9623748.*

✈ *Turin Airport of Caselle North : 15 km* ℘ *011 5676749 – Alitalia, via Lagrange 35* ⊠ *10123* ℘ *011 57691, Fax 011 5769220.*

🚗 ℘ *011 6651111-int. 2611.*

🅑 *via Roma 226 (piazza C.L.N.)* ⊠ *10121* ℘ *011 535901, Fax 011 530070 – Porta Nuova Railway Station* ⊠ *10125* ℘ *011 531327.*

A.C.I. *via Giovanni Giolitti 15* ⊠ *10123* ℘ *011 57791.*

Roma 669 – Briançon 108 – Chambéry 209 – Genève 252 – Genova 170 – Grenoble 224 – Milano 140 – Nice 220.

Turin Palace Hotel, via Sacchi 8 ✉ 10128 ℰ 011 5625511, Fax 011 5612187 – 📶 🗏 📺 ☎ 🕭 🚗 – 🛎 200. AE ⑤ ⓞ E VISA. 🛠 rest CY u
Meals *(closed August)* a la carte 60/105000 – **120 rm** 🗇 320/410000, suite.

Le Meridien Lingotto M, via Nizza 262 ✉ 10126 ℰ 011 6642000, Fax 011 6642001, 🛥 – 📶, 🖢 rm, 🗏 📺 ☎ 🕭 🕭 🚗 P – 🛎 35. AE ⑤ ⓞ E VISA JCB. 🛠 rest by via Nizza CZ
Meals *le Rivoli* Rest. *(closed Monday and 9 to 22 August)* a la carte 75/130000 – **229 rm** 🗇 450000, 15 suites.

Jolly Hotel Principi di Piemonte, via Gobetti 15 ✉ 10123 ℰ 011 5629693, Fax 011 5620270 – 📶, 🖢 rm, 🗏 📺 ☎ – 🛎 300. AE ⑤ ⓞ E VISA. 🛠 rest CY z
Meals *L'Gentilom* Rest. a la carte 75/115000 – **107 rm** 🗇 430/450000, 8 suites.

Gd H. Sitea, via Carlo Alberto 35 ✉ 10123 ℰ 011 5170171, Fax 011 548090 – 📶, 🖢 rm, 🗏 📺 ☎ – 🛎 100. AE ⑤ ⓞ E VISA. 🛠 rest CY t
Meals *Carignano* Rest. *(closed Saturday dinner, Sunday and August)* a la carte 65/105000 – **116 rm** 🗇 310/420000, 2 suites.

Jolly Hotel Ambasciatori, corso Vittorio Emanuele II 104 ✉ 10121 ℰ 011 5752, Fax 011 544978 – 📶, 🖢 rm, 🗏 📺 ☎ 🚗 – 🛎 400. AE ⑤ ⓞ E VISA. 🛠 rest BX a
Meals *Il Diplomatico* Rest. a la carte 65/105000 – **199 rm** 🗇 310/360000, 4 suites.

Jolly Hotel Ligure M, piazza Carlo Felice 85 ✉ 10123 ℰ 011 55641, Fax 011 535438 – 📶 🗏 📺 ☎ – 🛎 200. AE ⑤ ⓞ E VISA. 🛠 rest CY b
Meals *Birichino* Rest. a la carte 55/100000 – **167 rm** 🗇 325/380000, 2 suites.

Starhotel Majestic without rest., corso Vittorio Emanuele II 54 ✉ 10123 ℰ 011 539153, Fax 011 534963 – 📶 🖢 🗏 📺 ☎ 🕭 – 🛎 600. AE ⑤ ⓞ E VISA JCB. 🛠 CY e
148 rm 🗇 365/470000, suite.

Relais Villa Sassi 🦢, strada al Traforo del Pino 47 ✉ 10132 ℰ 011 8980556, Fax 011 8980095, 🌳, « 18C country house in extensive parkland » – 📶 🗏 📺 ☎ P – 🛎 200. AE ⑤ ⓞ E VISA. 🛠 rest by corso Casale DY
closed August – Meals *Villa Sassi* Rest. *(closed Sunday)* a la carte 80/125000 – **17 rm** 🗇 300/440000.

City, via Juvarra 25 ✉ 10122 ℰ 011 540546, Fax 011 548188 – 📶 🗏 📺 ☎ 🕭 🚗 – 🛎 60. AE ⑤ ⓞ E VISA. 🛠 BV e
Meals *(closed Saturday and Sunday)* (dinner only) 45/60000 – **57 rm** 🗇 180/250000, 11 suites.

Boston without rest., via Massena 70 ✉ 10128 ℰ 011 500359, Fax 011 599358, 🛥 – 📶 🗏 📺 ☎ 🚗 – 🛎 50. AE ⑤ ⓞ E VISA BZ c
86 rm 🗇 185/240000, 5 suites.

Victoria without rest., via Nino Costa 4 ✉ 10123 ℰ 011 5611909, Fax 011 5611806, « Elegant and personal ambience » – 📶 🗏 📺 ☎. AE ⑤ ⓞ E VISA. 🛠 CY v
90 rm 🗇 190/270000.

Holiday Inn Turin City Centre M, via Assietta 3 ✉ 10128 ℰ 011 5167111, Fax 011 5167699 – 📶, 🖢 rm, 🗏 📺 ☎ 🕭 🕭 🚗 – 🛎 40. AE ⑤ ⓞ E VISA JCB. 🛠 rest CY a
Meals *Camerana* Rest. (dinner only) a la carte 35/60000 – 🗇 25000 – **57 rm** 260/360000.

Genio without rest., corso Vittorio Emanuele II 47 ✉ 10125 ℰ 011 6505771, Fax 011 6508264 – 📶 🖢 🗏 📺 ☎ – 🛎 25. AE ⑤ ⓞ E VISA JCB CYZ w
93 rm 🗇 185/240000, 3 suites.

Concord, via Lagrange 47 ✉ 10123 ℰ 011 5176756, Fax 011 5176305 – 📶 🗏 📺 ☎ – 🛎 180. AE ⑤ ⓞ E VISA. 🛠 rest CY s
Meals a la carte 50/75000 – **135 rm** 🗇 305/360000, 4 suites.

Royal, corso Regina Margherita 249 ✉ 10144 ℰ 011 4376777, Fax 011 4376393 – 📶 🗏 📺 ☎ 🕭 🚗 P – 🛎 600. AE ⑤ ⓞ E VISA JCB BV u
closed 1 to 28 August – Meals a la carte 45/75000 – **70 rm** 🗇 190/240000.

Genova e Stazione without rest., via Sacchi 14/b ✉ 10128 ℰ 011 5629400, Fax 011 5629896 – 📶 🗏 📺 ☎ 🕭 – 🛎 60. AE ⑤ ⓞ E VISA. 🛠 CZ b
closed 1 to 24 August – **59 rm** 🗇 180/240000.

President without rest., via Cecchi 67 ✉ 10152 ℰ 011 859555, Fax 011 2480465 – 📶 🗏 📺 ☎ – 🛎 60. AE ⑤ ⓞ E VISA. 🛠 CV s
72 rm 🗇 180/200000.

Alexandra without rest., lungo Dora Napoli 14 ✉ 10152 ℰ 011 858327, Fax 011 2483805 – 📶 🗏 📺 ☎ 🚗. AE ⑤ ⓞ E VISA. 🛠 CV c
57 rm 🗇 220/290000.

TORINO

Traffic restricted
in the town centre

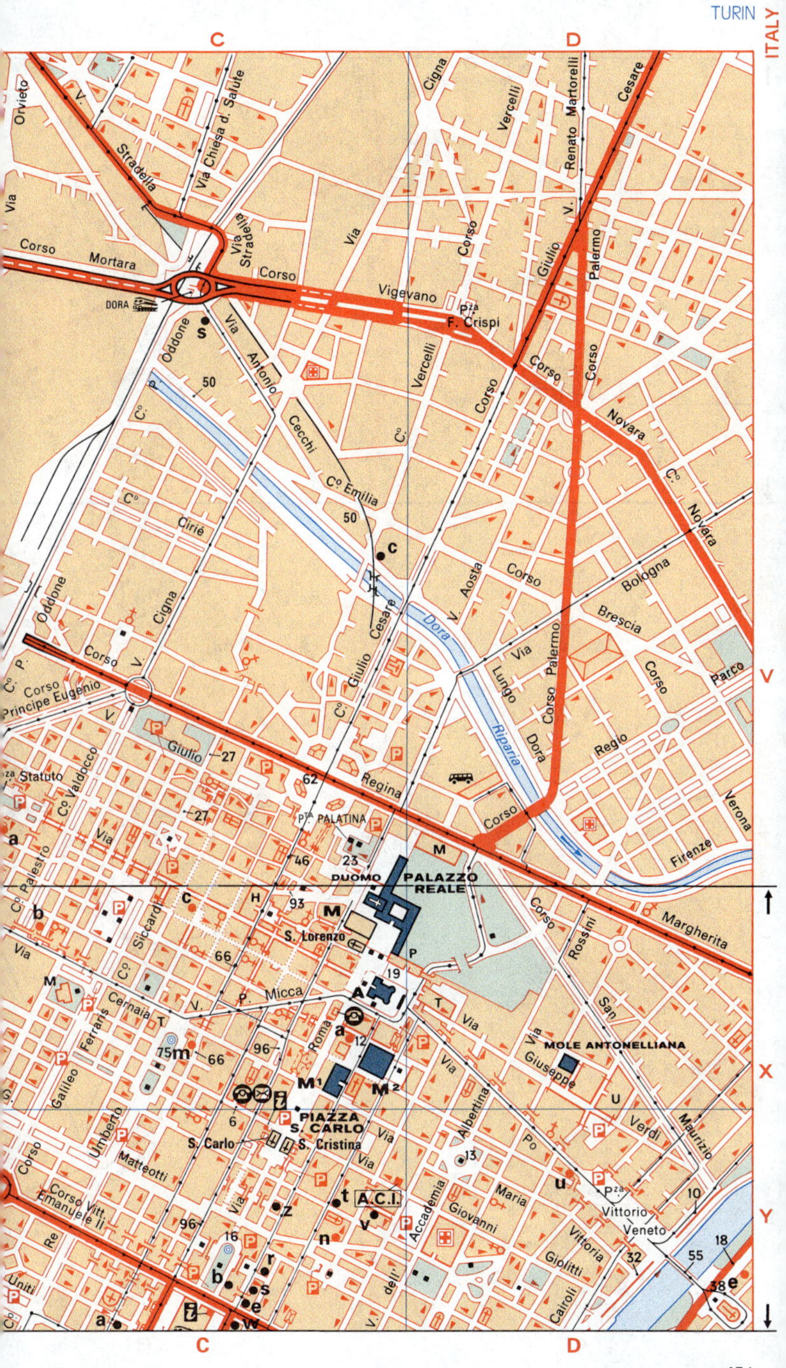

TURIN
ITALY
C   D
Orvieto
V.
Stradella
Via Chiesa d. Salute
Via
Corso   Mortara
Corso
DORA
Vigevano
P.za
F. Crispi
Cigna
Vercelli
Renato Martorelli
Cesare
Giulio   V.
Palermo
Corso
Corso
S
Oddone
Via Antonio
Cecchi
50
C.°
Via
C.° Emilia
50
C.°
c
Cirié
C.°
Cigna
Oddone
C.°
Giulio Cesare
Vercelli
Corso
Corso
Corso
Novara
Aosta
V.
Dora
Corso
Bologna
Brescia
V.
Novara
C.°
V.
Corso Palermo
Lungo   Dora
Riparia
Corso
Regio
Parco
Verona
Firenze
C.° P.
Corso
Principe Eugenio
V.
Giulio
27
62
27
P.za Statuto
Via
P.za Statuto
C.° Valdocco
C.° Palesto
P.ta PALATINA
46
23
DUOMO
PALAZZO
REALE
M
Corso
Margherita
Via
C
Siccardi
H
93
M
S. Lorenzo
66
Rossini
San
M
Cernaia
N.
P. Micca
T
Via
Via
Galileo
Ferraris
75 m
66
96
Roma
A
a
12
MOLE ANTONELLIANA
Giuseppe
Via
M¹
M²
Umberto
6
PIAZZA
S. CARLO
S. Carlo
S. Cristina
Via
Via
Albertina
Verdi
Maurizio
Matteotti
Po
u
P.za
Vittorio
Veneto
10
Corso
Corso Vitt.
Emanuele II
t   A.C.I.
z
v
Maria
Giovanni
Vittorio
32
55
18
Re
96
16
n
dell'
V.
Giolitti
38   e
Uniti
b
r
s
e
w
a
C.°
Accademia
Cairoli
C   D
451

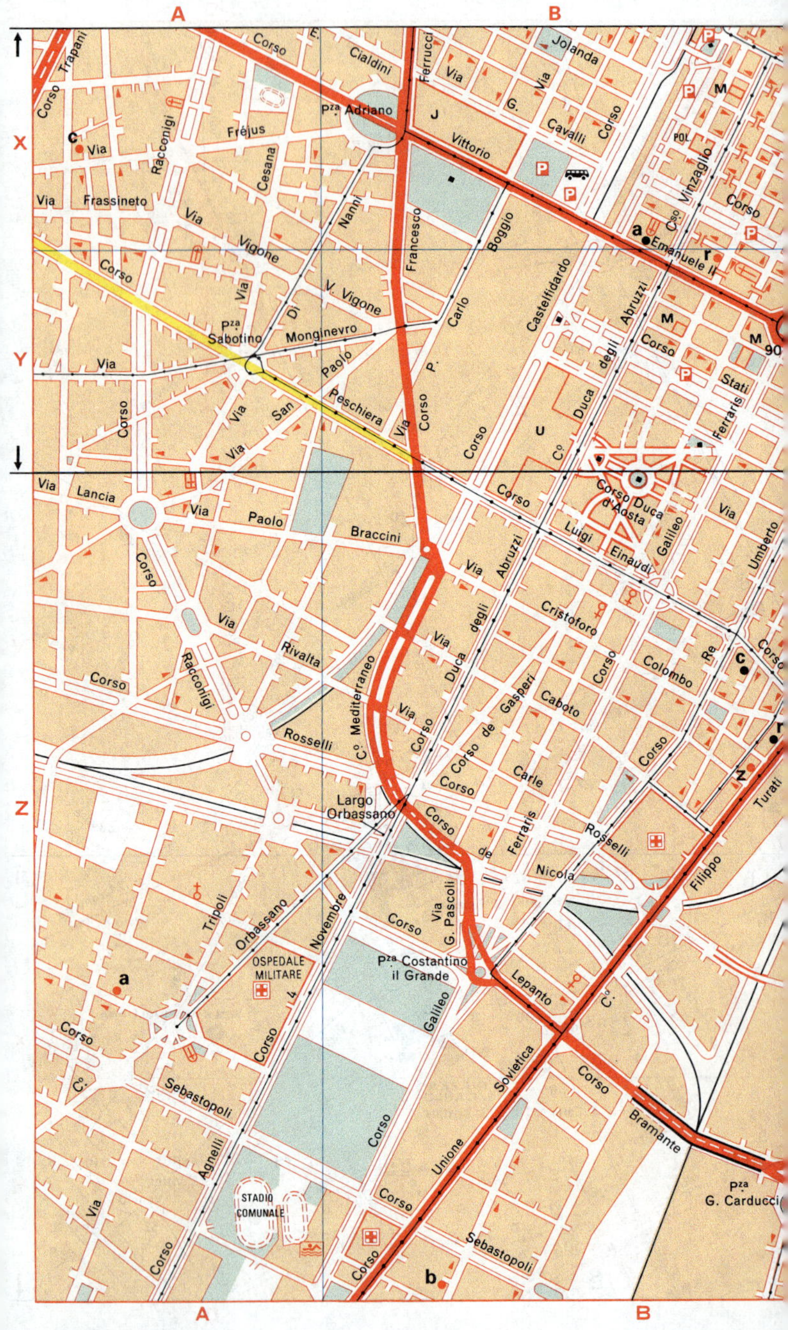
Corso Trapani
Corso
Cialdini
Ferrucci
Jolanda
Via
Via
G.
Cavalli
Corso
P
M
POL
Pza Adriano
J
Vittorio
P
Cso Vinzaglio
Corso
c
Via
Racconigi
Fréjus
P
a
Emanuele II
r
Via Frassineto
Cesana
Nanni
Francesco
Boggio
Castelfidardo
Abruzzi
M
r
Corso
Via
Vigone
Carlo
Duca degli
Corso
M
M 90
V. Vigone
Di
Pza Sabotino
Monginevro
Paolo
P.
Corso
Stati
P
Ferraris
Via
Peschiera
San
Via
Via
Corso
U
Cº
Corso Duca d'Aosta
Via
Corso
Via
Lancia
Via
Paolo
Braccini
Corso
Luigi
Einaudi
Galileo
Umberto
Racconigi
Corso
Via
Rivalta
Via
Abruzzi
Cristoforo
c
Corso
Cº Mediterraneo
Rosselli
Via
Duca degli
Corso
Colombo
Re
Corso
Corso
Via
Corso de Gasperi
Caboto
r
Corso
Largo Orbassano
Corso
Carle
Z
Turati
Tripoli
Orbassano
Novembre
Corso
Via G. Pascoli
Ferraris
Nicola
Rosselli
Filippo
Cº
OSPEDALE MILITARE
Pza Costantino il Grande
Galileo
Lepanto
Cº
a
Agnelli
Corso
Sovietica
Corso
Corso
Cº
Sebastopoli
Bramante
Via
STADIO COMUNALE
Corso
Unione
Sebastopoli
Pza G. Carducci
Corso
b
A
B

TORINO

Traffic restricted
in the town centre

Crimea without rest., via Mentana 3 ✉ 10133 ✆ 011 6604700, *Fax 011 6604912* – 🛗 TV ☎ 🚗 – 🔺 35. AE ⑤ ① E *VISA* JCB. 🛠
DZ e
48 rm ⮔ 185/240000, suite.

Gran Mogol without rest., via Guarini 2 ✉ 10123 ✆ 011 5612120, *Fax 011 5623160* – 🛗 ✂ ▤ TV ☎. AE ⑤ ① E *VISA* JCB
CY r
closed August and 23 December-3 January – **45 rm** ⮔ 185/240000.

Giotto without rest., via Giotto 27 ✉ 10126 ✆ 011 6637172, *Fax 011 6637173* – 🛗 ▤ TV ☎ 🦽 – 🔺 50. AE ⑤ ① E *VISA*
CZ c
50 rm ⮔ 140/160000

Piemontese without rest., via Berthollet 21 ✉ 10125 ✆ 011 6698101, *Fax 011 6690571* – 🛗 ✂ ▤ TV ☎ 🅿. AE ⑤ ① E *VISA*. 🛠
CZ x
40 rm ⮔ 160/220000.

Lancaster without rest., corso Filippo Turati 8 ✉ 10128 ✆ 011 5681982, *Fax 011 5683019* – 🛗 ▤ TV ☎ 🦽 – 🔺 40. AE ⑤ ① E *VISA*
BZ r
closed 5 to 31 August – **77 rm** ⮔ 165/210000.

Due Mondi without rest., via Saluzzo 3 ✉ 10125 ✆ 011 6698981, *Fax 011 6699383* – ▤ TV ☎. AE ⑤ ① E *VISA* JCB
CZ k
closed 10 to 20 August – ⮔ 15000 – **43 rm** 150/180000.

Cairo without rest., via La Loggia 6 ✉ 10134 ✆ 011 3171555, *Fax 011 3172027* – 🛗 TV ☎ 🅿. AE ⑤ ① E *VISA*. 🛠
by corso Unione Sovietica BZ
closed 1 to 28 August – ⮔ 20000 – **50 rm** 150/200000.

Tourist without rest., via Alpignano 3 angolo corso Francia 92 ✉ 10143 ✆ 011 7761740, *Fax 011 7493431* – 🛗 ▤ TV ☎. AE ⑤ ① E *VISA*
AV a
closed 28 July-5 September – **28 rm** ⮔ 170/220000.

Del Cambio, piazza Carignano 2 ✉ 10123 ✆ 011 543760, *Fax 011 535282*, Historic traditional restaurant, « 19C decor » – ▤. AE ⑤ ① E *VISA*. 🛠
CX a
closed Sunday, 8 to 31 August and 1 to 6 January – **Meals** (booking essential) 70/100000 (lunch) 90/110000 (dinner) and a la carte 75/125000 (15 %).

Balbo, via Andrea Doria 11 ✉ 10123 ✆ 011 8395775, *Fax 011 8151042* – ▤. AE ⑤ ① E *VISA*. 🛠
CY n
closed Monday and 25 July-20 August – **Meals** (booking essential) a la carte 100/165000
Spec. Filetto di fassone crudo con robiola, funghi e tartufo bianco (autumn). Carrè d'agnello in crosta d'erbe aromatiche con salsa allo scalogno (autumn-spring). Tortino di seirass (ricotta) e amaretti con salsa al Brachetto (autumn-spring).

Rendez Vous, corso Vittorio Emanuele II 38 ✉ 10123 ✆ 011 887666, *Fax 011 889362* – ▤. AE ⑤ ① E *VISA*. 🛠
CZ g
closed Saturday lunch and Sunday – **Meals** (booking essential for dinner)40/70000 (lunch) 65/90000 (dinner) and a la carte 70/100000.

Villa Somis, strada Val Pattonera 138 ✉ 10133 ✆ 011 6613086, *Fax 011 6614626*, ≼, « 18C house with summer service in park under a pergola » – 🅿. AE ⑤ ① E *VISA*
HU e
closed 9 to 25 August, 26 December-7 January, Monday and lunch October-May (except weekends) – **Meals** (booking essential) a la carte 50/80000.

La Prima Smarrita, corso Unione Sovietica 244 ✉ 10134 ✆ 011 3179657, *Fax 011 3179191* – ▤. AE ⑤ ① E *VISA*. 🛠
GU c
closed August – **Meals** (booking essential) Mediterranean cuisine a la carte 40/105000
Spec. Gamberi in agrodolce. Ravioli al ragù d'anatra. Rombo ai porcini.

La Cloche, strada al Traforo del Pino 106 ✉ 10132 ✆ 011 8994213, *Fax 011 8981522* – 🅿 – 🔺 100. AE ⑤ ① E *VISA*
by corso Moncalieri CDZ
closed Sunday dinner, Monday and 10 to 24 August – **Meals** (surprise menu) 25/50000 (lunch) 35/60000 (dinner) and a la carte 50/115000.

Marco Polo, via Marco Polo 38 ✉ 10129 ✆ 011 500096, *Fax 011 599900* – ▤. AE ⑤ ① E *VISA* JCB
BZ t
closed Monday and lunch (except Sunday) – **Meals** (booking essential) seafood 80000.

Al Gatto Nero, corso Filippo Turati 14 ✉ 10128 ✆ 011 590414, *Fax 011 502245* – ▤. AE ⑤ ① E *VISA*. 🛠
BZ z
closed Sunday and August – **Meals** a la carte 70/90000.

Porta Rossa, via Passalacqua 3/b ✉ 10122 ✆ 011 530816 – ▤. AE ⑤ ① E *VISA*. 🛠
CV a
closed Saturday lunch, Sunday, 4 to 10 April, August and 26 December-10 January – **Meals** 25/45000 (lunch only) and a la carte 55/100000.

Al Bue Rosso, corso Casale 10 ✉ 10131 ✆ 011 8191393 – ▤. AE ⑤ ① E *VISA*. 🛠
DY e
closed Saturday lunch, Monday and August – **Meals** a la carte 65/85000 (10 %).

XX **Perbacco,** via Mazzini 31 ⊠ 10123 ✆ 011 882110, Late night dinners – 🖃. AE 🖫 ⓪ E VISA
closed Sunday and August – **Meals** (dinner only) (booking essential) 40000.
DZ x

XX **Galante,** corso Palestro 15 ⊠ 10122 ✆ 011 537757 – 🖃. AE 🖫 ⓪ E VISA JCB
closed Saturday lunch, Sunday and August – **Meals** a la carte 55/90000.
CX b

XX **Il Porticciolo,** via Barletta 58 ⊠ 10136 ✆ 011 321601 – 🖃. AE 🖫 ⓪ E VISA
closed Saturday lunch, Monday and August – **Meals** (booking essential) seafood a la carte 70/95000.
AZ a

XX **Il 58,** via San Secondo 58 ⊠ 10128 ✆ 011 505566, Fax 011 505566 – 🖃. 🖫 E VISA.
closed Monday and 10 to 24 August – **Meals** seafood a la carte 45/65000.
CZ a

X **Trômlin,** via alla Parrocchia 7, a Cavoretto ⊠ 10133 ✆ 011 6613050
closed lunch (except Bank Holidays), Monday and 10 to 25 August – **Meals** (booking essential) (surprise Piemontese menu) 55000 b.i.
by corso Moncalieri DZ

X **Ristorantino Tefy,** corso Belgio 26 ⊠ 10153 ✆ 011 837332, Fax 011 837332 – 🖃.
AE 🖫 E VISA JCB
by corso Novara CZDV p
closed Sunday – **Meals** Umbrian rest. a la carte 45/90000.

VENICE (VENEZIA) 30100 🅿 988 ⑤, 429 F 19 *G. Venice* – *pop. 293 731.*

See : *St. Marks Square★★★ FKZ : Basilica★★★ LZ – Doges Palace★★★ LZ – Campanile★★ : ☀★★ KLZ Q – Correr Museum★★ KZ M1 – Bridge of Sighs★★ LZ Grand Canal★★★ : Rialto Bridge★★ KY – Ca' d'Oro★★★ JX – Academy of Fine Arts★★★ BV – Cà Dario★ DV – Cà Rezzonico★★ BV – Grassi Palace★ BV – Peggy Guggenheim Collection★★ in Palace Venier dei Leoni DV M¹ – Vendramin-Calergi Palace★ CT – Cà Pesaro★ JX.*
Churches : Santa Maria della Salute★★ DV – St. Giorgio Maggiore★ : ☀★★★ from campanile FV – St. Zanipolo★★ LX – Santa Maria Gloriosa dei Frari★★★ BTU – St. Zaccaria★★ LZ – Interior decoration★★ by Veronese in the Church of St. Sebastiano BV – Ceiling★ of the Church of St. Pantaleone BU – Santa Maria dei Miracoli★ KLX – St. Francesco della Vigna★ FT – Giudecca Island DV – Ghetto★★ BT.
Scuola di St. Rocco★★★ BU – Scuola di St. Giorgio degli Schiavoni★★★ FU – Scuola dei Carmini★ BV – Scuola di St. Marco★ LX – Palazzo Labia★★ BT.
Murano★★ : Glass Museum★, Church of Santi Maria e Donato★★ – Burano★★ - Torcello★★ : mosaics★★ in the basilica of Santa Maria Assunta.

🏌 *(closed Monday) at Lido Alberoni* ⊠ *30011* ✆ *041 731333, Fax 041 731339, 15 mn by boat and 9 km;*

🏌, 🏌 *Cà della Nave (closed Tuesday) at Martellago* ⊠ *30030* ✆ *041 5401555, Fax 041 5401555, North-West : 12 km;*

🏌, 🏌 *Villa Condulmer (closed Monday), at Zerman* ⊠ *31021* ✆ *041 457062, Fax 041 457202, North : 17 km.*

✈ *Marco Polo of Tessera, North-East : 13 km* ✆ *041 2606111 – Alitalia, via Sansovino 7 Mestre-Venezia* ⊠ *30173* ✆ *041 2581111, Fax 041 2581246.*

🚢 *to Lido-San Nicolò from piazzale Roma (Tronchetto) daily (35 mn); to island of Pellestrina-Santa Maria del Mare from Lido Alberoni daily (15 mn).*

🚢 *to Punta Sabbioni from Riva degli Schiavoni daily (40 mn) to islands of Burano (30 mn), Torcello (40 mn), Murano (1 h 10 mn) from Punta Sabbioni daily to islands of Murano (10 mn), Burano (50 mn), Torcello (50 mn) from Fondamenta Nuove daily; to Treporti-Cavallino from Fondamenta Nuove daily (1 h 10 mn); to Venezia-Fondamenta Nuove from Treporti-Cavallino (1 h 10 mn), to islands of Murano (1 h), Burano (20 mn), Torcello (25 mn) daily – Information : ACTV-Venetian Trasport Union, piazzale Roma* ⊠ *30135* ✆ *041 5287886, Fax 041 5207135.*

🛈 *Palazzetto Selva-Molo di San Marco 71/c* ⊠ *30124* ✆ *041 5226356, Fax 041 5298730 – Santa Lucia railway station* ⊠ *30121* ✆ *041 5298727, Fax 041 719078.*
Roma 528 ① – Bologna 152 ① – Milano 267 ① – Trieste 158 ①

Plans on following pages

🏨 **Cipriani** ⌂, isola della Giudecca 10 ⊠ 30133 ✆ 041 5207744, Fax 041 5203930, ≤, ♨, « Floral garden with heated 🏊 and Cip's Club Rest. summer service on terrace with ≤ Giudecca canal », ≘s, ✖ – 🛗 🖃 TV ☎ – 🔬 80. AE 🖫 ⓪ E VISA.
FV h
April-7 November – **Meals** a la carte 130/180000 – **59 rm** ⊒ 990/1650000, 12 suites (**Palazzo Vendramin** 7 apartments closed 7 November-20 February, **Il Palazzetto** 5 apartments closed 7 November-15 March and Meals **Cip's Club** Rest.).

🏨 **Danieli,** riva degli Schiavoni 4196 ⊠ 30122 ✆ 041 5226480, Fax 041 5200208, ≤ San Marco Canal, private pier, « Hall in a small Venetian style courtyard and summer rest. service on terrace with panoramic view » – 🛗 🖃 TV ☎ ✆ – 🔬 150. AE 🖫 ⓪ E VISA JCB.
LZ a
Meals a la carte 130/200000 – ⊒ 42000 – **221 rm** 570/1045000, 9 suites.

ITALY
A
B
S. Alvise
C
D
Madonna del Orto
Campo
S. Giobbe
Sinagoga
Spagnola
Museo ebraico
GHETTO
CANNAREGIO
27
Rio T. S. Leonardo
Pte d. Guglie
PAL. VENDRAMIN
CALERGI (CASINO)
27
Campo S. Geremia
PALAZZO
LABIA
Terà
b
GRANDE
e
di
31
a
Spagna
Rio
f
Lista
M5
CA'
D'ORO
Pte d. Scalzi
CA'
PESARO
TRONCHETTO
P
T
p
S. GIACOMO
DALL'ORIO
S. LUCIA
CANALE D.
GIUDECCA
66
76
34
CANAL
S. CROCE
MESTRE
P
A.C.I.
S. POLO
a
24
P
Piazzale
Roma
Campo
S. Polo
Ruga
d. Orefici
k
Campo
S. Silvestro
I FRARI
Terà
U
Rio
Pensieri
SCUOLA GRANDE
DI S. ROCCO
Campo
dei Frari
Pal.
Bernardo
CANAL GRANDE
dei
S. Pantalon
E
T
H
B
Pal.
Campo
Manin
Campo
S. Margherita
Ca' Foscari
Pal.
Mocenigo
Pal.
Fortuny
SCALA DEL
BOVOLO
SCUOLA GRANDE
DEI CARMINI
CA'
REZZONICO
PAL. GRASSI
70
82
C. del
Traghetto
SANTO
STEFANO
LA FENICE
DORSODURO
64
55
Angelo
Raffaele
C. Lunga S. Barnaba
S. MARCO
C. Larga
22 Marzo
V
S. SEBASTIANO
3
P
79
GALLERIE D.
ACCADEMIA
CANAL
CA' DARIO
FUSINA
Canal Grande
S. Trovaso
g
COLL.
P. GUGGENHEIM
b
d
S. MARIA
DELLA SALUTE
Rio Terà
A. Foscarini
ZATTERE
CANALE
ZATTERE
DELLA
Fondamenta
S. Eufemia
d
DELLA
ISOLA
A
B
C
D

P GIULIANO
Canal Grande
E
I. DI S. MICHELE
Torcello, Burano, S. Erasmo, Murano, S. Francesco d. deserto
F
G
Italy
VENEZIA
S. POLO
Limite e Nome di Sestiere
Linee e fermate dei vaporetti
0   300 m
T
LAGUNA
GESUITI
Fondamenta Nuove
Calle del Fumo
78
75
28
Campiello Widman
18
SCUOLA GRANDE DI S. MARCO
S. ZANIPOLO
S. MARIA D. MIRACOLI
43
A
Fondaco d. Tedeschi
P.TE DI RIALTO
S. FRANCESCO DELLA VIGNA
85
39
Salizz. S. Lio
Campo S. Maria Formosa
10
46
Campo S. Lorenzo
61
POL.
MERCERIE
67
C. dei Fabbri
FOND. QUERINI STAMPALIA
SCUOLA DI S. GIORGIO DEGLI SCHIAVONI
CASTELLO
49
31
N
21
SAN MARCO
S. ZACCARIA
d
ARSENALE
Torri d. Arsenale
M
6
S. GIOV. IN BRAGORA
S
P.ZZA S. MARCO
Q
52
P.TE DEI SOSPIRI
t
b
58
MUSEO CORRER
PAL. DUCALE
Riva d. Schiavoni
MUSEO STORICO NAVALE
T
BIBLIOTECA MARCIANA
Bacino di S. Marco
Campo S. Biagio
V. Garibaldi
GRANDE
Dogana da Mar
CANALE
Riva dei Z. Martiri
S. GIORGIO MAGGIORE
SAN
MARCO
DI
GIUDECCA
ISOLA DI S. GIORGIO MAGGIORE
TEATRO VERDE
h
GIUDECCA
S. Pietro, S. Elena
Lido, S. Servolo, S. Lazzaro d. Armeni
E
S. Clemente
S. Maria della Grazia
F
G

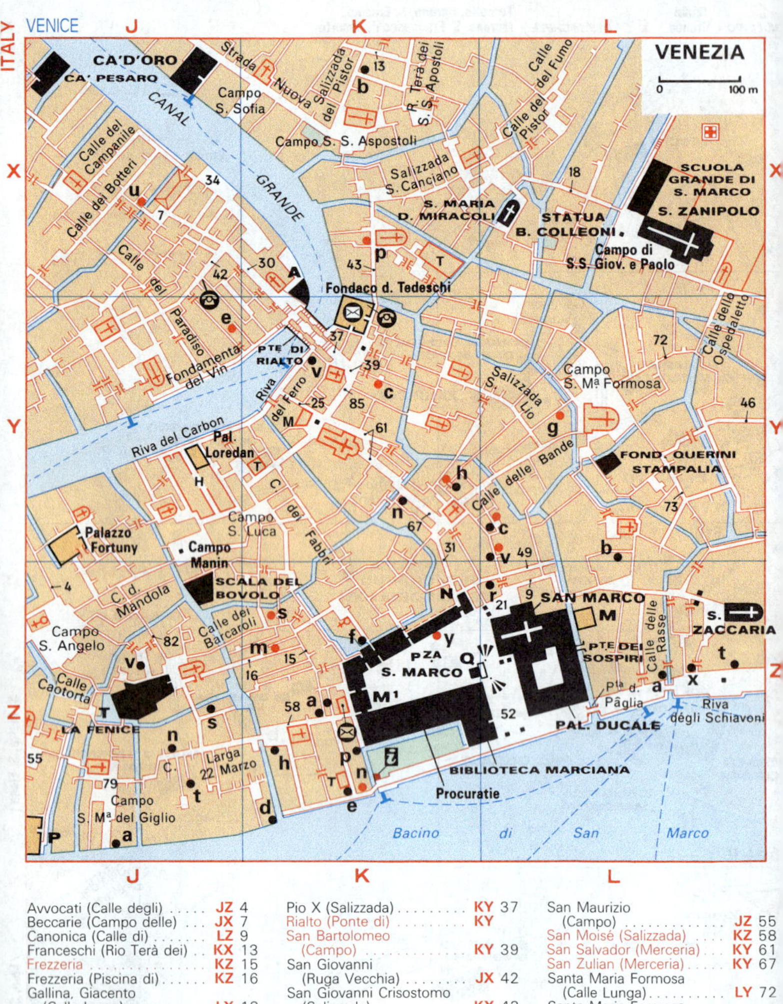

Gritti Palace, campo Santa Maria del Giglio 2467 ✉ 30124 ☎ 041 794611, *Fax 041 5200942,* ≤ Grand Canal, private pier, « Outdoor rest. summer service on the Grand Canal » – ‖, ☇ rm, ▤ TV ☎ ⅍ – ⚇ 100. AE ⑤ ⓪ Ε VISA JCB. ⋇   **JZ a**
Meals a la carte 140/215000 – ☕ 42000 – **87 rm** 705/1245000, 6 suites.

Bauer, campo San Moisè 1459 ✉ 30124 ☎ 041 5207022, *Fax 041 5207557,* « Summer rest. service on terrace with ≤ Grand Canal » – ‖, ☇ rm, ▤ TV ☎ – ⚇ 150. AE ⑤ ⓪ Ε VISA. ⋇ rest   **KZ h**
Meals a la carte 120/180000 – ☕ 35000 – **210 rm** 1000/1150000, 3 suites.

Londra Palace, riva degli Schiavoni 4171 ✉ 30122 ☎ 041 5200533, *Fax 041 5225032,* ≤ San Marco Canal, ⚘, private pier – ‖ ▤ TV ☎ ✆. AE ⑤ ⓪ Ε VISA JCB   **LZ t**
Meals *Do Leoni* Rest (Elegant rest., booking essential) a la carte 95/170000 – **53 rm** ☕ 750/850000.

Luna Hotel Baglioni, calle larga dell'Ascensione 1243 ⊠ 30124 ℘ 041 5289840, Fax 041 5287160 – |≉|, ≉ rm, ▤ TV ☎ – ♨ 150. AE ⑤ ① E VISA. ♨
KZ p
Meals 100/130000 and **Canova** Rest. (closed August and 1 to 15 January) a la carte 100/150000 – **111 rm** ⌣ 420/790000, 7 suites.

Europa e Regina, San Marco 2159 ⊠ 30124 ℘ 041 5200477, Fax 041 5231533, ≤ Grand Canal, private pier, « Outdoor rest. summer service on the Grand Canal » – |≉|, ≉ rm, ▤ TV ☎ – ♨ 120. AE ⑤ ① E VISA JCB. ♨ rest
KZ d
Meals **La Cusina** Rest. a la carte 90/120000 – ⌣ 65000 – **168 rm** 525/1050000, 13 suites.

Monaco e Grand Canal, calle Vallaresso 1325 ⊠ 30124 ℘ 041 5200211, Fax 041 5200501, ≤ Grand Canal and Santa Maria della Salute Church, « Outdoor rest. summer service on the Grand Canal » – |≉| ▤ TV ☎ ♿ – ♨ 40. AE ⑤ ① E VISA JCB. ♨
KZ e
Meals **Grand Canal** Rest. a la carte 115/165000 – **71 rm** ⌣ 490/850000, 2 suites.

Metropole, riva degli Schiavoni 4149 ⊠ 30122 ℘ 041 5205044, Fax 041 5223679, ≤ San Marco Canal, ♨, private pier, « Collection of period bric-a-brac » – |≉| ▤ TV ☎ – ♨ 100. AE ⑤ ① E VISA JCB
FV t
Meals **Buffet** Rest. 65/70000 – **73 rm** ⌣ 440/650000, 5 suites.

Sofitel M, Santa Croce 245, giardini Papadopoli ⊠ 30135 ℘ 041 710400, Fax 041 710394, private pier, « Service rest. in pleasant winter garden » – |≉|, ≉ rm, ▤ TV ☎ – ♨ 60. AE ⑤ ① E VISA. ♨
BT k
Meals a la carte 90/135000 – **92 rm** ⌣ 500/650000, 5 suites.

Starhotel Splendid-Suisse, San Marco-Mercerie 760 ⊠ 30124 ℘ 041 5200755, Fax 041 5286498 – |≉|, ≉ rm, ▤ TV ☎ – ♨ 50. AE ⑤ ① E VISA JCB. ♨ KY n
Meals (residents only) – **166 rm** ⌣ 580/760000.

Saturnia e International, calle larga 22 Marzo 2398 ⊠ 30124 ℘ 041 5208377, Fax 041 5207131, « 14C nobleman's town house » – |≉| ▤ TV ☎ – ♨ 60. AE ⑤ ① E VISA JCB
JZ n
Meals (see rest. **La Caravella** below) – **95 rm** ⌣ 420/660000.

Rialto, riva del Ferro 5149 ⊠ 30124 ℘ 041 5209166, Fax 041 5238958, ≤ Rialto bridge, ♨ – ▤ TV ☎. AE ⑤ ① E VISA JCB. ♨
KY v
Meals (closed Thursday and November-April) a la carte 55/90000 (12 %) – **79 rm** ⌣ 280/400000.

Gabrielli Sandwirth, riva degli Schiavoni 4110 ⊠ 30122 ℘ 041 5231580, Fax 041 5209455, ♨, private pier, « Small courtyard-garden and solarium terrace with ≤ San Marco Canal » – |≉| ▤ TV ☎. AE ⑤ ① E VISA JCB. ♨ rest
FV b
closed 28 November-31 December and January-5 February – Meals 50/75000 – **100 rm** ⌣ 370/620000.

Cavalletto without rest., calle del Cavalletto 1107 ⊠ 30124 ℘ 041 5200955, Fax 041 5238184, ≤ – |≉| ▤ TV ☎. AE ⑤ ① E VISA JCB
KZ f
95 rm ⌣ 430/550000.

Amadeus, Lista di Spagna 227 ⊠ 30121 ℘ 041 2206000 and rest. ℘ 041 715610, Fax 041 2206020, « Garden » – |≉| ▤ TV ☎ – ♨ 120. AE ⑤ ① E VISA JCB BT b
Meals **Il Papageno** Rest. (closed Wednesday except May-September) a la carte 60/85000 (12 %) – **63 rm** ⌣ 460/500000.

Bellini, Cannaregio 116-Lista di Spagna ⊠ 30121 ℘ 041 5242488, Fax 041 715193 – |≉| ▤ TV ☎. AE ⑤ ① E VISA JCB. ♨ rest
BT f
Meals 55/75000 – **64 rm** ⌣ 350/480000, 3 suites.

Concordia without rest., calle larga San Marco 367 ⊠ 30124 ℘ 041 5206866, Fax 041 5206775 – |≉| ▤ TV ☎. AE ⑤ ① E VISA. ♨
LZ r
57 rm ⌣ 400/600000.

Giorgione without rest., SS. Apostoli 4587 ⊠ 30131 ℘ 041 5225810, Fax 041 5239092, « Floral courtyard » – |≉| ▤ TV ☎. AE ⑤ ① E VISA. ♨ KX b
58 rm ⌣ 270/400000, 10 suites.

Montecarlo, calle dei Specchieri 463 ⊠ 30124 ℘ 041 5207144, Fax 041 5207789 – |≉| ▤ TV ☎. AE ⑤ ① E VISA JCB
LY c
Meals (see rest. **Antico Pignolo** below) – **48 rm** ⌣ 380/450000.

Flora ♨ without rest., calle larga 22 Marzo 2283/a ⊠ 30124 ℘ 041 5205844, Fax 041 5228217, « Small floral garden » – |≉| ▤ TV ☎. AE ⑤ ① E VISA JCB JZ t
44 rm ⌣ 260/340000.

La Fenice et des Artistes without rest., campiello de la Fenice 1936 ⊠ 30124 ℘ 041 5232333, Fax 041 5203721 – |≉| ▤ TV ☎. AE ⑤ ① E VISA. ♨
JZ v
70 rm ⌣ 200/360000, 3 suites.

Savoia e Jolanda, riva degli Schiavoni 4187 ⊠ 30122 ℘ 041 5206644, *Fax 041 5207494,* ≤ San Marco Canal, ☆ – ⧉ 🖭 ☎. AE S ① E VISA. ⊰ LZ x
Meals *(closed Tuesday)* 60000 (12 %) – **80 rm** ⊃ 240/350000.

Ai Due Fanali ⍋ without rest., Santa Croce 946 ⊠ 30135 ℘ 041 718490, *Fax 041 718344,* « Solarium terrace » – ⧉ 🖭 TV ☎. AE S ① E VISA. ⊰ BT p
closed January – **16 rm** ⊃ 250/330000.

Firenze without rest., San Marco 1490 ⊠ 30124 ℘ 041 5222858, *Fax 041 5202668*
– ⧉ 🖭 TV ☎. AE S E VISA JCB KZ a
25 rm ⊃ 260/560000.

Panada without rest., San Marco-calle dei Specchieri 646 ⊠ 30124 ℘ 041 5209088, *Fax 041 5209619* – ⧉ 🖭 TV ☎. AE S ① E VISA JCB LY v
48 rm ⊃ 350/450000.

Kette without rest., San Marco-piscina San Moisè 2053 ⊠ 30124 ℘ 041 5207766, *Fax 041 5228964* – ⧉ 🖭 TV ☎. AE S ① E VISA. ⊰ JZ s
70 rm ⊃ 260/360000.

Abbazia without rest., calle Priuli 68 ⊠ 30121 ℘ 041 717333, *Fax 041 717949,* « In an old monastery », ⛩ – 🖭 TV ☎. AE S ① E VISA. ⊰ BT a
39 rm ⊃ 290/330000.

Belle Arti without rest., Dorsoduro 912 ⊠ 30123 ℘ 041 5226230, *Fax 041 5280043,* ✗ – ⧉ 🖭 TV ☎ ⅃. S ① E VISA. ⊰ BV g
67 rm ⊃ 180/300000.

Bisanzio ⍋ without rest., calle della Pietà 3651 ⊠ 30122 ℘ 041 5203100, *Fax 041 5204114* – ⧉ 🖭 TV ☎ ✆. AE S ① VISA FV d
43 rm ⊃ 380/420000, 2 suites.

American without rest., San Vio 628 ⊠ 30123 ℘ 041 5204733, *Fax 041 5204048* –
🖭 TV ☎. AE S E VISA. ⊰ CV b
29 rm ⊃ 260/340000.

Castello without rest., Castello-calle Figher 4365 ⊠ 30122 ℘ 041 5230217, *Fax 041 5211023* – 🖭 TV ☎. AE S ① E VISA LY b
26 rm ⊃ 300/380000.

Calcina without rest., Dorsoduro 780 ⊠ 30123 ℘ 041 5206466, *Fax 041 5227045,* « Covered roof-terrace with view over the Giudecca canal » – 🖭 ☎. AE S ① E VISA JCB. ⊰ BV f
29 rm ⊃ 160/280000.

Caffè Quadri, piazza San Marco 120 ⊠ 30124 ℘ 041 5289299, *Fax 041 5208041* –
AE S ① E VISA JCB. ⊰ KZ y
closed Monday and Tuesday lunch – **Meals** (booking essential) 75/130000 (lunch) 130/190000 (dinner) and a la carte 100/170000.

Harry's Bar, calle Vallaresso 1323 ⊠ 30124 ℘ 041 5285777, *Fax 041 5208822,* American bar rest. – 🖭. AE S ① E VISA. ⊰ KZ n
Meals (booking essential) a la carte 145/200000 (10 %)
Spec. Tartare di tonno (spring-autumn). San Pietro ai capperi e pomodoro (spring-autumn). Pasticceria "della casa".

La Caravella - Hotel Saturnia e International, calle Larga 22 Marzo 2397 ⊠ 30124 ℘ 041 5208901, ⛩, Typical rest. – 🖭. AE S ① E VISA JCB. ⊰ JZ m
Meals (booking essential) a la carte 120/180000.

La Colomba, piscina di Frezzeria 1665 ⊠ 30124 ℘ 041 5221175, *Fax 041 5221468,* ⛩, « Collection of contemporary art » – 🖭 – ⛨ 60. AE S ① E VISA JCB. ⊰ KZ n
closed Wednesday except May-June and September-November – **Meals** 50/65000 (15 %) lunch and a la carte 100/180000 (15 %).

Do Forni, calle dei Specchieri 457/468 ⊠ 30124 ℘ 041 5237729, *Fax 041 5288132* – 🖭. AE S ① E VISA JCB LY c
Meals (booking essential) a la carte 80/115000 (12 %).

Osteria da Fiore, San Polo-calle del Scaleter 2202/A ⊠ 30125 ℘ 041 721308, *Fax 041 721343* – 🖭. AE S ① VISA CT a
closed Sunday, Monday, August and 24 December-12 January – **Meals** (booking essential) seafood a la carte 95/150000
Spec. Cappesante gratinate al timo. Ravioli di pesce. Filetto di branzino all'aceto balsamico.

Harry's Dolci, Giudecca 773 ⊠ 30133 ℘ 041 5224844, *Fax 041 5222322,* « Outdoor summer service on the Giudecca canal » – 🖭. AE S ① E VISA BV d
April-10 November, closed Tuesday – **Meals** 75/80000 (12 %) and a la carte 85/105000 (12 %).

Al Covo, campiello della Pescaria 3968 ⊠ 30122 ℘ 041 5223812 – ⊰ FV s
closed Wednesday, Thursday, 15 to 28 August and 15 December-15 January – **Meals** 50000 (lunch only) and a la carte 75/120000.

XX **Fiaschetteria Toscana,** San Giovanni Crisostomo 5719 ⊠ 30121 ℰ 041 5285281,
Fax 041 5285521, 🌿 – 🔲. AE ⑤ ⓪ E VISA   KX p
closed Tuesday and 6 July-2 August – **Meals** a la carte 60/95000.

XX **Ai Mercanti,** calle dei Fuseri-Corte Coppo 4346/A ⊠ 30124 ℰ 041 5238269,
Fax 041 5238269 – 🔲. AE ⑤ ⓪ E VISA. ✖   JX u
closed Sunday and Monday lunch – **Meals** a la carte 60/95000 (12 %).

XX **Antico Pignolo,** calle dei Specchieri 451 ⊠ 30124 ℰ 041 5228123, *Fax 041 5209007,*
🌿 – ✖ 🔲. AE ⑤ ⓪ E VISA JCB   LY v
closed Tuesday except May-June and September-October – **Meals** a la carte 75/120000
(12 %).

XX **Ai Gondolieri,** Dorsoduro-San Vio 366 ⊠ 30123 ℰ 041 5286396 – AE ⑤ ⓪
E VISA   DV d
closed Tuesday – **Meals** beef dishes only 90000 and a la carte 95/140000 (10 %).

XX **Da Ivo,** San Marco-calle dei Fuseri 1809 ⊠ 30124 ℰ 041 5285004, *Fax 041 5205889*
– 🔲. AE ⑤ ⓪ E VISA. ✖   KZ s
closed January and Sunday (except September-October) – **Meals** (booking essential) a la
carte 90/145000 (14 %).

XX **Da Mario-alla Fava,** San Bartolomeo-calle Stagneri 5242 e Galiazzo 5265 ⊠ 30124
ℰ 041 5285147 – AE ⑤ ⓪ E VISA   KY c
closed 7 to 20 January – **Meals** 30000 and a la carte 60/85000 (12 %).

XX **Vini da Gigio,** Cannaregio 3628/a-Fondamenta San Felice ⊠ 30131 ℰ 041 5285140,
Inn serving food – AE ⑤ ⓪ E VISA   DT e
closed Monday, 15 to 31 August and 15 to 31 January – **Meals** (booking essential) a la
carte 50/80000.

X **Trattoria alla Madonna,** calle della Madonna 594 ⊠ 30125 ℰ 041 5223824,
Fax 041 5210167, Venetian trattoria – AE ⑤ E VISA JCB. ✖   JY e
closed Wednesday, 4 to 17 August and 24 December-January – **Meals** a la carte 45/70000
(12 %).

X **Alle Testiere,** calle del Mondo Novo Castello 5801 ⊠ 30122 ℰ 041 5227220,
Fax 041 5227220, Inn serving food – 🔲. ⑤ E VISA   LY g
closed Sunday, August, Christmas and January – **Meals** (booking essential) a la carte
60/85000.

X **Al Conte Pescaor,** piscina San Zulian 544 ⊠ 30124 ℰ 041 5221483,
Fax 041 5221483, 🌿, Rustic rest. – 🔲. AE ⑤ ⓪ E VISA JCB. ✖   KY h
closed Sunday and 7 January-7 February – **Meals** a la carte 50/85000.

in Lido : *15 mn by boat from San Marco* KZ – ⊠ *30126 Venezia Lido.*
🛈 *Gran Viale S. M. Elisabetta 6* ℰ *041 5265721 :*

Excelsior, lungomare Marconi 41 ℰ 041 5260201, *Fax 041 5267276,* ≤, 🌿, ⤚, 🏖
🔞 – 🛗 🔲 TV ☎ 👤 🚗 🅿 – 🔺 600. AE ⑤ ⓪ E VISA JCB. ✖
15 March-15 November – **Meals** a la carte 160/230000 – **196 rm** ⊑ 800/850000.

Des Bains, lungomare Marconi 17 ℰ 041 5265921, *Fax 041 5260113,* ≤, 🌿, « Floral
park with heated 🏊 and ✖ », 🦶, ≘s, 🏖 – 🛗 🔲 TV ☎ 🅿 – 🔺 380. AE ⑤ ⓪ E
VISA JCB. ✖
15 March-15 November – **Meals** a la carte 130/170000 – **190 rm** ⊑ 700/870000,
suite.

Villa Mabapa, riviera San Nicolò 16 ℰ 041 5260590, *Fax 041 5269441,* « Summer
rest. service in garden » – 🛗 🔲 TV ☎ – 🔺 85. AE ⑤ ⓪ E VISA JCB.
✖ rest
Meals a la carte 60/90000 – **60 rm** ⊑ 270/420000.

Quattro Fontane ⚲, via 4 Fontane 16 ℰ 041 5260227, *Fax 041 5260726,*
« Summer rest. service in garden », ✖ – 🔲 TV ☎ 👤 – 🔺 40. AE ⑤ ⓪ E VISA.
✖ rest
April-14 November – **Meals** a la carte 110/165000 – **59 rm** ⊑ 500/520000.

Le Boulevard without rest., Gran Viale S. M. Elisabetta 41 ℰ 041 5261990,
Fax 041 5261917 – 🛗 🔲 TV ☎ 👤 🅿. AE ⑤ ⓪ E VISA JCB
50 rm ⊑ 290/390000.

Ca' del Borgo ⚲ without rest., piazza delle Erbe 8, località Malamocco Sud : 6 km
ℰ 041 770749, *Fax 041 770744,* ≤, « 16C mansion », � – 🔲 TV ☎ 👤. AE ⑤ ⓪ E
VISA
8 rm ⊑ 330/380000.

X **Trattoria Favorita,** via Francesco Duodo 33 ℰ 041 5261626, *Fax 041 5261626,*
« Outdoor summer service » – AE ⑤ ⓪ E VISA JCB
closed Monday and 15 January-1 March – **Meals** a la carte 60/85000.

in Murano *10 mn by boat from Fondamenta Nuove EFT and 1 h 10 mn by boat from Punta Sabbioni –* ✉ *30121 :*

⚑ **Ai Frati,** Fondamenta Venier 4 ☎ 041 736694, 🏮, « Outdoor terrace summer service on the canal »
closed Thursday and February – **Meals** seafood a la carte 45/75000 (12 %).

in Burano *50 mn by boat from Fondamenta Nuove EFT and 32 mn by boat from Punta Sabbioni –* ✉ *30012 :*

⚑ **Al Gatto Nero-da Ruggero,** ☎ 041 730120, Fax 041 735570, 🏮, Typical trattoria – ⁂ 𝕊 ⓞ Ⲉ *VISA*
closed Monday, 15 to 30 November and 15 to 31 January – **Meals** a la carte 50/85000.

in Torcello *45 mn by boat from Fondamenta Nuove EFT and 37 mn by boat from Punta Sabbioni –* ✉ *30012 Burano :*

⚑⚑ **Locanda Cipriani,** piazza Santa Fosca 29 ☎ 041 730150, Fax 041 735433, « Summer service in garden » – ▦. ⁂ 𝕊 ⓞ Ⲉ *VISA*
closed Tuesday and January-18 February – **Meals** 75000 and a la carte 95/135000.

Rubano *35030* **429** *F 17 – pop. 13 160 alt. 18.*
Roma 490 – Padova 8 – Venezia 49 – Verona 72 – Vicenza 27.

⚑⚑⚑ **Le Calandre,** strada statale 11, località Sarmeola ☎ 049 630303, Fax 049 633000 – ▦
❀❀ ℗. ⁂ 𝕊 ⓞ Ⲉ *VISA*. ⚒
closed 14-15 August, 1 to 11 January, Sunday dinner, Monday and Sunday lunch June-September – **Meals** (booking essential) a la carte 90/150000
Spec. Involtini di scampi fritti su salsa di lattuga. Baccalà mantecato con polenta bianca fritta e radicchio all'aceto balsamico (autumn-spring). "Trionfo" di desserts.

Verona *37100* ℙ **988** ④, **428**, **429** *F 14 G. Italy – pop. 254 748 alt. 59.*
🏌 *Parco della Musella (closed Monday and 20 December-2 January) Tenuta Mudella Cà dei Mori* ✉ *37036 San Martino Buon Albergo* ☎ *045 995144, Fax 045 994736, East : 7 km;*
🏌 *(closed Tuesday) at Sommacampagna* ✉ *37066* ☎ *045 510060, Fax 045 510242, West : 13 km.*
✈ *of Villafranca South-East : 14 km* ☎ *045 8095666, Fax 045 8619074 – Alitalia-Vacanze agency, corso Porta Nuova 7* ✉ *37122* ☎ *045 590977, Fax 045 8010491.*
🚗 ☎ *045 590688.*
🄱 *via Leoncino 61 (Barbieri Palace)* ✉ *37121* ☎ *045 592828, Fax 045 8003638 – piazza delle Erbe 42* ✉ *37121* ☎ *045 8000065 - Stazione Porta Nuova* ☎ *045 8000861.*
A.C.I. *via della Valverde 34* ✉ *37122* ☎ *045 595333.*
Roma 503 – Milano 157 – Venezia 114.

⚑⚑⚑ **Il Desco,** via Dietro San Sebastiano 7 ✉ 37121 ☎ 045 595358, Fax 045 590236 – ▦.
❀❀ ⁂ 𝕊 ⓞ Ⲉ *VISA*. ⚒
closed Sunday, Easter, 15 to 30 June, 25-26 December and 1 to 7 January – **Meals** (booking essential) a la carte 90/145000 (15 %)
Spec. Frutti di mare caldi con asparagi marinati. Risotto mantecato con tartufo bianco (autumn). Scampi e ostriche rosolati con fagiolini e rafano.

Norway

Norge

PRACTICAL INFORMATION

LOCAL CURRENCY

Norwegian Kroner: *100 NOK = 11,27 euros (€)*

TOURIST INFORMATION

The telephone number and address of the Tourist Information office is given in the text under ⚉.

National Holiday in Norway: *17 May.*

FOREIGN EXCHANGE

In the Oslo area banks are usually open between 8.15am and 3.30pm but in summertime, 15/5 - 31/8, they close at 3pm. Thursdays they are open till 5pm. Saturdays and Sundays closed.

Most large hotels, main airports and Tourist information office have exchange facilities. At Oslo Airport the bank is open from 6.30am to 8pm (weekdays), 6.30am to 6pm (Saturday), 7am to 8pm (Sunday), all year round.

MEALS

At lunchtime, follow the custom of the country and try the typical buffets of Scandinavian specialities.

At dinner, the a la carte and set menus will offer you more conventional cooking.

SHOPPING IN OSLO

Knitware and silverware

Your hotel porter should be able to help you with information.

CAR HIRE

The international car hire companies have branches in each major city. Your hotel porter should be able to give details and help you with your arrangements.

TIPPING IN NORWAY

A service charge is included in hotel and restaurant bills and it is up to the customer to give something in addition if he wants to.

The cloakroom is sometimes included in the bill, sometimes an extra charge is made. Taxi drivers and baggage porters don't expect to be tipped. It is up to you if you want to give a gratuity.

SPEED LIMITS

The maximum permitted speed within built-up areas is 50 km/h - 31mph. Outside these areas it is 80 km/h - 50mph. Where there are other speed limits (lower or higher) they are signposted.

SEAT BELTS

The wearing of seat belts in Norway is compulsory for drivers and all passengers.

OSLO

Norge 985 M 7 – *pop. 458 364.*

Hamburg 888 – København 583 – Stockholm 522.

❦ *Norwegian Information Centre Vestbaneplassen 1 ✆ 22 83 00 50, Fax 22 83 81 50 – KNA (Kongelig Norsk Automobilklub) Royal Norwegian Automobile Club, Drammensveien 20C ✆ 22 56 19 00 – NAF (Norges Automobil Forbund), Storg. 2 ✆ 22 34 14 00.*

☗ *Oslo Golfklubb ✆ 22 50 44 02.*

✈ *Oslo-Gardermden NE: 45 km ✆ 64 81 20 00 – SAS Head Office: Oslo City, Stenersg. 1 a ✆ 22 17 41 60 – Air Terminal: Galleri Oslo, Schweigaards gate 6.*

⛴ *Copenhagen, Frederikshavn, Kiel, Hirtshals : contact tourist information centre (see above).*

See: *Bygdøy* ABZ *Viking Ship Museum*★★★ *(Vikingskipshuset) ; Folk Museum*★★★ *(Norsk Folkemuseum) ; Fram Museum*★★ *(Frammuseet) ; Kon-Tiki Museum*★★ *(Kon-Tiki Museet) ; Maritime Museum*★★ *(Norsk Sjøfartsmuseum) – Munch Museum*★★ *(Munch-Museet)* DY *– National Gallery*★★ *(Nasjonalgalleriet)* CY **M¹** *– Vigelandsanlegget*★ *(Vigeland sculptures and museum)* AX *– Akershus Castle*★ *(Akershus Festning : Resistance Museum*★ *)* CZ **M²** *– Oslo Cathedral (Domkirke: views*★★ *from steeple)* CY.

Outskirts: *Holmenkollen*★ *(NW: 10 km): view from ski-jump tower and ski museum* BX *– Sonia Henie-Onstad Art Centre*★★ *(Sonia Henie-Onstad Kunstsenter) (W: 12 km)* AY.

NORWAY
OSLO
RING 3
A
Tryvannstårnet   Holmenkollen
B
VIGELANDS-PARKEN
Amaldus Nielsens plass
Bogstadveien
Sporveisgata
BISLE
161
Kirkeveien
Prof. Dahls gate
32
Bisle
Pilestredet
E 18
RING 2
Gyldenløves gate
Tidemands gate
51
57
Industigata
Holtegata
Uranienborg
v
b
Oscars gate
Parkveien
X
Arno Bergs plass
Frognerveien
Løvenskiolds gate
Briskebyveien
Camilla Colletts vei
32
t
Hegdehaugs veien
Wergelandsveien
66
60
veien
65
19
Gyldenløves gate
c
Juels gate
Oscars gate
52
Parkveien
SLOTTSPARKEN
Nordraaks plass
24
n
60
Colbjørnsens gate
Niels
Det Kongelige Slott
Kristi
Bygdøy
Frognerveien
Bygdøy allé
b
Juels gate
Gabels gate
NOBELINSTITUTTET
DRONNINGPARKEN
Drammensveien
Karl
National Theatret
Y
Strangs gate
x
Niels
Bygdøy allé
35
Cort
M
7 juni Plassen
42
Henie-Onstad Kunstsenter
Frederik
e
m
veien
Observatorie
U
k
f
39
gate
28
55
Olav Vs gate
KONSERTHUSET
Drammens
59
Parkveien
Adelers gate
42
42
DRAMMEN, BYGDØY
Frammesveien
42
36
Huitfeldts gate
55
Dokkveien
E 18
Oslo Tunnel
Aker Brygge
Filipstadveien
PIPERVIKA
KIEL
BYGDØY
OSLO
Museums
Strømsborgveien
STAVKIRKE
Dronninghavnveien
DRONNINGEN
0   200 m
Strømsborg
NORSK FOLKEMUSEUM
veien
aveny
Z
Strømsborgveien
7
Huk
Langviksbukta
FRAM MUSEET
BYGDØYNES
VIKINGSKIPSHUSET
Huk aveny
Langviks aveny
20
Bygdøynesveien
38
KON-TIKI MUSEET
NORSK SJØFARTSMUSEUM
A
B
NESODDEN

OSLO
NORWAY
C
D
X
Y
Z
ST. HANS HAUGEN
Sofies gate
Sofies plass
Sofies gate
Thranes gate
Ullevålsveien
Waldemar
Akersbakken
gate
Akersbakken
Akersbakken
Stensberggata
alsbergstien
Akersveien
Ullevålsveien
VÅR FRELSERS GRAVLUND
TEKNOLOGISK INSTITUTT
Maridalsveien
Helgesens gate
Thorvald Meyers gate
Toftes gate
Markveien
47
Nordre
Møllerveien
Akerselva
30
RIKSHOSPITALET
23
34
13
54
Fredensborgveien
Møllergata
67
Hausmanns gate
Christan Krohgs gate
17
68
h
St.
Olavs gate
gate
St. Olavs plass
M
41
Akersgata
Henrik Ibsens gate
Torggatta
33
RING 1
29
M¹
r
49
2
27
48
72
71
b
gate
Møllergata
RING 2
Munch-museet
POL
Johans
U
t gate
37
a
Grensen
Torggata
48
a
Storgata
Christian Krohgs gate
Grønland
IV's gate
Eidsvolls plass
53
T
21
62
k
c
Stortinget
Karl
73
Z
63
Johans
46
Jernbanetorget
b
Wessels plass
44
Domkirken
c
p
gate
5
45
Akersgata
S
73
Prinsens gate
Kirkegata
e
14
gate
31
Olsens gate
58
Rosenkrantz
Tollbugata
12
Rådhusgata
SKANSEN
9
44
e
Kongens gate
Tollbugata
f
Fred
S
64
BØRSEN
AKERSHUS FESTNING
M²
Myntgata
Rådhusgata
M
x
14
Akershusstranda
Oslo Tunnel
Skippergata
Kongens
M
BJØRVIKA
BISPEVIKA
OSLO
0   300 m
FREDRIKSHAVN, KIEL   C   KØBENHAVN
D   E 18 ASKIM   E 6
69
Møller-veien

STREET INDEX TO OSLO TOWN PLAN

Street	Grid	No.
Apotekergata	CY	2
Biskop Gunnerus' gate	DY	5
Bygdøy kappellvei	AZ	7
Christian Frederiks plass	DY	9
Christiania torv	CY	12
Damstredet	CDX	13
Dronningens gate	CYZ	14
Dronning Mauds gate	BY	16
Edvard Storm,s gate	CX	17
Elisenbergveien	AX	19
Fredriksborgveien	AZ	20
Fridtjof Nansens plass	CY	21
Frimanns gate	CX	23
Gimleveien	AX	24
Grensen	CY	
Grubbegata	CY	27
Haakon VII's gate	BY	28
Hammersborgtunnelen	CY	29
Holbergs gate	CX	30
Jernbanetorget	DY	31
Josefines gate	ABX	32
Karl Johans gate	BCDY	
Kristian Augusts gate	BCY	33
Langés gate	CX	34
Lapsetorvet	AY	35
Lassons gate	BY	36
Lille Grensen	CY	37
Løchenveien	ABZ	38
Løkkeveien	BY	39
Munchs gate	CXY	41
Munkedamsveien	ABY	42
Nedre Slottsgate	CYZ	44
Nedre Vollgate	CY	45
Nygata	DY	46
Olaf Ryes plass	DX	47
Pløens gate	DY	48
Professor Aschehougs pl.	CY	49
Professor Dahls gate	AX	51
Riddervolds gate	BX	52
Roald Amundsens gate	CY	53
Rosteds gate	DX	54
Ruseløkkveien	ABY	55
Rådhusplassen	BCY	56
Schives gate	AX	57
Schweigaards gate	DY	58
Skillebekk	AY	59
Skovveien	ABX	60
Stortingsgata	CY	62
Stortorvet	CY	63
Strandgata	DZ	64
Sven Bruns gate	BX	65
Thomas Heftyes gate	AX	66
Thor Olsens gate	CX	67
Torggata	CDY	
Tullins gate	CX	68
Uelands gate	DX	69
Vaterlandtunnelen	DY	71
Youngstorget	DY	72
Øvre Slottsgate	CY	73

Grand Hotel, Karl Johans Gate 31, ✉ 0101, ℘ 22 42 93 90, *Fax 22 42 12 25,* – rm, – 300. rest CY a
Julius Fritzner : **Meals** (dinner only) 495 and a la carte – ***Grand Café :*** **Meals** (buffet lunch) 170/500 and a la carte – **281 rm,** 1640/2840, 6 suites.

Continental, Stortingsgaten 24-26, ✉ 0161, ℘ 22 82 40 00, *Fax 22 42 96 89* – rm, – 200. CY n
closed 23 December-2 January – ***Annen Etage :*** **Meals** *(closed Sunday)* (dinner only) a la carte 480/645 – ***Lipp :*** **Meals** (dinner only) a la carte 345/445 (see also ***Theatercaféen*** below) – **151 rm,** 1660/2030, 8 suites.

Radisson SAS Plaza M, Sonja Henies Plass 3, ✉ 0134, ℘ 22 17 10 00, *Fax 22 17 73 00,* ← Oslo and Fjord, – rm, – 950. DY b
Abelone : **Meals** (dinner only) 195/425 and a la carte – **659 rm,** 1730/1930, 14 suites.

Clarion Royal Christiania M, Biskop Gunnerus' Gate 3, ✉ 0106, ℘ 23 10 80 00, *Fax 23 10 80 80,* – rm, – 400. DY p
closed Christmas and New Year – ***Lindgrens :*** **Meals** (dinner only and Sunday lunch)/dinner 325 and a la carte – ***Café Atrium :*** **Meals** *(closed 22 December-3 January)* (buffet lunch) 240 and a la carte 255/400 – **378 rm,** 1695/2195, 73 suites.

Radisson SAS Scandinavia M, Holbergsgate 30, ✉ 0166, ℘ 22 11 30 00, *Fax 22 11 30 17,* ← Oslo and Fjord, – rm, – 800. CX e
Meals *(closed Sunday dinner)* (buffet lunch) 255 and a la carte 270/655 – **479 rm,** 1790/1990, 9 suites.

Bristol, Kristian IV's Gate 7, ✉ 0164, ℘ 22 82 60 00, *Fax 22 82 60 01* – rm, – 100. CY b
Meals *(closed lunch Sunday and 26 December-1 January and 24-25 December)* a la carte 325/390 – **138 rm,** 1195/1795, 3 suites.

Rica Victoria M, Rosenkrantzgate 13, ✉ 0121, ℘ 22 42 99 40, *Fax 22 42 99 43* – rm, – 50. rest CY k
closed 23 to 26 December – **Meals** *(closed Sunday)* (buffet lunch) 115 and dinner a la carte 300/400 – **194 rm,** 1145/1360, 5 suites.

Rica Oslo, Karl Johans Gate 3, ✉ 0105, ℘ 23 10 42 00, *Fax 23 10 42 10,* – rm, – 60. DY c
Bjøvigen : **Meals** *(closed Sunday, Easter and Christmas)* (buffet lunch) 70 and a la carte 210/415 – **173 rm,** 1080/1350, 2 suites.

Noble House without rest., Kongens Gate 5, ✉ 0153, ℘ 23 10 72 00, *Fax 23 10 72 10,* – rm. CZ e
50 rm, 1350/1550, 19 suites.

Scandic H. K.N.A. M, Parkveien 68, ✉ 0202, ℘ 23 15 57 00, *Fax 23 15 50 01,* – rm, – 100. BY f
Meals a la carte 300/500 – **187 rm,** 995/1695, 2 suites.

Ambassadeur without rest., Camilla Colletts Vei 15, ✉ 0258, ℘ 22 44 18 35, *Fax 22 44 47 91,* – BX t
33 rm, 1130/1320, 8 suites.

Bøsparken without rest., Tollbugaten 4, ✉ 0152, ℘ 22 47 17 17, *Fax 22 47 17 18* – – 50. CDZ s
closed 22 December-3 January – **198 rm,** 930/1545.

Gabelshus ⟨S⟩, Gabelsgate 16, ✉ 0272, ✆ 22 55 22 60, Fax 22 44 27 30 – ⊠ ✉ TV ☎ P – ▲ 60. AE ① E VISA JCB. ✻
closed 26 March-6 April and 22 December-3 January – **Meals** *(closed Sunday lunch)* a la carte 300/375 – **43 rm**, ⊇ 1150/1350.
AY m

Ritz ⟨S⟩, Frederik Stangs Gate 3, ✉ 0272, ✆ 22 44 39 60, Fax 22 44 67 13 – ⊠, ✉ rm, TV ☎ P – ▲ 60. AE ① E VISA JCB. ✻ rest
closed 26 March-6 April and 22 December-3 January – **Meals** *(closed Sunday)* (lunch only) 175/400 – **48 rm**, ⊇ 910/1110.
AY e

Bastion without rest., Skippergaten 7, ✉ 0152, ✆ 22 47 77 00, Fax 22 33 11 80, ⒑ ⊜s – ⊠ ✉ ▤ TV ☎ P. AE ① E VISA
closed 23 December-4 January – **61 rm**, ⊇ 1195/1895.
CZ x

Europa M, St. Olavsgate 31, ✉ 0166, ✆ 22 20 99 90, Fax 22 11 27 27, ⟰ – ⊠, ✉ rm, TV ☎. AE ① E VISA JCB. ✻
Meals *(closed Sunday)* a la carte 110/185 – **162 rm**, ⊇ 875/975, 4 suites.
CX h

Spectrum M without rest., Brugate 7, ✉ 0186, ✆ 22 17 60 30, Fax 22 17 60 80 – ⊠ ✉ TV ☎ ♿. AE ① E VISA JCB. ✻
closed 23 December-3 January – **151 rm**, ⊇ 680/980.
DY a

Stefan M, Rosenkrantzgate 1, ✉ 0159, ✆ 22 42 92 50, Fax 22 33 70 22 – ⊠, ✉ rm, ▤ TV ☎ ♿ – ▲ 50. AE ① E VISA JCB. ✻
closed Easter and 22 December-4 January – **Meals** *(closed Sunday)* (buffet lunch) 185/325 and dinner a la carte – **138 rm**, ⊇ 885/1025.
CY r

Cecil M without rest., Stortingsgaten 8, ✉ 0161, *(entrance in Rosenkrantzgate)* ✆ 22 42 70 00, Fax 22 42 26 70 – ⊠ ✉ ▤ TV ☎ ✆ ♿. AE ① E VISA JCB. ✻
closed Easter, Christmas and New Year – **112 rm**, ⊇ 875/1050.
CY c

Gyldenløve M without rest., Bogstadveien 20, ✉ 0308, ✆ 22 60 10 90, Fax 22 60 33 90 – ⊠ ✉ TV ☎. AE ① E VISA JCB. ✻
closed Christmas – **168 rm**, ⊇ 670/870.
BX a

First H. Millennium, Tollbugaten 25, ✉ 0103, ✆ 23 00 30 00, Fax 23 00 30 30 – ⊠, ✉ rm, TV ☎ ♿. AE ① E VISA JCB. ✻
Meals *(closed Saturday lunch and Sunday)* (coffee shop) a la carte approx. 205/350 – **114 rm**, ⊇ 1295/1995.
CY s

Sjølyst without rest., Sjølyst plass 5, ✉ 0277, *West : 2 km by Drammens Veien* ✆ 23 15 51 00, Fax 23 15 51 01 – ⊠, ✉ rm, TV ☎ ✆ ♿ ⇌. AE ① E VISA. ✻
194 rm, ⊇ 1095/1295.

Norlandia Saga without rest., Eilert Sundtsgt. 39, ✉ 0259, ✆ 22 43 04 85, Fax 22 44 08 63 – ✉ TV ☎ – ▲ 25. AE ① E VISA
closed 20 December-3 January – **37 rm**, ⊇ 945/1095.
BX b

Vika Atrium M, Munkedamsveien 45, ✉ 0250, ✆ 22 83 33 00, Fax 22 83 09 57, ⒑ – ⊠, ✉ rm, ▤ TV ☎ – ▲ 240. AE ① E VISA JCB. ✻
Meals *(closed Friday dinner, Saturday and Sunday)* (buffet lunch) 140/300 and dinner a la carte – **91 rm**, ⊇ 830/1030.
BY d

Astoria M without rest., Dronningensgt. 21, ✉ 0102, ✆ 22 42 00 10, Fax 22 42 57 65 – ⊠ ✉ TV ☎ ♿. AE ① E VISA JCB. ✻
closed 23 December-3 January – **132 rm**, ⊇ 680/880.
CY e

Westside ⟨S⟩ without rest., Eilert Sundtsgt. 43, ✉ 0355, ✆ 22 56 87 70, Fax 22 56 63 20, ⊜s, ⟰ – ⊠, ✉ rm, ▤ rm, TV ☎ P. AE ① E VISA
31 rm, ⊇ 750/850.
BX v

XXX **Bagatelle** (Hellstrøm), Bygdøy Allé 3, ✉ 0257, ✆ 22 12 14 40, Fax 22 43 64 20 – AE ① E VISA JCB
❀❀
closed Sunday, 1 week Easter, 3 weeks July-August and 1 week Christmas – **Meals** (booking essential) (dinner only) 550/950 and a la carte 560/750
Spec. Noix de St. Jacques sautées, sauce gingembre. Chartreuse de homard et ris de veau à l'estragon. Perdrix de neige, sauce au foie gras.
AY x

XXX **Le Canard,** President Harbitz Gate 4, ✉ 0259, ✆ 22 54 34 00, Fax 22 54 34 10, ⟰,
❀ « Tastefully decorated 1900 villa » – AE ① E VISA JCB
closed Sunday, 29 March-6 April and 24 December-3 January – **Meals** (dinner only except May-September) 200/595 and a la carte 545/695
Spec. Fish and shellfish from the North Sea. Arctic char and lobster fricassee, mussel cream sauce. Veal tournedos and pigeon breast with pistachio cream and carrot confit.
AX c

XXX **Statholdergaarden** (Stiansen), Rådhusgate 11, *(entrance by Kirkegate)* 1st floor,
❀ ✉ 0151, ✆ 22 41 88 00, Fax 22 41 22 24 – ▤. AE ① E VISA
closed Sunday, 10 days Easter, 12 July-3 August and 10 days Christmas – **Meals** (booking essential) (dinner only) 570/630 and a la carte 450/560
Spec. Grilled Norway lobster with chilli and garlic, shellfish vinaigrette. Rack of lamb with fennel and squash timbale, wild mushrooms and sage sauce. Panna cotta with red berries.
CZ f

XXX **D'Artagnan,** Øvre Slottsgate 16 (1st floor), ⊠ 0157, ℘ 23 10 01 60, Fax 23 10 01 61 – 🖃. AE ⓞ E VISA JCB CY z
closed Sunday, Easter, 3 July-2 August and Christmas – **Meals** (dinner only) 495/625 and a la carte.

XX ❀ **Spisestedet Feinschmecker,** Balchensgate 5, ⊠ 0265, ℘ 22 44 17 77, Fax 22 56 11 39, « Tasteful decor » – 🖃. AE ⓞ E VISA AX n
closed Sunday, 1 week Easter, 3 weeks in summer and 1 week Christmas – **Meals** (booking essential) (dinner only) 395/450 and a la carte 460/570
Spec. Grilled scallops with Parmesan, celeriac and spinach coulis. Herb-crusted rack of lamb with mushrooms and creamed vegetables. Crème brûlée flavoured with basil.

XX **Det Blå Kjøkken,** Drammensveien 30, ⊠ 0202, ℘ 22 44 26 50, Fax 22 55 71 56 – 🖃. AE ⓞ E VISA BY k
closed Sunday, Easter, 5 to 26 July and Bank Holidays – **Meals** (dinner only) 455/595 and a la carte.

XX **Blom,** Paléet, Karl Johansgate 41b, ⊠ 0162, ℘ 23 13 95 00, Fax 23 13 95 01, « Collection of heraldic shields and paintings » – AE ⓞ E VISA CY t
closed Sunday and Bank Holidays – **Meals** (buffet lunch) 195/655 and a la carte.

XX **Babette's Gjestehus,** 1 Rådhuspassagen, Fridtjof Nansens Pl. 2, ⊠ 0160, ℘ 22 41 64 63, « Attractive decor » – 🖃. AE ⓞ E VISA BY f
closed Sunday and 24 to 27 December – **Meals** (booking essential) (dinner only) a la carte 405/490.

XX **Kastanjen,** Bygdøy Allé 18, ⊠ 0262, ℘ 22 43 44 67, Fax 22 55 48 72 – AE ⓞ E VISA JCB AY b
closed Sunday dinner, Easter, 1 and 17 May and 25 December – **Meals** (dinner only) 375 and a la carte.

XX **Theatercaféen** (at Continental H.), Stortingsgaten 24-26, ⊠ 0161, ℘ 22 82 40 50, Fax 22 41 20 94 – ⚒. AE ⓞ E VISA. ⚘ CY n
Meals (booking essential) a la carte 330/580.

at Fornebu Airport *Southwest : 8 km by E 18* AY *and Snarøyveien :*

▣ **Radisson SAS Park,** Fornebuparken, ⊠ 1324 *Lysaker,* ℘ 67 12 02 20, Fax 67 12 00 11, « Private beach and park », ₤₆, ≘s, ⚒ – ᕁ, ⚒ rm, 🖃 TV ☎ ✆ ₺ – ⚒ 150. AE ⓞ E VISA JCB. ⚘
Meals (buffet lunch) 185/325 and a la carte – **254 rm,** ⊑ 1440/1640.

at Sandvika *Southwest : 14 km by E 18* AY *exit E 68 :*

▣ **Oslofjord** Ⓜ, Sandviksveien 184, ⊠ 1300 *Sandvika,* ℘ 67 54 57 00, Fax 67 54 27 33, ₤₆, ≘s – ᕁ, ⚒ rm, 🖃 TV ☎ ₺ ⇔ 🅿 – ⚒ 350. AE ⓞ E VISA JCB. ⚘ rest
Fontaine : **Meals** (buffet lunch) 225/530 and a la carte – **Orchidee :** **Meals** (dinner only) 270/530 and a la carte – **227 rm,** ⊑ 980/1180, 15 suites.

at Holmenkollen *Northwest : 10 km by Bogstadveien* BX *Sørkedalsveien and Holmenkollveien :*

▣ **Holmenkollen Park** Ⓜ ⚘, Kongeveien 26, ⊠ 0390, ℘ 22 92 20 00, Fax 22 14 61 92, ← Oslo and Fjord, ≘s, ☒ – ᕁ, ⚒ rm, 🖃 TV ☎ ✆ ₺ ⇔ 🅿 – ⚒ 350. AE ⓞ E VISA JCB. ⚘ rest
closed 22 to 30 December and 1-2 January – **De Fem Stuer :** **Meals** (closed Sunday lunch) (buffet lunch) (dinner only in summer) 295/495 and dinner a la carte – **Galleriet :** **Meals** (buffet lunch) 245/450 and dinner a la carte – **210 rm,** ⊑ 1445/1945, 11 suites.

at Oslo Airport *Northeast : 45 km by E 6* DZ *at Gardermoen :*

▣ **Radisson SAS Airport,** ⊠ 2061, ℘ 63 93 30 00, Fax 63 93 30 30, ₤₆, ≘s – ᕁ, ⚒ rm, 🖃 TV ☎ ₺ 🅿 – ⚒ 120. AE ⓞ E VISA JCB. ⚘ rest
Meals (buffet lunch) 265/550 and a la carte – **350 rm,** ⊑ 1790/1990, 4 suites.

▣ **Clarion Oslo Airport,** West : 6 km, ⊠ 2060, ℘ 63 94 94 94, Fax 63 94 94 95, ₤₆, ≘s, ☒ – ᕁ, ⚒ rm, TV ☎ ₺ 🅿 – ⚒ 450. AE ⓞ E VISA. ⚘
Meals (buffet lunch) 250/495 and a la carte – **344 rm,** ⊑ 1450/1550, 2 suites.

Poland

Polska

Warsaw

PRACTICAL INFORMATION

LOCAL CURRENCY

Zloty : *100 PLN = 24,46 euros (€)*

National Holidays in Poland: *3 May and 11 November.*

PRICES

Prices may change if goods and service costs in Poland are revised and it is therefore always advisable to confirm rates with the hotelier when making a reservation.

FOREIGN EXCHANGE

It is strongly advised against changing money other than in banks, exchange offices or authorised offices such as large hotels and Kantor. Banks are usually open on weekdays from 8am to 6pm.

HOTEL RESERVATIONS

In case of difficulties in finding a room through our hotel selection, it is always possible to apply to the Tourist Office, ℰ 94 31, Fax (022) 27 11 23, open on weekdays from 8am to 7pm.

POSTAL SERVICES

Post offices are open from 8am to 8pm on weekdays.

The **General Post Office** *is open 7 days a week and 24 hours a day : Poczta Ctówna, Świetokrzyska 31/33.*

SHOPPING IN WARSAW

In the index of street names, those printed in red are where the principal shops are found. They are generally open from 10am to 7pm on weekdays and Saturday.

THEATRE BOOKING

Your hotel porter will be able to make your arrangements or direct you to a theatre booking office: Kasy Teatralne, Al Jerozolimskie 29 ℰ (022) 621 93 83, open from 11am to 2pm and 2.30pm to 6pm.

TIPPING

Hotel, restaurant and café bills often do not include service in the total charge. In these cases it is usual to leave the staff a gratuity which will vary depending upon the service given.

CAR HIRE

The international car hire companies have branches in Warsaw. Your hotel porter should be able to give details and help you with your arrangements.

BREAKDOWN SERVICE

A 24 hour breakdown service is operated calling ℰ 981.

SPEED LIMIT

On motorways, the maximum permitted speed is 110 km/h – 68 mph, 90 km/h – 56 mph on other roads and 60 km/h – 37 mph in built up areas.

SEAT BELTS

In Poland, the wearing of seat belts is compulsory for drivers and all passengers.

WARSAW

(Warsawa) *Polska* 970 *NO 4 – Pop. 1 700 000.*

Berlin 591 – Budapest 670 – Gdansk 345 – Kiev 795 – Moscow 1253 – Zagreb 993.

Warsaw Tourist Information Centre, Rynek Starego Miasta 28, ℘ 94-31, Pl. Powstańców Warszawy 2, ℘ 94-31, Al. Jerozolimskie 144, ℘ 94-31, Warsaw Airport (Arrivals Hall), ℘ 94-31.

First Warsaw Golf Club and Country Club, 05-110 Jabłonna ℘ (022) 782 45 55.
Okęcie (Warsaw Airport) SW 10 km, by Żwirki i Wigury ℘ 952 or 953.
Bus to airport: from major hotels in the town centre (ask the reception).
Polish Airlines (LOT) Al Jerozolmiskie 65/79, Warsaw ℘ 952 or 953.

SIGHTS

OLD TOWN★★★ (STARE MIASTO) BX

Castle Square★ (Plac Zamkowy) BX 33 – Royal Palace★★ (Zamek Królewski) BX – Beer Street (Ulica Piwna) BX – Ulica Świętojańska BX 57 – St John's Cathedral★ (Katedra Św. Jana) BX – Old Town Marketplace★★★ (Rynek Starego Miasta) BX 54 – Warsaw History Museum★ (Muzeum Historyczne Warsawy) BX M¹ – Barbakan BX A.

NEW TOWN★ (NOWE MIASTO) ABX

New Town Marketplace (Rynek Nowego Miasta) ABX 36 – Memorial to the Warsaw Uprising (Pomnik Powstania Warzszawskiego) AX D.

ROYAL WAY★ (TRAKT KRÓLEWSKI)

St Anne's Church (Kościół Św. Anny) BX – Krakow's District Street (Krakowskie Przedmieście) BXY – New World Street (Nowy Świat) BYZ – Holy Cross Church (Św. Krzyża) BY – National Museum★★ (Muzeum Narodowe) CZ.

LAZIENKI PARK★★★ (PARK ŁAZIENKOWSKI) FUV

Chopin Memorial (Pomnik Chopina) – Palace-on-the-Water★★ (Pałac na Wodzie) – Belvedere Palace (Belweder).

WILANÓW★★★ GV

ADDITIONAL SIGHTS

John Paul II Collection★★ (Muzeum Kolekcji im. Jana Pawła II) AY – Palace of Culture and Science (Pałac Kultury i Nauki): view★★ from panoramic gallery AZ.

POLAND
WARSAW
PŁOCK
OLSZTYN , GDAŃSK
OSTROŁĘKA
E 77
Modlińska
61
WÓLKA WĘGLOWA
MŁOCINY
PIEKIEŁKO
724
Arkuszowa
Wybrzeże
WAWRZYSZEW
Marymoncka
RADIOWO
BIELANY
PARK
Wólczyńska
LEŚNY
CHOMICZÓWKA
MARYMONT
BEMOWO
PIASKI
ŻOLIBORZ
Gdyńskie
Śląskich
CYTADELA
BOERNEROWO
NOWE MIASTO
POWĄZKI
ZOOL
BEMOWO
STARE MIAST
Okopowa
KOŁO
MURANÓW
Zamek Królew
MŁYNÓW
R
T
TRAKT
Warszawska
Górczewska
Solidarności
M
Towarowa
MIRÓW
Al.
JELONKI
Wolska
WOLA
ŚRÓDMIEŚCIE
f
Powstańców
46
34
U
c
2 E 30
66
a
Politechnika
Połczyńska
ODOLANY
POZNAŃ
Wawelska
Al.
ŁÓDŹ
b
OCHOTA
4
Pole Mokotowskie
S
STARE
Grójecka
Racławicka
Jerozolimskie
40
RAKÓW
WYGLĘDOW
Wierzbno
URSUS
Łopuszańska
Wigury
Al.
634
34
WŁOCHY
p
F.
Hynka
Wiland
719
Żwirki
30
OPACZ-KOLONIA
Krakowska
49
SŁUŻEWIEC
PRUSZKÓW
MICHELIN
Słuz
MICHAŁOWICE-OSIEDLE
7 E 77
WARSZAWA-OKĘCIE
RASZYN
Al.
WARSZAWA
0
2 km
8 E 67 WROCŁAW
KRAKÓW
Ur

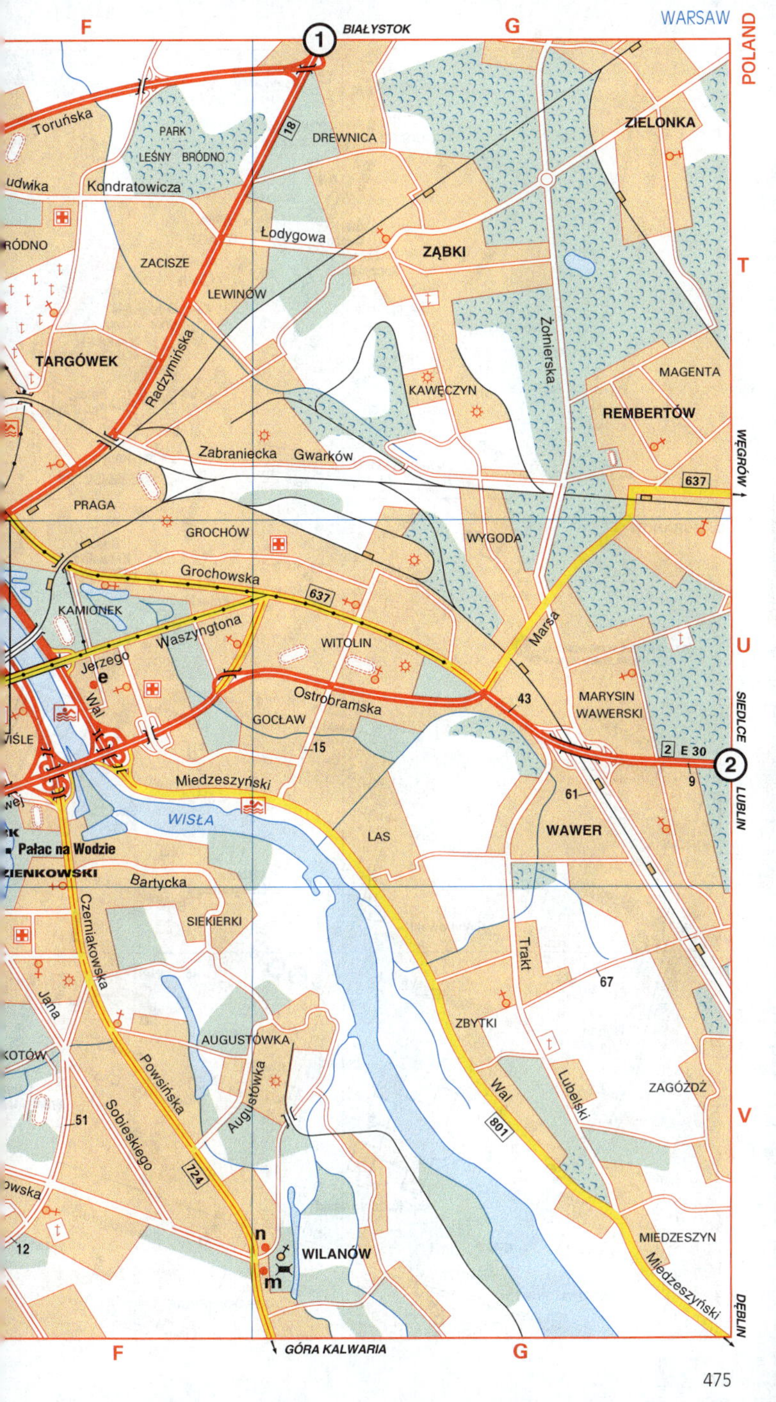

WARSAW
POLAND
BIAŁYSTOK
F
G
ZIELONKA
Toruńska
PARK
LEŚNY BRÓDNO
DREWNICA
udwika
Kondratowicza
RÓDNO
Łodygowa
ZACISZE
ZĄBKI
T
LEWINÓW
Żołnierska
MAGENTA
TARGÓWEK
Radzymińska
KAWĘCZYN
REMBERTÓW
WĘGRÓW
Zabraniecka
Gwarków
637
PRAGA
GROCHÓW
WYGODA
Grochowska
637
KAMIONEK
Marsa
Waszyngtona
WITOLIN
U
Jerzego
e
Wał
Ostrobramska
43
MARYSIN
WAWERSKI
SIEDLCE
GOCŁAW
15
2 E 30
2
Miedzeszyński
9
LUBLIN
61
WISŁA
WAWER
wej
Pałac na Wodzie
LAS
ZIENKOWSKI
Bartycka
Czerniakowska
SIEKIERKI
Trakt
67
Jana
ZBYTKI
Powsińska
AUGUSTÓWKA
Wał
Lubelski
ZAGÓŹDŹ
KOTÓW
Augustówka
V
51
Sobieskiego
801
724
12
MIEDZESZYN
n
Miedzeszyński
WILANÓW
m
DĘBLIN
F
GÓRA KALWARIA
G

A
B
X
Y
Z
Generala
Sapieżyńska
Franciszkańska
Ciasna
Władysława
Watowa
Bonifraterska
Świętojerska
NOWE
MIASTO
Nawiedzenia
Maryi Panny
M
Kościół
Sakramentek
36
52
6
724
Wybrzeże
Freta
M
Św. Jacka
33
Syrena
STARE
37
MIASTO
Św.
Ducha
Pałac
Raczyńskich
M
M
r
Gdańskie
PAŁAC
KRASIŃSKICH
24
D
Długa
Piwna
54
n
Kościół Jezuitów
ŚW. JANA
19
ZAMEK
KRÓLEWSKI
OGRÓD
KRASIŃSKICH
PAŁAC POD
CZTEREMA
WIATRAMI
Miodowa
Podwale
57
13
A
64
Pałac
Pod Blachą
Długa
Św. Anny
Dobra
MUZEUM
ARCHEOLOGICZNE
M
Al.
Solidarności
PAŁAC
PRYMASOWSKI
Krakowskie
MARIENSZTAT
Bednarska
t
Fumn
MURANÓW
Bielańska
Św. Anny
T
Kościół
Karmelitów
18
Al.
Solidarności
Senatorska
58
TEATR
WIELKI
Moliera
M
Pałac
Potockich
Pałac
Radziwiłłów
R
Pl.
Bankowy
Wierzbowa
M
HOTEL
BRISTOL
Kościół
Wizytek
MUZEUM KOLEKCJI
IM. JANA PAWŁA II
Przechodnia
HOTEL
EUROPEJSKI
TRAKT
Elektoralna
Ptasia
Ogród Saski
42
Królewska
U
Przedmieście
Pl. Mirowski
d
R. Traugutta
MIRÓW
M
Św.
Krzyża
22
Grzybowska
Królewska
25
31
T
Al. Jana Pawła II
Muzeum
Etnograficzne
10
Świętokrzyska
Z
Pl.
Grzybowski
Marszałkowska
Jasna
Nowy
f
45
Warecka
Świat
KRÓLEWSK
Twarda
T
Świętokrzyska
a
Górskiego
Chmielna
Rondo
Onz
FILHARMONIA
Pl.
Defilad
T
JUNIOR
Ordyn
Prosta
Złota
Zgoda
Pałac
Branickich
Emilii Plater
SAWA
n
Twarda
e
WARS
Sienna
Al. Jana Pawła II
P
Nowogrodzka
Żurawia
Złota
Pałac Kultury i Nauki
h
Chmielna
WARSZAWA CENTRALNA
Al.
Jerozolimskie
Nowogrodzka
b
ŚRÓDMIEŚCIE

STREET INDEX TO WARSZAWA TOWN PLANS

Bristol, Krakowskie Przedmieście 42-44, ⊠ 00 325, ℘ (022) 625 25 25, *Fax (022) 625 25 77*, « Late 19C facade, partly decorated in Art Nouveau style », ↦, ⇌, ⬛ – ⧉, ⇥ rm, ▤ ⦿ ☎ ⅋ – ⚲ 110. AE ⓞ E VISA JCB. ⅋
BY
Marconi : Meals - Mediterranean - a la carte 110/175 (see also **Malinowa** below
190 rm, ⌛ 1070/1330, 15 suites.

Sheraton Ⓜ, Ul. B. Prusa 2, ⊠ 00 493, ℘ (022) 657 61 00, *Fax (022) 657 62 00*,
⇌ – ⧉, ⇥ rm, ▤ ⦿ ☎ ⅋ ⅍ ⟷ – ⚲ 700. AE ⓞ E VISA. ⅋
CZ
The Oriental : Meals - Oriental - a la carte 90/150 – **Lalka** : Meals (buffet only) 8(
⌛ 40 – **336 rm**, 1085/1750, 14 suites.

Marriott Ⓜ, Al. Jerozolimskie 65-79, ⊠ 00 697, ℘ (022) 630 63 06, *Fax (022) 630*
39, ⩽ Warsaw, ↦, ⇌, ⬛ – ⧉ ⇥ ▤ ⦿ ☎ ⅋ ⅍ ⟷ – ⚲ 700. AE ⓞ E VISA J(
⅋ rest
AZ
closed Easter and Christmas – **Chicago Grill** : Meals 150/250 and dinner a la carte
Parmizzano's : Meals - Italian - (dinner only Saturday and Sunday June-August) 150/2
and a la carte – **Lila Weneda** : Meals (buffet lunch) 70/100 and a la carte – ⌛ 40 – **489 r**
950/1380, 34 suites.

Victoria Ⓜ, Ul. Królewska 11, ⊠ 00 065, ℘ (022) 657 80 11, *Fax (022) 657 80 57*,
⇌, ⬛ – ⧉, ⇥ rm, ▤ ⦿ ☎ ⅋ ⅍ ⟷ – ⚲ 300. AE ⓞ E VISA J(
⅋ rest
BY
Canaletto : Meals 120/305 and a la carte – **Opera** : Meals *(closed Sunday)* (dinner on
160/245 and a la carte – **Hetmańska** : Meals 100/205 and a la carte – **329 r**
⌛ 830/1200, 11 suites.

Jan III Sobieski Ⓜ, Plac Artura Zawiszy 1, ⊠ 02 025, ℘ (022) 658 44
Fax (022) 659 88 28, ↦, ⇶ – ⧉, ⇥ rm, ▤ ⦿ ☎ ⅍ ⟷ – ⚲ 180. AE ⓞ E VISA J(
⅋ rest
EU
Meals 100/150 and a la carte – **381 rm**, ⌛ 550/1035, 32 suites.

Holiday Inn Ⓜ, Ul. Złota 48-54, ⊠ 00 120, ℘ (022) 697 39 99, *Fax (022) 697 38 99*,
⇌ – ⧉, ⇥ rm, ▤ ⦿ ☎ ⅍ ⟷ Ⓟ – ⚲ 200. AE ⓞ E VISA JCB. ⅋ rest
AZ
Symfonia : Meals a la carte 110/140 – **Brasserie** : Meals (buffet only) 70 – ⌛ 4!
326 rm, 725/930, 10 suites.

Mercure Fryderyk Chopin Ⓜ, Al. Jana Pawła II 22, ⊠ 00 133, ℘ (022) 620 02
Fax (022) 620 87 79, ↦, ⇌ – ⧉, ⇥ rm, ▤ ⦿ ☎ ⅍ ⟷ Ⓟ – ⚲ 250. AE ⓞ E
JCB. ⅋ rest
AY
Balzac : Meals - French - *(closed lunch Saturday and Sunday)* 100/160 and a la cart
Stanislas : Meals (buffet lunch) 70/130 and a la carte – **242 rm**, ⌛ 640/705, 9 sui

Forum, Ul. Nowogrodzka 24-26, ⊠ 00 511, ℘ (022) 621 02 71, *Fax (022) 625 04*
– ⧉, ⇥ rm, ▤ ⦿ ☎ ⅍ – ⚲ 450. AE ⓞ E VISA JCB
BZ
Soplica : Meals a la carte 70/120 – **Maryla** : Meals (buffet only) 50 – **723 rm**, ⌛ 560/7
10 suites.

Europejski, Ul. Krakowskie Przedmieście 13, ⊠ 00 071, ℘ (022) 826 50 !
Fax (022) 826 11 11, ♨ – ⧉, ⇥ rm, ⦿ ☎ – ⚲ 180. AE ⓞ E VISA J(
⅋ rest
BY
Meals 70/80 and a la carte – **224 rm**, ⌛ 415/545, 13 suites.

Dom Chłopa, Pl. Powstancow Warszawy 2, ⊠ 00 030, ℘ (022) 625 15
Fax (022) 625 21 40 – ⧉, ▤ rest, ⦿ ☎ Ⓟ – ⚲ 400. AE ⓞ E VISA J(
⅋ rest
BZ
Polska Karczma : Meals a la carte approx. 50 – **212 rm**, ⌛ 320/360.

Vera, Ul. Bitwy Warszawskiej 1920 roku 16, ⊠ 02 366, ℘ (022) 822 74
Fax (022) 823 62 56, ↦ – ⧉, ⇥ rm, ▤ rest, ⦿ ☎ ⅍ Ⓟ – ⚲ 150. AE ⓞ E VISA J
Meals a la carte 50/100 – **154 rm**, ⌛ 430/510, 7 suites.
DU

MDM without rest., Pl. Konstytucji 1, ⊠ 00 647, ℘ (022) 621 62 11, *Fax (022) 621*
73 – ⧉ ⇥ ⦿ ☎ ⅍ – ⚲ 65. AE ⓞ E VISA JCB
EU
115 rm, ⌛ 340/450, 4 suites.

Belwederski, Ul. Sulkiewicza 11, ⊠ 00 758, ℘ (022) 840 40 11, *Fax (022) 840 08*
– ⧉ ▤ ⦿ ☎ ⅋ – ⚲ 100. AE E VISA. ⅋
FU
Meals 20/35 and a la carte – **42 rm**, ⌛ 300/350, 10 suites.

Reytan, Ul. Rejtana 6, ⊠ 02 516, ℘ (022) 646 31 66, *Fax (022) 646 29 89* – ⧉ ⦿
⅍ Ⓟ. AE E VISA. ⅋ rest
EU
Meals a la carte 40/70 – **84 rm**, ⌛ 250/300, 2 suites.

Karat, Ul. Sloneczna 37, ⊠ 00 789, ℘ (022) 601 44 11, *Fax (022) 49 52 94* – ⧉ ⦿
Ⓟ – ⚲ 25. AE E VISA
EU
Meals a la carte 45/80 – **40 rm**, ⌛ 250/330.

Malinowa (at Bristol H.), Krakowskie Przedmieście 42-44, ⊠ 00 325, ℘ (022) 625 25
Fax (022) 625 25 77 – ⇥ ▤. AE ⓞ E VISA JCB
BY
Meals - French - (dinner only) a la carte 155/280.

XXX **Dom Polski,** Ul. Francuska 11, ✉ 03 906, ✆ (022) 616 24 88, *Fax (022) 616 24 88* – ⤢ 🖩. AE ⓪ E *VISA* JCB
FU e
Meals a la carte 50/150.

XX **Belvedere,** Ul. Agrykoli 1A, ✉ 00 460, ✆ (022) 41 48 06, *Fax (022) 41 71 35*, ≤, ☂,
« Late 19C orangery in Łazienkowski park » – Ⓟ. AE ⓪ E *VISA*
FU d
closed 25 December-3 January – **Meals** 60 (lunch) and a la carte 110/230.

XX **Casa Valdemar,** Ul. Piękna 7-9, ✉ 00 539, ✆ (022) 628 81 40, *Fax (022) 622 88 96*,
☂, « Elegant Spanish style installation » – 🖩. AE ⓪ E *VISA* JCB
EU e
Meals - Spanish - a la carte 85/260.

XX **Restauracja Polska,** Ul. Nowy Świat 21 (in the basement of the Polish Sculptors Union's Gallery), ✉ 00 029, ✆ (022) 826 38 77, *Fax (022) 828 31 32*, ☂ – 🖩 Ⓟ. AE ⓪ E *VISA* JCB
BZ n
closed 25 December – **Meals** a la carte 50/140.

XX **Fukier,** Rynek Starego Miasta 27, ✉ 00 272, ✆ (022) 831 10 13, *Fax (022) 831 10 13*, ☂, « Traditional Polish decor » – ⤢. AE ⓪ E *VISA* JCB
BX n
closed 25 December – **Meals** a la carte 50/150.

XX **Kahlenberg,** Ul. Koszykowa 54, ✉ 00 675, ✆ (022) 630 88 50, *Fax (022) 630 88 50* – 🖩. AE ⓪ E *VISA* JCB
EU f
Meals a la carte 60/100.

XX **Montmartre,** Nowy Swiat 7, ✉ 00 496, ✆ (022) 628 63 15 – AE
BZ x
closed 15 to 31 August – **Meals** - French - a la carte 60/200.

XX **Świętoszek,** Ul. Jezuicka 6-8, ✉ 00 281, ✆ (022) 831 56 34, *Fax (022) 635 59 47*, « Vaulted cellar » – ⤢. AE ⓪ E *VISA* JCB
BX r
closed Easter Sunday, Christmas and New Year – **Meals** 45 (lunch) and a la carte 50/90.

XX **Flik,** Ul. Puławska 43, ✉ 02 508, ✆ (022) 49 44 34, *Fax (022) 49 44 34*, ☂ – ⤢ 🖩. AE ⓪ E *VISA* JCB
EV h
closed 25 December – Meals (buffet lunch) 45 and a la carte 35/85 – **Petit Flik** : Meals a la carte 25/55.

XX **Tsubame,** Ul. Foksal 16, ✉ 00 372, ✆ (022) 826 51 27, *Fax (022) 826 48 51*, Japanese decor – 🖩. AE E *VISA* JCB
BZ s
closed 24-25 December and 1 January – **Meals** - Japanese - 25/65 and a la carte.

XX **Pod Retmanem,** Ul. Bednarska 9, ✉ 00 310, ✆ (022) 826 87 58, *Fax (022) 826 87 58*, « Fresco depicting the old port of Gdansk » – AE ⓪ E *VISA* JCB
BY t
Meals (music Thursday to Saturday evening) a la carte 50/200.

X **Kuchcik,** Ul. Nowy Swiat 64, ✉ 00 357, ✆ (022) 826 93 53, *Fax (022) 827 39 00* – ⤢ 🖩. AE ⓪ E *VISA* JCB
BY z
Meals a la carte 40/75 – **Pod Kuchcikiem** (wine bar in cellar) : Meals (dinner only) a la carte 25/45.

to the South :

Wilanów *South : 9 km at PaŁac Wilanowski entrance :*

XX **Wilanów,** Ul. Stanislawa Kostki Potockiego 27, ✉ 02 952, ✆ (022) 42 13 63, *Fax (022) 42 18 52*, « Hunting atmosphere » – AE ⓪ E *VISA* JCB
GV m
Meals a la carte 60/90.

X **Kuźnia Królewska,** Ul. Stanislawa Kostki Potockiego 24, ✉ 02 958, ✆ (022) 42 31 71, ☂ – AE ⓪ E *VISA* JCB
GV n
Meals a la carte 35/105.

to the Southwest :

🏨 **Novotel,** Ul. Sierpnia 1, ✉ 02 134, *6 km on airport rd* ✆ (022) 846 40 51, *Fax (022) 846 36 86*, ☂, ☀ – |≣|, ⤢ rm, 🖩 rest, TV ☎ & Ⓟ – 🔺 200. AE ⓪ E *VISA* JCB. ⌘ rest
EV p
Meals a la carte 40/80 – **146 rm,** ⌑ 385/425.

Portugal

PRACTICAL INFORMATION

LOCAL CURRENCY

Escudo: *100 PTE = 0,50 euro (€)*
National Holiday in Portugal: *10 June.*

FOREIGN EXCHANGE

Hotels, restaurants and shops do not always accept foreign currencies and the tourist is therefore advised to change cheques and currency at banks, saving banks and exchange offices. The general opening times are as follows: banks 8.30am to 3pm (closed on Saturdays, Sundays, and Bank Holidays), money changers 9.30am to 6pm (usually closed on Sundays and Bank Holidays).

TRANSPORT

Taxis may be hailed when showing the green light or "Livre" sign on the windscreen. Metro (subway) network. In each station complete information and plans will be found.

SHOPPING IN LISBON

Shops and boutiques are generally open from 9am to 2.30pm and 3 to 7pm. In Lisbon, the main shopping streets are: Rua Augusta, Rua do Carmo, Rua Garrett (Chiado), Rua do Ouro, Rua da Prata, Av. de Roma, Av. da Liberdade, Shopping Center Amoreiras, Shopping Center Colombo.

TIPPING

Hotels, restaurants and cafés bills include service in the total charge. It is usual, however, to give an additional tip for personal service; 10 % of the fare or ticket price is also the usual amount given to taxi drivers and cinema and theatre usherettes.

SPEED LIMITS

The speed limit on motorways is 120 km/h - 74 mph, on other roads 90 km/h - 56 mph and in built up areas 50 km/h - 37 mph.

SEAT BELTS

The wearing of seat belts is compulsory for drivers and all passengers.

THE FADO

The Lisbon Fado (songs) can be heard in restaurants in old parts of the town such as the Alfama, the Bairro Alto and the Mouraria. A selection of fado cabarets will be found at the end of the Lisbon restaurant list.

LISBON

(LISBOA) *1100* P 940 P 2 – *Pop. 662 782 – alt. 111.*

Paris 1820 – Madrid 658 – Bilbao/Bilbo 907 – Porto 314 – Sevilla 417.

Palácio Foz, Praça dos Restaudores ⊠ *1200* ☎ *(01) 346 63 07, Fax (01) 346 87 72 –
Rua Jardim do Regedor 50* ⊠ *1200,* ☎ *(01) 343 36 72, Fax (01) 343 36 73, and airport*
☎ *(01) 849 43 23, Fax (01) 848 59 74 – A.C.P. Rua Rosa Araújo 24,* ⊠ *1200,*
☎ *(01) 356 39 31, Fax (01) 357 47 32.*

9 , 18 Estoril Golf Club W : 25 km ☎ *(01) 468 01 76 – 18 Lisbon Sports Club NW : 20 km*
☎ *(01) 431 00 77 – 18 Club de Campo da Aroeira S : 15 km* ☎ *(01) 297 13 14 Aroeira,
Monte da Caparica*

Lisbon Airport N : 8 km from city centre ☎ *(01) 841 35 00 – T.A.P., Praça Marquês
de Pombal 3,* ⊠ *1200,* ☎ *(01) 317 91 00 and airport* ☎ *(01) 841 50 00.*
Santa Apolónia ☎ *(01) 888 40 25* MX.
to Madeira : E.N.M., Rua de São Julião 5-1°, ⊠ *1100,* ☎ *(01) 887 01 21.*

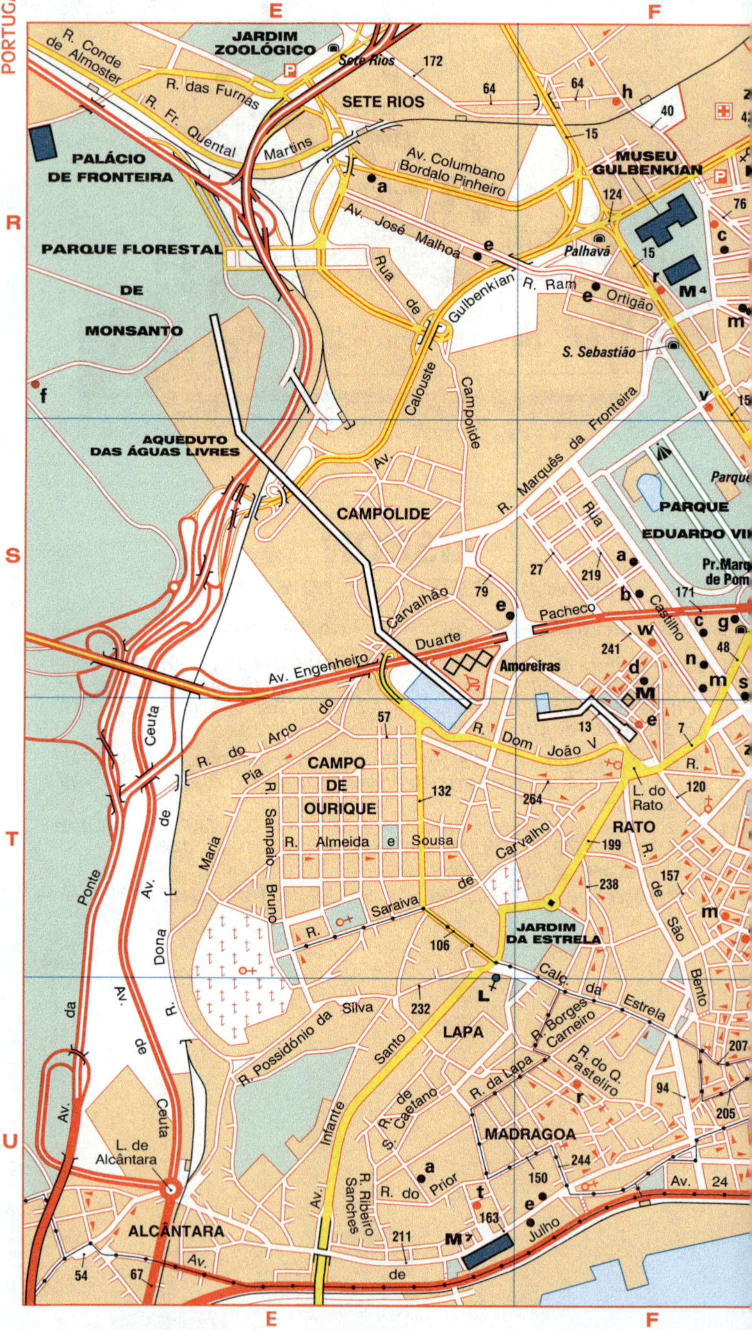

PORTUGAL

JARDIM ZOOLÓGICO
Sete Rios
172
64
64
h
40
SETE RIOS
15
R. Conde de Almoster
R. das Furnas
R. Fr. Quental
Martins
Av. Columbano Bordalo Pinheiro
a
MUSEU GULBENKIAN
124
PALÁCIO DE FRONTEIRA
Av. José Malhoa
e
Palhavã
15
76
c
PARQUE FLORESTAL DE MONSANTO
Rua de Gulbenkian
R. Ram
e
Ortigão
M 4
m
S. Sebastião
f
v
15
AQUEDUTO DAS ÁGUAS LIVRES
Calouste
Campolide
R. Marquês da Fronteira
Parque
PARQUE EDUARDO VII
Pr. Marq de Pom
Av
CAMPOLIDE
R. Marquês da Fronteira
Rua
a
27
219
171
Carvalhão
79
b
Castilho
c
g
48
e
Pacheco
w
n
m
s
Duarte
Amoreiras
241
d
M
e
Av. Engenheiro
R. Dom João V
13
7
57
R. do Arco do
Pia
CAMPO DE OURIQUE
Maria
Sampaio
Bruno
132
R. Almeida e Sousa
264
L. do Rato
120
RATO
de
Carvalho
199
R. de
157
Saraiva
238
m
106
JARDIM DA ESTRELA
232
L
Calç. da Estrela
São
Bento
Ponte
Av.
Dona
R. de Caetano
LAPA
R. Borges Carneiro
R. da Lapa
R. do Q. Pasteliro
207
94
r
205
Av. da
Ceuta
Av. de
Ceuta
Infante Santo
R. Possidônio da Silva
R. Ribeiro Sanches
MADRAGOA
150
244
L. de Alcântara
a
Prior
t
Av. 24
e
Julho
163
ALCÂNTARA
211
M
Av.
54
67
de

LISBON

PORTUGAL

LISBOA

0   500 m

Praça de Touros
Areeiro
Pr. Sá Carneiro
W
de
João   XXI
Av.
Afonso
Costa
114
C. Pequeno
Av.
Pr. de Londres
Reis
z
Olaias
da
25
CAIXA GERAL DE DEPÓSITOS
t
c
18
178
e
93
R.
Barão
Rotunda das Olaias
República
109
Alameda
de
ALTO DO PINA
186
Duque   de   Ávila
r
22
Almirante
Sabrosa
112   Saldanha
222
Arroios
R. de Dona
66
Rua
Morais
R.   Pascoal de Melo
204
Soares
Picoas
Pr. J. Fontana
198
Estefânia
Av.
Afonso
T
e
R. da Penha de França
Roçadas
Mouzinho
111   z
Gomes   Freire
Avenida
Anjos
General
B. LOPES
S
78
k   162
129
147
de
SAPADORES
117
180
R. A. Vidal
7
195
Intendente
R. dos Sapodores
Albuquerque
DA
R. da Palma
R. da Graça
Calç. dos Barbadinhos
litre
LIBERDADE
GRAÇA
M 8
DIM ÂNICO
R. D. Pedro V
Pr. dos Restauradores
Henrique
SÃO ROQUE
ROSSIO
CASTELO DE SÃO JORGE
CAMPO DE STA CLARA
BAIRRO ALTO
R. do Ouro
D.
CHIADO
R. GARRETT
BAIXA
R. da Prata
ALFAMA
M 10
lç. do mbro
H
SÉ
R. de S. Paulo
Infante
Av. da Ribeira das Naus
PR. DO COMÉRCIO
Estação do Sul e Sueste
TEJO
CACILHAS
BARREIRO , MONTIJO , SEIXAL

G   H
R
S
T
U

485

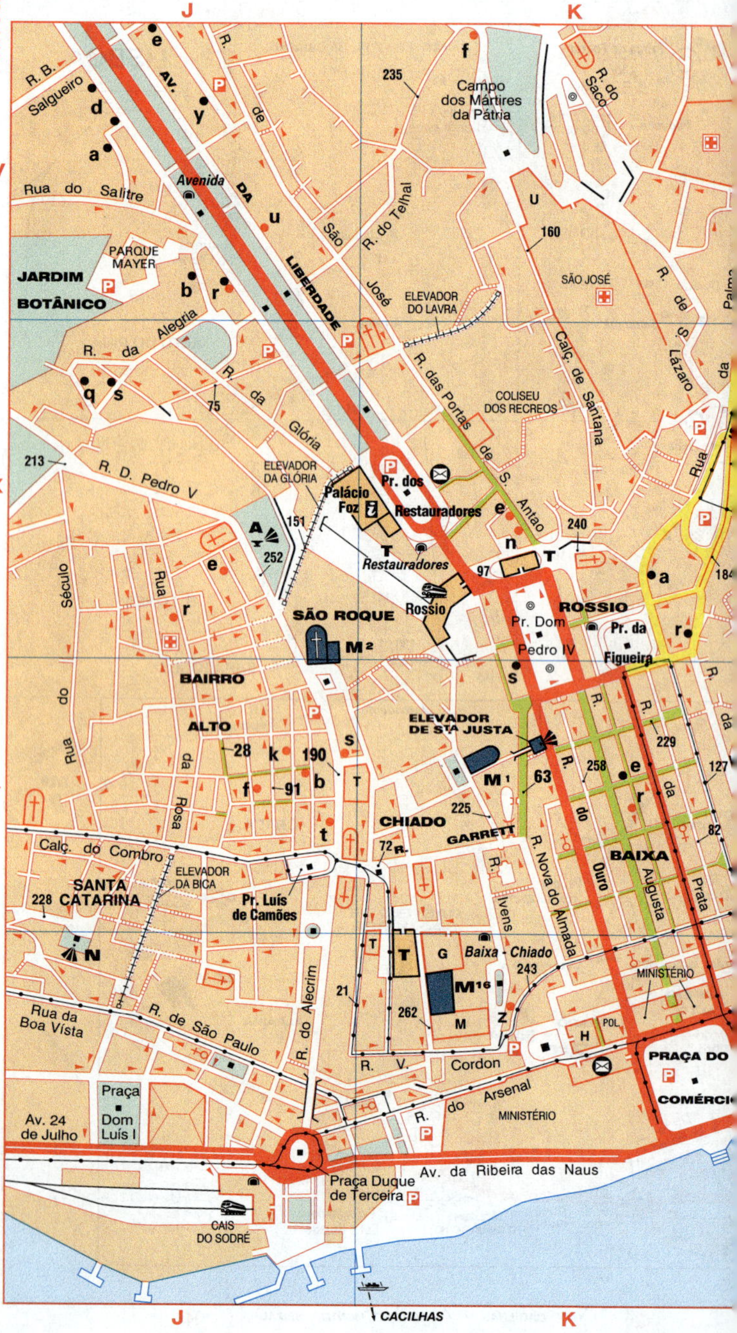

J
K
V
X
Y
N
R. B. Salgueiro
Rua do Salitre
JARDIM BOTÂNICO
PARQUE MAYER
Avenida
AV.
LIBERDADE
DA
de
São José
R. da Alegria
R. da Glória
R. D. Pedro V
Século
Rua
Rua do
ELEVADOR DA GLÓRIA
Palácio Foz
Pr. dos Restauradores
Restauradores
Rossio
SÃO ROQUE
BAIRRO
ALTO
da Rosa
Calç. do Combro
ELEVADOR DA BICA
SANTA CATARINA
Pr. Luís de Camões
Rua da Boa Vista
R. de São Paulo
R. do Alecrim
Av. 24 de Julho
Praça Dom Luís I
CAIS DO SODRÉ
Praça Duque de Terceira
CACILHAS
Campo dos Mártires da Pátria
R. do Telhal
ELEVADOR DO LAVRA
SÃO JOSÉ
COLISEU DOS RECREOS
Calç. de Santana
R. das Portas de S. Antão
Pr. dos Restauradores
R. do Saco
R. de S. Lázaro
Rua
ROSSIO
Pr. Dom Pedro IV
Pr. da Figueira
ELEVADOR DE Sta JUSTA
CHIADO
GARRETT
R. Nova do Almada
R. Ivens
R. do Ouro
R. da Prata
Augusta
BAIXA
Baixa - Chiado
MINISTÉRIO
POL.
PRAÇA DO COMÉRCIO
R. do Arsenal
R. V. Cordon
MINISTÉRIO
Av. da Ribeira das Naus
235
160
240
97
151
252
213
75
28
190
91
72
21
262
243
225
63
258
229
127
82
184

LISBON
PORTUGAL
L
M
SAPADORES
R. dos Sapadores
Calç. dos Barbadinhos
R. Maria da Fonte
Bombarda
R. Damasceno Monteiro
R. A. Vidal
Rua da Graça
V
R. Vale de S.to António
Senhora da Glória
Miradouro da Senhora do Monte
c
d
GRAÇA
R. Leite de Vasconcelos
Largo da Graça
Convento N.S. da Graça
R. da Verónica
R. do Mirante
R. dos Lagares
Calç. de Sto André
Calç. de Sto André
R. Voz do Operário
CAMPO DE STA CLARA
X
URARIA
CASTELO DE SÃO JORGE
São Vicente de Fora
SANTA ENGRÁCIA
Castelo
153
R. de S. Vicente
256
R. do Paraíso
n
SANTA APOLÓNIA
M
220
255
85
s
b
CASTELO
118
226
270
Remédios
M 10
Henrique
70
148
210
154
214
Sto Estêvão
236
R. dos 165
36
L. dos Lóios
231
M 3
ALFAMA
249
ALFÂNDEGA
Infante
Av.
253
C
250
S. Miguel
R. da Saudade
175
193
267
Largo do Chafariz de Dentro
Doca do Terreiro do Trigo
31
SÉ
33
166
ALFÂNDEGA
234
90
246
49
Henrique
D.
10
Campo das Cebolas
Infante
P
Doca da Marinha
Av.
T E J O
N
Estação do Sul e Sueste
(TERREIRO DO PAÇO)
DEGA
DA
STÉRIO
LISBOA
0   300 m
CACILHAS   L
BARREIRO, MONTIJO, SEIXAL
M

STREET INDEX TO LISBOA TOWN PLANS

SIGHTS

VIEWS OVER LISBON

★★ *from the Suspension Bridge (Ponte 25 de Abril★) S: by Av. da Ponte* EU *–* ☀★★ *from Christ in Majesty (Cristo Rei) S: by Av. da Ponte* EU *– St. Georges Castle★★ (Castelo de São Jorge:* ≼★★★*)* LX *– Santa Luzia Belvedere★ (Miradouro de Santa Luzia):* ≼★★ LY C *– Santa Justa Lift★ (Elevador de Santa Justa):* ≼★ KY *– São Pedro de Alcântara Belvedere★ (Miradouro de São Pedro de Alcâtara):* ≼ JX A *– Alto de Santa Catarina Belvedere★* JZ N *– Senhora do Monte Belvedere (Miradouro da Senhora do Monte):* ☀★★★ LV *– Largo das Portas do Sol★ :* ≼ LY *– Nossa Senhora da Graça Belvedere (Miradouro):* ≼★ LX

MUSEUMS

Museum of Ancient Art★★★ (Museum Nacional de Arte Antiga; polyptych da Adoração de São Vicente★★★, Tentação de Santo Antão★★★, Japanese folding screens★★, Twelve' Apostles★, Anunciação★, Chapel★) EU M[7] *– Gulbenkian Foundation (Calouste Gulbenkian Museum★★★* FR, *Modern Art Centre★* FR M[4]*) – Maritime Museum★★ (Museu de Marinha: model boats★★★)* W*: by Av. 24 de Julho* EU *– Coach Museum★★ (Museu Nacional dos Coches)* W*: by Av. 24 de Julho* EU *– Azulejo Museum★★ (Madre de Deus Convent: Church★★, chapter house★)* NE*: by Av. Infante D. Henrique* MX *– Water Museum EPAL★ (Museu da Água da EPAL)* HT M[8] *– Costume Museum★ (Museu Nacional do Traje)* N*: by Av. da República* GR *– Theatre Museum★ (Museu Nacional do Teatro)* N*: by Av. da República* GR *– Military Museum (Museu Militar; cellings★)* MY M[10] *– Museum of Decorative Arts★★ (Museu de Artes Decorativas: Fundação Ricardo do Espírito Santo Silva)* LY M[3] *– Archaeological Museum – Carmelite Church (Igreja do Carmo★)* KY M[1] *– São Roque Arte Sacra Museum★ (vestments★)* JKX M[2] *– Chiado Museum★ (Museu Nacional do Chiado)* KZ M[16] *– Music Museum★ (Museu da Música)* N*: by Av. da República* GR *– Rafael Bordalo Pinheiro Museum (ceramics★)* N*: by av. da Republica* GR

CHURCHES AND MONASTERIES

Cathedral★★ (See: gothic tombs★, grille★, tresor★) LY *– Hieronymite Monastery★★★ (Monasteiro dos Jerónimos): Santa Maria Church★★★ (vaulting★★, cloister★★★ ; Archaeological Museum: treasury★)* W*: by Av. 24 de Julho* EU *– São Roque Church★ (São João Baptista Chapel★★, interior★)* JX *– São Vicente de Fora Church (azulejos★)* MX *– Our Lady of Fátima Church (Igraja de Nossa Senhora de Fátima: windows★)* FR K *– Estrela Basilica★ (garden★)* EU L *– Old Conception Church (Igreja da Conceição Velha: south front★)* LZ V *– Santa Engrácia Church★* MX

HISTORIC QUARTERS

Belém★★ (Culture Centre★) W*: by Av. 24 de Julho* EU *– The Baixa★★* JKXYZ *– Alfama★★* LY *– Chiado and Bairro Alto★* JKY

PLACES OF INTEREST

Praça do Comércio★★ (or Terreiro do Paço) KZ *– Belém Tower★★★ (Torre de Belém)* W*: by Av. 24 de Julho* EU *– Marquis Fronteira Palace★★ (Palácio dos Marqueses de Fronteira: azulejos★★)* ER *– Rossio★ (station: neo-manuelina façade★)* KX *– Do Carmo st. and Garrett st. (Rua do Carmo and Rua Garrett)* KY *– Liberdade Ave★ (Avenida da Liberdade)* JV *– Edward VII Park★ (Parque Eduardo VII:* ≼★*, greenhouse★)* FS *– Zoological Garden★★ (Jardin Zoológico)* ER *– Águas Livres Aqueduct★ (Aqueduto das Águas Livres)* ES *– Botanic Garden★ (Jardim Botánico)* JV *– Monsanto Park★ (Parque Florestal de Monsanto): Belvedere (Miradouro):* ☀★ *)* ER *– Campo de Santa Clara★* MX *– Santo Estêvão stiarway and terrace★ (*≼★*)* MY *– Ajuda Palace★ (Palacio da Ajuda)* M*: by Av. 24 de Julho* EU *– Arpad Szenes-Vieira da Silva Foundation★* EFS *– Boat trip on the river Tagus★ (*≼★★*)*

Centre : Av. da Liberdade, Rua Augusta, Rua do Ouro, Praça do Comércio, Praça D
Pedro IV (Rossio), Praça dos Restauradores

Tivoli Lisboa, Av. da Liberdade 185, ⊠ 1250, ℘ (01) 353 01 81, Fax (01) 357 94
⌂, « Terrace with ≤ town », 丁 heated, ✗ – |≑| ▤ ▣ ☎ ⇔ – 齊 40/200. ㏂
▣ VISA JCB. ✗ JV
Grill Terraço : Meals a la carte 5050/9100 - **Zodíaco** : Meals a la carte 3100/5100
298 rm ⊇ 38000/42000, 29 suites.

Sofitel Lisboa, Av. da Liberdade 127, ⊠ 1250, ℘ (01) 342 92 02, Telex 425.
Fax (01) 342 92 22 – |≑| ▤ ▣ ☎ ♿ ⇔ – 齊 25/300. ㏂ ⓪ ▣ VISA JV
Meals (see rest. **Cais da Avenida** below) – ⊇ 2500 – **166 rm** 32000/35000, 4 suit

Lisboa Plaza, Travessa do Salitre 7, ⊠ 1250, ℘ (01) 346 39 22, Fax (01) 347 16
– |≑| ▤ ▣ ☎ – 齊 25/140. ㏂ ⓪ ▣ VISA JCB. ✗ JV
Meals a la carte 4800/5900 – **94 rm** ⊇ 25600/28400, 12 suites.

Mundial, Rua D. Duarte 4, ⊠ 1100, ℘ (01) 886 31 01, Fax (01) 887 91 29, ≤ – |≑|
▣ ☎ ⇔ – 齊 25/120. ㏂ ⓪ ▣ VISA. ✗ KX
Meals 3500 – **245 rm** ⊇ 19100/23200, 10 suites.

Tivoli Jardim, Rua Julio Cesar Machado 7, ⊠ 1250, ℘ (01) 353 99 71, Fax (01) 355 65
丁 heated, ✗ – |≑| ▤ ▣ ☎ ⇔ ℗ – 齊 25/40. ㏂ ⓪ ▣ VISA JCB. ✗ JV
Meals a la carte approx. 5500 – **119 rm** ⊇ 25000/29000.

Lisboa coffee shop only, Rua Barata Salgueiro 5, ⊠ 1150, ℘ (01) 355 41
Fax (01) 355 41 39 – |≑| ▤ ▣ ☎ ⇔. ㏂ ⓪ ▣ VISA. ✗ JV
55 rm ⊇ 25000/30000, 6 suites.

Britânia without rest, Rua Rodrigues Sampaio 17, ⊠ 1150, ℘ (01) 315 50
Fax (01) 315 50 21 – |≑| ▤ ▣ ☎. ㏂ ⓪ ▣ VISA JCB. ✗ JV
30 rm ⊇ 22200/23500.

Veneza without rest, Av. da Liberdade 189, ⊠ 1250, ℘ (01) 352 26
Fax (01) 352 66 78, « Old palace » – |≑| ▤ ▣ ☎ ℗. ㏂ ⓪ ▣ VISA JCB. ✗ JV
36 rm ⊇ 18000/20000.

Príncipe Real, Rua da Alegria 53, ⊠ 1250, ℘ (01) 346 01 16, Fax (01) 342 21 04
|≑| ▤ ▣ ☎. ㏂ ⓪ ▣ VISA JCB. ✗ JX
Meals 3400 – **24 rm** ⊇ 20500/24000.

Metropole without rest, Praça do Rossio 30, ⊠ 1100, ℘ (01) 346 91
Fax (01) 346 91 66 – |≑| ▤ ▣ ☎. ㏂ ⓪ ▣ VISA JCB KY
36 rm ⊇ 22000/25000.

Botánico without rest, Rua Mãe de Água 16, ⊠ 1250, ℘ (01) 342 03
Fax (01) 342 01 25 – |≑| ▤ ▣ ☎. ㏂ ⓪ ▣ VISA JCB. ✗ JX
30 rm ⊇ 14000/17000.

Albergaria Senhora do Monte without rest, Calçada do Monte 39, ⊠ 1170, ℘ (
886 60 02, Fax (01) 887 77 83, ≤ São Jorge castle, town and river Tejo – |≑| ▤ ▣
㏂ ⓪ ▣ VISA. ✗ LV
28 rm ⊇ 16000/27500.

Lisboa Tejo without rest, Poço do Borratém 4, ⊠ 1100, ℘ (01) 886 61
Fax (01) 886 51 63 – |≑| ▤ ▣ ☎. ㏂ ⓪ ▣ VISA. ✗ KX
58 rm ⊇ 15000/18000.

Insulana without rest, Rua da Assunção 52, ⊠ 1100, ℘ (01) 342 76
Fax (01) 342 89 24 – |≑| ▤ ▣ ☎. ㏂ ⓪ ▣ VISA. ✗ KY
32 rm ⊇ 10000/12000.

Tágide, Largo da Académia Nacional de Belas Artes 18, ⊠ 1200, ℘ (01) 342 07
Fax (01) 347 18 80, ≤ – ▤. ✗ KZ
closed Saturday and Sunday – Meals a la carte 6800/8100.

Clara, Campo dos Mártires da Pátria 49, ⊠ 1150, ℘ (01) 885 30 53, Fax (01) 885 20
⌂, « Garden terrace » – ▤. ㏂ ⓪ ▣ VISA JCB. ✗ KV
closed Saturday lunch, Sunday and 1 to 15 August – Meals a la carte 4450/5250.

Tavares, Rua da Misericórdia 37, ⊠ 1200, ℘ (01) 342 11 12, Fax (01) 347 81 25, « L
19C decor » – ▤. ㏂ ⓪ ▣ VISA. ✗ JY
closed Saturday and Sunday lunch – Meals a la carte approx. 8500.

Bachus, Largo da Trindade 9, ⊠ 1200, ℘ (01) 342 28 28, Fax (01) 342 12 60 – ▤.
⓪ ▣ VISA JCB. ✗ JY
closed Saturday lunch and Sunday – Meals a la carte 5050/6450.

Gambrinus, Rua das Portas de Santo Antão 25, ⊠ 1150, ℘ (01) 342 14
Fax (01) 346 50 32 – ▤. ㏂ ⓪ ▣ VISA. ✗ KX
Meals a la carte 11000/14000.

Escorial, Rua das Portas de Santo Antão 47, ⊠ 1100, ℘ (01) 346 44
Fax (01) 346 37 58 – ▤. ㏂ ⓪ ▣ VISA JCB. ✗ KX
Meals a la carte approx. 5840.

XXX **Cais da Avenida** - *Hotel Sofitel Lisboa*, Av. da Liberdade 123, ⊠ 1250, ℰ (01) 342 92 24, Fax (01) 342 92 22 – 🗐 🚗. 🖭 ⓄⒹ Ⓔ VISA JCB. ⅏
JV r
Meals a la carte 4050/5600.

XXX **Jardim Tropical,** Av. da Liberdade 144, ⊠ 1250, ℰ (01) 346 88 39, *Fax (01) 342 31 24*, « Tropical conservatory » – 🗐 🚗. 🖭 ⓄⒹ Ⓔ VISA JCB. ⅏
JV u
Meals a la carte 3350/7300.

XXX **Casa do Leão,** Castelo de São Jorge, ⊠ 1100, ℰ (01) 887 59 62, *Fax (01) 887 63 29*, ≼ – 🗐. 🖭 ⓄⒹ VISA. ⅏
LXY s
Meals a la carte 5800/7400.

XX **Via Graça,** Rua Damasceno Monteiro 9-B, ⊠ 1170, ℰ (01) 887 08 30, *Fax (01) 887 03 05*, ≼ *São Jorge castle, town and river Tejo* – 🗐. 🖭 ⓄⒹ Ⓔ VISA JCB. ⅏ *closed Saturday lunch and Sunday* – **Meals** a la carte 3300/4980.
LV d

XX **O Faz Figura,** Rua do Paraíso 15-B, ⊠ 1100, ℰ (01) 886 89 81, ≼, 🏮 – 🗐. 🖭 ⓄⒹ Ⓔ VISA JCB. ⅏
MX n
closed Sunday – **Meals** a la carte 4000/5500.

X **Porta Branca,** Rua do Teixeira 35, ⊠ 1250, ℰ (01) 342 10 24, *Fax (01) 347 92 57* – 🗐. 🖭 Ⓔ VISA. ⅏
JX e
closed Sunday – **Meals** a la carte 3480/5980.

X **Mercado de Santa Clara,** Campo de Santa Clara (at market), ⊠ 1170, ℰ (01) 887 39 86, *Fax (01) 887 39 86*, ≼ – 🗐. 🖭 ⓄⒹ Ⓔ VISA. ⅏
MX c
closed Sunday dinner and Monday – **Meals** a la carte 4000/5000.

X **O Múni,** Rua dos Correeiros 115, ⊠ 1100, ℰ (01) 342 89 82 – 🗐. 🖭 ⓄⒹ Ⓔ VISA. ⅏
KY r
closed Saturday, Sunday and September – **Meals** a la carte 2900/3650.

East : Av. da Liberdade, Av. Almirante Reis, Av. Estados Unidos de América, Av. de Roma, Av. João XXI, Av. da República, Praça Marquês de Pombal

🏨 **Radisson SAS,** Av. Marechal Craveiro Lopes 390, ⊠ 1700, ℰ (01) 759 96 39, *Telex 61170, Fax (01) 758 66 05*, 𝓕𝓼 – 🛗 🗐 📺 ☎ 🔔 🚗 – 🕍 25/200. 🖭 ⓄⒹ Ⓔ VISA JCB. ⅏
North : by Av. da República GR
Meals a la carte 4800/7300 – 🍵 1800 – **205 rm** 35000/37000, 16 suites.

🏨 **Altis Park H.,** Av. Engenheiro Arantes e Oliveira 9, ⊠ 1900, ℰ (01) 846 08 66, *Fax (01) 846 08 38* – 🛗 🗐 📺 ☎ 🔔 🚗 – 🕍 25/600. 🖭 ⓄⒹ Ⓔ VISA JCB. ⅏ rest
HR z
Meals 3100 – **285 rm** 🍵 22000/24500, 15 suites.

🏨 **Meliá Confort Lisboa,** Av. Duque de Loulé 45, ⊠ 1050, ℰ (01) 353 21 08, *Fax (01) 353 18 65*, ⅀ – 🛗 🗐 📺 ☎ 🔔 🚗 – 🕍 25/50. 🖭 ⓄⒹ Ⓔ VISA JCB. ⅏
GS z
Meals *(closed Sunday)* a la carte 2800/5400 – **80 rm** 🍵 28000/30000, 4 suites.

🏨 **Holiday Inn Lisboa,** Av. António José de Almeida 28-A, ⊠ 1000, ℰ (01) 793 52 22, *Fax (01) 793 66 72*, 𝓕𝓼 – 🛗 🗐 📺 ☎ 🔔 🚗 – 🕍 25/300. 🖭 ⓄⒹ Ⓔ VISA JCB. ⅏
GR c
Meals a la carte 4650/6100 – **161 rm** 🍵 35000/40000, 8 suites.

🏨 **Lutécia,** Av. Frei Miguel Contreiras 52, ⊠ 1700, ℰ (01) 840 31 21, *Telex 12457, Fax (01) 840 78 18*, ≼ – 🛗 🗐 📺 ☎ – 🕍 25/100. 🖭 ⓄⒹ Ⓔ VISA JCB. ⅏
North : by Av. Almirante Reis HR
Meals a la carte 3700/5450 – **143 rm** 🍵 18000/21000, 8 suites.

🏨 **Alif** without rest, Campo Pequeno 51, ⊠ 1000, ℰ (01) 795 24 64, *Telex 64460, Fax (01) 795 41 16* – 🛗 🗐 📺 ☎ 🔔 🚗 – 🕍 25/40. 🖭 Ⓓ Ⓔ VISA. ⅏ GR w
107 rm 🍵 12900/14900, 8 suites.

🏨 **Roma,** Av. de Roma 33, ⊠ 1700, ℰ (01) 796 77 61, *Fax (01) 793 29 81*, ≼, 🖼 – 🛗 🗐 📺 ☎ 🔔 – 🕍 25/230. 🖭 ⓄⒹ Ⓔ VISA. ⅏
North : by Av. Almirante Reis HR
Meals 2900 – **263 rm** 🍵 12500/15000.

🏨 **A.S. Lisboa** without rest, Av. Almirante Reis 188, ⊠ 1000, ℰ (01) 847 30 25, *Fax (01) 847 30 34* – 🛗 🗐 📺 ☎ – 🕍 25/80. 🖭 ⓄⒹ Ⓔ VISA. ⅏
HR e
75 rm 🍵 15000/17000.

🏨 **Presidente** coffee shop only, Rua Alexandre Herculano 13, ⊠ 1150, ℰ (01) 353 95 01, *Fax (01) 352 02 72* – 🛗 🗐 📺 ☎ – 🕍 25/40. 🖭 ⓄⒹ Ⓔ VISA JCB. ⅏
GS t
59 rm 🍵 16200/18800.

🏨 **Dom Carlos** coffee shop only, Av. Duque de Loulé 121, ⊠ 1050, ℰ (01) 353 90 71, *Fax (01) 352 07 28* – 🛗 🗐 📺 ☎ – 🕍 25/40. 🖭 ⓄⒹ Ⓔ VISA JCB. ⅏
GS n
76 rm 🍵 17500/20800.

🏨 **Dom João** without rest, Rua José Estêvão 43, ⊠ 1150, ℰ (01) 314 41 71, *Fax (01) 352 45 69* – 🛗 🗐 📺 ☎. 🖭 ⓄⒹ Ⓔ VISA. ⅏
HS e
18 rm 🍵 8000/10000.

XXXX **Antonio Clara-Clube de Empresários,** Av. da República 38, ✉ 1050, ℰ (0
796 63 80, *Fax (01) 797 41 44,* « *Former palace* » – 🖿 🅿. AE ① E VISA JCB. ⇙GR
closed Sunday and 23 to 31 August – **Meals** a la carte approx. 6200.

X **Chez Armand,** Rua Carlos Mardel 38, ✉ 1900, ℰ (01) 847 57 70, *Fax (01) 887 19
– 🖿. AE E VISA. ⇙   HR
closed Sunday and August – **Meals** - French rest - a la carte approx. 4700.

X **D'Avis,** Rua do Grilo 98, ✉ 1900, ℰ (01) 868 13 54, *Fax (01) 868 13 54,* « *Typical rest*
– 🖿. E VISA. ⇙   East : Av. Infante D. Henrique   MX
closed Sunday and 1 to 15 August – Meals - Alentejo rest - a la carte 2150/3600.

X **Celta,** Rua Gomes Freire 148, ✉ 1150, ℰ (01) 357 30 69, *Fax (01) 357 30 69* – 🖿.
E VISA   GS
closed Sunday – **Meals** a la carte 1980/3840.

West : Av. da Liberdade, Av. 24 de Julho, Av. da India, Av. Infante Santo, Av. de Ber
Av. António Augusto de Aguiar, Largo de Alcântara, Praça Marquês de Pombal, Praça
Espanha

🏛 **Four Seasons H. The Ritz Lisbon,** Rua Rodrigo da Fonseca 88, ✉ 1093, ℰ (0
383 20 20, *Fax (01) 383 17 83,* ≼, 🌿, 🛌 – 🛗 🖿 TV ☎ ⴲ ⇔ 🅿 – 🛋 25/600.
① E VISA JCB. ⇙ rest   FS
Varanda : **Meals** a la carte 6950/13850 – ⌑ 2800 – **262 rm** 46200/50600, 20 suit

🏛 **Sheraton Lisboa H.,** Rua Latino Coelho 1, ✉ 1069, ℰ (01) 312 00 00, *Telex 127.*
Fax (01) 354 71 64, ≼, 🛌, 🛋 heated – 🛗 🖿 TV ☎ ⴲ ⇔ – 🛋 25/550. AE ① E
JCB. ⇙   GR
Alfama Grill (closed Saturday, Sunday and August) **Meals** a la carte 8100/12000 - *Ca*
vela : **Meals** a la carte 5250/7900 – ⌑ 3000 – **374 rm** 36000/39000, 7 suites.

🏛 **Da Lapa** ⇙, Rua do Pau de Bandeira 4, ✉ 1200, ℰ (01) 395 00 05, *Fax (01) 395 06*
≼, 🌿, « *Park with waterfall and* 🛋 », 🛌, 🛋 – 🛗 🖿 TV ☎ ⴲ ⇔ 🅿 – 🛋 25/2
AE ① E VISA. ⇙   EU
Embaixada : **Meals** a la carte 6150/7550 – ⌑ 2350 – **86 rm** 45000/47500, 8 suit

🏛 **Dom Pedro Lisboa,** Av. Engenheiro Duarte Pacheco 24, ✉ 1070, ℰ (01) 389 66 (
Fax (01) 389 66 01, ≼, 🌿 – 🛗 🖿 TV ☎ ⇔ – 🛋 25/500. AE ① E VISA J
⇙   ES
Meals a la carte 4000/5700 – ⌑ 2500 – **254 rm** 45000/50000, 9 suites.

🏛 **Le Meridien Park Atlantic Lisboa,** Rua Castilho 149, ✉ 1070, ℰ (01) 381 87 (
Fax (01) 383 32 31, ≼ – 🛗 🖿 TV ☎ ⴲ ⇔ – 🛋 25/550. AE ① E VISA J
⇙   FS
Brasserie des Amis : **Meals** a la carte 4450/5470 – ⌑ 2300 – **313 rm** 41000/4400
17 suites.

🏛 **Altis,** Rua Castilho 11, ✉ 1250, ℰ (01) 314 24 96, *Telex 13314, Fax (01) 354 86 96,*
🛋 – 🛗 🖿 TV ☎ ⇔ – 🛋 25/700. AE ① E VISA JCB. ⇙   FT
Girassol : **Meals** a la carte approx. 7500 - *Grill Dom Fernando :* **Meals** a la ca
4700/8000 – **290 rm** ⌑ 32000/35000, 53 suites.

🏛 **Alfa Lisboa,** Av. Columbano Bordalo Pinheiro, ✉ 1070, ℰ (01) 726 21 21, *Telex 184*
Fax (01) 726 30 31, ≼, 🛌, 🛋 – 🛗 🖿 TV ☎ ⇔ – 🛋 25/700. AE ① E VISA JCB.
A Aldeia : **Meals** a la carte 3200/6150 – **440 rm** ⌑ 55000/57000.   ER

🏛 **Holiday Inn Lisboa-Continental,** Rua Laura Alves 9, ✉ 1050, ℰ (01) 793 50 (
Telex 65632, Fax (01) 797 36 69 – 🛗 🖿 TV ☎ ⇔ – 🛋 25/180. AE ① E VISA J
⇙   FR
Meals 3900 – ⌑ 1700 – **210 rm** 30000/35000, 10 suites.

🏛 **Real Parque,** Av. Luís Bívar 67, ✉ 1050, ℰ (01) 357 01 01, *Fax (01) 357 07 50* –
🖿 TV ☎ ⴲ ⇔ – 🛋 25/100. AE ① E VISA JCB. ⇙   FR
Meals 4900 - *Cozinha do Real :* **Meals** a la carte 4900/6800 – **147 rm** ⌑ 34000/380
6 suites.

🏛 **Lisboa Penta,** Av. dos Combatentes, ✉ 1600, ℰ (01) 726 40 54, *Fax (01) 726 42*
≼, 🛌, 🛋, 🌿 – 🛗 🖿 TV ☎ ⇔ 🅿 – 🛋 25/600. AE ① E VISA J
⇙ rest   North-West : by Av. A. Augusto de Aguiar   FR
Grill Passarola : **Meals** a la carte approx. 6600 - *Verde Pino :* **Meals** a la carte appr
3750 – **588 rm** ⌑ 22000/26000, 4 suites.

🏛 **Metropolitan Lisboa H.,** Rua Soeiro Gomes-parcela 2, ✉ 1600, ℰ (01) 798 25 (
Fax (01) 795 08 64 – 🛗 🖿 TV ☎ ⴲ ⇔ – 🛋 25/250. AE ① E VISA. ⇙
Meals 4200 – **315 rm** ⌑ 19000/23000.   North : by Av. da República   GR

🏛 **Fénix,** Praça Marquês de Pombal 8, ✉ 1250, ℰ (01) 386 21 21, *Telex 121.*
Fax (01) 386 01 31 – 🛗 🖿 TV ☎ ⴲ – 🛋 25/100. AE ① E VISA. ⇙ rest   FS
Bodegón : **Meals** a la carte 4050/6100 – **119 rm** ⌑ 22000/25000, 4 suites.

🏛 **Do Reno** coffee shop only, Av. Duque d'Ávila 195-197, ✉ 1050, ℰ (01) 313 50 (
Fax (01) 313 50 01, 🛋 – 🛗 🖿 TV ☎ ⴲ ⇔ – 🛋 25/115. AE ① E VISA. ⇙   FR
89 rm ⌑ 40000, 3 suites.

Zurique, Rua Ivone Silva 18, ✉ 1050, ✆ (01) 793 71 11, *Fax (01) 793 72 90*, ⚊ – ⦵ ▤ TV ☎ ⇋ – ☖ 25/150. AE ⓪ E *VISA*. ✵   FR s
Meals 3000 – **248 rm** ☕ 15000/17000, 4 suites.

Diplomático, Rua Castilho 74, ✉ 1250, ✆ (01) 386 20 41, *Fax (01) 386 21 55* – ⦵ ▤ TV ☎ – ☖ 25/80. AE ⓪ E *VISA* JCB. ✵ rest   FS c
Meals a la carte 3000/4250 – **90 rm** ☕ 17500/20000.

Novotel Lisboa, Av. José Malhoa 1642, ✉ 1070, ✆ (01) 726 60 22, *Fax (01) 726 64 96*, ≤, ⚊ – ⦵ ▤ TV ☎ ⅋ ⇋ – ☖ 25/300. AE ⓪ E *VISA* JCB   ER e
Meals 3100 – ☕ 1200 – **246 rm** 12400.

Barcelona without rest, Rua Laura Alves 10, ✉ 1050, ✆ (01) 795 42 73, *Fax (01) 795 42 81* – ⦵ ▤ TV ☎ ⅋ ⇋ – ☖ 25/230. AE ⓪ E *VISA* JCB. ✵   FR z
120 rm ☕ 17000/19000, 5 suites.

Quality H., Campo Grande 7, ✉ 1700, ✆ (01) 795 75 55, *Fax (01) 795 75 00*, ₣ⱪ – ⦵ ▤ TV ☎ ⅋ ⇋ – ☖ 25/70. AE ⓪ E *VISA* JCB. ✵
Meals 3200 – **80 rm** ☕ 15000/16000, 2 suites.   North : by Av. da República   GR

Amazónia Lisboa without rest, Travessa Fábrica dos Pentes 12, ✉ 1250, ✆ (01) 387 70 06, *Telex 66361, Fax (01) 387 90 90*, ⚊ heated – ⦵ ▤ TV ☎ ⅋ ⇋ – ☖ 25/200. AE ⓪ E *VISA*. ✵   FS d
192 rm ☕ 14000/16000.

Dom Rodrigo Suite H. coffee shop only, Rua Rodrigo da Fonseca 44, ✉ 1250, ✆ (01) 386 38 00, *Fax (01) 386 30 00*, ⚊ – ⦵ ▤ TV ☎ ⇋. AE ⓪ E *VISA* JCB. ✵   FS m
☕ 900 – **57 suites** 21000/26000.

York House, Rua das Janelas Verdes 32, ✉ 1200, ✆ (01) 396 25 44, *Fax (01) 397 27 93*, ⍥, « Former 16C convent. Portuguese decor » – TV ☎. AE ⓪ E *VISA* JCB. ✵   FU e
Meals a la carte 3650/5800 – **31 rm** ☕ 27500/38500, 3 suites.

Dom Manuel I without rest, Av. Duque d'Ávila 189, ✉ 1050, ✆ (01) 357 61 60, *Fax (01) 357 69 85* – ⦵ ▤ TV ☎. AE ⓪ E *VISA*. ✵   FR p
64 rm ☕ 12500/15000.

Executive Inn without rest, Av. Conde Valbom 56, ✉ 1050, ✆ (01) 795 11 57, *Fax (01) 795 11 66* – ⦵ ▤ TV ☎ ⇋ – ☖ 25/55. AE ⓪ E *VISA*. ✵   FR g
72 rm ☕ 20000/22000.

Miraparque, Av. Sidónio Pais 12, ✉ 1050, ✆ (01) 352 42 86, *Fax (01) 357 89 20* – ⦵ ▤ TV ☎. AE ⓪ E *VISA*. ✵   FS k
Meals 3200 – **101 rm** ☕ 13000/14000.

Eduardo VII, Av. Fontes Pereira de Melo 5, ✉ 1050, ✆ (01) 353 01 41, *Fax (01) 353 38 79*, ≤ – ⦵ ▤ TV ☎ – ☖ 25/120. AE ⓪ E *VISA*. ✵   FS p
Varanda : Meals a la carte 3500/4500 – **127 rm** ☕ 16800/19200, 2 suites.

Marquês de Sá, Av. Miguel Bombarda 130, ✉ 1050, ✆ (01) 791 10 14, *Fax (01) 793 69 86* – ⦵ ▤ TV ☎ ⇋ – ☖ 25/150. AE ⓪ E *VISA*. ✵   FR c
Meals 3250 – **97 rm** ☕ 16000/18000.

Amazónia Jamor, Av. Tomás Ribeiro 129 Queijas, ✉ 2795 Linda-A-Pastora, ✆ (01) 417 56 38, *Fax (01) 417 56 30*, ≤, ₣ⱪ, ⚊, ⍉ – ⦵ ▤ TV ☎ ⅋ Ⓟ – ☖ 25/200. AE ⓪ E *VISA*. ✵   West : 10 km by Av. Engenheiro Duarte Pacheco   ES
Meals 3500 – **93 rm** ☕ 14700, 4 suites.

As Janelas Verdes without rest, Rua das Janelas Verdes 47, ✉ 1200, ✆ (01) 396 81 43, *Fax (01) 396 81 44*, « Late 18C house with attractive courtyard » – ▤ TV ☎. AE ⓪ E *VISA* JCB. ✵   FU e
17 rm ☕ 27600/29900.

Nacional without rest, Rua Castilho 34, ✉ 1250, ✆ (01) 355 44 33, *Fax (01) 356 11 22* – ⦵ ▤ TV ☎ ⇋. AE ⓪ E *VISA*. ✵   FST s
59 rm ☕ 12900/15100, 2 suites.

Rex, Rua Castilho 169, ✉ 1070, ✆ (01) 388 21 61, *Fax (01) 388 75 81* – ⦵ ▤ TV ☎ – ☖ 25/50. AE ⓪ E *VISA*. ✵   FS a
Meals 4500 – **68 rm** ☕ 20000/22000.

Da Torre, Rua dos Jerónimos 8, ✉ 1400, ✆ (01) 363 62 62, *Fax (01) 364 59 95* – ⦵ ▤ TV ☎ – ☖ 25/50. AE ⓪ E *VISA* JCB   West : by Av. 24 de Julho   EU
Meals (see rest. *São Jerónimo* below) – **50 rm** ☕ 13000/15500.

Berna without rest, Av. António Serpa 13, ✉ 1050, ✆ (01) 793 67 67, *Telex 62516, Fax (01) 793 62 78* – ⦵ ▤ TV ☎ ⇋ – ☖ 25/180. AE ⓪ E *VISA*. ✵   GR a
240 rm ☕ 10000/12000.

Real Residência, Rua Ramalho Ortigão 41, ✉ 1070, ✆ (01) 382 29 00, *Fax (01) 382 29 30* – ⦵ ▤ TV ☎ – ☖ 25/70. AE ⓪ E *VISA* JCB. ✵   FR e
Meals 3600 – ☕ 1000 – **24 suites** 28000.

XXXX **Casa da Comida**, Travessa das Amoreiras 1, ⊠ 1250, ℰ (01) 388 53 7
Fax (01) 387 51 32, « Patio with plants » – ▤. AE ① E VISA JCB. ⅏   FT
closed Saturday lunch and Sunday – **Meals** a la carte 5700/11200.

XXX **Pabe**, Rua Duque de Palmela 27-A, ⊠ 1250, ℰ (01) 353 74 84, Fax (01) 353 64 3
« English pub style » – ▤. AE ① E VISA. ⅏   FS
Meals a la carte 5600/7700.

XXX **Conventual**, Praça das Flores 45, ⊠ 1200, ℰ (01) 390 91 96, Fax (01) 390 91 96
▤. AE ① E VISA   FT
closed Saturday lunch, Bank Holidays lunch, Sunday and Monday lunch – **Meals** a la car
4100/6300.

XXX **São Jerónimo** - Hotel Da Torre, Rua dos Jerónimos 12, ⊠ 1400, ℰ (01) 364 87 9
Fax (01) 363 26 92, « Modern decor » – ▤. AE ① E VISA JCB. ⅏
Meals a la carte 4950/6350.   West : by Av. 24 de Julho   EU

XXX **Chester**, Rua Rodrigo da Fonseca 87-D, ⊠ 1250, ℰ (01) 385 73 47, Fax (01) 388 78
– ▤. AE ① E VISA JCB. ⅏   FS
closed Saturday lunch and Sunday – **Meals** - Meat specialities - a la carte 4200/620

XXX **T Clube**, Av. de Brasília, ⊠ 1400, ℰ (01) 301 66 52, Fax (01) 301 58 81 – ▤. AE
E VISA. ⅏   West : by Av. 24 de Julho   EU
closed Sunday – **Meals** a la carte 5250/11100.

XX **Saraiva's**, Rua Engenheiro Canto Resende 3, ⊠ 1050, ℰ (01) 354 06 0
Fax (01) 353 19 87, « Modern decor » – ▤. AE ① E VISA JCB. ⅏   FR
closed Saturday and Bank Holidays – **Meals** a la carte 3500/ 5650.

XX **Espelho d'Água**, Av. de Brasília, ⊠ 1400, ℰ (01) 301 73 73, Fax (01) 363 26 5
≤, 🌿, « Lakeside setting » – ▤. AE ① E VISA JCB. ⅏
closed Saturday lunch and Sunday – **Meals** a la carte 5350/6650.
    West : by Av. 24 de Julho   EU

XX **Adega Tia Matilde**, Rua da Beneficéncia 77, ⊠ 1600, ℰ (01) 797 21 7
Fax (01) 793 90 00 – ▤. AE ① E VISA. ⅏   FR
closed Saturday dinner and Sunday – **Meals** a la carte 4000/6173.

XX **O Nobre**, Rua das Mercês 71, ⊠ 1300, ℰ (01) 363 38 27, Fax (01) 362 21 06 – ▤.
VISA. ⅏   West : by Av. 24 de Julho   EU
closed Saturday lunch and Sunday – **Meals** a la carte 4840/6440.

XX **O Mercado do Peixe**, Estrada do Casal Pedro Teixeira-Caramão da Ajuda, ⊠ 140
ℰ (01) 362 31 40, Fax (01) 362 30 23 – ▤. AE ① E VISA. ⅏
closed Sunday dinner and Monday – **Meals** - Seafood - a la carte approx. 8900.
    West : by Av. 24 de Julho   EU

XX **O Polícia**, Rua Marquês Sá da Bandeira 112, ⊠ 1050, ℰ (01) 796 35 0
Fax (01) 796 02 19 – ▤. AE E VISA. ⅏   FR
closed Saturday dinner and Sunday – **Meals** a la carte 3450/4100.

X **Sua Excelência**, Rua do Conde 34, ⊠ 1200, ℰ (01) 390 36 14, Fax (01) 396 75 8
▤. AE ① E VISA JCB   EU
closed Saturday lunch, Sunday lunch, Wednesday and September – **Meals** a la car
4000/7000.

X **Frei Contente**, Rua de São Marçal 94, ⊠ 1200, ℰ (01) 347 59 22 – ▤. AE E V
⅏   FT
closed Saturday lunch, Sunday and August – Meals a la carte 2800/3500.

The fado restaurants :

XX **O Faia**, Rua da Barroca 56, ⊠ 1200, ℰ (01) 342 67 42, Fax (01) 342 19 23 – ▤. AE
E VISA JCB. ⅏   JY
closed Sunday – **Meals** - dinner only - a la carte 5300/8500.

XX **Sr. Vinho**, Rua do Meio-à-Lapa 18, ⊠ 1200, ℰ (01) 397 74 56, Fax (01) 395 20 7
▤. ① E VISA JCB. ⅏   FU
closed Sunday – **Meals** - dinner only - a la carte 5980/8940.

XX **A Severa**, Rua das Gáveas 51, ⊠ 1200, ℰ (01) 342 83 14, Fax (01) 346 40 06 – ▤.
① E VISA JCB. ⅏   JY
closed Thursday – **Meals** a la carte 6300/9100.

X **Adega Machado**, Rua do Norte 91, ⊠ 1200, ℰ (01) 322 46 40, Fax (01) 346 75
– ▤. AE ① E VISA JCB. ⅏   JY
closed Monday – **Meals** - dinner only - a la carte 5850/7600.

Spain

España

MADRID – BARCELONA – BILBAO
MÁLAGA – SEVILLA – VALENCIA

PRACTICAL INFORMATION

LOCAL CURRENCY

Peseta: *100 ESP = 0,60 euro (€)*

National Holiday in Spain: *12 October*

TOURIST INFORMATION

The telephone number and address of the Tourist Information offices is given in the text of the towns under 🛈.

FOREIGN EXCHANGE

Banks are usually open fron 8.30am to 2pm (closed on Saturdays and Sundays in summer).

Exchange offices in Sevilla and Valencia airports open from 9am to 2pm, in Barcelona airport from 9am to 2pm and 7 to 11pm. In Madrid and Málaga airports, offices operate a 24-hour service.

TRANSPORT

Taxis may be hailed when showing the green light or "Libre" sign on the windscreen. Madrid, Barcelona, Bilbao and Valencia have a Metro (subway) network. In each station complete information and plans will be found.

SHOPPING

In the index of street names, those printed in red are where the principal shops are found.

The big stores are easy to find in town centres; they are open from 10am to 9.30pm. Exclusive shops and boutiques are open from 10am to 2pm and 5 to 8pm. In Madrid they will be found in Serrano, Princesa and the Centre; in Barcelona, Passeig de Gràcia, Diagonal and the Rambla de Catalunya.

Second-hand goods and antiques: El Rastro (Flea Market), Las Cortes, Serrano in Madrid; in Barcelona, Les Encantes (Flea Market), Gothic Quarter.

TIPPING

Hotel, restaurant and café bills always include service in the total charge. Nevertheless it is usual to leave the staff a small gratuity which may vary depending upon the district and the service given. Doormen, porters and taxi-drivers are used to being tipped.

SPEED LIMITS

The maximum permitted speed on motorways is 120 km/h - 74 mph, and 90 km/h - 56 mph on other roads.

SEAT BELTS

The wearing of seat belts is compulsory for drivers and all passengers.

"TAPAS"

Bars serving "tapas" (typical Spanish food to be eaten with a glass of wine or an aperitif) will usually be found in central, busy or old quarters of towns. In Madrid, search out the Calle de Cuchilleros (Plaza Mayor). In Sevilla, search out the Barrio de Santa Cruz, El Arenal and Triana.

MADRID

Madrid 28000 **P** **444** K 19 – Pop. 3 084 673 – alt. 646.

Paris (by Irún) 1310 – Barcelona 627 – Bilbao/Bilbo 397 – La Coruña/A Coruña 603 – Lisboa 653 – Málaga 548 – Porto 599 – Sevilla 550 – Valencia 351 – Zaragoza 322.

B Duque de Medinaceli 2, ⊠ 28014, ℰ (91) 429 49 51, Pl. Mayor 3, ⊠ 28012, ℰ (91) 588 16 36, Puerta de Toledo Market, ⊠ 28005, ℰ (91) 364 18 76, Chamartín Station, ⊠ 28036, ℰ (91) 315 99 76 and Madrid-Barajas airport ℰ (91) 305 86 56 – R.A.C.E. José Abascal 10, ⊠ 28003, ℰ (91) 447 32 00, Fax (91) 447 79 48.

[18] [18] Puerta de Hierro, North-west by Av. de la Victoria ℰ (91) 316 17 45 DU
[18] [18] [9] Club de Campo-Villa de Madrid, North-west by Av. de la Victoria ℰ (91) 357 21 32 DU
[18] [18] La Moraleja, North : 11 km by Pas. de la Castellana ℰ (91) 650 07 00 GR– [9] Club Barberán, South-west : 10 km by Av. de Portugal ℰ (91) 509 11 40 DX
[18] [9] Las Lomas – El Bosque, South-west : 18 km by Av. de Portugal and detour to Boadilla del Monte ℰ (91) 616 75 00 DX
[18] Real Automóvil Club de España, North : 28 km by Pas. de la Castellana ℰ (91) 657 00 11 GR
[18] Nuevo Club de Madrid, Las Matas, West : 26 km by Av. de la Victoria ℰ (91) 630 08 20 DU
[9] Somosaguas, West : 10 km Puente del Rey ℰ (91) 352 16 47 DX
[18] Club Olivar de la Hinojosa, North-east by Av. de América and detour to M 40 ℰ (91) 721 18 89 JT
[18] La Dehesa, Villanueva de la Cañada, West : 28 km by Av. de la Victoria and detour to El Escorial ℰ (91) 815 70 22 DU
[18] [18] Real Sociedad Hipica Española Club de Campo, North : 28 km by Pas. de la Castellana ℰ (91) 657 10 18 GR.
✈ Madrid-Barajas E : 13 km ℰ (91) 393 60 00 – Iberia : Velázquez 130, ⊠ 28006, ℰ (91) 587 87 87 HUV at airport, ⊠ 28042, ℰ (91) 587 42 77, and Aviaco, Maudes 51, ⊠ 28003, ⊠ 534 42 00 ET.
Chamartín 🚗 ℰ (91) 733 11 22 HR.

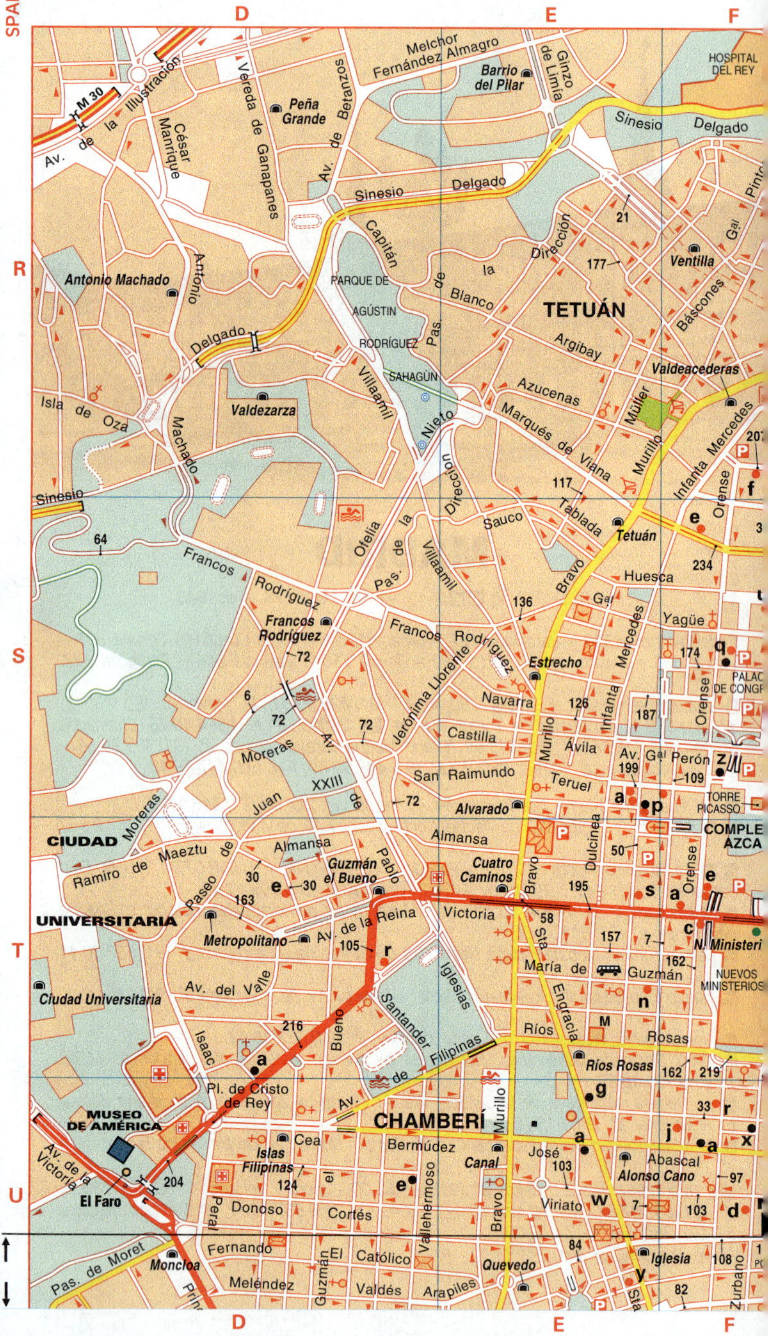

D · **E** · **F**

HOSPITAL DEL REY

Melchor Fernández Almagro

Barrio del Pilar

Ginzo de Limia

Sinesio Delgado

R

Peña Grande

Vereda de Ganapanes

César Manrique

Av. de la Ilustración

Av. de Betanzos

Sinesio Delgado

Antonio Machado

Antonio

Machado

Delgado

Isla de Oza

PARQUE DE AGÚSTIN RODRÍGUEZ SAHAGÚN

Capitán Blanco

Pas. de la Dirección

Villaamil

Nieto

la Dirección

TETUÁN

Ventilla

Báscones

Valdeacederas

21

177

Argibay

Azucenas

Marqués de Viana

Müller

Murillo

Infanta Mercedes

Orense

S

Sinesio

64

Francos Rodríguez

Valdezarza

Otelia

Pas.

de la

Villaamil

Dirección

Sauco

Tablada

Bravo

Huesca

Gal

Yagüe

117

Tetuán

234

136

Estrecho

Navarra

Castilla

Ávila

Infanta Mercedes

Murillo

Orense

174

187

PALAC DE CONGR

f

e

3

q

Francos Rodríguez

72

6

72

72

Moreras

Jerónima Llorente

Francos Rodríguez

San Raimundo

Teruel

Alvarado

Av. Gal Perón

199

126

109

TORRE PICASSO

z

a

p

COMPLE AZCA

CIUDAD

Ramiro de Maeztu

Moreras

Paseo de

Almansa

30

163

30

Guzmán el Bueno

Pablo

Almansa

Cuatro Caminos

Dulcinea

Bravo

50

195

e

s

a

e

UNIVERSITARIA

Metropolitano

Av. de la Reina

105

Victoria

58

157

7

162

c

N. Ministeri

NUEVOS MINISTERIOS

r

Ciudad Universitaria

Juan

XXIII

de

Av. del Valle

Isaac

216

Bueno

Santander

Iglesias

de Filipinas

María de

Sta.

Guzmán

Engracia

Ríos

M

n

T

a

Pl. de Cristo de Rey

MUSEO DE AMÉRICA

Av.

Murillo

CHAMBERÍ

Ríos Rosas

162

219

g

U

Av. de la Victoria

204

El Faro

Peral

Cea

Islas Filipinas

124

Donoso

Cortés

Bermúdez

Canal

Vallehermoso

José

103

Viriato

Bravo

Sta.

33

j

a

w

7

Abascal

Alonso Cano

97

103

r

x

a

d

Pas. de Moret

Moncloa

Prín

Fernando

Meléndez

Guzmán

El Católico

Valdés

Arapiles

Quevedo

84

Zurbano

Iglesia

108

82

v

D · **E** · **F**

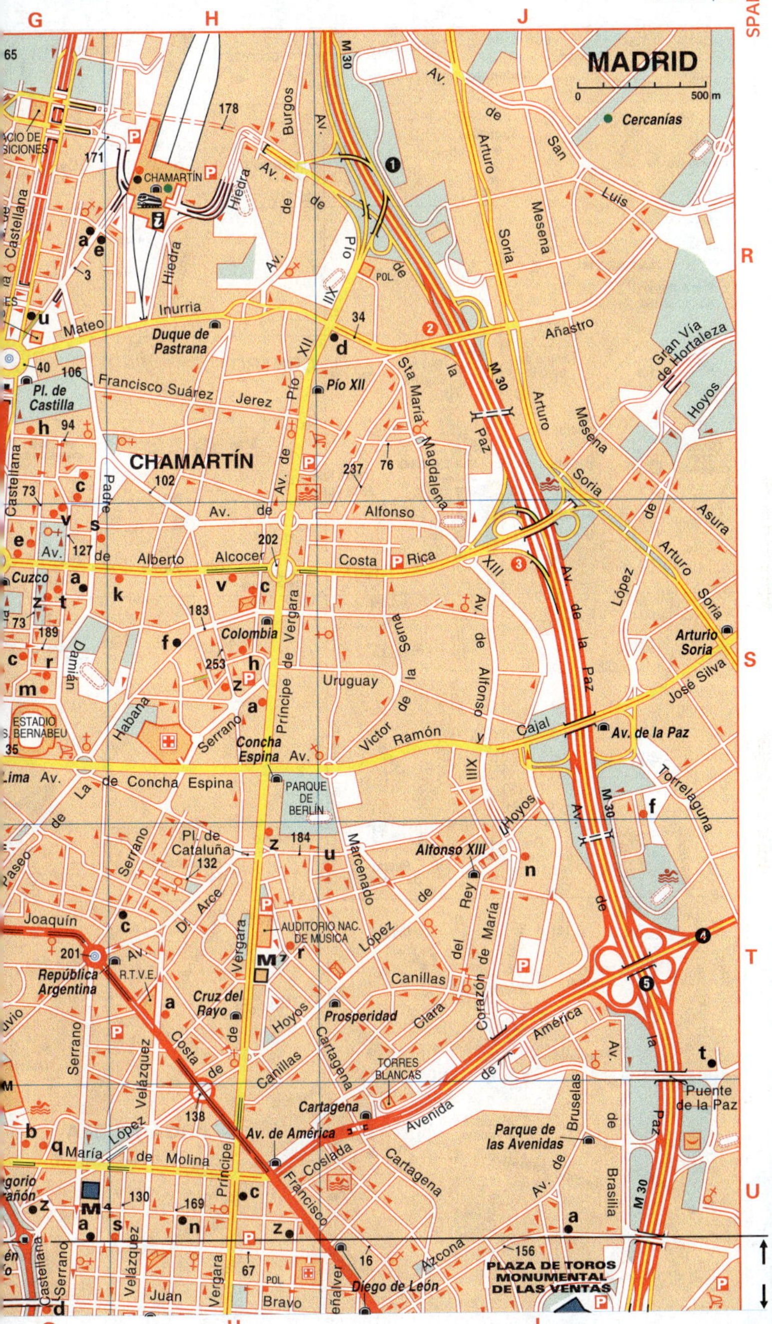

SPAIN
MADRID
0 500 m
Cercanías
G H J
R
S
T
U
65
ACIO DE
SICIONES
171
178
CHAMARTÍN
Hiedra
Burgos
Av. de
Av. de
Av. de
M 30
Av. de
Pío
POL.
XII
34
Mateo
Inurria
Duque de
Pastrana
40
106
Francisco Suárez
Jerez
Pío XII
Pío XII
Sta. María
Magdalena
d
Pl. de
Castilla
Castellana
h
94
CHAMARTÍN
102
73
c
Av. de
Alfonso
237
76
la
Paz
Arturo
Soria
Mesena
Mesena
San
Luis
Soria
Añastro
Gran Vía
de Hortaleza
Hoyos
Soria
de
Asura
Arturio
Soria
José Silva
v
s
e
Av.
127
de
Alberto
Alcocer
202
Costa
Rica
XIII
Arturo Soria
López
Cuzco
z
t
a
k
v
c
183
XIII
Av. de la Paz
73
189
Colombia
Damián
253
h
f
z
a
Uruguay
Príncipe de Vergara
Serrano
de
la
Serna
Av. de Alfonso y
Cajal
Av. de la Paz
f
ESTADIO
S BERNABEU
35
m
c
r
Habana
Concha
Espina
Serrano
Victor
Ramón
Av. de Alfonso
XIII
Torrelaguna
Lima
Av.
de
La
de Concha Espina
PARQUE
DE
BERLÍN
z
184
u
Marcenado
Alfonso XIII
Hoyos
Av.
M 30
de
Paseo
Serrano
Pl. de
Cataluña
132
de
del
Rey
n
Joaquín
c
Dr. Arce
AUDITORIO NAC.
DE MUSICA
López
Corazón de María
201
República
Argentina
R.T.V.E.
Av.
M
r
Vergara
Canillas
Clara
América
4
5
República
Argentina
a
Cruz del
Rayo
Hoyos
Prosperidad
Bruselas
t
uvio
Serrano
Costa
de
Canillas
Cartagena
TORRES
BLANCAS
Avenida
de
la
Puente
de la Paz
M
b
q
María
López
de Molina
de
Velázquez
138
Cartagena
Av. de América
Coslada
Cartagena
Parque de
las Avenidas
Brasilia
Paz
M 30
gorio
rañón
z
M
a
s
130
169
n
Príncipe
Francisco
c
z
Av.
a
en
s
Castellana
Serrano
Velázquez
Vergara
67
POL.
16
Azcona
Diego de León
Juan
Bravo
156
PLAZA DE TOROS
MONUMENTAL
DE LAS VENTAS
G H J
1 2 3 4 5

D
E
F
Fernando
Moncloa
Quevedo
Iglesia
84
108
Pas. de Moret
Meléndez
Guzmán El Católico
Valdés
Arapiles
82
y
Zurbano
Pas. del Pintor
Princesa
Argüelles
Alberto
Aguilera
b
San Bernardo
e
Bilbao
k
c
PARQUE
Ferraz
150
P
Z
c
208
Carranza
v
v
p
Luchana
Caracas
DEL
Princesa
Carranza
166
Sagasta
Almagro
V
OESTE
TELEFÉRICO
POL
Bernardo
Fuencarral
Génova
La Rosaleda
San Antonio
de la Florida
Ferraz
Rosales
M
Pl. de
España
Gran
San
CENTRO
Hortaleza
Templo de
Debod
Vía
15
100
Vicente
Torija
Gran
Gran Vía
PL. DE
CIBELES
M 30
Príncipe Pío
PALACIO
REAL
Teatro Real
de la Opera
Vía
Montera
147
Cuesta de S.
CASA
DE
CAMPO
18
M 1
Bailén
Arenal
Alcalá
M
PASEO
Puente
del Rey
CAMPO
DEL
MORO
Mayor
Pl. de la
Puerta del Sol
M
Av.
de
Portugal
PLAZA
MAYOR
Prado
DEL
Pte de
Segovia
Segovia
H
Huertas
MUSEO
DEL PRADO
93
Segovia
Segovia
Toledo
Atocha
PRADO
M 30
258
Ronda
Bailén
Gran Vía de
S. Francisco
Toledo
Ribera
Lavapiés
Sta Isabel
Atocha
Y
Av.
del Santo
Pas.
de
Segovia
de
Embajadores
de Curtidores
CASINO
DE LA REINA
242
22
Pas. de los Melancólicos
Gta de Puerta
de Toledo
P
Z
V
Puerta
de Toledo
Embajadores
85
243
Pas. de la Ermita del Manzanares
Puente de
San Isidro
181
181
Imperial
Toledo
Pirámides
las
Acacias
Acacias
235
87
172
n
Palos de
la Frontera
r
de
Pas. del Dr. Vallejo
Nágera
Ferrocarril
ESTADIO
V. CALDERÓN
Pirámides
Pas.
Pas.
de
87
228
Delicias
Pas. del Manzanares
15
PARQUE
DE LA
ARGANZUELA
Yeserías
Av.
María
e
Z
Pas. del Quince de Mayo
Marqués
de Vadillo
Antonio
M 30
2
ARGANZUELA
121
28
General Ricardos
Jacinto Verdaguer
Av.
14
u
López
v
P
Manzanares
Pas.
Urgel
Mercedes Arteaga
Antonio Leyva
Pas. de Santa
López
PALACIO
DE CRISTAL
Legazp
Embajadores
de las
Pl. de
Legaz
0   500 m
240
Manzanares
D
E
F

G
H
J
PLAZA DE TOROS
MONUMENTAL
DE LAS VENTAS
156
16
Azcona
Diego de León
Peñalver
67
POL.
Vergara
Velázquez
Juan
Serrano
Castellana
El Carmen
Alcalá
P
d
w
r
m
t
N. de Balboa
Bravo
Av. de los
Toreros
129
Ventas
63
6
48
130
f
169
de
Lista
t
Ventas
V
y
José
Ortega
148
e
y
SALAMANCA
Gasset
75
Pl. de Manuel
Becerra
Alcalá
Ayala
75
N. de Balboa
Ayala
4
POL.
Manuel Becerra
Hermosilla
151
Parque de la
Quinta
Fuente del Berro
u
k
Hermosilla
Conde
Alcalá
Serrano
Goya
Velázquez
Goya
P
PALACIO
DE LOS
DEPORTES
Paz
48
Jorge
Goya
Juan
g
Goya
210
Jorge Juan
O'Donnell
v
h
130
P
e
Alcalá
Jorge
x
Juan
Esguerra
TORRE
ESPAÑA
Baranda
t
d
P. de
Vergara
96
O'Donnell
R.T.V.E.
W
O'Donnell
70
X
UERTA
ALCALÁ
Retiro
Av. Menéndez
Ibiza
Ibiza
de
Sáinz
Juan Esplandiú
4
7
Alfonso
Estanque
s
Alcalde
PARQUE
DE
ROMA
XII
EL PARTERRE
Alfonso XII
POL.
Sáinz
de Baranda
M
PARQUE
DEL BUEN RETIRO
Pelayo
69
RETIRO
Alfonso
XII
Palacio
de Cristal
180
x
175
55
LA CHOPERA
de Nazaret
Astros
90
37
Av.
Doctor
Estrella
Y
OBSERVATORIO
ASTRONÓMICO
90
55
19
Pl. de Mariano
de Cavia
Pl. Corregidor
Alonso de Aguilar
Pelayo
Conde de Casal
Pl. Conde
de Casal
Atocha Renfe
198
a
Avenida
a
del
A 3
PANTEÓN
Cavanilles
Esguerdo
P
9
3
Mediterráneo
TOCHA
Av.
de
Menéndez
Pelayo
Valderribas
Doctor
la
Ciudad
Valderribas
Camino
Comercio
la
Bosch
de
Pacífico
139
de
Sierra
Toledana
Barcelona
Valderribas
Álvaro
10
P.º de Vallecas
193
ustamante
Méndez
Pedro
Z
ARQUE
Méndez
Álvaro
Méndez
Álvaro
155
Nueva Numancia
DE LAS
P
de
la
DELICIAS
M
Iguelda
155
Arroyo del Olivar
Albufera
Portazgo
P
PLANETARIO
CINE IMAX
11
Av. de la Paz
Monte
Monte
Perdido
155
POL.
var
G
H
J
Z

K L

MALASAÑA

Princesa

Montserrat

Divino

a

Glorieta
de Bilbao

Bilbao

Sagas

Pl. Dos
de Mayo

Pastor

159

Apodaca

Barceló

t Palacio de Liria

Conde Duque

Amaniel

Palma

Bernardo

Palma

Espíritu

Santo

Tribunal

M

San Mateo

V

d

250

Princesa

211

Noviciado

San

Pez

de San Pablo

2

TORRE
DE MADRID

Ferraz

EDIFICIO
ESPAÑA

Reyes

Luna

123

Madera

Colón

MUSEO
CERRALBO

s

r

u **f** **z**

POL

Pizarro

Pez

Baja

T

246

24

Plaza
de España

Río

v

Leganitos

c

Gran Vía

g

Corredera

Barco

Puebla

Fuencarral

Hortaleza

Cuesta
de San Vicente

y

T

n

133

238

Jardines de
Sabatini

Bailén

Torija

Santo Domingo

a

e **e** Gran Vía

Gran Vía

Infantas

X

r

Bola

k

231

z

36

Callao

q

T

p

256

Jardines

PALACIO REAL

LA ENCARNACIÓN

18

Teatro Real
de la Opera

LAS DESCALZAS
REALES

v

Carmen

c

P

Montera

M²

v

Pl. de la
Armería

h

Pl. de
Oriente

Pl. de
Isabel II

f

186

Alcalá

232

Pl. del
Canal

W

252

Ópera

Arenal

Sol

218

u

Catedral
N. S. de la Almuneda

e

g

115

r

Mayor

Pl. de la
Puerta del Sol

88

Cruz

T

168

9

8

Mayor

31

POL

Carretas

s

Y

PL. DE LA
VILLA

c

45

**PLAZA
MAYOR**

Pl. de
la Provincia

P

T

Bailén

H

m

d

Pl. J.
Benavente

Atocha

Huertas

Sacramento

Arco de
Cuchilleros

S. MIGUEL

n

z

60

52

53

T

54

San Pedro

190

220

Jardines

de las

Pl. de la
Paja

Capilla
del Obispo

c

v S. Isidro

Colegiata

Magdalena

Antón M

Vistillas

43

Toledo

Pl. de Tirso
de Molina

Jesús

María

Lavapiés

Olivar

y

42

91

78

Ave

María

Don Pedro

e

192

T

La Latina

225

Mesón

de

a

San Francisco
el Grande

Pl. de
Cascorro

Paredes

N

214

Pl. de la
Cebada

Ribera de Curtidores

Embajadores

Calatrava

112

Gran Vía de
San Francisco

Toledo

el Rastro

Lavapiés

Argum

Valencia

T

0 200 m

● Cercanías

K L

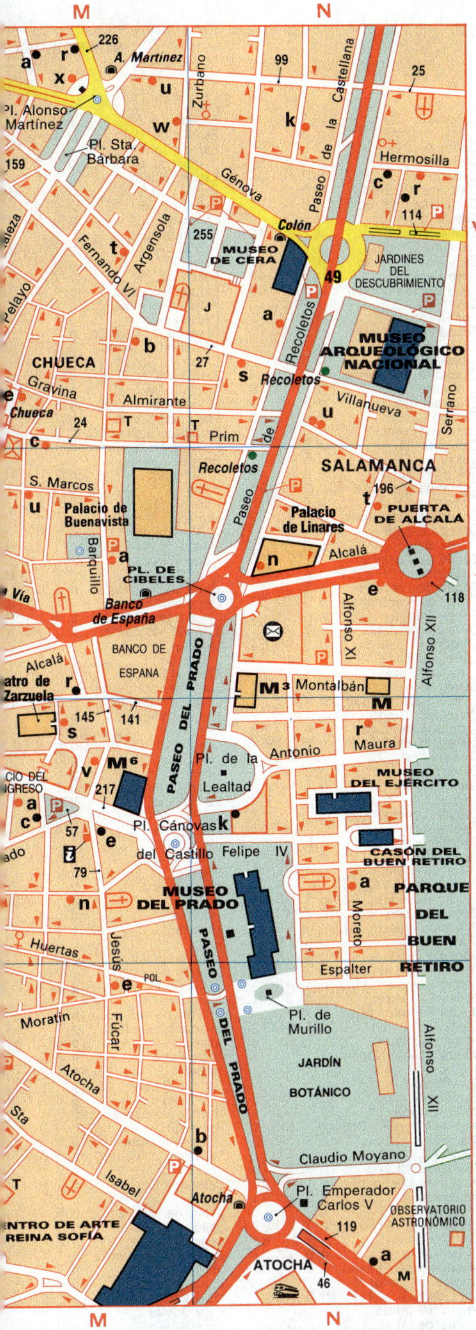

MADRID

Alcalá	MX	
Alvarez Gato	LY	9
Arenal	KY	
Arrieta	KX	18
Augusto Figueroa	MV	24
Ayala	NV	25
Bárbara de Braganza	NV	27
Bordadores	KY	31
Callao (Pl. del)	LX	36
Carmen	LX	
Cava Alta	KZ	42
Cava Baja	KZ	43
Cava de San Miguel	KY	45
Ciudad de Barcelona (Av. de la)	NZ	46
Colón (Pl. de)	NV	49
Concepción Jerónima	LY	52
Conde de Romanones	LY	53
Cordón (Pl. del)	KY	54
Cortes (Pl. de las)	MY	57
Cuchilleros	KY	60
Duque de Alba	LZ	78
Duque de Medinaceli	MY	79
Echegaray	LY	81
Espoz y Mina	LY	88
Estudios	KZ	91
Felipe IV	NY	
Fernando el Santo	NV	99
Fuencarral	LV	
General Vara del Rey (Pl. del)	KZ	112
Goya	NV	114
Gran Vía	LX	
Herradores (Pl. de los)	KY	115
Hortaleza	LX	
Independencia (Pl. de la)	NX	118
Infanta Isabel (Pas. de la)	NZ	119
Jesús del Valle	LV	123
Libreros	KX	133
Madrazo	MY	141
Marqués de Cubas	MY	145
Mayor	KY	
Mayor (Pl.)	KY	
Mejía Lequerica	LMV	159
Montera	LX	
Núñez de Arce	LY	168
Preciados	LX	186
Puerta Cerrada (Pl. de)	KY	190
Puerta de Moros (Pl. de)	KZ	192
Puerta del Sol (Pl. de la)	LY	
Recoletos	NX	196
San Bernardino	KV	211
San Francisco (Carrera de)	KZ	214
San Jerónimo (Carrera de)	LMY	218
San Justo	KY	220
San Lorenzo	LV	222
San Millán	KZ	225
Santa Engracia	MV	226
Santo Domingo (Cuesta, Pl. de)	KX	231
Sevilla	LY	232
Tudescos	LX	238
Valverde	LV	246
Ventura de la Vega	LY	249
Ventura Rodríguez	KV	250
Vergara	KY	252
Villa de París (Pl. de la)	NV	255
Virgen de los Peligros	LX	256

Michelin
pone sus mapas
constantemente al día.
Llévelos en su coche
y no tendrá Vd. sorpresas
desagradables
en carretera.

MADRID TOWN PLAN

SIGHTS

VIEW OVER MADRID

Moncloa Beacon (Faro de Moncloa): ☀︎★★ DU

MUSEUMS

Prado-Museum★★★ NY – *Thyssen Bornemisza Museum*★★★ MY **M⁶** – *Royal Palace*★★ *(Palacio Real)* KX *(Palace*★*; Throne Room*★*; Royal Armoury*★★*; Royal Carriage Museum*★ DX **M¹**) – *National Archaeological Museum*★★ *(Dama de Elche*★★★*)* NV – *Lázaro Galdiano Museum*★★ *(collection of enamels and ivories*★★★*)* GU **M⁴** – *Casón del Buen Retiro*★ *(annexe to the Prado)* NY – *Reina Sofia Art Museum*★ *(Picasso's Guernica*★★★*)* MZ – *Army Museum*★ *(Museo del Ejército)* NY – *Museum of the Americas*★ *(Museo de América; Treasure of Los Quimbayas*★*, Cortesano Manuscript*★★★*)*, DU – *San Fernando Royal Fine Arts Academy*★ *(Real Academia de Bellas Artes de San Fernando)* LX **M²** – *Cerralbo Museum*★ KV – *Sorolla Museum*★ FU **M⁵** – *City Museum (Museo de la Ciudad Models*★*)* HUT **M⁷** – *Waxworks Museum* ★ *(Museo de Cera)* NV – *Naval Museum (ship models*★*, map of Juan de la Cosa*★★*)* NXY **M³**

CHURCHES AND MONASTERIES

Descalzas Reales Monastery★★ KLX – *San Francisco el Grande Church (stall*★ *in chancel and sacristy)* KZ – *Royal Convent of the Incarnation*★ *(Real Monasterio de la Encarnatión)* KX – *San Antonio de la Florida Chapel (frescoes*★★*)* DV – *Sant Michael Church*★ KY

THE OLD TOWN

Eastern Quarter★★ *(Barrio de Oriente)* KVXY – *Bourbon Madrid*★★ MNXYZ – *Old Madrid*★ KYZ

PLACES OF INTEREST

Plaza Mayor★★ KY – *Buen Retiro Park*★★ HY – *Zoo*★★ *West : by Casa de Campo Park*★ DX – *Plaza de la Villa*★ KY – *Vistillas Gardens (*☀︎*)* KYZ – *Campo del Moro Winter Garden*★ DX – *University City*★ *(Ciudad Universitaria)* DT – *Plaza de Cibeles*★ MNX – *Paseo del Prado*★ MNXYZ – *Alcalá Arch*★ *(Puerta de Alcalá)* NX – *Bullring*★ *(Plaza Monumental de las Ventas)* JUV – *West Park*★ *(Parque del Oeste)* DV

Centre : Paseo del Prado, Puerta del Sol, Gran Vía, Alcalá, Paseo de Recoletos, Plaza Mayor

Palace, pl. de las Cortes 7, ⊠ 28014, ℘ (91) 360 80 00, *Fax (91) 360 81 00* – 📶 🚇 📺 ☎ 🕭 🚗 – 🛎 25/450. AE ⑩ E VISA JCB. ⋘ rest — MY e
La Cupola (dinner only closed Sunday, Monday and August) **Meals** a la carte 4900/6300 – ⊇ 3100 – **400 rm** 65000/72000, 40 suites.

Husa Princesa, Princesa 40, ⊠ 28008, ℘ (91) 542 21 00, *Fax (91) 542 73 28*, 📳, ▨ – 📶 🚇 📺 ☎ 🕭 🚗 – 🛎 25/825. AE ⑩ E VISA JCB. ⋘ — DV z
Meals 2900 – ⊇ 2150 – **263 rm** 28100/34250, 12 suites.

Villa Real, pl. de las Cortes 10, ⊠ 28014, ℘ (91) 420 37 67, *Fax (91) 420 25 47*, « Tasteful decor » – 📶 🚇 📺 ☎ 🚗 – 🛎 35/100. AE ⑩ E VISA JCB. ⋘ rest — MY c
Meals a la carte 5300/5850 – ⊇ 2000 – **96 rm** 26400/33000, 19 suites.

Crowne Plaza, pl. de España, ⊠ 28013, ℘ (91) 547 12 00, *Fax (91) 548 23 89*, ≤, 📳 – 📶 🚇 📺 ☎ 🕭 – 🛎 25/350. AE ⑩ E VISA JCB. ⋘ — KV s
Meals 4400 – ⊇ 1925 – **295 rm** 21200/24400, 11 suites.

Tryp Ambassador, Cuesta de Santo Domingo 5, ⊠ 28013, ℘ (91) 541 67 00, *Fax (91) 559 10 40* – 📶 🚇 📺 ☎ – 🛎 25/280. AE ⑩ E VISA JCB. ⋘ — KX k
Meals a la carte 3600/5000 – ⊇ 1650 – **163 rm** 20000/25000, 18 suites.

NH Nacional, paseo del Prado 48, ⊠ 28014, ℘ (91) 429 66 29, *Fax (91) 369 15 64* – 📶 🚇 📺 ☎ 🕭 🚗 – 🛎 25/200. AE ⑩ E VISA JCB. ⋘ — NZ r
Meals 2000 – ⊇ 1800 – **214 rm** 18500/22000, 1 suite.

Liabeny, Salud 3, ⊠ 28013, ℘ (91) 531 90 00, *Fax (91) 532 74 21* – 📶 🚇 📺 ☎ 🚗 – 🛎 25/125. AE ⑩ E VISA. ⋘ — LX c
Meals 3000 – ⊇ 1600 – **222 rm** 11200/15400.

Moncloa Garden without rest, Serrano Jover 1, ⊠ 28015, ℘ (91) 542 45 82, *Fax (91) 542 71 69* – 📶 🚇 📺 ☎ – 🛎 25/80. AE ⑩ E VISA JCB. ⋘ — DV c
⊇ 1000 – **103 rm** 14900/17100, 20 suites.

Emperador without rest, Gran Vía 53, ⊠ 28013, ℘ (91) 547 28 00, *Fax (91) 547 28 17*, 📳, ▨ – 📶 🚇 📺 ☎ – 🛎 25/150. AE ⑩ E VISA JCB — KX n
⊇ 1950 – **232 rm** 18700/23400.

Arosa coffee shop only, Salud 21, ⊠ 28013, ℘ (91) 532 16 00, *Telex 43618, Fax (91) 531 31 27* – 📶 🚇 📺 ☎ 🚗 – 🛎 25/60. AE ⑩ E VISA JCB — LX q
⊇ 1350 – **139 rm** 13750/21250.

Santo Domingo, pl. de Santo Domingo 13, ⊠ 28013, ℘ (91) 547 98 00, *Fax (91) 547 59 95* – 📶 🚇 📺 ☎ – 🛎 25/60. AE ⑩ E VISA JCB. ⋘ — KX a
Meals 3850 – ⊇ 1450 – **120 rm** 16925/24625.

Mayorazgo, Flor Baja 3, ⊠ 28013, ℘ (91) 547 26 00, *Fax (91) 541 24 85* – 📶 🚇 📺 ☎ 🚗 – 🛎 25/250. AE ⑩ E VISA JCB. ⋘ — KV c
Meals a la carte 2925/4125 – ⊇ 1300 – **200 rm** 13750/18000.

Gaudí, Gran Vía 9, ⊠ 28013, ℘ (91) 531 22 22, *Fax (91) 531 54 69*, 📳 – 📶 🚇 📺 ☎ – 🛎 25/120. AE ⑩ E VISA JCB. ⋘ — LX s
Meals 2500 – ⊇ 1500 – **88 rm** 20000/24000.

G.H. Reina Victoria, pl. de Santa Ana 14, ⊠ 28012, ℘ (91) 531 45 00, *Fax (91) 522 03 07* – 📶 🚇 📺 ☎ 🚗 – 🛎 25/350. AE ⑩ E VISA JCB. ⋘ — LY s
Meals 4800 – ⊇ 1800 – **195 rm** 21000/26250, 6 suites.

El Coloso, Leganitos 13, ⊠ 28013, ℘ (91) 559 76 00, *Fax (91) 547 49 68* – 📶 🚇 📺 ☎ 🚗 – 🛎 25/200. AE ⑩ E VISA JCB. ⋘ — KX y
Meals 1975 – ⊇ 1500 – **84 rm** 18975/22860.

Suecia, Marqués de Casa Riera 4, ⊠ 28014, ℘ (91) 531 69 00, *Fax (91) 521 71 41* – 📶 🚇 📺 ☎ – 🛎 25/150. AE ⑩ E VISA JCB. ⋘ — MX r
Meals 3500 – ⊇ 1500 – **119 rm** 19200/24200, 9 suites.

Tryp Menfis, Gran Vía 74, ⊠ 28013, ℘ (91) 547 09 00, *Fax (91) 547 51 99* – 📶 🚇 📺 ☎. AE ⑩ E VISA JCB. ⋘ — KV u
Meals 1800 – ⊇ 1300 – **116 rm** 16275/20475.

Atlántico without rest, Gran Vía 38-1°, ⊠ 28013, ℘ (91) 522 64 80, *Fax (91) 531 02 10* – 📶 🚇 📺 ☎. AE ⑩ E VISA JCB. ⋘ — LX e
⊇ 850 – **81 rm** 11100/14670.

Regina without rest, Alcalá 19, ⊠ 28014, ℘ (91) 521 47 25, *Telex 27500, Fax (91) 522 40 88* – 📶 🚇 📺 ☎. AE ⑩ E VISA. ⋘ — LX v
142 rm ⊇ 9950/14400.

Casón del Tormes without rest, Río 7, ⊠ 28013, ℘ (91) 541 97 46, *Fax (91) 541 18 52* – 📶 🚇 📺 ☎. E VISA. ⋘ — KV v
⊇ 690 – **63 rm** 10200/14000.

El Prado without rest, Prado 11, ⊠ 28014, ℘ (91) 369 02 34, *Fax (91) 429 28 29* – 📶 🚇 📺 ☎ – 🛎 25/50. AE ⑩ E VISA JCB — LY a
⊇ 500 – **47 rm** 15600/19700.

Mercator coffee shop only, Atocha 123, ⊠ 28012, ℘ (91) 429 05 0
Fax (91) 369 12 52 – 🛗 📺 ☎ 🅿. 🄰🄴 🕪 ℂ *VISA*. 🛇
☕ 800 – **89 rm** 8800/12300.
NZ

Carlos V without rest, Maestro Vitoria 5, ⊠ 28013, ℘ (91) 531 41 0
Fax (91) 531 37 61 – 🛗 🖿 📺 ☎. 🄰🄴 🕪 ℂ *VISA* 🄹🄲🄱. 🛇
67 rm ☕ 11570/14565.
LX

Tryp Washington, Gran Vía 72, ⊠ 28013, ℘ (91) 541 72 27, *Telex 4877*
Fax (91) 547 51 99 – 🛗 🖿 📺 ☎. 🄰🄴 🕪 ℂ *VISA* 🄹🄲🄱. 🛇
Meals (at Hotel *Tryp Menfis*) – ☕ 1100 – **120 rm** 13675/17150.
KV

Los Condes without rest, Los Libreros 7, ⊠ 28004, ℘ (91) 521 54 5
Fax (91) 521 78 82 – 🛗 🖿 📺 ☎. 🄰🄴 🕪 ℂ *VISA* 🄹🄲🄱. 🛇
☕ 650 – **68 rm** 7850/10990.
KLV

California without rest, Gran Vía 38, ⊠ 28013, ℘ (91) 522 47 03, *Fax (91) 531 61 0*
– 🛗 🖿 📺 ☎. 🄰🄴 🕪 ℂ *VISA*. 🛇
☕ 485 – **26 rm** 8200/10500.
LX

Alexandra without rest, San Bernardo 29, ⊠ 28015, ℘ (91) 542 04 0
Fax (91) 559 28 25 – 🛗 🖿 📺 ☎. 🄰🄴 🕪 ℂ *VISA* 🄹🄲🄱. 🛇
☕ 855 – **68 rm** 9600/12000.
KV

XXX **Teatro Real,** Felipe V-2º, ⊠ 28013, ℘ (91) 516 06 70, *Fax (91) 559 96 29*, « With
the Teatro Real » – 🖿. 🄰🄴 🕪 ℂ *VISA*. 🛇
closed Monday and August – **Meals** - dinner only - a la carte 5400/6450.
KX

XXX **San Carlo,** Barquillo 10, ⊠ 28004, ℘ (91) 522 79 88, *Fax (91) 522 73 01*, « Tastef
decor » – 🖿. 🄰🄴 🕪 ℂ *VISA* 🄹🄲🄱. 🛇
Meals - Italian rest - a la carte 3800/5700.
MX

XXX **Paradis Madrid,** Marqués de Cubas 14, ⊠ 28014, ℘ (91) 429 73 0
Fax (91) 429 32 95 – 🖿. 🄰🄴 🕪 ℂ *VISA*. 🛇
closed Saturday lunch, Sunday and August – **Meals** a la carte 4725/6300.
MY

XXX **El Landó,** pl. Gabriel Miró 8, ⊠ 28005, ℘ (91) 366 76 81, *Fax (91) 366 76 81*, « Tastef
decor » – 🖿. 🄰🄴 🕪 ℂ *VISA*. 🛇
closed Sunday, Bank Holidays and August – **Meals** a la carte 4200/6500.
KZ

XXX **Moaña,** Hileras 4, ⊠ 28013, ℘ (91) 548 29 14, *Fax (91) 541 65 98* – 🖿 🚗. 🄰🄴
ℂ *VISA* 🄹🄲🄱. 🛇
closed Sunday dinner – **Meals** - Galician rest - a la carte 4140/5600.
KY

XXX **Bajamar,** Gran Vía 78, ⊠ 28013, ℘ (91) 548 48 18, *Fax (91) 559 13 26* – 🖿. 🄰🄴
ℂ *VISA* 🄹🄲🄱. 🛇
Meals - Seafood - a la carte 4600/7100.
KV

XX **El Espejo,** paseo de Recoletos 31, ⊠ 28004, ℘ (91) 308 23 47, *Fax (91) 593 22 2*
« Old Parisian style café » – 🖿. 🄰🄴 ℂ *VISA*. 🛇
closed Saturday lunch – **Meals** a la carte approx. 2850.
NV

XX **Errota-Zar,** Jovellanos 3-1º, ⊠ 28014, ℘ (91) 531 25 64, *Fax (91) 531 25 64* – 🖿. 🄰
🕪 ℂ *VISA*
closed Sunday and 10 to 16 August – **Meals** a la carte 4300/6200.
MY

XX **Ainhoa,** Bárbara de Braganza 12, ⊠ 28004, ℘ (91) 308 27 26 – 🖿. 🄰🄴 ℂ *VISA*. 🛇
closed Sunday and August – **Meals** - Basque rest - a la carte 4800/5900.
NV

XX **Café de Oriente,** pl. de Oriente 2, ⊠ 28013, ℘ (91) 541 39 74, *Fax (91) 547 77 0*
« In a bodega » – 🖿. 🄰🄴 🕪 ℂ *VISA*. 🛇
Meals a la carte 4900/6050.
KXY

XX **La Gastroteca de Stéphane y Arturo,** pl. de Chueca 8, ⊠ 28004, ℘ (91
532 25 64 – 🖿. 🄰🄴 🕪 ℂ *VISA*. 🛇
closed Saturday lunch, Bank Holidays and August – **Meals** - French rest - a la cart
5500/6500.
MV

XX **El Asador de Aranda,** Preciados 44, ⊠ 28013, ℘ (91) 547 21 56, *Fax (91) 556 62 0*
« Castilian decor » – 🖿. 🄰🄴 🕪 ℂ *VISA* 🄹🄲🄱. 🛇
closed Monday dinner and 21 July-12 August – **Meals** - Roast lamb - a la carte appro
4000.
KX

XX **Arce,** Augusto Figueroa 32, ⊠ 28004, ℘ (91) 522 04 40, *Fax (91) 522 59 13* – 🖿. 🄰
🕪 ℂ *VISA*. 🛇
closed Saturday lunch, Sunday, Holy Week and 15 to 31 August – **Meals** a la cart
5930/6840.
MV

XX **El Mentidero de la Villa,** Santo Tomé 6, ⊠ 28004, ℘ (91) 308 12 85
Fax (91) 319 87 92, « Original decor » – 🖿. 🄰🄴 🕪 ℂ *VISA* 🄹🄲🄱. 🛇
closed Saturday lunch, Sunday and 15 to 31 August – **Meals** a la carte 3650/5200.
MV

XX **Julián de Tolosa,** Cava Baja 18, ⊠ 28005, ℘ (91) 365 82 10, « Neorustic decor »
🖿. 🄰🄴 🕪 ℂ *VISA*
closed Sunday – **Meals** - Braised meat specialities - a la carte 4200/5100.
KZ

XX **Casa Gallega,** pl. de San Miguel 8, ⊠ 28005, ℘ (91) 547 30 55 – 🗐. AE ① E *VISA* JCB. ⪢
KY c
Meals - Galician rest - a la carte 3650/5600.

XX **La Ópera de Madrid,** Amnistía 5, ⊠ 28013, ℘ (91) 559 50 92, Fax (91) 559 50 92,
« Welcoming ambience » – 🗐. AE ① E *VISA* JCB. ⪢
KY g
closed Sunday and August – **Meals** a la carte 3125/4175.

XX **Casa Parrondo,** Trujillos 4, ⊠ 28013, ℘ (91) 522 62 34 – 🗐. AE ① E *VISA* JCB. ⪢
KX v
Meals - Asturian rest - a la carte 4000/8000.

XX **El Rincón de Esteban,** Santa Catalina 3, ⊠ 28014, ℘ (91) 429 92 89,
Fax (91) 365 87 70 – 🗐. AE ① E *VISA* JCB. ⪢
MY a
closed Sunday and 15 to 31 August – **Meals** a la carte 4700/6500.

X **La Barraca,** Reina 29, ⊠ 28004, ℘ (91) 532 71 54, Fax (91) 521 58 96 – 🗐. AE ①
E *VISA* JCB. ⪢
LX a
Meals - Rice dishes - a la carte 3475/4250.

X **Robata,** Reina 31, ⊠ 28004, ℘ (91) 521 85 28, Fax (91) 531 30 63 – 🗐. AE ① *VISA*
JCB. ⪢
LX a
closed Tuesday – **Meals** - Japanese rest - a la carte 4100/5100.

X **La Vaca Verónica,** Moratín 38, ⊠ 28014, ℘ (91) 429 78 27 – 🗐. AE ① E
VISA JCB
MZ e
closed Saturday lunch and Sunday – **Meals** a la carte 3550/4150.

X **Casa Vallejo,** San Lorenzo 9 ℘ (91) 308 61 58 – 🗐. E *VISA* JCB. ⪢
LV f
closed Sunday, Monday dinner, Bank Holidays and August – **Meals** a la carte 2600/
3550.

X **Ciao Madrid,** Argensola 7, ⊠ 28004, ℘ (91) 308 25 19 – 🗐. AE ① E
VISA JCB
MV t
closed Saturday lunch, Sunday and August – **Meals** - Italian rest - a la carte 2600/
3950.

X **La Bola,** Bola 5, ⊠ 28013, ℘ (91) 547 69 30, Fax (91) 547 04 63 – 🗐. ⪢
KX r
closed Saturday dinner (July-August) and Sunday – **Meals** - Madrid style stew - a la carte
3700/4400.

X **Taberna Carmencita,** Libertad 16, ⊠ 28004, ℘ (91) 531 66 12, « Typical taverna »
– 🗐. AE ① E *VISA* JCB. ⪢
MX u
closed Saturday lunch and Sunday – **Meals** a la carte 3000/4400.

X **Donzoko,** Echegaray 3, ⊠ 28014, ℘ (91) 429 57 20, Fax (91) 429 57 20 – 🗐. AE ①
E *VISA* JCB. ⪢
LY z
closed Sunday – **Meals** - Japanese rest - a la carte 2950/5100.

X **La Esquina del Real,** Amnistía 2, ⊠ 28013, ℘ (91) 559 43 09 – 🗐. AE E *VISA*. ⪢
KY e
closed Saturday lunch, Sunday and August – **Meals** a la carte 4675/6050.

X **Ciao Madrid,** Apodaca 20, ⊠ 28004, ℘ (91) 447 00 36 – 🗐. AE ①
VISA. ⪢
LV d
closed Saturday lunch, Sunday and September – **Meals** - Italian rest - a la carte 2950/4200.

X **El Ingenio,** Leganitos 10, ⊠ 28013, ℘ (91) 541 91 33, Fax (91) 547 35 34 – 🗐. AE ①
E *VISA* JCB. ⪢
KX y
closed Sunday and Bank Holidays – **Meals** a la carte 2500/3250.

Typical atmosphere :

XX **Posada de la Villa,** Cava Baja 9, ⊠ 28005, ℘ (91) 366 18 60, Fax (91) 366 18 80,
« Castilian decor » – 🗐. ① E *VISA*. ⪢
KZ v
closed Sunday dinner and August – **Meals** a la carte 3375/4875.

XX **Botín,** Cuchilleros 17, ⊠ 28005, ℘ (91) 366 42 17, Fax (91) 366 84 94, « Old Madrid
decor. typical bodega » – 🗐. AE ① E *VISA* JCB. ⪢
KY n
Meals a la carte 4160/6100.

X **Casa Lucio,** Cava Baja 35, ⊠ 28005, ℘ (91) 365 32 52, Fax (91) 366 48 66, « Castilian
decor » – 🗐. AE ① *VISA*. ⪢
KZ y
closed Saturday lunch and August – **Meals** a la carte 4900/6000.

X **Las Cuevas de Luis Candelas,** Cuchilleros 1, ⊠ 28005, ℘ (91) 366 54 28,
Fax (91) 366 49 37, « Old Madrid decor. staff in bandit costumes » – 🗐. ① E *VISA*. ⪢
KY m
Meals a la carte 3375/5325.

X **Zerain,** Quevedo 3, ⊠ 28014, ℘ (91) 429 79 09, Fax (91) 429 17 20, Basque cider press
– 🗐. AE ① E *VISA*. ⪢
MY x
closed Sunday and August – **Meals** a la carte 3300/4500.

X **Taberna del Alabardero,** Felipe V-6, ⊠ 28013, ℘ (91) 547 25 77,
Fax (91) 547 77 07, « Typical taverna » – 🗐. AE ① E *VISA* JCB. ⪢
KX h
Meals - Basque rest - a la carte 4100/4850.

Retiro, Salamanca, Ciudad Lineal : Paseo de la Castellana, Velázquez, Serrano, Goy
Príncipe de Vergara, Narváez, Don Ramón de la Cruz

Ritz, pl. de la Lealtad 5, ⊠ 28014, ℰ (91) 521 28 57, Fax (91) 532 87 76, 佘, ⅃ઠ –
▤ TV ☎ – 諡 25/280. AE ① E VISA JCB. ⅙ rest
Meals a la carte approx. 6750 – ⍁ 3500 – **130 rm** 49000/60900, 29 suites.
NY

Villa Magna, paseo de la Castellana 22, ⊠ 28046, ℰ (91) 587 12 34, Fax (91) 431 22 8
, ⅃ઠ – ៛ ▤ TV ☎ ⇌ – 諡 25/250. AE ① E VISA JCB. ⅙
Meals 5000 - **Le Divellec :** Meals a la carte 6300/8100 - **Tsé Yang** (Chinese rest) Mea
a la carte 4400/6200 – ⍁ 3100 – **164 rm** 55000/60000, 18 suites.
GV

Wellington, Velázquez 8, ⊠ 28001, ℰ (91) 575 44 00, Telex 2270
Fax (91) 576 41 64, ⍅ – ៛ ▤ TV ☎ ⇌ – 諡 25/300. AE ① E VIS
JCB. ⅙
Meals (see rest. **El Fogón** below) – ⍁ 2200 – **198 rm** 29000/36250, 25 suites.
HX

Meliá Confort Los Galgos, Claudio Coello 139, ⊠ 28006, ℰ (91) 562 66 00
Fax (91) 561 76 62 – ៛ ▤ TV ☎ ⇌ – 諡 25/300. AE ① E VISA JCB. ⅙
Diábolo : Meals a la carte 3325/4975 – ⍁ 1550 – **357 rm** 17200/28950.
GU

Tryp Fénix, Hermosilla 2, ⊠ 28001, ℰ (91) 431 67 00, Fax (91) 576 06 61 – ៛ ▤ T
☎ ⇌ – 諡 25/100. AE ① E VISA JCB. ⅙
Meals 2750 – ⍁ 1735 – **213 rm** 25305/31655, 13 suites.
NV

Meliá Avenida América, Juan Ignacio Luca de Tena 36, ⊠ 28027, ℰ (91) 320 30 30
Fax (91) 320 14 40, ⅃ઠ, ⍅, ⍆ – ៛ ▤ TV ☎ & ⇌ – 諡 25/1500. AE ① E VIS
JCB. ⅙
Meals a la carte 4650/5800 – ⍁ 1800 – **285 rm** 22700/28000, 18 suites.
North-East : by Av. de América   JT

Sofitel Madrid-Aeropuerto, Campo de las Naciones, ⊠ 28042, ℰ (91) 721 00 70
Fax (91) 721 05 15, ⍆ – ៛ ▤ TV ☎ & ⇌ – 諡 50/120. AE ① VISA JC
⅙ rest
North-East : by Av. de América   JT
Meals a la carte 5460/6580 – ⍁ 2035 – **178 rm** 28000/32000, 3 suites.

NH Príncipe de Vergara, Príncipe de Vergara 92, ⊠ 28006, ℰ (91) 563 26 95
Fax (91) 563 72 53, ⅃ઠ – ៛ ▤ TV ☎ ⇌ – 諡 25/200. AE ① E VIS
JCB. ⅙
Meals a la carte 5150/5650 – ⍁ 1900 – **170 rm** 18300/19800, 3 suites.
HU

Emperatriz, López de Hoyos 4, ⊠ 28006, ℰ (91) 563 80 88, Fax (91) 563 98 04 –
▤ TV ☎ – 諡 25/150. AE ① E VISA JCB. ⅙
Meals 3000 – ⍁ 1750 – **155 rm** 22500/27000, 3 suites.
GU

NH Sanvy, Goya 3, ⊠ 28001, ℰ (91) 576 08 00, Fax (91) 575 24 43 – ៛ ▤ TV ☎
諡 25/150. AE ① E VISA JCB. ⅙
Meals (see rest. **Sorolla** below) – ⍁ 2200 – **144 rm** 28440, 15 suites.
NV

Agumar coffee shop only, paseo Reina Cristina 7, ⊠ 28014, ℰ (91) 552 69 00
Fax (91) 433 60 95 – ៛ ▤ TV ☎ ⇌ – 諡 25/150. AE ① E VIS
JCB. ⅙
⍁ 1500 – **239 rm** 16200/20500, 6 suites.
HY

Novotel Madrid-Puente de La Paz, Albacete 1, ⊠ 28027, ℰ (91) 405 46 00
Fax (91) 404 11 05, ⍆ – ៛ ▤ TV ☎ & ⇌ ⑫ – 諡 25/250. AE ① E VISA
JT
Meals 1950 – ⍁ 1500 – **236 rm** 15700/17100.

Conde de Orgaz, av. Moscatelar 24, ⊠ 28043, ℰ (91) 388 40 99, Fax (91) 388 00 0
– ៛ ▤ TV ☎ ⇌ – 諡 25/140. AE ① VISA. ⅙   North-East : by José Silva   JS
Meals 3500 – ⍁ 1400 – **90 rm** 16000/19200.

NH Parque Avenidas, Biarritz 2, ⊠ 28028, ℰ (91) 361 02 88, Fax (91) 361 21 38
⍆ – ៛ ▤ TV ☎ & ⇌ – 諡 25/400. AE ① E VISA JCB
JU
Meals a la carte 3900/5400 – ⍁ 1700 – **198 rm** 17800, 1 suite.

NH Alcalá, Alcalá 66, ⊠ 28009, ℰ (91) 435 10 60, Fax (91) 435 11 05 – ៛ ▤ TV
⇌ – 諡 25/100. AE ① E VISA. ⅙
HX V
Meals (closed Saturday, Sunday and August) 3000 – ⍁ 1800 – **146 rm** 19500,
20600.

El Madroño, General Díaz Porlier 101, ⊠ 28006, ℰ (91) 562 52 92, Fax (91) 563 06 9
– ៛ ▤ TV ☎ ⇌ – 諡 25/300. AE ① E VISA. ⅙
HU
Meals 2650 – ⍁ 1500 – **66 rm** 16720/20900.

G.H. Colón, Pez Volador 1-11, ⊠ 28007, ℰ (91) 573 59 00, Fax (91) 573 08 09, ⅃ઠ,
– ៛ ▤ TV ☎ ⇌ – 諡 25/250. AE ① E VISA JCB. ⅙
JY
Meals 1850 – ⍁ 1150 – **380 rm** 9900/14900.

Novotel Madrid-Campo de las Naciones, Campo de las Naciones, ⊠ 28042
ℰ (91) 721 18 18, Fax (91) 721 11 22, 佘, ⍆ – ៛ ▤ TV ☎ & ⇌ – 諡 25/400. A
① E VISA JCB. ⅙ rest
North-East : by Av. de América   JT
Meals a la carte 3540/5145 – ⍁ 1545 – **240 rm** 18000/19115, 6 suites.

NH Balboa, Núñez de Balboa 112, ✉ 28006, ℰ (91) 563 03 24, *Fax (91) 562 69 80* – HU n
🛗 ▤ 📺 ☎ – 🏔 25/30. AE ① E VISA JCB. ⛔
a la carte 3300/4850 – ⊡ 1600 – **120 rm** 17500/21000.

NH Sur without rest, paseo Infanta Isabel 9, ✉ 28014, ℰ (91) 539 94 00, NZ a
Fax (91) 467 09 96 – 🛗 ▤ 📺 ☎ – 🏔 25/30. AE ① E VISA JCB
⊡ 1500 – **68 rm** 14500/17500.

Horcher, Alfonso XII-6, ✉ 28014, ℰ (91) 522 07 31, *Fax (91) 523 34 90*, « Tasteful NX y
decor » – ▤. AE ① VISA. ⛔
closed Saturday lunch, Sunday, Holy Week and August – **Meals** a la carte 7275/8925.

Club 31, Alcalá 58, ✉ 28014, ℰ (91) 531 00 92, *Fax (91) 531 00 92* – ▤. AE ① E VISA NX e
JCB. ⛔
closed August – **Meals** a la carte 5050/7700.

El Amparo, Puigcerdá 8, ✉ 28001, ℰ (91) 431 64 56, *Fax (91) 575 54 91*, « Original HX h
decor » – ▤. AE E VISA. ⛔
closed Saturday lunch, Sunday, Holy Week and 10 to 16 August – **Meals** a la carte
7200/8225
Spec. Milhojas de manzana ácida con pescado ahumado y foie gras. Cigalas salteadas con
raviolis cremosos de maíz al aceite de vainilla y reducción de Módena. Rabo de buey guisado
al vino tinto.

Combarro, José Ortega y Gasset 40, ✉ 28020, ℰ (91) 577 82 72, *Fax (91) 435 95 12* HV e
– ▤. AE ① E VISA JCB. ⛔
closed Sunday dinner and August – **Meals** - seafood - a la carte 4400/7500.

El Fogón - Hotel Wellington, Villanueva 34, ✉ 28001, ℰ (91) 575 44 00, *Telex 22700,* HX t
Fax (91) 576 41 64 – ▤. AE ① E VISA JCB. ⛔
Meals a la carte 6100/7400.

Sorolla - Hotel NH Sanvy, Hermosilla 4-1º, ✉ 28001, ℰ (91) 431 27 15, NV r
Fax (91) 575 24 43 – ▤. AE ① E VISA. ⛔
closed Sunday and August – **Meals** a la carte 4100/4850.

Suntory, paseo de la Castellana 36, ✉ 28046, ℰ (91) 577 37 34, *Fax (91) 577 44 55* GU d
– ▤ 🚗. AE ① E VISA JCB. ⛔
closed Sunday, Bank Holidays and Holy Week – **Meals** - Japanese rest - a la carte 5750/8000.

Balzac, Moreto 7, ✉ 28014, ℰ (91) 420 01 77, *Fax (91) 429 83 70* – ▤. AE ① E VISA. NY a
⛔
closed Sunday, Bank Holidays, Holy Week and August – **Meals** a la carte 4960/5790.

Pedro Larumbe, Serrano 61-ático 2nd floor, ✉ 28006, ℰ (91) 575 11 12, GV r
Fax (91) 576 60 19 – 🛗 ▤. AE ① E VISA. ⛔
closed Saturday lunch, Sunday, Holy Week and 13 to 23 August – **Meals** a la carte
4150/6950.

Paradis Casa América, paseo de Recoletos 2, ✉ 28001, ℰ (91) 575 45 40, NX n
Fax (91) 576 02 15, 🏛, « Within the Palacio de Linares » – ▤. AE ①
VISA. ⛔
closed Saturday lunch and Sunday – **Meals** a la carte 5250/5900.

Ponteareas, Claudio Coello 96, ✉ 28006, ℰ (91) 575 58 73, *Fax (91) 431 99 57* – ▤ GV w
🚗. AE ① E VISA JCB. ⛔
closed Sunday, Bank Holidays and 20 days in August – **Meals** - Galician rest - a la carte
4140/5795.

Castelló 9, Castelló 9, ✉ 28001, ℰ (91) 435 00 67, *Fax (91) 435 91 34* – ▤. AE ① HX e
E VISA. ⛔
closed Sunday and 15 to 31 August – **Meals** a la carte 4950/6050.

La Paloma, Jorge Juan 39, ✉ 28001, ℰ (91) 576 86 92 – ▤. AE ① E VISA. ⛔
closed Sunday, Bank Holidays, Holy Week and August – **Meals** 7500 and a la carte
4700/6350 HX g
Spec. Lasagna de txangurro y espinacas con salsa de berros. Rodaballo al horno sobre
verduras con salsa de vino tinto. Tarta fina de hojaldre con manzana.

Viridiana, Juan de Mena 14, ✉ 28014, ℰ (91) 523 44 78, *Fax (91) 532 42 74* – ▤. AE NY r
VISA
closed Sunday, Holy Week and August – **Meals** a la carte 5600/8400.

Al Mounia, Recoletos 5, ✉ 28001, ℰ (91) 435 08 28, « Oriental atmosphere » – ▤. NV u
AE ① E VISA. ⛔
closed Sunday, Monday, Holy Week and August – **Meals** - North African rest - a la carte
4400/4900.

Teatriz, Hermosilla 15, ✉ 28001, ℰ (91) 577 53 79, *Fax (91) 577 91 98*, « Housed in GV u
an old theatre » – ▤. AE ① E VISA. ⛔
closed August – **Meals** - Italian rest - a la carte 3500/4200.

XX **El Chiscón de Castelló**, Castelló 3, ✉ 28001, ℘ (91) 575 56 62, « Welcoming ambience » – 🗏. 𝔸𝔼 Ⓞ 🄴 𝑉𝐼𝑆𝐴. ⌘
closed Sunday, Bank Holidays and August – **Meals** a la carte 3100/4475.
HX

XX **Rafa**, Narváez 68, ✉ 28009, ℘ (91) 573 10 87, Fax (91) 573 82 98, ☂ – 🗏 🚗.
Ⓞ 🄴 𝑉𝐼𝑆𝐴 𝐽𝐶𝐵. ⌘
Meals a la carte 4600/6700.
HX

XX **El Asador de Aranda**, Diego de León 9, ✉ 28006, ℘ (91) 563 02 4
Fax (91) 556 62 02 – 🗏. 𝔸𝔼 Ⓞ 🄴 𝑉𝐼𝑆𝐴 𝐽𝐶𝐵. ⌘
closed Sunday dinner and August – **Meals** - Roast lamb - a la carte approx. 4000.
HU

XX **Guisando**, Núñez de Balboa 75, ✉ 28006, ℘ (91) 575 09 00 – 🗏. 𝔸𝔼 Ⓞ 🄴 𝑉𝐼𝑆𝐴.
closed Saturday lunch, Sunday, Holy Week and August – **Meals** a la carte 3450/
4300.
HV

XX **St. James**, Juan Bravo 26, ✉ 28006, ℘ (91) 575 00 69, ☂ – 🗏. 𝔸𝔼 𝑉𝐼𝑆𝐴.
closed Sunday – **Meals** - Rice dishes - a la carte 4000/5000.
HV

XX **Casa Domingo**, Alcalá 99, ✉ 28009, ℘ (91) 576 01 37, Fax (91) 575 78 62, ☂ – 🗏
𝔸𝔼 🄴 𝑉𝐼𝑆𝐴. ⌘
Meals a la carte 2550/4550.
HX

XX **Nicolás**, Villalar 4, ✉ 28001, ℘ (91) 431 77 37, Fax (91) 431 77 37 – 🗏. 𝔸𝔼 Ⓞ 🄴 𝑉𝐼𝑆
⌘
closed Sunday, Monday, Holy Week and August – **Meals** a la carte 3625/4450.
NX

X **Casa d'a Troya**, Emiliano Barral 14, ✉ 28043, ℘ (91) 416 44 55 – 🗏. Ⓞ 🄴 𝑉𝐼𝑆𝐴.
closed Sunday, Bank Holidays, Christmas and 15 July-1 September – **Meals** *(booking essen-tial)* - Galician rest, seafood - a la carte 3400/4850
Spec. Pulpo a la gallega. Merluza a la gallega. Tarta de Santiago.
JS

X **La Giralda IV**, Claudio Coello 24, ✉ 28001, ℘ (91) 576 40 69 – 🗏. 𝔸𝔼 Ⓞ 𝑉𝐼𝑆𝐴.
closed Sunday (July-August) and Sunday dinner the rest of the year – **Meals** - Andalusia
rest - a la carte approx. 5550.
GX

X **Asador Velate**, Jorge Juan 91, ✉ 28009, ℘ (91) 435 10 24, Fax (91) 574 38 54 –
𝔸𝔼 Ⓞ 🄴 𝑉𝐼𝑆𝐴 𝐽𝐶𝐵. ⌘
closed Sunday and August – **Meals** - Basque rest - a la carte 4750/6450.
JX

X **Pelotari**, Recoletos 3, ✉ 28001, ℘ (91) 578 24 97, Fax (91) 431 60 04 – 🗏. 𝔸𝔼 Ⓞ
𝑉𝐼𝑆𝐴. ⌘
closed Sunday – **Meals** a la carte 4215/5925.
NV

X **La Trainera**, Lagasca 60, ✉ 28001, ℘ (91) 576 05 75, Fax (91) 575 06 31 – 🗏. 𝔸𝔼 Ⓞ
🄴 𝑉𝐼𝑆𝐴 𝐽𝐶𝐵. ⌘
closed Sunday and August – **Meals** - Seafood - a la carte 4700/5400
Spec. Salpicón de marisco. Dorada a la plancha. Langosta a la americana.
GHV

X **El Pescador**, José Ortega y Gasset 75, ✉ 28006, ℘ (91) 402 12 90, Fax (91) 401 30 2
– 🗏. 🄴 𝑉𝐼𝑆𝐴. ⌘
closed Sunday, Holy Week and August – **Meals** - Seafood - a la carte 4800/5900
Spec. Almejas a la marinera. Lenguado Evaristo. Mero Pescador.
JV

Arganzuela, Carabanchel, Villaverde : Antonio López, Paseo de Las Delicias, Pase
Santa María de la Cabeza

🏨 **Rafael Pirámides**, paseo de las Acacias 40, ✉ 28005, ℘ (91) 517 18 28
Fax (91) 517 00 90 – 📶 🗏 📺 ☎ 👤 🚗. 𝔸𝔼 Ⓞ 🄴 𝑉𝐼𝑆𝐴. ⌘ rest
DZ
Meals *(closed Saturday, Sunday and August)* 1300 – ☕ 1175 – **84 rm** 11850/14600
9 suites.

🏨 **Carlton**, paseo de las Delicias 26, ✉ 28045, ℘ (91) 539 71 00, Telex 44571
Fax (91) 527 85 10 – 📶 🗏 📺 ☎. 𝔸𝔼 Ⓞ 🄴 𝑉𝐼𝑆𝐴. ⌘
FZ
Meals 3465 – ☕ 1500 – **105 rm** 18300/22800, 7 suites.

🏨 **Praga** coffee shop only, Antonio López 65, ✉ 28019, ℘ (91) 469 06 00
Fax (91) 469 83 25 – 📶 🗏 📺 ☎ 🚗 – 🔔 25/350. 𝔸𝔼 Ⓞ 🄴 𝑉𝐼𝑆𝐴 𝐽𝐶𝐵. ⌘
DZ
☕ 1100 – **428 rm** 12500/16000.

🏨 **Aramo**, paseo Santa María de la Cabeza 73, ✉ 28045, ℘ (91) 473 91 11
Fax (91) 473 92 14 – 📶 🗏 📺 ☎ 🚗. 𝔸𝔼 Ⓞ 🄴 𝑉𝐼𝑆𝐴. ⌘ rest
EZ
Meals 1500 – ☕ 1000 – **105 rm** 9600/12000.

🏨 **Puerta de Toledo**, glorieta Puerta de Toledo 4, ✉ 28005, ℘ (91) 474 71 00
Fax (91) 474 07 47 – 📶 🗏 📺 ☎ 🚗 – 🔔 25/30. 𝔸𝔼 Ⓞ 🄴 𝑉𝐼𝑆𝐴 𝐽𝐶𝐵. ⌘
DY
Meals *(see rest. **Puerta de Toledo** below)* – ☕ 930 – **152 rm** 7800/12100.

XX **Hontoria**, pl. del General Maroto 2, ✉ 28045, ℘ (91) 473 04 25 – 🗏. 𝔸𝔼 Ⓞ 🄴 𝑉𝐼𝑆𝐴
⌘
EZ
closed Sunday, Bank Holidays, Holy Week and August – **Meals** a la carte 3675/4800.

XX **Puerta de Toledo** - Hotel Puerta de Toledo, glorieta Puerta de Toledo 4, ✉ 28005
℘ (91) 474 12 69, Fax (91) 474 30 35 – 🗏. Ⓞ 🄴 𝑉𝐼𝑆𝐴. ⌘
DY
Meals a la carte 2550/3800.

SPAIN

Moncloa : Princesa, Paseo del Pintor Rosales, Paseo de la Florida, Casa de Campo

Meliá Madrid, Princesa 27, ⊠ 28008, ℰ (91) 541 82 00, *Telex 22537, Fax (91) 541 19 88*, ⟂ – 🛗 ▤ 📺 ☎ – 🔺 25/200. 🝙 ⓪ Ε *VISA* JCB. ✦   KV t
Meals a la carte 3400/4150 – ⊑ 2000 – **253 rm** 29500/33900, 23 suites.

Tryp Monte Real ⤂, Arroyofresno 17, ⊠ 28035, ℰ (91) 316 21 40, *Fax (91) 316 39 34*, « Garden », 🛆 – 🛗 ▤ 📺 ☎ ⌘ ℗ – 🔺 25/250. 🝙 ⓪
VISA. ✦   North-West : 8 km by Av. de la Victoria   DU
Meals a la carte 3800/5500 – ⊑ 1750 – **76 rm** 19270/24150, 4 suites.

Sofitel-Plaza de España without rest, Tutor 1, ⊠ 28008, ℰ (91) 541 98 80, *Fax (91) 542 57 36* – 🛗 ▤ 📺 ☎ 🅯 – 🔺 25/30. 🝙 ⓪ Ε *VISA*   KV d
⊑ 2000 – **97 rm** 30000/34000.

Sal Gorda, Beatriz de Bobadilla 9, ⊠ 28040, ℰ (91) 553 95 06 – ▤. 🝙 ⓪ Ε *VISA*. ✦
closed Sunday and August – **Meals** a la carte 3540/4200.   DT e

Currito, Casa de Campo-Pabellón de Vizcaya, ⊠ 28011, ℰ (91) 464 57 04, *Fax (91) 479 72 54*, ☂ – ▤ ℗. 🝙 ⓪ *VISA*. ✦   West : by Av. de Portugal   DX
closed Sunday dinner – **Meals** - Basque rest - a la carte 5000/6400.

Chamberí : San Bernardo, Fuencarral, Alberto Aguilera, Santa Engracia

Santo Mauro, Zurbano 36, ⊠ 28010, ℰ (91) 319 69 00, *Fax (91) 308 54 77*, « Elegant palace with garden », ⟂ – 🛗 ▤ 📺 ☎ ⌘ – 🔺 25/70. 🝙 ⓪ *VISA*
JCB. ✦   FV e
Meals 8000 - *Belagua* : Meals a la carte 4800/6500 – ⊑ 2500 – **33 rm** 32000/38000, 4 suites.

Miguel Ángel, Miguel Ángel 31, ⊠ 28010, ℰ (91) 442 00 22, *Fax (91) 442 53 20*, ☂, 🛆, ⟂ – 🛗 ▤ 📺 ☎ ⌘ – 🔺 25/300. 🝙 ⓪ Ε *VISA* JCB. ✦   FU c
Florencia : Meals a la carte 5400/6700 – ⊑ 2400 – **251 rm** 26500/37000, 20 suites.

Castellana Inter-Continental, paseo de la Castellana 49, ⊠ 28046, ℰ (91) 310 02 00, *Fax (91) 319 58 53*, ☂, « Garden », 🛆 – 🛗 ▤ 📺 ☎ ⌘ – 🔺 25/550. 🝙 ⓪ Ε *VISA* JCB. ✦   GU v
Meals a la carte 3840/7140 – ⊑ 2600 – **278 rm** 37900/45800, 27 suites.

Mindanao, San Francisco de Sales 15, ⊠ 28003, ℰ (91) 549 55 00, *Telex 22631, Fax (91) 544 55 96*, ⟂, ⟂ – 🛗 ▤ 📺 ☎ 🅯 ⌘ – 🔺 25/250. 🝙 ⓪ Ε *VISA* JCB. ✦
Meals 3750 - *El Candelabro* (closed August) Meals a la carte 4600/6000 – ⊑ 1825 –
272 rm 15000/18900, 9 suites.   DT a

Gran Versalles coffee shop only, Covarrubias 4, ⊠ 28010, ℰ (91) 447 57 00, *Telex 49150, Fax (91) 446 39 87* – 🛗 ▤ 📺 ☎ – 🔺 25/120. 🝙 ⓪ Ε
VISA. ✦   MV a
⊑ 1400 – **143 rm** 17500/24500, 2 suites.

NH Zurbano, Zurbano 79-81, ⊠ 28003, ℰ (91) 441 45 00, *Fax (91) 441 32 24* – 🛗 ▤ 📺 ☎ ⌘ – 🔺 25/250. 🝙 ⓪ Ε *VISA* JCB. ✦   FU x
Meals a la carte 3400/4600 – ⊑ 1600 – **255 rm** 19710/26700, 12 suites.

NH Abascal, José Abascal 47, ⊠ 28003, ℰ (91) 441 00 15, *Fax (91) 442 22 11*, 🛆 – 🛗 ▤ 📺 ☎ 🅯 ⌘ – 🔺 25/180. 🝙 ⓪ Ε *VISA* JCB. ✦   FU a
Meals a la carte 4500/6000 – ⊑ 1900 – **181 rm** 25900/31000, 3 suites.

NH Embajada, Santa Engracia 5, ⊠ 28010, ℰ (91) 594 02 13, *Fax (91) 447 33 12*, « Spanish style building » – 🛗 ▤ 📺 ☎ – 🔺 25/45. 🝙 ⓪ Ε *VISA*. ✦   MV r
Meals (closed Saturday, Sunday and July-August) 2100 – ⊑ 1600 – **101 rm** 21900/27400.

NH Prisma, Santa Engracia 120, ⊠ 28003, ℰ (91) 441 93 77, *Fax (91) 442 58 51* – 🛗 ▤ 📺 ☎ – 🔺 25/70. 🝙 ⓪ Ε *VISA* JCB. ✦   EU g
Meals (closed August) a la carte approx. 4000 – ⊑ 1600 – **103 suites** 21000.

NH Argüelles coffee shop only, Vallehermoso 65, ⊠ 28015, ℰ (91) 593 97 77, *Fax (91) 594 27 39* – ▤ 📺 ☎ ⌘. 🝙 ⓪ Ε *VISA*. ✦   DU e
⊑ 1500 – **75 rm** 20900.

Sol Inn Alondras coffee shop only, José Abascal 8, ⊠ 28003, ℰ (91) 447 40 00, *Fax (91) 593 88 00* – 🛗 ▤ 📺 ☎. 🝙 ⓪ Ε *VISA* JCB. ✦   EU a
⊑ 1095 – **72 rm** 16400/19800.

Jockey, Amador de los Ríos 6, ⊠ 28010, ℰ (91) 319 24 35, *Fax (91) 319 24 35* – ▤. 🝙 ⓪ Ε *VISA* JCB. ✦   NV k
closed Saturday lunch, Sunday, Bank Holidays and August – **Meals** a la carte 6350/9350
Spec. Vieiras marinadas al aceite virgen y trufa. Esturión fresco a la vinagreta de balsámico y soja. Pichón de Navaz a la parrilla con fideos de arroz.

Las Cuatro Estaciones, General Ibáñez de Íbero 5, ⊠ 28003, ℰ (91) 553 63 05, *Fax (91) 553 32 98* – ▤. 🝙 ⓪ Ε *VISA* JCB. ✦   DT r
closed Saturday lunch, Sunday and August – **Meals** 4500 and a la carte 4500/5750
Spec. Verduras a la plancha. Arroz negro con anillas de chipirones. Foie caliente al Pedro Ximénez.

513

SPAIN

Lur Maitea, Fernando el Santo 4, ⊠ 28010, ℘ (91) 308 03 50, Fax (91) 308 03 93 ▤. AE ⓘ E VISA. ⌾
MV
closed Saturday lunch, Sunday, Bank Holidays and August – **Meals** - Basque rest - a la car
5000/6050.

Annapurna, Zurbano 5, ⊠ 28010, ℘ (91) 308 32 49, Fax (91) 308 32 49 – ▤. AE ⓘ
E VISA. ⌾
MV
closed Saturday lunch, Sunday and Bank Holidays – **Meals** - Indian rest - a la car
3500/5200.

Solchaga, pl. Alonso Martínez 2, ⊠ 28004, ℘ (91) 447 14 96, Fax (91) 593 22 23 – ▤
AE E VISA. ⌾
MV
closed Saturday lunch, Sunday, Bank Holidays and August – **Meals** a la carte 4100/550

La Vendimia, pl. del Conde del Valle de Suchil 7, ⊠ 28015, ℘ (91) 445 73 77 – ▤.
ⓘ E VISA. ⌾
DV
closed Sunday dinner – **Meals** a la carte 3300/4650.

Kulixka, Fuencarral 124, ⊠ 28010, ℘ (91) 447 25 38 – ▤. AE ⓘ E VISA. ⌾
EV
closed Sunday and August – **Meals** - Seafood - a la carte 4200/5800.

Polizón, Viriato 39, ⊠ 28010, ℘ (91) 593 39 19 – ▤. AE ⓘ E VISA JCB. ⌾
EU
closed Sunday in summer, Sunday dinner the rest of the year and August – **Meals** - Seafoo
- a la carte 3475/4350.

La Plaza de Chamberí, pl. de Chamberí 10, ⊠ 28010, ℘ (91) 446 06 97 – ▤.
ⓘ E VISA JCB. ⌾
FV
closed Sunday – **Meals** a la carte 3700/4225.

La Fuente Quince, Modesto Lafuente 15, ⊠ 28003, ℘ (91) 399 14 7
Fax (91) 441 10 43 – ▤. AE ⓘ E VISA. ⌾
FU
closed Saturday lunch, Sunday, Holy Week and August – **Meals** a la carte 3000/3725

Doña, Zurbano 59, ⊠ 28010, ℘ (91) 319 25 51, Fax (91) 441 90 20 – ▤. AE ⓘ VIS
⌾
FU
closed Sunday dinner and 15 to 31 August – **Meals** a la carte 3000/3750.

Pinocchio, Orfila 2, ⊠ 28010, ℘ (91) 308 16 47, Fax (91) 766 98 04 – ▤. AE ⓘ
VISA. ⌾
NV
closed Sunday and August – **Meals** - Italian rest - a la carte 2950/3335.

Balear, Sagunto 18, ⊠ 28010, ℘ (91) 447 91 15, Fax (91) 445 19 97 – ▤. AE E VIS
⌾
EU
closed Sunday dinner and Monday dinner – **Meals** - Rice dishes - a la carte 3150/450

Villa de Foz, Gonzálo de Córdoba 10, ⊠ 28010, ℘ (91) 446 89 93 – ▤. AE VISA. ⌾
closed Sunday and August – **Meals** - Galician rest - a la carte 3400/5200.
EV

La Despensa, Cardenal Cisneros 6, ⊠ 28010, ℘ (91) 446 17 94 – ▤. AE ⓘ E VIS
⌾
EV
closed Sunday dinner, Monday and 22 August-19 September – **Meals** a la carte 2425/320

Chamartín, Tetuán : Paseo de la Castellana, Capitán Haya, Orense, Alberto Alcoce
Paseo de la Habana

Meliá Castilla, Capitán Haya 43, ⊠ 28020, ℘ (91) 567 50 00, Fax (91) 567 50 51,
– ⧌ ▤ TV ☎ ఉ ⇔ – ⌂ 25/800. AE ⓘ E VISA JCB. ⌾
FR
Meals (see rest. **L'Albufera** and rest. **La Fragata** below) – ☕ 2500 – **891 r**
29000/33000, 14 suites.

Crowne Plaza Madrid City Centre, pl. Carlos Trías Beltrán 4 (entrance by Orens
22-24), ⊠ 28020, ℘ (91) 456 80 00, Fax (91) 456 80 01, ⬚, ⬚ – ⧌ ▤ TV ☎ ఉ
⌂ 25/400. AE ⓘ E VISA JCB. ⌾ rest
FS
La Terraza (lunch only, closed 15 July-1 September) **Meals** a la carte approx. 3275 - **Bi**
Blue : **Meals** a la carte 2595/4725 – ☕ 2350 – **282 rm** 29100/32100, 31 suites.

NH Eurobuilding, Padre Damián 23, ⊠ 28036, ℘ (91) 345 45 00, Fax (91) 345 45 76
« Garden and terrace with ⬚ », ⬚ – ⧌ ▤ TV ☎ ⇔ – ⌂ 25/900. AE ⓘ E VISA
GS
La Taberna : Meals a la carte approx. 5700 - **Le Relais : Meals** a la carte approx. 450
– ☕ 2200 – **416 rm** 28500, 84 suites.

Cuzco coffee shop only, paseo de la Castellana 133, ⊠ 28046, ℘ (91) 556 06 0
Fax (91) 556 03 72, ⬚ – ⧌ ▤ TV ☎ ⇔ ⓟ – ⌂ 25/450. AE ⓘ E VISA. ⌾
FS
☕ 1300 – **322 rm** 20580/25725, 8 suites.

Chamartín, Chamartín railway station, ⊠ 28036, ℘ (91) 334 49 00, Fax (91) 733 02 1
– ⧌ ▤ TV ☎ – ⌂ 25/500. AE ⓘ E VISA JCB. ⌾
HR
Meals (see rest. **Cota 13** below) – ☕ 1400 – **360 rm** 18900/21900, 18 suites.

NH La Habana, paseo de la Habana 73, ⊠ 28036, ℘ (91) 345 82 84, Fax (91) 457 75 7
– ⧌ ▤ TV ☎ ⇔ – ⌂ 25/250. AE ⓘ E VISA JCB. ⌾ rest
HS
Meals 3000 – ☕ 1600 – **156 rm** 16500/21000.

Orense, Pedro Teixeira 5, ⊠ 28020, ℰ (91) 597 15 68, *Fax (91) 597 12 95* – 🛗 ▤ 📺 ☎ 🚗. AE ⓞ E *VISA* JCB. ⌗   FS q
Meals 2500 – ⌑ 1350 – **140 rm** 21150/25575.

Foxá 32, Agustín de Foxá 32, ⊠ 28036, ℰ (91) 733 10 60, *Fax (91) 314 11 65* – 🛗 ▤ 📺 ☎ 🚗 – 🍽 25/250. AE ⓞ E *VISA*. ⌗   GR u
Meals a la carte 2600/3500 – ⌑ 1200 – **63 rm** 19000, 98 suites.

Foxá 25, Agustín de Foxá 25, ⊠ 28036, ℰ (91) 323 11 19, *Fax (91) 314 53 11* – 🛗 ▤ 📺 ☎ 🚗. AE ⓞ E *VISA*. ⌗   GR a
Meals a la carte 2600/3500 – ⌑ 1200 – **121 suites** 19000.

Castilla Plaza, paseo de la Castellana 220, ⊠ 28046, ℰ (91) 323 11 86, *Fax (91) 315 54 06* – 🛗 ▤ 📺 ☎ 🚗 – 🍽 25/150. AE ⓞ E *VISA*. ⌗   GR u
Meals 2750 – ⌑ 2000 – **147 rm** 24450/27300.

El Gran Atlanta without rest, Comandante Zorita 34, ⊠ 28020, ℰ (91) 553 59 00, *Fax (91) 533 08 58*, 🛌 – 🛗 ▤ 📺 ☎ 🚗 – 🍽 25/120. AE ⓞ E *VISA*. ⌗   ES p
⌑ 1200 – **180 rm** 11900/16450.

Aristos, av. Pío XII-34, ⊠ 28016, ℰ (91) 345 04 50, *Fax (91) 345 10 23* – 🛗 ▤ 📺 ☎. AE ⓞ E *VISA*. ⌗   JR d
Meals (see rest. **El Chaflán** below) – ⌑ 950 – **24 rm** 14750/19750, 1 suite.

La Residencia de El Viso 🌳, Nervión 8, ⊠ 28002, ℰ (91) 564 03 70, *Fax (91) 564 19 65* – 🛗 ▤ 📺 ☎. AE ⓞ E *VISA*. ⌗   HT c
Meals 1700 – ⌑ 750 – **12 rm** 9000/16000.

Zalacaín, Álvarez de Baena 4, ⊠ 28006, ℰ (91) 561 48 40, *Fax (91) 561 47 32* – ▤. AE ⓞ E *VISA* JCB. ⌗   GU b
closed Saturday lunch, Sunday, Bank Holidays, Holy Week and August – **Meals** 9500 and a la carte 6350/8825
Spec. Cazoleta de almejas con pasta al Jerez y pistachos asados. Rodaballo sobre puré de espárragos a la vinagreta de tomate. Pequeño volcán de chocolate caliente al café.

Príncipe y Serrano, Serrano 240, ⊠ 28016, ℰ (91) 458 62 31, *Fax (91) 458 62 31* – ▤. AE ⓞ *VISA*. ⌗   HS a
closed Saturday lunch, Sunday and August – **Meals** a la carte 4900/5700.

La Máquina, Sor Ángela de la Cruz 22, ⊠ 28020, ℰ (91) 572 33 18, *Fax (91) 570 44 09* – ▤. AE ⓞ E *VISA*. ⌗   FS e
closed Sunday dinner – **Meals** a la carte 4050/5350.

El Bodegón, Pinar 15, ⊠ 28006, ℰ (91) 562 88 44, *Fax (91) 562 97 25* – ▤. AE ⓞ E *VISA*. ⌗   GU q
closed Saturday lunch, Sunday, Bank Holidays and August – **Meals** a la carte 6200/7050.

Príncipe de Viana, Manuel de Falla 5, ⊠ 28036, ℰ (91) 457 15 49, *Fax (91) 457 52 83* – ▤. AE ⓞ E *VISA* JCB. ⌗   GS c
closed Saturday lunch, Sunday, Holy Week and August – **Meals** - Basque rest - a la carte 5650/6725
Spec. Menestra de verduras (season). Bacalao al ajoarriero. Tarta de arroz.

Nicolasa, Velázquez 150, ⊠ 28002, ℰ (91) 561 99 85, *Fax (91) 564 32 75* – ▤. AE ⓞ *VISA*. ⌗   HT a
Meals a la carte 4950/6350.

O'Pazo, Reina Mercedes 20, ⊠ 28020, ℰ (91) 553 23 33, *Fax (91) 554 90 72* – ▤. E *VISA*. ⌗   EFS p
closed Sunday, Holy Week and August – **Meals** - Seafood - a la carte 4800/5900
Spec. Centollo gallego. Langosta del Cantábrico a la americana. Rodaballo al horno.

L'Albufera - *Hotel Meliá Castilla*, Capitán Haya 43, ⊠ 28020, ℰ (91) 567 51 97, *Fax (91) 567 50 51* – ▤ 🚗. AE ⓞ E *VISA* JCB. ⌗   FR c
Meals - Rice dishes - a la carte 4900/6500.

La Fragata - *Hotel Meliá Castilla*, Capitán Haya 43, ⊠ 28020, ℰ (91) 567 51 96 – ▤ 🚗. AE ⓞ E *VISA* JCB. ⌗   FR c
closed Bank Holidays and August – **Meals** a la carte 4990/6490.

José Luis, Rafael Salgado 11, ⊠ 28036, ℰ (91) 457 50 36, *Fax (91) 344 18 37* – ▤. AE ⓞ E *VISA*. ⌗   GS m
closed Sunday and August – **Meals** a la carte 3025/4350.

La Misión, Comandante Zorita 6, ⊠ 28020, ℰ (91) 533 27 57, *Fax (91) 534 50 90* – ▤. AE ⓞ *VISA*. ⌗   ET s
closed Saturday lunch and Sunday – **Meals** a la carte 3400/4650.

Bogavante, Capitán Haya 20, ⊠ 28020, ℰ (91) 556 21 14, *Fax (91) 597 00 79* – ▤. AE ⓞ E *VISA* JCB. ⌗   FS d
closed Sunday dinner – **Meals** - Seafood - a la carte 2900/6200.

XXX **Señorío de Alcocer,** av. de Alberto Alcocer 1, ⊠ 28036, ℘ (91) 345 16 9
Fax (91) 345 16 96 – 🖥. 🆎 ⓓ 🅴 *VISA*. ⅍ GS
closed Saturday lunch, Sunday, Bank Holidays and 7 to 24 August – **Meals** a la car
5550/6250.

XXX **El Olivo,** General Gallegos 1, ⊠ 28036, ℘ (91) 359 15 35, *Fax (91) 345 91 83* – 🖥.
❀ ⓓ 🅴 *VISA* JCB GR
closed Sunday, Monday and 15 to 31 August – **Meals** 5600 and a la carte 4800/590
Spec. Sardinas marinadas sobre caviar de berenjenas. Ensalada templada de bogavante
su vinagreta de finas hierbas. Pichón en dos cocciones sobre verduritas y su jugo trufac

XXX **Goizeko Kabi,** Comandante Zorita 37, ⊠ 28020, ℘ (91) 533 01 85, *Fax (91) 533 02*
❀ – 🖥. 🆎 ⓓ 🅴 *VISA*. ⅍ ES
closed Saturday lunch (July-August) and Sunday – **Meals** - Basque rest - a la car
6150/7200
Spec. Menestra de setas (autumn-spring). Tártaro de salmón al queso y vinagreta de rem
lacha. Solomillo braseado con sal gorda y aceite de oliva.

XXX **Cabo Mayor,** Juan Ramón Jiménez 37, ⊠ 28036, ℘ (91) 350 87 76, *Fax (91) 359 16 2*
– 🖥. 🆎 ⓓ 🅴 *VISA* JCB. ⅍ GS
closed Sunday, 25 December-1 January, Holy Week and two weeks in August – **Mea**
a la carte 5400/7200.

XXX **Blanca de Navarra,** av. de Brasil 13, ⊠ 28020, ℘ (91) 555 10 29 – 🖥. 🆎 ⓓ 🅴 *VISA*. ⅍
closed August – **Meals** a la carte 4500/5400. FS

XXX **Lutecia,** Corazón de María 78, ⊠ 28002, ℘ (91) 519 34 15 – 🖥. 🆎 ⓓ 🅴 *VISA*. ⅍ JT
closed Sunday and August – **Meals** a la carte 3300/4500.

XXX **Aldaba,** av. de Alberto Alcocer 5, ⊠ 28036, ℘ (91) 345 21 93 – 🖥. 🆎 ⓓ 🅴 *VISA*. ⅍
closed Saturday lunch, Sunday and August – **Meals** a la carte 4425/6000. GS

XXX **El Foque,** Suero de Quiñones 22, ⊠ 28002, ℘ (91) 519 25 72, *Fax (91) 519 52 61*
🖥. 🆎 ⓓ 🅴 *VISA*. ⅍ HT
closed Sunday – **Meals** - Cod dishes - a la carte 4500/5300.

XX **Combarro,** Reina Mercedes 12, ⊠ 28020, ℘ (91) 554 77 84, *Fax (91) 534 25 01* –
🆎 ⓓ 🅴 *VISA* JCB. ⅍ ES
closed Sunday dinner and August – **Meals** - Seafood - a la carte 5075/7500.

XX **La Tahona,** Capitán Haya 21 (side), ⊠ 28020, ℘ (91) 555 04 41, *Fax (91) 556 62 0*
« Castilian medieval decor » – 🖥. 🆎 ⓓ 🅴 *VISA* JCB. ⅍ FS
closed Sunday dinner and August – **Meals** - Roast lamb - a la carte approx. 4000.

XX **De Funy,** Serrano 213, ⊠ 28016, ℘ (91) 457 95 22, *Fax (91) 458 85 84*, � – 🖥. L
ⓓ 🅴 *VISA*. ⅍ HS
Meals - Lebanese rest - a la carte 4050/5300.

XX **Gaztelupe,** Comandante Zorita 32, ⊠ 28020, ℘ (91) 534 90 28, *Fax (91) 554 65 6*
– 🖥. 🆎 ⓓ *VISA*. ⅍ ES
closed Sunday in July-August and Sunday lunch in winter – **Meals** - Basque rest - a la car
5150/6050.

XX **Asador Frontón II,** Pedro Muguruza 8, ⊠ 28036, ℘ (91) 345 36 9
Fax (91) 350 95 33 – 🖥. 🆎 ⓓ 🅴 *VISA*. ⅍ GR
closed Sunday – **Meals** a la carte 4000/5025.

XX **Carta Marina,** Padre Damián 40, ⊠ 28036, ℘ (91) 458 68 26, *Fax (91) 458 68 26*
🖥. 🆎 ⓓ 🅴 *VISA* JCB. ⅍ HS
closed Sunday and August – **Meals** - Galician rest - a la carte 4400/5450.

XX **El Telégrafo,** Padre Damián 44, ⊠ 28036, ℘ (91) 350 61 19, *Fax (91) 401 34 43*, �
« Resembles the inside of a boat » – 🖥. 🆎 ⓓ 🅴 *VISA* JCB. ⅍ GS
Meals - Seafood - a la carte approx. 5100.

XX **De María,** Félix Boix 5, ⊠ 28036, ℘ (91) 359 65 07, *Fax (91) 345 22 94* – 🖥. 🆎 ⓓ
VISA. ⅍ GR
Meals - Braised fish and meat specialities - a la carte 4050/6875.

XX **Sacha,** Juan Hurtado de Mendoza 11 (back), ⊠ 28036, ℘ (91) 345 59 52, �, Bistr
– 🖥. 🆎 ⓓ *VISA*. ⅍ GS
closed Sunday, Holy Week and 10 to 31 August – **Meals** a la carte 3500/5250.

XX **Rianxo,** Oruro 11, ⊠ 28016, ℘ (91) 457 10 06, *Fax (91) 457 22 04* – 🖥. 🆎 ⓓ 🅴 *VIS*
⅍ HS
closed Sunday dinner – **Meals** - Galician rest - a la carte 4050/6700.

XX **El Chaflán** - *Hotel Aristos,* av. Pío XII-34, ⊠ 28016, ℘ (91) 350 61 9
Fax (91) 345 10 23, � – 🖥. 🆎 ⓓ 🅴 *VISA*. ⅍ JR
closed Sunday dinner and Holy Week – **Meals** a la carte 3500/5175.

XX **Cota 13** - *Hotel Chamartín,* Chamartín railway station, ⊠ 28036, ℘ (91) 314 95 0
Fax (91) 733 02 14 – 🖥. 🆎 ⓓ 🅴 *VISA* JCB. ⅍ HR
Meals a la carte 2450/4650.

XX **La Broche,** Dr. Fleming 36, ✉ 28036, ☎ (91) 457 99 60, *Fax (91) 344 15 03* – ▤. AE
☼ ⓪ E *VISA*. ✗ – *closed Saturday lunch, Sunday, Bank Holidays, Holy Week and August* –
Meals a la carte 4550/6600   GS t
Spec. Carpaccio de ceps con pasta y piñones. Lomo de conejo con caracoles de mar y
montaña. Espuma quemada de crema catalana avainillada.

XX **Asador de Roa,** Pintor Juan Gris 5, ✉ 28020, ☎ (91) 555 38 17, *Fax (91) 555 86 29*
    – ▤. AE ⓪ *VISA*. ✗   FS d
Meals a la carte 4000/4500.

X   **La Ancha,** Príncipe de Vergara 204, ✉ 28002, ☎ (91) 563 89 77, *Fax (91) 563 89 77,*
    ⛲ – ▤. AE ⓪ E *VISA*. ✗   HT z
closed Sunday, Bank Holidays, Holy Week and Christmas – **Meals** a la carte 3350/4500.

X   **El Asador de Aranda,** pl. de Castilla 3, ✉ 28046, ☎ (91) 733 87 02,
Fax (91) 556 62 02, « Castilian decor » – ▤. AE ⓪ E *VISA*. ✗   GR b
closed Sunday dinner and 17 August-13 September – **Meals** - Roast lamb - a la carte approx.
4000.

X   **Zacarías de Santander,** Rosario Pino 17, ✉ 28020, ☎ (91) 571 28 86,
Fax (91) 571 28 86, ⛲ – ▤. AE ⓪ E *VISA*. ✗   FR f
Meals a la carte 4100/7200.

X   **Casa Benigna,** Benigno Soto 9, ✉ 28002, ☎ (91) 416 93 57, *Fax (91) 413 33 56* – ▤.
    AE ⓪ E *VISA*. ✗   JT u
Meals a la carte 5650/6450.

X   **El Cenachero,** Manuel de Falla 8, ✉ 28036, ☎ (91) 457 59 04, *Fax (91) 457 59 04* –
    ▤. AE ⓪ E *VISA*. ✗   GS r
closed Saturday lunch, Sunday, Holy Week and 15 to 30 August – **Meals** a la carte
2925/4850.

Environs

n the road to the airport *East : 12,5 km –* ✉ *28042 Madrid :*

🏨 **Tryp Diana,** Galeón 27 (Alameda de Osuna) ☎ (91) 747 13 55, *Telex 45688,*
Fax (91) 747 97 97, ⏋ – ▤ TV ☎ – 25/220. AE ⓪ E *VISA* JCB. ✗ rest
Meals 2400 - *Asador Duque de Osuna* (*closed Sunday and Bank Holidays*) **Meals** a la carte
3400/5500 - *El Pato Mudo* (*closed Monday*) **Meals** a la carte approx. 4900 – ⌛ 1600
– **228 rm** 15200/18100, 42 suites.

y motorway N VI – ✉ *28023 Madrid :*

🏠 **Concordy** coffee shop only, at the junction of the N VI and M 40 - El Plantío, North-West :
11,7 km ☎ (91) 307 65 54, *Fax (91) 372 81 95* – ▤ TV ☎ ⓟ. E *VISA*. ✗
⌛ 350 – **22 rm** 6420/9630.

XXX **Gaztelubide,** Sopelana 13 - La Florida - North-West : 12,8 km ☎ (91) 372 85 44,
Fax (91) 372 84 19, ⛲ – ▤ ⓟ. AE ⓪ E *VISA*. ✗
closed Sunday dinner – **Meals** - Basque rest - a la carte 5000/7000.

XX **Los Remos,** La Florida - North-West : 13 km ☎ (91) 307 72 30, *Fax (91) 372 84 35* –
    ▤ ⓟ. AE ⓪ E *VISA*. ✗
Meals - Seafood - a la carte 4700/5400.

y motorway N I *North : 13 km –* ✉ *28100 Alcobendas :*

🏨 **La Moraleja** without rest, av. de Europa 17 - parque empresarial La Moraleja ☎ (91)
661 80 55, *Fax (91) 661 21 88,* 🏋, ⏋ – ▤ TV ☎ 🚗 ⓟ. AE ⓪ *VISA*. ✗
⌛ 1350 – **37 suites** 32000.

t Barajas *East : 14 km –* ✉ *28042 Madrid :*

🏨 **Barajas,** av. de Logroño 305 ☎ (91) 747 77 00, *Fax (91) 747 87 17,* ⛲, 🏋, ⏋, 🍴 –
    ▤ TV ☎ ⓟ – 25/675. AE ⓪ E *VISA*. ✗ rest
Meals 5500 – ⌛ 1850 – **218 rm** 23200/29000, 12 suites.

🏨 **Alameda,** av. de Logroño 100 ☎ (91) 747 48 00, *Fax (91) 747 89 28,* 🍴 – ▤ TV ☎
    ⓟ – 25/280. AE ⓪ E *VISA* JCB. ✗ rest
Meals a la carte approx. 4600 – ⌛ 1400 – **136 rm** 19200/24000, 9 suites.

Moralzarzal *28411 Madrid* 444 *J 18 – pop. 2 248 alt. 979.*
Madrid 42.

XXX **El Cenador de Salvador** with rm, av. de España 30 ☎ (91) 857 77 22,
☼ *Fax (91) 857 77 80,* ⛲, « Garden terrace » – ▤ TV ☎ ⓟ. AE ⓪ *VISA*. ✗
Meals a la carte 5775/8075 – ⌛ 2000 – **7 rm** 25000/40000
Spec. Ensalada de hierbas aromáticas y flores de mi huerta con vinagreta Cabernet Sau-
vignon (spring-summer). Cabecita de pata de cordero lechal con frito de garbanzos blancos.
Burbujas de Vichy con leche de coco y mermelada de naranja.

BARCELONA 08000 ℗ 443 H36 – pop. 1 681 132.

See : Gothic Quarter★★ (Barri Gòtic : Ardiaca House★ MX **A**, Cathedral★ MX, No 10 Car.
del Paradis (Roman columns★) MX **135**, Plaça del Rei★★ MX **149**, Museum of the Cit
History★ (The Roman City★★) MX **M'**, Santa Ágata Chapel★ (Altarpiece of t
Constable★★) MX **F**, Rei Martí Belvedere ≤★★ MX**K** – Frederic Marès Museum★ MX **I**
La Rambla★★ : Barcelona Contemporary Art Museum★★ (MACBA) HX **M¹⁰**, Barcelo
Contemporary Culture Centre (CCCB) : patio★ HX **R**, (Former) Hospital of Santa Creu (Got
patio★) LY, Santa Maria del Pi Church★ LX, Güell Palace★★ LY, Plaça Reial★★ MY – T
Sea Front★ : Shipyards (Drassanes) and Maritime Museum★★ MY, Old Harbour★ (Port V
NY, Mercè Basilica★ NY, La Llotja★ (Gothic Hall★★) NX, França Station★ NVX, Ciutade
Park★ NV, KX (Three Dragons Pavilion★★ NV **M⁷**, Zoology Museum★ NV **M⁷**, Zoo★ KX
La Barceloneta★ KXY, Vila Olímpica★ (marina★★, twin towers ✳★★★) East : by Av. D'Icà
KX, Carrer de Montcada★★ : Picasso Museum★ NV, Santa Maria del Mar Church★★ (ro
window★) NX – Montjüic★ (≤★ from castle terraces) South : by Av. de la Reina Ma
Cristina GY : Mies van der Rohe Pavilion★★, National Museum of Catalonian Art★★★, Span
Village★ (Poble Espanyol), Anella Olímpica★ (Olympic Stadium★, Sant Jordi Spor
Centre★★) – Joan Miró Foundation★★★, Greek Theatre★, Archaeological Museum★ – E
ample District★★ : La Sagrada Familia Church★★★ (East or Nativity Façade★★, ≤★★ fro
east spire) JU, Hospital Sant Pau★ North : by Padilla JU, Passeig de Gràcia★★ HV (Lleó a
Morera House★ HV **Y**, Amatller House★ HV **Y**, Batlló House★★ HV **Y**, La Pedrera or M
House★★★ HV **P**) – Terrades House (les Punxes★) HV **Q**, Güell Park★★ (rolling bench★
North : by Padilla JU – Catalonian Concert Hall★★ (Palau de la Mìsica Catalana : façade
inverted cupola★★) MV - Antoni Tàpies Foundation★★ HV **S**.

Additional sights : Santa Maria de Pedralbes Monastery★★ (Church★, Cloister★, Sa
Miquel Chapel frescoes★★★, Thyssen Bornemisza Collection★) West : by Av. de Pedralb
EX – Pedralbes Palace (Decorative Arst Museum★ EX, Güell Stables★ (Pabellones) EX, Sa
Pau del Camp Church (Cloister★) LY, Science Museum★ North-West : by Balmes FU.

🛫, 🛫 Prat, South-West : 16 km ℘ (93) 379 02 78 – 🛫 Sant Cugat, North-West : 20 k
℘ (93) 674 39 08 Fax (93) 675 51 52.

✈ Barcelona, South-West : 12 km ℘ (93) 298 38 38 – Iberia : Diputació 258, ✉ 0800
℘ (93) 401 32 82 HV – Aviaco : Airport ℘ (93) 478 24 11.

🚗 Sants ℘ (93) 490 75 91.

⛴. to the Balearic Islands : Cia. Trasmediterránea, Moll de Sant Beltrà - Estació Marítim
✉ 08039, ℘ (93) 295 91 00, Fax (93) 295 91 34.

🛈 pl. de Catalunya 17-S ✉ 08002 ℘ (93) 304 31 35 Fax (93) 304 31 55 passeig de Gràc
107 ✉ 08008 ℘ (93) 238 40 00 Fax (93) 238 40 10, Sants Estació ✉ 08014 ℘ (9
491 44 31 and at Airport ℘ (93) 478 05 65 (Terminal A) and ℘ (93) 478 47 04 (Termir
B) – R.A.C.C. Parc de Negocis Mas Blau (edif. Muntadas 1º 4-esc. B) ✉ 08820 El Prat
Llobregat, ℘ (93) 478 77 05 Fax (93) 478 77 36.

Madrid 627 – Bilbao/Bilbo 607 – Lérida/Lleida 169 – Perpignan 187 – Tarragona 109
Toulouse 388 – Valencia 361 – Zaragoza 307.

Plans on following pages

Old Town and the Gothic Quarter : Ramblas, Pl. de Catalunya, Via Laietana, Pl. S
Jaume, Passeig de Colom, Passeig de Joan Borbó Comte de Barcelona

Le Meridien Barcelona, La Rambla 111, ✉ 08002, ℘ (93) 318 62 00, Telex 5463
Fax (93) 301 77 76 – 🛗 🗎 📺 ☎ 🚻 ⟲ – 🔔 25/200. AE ① E VISA JCB   LX
Meals a la carte 4000/5375 – ☕ 2350 – **197 rm** 30000/36000, 7 suites.

Colón, av. de la Catedral 7, ✉ 08002, ℘ (93) 301 14 04, Fax (93) 317 29 15 – 🛗
📺 ☎ 🚻 – 🔔 25/120. AE ① E VISA JCB   MV
Meals 3800 – ☕ 1800 – **138 rm** 17000/25500, 9 suites.

Royal coffee shop only, La Rambla 117, ✉ 08002, ℘ (93) 301 94 00, Fax (93) 317 31 7
– 🛗 🗎 📺 ☎ ⟲ – 🔔 25/100. AE ① VISA JCB. ✀   LX
☕ 1600 – **108 rm** 14000/18500.

Meliá Confort Apolo coffee shop only, av. del Paral.lel 57, ✉ 08004, ℘ (93) 443 11 2
Fax (93) 443 00 59 – 🛗 🗎 📺 ☎ 🚻 ⟲ – 🔔 25/500. AE ① E VISA JCB. ✀   LY
☕ 1050 – **314 rm** 16000/20000.

Ambassador, Pintor Fortuny 13, ✉ 08001, ℘ (93) 412 05 30, Telex 9922
Fax (93) 317 20 38, ⅃₅, ☒ – 🛗 🗎 📺 ☎ 🚻 ⟲ – 🔔 25/200. AE ① E VISA JCB. ✀
Meals 3000 – ☕ 1600 – **96 rm** 22000/28000, 9 suites.   LX

Duques de Bergara, Bergara 11, ✉ 08002, ℘ (93) 301 51 51, Fax (93) 317 34 4
☒ – 🛗 🗎 📺 ☎ 🚻 – 🔔 25/400. AE ① E VISA JCB. ✀   LV
Meals 1950 – ☕ 1500 – **149 rm** 18600/22900.

G.H. Barcino without rest, Jaume I-6, ✉ 08002, ℘ (93) 302 20 12, Fax (93) 301 42 4
– 🛗 🗎 📺 ☎ 🚻. AE ① E VISA JCB   MX
☕ 1800 – **53 rm** 18745/27000.

Mercure Barcelona Rambla without rest, La Rambla 124, ✉ 08002, ℘ (9
412 04 04, Fax (93) 318 73 23 – 🛗 🗎 📺 ☎ 🚻 ⟲. AE ① E VISA. ✀   LX
☕ 1400 – **74 rm** 9500/16400, 1 suite.

Allegro without rest, av. Portal de l'Àngel 15-17, ⊠ 08002, ℰ (93) 318 41 41, *Fax (93) 301 26 31*, « In the ancient Rocamora palace » – |**≑**| ▤ 🖵 ☎ 🕭. 🗛 ⓪ 🖪 *VISA* JCB. 🕸
☑ 950 – **74 rm** 20900/22900.
LV a

Gravina coffee shop only, Gravina 12, ⊠ 08001, ℰ (93) 301 68 68, *Fax (93) 317 28 38* – |**≑**| ▤ 🖵 ☎ 🕭 – 🔼 25/50. 🗛 ⓪ 🖪 *VISA*. 🕸
☑ 1400 – **81 rm** 12000/18000, 5 suites.
HX d

Guitart Almirante without rest, Via Laietana 42, ⊠ 08003, ℰ (93) 268 30 20, *Fax (93) 268 31 92* – |**≑**| ▤ 🖵 ☎ ⇔ – 🔼 25/40. 🗛 ⓪ 🖪 *VISA* JCB. 🕸
76 rm ☑ 17180/22900.
MV d

Regina coffee shop only, Bergara 2, ⊠ 08002, ℰ (93) 301 32 32, *Telex 59380*, *Fax (93) 318 23 26* – |**≑**| ▤ 🖵 ☎. 🗛 ⓪ 🖪 *VISA* JCB. 🕸
☑ 1500 – **102 rm** 14300/21800.
LV r

Reding, Gravina 5, ⊠ 08001, ℰ (93) 412 10 97, *Fax (93) 268 34 82* – |**≑**| ▤ 🖵 ☎ 🕭. 🗛 ⓪ 🖪 *VISA* JCB. 🕸
Meals *(closed Sunday and Bank Holidays)* 2450 – ☑ 1300 – **44 rm** 16200/20000.
HX d

Catalunya Plaza coffee shop only, pl. de Catalunya 7, ⊠ 08002, ℰ (93) 317 71 71, *Fax (93) 317 78 55* – |**≑**| ▤ 🖵 ☎ – 🔼 25. 🗛 ⓪ 🖪 *VISA* JCB. 🕸
☑ 1500 – **46 rm** 20000/23000.
LV g

Atlantis without rest, Pelai 20, ⊠ 08001, ℰ (93) 318 90 12, *Fax (93) 412 09 14* – |**≑**| ▤ 🖵 ☎ 🕭. 🗛 ⓪ 🖪 *VISA*. 🕸
☑ 1000 – **42 rm** 10000/13000.
HX a

Metropol without rest, Ample 31, ⊠ 08002, ℰ (93) 310 51 00, *Fax (93) 319 12 76* – |**≑**| ▤ 🖵 ☎. 🗛 ⓪ 🖪 *VISA*
☑ 1000 – **68 rm** 11700/12900.
NY r

Gaudí coffee shop only, Nou de la Rambla 12, ⊠ 08001, ℰ (93) 317 90 32, *Fax (93) 412 26 36* – |**≑**| ▤ 🖵 ☎ ⇔. 🗛 ⓪ 🖪 *VISA* JCB
☑ 1000 – **73 rm** 12000/15000.
LY q

Lleó coffee shop only, Pelai 22, ⊠ 08001, ℰ (93) 318 13 12, *Fax (93) 412 26 57* – |**≑**| ▤ 🖵 ☎ 🕭 – 🔼 25/150. 🗛 🖪 *VISA* JCB
☑ 1150 – **80 rm** 11600/14500.
HX a

Turín, Pintor Fortuny 9, ⊠ 08001, ℰ (93) 302 48 12, *Fax (93) 302 10 05* – |**≑**| ▤ 🖵 ☎ 🕭. 🗛 ⓪ *VISA*. 🕸
Meals *(closed Saturday)* 1200 – ☑ 1000 – **60 rm** 10500/14500.
LX v

Ramblas H. without rest, Rambles 33, ⊠ 08002, ℰ (93) 301 57 00, *Fax (93) 412 25 07* – |**≑**| ▤ 🖵 ☎ – 🔼 25. 🗛 *VISA*
70 rm ☑ 18000/20000.
MY z

Rialto coffee shop only, Ferran 42, ⊠ 08002, ℰ (93) 318 52 12, *Fax (93) 318 53 12* – |**≑**| ▤ 🖵 ☎. 🗛 ⓪ 🖪 *VISA* JCB
☑ 1450 – **163 rm** 12400/16100, 2 suites.
MX s

Park H., av. Marquès de l'Argentera 11, ⊠ 08003, ℰ (93) 319 60 00, *Fax (93) 319 45 19* – |**≑**| ▤ 🖵 ☎ 🕭. 🗛 ⓪ 🖪 *VISA*. 🕸
Meals 2950 – ☑ 1150 – **87 rm** 11500/14500.
NX e

Regencia Colón without rest, Sagristans 13, ⊠ 08002, ℰ (93) 318 98 58, *Fax (93) 317 28 22* – |**≑**| ▤ 🖵 ☎. 🗛 ⓪ 🖪 *VISA*
☑ 1200 – **55 rm** 9500/16000.
MV r

Continental without rest, Rambles 138-2°, ⊠ 08002, ℰ (93) 301 25 70, *Fax (93) 302 73 60* – |**≑**| 🖵 ☎. 🗛 ⓪ 🖪 *VISA*
☑ 550 – **35 rm** 6950/11250.
LV b

Hofmann, Argenteria 74-78 (1°), ⊠ 08003, ℰ (93) 319 58 89, *Fax (93) 319 58 89*, « Pleasant setting amongst plants » – ▤. 🗛 ⓪ 🖪 *VISA*. 🕸
closed Saturday, Sunday, Holy Week and August – **Meals** a la carte 4725/6290.
NX v

Agut d'Avignon, Trinitat 3, ⊠ 08002, ℰ (93) 302 60 34, *Fax (93) 302 53 18* – ▤. 🗛 ⓪ 🖪 *VISA* JCB. 🕸
Meals a la carte 5090/5965.
MY n

Flo, Jonqueres 10, ⊠ 08003, ℰ (93) 319 31 02, *Fax (93) 268 23 95* – ▤. 🗛 ⓪ 🖪 *VISA*. 🕸
Meals a la carte 3950/5760.
LV m

Reial Club Marítim, Moll d'Espanya, ⊠ 08039, ℰ (93) 221 71 43, *Fax (93) 221 44 12*, ≼, 🏯, « In the sports complex » – ▤. 🖪 *VISA* JCB
closed Sunday dinner – **Meals** a la carte 3450/4850.
NY a

Senyor Parellada, Argenteria 37, ⊠ 08003, ℰ (93) 310 50 94 – ▤. 🗛 ⓪ 🖪 *VISA* JCB. 🕸
closed Sunday and Bank Holidays – **Meals** a la carte 3160/3590.
NX t

BARCELONA
0   300 m

E   F
U
V
X
Y

Pl. de la Bonanova
Escoles
Bonanova
Balmes
El Putget
Muntaner
t
u
Mitre
a
TURÓ DE
MONTEROL
Santaló
Vallmajor
Vico
General
Mandri
Ganduxer
Calatrava
Pies
Angli
n
s
la
t
r
de
Major
SARRIÀ
d   a
Pas.
Via
Sarrià
M c
c
Vergós
Les Tres
Torres
La Bonanova
Reina
Elisenda
Augusta
Via
Augusta
88
136
Sarrià
Pas. Sant Joan Bosco
Ronda
100
JARDINS
E. MARQUINA
59
187
Ganduxer
i
Fontestà
e
Bosch i Gimpera
Pl. de
Fra Eloi
de Bianya
b
Capità
Marquès
de
Mulhacén
Manuel
Girona
Av.   de   Sarrià
Mata
n
e
M
t
f
Gran
Av.
c
Entença
PAVELLÓ
GÜELL
Pas.
de
Pedralbes
z
57
r
Arenas
153
Diagonal
Deu
u
U
Palau
de Pedralbes
Pl. Pius XII
M
Maria Cristina
n
V
Numància
Palau Reial
X
158
Via
de
Europa
Galileo
Corts
a
t
Sentmenat
Berlin
Zona
Universitària
Av. Joan XXIII
TORRES
TRADE
Joan
Marquès Vallespir
de
Les Corts
z
Aristides
Carles III
les
Madrid
Pl. del Centre
Sants-Estació
CAMP
NOU
de
b
Güell
Vallespir
Galileo
SANTS
63
44
de
Sant Antón
P
Maillol
Arizala
Brasil
Roses
Pl.
de Sants
Y
177
Travessera
Riera
Av.
Roger
Badal
Mercat Nou
Collblanc
Collblanc
Blanca
Sants
Sants
Badal
Sants

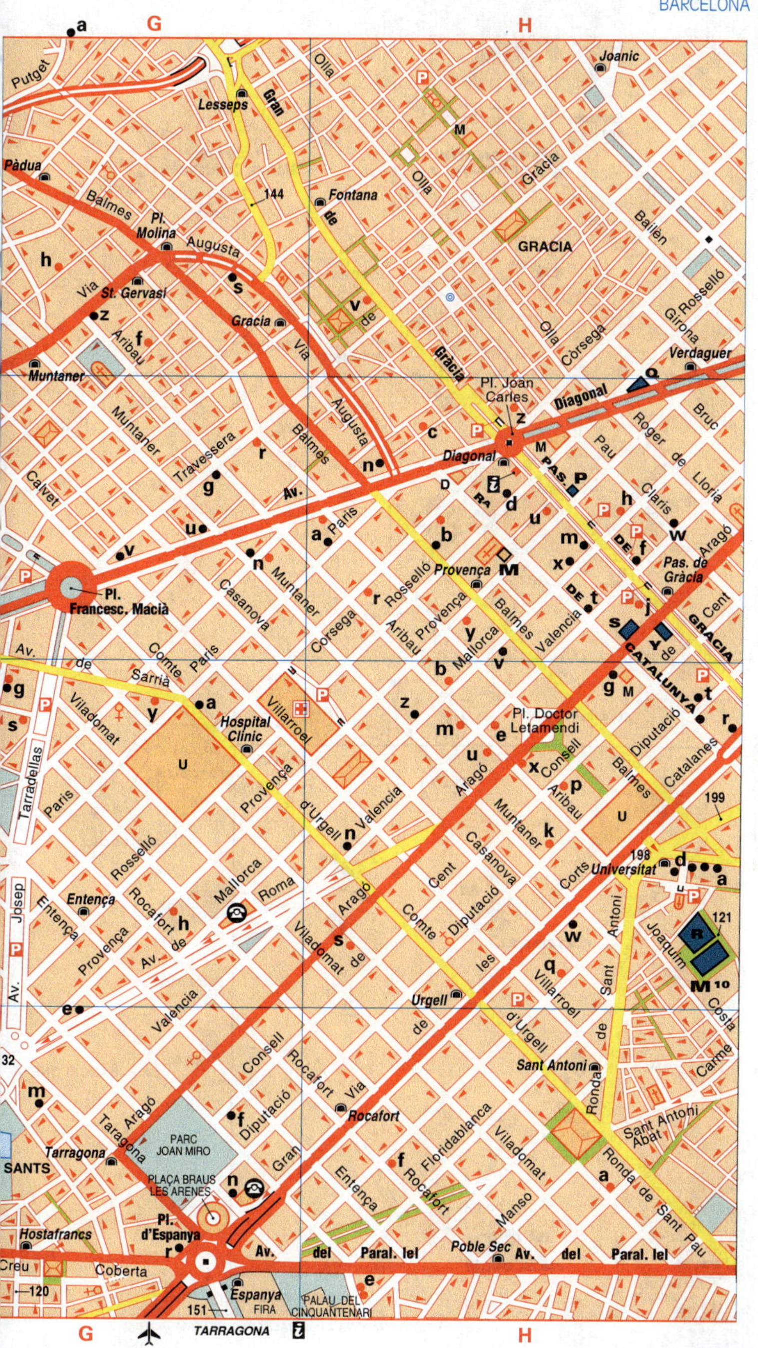

BARCELONA
SPAIN
G
H
a
Putget
Lesseps
Gran
Olla
Joanic
Pàdua
Balmes
Pl. Molina
Augusta
de
Fontana
Olla
Gracia
GRACIA
Bailèn
h
Via
St. Gervasi
Gracia
Aribau
z
f
Muntaner
Gràcia
Pl. Joan Carles
Diagonal
Roger
Bruc
Rosselló
Girona
Verdaguer
Còrsega
de
Lloria
Muntaner
Travessera
Balmes
Augusta
Pl. Joan Carles
c
Diagonal
M
Q
Calvet
r
Av.
n
Diagonal
PAS.
P
Pau
Claris
Aragó
g
D
d
h
w
u
Paris
a
b
RA
u
m
DE
f
Pas. de Gràcia
v
n
Muntaner
Rosselló
Provença
M
x
DE
t
j
Casanova
Corsega
Aribau
Provença
y
Balmes
Valencia
Cent
Pl. Francesc. Macià
r
Mallorca
S
Y
de
GRACIA
CATALUNYA
Av.
de
Comte
Paris
b
v
g
M
CATALUNYA
g
Sarrià
Viladomat
a
Villarroel
z
Pl. Doctor Letamendi
Diputació
t
r
s
y
Hospital Clinic
m
u
Consell
x
p
199
Tarradellas
Paris
U
Provença
d'Urgell
n
Valencia
Aragó
Muntaner
p
Balmes
U
Catalanes
Rosselló
Mallorca
Roma
Casanova
Aribau
k
198
Universitat
d
a
Entença
Rocafort
de
h
Cent
Corts
Diputació
w
u
P
Jossep
Entença
Provença
Av
Viladomat
s
de
Comte
Diputació
Sant Antoni
Joaquim
121
R
Av.
Valencia
Aragó
les
q
Villarroel
M
10
e
Urgell
de
d'Urgell
Carme
32
Consell
Rocafort
Via
Sant Antoni
Ronda
m
Aragó
Diputació
f
Rocafort
Floridablanca
Viladomat
Sant Antoni Abat
Tarragona
Taragona
PARC JOAN MIRO
Gran
Entença
Rocafort
f
Manso
Ronda de Sant Pau
SANTS
PLAÇA BRAUS LES ARENES
n
a
Hostafrancs
Pl. d'Espanya
Creu
Coberta
r
Av.
del
Paral. lel
Poble Sec
Av.
del
Paral. lel
120
Espanya
FIRA
e
PALAU DEL CINQUANTENARI
151
G
TARRAGONA
H
144
151
198
199

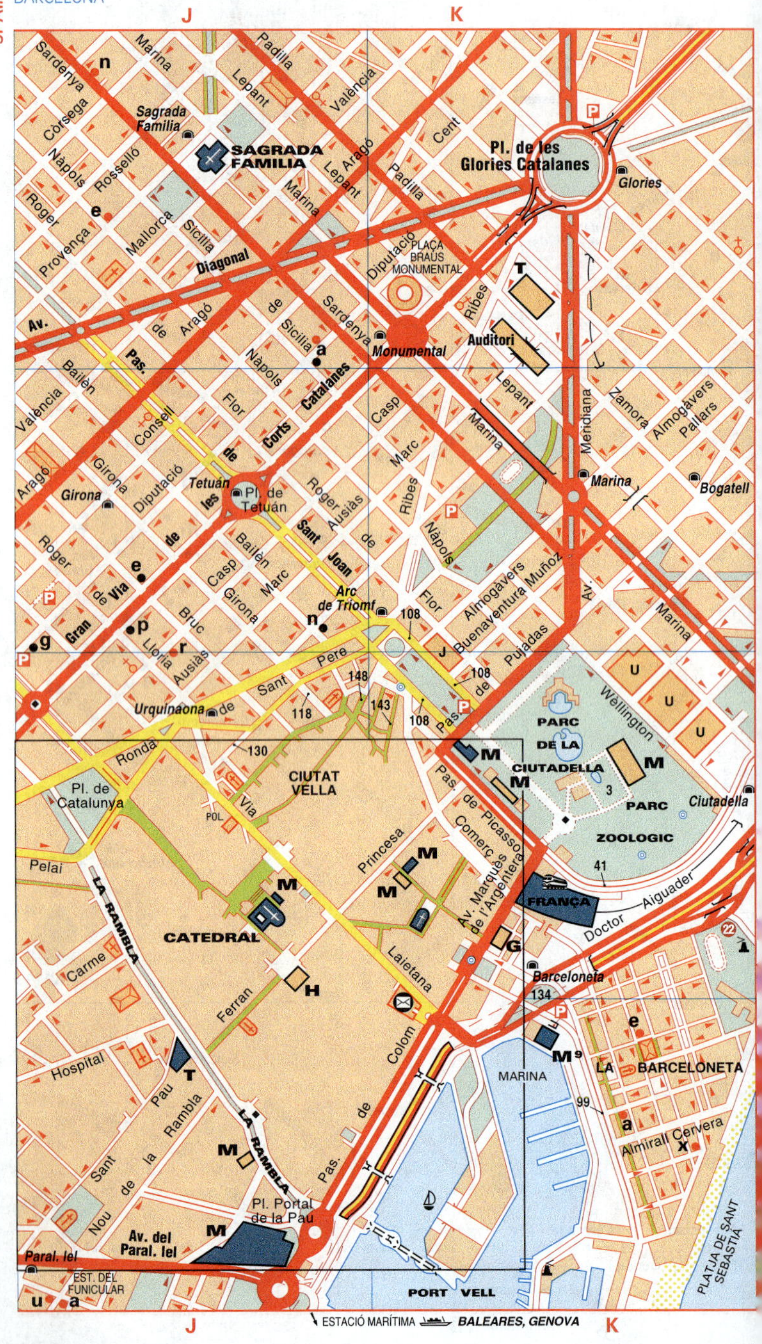
J
K
Sardenya
Marina
Padilla
Lepant
València
Cent
Pl. de les
Glories Catalanes
P
Glories
Còrsega
Nàpols
Rosselló
Sagrada
Familia
SAGRADA
FAMILIA
Le Aragó
Lepant
Padilla
Roger
Provença
Mallorca
Sicilia
Diagonal
Marina
Diputació
PLAÇA
BRAUS
MONUMENTAL
T
Av.
Bailèn
Pas.
de Aragó
de Sicilia
Sardenya
Monumental
Auditori
Ribes
Lepant
Meridiana
Zamora
Almogàvers
Pallars
València
Consell
Corts
Catalanes
Nàpols
Casp
Marc
Casp
Ribes
Marina
Marina
Bogatell
Aragó
Girona
Diputació
de
les
Tetuán
Pl. de
Tetuán
Roger
Ausiàs
de
Flor
Nàpols
Marina
Roger
Via
de
Bailèn
Casp
Marc
Girona
Sant
Joan
Arc
de Triomf
108
Almogàvers
Buenaventura Muñoz
Pujadas
Av.
P
g
p
Bruc
Lloria
r
Ausiàs
n
Sant
Pere
108
de
Flor
J
108
de
Pas.
Wellington
U
U
U
U
Urquinaona
de
Sant
148
118
143
108
P
PARC
DE LA
CIUTADELLA
M
M
3
PARC
ZOOLOGIC
M
Ciutadella
Ronda
130
CIUTAT
VELLA
Via
POL
Princesa
Comerç
Av. Marquès
de l'Argentera
M
M
M
41
FRANÇA
Doctor
Aiguader
Pl. de
Catalunya
Pelai
Pas. de Picasso
CATEDRAL
M
Laietana
G
Barceloneta
134
22
Carme
Ferran
Colom
M 9
MARINA
LA BARCELONETA
e
Hospital
Pau
T
LA RAMBLA
de la Rambla
Sant
Nou
M
LA RAMBLA
Pl. Portal
de la Pau
Pas.
99
a
Almirall Cervera
X
PLATJA DE SANT
SEBASTIÀ
Paral. lel
EST. DEL
FUNICULAR
u
a
Av. del
Paral. lel
M
J
K
ESTACIÓ MARÍTIMA   BALEARES, GENOVA
PORT VELL

STREET INDEX TO BARCELONA TOWN PLAN

EUROPE on a single sheet
Michelin map n° **970**.

BARCELONA

Bacardí (Pas.) . . . . MY 4
Banys Nous . . . . MX 7
Bergara . . . . LV 10
Bisbe Irurita . . . . MX 15
Bòria . . . . MV 18
Born (Pas. del) . . . . NX 20
Boters . . . . MX 23
Canaletes
(Rambla de) . . . . LV 27
Canonge Colom (Pl.) . . . . . LY 28
Canvis Vells . . . . NX 32
Caputxins
(Rambla dels) . . . . MY 35
Cardenal Casañas . . . . LX 36
Catalunya (Pl. de) LV
Catedral (Av.) . . . . MV 40
Ciutat . . . . MX 43
Comercial (Pl.) . . . . NV 45
Cucurella . . . . LX 55
Doctor Joaquim Pou . . . . . MV 61
Escudellers . . . . MY
Estudis (Rambla dels) LX
Francesc Cambó
(Av.) . . . . MV 79
Garriga i Bach . . . . MX 81
Isabel II (Pas. d') . . . . NX 98
Montcada . . . . NX 122
Montjuïc del Bisbe . . . . MX 123
Nou de Sant Francesc . . . . MY 126
Nova (Pl.) . . . . MX 128
Paradís . . . . MX 133
Pi (Pl. del) . . . . LX 137
Pintor Fortuny . . . . LX 140
Portal de Santa
Madrona . . . . MY 142
Ramon Berenguer
el Gran (Pl.) . . . . MX 147
Rei (Plaça del) . . . . MX 149
Sant Felip Neri (Pl.) . . . . . . MX 163
Sant Josep (Rambla de) . . . LX 168
Sant Miquel (Pl. de) . . . . . . MX 173
Sant Sever . . . . MX 181
Santa Anna . . . . LV 182
Santa Maria (Pl.) . . . . NX 189
Seu (Pl. de la) . . . . MX 192
Tapineria . . . . MX 193
Santa Mònica
(Rambla de) . . . . MY
Universitat
(Ronda de la) . . . . LV 199

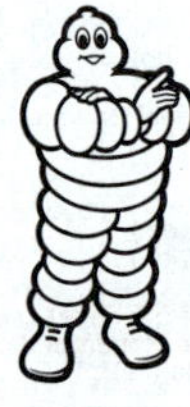

We suggest:

For a successful tour, that you prepare it in advance. Michelin maps *and* guides *will give you much useful information on route planning, places of interest, accommodation, prices, etc.*

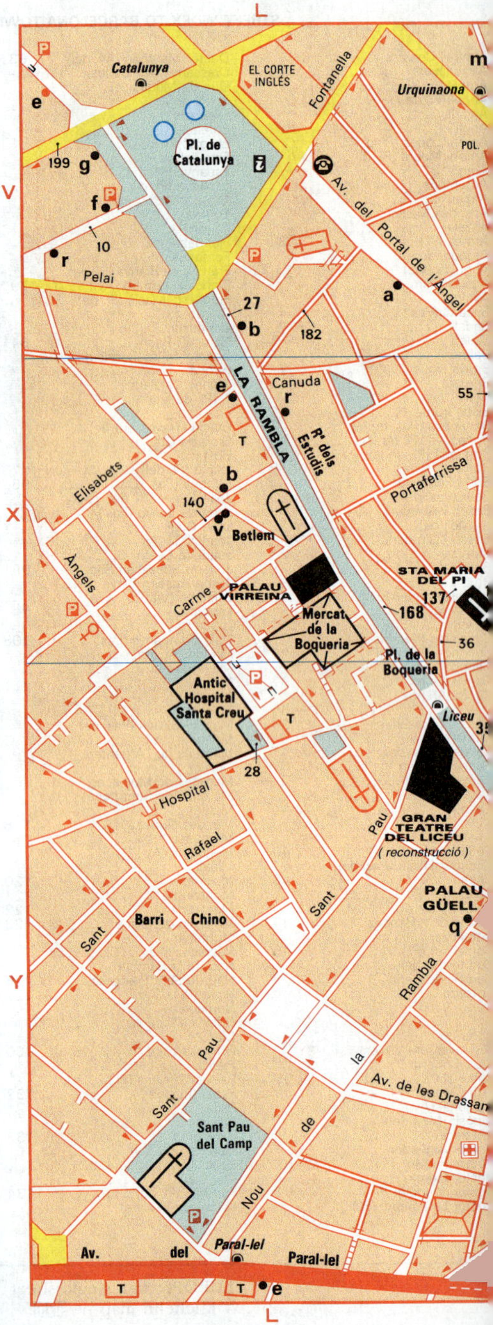

BARCELONA
SPAIN
PALAU DE LA MÚSICA CATALANA
PARC DE LA CIUTADELLA
M 7
M 13
LA RIBERA
Alt
St. Pere més Baix
Sant Pere més
St Pere més Alt
Laietana
Sant
més
Carders
Assaonadors
Mercaders
Princesa
Pg. de Comerç
Picasso
l'Argentera
d
79
61
Pl. d'Antoni Maura
40
e
r
e
18
Mercat del Born
45
P
P
c
MUSEU PICASSO
122
M
M 2
193
192
F 147
170
149
128
A
123
M 1
e
20
ESTACIÓ DE FRANÇA
e de
CATEDRAL
a
STA MARIA DEL MAR
G
M
81
181
163
15
BARRI GÒTIC
Pl. de l'Angel
Mirallers
t
Jaume 1
Argenteria
Via Laietana
v
189
Av. Marquès
7
Pl. St Jaume
133
r
Palau de la Generalitat
43
H
173
S
32
Pl. del Palau
LA LLOTJA
s
98
n
Pl. A. López
Moll del Dipòsit
PALAU DE MAR
Avinyó
r
e
Ample
Colom
P
MARINA
PLAÇA REIAL
Serra
k
LA MERCÈ
4
35
Escudellers
126
Pl. del Teatre
RAMBLA
Ample
de
LITORAL
DEL
Bosch i Alsina
(Moll de la Fusta)
Pl. del Ictinio
Clavé
Pl. del Duc de Medinaceli
RONDA
Moll de
Imax
Josep A.
Passeig
M
REAL CLUB NAUTICO
Sta. Mónica
M
142
Pl. Portal de la Pau
PORT VELL
L'Aquàrium
DUANES
Monument a Colom
Pl. de la Odisea
Moll d'Espanya
DRASSANES i MUSEU MARÍTIM
REAL CLUB MARITIMA
a
MAREMAGNUM
Rambla de Mar
m
0   100 m
M
N
V
X
Y

XX **7 Portes**, passeig d'Isabel II-14, ⊠ 08003, ℘ (93) 319 30 33, Fax (93) 319 30 46 – 🗉
AE ⓘ E VISA. 🐾
Meals a la carte approx. 3300.
NX s

XX **Tikal**, Rambla de Catalunya 5, ⊠ 08007, ℘ (93) 302 22 21 – 🗉. AE ⓘ E VISA
JCB. 🐾
LV e
closed Saturday lunch, Sunday dinner and 8 to 23 August – **Meals** a la carte 2870/4280

X **Can Ramonet**, Maquinista 17, ⊠ 08003, ℘ (93) 319 30 64, Fax (93) 319 70 14 – 🗉
AE ⓘ E VISA JCB. 🐾
KY e
Meals - Seafood - a la carte 3175/4500.

X **Pitarra**, Avinyó 56, ⊠ 08002, ℘ (93) 301 16 47, Fax (93) 301 85 62, « Period decor
and memorabilia of the poet Pitarra » – 🗉. AE ⓘ E VISA JCB
NY e
closed Sunday and August – **Meals** a la carte 2400/3475.

X **L'Elx al Moll**, Moll d'Espanya-Maremagnun, Local 9, ⊠ 08039, ℘ (93) 225 81 17
Fax (93) 225 81 20, ≤, 🌴, « At the pleasure harbour » – 🗉. AE E VISA
NY m
Meals - Rice dishes - a la carte approx. 3840.

X **Can Majó**, Almirall Aixada 23, ⊠ 08003, ℘ (93) 221 54 55, Fax (93) 221 54 55, 🌴
🗉. AE ⓘ E VISA
KY x
closed Sunday dinner and Monday except Bank Holidays – **Meals** - Seafood - a la carte
approx. 3840.

X **Can Solé**, Sant Carles 4, ⊠ 08003, ℘ (93) 221 50 12, Fax (93) 221 58 15 – 🗉. AE ⓘ
E VISA. 🐾
KY a
closed Sunday dinner, Monday and 15 days in August – **Meals** a la carte 3250/4900.

South of Av. Diagonal : Gran Via de les Corts Catalanes, Passeig de Gràcia, Balmes
Muntaner, Aragó

Arts 🐦, Marina 19, ⊠ 08005, ℘ (93) 221 10 00, Fax (93) 221 10 70, ≤, 🌴, 🎡,
– 🛗 🗉 📺 ☎ 🚗 – 🔬 25/900. AE ⓘ E VISA JCB. 🐾
Newport Room (closed Sunday lunch and August) **Meals** a la carte approx. 6100
🍵 3100 – **397 rm** 45000, 58 suites.
East : by Av. d'Icària KX

Rey Juan Carlos I 🐦, av. Diagonal 661, ⊠ 08028, ℘ (93) 448 08 08
Fax (93) 448 06 07, ≤ city, 🌴, « Modern facilities. park with lake and 🎡 », 🎡, 🏊,
– 🛗 🗉 📺 ☎ 🚗 ⓟ – 🔬 25/1000. AE ⓘ E VISA JCB. 🐾
Chez Vous (closed Sunday) **Meals** a la carte 4750/6750 - **Café Polo** : **Meals** a la carte approx
4650 – 🍵 2300 – **375 rm** 30000/40000, 37 suites.
West : by Av. Diagonal EX

Ritz, Gran Via de les Corts Catalanes 668, ⊠ 08010, ℘ (93) 318 52 00
Fax (93) 318 01 48, 🌴 – 🛗 🗉 📺 ☎ – 🔬 25/280. AE ⓘ E VISA JCB. 🐾
JV
Meals a la carte 5800/7600 – 🍵 2450 – **148 rm** 30000/38000, 13 suites.

Claris 🐦, Pau Claris 150, ⊠ 08009, ℘ (93) 487 62 62, Fax (93) 215 79 70, « Moder
facilities with antiques. Archaelogical museum », 🎡, 🏊 – 🛗 🗉 📺 ☎ 🚗 – 🔬 25/60
AE ⓘ E VISA JCB
HV v
Meals 6000 - **Beluga** (closed Sunday) **Meals** a la carte approx. 8100 – 🍵 2400 – **102 rm**
27300/34100, 18 suites.

G.H. Havana, Gran Via de les Corts Catalanes 647, ⊠ 08010, ℘ (93) 412 11 15
Fax (93) 412 26 11 – 🛗 🗉 📺 ☎ 🚗 – 🔬 25/250. AE ⓘ E VISA JCB
🐾 rest
JV
Meals a la carte approx. 4300 – 🍵 1800 – **141 rm** 20500/22500, 4 suites.

Meliá Barcelona, av. de Sarrià 50, ⊠ 08029, ℘ (93) 410 60 60, Fax (93) 321 51 75
≤ – 🛗 🗉 📺 ☎ 🚗 – 🔬 25/500. AE ⓘ E VISA JCB. 🐾
FV
Meals (closed Sunday lunch) a la carte 5050 – 🍵 2100 – **296 rm** 28500/32750
4 suites.

Majestic, passeig de Gràcia 70, ⊠ 08008, ℘ (93) 488 17 17, Telex 52211
Fax (93) 488 18 80, 🏊 – 🛗 🗉 📺 ☎ 🚗 – 🔬 25/400. AE ⓘ E VIS
JCB. 🐾
HV
Meals 2800 – 🍵 2000 – **310 rm** 26000/34000, 9 suites.

Fira Palace, av. Rius i Taulet 1, ⊠ 08004, ℘ (93) 426 22 23, Fax (93) 424 86 79, 🎡
🏊 – 🛗 🗉 📺 ☎ 🚗 – 🔬 25/1300. AE ⓘ E VISA JCB. 🐾
Meals 2800 - **El Mall** : **Meals** a la carte 3290/4400 – 🍵 1550 – **258 rm** 25000/30000
18 suites.
South : by Lleida HY

Princesa Sofía Inter-Continental, pl. Pius XII-4, ⊠ 08028, ℘ (93) 330 71 11
Telex 51032, Fax (93) 330 76 21, ≤, 🎡, 🏊 – 🛗 🗉 📺 ☎ 🚗 – 🔬 25/1200. AE ⓘ
E VISA JCB. 🐾
EX
Meals 3200 – 🍵 2500 – **482 rm** 28000/34000, 21 suites.

Barcelona Hilton, av. Diagonal 589, ⊠ 08014, ℘ (93) 495 77 77, Fax (93) 495 77 00
🌴, 🎡 – 🛗 🗉 📺 ☎ 🚗 – 🔬 25/600. AE ⓘ E VISA JCB
FX
Meals 3750 – 🍵 2400 – **284 rm** 32000/36500, 2 suites.

NH Calderón, Rambla de Catalunya 26, ⊠ 08007, ℰ (93) 301 00 00, Fax (93) 317 31 57, 🛋, ≋, ☒ – 🛗 ≣ 📺 ☎ 🚗 – 🛎 25/200. 🖭 ⑩ Ε 𝘝𝘐𝘚𝘈 𝒿𝒸ʙ. ⌘ rest
Meals a la carte approx. 4800 – ⊇ 2100 – **224 rm** 23500, 29 suites.   HX t

Barcelona Plaza H., pl. d'Espanya 6, ⊠ 08014, ℰ (93) 426 26 00, Fax (93) 426 04 00, 🛋, ≋ – 🛗 ≣ 📺 ☎ ♿ 🚗 – 🛎 25/600. 🖭 ⑩ Ε 𝘝𝘐𝘚𝘈. ⌘   GY r
Meals 3500 - **Gourmet Plaza** : Meals a la carte 4800/5800 – ⊇ 1700 – **338 rm** 28900/32900, 9 suites.

Barceló Sants, pl. dels Països Catalans (Barcelona Sants railway station), ⊠ 08014, ℰ (93) 490 95 95, Fax (93) 490 60 45, ⇜ – 🛗 ≣ 📺 ☎ ♿ ℗ – 🛎 25/1500. 🖭 ⑩ Ε 𝘝𝘐𝘚𝘈. ⌘   FY
Meals 4100 – ⊇ 1750 – **364 rm** 22500/25000, 13 suites.

Condes de Barcelona (Monument and Centre), passeig de Gràcia 75, ⊠ 08008, ℰ (93) 488 11 52, Telex 51531, Fax (93) 487 14 42 – 🛗 ≣ 📺 ☎ ♿ 🚗 – 🛎 25/200. 🖭 ⑩ Ε 𝘝𝘐𝘚𝘈 𝒿𝒸ʙ. ⌘   HV m
Meals 2500 - **Thalassa** : Meals a la carte 2600/3800 – ⊇ 2000 – **180 rm** 26000/28000, 2 suites.

G.H. Catalonia, Balmes 142, ⊠ 08008, ℰ (93) 415 90 90, Telex 98718, Fax (93) 415 22 09 – 🛗 ≣ 📺 ☎ ♿ 🚗 – 🛎 50/260. 🖭 ⑩ Ε 𝘝𝘐𝘚𝘈 𝒿𝒸ʙ. ⌘   HV b
Meals 2700 – ⊇ 1500 – **82 rm** 28900/32900, 2 suites.

Avenida Palace, Gran Via de les Corts Catalanes 605, ⊠ 08007, ℰ (93) 301 96 00, Fax (93) 318 12 34 – 🛗 ≣ 📺 ☎ – 🛎 25/350. 🖭 ⑩ Ε 𝘝𝘐𝘚𝘈 𝒿𝒸ʙ. ⌘ rest   HX r
Meals 3500 – ⊇ 1700 – **146 rm** 20000/29000, 14 suites.

L'Illa, av. Diagonal 555, ⊠ 08029, ℰ (93) 410 33 00, Fax (93) 410 88 92 – 🛗 ≣ 📺 ☎ ♿ – 🛎 25/100. 🖭 ⑩ Ε 𝘝𝘐𝘚𝘈. ⌘   FX c
Meals (closed Saturday, Sunday and August) 2300 – ⊇ 1500 – **93 rm** 24000/29500, 10 suites.

Gallery H., Rosselló 249, ⊠ 08008, ℰ (93) 415 99 11, Telex 97518, Fax (93) 415 91 84, 🌳, 🛋 – 🛗 ≣ 📺 ☎ ♿ 🚗 – 🛎 25/200. 🖭 ⑩ Ε 𝘝𝘐𝘚𝘈. ⌘   HV d
Meals 2550 – ⊇ 2500 – **108 rm** 25000/29000, 5 suites.

St. Moritz, Diputació 264, ⊠ 08007, ℰ (93) 412 15 00, Telex 97340, Fax (93) 412 12 36 – 🛗 ≣ 📺 ☎ ♿ 🚗 – 🛎 25/200. 🖭 ⑩ Ε 𝘝𝘐𝘚𝘈 𝒿𝒸ʙ   JV g
Meals a la carte 3400/4600 – ⊇ 2100 – **92 rm** 21400/26800.

Gran Derby without rest, Loreto 28, ⊠ 08029, ℰ (93) 322 20 62, Fax (93) 419 68 20 – 🛗 ≣ 📺 ☎ 🚗 – 🛎 25/100. 🖭 ⑩ Ε 𝘝𝘐𝘚𝘈 𝒿𝒸ʙ   GX g
⊇ 1950 – **29 rm** 21670/24700, 12 suites.

City Park H., Nicaragua 47, ⊠ 08029, ℰ (93) 419 95 00, Fax (93) 419 71 63 – 🛗 ≣ 📺 ☎ 🚗 – 🛎 25/75. 🖭 ⑩ Ε 𝘝𝘐𝘚𝘈 𝒿𝒸ʙ. ⌘   FX z
Meals 2500 – ⊇ 1600 – **80 rm** 15600/22000.

NH Podium, Bailén 4, ⊠ 08010, ℰ (93) 265 02 02, Fax (93) 265 05 06, 🛋, ≋ – 🛗 ≣ 📺 ☎ ♿ 🚗 – 🛎 25/240. 🖭 ⑩ Ε 𝘝𝘐𝘚𝘈 𝒿𝒸ʙ. ⌘ rest   JV n
Meals 2500 – ⊇ 1800 – **140 rm** 16500/20000, 5 suites.

Balmes, Mallorca 216, ⊠ 08008, ℰ (93) 451 19 14, Fax (93) 451 00 49, « Terrace with ≋ » – 🛗 ≣ 📺 ☎ 🚗 – 🛎 25/30. 🖭 ⑩ Ε 𝘝𝘐𝘚𝘈 𝒿𝒸ʙ   HV v
Meals 1800 – ⊇ 1700 – **92 rm** 20150/22390, 8 suites.

Derby coffee shop only, Loreto 21, ⊠ 08029, ℰ (93) 322 32 15, Fax (93) 410 08 62 – 🛗 ≣ 📺 ☎ 🚗 – 🛎 25/60. 🖭 ⑩ Ε 𝘝𝘐𝘚𝘈 𝒿𝒸ʙ   FX e
⊇ 1950 – **107 rm** 19970/22390, 4 suites.

Alexandra, Mallorca 251, ⊠ 08008, ℰ (93) 467 71 66, Telex 81107, Fax (93) 488 02 58 – 🛗 ≣ 📺 ☎ ♿ 🚗 – 🛎 25/100. 🖭 ⑩ Ε 𝘝𝘐𝘚𝘈 𝒿𝒸ʙ. ⌘   HV x
Meals 2800 – ⊇ 2100 – **73 rm** 29000/33000, 2 suites.

NH Master, València 105, ⊠ 08011, ℰ (93) 323 62 15, Fax (93) 323 43 89 – 🛗 ≣ 📺 ☎ 🚗 – 🛎 25/100. 🖭 ⑩ 𝘝𝘐𝘚𝘈. ⌘ rest   HX n
Meals (closed Saturday, Sunday and Bank Holiday weekends) a la carte 3650/4050 – ⊇ 1400 – **80 rm** 18900, 1 suite.

Cristal, Diputació 257, ⊠ 08007, ℰ (93) 487 87 78, Telex 54560, Fax (93) 487 90 30 – 🛗 ≣ 📺 ☎ 🚗 – 🛎 25/100. 🖭 ⑩ Ε 𝘝𝘐𝘚𝘈 𝒿𝒸ʙ. ⌘ rest   HX t
Meals 1495 – ⊇ 1250 – **148 rm** 14000/21000.

NH Sant Angelo coffe shop dinner only, Consell de Cent 74, ⊠ 08015, ℰ (93) 423 46 47, Fax (93) 423 88 40 – 🛗 ≣ 📺 ☎ ♿ 🚗 – 🛎 25. 🖭 ⑩ Ε 𝘝𝘐𝘚𝘈 𝒿𝒸ʙ. ⌘
⊇ 1400 – **50 rm** 18900/19400.   GY f

Núñez Urgell, Comte d'Urgell 232, ⊠ 08036, ℰ (93) 322 41 53, Fax (93) 419 01 06 – 🛗 ≣ 📺 ☎ 🚗 – 🛎 25/150. 🖭 ⑩ Ε 𝘝𝘐𝘚𝘈 𝒿𝒸ʙ. ⌘   GX a
Meals (closed Saturday and Sunday) 3500 – ⊇ 1650 – **106 rm** 16000/17500, 2 suites.

🏨 **Guitart Grand Passage**, Muntaner 212, ✉ 08036, 📞 (93) 201 03 06
Fax (93) 201 00 04 – [⇕] ▤ 📺 ☎ – 🔊 25/80. AE ⓘ E *VISA*. ⊯ rest   GV r
Come Prima (closed Sunday) Meals a la carte 3250/4550 – ⊊ 1300 – **40 suites**
17280/21600.

🏨 **Expo H. Barcelona**, Mallorca 1, ✉ 08014, 📞 (93) 325 12 12, Fax (93) 325 11 44, ⊑
– [⇕] ▤ 📺 ☎ ⟷ – 🔊 25/300. AE ⓘ E *VISA* JCB ⊯   GY m
Meals 1900 – ⊊ 1200 – **435 rm** 15000/18000.

🏨 **Dante** coffee shop dinner only, Mallorca 181, ✉ 08036, 📞 (93) 323 22 54
Fax (93) 323 74 72 – [⇕] ▤ 📺 ☎ ⟷ – 🔊 25/70. AE ⓘ E *VISA*. ⊯   HX
⊊ 1400 – **81 rm** 16800/22700.

🏨 **Regente** without rest, Rambla de Catalunya 76, ✉ 08008, 📞 (93) 487 59 89
Telex 51939, Fax (93) 487 32 27, ⊑ – [⇕] ▤ 📺 ☎ ⅓ – 🔊 25/120. AE ⓘ E *VISA* JCB
⊊ 2100 – **79 rm** 21400/26800.   HV

🏨 **NH Forum**, Ecuador 20, ✉ 08029, 📞 (93) 419 36 36, Fax (93) 419 89 10 – [⇕] ▤ 📺
☎ ⟷ – 🔊 25/50. AE ⓘ E *VISA*. ⊯   FX
Meals (closed August) 3500 – ⊊ 1400 – **47 rm** 18000, 1 suite.

🏨 **NH Rallye**, Travessera de les Corts 150, ✉ 08028, 📞 (93) 339 90 50
Fax (93) 411 07 90, ⅙, ⊑ – [⇕] ▤ 📺 ☎ ⅓ ⟷ – 🔊 25/300. AE ⓘ E *VISA* JCB ⊯ res
Meals 1950 – ⊊ 1400 – **105 rm** 14000, 1 suite.   EY

🏨 **NH Les Corts** coffee shop dinner only, Travessera de les Corts 292, ✉ 08029
📞 (93) 322 08 11, Fax (93) 322 09 08 – [⇕] ▤ 📺 ☎ ⟷ – 🔊 25/80. AE ⓘ E *VISA* JC
⊊ 1400 – **80 rm** 14000, 1 suite.   FX

🏨 **Caledonian** without rest, Gran Via de les Corts Catalanes 574, ✉ 08011
📞 (93) 453 02 00, Fax (93) 451 77 03 – [⇕] ▤ 📺 ☎ ⅓ ⟷. AE ⓘ E *VISA*. ⊯
⊊ 1100 – **44 rm** 10900/17300.   HX v

🏨 **Onix** without rest, Llançà 30, ✉ 08015, 📞 (93) 426 00 87, Fax (93) 426 19 81 – [⇕]
📺 ☎ ⟷ – 🔊 25/70. AE ⓘ *VISA*. ⊯
⊊ 1100 – **80 rm** 12000/15000.   GY

🏨 **Astoria** without rest, París 203, ✉ 08036, 📞 (93) 209 83 11, Telex 81129
Fax (93) 202 30 08 – [⇕] ▤ 📺 ☎ – 🔊 25/30. AE E *VISA* JCB   HV
⊊ 1550 – **114 rm** 17200/20350, 3 suites.

🏨 **Abbot** without rest, av. de Roma 23, ✉ 08029, 📞 (93) 430 04 05, Fax (93) 419 57 4
– [⇕] ▤ 📺 ☎ ⟷ – 🔊 25/100. AE ⓘ E *VISA*. ⊯   GXY
⊊ 1250 – **35 rm** 11900/14900, 4 suites.

🏠 **Antibes** without rest, Diputació 394, ✉ 08013, 📞 (93) 232 62 11, Fax (93) 265 74 4
– [⇕] ▤ 📺 ☎ ⟷. E *VISA*   JVU
⊊ 575 – **71 rm** 6500/8500.

XXXX **La Dama**, av. Diagonal 423, ✉ 08036, 📞 (93) 202 06 86, Fax (93) 200 72 99, « House
❀ in a Modernist style building » – ▤. AE ⓘ E *VISA*. ⊯   HV
Meals a la carte 5350/7500
Spec. Ensalada de judías verdes y mariscos La Dama. Hígado de pato fresco sobre fond
de manzanas al vinagre de higos. Carro de pastelería de elaboración propia.

XXXX **Beltxenea**, Mallorca 275, ✉ 08008, 📞 (93) 215 30 24, Fax (93) 487 00 81, 🌳, « Ear
20C manor house » – ▤   HV

XXX **Casa Calvet**, Casp 48, ✉ 08010, 📞 (93) 412 40 12, Fax (93) 412 43 36 – ▤. AE ⓘ
E *VISA*. ⊯   JVX
closed Sunday, Bank Holidays and 15 to 31 August – **Meals** a la carte 4600/5525.

XXX **Jaume de Provença**, Provença 88, ✉ 08029, 📞 (93) 430 00 29, Fax (93) 439 29 5
❀ – ▤. AE ⓘ E *VISA* JCB. ⊯ – closed Sunday dinner, Monday, Holy Week, August an
Christmas – **Meals** 7000 and a la carte 5250/6400   GX
Spec. Huevo mollet en camisa de jamón serrano y espinacas catalana. Poti poti de bacala
con hortalizas confitadas y vinagreta remolacha. Crujiente de manitas de cerdo con fo
gras y trufas.

XXX **Windsor**, Còrsega 286, ✉ 08008, 📞 (93) 415 84 83, Fax (93) 217 42 65 – ▤. AE ⓘ
E *VISA* JCB. ⊯   HV
closed Sunday and August – **Meals** a la carte 4500/5550.

XXX **Oliver y Hardy**, av. Diagonal 593, ✉ 08014, 📞 (93) 419 31 81, Fax (93) 419 18 9
🌳 – ▤. AE ⓘ E *VISA*. ⊯   FX
closed Saturday lunch, Sunday and Holy Week – **Meals** a la carte approx. 5400.

XXX **Talaia Mar**, Marina 16, ✉ 08005, 📞 (93) 221 90 90, Fax (93) 221 89 89, ≼ – ▤ ⟷
AE ⓘ E *VISA* JCB   East : by Av. d'Icària KX
Meals a la carte 4750/6800.

XXX **El Tragaluz**, passatge de la Concepció 5-1°, ✉ 08008, 📞 (93) 487 01 9
Fax (93) 217 06 50, « Original decor with glass roof » – ▤. AE ⓘ E *VISA* JCB. ⊯   HV
Meals a la carte approx. 4300.

XXX **Els Pescadors,** pl. Prim 1, ✉ 08005, ✆ (93) 225 20 18, *Fax (93) 225 20 18*, 🌳 – 🍽.
AE ⓞ E VISA JCB   East : by Av. d'Icària   KX
closed Holy Week – **Meals** a la carte 3385/5400.

XXX **El Asador de Aranda,** Londres 94, ✉ 08036, ✆ (93) 414 67 90, *Fax (93) 414 67 90*
– 🍽. AE ⓞ E VISA. �належ   GV   n
closed Sunday dinner and 15 to 30 August – **Meals** - Roast lamb - a la carte approx. 3800.

XXX **Rías de Galicia,** Lleida 7, ✉ 08004, ✆ (93) 424 81 52, *Fax (93) 426 13 07* – 🍽. AE ⓞ
E VISA JCB. �   HY   e
Meals - Seafood - a la carte 4800/6500.

XXX **La Provença,** Provença 242, ✉ 08008, ✆ (93) 323 23 67, *Fax (93) 323 57 87* – 🍽.
AE ⓞ E VISA   HV   y
Meals a la carte 2770/3270.

XXX **Boix de la Cerdanya,** passeig de Gràcia 51, ✉ 08007, ✆ (93) 487 38 20,
Fax (93) 487 97 85 – 🍽. AE E VISA. ✳   HV   j
closed Sunday and Bank Holidays – **Meals** a la carte 2790/3850.

XXX **Vinya Rosa-Magí,** av. de Sarrià 17, ✉ 08029, ✆ (93) 430 00 03, *Fax (93) 430 00 41*
– 🍽. AE ⓞ E VISA   GX   y
closed Saturday lunch and Sunday – **Meals** a la carte approx. 5480.

XXX **Gorría,** Diputació 421, ✉ 08013, ✆ (93) 245 11 64, *Fax (93) 232 78 57* – 🍽. AE ⓞ E
VISA JCB. ✳   JU   a
closed Sunday, Bank Holidays dinner, Holy Week and August – **Meals** - Basque rest -
a la carte 4950/5750.

XXX **La Llotja,** Aribau 55, ✉ 08011, ✆ (93) 453 89 58, *Fax (93) 453 89 58* – 🍽. AE ⓞ E
VISA. ✳   HX   u
closed Sunday and August – **Meals** - Meat, braised fish and cod specialities - a la carte
2600/3775.

XXX **Casa Darío,** Consell de Cent 256, ✉ 08011, ✆ (93) 453 31 35, *Fax (93) 451 33 95* –
🍽. AE ⓞ E VISA JCB. ✳   HX   p
closed Sunday and August – **Meals** a la carte 3640/5950.

XXX **El Túnel del Port,** Moll de Gregal 12 (Port Olímpic), ✉ 08005, ✆ (93) 221 03 21,
Fax (93) 221 35 86, ≤, 🌳 – 🍽. AE ⓞ E VISA. ✳   East : by Av. d'Icària   KX
closed Sunday dinner and Monday – **Meals** a la carte 3400/4300.

X **El Celler de Casa Jordi,** Rita Bonnat 3, ✉ 08029, ✆ (93) 430 10 45 – 🍽. AE ⓞ E
VISA JCB. ✳   GX   s
closed Saturday, Sunday and August – **Meals** a la carte 2350/3750.

X **Nervión,** Còrsega 232, ✉ 08036, ✆ (93) 218 06 27 – 🍽. AE E VISA
JCB. ✳   HV   r
closed Sunday, Bank Holidays, Holy Week and August – **Meals** - Basque rest - a la carte
3100/5600.

X **Rosamar,** Sepúlveda 159, ✉ 08011, ✆ (93) 453 31 92 – 🍽. AE ⓞ
E VISA   HX   q
closed Sunday dinner, Monday, Holy Week and August – **Meals** a la carte 2600/3900.

X **Chicoa,** Aribau 73, ✉ 08036, ✆ (93) 453 11 23, « Rustic decor » – 🍽. AE E
VISA. ✳   HX   m
closed Sunday, Bank Holidays and 3 weeks in August – **Meals** a la carte 3300/
4925.

X **Elche,** Vila i Vilà 71, ✉ 08004, ✆ (93) 441 30 89, *Fax (93) 329 40 12* – 🍽. AE ⓞ E VISA.
✳   JY   a
Meals - Rice dishes - a la carte 2560/3680.

X **Cañota,** Lleida 7, ✉ 08004, ✆ (93) 325 91 71, *Fax (93) 426 13 07* – 🍽. E
VISA. ✳   HY   e
Meals - Braised meat specialities - a la carte 2450/3850.

North of Av. Diagonal : Via Augusta, Capità Arenas, Ronda General Mitre, Passeig de
la Bonanova, Av. de Pedralbes

🏨 **Tryp Presidente,** av. Diagonal 570, ✉ 08021, ✆ (93) 200 21 11, *Fax (93) 209 51 06*
– 🛗 🖥 📺 ☎ – 🕴 25/420. AE ⓞ E VISA. ✳   GV   u
Meals 2300 – ☕ 1300 – **155 rm** 21000/27000.

🏨 **Alimara,** Berruguete 126, ✉ 08035, ✆ (93) 427 00 00, *Fax (93) 427 92 92* – 🛗 🖥 📺
☎ ♿ 🚗 – 🕴 25/470. AE ⓞ E VISA. ✳ rest   North : by Padilla   JU
Meals 2500 – ☕ 1500 – **156 rm** 16500/19000.

🏨 **Hesperia** coffee shop only, Vergós 20, ✉ 08017, ✆ (93) 204 55 51, *Fax (93) 204 43 92*
– 🛗 🖥 📺 ☎ 🚗 – 🕴 25/150. AE ⓞ E VISA. ✳   EU   c
Meals 2800 – ☕ 1400 – **134 rm** 19100/23100.

Suite H., Muntaner 505, ✉ 08022, ☎ (93) 212 80 12, Fax (93) 211 23 17 – |‡| 🗏 TV ☎ 🚗 – 🔏 25/90. AE ⓓ E VISA JCB. ✻
FU
Meals 1800 – ☕ 1200 – **77 suites** 20900/22900.

Balmoral coffee shop only, Via Augusta 5, ✉ 08006, ☎ (93) 217 87 00
Fax (93) 415 14 21 – |‡| 🗏 TV ☎ 🚗 – 🔏 25/200. AE ⓓ E VISA. ✻
HV
☕ 1250 – **106 rm** 14300/21450.

Turó de Vilana without rest, Vilana 7, ✉ 46817, ☎ (93) 434 03 63, Fax (93) 418 89 0
– |‡| 🗏 TV ☎ 🚗. AE ⓓ E VISA. ✻
EU
☕ 1200 – **20 rm** 14500/18200.

NH Cóndor, Via Augusta 127, ✉ 08006, ☎ (93) 209 45 11, Fax (93) 202 27 13 – |‡|
🗏 TV ☎ – 🔏 25/50. AE ⓓ E VISA
GU
Meals (closed Saturday, Sunday and August) 2200 – ☕ 1300 – **78 rm** 15000, 12 suites

Arenas coffee shop only, Capità Arenas 20, ✉ 08034, ☎ (93) 280 03 03
Fax (93) 280 33 92 – |‡| 🗏 TV ☎ 🕭 – 🔏 25/50. AE ⓓ E VISA. ✻
EX
☕ 1500 – **58 rm** 17500/22000, 1 suite.

Park Putxet, Putxet 68, ✉ 08023, ☎ (93) 212 51 58, Fax (93) 418 58 17 – |‡| 🗏 TV
☎ 🚗 – 🔏 25/200. AE ⓓ VISA JCB. ✻
GU
Meals 1800 – ☕ 950 – **141 rm** 15900/17900.

NH Belagua coffe shop dinner only, Via Augusta 89, ✉ 08006, ☎ (93) 237 39 40
Fax (93) 415 30 62 – |‡| 🗏 TV ☎ – 🔏 25/50. AE ⓓ E VISA JCB. ✻
GU
☕ 1400 – **72 rm** 18900.

Mitre without rest, Bertràn 9, ✉ 08023, ☎ (93) 212 11 04, Fax (93) 418 94 81 – |‡| 🗏
TV ☎. AE ⓓ E VISA JCB
FU
☕ 1000 – **57 rm** 14300/18300.

Condado without rest, Aribau 201, ✉ 08021, ☎ (93) 200 23 11, Fax (93) 200 25 8
– |‡| 🗏 TV ☎. AE ⓓ E VISA
GV
☕ 1200 – **88 rm** 13000/14000.

NH Pedralbes coffee shop dinner only, Fontcuberta 4, ✉ 08034, ☎ (93) 203 71 12
Fax (93) 205 70 65 – |‡| 🗏 TV ☎ – 🔏 25. AE ⓓ E VISA JCB. ✻
EV
☕ 1500 – **30 rm** 16000.

Covadonga without rest, av. Diagonal 596, ✉ 08021, ☎ (93) 209 55 11
Fax (93) 209 58 33 – |‡| 🗏 TV ☎. AE ⓓ E VISA JCB
GV
☕ 1600 – **85 rm** 16900/21000.

Albéniz without rest, Aragó 591, ✉ 08026, ☎ (93) 265 26 26, Fax (93) 265 40 07
|‡| 🗏 TV ☎ 🕭 – 🔏 25/40. AE ⓓ E VISA. ✻
☕ 950 – **47 rm** 15900/17900.North-East : by Gran Via de les Corts Catalanes HX

Via Veneto, Ganduxer 10, ✉ 08021, ☎ (93) 200 72 44, Fax (93) 201 60 95, « Early 20
style » – 🗏. AE ⓓ E VISA. ✻
FV
closed Saturday lunch, Sunday and 1 to 20 August – **Meals** 7500 and a la carte 5980/881
Spec. Huevos escalfados con hígado de pato fresco y espinacas a la crema. Colita de rap
dorada al horno con semilla de sésamo y garbanzos crujientes al vinagre balsámico. Ravic
de plátanos en infusión de frutos rojos y su sorbete.

Reno, Tuset 27, ✉ 08006, ☎ (93) 200 91 29, Fax (93) 414 41 14 – 🗏. AE ⓓ E VIS
JCB. ✻
GV
closed Saturday lunch and Monday except Bank Holidays – **Meals** a la carte approx. 8000

Neichel, Beltran i Rózpide 16 bis, ✉ 08034, ☎ (93) 203 84 08, Fax (93) 205 63 69
🗏. AE ⓓ E VISA. ✻ – closed Saturday lunch, Sunday, Holy Week and August – **Mea**
7800 and a la carte 6900/8100
EX
Spec. Gambas de Palamós, alcachofas del país, vinagreta de aceitunas y pesto. Tronco d
lenguado y ajo tierno al vinagre de Chardonnay con laurel. Manzana caramelizada co
helado a la miel de tomillo.

Jean Luc Figueras, Santa Teresa 10, ✉ 08012, ☎ (93) 415 28 77, Fax (93) 218 92 6
« Tasteful decor » – 🗏. AE E VISA. ✻ – closed Saturday lunch, Sunday, Holy Week an
12 to 16 August – **Meals** a la carte 6100/9500
HV
Spec. Ensalada de gambas de Palamós, crema de calabaza, jenjibre y naranja confitad
Dorada sobre su piel, sopita de moluscos y macedonia de frutas. Pastel de chocolate
momento, helado de pan de especies y gelée de cacao.

Gaig, passeig de Maragall 402, ✉ 08031, ☎ (93) 429 10 17, Fax (93) 429 70 02, 🏠
🗏. AE ⓓ E VISA   North : by Travessera de Gràcia HU
closed Monday, Bank Holidays dinner, Holy Week and August – **Meals** 8900 and a la car
5520/7280
Spec. Ensalada de gambas con gelatina de tomates. Rodaballo rostit con percebes. Carr
de cordero al enebro.

Botafumeiro, Gran de Gràcia 81, ✉ 08012, ☎ (93) 218 42 30, Fax (93) 415 58 48
🗏. AE ⓓ E VISA JCB. ✻
HU
closed 3 weeks in August – **Meals** - Seafood - a la carte 4900/7900.

XX **El Trapío,** Esperanza 25, ✉ 08017, ℰ (93) 211 58 17, *Fax (93) 417 10 37*, ✿,
« Terrace » – 🍽. AE ① VISA. ✄   EU t
closed Sunday dinner – **Meals** a la carte approx. 3800.

XX **La Petite Marmite,** Madrazo 68, ✉ 08006, ℰ (93) 201 48 79, *Fax (93) 202 23 43* –
🍽. AE ① E VISA. ✄   GU f
closed Sunday, Bank Holidays, Holy Week and August – **Meals** a la carte 3000/
4275.

XX **Can Cortada,** av. de l'Estatut de Catalunya, ✉ 08035, ℰ (93) 427 23 15,
Fax (93) 427 02 94, ✿, « 16C farm » – |≋| 🍽 P. AE ① E VISA JCB. ✄
Meals a la carte approx. 3200.   North : by Padilla JU

XX **El Asador de Aranda,** av. del Tibidabo 31, ✉ 08022, ℰ (93) 417 01 15,
Fax (93) 212 24 82, ✿, « Former palace » – AE ① E VISA. ✄
closed Sunday dinner and Holy Week – **Meals** - Roast lamb - a la carte approx.
3690.   North-West : by Balmes FU

XX **Paradis Barcelona** with buffet, passeig Manuel Girona 7, ✉ 08034, ℰ (93) 203 76 37,
Fax (93) 203 61 94 – 🍽. AE ① E VISA. ✄   EVX t
Meals a la carte approx. 4000.

XX **El Racó d'en Freixa,** Sant Elíes 22, ✉ 08006, ℰ (93) 209 75 59, *Fax (93) 209 79 18*
– 🍽. AE ① E VISA. ✄   GU h
closed Bank Holidays dinner, Holy Week and August – **Meals** 6850 and a la carte 5500/
7500
Spec. Sopa de bacalao con miel y buñuelo de romesco con calamar. Liebre a la Royal (winter).
Caneton a las especies con tatin de berenjena e higos.

XX **Roig Robí,** Sèneca 20, ✉ 08006, ℰ (93) 217 97 38, *Fax (93) 415 78 42*, ✿, « Garden
terrace » – 🍽. AE ① E VISA   HV c
closed Saturday lunch, Sunday and 15 days in August – **Meals** a la carte 4750/6450.

XX **Tram-Tram,** Major de Sarrià 121, ✉ 08017, ℰ (93) 204 85 18, ✿ – 🍽. AE ① E VISA.
✄   EU d
closed Saturday lunch, Sunday, 23 to 30 December, Holy Week and 15 to 31 August –
Meals a la carte 4350/6500.

XX **St. Rémy,** Iradier 12, ✉ 08017, ℰ (93) 418 75 04, *Fax (93) 434 04 34* – 🍽. AE ① E
VISA. ✄   EU n
closed Sunday dinner – **Meals** a la carte 2870/3370.

X **Vivanda,** Major de Sarrià 134, ✉ 08017, ℰ (93) 205 47 17, *Fax (93) 203 19 18*, ✿ –
🍽. ① E VISA. ✄   EU a
closed Sunday and Monday lunch – **Meals** a la carte 3075/4775.

X **La Venta,** pl. Dr. Andreu, ✉ 08035, ℰ (93) 212 64 55, *Fax (93) 212 51 44*, ✿,
« Former cafe » – AE ① E VISA. ✄   North-West : by Balmes FU
closed Sunday – **Meals** a la carte 4200/4900.

X **Sal i Pebre,** Alfambra 14, ✉ 08034, ℰ (93) 205 36 58, *Fax (93) 205 56 72* – 🍽. AE
① E VISA JCB. ✄   West : by Pas. de Manuel Girona EX
Meals a la carte approx. 2625.

X **La Taula,** Sant Màrius 8-12, ✉ 08022, ℰ (93) 417 28 48 – 🍽. AE ① E VISA JCB. ✄
closed Saturday lunch, Sunday, Bank Holidays and August – **Meals** a la carte 2300/
3400.   FU u

X **La Yaya Amelia,** Sardenya 364, ✉ 08025, ℰ (93) 456 45 73 – 🍽. AE E VISA
JCB. ✄   JU n
closed Sunday, Holy Week and August – **Meals** a la carte 3275/4780.

Typical atmosphere :

XX **La Bona Cuina,** Pietat 12, ✉ 08002, ℰ (93) 268 23 94, *Fax (93) 315 07 98* – 🍽. AE
① E VISA JCB. ✄   MX e
Meals a la carte 3550/5975.

X **Can Culleretes,** Quintana 5, ✉ 08002, ℰ (93) 317 64 85, *Fax (93) 317 64 85*, « Typical
rest » – 🍽. E VISA JCB. ✄   MY c
closed Sunday dinner, Monday and 1 to 21 July – **Meals** a la carte 2150/3200.

X **Los Caracoles,** Escudellers 14, ✉ 08002, ℰ (93) 302 31 85, *Fax (93) 302 07 43*,
« Typical rest. rustic regional decor » – 🍽. AE ① E VISA JCB. ✄   MY k
Meals a la carte 3300/5150.

X **Pá i Trago,** Parlament 41, ✉ 08015, ℰ (93) 441 13 20, *Fax (93) 441 13 20*, « Typical
rest » – 🍽. AE ① E VISA   HY a
closed Monday and 20 June-15 July – **Meals** a la carte 2600/4050.

X **A la Menta,** passeig Manuel Girona 50, ✉ 08034, ℰ (93) 204 15 49, « Typical taverna »
– 🍽. AE ① E VISA. ✄   EV f
closed Sunday and Bank Holidays dinner – **Meals** a la carte 3750/4750.

Environs

at Esplugues de Llobregat *West : 5 km –* ✉ *08950 Esplugues de Llobregat :*

XXX **La Masía,** av. Països Catalans 58 ☎ (93) 371 00 09, *Fax (93) 372 84 00,* 🌳, « Terrace under pine trees » – ▤ ℗. AE ⓪ Ⓔ VISA JCB. ⚸
closed Sunday dinner – **Meals** a la carte 3675/5475.

at Sant Just Desvern *West : 6 km –* ✉ *08960 Sant Just Desvern :*

🏨 **Sant Just,** Frederic Mompou 1 ☎ (93) 473 25 17, *Fax (93) 473 24 50,* ≤, ₤ఠ – 🛗 ▤
📺 ☎ ⇔ – 🛠 25/450. AE ⓪ Ⓔ VISA. ⚸
Meals 3000 - *Alambí :* **Meals** a la carte 2850/4950 – ☕ 1300 - **144 rm** 13900/14900
6 suites.

XX **El Mirador de Sant Just,** av. Indústria 12 ☎ (93) 499 03 42, *Fax (93) 499 04 41,* ≤
« Hanging in the chimney of an old factory » – ▤. AE ⓪ Ⓔ VISA
closed Sunday dinner and 16 to 31 August – **Meals** a la carte 3300/4350.

at Sant Joan Despí *West : 7 km –* ✉ *08970 Sant Joan Despí :*

🏨 **Sant Joan** coffee shop only, Josep Trueta 2 ☎ (93) 477 30 03, *Fax (93) 477 33 88,* ₤ఠ
🏊 – 🛗 ▤ 📺 ☎ & ⇔ – 🛠 25/90. AE ⓪ Ⓔ VISA. ⚸
☕ 1000 – **128 rm** 11000/13600.

at Sant Cugat del Vallès *North-West : 18 km –* ✉ *08190 Sant Cugat del Vallès :*

🏨 **Novotel Barcelona-Sant Cugat** 🦅, pl. Xavier Cugat, ✉ 08190 apartado 122
☎ (93) 589 41 41, *Fax (93) 589 30 31,* ≤, 🌳, 🏊 – 🛗 ▤ 📺 ☎ & ⇔ ℗ – 🛠 25/300
AE ⓪ Ⓔ VISA
Meals 2135 – ☕ 1580 – **146 rm** 14300/16500, 4 suites.

Rosas o **Roses** 17480 Gerona 443 *F 39 – pop. 10 303 – Seaside resort.*
See : *Ciudadela★.*
🛈 Av. de Rhode 101 ☎ (972) 25 73 31 Fax (972) 15 11 50.
Madrid 763 – Barcelona 153 – Gerona/Girona 56.

at Cala Montjoi *South-East : 7 km –* ✉ *17480 Rosas :*

XXX **El Bulli,** ✉ apartado 30, ☎ (972) 15 04 57, *Fax (972) 15 07 17,* 🌳, « Pleasant rusti
❀❀❀ villa overlooking a creek » – ▤ ℗. AE ⓪ Ⓔ VISA
15 March-15 October – **Meals** *(closed Monday and Tuesday except July-September)* 14500
and a la carte 7850/12200
Spec. Menestra en texturas. Espardenyes en agridulce. Tuétano con caviar.

San Celoni o **Sant Celoni** 08470 Barcelona 443 *G 37 – pop. 11 937 alt. 152.*
Envir. : *North-West : Sierra de Montseny★ : itinerary★★ from San Celoni to Santa Fé de*
Montseny – Road★ from San Celoni to Tona by Montseny.
Madrid 662 – Barcelona 49 – Gerona/Girona 57.

XXX **El Racó de Can Fabes,** Sant Joan 6 ☎ (93) 867 28 51, *Fax (93) 867 38 61,* « Rusti
❀❀❀ decor » – ▤ ⇔. AE ⓪ Ⓔ VISA JCB. ⚸
closed Sunday dinner, Monday, 1 to 15 February and 21 June-5 July – **Meals** 15500 an
a la carte 9850/13100
Spec. Espardenyes con amouretes y un caviar de arenque. Gigot de cabrito caramelizad
a la salvia. Buñuelos de chocolate con helado de coco.

San Pol de Mar o **Sant Pol de Mar** 08395 Barcelona 443 *H 37 – pop. 2 383 – Seasid*
resort.
Madrid 679 – Barcelona 44 – Gerona/Girona 53.

XXX **Sant Pau,** Nou 10 ☎ (93) 760 06 62, *Fax (93) 760 09 50 –* ▤ ℗. AE Ⓔ VISA. ⚸
❀❀ *closed Sunday dinner, Monday, 8 to 24 March and 1 to 18 November –* **Meals** 8900 an
a la carte 7500/8700
Spec. El gazpacho de fresones con atillos de hojas de pimiento y bonito (July-September
La brochette de vieiras sobre fondant de cebolla tierna. La dentelle de naranja con garnach
de chocolate.

Pleasant hotels and restaurants
are shown in the Guide by a red sign.
Please send us the names
of any where you have enjoyed your stay.
Your Michelin Guide will be even better.

🏨 ... 🏠

XXXXX ... X

BILBAO o **BILBO** 48000 🅿 Vizcaya **442** C 20 – pop. 372 054.

See : Guggenheim Bilbao Museum★★★ DX – Museo de Bellas Artes★ (Fine Arts Museum : Antique Art Collection★★) DY **M**.

🏌 Laukariz, carret de Munguía North-East by railway Bl 631 (FYZ) ℘ (94) 674 04 62.

✈ de Bilbao, Sondica, North-East : 11 km by railway Bl 631 ℘ (94) 486 93 01 – Iberia : Ercilla 20 ✉ 48009 ℘ (94) 471 12 10 DY.

🚗 Abando ℘ (94) 423 06 17.

⛴. Cía Trasmediterránea, Colón de Larreategui 30 ✉ 48009 ℘ (94) 423 43 00 Fax (94) 424 74 59 EY.

🛈 paseo del Arenal 1 ✉ 48005 ℘ (94) 479 57 60 Fax (94) 479 57 61 – R.A.C.V.N. (R.A.C. Vasco Navarro) Rodriguez Arias 59 bis ✉ 48013 ℘ (94) 442 58 08 Fax (94) 441 27 12.

Madrid 397 – Barcelona 607 – La Coruña/A Coruña 622 – Lisboa 907 – San Sebastián/Donostia 100 – Santander 116 – Toulouse 449 – Valencia 606 – Zaragoza 305.

Plans on following pages

López de Haro, Obispo Orueta 2, ✉ 48009, ℘ (94) 423 55 00, Telex 34787, Fax (94) 423 45 00 – 📶 ▤ 📺 ☎ 🚗 – 🕴 25/40. AE ◑ E VISA. ✀ rest   EY r
Meals 4000 - **Náutico** (closed Saturday lunch, Sunday and 15 July-15 August) Meals a la carte 4700/6100 – ☕ 1550 – **49 rm** 20850/28000, 4 suites.

Carlton, pl. de Federico Moyúa 2, ✉ 48009, ℘ (94) 416 22 00, Fax (94) 416 46 28 – 📶 ▤ 📺 ☎ 🚗 – 🕴 25/200. AE ◑ VISA. ✀   DY x
Meals 3000 – ☕ 1500 – **141 rm** 15200/19200, 7 suites.

Indautxu, pl. Bombero Etxaniz 2, ✉ 48010, ℘ (94) 421 11 98, Fax (94) 422 13 31 – 📶 ▤ 📺 ☎ ♿ 🚗 – 🕴 25/400. AE ◑ E VISA   DZ b
Meals (see rest. **Etxaniz** below) – ☕ 1700 – **181 rm** 21350/23500, 3 suites.

G.H. Ercilla, Ercilla 37, ✉ 48011, ℘ (94) 470 57 00, Fax (94) 443 93 35 – 📶 ▤ 📺 ☎ 🚗 – 🕴 25/400. AE ◑ E VISA JCB   DY a
Meals (see rest. **Bermeo** below) – ☕ 1525 – **338 rm** 16745/21000, 8 suites.

Abando, Colón de Larreategui 9, ✉ 48001, ℘ (94) 423 62 00, Fax (94) 424 55 25 – 📶 ▤ 📺 ☎ 🚗 – 🕴 25/150. AE ◑ E VISA JCB. ✀   EY b
Meals (closed Sunday and Bank Holidays) 2750 – ☕ 1400 – **142 rm** 11200/18500, 3 suites.

NH Villa de Bilbao, Gran Vía de Don Diego López de Haro 87, ✉ 48011, ℘ (94) 441 60 00, Fax (94) 441 65 29 – 📶 ▤ 📺 ☎ 🚗 – 🕴 25/250. AE ◑ E VISA JCB. ✀
Meals 3250 - **La Pérgola** : Meals 5500 – ☕ 1800 – **139 rm** 20000/30000, 3 suites.   CY n

Nervión, paseo Campo de Volantín 11, ✉ 48007, ℘ (94) 445 47 00, Fax (94) 445 56 08 – 📶, ▤ rest, 📺 ☎ ♿ 🚗 – 🕴 25/250. AE ◑ E VISA. ✀   EX m
Meals (closed Sunday) 2000 – ☕ 1250 – **324 rm** 13200/16500, 24 suites.

NH de Deusto without rest, Francisco Maciá 9, ✉ 48014, ℘ (94) 476 00 06, Fax (94) 476 21 99 – 📶 ▤ 📺 ☎ 🚗 – 🕴 25/90. AE ◑ E VISA JCB   CX f
☕ 1200 – **70 rm** 12900.

Conde Duque, paseo Campo de Volantín 22, ✉ 48007, ℘ (94) 445 60 00, Fax (94) 445 60 66 – 📶 ▤ 📺 ☎ 🚗 – 🕴 25/120. AE ◑ E VISA. ✀   EX m
Meals 1600 – ☕ 1200 – **65 rm** 12000/18000, 2 suites.

Meliá Confort Arenal, Fueros 2, ✉ 48005, ℘ (94) 415 31 00, Fax (94) 415 63 95 – 📶 ▤ 📺 ☎ – 🕴 25/80. AE ◑ E VISA. ✀   EYZ m
Meals a la carte 3900/4900 – ☕ 1100 – **40 rm** 15000/19000.

Vista Alegre without rest, Pablo Picasso 13, ✉ 48012, ℘ (94) 443 14 50, Fax (94) 443 14 54 – 📺 ☎ 🚗. E VISA. ✀   DZ t
☕ 500 – **35 rm** 6000/8000.

Zabálburu without rest, Pedro Martínez Artola 8, ✉ 48012, ℘ (94) 443 71 00, Fax (94) 410 00 73 – 📺 ☎ 🚗. AE E VISA. ✀   DZ d
☕ 425 – **38 rm** 5800/7800.

XXXXX **Zortziko**, Alameda de Mazarredo 17, ✉ 48001, ℘ (94) 423 97 43, Fax (94) 423 56 87 – ▤. AE ◑ VISA. ✀   EY e
❀ closed Sunday, Monday dinner and 23 August-5 September – **Meals** 6950 and a la carte 6200/7200
Spec. Copa de foie en gelée de tempranillo. Risotto de bacalao y trufas. Pichón a la moda Zor cinco cocciones.

XXXX **Guria**, Gran Vía de Don Diego López de Haro 66, ✉ 48011, ℘ (94) 441 05 43, Fax (94) 441 85 64 – ▤. AE ◑ E VISA. ✀   CY s
closed Sunday dinner – **Meals** a la carte 6050/8700.

XXXX **Bermeo** - Hotel G.H. Ercilla, Ercilla 37, ✉ 48011, ℘ (94) 470 57 00, Fax (94) 443 93 35 – ▤. AE ◑ E VISA JCB. ✀   DY a
closed Saturday lunch and Sunday dinner – **Meals** a la carte approx. 5600.

BILBAO o BILBO

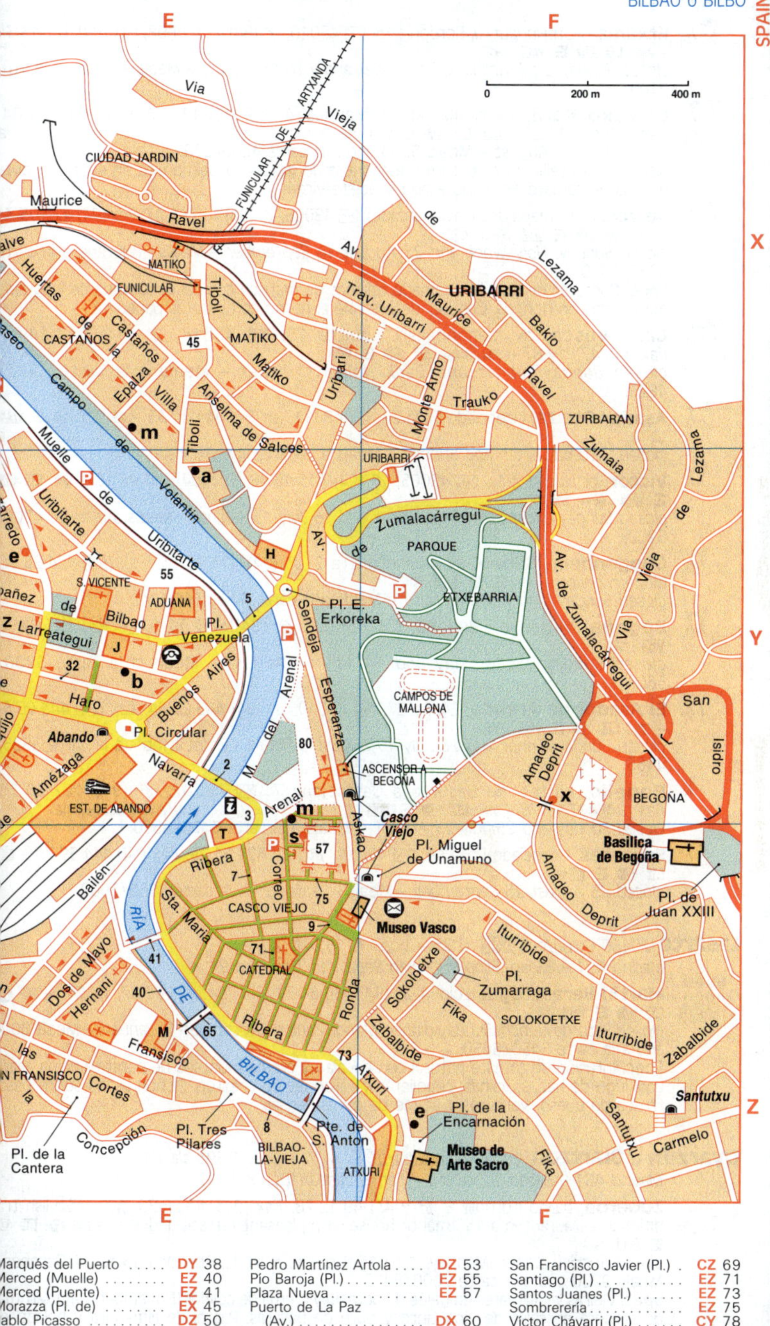
E
F
X
Y
Z
Via
DE
FUNICULAR
ARTXANDA
Vieja
Via
de
CIUDAD JARDIN
Maurice
Ravel
Av.
MATIKO
FUNICULAR
Tiboli
MATIKO
Matiko
Trav. Uríbarri
Maurice
URIBARRI
Lezama
Bakio
Ravel
45
Uribari
Trauko
ZURBARAN
Zumaia
Huertas
de
CASTAÑOS
Castaños
la
Epalza
Villa
Tiboli
Anselma de Salces
Monte Amo
Zumalacárregui
Lezama
m
Paseo
Campo
Muelle
de
Volantin
de
Uribitarte
URIBARRI
a
Uribitarte
arredo
de
PARQUE
ETXEBARRIA
Av. de Zumalacárregui
Via
de
Vieja
Av.
de
Sendeja
PI. E.
Erkoreka
P
e
S. VICENTE
Arenal
55
ADUANA
5
H
Zalbide
P
ñez
Bilbao
PI.
Venezuela
de
del
Esperanza
Buenos Aires
CAMPOS DE
MALLONA
San
Z Larreategui
J
32
b
Haro
Arenal
80
ASCENSOR A
BEGOÑA
Amadeo
Deprit
BEGOÑA
Abando
PI. Circular
Navarra
2
Arenal
m
Casco
Viejo
X
Basilica
de Begoña
Amé_aga
EST. DE ABANDO
3
Askao
PI. Miguel
de Unamuno
Amadeo
Deprit
Bailén
T
P
S
57
PI. de
Juan XXIII
Ribera
7
Correo
75
Museo Vasco
Iturribide
Sta. María
CASCO VIEJO
9
Sokoetxe
PI.
Zumarraga
RIA
71
CATEDRAL
Ronda
Fika
SOLOKOETXE
Iturribide
Zabalbide
Dos de Mayo
Hernani
41
40
M
DE
65
Ribera
Zabalbide
Zaballbide
Fransisco
73
Atxuri
Santutxu
N FRANSISCO
Cortes
BILBAO
e
PI. de la
Encarnación
Santutxu
Carmelo
la
Concepción
PI. Tres
Pilares
8
Pte. de
S. Antón
BILBAO-
LA-VIEJA
Museo de
Arte Sacro
Fika
PI. de la
Cantera
ATXURI
0   200 m   400 m

XXX **Etxaniz** - *Hotel Indautxu*, Gordoniz 15, ⊠ 48010, ℰ (94) 421 11 98, *Fax (94) 422 13 31* – 🗏. 🕮 ⓘ 🅔 *VISA*. 🗶   DZ b
closed Sunday, Bank Holidays, Holy Week and 1 to 15 August – **Meals** a la carte approx. 5100.

XXX ❀ **Goizeko Kabi,** Particular de Estraunza 4, ⊠ 48011, ℰ (94) 441 50 04, *Fax (94) 442 11 29* – 🗏. 🕮 ⓘ 🅔 *VISA*. 🗶   CDY a
closed 1 to 15 August – **Meals** 5200 and a la carte 4200/6200
Spec. Patata rellena de centollo y mahonesa de gazpacho. Salmonete sin espinas y puré natural de tomate. Solomillo asado al aceite virgen.

XXX ❀ **Gorrotxa,** Alameda Urquijo 30 (arcade), ⊠ 48008, ℰ (94) 443 49 37, *Fax (94) 422 05 35* – 🗏. 🕮 ⓘ 🅔 *VISA* ᴊᴄʙ. 🗶   DY
closed Sunday, Holy Week and 25 August-14 September – **Meals** 5800 and a la carte 5350/7350
Spec. Cornetes de salmón ahumado rellenos de marisco con caviar. Corona de lenguado mariscado con hongos. Costillar de pré-salé al horno con patatas panadera.

XXX **Casa Vasca,** av. Lehendakari Aguirre 13, ⊠ 48014, ℰ (94) 448 39 80, *Fax (94) 476 14 87* – 🗏 🚗. 🕮 ⓘ 🅔 *VISA*   CX c
closed Sunday dinner and Bank Holidays dinner – **Meals** a la carte 3775/4625.

XX **Asador Oteiza,** Licenciado Poza 27, ⊠ 48011, ℰ (94) 441 41 33 – 🗏. 🕮 ⓘ 🅔 *VISA* 🗶   DY e
closed Saturday lunch and Sunday – **Meals** a la carte approx. 4900.

XX **Víctor,** pl. Nueva 2-1º, ⊠ 48005, ℰ (94) 415 16 78, *Fax (94) 415 06 16* – 🗏. 🕮 ⓘ 🅔 *VISA* ᴊᴄʙ. 🗶   EZ s
closed Sunday except May, Holy Week and 15 July-15 August – **Meals** a la carte 4700/6200.

XX **Guggenheim Bilbao,** av. Abandoibarra 2 ℰ (94) 423 93 33, *Fax (94) 424 25 60* Modern decor – 🗏. 🕮 🅔 *VISA*. 🗶   DX
closed Sunday dinner and Monday – **Meals** a la carte 4100/5600.

XX **Begoña,** Virgen de Begoña, ⊠ 48006, ℰ (94) 412 72 57 – 🗏. 🕮 ⓘ 🅔 *VISA*. 🗶   FY
closed Sunday except May and 14 July-14 August – **Meals** a la carte 3800/5600.

XX **El Asador de Aranda,** Egaña 27, ⊠ 48010, ℰ (94) 443 06 64, *Fax (94) 443 06 64* – 🗏. 🕮 ⓘ 🅔 *VISA*. 🗶   DZ
closed Sunday dinner and 20 July-10 August – **Meals** - Roast lamb - a la carte 3525/4165.

X **Rogelio,** carret. de Basurto a Castrejana 7, ⊠ 48002, ℰ (94) 427 30 21, *Fax (94) 427 17 78* – 🗏. 🕮 ⓘ 🅔 *VISA*   by Av. Autonomía CZ
closed Sunday and 25 July-23 August – **Meals** a la carte 3350/5500.

X **Serantes,** Licenciado Poza 16, ⊠ 48011, ℰ (94) 421 21 29, *Fax (94) 444 59 79* – 🗏 🕮 ⓘ 🅔 *VISA*   DY
closed 25 August-25 September – **Meals** - Seafood - a la carte 4850/5900.

Lasarte *20160 Guipúzcoa* 442 *C 23* – *pop. 18 165 alt. 42.*
Madrid 491 – Bilbao/Bilbo 98 – San Sebastián/Donostia 9.

XXXX ❀❀ **Martín Berasategui,** Loidi 4 ℰ (943) 36 64 71, *Fax (943) 36 61 07,* ≤, 🌿 – 🗏 🅿 🕮 ⓘ 🅔 *VISA*. 🗶
closed Saturday lunch, Sunday dinner, Monday and 13 December-13 January – **Meals** 8000 and a la carte 5450/6650
Spec. Infusión de tomate natural con bacalao y crema montada de patata. Lubina asada con jugo de habas, vainas, cebolletas y tallarines de chipirón. Pichón asado sobre pasta fresca de queso, verduras y aceite de olivas negras.

Oyarzun u **Oiartzun** *20180 Guipúzcoa* 442 *C 24* – *pop. 8 393 alt. 81.*
Madrid 481 – Bilbao/Bilbo 113 – San Sebastián/Donostia 13.

XXX ❀❀ **Zuberoa,** barrio Iturriotz 8 ℰ (943) 49 12 28, *Fax (943) 49 26 79,* 🌿, « *Stylish traditional restaurant in a 15C manor house with pleasant terrace and* ≤ » – 🗏 🅿. 🕮 ⓘ 🅔 *VISA*. 🗶
closed Sunday dinner, Monday, 1 to 15 January, 5 to 19 April and 15 to 31 October – **Meals** 9000 and a la carte 7000/8400
Spec. Vieiras y calamares en gelée de pomelo y crema de coliflor (November-May). Milhoja de ternera en salsa de vino tinto y puré de patatas. Pastel de almendra y helado de yogurt.

San Sebastián o **Donostia** 20000 P *Guipúzcoa* 442 *C 24 – pop. 176 019 – Seaside resort.*
See : *Location and bay*★★★ – *Monte Igueldo* ≤★★★ – *Monte Urgull* ≤★★.
Envir. : *Monte Ulía* ≤★ *North-East : 7 km by N I.*

🛆₁₈ *of San Sebastián Jaizkíbel, East : 14 km by N I ℰ (943) 61 68 45.*

✈ *of San Sebastián, Fuenterrabía, North-East : 20 km ℰ (943) 64 12 67 – Iberia : Bengoetxea 3 ✉ 20004 ℰ (943) 42 35 86 and Aviaco airport ℰ (943) 64 12 67.*

🅱 *Reina Regente ✉ 20003 ℰ (943) 48 11 66 Fax (943) 48 11 72 and Fueros 1 ✉ 20005 ℰ (943) 42 62 82 Fax (943) 43 17 46 – R.A.C.V.N. (R.A.C. Vasco Navarro) Echaide 12 ✉ 20005 ℰ (943) 43 08 00 Fax (943) 42 91 50.*

Madrid 488 – Bayonne 54 – Bilbao/Bilbo 100 – Pamplona/Iruñea 94 – Vitoria/Gasteiz 115.

María Cristina, Okendo 1, ✉ 20004, ℰ (943) 42 49 00, Fax (943) 42 39 14, ≤ – 🛗 ▤ TV ☎ – 🛐 25/300. AE ⓞ E VISA JCB. ✼ rest
Meals 3700 - *Easo* : **Meals** a la carte 4900/6600 – ⬜ 2500 – **108 rm** 32000/46000, 28 suites.

Arzak, alto de Miracruz 21, ✉ 20015, ℰ (943) 27 84 65, Fax (943) 27 27 53 – ▤ ⓟ AE ⓞ E VISA JCB. ✼
closed Sunday dinner, Monday, 13 to 30 June and 7 November-1 December – **Meals** 9900 and a la carte 9200/10800
Spec. Carabineros con relieve de pistachos, almendras, pipas verdes y pan de cocido. Arraitxikis horneados con pomada de crustáceos y cereales (July-November). Sopa de chufas con pan de frutas.

Akelañe, paseo del Padre Orcolaga 56 - barrio de Igueldo : 7,5 km, ✉ 20008, ℰ (943) 21 20 52, Fax (943) 21 92 68, ≤ sea – ▤ ⓟ AE ⓞ E VISA. ✼
closed Sunday dinner, Monday except Bank Holiday weekends, February and 1 to 15 October – **Meals** 8700 and a la carte 7000/8500
Spec. Lascas de bacalao asado con patatitas y crema de espárragos verdes y blancos. Lubina al horno con ajoblanco y coco, extracto del refrito con piquillo. Gin tonic helado.

MÁLAGA 29000 446 *V 16 – pop. 534 683 – Seaside resort.*
See : *Gibralfaro :* ≤★★ DY – *Alcazaba*★ *(Archaelogical Museum*★*)* DY – *Cathedral*★ CZ – *El Sagrario Church (marienista altarpiece*★*)* CY.
Envir. : *Finca de la Concepción*★ *North : 7 km.*

🛆₁₈ *Málaga, South-West : 9 km ℰ (95) 237 66 77 Fax (95) 237 66 12 –* 🛆₉ *El Candado, East : 5 km ℰ (95) 229 93 40 Fax (95) 229 08 45.*

✈ *Málaga, South-West : 9 km ℰ (95) 204 84 84 – Iberia : Molina Larios 13, ✉ 29015, ℰ (95) 213 61 48 CY and Airport ℰ (95) 204 84 84.*

🚗 *ℰ (95) 212 82 25.*

⚓ *. to Melilla : Cía Trasmediterránea, Estación Marítima, Local E-1 ✉ 29016 CZ, ℰ (95) 222 43 91, Fax (95) 222 48 83.*

🅱 *Pasaje de Chinitas 4 ✉ 29015 ℰ (95) 221 34 45 Fax (95) 222 94 21 and av. Cervantes 1 ✉ 28016 ℰ (95) 260 44 10 Fax (95) 221 41 20 – R.A.C.E. Calderería (galerías Goya 5º-1) ✉ 29008, ℰ (95) 221 42 60 Fax (95) 221 20 32.*

Madrid 548 – Algeciras 133 – Córdoba 175 – Sevilla 217 – Valencia 651.

Plan on next page

Parador de Málaga-Gibralfaro 🐾, Castillo de Gibralfaro, ✉ 29016, ℰ (95) 222 19 02, Fax (95) 222 19 04, « Magnificent setting with ≤ Málaga and sea »,
🏊 – 🛗 ▤ TV ☎ & ⓟ – 🛐 25/60. AE ⓞ E VISA JCB. ✼   DY
Meals 3700 – ⬜ 1300 – **38 rm** 15200/19000.

Larios, Marqués de Larios 2, ✉ 29005, ℰ (95) 222 22 00, Fax (95) 222 24 07 – 🛗 ▤ TV ☎ – 🛐 25/150. AE ⓞ E VISA. ✼   CY s
Meals *(closed Sunday)* 3500 – ⬜ 1300 – **40 rm** 15000/19000.

Don Curro coffee shop only, Sancha de Lara 7, ✉ 29015, ℰ (95) 222 72 00, Fax (95) 221 59 46 – 🛗 ▤ TV ☎ – 🛐 25/60. AE ⓞ E VISA JCB   CZ e
⬜ 650 – **118 rm** 9270/13604.

Los Naranjos without rest, paseo de Sancha 35, ✉ 29016, ℰ (95) 222 43 19, Fax (95) 222 59 75 – 🛗 ▤ TV ☎ 🚗. AE ⓞ E VISA. ✼
⬜ 950 – **40 rm** 10800/15200, 1 suite.   East : by Pas. Cánovas del Castillo DZ

Don Paco without rest, Salitre 53, ✉ 29002, ℰ (95) 231 90 08, Fax (95) 231 90 62 – 🛗 ▤ TV ☎ 🚗. E VISA. ✼   South-West : by Alameda Principal CZ
⬜ 375 – **25 rm** 6740/8560.

Café de París, Vélez Málaga 8, ✉ 29016, ℰ (95) 222 50 43, Fax (95) 260 38 64 – ▤ ⓟ. AE ⓞ E VISA JCB. ✼   East : by Pas. Cánovas del Castillo DZ
closed Sunday and 1 to 15 July – **Meals** a la carte 4100/4800.

MÁLAGA

Aduana (Pl. de la) . . . . . **DY** 2
Arriola (Pl. de la) . . . . **CZ** 5
Atocha (Pasillo) . . . . **CZ** 8
Calderería . . . . **CY** 13
Cánovas del Castillo
(Pas.) . . . . **DZ** 18
Cárcer . . . . **CY** 27
Casapalma . . . . **CY** 30
Colón (Alameda de) . . . . . **CZ** 32

Comandante Benítez (Av. del) **CZ** 35
Compañía . . . . **CY** 37
Constitución . . . . **CY** 40
Cortina del Muelle . . . . **CZ** 42
Especerías . . . . **CY** 56
Frailes . . . . **CDY** 61
Granada . . . . **CDY**
Huerto del Conde . . . . **DY** 67
Mariblanca . . . . **CY** 77
Marina (Pl. de la) . . . . **CZ** 80
Marqués de Larios . . . . . . **CYZ** 84
Martínez . . . . **CZ** 86

Molina Larios . . . . **CYZ** 95
Nueva . . . . **CYZ**
Postigo de los Abades . . **CDZ** 106
Reding (Paseo de) . . . . **DY** 110
Santa Isabel (Pasillo de) . **CYZ** 120
Santa Lucía . . . . **CY** 123
Santa María . . . . **CY** 125
Sebastián Souvirón . . . . . **CZ** 130
Strachan . . . . **CZ** 133
Teatro (Pl. del) . . . . **CY** 135
Tejón y Rodríguez . . . . . . **CY** 138
Tetuán (Puente de) . . . . . **CZ** 140

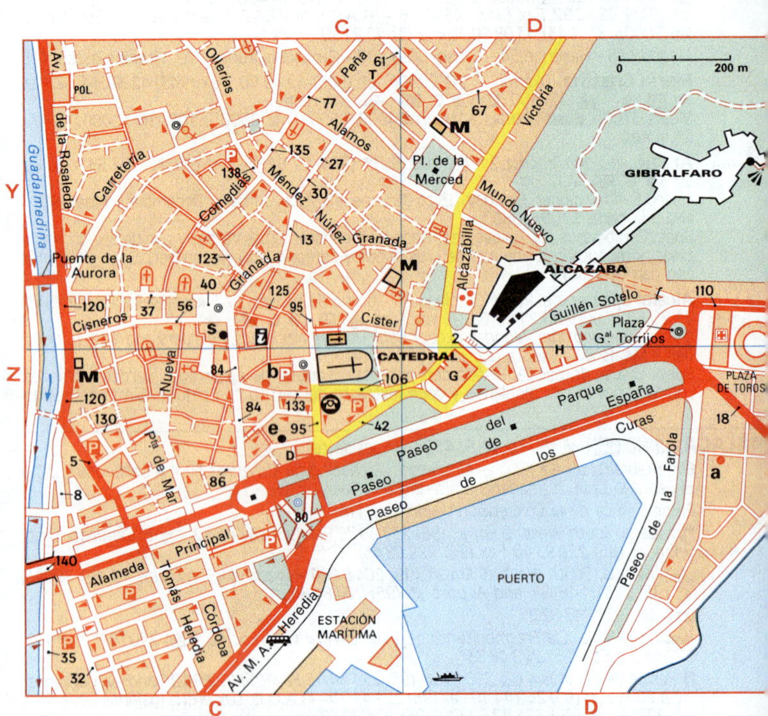

XX **Adolfo,** paseo Marítimo Pablo Ruiz Picasso 12, ⊠ 29016, ℰ (95) 260 19 14
Fax (95) 260 19 14 – 🗐. **E** **VISA**. 🍽️   East : by Pas. Cánovas del Castillo   **DZ**
closed Sunday – **Meals** a la carte 2400/4200.

XX **Doña Pepa,** Vélez Málaga 6, ⊠ 29016, ℰ (95) 260 34 89 – 🗐. **AE E VISA**. 🍽️   **DZ**
closed Sunday and September – **Meals** a la carte 2400/4250.

X **El Refectorium,** Cervantes 8, ⊠ 29016, ℰ (95) 221 89 90 – 🗐. **AE ⊙ E VISA**. 🍽️
closed Sunday and 1 to 15 June – **Meals** a la carte approx. 4300.
East : by Pas. Cánovas del Castillo   **DZ**

at Club de Campo South-West : 9 km – ⊠ 29000 Málaga :

Parador de Málaga del Golf, at the golf course, ⊠ 29080 apartado 324 Málaga
ℰ (95) 238 12 55, Fax (95) 238 89 63, ≤, 🌳, « Overlooking the golf course », 🏊, 🍽️
🔳 – 🗐 **TV** ☎ **P** – 🔥 25/70. **AE ⊙ E VISA**. 🍽️
Meals 3500 – ☕ 1300 – **56 rm** 14000/17500, 4 suites.

at Urbanización Mijas Golf South-West : 30 km by N 340 – ⊠ 29640 Fuengirola :

Byblos Andaluz 🍳, ℰ (95) 246 02 50, Fax (95) 247 67 83, ≤ golf course and mountains, 🌳, Thalassotherapy facilities, « Tasteful Andalusian style situated between two golf courses », 🏋️, 🏊, 🏊, 🎾, 🍽️, 🔳 🔳 – 🛗 🗐 **TV** ☎ **P** – 🔥 20/170. **AE ⊙ E VISA**
JCB. 🍽️ rest
Meals 6000 - **Le Nailhac** (closed Wednesday and January) **Meals** a la carte 7000/8200
- **El Andaluz** : **Meals** a la carte 4700/5650 – ☕ 2350 – **108 rm** 34000/40100, 36 suites

Marbella 29600 Málaga **446** W 15 – pop. 84 410 – Seaside resort.

See : The Old town★.

Envir. : Puerto Banús (Pleasure harbour★) by ② : 8 km.

Río Real, by ① : 5 km 𝄐 (95) 277 95 09 Fax (95) 277 21 40 – Los Naranjos, by ② : 7 km 𝄐 (95) 281 24 28 – Aloha, urb. Aloha by ② : 8 km 𝄐 (95) 281 23 88 – Las Brisas, Nueva Andalucía by ② : 11 km, 𝄐 (95) 281 08 75.

Glorieta de la Fontanilla 𝄐 (95) 277 14 42 Fax (95) 277 94 57 and Pl. de los Naranjos 𝄐 (95) 282 35 50 Fax (95) 277 36 21.

Madrid 602 ① – Algeciras 77 ② – Cádiz 201 ② – Málaga 56 ①

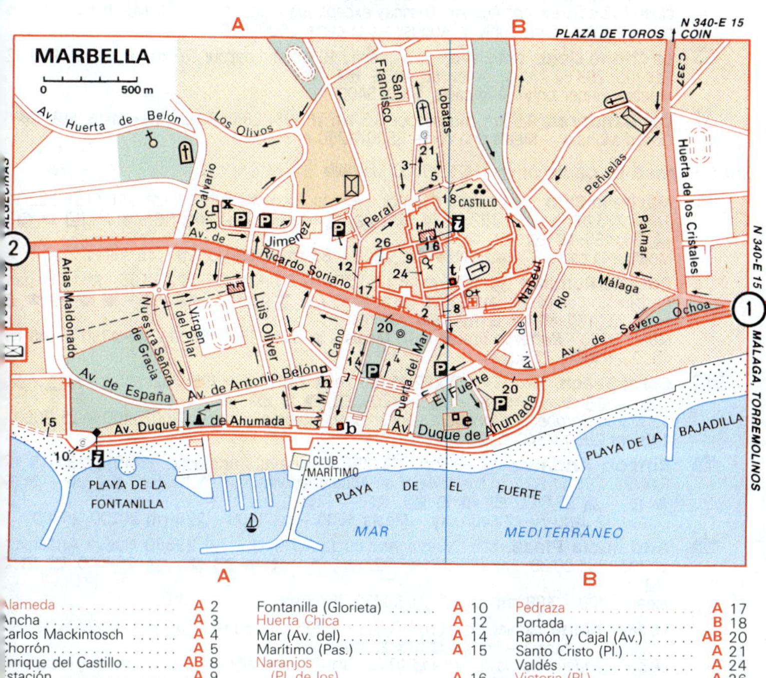

Gran Meliá Don Pepe ⑤, José Meliá 𝄐 (95) 277 03 00, Fax (95) 277 99 54, ≤ sea and mountains, « Subtropical plants », 🔥, 🏊, 🏊, 🏖, 🌿, ✕ – 🛗 ▤ TV ☎ 🦽 P – 🅿 25/300. AE ① E VISA. ✕ — by ②
Meals 6800 - **Grill La Farola** : Meals a la carte 5200/9730 – ☕ 2600 – **199 rm** 38000/41000, 3 suites.

El Fuerte, av. del Fuerte 𝄐 (95) 286 15 00, Fax (95) 282 44 11, ≤, 🌿, « Terraces with garden and palm trees », 🔥, 🏊 heated, 🏊, 🏖, ✕ – 🛗 ▤ TV ☎ 🦽 🚗 P – 🅿 25/500. AE ① E VISA. ✕ rest — AB e
Meals - dinner only except July-August - a la carte 4550/5800 – ☕ 1600 – **249 rm** 12000/21000, 14 suites.

Lima without rest, av. Antonio Belón 2 𝄐 (95) 277 05 00, Fax (95) 286 30 91 – 🛗 TV ☎. AE ① E VISA. ✕ — A h
☕ 495 – **64 rm** 9600/12000.

Santiago, av. Duque de Ahumada 5 𝄐 (95) 277 43 39, Fax (95) 282 45 03, 🌿 – ▤. AE ① E VISA JCB. ✕ — A b
closed November – Meals - Seafood - a la carte 4050/4750.

Triana, Gloria 11 𝄐 (95) 277 99 62 – ▤. AE ① E VISA. ✕ — B t
closed Monday and 7 January-7 March – Meals - Rice dishes - a la carte 3000/5000.

Cenicienta, av. Cánovas del Castillo 52 (by pass) 𝄐 (95) 277 43 18, 🌿 – ① E VISA
closed November - Meals - dinner only - a la carte 3400/4450. — by ②

on the road to Málaga *by ① –* ✉ *29600 Marbella :*

Don Carlos ⑤, exit Elviria : 10 km ℘ (95) 283 11 40, *Fax (95) 283 34 29,* ≤, 🏖
« Extensive gardens », 🏋, ⏞ heated, ✗ – 🛗 ▤ 📺 ☎ & 🅿 – 🛁 25/1200. AE ⑩ E
VISA JCB. ❄
Los Naranjos : Meals a la carte 4500/7500 – ☕ 2400 – **225 rm** 31000/36500, 14 suites.

Artola without rest, 12,5 km ℘ (95) 283 13 90, *Fax (95) 283 04 50,* ≤, « On a golf
course », ⏞, 🚣, ⛳ – 🛗 📺 ☎ 🚗 🅿. AE E VISA
29 rm ☕ 9400/14800, 2 suites.

La Hacienda, exit Las Chapas : 11,5 km and detour 1,5 km ℘ (95) 283 12 67,
Fax (95) 283 33 28, 🏖, « Rustic decor. patio » – 🅿. AE ⑩ E VISA JCB. ❄
closed Monday except August, Tuesday except July-August and 15 November-20 Decem-
ber – **Meals** - dinner only in August - a la carte 5900/6800.

Le Chêne Liège, exit Elviria - La Mairena : 10 km and detour 5,5 km ℘ (95) 283 60 92,
Fax (95) 283 62 23, 🏖 – ▤. AE ⑩ E VISA. ❄
Meals - dinner only - a la carte 3100/5400.

Las Banderas, 9,5 km and detour 0,5 km ℘ (95) 283 18 19, 🏖 – AE E VISA. ❄
closed Monday – **Meals** a la carte 2500/4250.

on the road to Cádiz *by ② –* ✉ *29600 Marbella :*

Marbella Club ⑤, Boulevard Príncipe Alfonso de Hohenlohe : 3 km ℘ (95) 282 22 11,
Telex 77319, Fax (95) 282 98 84, 🏖, 🏋, ⏞ heated, 🏖, 🚣, ✗ – 🛗 ▤ 📺 ☎ 🅿 –
🛁 25/180. AE ⑩ VISA. ❄
Meals a la carte 8715/10815 – ☕ 2800 – **83 rm** 45000/55000, 46 suites.

Puente Romano ⑤, 3,5 km ℘ (95) 282 09 00, *Fax (95) 277 57 66,* 🏖, « Elegant
Andalusian complex in attractive gardens », 🏋, ⏞ heated, 🏖, 🚣, ✗ – 🛗 ▤ 📺 ☎ 🅿
– 🛁 25/170. AE ⑩ E VISA JCB. ❄ rest
Meals 5900 - **Roberto** *(Italian rest)* **Meals** a la carte 3600/6900 – ☕ 2750 – **149 rm**
40000/53000, 77 suites.

Coral Beach, 5 km ℘ (95) 282 45 00, *Telex 79816, Fax (95) 282 62 57,* 🏋, ⏞, 🏖
– 🛗 ▤ 📺 ☎ & 🚗 🅿 – 🛁 25/200. AE ⑩ E VISA. ❄
15 March-October – **Florencia** *(dinner only)* **Meals** a la carte 4200/6400 – ☕ 2050 –
148 rm 29000/34000, 22 suites.

Rincón Andaluz ⑤, 8 km, ✉ 29660 Nueva Andalucía, ℘ (95) 281 15 17,
Fax (95) 281 41 80, « In the style of an Andalusian village », ⏞ heated, 🏖, 🚣 – ▤ 📺
☎ 🅿 – 🛁 25/100. AE ⑩ E VISA. ❄
closed 12 January-12 February – **Meals** 3500 – ☕ 1400 – **224 rm** 20200/26500.

Andalucía Plaza, urb. Nueva Andalucía - 7,3 km, ✉ 29660 Nueva Andalucía,
℘ (95) 281 20 00, *Fax (95) 281 47 92,* 🏖, ⏞ – 🛗 ▤ 📺 ☎ – 🛁 25/600. AE ⑩ E
VISA. ❄
Meals 3700 – **388 rm** ☕ 22050/30450, 2 suites.

La Meridiana, camino de la Cruz : 3,5 km ℘ (95) 277 61 90, *Fax (95) 282 60 24,* ≤, 🏖
« Garden terrace » – ▤ 🅿. AE ⑩ E VISA
closed Monday, Tuesday lunch and 10 January-27 February – **Meals** - dinner only in summer
- a la carte 5100/7250.

Villa Tiberio, 2,5 km ℘ (95) 277 17 99, *Fax (95) 282 47 72,* 🏖, « Garden terrace »
– 🅿. AE ⑩ E VISA. ❄
closed Sunday except August – **Meals** - dinner only - a la carte 5100/6800.

El Portalón, 3 km ℘ (95) 282 78 80, *Fax (95) 277 71 04* – ▤ 🅿. AE ⑩ E VISA. ❄
Meals - Braised meat specialities - a la carte 5200/7200.

at Puerto Banús *West : 8 km –* ✉ *29660 Nueva Andalucía :*

Cipriano, av. Playas del Duque - edificio Sevilla ℘ (95) 281 10 77, *Fax (95) 281 10 77,*
🏖 – ▤ 🅿. AE ⑩ E VISA. ❄
closed 15 November-15 December – **Meals** a la carte 5100/7050.

Taberna del Alabardero, muelle Benabola ℘ (95) 281 27 94, *Fax (95) 281 86 30,* 🏖
– ▤. AE ⑩ E VISA. ❄
Meals a la carte 3125/6000.

Don't confuse :

Comfort of hotels : 🏨 ... 🏠

Comfort of restaurants : XXXXX ... X

Quality of the cuisine : ✿✿✿, ✿✿, ✿, 🍽 Meals

SEVILLA 41000 P 446 T 11 y 12 – pop. 704 857 alt. 12.

See : La Giralda★★★ (✳★★) BX – Cathedral★★★ (Capilla Mayor altarpiece★★★, Capilla Real★★) BX – Reales Alcázares★★★ BXY (Admiral Apartment : Virgin of the Mareantes altarpiece★ ; Pedro el Cruel Palace★★★ : Ambassadors room vault★★ ; Carlos V Palace : tapestries★★, gardens★) – Santa Cruz Quarter★★ BCX (Venerables Hospital★) – Fine Arts Museum★★ (room V★★★, room X★★) AV – Pilate's House★★ (Azulejos★★, staircase★ : cupule★) CX – Maria Luisa Park★★ (España Square★, Archaelogical Museum : Carambolo tresor★) South : by Paseo de las Delicias BY.

Other curiosities : Charity hospital★ BY - Santa Paula Convent★ CV (front★ church) – Salvador Church★ BX (baroque altarpieces★) – Sant Josep Chappel★ BX – Town Hall (Ayuntamiento) : east front★ BX – Isla Mágica★ North : by Torneo AV.

⛳ Pineda, South-East : 3 km ℰ (95) 461 14 00.

✈ Sevilla - San Pablo, North-East : 14 km ℰ (95) 444 90 00 – Iberia : Almirante Lobo 2, ✉ 41001, ℰ (95) 422 89 01 BX.

🚗 Santa Justa ℰ (95) 453 86 86.

🛈 Av. de la Constitución 21 B ✉ 41004 ℰ (95) 422 14 04 Fax (95) 422 97 53 and Paseo de las Delicias 9 ✉ 41012 ℰ (95) 423 44 65 – R.A.C.E. Av. Eduardo Dato 22, ✉ 41018 ℰ (95) 463 13 50, Fax (95) 465 96 04.

Madrid 550 – La Coruña/A Coruña 950 – Lisboa 417 – Málaga 217 – Valencia 682.

Plans on following pages

Alfonso XIII, San Fernando 2, ✉ 41004, ℰ (95) 422 28 50, Fax (95) 421 60 33, 🌸, « Magnificent Andalusian building », ⅃, 🚗 – 🛗 ☰ TV ☎ 🚗 P – 🔶 25/500. AE ⓘ E VISA JCB. ✗
BY c
Meals a la carte 6800/7600 – ⊊ 2750 – **127 rm** 39000/51000, 19 suites.

Tryp Colón, Canalejas 1, ✉ 41001, ℰ (95) 422 29 00, Fax (95) 422 09 38, ⌀ – 🛗 ☰ TV ☎ ᕒ – 🔶 25/200. AE ⓘ E VISA. ✗
AX s
Meals (see rest. **El Burladero** below) – ⊊ 1700 – **204 rm** 19450/24300, 14 suites.

Occidental Porta Coeli, av. Eduardo Dato 49, ✉ 41018, ℰ (95) 453 35 00, Fax (95) 453 23 42, ⅃ – 🛗 ☰ TV ☎ P – 🔶 25/600. AE ⓘ E VISA. ✗
Meals (see rest. **Florencia** below) – ⊊ 1500 – **241 rm** 23000/30000, 3 suites.
East : by Demetrio de los Ríos CXY

Meliá Sevilla, Doctor Pedro de Castro 1, ✉ 41004, ℰ (95) 442 15 11, Fax (95) 442 29 77, ⌀, ⅃ – 🛗 ☰ TV ☎ ᕒ 🚗 – 🔶 25/1000. AE ⓘ E VISA JCB. ✗
South-East : by Av. de Portugal CY
closed July-August – **Meals** 3500 – ⊊ 1500 – **359 rm** 25200/28300, 5 suites.

Meliá Lebreros, Luis Morales 2, ✉ 41018, ℰ (95) 457 94 00, Fax (95) 458 27 26, 🌸, ⌀, ⅃ – 🛗 ☰ TV ☎ ᕒ 🚗 – 🔶 25/600. AE ⓘ VISA. ✗
Meals (see rest. **La Dehesa** below) – ⊊ 1500 – **431 rm** 17300/21300, 6 suites.
East : by La Florida CX

Meliá Confort Macarena, San Juan de Ribera 2, ✉ 41009, ℰ (95) 437 58 00, Fax (95) 438 18 03, ⅃ – 🛗 ☰ TV ☎ ᕒ – 🔶 25/700. AE ⓘ E VISA JCB. ✗
North : by María Auxiliadora CV
Meals 3200 – ⊊ 1500 – **323 rm** 13700/16900, 10 suites.

Occidental Sevilla coffee shop only, av. Kansas City, ✉ 41018, ℰ (95) 458 20 00, Fax (95) 458 46 15, ⅃ – 🛗 ☰ TV ☎ ᕒ – 🔶 25/320. AE ⓘ E VISA JCB. ✗
⊊ 1600 – **228 rm** 25000/32000, 14 suites.
East : by La Florida CX

Inglaterra, pl. Nueva 7, ✉ 41001, ℰ (95) 422 49 70, Fax (95) 456 13 36 – 🛗 ☰ TV ☎ 🚗 – 🔶 25/200. AE ⓘ E VISA JCB. ✗ rest
AX r
Meals 3000 – ⊊ 1500 – **105 rm** 17000/22000, 4 suites.

Los Seises, Segovias 6, ✉ 41004, ℰ (95) 422 94 95, Fax (95) 422 43 34, « On the 3rd patio of the Archbishop's palace », ⅃ – 🛗 ☰ TV ☎ – 🔶 25/100. AE ⓘ E VISA. ✗
Meals a la carte 3350/5800 – ⊊ 2000 – **43 rm** 20000/27000.
BX f

Ciudad de Sevilla, av. Manuel Siurot 25, ✉ 41013, ℰ (95) 423 05 05, Fax (95) 423 85 39, ⅃ – 🛗 ☰ TV ☎ 🚗 – 🔶 25/300. AE ⓘ E VISA JCB. ✗
South-East : by Paseo de las Delicias BY
Meals 2800 – ⊊ 1400 – **91 rm** 30000/32000, 3 suites.

NH Plaza de Armas, av. Marqués de Paradas, ✉ 41001, ℰ (95) 490 19 92, Fax (95) 490 12 32, ⅃ – 🛗 ☰ TV ☎ ᕒ – 🔶 25/250. AE ⓘ E VISA JCB. ✗ AV c
Meals 3800 – ⊊ 1500 – **260 rm** 13500/14100, 2 suites.

Bécquer coffee shop only, Reyes Católicos 4, ✉ 41001, ℰ (95) 422 89 00, Fax (95) 421 44 00 – 🛗 ☰ TV ☎ 🚗 – 🔶 25/45. AE ⓘ E VISA. ✗
AX v
⊊ 1200 – **116 rm** 15000/18900, 2 suites.

Sevilla Congresos, av. Alcalde Luis Uruñuela, ✉ 41020, ℰ (95) 425 90 00, Fax (95) 425 95 00, ⌀, ⅃ – 🛗 ☰ TV ☎ 🚗 P – 🔶 25/270. AE ⓘ E VISA. ✗ rest
North-East : by La Florida CX
Meals a la carte 3725/4600 – **217 rm** ⊊ 10500/13500, 1 suite.

SEVILLA

*Inclusion in the
Michelin Guide
cannot be achieved
by pulling strings
or by offering favours.*

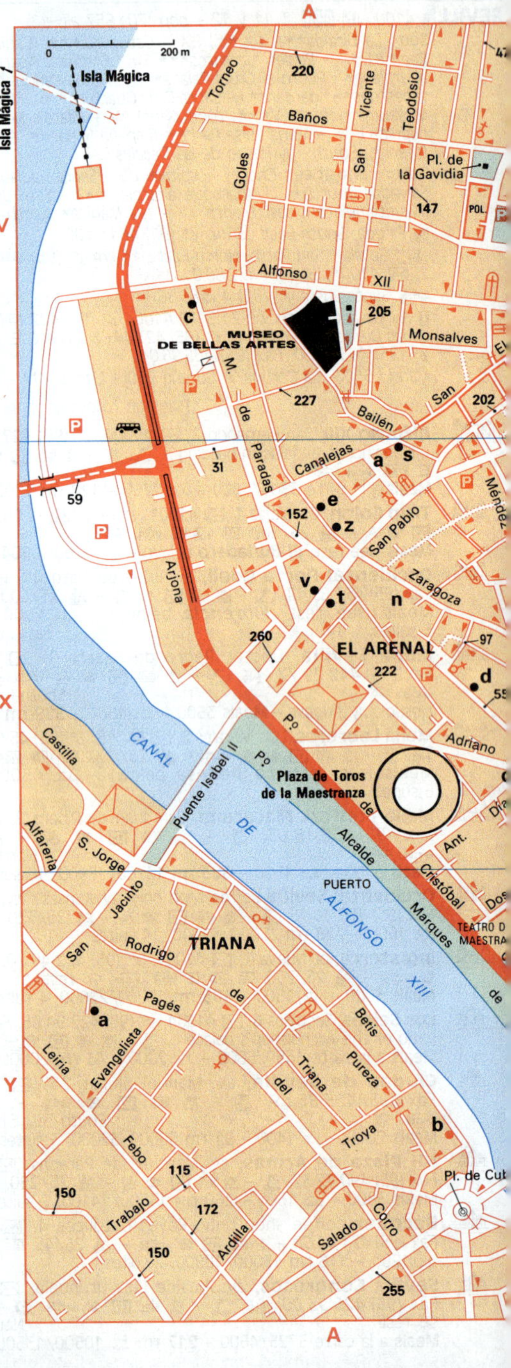

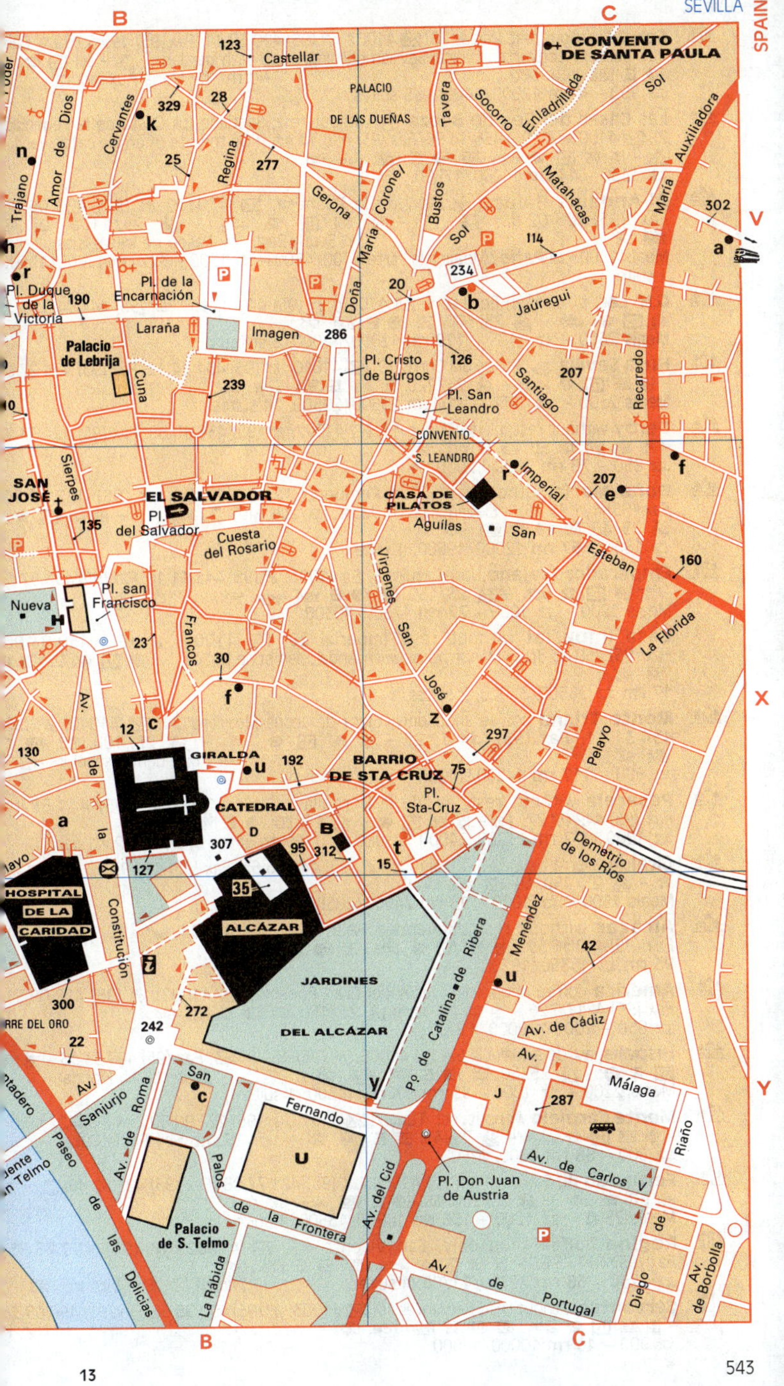

SEVILLA
SPAIN
B
C
V
X
Y
CONVENTO DE SANTA PAULA
123
Castellar
329
28
PALACIO
DE LAS DUEÑAS
k
25
277
Regina
Gerona
Doña Maria Coronel
Bustos
Tavera
Socorro
Enladrillada
Sol
Maria Auxiliadora
302
a
n
Amor de Dios
Trajano
n
r
Pl. Duque
de la
Victoria
190
Pl. de la
Encarnación
Laraña
Imagen
286
20
234
114
b
Jaúregui
Recaredo
Palacio
de Lebrija
Cuna
239
Pl. Cristo
de Burgos
126
Pl. San
Leandro
Santiago
207
f
CONVENTO
S. LEANDRO
San
José
Sierpes
EL SALVADOR
Pl.
del Salvador
Cuesta
del Rosario
CASA DE
PILATOS
r
Imperial
Aguilas
San
e
207
Esteban
160
135
Pl. san
Francisco
Francos
Virgenes
San
La Florida
Nueva
H
23
30
f
José
Z
297
12
c
GIRALDA
u
192
BARRIO
DE STA CRUZ
75
Pelayo
130
de
CATEDRAL
Pl.
Sta-Cruz
a
la
D
B
t
307
95
312
15
Dematrio
de los Ríos
Menéndez
Pelayo
127
HOSPITAL
DE LA
CARIDAD
Constitución
35
ALCÁZAR
42
300
272
JARDINES
u
RRE DEL ORO
22
242
DEL ALCÁZAR
Av. de Cádiz
Av.
San
c
Sanjurjo
Av. de Roma
Fernando
Palos
U
de
la
Frontera
y
Po. de Catalina de Ribera
Av. del Cid
Málaga
J
287
Riaño
Pl. Don Juan
de Austria
Palacio
de S. Telmo
La Rábida
Paseo de las Delicias
Av.
de
Portugal
Diego de
Av. de Borbolla
Av. de Carlos V
B
C
13
543

San Gil without rest, Parras 28, ✉ 41002, ☎ (95) 490 68 11, *Fax (95) 490 69 39*, « Earl
20C partially converted typical Sevilian building. patio with garden », 🏊 – 🖥 TV ☎. A
⓪ E VISA JCB. ✲
North : by María Auxiliadora   CV
☕ 950 – **4 rm** 12000/14000, 35 suites.

Las Casas del Rey de Baeza ⌂ without rest, Santiago (pl. Cristo de la Redenció
2), ✉ 41003, ☎ (95) 456 14 96, *Fax (95) 456 14 41*, « On the site of an old cattle yard »
🏊 – 🛗 🖥 TV ☎ ⟵. AE ⓪ E VISA JCB. ✲
CV
☕ 1350 – **44 rm** 14000/17800.

Al-Andalus Palace ⌂, av. de la Palmera, ✉ 41012, ☎ (95) 423 06 0C
Fax (95) 423 02 00, 🏋, 🏊 – 🛗 🖥 TV ☎ ⟵ – 🛶 25/1100. AE ⓪
VISA. ✲
South-East : by Paseo de las Delicias   BY
Meals 1900 - *El Patio :* Meals a la carte 3100/4500 – ☕ 1500 – **327 rm** 15600/1950C
1 suite.

G.H. Lar, pl. Carmen Benítez 3, ✉ 41003, ☎ (95) 441 03 61, *Fax (95) 441 04 52* – 🛗
🖥 TV ☎ ⟵ – 🛶 25/300. AE ⓪ E VISA. ✲
CX
Meals 2600 – ☕ 1125 – **129 rm** 12000/18000, 8 suites.

Husa Sevilla ⌂, Pagés del Corro 90, ✉ 41010, ☎ (95) 434 24 12, *Fax (95) 434 27 0*
– 🛗 🖥 TV ☎ ⟵ – 🛶 25/220. AE ⓪ E VISA JCB. ✲
AY
Meals 2300 – ☕ 1250 – **114 rm** 25600/29500, 14 suites.

Derby without rest, pl. del Duque 13, ✉ 41002, ☎ (95) 456 10 88, *Fax (95) 421 33 9*
– 🛗 🖥 TV ☎. AE ⓪ E VISA. ✲
BV
☕ 850 – **75 rm** 9000/12000.

Doña María without rest, Don Remondo 19, ✉ 41004, ☎ (95) 422 49 90
Fax (95) 421 95 46, « Elegant classic decor. terrace with 🏊 and ≤ » – 🛗 🖥 TV ☎
🛶 25/40. AE ⓪ E VISA. ✲
BX
☕ 1500 – **67 rm** 12000/19500, 1 suite.

Emperador Trajano, José Laguillo 8, ✉ 41003, ☎ (95) 441 11 11, *Fax (95) 453 57 0*
– 🛗 🖥 TV ☎ ⟵ – 🛶 25/150. AE ⓪ E VISA JCB. ✲
CV
Meals 1900 – ☕ 1000 – **77 rm** 17300/20300.

Casa Imperial without rest, Imperial 29, ✉ 41003, ☎ (95) 450 03 00
Fax (95) 450 03 30, « Manor house with Andalusian style patios » – 🖥 TV ☎. AE ⓪ E
VISA. ✲
CX
17 rm ☕ 26500/35000, 7 suites.

Monte Triana coffee shop only, Clara de Jesús Montero 24, ✉ 41010, ☎ (95
434 31 11, *Fax (95) 434 33 28* – 🛗 🖥 TV ☎ ⟵ – 🛶 25/100. AE ⓪ E
VISA. ✲
West : by Puente Isabel II   AX
☕ 900 – **117 rm** 11200/14000.

Pasarela without rest, av. de la Borbolla 11, ✉ 41004, ☎ (95) 441 55 11
Fax (95) 442 07 27, 🏋 – 🛗 🖥 TV ☎ – 🛶 25. AE ⓪ E VISA. ✲
☕ 1200 – **77 rm** 13000/24000, 5 suites.   South-East : by Av. de Portugal   CY

Giralda, Sierra Nevada 3, ✉ 41003, ☎ (95) 441 66 61, *Fax (95) 441 93 52* – 🛗 🖥 TV
☎ – 🛶 25/250. AE ⓪ VISA. ✲
CX
Meals 1500 – ☕ 1000 – **98 rm** 24000/28500.

Alcázar without rest, Menéndez Pelayo 10, ✉ 41004, ☎ (95) 441 20 11
Fax (95) 442 16 59 – 🛗 🖥 TV ☎ ⟵. AE ⓪ E VISA. ✲
CY
93 rm ☕ 15350/19700.

América coffee shop only, Jesús del Gran Poder 2, ✉ 41002, ☎ (95) 422 09 51
Fax (95) 421 06 26 – 🛗 🖥 TV ☎ – 🛶 25/150. AE ⓪ E VISA. ✲
BV
☕ 850 – **100 rm** 8000/11000.

Hispalis, av. de Andalucía 52, ✉ 41006, ☎ (95) 452 94 33, *Fax (95) 467 53 13* – 🛗 🖥
TV ☎ Ⓟ – 🛶 25/50. AE ⓪ E VISA JCB. ✲
East : by La Florida   CX
Meals 2200 – ☕ 1000 – **99 rm** 12000/14500, 1 suite.

Monte Carmelo without rest, Turia 7, ✉ 41011, ☎ (95) 427 90 00, *Fax (95) 427 10 04*
– 🛗 🖥 TV ☎ ⟵ – 🛶 25/35. AE E VISA. ✲
South : by Pl. de Cuba   AY
☕ 800 – **68 rm** 8000/12500.

Fernando III, San José 21, ✉ 41004, ☎ (95) 421 77 08, *Fax (95) 422 02 46*, 🏊 – 🛗
🖥 TV ☎ ⟵ – 🛶 25/250. AE ⓪ E VISA JCB. ✲ rest
CX
Meals 2500 – ☕ 1200 – **156 rm** 10800/13500, 1 suite.

Regina coffee shop only, San Vicente 97, ✉ 41002, ☎ (95) 490 75 75
Fax (95) 490 75 62 – 🛗 🖥 TV ☎ ⟵. AE ⓪ E VISA. ✲
☕ 1250 – **68 rm** 20700/21700, 4 suites.
North : by San Vicente   AV

Cervantes without rest, Cervantes 10, ✉ 41003, ☎ (95) 490 05 52, *Fax (95) 490 05 36*
– 🛗 🖥 TV ☎ ⟵. AE ⓪ E VISA JCB. ✲
BV
☕ 900 – **46 rm** 10000/14000.

🏠 **Puerta de Triana** without rest, Reyes Católicos 5, ⊠ 41001, ℘ (95) 421 54 04, *Fax (95) 421 54 01* – 🛗 🗐 📺 ☎. 🖭 ⓞ ⅇ 𝑉𝐼𝑆𝐴 𝐽𝐶𝐵. ⁓ AX t
65 rm 🍵 8500/12000.

🏠 **La Rábida**, Castelar 24, ⊠ 41001, ℘ (95) 422 09 60, *Telex 73062, Fax (95) 422 43 75* AX d
– 🛗, 🗐 rm, 📺 ☎. 🖭 ⓞ ⅇ 𝑉𝐼𝑆𝐴. ⁓ rest
Meals 1950 – 🍵 500 – **100 rm** 5900/9000.

🏠 **Baco**, pl. Ponce de León 15, ⊠ 41003, ℘ (95) 456 50 50, *Fax (95) 456 36 54* – 🛗 🗐 CV b
📺 ☎. 🖭 ⓞ ⅇ 𝑉𝐼𝑆𝐴 𝐽𝐶𝐵
Meals (see rest. *El Bacalao* below) – 🍵 600 – **25 rm** 6500/9000.

🏠 **Montecarlo** (annexe 🏠), Gravina 51, ⊠ 41001, ℘ (95) 421 75 03, *Fax (95) 421 68 25* AX e
– 🛗 🗐 📺 ☎. 🖭 ⓞ ⅇ 𝑉𝐼𝑆𝐴. ⁓
Meals *(closed January-15 February)* 1950 – 🍵 650 – **51 rm** 8000/11000.

🏠 **Reyes Católicos** without rest, no 🍵, Gravina 57, ⊠ 41001, ℘ (95) 421 12 00, *Fax (95) 421 63 12* – 🛗 🗐 📺 ☎. 🖭 ⓞ ⅇ 𝑉𝐼𝑆𝐴. ⁓ AX z
27 rm 8000/11000.

𝗫𝗫𝗫 **Egaña Oriza**, San Fernando 41, ⊠ 41004, ℘ (95) 422 72 54, *Fax (95) 421 04 29*, CY y
❀ « Winter garden » – 🗐. 🖭 ⓞ ⅇ 𝑉𝐼𝑆𝐴 𝐽𝐶𝐵. ⁓
closed Saturday lunch, Sunday and August – **Meals** 6000 and a la carte 5000/6400
Spec. Caña de lomo en ensalada con láminas de patata a la vinagreta de tomate. Salmorejo con ostras y virutas de jamón al aceite virgen (autumn-winter). Suprema de lubina con crema de patata y salsa de trufas.

𝗫𝗫𝗫 **Florencia** - *Hotel Porta Coeli*, av. Eduardo Dato 49, ⊠ 41018, ℘ (95) 453 35 00, *Fax (95) 453 23 42*, « Tasteful decor » – 🗐 🅿. 🖭 ⓞ ⅇ 𝑉𝐼𝑆𝐴 𝐽𝐶𝐵. ⁓
closed August – **Meals** a la carte 3850/6600.   East : by Demetrio de los Ríos CXY

𝗫𝗫𝗫 **Taberna del Alabardero** with rm, Zaragoza 20, ⊠ 41001, ℘ (95) 456 06 37, AX n
❀ *Fax (95) 456 36 66*, « Former palace » – 🛗 🗐 📺 ☎ 🚗. 🖭 ⓞ ⅇ 𝑉𝐼𝑆𝐴 𝐽𝐶𝐵. ⁓
closed August – **Meals** a la carte 4350/6250 – **7 rm** 🍵 21000/30000
Spec. Ensalada de aguacate con langostinos de Sanlúcar al vinagre de Jerez. Lomos de merluza con almejas en salsa verde. Solomillo de buey con tuétano al vino de Rioja.

𝗫𝗫𝗫 **El Burladero** - *Hotel Tryp Colón*, Canalejas 1, ⊠ 41001, ℘ (95) 422 29 00, *Telex 72726, Fax (95) 422 09 38*, « Bullfighting theme » – 🗐. 🖭 ⓞ ⅇ 𝑉𝐼𝑆𝐴. ⁓ AX a
closed August – **Meals** a la carte 6000/6500.

𝗫𝗫𝗫 **La Dehesa** - *Hotel Meliá Lebreros*, Luis Morales 2, ⊠ 41018, ℘ (95) 457 62 04, *Fax (95) 458 23 09*, 🌳, « Typical Andalusian decor » – 🗐. 🖭 ⓞ 𝑉𝐼𝑆𝐴. ⁓
Meals - Braised meat specialities - a la carte approx. 4100.   East : by La Florida CX

𝗫𝗫𝗫 **Marea Grande**, Diego Angulo Íñiguez 16 - edificio Alcázar, ⊠ 41018, ℘ (95) 453 80 00, *Fax (95) 453 80 00* – 🗐. 🖭 ⓞ ⅇ 𝑉𝐼𝑆𝐴. ⁓   East : by Demetrio de los Ríos CXY
closed Sunday and 15 to 31 August – **Meals** - Seafood - a la carte 3900/5125.

𝗫𝗫 **Al-Mutamid**, Alfonso XI-1, ⊠ 41005, ℘ (95) 492 55 04, *Fax (95) 492 25 02*, 🌳 – 🗐.
🖭 ⓞ ⅇ 𝑉𝐼𝑆𝐴 𝐽𝐶𝐵. ⁓   East : by Demetrio de los Ríos CXY
Meals a la carte 3700/4700.

𝗫𝗫 **La Albahaca**, pl. Santa Cruz 12, ⊠ 41004, ℘ (95) 422 07 14, *Fax (95) 456 12 04*, 🌳 CX t
« Former manor house » – 🗐. 🖭 ⓞ ⅇ 𝑉𝐼𝑆𝐴 𝐽𝐶𝐵. ⁓
closed Sunday – **Meals** a la carte 4100/5400.

𝗫𝗫 **Rincón de Casana**, Santo Domingo de la Calzada 13, ⊠ 41018, ℘ (95) 453 17 10, *Fax (95) 453 78 37*, « Regional decor » – 🗐. 🖭 ⓞ ⅇ 𝑉𝐼𝑆𝐴. ⁓
closed Sunday (14 June-13 September) and Sunday dinner the rest of the year – **Meals** a la carte 3500/5100.   East : by Demetrio de los Ríos CXY

𝗫𝗫 **La Isla**, Arfe 25, ⊠ 41001, ℘ (95) 421 26 31, *Fax (95) 456 22 19* – 🗐. 🖭 ⓞ 𝑉𝐼𝑆𝐴. ⁓ BX a
closed August – **Meals** a la carte 4750/6900.

𝗫𝗫 **El Asador de Aranda**, Luis Montoto 150, ⊠ 41005, ℘ (95) 457 81 41, *Fax (95) 457 81 41*, 🌳 – 🗐 🅿. 🖭 ⅇ 𝑉𝐼𝑆𝐴. ⁓   East : by La Florida CX
closed Sunday dinner and August – **Meals** - Roast lamb - a la carte 3175/4025.

𝗫𝗫 **Ox's**, Betis 61, ⊠ 41010, ℘ (95) 427 95 85, *Fax (95) 427 84 65* – 🗐. 🖭 ⓞ ⅇ 𝑉𝐼𝑆𝐴 𝐽𝐶𝐵. AY b
⁓
closed Sunday dinner, Monday and August – **Meals** - Basque rest - a la carte 4200/5100.

𝗫𝗫 **Casa Robles**, Álvarez Quintero 58, ⊠ 41004, ℘ (95) 456 32 72, *Fax (95) 456 44 79* – BX c
🗐. 🖭 ⓞ ⅇ 𝑉𝐼𝑆𝐴 𝐽𝐶𝐵. ⁓
Meals a la carte 3650/5400.

𝗫 **El Bacalao** - *Hotel Baco*, pl. Ponce de León 15, ⊠ 41003, ℘ (95) 421 66 70, *Fax (95) 422 49 12* – 🗐. 🖭 ⓞ ⅇ 𝑉𝐼𝑆𝐴. ⁓ CV b
closed Sunday dinner and August – **Meals** - Cod specialities - a la carte 3400/4600.

𝗫 **Horacio**, Antonia Díaz 9, ⊠ 41001, ℘ (95) 422 53 85, *Fax (95) 421 79 27* – 🗐. 🖭 ⓞ AX c
ⅇ 𝑉𝐼𝑆𝐴 𝐽𝐶𝐵. ⁓
Meals a la carte 3075/4000.

SPAIN

at San Juan de Aznalfarache *West : 4 km –* ✉ *41920 San Juan de Aznalfarache :*

Alcora ⑤, carret. de Tomares ℘ (95) 476 94 00, Fax (95) 476 94 98, ≤, « Patio with plants », ⬛, ⬛ – ⬛ ⬛ ⬛ ☎ ⬛ ⬛ ⬛ – ⬛ 25/1200. ⬛ ⬛ ⬛ ⬛. ⬛
Meals 3300 - **Don Aníbal** *(closed August)* **Meals** a la carte approx. 4100 – ⬛ 1600 –
331 rm 22000/27500, 70 suites.

at Castilleja de la Cuesta *West : 5 km –* ✉ *41950 Castilleja de la Cuesta :*

Hacienda San Ygnacio, Real 194 ℘ (95) 416 04 30, Fax (95) 416 14 37, ⬛, « In an old hacienda », ⬛, ⬛ – ⬛ ⬛ ☎ ⬛ – ⬛ 25/200. ⬛ ⬛ ⬛ ⬛ ⬛. ⬛ rest
Almazara *(closed Monday and August)* **Meals** a la carte 2250/2850 – ⬛ 1000 – **16 rm**
14000/19000.

at Benacazón *West : 23 km –* ✉ *41805 Benacazón :*

Andalusi Park H., autopista A 49 - exit 6 ℘ (95) 570 56 00, Fax (95) 570 50 79,
« Arabian style building. garden », ⬛, ⬛ – ⬛ ⬛ ⬛ ☎ ⬛ ⬛ – ⬛ 25/500. ⬛ ⬛ ⬛
⬛. ⬛
Meals 4000 – ⬛ 1500 – **189 rm** 16700/20900, 11 suites.

at Sanlúcar la Mayor *West : 27 km –* ✉ *41800 Sanlúcar la Mayor :*

Hacienda Benazuza ⑤, Virgen de las Nieves ℘ (95) 570 33 44, Fax (95) 570 34 10,
≤, « In a 10C Arabian farmhouse », ⬛, ⬛, ⬛ – ⬛ ⬛ ⬛ ☎ ⬛ – ⬛ 25/400. ⬛ ⬛
⬛ ⬛. ⬛ rest
closed 15 July-August – **Meals** 6500 - **La Alquería :** **Meals** a la carte 5500/9100 –
⬛ 1500 – **26 rm** 36000/44000, 18 suites.

VALÈNCIA 46000 ℗ **445** *N 28 y 29 – pop. 777 427 alt. 13.*

See : *The Old town★ : Cathedral★ (El Miguelete★, Capilla del Santo Cáliz★)* EX *– Palacio de la Generalidad★ (golden room : ceiling★)* EX D *– Lonja★ (silkhall★★)* DY.

Other curiosities : *Ceramic Museum★★ (Palacio del Marqués de Dos Aguas★)* EY M[1] *– San Pío V Museum★ (valencian primitifs★★)* FX *– Patriarch College or of the Corpus Christi★ (Passion triptych★)* EY N *– Serranos Towers★* EX.

⬛ *Manises, East : 12 km,* ℘ *(96) 152 38 04 –* ⬛ *Club Escorpión, North-West : 19 km by road to Liria* ℘ *(96) 160 12 11 –* ⬛ *El Saler-Parador de El Saler, South-East : 15 km* ℘ *(96) 161 11 86.*

⬛ *Valencia - Manises Airport, East : 9,5 km* ℘ *(96) 159 85 00 – Iberia : Paz 14,* ✉ *46003* ℘ *(96) 902 40 05 00* EFY.

⬛ . *To the Balearic Islands : Estación Marítima* ✉ *46024* ℘ *(96) 367 65 12 Fax (96) 367 06 44 by Av. Regne de València* FZ.

🛈 *Pl. del Ayuntamiento 1,* ✉ *46002* ℘ *(96) 351 04 17 Fax (96) 352 58 12, Paz 48* ✉ *46003* ℘ *(96) 398 64 22 and Xàtiva 24 (North Station)* ✉ *46007* ℘ *(96) 352 85 73 –* R.A.C.E. *(R.A.C. de València) Av. Regne de València 64,* ✉ *46005,* ℘ *(96) 374 94 05 Fax (96) 373 71 06.*

Madrid 351 – Albacete 183 – Alicante/Alacant (by coast) 174 – Barcelona 361 – Bilbao/Bilbo 606 – Castellón de la Plana/Castelló de la Plana 75 – Málaga 651 – Sevilla 682 – Zaragoza 330.

Plans on following pages

Meliá Valencia Palace ⑤, paseo de la Alameda 32, ✉ 46023, ℘ (96) 337 50 37,
Fax (96) 337 55 32, ≤, ⬛, ⬛ – ⬛ ⬛ ⬛ ☎ ⬛ ⬛ – ⬛ 25/800. ⬛ ⬛ ⬛ ⬛ ⬛
⬛   East : by Puente de Aragón FZ
Meals a la carte 4100/5050 – ⬛ 1605 – **183 rm** 19155/21295, 16 suites.

Meliá Rey Don Jaime, av. Baleares 2, ✉ 46023, ℘ (96) 337 50 30, Fax (96) 337 15 72,
⬛ – ⬛ ⬛ ⬛ ☎ ⬛ – ⬛ 25/250. ⬛ ⬛ ⬛ ⬛ ⬛. ⬛
Meals a la carte 3600/4650 – ⬛ 1500 – **318 rm** 19350/24200.
                                          East : by Puente de Aragón FZ

Astoria Palace, pl. Rodrigo Botet 5, ✉ 46002, ℘ (96) 352 67 37, Fax (96) 352 80 78,
– ⬛ ⬛ ⬛ ☎ ⬛ – ⬛ 25/500. ⬛ ⬛ ⬛ ⬛ ⬛. ⬛   EY p
Vinatea : **Meals** a la carte 3900/6200 – ⬛ 1600 – **196 rm** 21500/27000, 7 suites.

Acteón Plaza without rest, Islas Canarias 102, ✉ 46023, ℘ (96) 331 07 07,
Fax (96) 330 22 30, ⬛ – ⬛ ⬛ ⬛ ☎ ⬛ – ⬛ 25/400. ⬛ ⬛ ⬛ ⬛. ⬛
⬛ 1400 – **182 rm** 18400/23000, 5 suites.   East : by Av. Regne de València FZ

Turia, Profesor Beltrán Baguena 2, ✉ 46009, ℘ (96) 347 00 00, Fax (96) 347 32 44 –
⬛ ⬛ ⬛ ☎ ⬛ – ⬛ 25/300. ⬛ ⬛ ⬛. ⬛
Meals 3000 – ⬛ 600 – **160 rm** 10000/14500, 10 suites.
                          North-West : by Gran Vía Fernando el Católico DY

Mercure Conqueridor, Cervantes 9, ✉ 46007, ℘ (96) 352 29 10, *Fax (96) 352 28 83* – |♯| 🗏 TV ☎ 🚗 – 🔬 25/80. AE ① E VISA. ✄
DZ b
Meals 2700 – ☕ 1500 – **55 rm** 14600/22800, 4 suites.

Inglés, Marqués de Dos Aguas 6, ✉ 46002, ℘ (96) 351 64 26, *Fax (96) 394 02 51,* « In the Duke of Cardona's 18C palace » – |♯| 🗏 TV ☎ – 🔬 25/60. AE ① E VISA JCB. ✄
EY e
Meals 1925 – ☕ 1000 – **63 rm** 15000/19000.

Dimar coffee shop only, Gran Vía Marqués del Turia 80, ✉ 46005, ℘ (96) 395 10 30, *Fax (96) 395 19 26* – |♯| 🗏 TV ☎ – 🔬 25/50. AE ① E VISA. ✄
FZ q
☕ 1300 – **103 rm** 13800/22900, 1 suite.

Reina Victoria, Barcas 4, ✉ 46002, ℘ (96) 352 04 87, *Fax (96) 352 27 21* – |♯| 🗏 TV ☎ – 🔬 25/75. AE ① E VISA. ✄
EY s
Meals 3000 – ☕ 1200 – **94 rm** 13000/20500, 3 suites.

NH Center, Ricardo Micó 1, ✉ 46009, ℘ (96) 347 50 00, *Fax (96) 347 62 52,* ⅃₅, ⅃ heated – |♯| 🗏 TV ☎ ♿ 🚗 – 🔬 25/400. AE ① E VISA JCB. ✄
Meals 2500 – ☕ 1500 – **190 rm** 15500, 3 suites.

North : by Gran Vía Fernando el Católico DY

NH Ciudad de Valencia, av. del Puerto 214, ✉ 46023, ℘ (96) 330 75 00, *Fax (96) 330 98 64* – |♯| 🗏 TV ☎ 🚗 – 🔬 30/80. AE ① VISA JCB. ✄
Meals *(closed Sunday)* 2800 – ☕ 1000 – **147 rm** 12000, 2 suites.

East : by Puente de Aragón FZ

Cónsul del Mar, av. del Puerto 39, ✉ 46021, ℘ (96) 362 54 32, *Fax (96) 362 16 25,* « Old manor house » – |♯| 🗏 TV ☎ Ⓟ – 🔬 25/50. AE ① E VISA
Meals 1250 – ☕ 700 – **45 rm** 10500/16000.   East : by Puente de Aragón FZ

NH Abashiri, av. Ausias March 59, ✉ 46013, ℘ (96) 373 28 52, *Fax (96) 373 49 66* – |♯| 🗏 TV ☎ 🚗 – 🔬 30/250. AE ① E VISA JCB. ✄
Meals 2500 – ☕ 1100 – **105 rm** 10500/12600.   South : by Av. Regne de València FZ

NH Villacarlos without rest, av. del Puerto 60, ✉ 46023, ℘ (96) 337 50 25, *Fax (96) 337 50 74* – |♯| 🗏 TV ☎ 🚗. AE ① E VISA. ✄
☕ 1200 – **51 rm** 14500/18125.   East : by Puente de Aragón FZ

Ad-Hoc, Boix 4, ✉ 46003, ℘ (96) 391 91 40, *Fax (96) 391 36 67,* « Attractive 19C building » – |♯| 🗏 TV ☎. AE ① E VISA
FX a
Meals (see rest. ***Chust Godoy*** below) – ☕ 850 – **28 rm** 11900/16700.

Renasa coffee shop only, av. de Cataluña 5, ✉ 46010, ℘ (96) 369 24 50, *Fax (96) 393 18 24* – |♯| 🗏 TV ☎ – 🔬 25/75. AE ① E VISA
69 rm ☕ 6800/11000, 4 suites.   East : by Puente del Real FX

Llar without rest, Colón 46, ✉ 46004, ℘ (96) 352 84 60, *Fax (96) 351 90 00* – |♯| 🗏 TV ☎ – 🔬 25/30. AE ① E VISA. ✄
FZ u
☕ 1000 – **50 rm** 10200/12750.

Sorolla without rest, no ☕, Convento de Santa Clara 5, ✉ 46002, ℘ (96) 352 33 92, *Fax (96) 352 14 65* – |♯| 🗏 TV ☎. AE ① E VISA JCB. ✄
EZ z
50 rm 6700/11700.

Rías Gallegas, Cirilo Amorós 4, ✉ 46004, ℘ (96) 352 51 11, *Fax (96) 351 99 10* – 🗏 Ⓟ. AE ① E VISA JCB
EZ r
closed Sunday and 9 to 22 August – **Meals** 4650 and a la carte 4650/6500
Spec. Lamprea estilo Arbo (January-April). Merluza a la gallega. Solomillo de buey al queso Cabrales.

Eladio, Chiva 40, ✉ 46018, ℘ (96) 384 22 44, *Fax (96) 384 22 44* – 🗏. AE ① E VISA. ✄
West : by Ángel Guimerá DY
closed Sunday and August – **Meals** a la carte 4050/5150.

Óscar Torrijos, Dr. Sumsi 4, ✉ 46005, ℘ (96) 373 29 49 – 🗏. AE ① E VISA. ✄   FZ h
closed Sunday and 15 August-15 September – **Meals** 6500 and a la carte 5100/5900
Spec. Arroz con pintada y alcachofas (November-May). Tartaleta de bacalao con trufas (December-March). Crujiente de chocolate con salsa suzette.

Albacar, Sorní 35, ✉ 46004, ℘ (96) 395 10 05, *Fax (96) 395 10 05* – 🗏. AE ① E VISA. ✄
FY s
closed Saturday lunch, Sunday, Bank Holidays, Holy Week and 7 August-7 September – **Meals** a la carte 4400/5500.

La Sucursal, av. Navarro Reverter 16, ✉ 46004, ℘ (96) 374 66 65, *Fax (96) 374 66 65* – 🗏. AE ① E VISA. ✄
FY n
closed Saturday lunch, Sunday and 15 to 30 August – **Meals** a la carte 3250/5050.

El Ángel Azul, Conde de Altea 33, ✉ 46005, ℘ (96) 374 56 56, *Fax (96) 374 56 56* – 🗏. ① E VISA. ✄
FZ e
closed Sunday, Monday lunch, Holy Week and 15 August-15 September – **Meals** a la carte approx. 4200.

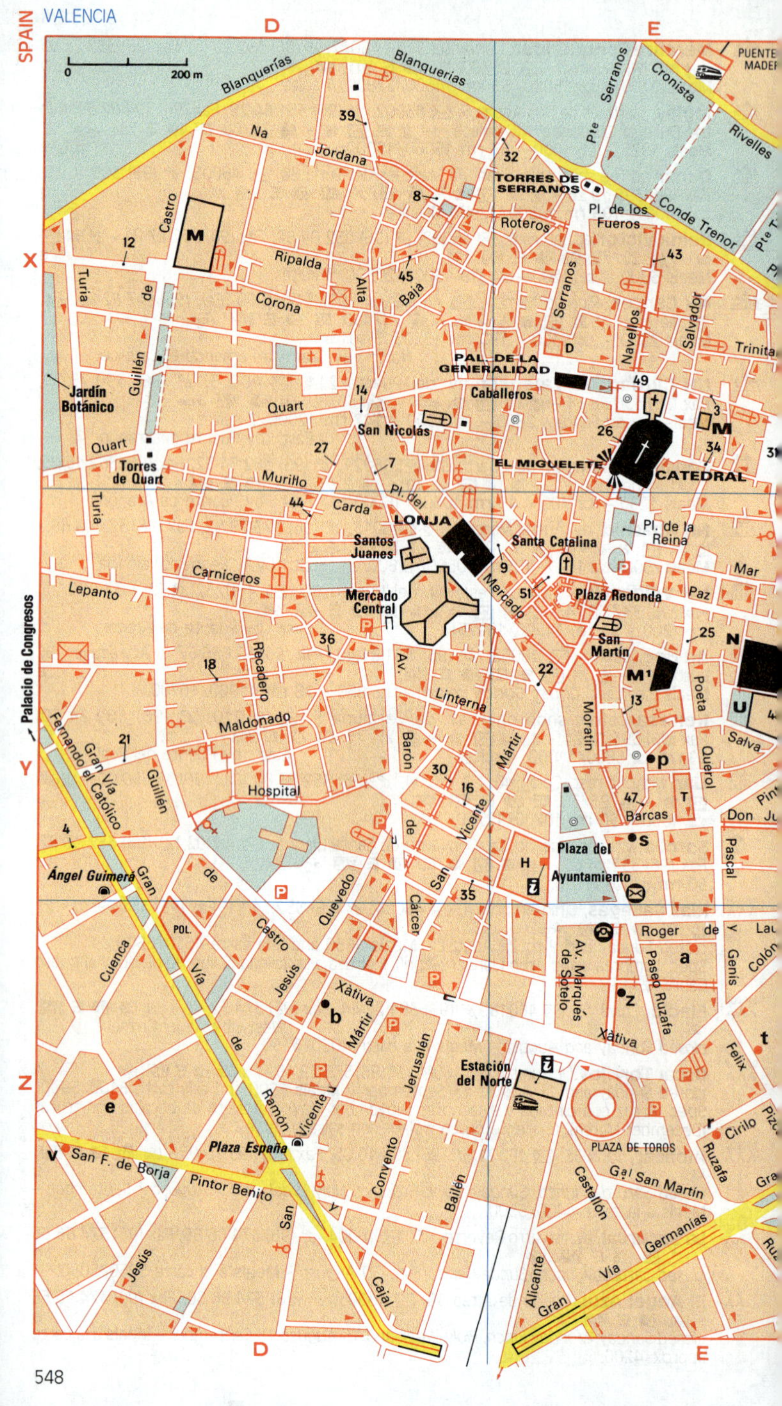

SPAIN
VALENCIA
0   200 m
D
E
Blanquerías
Blanquerías
Na
Jordana
39
32
Castro
M
Ripalda
TORRES DE
SERRANOS
8
Roteros
Pl. de los
Fueros
Pte Serranos
Cronista
Rivelles
PUENTE
MADER
Conde Trenor
Pte T
Pl
12
de
Guillén
Alta
Baja
45
Serranos
43
X
Turia
Corona
Navellos
Salvador
Trinita
PAL. DE LA
GENERALIDAD
D
Caballeros
49
Jardín
Botánico
Quart
14
San Nicolás
26
3
M
34
Quart
27
7
EL MIGUELETE
CATEDRAL
3
Torres
de Quart
Murillo
Pl. del
44
Carda
LONJA
Pl. de la
Reina
Turia
Santos
Juanes
Santa Catalina
9
Mar
Lepanto
Carniceros
Mercado
Central
Mercado
51
Plaza Redonda
Paz
P
36
San
Martín
25
N
18
Recadero
Av.
22
M¹
Maldonado
Linterna
13
Poeta
U
4
21
Gran Vía
Hospital
Barón
Mártir
Moratín
Querol
Salva
p
Palacio de Congresos
Fernando el Católico
Guillén
Pu
de
San
Vicente
30
16
47
Barcas
T
Pint
Don Ju
4
Ángel Guimerá
Gran
de
Quevedo
Cárcel
35
H
Plaza del
Ayuntamiento
S
Pascal
POL.
Vía
Castro
Jesús
Roger de
y
Genis
a
Colón
Cuenca
de
Xàtiva
b
Mártir
Jerusalén
Av. Marqués
de Sotelo
z
Paseo Ruzafa
Z
t
e
Ramón
Vicente
Convento
Bailén
Xàtiva
Estación
del Norte
Felix
P
r
Ruzafa
Cirilo
Pizo
V
San F. de Borja
Plaza España
PLAZA DE TOROS
Pintor Benito
San
Jesús
Cajal
Alicante
Castellón
Gral San Martín
Germanías
Vía
Gran
Gra
Ru
D
E
548

VALENCIA

SPAIN

We suggest:
For a successful tour,
that you prepare it
in advance.
Michelin maps
and guides
will give you much
useful information
on route planning,
places of interest,
accommodation,
prices, etc.

XX **Kailuze,** Gregorio Mayáns 5, ⊠ 46005, ℘ (96) 374 39 99 – ▤. **AE**
VISA. ⊘   FZ
closed Saturday lunch, Sunday, Holy Week and August – **Meals** - Basque rest - a la cart
5050/5850.

XX **El Gastrónomo,** av. Primado Reig 149, ⊠ 46020, ℘ (96) 369 70 36 – ▤. **AE E** *VISA*
⊘   North-East : by Puente del Real   FX
closed Sunday dinner, Monday dinner, Holy Week and August – **Meals** a la carte 3650/465(

XX **Joaquín Schmidt,** Visitación 7, ⊠ 46009, ℘ (96) 340 17 10, *Fax (96) 340 17 10,*
« In an old house with patio » – ▤. **① E** *VISA*. ⊘
closed Sunday, Monday lunch and 5 to 19 April – **Meals** a la carte 4750
5950.   North : by Cronista Rivelles   EX

XX **El Gourmet,** Martí 3, ⊠ 46005, ℘ (96) 395 25 09 – ▤. **AE ① E** *VIS*
JCB. ⊘   FZ
closed Sunday and Holy Week – **Meals** a la carte 2550/3600.

XX **Civera,** Lérida 11, ⊠ 46009, ℘ (96) 347 59 17, *Fax (96) 348 46 38* – ▤. **AE ① E** *VISA*
⊘   North : by Cronista Rivelles   EX
closed Sunday dinner, Monday and August – **Meals** - Seafood - a la carte 4200/5500.

XX **Río Sil Civera,** Mosén Femades 10, ⊠ 46002, ℘ (96) 352 97 64, *Fax (96) 351 38 3*
– ▤. **AE ① E** *VISA*. ⊘   EZ
closed 15 June-15 July – **Meals** - Seafood - a la carte 3400/5800.

XX **El Cabanyal,** Reina 128, ⊠ 46011, ℘ (96) 356 15 03, *Fax (96) 356 15 03* – ▤. **AE ①**
E *VISA*. ⊘   East : by Puente de Aragón   FZ
closed Sunday and 15 August-15 September – **Meals** a la carte 3900/5250.

XX **Chust Godoy** - Hotel Ad-Hoc, Boix 6, ⊠ 46003, ℘ (96) 391 38 15, *Fax (96) 391 36 6*
– ▤. **AE E** *VISA*. ⊘   FX
closed Saturday lunch, Sunday and August – **Meals** a la carte 3400/5200.

XX **José Mari,** Estación Marítima 1º, ⊠ 46024, ℘ (96) 367 20 15, ← – ▤. **AE ① E** *VISA*
⊘   South-East : by Puente de Aragón   FZ
closed Sunday and August – **Meals** - Basque rest - a la carte 3200/4800.

X **Montes,** pl. Obispo Amigó 5, ⊠ 46007, ℘ (96) 385 50 25 – ▤. **AE ① E**
VISA. ⊘   DZ
closed Sunday dinner, Monday and August – **Meals** a la carte 2740/4450.

X **Mey Mey,** Historiador Diago 19, ⊠ 46007, ℘ (96) 384 07 47 – ▤. **A**
VISA. ⊘   DZ
closed Holy Week and the last three weeks in August – **Meals** - Chinese rest - a la cart
2180/3650.

X **El Plat,** Ciscar 3, ⊠ 46005, ℘ (96) 374 12 54 – ▤.
AE E *VISA*   FZ
closed Holy Week – **Meals** a la carte 3850/4500.

X **Eguzki,** av. Baleares 1, ⊠ 46023, ℘ (96) 337 50 33 – ▤. **E** *VISA*. ⊘
closed Sunday and August – **Meals** - Basque rest - a la carte 3100/5650.
    East : by Puente de Aragón   FZ

X **Palace Fesol,** Hernán Cortés 7, ⊠ 46004, ℘ (96) 352 93 23, *Fax (96) 352 93 23*
« Regional decor » – ▤. **AE ① E** *VISA*. ⊘   FZ
closed Saturday and Sunday in summer, Monday the rest of the year, Holy Week and 1
days in August – **Meals** a la carte 2400/4400.

X **Bazterretxe,** Maestro Gozalbo 25, ⊠ 46005, ℘ (96) 395 18 94 – ▤. **AE**
VISA. ⊘   FZ
closed Sunday dinner and August – **Meals** - Basque rest - a la carte 2300/3550.

X **El Romeral,** Gran Vía Marqués del Turia 62, ⊠ 46005, ℘ (96) 395 15 17 – ▤. **AE ①**
E *VISA*. ⊘   FZ
closed Monday, Holy Week and August – **Meals** a la carte 3600/4600.

X **Olabarrieta,** La Barraca 35, ⊠ 46011, ℘ (96) 367 07 79 – ▤. *VISA*. ⊘
closed Sunday and August – **Meals** a la carte approx. 3500.
    East : by Puente de Aragón   FZ

by road C 234 *North-West : 8,5 km* – ⊠ 46035 Valencia :

🏨 **Feria,** av. de las Ferias 2 ℘ (96) 364 44 11, *Fax (96) 364 54 83* – ▨ ▤ **TV** ☎ 🚗
🛁 25/200. **AE ① E** *VISA*. ⊘ rest   by Gran Vía Fernando el Católico   DY
Meals a la carte 3250/4450 – **136 suites** ⊇ 16750/28750.

at Almàssera *North-East : 9 km* – ⊠ 46132 Almàssera :

XX **Lluna de València,** Camí del Mar 56 ℘ (96) 185 10 86, *Fax (96) 185 10 06,* « Ol
farmhouse » – ▤ **℗**. **AE ① E** *VISA*. ⊘   by Puente del Real   FX
closed Saturday lunch, Sunday and Holy Week – **Meals** a la carte 2700/3775.

at El Saler *South : 8 km –* ⊠ *46012 Valencia :*

🏠 **Parador de El Saler** ♨ , 7 km ℘ (96) 161 11 86, *Fax (96) 162 70 16*, ≤, « In the middle of the golf course », ⌕, ⅂₈ – |♿| ▤ TV ☎ P – ☒ 25/200. AE ⓓ E VISA. ⅏
Meals 3700 – ⌣ 1300 – **58 rm** 15600/19500.

🏠 **Sidi Saler** ♨ , beach - 3 km ℘ (96) 161 04 11, *Fax (96) 161 08 38*, ≤, ⛱, ⅂₈, ⌕, ⌕,
⇆, ✕ – |♿| ▤ TV ☎ P – ☒ 25/300. AE ⓓ E VISA. ⅏ rest
Meals 3550 - *Grill Bendinat :* Meals a la carte 3550/5400 – ⌣ 1700 – **260 rm** 20150/25200, 17 suites.

at Manises *on the airport road - East : 9,5 km –* ⊠ *46940 Manises :*

🏠 **Meliá Confort Azafata**, autopista del aeropuerto 15 ℘ (96) 154 61 00, *Fax (96) 153 20 19*, ⅂₈ – |♿| ▤ TV ☎ ⇆ P – ☒ 25/300. AE ⓓ E VISA. ⅏ rest
Meals 2900 – ⌣ 1200 – **124 rm** 13700/17000, 4 suites.

at Puçol *North : 25 km by motorway A 7 –* ⊠ *46760 Puçol :*

🏠 **Monte Picayo** ♨ , urb. Monte Picayo ℘ (96) 142 01 00, *Fax (96) 142 21 68*, ⛱, « On a hillside with ≤ », ⌕, ⇆, ✕ – |♿| ▤ TV ☎ P – ☒ 25/800. AE ⓓ E VISA. ⅏
Meals 4000 – ⌣ 1500 – **79 rm** 19600/23500, 4 suites.

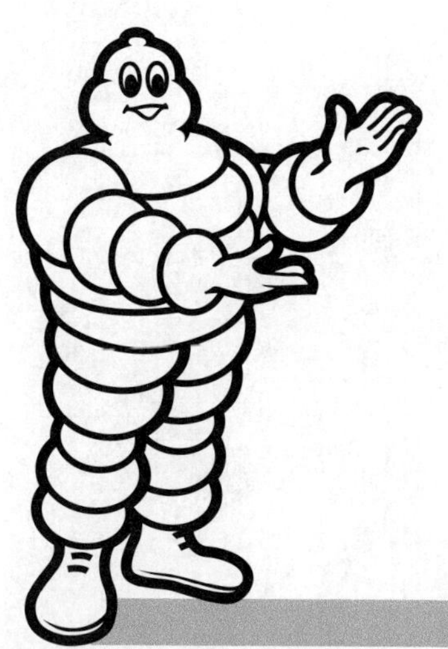

Sweden

Sverige

PRACTICAL INFORMATION

LOCAL CURRENCY

Swedish Kronor: *100 SEK = 10,54 euros (€)*

TOURIST INFORMATION

In Stockholm, the Tourist Centre is situated in Sweden House, entrance from Kungsträdgården at Hamngatan. Open Mon-Fri 9am-6pm. Sat. and Sun. 9am-3pm. Telephone weekdays (08) 789 24 00, weekends to Excursion Shop and Tourist Centre. For Gothenburg, see information in the text of the town under 🛈.

National Holiday in Sweden: *6 June.*

FOREIGN EXCHANGE

Banks are open between 9.30am and 3pm on weekdays only. Some banks in the centre of the city are usually open weekdays 9am to 6pm. Most large hotels and the Tourist Centre have exchange facilities. Arlanda airport has banking facilities between 7am to 10pm seven days a week.

MEALS

At lunchtime, follow the custom of the country and try the typical buffets of Scandinavian specialities (Smörgåsbord).
At dinner, the a la carte and set menus will offer you more conventional cooking.

SHOPPING

In the index of street names, those printed in red are where the principal shops are found.
The main shopping streets in the centre of Stockholm are: Hamngatan, Biblioteksgatan, Drottninggatan.
In the Old Town mainly Västerlånggatan.

THEATRE BOOKINGS

Your hotel porter will be able to make your arrangements or direct you to Theatre Booking Agents.

CAR HIRE

The international car hire companies have branches in Stockholm, Gothenburg, Arlanda and Landvetter airports. Your hotel porter should be able to give details and help you with your arrangements.

TIPPING

Hotels and restaurants normally include a service charge of 15 per cent. Doormen, baggage porters etc. are generally given a gratuity.
Taxis include 10 % tip in the amount shown on the meter.

SPEED LIMITS - SEAT BELTS

The maximum permitted speed on motorways and dual carriageways is 110 km/h - 68 mph, 90 km/h - 56 mph on other roads except where a lower speed limit is indicated and in built up areas 50 km/h - 31 mph.
The wearing of seat belts is compulsory for drivers and all passengers.
In Sweden, drivers must not drink alcoholic beverages at all.

BREAKDOWN SERVICE

A 24 hour breakdown service is operated ☎ 112.

STOCKHOLM

Sverige 985 *M 15 – pop. 674 459 Greater Stockholm 1 491 726.*

Hamburg 935 – Copenhagen 630 – Oslo 522.

ℹ *Stockholm Information Service, Tourist Centre, Sverigehuset, Hamngatan 27 ℘ (08) 789 24 00 – Motormännens Riksförbund ℘ (08) 690 38 00 – Kungliga. Automobilklubben (Royal Automobile Club) Gyllenstiernsgatan 4 ℘ (08) 660 00 55.*

₁₈ *Svenska Golfförbundet (Swedish Golf Federation) ℘ (08) 622 15 00.*

✈ *Stockholm-Arlanda NW : 40 km ℘ (08) 797 61 00 – SAS : Flygcity, Stureplan 8 ℘ (08) 797 41 75, Reservations (020) 727 727 – Air-Terminal : opposite main railway station.*

🚢 *Motorail for Southern Europe : Ticket Travel-Agency, Kungsgatan 60 ℘ (08) 24 00 90.*

🚢 *To Finland : contact Silja Line ℘ (08) 22 21 40 or Viking Line ℘ (08) 714 57 70 – Excursions by boat : contact Stockholm Information Service (see below).*

See: *Old Town★★★ (Gamla Stan)* AZ *– Vasa Museum★★★ (Vasamuseet)* DY *– Skansen Open-Air Museum★★★* DY.
Royal Palace★★ (Kungliga Slottet) AZ *; Royal Apartments★★ ; Royal Armoury★ ; Royal Treasury★★ – Stockholm Cathedral★★ (Storkyrkan)* AZ *– City Hall★★ (Stadhuset) : Blue Hall★★★, Golden Hall★★★ ; ❋★★★* BY **H** *– Prins Eugens Waldemarsudde★★ (house and gallery)* DY *– Thiel Gallery★★ (Thielska Galleriet)* DZ.
House of the Nobility★ (Riddarhuset) AZ **R** *– Riddarholmen Church★ (Riddarholmskyrkan)* AZ **K¹** *– Österlånggatan★* AZ.
Kaknäs TV Tower (Kaknästornet) ❋★★★ DY *– Stigberget : Fjällgatan ❋★* DZ *– Skinnerviksberget : ❋★* BZ.

Museums: *National Art Gallery★★ (Nationalmuseum)* DY **M⁵** *– Nordic Museum★★ (Nordiska Museet)* DY *– Museum of National Antiquities★★ (Historiska Museet)* DY *– Museum of Medieval Stockholm★★ (Stockholms Medeltidsmuseet)* CY **M¹** *– Museum of Far Eastern Antiquities★ (Östasiatiska Museet)* DY **M⁶** *– Hallwyl Collection★ (Hallwylska Museet)* CY **M³** *– Museum of Modern Art (Moderna Museet)* DY **M⁴** *– Strindberg Museum★ (Strindbergsmuseet)* BX **M²**.

Outskirts : *Drottningholm Palace★★★ (Drottningholm Slott) W : 12 km* BY *– Stockholm Archipelago★★★ – Millesgården★★ (house and gallery) E : 4 km* BX *– Skogskyrkogården (UNESCO World Heritage Site).*

Excursions : *Gripsholms Slott★★ – Skokloster★★ – Ulriksdal★ – Birka★ – Strängnas★ – Sigtuna★ – Uppsala★★.*

STOCKHOLM

Biblioteksgatan	CY	2
Birger Jarlsgatan	CXY	3
Brunkebergstorg	CY	5
Brunnsgränd	AZ	6
Bryggargatan	BY	7
Brända Tomten	AZ	8
Djurgårdsbron	DY	9
Drottninggatan	BX, CY	10
Evert Taubes Terrass	AZ	13
Gallerian	CY	14
Grev Turegatan	CY	18
Gustav Adolfs Torg	CY	16
Hamngatan	CY	
Herkulesgatan	CY	19
Hötorget	CY	20
Järntorget	AZ	21
Järntorgsgatan	AZ	23
Kindstugatan	AZ	24
Klarabergsgatan	CY	25
Klarabergsviadukten	BY	27
Kornhamnstorg	AZ	28
Kungsgatan	BCY	
Kungsträdgårdsgatan	CY	32
Köpmangatan	AZ	35
Lilla Nygatan	AZ	36
Mosebacke Torg	CZ	39
Munkbrogatan	AZ	40
Myntgatan	AZ	41
Mäster Mikaels Gata	DZ	42
Norrbro	CY	43
Norrlandsgatan	CY	44
Nybroplan	CY	45
Olof Palmes Gata	BY	47
Österlånggatan	AZ	
Prästgatan	AZ	48
Riddarhusgränd	AZ	49
Riddarhustorget	AZ	50
Rådhusgränd	AZ	52
Sergelgatan	CY	53
Sergels Torg	CY	54
Sista Styverns Trappor	DZ	55
Slottskajen	AZ	56
Slussplan	AZ	57
Stallgatan	CY	59
Stigbergsgatan	DZ	60
Storkyrkobrinken	AZ	61
Strömbron	CY	62
Strömgatan	CY	63
Södermalmstorg	CZ	64
Södra Blasieholmshamnen	CY	66
Tegelbacken	CY	67
Tegnérlunden	BX	69
Triewaldsgränd	AZ	70
Tyska Brinken	AZ	73
Urvädersgränd	CZ	74
Västerlånggatan	AZ	
Östermalmstorg	DY	76
Östra Järnvägsgatan	BY	78

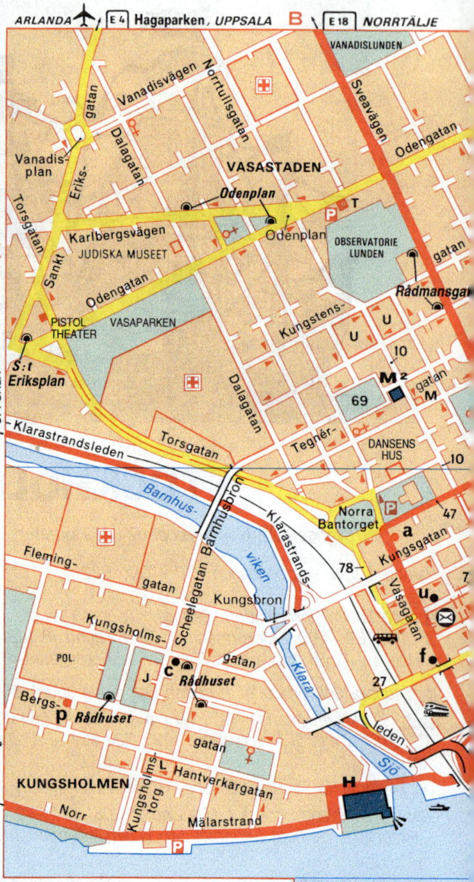

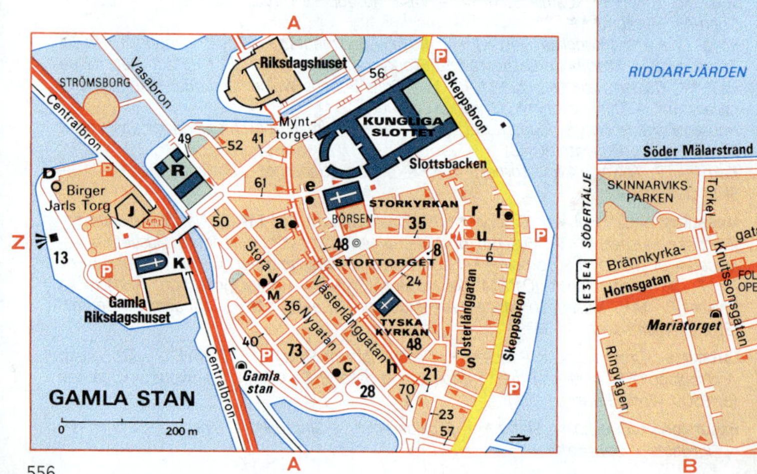

STOCKHÖLM
SWEDEN
Naturhistoriska Riksmuseet
VÄRTAHAMNEN
Millesgården (LIDINGÖ)
277
TEKNISKA HÖGSKOLAN
Valhallavägen
Odengatan
Tekniska Högskolan
Östermalms-
Lill-Jans Plan
Lidingövägen
STADION
Erik Dahlbergsgatan
Gärdet
X
Valhallavägen
Stadion
TESSIN PARKEN
Nybrogatan
Östermalms-
Värtavägen
Karlavägen
Valhallavägen
HUMLEGÅRDEN
Stadion
Karlaplan
Sture
KUNGLIGA BIBLIOTEKET
Karlavägen
Artilleri-
ÖSTERMALM
Karlaplan
G. ADOLFS-PARKEN
Humlegårdsgatan
Linnégatan
Banérgatan
Karlavägen
Hötorget
Kungsgatan
Sture-gallerian
76
Hedvig Eleonora Kyrka
HISTORISKA MUSEET
Narvavägen
Kaknästornet
Sjöhistoriska Museet
Regeringsgatan
Östermalmstorg
Linnégatan
NORRMALM
Artillerigatan
Storgatan
Strandvägen
Hamngatan
Regerings-
Styrmansgatan
STADSTEATERN
centralen
Strandvägen
Nobel-Parken
Kulturhuset
Kungs-trädgården
Nybrokajen
JUNIBACKEN
Lejon-slätten
Jakobsgatan
OPERAN
BLASIEHOLMEN
NORDISKA MUSEET
SKANSEN
HELGEANDS-HOLMEN
Skeppsholms-bron
VASAMUSEET
Djurgårdsvägen
Djurgården
RIDDAR-HOLMEN
GAMLA STAN
AF CHAPMAN
SKEPPSHOLMEN
Gröna Lunds Tivoli
Centralbron
KASTELL HOLMEN
Söder
Slussen
SALTSJÖN
BECK-HOLMEN
Mälarstrand
Katarinahissen
Z
Hornsgatan
Slussen
Stadsgården
Maria-torget
Katarinavägen
Söderleden
gatan
Högbergs-
Katarina Kyrka
42
Fjällgatan
55
Stadsgården
Mariatorget
60
NACKA
SÖDERMALM
Högbergs-
Götgatan
Renstiernas Gata
Folkungagatan
222
Medborgar-platsen
Folkungagatan
0   300 m
Medborgarplatsen
NYNÄSHAMM
73

557

Grand Hotel, Södra Blasieholmshamnen 8, ⊠ S-103 27, ℘ (08) 679 35 00, *Fax (08) 611 86 86,* « Elegant late 19C hotel on the waterfront overlooking Royal Palace and Old Town », ₤₆, ≘s – |≢|, ⇥ rm, ▤ rest, ⊺⊽ ☎ ⅙ ☞ – ⚿ 600. ᴁ ◑ ᴇ *VISA*. JCB. ⇶ rest
CY
Verandan (℘ (08) 679 35 86) : Meals (buffet lunch) 225/295 and a la carte (see also **Franska Matsalen** below) – **285 rm** �@ 1770/3670, 21 suites.

Sheraton Stockholm H. and Towers Ⓜ, Tegelbacken 6, ⊠ S-101 23, ℘ (08) 412 34 00, *Fax (08) 412 34 09,* ≼, ≘s – |≢|, ⇥ rm, ▤ ⊺⊽ ☎ ⅙ Ⓟ – ⚿ 380. ᴁ ◑ ᴇ *VISA*. ⇶ rest
CY
Die Ecke : Meals - German Bierstub - (closed Saturday lunch, Sunday and Bank Holidays) a la carte 310/420 – �@ 90 – **453 rm** 1975/2175, 6 suites.

Radisson SAS Royal Viking Ⓜ, Vasagatan 1, ⊠ S-101 24, ℘ (08) 14 10 00, *Fax (08) 10 81 80,* « Panoramic Sky Bar on 9th floor with ≼ Stockholm », ≘s, ⬗ – |≢|, ⇥ rm, ▤ ⊺⊽ ☎ ⅙ ☞ – ⚿ 140. ᴁ ◑ ᴇ *VISA* JCB. ⇶
BY
Stockholm Fisk : Meals - Seafood - (closed Sunday lunch) 195/450 and a la carte – **315 rm** �@ 2150/3100, 4 suites.

Provobis Sergel Plaza Ⓜ, Brunkebergstorg 9, ⊠ S-103 27, ℘ (08) 22 66 00, *Fax (08) 21 50 70,* ≘s – |≢|, ⇥ rm, ▤ ⊺⊽ ☎ ⅙ ☞ – ⚿ 200. ᴁ ◑ ᴇ *VISA* JCB. ⇶ rest
Anna Rella : Meals (closed Saturday lunch, Sunday and Bank Holidays) a la carte 335/480 – **Mongolian Barbecue** : (℘ (08) 24 36 55) : Meals - Chinese - a la carte approx. 200 – **405 rm** �@ 1745/2400.
CY

Radisson SAS Strand Ⓜ, Nybrokajen 9, ⊠ S-103 27, ℘ (08) 678 78 00, *Fax (08) 611 24 36,* « Attractive old world architecture, overlooking the harbour », ≘s – |≢|, ⇥ rm, ⊺⊽ ☎ – ⚿ 90. ᴁ ◑ ᴇ *VISA*. ⇶
CDY
Meals 300/600 (dinner) and a la carte 170/185 – **136 rm** ⊚ 2500/3590, 12 suites.

Diplomat, Strandvägen 7c, ⊠ S-104 40, ℘ (08) 459 68 00, *Fax (08) 459 68 20,* « Elegant Art Nouveau style former diplomatic lodgings, overlooking the harbour », ≘s – |≢|, ⇥ rm, ⊺⊽ ☎. ᴁ ◑ ᴇ *VISA*. ⇶
DY
closed Christmas – **Meals** (closed Sunday dinner) 205 and a la carte – **126 rm** ⊚ 1595/2295, 2 suites.

Berns, Näckströmsgatan 8, Berzelii Park, ⊠ S-111 47, ℘ (08) 566 322 00, *Fax (08) 566 322 01,* ⌖, « Meticulously restored 19C ballroom restaurant and salons » – |≢|, ⇥ rm, ▤ rm, ⊺⊽ ☎ – ⚿ 180. ᴁ ◑ ᴇ *VISA*. ⇶
CY
closed 22 to 27 December – **Meals** (closed Sunday) 295/550 and a la carte – **62 rm** ⊚ 1690/2340, 3 suites.

Stockholm Plaza, Birger Jarlsgatan 29, ⊠ S-103 95, ℘ (08) 566 220 00, *Fax (08) 566 220 20,* ⌖, ≘s – |≢|, ⇥ rm, ▤ rest, ⊺⊽ ☎ ⅙ – ⚿ 45. ᴁ ◑ ᴇ *VISA*. ⇶
Meals (closed lunch Saturday and Sunday) a la carte 270/335 – **147 rm** ⊚ 1395/1795, 4 suites.
CX

First H. Amaranten Ⓜ, Kungsholmsgatan 31, ⊠ S-104 20, ℘ (08) 654 10 60, *Fax (08) 652 62 48,* ≘s – |≢|, ⇥ rm, ▤ rest, ⊺⊽ ☎ ⅙ ☞ – ⚿ 85. ᴁ ◑ ᴇ *VISA* JCB. ⇶
BY
Amaryllis : Meals (closed Sunday) (dinner only) 185/425 and a la carte – **Nordquist &** **Ciao-Ciao** : Meals (closed lunch Saturday, Sunday and Monday) 365/530 and dinner a la carte – **422 rm** ⊚ 1345/1985, 1 suite.

Scandic H. Park Ⓜ, Karlavägen 43, ⊠ S-102 46, ℘ (08) 22 96 20, *Fax (08) 21 62 68,* ⌖, ≘s – |≢|, ⇥ rm, ▤ rm, ⊺⊽ ☎ ⅙ ☞ – ⚿ 100. ᴁ ◑ ᴇ *VISA*. ⇶
CX
Park Village : Meals 245/295 and a la carte – **195 rm** ⊚ 1500/2280, 3 suites.

Birger Jarl Ⓜ without rest., Tulegatan 8, ⊠ S-104 32, ℘ (08) 674 10 00, *Fax (08) 673 73 66,* ≘s – |≢| ⇥ ⊺⊽ ☎ ⅙ ☞ – ⚿ 150. ᴁ ◑ ᴇ *VISA*
CX
closed 23 December-1 January – **221 rm** ⊚ 1285/1610, 4 suites.

Comfort Home H. Tapto, Jungfrugatan 57, ⊠ S-115 31, ℘ (08) 664 50 00, *Fax (08) 664 07 00,* « Military exhibits depicting the history of the Swedish army », ≘s – |≢| ⇥ ⊺⊽ ☎ ⅙. ᴁ ◑ ᴇ *VISA*. ⇶
DX
closed 23 to 26 December and restricted opening 27 December-2 January – **Meals** (buffet dinner residents only) – **86 rm** ⊚ (dinner included) 1350/1490.

Rica City, Slöjdgatan 7, Hötorget, ⊠ S-111 81, ℘ (08) 723 72 00, *Fax (08) 723 72 09,* ≘s – |≢|, ⇥ rm, ▤ rest, ⊺⊽ ☎ ⅙ – ⚿ 65. ᴁ ◑ ᴇ *VISA* JCB. ⇶
CY
closed 23 to 29 December – **Meals** (closed Saturday and Sunday) (buffet lunch only) (unlicensed) approx. 95 – **292 rm** ⊚ 1200/1800.

Mornington, Nybrogatan 53, ⊠ S-102 44, ℘ (08) 663 12 40, *Fax (08) 662 21 79,* ≘s – |≢|, ⇥ rm, ⊺⊽ ☎ ☞. ᴁ ◑ ᴇ *VISA*. ⇶
DX
closed 23 December-3 January – **Meals** (closed lunch Saturday and Sunday) 245/345 (dinner) and a la carte 245/345 – **141 rm** ⊚ 1445/1745.

Wellington Ⓜ without rest., Storgatan 6, ⊠ S-114 51, ℘ (08) 667 09 10, *Fax (08) 667 12 54,* ≘s – |≢|, ⇥ rm, ⊺⊽ ☎ ☞. ᴁ ◑ ᴇ *VISA* JCB
DY
closed 23 to 27 December – **59 rm** ⊚ 1195/1495, 1 suite.

Castle without rest., Riddargatan 14, ✉ S-114 35, ☎ (08) 679 57 00, *Fax (08) 611 20 22* – 📶, 🍴 rest, 📺 ☎ 🚻 – 🔨 30. 🆎 ① ⓔ 𝗩𝗜𝗦𝗔 JCB. 🛪   CY e
48 rm ☕ 1250/1650, 2 suites.

Freys, Bryggargatan 12, ✉ S-101 31, ☎ (08) 50 62 13 00, *Fax (08) 50 62 13 13* – 📶, 🛪 rm, 📺 ☎ 🚻. 🆎 ① ⓔ 𝗩𝗜𝗦𝗔. 🛪 rest   BY u
closed Christmas – **Meals** *(closed Saturday and Sunday lunch)* (light lunch)/dinner 250/400 and a la carte – **112 rm** ☕ 1290/1990.

Operakällaren, Operahuset, Karl XII's Torg, ✉ S-111 86, ☎ (08) 676 58 00, *Fax (08) 676 58 72,* ≼, « Historic late 19C restaurant situated in the Opera House, baroque decor » – 🍴. 🆎 ① ⓔ 𝗩𝗜𝗦𝗔 JCB   CY d
closed July, 25-26 December and 1 January – **Meals** (dinner only) 590/685 and a la carte 550/685
Spec. Sea urchin soup with crab and oysters. Poached lobster with pesto and ragoût of squid. Pepper glazed knuckle of veal with seasonal vegetables and confit of shallots.

Franska Matsalen (at Grand Hotel), Södra Blasieholmshamnen 8, ✉ S-103 27, ☎ (08) 679 35 84, *Fax (08) 611 86 86,* « Elegant Jacobean style dining room, ≼ Royal Palace and Old Town » – 🍴. 🆎 ① ⓔ 𝗩𝗜𝗦𝗔 JCB   CY r
closed Saturday and Sunday – **Meals** (dinner only) 695/985 and a la carte.

Paul and Norbert (Lang), Strandvägen 9, ✉ S-114 56, ☎ (08) 663 81 83, *Fax (08) 661 72 36* – 🆎 ① ⓔ 𝗩𝗜𝗦𝗔 JCB. 🛪   DY m
closed 22 December-8 January – **Meals** (booking essential) 235/650 and a la carte 540/690
Spec. Port wine marinated goose liver. Creamy morel soup with sherry and pheasant quenelles. Juniper berry marinated elk steak with a creamy Roquefort sauce.

Riche, Birger Jarlsgatan 4, ✉ S-114 34, ☎ (08) 679 68 40, *Fax (08) 611 32 06* – 🆎 ①
ⓔ 𝗩𝗜𝗦𝗔   CY v
closed Sunday and 24 to 27 December – **Meals** 175/450 and a la carte – **Veranda** : **Meals** 175/450 and a la carte.

Pica Pica, Regeringsgatan 111, ✉ S-111 39, ☎ (08) 660 60 60, *Fax (08) 10 76 35,* « Modern interior design » – 🍴. 🆎 ① ⓔ 𝗩𝗜𝗦𝗔 JCB   CX n
closed Saturday lunch, Sunday, July and Christmas – **Meals** 295/350 and a la carte.

Fredsgatan 12 (Andersson), Fredsgatan 12, ✉ S-111 52, ☎ (08) 24 80 52, *Fax (08) 411 73 48,* « Modern decor » – 🆎 ① ⓔ 𝗩𝗜𝗦𝗔   CY f
closed Saturday lunch, Sunday, July and Christmas – **Meals** (booking essential) (light lunch)/dinner 230/515 and a la carte 350/465
Spec. Caviar "taco". Antipasto. Venison bourguignon with pumpkin and chipotle chilli.

Bon Lloc (Dahlgren), Bergsgatan 33, ✉ S-112 28, ☎ (08) 650 50 82, *Fax (08) 650 50 83* – 🆎 ① ⓔ 𝗩𝗜𝗦𝗔   BY p
closed Saturday lunch, Sunday, 28 June-1 August, Christmas and Bank Holidays – **Meals** - Catalonian influences - (booking essential) (light lunch) 185/500 and a la carte 185/500
Spec. Duck terrine with apple purée. Escalope of monkfish with seafood paella. Crema Barcelona.

Wedholms Fisk, Nybrokajen 17, ✉ S-111 48, ☎ (08) 611 78 74, *Fax (08) 678 60 11* – 🍴. 🆎 ① ⓔ 𝗩𝗜𝗦𝗔   CY s
closed Saturday lunch, Sunday and Bank Holidays – **Meals** - Seafood - (light lunch) (dinner only Monday to Friday 25 June-23 August) a la carte 325/585
Spec. Fricassee of sole, turbot, lobster and scallops with Champagne sauce. Boiled turbot with melted butter and horseradish. Tartare of salmon and salmon roe with crème fraîche.

Clas På Hörnet with rm, Surbrunnsgatan 20, ✉ S-113 48, ☎ (08) 16 51 30, *Fax (08) 612 53 15,* 🌳, « Characterful 18C inn, antique furnishings » – 📶 📺 ☎. 🆎 ① ⓔ 𝗩𝗜𝗦𝗔 JCB. 🛪 rest   CX f
closed 5 July-1 August and 24 to 27 December – **Meals** *(closed lunch Saturday and Sunday)* 200/420 (dinner) and a la carte 205/420 – **10 rm** ☕ 1090/1290.

Eriks Bakficka, Frederikshovsgatan 4, ✉ S-115 23, ☎ (08) 660 15 99, *Fax (08) 663 25 67,* 🌳 – 🍴. 🆎 ① ⓔ 𝗩𝗜𝗦𝗔   DY r
closed lunch Saturday and Sunday, 3 July-3 August and 23 December-5 January – **Meals** - Bistro - 145/410 and a la carte.

Norrlands Bar & Grill, Norrlandsgatan 24, ✉ S-111 43, ☎ (08) 611 88 10, *Fax (08) 611 88 30,* 🌳 – 🆎 ① ⓔ 𝗩𝗜𝗦𝗔   CY k
closed Saturday lunch, Monday dinner, Sunday and 23 December-12 January – **Meals** 250/520 and a la carte.

Greitz, Vasagatan 50, ✉ S-111 20, ☎ (08) 23 48 20, *Fax (08) 24 20 93,* « Late 19C bistro » – 🆎 ① ⓔ 𝗩𝗜𝗦𝗔 JCB   BY a
closed Saturday lunch, Sunday and 23 December-4 January – **Meals** 230/450 and a la carte – **Pressklubben** : **Meals** 220 and a la carte.

576 16000

KB, Smålandsgatan 7, ⊠ S-111 46, ℘ (08) 679 60 32, Fax (08) 611 82 83, « 19C building modern art display » – AE ① E VISA JCB   CY
closed Saturday lunch, Sunday, 19 June-12 August, 24-25 and 31 December and 1 Januar – Meals 195/565 and a la carte 255/370.

Prinsen, Mäster Samuelsgatan 4, ⊠ S-111 44, ℘ (08) 611 13 31, Fax (08) 611 70 7 – AE ① E VISA JCB   CY
closed Sunday lunch – Meals (lunch booking essential) 230 (dinner) and a la carte 230/42

Sturehof, Stureplan 2-4, ⊠ S-114 46, ℘ (08) 440 57 30, Fax (08) 678 11 01, 🌴 – A ① E VISA   CY
Meals a la carte 250/470.

Grodan, Grev Turegatan 16, ⊠ S-114 46, ℘ (08) 679 61 00, Fax (08) 679 61 10 – A ① E VISA JCB   CY
closed Sunday, 26 June and 24-25 December – Meals 305 (dinner) and a la carte 190/39

at Gamla Stan (Old Stockholm) :

Reisen, Skeppsbron 12, ⊠ S-111 30, ℘ (08) 22 32 60, Fax (08) 20 15 59, ≤, « 18C hote on waterfront with original maritime decor », ⊆s – 🛗, ⇤ rm, TV ☎ ዿ. AE ① E VISA ⊁ rest   AZ
Primo Chao-Chao : Meals (dinner only Saturday and Sunday) a la carte 195/410 – **111 rr** ☲ 1695/2195, 3 suites.

Victory, Lilla Nygatan 5, ⊠ S-111 28, ℘ (08) 14 30 90, Fax (08) 20 21 77, « 17C hote with Swedish rural furnishings and maritime antiques », ⊆s – 🛗, ⇤ rm, TV ☎ – 🔏 8C AE ① E VISA JCB. ⊁   AZ
closed Christmas and 31 December – Meals (see **Leijontornet** below) – **45 rn** ☲ 1890/2190, 3 suites.

Lady Hamilton without rest., Storkyrkobrinken 5, ⊠ S-111 28, ℘ (08) 23 46 8C Fax (08) 411 11 48, « 15C house, Swedish rural antiques », ⊆s – 🛗 ⇤ TV ☎. AE ① E VISA JCB. ⊁   AZ
34 rm ☲ 1790/2090.

Rica City H. Gamla Stan without rest., Lilla Nygatan 25, ⊠ S-111 28, ℘ (08) 723 72 5C Fax (08) 723 72 59, « 17C house » – 🛗 ⇤ TV ☎ – 🔏 30. AE ① E VISA JCB. ⊁   AZ
50 rm ☲ 1250/1490, 1 suite.

Lord Nelson without rest., Västerlånggatan 22, ⊠ S-111 29, ℘ (08) 23 23 90 Fax (08) 10 10 89, « Late 17C house with ship style installation and maritime antiques » ⊆s – 🛗 ⇤ TV ☎. AE ① E VISA JCB. ⊁   AZ
closed Christmas and New Year – **31 rm** ☲ 1420/1770.

Pontus in the Green House, Österlånggatan 17, ⊠ S-112 61, ℘ (08) 23 85 00 Fax (08) 796 60 69, « 15C house » – AE ① E VISA   AZ
closed Sunday, 3 weeks late July-early August, 24 December-3 January and Bank Holiday. – Meals - mainly Seafood - (booking essential) (dinner only mid July and mid August 400/1000 and a la carte 450/695.

Leijontornet (at Victory H.), Lilla Nygatan 5, ⊠ S-111 28, ℘ (08) 14 23 55 Fax (08) 406 08 14, « Remains of a 14C fortification tower in the dining room » – AE ① E VISA JCB   AZ
closed Sunday, July, 23 December-7 January and Bank Holidays – Meals (booking essential (dinner only) 395/540 and a la carte – **Loherummet :** Meals - Bistro - (dinner only 250/350 and a la carte.

Fem Små Hus, Nygränd 10, ⊠ S-111 30, ℘ (08) 10 87 75, Fax (08) 14 96 95, « 17C cellars, antiques » – AE ① E VISA JCB   AZ
Meals (dinner only) 325/455 and a la carte.

Den Gyldene Freden, Österlånggatan 51, ⊠ S-103 17, ℘ (08) 24 97 60 Fax (08) 21 38 70, « Early 18C inn with vaulted cellars » – AE ① E VISA   AZ s
closed Sunday, July and Bank Holidays – Meals (dinner only and Saturday lunch)/dinner 425/575 and a la carte 345/585.

Mårten Trotzig, Västerlånggatan 79, ⊠ S-103 15, ℘ (08) 24 02 31, Fax (08) 24 02 51 🌴, « Contemporary decor in 17C house » – AE ① E VISA   AZ H
closed lunch Saturday and Sunday, dinner Bank Holidays and 23 December-6 January – Meals 295/415 and a la carte.

at Djurgården :

Scandic H. Hasselbacken M, Hazeliusbacken 20, ⊠ S-100 55, ℘ (08) 670 50 00 Fax (08) 663 84 10, 🌴, « Historic summer restaurant in former royal park », ⊆s – 🛗 ⇤ rm, 🖥 TV ☎ ዿ ⇌ P – 🔏 100. AE ① E VISA. ⊁ rest   DZ e
Meals (booking essential) 300/360 and a la carte – **109 rm** ☲ 1580/2190, 2 suites.

XX **Ulla Winbladh,** Rosendalsvägen 8, ⊠ S-115 21, ℰ (08) 663 05 71, *Fax (08) 663 05 73,*
☶, « *Late 19C pavilion in former royal hunting ground* » – AE ① E VISA   DY a
closed 24 and 25 December – **Meals** (booking essential) a la carte 280/380.

at Södermalm :

🏨 **Scandic H. Slussen** M, Guldgränd 8, ⊠ S-104 65, ℰ (08) 517 353 00, *Fax (08) 517 353*
11, ≤, ☶, ⌂, ⊟s, ⊠ – ♦, ⇔ rm, ☰ TV ☎ ♿ ⇔ – ⚒ 300. AE ① E VISA. ⋙
Eken : **Meals** a la carte 230/315 – **253 rm** ⊒ 1710/2450, 11 suites.   CZ e

XX **Gondolen,** Stadsgården 6 (11th floor), ⊠ S-104 56, ℰ (08) 641 70 90,
Fax (08) 641 11 40, « Glass enclosed passageway with nautical decor, ☀ Stockholm and
water » – ☰. AE ① E VISA   CZ a
closed July lunch, Sunday, 24 to 26 December and 1 January – **Meals** 295/450 and a la carte.

XX **Nils Emil,** Folkungagatan 122, ⊠ S-116 30, ℰ (08) 640 72 09, *Fax (08) 640 37 25* – AE
① E VISA   DZ a
closed Sunday and July – **Meals** 390/440 (dinner) and a la carte 235/420.

XX **Gässlingen** (Grossmann), Brännkyrkagatan 93, ⊠ S-117 26, ℰ (08) 669 54 95,
☸ *Fax (08) 84 89 90* – AE ① E VISA   BZ
closed Sunday, Monday, 18 June-2 September and 21 December-12 January – **Meals** (booking essential) (dinner only) 495 and a la carte 305/705
Spec. Goose liver terrine. Tournedos "Rossini". Apple pancakes flamed in Calvados with
caramel ice cream.

to the North :

XX **Stallmästaregården,** Norrtull, ⊠ S-113 39, *North : 2 km by Sveavägen (at beginning*
of E 4) ℰ (08) 610 13 00, *Fax (08) 610 13 40,* ≤, « *17C inn, waterside setting* », ☶ –
☰ P. AE ① E VISA
Meals 250/530 and dinner a la carte.

to the Northeast :

at the Silja terminal in Värtahamnen *Northeast : 3 km by Värtavägen DX and Tegelud-*
dsvägen :

🏛 **Silja H. Ariadne** M, Sodra Kajen 37, ⊠ S-115 74, ℰ (08) 665 78 00, *Fax (08) 662 76 80,*
≤, ☶, ⊟s – ♦, ⇔ rm, ☰ TV ☎ ♿ P – ⚒ 250. AE ① E VISA. ⋙
Meals *(closed Saturday lunch and Sunday)* (buffet lunch) 135/500 and a la carte – **283 rm**
⊒ 1220/1395.

to the East :

at Ladugårdsgärdet :

XX **Villa Källhagen** ⧖ with rm, Djurgårdsbrunnsvägen 10, ⊠ S-115 27, *East : 3 km by*
Strandvägen ℰ (08) 665 03 00, *Fax (08) 665 03 99,* ≤, ☶, « *Waterside setting, stylish*
modern bedrooms », ⊟s, ☷ – ♦, ⇔ rm, ☰ TV ☎ P – ⚒ 55. AE ① E VISA. ⋙
closed Christmas – **Meals** 225 (lunch) and a la carte 285/510 – **18 rm** ⊒ 1560/1790,
2 suites.

at Fjäderholmarna Island *25 mn by boat, departure every hour from Nybroplan CY :*

XX **Fjäderholmarnas Krog,** Stora Fjäderholmen, ⊠ S-100 05, ℰ (08) 718 33 55,
Fax (08) 716 39 89, ☶, « *Waterside setting on archipelago island with* ≤ *neighbouring*
islands and sea » – AE ① E VISA JCB
closed 23 December-1 May and 26 September-1 December – **Meals** 175/385 and a la carte.

to the South :

at Johanneshov :

🏛 **Globe** M, Arenaslingan 7, ⊠ S-121 26, *South : 1 ½ km by Rd 73* ℰ (08) 686 63 00,
Fax (08) 686 63 01, ☶, ⊟s – ♦, ⇔ rm, ☰ TV ☎ ♿ ⇔ – ⚒ 220. AE ① E VISA JCB. ⋙
closed 23 to 26 December – **Arena** : **Meals** 245/450 and dinner a la carte – **Tabac** : **Meals**
a la carte 170/320 – **279 rm** ⊒ 1195/1395, 8 suites.

to the West :

at Bromma *West : 5 ½ km by Norr Mälarstrand BY and Drottningholmsvägen :*

XX **Sjöpaviljongen,** Tranebergs Strand 4, Alvik, ⊠ 167 40, *East : 1 ½ km* ℰ (08) 704 04 24,
Fax (08) 704 82 40, ≤, « *Attractive modern pavilion, waterside setting* » –, ⚓ P. AE ①
E VISA JCB
closed Saturday lunch, Sunday, 23 December-6 January and Bank Holidays – **Meals**
220/360 and a la carte 360/450 – **Bistro** ☶ : **Meals** 210 (dinner) and a la carte 185/320.

to the Northwest :

🏨 **Radisson SAS Royal Park** M ⧖, Frösundaviks Allé 15, ⊠ S-169 03, *Northwest : 5 km*
by Sveavägan and E 4, Exit Frösunda and Frösundavik rd ℰ (08) 624 55 00,
Fax (08) 85 85 66, ≤, ☶, « *Situated in Royal Park on shores of Brunnsvik Bay* », ⌂, ⊟s,
⊠, park – ♦, ☷, ⇔ rm, TV ☎ ♿ ⇔ P – ⚒ 280. AE ① E VISA JCB. ⋙
closed Christmas-early January – **Meals** 220/345 – **193 rm** ⊒ 1660/1910.

XXX **Ulriksdals Wärdshus,** ⊠ 170 79, Northwest : 8 km by Sveavägen and E 4, takir
E 18 towards Norrtälje, following signs for Ulriksdals Slott ℘ (08) 85 08 1!
Fax (08) 85 08 58, ≤, « 17C former inn in Royal Park », 🚗 – **P**. **AE ◑ E VIS**
⚡
closed dinner Sunday and Bank Holidays and 24 to 26 December – **Meals** 180/450 ar
a la carte 460/595.

at Sollentuna Northwest : 15 km by Sveavägen BX and E 4 (exit Sollentuna c) :

XXX **Edsbacka Krog** (Lingström), Sollentunavägen 220, ⊠ 191 35, ℘ (08) 96 33 0(
⚘ Fax (08) 96 40 19, « 17C inn » – **P**. **AE ◑ E VISA JCB**
closed Monday, Easter, Whitsun, 17 to 21 June and 10 July-3 August – **Meals** 265/75
and a la carte 465/875
Spec. Lightly smoked fillet of roe deer with Jerusalem artichoke. Seared scallops with puré
of smoked cod, duck liver sauce. Fillet of char with purée of pike and dill.

at Arlanda Airport Northwest : 40 km by Sveavägen BX and E 4 – ⊠ Arlanda :

🏛 **Radisson SAS Sky City** M, ⊠ 190 45 Stockholm-Arlanda, Sky City ℘ (08) 590 773 0(
Fax (08) 593 781 00, **Ⅰ**, ☎s – |≹|, ⚡ rm, 🖥 **TV** ☎ ⏃. **AE ◑ E VISA JCB**. ⚡
Meals a la carte 270/460 – **230 rm** ☕ 1695/1795.

🏛 **Radisson SAS Arlandia,** Benstocksvägen 1, ⊠ 190 45 Stockholm-Arlanda, Southeast
1 km ℘ (08) 593 618 00, Fax (08) 593 619 70, ☎s, 🏊 – |≹|, ⚡ rm, **TV** ☎ ⏃ **P** – 🛇 24!
AE ◑ E VISA. ⚡
Meals 230/400 and a la carte – **332 rm** ☕ 1395/1495, 2 suites.

GOTHENBURG (Göteborg) Sverige 985 0 8 – pop. 437 313.

See : Art Gallery★★ (Göteborgs Konstmuseet) CX M¹ – Castle Park★★ (Slottsskogen) A:
– Botanical Gardens★★ (Botaniska Trädgården) AX – East India House★★ (Ostindiska Huset
Göteborgs stadmuseum) BU M² Museum of Arts and Crafts★★ (Röhsska Konstlojdmuseet
BV M³ – Liseberg Amusement Park★★ (Liseberg Nöjespark) DX Horticultural Gardens★★
(Trädgårdsföreningen) CU – Natural History Museum★ (Naturhistoriska museet) AX – Mar
time Museum★ (Sjöfartsmuseet) AV – Kungsportsavenyn★ BCVX 22 – Götaplatsen (Ca
Milles Poseidon★★) CX – Seaman's Tower (Sjömanstornet) (✳★★) AV Göteborgs-Utkike
(✳★★) BT – Masthugg Church (Masthuggskyrkan) (interior★) AV.

Envir. : Öckerö Archipelago★ by boat or by car : N : 17 km by E 6 and road 155 – Nev
Älvsborg Fortress★ (Nya Älvsborgs Fästning) AU – Bohuslan★★ (The Golden Coast) N :
Halland coast to the south : Äskhult Open-Air Museum★ ; Tjolöholms Slott★ AX.

🏌 Albatross, Lillhagsvägen Hisings Backa ℘ (031) 55 19 01 – 🏌 Delsjö, Kallebäck ℘ (031
40 69 59 – 🏌 Göteborgs, Golfbanevägen, Hovås ℘ (031) 28 24 44.

✈ Scandinavian Airlines System : Svenska Mässan (vid Korsvägen) ℘ (031) 94 20 0(
Landvetter Airport : ℘ (031) 94 10 00.

🚢 To Denmark : contact Stena Line A/B ℘ (031) 775 00 00, Fax (031) 85 85 95 - Colc
SeaCat ℘ (031) 775 08 00 – To Continent : contact Scandinavian Seaways ℘ (031
65 06 50, Fax (031) 53 23 09.

🛈 Kungsportplatsen 2 ℘ (031) 10 07 40, Fax (031) 13 21 84.
Copenhagen 279 – Oslo 322 – Stockholm 500.

Plans on following pages

🏰 **Sheraton Göteborg H. and Towers,** Södra Hamngatan 59-65, ⊠ S-401 24
℘ (031) 80 60 00, Fax (031) 15 98 88, « Atrium courtyard », **Ⅰ**, ☎s, 🏊 – |≹|, ⚡ rm
🖥 **TV** ☎ ⏃ 🚗 – 🛇 450. **AE ◑ E VISA**. ⚡   BU
closed 22 December-3 January – **Frascati :** Meals (closed lunch Saturday and Sunday
(buffet lunch) 235/495 and a la carte – **333 rm** ☕ 2125/2350, 12 suites.

🏛 **Radisson SAS Park Avenue,** Kungsportsavenyn 36-38, ⊠ S-400 16, ℘ (031
17 65 20, Fax (031) 16 95 68, 🌴, **Ⅰ**, ☎s – |≹|, ⚡ rm, 🖥 rest, **TV** ☎ 🚗 – 🛇 550
AE ◑ E VISA JCB. ⚡
Parkbaren : Meals 235 (dinner) and a la carte approx. 265 – **301 rm** ☕ 1625/1875, 1;
suites.   CX

🏛 **Hotel 11,** Maskingatan 11, Eriksberg, ⊠ S-417 64, West : 6 km by Götaälvbron follow
signs for Torslanda and turn left at Shell garage, or boat from Lilla Bommens Hamn ℘ (031
779 11 11, Fax (031) 779 11 10, ≤, « Former shipbuilding warehouse, modern interio
design », ⚡ – |≹|, ⚡ rm, 🖥 **TV** ☎ 🚗 **P** – 🛇 200. **AE ◑ E VISA JCB**. ⚡ rest
closed 22 to 30 December – **Bar 67 :** Meals (dinner only Saturday, Sunday and July
155/195 and a la carte (see also **Westra Piren** below) – **132 rm** ☕ 1200/1370.

🏛 **Scandic H. Crown,** Polhemsplatsen 3, ⊠ S-411 11, ℘ (031) 751 51 00
Fax (031) 751 51 11, **Ⅰ**, ☎s – |≹|, ⚡ rm, 🖥 **TV** ☎ ⏃ 🚗 – 🛇 300. **AE ◑ E VISA**
⚡ rest   CU c
Meals 200/400 and a la carte – **315 rm** ☕ 1430/1660, 5 suites.

Scandic H. Opalen, Engelbrektsgatan 73, ⊠ S-402 23, ℘ (031) 751 53 00, Fax (031) 751 53 11, Ⅰ₅, ⊆s – 🛊|, ⇔ rm, 🍽 rest, 📺 & ⇔ 🅿 – 🔬 180. 🅰🅴 ⓓ 🇪 🆅🇮🇸🇦. ⅜ rest
DV u
Meals (dancing Thursday to Saturday evenings except in summer) (light lunch) 245/385 (dinner) and a la carte 290/400 – **237 rm** 1180/1660, 4 suites.

Gothia, Mässans Gata 24, ⊠ S-402 26, ℘ (031) 40 93 00, Fax (031) 18 98 04, ≤, « Panoramic restaurant on 18th floor », ⊆s – 🛊|, ⇔ rm, 🍽 📺 ☎ & – 🔬 1500. 🅰🅴 ⓓ 🇪 🆅🇮🇸🇦 🇯🇨🇧. ⅜
DX k
closed Christmas – **18 : E Våningen** : **Meals** (closed Saturday lunch) 150/205 and a la carte – **288 rm** 1390/1590, 2 suites.

Riverton, Stora Badhusgatan 26, ⊠ S-411 21, ℘ (031) 750 10 00, Fax (031) 750 10 01, « 12th floor restaurant with ≤ Göta Älv river and docks », ⊆s – 🛊|, ⇔ rm, 🍽 rest, 📺 ☎ & 🅿 – 🔬 300. 🅰🅴 ⓓ 🇪 🆅🇮🇸🇦. ⅜
AV c
Meals (closed Sunday dinner, 1 to 6 April, 1 and 22 to 25 May and 18 December-10 January) a la carte 320/390 – **187 rm** 1125/1425, 4 suites.

Europa, Köpmansgatan 38, ⊠ S-404 29, ℘ (031) 80 12 80, Fax (031) 15 47 55, ⊆s, 🔲 – 🛊|, ⇔ rm, 🍽 📺 ☎ & ⇔ – 🔬 60. 🅰🅴 ⓓ 🇪 🆅🇮🇸🇦. ⅜
BU a
Meals (closed Sunday) 185/315 and a la carte – **453 rm** 1360/1660, 7 suites.

Scandic H. Rubinen, Kungsportsavenyn 24, ⊠ S-400 14, ℘ (031) 81 08 00, Fax (031) 16 75 86 – 🛊|, ⇔ rm, 🍽 📺 ☎ – 🔬 60. 🅰🅴 ⓓ 🇪 🆅🇮🇸🇦
CV c
Meals (dinner only) a la carte 225/355 – **189 rm** 1180/2070, 1 suite.

Panorama, Eklandagatan 51-53, ⊠ S-400 22, ℘ (031) 767 70 00, Fax (031) 767 70 70, ⊆s – 🛊|, ⇔ rm, 🍽 📺 ☎ & ⇔ 🅿 – 🔬 120. 🅰🅴 ⓓ 🇪 🆅🇮🇸🇦. ⅜ rest
DX
closed 23 December-7 January – **Meals** (closed Sunday and Bank Holidays) (dinner only) 220 and a la carte – **339 rm** 1090/1490.

Mornington, Kungsportsavenyn 6, ⊠ S-411 36, ℘ (031) 17 65 40, Fax (031) 711 34 39, ⊆s – 🛊|, ⇔ rm, 🍽 📺 ☎ ⇔ – 🔬 45. 🅰🅴 ⓓ 🇪 🆅🇮🇸🇦 🇯🇨🇧. ⅜
BV e
Brasserie Lipp : **Meals** (closed Sunday October-March) 450 (dinner) and a la carte 315/445 – **91 rm** 1095/1895.

Novotel Göteborg, Klippan 1, ⊠ S-414 51, Southwest : 3 ½ km by Andréeg or boat from Lilla Bommens Hamn ℘ (031) 14 90 00, Fax (031) 42 22 32, ≤, 🌿, « Converted brewery on waterfront », ⊆s – 🛊|, ⇔ rm 🍽 📺 ☎ & 🅿 – 🔬 120. 🅰🅴 ⓓ 🇪 🆅🇮🇸🇦. ⅜ rest
Carnegie Kaj : **Meals** (buffet lunch) 145/365 and dinner a la carte – **144 rm** 1060/1210, 4 suites.

Victors, Skeppsbroplatsen 1, ⊠ S-411 18, ℘ (031) 17 41 80, Fax (031) 13 96 10, ≤ Göta Älv river and harbour, ⊆s – 🛊|, ⇔ rm, 🍽 📺 ☎ & – 🔬 40. 🅰🅴 ⓓ 🇪 🆅🇮🇸🇦 🇯🇨🇧. ⅜
AU b
Meals (closed Friday to Sunday) (dinner only) a la carte 225/405 – **35 rm** 1150/1350, 9 suites.

Tidbloms, Olskroksgatan 23, ⊠ S-416 66, Northeast : 2 ½ km by E 20 ℘ (031) 707 50 00, Fax (031) 707 50 99, ⊆s – 🛊|, ⇔ rm, 📺 ☎ & 🅿 – 🔬 70. 🅰🅴 ⓓ 🇪 🆅🇮🇸🇦. ⅜
closed 22 December-2 January – **Meals** (closed Saturday lunch) a la carte 240/330 – **42 rm** 1050/1350.

Liseberg Heden ⅜ without rest., Sten Sturegatan, ⊠ S-411 38, ℘ (031) 750 69 10, Fax (031) 750 69 30, ⊆s, 🚲 – 🛊 ⇔ 📺 ☎ & 🅿 – 🔬 70. 🅰🅴 ⓓ 🇪 🆅🇮🇸🇦
CV b
172 rm 995/1395.

Eggers, Drottningtorget, ⊠ S-401 25, ℘ (031) 80 60 70, Fax (031) 15 42 43, « Characterful late 19C ambience » – 🛊|, ⇔ rm, 📺 ☎ – 🔬 30. 🅰🅴 ⓓ 🇪 🆅🇮🇸🇦 🇯🇨🇧. ⅜
closed 23 to 27 December – **Meals** (closed Sunday) (dinner only except Saturday in July) 245/295 and a la carte – **67 rm** 1115/1660.
BU e

Poseidon without rest., Storgatan 33, ⊠ S-411 33, ℘ (031) 10 05 50, Fax (031) 13 83 91, « Late 19C », ⊆s – 🛊 ⇔ 📺 ☎. 🅰🅴 ⓓ 🇪 🆅🇮🇸🇦 🇯🇨🇧. ⅜
BV a
48 rm 940/1150.

Onyxen without rest., Sten Sturegatan 23, ⊠ S-412 52, ℘ (031) 81 08 45, Fax (031) 165 67 21 – 🛊|, ⇔ rm, 📺 ☎ 🅿. 🅰🅴 ⓓ 🇪 🆅🇮🇸🇦 🇯🇨🇧
DX a
closed Christmas – **34 rm** 990/1290.

Westra Piren (Öster), Eriksberg, Dockepiren, (on Pier No. 4), ⊠ S-417 64, West : 6 km by Götaälvbron, follow signs for Torslanda and turn left at Shell garage, or boat from Lilla Bommens Hamn ℘ (031) 51 95 55, Fax (031) 23 99 40, « Dockside setting, ≤ Göta Älv river and harbour » – 🅿. 🅰🅴 ⓓ 🇪 🆅🇮🇸🇦 🇯🇨🇧
closed Sunday, 7 July-9 August, 23 December-10 January and Bank Holidays – **Meals** (booking essential) (dinner only) 425/640 and a la carte 500/640 (see also **Brasserie** below)
Spec. Assiette de fruits de mer, sauce au safran. Canard sauvage, sauce au Calvados et champignons des bois. Charlotte des framboises avec sorbet aux poires.

SWEDEN
GOTHENBURG
GÖTEBORG
0   500 m
E 6   OSLO
GÖTA   ÄLV
Götaälvbron
BARKEN VIKING
Göteborgs-Utkiken
Hamntorget
53
Lilla Bommens Hamn
FRIHAMNEN
Göteborgs Operan
LUNDBYVASSEN
Göteborgs Maritima Centrum
P
16
29
P
33
Nils Ericso plats
52
Östra
Torggatan
NORDSTADEN
Nordstads-torget
51
23
M
39
a
e
Stenpiren
P
P
23
35
M
H
23
G. Adolfs Torg
VINGA
Nya Älvsborgs Fästning
35
M
Hamn   kanalen
60
b
Stora
Hamn
60
b
54
f
Lilla Torget
M 4
55
Korsg.
Hamngatan
12
Skeppsbron
Magasins-
Västra
DOMKYRKAN
c
INOM VALLGRAVEN
Kungsgatan
Kungsports-platsen
e
Hamngatan
r
Kungsgatan
Masthuggskajen
3
Kungstorget
STENA-TERMINALEN
gatan
KUNGSPARKEN
Stora Teatern
P
2
P
T
20
Feskekörka
45
47
Allén
gatan
22
32
17
Nya
a
56
Vasagatan
159
34
P
Park-
U
Första Långg
19
PUSTERVIK
34
M 3
Södra
Allégatan
Viktoria
56
15
b
Haga
Nygata
Kyrkogata
Vasagatan
HAGA
25
Sprängkullsg.
VASASTADEN
VASAPARKEN
U
8
U
Haga
gatan
Ascheberge
P
Haga
8
SKANSENPARKEN
U
Utsikts-platsen
U
31
Skansen Kronan
P
U
gatan
a
44
Föreningsgatan
Husargatan
Sveagatan
Linnégatan
Övre
Brunnsgatan
Älvsborgsbron, Sjömanstornet
Masthuggskyrkan, Sjöfartsmuseet
E 6-E 20   158
Slottsskogen, Botaniska Trädgården
Naturhistoriska museet
A   B

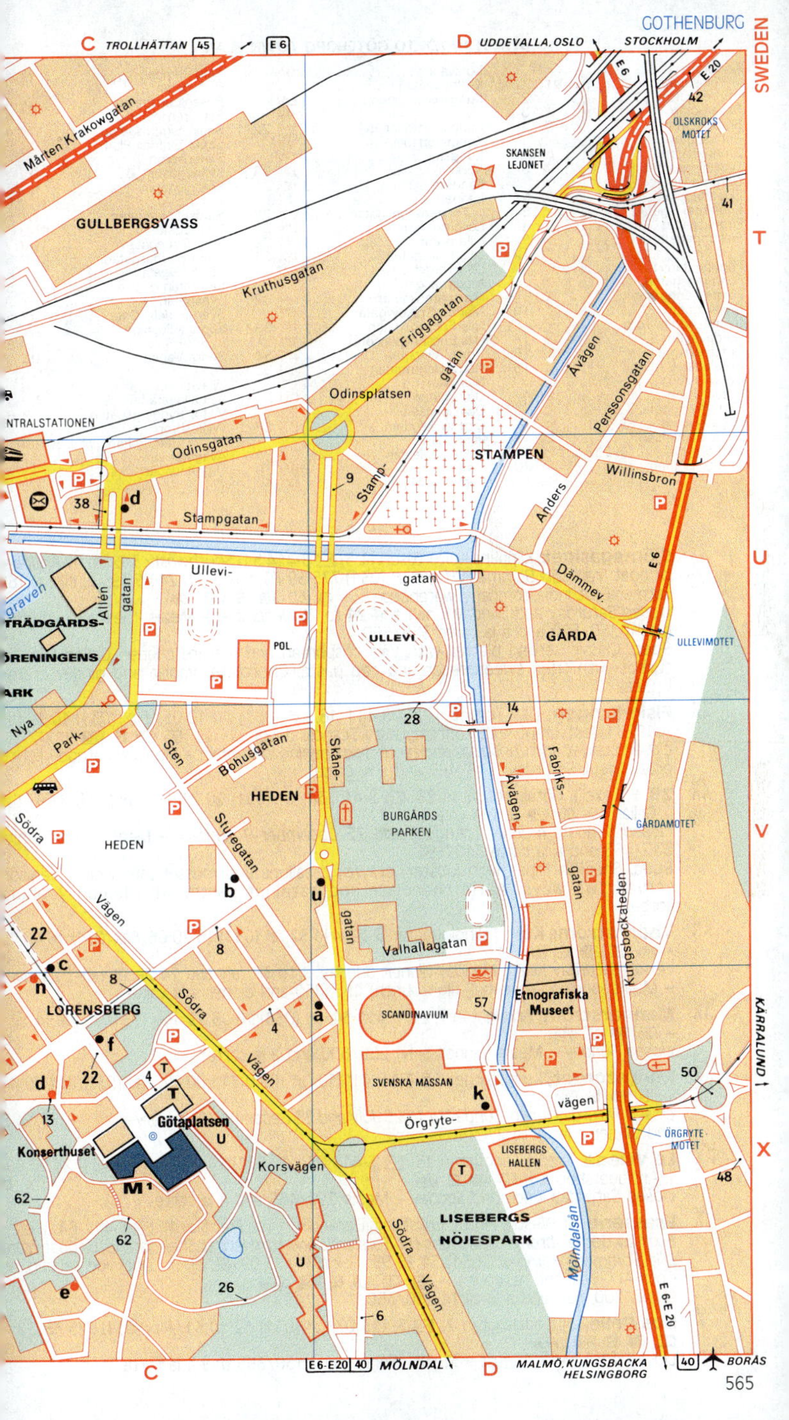

GOTHENBURG
SWEDEN
C TROLLHÄTTAN 45 E 6
D UDDEVALLA, OSLO STOCKHOLM
E 6
E 20
42
OLSKROKS MOTET
41
Mårten Krakowgatan
GULLBERGSVASS
SKANSEN LEJONET
T
Kruthusgatan
Friggagatan
gatan
Odinsplatsen
Åvägen
Perssonsgatan
NTRALSTATIONEN
Odinsgatan
9
Stamp-
STAMPEN
Willinsbron
38
d
Stampgatan
Anders
Dämmev.
E 6
U
graven
TRÄDGÅRDS-
ÖRENINGENS
ARK
Allén
gatan
Ullevi-
gatan
GÅRDA
ULLEVIMOTET
P
POL.
ULLEVI
Nya
Park-
28
14
Bohusgatan
Åvägen
Fabriks-
GÅRDAMOTET
Sten
Skåne-
HEDEN
BURGÅRDS PARKEN
Södra
HEDEN
Stureatan
gatan
gatan
b
u
Kungsbackaleden
Valhallagatan
Vägen
22
8
c
8
57
Etnografiska Museet
n
LORENSBERG
Södra
4
a
SCANDINAVIUM
KÄRRALUND
f
22
Vägen
d
4
T
T
SVENSKA MASSAN
k
50
13
Götaplatsen
U
vägen
ÖRGRYTE MOTET
Konserthuset
Örgryte-
62
Korsvägen
LISEBERGS HALLEN
X
M¹
T
48
62
Södra
LISEBERGS NÖJESPARK
Mölndalsån
e
U
26
Vägen
6
E 6·E 20
C
E 6-E 20 40 MÖLNDAL D MALMÖ, KUNGSBACKA HELSINGBORG 40 BORÅS

STREET INDEX TO GÖTEBORG TOWN PLAN

Sjömagasinet, Klippans Kulturreservat 5, ⊠ S-414 51, Southwest : 3 ½ km by Andrée or boat from Lilla Bommens Hamn ℘ (031) 775 59 20, Fax (031) 24 55 39, ≤, 🌂, « 18 former East India company warehouse » – **P**. **AE** **①** **E** **VISA**. 🍴
closed Saturday and Sunday lunch and 24 to 26 December – **Meals** - Seafood - (buffe lunch) 150/510 and a la carte 355/560
Spec. Classic herring platter with Vika crispbread and mature cheese. Grilled fillet o turbot with fried sweetbreads and cep pasta. Chocolate, vanilla and ginger crèm brûlées.

Fiskekrogen, Lilla Torget 1, ⊠ S-411 18, ℘ (031) 10 10 05, Fax (031) 10 10 06 « 1920's restaurant with contemporary Scandic decor » – ▤. **AE** **①** **E** **VISA**   AU
closed Sunday and Christmas and restricted opening in summer – **Meals** - Seafood - (lunch only except Saturday) 240/495 and a la carte.

28 + (Lyxell), Götabergsgatan 28, ⊠ S-411 34, ℘ (031) 20 21 61, Fax (031) 81 97 57 « Cellar » – **AE** **①** **E** **VISA** **JCB**   BX
closed Sunday, 4 July-11 August and 22 December-8 January – **Meals** (dinner only 335/465 and a la carte 310/595
Spec. Shellfish tapas with lobster, crayfish, scallops and mussel cappuccino. Venison served two ways. Warm chocolate and hazelnut pastry with lemon yoghur sorbet.

Thörnströms Kök, Teknologgatan 3, ⊠ 411 32, ℘ (031) 16 20 66, Fax (031) 16 40 1 – ▤. **AE** **①** **E** **VISA**   CX
closed Saturday lunch, Monday dinner, Sunday, 1 to 30 July and 24 December-3 January – **Meals** (booking essential) (light lunch) 165/450 and dinner a la carte.

Mannerström, Arkivgatan 7, ⊠ S-411 34, ℘ (031) 16 03 33, Fax (031) 16 78 54, 🌂 – **AE** **①** **E** **VISA**   CX
closed Sunday – **Meals** (dinner only) 265/500 and a la carte.

Kungstorget, Kungstorget 14, ⊠ S-411 10, ℘ (031) 711 00 22, Fax (031) 711 00 44 – **AE** **①** **E** **VISA**   BV
closed Saturday lunch, Sunday, 4 to 25 July and 23 December-2 January – **Meals** 225/625 and dinner a la carte 210/485.

Le Village, Tredje Långgatan 13, ⊠ S-413 03, ℘ (031) 24 20 03, Fax (031) 24 20 69 « Antique shop » – **AE** **①** **E** **VISA**   AX
closed Saturday lunch and Sunday – **Meals** 250/465 and a la carte.

Brasserie (at Westra Piren), Eriksberg, Dockepiren, (on Pier No. 4), ⊠ S-417 64, West 6 km by Götaälvbron, follow signs for Torslanda and turn left at Shell garage, or boat from Lilla Bommens Hamn ℘ (031) 51 95 55, Fax (031) 23 99 40, 🌂, « Dockside setting, ≤ Gota Alv river and harbour » – **P**. **AE** **①** **E** **VISA** **JCB**
Meals 200/425 and a la carte 280/350.

Hos Pelle, Djupedalsgatan 2, ⊠ S-413 07, ℘ (031) 12 10 31, Fax (031) 775 38 32 - **AE** **①** **E** **VISA** **JCB**   AX
closed 10 July-15 August – **Meals** (dinner only) 150/395 and a la carte.

LOCAL ATMOSPHERE BRASSERIE

X **Tvåkanten,** Kungsportavenyn 27, ✉ S-411 36, ✆ (031) 18 21 15, *Fax (031) 81 11 98* – ⇔ ▤. AE ◑ E VISA CX n
closed Sunday lunch, 25-26 June and 22 December-6 January – **Meals** 365/415 and a la carte 240/415.

at Landvetter Airport *East : 30 km by Rd 40* DX – ✉ *S-438 13 Landvetter :*

Landvetter Airport H., ✉ S-438 13, ✆ (031) 97 75 50, *Fax (031) 94 64 70,* ⛱, ≘s – |‡|, ⇔ rm ▣ ☎ ♿ Ⓟ – 🏟 25. AE ◑ E VISA. ✂
closed 23 to 26 December and 31 December-2 January – **Meals** *(closed lunch Saturday and Sunday)* a la carte 275/350 – **62 rm** ☕ 1095/1250, 3 suites.

Switzerland

Suisse
Schweiz
Svizzera

BERNE – BASLE – GENEVA – ZÜRICH

PRACTICAL INFORMATION

LOCAL CURRENCY – PRICES

Swiss Franc: *100 CHF = 62,20 euros (€)*

National Holiday in Switzerland: *1st August.*

LANGUAGES SPOKEN

German, French and Italian are usually spoken in all administrative departments, shops, hotels and restaurants.

AIRLINES

SWISSAIR: *Genève-Airport, 1215 Genève 15, ✆ 157 15 00, Fax (022) 799 31 38. Hirschengraben 84, 8001 Zürich, ✆ (0848) 80 07 00, Fax (01) 258 34 40.*

AIR FRANCE: *15 rte de l'Aéroport, 1215 Genève 15, ✆ (022) 798 05 05, Fax (022) 788 50 40.*
Kanalstr. 31, 8152 Glattbrugg, ✆ (01) 809 46 46, Fax (01) 809 46 11.

ALITALIA: *rue Lausanne 36, 1201 Genève, ✆ (022) 731 66 50, Fax (022) 732 40 29. Forchstr. 51, 8032 Zürich, ✆ (01) 389 61 11.*

AMERICAN AIRLINES: *Löwenstr. 25, 8001 Zürich, ✆ (01) 225 16 16, Fax (01) 221 39 59.*

BRITISH AIRWAYS: *Chantepoulet 13, 1201 Genève, ✆ (0848) 80 10 10, Zürich-Airport, 8058 Zürich, ✆ (0848) 84 58 45.*

LUFTHANSA: *Chantepoulet 1-3, 1201 Genève, ✆ (022) 908 01 80, Fax (022) 908 01 88.*
Gutenbergstr. 10, 8002 Zürich, ✆ (01) 447 99 66, Fax (01) 286 72 07.

POSTAL SERVICES

In large towns, post offices are open from 7.30am to noon and 1.45pm to 6pm, and Saturdays until 11am. The telephone system is fully automatic.
Many public phones are equipped with phone card facilities. Prepaid phone cards are available from post offices, railway stations and tobacconist's shops.

SHOPPING

Department stores are generally open from 8.30am to 6.30pm, except on Saturdays when they close at 4 or 5pm. They are closed on Monday mornings.
In the index of street names, those printed in red are where the principal shops are found.

TIPPING

In hotels, restaurants and cafés the service charge is generally included in the prices.

SPEED LIMITS – MOTORWAYS

The speed limit on motorways is 120 km/h - 74 mph, on other roads 80 km/h - 50 mph, and in built up areas 50 km/h - 31 mph.
Driving on Swiss motorways is subject to the purchase of a single rate annual road tax (vignette) obtainable from border posts, tourist offices and post offices.

SEAT BELTS

The wearing of seat belts is compulsory in all Swiss cantons for drivers and all passengers.

Town plans of Berne, Basle, Geneva and Zürich : with the permission
of Federal directorate for cadastral surveys.

BERNE

3000 Bern **927** ⑬, **217** ⑥ – *pop. 130 069 – alt. 548.*

Basle 100 – Lyons 315 – Munich 435 – Paris 556 – Strasbourg 235 – Turin 311.

B *Tourist Office, Railway Station* ☎ *(031) 311 66 11, Fax (031) 312 12 33 – T.C.S., Thunstr. 63,* ☎ *(031) 352 22 22, Fax (031) 352 22 29 – A.C.S., Theaterplatz 13,* ☎ *(031) 311 38 13, Fax (031) 311 26 37.*

18 *Blumisberg,* ✉ *3184 Wünnewil (mid-March-mid-November),* ☎ *(026) 496 34 38, Fax (026) 496 35 23, SW : 18 km.*

Bern-Belp, ☎ *(031) 960 21 11, Fax (031) 960 21 12.*

See: *Old Berne*★★ *: Marktgasse*★ DZ *; Clock Tower*★ EZ **C** *; Kramgasse*★ EZ *; views*★ *from the Nydegg Bridge* FY *; Bear Pit*★ FZ *; Cathedral of St Vincent*★ EZ *: tympanum*★★*, panorama*★★ *from the tower* EZ *– Rosengarden* FY *: view*★ *of the Old Berne – Botanical Garden*★ DY *– Dählhölzli Zoo*★ *– Church of St Nicholas*★*.*

Museums: *Fine Arts Museum*★★ *: Paul Klee Collection* DY *– Natural History Museum*★★ EZ *– Bernese Historical Museum*★★ EZ *– Alpine Museum*★★ EZ *– Swiss Postal Museum*★ EZ*.*

Excursions: *The Gurten*★★*.*

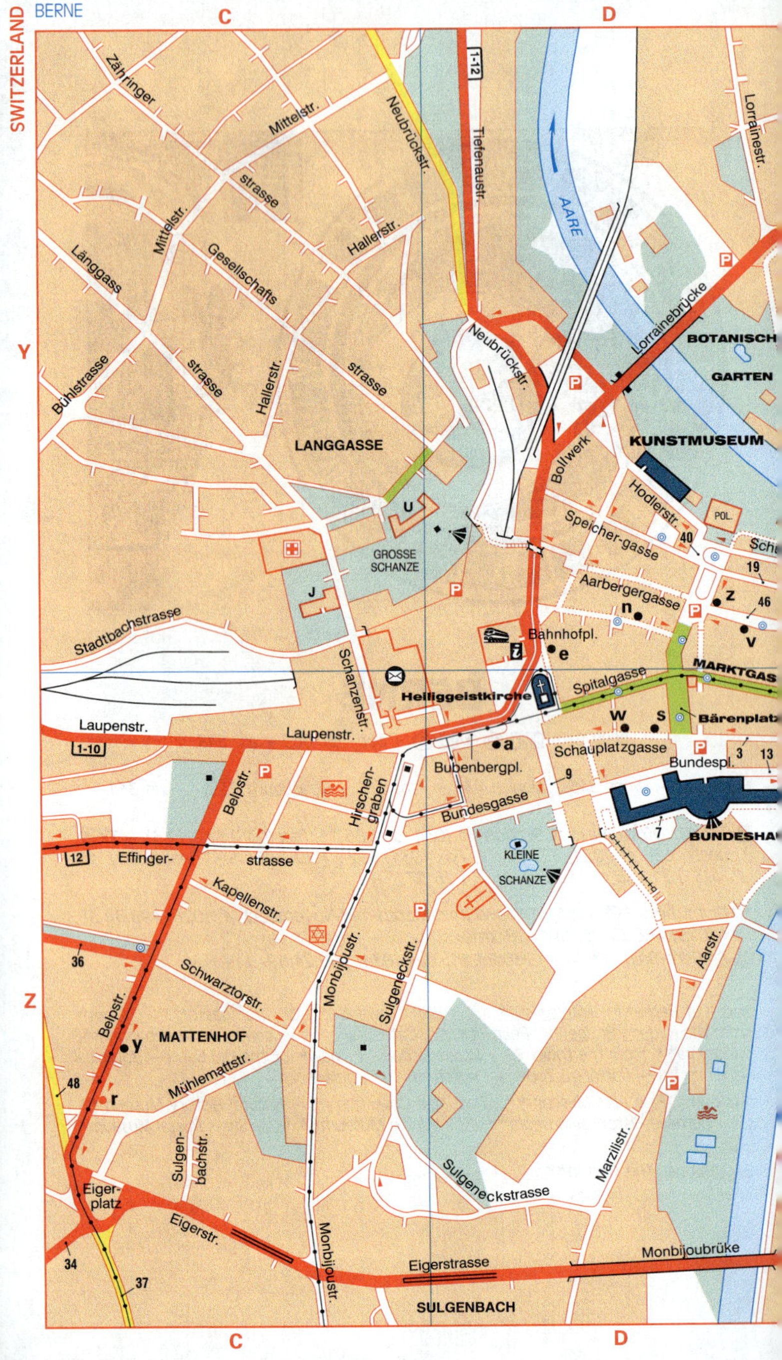

SWITZERLAND
BERNE
C
D
Zähringer
Mittelstr.
strasse
Hallerstr.
Neubrückstr.
1-12
Tiefenaustr.
AARE
Lorrainestr.
Mittelstr.
Gesellschafts
Hallerstr.
strasse
Neubrückstr.
Lorrainebrücke
BOTANISCH
Y
Bühlstrasse
strasse
Hallerstr.
strasse
Langgass
LANGGASSE
Bollwerk
P
GARTEN
KUNSTMUSEUM
Hodlerstr.
POL.
U
Speicher-gasse
40
Sch
GROSSE
SCHANZE
Aarbergergasse
19
Z
46
J
P
n
V
Stadtbachstrasse
Schanzenstr.
Bahnhofpl.
e
MARKTGAS
Laupenstr.
1-10
Laupenstr.
Heiliggeistkirche
Spitalgasse
W
S
Bärenplatz
a
Schauplatzgasse
3
13
Belpstr.
Hirschen-graben
Bubenbergpl.
9
Bundespl.
P
Bundesgasse
7
BUNDESHA
12
Effinger-
strasse
KLEINE
SCHANZE
Kapellenstr.
P
36
Monbijoustr.
Sulgeneckstr.
Aarstr.
Z
Schwarztorstr.
MATTENHOF
y
Belpstr.
Mühlemattstr.
Marzilistr.
48
r
Sulgen-bachstr.
Eiger-platz
Sulgeneckstrasse
P
34
Eigerstr.
Monbijoustr.
Eigerstrasse
Monbijoubrüke
37
SULGENBACH
C
D

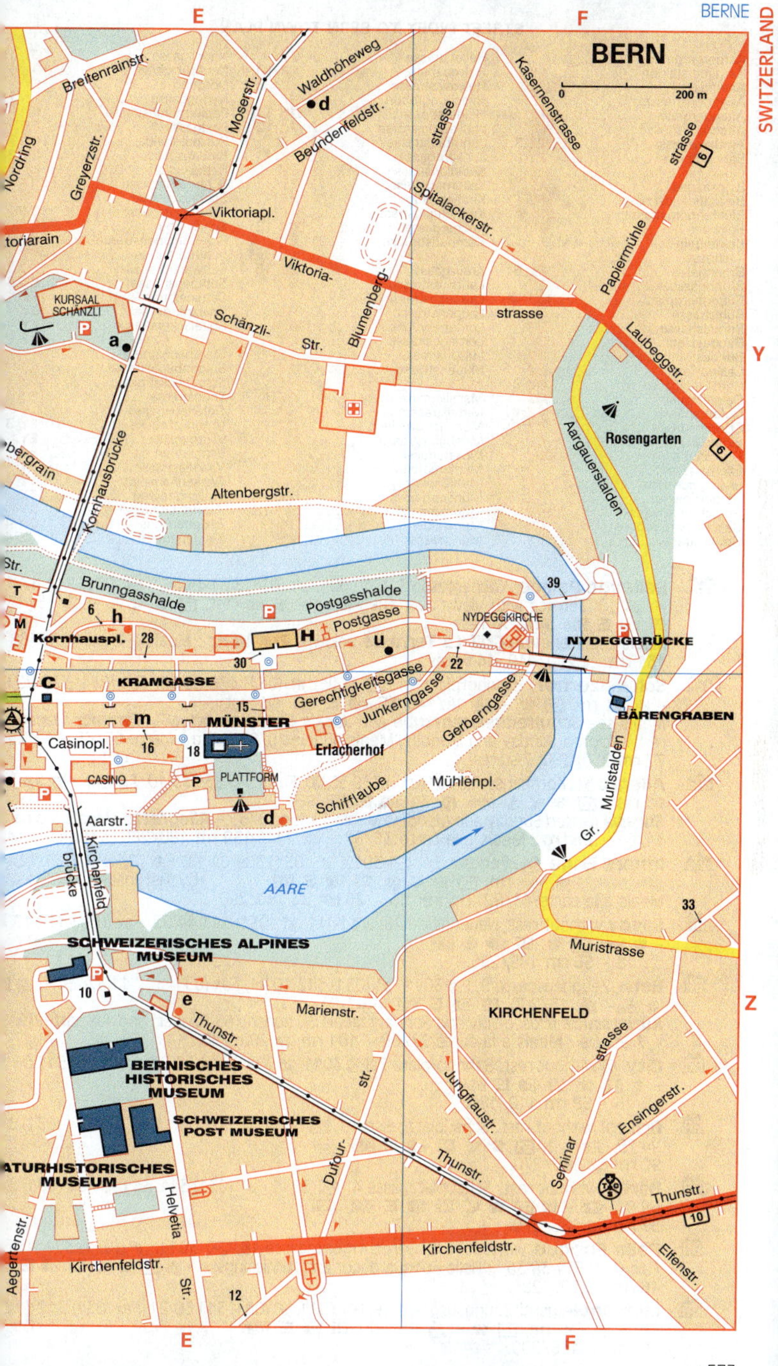

BERNE
SWITZERLAND
BERN
0   200 m
E
F
Y
Z
Breitenrainstr.
Nordring
Greyerzstr.
toriarain
Moserstr.
Waldhöheweg
d
Beundenfeldstr.
Viktoriapl.
Viktoria-
Schänzli-
Str.
Blumenberg-
strasse
strasse
Spitalackerstr.
Kasernenstrasse
Papiermühle
strasse
6
Laubeggstr.
6
KURSAAL
SCHÄNZLI
P
a
Kornhausbrücke
...bergrain
Altenbergstr.
Aargauerstalden
Rosengarten
Str.
Brunnggasshalde
Postgasshalde
P
Postgasse
39
T
M
6
h
Postgasse
NYDEGGKIRCHE
P
Kornhauspl.
28
H
NYDEGGBRÜCKE
30
u
22
c
KRAMGASSE
Gerechtigkeitsgasse
Junkerngasse
Gerberngasse
BÄRENGRABEN
15
MÜNSTER
m
Casinopl.
16
18
Erlacherhof
Mühlenpl.
Muristalden
CASINO
P
PLATTFORM
Schifflaube
Aarstr.
d
Kirchenfeld
AARE
Gr.
33
brücke
Muristrasse
SCHWEIZERISCHES ALPINES
MUSEUM
P
10
e
Thunstr.
Marienstr.
KIRCHENFELD
str.
strasse
BERNISCHES
HISTORISCHES
MUSEUM
Jungfraustr.
Ensingerstr.
SCHWEIZERISCHES
POST MUSEUM
Thunstr.
Seminar
...ATURHISTORISCHES
MUSEUM
Dufour-
Thunstr.
10
Helvetia
Aegertenstr.
Kirchenfeldstr.
Str.
Kirchenfeldstr.
Elfenstr.
12
E
F

STREET INDEX TO BERN TOWN PLAN

Bellevue Palace, Kochergasse 3, ⊠ 3001, ℘ (031) 320 45 45, Fax (031) 311 47 4. ≼, 🌣, « Terrace with views over the Aare » – ⒮, ▤ rest, ⊺⊽ ☎ ℭ ⅙ – 🏊 15/15 ⒜ ⓞ Ⓔ *VISA* JCB. 彩 rest   EZ
Meals see *Bellevue-Grill/La Terrasse* below – *Zur Münz :* Meals a la carte 35/88
131 rm 290/430, 14 suites.

Schweizerhof, Bahnhofplatz 11, ⊠ 3001, ℘ (031) 326 80 80, Fax (031) 326 80 9 – ⒮, ▤ rm, ⊺⊽ ☎ – 🏊 15/140. ⒜ ⓞ Ⓔ *VISA*. 彩 rest   DY
Meals see *Schultenheissenstube* and *Jack's Brasserie* below – **Yamato** - Japanes rest. - *(closed Sunday and Monday)* Meals 45 (lunch)/92 and a la carte 63/88 – 25
77 rm 260/380, 7 suites.

Allegro Ⓜ, Kornhausstr. 3, ℘ (031) 339 55 00, Fax (031) 339 55 10, ₤, 🛋 – ⒮, 彩 c ▤ rest, ⊺⊽ ☎ ℭ ⅙ 🚗 ⓟ. ⒜ ⓞ Ⓔ *VISA* JCB   EY
Eurasia (closed Sunday and Monday) Meals 45 (lunch)/65 – *Allegretto :* Meals a la cart 31/69 – *Bistro :* Meals a la carte 35/82 – 21 – **159 rm** 180/280, 3 suites.

Innere Enge ⌂, Engestr. 54, ⊠ 3012, ℘ (031) 309 61 11, Fax (031) 309 61 12, 🌣, park – ⒮, 彩 rm, ⊺⊽ ☎ ℭ ⓟ. ⒜ ⓞ Ⓔ *VISA*   by Tiefenaustrasse   AX
Meals a la carte 43/82, children 13 – **26 rm** 180/290.

Savoy without rest, Neuengasse 26, ⊠ 3011, ℘ (031) 311 44 05, Fax (031) 312 19 7 – ⒮ 彩 ⊺⊽ ☎. ⒜ ⓞ Ⓔ *VISA*   DY
18 – **56 rm** 185/295.

Bern, Zeughausgasse 9, ⊠ 3011, ℘ (031) 312 10 21, Fax (031) 312 11 47, 🌣 – ⒮ ☎ ⅙ – 🏊 15/200. ⒜ ⓞ Ⓔ *VISA* JCB   EY
Kurierstube (closed July and Sunday) Meals 30 (lunch)/65 (dinner) and a la carte 49/9 – *7 Stube :* Meals a la carte 27/68 – **101 rm** 200/280.

City Ⓜ without rest, Bahnhofplatz 7, ⊠ 3011, ℘ (031) 311 53 77, Fax (031) 311 06 3 – ⒮ ⊺⊽ ☎. ⒜ ⓞ Ⓔ *VISA*   DZ
16 – **58 rm** 110/180.

Bristol without rest, Schauplatzgasse 10, ⊠ 3011, ℘ (031) 311 01 01, Fax (031) 31 94 79, 🛋 – ⒮ ⊺⊽ ☎ ℭ. ⒜ ⓞ Ⓔ *VISA* JCB   DZ
92 rm 185/270.

Bären without rest, Schauplatzgasse 4, ⊠ 3011, ℘ (031) 311 33 67, Fax (031) 31 69 83, 🛋 – ⒮ ⊺⊽ ☎ ℭ. ⒜ ⓞ Ⓔ *VISA* JCB   DZ
57 rm 185/270.

Belle Epoque without rest, Gerechtigkeitsgasse 18, ⊠ 3011, ℘ (031) 311 43 3 Fax (031) 311 39 36, « Belle Epoque decor and furnishings » – ⒮ ⊺⊽ ☎ ℭ. ⒜ ⓞ Ⓔ *V* EY
16 rm 200/285.

Metropole garni, Zeughausgasse 26, ⊠ 3011, ℘ (031) 311 50 21, Fax (031) 312 11 5 🌣 – ⒮, 彩 rm, ⊺⊽ ☎ – 🏊 15/100. ⒜ ⓞ Ⓔ *VISA*   DY
59 rm 136/200.

SWITZERLAND

🏠 **Kreuz,** Zeughausgasse 41, ℘ (031) 311 11 62, *Fax (031) 311 37 47* – 🛗 📺 ☎ – ♨ 15/120. 🆎 ⓸ 🄴 *VISA* ᴶᶜᴮ DY v
Meals *(closed Saturday and Sunday)* a la carte 28/73 – **103 rm** ⊇ 136/200.

🏠 **La Pergola** without rest, Belpstr. 43, ✉ 3007, ℘ (031) 381 91 46, *Fax (031) 381 50 54* – 🛗 📺 ☎. 🆎 🄴 *VISA* CZ y
closed 23 December - 4 January – **55 rm** ⊇ 140/185.

🏠 **Waldhorn** without rest, Waldhöheweg 2, ✉ 3013, ℘ (031) 332 23 43, *Fax (031) 332 18 69* – 🛗 📺 ☎ 🚗. 🆎 ⓸ 🄴 *VISA* EY d
46 rm ⊇ 120/175.

XXXX **Bellevue Grill / Bellevue Terrasse** - Hotel Bellevue Palace, Kochergasse 3, ✉ 3001, ℘ (031) 320 45 45, *Fax (031) 311 47 43*, 🌲, « Terrace with views over the Aare » – 🍽. 🆎 ⓸ 🄴 *VISA* ᴶᶜᴮ. ✈ EZ p
Grill : closed June - September and lunch ; Terrasse : closed dinner in winter – **Meals** 66/114 and a la carte 74/140.

XXX **Schultheissenstube** - Hotel Schweizerhof, Bahnhofplatz 11 (1st floor), ✉ 3001, ℘ (031) 326 80 80, *Fax (031) 326 80 90* – 🍽. 🆎 ⓸ 🄴 *VISA* ᴶᶜᴮ. ✈ DY e
closed 4 July - 8 August and Sunday – **Meals** 75/120 and a la carte 70/117.

XX **Jack's Brasserie** - Hotel Schweizerhof, Bahnhofplatz 11, ✉ 3001, ℘ (031) 326 80 80, *Fax (031) 326 80 90*, 🌲 – 🍽. 🆎 ⓸ 🄴 *VISA* ᴶᶜᴮ. ✈ DY e
Meals 74 and a la carte 43/106.

XX **Kirchenfeld,** Thunstr. 5, ✉ 3005, ℘ (031) 351 02 78, *Fax (031) 351 84 16*, 🌲 – 🆎 🄴 *VISA* EZ e
closed Sunday and Monday – **Meals** 35 (lunch)/55 and a la carte 41/76.

XX **Ermitage,** Amtshausgasse 10, ✉ 3011, ℘ (031) 311 35 41, *Fax (031) 311 35 42* – 🆎 🄴 *VISA* EZ g
closed mid July - mid August, Saturday dinner and Sunday – **Meals** (booking essential) 55 and a la carte 37/94.

X **Frohegg,** Belpstr. 51, ✉ 3007, ℘ (031) 382 25 24, *Fax (031) 382 25 27*, 🌲 – 🆎 ⓸ 🄴 *VISA* CZ r
closed Sunday – **Meals** (booking essential) 48 and a la carte 40/89.

X **Zimmermania,** Brunngasse 19, ✉ 3011, ℘ (031) 311 15 42, *Fax (031) 312 28 22*, Old Bernese bistro – 🆎 🄴 *VISA* EY h
closed 10 July - 10 August, Sunday and Monday – **Meals** (booking essential) 39 (lunch)/85 (dinner) and a la carte 40/88.

X **Frohsinn,** Münstergasse 54, ✉ 3011, ℘ (031) 311 37 68, *Fax (031) 311 37 68*, 🌲 – 🆎 🄴 *VISA* EZ m
closed 11 July - 2 August, Monday (except December) and Sunday – **Meals** 68 and a la carte 45/86.

X **Zum Zähringer,** Badgasse 1, ✉ 3011, ℘ (031) 311 32 70, 🌲 – 🆎 ⓸ 🄴 *VISA* EZ d
closed Sunday – **Meals** 26 (lunch) and a la carte 40/89.

t Muri *SE : 3,5 km by Thunstrasse – alt. 560 – ✉ 3074 Muri bei Bern :*

🏠🏠 **Sternen,** Thunstr. 80, ℘ (031) 950 71 11, *Fax (031) 950 71 00*, 🌲 – 🛗 ⊁ 📺 ☎ 🚻 🚗 – ♨ 15/120. 🆎 ⓸ 🄴 *VISA* ᴶᶜᴮ BX a
Läubli : Meals 39 (lunch)/60 and a la carte 48/77 – **Da Pietro** - Italian rest. - *(closed 4 July - 8 August, Saturday lunch, Sunday lunch and Bank Holidays)* **Meals** a la carte 37/73 – **44 rm** ⊇ 170/245.

t Liebefeld *SW : 3 km direction Schwarzenburg – alt. 563 – ✉ 3097 Liebefeld :*

XX **Landhaus,** Schwarzenburgstr. 134, ℘ (031) 971 07 58, *Fax (031) 972 02 49*, 🌲 – 🅿. 🆎 ⓸ 🄴 *VISA* AX s
closed Sunday and Bank Holidays – **Rôtisserie :** Meals 54 (lunch)/120 and a la carte 58/109 – **Taverne Alsacienne :** Meals a la carte 40/79.

BASLE (BASEL) 927 ④, 216 ④, 66 ⑩ – *pop. 175 510 – alt. 273 –* ☼ *Basle and environs ; fror France 0041-61 from Switzerland 061.*

See : *Old town★ : Cathedral★★ (Münster) : ≼★ CY – Fish Market Fountain★ (Fischmark brunnen) BY – Old Streets★ BY – Zoological Garden★★★ AZ – The Port (Hafen) ⚹★, "Fror Basle to the High Seas"★ Exhibition.*

Museums : *Fine Arts★★★ (Kunstmuseum) CY – Historical★★ (Historisches Museum) BY Ethnographic★★ (Museum für Kulturen) BY M' – Antiquities★ (Antikenmuseum) CY Paper Museum★ (Basler Papiermühle) DY M⁶ – Haus zum Kirschgarten★ BZ – Jean Tingue Museum★.*

Envir : *⚹★ from Bruderholz Water Tower S : 3,5 km – Chapel of St.-Chrischona★ NE : 8 kr – Augst Roman Ruins★★ SE : 11 km – Beyeler Foundation★★ NW : 6 km at Riehen.*

🏌 *at Hagenthal-le-Bas,* ✉ *F-68220 (March - November), SW : 10 km,* ℘ *(003. 389 68 50 91, Fax (0033) 389 68 55 66.*

✈ *Euro-Airport,* ℘ *(061) 325 31 11, Basle (Switzerland) by Flughafenstrasse 8 km ar – at Saint-Louis (France),* ℘ *(0033) 389 90 31 11.*

🛈 *Tourist Office, Schifflände 5,* ℘ *(061) 268 68 68, Fax (061) 268 68 70 – T.C.S., Steiner torstr. 13,* ℘ *(061) 205 99 99, Fax (061) 205 99 70 – A.C.S., Birsigstr.* ℘ *(061) 272 39 33, Fax (061) 281 36 57.*

Berne 100 – Freiburg im Breisgau 72 – Lyons 401 – Mulhouse 35 – Paris 554 – Stra bourg 145.

Plans on following pages

Drei Könige, Blumenrain 8, ✉ 4001, ℘ (061) 261 52 52, Fax (061) 261 21 53, ≼, 🌳 – 🛗, ☰ rm, 📺 ☎ 🅿 – 🏛 15/80. 🆎 ⓞ Ⅼ 𝒱𝐼𝒮𝒜 🅹🅲🅱   BY
Rôtisserie des Rois : Meals 88/105 and a la carte 74/135 – *Königsbrasserie* : Mea a la carte 36/86, children 14 – ☕ 29 – **82 rm** 255/590, 6 suites.

Plaza Ⓜ, Messeplatz 25, ✉ 4021, ℘ (061) 690 33 33, Fax (061) 690 39 70, ⇌s, 🔲 🛗, ⇥ rm, ☰ 📺 ☎ 📞 ⅙ ⇔ – 🏛 35. 🆎 ⓞ Ⅼ 𝒱𝐼𝒮𝒜 🅹🅲🅱   DX
Le Monet (closed 26 June - 29 August) Meals 48 (lunch)/85 and a la carte 58/101 *Le Provence* : Meals 23 and a la carte 39/86 – **218 rm** ☕ 389/55 20 Suiten.

Hilton Ⓜ, Aeschengraben 31, ✉ 4002, ℘ (061) 275 66 00, Fax (061) 275 66 5 ⇌s, 🔲 – 🛗, ⇥ rm, ☰ 📺 video ☎ 📞 ⅙ 🅿 – 🏛 15/300. 🆎 ⓞ 𝒱𝐼𝒮𝒜 🅹🅲🅱   CZ
Le Wettstein : Meals 43 (lunch)/57 (dinner) and a la carte 42/100 – ☕ 27 – **204 r** 280/450, 10 suites.

Europe Ⓜ, Clarastr. 43, ✉ 4005, ℘ (061) 690 80 80, Fax (061) 690 88 80 – 🛗, ⇥ rr ☰ 📺 video ☎ 📞 ⇔ – 🏛 15/180. 🆎 ⓞ Ⅼ 𝒱𝐼𝒮𝒜 🅹🅲🅱. ⚡ rest   CX
Meals see *Les Quatre Saisons* below – *Bajazzo* (Brasserie) Meals a la carte 43/73, chil ren 15 – **166 rm** ☕ 310/410.

Radisson SAS, Steinentorstr. 25, ✉ 4001, ℘ (061) 227 27 27, Fax (061) 227 28 2 ♿, ⇌s, 🔲 – 🛗 ⇥, ☰ rm, 📺 video ☎ 📞 ⅙ ⇔ – 🏛 15/150. 🆎 ⓞ 𝒱𝐼𝒮𝒜 🅹🅲🅱   BZ
Steinenpick (Brasserie) Meals 45 (dinner) and a la carte 38/90 – *Kaffi Mühli* : Meals la carte 36/70, children 12 – **205 rm** ☕ 430/560.

Basel Ⓜ, Münzgasse 12, ✉ 4001, ℘ (061) 264 68 00, Fax (061) 264 68 11 – 🛗 ⇥ ☰ rest, 📺 ☎ 📞 – 🏛 25. 🆎 ⓞ Ⅼ 𝒱𝐼𝒮𝒜 🅹🅲🅱   BY
Basler Keller (closed 3 July - 8 August, Saturday lunch and Sunday) Meals 38 (lunch)/ (dinner) and a la carte 54/106 – *Brasserie Steiger* : Meals a la carte 31/64, children – **72 rm** ☕ 275/355.

Palazzo Ⓜ without rest, Grenzacherstr. 6, ℘ (061) 690 64 64, Fax (061) 690 64 10, – 🛗 ⇥ ☰ 📺 ☎ 📞 ⅙ ⇔. 🆎 ⓞ Ⅼ 𝒱𝐼𝒮𝒜   DY
28 rm ☕ 200/320.

Der Teufelhof Ⓜ, Leonhardsgraben 47, ✉ 4051, ℘ (061) 261 10 10, Fax (061) 2 10 04 – 🛗, ⇥ rm, 📺 ☎ ⅙. 🆎 ⓞ Ⅼ 𝒱𝐼𝒮𝒜   BY
Meals see *Der Teufelhof* below – **29 rm** ☕ 195/315, 4 suites.

Schweizerhof, Centralbahnplatz 1, ✉ 4002, ℘ (061) 271 28 33, Fax (061) 271 29 1 🌳 – 🛗, ☰ rm, 📺 ☎ 🅿 – 🏛 15/80. 🆎 ⓞ Ⅼ 𝒱𝐼𝒮𝒜   BZ
Meals 49/69 and a la carte 48/107 – **75 rm** ☕ 170/300.

St. Gotthard Ⓜ without rest, Centralbahnstr. 13, ✉ 4002, ℘ (061) 271 52 5 Fax (061) 271 52 14 – 🛗 ⇥ 📺 ☎ 📞. 🆎 ⓞ Ⅼ 𝒱𝐼𝒮𝒜 🅹🅲🅱   BZ
62 rm ☕ 220/320.

Merian, Rheingasse 2, ✉ 4005, ℘ (061) 681 00 00, Fax (061) 681 11 01, ≼, 🌳 – 📺 ☎ ⅙ ⇔ – 🏛 15/100. 🆎 ⓞ Ⅼ 𝒱𝐼𝒮𝒜 🅹🅲🅱   BY
Café Spitz - Fish specialities - Meals 49/75 and a la carte 47/78 – **62 rm** ☕ 16 270.

Admiral, Rosentalstr. 5 (on Messeplatz), ⊠ 4021, ℘ (061) 691 77 77, Fax (061) 691 77 89, ⅂₆, ⊡ – ⧉, ⇥ rm, TV ☎ – ⚐ 25. AE Ⓞ E VISA   DX m
closed 23 December - 3 January – **Meals** (closed Saturday except fairs) a la carte 32/68 – **140 rm** ⊇ 150/350.

Victoria without rest, Centralbahnplatz 3, ⊠ 4002, ℘ (061) 270 70 70, Fax (061) 270 70 77 – ⧉ TV ☎ 🅿 – ⚐ 15/80. AE Ⓞ E VISA JCB   BZ d
41 rm ⊇ 280/380.

Wettstein without rest, Grenzacherstr. 8, ⊠ 4058, ℘ (061) 690 69 69, Fax (061) 691 05 45 – ⧉ ⇥ TV ☎ 📞. AE Ⓞ E VISA   DY q
40 rm ⊇ 145/210.

Steinenschanze without rest, Steinengraben 69, ⊠ 4051, ℘ (061) 272 53 53, Fax (061) 272 45 73 – ⧉ TV ☎ 📞. AE Ⓞ E VISA   BY s
54 rm ⊇ 180/250.

XXXX **Bruderholz**, Bruderholzallee 42, ⊠ 4059, ℘ (061) 361 82 22, Fax (061) 361 82 03, 🌺,
❀ « Flowered garden », 🚿 – 🅿. AE Ⓞ E VISA   U z
closed 3 to 18 January, Sunday and Monday except fairs – **Meals** 67 (lunch)/185 and a la carte 117/195
Spec. Fricassée de queues de langoustines à l'amigne flétrie et truffe noire (15 December - 15 March). Chausson de suprême de pigeon de Toscane aux morilles fraîches et asperges (15 March - 15 June). Feuillantine aux fruits de la passion et glace Pinacolada.

XXX **Les Quatre Saisons** Hotel Europe, Clarastr. 43 (1st floor), ⊠ 4005, ℘ (061) 690 87 20,
❀ Fax (061) 690 88 80 – ▤. AE Ⓞ E VISA JCB. ⌺   CX k
closed 12 July - 8 August and Sunday (except fairs) – **Meals** 55 (lunch)/165 and a la carte 87/145, children 30
Spec. Foie d'oie mi-cuit en robe de pommes. Gaspacho aux gnocchi piémontais. Mousseline de babeurre glacée aux baies des bois.

XXX **Der Teufelhof** - Hotel Der Teufelhof, Leonhardsgraben 47, ⊠ 4051, ℘ (061) 261
❀ 10 10, Fax (061) 261 10 04, 🌺 – ⇥. AE Ⓞ E VISA   BY g
Bel Etage closed 2 weeks in October, 1 to 11 January, 22 February - 8 March, Sunday and Monday (except fairs) **Meals** 75 (lunch)/180 and a la carte 86/169 – **Weinstube** : **Meals** 70 and a la carte 60/112
Spec. Sommerbockschinken mit Tannenwipfelvinaigrette und Pfifferlingssalat (summer). Gratiniertes Zackenbarschfilet mit Krustentieren in Estragonsauce. Limonen - Tiramisu mit marinierten Beeren und Spinetta - Eis.

XXX **Chez Donati**, St. Johanns-Vorstadt 48, ⊠ 4056, ℘ (061) 322 09 19, Fax (061) 322
09 81, 🌺, Typical bistro installation from the turn of the century   BX p
closed 12 July - 10 August, Monday and Tuesday – **Meals** - Italian rest. - a la carte 60/113.

XX **Schlüsselzunft**, Freie Strasse 25, ⊠ 4001, ℘ (061) 261 20 46, Fax (061) 261 20 56,
« 15C house » – AE E VISA JCB   BY r
closed Sunday and Bank Holidays – **Meals** 48 (lunch)/58 and a la carte 45/98 – **Höfli** : **Meals** a la carte 36/60, children 10.

XX **St. Alban-Eck**, St. Alban-Vorstadt 60, ⊠ 4052, ℘ (061) 271 03 20 – AE E
VISA. ⌺   CDY t
closed 10 July - 8 August, Saturday except dinner from late September - June, Sunday and Bank Holidays – **Meals** 37 (lunch)/79 and a la carte 65/110.

XX **Charon**, Schützengraben 62, ⊠ 4051, ℘ (061) 261 99 80, Fax (061) 261 99 09, Bistro atmosphere – AE E VISA JCB   AY s
closed Easter, July, Christmas, Sunday - Monday from October - April and Saturday - Sunday from May - September – **Meals** 40 (dinner)/90 and a la carte 67/111.

XX **Hong Kong**, Riehenring 91, ℘ (061) 691 88 14, Fax (061) 691 88 36. AE Ⓞ
E VISA   CX w
closed July – **Meals** - Chinese rest. - 43 (lunch)/102 and a la carte 33/78.

X **St. Alban-Stübli**, St. Ablan-Vorstadt 74, ⊠ 4052, ℘ (061) 272 54 15, Fax (061) 272
☺ 04 88, 🌺 – E VISA   DY a
closed 24 December - 11 January, Saturday lunch and Sunday – **Meals** 32/75 and a la carte 50/100.

X **Sakura**, Centralbahnstr. 14, ⊠ 4051, ℘ (061) 272 05 05, Fax (061) 295 39 88, Japanese rest. – ▤. AE Ⓞ E VISA   BZ k
closed 11 July - 22 August, Saturday lunch, Sunday and Bank Holidays – **Teppanyaki** : **Meals** 58/99 and a la carte 37/81, children 30 – **Yakitori** (Grill) **Meals** 44/82 and a la carte 50/71.

t Riehen by ② : 5 km – alt. 288 – ⊠ 4125 Riehen :

XX **Schürmann's**, Äussere Baselstr. 159, ℘ (061) 643 12 10, Fax (061) 643 12 10, 🌺 –
AE E VISA
closed 22 to 24 February, Saturday lunch, Monday lunch and Sunday – **Meals** 50 (lunch)/85 (dinner) and a la carte 54/114.

SWITZERLAND
BASLE (BASEL)
Kannenfeldpl.
Ring
St.
Feldbergs
Klybecks
0   200 m
Metzerstr.
Johanns-
Johanns-
Johanniterbrücke
Spital
M
St. Antonius-Kirche
St.
Schanzenstr.
Vorstadt
P
46
FRAUENSPITAL
str.
Blumen- a
rain
M
G
Klingelbergstr.
KANTONSSPITAL
graben
Petersgasse
Mittlere
Rheinbrüc
Burgfelderplatz
Str.
12
G
28
Rhein-
P
Peterskirche
Petersgasse
61
Nonnenweg
Missionsstr.
Peterspl.
FISCHMARKT-BRUNNEN
24
sprung
Birmannsgasse
84
U
5
M
87
H
Spalentor
Peters-
82
Marktpl.
Ahornstr.
Spalenring
Socinstr.
Schützen-
85
Spalenberg
X
76
r   M¹
31
M
P
S
graben
Heuberg
93
70
Allschwilerstr.
Socinstr.
Eulerstr.
str.
55
g
27
Austr.
Steinengraben
M
90
Schützenmatt
Holbeinstr.
M
57
51
7
Weiherweg
Austr.
HISTORISC MUSEUM
Steinen
SCHÜTZENMATT-PARK
Leimenstr.
S
52
92
T
Steinenvorstadt
Brennerstr.
Bundesstr.
Steinenring
Auberg
HAUS ZUM KIRSCHGARTEN
Arnold Böcklin-Str.
Holbeinstr.
Birsigstr.
88
49
Bundespl.
Birsigstr.
b
Rütimeyer
str.
A
P
P
63
Viaduktstr.
43
Bachlettenstr.
Vivarium
18
16
Bernerring
Binningerstr.
25
k
Oberwiler
str.
ZOOLOGISCHER GARTEN
Margarethenstr.
Dornacherstr.
Güterstr.

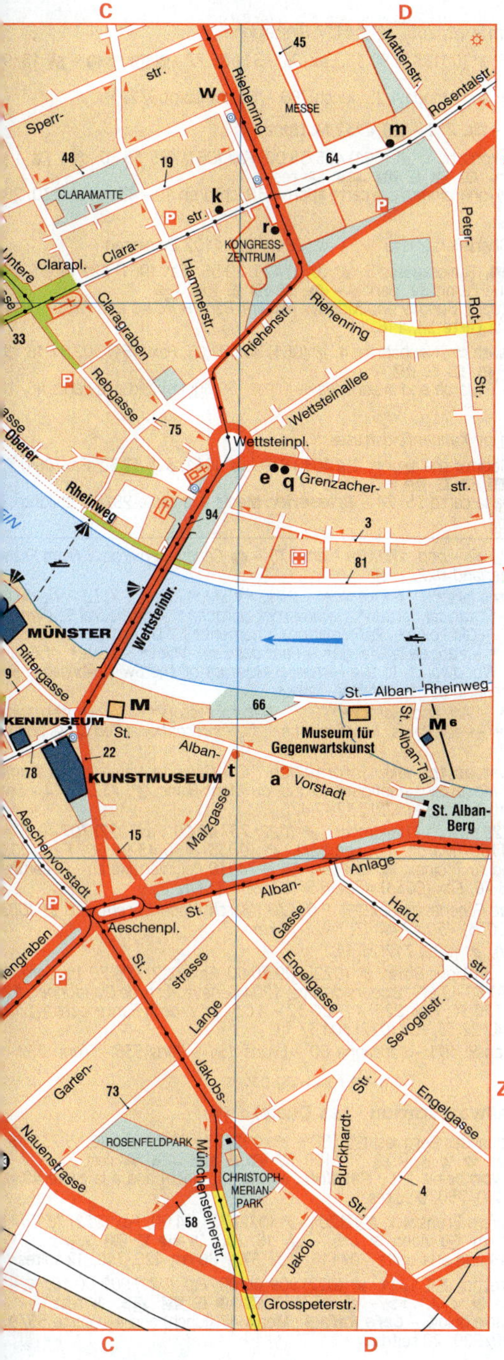

BASEL

The names of main shopping streets are printed in red at the beginning of the list of streets.

BASLE (BASEL)

at Birsfelden *E by ④ : 3 km – alt. 260 –* ✉ *4127 Birsfelden :*

🏠 **Alfa** Ⓜ, Hauptstr. 15, ☎ *(061) 311 80 15, Fax (061) 311 05 77 –* 📶 📺 ☎ 🅿 – 🏋 15/9
AE ⓪ E VISA
Meals *(closed Sunday and Monday)* 25 (lunch)/60 – **55 rm** � 105/225.

at Muttenz *by ⑤ : 4,5 km – alt. 271 –* ✉ *4132 Muttenz :*

🏨 **Baslertor** Ⓜ, St. Jakobsstr. 1, ☎ *(061) 465 55 00, Fax (061) 465 55 50,* 🌿, 🎰 – 🗎
🍴 rm, 📺 ☎ 📞 🚗. AE ⓪ E VISA JCB. ✗ rest
Meals *(closed Sunday) (only dinner)* a la carte approx. 38, children 10 – **43 rm** ⊔ 230/28
4 suites.

at Binningen *S : 2 km by Oberwilerstrasse* AZ *– alt. 284 –* ✉ *4102 Binningen :*

XXX **Schloss Binningen,** Schlossgasse 5, ☎ *(061) 421 20 55, Fax (061) 421 06 35,* 🌿
« *Old mansion, antique furniture, park* » – 🅿. AE ⓪ E VISA JCB U
closed 14 to 28 February, Sunday and Monday (except Bank Holidays and fairs) – **Mea**
45 (lunch)/95 and a la carte 54/116.

XX **Gasthof Neubad** with rm, Neubadrain 4, ☎ *(061) 302 07 05, Fax (061) 302 81 16,* 🌿
🚗 – 🍴 rm, 📺 ☎ 🅿. AE E VISA U
closed 13 February - 3 March and Wednesday – **Meals** 50 (lunch) and a la carte 46/10
– **6 rm** ⊔ 90/170.

at Euro-Airport *NW : 8 km by Kannenfeldstrasse* AX :

XX **Euroairport,** 5th floor of the airport, ✉ *4030 Basel,* ☎ *(061) 325 32 32, Fax (061) 3*
32 65, ← – 🍴 🗎. AE ⓪ E VISA
***Grill :* Meals** 45 and a la carte 35/74 – ***Brasserie :* Meals** a la carte 28/59, children 1

GENEVA 927 ⑪, 217 ⑪, 74 ⑥ *– pop. 170 189 – alt. 375 –* ✪ *Geneva, environs : from Fran*
0041-22, from Switzerland 022.

See : *The Shores of the lake*★★ : ←★★★ FGY *– Parks*★★ : *Mon Repos* GX, *La Perle du L*
and Villa Barton★★ *– Botanical Garden*★ : *alpine rock-garden*★★ *– Cathedral St-Pierre*★
north Tower ✳★★ FZ *– Old Town*★ : *Reformation Monument*★ FZ D ; *Archaeological Site*
– Palais des Nations★★ *– Parc de la Grange*★ *– Parc des Eaux-Vives*★ *– Nave*★ *of Chur*
of Christ the King – Woodwork★ *in the Historical Museum of the Swiss Abroad – Ba*
Collection★ *(in 19C mansion)* GZ *– Maison Tavel*★ FZ.

Museums : *Ariana*★★ *– Art and History*★★ GZ *– Natural History*★★ GZ *– Internation*
Automobile Museum★ *– Petit Palais : Modern Art*★★ GZ *– International Red Cross and R*
Crescent Museum★.

Excursions : *by boat on the lake, Information : Cie Gén. de Nav., Jardin Angl.*
☎ *(022) 312 52 23- Mouettes genevoises, 8 quai du Mont-Blanc,* ☎ *732 29 44 - Sw*
Boat, 4 quai du Mont-Blanc, ☎ *(022) 732 47 47.*

⛳ *at Cologny* ✉ *1223 (March - December),* ☎ *(022) 707 48 00, Fax (022) 707 48 20 ;*
at Bossey ✉ *F-74160 (March - December),* ☎ *(0033) 450 43 95 50, Fax (003*
450 95 32 57 by road to Troinex ; ⛳ *at Esery* ✉ *F-74930 Reignier (March - Decembe*
☎ *(0033) 450 36 58 70, Fax (0033) 450 36 57 62, SE : 15 km.*

⛳ *Maison Blanche at Echenevex-Gex* ✉ *F-01170 (March - mid December),* ☎ *(003*
450 42 44 42, Fax (0033) 450 42 44 43, NW : 17 km.

✈ *Genève-Cointrin,* ☎ *(022) 717 71 11.*

🛈 *Tourist Office, 3 r. du Mont Blanc,* ☎ *(022) 909 70 00, Fax (022) 909 70 11, Gare Co*
navin, ☎ *(022) 909 70 50 – T.C.S., 8 cours de Rive, 1204 Genève, 4 ch. de Blandonnet, 12*
Vernier, ☎ *(022) 417 20 30, Fax (022) 417 20 32 – A.C.S., 21 r. de la Fontenette* ✉ *12*
Carouge, ☎ *(022) 342 22 33, Fax (022) 301 37 11.*

Berne 164 – Bourg-en-B. 101 – Lausanne 60 – Lyons 151 – Paris 538 – Turin 252.

Plans on following pages

Right Bank (Cornavin Railway Station - Les Quais) :

🏨 **Des Bergues,** 33 quai des Bergues, ✉ *1201,* ☎ *(022) 731 50 50, Fax (022) 732 19*
– 📶, 🗎 rm, 📺 video ☎ 📞 🚗 ♿ – 🏋 15/190. AE ⓪ E VISA JCB. ✗ rest FY
Meals see **Amphitryon** below – ***Le Pavillon :* Meals** 48 (lunch) and a la carte 49/1
– ⊔ 35 – **109 rm** 450/750, 9 suites.

🏨 **Le Richemond,** Jardin Brunswick, ✉ *1201,* ☎ *(022) 731 14 00, Fax (022) 731 67*
←, 🌿, 🎰 – 📶, 🗎 rm, 📺 video ☎ 🚗 – 🏋 15/200. AE ⓪ E VISA JCB FY
***Le Jardin :* Meals** 48 and a la carte 70/116 – ⊔ 37 – **86 rm** 420/740, 12 suites.

🏨 **Rhône,** 1 quai Turrettini, ✉ *1211,* ☎ *(022) 909 00 00, Fax (022) 909 00 10,* ← –
🍴 rm, 🗎 📺 video ☎ 📞 🚗 ♿ 🚗 – 🏋 15/150. AE ⓪ E VISA JCB. ✗ rest FY
Meals see ***Le Neptune*** below – ***Café Rafael :* Meals** 47 (lunch) and a la carte 55/97
⊔ 30 – **169 rm** 450/520, 20 suites.

Noga Hilton, 19 quai du Mont-Blanc, ⊠ 1201, ℰ (022) 908 90 81, *Fax (022) 908 90 90*, ≤, ☷, ℔, ≦s, ⊠ – ⧠, ⇥ rm, ▤ rm, ▥ video ☎ ℓ ⅙ – ⚐ 15/440. 匯 ⓪ ⴹ 𝗩𝗜𝗦𝗔 ᴊᴄʙ   GY y
Meals see *Le Cygne* below – *La Grignotière* : Meals a la carte 42/82 – ⌸ 32 – **390 rm** 405/670, 20 suites.

Président Wilson Ⓜ, 47 quai Wilson, ⊠ 1211, ℰ (022) 906 66 66, *Fax (022) 906 66 67*, ≤, ≦s, ⧖ – ⧠, ⇥ rm, ▤ ▥ ☎ ℓ ⅙ – ⚐ 15/600. 匯 ⓪ ⴹ 𝗩𝗜𝗦𝗔 ᴊᴄʙ. ⊗ rest   GX d
Le Cirque : (closed Saturday and Sunday in July - August) **Meals** 75 (dinner) and a la carte 67/123 – *L'Arabesque* - Liebanese rest. - **Meals** a la carte 50/83 – ⌸ 32 – **234 rm** 540/800, 21 suites.

Beau-Rivage, 13 quai du Mont-Blanc, ⊠ 1201, ℰ (022) 716 66 66, *Fax (022) 716 60 60*, ≤, ☷ – ⧠, ⇥ rm, ▤ rm, ▥ video ☎ ℓ ⅙ – ⚐ 15/250. 匯 ⓪ ⴹ 𝗩𝗜𝗦𝗔 ᴊᴄʙ. ⊗   FY d
Meals see *Le Chat Botté* below – *Le Quai 13*, ℰ (022) 716 69 25 **Meals** a la carte 37/83 – ⌸ 34 – **91 rm** 430/740, 6 suites.

Angleterre Ⓜ, 17 quai du Mont-Blanc, ⊠ 1201, ℰ (022) 906 55 55, *Fax (022) 906 55 56*, ≤, « Atmosphere of a fine English residence », ℔, ≦s – ⧠ ▤ ▥ video ☎ ℓ ⅙ – ⚐ 35. 匯 ⓪ ⴹ 𝗩𝗜𝗦𝗔 ᴊᴄʙ   FGY n
Tea Roux : Meals 37 (lunch)/50 and a la carte 53/103 – ⌸ 32 – **45 rm** 410/750.

Bristol, 10 r. du Mont-Blanc, ⊠ 1201, ℰ (022) 732 38 00, *Fax (022) 738 90 39*, ℔, ≦s – ⧠ ▤ ▥ ☎ ℓ – ⚐ 15/90. 匯 ⓪ ⴹ 𝗩𝗜𝗦𝗔 ᴊᴄʙ. ⊗ rest   FY w
Meals 41 and a la carte 45/77 – ⌸ 27 – **93 rm** 275/470, 5 suites.

Ramada Genève, 19 r. de Zürich, ⊠ 1211, ℰ (022) 909 90 00, *Fax (022) 909 90 01* – ⧠, ⇥ rm, ▤ ▥ video ☎ ℓ ⅙ – ⚐ 15/80. 匯 ⓪ ⴹ 𝗩𝗜𝗦𝗔 ᴊᴄʙ   FX s
The Taj - Indian and International rest. - **Meals** 39 (lunch) and a la carte 42/92 – ⌸ 28 – **194 rm** 295/510, 11 suites.

Sofitel, 18 r. du Cendrier, ⊠ 1201, ℰ (022) 908 80 80, *Fax (022) 908 80 81*, ☷ – ⧠, ⇥ rm, ▤ ▥ ☎ ℓ. 匯 ⓪ ⴹ 𝗩𝗜𝗦𝗔. ⊗ rest   FY t
Meals (closed 22 December - 4 January) 43 and a la carte 49/100 – ⌸ 31 – **85 rm** 350/390, 10 suites.

Warwick, 14 r. de Lausanne, ⊠ 1201, ℰ (022) 731 62 50, *Fax (022) 738 99 35* – ⧠, ⇥ rm, ▤ ▥ video ☎ ℓ – ⚐ 15/140. 匯 ⓪ ⴹ 𝗩𝗜𝗦𝗔 ᴊᴄʙ. ⊗ rest   FY c
Les 4 Saisons (closed 20 July - 10 August, Saturday lunch and Sunday) **Meals** 40 (lunch)/70 and a la carte 58/98 – *La Bonne Brasserie* : **Meals** a la carte 40/75, children 15 – ⌸ 27 – **169 rm** 320/480.

Grand Pré without rest, 35 r. du Grand-Pré, ⊠ 1202, ℰ (022) 918 11 11, *Fax (022) 734 76 91* – ⧠ ▤ ▥ ☎ ℓ – ⚐ 25. 匯 ⓪ ⴹ 𝗩𝗜𝗦𝗔   by rue du Fort-Barreau CU s
89 rm ⌸ 225/325.

Eden, 135 r. de Lausanne, ⊠ 1202, ℰ (022) 732 65 40, *Fax (022) 731 52 60* – ⧠ ▤ ▥ ☎ ℓ. 匯 ⓪ ⴹ 𝗩𝗜𝗦𝗔 ᴊᴄʙ   CU t
Meals (closed Saturday and Sunday) 29 and a la carte 30/62 – **54 rm** ⌸ 185/245.

Cornavin without rest, 23 bd James-Fazy, ⊠ 1201, ℰ (022) 732 21 00, *Fax (022) 732 88 43* – ⧠ ▤ ▥ video ☎ ℓ. 匯 ⓪ ⴹ 𝗩𝗜𝗦𝗔   FY a
⌸ 16 – **155 rm** 215/310, 5 suites.

du Midi, 4 pl. Chevelu, ⊠ 1211, ℰ (022) 731 78 00, *Fax (022) 731 00 20* – ▥ ☎ ℓ. 匯 ⓪ ⴹ 𝗩𝗜𝗦𝗔   FY v
Meals (closed Saturday and Sunday) 39 and a la carte 38/70 – ⌸ 15 – **89 rm** 185/260.

Carlton, 22 r. Amat, ⊠ 1202, ℰ (022) 908 68 50, *Fax (022) 908 68 68* – ⧠, ▤ rest, ▥ ☎ ℓ ⅙. 匯 ⓪ ⴹ 𝗩𝗜𝗦𝗔 ᴊᴄʙ   FX a
Meals a la carte 40/80 – **121 rm** ⌸ 214/268.

Strasbourg without rest, 10 r. Pradier, ⊠ 1201, ℰ (022) 906 58 00, *Fax (022) 738 42 08* – ⧠ ▥ ☎ ℓ. 匯 ⓪ ⴹ 𝗩𝗜𝗦𝗔. ⊗   FY q
51 rm ⌸ 170/230.

Le Cygne - Hôtel Noga Hilton, 19 quai du Mont-Blanc, ⊠ 1201, ℰ (022) 908 90 85, *Fax (022) 908 90 90*, ≤ – ▤. 匯 ⓪ ⴹ 𝗩𝗜𝗦𝗔 ᴊᴄʙ. ⊗   GY y
closed 2 to 12 April, 5 to 26 July and 1st to 9 January – **Meals** 59 (lunch)/108 and a la carte 75/134
Spec. Ragoût de racines d'hiver aux truffes et foie gras (winter). Bar cuit à la fumée de bois et vinaigrette aux truffes. Déclinaison de poissons bleus lamparo (spring - summer).

Le Chat Botté - Hôtel Beau-Rivage, 13 quai du Mont-Blanc, ⊠ 1201, ℰ (022) 716 69 20, *Fax (022) 716 60 60*, ☷ – 匯 ⓪ ⴹ 𝗩𝗜𝗦𝗔 ᴊᴄʙ. ⊗   FY d
closed Christmas - New Year, Saturday, Sunday and Bank Holidays – **Meals** 60 (lunch)/145 and a la carte 78/128
Spec. Filets de perche du lac en vinaigrette aux appétits (summer). Bar grillé aux herbes. Filet d'agneau moutardé en verdure.

SWITZERLAND

PARC MON REPOS

LAC LÉMAN

0 200 m

LE PRIEURÉ

LES PÂQUIS

Rue du Valais

Rue de Lausanne

R. des Buis

Pâquis

Quai Wilson

CASINO

Plantamour

Mont-Blanc

R. des Gares

Montbrillant

LES CROPETTES

CORNAVIN

James Fazy

Bd. James Fazy

PROM DE ST-JEAN

RHÔNE

Berne

R. des Alpes

R. Rousseau

Quai du Mont-Blanc

ÎLE J. J. ROUSSEAU

Pt. du Mont-Blanc

Jet d'eau

PIERRE DU NITON

Quai Gustave Ador

Jardin Anglais

Guisan

Quai du Général Guisan

Rhône

R. de la Scie

R. des Eaux-Vives

POL.

Musée Rath

Grand' Rue

MAISON TAVEL

CATH. ST-PIERRE

R. de Rive

Bd. Helvétique

MUSEUM D'HISTOIRE NATURELLE

PLAINE DE PLAINPALAIS

Av. Henri Dunant

Georges Favor

PI. Neuve

VIEILLE VILLE

Prom. des Bastions

R. de la Croix Rouge

Bibliothèque Universitaire

Dalcroze

Hodler

MUSÉE D'ART ET D'HISTOIRE

COLLECTIONS BAUR

Musée de l'Horlogerie

PETIT PALAIS

LES TRANCHÉES

R. de Contamines

R. des Tranchées

Av. du Mail

Quai

Rd. Point de Plainpalais

Bd. du Pont d'Arve

PLAINPALAIS

Bd. des Philosophes

PI. Ed. Claparède

R. de Florissant

Jardin

STREET INDEX TO GENEVE TOWN PLAN

XXXX **Amphitryon** - Hotel Des Bergues, 33 quai des Bergues, ✉ 1201, ℘ (022) 731 50 50,
Fax (022) 732 19 89 – AE ① E VISA JCB. ✀   FY k
closed July - August and 24 December - 2 January – **Meals** 63 (lunch)/150 and a la carte
71/126.

XXX **Le Neptune** - Hôtel du Rhône, 1 quai Turrettini, ✉ 1211, ℘ (022) 909 00 06,
✿ *Fax (022) 909 00 10* – ▣. AE ① E VISA JCB. ✀   FY r
closed August, Saturday, Sunday and Bank Holidays – **Meals** 65/125 and a la carte 91/137
Spec. Epicé de rouget Barbet à l'émulsion d'aubergine. Poissons du lac Léman (February
- October). Blanc de turbot poêlé et croustillant d'épinards à l'aneth.

XXX **La Perle du Lac,** 126 r. de Lausanne, ✉ 1202, ℘ (022) 731 79 35, *Fax (022) 731 49 79*,
⏛, « Chalet in a park ≤ lake » – Ⓟ. AE ① E VISA. ✀   CU f
closed 21 December - 10 January and Monday – **Meals** 58 (lunch)/112 and a la carte
75/149.

XXX **Tsé Yang,** 19 quai du Mont-Blanc, ✉ 1201, ℘ (022) 732 50 81, *Fax (022) 731 05 82*,
≤, « Elegant installation » – ▣. AE ① E VISA JCB   GY e
Meals - Chinese rest. - 42 (lunch)/125 and a la carte 64/134.

X **Brasserie Victoria,** 2 r. Bovy Lysberg, pl. du Cirque, ✉ 1204, ℘ (022) 807 11 99,
⊛ *Fax (022) 807 11 98* – ▣. AE E VISA   FZ p
Meals (booking essential) 39/49 (lunch) and a la carte 45/89.

X **Bœuf Rouge,** 17 r. Alfred-Vincent, ✉ 1201, ℘ (022) 732 75 37, *Fax (022) 731 46 84*
– AE ① E VISA   FY z
closed Saturday and Sunday – **Meals** - Specialities of Lyons - 45 and a la carte 46/
88.

Left Bank (Commercial Centre) :

🏨 **Métropole,** 34 quai Général-Guisan, ✉ 1204, ℘ (022) 318 32 00, *Fax (022) 318 33 00*,
⏛ – 🛗 ▤ TV video ☎ ℡ – 🔔 15/120. AE ① E VISA JCB   GY a
Le Grand Quai : **Meals** a la carte 44/81 – ☕ 23 – **120 rm** 245/510, 7 suites.

🏨 **La Cigogne,** 17 pl. Longemalle, ✉ 1204, ℘ (022) 818 40 40, *Fax (022) 818 40 50*,
« Tastefully decorated and furnished » – 🛗 ▤ TV video ☎ ℡ – 🔔 20. AE ① E VISA.
✀ rest   FGY j
Meals 56 (lunch)/90 and a la carte 75/109 – **45 rm** ☕ 325/420, 7 suites.

🏨 **Les Armures** ✀, 1 r. du Puits-Saint-Pierre, ✉ 1204, ℘ (022) 310 91 72, *Fax (022) 310
98 46*, ⏛, « Attractive rustic furnishings in a 17C house » – 🛗, ▤ rm, TV video ☎. AE
① E VISA JCB   FZ g
Meals *(closed Easter, Christmas and New Year)* 45 and a la carte 35/79, children 17 – **28 rm**
☕ 290/440.

🏨 **Century** without rest, 24 av. de Frontenex, ✉ 1207, ℘ (022) 736 80 95, *Fax (022) 786
52 74* – 🛗 ✂ TV ☎ Ⓟ – 🔔 35. AE ① E VISA JCB   GZ p
117 rm ☕ 215/440, 14 suites.

🏨 **Tiffany** Ⓜ, 18 r. de l'Arquebuse, ✉ 1204, ℘ (022) 329 33 11, *Fax (022) 320 89 91* –
🛗, ▤ rm, TV video ☎. AE ① E VISA JCB   FZ v
Meals *(closed Easter, Christmas and New Year)* a la carte 40/85 – **28 rm** ☕ 205/
350.

Le Béarn (Goddard), 4 quai de la Poste, ⊠ 1204, ℘ (022) 321 00 28, Fax (022) 781 31 1*
– ▣. ᴀᴇ Ⓞ Ɛ 𝗩𝗜𝗦𝗔   FY
*closed 12 July - 15 August, 14 to 21 February, Saturday except dinner October - May and
Sunday* – **Meals** 53 (lunch)/160 and a la carte 91/150
Spec. Les trois gourmandises de l'été : homard, cappuccino et rillettes de tourteau. Souffle
aux truffes (winter). Saint-Pierre rôti à la feuille de laurier, pomme verte et céleri (spring)

Parc des Eaux-Vives, 82 quai G.-Ador, ⊠ 1207, ℘ (022) 735 41 40, Fax (022) 78*
87 65, ≤, 🏡, « Pleasant setting in extensive park » – Ⓟ. ᴀᴇ Ɛ 𝗩𝗜𝗦𝗔
*closed 4 to 13 April, 26 December - 25 January, Sunday except lunch in summer and
Monday* – **Meals** 48 (lunch)/132 and a la carte 76/148.   by quai G. Ador   CU

Baron de la Mouette (Mövenpick Fusterie), 40 r. du Rhône, ⊠ 1204
℘ (022) 311 88 55, Fax (022) 310 93 22 – ᴀᴇ Ⓞ Ɛ 𝗩𝗜𝗦𝗔 𝗝𝗖𝗕   FY
closed Saturday, Sunday, Bank Holidays and dinner – **Meals** a la carte 50/106.

Roberto, 10 r. Pierre-Fatio, ⊠ 1204, ℘ (022) 311 80 33, Fax (022) 311 84 66 – ▣. A
Ɛ 𝗩𝗜𝗦𝗔   GZ
closed Saturday dinner and Sunday – **Meals** - Italian rest. - 68/93 and a la carte 56/105

Le Patio, 19 bd Helvétique, ℘ (022) 736 66 75, Fax (022) 786 40 74 – ᴀᴇ Ⓞ Ɛ 𝗩𝗜𝗦𝗔   GZ
closed 18 July - 8 August, Saturday and Sunday – **Meals** 39 (lunch) and a la carte 58/9*

Brasserie Lipp, 8 r. de la Confédération (2nd floor), ⊠ 1204, ℘ (022) 311 10 1*
Fax (022) 312 01 04, 🏡 – ✂ ▣. ᴀᴇ Ⓞ Ɛ 𝗩𝗜𝗦𝗔   FY
Meals a la carte 39/88.

La Favola, 15 r. Jean-Calvin, ⊠ 1204, ℘ (022) 311 74 37, 17C house – ✂   FZ
closed 26 July - 8 August, Saturday lunch and Sunday – **Meals** - Italian rest. - (booking
essential) a la carte 64/81.

Environs
to the North :

Palais des Nations :   *by quai Wilson* FGX :

Intercontinental, 7 chemin du Petit-Saconnex, ⊠ 1209, ℘ (022) 919 39 39
Fax (022) 919 38 38, ≤, 🏡, 🛋 – 🔌 ▣ 📺 ☎ & 🚗 Ⓟ – 🔏 15/400. ᴀᴇ Ⓞ Ɛ 𝗩𝗜𝗦
𝗝𝗖𝗕. ✂ rest   BT
Meals see **Les Continents** below – **La Pergola :** Meals a la carte 51/91 – ☕ 23 – **285 r**
420/540, 60 suites.

Les Continents - Hotel Intercontinental, 7 chemin du Petit-Saconnex, ⊠ 1209
℘ (022) 919 33 50, Fax (022) 919 38 38 – ▣ Ⓟ. ᴀᴇ Ⓞ Ɛ 𝗩𝗜𝗦𝗔 𝗝𝗖𝗕. ✂   BT
closed Christmas to New Year, Saturday and Sunday – **Meals** 55 (lunch)/112 and a la cart
74/124
Spec. Raviole de ris de veau aux asperges et champignons. Filets de perche en salade a
jambon de Parme et vinaigre au vin vieux. Noisettes d'agneau rôties, gâteau de bette
et chanterelles.

at Chambésy *5 km* - CT – *alt. 389* – ⊠ *1292 Chambésy :*

Relais de Chambésy, 8 pl. de Chambésy, ℘ (022) 758 11 05, Fax (022) 758 02 3*
🏡 – ᴀᴇ Ⓞ Ɛ 𝗩𝗜𝗦𝗔   CT
closed Saturday lunch and Sunday – Meals 29 (lunch)/75 and a la carte 41/83.

at Bellevue :   *by road to Lausanne* FX : *6 km – alt. 380* – ⊠ *1293 Bellevue :*

La Réserve, 301 rte de Lausanne, ℘ (022) 959 86 88, Fax (022) 959 85 88, ≤, 🏡, Par
🛋, ≋s, 🛋, 🛋, ✕, 🛋 – 🔌 ▣ 📺 video ☎ 🚗 Ⓟ – 🔏 15/80. ᴀᴇ Ⓞ Ɛ 𝗩𝗜𝗦𝗔 𝗝𝗖𝗕   CT
Meals see **Tsé Fung** below – **La Closerie :** *(closed Saturday)* Meals 55 (lunch)/85 and
la carte 44/103 – **Mikado** - Japanese rest. - *(closed at lunch)* Meals 70/95 and a la car
41/110 – **Chez Gianni** - Italian rest. - Meals 55 (lunch)/70 and a la carte 45/118 – ☕ 2
– **108 rm** 300/500, 6 suites.

Tsé Fung - Hotel La Réserve, 301 rte de Lausanne, ℘ (022) 959 86 88, Fax (022) 9*
85 88, 🏡 – ▣ Ⓟ. ᴀᴇ Ⓞ Ɛ 𝗩𝗜𝗦𝗔 𝗝𝗖𝗕   CT
Meals - Chinese rest. - 80/125 and a la carte 66/108.

to the East by road to Evian :

at Cologny :   *by Quai Gustave Ador* GY : *3,5 km – alt. 432* – ⊠ *1223 Cologny :*

Auberge du Lion d'Or (Byrne/Dupont), 5 pl. Pierre-Gautier, ℘ (022) 736 44 3
Fax (022) 786 74 62, 🏡, « Overlooking the lake and Geneva » – ᴀᴇ Ɛ 𝗩𝗜𝗦𝗔   DU
closed 20 December - 20 January, Saturday except dinner from 15 June - 15 August a
Sunday – **Meals** 56 (lunch)/140 and a la carte 90/135 – **Bistro de Cologny :** Meals *
(lunch) and a la carte 51/74
Spec. Sashimi de thon rouge saisi aux poivres et herbes, beignets de tourteau. Langou
tines poêlées, cannelloni d'aubergines, émulsion de fenouil. Agneau de lait de Sisteron rô
au romarin et ail nouveau.

at Anières : *by road to Hermance : 7 km – alt. 410 – ⊠ 1247 Anières :*

XXX **Auberge de Floris** (Legras), 287 rte d'Hermance, ℘ (022) 751 20 20, Fax (022) 751 22 50, 🌿, « terrace ≤ lake » – 🅿. 🆎 🇪 *VISA* – *closed 11 to 26 April, 24 October - 6 November, 20 December - 5 January, Sunday and Monday* – **Meals** 54 (lunch)/105 and a la carte 74/140 – **Le Café :** Meals 34 and a la carte 50/78
Spec. Nougat de foie gras aux fruits secs. Coussinet d'omble du lac à la crème de parmesan. Bouillabaisse (except July - August).

to the East by road to Annemasse :

at Thônex : *by rte de Chêne GZ : 5 km – alt. 414 – ⊠ 1226 Thônex :*

XX **Le Cigalon** (Bessire), 39 rte d'Ambilly, at the customs border of Pierre-à-Bochet, ℘ (022) 349 97 33, Fax (027) 349 97 33, 🌿 – 🅿. 🆎 🇪 *VISA* DU f
closed 11 July - 3 August, 24 to 28 December, 14 to 22 February, Saturday lunch, Sunday dinner and Monday – **Meals** 42 (lunch)/95 and a la carte 65/111
Spec. Gaspacho aux médaillons de homard (summer). Tartare de thon à la tomate séchée (summer). Bar de ligne rôti en écailles.

to the South :

at Conches *SE : 5 km – alt. 419 – ⊠ 1231 Conches :*

X **Le Vallon,** 182 rte de Florissant, ℘ (022) 347 11 04, Fax (022) 347 63 81, 🌿, « Bistro style » – 🅿
closed 2 to 10 April, 21 June - 12 July, 23 December - 4 January, Saturday and Sunday – **Meals** la carte 41/86.

at Vessy : *by road to Veyrier : 4 km – alt. 419 – ⊠ 1234 Vessy :*

XX **Alain Lavergnat,** 130 rte de Veyrier, ℘ (022) 784 26 26, Fax (022) 784 13 34, 🌿 – 🅿. 🆎 🇪 *VISA* CV z
closed 25 July - 10 August, 19 December - 4 January, Sunday and Monday – **Meals** 48 (lunch)/90 and a la carte 85/117.

at Carouge : *by Av. Henri-Dunant FZ : 3 km – alt. 382 – ⊠ 1227 Carouge :*

XX **L'Olivier de Provence,** 13 r. Jacques-Dalphin, ℘ (022) 342 04 50, Fax (022) 342 88 80, 🌿 – 🆎 🅾 🇪 *VISA* 🇯🇨🇧 CV a
closed 2 to 11 April, 24 December - 10 January, Saturday lunch, Sunday and Bank Holidays – **Meals** 43 (lunch)/98 and a la carte 69/94 – **Le Bistrot :** Meals 27 (lunch)/34 and a la carte 36/64.

XX **Auberge de Pinchat** with rm, 33 chemin de Pinchat, ℘ (022) 342 30 77, Fax (022) 300 22 19, 🌿 – 📺 ☎ 🅿. 🆎 🇪 *VISA* CV k
closed 28 March - 5 April, 31 August - 13 September, 20 December - 4 January, Sunday and Monday – **Meals** 45 (lunch)/90 and a la carte 64/123 – **5 rm** � 120/145.

t Petit-Lancy : *by Av. Henri-Dunant FZ : 3 km – alt. 426 – ⊠ 1213 Petit-Lancy :*

🏰 **Hostellerie de la Vendée,** 28 chemin de la Vendée, ℘ (022) 792 04 11, Fax (022) 792 05 46, 🌿, Winter garden – 📶 🔲 📺 ☎ 📞 🚗 – 🛁 15/60. 🆎 🅾 🇪 *VISA* BV q
closed Easter and 24 December - 5 January – **Meals** *(closed Saturday lunch and Sunday)* 50 (lunch)/120 and a la carte 72/124 – **Bistro** *(closed Saturday and Sunday)* Meals 36 and a la carte 39/60 – **34 rm** ⊇ 160/275
Spec. Langoustines grillées, tartare d'avocats à l'huile d'olive vierge (spring). Loup de ligne en croûte de sel, pousses d'épinards à la crème (summer). Côte de veau poêlée aux miettes de truffes (autumn - winter).

Lully *SW : 8 km by road to Bernex – alt. 430 – ⊠ 1233 Bernex :*

XX **La Colombière** (Lonati), 122 rte de Soral, ℘ (022) 757 10 27, Fax (022) 757 65 49, 🌿 – 🅿. 🆎 🅾 🇪 *VISA* AV b
closed 21 August - 21 September, 20 December - 11 January, Saturday and Sunday – **Meals** (booking essential) 42 (lunch)/82 and a la carte 68/102
Spec. Tartare de canard aux épices et ses rôties à l'huile d'olive de Baux. Cannellons de langoustines à l'infusion de thym et huile d'olive toscane. Parmentier de rôti de veau à la truffe noire.

to the West :

t Peney-Dessus *by road to Satigny and private lane : 10 km – ⊠ 1242 Satigny :*

XXXX **Domaine de Châteauvieux** (Chevrier) 🦢 with rm, ℘ (022) 753 15 11, Fax (022) 753 19 24, ≤, 🌿, « Beautiful country inn, in a former farm » – 📺 ☎ 🅿 – 🛁 15. 🆎 🇪 *VISA*
closed 1st to 15 August, 24 December - 8 January – **Meals** *(closed Sunday and Monday)* 72 (lunch)/180 and a la carte 126/186 – **19 rm** ⊇ 175/275
Spec. Filets de rouget de roche en papillote aux champignons et thym citronné (April - September). Carré d'agneau d'Ecosse cuit dans le foin et les herbes aromatiques en cocotte lutée (May - October). Gibier à plumes (October - November).

SWITZERLAND

at Cointrin : *by road to Lyons : 4 km – alt. 428 –* ✉ *1216 Cointrin :*

Mövenpick Genève Ⓜ, 20 rte Pré-Bois, ✉ 1215 Genève, ℘ (022) 798 75 75, Fax (022) 791 02 84, ≤ – 📶, ✸ rm, ▤ 📺 video ☎ ✆ 👤 Ⓟ – 🔺 15/250. 🆎 ⓞ Ⓔ VISA JCB
BU
La Brasserie : Meals a la carte 44/115 – **Kamome** - Japanese rest. - *(closed mid July - mid August, Saturday lunch, Monday lunch and Sunday)* **Meals** 45/105 and a la carte 46/86, children 22 – ☕ 25 – **344 rm** 275/395, 6 suites.

Forum Park, 75 av. Louis-Casaï, ℘ (022) 710 30 00, Fax (022) 710 31 00, 🔽, ⊆s – 📶, ✸ rm, ▤ 📺 video ☎ ✆ 👤 Ⓟ – 🔺 15/600. 🆎 ⓞ Ⓔ VISA JCB. ✸ rest
BT
La Récolte : Meals a la carte 41/90 – ☕ 26 – **302 rm** 280/390, 6 suites.

Canonica, 2nd floor at the airport, ℘ (022) 717 76 76, Fax (022) 798 77 68, ≤, Restaurants arranged around an aircraft cabin – ▤. 🆎 ⓞ Ⓔ VISA
BT
Plein Ciel *(closed Sunday except lunch in winter and Saturday)* **Meals** 47 (lunch)/98 and a la carte 61/124 – **L'Avion** (Brasserie) **Meals** 29 and a la carte 33/80, children 14.

at Palais des Expositions : *by quai Wilson* FGX *: 5 km – alt. 452 –* ✉ *1218 Grand Saconnex :*

Holiday Inn Crowne Plaza Ⓜ, 26 voie de Moëns, ℘ (022) 791 00 11, Fax (022) 79. 92 73, 🔽, ⊆s, ▨ – 📶, ✸ rm, ▤ 📺 video ☎ ✆ 👤 Ⓟ – 🔺 15/140. 🆎 ⓞ Ⓔ VISA JCB
BT
L'Intervista - Italian rest. - *(closed Saturday lunch)* **Meals** a la carte 32/88 – ☕ 26 – **305 rm** 290/420.

Vufflens-le-Château 1134 Vaud **927** ⑪, **217** ② – *pop. 576 – alt. 471.*
Berne 118 – Geneva 53 – Lausanne 14 – Morges 3 – Pontarlier 72 – Yverdon-les-Bains 4

L'Ermitage (Ravet) 🦢 with rm, ℘ (021) 804 68 68, Fax (021) 802 22 40, « Beautiful residence in a garden, pond » – 📺 ☎ ✆ Ⓟ. ⓞ Ⓔ VISA
closed 1st to 24 August, 24 December - 11 January, Sunday and Monday – **Meals** 7 (lunch)/185 and a la carte 142/196 – **9 rm** ☕ 300
Spec. Dinette de foies gras d'oie et de canard. Fraîcheur de homard bleu, millefeuille d bricelets au tourteau. Canard de Barbarie doré à la broche et confit au jus de pamplemouss et gentiane.

In this Guide,
a symbol or a character, printed in red or black,
does not have the same meaning.
Please read the explanatory pages carefully.

COSSONAY 1304 Vaud (VD) **927** ⑪ **217** ③ – *pop. 2 203 – alt. 565.*
Bern 107 – Lausanne 16 – Fribourg 78 – Genève 62 – Yverdon-les-Bains 28.

Cerf (Crisci), 10 r. du Temple, ℘ (021) 861 26 08, Fax (021) 861 26 27, « 16C house – 🆎 Ⓔ VISA
closed 10 July - 3 August, 23 December - 4 January, Sunday and Monday – **Meals** 5 (lunch)/168 and a la carte 95/155
Spec. Foie gras luté aux truffes (December - February). Truffes blanches et purée de ratte (November). Pigeon en vessie parfumé à la benoîte et racines de raiponce.

Crissier 1023 Vaud **927** ⑪ **217** ③ – *pop. 5 245 – alt. 470.*
Berne 111 – Lausanne 6 – Montreux 40 – Nyon 50 – Pontarlier 64.

Hôtel de Ville (Rochat), 1 r. d'Yverdon, ℘ (021) 634 05 05, Fax (021) 634 24 6 « Elegant decor » – 🆎 ⓞ Ⓔ VISA
closed 31 July - 23 August, 18 December - 3 January, Sunday and Monday – **Meals** 195/2 and a la carte 120/240
Spec. Œuf en surprise aux truffes blanches d'Alba (autumn). Truite du Lac en cour bouillon, mousseline à l'estragon (summer). Canard nantais cuit rosé au vin de Brouilly

Brent Vaud **217** ⑭ – *alt. 569.*
Berne 85 – Geneva 89 – Lausanne 25 – Martigny 47 – Montreux 5.

Le Pont de Brent (Rabaey), ℘ (021) 964 52 30, Fax (021) 964 55 30, « Elegant decor – ▤ Ⓟ. Ⓔ VISA
closed 18 July - 9 August, 24 December - 11 January, Sunday and Monday – **Meals** 8 (lunch)/185 and a la carte 98/165
Spec. Charlotte de grenouilles aux truffes blanches (September - December). Cœur cabillaud au genièvre, chou rouge braisé (winter). Savarin aux cerises, glace pistache (M - July).

ZÜRICH 927 ⑥, 216 ⑱ – pop. 345 235 – alt. 409.

See : The Quays★★ : ≤★ FZ ; Mythenquai : ≤★ CX – Fraumünster cloisters★ (Alter Kreuzgang des Fraumünsters), windows★ EZ – Church of SS. Felix and Regula★ – Cathedral★ (Grossmünster) – Fine Arts Museum★★ (Kunsthaus) FZ – Zoological Gardens★ (Zoo Dolder) – Bührle Collection★★ (Sammlung Bührle).

Museums : Swiss National Museum★★★ (Schweizerisches Landesmuseum) EY – Rietberg Museum★★ CX M².

Envir : Uetliberg★★ SW : by rail – Albis Pass Road★ SW by the Bederstrasse – Former Abbey of Kappel★ SW : 22 km – Eglisau : site★ N : 27 km.

Excursions : Boat Trips, Information : Zürichsee-Schiffahrtsgesellschaft, Bürkliplatz 10, ℰ (01) 487 13 33, Fax (01) 487 13 20.

ᵢ₉ Dolder (April-15 Nov.), ℰ (01) 261 50 45, Fax (01) 261 53 02 ; ᵢ₁₈ at Zumikon, ✉ 8126 (April-Oct.), ℰ (01) 918 00 50, Fax (01) 918 00 37, SE : 9 km ; ᵢ₁₈ at Hittnau, ✉ 8335 (April-Oct.), ℰ (01) 950 24 42, Fax (01) 951 01 66 E : 33 km, ᵢ₁₈ at Breitenloo, ✉ 8309 Nürensdorf (April-Oct.), ℰ (01) 836 40 80, Fax (01) 837 10 85 N : 22 km.

✈ Zürich-Kloten, ℰ (01) 816 22 11.

🛈 Tourist Office, Bahnhofbrücke 1, ℰ (01) 215 40 00, Fax (01) 215 40 44 – T.C.S., Alfred Escher-Str. 38, ℰ (01) 286 86 86, Fax (01) 286 86 87 – A.C.S., Forchstr. 95, ℰ (01) 422 15 00, Fax (01) 422 15 37.

Berne 125 – Basle 109 – Geneva 278 – Innsbruck 288 – Milan 304.

Plans on following pages

n the right bank of river Limmat (University, Fine Arts Museum) :

Dolder Grand Hotel ⑤, Kurhausstr. 65, ✉ 8032, ℰ (01) 269 30 00, Fax (01) 269 30 01, 🌳, ᵢ₉ Park, « Overlooking Zurich lake, city and mountains », ⌇, ✗ – ⧮, 🖩 rest, 📺 ☎ ✆ 🚗 – 🏊 15/250. AE ① E VISA JCB. ✗ rest
La Rotonde : Meals 85/125 (dinner) and a la carte 60/138 – **173 rm** ⌷ 390/580, 11 suites.
by Gloriastrasse BU f

Zürich Marriott, Neumühlequai 42, ✉ 8001, ℰ (01) 360 70 70, Fax (01) 360 77 77, ≤, 🛌, ⌷s, ⌇ – ⧮, ✗ rm, 🖩 rm, 📺 video ☎ ✆ 🚗 – 🏊 15/250. AE ① E VISA. ✗ rest
EY c
White Elephant - Thaï rest. - (closed Sunday) Meals 38/85 and a la carte 48/87 – *La Brasserie* : Meals a la carte 43/90 – ⌷ 31 – **251 rm** 305, 9 suites.

Eden au Lac, Utoquai 45, ✉ 8023, ℰ (01) 266 25 25, Fax (01) 266 25 00, ≤, ⌷s – ⧮ 🖩 📺 ☎ ✆ Ⓟ. AE ① E VISA JCB. ✗ rest
DX a
Meals 105 and a la carte 48/138 – **56 rm** ⌷ 330/610.

Dolder Waldhaus ⑤, Kurhausstr. 20, ✉ 8032, ℰ (01) 269 10 00, Fax (01) 269 10 01, ≤ Zürich and lake, 🌳, ᵢ₉, ⌷s, ⌇, ✗ – ⧮, 🖩 rest, 📺 ☎ ✆ 🚗 Ⓟ – 🏊 35. AE ① E VISA JCB
by Gloriastrasse BU r
Meals 49 and a la carte 41/94 – ⌷ 16 – **71 rm** 220/430.

Sofitel, Stampfenbachstr. 60, ✉ 8035, ℰ (01) 360 60 60, Fax (01) 360 60 61 – ⧮, ✗ rm, 🖩 📺 ☎ ✆ 🚗 – 🏊 15/30. AE ① E VISA JCB. ✗ rest
FY b
Diff (closed Saturday lunch and Sunday lunch) Meals 58 (lunch)/87 and a la carte 58/133 – ⌷ 29 – **168 rm** 320/400.

Central Plaza M, Central 1, ✉ 8001, ℰ (01) 251 55 55, Fax (01) 251 85 35 – ⧮, ✗ rm, 🖩 rm, 📺 video ☎ ✆ – 🏊 35. AE ① E VISA JCB
FY z
Cascade : Meals a la carte 46/86 – ⌷ 24 – **94 rm** 320/380, 6 suites.

Florhof ⑤, Florhofgasse 4, ✉ 8001, ℰ (01) 261 44 70, Fax (01) 261 46 11, 🌳, « Tasteful installation » – ⧮, ✗ rm, 📺 ☎. AE ① E VISA JCB
FZ k
Meals (closed 24 December - 10 January, Saturday, Sunday and Bank Holidays) 75 (lunch) and a la carte 59/99 – **33 rm** ⌷ 225/340.

Europe, Dufourstr. 4, ✉ 8008, ℰ (01) 261 10 30, Fax (01) 251 03 67, 🌳 – ⧮, 🖩 rm, 📺 ☎ ✆. AE ① E VISA
FZ u
Quaglinos : Meals a la carte 44/88 – ⌷ 17 – **40 rm** 180/280.

Opera without rest, Dufourstr. 5, ✉ 8008, ℰ (01) 251 90 90, Fax (01) 251 90 01 – ⧮ 🖩 📺 video ☎ ✆. AE ① E VISA JCB
FZ b
closed 22 December - 4 January – **66 rm** ⌷ 220/360.

Ambassador, Falkenstr. 6, ✉ 8008, ℰ (01) 261 76 00, Fax (01) 251 23 94 – ⧮, ✗ rm, 🖩 rm, 📺 video ☎ ✆. AE ① E VISA JCB
FZ a
Meals a la carte 44/107 – **46 rm** ⌷ 210/360.

Krone Unterstrass, Schaffhauserstr. 1, ✉ 8006, ℰ (01) 360 56 56, Fax (01) 360 56 00 – ⧮, 🖩 rm, 📺 ☎ ✆ Ⓟ – 🏊 15/90. AE ① E VISA
CV b
Grill : Meals a la carte 41/77 – *Wirtschaft* : Meals a la carte 35/71 – **57 rm** ⌷ 158/225.

ZÜRICH

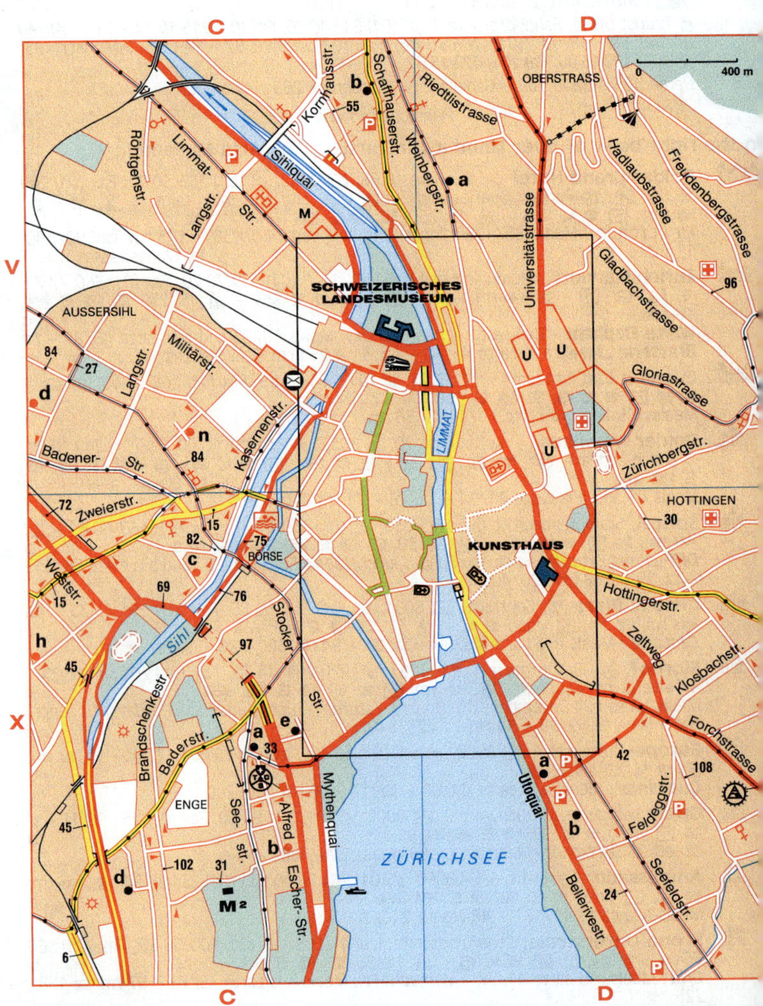

ZÜRICH
SWITZERLAND
E
F
Y
Z
36
c
88
52
d
Sihlquai
Limmatstr.
81
21
Neumühlequai
Weinberg-
Sonneggstrasse
b
LIMMAT
Sihl
f
40
k
79
19
Universitätstrasse
U
U
Zollstr.
r
c
strasse
SCHWEIZERISCHES
LANDESMUSEUM
103
Leonhard-
49
Walche-
brücke
Museumstr.
P
19
U
HAUPTBAHNHOF
81
91
Bahnhof-
pl.
P
EIDG.
TECHN.
HOCHSCHULE
str.
e
Bahnhof-
brücke
z
K.Schmidstr.
Gessnerallee
a
Waisenhaus-
Bahnhofquai
a
Hirschen-
Seiler-
Künstler-
U
Gloria-
str.
Gessner-
br.
strasse
strasse
quai
Niederdorf-
Rämistr.
Löwenpl.
100
Werdmühlestr.
POL.
Rudolf Brun-
Brücke
Mühleg.
str.
PREDIGER-KIRCHE
graben
gasse
Urania-
str.
d
Oetenbachg.
63
Limmat-
w
s
Hirschen-
Platz
54
k
Sihl-
St. Annag.
b
Lindenhof
r
64
n
39
Nüschelerstr.
Pelikanstr.
9
v
z
87
G
46
J
P
Rämistr.
Weinpl.
60
H
Münsterg.
Bahnhof-
u
z
Heimpl.
85
c
Zwinglipl.
Kirchg.
Tal-
90
x
M
Zwinglipl.
KUNSTHAUS
T
48
Münsterbr.
M
GROSSMÜNSTER
Hottinger-
str.
ohnmuseum
10
strasse
r
58
Fraumünster
Wasserkirche
v
Oberdorfstr.
Heimpl.
Paradeplatz
Bleicherweg
Tal-
28
Stadthausquai
Limmat-
graben
Rämistr.
Zeltweg
Z
strasse
STADTHAUS
ANLAGE
12
f
t
78
Stocker-
Dreikönigstr.
18
a
Bellevuepl.
e
STADELHOFEN
Bürklipl.
93
Kreuzbühlstr.
Gotthardstr.
str
KONGRESSGEB.
Quaibrücke
Sechseläuten-
platz
Utoquai
Stadelhoferpl.
m
d
Quai
Guisan-
ZÜRICHSEE
T
Falkenstr.
Seefeldstr.
G.
a
y
b
0
200 m
u
E
F

589

Adler M, Rosengasse 10, at Hirschplatz, ℘ (01) 266 96 96, *Fax (01) 266 96 69*, *Mural of Zürich by Heinz Blum, in the rooms* – |阁|, ⇥ rm, TV ☎ ✆. AE ① E
VISA JCB
Meals a la carte 35/91 – **52 rm** ☑ 130/200.

Wellenberg M without rest, Niederdorfstr. 10, ⊠ 8001, ℘ (01) 262 43 00, *Fax (01) 251 31 30* – |阁| ⇥ TV ☎ ✆. AE ① E *VISA*
45 rm ☑ 250/340.

Helmhaus without rest, Schifflände 30, ⊠ 8001, ℘ (01) 251 88 10, *Fax (01) 251 04 3* – |阁| ⇥ ▤ TV ☎ ✆. AE ① E *VISA* JCB
25 rm ☑ 220/330.

Rütli without rest, Zähringerstr. 43, ⊠ 8001, ℘ (01) 251 54 26, *Fax (01) 261 21 53* |阁| TV ☎. AE ① E *VISA*
62 rm ☑ 180/260.

Seegarten, Seegartenstr. 14, ⊠ 8008, ℘ (01) 388 37 37, *Fax (01) 383 37 38*, ☂ |阁| TV video ☎ ✆. AE ① E *VISA*
Latino - Italian rest. - (*closed Saturday lunch and Sunday lunch*) **Meals** a la carte 40/7 – **28 rm** ☑ 168/288.

Rex M, Weinbergstr. 92, ⊠ 8006, ℘ (01) 360 25 25, *Fax (01) 360 25 52*, ☂ – |阁| ⇥ rm, TV ☎ ℗. AE ① E *VISA* JCB
Blauer Apfel (*closed Saturday lunch and Sunday*) **Meals** a la carte 35/83 – **37 rm** ☑ 140/190.

XX **Kronenhalle**, Rämistr. 4, ⊠ 8001, ℘ (01) 251 02 56, *Fax (01) 251 66 81*, « *Collectio of exceptional works of art* » – ▤. AE ① E *VISA*
Meals a la carte 59/140.

XX **Jacky's Stapferstube**, Culmannstr. 45, ⊠ 8006, ℘ (01) 361 37 48, *Fax (01) 36 00 60*, ☂, « *Rustic decor* » – ℗. AE ① E *VISA*
closed mid July - mid August, Sunday and Monday – **Meals** - veal and beef specialities (booking essential) a la carte 72/146.

XX **Königstuhl**, Stüssihofstatt 3, ⊠ 8001, ℘ (01) 261 76 18, *Fax (01) 262 71 23*, ☂ AE ① E *VISA*
Meals (1st floor) (*closed 12 July - 15 August, Sunday and Monday*) 39 (lunch)/95 and la carte 59/121.

XX **Wirtschaft Flühgass**, Zollikerstr. 214, ⊠ 8008, ℘ (01) 381 12 15, *Fax (01) 42 75 32*, « *16C inn* » – ℗. AE E *VISA*   by Zollikerstrasse **BU**
closed 10 July - 8 August, 23 December - 3 January, Saturday except dinner from Nover ber - December and Sunday – **Meals** (booking essential) 52 (lunch)/115 and a la car 54/109.

XX **Haus zum Rüden**, Limmatquai 42 (1st floor), ⊠ 8001, ℘ (01) 261 95 66, *Fax (01) 26 18 04*, « *13C guild house* » – |阁| ▤. AE ① E *VISA* JCB
closed Saturday and Sunday – **Meals** 52 (lunch)/93 and a la carte 68/112.

XX **Zunfthaus zur Zimmerleuten**, Limmatquai 40 (1st floor), ⊠ 8001, ℘ (01) 2 08 34, *Fax (01) 252 08 48*, « *18C guild house* » – AE ① E *VISA*
closed 18 July - 15 August, Sunday and Bank Holidays – **Meals** a la carte 43/102.

XX **Conti-da Bianca**, Dufourstr. 1, ⊠ 8008, ℘ (01) 251 06 66, *Fax (01) 251 06 86* – ① E *VISA*
closed mid July - mid August, Saturday lunch and Sunday – **Meals** - Italian rest. - 52/ and a la carte 51/105.

XX **Riesbächli**, Zollikerstr. 157, ⊠ 8008, ℘ (01) 422 23 24, *Fax (01) 422 29 41* – AE E *VISA*   by Zollikerstrasse **BU**
closed 24 July - 15 August, 24 December - 5 January, Saturday except dinner from Nove ber - March and Sunday – **Meals** 55 (lunch)/135 and a la carte 58/136.

XX **Casa Ferlin**, Stampfenbachstr. 38, ⊠ 8006, ℘ (01) 362 35 09, *Fax (01) 362 35 34* – ▤. AE ① E *VISA*
closed mid July - mid August, Saturday and Sunday – **Meals** - Italian rest. - (booking esse tial) 48 (lunch) and a la carte 61/128.

X **Oepfelchammer**, Rindermarkt 12, ⊠ 8001, ℘ (01) 251 23 36, *Fax (01) 262 75 3* ☂, « *14C inn with original wine tavern* » – AE ① E *VISA*
closed 19 July - 11 August and 22 to 31 December – **Meals** 98 and a la carte 49/9

X **Blaue Ente**, Seefeldstr. 223 (Mühle Tiefenbrunnen), ⊠ 8008, ℘ (01) 388 68 4 *Fax (01) 422 77 41*, ☂ – AE ① E *VISA*   by Zollikerstrasse **BU**
closed 19 July - 11 August and 24 December - 5 January – **Meals** a la carte 56/92.

X **Rosaly's**, Freieckgasse 7, ℘ (01) 261 44 30, *Fax (01) 261 44 13* – AE E *VISA*
closed Saturday lunch and Sunday lunch – **Meals** a la carte 32/75.

On the left bank of the river Limmat *(Main railway station, Business centre)* :

Baur au Lac, Talstr. 1, ⊠ 8022, ℰ (01) 220 50 20, *Fax (01) 220 50 45*, 🌿, « Lakeside setting and garden », 🦢 – 🛗 ▤ TV ☎ 📞 ♿ 🚗 – 🔥 15/60. AE ⓓ E *VISA* JCB. 🦃 *Pavillon* : Meals 74/92 and a la carte 74/142 – *rive gauche* *(closed Sunday)* Meals a la carte 57/116 – 🍵 28 – **107 rm** 430/720, 18 suites.　　　　　　　　　EZ **a**

Widder Ⓜ, Rennweg 7, ⊠ 8001, ℰ (01) 224 25 26, *Fax (01) 224 24 24*, « Restored old town houses with contemporary interiors » – 🛗 ▤ TV ☎ 📞 ♿ 🚗 – 🔥 15/170. AE ⓓ E *VISA* JCB. 🦃 rest
Meals 58 (lunch)/85 and a la carte 59/115 – **42 rm** 🍵 370/640, 7 suites.　　EZ **v**

Savoy Baur en Ville Ⓜ, am Paradeplatz, ⊠ 8022, ℰ (01) 215 25 25, *Fax (01) 215 25 00*, « Elegant modern decor » – 🛗 ▤ TV ☎ 📞 ♿ – 🔥 15/70. AE ⓓ E *VISA* JCB. 🦃　EZ **r**
Savoy (1st floor) Meals 64 (lunch) and a la carte 70/120 – *Orsini* (am Münsterhof) - Italian rest. - *(booking essential)* Meals 62 (lunch)/95 and a la carte 78/137 – **104 rm** 🍵 430/650, 8 suites.

Schweizerhof, Bahnhofplatz 7, ⊠ 8001, ℰ (01) 218 88 88, *Fax (01) 218 81 81* – 🛗, 🍴 rm, ▤ rm, TV ☎ 📞 – 🔥 40. AE ⓓ E *VISA* JCB. 🦃 rest　　　　　EY **a**
La Soupière (1st floor) *(closed 25 July - 9 August, Saturday lunch and Sunday)* Meals 65/92 and a la carte 75/121 – **115 rm** 🍵 350/550.

Ascot Ⓜ, Tessinerplatz 9, ⊠ 8002, ℰ (01) 208 14 14, *Fax (01) 208 14 20*, 🌿 – 🛗, 🍴 rm, TV ☎ 📞 🚗 – 🔥 15/50. AE ⓓ E *VISA* JCB　　　　　　　　CX **a**
Lawrence : Meals 48 (lunch) and a la carte 53/101 – *Fujiya of Japan* ℰ (01) 208 15 55 *(closed Sunday and Monday)* Meals 48 (lunch)/85 and a la carte 55/91 – **73 rm** 🍵 320/450.

Neues Schloss Ⓜ, Stockerstr. 17, ⊠ 8022, ℰ (01) 286 94 00, *Fax (01) 286 94 45*, 🌿 – 🛗, 🍴 rm, ▤ TV video ☎ 📞 – 🔥 25. AE ⓓ E *VISA* JCB. 🦃 rest　　　EZ **m**
Le Jardin *(closed Saturday lunch)* *(Sunday and Bank Holidays dinner only for residents)* Meals 48 (lunch)/95 and a la carte 59/111 – **58 rm** 🍵 265/420.

Splügenschloss, Splügenstr. 2 / Genferstrasse, ⊠ 8002, ℰ (01) 289 99 99, *Fax (01) 289 99 98* – 🛗, 🍴 rm, ▤ rm, TV ☎ 📞 Ⓟ – 🔥 20. AE ⓓ E *VISA* JCB　　CX **e**
Meals 59/95 and a la carte 67/135 – **52 rm** 🍵 260/560.

Atlantis Sheraton, Döltschiweg 234, ℰ (01) 454 54 54, *Fax (01) 454 54 00*, ≤, 🌿, Park, 🏋, ♨ – 🛗, 🍴 rm, TV ☎ 📞 Ⓟ – 🔥 300. AE ⓓ E *VISA* JCB　　　AU **z**
Quatre Saisons *(closed 11 July - 2 August, Saturday dinner and Sunday dinner)* Meals 59 and a la carte 59/105 – *Döltschistube* : Meals 38 and a la carte 38/90, children 14 – 🍵 29 – **161 rm** 430/475.

Inter-Continental Zürich Ⓜ, Badenerstr. 420, ⊠ 8040, ℰ (01) 404 44 44, *Fax (01) 404 44 40*, 🏋, ♨, 🏊 – 🛗, 🍴 rm, ▤ TV ☎ 📞 ♿ 🚗 – 🔥 15/500. AE ⓓ
E *VISA* JCB. 🦃 rest　　　　　　　　　　　　　　　　　　AT **c**
Meals 42 and a la carte 43/97 – 🍵 26 – **364 rm** 270/430.

Zum Storchen, Weinplatz 2, ⊠ 8001, ℰ (01) 227 27 27, *Fax (01) 227 27 00*, ≤ River Limmat and City, 🌿, « Riverside setting » – 🛗 TV ☎ 📞 – 🔥 25. AE ⓓ E *VISA* JCB. 🦃 rest
Rôtisserie : Meals 55 (lunch)/88 and a la carte 62/103 – **73 rm** 🍵 305/550.　EZ **u**

Stoller Ⓜ, Badenerstr. 357, ⊠ 8040, ℰ (01) 405 47 47, *Fax (01) 405 48 48*, 🌿 – 🛗
🍴 TV ☎ 📞 Ⓟ – 🔥 25. AE ⓓ E *VISA* JCB　　　　by Badenerstrasse AU **x**
Meals a la carte 37/84 – **79 rm** 🍵 260/380.

Glärnischhof Ⓜ, Claridenstr. 30, ⊠ 8022, ℰ (01) 286 22 22, *Fax (01) 286 22 86* – 🛗,
🍴 rm, ▤ rm, TV ☎ 📞 – 🔥 25. AE ⓓ E *VISA* JCB　　　　　　　EZ **f**
Le Poisson *(closed Saturday and Sunday)* Meals 53 (lunch)/95 and a la carte 61/107 – *Vivace* : Meals a la carte 40/72 – **62 rm** 🍵 250/450.

Glockenhof, Sihlstr. 31, ⊠ 8023, ℰ (01) 211 56 50, *Fax (01) 211 56 60*, 🌿 – 🛗,
🍴 rm, ▤ rest, TV ☎ 📞. AE ⓓ E *VISA*　　　　　　　　　　EZ **b**
Meals a la carte 38/90 – **106 rm** 🍵 230/380.

Engimatt, Engimattstr. 14, ⊠ 8002, ℰ (01) 284 16 16, *Fax (01) 201 25 16*, 🌿, 🍴
– 🛗 TV ☎ 📞 🚗 – 🔥 15. AE ⓓ E *VISA* JCB　　　　　　　　CX **d**
Meals a la carte 35/90, children 15 – **80 rm** 🍵 190/300.

Walhalla Ⓜ, Limmatstr. 5, ⊠ 8005, ℰ (01) 446 54 00, *Fax (01) 446 54 54*, 🌿 – 🛗,
🍴 rm, TV ☎ 📞 🚗 – 🔥 15. AE ⓓ E *VISA* JCB　　　　　　　EY **r**
Meals a la carte 38/71 – 🍵 13 – **48 rm** 130/180.

Kindli Ⓜ, Pfalzgasse 1, ⊠ 8001, ℰ (01) 211 59 17, *Fax (01) 211 65 28*, 🌿, « English country house style installation » – 🛗 TV ☎. AE ⓓ E *VISA*　　　　EZ **z**
Opus ℰ (01) 211 41 82 *(closed Bank Holidays)* Meals 39 (lunch)/48 and a la carte 43/90 – **21 rm** 🍵 190/290.

Montana, Konradstr. 39, ⊠ 8005, ℰ (01) 271 69 00, *Fax (01) 272 30 70*, 🌿 – 🛗 TV
☎ 📞 ♿. AE ⓓ E *VISA* JCB　　　　　　　　　　　　EY **f**
Bistro le Lyonnais *(closed Christmas, Saturday lunch and Sunday)* Meals 40 and a la carte 41/83 – **74 rm** 🍵 170/290.

SWITZERLAND

XXX ⊕ **Sukhothai** (Wanphen Heymann-Sukphan), Erlachstr. 46, ⊠ 8003, ℰ (01) 462 66 22, Fax (01) 462 66 54 – 🗏. 🗛 ⓪ E. ⬧ CX
closed Easter, 11 July - 10 August, Sunday, Monday and Bank Holidays – **Meals** - Thai rest. - (booking essential) 90/145 and a la carte 86/142
Spec. Bärenkrebse und Königskrabben gebraten, drei Saucen. Junge Kokosnuss gefül mit Perlhuhnbrust an roter Currypaste. Rindsfiletstreifen gebraten mi Krachaiwurzeln.

XX **Accademia Piccoli,** Rotwandstr. 48, ⊠ 8004, ℰ (01) 241 62 43 – 🗏. 🗛 ⓪ E VISA ⬧ CV
closed Saturday and Sunday – **Meals** - Italian rest. - a la carte 60/115.

XX **Zunfthaus zur Waag,** Münsterhof 8, ⊠ 8001, ℰ (01) 211 07 30, Fax (01) 212 01 69 Linen weaver's and hatter's guildhall – 🗛 ⓪ E VISA JCB EZ
Meals a la carte 61/108.

XX **Intermezzo** - Kongresshaus Zürich, General Guisan-Quai, ⊠ 8022, ℰ (01) 206 36 36 Fax (01) 206 36 59 – 🗏. 🗛 ⓪ E VISA EZ
closed mid July - mid August, Saturday and Sunday – **Meals** 48 and a la carte 56, 90.

XX **Sala of Tokyo,** Limmatstr. 29, ⊠ 8005, ℰ (01) 271 52 90, Fax (01) 271 78 07, 🌫 – 🗛 ⓪ E VISA JCB EY
closed 24 July - 9 August, 20 December - 4 January, Sunday and Monday – **Meals** - Japanes rest. - 110 and a la carte 47/98.

XX **da Bernasconi,** Lavaterstr. 87, ⊠ 8002, ℰ (01) 201 16 13, Fax (01) 201 16 49, 🌫 – 🗛 ⓪ E VISA CX
Meals - Italian rest. - a la carte 50/94.

XX **Il Giglio,** Weberstr. 14, ⊠ 8004, ℰ (01) 242 85 97, Fax (01) 291 01 83 – 🗛 ◁ E VISA CX
closed mid July - mid August, 2 to 10 January, Saturday lunch and Sunday – **Meals** - Italia rest. - 40 (lunch)/95 and a la carte 44/105.

X **Brasserie Lipp,** Uraniastr. 9, ⊠ 8001, ℰ (01) 211 11 55, Fax (01) 212 17 26, 🌫 – 🗏 🗛 ⓪ E VISA EY
closed Sunday in July – August – **Meals** a la carte 35/104.

X **Caduff's Wine Loft,** Kanzleistr. 126, ℰ (01) 240 22 55, Fax (01) 240 22 56 – 🗛 ⓪ E VISA CV
closed Saturday lunch and Sunday lunch – **Meals** (booking essential) a la carte 38, 84.

at Zürich-Oerlikon : N : by Universitätstrasse DV : 5 km – alt. 442 – ⊠ 8050 Zürich-Oerlikon

🏨 **Swissôtel Zürich** M, Am Marktplatz, ℰ (01) 311 43 41, Fax (01) 312 44 68, ≤, 🌫 🖅, 🏊 – 🛗, 🗏 rm, 📺 video ☎ 📞 👌 🚗 – 🔬 15/400. 🗛 ⓪ E VISA ⬧ rm BT
Szenario : **Meals** a la carte 41/96 – 🍵 23 – **336 rm** 280/380, 11 suites.

at Zürich-Seebach : N : by Schaffenhauserstrasse CV – alt. 442 – ⊠ 8052 Zürich-Seebach

🏠 **Landhus,** Katzenbachstr. 10, ℰ (01) 308 34 00, Fax (01) 308 34 51, 🍴 – 🛗 📺 ☎ 📞 – 🔬 15/300. 🗛 ⓪ E VISA. ⬧ rm BT
Meals 22 (lunch) and a la carte 42/72 – **28 rm** 🍵 115/145.

at Glattbrugg : N : by Universitätstrasse DV : 8 km – alt. 432 – ⊠ 8152 Glattbrugg :

🏨 **Renaissance Zürich** M, Talackerstr. 1, ℰ (01) 810 85 00, Fax (01) 810 87 55, 🖅, ≦s 🏊 – 🛗, 🌫 rm, 🗏 📺 ☎ 📞 🚗 – 🔬 15/300. 🗛 ⓪ E VISA JCB
Asian Place - Asian rest. - (closed Saturday lunch and Sunday lunch) **Meals** 25 (lunch) an a la carte 43/151 – **Brasserie La Noblesse** (closed Saturday and Sunday) (lunch only) **Meals** 43 and a la carte 39/88 – 🍵 28 – **198 rm** 310/350, 6 suites.

🏨 **Hilton,** Hohenbühlstr. 10, ℰ (01) 828 50 50, Fax (01) 828 51 51, 🌫, ≦s – 🛗, 🌫 rm 🗏 📺 ☎ 📞 🅿 – 🔬 15/280. 🗛 ⓪ E VISA JCB
Harvest Grill (closed July - August, Saturday lunch and Sunday lunch) **Meals** 3 (lunch)/68 and a la carte 53/124 – **Taverne** (closed 20 December - 10 January Sunday except dinner from May - September and Saturday lunch) **Meals** a la carte 41/7 – **Market Place** : **Meals** 39 and a la carte 43/92 – 🍵 31 – **270 rm** 275/385 11 suites.

🏨 **Mövenpick** M, Walter Mittelholzerstr. 8, ℰ (01) 808 88 88, Fax (01) 808 88 77 – 🛗 🌫 rm, 🗏 📺 ☎ 📞 👌 🅿 – 🔬 15/220. 🗛 ⓪ E VISA JCB
Appenzeller Stube (closed mid July - mid August and Saturday lunch) **Meals** 40 (lunch)/7 and a la carte 48/102 – **Mövenpick Rest.** : **Meals** a la carte 30/76 – **Dim Sum** - Chines rest. - (closed 3 weeks in July, Saturday lunch and Sunday lunch) **Meals** 58 and a la cart 39/92 – 🍵 23 – **335 rm** 265/370.

🏨 **Novotel Zürich Airport,** Talackerstr. 21, 🖊 (01) 829 90 00, Fax (01) 829 99 99, 🌿 – 📶, ⟷ rm, 🔲 📺 ☎ 🔾 🔾 ⟷ 🅿 – 🔾 15/150. AE ⓪ E VISA JCB. 🕸 rest
Meals a la carte 38/76, children 15 – ☕ 21 – **256 rm** 195/219.

🏨 **Airport,** Oberhauserstr. 30, 🖊 (01) 809 47 47, Fax (01) 809 47 74 – 📶, ⟷ rm, 📺 ☎ 🔾 🅿. AE ⓪ E VISA JCB. 🕸 rest
Edo Garden : Meals 67/75 and a la carte 50/89 – **Fujiya of Japan** (closed Saturday lunch and Sunday lunch) Meals 48 (lunch)/97 and a la carte 60/99 – **44 rm** ☕ 160/235.

🍴 **Bruno's Rest.,** Europastr. 2, 🖊 (01) 811 03 01, Fax (01) 811 03 21, 🌿, Elegant modern decor – 🔲 🅿. AE E VISA. 🕸
closed end of July - 7 August, 22 December - 4 January and Sunday – **Meals** 59 (lunch)/98 and a la carte 53/110, children 20.

at Nürensdorf : *NE by Universitätstrasse and road to Bassersdorf : 19 km – alt. 505 – ✉ 8309 Nürensdorf :*

🍴 **Zum Bären** with rm, Alte Winterthurerstr. 45, 🖊 (01) 838 36 36, Fax (01) 838 36 46, 🌿 – 📺 ☎ ⟷ 🅿. AE ⓪ E VISA. 🕸 rest
closed 17 July - 3 August, 24 December - 5 January, Sunday and Monday (except hotel) – **Meals** 49 (lunch)/104 and a la carte 62/119 – **Beizli :** Meals a la carte 42/80 – **14 rm** ☕ 150/215
Spec. Gebratene Entenlebermedaillons mit Portweinrosinen und karamelisierten Apfelschnitzeln. Pyrenäen Milchlamm mit Bärlauch und Morchelragout (spring). Rehfilet im Zimtcrêpemantel an Portweinjus (autumn).

at Kloten : *N : by Universitätstrasse DV : 12 km – alt. 447 – ✉ 8302 Kloten :*

🏨 **Fly Away** M, Marktgasse 19, 🖊 (01) 813 66 13, Fax (01) 813 51 25, 🌿 – 📶, 🔲 rm, 📺 ☎ 🔾 ⟷ 🅿. AE ⓪ E VISA
Meals - Italian rest. - a la carte 37/69 – ☕ 14 – **42 rm** 150/188.

🍴 **Top-Air,** at the airport (Terminal A), 🖊 (01) 816 60 60, Fax (01) 816 41 91, ⟨ – 🔲. AE ⓪ E VISA
Meals 35 (lunch)/74 and a la carte 50/107, children 17.

at Küsnacht : *SE : by Bellerivestrasse DX : 8 km – alt. 415 – ✉ 8700 Küsnacht :*

🍴 **Ermitage am See** M with rm, Seestr. 80, 🖊 (01) 910 52 22, Fax (01) 910 52 44, ⟨ Zurich lake, 🌿, « Lakeside setting, terrace and garden », 🚤, ⚓ – 📶 📺 ☎ 🔾 🅿. AE ⓪ E VISA. 🕸 rest
Meals 62 (lunch)/150 and a la carte 80/136 – ☕ 17 – **22 rm** 160/340, 4 suites
Spec. Pavé de loup à la niçoise, courgettes et leurs fleurs en beignets. Carré d'agneau de Sisteron rôti aux aubergines et tomates (June - December). Dentelle au thym et romarin, sauté d'abricots aux amandes (June - September).

🍴 **Petermann's Kunststuben,** Seestr. 160, 🖊 (01) 910 07 15, Fax (01) 910 04 95, 🌿 – 🔲 🅿. AE ⓪ E VISA
closed 24 August - 12 September, 10 to 24 February, Sunday and Monday – **Meals** (dinner : booking essential) 78 (lunch)/185 and a la carte 113/192
Spec. Noix de St-Jacques grillées, jus de persil et oursins (winter). Gaspacho d'écrevisses au confit de fenouil (summer). Cœur de perdreau et sa jambonnette sur chou aux raisins secs et jambon de Parme (autumn).

at Uetikon am See : *SE by Bellerivestrasse : 18 km – alt. 414 – ✉ 8707 Uetikon am See :*

🍴 **Wirtschaft zum Wiesengrund** (Hussong), Kleindorfstr. 61, 🖊 (01) 920 63 60, Fax (01) 921 17 09, 🌿 – 🅿. AE ⓪ E VISA. 🕸
closed 1st to 23 August, 1st to 16 February, Sunday and Monday – **Meals** (booking essential) 55 (lunch)/135 and a la carte 91/140
Spec. Langustinen in Olivenöl gebraten auf Auberginenkaviar. Millefeuille von roh mariniertem Blue-Marlin an Olivenöl-Zitronensauce. Ganze Ente gefüllt mit Zitronen an Sesamsauce.

at Unterengstringen : *NW : by Sihlquai CV : 10 km – alt. 405 – ✉ 8103 Unterengstringen :*

🍴 **Witschi's,** Zürcherstr. 55, 🖊 (01) 750 44 60, Fax (01) 750 19 68, 🌿, « Elegant modern installation » – ⟷ 🅿. AE ⓪ E VISA JCB
closed 27 July - 10 August, 20 December - 5 January, Sunday and Monday – **Meals** 69 (lunch)/195 and a la carte 111/155
Spec. Lasagnes de primeurs aux ris de veau et langoustines (spring). Bouchées de sandre à la mousseline de céleri et petits légumes à l'huile vierge (summer). Perdreau rôti au chou vert à l'ananas et jus de truffes (autumn).

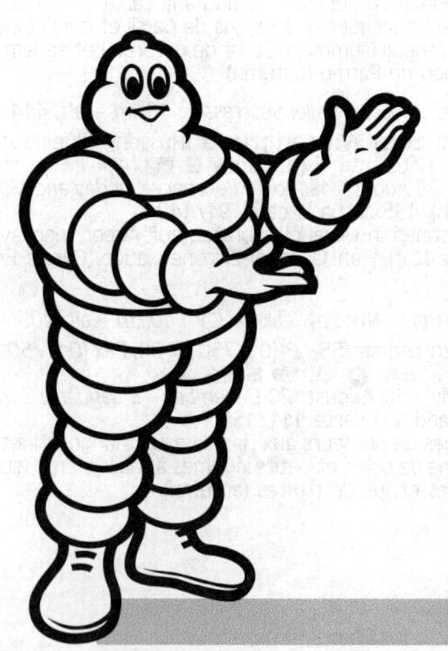

United Kingdom

**LONDON – BIRMINGHAM – EDINBURGH
GLASGOW – LEEDS – LIVERPOOL
MANCHESTER**

PRACTICAL INFORMATION

LOCAL CURRENCY

Pound Sterling: *1 GBP = 1,42 euro (€)*

TOURIST INFORMATION

Tourist information offices exist in each city included in the Guide. The telephone number and address is given in each text under **i**

FOREIGN EXCHANGE

Banks are usually open between 9.00am and 4.3pm on weekdays only and some open on Saturdays. Most large hotels have exchange facilities. Heathrow and Gatwick Airports have 24-hour banking facilities.

SHOPPING

In London: *Oxford St./Regent St. (department stores, exclusive shops) Bond St. (exclusive shops, antiques)*
Knightsbridge area (department stores, exclusive shops, boutiques)
For other towns see the index of street names; those printed in red are where the principal shops are found.

THEATRE BOOKINGS IN LONDON

Your hotel porter will be able to make your arrangements or direct you to Theatre Booking Agents.
In addition there is a kiosk in Leicester Square selling tickets for the same day's performances at half price plus a booking fee. It is open 12 noon-6.30pm.

CAR HIRE

The international car hire companies have branches in each major city. Your hotel porter should be able to give details and help you with your arrangements.

TIPPING

Many hotels and restaurants include a service charge but where this is not the case an amount equivalent to between 10 and 15 per cent of the bill is customary. Additionally doormen, baggage porters and cloakroom attendants are generally given a gratuity.
Taxi drivers are customarily tipped between 10 and 15 per cent of the amount shown on the meter in addition to the fare.

SPEED LIMITS

The maximum permitted speed on motorways and dual carriageways is 70 mph (113 km/h.) and 60 mph (97 km/h.) on other roads except where a lower speed limit is indicated.

SEAT BELTS

The wearing of seat belts in the United Kingdom is compulsory for drivers, front seat passengers and rear seat passengers where seat belts are fitted. It is illegal for front seat passengers to carry children on their lap.

ANIMALS

It is forbidden to bring domestic animals (dogs, cats...) into the United Kingdom.

LONDON

404 *folds* ㊷ *to* ㊹ *- pop. 6 679 699*

🛈 *British Travel Centre, 12 Regent St. Piccadilly Circus, SW1Y 4 PQ, ℰ (0171) 971 0026. Victoria Station Forecourt, SW1, ℰ (0171) 730 3488.*

🛪 *Heathrow, ℰ (0181) 759 4321 –* **Terminal** *: Airbus (A1) from Victoria, Airbus (A2) from Paddington – Underground (Piccadilly line) frequent service daily.*

🛪 *Gatwick, ℰ (01293) 535353, and ℰ (0181) 763 2020, by A 23 and M 23 –* **Terminal** *: Coach service from Victoria Coach Station (Flightline 777, hourly service) – Railink (Gatwick Express) from Victoria (24 h service).*

🛪 *London City Airport, ℰ (0171) 646 0000.*

🛪 *Stansted, at Bishop's Stortford, ℰ (01279) 680500, NE : 34 m. by M 11 and A 120.*
British Airways, Victoria Air Terminal *: 115 Buckingham Palace Rd., SW1, ℰ (0171) 707 4750, p. 16.*

SIGHTS

HISTORIC BUILDINGS AND MONUMENTS

Palace of Westminster★★★ *p. 10* LY – *Tower of London*★★★ *p. 11* PVX – *Banqueting House*★★ *p. 10* LX – *Buckingham Palace*★★ *p. 16* BVX – *Kensington Palace*★★ *p. 8* FX – *Lincoln's Inn*★★ *p. 17* EV – *Lloyds Building*★★ *p. 7* PV – *Royal Hospital Chelsea*★★ *p. 15* FU – *St. James's Palace*★★ *p. 13* EP – *Somerset House*★★ *p. 17* EXY – *South Bank Arts Centre*★★ *p. 10* MX – *Spencer House*★★ *p. 13* DP – *The Temple*★★ *p. 6* MV – *Tower Bridge*★★ *p. 11* PX – *London Bridge*★ *p. 11* PVX – *Albert Memorial*★ *p. 14* CQ – *Apsley House*★ *p. 12* BP – *George Inn*★, *Southwark p. 11* PX – *Guildhall*★ *p. 7* OU – *International Shakespeare Globe Centre*★ *p. 11* OX **T** – *Dr Johnson's House*★ *p. 6* NUV **A** – *Leighton House*★ *p. 8* EY – *The Monument*★ (❊★) *p. 7* PV **G** – *Royal Albert Hall*★ *p. 14* CQ – *Royal Opera Arcade*★ *p. 13* FGN – *Staple Inn*★ *p. 6* MU **Y** – *Theatre Royal*★ (Haymarket) *p. 13* GM – *Westminster Bridge*★ *p. 10* LY.

CHURCHES

The City Churches – *St. Paul's Cathedral*★★★ (Dome ≼★★★) *p. 7* NOV – *St. Bartholomew the Great*★★ *p. 7* OU **K** – *St. Mary-at-Hill*★★ *p. 7* PV **B** – *Temple Church*★★ *p. 6* MV – *All Hallows-by-the-Tower* (font cover★★, brasses★) *p. 7* PV **Y** – *St. Bride*★ (steeple★★) *p. 7* NV **J** – *St. Giles Cripplegate*★ *p. 7* OU **N** – *St. Helen Bishopsgate*★ (monuments★★) *p. 7* PUV **R** – *St. James Garlickhythe* (tower and spire★, sword rests★) *p. 7* OV **R** – *St. Margaret Lothbury*★ *p. 7* PU **S** – *St. Margaret Pattens* (spire★, woodwork★) *p. 7* PV **N** – *St. Mary Abchurch*★ *p. 7* PV **X** – *St. Mary-le-Bow* (tower and steeple★★) *p. 7* OV **G** – *St. Michael Paternoster Royal* (tower and spire★) *p. 7* OV **D** – *St. Olave*★ *p. 7* PV **S**.

Other Churches – *Westminster Abbey*★★★ *p. 10* LY – *Southwark Cathedral*★★ *p. 11* PX – *Queen's Chapel*★ *p. 13* EP – *St. Clement Danes*★ *p. 17* EX – *St. James's*★ *p. 13* EM – *St. Margaret's*★ *p. 10* LY **A** – *St. Martin in-the-Fields*★ *p. 17* DY – *St. Paul's*★ (Covent Garden) *p. 17* DX – *Westminster Roman Catholic Cathedral*★ *p. 10* KY **B**.

STREETS – SQUARES – PARKS

The City★★★ *p. 7* NV – *Regent's Park*★★★ (Terraces★★, Zoo★★) *p. 5* HIST – *Belgrave Square*★★ *p. 16* AVX – *Burlington Arcade*★★ *p. 13* DM – *Covent Garden*★★ (The Piazza★★) *p. 17* DX – *Hyde Park*★★ *pp. 8 and 9* GHVX – *The Mall*★★ *p. 13* FP – *St. James's Park*★★ *p. 10* KXY – *Trafalgar Square*★★ *p. 17* DY – *Whitehall*★★ (Horse Guards★) *p. 10* LX – *Barbican*★ *p. 7* OU – *Bloomsbury*★ *p. 6* LMU – *Bond Street*★ *pp. 12-13* CK-DM – *Cheyne Walk*★ *p. 9* GHZ – *Jermyn Street*★ *p. 13* EN – *Leicester Square*★ *p. 13* GM – *Neal's Yard*★ *p. 17* DV – *Piccadilly Arcade*★ *p. 13* DEN – *Piccadilly Circus*★ *p. 13* FM – *Queen Anne's Gate*★ *p. 10* KY – *Regent Street*★ *p. 13* EM – *St. James's Square*★ *p. 13* FN – *St. James's Street*★ *p. 13* EN – *Shepherd Market*★ *p. 12* CN – *Soho*★ *p. 13* – *Strand*★ *p. 17* DY – *Victoria Embankment gardens*★ *p. 17* DEXY – *Waterloo Place*★ *p. 13* FN.

MUSEUMS

British Museum★★★ *p. 6* LU – *National Gallery*★★★ *p. 13* GM – *Science Museum*★★★ *p. 14* CR – *Tate Gallery*★★★ *p. 10* LZ – *Victoria and Albert Museum*★★★ *p. 15* DR – *Wallace Collection*★★★ *p. 12* AH – *Courtauld Institute of Art*★★ (Somerset House) *p. 17* EXY – *Museum of London*★★ *p. 7* OU **M** – *National Portrait Gallery*★★ *p. 13* GM – *Natural History Museum*★★ *p. 14* CS – *Sir John Soane's Museum*★★ *p. 6* MU **M** – *Imperial War Museum*★ *p. 10* NY – *London Transport Museum*★ *p. 17* DX – *Madame Tussaud's*★ *p. 5* IU **M** – *Planetarium*★ *p. 5* IU **M** – *Wellington Museum*★ (Apsley House) *p. 12* BP.

Alphabetical list of areas included

LONDON CENTRE

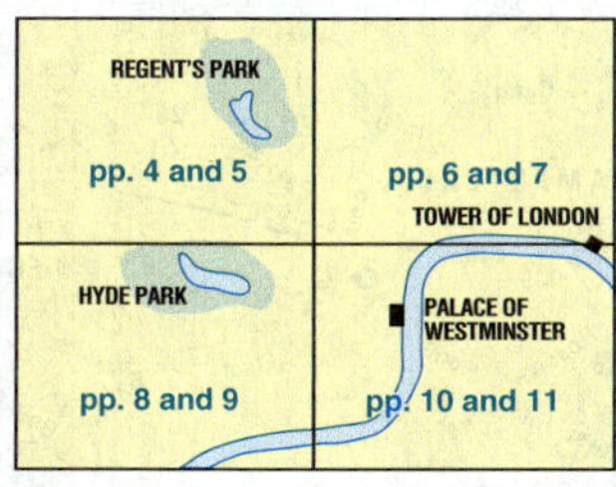

STREET INDEX TO LONDON CENTRE TOWN PLANS

Abingdon Rd — EY 2	Great Eastern St. — PT 192	Parry St. — LZ 341
Addison Crescent — EY 3	Great George St. — LY 193	Pembroke Gardens — EY 342
Allsop Pl. — HU 4	Great Smith St. — LY 196	Penn St. — PS 343
Appold St. — PU 5	Great Tower St. — PV 197	Penton Rise — MT 344
Atterbury St. — LZ 9	Greycoat Pl. — KY 200	Penton St. — MT 345
Bartholomew Rd — KS 16	Gunter Grove — FZ 202	Penywern Rd — FZ 347
Battersea Park Rd — JS 19	Gunterstone Rd — EZ 203	Philbeach Gardens — EZ 348
Beauchamp Place — ER	Hampstead Grove — ES 208	Piccadilly — EM
Belsize Crescent — ES 22	Hampstead High St. — ES 209	Pilgrimage St. — PY 349
Belvedere Rd — MX 23	Harleyford St. — MZ 211	Poole St. — PS 350
Bernard St. — LT 25	Herbrand St. — LT 218	Porchester Rd — FU 351
Bessborough St. — KZ 30	Hercules Rd — MY 219	Portobello Road — EV
Bethnal Green Rd — PT 32	Holland Park Gardens — EX 224	Poultry — OV 352
Bevis Marks — PU 34	Holland Walk — EY 225	Princes St. — PV 357
Bishopsgate — PU 36	Hollybush Hill — ES 227	Queen's Circus — IZ 361
Blackfriars Bridge — NV 38	Horseguards Av. — LX 228	Queen St. — OV 365
Bloomsbury St. — LU 39	Hornton St. — FY 229	Randolph St. — KS 366
Bowling Green Lane — NT 43	Howland St. — KU 232	Regent Street — EM
Bridgefoot — LZ 49	Hunter St. — LT 233	Rossmore Rd — HT 369
Broad Sanctuary — LY 52	Hyde Rd — PS 235	Royal Crescent — EX 371
Brompton Road — DS	Jermyn Street — EN	St. Andrew St. — NU 372
Burlington Arcade — DM	Keat's Grove — ES 236	St. Bride St. — NV 376
Byward St. — PV 62	Kensington High Street — EY	St. John's Wood High St. — GT 378
Calthorpe St. — MT 65	Kenway Rd — FZ 245	St. John's Wood Park — GS 379
Camden Passage — NS 70	King Edward St. — OU 247	St. Martin's-le-Grand — OU 380
Camomile St. — PU 71	King's Road — DU	Shoreditch High St. — PT 384
Carnaby Street — EK	King William St. — PV 250	Sidmouth St. — LT 385
Carriage Drive North — IZ 75	Knightsbridge — EQ	Sloane Street — FR
Charlbert St. — HT 79	Leadenhall St. — PV 260	Snows Fields — PX 386
Charterhouse Square — OU 81	Little Britain — OU 264	Southampton Row — LU 387
Charterhouse St. — NU 83	Lloyd Baker St. — MT 265	South Hill — ES 390
Churton St. — KZ 91	Lombard St. — PV 268	South Pl. — PU 391
Constantine Rd — ES 106	Long Lane CITY — OU 270	Southwark Bridge — OV 395
Cornwall Crescent — EV 107	Lothbury — PU 273	Spencer St. — NT 398
Cornwall Rd — MX 108	Lower Marsh — MY 277	Spital Square — PU 399
Corporation Row — NT 110	Lower Thames St. — PV 278	Storeys Gate — LY 402
Cowcross St. — NU 113	Mansell St. — PV 282	Tabard St. — OY 408
Crawford Pl. — HU 116	Middlesex Street — PU	Tavistock Square — LT 409
Cromwell Crescent — EZ 119	Miles St. — LZ 290	Templeton Pl. — EZ 410
Crucifix Lane — PX 125	Moreland St. — OT 293	Threadneedle St. — PV 417
Curtain Rd — PT 126	Myddelton St. — NT 296	Throgmorton St. — PU 418
Dante Rd — NZ 129	Nassington St. — ES 297	Tower Hill — PV 425
Downshire Hill — ES 139	Nevern Pl. — ES 298	Trebovir Rd — FZ 426
Dufferin St. — OT 141	Nevern Square — EZ 299	Upper Ground — NX 428
Duke's Pl. — PV 145	New Bond Street — CK	Upper Thames St. — OV 431
Durham St. — MZ 150	New Bridge St. — NV 301	Upper Woburn Pl. — LT 432
Eardley Crescent — EZ 151	New Change — OV 304	Vincent St. — LZ 436
Eastcheap — PV 154	New End Square — ES 305	Warwick Av. — FU 441
Ebury Bridge — IZ 156	Newington Butts — OZ 306	Westbourne Park Villas — FU 449
Edwardes Square — EY 158	Newington Causeway — OY 307	Westbourne Terrace Rd — FU 452
Elephant Rd — OZ 163	Northumberland Av. — LX 317	West Smithfield — NU 454
Fann St. — OU 166	Old Bailey — NV 318	Wharfdale Rd — LS 455
Farringdon St. — NU 168	Old Bond Street — DM	Whitechapel High St. — PU 456
Fetter Lane — NU 169	Old Broad St. — PU 319	Whitehall Court — LX 460
Frognal Rise — ES 171	Old Marylebone Rd — HU 324	Whitehall Pl. — LX 462
Garden Row — NY 173	Olympia Way — EY 326	Whitmore Rd — PS 464
Giltspur St. — OU 178	Ornan Rd — ES 331	Willoughby Rd — ES 470
Gliddon Rd — EZ 182	Oxford Street — BK	Wormwood St. — PU 472
Goodge St. — KU 184	Paddington St. — IU 333	
Gracechurch St. — PV 187	Park Crescent — IU 337	
	Parliament St. — LY 340	

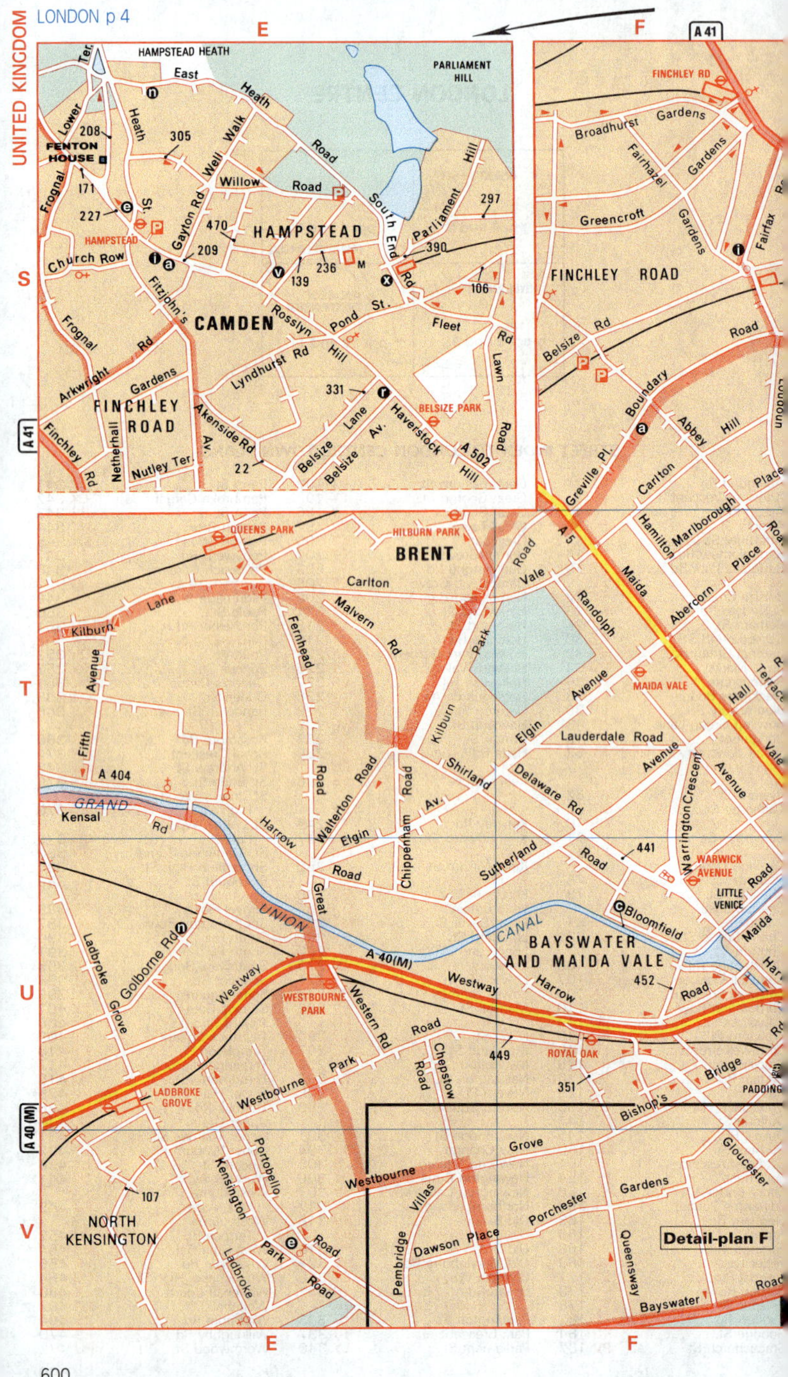
UNITED KINGDOM
A 41
E
F
A 41
HAMPSTEAD HEATH
East
Heath
PARLIAMENT HILL
FINCHLEY RD
Lower Ter.
Heath
Well Walk
Willow
Road
297
Broadhurst Gardens
Fairhazel Gardens
FENTON HOUSE
208
305
South End
Parliament Hill
Greencroft Gardens
Fairfax
171
Frognal
Willow Road
HAMPSTEAD
390
FINCHLEY ROAD
227
St.
470
209
HAMPSTEAD
236
M
139
106
Belsize Rd
Road
Boundary
London
Church Row
Fitzjohn's
Rosslyn Hill
Pond St.
Fleet Rd
Belsize Rd
Abbey
Hill
Place
CAMDEN
Lyndhurst Rd
Lawn Road
Greville Pl.
Carlton
FINCHLEY ROAD
Frognal
Arkwright
Gardens
Akenside Rd
331
Belsize Park
Hamilton
Marlborough
Road
Netherhall
Av.
Belsize Lane
Belsize Av.
Haverstock Hill
A 502
Abercorn
Place
Finchley Rd
Nutley Ter.
22
BELSIZE PARK
A 41
QUEENS PARK
HILBURN PARK
Road
Vale
A 5
Maida
BRENT
Carlton
Malvern Rd
Park
Randolph
Abercorn
Terrace
Lane
Fernhead
Kilburn
Avenue
MAIDA VALE
Hall
Vale
Kilburn
Avenue
Elgin
Lauderdale Road
Avenue
Avenue
Fifth
Road
Walterton Road
Shirland
Delaware Rd
A 404
Chippenham Road
Warrington Crescent
441
WARWICK AVENUE
GRAND
Harrow
Elgin
Av.
Sutherland
Road
LITTLE VENICE
Kensal
Rd
Road
Great
Bloomfield
Maida
UNION
A 40(M)
CANAL
BAYSWATER
AND MAIDA VALE
Ladbroke Grove
Golborne Rd
Westway
Westway
Harrow
452
Road
Hall
WESTBOURNE PARK
Western Rd
Road
449
ROYAL OAK
Bridge
Rd
A 40(M)
LADBROKE GROVE
Park
Chepstow Road
351
Bishop's
PADDING
Westbourne
Grove
Gloucester
107
Portobello
Kensington
Westbourne
Villas
Porchester
Gardens
NORTH KENSINGTON
Park
Road
Pembridge
Dawson Place
Queensway
Detail-plan F
Ladbroke
Road
Bayswater
Road
E
F

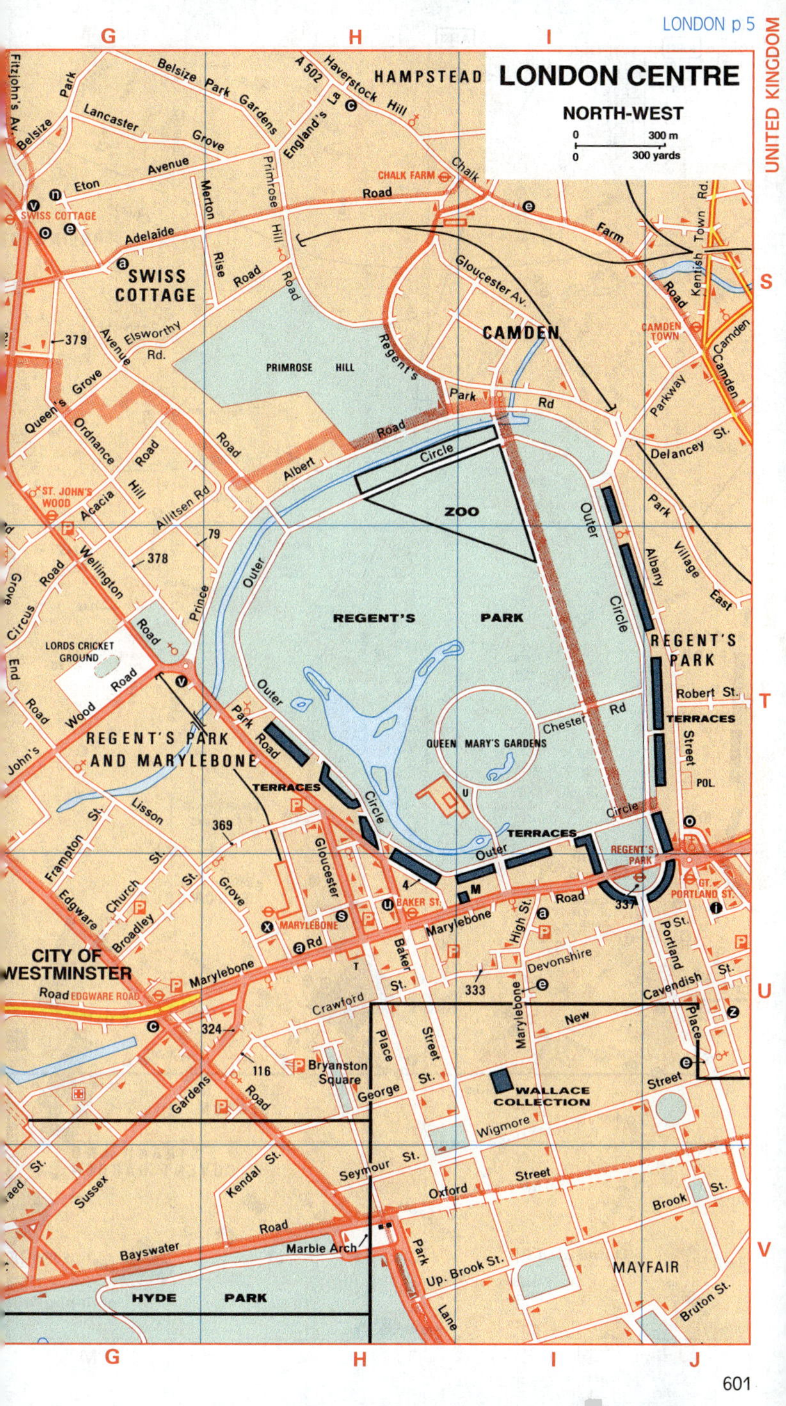

UNITED KINGDOM
LONDON CENTRE
NORTH-WEST
0   300 m
0   300 yards
G
H
I
HAMPSTEAD
Belsize Park Gardens
Belsize Park
Lancaster Grove
A 502
Haverstock Hill
England's La
Fitzjohn's Av.
Belsize Av.
Eton
Adelaide
Avenue
Merton Rise
Primrose Hill Road
CHALK FARM
Road
Chalk
Farm
Kentish Town Rd.
Camden
SWISS COTTAGE
SWISS COTTAGE
Elsworthy Rd.
Regent's
Park
Rd
CAMDEN
CAMDEN TOWN
Camden
379
Avenue
Queen's Grove
Ordnance Hill
Acacia Road
Allitsen Rd
Road
Road
Albert
Circle
PRIMROSE HILL
Road
Delancey
ST. JOHN'S WOOD
79
378
Prince
Outer
ZOO
Outer
Circle
Park
Village
East
Albany St.
REGENT'S PARK
Grove End Road
Wellington
Circus
Road
Wood
LORDS CRICKET GROUND
Park Road
REGENT'S PARK
Outer
REGENT'S PARK
REGENT'S PARK AND MARYLEBONE
Robert St.
TERRACES
Street
Lisson
John's
Frampton St.
Church St.
Broadley St.
Edgware
369
Grove
St.
Gloucester Place
TERRACES
Circle
REGENT'S PARK AND MARYLEBONE
QUEEN MARY'S GARDENS
Chester Rd
Outer
Circle
TERRACES
POL.
REGENT'S PARK
CITY OF WESTMINSTER
MARYLEBONE
BAKER ST.
Marylebone
Baker
St.
High St.
Road
Devonshire
Portland
St.
GT. PORTLAND ST.
337
Marylebone
Road
Marylebone Rd
333
Cavendish St.
Road
EDGWARE ROAD
324
Crawford St.
Place
Street
St.
New
Cavendish Place
116
Bryanston Square
George St.
WALLACE COLLECTION
Street
Gardens
Seymour St.
Wigmore
Street
Kendal St.
Sussex Gardens
Road
Oxford
Street
Brook St.
Bayswater Road
Marble Arch
Up. Brook St.
Park
Lane
MAYFAIR
Bruton St.
HYDE PARK
G
H
I
J
S
T
U
V

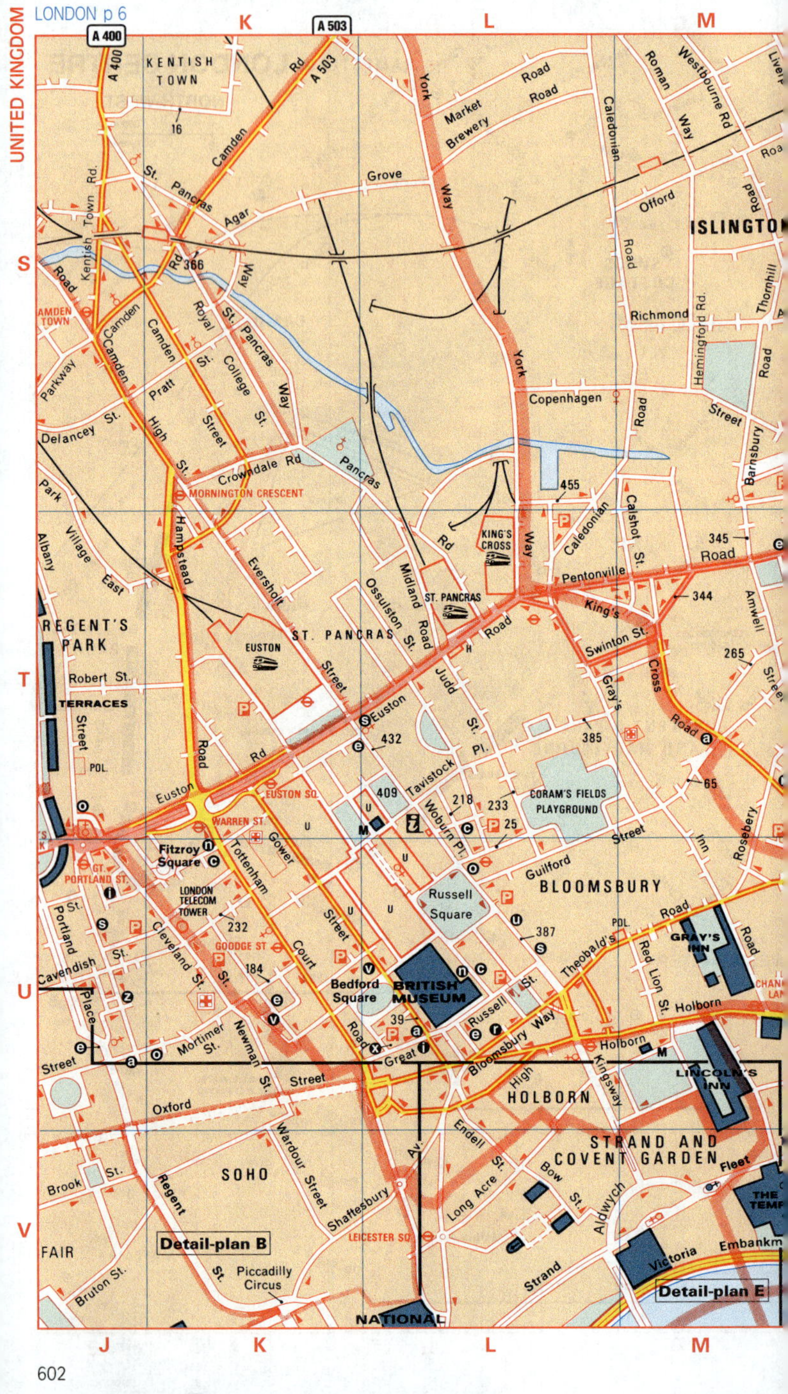

LONDON p 6
UNITED KINGDOM
A 400
A 503
K
L
M
KENTISH TOWN
16
Rd
A 503
York
Market
Brewery
Road
Road
Caledonian
Roman
Westbourne Rd
Way
Liver
Camden
St. Pancras
Agar
Grove
Way
Offord
Road
ISLINGTON
Roa
S
Road
Kentish Town Rd.
Rd 366
Way
York
Copenhagen
Road
Richmond
Hemingford Rd.
Thornhill
Barnsbury
Road
AMDEN TOWN
Camden
Camden
Royal
St. Pancras
Way
Pancras
455
Calshot St.
345
Road
Parkway
Camden
Pratt
College
St.
Street
Crowndale Rd
King's Cross
Caledonian
Pentonville
344
Amwell
Delancey
St.
High
St.
MORNINGTON CRESCENT
Rd
King's
Swinton St.
265
Street
Park
Albany
Village
East
Eversholt
Ossulston St.
Midland Road
St. PANCRAS
St. PANCRAS
Road
Gray's
Cross
Road
REGENT'S PARK
EUSTON
ST. PANCRAS
Judd
385
65
Robert St.
Street
Euston
St.
Woburn Pl.
Rosebery
TERRACES
Street
POL.
Euston
Rd
EUSTON
432
409
Tavistock
218
233
25
CORAM'S FIELDS PLAYGROUND
Inn
Street
o
EUSTON SQ.
WARREN ST.
Woburn
Guilford
Street
GT. PORTLAND ST.
Fitzroy Square
Tottenham
Russell Square
BLOOMSBURY
Road
Portland
St.
LONDON TELECOM TOWER
Cleveland St.
232
GOODGE ST.
Court
Street
387
Theobald's
POL.
Red Lion St.
GRAY'S INN
Road
CHAN LA
Cavendish
Place
184
Bedford Square
BRITISH MUSEUM
Russell
St.
Holborn
LINCOLN'S INN
Street
Mortimer St.
Newman St.
Street
39
Great
Russell
Bloomsbury Way
High
Kingsway
Holborn
M
Oxford
Wardour Street
Road
HOLBORN
STRAND AND COVENT GARDEN
Fleet
SOHO
Shaftesbury
Av.
Endell St.
Long Acre
Bow St.
Aldwych
THE TEMPLE
Brook St.
Regent
St.
LEICESTER SQ
Strand
Victoria
Embankm
FAIR
Detail-plan B
Bruton St.
Piccadilly Circus
NATIONAL
Detail-plan E
J
K
L
M
602

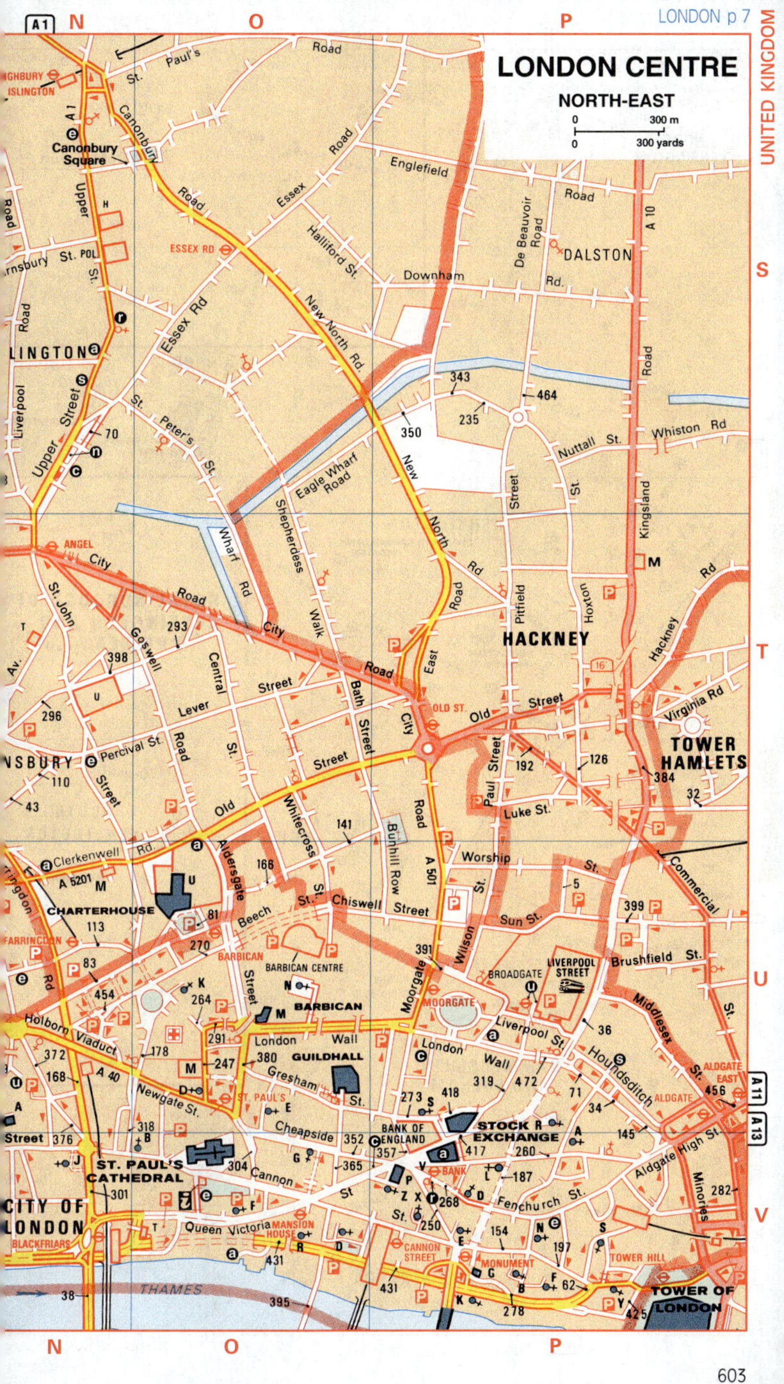

LONDON p 7
UNITED KINGDOM
LONDON CENTRE
NORTH-EAST
0   300 m
0   300 yards
A1
N   O   P
S
T
U
V
Canonbury Square
ISLINGTON
DALSTON
HACKNEY
TOWER HAMLETS
CHARTERHOUSE
BARBICAN
BARBICAN CENTRE
GUILDHALL
LIVERPOOL STREET
BROADGATE
MOORGATE
ALDGATE
ALDGATE EAST
STOCK EXCHANGE
BANK OF ENGLAND
ST. PAUL'S CATHEDRAL
CITY OF LONDON
BLACKFRIARS
MANSION HOUSE
MONUMENT
TOWER HILL
TOWER OF LONDON
THAMES
ANGEL
CLERKENWELL
FARRINGDON
Paul's
Road
St.
Canonbury
Upper
Street
Essex Rd
Essex
Road
Halliford St.
New North Rd.
Englefield
Road
De Beauvoir Road
A 10
Kingsland
Road
Whiston Rd
Nuttall St.
Downham
Eagle Wharf Road
Shepherdess
Wharf
Road
City
Road
Walk
Bath Street
City Road
East Road
New North Rd
Pitfield Street
Hoxton
Hackney Rd
St. John
Goswell
Central Street
Lever Street
Old Street
City Road
Old St.
Paul Street
Luke St.
Worship St.
Sun St.
Virginia Rd
Commercial
Whitecross Street
Bunhill Row
A 501
Moorgate
Wilson
Brushfield St.
Middlesex St.
Houndsditch
Aldersgate Street
Beech St.
Chiswell Street
London Wall
Liverpool St.
London Wall
Gresham St.
Newgate St.
Cheapside
Cannon St.
Queen Victoria Street
Fenchurch St.
Aldgate High St.
Minories
Cannon Street
A 40
Holborn Viaduct
A 5201
A 11
A 13
CANONBURY
ESSEX RD
OLD ST.
CHARTERHOUSE
BARBICAN
ST. PAUL'S
BANK
MONUMENT
TOWER HILL
HIGHBURY ISLINGTON
70
343
464
235
350
293
398
296
110
43
141
166
81
270
113
83
454
264
178
291
247
380
273
418
319
472
71
34
145
352
357
365
417
260
187
304
301
318
376
372
168
391
399
384
32
126
192
5
36
456
282
250
154
197
62
278
425
395
431
431
38
268

NORTH KENSINGTON
Detail-plan F
107
Portobello
Kensington
Park
Road
Ladbroke
Grove
Westbourne
Pembridge Villas
Dawson Place
Porchester
Gardens
Gloucester
Gardens
Queensway
Bayswater
Road
Grove
Clarendon Rd
Lansdowne
Walk
Park
Avenue
Notting Hill Gate
Campden
Kensington
Kensington
Palace
Gardens
Bayswater
ROUND POND
KENSINGTO
HOLLAND PARK
Holland
Holland
Park
371
A 40
(M 41)
224
Holland Villas
Addison
Abbotsbury
Road
Sheffield Ter.
Hill
Church
Street
A
KENSINGTON PALACE
HOLLAND PARK
KENSINGTON
LINLEY SAMBOURNE HOUSE
225
Holland
Street
229
High
Street
HIGHT STREET KENSINGTON
Sinclair
Holland
A 3220
Road
KENSINGTON OLYMPIA
326
Melbury Rd
LEIGHTON HOUSE
Kensington
Road
High
St.
POL.
158
342
Kensington
2
Scarsdale Villas
ROYAL BOROUGH OF KENSINGTON AND CHELSEA
Elvaston Pl.
Gloucester
Road
Queen's
Marloes
Road
A 315
207
Edith
North
End
Road
Road
OLYMPIA
Warwick
Rd
Pembroke
Earl's
Rd
119
Cromwell
Road
EARL S COURT
298
299
410
426
245
Cromwell
Road
347
SOUTH KENSINGTON
Brompton
Collingham Rd
Drayton Gard
Gliston Rd
182
203
Talgarth
Rd
A 4
BARONS COURT
Baron's Court Rd
North
End
Road
WEST KENSINGTON
Star Road
West
348
151
EARLS COURT EXHIBITION BLDG
Redcliffe
Finborough
Gardens
Road
WEST BROMPTON
Greyhound
Road
Musard Rd
Lillie
Ryston Rd
Road
End
Road
Seagrave
Road
Old
Road
BROMPTON CEMETERY
Fulham
Road
Edith Grove
202
HAMMERSMITH AND FULHAM
Lillie
Road
Dawes Rd
Estcourt Rd
FULHAM
Halford Rd
Bishops Rd
Vanston Pl.
FULHAM BROADWAY
Munster
Road
Filmer Rd
Dawes
Rd
Fulham Rd
A 304
Harwood
Rd
King's
A 217
Lots Rd
Lots

LONDON p 9
LONDON CENTRE
SOUTH-WEST
0   300 m
0   300 yards
G
H
I
J
V
X
Y
Z
Sussex
Bayswater
Road
Kendal St.
Seymour St.
Oxford
Marble Arch
HYDE   PARK
Up. Brook St.
Park
Lane
Park
Lane
South
Audley
St.
Curzon
Bruton St.
Berkeley St.
St.
Piccadilly
GREEN PARK
Constitution
Hill
The Long Water
CITY OF WESTMINSTER
Serpentine
The   Serpentine
Road
ARDENS
HYDE PARK AND KNIGHTSBRIDGE
HYDE PARK
CORNER
Grosvenor
Road
Knightsbridge
ensington
Exhibition
Road
Road
Road
Sloane
Belgrave
Square
Chapel St.
Pl.
Detail-plan D
BELGRAVIA
VICTORIA
AND
ALBERT
MUSEUM
Brompton
Street
Pont
Street
Cadogan Sq.
Cadogan Gdns.
Lyall
St.
King's
Road
Street
Street
VICTORIA
Buckingham Palace Rd.
Belgrave
CIENCE
MUSEUM
Road
Walton
Street
Pelham   Street
Road
Detail-plan C
Onslow
Gdns
Rd.
Sydney
Cale
Street
Sloane
Avenue
Street
CHELSEA
Road
Ebury
Pimlico
Rd
156
e
a
c
Warwick
Way
Saint
Sutherland St.
Gloucester
ulham
Old
Street
Church
King's
Smith Street
Street
Flood
Street
Royal
Royal
Chelsea
Bridge
Road
Chelsea
Bridge
Lupus
ROYAL
HOSPITAL
CHELSEA
Hospital
Road
14'9
Grosvenor
Beaufort
Street
Oakley
Street
Chelsea
Embankment
Chelsea
Bridge
Z
Walk
Cheyne
Walk
Walk
Cheyne
Battersea
Bridge
Battersea
Bridge Rd
Albert
Bridge
Albert Bridge Rd.
Parkgate
Rd
C
75
The
Parade
Carriage
Drive
East
BATTERSEA PARK
WANDSWORTH
Queenstown
Road
75
361
19
e

J
K
L
M
STRAND AND COVENT GARDEN
Fleet
Brook St.
SOHO
Wardour Street
Shaftesbury
Long Acre
Bow St.
Aldwych
THE TEMPLE
Regent
Av.
LEICESTER SQ.
Strand
Victoria
Embankment
FAIR
Detail-plan B
St.
Piccadilly Circus
Detail-plan E
Bruton St.
Berkeley St.
Regent St.
NATIONAL GALLERY
CHARING CROSS
Piccadilly
St. James's St.
Trafalgar Square
317
e
SOUTH BANK ARTS CENTRE
ST. JAMES'S
Pall
Mall
OLD ADMIRALTY
Whitehall
462
460
a
Stamf
108
Mall
HORSE GUARDS
228
GREEN PARK
The
ST. JAMES'S PARK
BANQUETING HOUSE
23
WATERLOO
Constitution Hill
340
WESTMINSTER
COUNTY HALL
u
a
York Road
WATERL
BUCKINGHAM PALACE
Birdcage Walk
Queen Anne's Gate
193
A
WESTMINSTER BRIDGE
Westminster
277
Bavlis Rd.
Petty France
Tothill St.
402
52
M
Palace Rd.
14'6
LAMBETH NORTH
Buckingham Gate
ST. JAMES'S PARK
St.
WESTMINSTER ABBEY
PALACE OF WESTMINSTER
Victoria
NEW SCOTLAND YARD
196
Lambeth
LAMBETH
H
Great
Peter Street
LAMBETH PALACE
219
Lambeth
VICTORIA
Francis
Rochester Row
200
Marsham
S
Millbank
M
Walk
Palace Rd.
St.
Vincent Sq.
Horseferry
Page St.
Rd.
Lambeth Bridge
a
Fitzalan St.
Belgrave
Wilton Rd
VICTORIA
Vincent Bridge
Regency
St.
Islip St.
Lambeth
Embankment
Black Prince Road
LAMBET
Saint
Warwick Way
St. George's
Denbigh St.
Tachbrook Street
436
Z
TATE GALLERY
C
John Millbank
THAMES
Vauxhall Walk
Tyers St.
Newburn St.
Sutherland St.
Gloucester
Drive
Street
30
PIMLICO
Vauxhall Bridge
49
Albert
Kennington
Lupus
Claverton St.
a
St. George's Square
Rd.
150
Street
Kennington Lane
14'9
Grosvenor
VAUXHALL
341
Harleyford Road
Kennington Oval
THE OVAL
Clayton St.
Kennington
290
SOUTH LAMBETH
211
OVAL
Elms
Lane
Lambeth
Fentiman
Road
Oval
Road
61
19
Nine
NEW COVENT GARDEN MARKET
Wandsworth
South
Dorset
Rd
Clapham
Brixton Rd
A 3
A 2

LONDON CENTRE
SOUTH-EAST
0   300 m
0   300 yards
CITY OF LONDON
ST. PAUL'S CATHEDRAL
BLACKFRIARS
Cannon
Queen Victoria
MANSION HOUSE
CANNON STREET
BANK
ENGLAND
MONUMENT
TOWER HILL
TOWER OF LONDON
TOWER BRIDGE
THAMES
Blackfriars
LONDON BRIDGE
SOUTHWARK CATHEDRAL
Sumner
Southwark
Street
Street
St.
Road
Tooley
LONDON BRIDGE
St. Thomas
George Inn
Newcomen
St.
The Cut
Union
Suffolk
Bridge
High
Street
St.
Street
Weston
Lane
Bermondsey Street
Druid
St.
Webber
Street
BOROUGH
Borough
St.
Long
Great
Road
Trinity
St.
Dover
349
Abbey
St.
Trinity Church Square
Merrick Square
Harper
Street
SOUTHWARK
Grange
Southwark
Road
London
Imperial War Museum
St. George's Road
Elephant and Castle
New
Kent
Falmouth
Rd.
Road
Tower
Page's Walk
Willow Walk
Spa Rd
Road
H
Drive
Brook
Heygate St.
Rodney Rd
WALWORTH
Old
Dunton
Road
A 200
A2
Walworth
East
Street
Flint St.
East
St.
Kent
Thurlow
Road
KENNINGTON
Lane
Penton Pl.
Manor
Pl.
Portland
St.
East
Street
Braganza St.
Chapter Rd
Ruskin
St.
Albany
Neate
St.
Wells Rd
Trafalgar
Av.
KENNINGTON PARK
Camberwell
Foxley Rd
New
Rd
Wyndham
Road
A 202
John
Road
Camberwell
New
Church
Southampton
Way
A 202

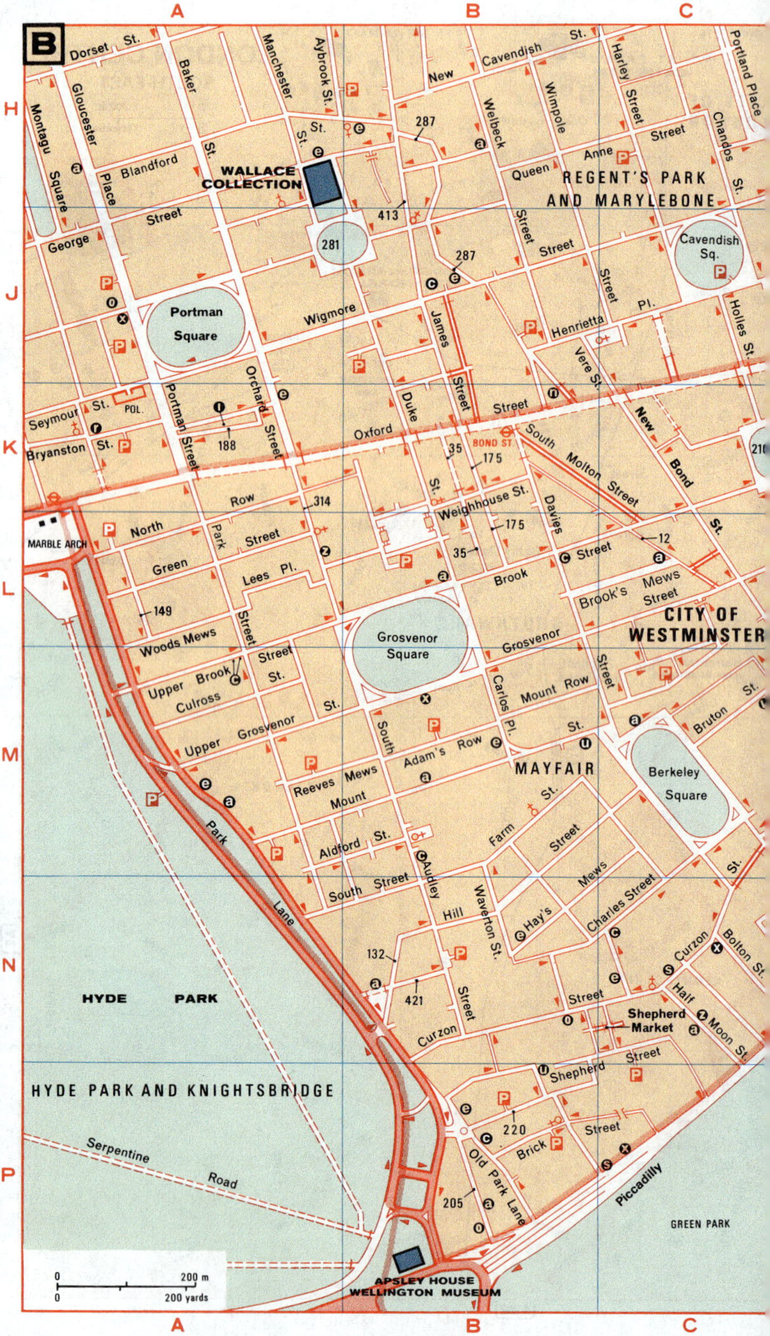
B
A
B
C
H
J
K
L
M
N
P
Dorset St.
Baker St.
Manchester St.
Aybrook St.
New Cavendish St.
Harley Street
Portland Place
Montagu Square
Gloucester Place
Blandford Street
WALLACE COLLECTION
Welbeck Street
Wimpole Street
Queen Anne Street
Chandos St.
REGENT'S PARK AND MARYLEBONE
George Street
Cavendish Sq.
Portman Square
Wigmore Street
James Street
Henrietta Pl.
Holles St.
Vere St.
Seymour St.
Bryanston St.
POL.
Portman Street
Orchard Street
Duke Street
Oxford Street
BOND ST.
South Molton Street
New Bond St.
MARBLE ARCH
North Row
Park Street
Green Street
Lees Pl.
Weighhouse St.
Davies Street
Brook Street
Brook's Mews
CITY OF WESTMINSTER
Grosvenor Square
Grosvenor Street
Woods Mews
Upper Brook Street
Culross St.
Carlos Pl.
Mount Row
Upper Grosvenor St.
South St.
Adam's Row
Bruton St.
Berkeley Square
MAYFAIR
Reeves Mews
Mount St.
Farm Street
Aldford St.
South Street
Audley St.
Hill St.
Waverton St.
Hay's Mews
Charles Street
Curzon Street
Bolton St.
Half Moon St.
Park Lane
HYDE PARK
Shepherd Market
Shepherd Street
Curzon Street
HYDE PARK AND KNIGHTSBRIDGE
Serpentine Road
Brick Street
Old Park Lane
Piccadilly
GREEN PARK
APSLEY HOUSE WELLINGTON MUSEUM
0 200 m
0 200 yards
287
413
281
188
314
175
35
12
149
132
421
220
205
210

CAMDEN
St. Giles Circus
TOTTENHAM COURT RD
BLOOMSBURY
Margaret Street
Eastcastle St.
Wells St.
Oxford Street
Regent St.
286
189
Oxford Circus
Poland Street
Noel St.
D'Arblay Street
Wardour Street
Dean Street
Soho Square
Charing Cross Road
134
Prince's St.
Hanover St.
Argyll St.
Great Marlborough Street
Marshall Street
26
Frith St.
198
323
Cambridge Circus
Maddox Street
Kingly Street
Carnaby Street
Broadwick St.
SOHO
Street
323
368
St. George Street
Conduit Street
Beak St.
James St.
Golden Square
Great Windmill St.
Rupert St.
Shaftesbury Avenue
Lisle Street
174
Cranbourn St.
261
New Bond St.
Clifford St.
Saville Row
444
Brewer St.
179
133
Coventry St.
Whitcomb St.
NATIONAL PORTRAIT GALLERY
Dover St.
Cork St.
Old Bond St.
322
Vigo St.
Regent St.
Piccadilly Circus
336
Orange St.
NATIONAL GALLERY
Burlington Arc.
BURLINGTON HOUSE
Sackville Street
Piccadilly
Haymarket Street
Trafalgar Square
Berkeley St.
ST. JAMES'S
Jermyn St.
Piccadilly Arcade
143
Charles II St.
NEW ZEALAND HOUSE
Cockspur St.
Bratton St.
St.
146
6
ST. JAMES'S
St. James's Square
Mall
Waterloo Place
House Ter.
CARLTON HOUSE TERRACE
GREEN PARK
Bury St.
King Street
Pall Mall
Carlton House
VICTORIA
OLD ADMIRALTY
Queen's Walk
St. James's Pl.
74
St. James's St.
QUEEN'S CHAPEL
GREEN PARK
ST. JAMES'S PALACE
The Mall
ST. JAMES'S PARK
LANCASTER HOUSE
Oxford Street is closed to private traffic, Mondays to Saturdays :
from 7 am to 9 pm between Portman Street and St. Giles Circus

C
HYDE PARK AND KNIGHTSBRIDGE
KENSINGTON GARDENS
ALBERT MEMORIAL
Kensington High St
Young St.
241
241
242
Kensington Square
KENSINGTON
St. Alban's Grove
Victoria Rd
De Vere Gardens
Palace Gate
Victoria Grove
Kensington Road
Kensington Gore
Kensingt
ROYAL ALBERT HALL
Prince Consort Rd
Exhibition
356
Queen's Gate Terrace
Queen's Gate
Gloucester
259
Elvaston Place
IMPERIAL COLLEGE OF SCIENCE AND TECHNOLOGIE
ROYAL COLLEGE OF ART
363
Cornwall Gardens
Gardens
Grenville Place
Gate Gardens
SCIENCE MUSEUM
NATURAL HISTORY MUSEUM
Road
Cromwell
Lexham Gardens
Lexham Gdns
Road
120
420
360
SOUTH KENSINGTON
Cromwell
Ashburn
Rd
GLOUCESTER RD
Stanhope Gardens
Queen's
215
59
180
Knaresborough Place
Courtfield Gdns
101
14
Courtfield Road
Courtfield Gdns
Harrington
Courtfield Place Gdns
Gardens
Gloucester
SOUTH KENSINGTON
Gate
Rd
Sumner Square
Onslow
Wetherby
Bina Gdns
Gardens
Old
Rd
Brompton
Onslow Gardens
Onslow Gdns
170
Bramham Gdns
99
Gardens
Road
Drayton
Roland Gardens
Cranley Gdns
300
South Para
Bolton
Brompton
Earl's Court Rd
Old
EARL'S COURT
Redcliffe
The Boltons
The Boltons
Gilston
Gardens
Evelyn Gdns
Rds
Elm Park Gdns
Old
South Pa
Square
Harcourt Ter.
Little Boltons
Road
Road
Gardens
Onslow Gdns
Elm Park Gdns
Road
The Vale
Finborough
Redcliffe
Tregunter
Hollywood
Road
Fulham
Beaufort Park
Elm
Park
Street
Cho
Oldfield Road
Road
Gardens
Fulham
Walk
BROMPTON CEMETERY

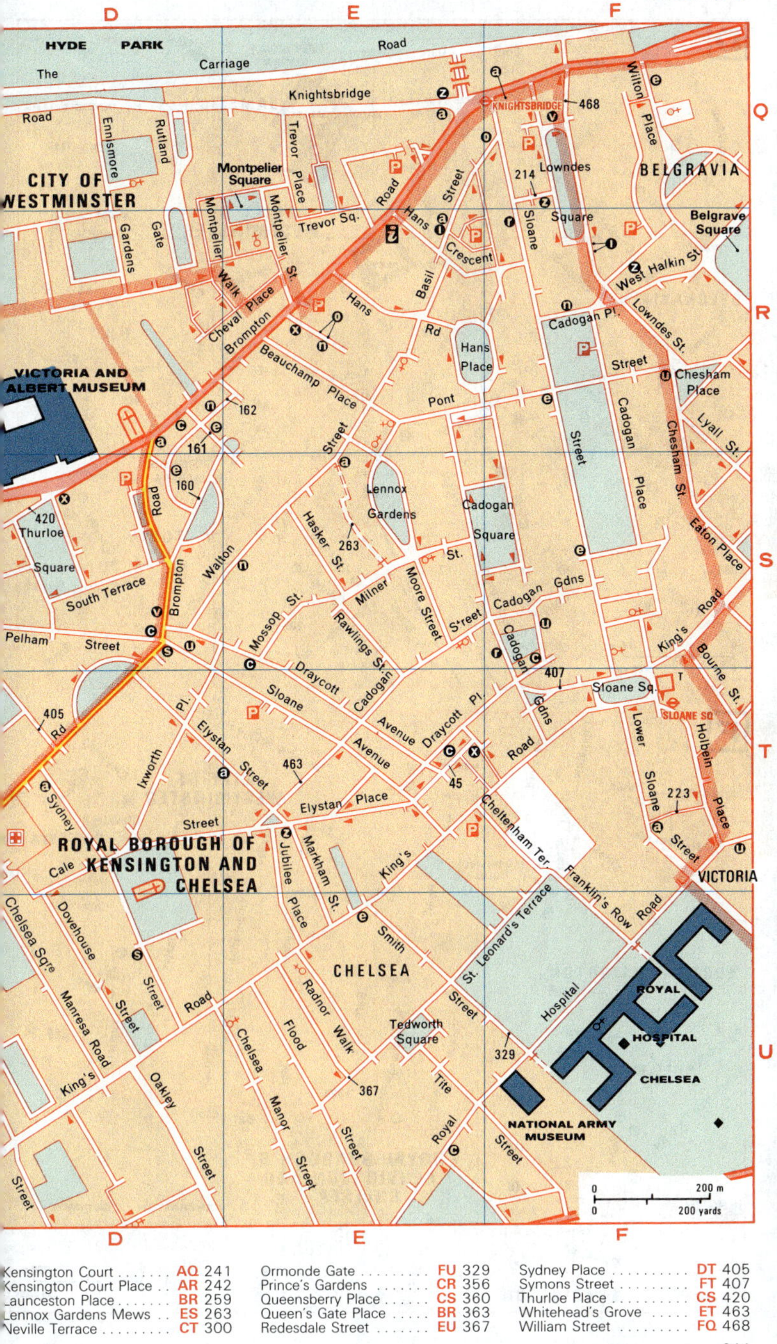
HYDE PARK
The Carriage Road
Knightsbridge
Trevor Place
CITY OF WESTMINSTER
Ennismore Gardens
Rutland Gate
Montpelier Square
Montpelier Place
Montpelier St.
Trevor Sq.
Cheval Place
Brompton
Walk
Hans Road
Hans Street
Basil Street
Crescent
Hans Place
Sloane Street
KNIGHTSBRIDGE
468
214
Lowndes Square
BELGRAVIA
Belgrave Square
West Halkin St.
Lowndes St.
Cadogan Pl.
Chesham Place
Lyall St.
Wilton Place
VICTORIA AND ALBERT MUSEUM
Beauchamp Place
162
161
160
420 Thurloe Square
South Terrace
Pont Street
Cadogan Square
Cadogan Place
Chesham St.
Eaton Place
Brompton Road
Walton Street
Hasker St.
Lennox Gardens
263
Cadogan Gdns
Milner Street
Moore Street
Rawlings St.
Mossop St.
Cadogan Street
Cadogan Gdns
King's Road
Bourne St.
Holbein Place
Pelham Street
Draycott
Sloane
Avenue
Avenue
Draycott Pl.
407
Sloane Sq.
SLOANE SQ
405
Ixworth
Elystan Street
463
45
Sloane
Lower Sloane Street
223
VICTORIA
Elystan Place
Sydney
Cale
ROYAL BOROUGH OF KENSINGTON AND CHELSEA
Jubilee Place
Markham St.
King's Road
Smith Street
Cheltenham Ter.
Franklin's Row
St. Leonard's Terrace
ROYAL HOSPITAL CHELSEA
Chelsea Sq.
Dovehouse Street
Manresa Road
Chelsea Manor Street
Flood Street
Radnor Walk
CHELSEA
Tedworth Square
329
367
Tite Street
Royal Hospital Road
NATIONAL ARMY MUSEUM
King's Road
Oakley Street
0   200 m
0   200 yards

D

WELLINGTON ARCH
142
Constitution Hill
GREEN PARK
QUEEN VICTORIA MEMORIAL
The Mall
St. James's Park Lake
ST. JAMES'S
ST. JAMES'S PARK
BUCKINGHAM PALACE GARDENS
BUCKINGHAM PALACE
Birdcage Walk
M
Grosvenor Cres.
Halkin St.
Chapel St.
Grosvenor Place
Chester St.
Belgrave Square
Upper Belgrave St.
BELGRAVIA
56
CITY OF WESTMINSTER
56
Petty France
Palmer St.
PASSPORT OFFICE
ROYAL MEWS
Palace Street
Castle La.
56
H Victoria St.
Wilton St.
Hobart Pl.
Grosvenor Gdns.
274
Rd
48
Howick Pl.
8
Belgrave Place
Belgrave Place
Square
Road
Lower Belgrave St.
88
Victoria St.
412
St. James's St.
Ashley Pl.
416
Row
Eaton Place
Eaton Square
Palace Street
Carlisle Place
WESTMINSTER CATHEDRAL
Eccleston Street
King's Road
Eaton
88
Elizabeth Street
Palace Street
VICTORIA
Vauxhall Bridge Road
Francis Street
Rochester Row
VICTORIA
Vincent Square
389
Chester Row
389
Ebury Street
157
Buckingham Palace Road
Hugh Street
Gillingham Street
Hudson's Pl.
Wilton Road
Belgrave Rd
Eccleston Square
201
Tachbrook Street
Warwick Way
Road
VICTORIA COACH STATION
0   200 m
0   200 yards

F

Chepstow Road
Hereford Road
Newton Road
Bishop's Bridge Rd
CITY OF WESTMINSTER
Cleveland Ter.
Gloucester Terrace
90
Artesian Road
Westbourne
Chepstow Rd
Grove
Garway Road
Queensway
Inverness Terrace
Leinster Gdns
84
Cleveland Square
BAYSWATER
136
Leinster Square
Leinster Square
Road
243
Porchester Gardens
Queensborough Terrace
Porchester Terrace
362
84
Pembridge Villas
Pembridge Road
Moscow Road
St. Petersburgh Place
Bark Pl.
Queensway
BAYSWATER
Craven Hill
Leinster Ter.
256
NORTH KENSINGTON
Dawson Place
Pembridge Place
Pembridge Square
Palace Court
328
Bayswater Road
Portobello Rd
Kensington Park Rd
Pembridge Gdns
Gate
Kensington Palace Gardens
ROYAL BOROUGH OF KENSINGTON AND CHELSEA
Bayswater
Queensway
The Broad Walk
KENSINGTON GARDENS
Hill
Notting Hill Gate
Notting
238
335
Place
KENSINGTON
0   200 m
0   200 yards

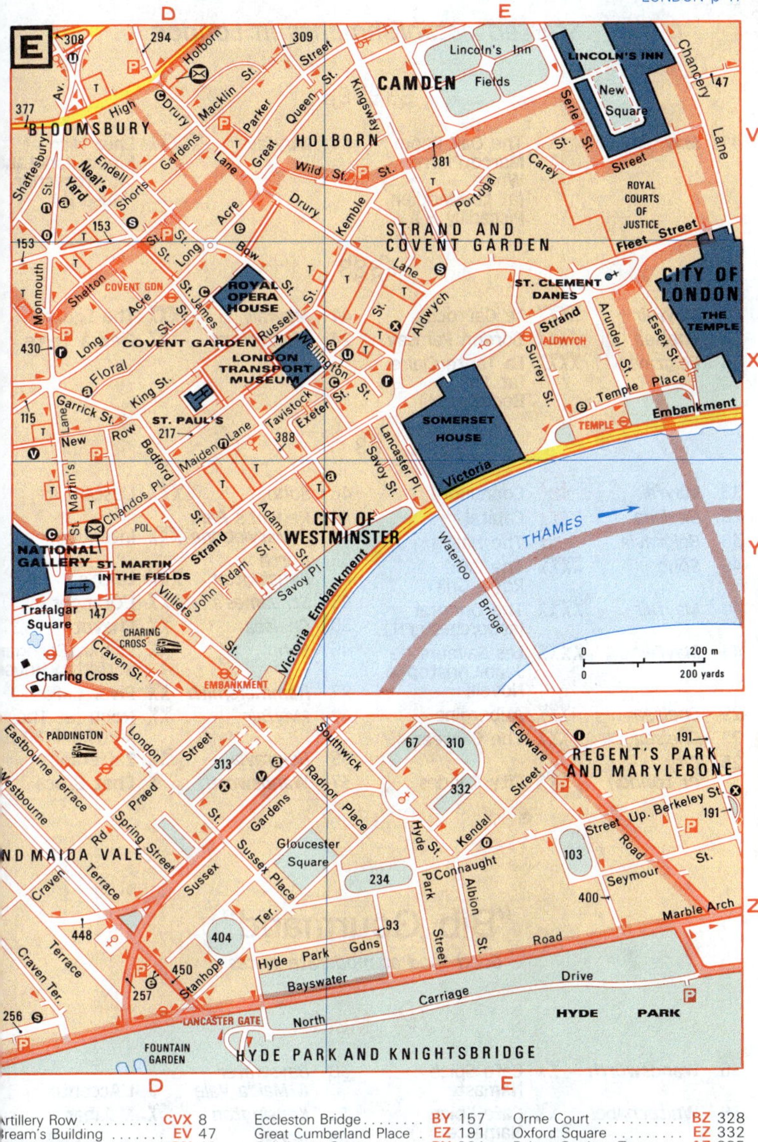
E
CAMDEN
Lincoln's Inn
Fields
LINCOLN'S INN
New Square
Chancery Lane
BLOOMSBURY
HOLBORN
Neal's Yard
STRAND AND
COVENT GARDEN
ST. CLEMENT DANES
ROYAL COURTS OF JUSTICE
Fleet Street
CITY OF LONDON
THE TEMPLE
COVENT GDN.
ROYAL OPERA HOUSE
COVENT GARDEN
LONDON TRANSPORT MUSEUM
Strand
ALDWYCH
Aldwych
Essex St.
Arundel St.
Surrey St.
Temple Place
Embankment
TEMPLE
ST. PAUL'S
SOMERSET HOUSE
Victoria
CITY OF WESTMINSTER
THAMES
Victoria Embankment
Waterloo Bridge
NATIONAL GALLERY
ST. MARTIN IN THE FIELDS
Trafalgar Square
CHARING CROSS
Charing Cross
EMBANKMENT
0   200 m
0   200 yards
PADDINGTON
London Street
Southwick
Edgware
REGENT'S PARK AND MARYLEBONE
Up. Berkeley St.
Eastbourne Terrace
Westbourne Terrace
MAIDA VALE
Praed Street
Spring Street
Gloucester Square
Sussex Place
Radnor Place
Hyde St.
Kendal Street
Connaught
Albion
Seymour
Marble Arch
Craven Terrace
Sussex Square
Stanhope Place
Hyde Park Gdns
Bayswater Road
Carriage Drive
North
HYDE PARK
Lancaster Gate
FOUNTAIN GARDEN
HYDE PARK AND KNIGHTSBRIDGE

Starred establishments in London

✿✿✿

| 41 | *Mayfair* | XXXX | The Oak Room Marco Pierre White (at Le Meridien Piccadilly H.) | 41 | *Mayfair* | XXXXX | Chez Nico at Ninety Park Lane (at Grosvenor House H.) |

✿✿

41	*Mayfair*	XXXX	Le Gavroche	41	*Mayfair*	XXX	The Square
29	*Chelsea*	XXXX	Gordon Ramsay	24	*Bloomsbury*	XX	Pied à Terre
38	*Belgravia*	XXXX	La Tante Claire (at The Berkeley H.)				

✿

39	*Mayfair*	🏛	Connaught	46	*Soho*	XXX	L'Escargot
28	*Chelsea*	🏛	Capital	44	*Regent's Park & Marylebone*	XXX	Interlude
38	*Belgravia*	🏛	The Halkin	33	*North Kensington*	XXX	Leith's
46	*Soho*	XXXX	The Café Royal Grill	45	*St. James's*	XX	L'Oranger
41	*Mayfair*	XXXX	The Oriental (at Dorchester H.)	30	*Chelsea*	XX	Chavot
41	*Mayfair*	XXXX	Les Saveurs de Jean-Christophe Novelli	46	*Soho*	XX	Richard Corrigan at Lindsay House
29	*Chelsea*	XXX	Aubergine	27	*Hammersmith*	XX	River Café
29	*Chelsea*	XXX	The Canteen	42	*Mayfair*	XX	Nobu (at The Metropolitan H.)
25	*City of London*	XXX	City Rhodes	39	*Belgravia*	XX	Zafferano
				37	*Wandsworth*	X	Chez Bruce

"Bib Gourmand"

Good food at moderate prices

 Meals

36	*Wandsworth*	XX	Cafe Spice Namaste	38	*Bayswater & Maida Vale*	X	L'Accento
36	*Whitechapel*	XX	Cafe Spice Namaste	32	*Kensington*	X	Malabar
				33	*North Kensington*	X	Woz

UNITED KINGDOM

Restaurants classified according to type

Chinese

41	*Mayfair*	XXXX	✿ The Oriental (at Dorchester H.)
41	*Mayfair*	XXX	Princess Garden
29	*Chelsea*	XXX	L'Oriental (at La Belle Epoque)
31	*Chelsea*	XX	Good Earth
49	*Victoria*	XX	Hunan
26	*City of London*	XX	Imperial City
49	*Victoria*	XX	Ken Lo's Memories of China
26	*Fulham*	XX	Mao Tai
32	*Kensington*	XX	Memories of China
38	*Bayswater & Maida Vale*	XX	Poons
31	*Chelsea*	XX	Red of Knightsbridge
38	*Bayswater & Maida Vale*	XX	Royal China
37	*Putney*	XX	Royal China
24	*Hampstead*	XX	Vegetarian Cottage
24	*Hampstead*	XX	ZeNW3
47	*Soho*	X	Fung Shing
47	*Soho*	X	Jen
47	*Kensington*	X	Mandarin
47	*Soho*	X	Wok Wok

English

41	*Mayfair*	XXXX	Grill Room (at Dorchester H.)
49	*Victoria*	XXX	Shepherd's
30	*Chelsea*	XX	English Garden
47	*Strand & Covent Garden*	XX	Rules
24	*Bloomsbury*	X	Alfred

French

41	*Mayfair*	XXXXX	✿✿✿ Chez Nico at Ninety Park Lane
41	*Mayfair*	XXXX	✿✿ (Le) Gavroche
41	*Mayfair*	XXXX	✿ (Les) Saveurs de Jean-Christophe Novelli
38	*Belgravia*	XXXX	✿✿ (La) Tante Claire
49	*Victoria*	XXX	Auberge de Provence
33	*North Kensington*	XXX	Chez Moi
30	*Chelsea*	XX	Brasserie St. Quentin
30	*Chelsea*	XX	✿ Chavot
30	*Chelsea*	XX	(Le) Colombier
32	*Kensington*	XX	(L') Escargot Doré
48	*Strand & Covent Garden*	XX	(L') Estaminet
30	*Chelsea*	XX	Poissonnerie de l'Avenue
26	*City of London*	XX	(Le) Quai
39	*Belgravia*	XX	Vong (French Thai)
48	*Stand & Covent Garden*	X	Magno's Brasserie
49	*Victoria*	X	(La) Poule au Pot

Hungarian

46	*Soho*	XX	Gay Hussar

UNITED KINGDOM

Indian & Pakistani

35	*Bermondsey*	XXX	Bengal Clipper
34	*South Kensington*	XXX	Bombay Brasserie
30	*Chelsea*	XXX	Chutney Mary (Anglo-Indian)
34	*South Kensington*	XX	Café Lazeez
36	*Battersea*	XX	Cafe Spice Namaste
36	*Whitechapel*	XX	Cafe Spice Namaste
42	*Mayfair*	XX	Chor Bizarre
34	*South Kensington*	XX	Delhi Brasserie
44	*Regent's Park & Marylebone*	XX	Gaylord
46	*Soho*	XX	Gopal's
34	*South Kensington*	XX	Khan's of Kensington
24	*Bloomsbury*	XX	Malabar Junction
34	*South Kensington*	XX	Memories of India
44	*Regent's Park & Marylebone*	XX	(La) Porte des Indes
46	*Soho*	XX	Red Fort
26	*City of London*	XX	Sri India
37	*Wandsworth*	XX	Tabaq
42	*Mayfair*	XX	Tamarind
27	*Hammersmith*	XX	Tandoori Nights
30	*Chelsea*	XX	Vama
37	*Wandsworth*	X	Bombay Bicycle Club
32	*Kensington*	X	Malabar
47	*Soho*	X	Soho Spice

Irish

44	*Regent's Park & Marylebone*	XX	Ard-ri at the O'Conor Don

Italian

38	*Belgravia*	⌂ ❀	(The) Halkin
30	*Chelsea*	XXX	Grissini
49	*Victoria*	XXX	(L') Incontro
49	*Victoria*	XXX	Santini
41	*Mayfair*	XXX	Sartoria
38	*Bayswater & Maida Vale*	XX	Al San Vincenzo
44	*Regent's Park & Marylebone*	XX	Bertorelli's
48	*Strand & Covent Garden*	XX	Bertorelli's
44	*Regent's Park & Marylebone*	XX	Caldesi
30	*Chelsea*	XX	Caraffini
30	*Chelsea*	XX	Daphne's
36	*Dulwich*	XX	Luigi's
33	*North Kensington*	XX	Orsino
27	*Hammersmith*	XX ❀	River Café
42	*Mayfair*	XX	Teca
35	*Bermondsey*	XX	Tentazioni
31	*Chelsea*	XX	Toto's
39	*Belgravia*	XX ❀	Zafferano
38	*Bayswater & Maida Vale*	X	(L') Accento
38	*Bayswater & Maida Vale*	X	Assaggi
35	*Bermondsey*	X	Cantina Del Ponte
32	*Kensington*	X	Cibo
44	*Regent's Park & Marylebone*	X	Ibla
49	*Victoria*	X	Olivo

Japanese

45	*St. James's*	XXX	Suntory
26	*City of London*	XXX	Tatsuso
44	*Regent's Park & Marylebone*	XX	Asuka
30	*Chelsea*	XX	Benihana
42	*Mayfair*	XX	Benihana
42	*Mayfair*	XX ❀	Nobu
45	*St. James's*	XX	Matsuri
26	*City of London*	XX	Miyama
42	*Mayfair*	XX	Shogun

Lebanese

39	*Belgravia*	XX	(Al) Bustan
31	*Chelsea*	XX	Beit Eddine
32	*Kensington*	XX	Phoenicia

Pubs

27	*Hammersmith*	Anglesea Arms
31	*Chelsea*	Chelsea Ram
37	*Battersea*	Duke of Cambridge
27	*Shepherd's Bush*	Havelock Tavern
27	*Finsbury*	Peasant
25	*Primrose Hill*	(The) Queens
31	*Chelsea*	Swag and Tails

Seafood

30	*Chelsea*	XXX	One-O-One
32	*Mayfair*	XXX	Scotts
32	*Mayfair*	XX	Bentley's
34	*South Kensington*	XX	Downstairs at One Ninety
38	*Bayswater & Maida Vale*	XX	Jason's
30	*Chelsea*	XX	Poissonnerie de l'Avenue
48	*Strand & Covent Garden*	XX	Sheekey's

Spanish

34	*South Kensington*	XX	Cambio de Terci
34	*South Kensington*	XX	Pasha

Thai

26	*Fulham*	XX	Blue Elephant
31	*Chelsea*	XX	Busabong Too
37	*Battersea*	XX	Chada
38	*Bayswater & Maida Vale*	XX	Nipa
26	*City of London*	XX	Sri Siam City
39	*Belgravia*	XX	Vong (French Thai)
47	*Soho*	X	Sri Siam

Vegetarian

24	*Hampstead*	XX	Vegetarian Cottage

Vietnamese

47	*Soho*	X	Saigon

617

UNITED KINGDOM

Greater London is divided, for administrative purposes, into 32 boroughs plus the City; thes
sub-divide naturally into minor areas, usually grouped around former villages or quarters, whic
often maintain a distinctive character.

of Greater London: **0171** *or* **0181** *except special cases.*

LONDON AIRPORTS

Heathrow *Middx. West : 17 m. by A 4, M 4* **Underground** *Piccadilly line direct.*
$\quad$ *(0181) 759 4321 –* **Terminal** : *Airbus (A 1) from Victoria, Airbus (A 2) from Pad*
dington.
$\quad$ *Underground Station Concourse, Heathrow Airport, TW6 2JA* *(017*
824 8844/(0839) 123456.

Radisson Edwardian, 140 Bath Rd, Hayes, UB3 5AW, *(0181) 759 631*
Fax (0181) 759 4559, – rm, 550. *.*
Henleys : Meals *(closed Saturday and Sunday lunch and Bank Holidays)* 30.00 **st.** and
la carte 12.00 – *Brasserie* : Meals 16.50 **t.** (lunch) and a la carte 18.75/24.75 **t.** 8.0
– 13.50 – **442 rm** 185.00/235.00 **st.,** 17 suites.

Crowne Plaza Heathrow London, Stockley Rd, West Drayton, UB7 9NA, *(0189*
445555, Fax (01895) 445122, – 20
Concha Grill : Meals 18.50 **st.** and a la carte (see also *Simply Nico Heathrow* belov
– 15.00 – **457 rm** 125.00/235.00 **st.,** 1 suite.

Sheraton Skyline, Bath Rd, Hayes, UB3 5BP, *(0181) 759 2535, Fax (0181) 750 915*
– rm, 500. *.*
Colony Room : Meals *(dinner only)* a la carte 25.25/41.75 **t.** 11.50 – *Le Jardin* : Mea
(lunch only) a la carte 26.00/35.75 **st.** 11.50 – 15.50 – **346 rm** 198.00/208.00 st
5 suites.

Hilton Heathrow, Terminal 4, TW6 3AF, *(0181) 759 7755, Fax (0181) 759 757.*
– rm, 240. *.*
Brasserie : Meals 22.50/24.50 **st.** and a la carte 12.50 – *Zen Oriental* : Meals - Chines
- 29.00/35.00 **t.** and a la carte 14.80 – 15.95 – **390 rm** 205.00 **st.,** 5 suites – S

Excelsior Heathrow, Bath Rd, West Drayton, UB7 0DU, *(0181) 759 661*
Fax (0181) 759 3421, – rm, 700. *.*
Meals *(carving rest.)* 18.95/19.95 **st.** and dinner a la carte 5.50 – *Wheeler's* : Mea
- Seafood - *(closed lunch Saturday and Sunday and Bank Holidays)* a la carte 23.50/38.00
6.00 – 14.95 – **810 rm** 135.00/145.00 **st.,** 20 suites – SB.

Forte Crest, Sipson Rd, West Drayton, UB7 0JU, *(0181) 759 2323*
Fax (0181) 897 8659 – rm, 100. *.*
Meals *(closed Saturday lunch)* (carving rest.) 17.50 **t.** 8.95 – *Sampans* : Meals - Chines
- (dinner only) 18.95 **t.** and a la carte 8.75 – 11.95 – **604 rm** 155.00/165.00 st
6 suites – SB.

Renaissance London Heathrow, Bath Rd, TW6 2AQ, *(0181) 897 636*
Fax (0181) 897 1113, – rm, 550. *.*
Meals 17.50/20.50 **st.** and a la carte 6.50 – 14.50 – **644 rm** 145.00 **st.,** 6 suite

Sheraton Heathrow, Colnbrook bypass, West Drayton, UB7 0HJ, *(0181) 759 242*
Fax (0181) 759 2091 – rm, 70. *.*
Meals 19.95 **t.** and a la carte 13.00 – 14.95 – **425 rm** 180.00/190.00 **t.,** 6 suite

Forte Posthouse Heathrow, Bath Rd, Hayes, UB3 5AJ, *(0181) 759 255.*
Fax (0181) 564 9265 – rm, 50. *.*
Meals a la carte 15.85/24.85 **t.** – 11.50 – **186 rm** 119.00 **st.**

Simply Nico Heathrow (at Crowne Plaza Heathrow London H.), Stockley Rd, Wes
Drayton, UB7 9NA, *(01895) 437564, Fax (01895) 437565 –* .
closed Saturday lunch, Sunday and 25 December – **Meals** 25.00 **st.** 8.00.

Gatwick *W. Sussex South : 28 m. by A 23 and M 23 -* **Train** *from Victoria : Gatwick Express* 40
$\quad$ *T 30 – Crawley.*
$\quad$ *(01293) 535353.*
$\quad$ *International Arrivals Concourse, South Terminal, RH6 0NP* *(01293) 560108.*

London Gatwick Airport Hilton, South Terminal, RH6 0LL, *(01293) 51808*
Fax (01293) 528980, – rm, 500.
.
Meals 15.95/25.95 **t.** and a la carte 9.00 – 13.95 – **547 rm** 187.00/220.00 st
3 suites.

Le Meridien London Gatwick, Gatwick Airport (North Terminal), RH6 0PH, ℰ (01293) 567070, *Fax (01293) 567739*, ℔, ⊆s, ☒ – |≑|, ↫ rm, ▤ TV ☎ ৬ ℗ – ⚐ 350. ⑩ ⒜ ⓪ VISA
Gatwick Oriental : Meals - Asian - *(closed Saturday lunch)* a la carte 22.00/34.00 t. ♌ 8.50 – *Brasserie* : Meals 14.50/18.95 t. and a la carte ♌ 6.95 – ☕ 10.95 – **468 rm** 175.00 st., 6 suites – SB .

Ramada H. Gatwick, Povey Cross Rd, RH6 0BE, ℰ (01293) 820169, *Fax (01293) 820259*, ℔, ⊆s, ☒, squash – |≑|, ↫ rm, ▤ TV ☎ ℗ – ⚐ 180. ⑩ ⒜ ⓪ VISA. ⌘
Meals *(closed lunch Saturday and Sunday)* 16.50/18.50 st. and dinner a la carte ♌ 7.50 – ☕ 11.50 – **253 rm** 105.00 st., 2 suites.

Forte Posthouse Gatwick, Povey Cross Rd, RH6 0BA, ℰ (01293) 771621, *Fax (01293) 771054* – |≑|, ↫ rm, ▤ rest, TV ☎ ℗ – ⚐ 170. ⑩ ⒜ ⓪ VISA
Meals 14.95 t. (dinner) and a la carte 22.00/30.00 t. ♌ 7.95 – ☕ 11.50 – **210 rm** 119.00 st. – SB .

Gatwick Moat House, Longbridge Roundabout, Povey Cross Rd, RH6 0AB, ℰ (01293) 899988, *Fax (01293) 785991*, ℔ – ↫ rm TV ☎ ৬ ℗ – ⚐ 150. ⑩ ⒜ ⓪ VISA. ⌘
Meals (bar lunch)/dinner a la carte 14.85/21.95 st. ♌ 6.95 – ☕ 9.95 – **124 rm** 105.00 st. – SB.

CAMDEN *Except where otherwise stated see pp. 4-7.*

Bloomsbury – ✉ NW1/W1/WC1.
🛈 34-37 Woburn Pl. WC1H 0JR ℰ (0171) 580 4599.

Holiday Inn Kings Cross, 1 Kings Cross Rd, WC1X 9HX, ℰ (0171) 833 3900, *Fax (0171) 917 6163*, ⩽, ℔, ⊆s, ☒, squash – |≑|, ↫ rm, ▤ TV ☎ ৬ – ⚐ 220. ⑩ ⒜ ⓪ VISA JCB. ⌘
MT a
Meals *(closed Saturday lunch)* 17.95 st. (dinner) and a la carte 15.85/19.85 st. ♌ 6.00 – **403 rm** ☕ 170.00 st., 2 suites – SB.

Marlborough, 9-14 Bloomsbury St., WC1B 3QD, ℰ (0171) 636 5601, *Fax (0171) 240 3540* – |≑|, ↫ rm, ▤ rest, TV ☎ ৬ – ⚐ 200. ⑩ ⒜ ⓪ VISA. ⌘ LU i
Brasserie Saint Martin : Meals (bar lunch Saturday) a la carte approx. 20.50 st. ♌ 8.00 – ☕ 15.00 – **166 rm** 169.00/195.00 s., 7 suites.

Russell, Russell Sq., WC1B 5BE, ℰ (0171) 837 6470, *Fax (0171) 837 2857* – |≑|, ↫ rm, ▤ rest, TV ☎ – ⚐ 400. ⑩ ⒜ ⓪ VISA JCB. ⌘ LU o
Fitzroy Doll's : Meals 14.95/15.95 t. and dinner a la carte ♌ 8.95 – *Virginia Woolf's* : Meals a la carte 13.00/26.70 t. ♌ 7.50 – ☕ 12.95 – **327 rm** 139.00/204.00 st., 2 suites – SB .

Grafton, 130 Tottenham Court Rd, W1P 9HP, ℰ (0171) 388 4131, *Fax (0171) 387 7394* – |≑|, ↫ rm, ▤ rest, TV ☎ ☏ – ⚐ 100. ⑩ ⒜ ⓪ VISA JCB. ⌘ KU n
Cliveden Room : Meals 19.50 t. and a la carte ♌ 7.50 – ☕ 12.00 – **320 rm** 145.00/165.00 s., 4 suites.

Montague, 15 Montague St., WC1B 5BJ, ℰ (0171) 637 1001, *Fax (0171) 637 2516*, 🌱, 🛋 – |≑|, ↫ rm, ▤ rest, TV ☎ ☏ ৬ – ⚐ 120. ⑩ ⒜ ⓪ VISA JCB. ⌘ LU c
Blue Door Bistro : Meals *(closed lunch Saturday and Sunday)* a la carte 16.95/27.85 t. ♌ 15.00 – ☕ 12.50 – **102 rm** 140.00/210.00 s., 2 suites.

Mountbatten, 20 Monmouth St., WC2H 9HD, ℰ (0171) 836 4300, *Fax (0171) 240 3540* – |≑|, ↫ rm, ▤ rest, TV ☎ – ⚐ 75. ⑩ ⒜ ⓪ VISA. ⌘ p. 17 DV o
The Ad-Lib : Meals 22.50 t. and a la carte ♌ 7.50 – ☕ 15.00 – **120 rm** 215.00/245.00 s., 7 suites.

Covent Garden, 10 Monmouth St., WC2H 9HB, ℰ (0171) 806 1000, *Fax (0171) 806 1100*, ℔ – |≑| ▤ TV ☎ ☏. ⑩ ⒜ VISA. ⌘ p. 17 DV n
Brasserie Max : Meals (booking essential) a la carte 25.00/28.95 t. – ☕ 15.50 – **48 rm** 175.00/255.00 s., 2 suites.

Thistle Kingsley, Bloomsbury Way, WC1A 2SD, ℰ (0171) 242 5881, *Fax (0171) 831 0225* – |≑|, ↫ rm, TV ☎ ৬ – ⚐ 90. ⑩ ⒜ ⓪ VISA JCB. ⌘ LU r
Meals *(closed lunch Saturday, Sunday and Bank Holidays)* 18.50 t. and a la carte ♌ 6.10 – ☕ 12.50 – **138 rm** 150.00/240.00 st.

Forte Posthouse Bloomsbury, Coram St., WC1N 1HT, ℰ (0171) 837 1200, *Fax (0171) 837 5374* – |≑|, ↫ rm, ▤ rest, TV ☎ ৬ – ⚐ 300. ⑩ ⒜ ⓪ VISA JCB. ⌘
Meals 16.95 t. (dinner) and a la carte 17.00/28.00 t. ♌ 8.95 – ☕ 11.95 – **281 rm** 139.00/169.00 st., 3 suites – SB . LT c

Kenilworth, 97 Great Russell St., WC1B 3LB, ℰ (0171) 637 3477, *Fax (0171) 631 3133* – |≑|, ↫ rm, ▤ rest, TV ☎ – ⚐ 65. ⑩ ⒜ ⓪ VISA JCB. ⌘ LU a
Meals 14.50 st. and a la carte ♌ 9.00 – ☕ 12.00 – **187 rm** 140.00/165.00 s.

Blooms without rest., 7 Montague St., WC1B 5BP, ℘ (0171) 323 1717
Fax (0171) 636 6498 – ⓘ TV ☎. ⓂⓄ ⒶⒺ Ⓞ VISA JCB. ⅗   LU
27 rm ☑ 125.00/195.00 st.

Bonnington in Bloomsbury, 92 Southampton Row, WC1B 4BH, ℘ (0171) 242 2828
Fax (0171) 831 9170 – ⓘ, ⅙ rm, ▤ rest, TV ☎ ⅙ – ⚐ 250. ⓂⓄ ⒶⒺ Ⓞ VISA JCB   LU
Meals (bar lunch Saturday and Sunday) 11.50/19.75 st. and a la carte ⓘ 7.80 – 215 rm
☑ 110.00/140.00 st.

Bloomsbury Park, 126 Southampton Row, WC1B 5AD, ℘ (0171) 430 0434
Fax (0171) 242 0665 – ⓘ, ⅙ rm, TV ☎ – ⚐ 25. ⓂⓄ ⒶⒺ Ⓞ VISA JCB. ⅗   LU
Meals a la carte 13.85/17.95 t. ⓘ 4.95 – ☑ 11.95 – 95 rm 110.00/140.00 st. – SB.

Pied à Terre, 34 Charlotte St., W1P 1HJ, ℘ (0171) 636 1178, Fax (0171) 916 1171
▤. ⓂⓄ ⒶⒺ Ⓞ VISA JCB   KU
❀❀   closed Saturday lunch, Sunday, last 2 weeks August, 2 weeks Christmas-New Year and Bank
Holidays – Meals 23.00/35.50-49.00 t. ⓘ 11.00
Spec. Roasted langoustines with tomato and langoustine millefeuille, fennel purée. Venison
fillet with beetroot gratin and purée, port sauce. Lime parfait with warm ginger savarin
and lime sauce.

Neal Street, 26 Neal St., WC2H 9PS, ℘ (0171) 836 8368, Fax (0171) 240 3964 – ⓂⓄ
ⒶⒺ Ⓞ VISA JCB   p. 17   DV
closed Sunday, Christmas-New Year and Bank Holidays – Meals 27.00 t. (lunch) and a la
carte 25.00/42.00 t. ⓘ 12.75.

The Birdcage, 110 Whitfield St., W1P 5RU, ℘ (0171) 383 3346, Fax (0171) 350 159.
– ⓂⓄ ⒶⒺ VISA   KU
closed Saturday lunch and Sunday – Meals 18.00/32.00 t. and·a la carte.

Malabar Junction, 107 Great Russell St., WC1B 3NA, ℘ (0171) 580 5230
Fax (0171) 436 9942 – ▤. ⓂⓄ ⒶⒺ VISA   LU
closed 25 and 26 December – Meals - South Indian - 8.90 t. (lunch) and a la carte
12.00/26.00 t. ⓘ 8.00.

Mon Plaisir, 21 Monmouth St., WC2H 9DD, ℘ (0171) 836 7243, Fax (0171) 240 477.
– ⓂⓄ ⒶⒺ Ⓞ VISA JCB   p. 17   DV
closed Saturday lunch, Sunday, 1 week Christmas-New Year, Easter and Bank Holidays
Meals - French - 14.95/13.95 t. and a la carte ⓘ 6.20.

Alfred, 245 Shaftesbury Av., WC2H 8EH, ℘ (0171) 240 2566, Fax (0171) 497 0672,
– ▤. ⓂⓄ ⒶⒺ Ⓞ VISA   p. 17   DV
closed Sunday, 24 December-2 January and Bank Holidays – Meals - English - 15.90 t.
(lunch) and a la carte.

Museum Street Cafe, 47 Museum St., WC1A 1LY, ℘ (0171) 405 3211
Fax (0171) 405 3211 – ⅙. ⓂⓄ ⒶⒺ VISA   LU
closed 1 week in summer and 2 weeks Christmas – Meals (lunch only) a la carte
14.00/18.00 t. ⓘ 9.00.

Euston – ✉ WC1.

Euston Plaza, 17/18 Upper Woburn Pl., WC1H 0HT, ℘ (0171) 383 4105
Fax (0171) 383 4106, Ⓕ, ⇌ – ⓘ, ⅙ rm, ▤ TV ☎ ⅙ – ⚐ 150. ⓂⓄ ⒶⒺ Ⓞ VISA JCB
⅗   KLT
Three Crowns : Meals 13.95/17.95 t. and dinner a la carte ⓘ 5.90 – Terrace : Meal
a la carte 11.40/19.05 t. ⓘ 5.90 – ☑ 11.95 – 150 rm 149.00/165.00 st. – SB.

London Euston Travel Inn Capital, 141 Euston Rd, NW1 2AU, ℘ (0171) 554 3400
Fax (0171) 554 3419 – ⓘ, ⅙ rm, ▤ rest TV ⅙. ⓂⓄ ⒶⒺ Ⓞ VISA. ⅗   LT
Meals (grill rest.) – 220 rm 55.00 t.

Hampstead – ✉ NW3.

Ⓖ Winnington Rd, Hampstead ℘ (0181) 455 0203.

Forte Posthouse Hampstead, 215 Haverstock Hill, NW3 4RB, ℘ (0171) 794 8121
Fax (0171) 435 5586 – ⓘ, ⅙ rm, ▤ rest, TV ☎ ⓟ – ⚐ 30. ⓂⓄ ⒶⒺ Ⓞ VISA JCB. ⅗
Meals (bar lunch Monday to Saturday)/dinner a la carte 16.30/25.90 st. ⓘ 8.00 – ☑ 10.9
– 140 rm 129.00 st. – SB.   ES

Byron's, 3a Downshire Hill, NW3 1NR, ℘ (0171) 435 3544, Fax (0171) 431 3544 – ⓂⓄ
ⒶⒺ VISA   ES
closed 25 December – Meals (dinner only) a la carte 19.75/34.65 t.

ZeNW3, 83-84 Hampstead High St., NW3 1RE, ℘ (0171) 794 7863, Fax (0171) 794 695.
– ▤. ⓂⓄ ⒶⒺ Ⓞ VISA JCB   ES
closed Christmas – Meals - Chinese - 16.50/27.50 t. and a la carte.

Vegetarian Cottage, 91 Haverstock Hill, NW3 4RL, ℘ (0171) 586 1257 – ▤. ⓂⓄ VIS.
closed Tuesday and 25-26 December – Meals - Chinese Vegetarian - (dinner only and
Sunday lunch)/dinner 11.80 t. and a la carte ⓘ 5.00.   HS

Hatton Garden – ✉ EC1.

XX **Bleeding Heart,** Bleeding Heart Yard, EC1N 8SJ, *off Greville St., Hatton Garden* ℰ (0171) 242 2056, Fax (0171) 831 1402, ☂ – 🅼🅒 🅰🅔 🅞 🆅🅘🆂🅰 🅹🅒🅱   NU e
closed Saturday, Sunday, 24 December-5 January and Bank Holidays – **Meals** a la carte 21.85/26.70 **t.** ⓘ 6.95.

Holborn – ✉ WC2.

🏨 **Drury Lane Moat House,** 10 Drury Lane, High Holborn, WC2B 5RE, ℰ (0171) 208 9988, Fax (0171) 831 1548, 🗲 – ⊞, ⇥ rm, 🔲 📺 ☎ & 🅿 – ⚞ 60. 🅼🅒 🅰🅔 🅞 🆅🅘🆂🅰. ⌧
Meals 14.00/16.00 **st.** and a la carte ⓘ 5.60 – ☕ 10.75 – **163 rm** 155.00/175.00 **st.** –
SB.   p. 17 DV c

Primrose Hill – ✉ NW1.

XX **Odette's,** 130 Regent's Park Rd, NW1 8XL, ℰ (0171) 586 5486, Fax (0171) 586 2575 – 🅼🅒 🅰🅔 🅞 🆅🅘🆂🅰   HS i
closed Saturday lunch, Sunday, 1 week Christmas and Bank Holidays – **Meals** 10.00 **t.** (lunch) and a la carte 17.25/31.25 **t.** ⓘ 6.95 (see also **Odette's Wine Bar** below).

X **Odette's Wine Bar** (at Odette's), 130 Regent's Park Rd, NW1 8XL, ℰ (0171) 722 5388, Fax (0171) 586 2575 – 🅼🅒 🅰🅔 🅞 🆅🅘🆂🅰   HS i
closed Sunday dinner, 1 week Christmas and Bank Holidays – **Meals** (booking essential) 10.00 **t.** (lunch) and a la carte 13.00/18.45 **t.** ⓘ 6.95.

🍺 **The Queens,** 49 Regent's Park Rd, NW1 8XE, ℰ (0171) 586 0408, Fax (0171) 586 5677, ☂ – 🅼🅒 🆅🅘🆂🅰   HS a
Meals a la carte 15.85/20.85 ⓘ 5.95.

Regent's Park – ✉ NW1.

🏨 **White House,** Albany St., NW1 3UP, ℰ (0171) 387 1200, Fax (0171) 388 0091, 🗲, ⇌s – ⊞, ⇥ rm, 🔲 rest, 📺 ☎ – ⚞ 110. 🅼🅒 🅰🅔 🅞 🆅🅘🆂🅰 🅹🅒🅱. ⌧   JT o
The Restaurant : Meals a la carte approx. 35.00 **t.** ⓘ 8.00 – **Garden Cafe :** Meals *(closed Saturday lunch and Sunday)* a la carte approx. 35.00 **t.** – ☕ 12.00 – **580 rm** 152.00/201.00 **st.**, 2 suites.

Swiss Cottage – ✉ NW3.

🏨 **Regents Park Marriott,** 128 King Henry's Rd, NW3 3ST, ℰ (0171) 722 7711, Fax (0171) 586 5822, 🗲, ⇌s, ▨ – ⊞, ⇥ rm, 🔲 📺 ☎ & 🅿 – ⚞ 400. 🅼🅒 🅰🅔 🅞 🆅🅘🆂🅰 🅹🅒🅱. ⌧   GS a
Meals 18.95 **st.** and a la carte ⓘ 6.00 – ☕ 13.95 – **298 rm** 180.00/200.00 **s.**, 5 suites – SB.

🏨 **Swiss Cottage** without rest., 4 Adamson Rd, NW3 3HP, ℰ (0171) 722 2281, Fax (0171) 483 4588 – ⊞ 📺 ☎ – ⚞ 50. 🅼🅒 🅰🅔 🅞 🆅🅘🆂🅰. ⌧   GS n
☕ 5.00 **48 rm** 87.50/143.00 **st.**, 6 suites.

XX **Peter's Chateaubriand,** 65 Fairfax Rd, NW6 4EE, ℰ (0171) 624 5804 – 🔲. 🅼🅒 🆅🅘🆂🅰   FS i
closed Saturday lunch, 26 December and 1 January – **Meals** a la carte 17.45/28.40 **t.**

XX **Bradley's,** 25 Winchester Rd, NW3 3NR, ℰ (0171) 722 3457, Fax (0171) 431 4776 – 🔲. 🅼🅒 🅰🅔 🆅🅘🆂🅰   GS e
closed Saturday lunch, 25-26 December and 1 January – **Meals** 10.00 **t.** (lunch) and a la carte 22.00/29.00 **t.** ⓘ 9.00.

XX **Globe,** 100 Avenue Rd, NW3 3HF, ℰ (0171) 722 7200, Fax (0171) 722 7676 – 🔲. 🅼🅒 🆅🅘🆂🅰 🅹🅒🅱   GS v
closed Saturday lunch – **Meals** 13.50 **t.** (lunch) and a la carte 18.00/20.50 **t.**

XX **Benihana,** 100 Avenue Rd, NW3 3HF, ℰ (0171) 586 9508, Fax (0171) 586 6740 – 🔲. 🅼🅒 🅰🅔 🅞 🆅🅘🆂🅰 🅹🅒🅱   GS o
closed 25 December – **Meals** - Japanese (Teppan-Yaki) - 8.50/14.00 **t.** and a la carte.

CITY OF LONDON *Except where otherwise stated see* p. 7.

XXX **Gladwins,** Minister Court, Mark Lane, EC3R 7AA, ℰ (0171) 444 0004, Fax (0171) 444 0001 – 🔲. 🅼🅒 🅰🅔 🆅🅘🆂🅰   PV e
closed Saturday, Sunday and 23 December-4 January – **Meals** (lunch only) 33.00 **t.**

XXX **City Rhodes,** 1 New Street Sq., EC4A 3BF, ℰ (0171) 583 1313, Fax (0171) 353 1662 ❀ – 🔲. 🅼🅒 🅰🅔 🅞 🆅🅘🆂🅰   NU u
closed Saturday, Sunday, Christmas, New Year and Bank Holidays – **Meals** a la carte 29.00/47.00 **t.** ⓘ 9.00
Spec. Seared scallops and roasted chicory, sweet carrot and foie gras sauce. Braised pig's trotter "Bourguignonne". Bread and butter pudding.

UNITED KINGDOM

XXX **Coq d'Argent,** No.1 Poultry, EC2R 8EJ, ✆ (0171) 395 5000, *Fax (0171) 395 5050*, ⛓
– 📧. ⓂⒸ ⒶⒺ ⓪ 𝑉𝐼𝑆𝐴 🄹🄲🄱
PV
closed Saturday lunch and 25 December – **Meals** a la carte 30.00/43.00 **t.** ⬧ 12.50.

XXX **Tatsuso,** 32 Broadgate Circle, EC2M 2QS, ✆ (0171) 638 5863, *Fax (0171) 638 5864*
📧. ⓂⒸ ⒶⒺ ⓪ 𝑉𝐼𝑆𝐴 🄹🄲🄱
PU
closed Saturday, Sunday and Bank Holidays – **Meals** - Japanese - (booking essential) a l
carte 35.00/80.00 **t.**

XXX **1 Lombard Street (Restaurant),** 1 Lombard St., EC2V 9AA, ✆ (0171) 929 661
Fax (0171) 929 6622 – ⓂⒸ ⒶⒺ 𝑉𝐼𝑆𝐴 🄹🄲🄱
PV
closed Saturday, Sunday and Bank Holidays – **Meals** 27.50/38.00 **t.** and a la carte (see als
1 Lombard Street (Brasserie) below).

XX **1 Lombard Street (Brasserie),** 1 Lombard St., EC2V 9AA, ✆ (0171) 929 661
Fax (0171) 929 6622 – ⓂⒸ ⒶⒺ ⓪ 𝑉𝐼𝑆𝐴 🄹🄲🄱
PV
closed Saturday, Sunday and Bank Holidays – **Meals** a la carte 17.95/28.40 **t.**

XX **10,** Cutlers Gardens Arcade, Devonshire Sq., EC2M 4EY, ✆ (0171) 283 7888
Fax (0171) 626 4859 – 📧. ⓂⒸ ⒶⒺ ⓪ 𝑉𝐼𝑆𝐴 🄹🄲🄱
PU
closed Saturday, Sunday and Bank Holidays – **Meals** 15.95 (dinner) and a la cart
21.75/39.75.

XX **Brasserie Rocque,** 37 Broadgate Circle, EC2M 2QS, ✆ (0171) 638 7919
Fax (0171) 628 5899, ⛱ – 📧. ⓂⒸ ⒶⒺ ⓪ 𝑉𝐼𝑆𝐴
PU
closed Saturday, Sunday and Bank Holidays – **Meals** (lunch only) 29.50 **t.** ⬧ 5.00.

XX **Le Quai,** Riverside, 1 Paul's Walk, High Timber St., EC4V 3QH, ✆ (0171) 236 6480
Fax (0171) 236 6479 – 📧. ⓂⒸ ⒶⒺ ⓪ 𝑉𝐼𝑆𝐴 🄹🄲🄱
OV
closed Saturday, Sunday, 2 weeks Christmas-New Year and Bank Holidays – **Meals** - Frenc
- (dinner booking essential) 32.50 **st.** ⬧ 13.20.

XX **Miyama,** 17 Godliman St., EC4V 5BD, ✆ (0171) 489 1937, *Fax (0171) 236 0325* – 📧
ⓂⒸ ⒶⒺ ⓪ 𝑉𝐼𝑆𝐴 🄹🄲🄱
OV
closed Saturday dinner, Sunday, 20 December-3 January and Bank Holidays – **Meals** - Japa
nese - 35.00/45.00 **t.** and a la carte.

XX **Imperial City,** Royal Exchange, Cornhill, EC3V 3LL, ✆ (0171) 626 3437
Fax (0171) 338 0125 – 📧. ⓂⒸ ⒶⒺ ⓪ 𝑉𝐼𝑆𝐴
PV
closed Saturday, Sunday, 25-26 December and Bank Holidays – **Meals** - Chinese
15.95/30.00 **t.** and a la carte.

XX **Sri Siam City,** 85 London Wall, EC2M 7AD, ✆ (0171) 628 5772, *Fax (0171) 628 339*
– 📧. ⓂⒸ ⒶⒺ ⓪ 𝑉𝐼𝑆𝐴
PU
closed Saturday, Sunday, 25-26 December and Bank Holidays – **Meals** - Thai
15.95/29.95 **t.** and a la carte ⬧ 8.00.

XX **Sri India,** 7 Bishopgate Churchyard, EC2M 3TJ, ✆ (0171) 628 7888
Fax (0171) 628 8282, ⛱ – 📧. ⓂⒸ ⒶⒺ ⓪ 𝑉𝐼𝑆𝐴
PU
closed Saturday, Sunday, 25-26 December and Bank Holidays – **Meals** - Indian - 15.50 t
and a la carte.

HAMMERSMITH AND FULHAM *pp. 8 and 9.*

Fulham – ✉ SW6.

🏨 **La Reserve,** 422-428 Fulham Rd, SW6 1DU, ✆ (0171) 385 8561, *Fax (0171) 385 766*
– 📶, ✳ rm, 📺 ☎. ⓂⒸ ⒶⒺ ⓪ 𝑉𝐼𝑆𝐴. 🚫
FZ
Meals 10.00/12.00 and a la carte ⬧ 9.95 – ☕ 4.50 – **43 rm** 79.00/110.00 **t.**

🏠 **London Putney Bridge Travel Inn Capital,** 3 Putney Bridge Approach, SW6 3J
✆ (0171) 471 8300, *Fax (0171) 471 8315* – 📶, ✳ rm, 📺 &. ⓂⒸ ⒶⒺ ⓪
𝑉𝐼𝑆𝐴. 🚫
Meals (grill rest.) – **154 rm** 55.00 **t.**

XX **Blue Elephant,** 4-6 Fulham Broadway, SW6 1AA, ✆ (0171) 385 6595
Fax (0171) 386 7665 – 📧. ⓂⒸ ⒶⒺ ⓪ 𝑉𝐼𝑆𝐴
EZ
closed Saturday lunch and 24 to 27 December – **Meals** - Thai - (booking essential) 29.00
and a la carte ⬧ 6.25.

XX **755,** 755 Fulham Rd, SW6 5UU, ✆ (0171) 371 0755, *Fax (0171) 371 0695* – 📧. ⓂⒸ Ⓐ
𝑉𝐼𝑆𝐴
closed Sunday dinner, Monday, 2 weeks August and 1 week Christmas – **Meal**
16.00/22.00 **t.** and a la carte ⬧ 9.00.

XX **Mao Tai,** 58 New Kings Rd., Parsons Green, SW6 4UG, ✆ (0171) 731 2520 – 📧. ⓂⒸ Ⓐ
⓪ 𝑉𝐼𝑆𝐴
closed 25 and 26 December – **Meals** - Chinese (Szechuan) - a la carte 11.90/17.80 st
⬧ 15.00.

Hammersmith – ✉ W6/W12/W14.

River Café (Ruth Rogers/Rose Gray), Thames Wharf, Rainville Rd, W6 9HA, ℘ (0171) 381 8824, Fax (0171) 381 6217, 🌳 – ⓂⒸ 🄰🄴 ⓄⒹ 𝖵𝖨𝖲𝖠 𝖩𝖢𝖡
closed Sunday dinner, 1 week Christmas-New Year and Bank Holidays – **Meals** - Italian - (booking essential) a la carte 33.50/45.00 **t.** ⅄ 8.50.
Spec. Chargrilled squid with red chilli and rocket. Wood roasted tranche of turbot, grilled zucchini, peppers and aubergine. "Chocolate nemesis".

Tandoori Nights, 319-321 King St., W6 9NH, ℘ (0181) 741 4328, Fax (0181) 741 4328 – ▤. ⓂⒸ 🄰🄴 ⓄⒹ 𝖵𝖨𝖲𝖠 𝖩𝖢𝖡
closed 25 and 26 December – **Meals** - Indian - a la carte 12.65/23.25 **t.** ⅄ 6.95.

Snows on the Green, 166 Shepherd's Bush Rd, Brook Green, W6 7PB, ℘ (0171) 603 2142, Fax (0171) 602 7553 – ⓂⒸ 🄰🄴 ⓄⒹ 𝖵𝖨𝖲𝖠
closed Saturday lunch, Sunday dinner, 1 week Christmas and Bank Holiday Mondays – **Meals** 15.50 **t.** (lunch) and a la carte 20.20/25.95 **t.** ⅄ 6.95.

The Brackenbury, 129-131 Brackenbury Rd, W6 0BQ, ℘ (0181) 748 0107, Fax (0181) 741 0905, 🌳 – ⓂⒸ 🄰🄴 𝖵𝖨𝖲𝖠
closed Saturday lunch, Sunday dinner and Bank Holidays – **Meals** 10.50 **t.** (lunch) and a la carte 16.00/23.00 **t.** ⅄ 8.50.

Anglesea Arms, 35 Wingate Rd, W6 0UR, ℘ (0181) 749 1291, Fax (0181) 749 1254 – ⓂⒸ 𝖵𝖨𝖲𝖠
closed 24 to 31 December – **Meals** (bookings not accepted) a la carte 15.95/25.70 **t.** ⅄ 8.50.

Shepherd's Bush – ✉ W14.

Chinon, 23 Richmond Way, W14 0AS, ℘ (0171) 602 5968, Fax (0171) 602 4082 – ▤. ⓂⒸ 🄰🄴 𝖵𝖨𝖲𝖠
closed Sunday, 25 December and 3 days Easter – **Meals** (dinner only) 20.00 **t.** and a la carte.

Havelock Tavern, 57 Masbro Rd, W14 0LS, ℘ (0171) 603 5374, Fax (0171) 602 1163, 🌳
closed 29-30 August and 21-27 December – **Meals** (bookings not accepted) a la carte approx. 16.00 ⅄ 4.50.

ISLINGTON *pp. 4-7.*

Clerkenwell – ✉ EC1.

Maison Novelli, 29 Clerkenwell Green, EC1R 0DU, ℘ (0171) 251 6606, Fax (0171) 490 1083 – ⓂⒸ 🄰🄴 ⓄⒹ 𝖵𝖨𝖲𝖠   NU a
closed Saturday lunch and Sunday – **Meals** a la carte 29.75/41.75 **t.** ⅄ 12.65.

Novelli EC1, 30 Clerkenwell Green, EC1R 0DU, ℘ (0171) 251 6606, Fax (0171) 490 1083 – ⓂⒸ 🄰🄴 ⓄⒹ 𝖵𝖨𝖲𝖠   NU a
closed Saturday lunch and Sunday – **Meals** a la carte 22.50/29.45 **t.** ⅄ 10.50.

Finsbury – ✉ EC1.

Simply Nico, 7 Goswell Rd, EC1N 7AH, ℘ (0171) 336 7677, Fax (0171) 336 7690 – ▤. ⓂⒸ 🄰🄴 ⓄⒹ 𝖵𝖨𝖲𝖠 𝖩𝖢𝖡   OUT a
closed Saturday lunch and Sunday – **Meals** 25.00/27.00 **st.** ⅄ 8.00.

Peasant, 240 St. John St., EC1V 4PH, ℘ (0171) 336 7726, Fax (0171) 251 4476 – ⓂⒸ 🄰🄴 𝖵𝖨𝖲𝖠   NT e
closed Saturday lunch, Sunday, 24 December-3 January and Bank Holidays – **Meals** a la carte 16.80/22.00 **st.**

Islington – ✉ N1.

Stakis London Islington, 53 Upper St., N1 0UY, ℘ (0171) 354 7700, Fax (0171) 354 7711 – 🛗, ✳ rm, ▤ 📺 ☎ ᵔ – 🔬 35. ⓂⒸ 🄰🄴 ⓄⒹ 𝖵𝖨𝖲𝖠 𝖩𝖢𝖡. ✳   NS s
Meals 18.65 **t.** (dinner) and a la carte 15.40/28.30 **t.** – ☕ 12.50 – **177 rm** 160.00/210.00 **st.,** 6 suites.

Jurys London Inn, 60 Pentonville Rd, N1 9LA, ℘ (0171) 282 5500, Fax (0171) 282 5511 – 🛗, ✳ rm, ▤ 📺 ☎ ᵔ – 🔬 30. ⓂⒸ 🄰🄴 ⓄⒹ 𝖵𝖨𝖲𝖠. ✳   MT e
closed 24 to 27 December – **Meals** (carving lunch Monday to Friday)/dinner 15.00 **st.** and a la carte ⅄ 4.75 – ☕ 8.00 – **229 rm** 85.00 **st.**

XX **Frederick's,** Camden Passage, N1 8EG, ℘ (0171) 359 2888, *Fax (0171) 359 5173,* 🍃
🚗 – 🍽. 💳 AE ① VISA JCB.
NS
closed Sunday, Christmas and Bank Holidays – **Meals** a la carte 25.00/30.00 t. ⚶ 6.95

XX **Lola's,** 359 Upper St., N1 0PD, ℘ (0171) 359 1932, *Fax (0171) 359 2209* – 💳 AE ①
VISA
NS
Meals a la carte 23.25/26.00 t. ⚶ 7.75.

XX **White Onion,** 297 Upper St., N1 2TU, ℘ (0171) 359 3533, *Fax (0171) 359 3533* – 🍽
💳 AE VISA
NS
closed Monday lunch, 25 December and 1 January – **Meals** 14.50 t. (lunch) and dinner
la carte 25.00/28.90 t. ⚶ 9.50.

KENSINGTON and CHELSEA (Royal Borough of).

Chelsea – ✉ SW1/SW3/SW10 – *Except where otherwise stated see pp. 14 and 15.*

Hyatt Carlton Tower, 2 Cadogan Pl., SW1X 9PY, ℘ (0171) 235 1234,
Fax (0171) 235 9129, ≤, 🏋, ⛷s, 🔲, 🚗, ✂ – 🛗, 🍽 rm, 🍽 TV ☎ 📞 🚗 – 🔏 25.
💳 AE ① VISA JCB. 🚭
FR
Rib Room (℘ (0171) 824 7053) : **Meals** 28.00/34.00 t. and a la carte ⚶ 16.00 (see als
Grissini below) – ☕ 18.50 – **191 rm** 267.50/372.75 s., 29 suites – SB .

Conrad International London, Chelsea Harbour, SW10 0XG, ℘ (0171) 823 3000
Fax (0171) 351 6525, ≤, 🏋, ⛷s, 🔲 – 🛗, 🍽 rm, 🍽 TV ☎ 📞 ⅙ 🚗 – 🔏 180. 💳
AE ① VISA JCB. 🚭
The Brasserie : **Meals** 18.00 t. (lunch) and a la carte 28.50/34.00 t. – ☕ 19.00, **159 suite**
160.00/1600.00.

Sheraton Park Tower, 101 Knightsbridge, SW1X 7RN, ℘ (0171) 235 8050
Fax (0171) 235 8231, ≤ – 🛗, 🍽 rm, 🍽 TV ☎ ⅙ 🚗 – 🔏 60. 💳 AE ①
VISA. 🚭
FQ
Meals (see *One-O-One* below) – ☕ 18.50 – **267 rm** 285.00/305.00 s
22 suites.

Capital, 22-24 Basil St., SW3 1AT, ℘ (0171) 589 5171, *Fax (0171) 225 0011* – 🛗 🍽 ☐
❀
☎ 🚗 – 🔏 25. 💳 AE ① VISA JCB. 🚭
ER
Meals (booking essential) 28.00/60.00 t. and a la carte 52.50/56.00 t. ⚶ 9.00 – ☕ 16.5
– **48 rm** 167.00/320.00 s.
Spec. Mozzarella and tomato pizza with basil oil. Pigeon pie. Chocolate box with hazelnut
and cinnamon sauce.

Cadogan, 75 Sloane St., SW1X 9SG, ℘ (0171) 235 7141, *Fax (0171) 245 0994,* 🚗,
– 🛗, 🍽 rm, 🍽 rest, TV ☎ 📞 – 🔏 40. 💳 AE VISA. 🚭
FR
Meals *(closed Saturday lunch)* 17.90/25.50 st. ⚶ 6.75 – ☕ 15.50 – **61 rr**
150.00/230.00 st., 4 suites – SB.

Durley House, 115 Sloane St., SW1X 9PJ, ℘ (0171) 235 5537, *Fax (0171) 259 697*
« Georgian town house », 🚗, ✂ – 🛗 TV ☎. 💳 AE VISA. 🚭
FS
Meals (room service only) a la carte 20.00/31.50 t. ⚶ 19.00 – ☕ 15.00, **11 suite**
240.00/435.00.

Cliveden Town House, 26 Cadogan Gdns., SW3 2RP, ℘ (0171) 730 6466
Fax (0171) 730 0236, 🚗 – 🛗, 🍽 rm, TV ☎ 📞. 💳 AE ① VISA JCB
FS
Meals (room service only) a la carte 35.00/45.00 st. ⚶ 20.00 – ☕ 18.50 – **31 rr**
125.00/260.00 s., 4 suites.

Millenium Chelsea, 17-25 Sloane St., SW1X 9NU, ℘ (0171) 235 4377
Fax (0171) 235 3705 – 🛗, 🍽 rm, 🍽 TV ☎ – 🔏 100. 💳 AE ① VIS
JCB. 🚭
FR
The Restaurant : **Meals** *(closed Sunday)* a la carte 23.45/36.45 t. – ☕ 15.50 – **220 rr**
190.00/230.00 s., 4 suites.

Franklin, 22-28 Egerton Gdns., SW3 2DB, ℘ (0171) 584 5533, *Fax (0171) 584 5449*
« Tastefully furnished Victorian town house », 🚗 – 🛗 🍽 TV ☎ 📞. 💳 AE ①
VISA. 🚭
DS
Meals (room service only) – ☕ 14.00 – **46 rm** 150.00/295.00 s., 1 suite.

Basil Street, 8 Basil St., SW3 1AH, ℘ (0171) 581 3311, *Fax (0171) 581 3693* – 🛗 ☐
☎ – 🔏 55. 💳 AE ① VISA JCB. 🚭
FQ
Meals 16.50/19.50 t. and a la carte ⚶ 8.50 – ☕ 13.50 – **93 rm** 120.00/179.00 t.

Chelsea Village, Fulham Rd, SW6 1HS, ℘ (0171) 565 1400, *Fax (0171) 565 1450*
« Adjacent to Chelsea Football Club » – 🛗, 🍽 rm, 🍽 TV ☎ 📞 ⅙ 🅿 – 🔏 50. 💳 A
① VISA. 🚭
p. 8 FZ
Kings brasserie : **Meals** a la carte 20.70/35.50 t. ⚶ 14.50 – *Fishnets* : **Meals** - Seafoo
- a la carte 24.25/30.75 t. ⚶ 12.50 – *Arkles* : **Meals** - Irish - 21.00 t. (lunch) and dinne
a la carte 24.50/33.25 t. ⚶ 6.50 – ☕ 12.95 – **160 rm** 135.00/155.00 st.

UNITED KINGDOM

Egerton House, 17-19 Egerton Terr., SW3 2BX, ℘ (0171) 589 2412, Fax (0171) 584 6540, « Tastefully furnished Victorian town house » – ▯ ▯ TV ☎ ✆. ⓂⓄ AE Ⓞ VISA. ⌘
DR e
Meals (room service only) – ☕ 14.00 – **29 rm** 130.00/210.00 **s.**

Sydney House, 9-11 Sydney St., SW3 6PU, ℘ (0171) 376 7711, Fax (0171) 376 4233, « Tastefully furnished Victorian town house » – ▯ TV ☎ ✆. ⓂⓄ AE Ⓞ VISA
DT a
Meals (room service only) – ☕ 14.10 – **21 rm** 150.00/200.00 **s.**

The Sloane, 29 Draycott Pl., SW3 2SH, ℘ (0171) 581 5757, Fax (0171) 584 1348, « Victorian town house, antiques » – ▯ ▯ TV ☎. ⓂⓄ AE Ⓞ VISA JCB. ⌘
ET c
Meals (room service only) – ☕ 12.00 – **12 rm** 140.00/225.00 **s.**

The London Outpost of the Carnegie Club without rest., 69 Cadogan Gdns., SW3 2RB, ℘ (0171) 589 7333, Fax (0171) 581 4958, ⛟ – ▯ ⤬ ▯ TV ☎. ⓂⓄ AE Ⓞ VISA. ⌘
FS r
☕ 16.75 – **11 rm** 150.00/250.00.

Eleven Cadogan Gardens, 11 Cadogan Gdns., SW3 2RJ, ℘ (0171) 730 7000, Fax (0171) 730 5217, ♨ – ▯ TV ☎. ⓂⓄ AE Ⓞ VISA JCB. ⌘
FS u
Meals (room service only) – ☕ 11.75 – **55 rm** 160.00/260.00 **st.**, 5 suites.

Parkes without rest., 41 Beaufort Gdns., SW3 1PW, ℘ (0171) 581 9944, Fax (0171) 581 1999 – ▯ ▯ TV ☎ ✆. ⓂⓄ AE Ⓞ VISA JCB. ⌘
ER x
☕ 5.00 – **18 rm** 130.00/180.00 **s.**, 15 suites 210.00/265.00 **s.**

Beaufort without rest., 33 Beaufort Gdns., SW3 1PP, ℘ (0171) 584 5252, Fax (0171) 589 2834, « English floral watercolour collection » – ▯ ▯ TV ☎ ✆. ⓂⓄ AE Ⓞ VISA JCB. ⌘
ER n
28 rm 160.00/295.00 **s.**

L'Hotel, 28 Basil St., SW3 1AS, ℘ (0171) 589 6286, Fax (0171) 823 7826 – ▯ TV ☎. ⓂⓄ AE Ⓞ VISA JCB. ⌘
ER i
Le Metro : **Meals** a la carte 15.00/19.70 **t.** – ☕ 6.50 – **12 rm** 140.00/160.00 **s.**

Claverley without rest., 13-14 Beaufort Gdns., SW3 1PS, ℘ (0171) 589 8541, Fax (0171) 584 3410 – ▯ TV ☎. ⓂⓄ AE Ⓞ VISA JCB. ⌘
ER o
30 rm ☕ 85.00/215.00 **st.**

Knightsbridge, 12 Beaufort Gdns., SW3 1PT, ℘ (0171) 589 9271, Fax (0171) 823 9692, ♨, ⇌ – ▯ TV ☎. ⓂⓄ AE Ⓞ VISA JCB. ⌘
ER o
Meals (room service only) – **44 rm** ☕ 110.00/145.00 **t.**, 6 suites.

Gordon Ramsay, 68-69 Royal Hospital Rd, SW3 4HP, ℘ (0171) 352 4441, Fax (0171) 352 3334 – ▯. ⓂⓄ AE Ⓞ VISA JCB
EU c
closed Saturday, Sunday, 2 weeks August, 1 week Christmas and Bank Holidays – **Meals** (booking essential) 25.00/50.00 **t.** ♨ 11.00
Spec. Panaché of roasted sea scallops with cauliflower purée. Bresse pigeon poached in a bouillon of ceps with chou farci. Crème brûlée with a Granny Smith jus.

Aubergine, 11 Park Walk, SW10 0AJ, ℘ (0171) 352 3449, Fax (0171) 351 1770 – ▯. ⓂⓄ AE Ⓞ VISA
CU r
closed Saturday lunch, Sunday, 2 to 6 April and 23 December-4 January – **Meals** (booking essential) 23.50/39.50 **t.** ♨ 19.00
Spec. Brandade of cod with roast scallops and watercress sauce. Roasted veal sweetbreads with caramelised onion purée and a cep casserole. Millefeuille of caramelised pineapple with coconut ice cream.

The Canteen, Harbour Yard, Chelsea Harbour, SW10 0XD, ℘ (0171) 351 7330, Fax (0171) 351 6189 – ▯. ⓂⓄ AE Ⓞ VISA
closed Saturday lunch, Sunday dinner, 24 December-4 January and Bank Holidays – **Meals** 19.50 **t.** (lunch) and a la carte 24.45/27.40 **t.** ♨ 7.50
Spec. Velouté of sweetcorn, coriander and red pepper. Lobster tempura, Asian greens, Chinese noodles and ginger dressing. Chump of lamb with casserole of lentils and potatoes.

Bibendum, Michelin House, 81 Fulham Rd, SW3 6RD, ℘ (0171) 581 5817, Fax (0171) 823 7925 – ▯. ⓂⓄ AE Ⓞ VISA
DS s
closed 24 to 26 December – **Meals** 28.00 **t.** (lunch) and dinner a la carte 30.00/51.00 **t.** ♨ 7.25.

Fifth Floor (at Harvey Nichols), Knightsbridge, SW1X 7RJ, ℘ (0171) 235 5250, Fax (0171) 823 2207 – ▯. ⓂⓄ AE Ⓞ VISA JCB
FQ a
closed dinner Sunday and Bank Holidays and 24 to 26 December – **Meals** 23.50 **t.** (lunch) and dinner a la carte 29.50/37.50 **t.** ♨ 10.00.

La Belle Epoque, 151 Draycott Av., SW3 3AL, ℘ (0171) 460 5000, Fax (0171) 460 5001 – ▯. ⓂⓄ AE Ⓞ VISA JCB
ES c
closed 25-26 December and 1 January – **La Salle :** **Meals** a la carte 19.00/31.45 **t.** (see also **L'Oriental** below).

XXX **L'Oriental** (at La Belle Epoque), 151 Draycott Av., SW3 3AL, ℰ (0171) 460 5010
Fax (0171) 460 5001 – 🔲. 💳 AE ① VISA JCB
 ES
closed Sunday – **Meals** - Eastern specialities - (dinner only) a la carte 29.00/35.00 t.

XXX **Grissini** (at Hyatt Carlton Tower H.), Cadogan Pl., SW1X 9PY, ℰ (0171) 858 7171
Fax (0171) 235 9129, ⪡ – 🔲. 💳 AE ① VISA JCB
 FR
closed Saturday lunch and Sunday – **Meals** - Italian - 22.50/28.50 t. 🍶 12.00.

XXX **Turner's,** 87-89 Walton St., SW3 2HP, ℰ (0171) 584 6711, *Fax (0171) 584 4441 –* 🔲
💳 AE ① VISA
 ES
closed Saturday lunch, 25-26 December and Bank Holidays – **Meals** 15.00/29.50 t. and a
la carte.

XXX **One-O-One** (at Sheraton Park Tower H.), William St., SW1X 7RN, ℰ (0171) 290 7101
Fax (0171) 235 6196 – 🔲. 💳 AE ① VISA
 FQ
Meals - Seafood - 25.00 t. (lunch) and a la carte 34.50/47.50 t. 🍶 10.95.

XXX **Chutney Mary,** 535 King's Rd, SW10 0SZ, ℰ (0171) 351 3113, *Fax (0171) 351 7694*
– 🔲. 💳 AE ① VISA JCB
 p. 8 FZ
closed dinner 25 December – **Meals** - Anglo-Indian - a la carte 19.00/28.25 t.

XX **Chavot,** 257-259 Fulham Rd, SW3 6HY, ℰ (0171) 351 7823, *Fax (0171) 376 4971 –* 🔲
❀ 💳 AE ① VISA JCB
 CU
closed Saturday lunch, Sunday and 1 week Christmas – **Meals** - French - 18.50 t. (lunch)
and a la carte 36.00/43.00 t. 🍶 9.50
Spec. Tarte Tatin of endives with pan-fried foie gras. Stuffed saddle of rabbit with squid
Provençal, pearl barley risotto. White and dark chocolate marbré.

XX **Bluebird,** 350 King's Rd, SW3 5UU, ℰ (0171) 559 1000, *Fax (0171) 559 1111 –* 📶 🔲
💳 AE ① VISA JCB
 CU
closed 25 December and lunch 31 December – **Meals** 15.75 t. (lunch) and a la carte
19.50/36.90 🍶 5.90.

XX **English Garden,** 10 Lincoln St., SW3 2TS, ℰ (0171) 584 7272, *Fax (0171) 581 2844*
– 🔲. 💳 AE ① VISA JCB
 ET
closed 25 and 26 December – **Meals** - English - 16.75 t. (lunch) and a la carte 25.50/32.50 t.
🍶 5.50.

XX **Benihana,** 77 King's Rd, SW3 4NX, ℰ (0171) 376 7799, *Fax (0171) 376 7377 –* 🔲. 💳
AE ① VISA JCB
 EU
closed 25 December – **Meals** - Japanese (Teppan-Yaki) - 8.50/14.00 t. and a la carte.

XX **Brasserie St. Quentin,** 243 Brompton Rd, SW3 2EP, ℰ (0171) 589 8005
Fax (0171) 584 6064 – 🔲. 💳 AE ① VISA JCB
 DR
Meals - French - 14.50/16.50 t. and a la carte 🍶 8.50.

XX **Daphne's,** 112 Draycott Av., SW3 3AE, ℰ (0171) 589 4257, *Fax (0171) 581 2232 –* 🔲
💳 AE ① VISA
 DS
closed 24 December-3 January – **Meals** - Italian - a la carte 26.50/39.50 t. 🍶 14.00.

XX **Poissonnerie de l'Avenue,** 82 Sloane Av., SW3 3DZ, ℰ (0171) 589 2457
Fax (0171) 581 3360 – 🔲. 💳 AE ① VISA JCB
 DS
closed Sunday, 24 December-3 January and Bank Holidays – **Meals** - French Seafood
18.50 t. (lunch) and a la carte 28.00/37.00 t. 🍶 7.00.

XX **Simply Nico,** 7 Park Walk, SW10 0AJ, ℰ (0171) 349 8866, *Fax (0171) 349 8867 –* 🔲
💳 AE ① VISA
 BU
closed lunch Saturday and Monday, Sunday dinner, 25-26 December and Bank Holidays –
Meals 15.50/25.00 st.

XX **Icon,** 21 Elystan St., SW3 3NT, ℰ (0171) 589 3718, *Fax (0171) 584 1789,* 🌿 – 💳 AE
① VISA JCB
 DET
closed Sunday, 24 December-4 January and Bank Holidays – **Meals** 18.00 t. (lunch) and a
la carte 23.00/36.00 t. 🍶 12.50.

XX **Vama,** 438 King's Rd, SW10 0LJ, ℰ (0171) 351 4118, *Fax (0171) 565 8501 –* 💳 AE VISA
Meals - Indian - 10.00 st. (lunch) and a la carte 18.50/30.75 st.
 p. 9 GZ

XX **Caraffini,** 61-63 Lower Sloane St., SW1W 8DH, ℰ (0171) 259 0235, *Fax (0171) 259 0236*
– 🔲. 💳 AE VISA
 FT
closed Sunday, Easter Saturday and Bank Holidays – **Meals** - Italian - a la carte
18.50/28.00 t. 🍶 7.75.

XX **The Collection,** 264 Brompton Rd, SW3 2AS, ℰ (0171) 225 1212, *Fax (0171) 225 1050*
– 🔲. 💳 AE ① VISA JCB
 DS
closed Sunday dinner and 25-26 December – **Meals** 39.50 t. (dinner) and a la carte
25.00/33.00 t. 🍶 5.75.

XX **Le Colombier,** 145 Dovehouse St., SW3 6LB, ℰ (0171) 351 1155, *Fax (0171) 351 0077*
🌿. 💳 AE VISA
 DT
Meals - French - 15.50 t. (lunch) and a la carte 18.60/30.90 t. 🍶 5.30.

UNITED KINGDOM

XX **Pelham Street,** 93 Pelham St., SW7 2NJ, ℘ (0171) 584 4788, Fax (0171) 584 4796 –
🖃. Ⓜ️ⓒ ᴬᴱ Ⓞ 𝑉𝐼𝑆𝐴   DS c
closed Sunday, 25 December and 1 January – **Meals** 15.95 **t.** (lunch) and dinner a la carte
approx. 28.00 **t.** 🗍 10.50.

XX **Busabong Too,** 1a Langton St., SW10 0JL, ℘ (0171) 352 7414, Fax (0171) 352 7414
– 🖃. Ⓜ️ⓒ ᴬᴱ Ⓞ 𝑉𝐼𝑆𝐴 𝐉𝐂𝐁   p. 8 FZ x
closed 24 to 26 December – **Meals** - Thai - (dinner only) 22.25 **t.** and a la carte.

XX **Toto's,** Walton House, Walton St., SW3 2JH, ℘ (0171) 589 0075, Fax (0171) 581 9668
– 🖃. Ⓜ️ⓒ ᴬᴱ Ⓞ 𝑉𝐼𝑆𝐴 𝐉𝐂𝐁   ES a
closed 25 to 27 December – **Meals** - Italian - 19.50/33.00 **st.** and a la carte 🗍 11.00.

XX **Red of Knightsbridge,** 8 Egerton Garden Mews, SW3 2EH, ℘ (0171) 584 7007 – Ⓜ️ⓒ
ᴬᴱ Ⓞ 𝑉𝐼𝑆𝐴 𝐉𝐂𝐁   DR n
Meals - Chinese - 12.50/15.50 **t.** and a la carte 🗍 4.50.

XX **Good Earth,** 233 Brompton Rd, SW3 2EP, ℘ (0171) 584 3658, Fax (0171) 823 8769
– 🖃. Ⓜ️ⓒ ᴬᴱ Ⓞ 𝑉𝐼𝑆𝐴 𝐉𝐂𝐁   DR c
closed 24 to 27 December – **Meals** - Chinese - 12.25/19.90 **st.** and a la carte.

XX **Dan's,** 119 Sydney St., SW3 6NR, ℘ (0171) 352 2718, Fax (0171) 352 3265, 🌴 – Ⓜ️ⓒ
ᴬᴱ 𝑉𝐼𝑆𝐴   DU s
closed Saturday lunch, Sunday and 25 December-2 January – **Meals** 16.00 **t.** (lunch) and
dinner a la carte 20.50/27.00 **t.**

XX **Beit Eddine,** 8 Harriet St., SW1X 9JW, ℘ (0171) 235 3969, Fax (0171) 245 6335 – Ⓜ️ⓒ
ᴬᴱ Ⓞ 𝑉𝐼𝑆𝐴   FQ z
closed 25 December – **Meals** - Lebanese - a la carte approx. 25.00 **t.** 🗍 7.50.

🍺 **Chelsea Ram,** 32 Burnaby St., SW10 0PL, ℘ (0171) 351 4008, Fax (0171) 349 0884 –
Ⓜⓒ 𝑉𝐼𝑆𝐴   p. 8 FZ r
closed Christmas – **Meals** (bookings not accepted) a la carte 12.00/21.00 **t.**

🍺 **Swag and Tails,** 10-11 Fairholt St., SW7 1EG, ℘ (0171) 584 6926, Fax (0171) 581 9935
– Ⓜⓒ ᴬᴱ 𝑉𝐼𝑆𝐴 𝐉𝐂𝐁   DR r
closed Saturday, Sunday and Bank Holidays – **Meals** a la carte 16.00/21.00 **t.** 🗍 9.75.

Earl's Court – ✉ SW5 – *Except where otherwise stated see pp. 14 and 15.*

🏨 **Barkston Gardens,** 34-44 Barkston Gdns., SW5 0EW, ℘ (0171) 373 7851,
Fax (0171) 370 6570 – 🛗, ⇛ rm, 📺 ☎ – 🛐 100. Ⓜⓒ ᴬᴱ Ⓞ 𝑉𝐼𝑆𝐴. 🞨   AT e
Meals *(closed Sunday lunch)* 10.00 **st.** (dinner) and a la carte 14.00/23.00 **st.** 🗍 5.50 –
⬚ 8.75 – **93 rm** 85.00/99.00 **st.**

XX **Langan's Coq d'Or,** 254-260 Old Brompton Rd, SW5 9HR, ℘ (0171) 259 2599,
Fax (0171) 370 7735, 🌴 – 🖃. Ⓜⓒ ᴬᴱ Ⓞ 𝑉𝐼𝑆𝐴 𝐉𝐂𝐁   AU e
closed Monday, Easter and 25-26 December – **Meals** a la carte 22.00/27.50 **t.**

Kensington – ✉ SW7/W8/W11/W14 – *Except where otherwise stated see pp. 8-11.*

🏛 **Royal Garden,** 2-24 Kensington High St., W8 4PT, ℘ (0171) 937 8000,
Fax (0171) 937 1991, ≤, 🎞, 🇸 – 🛗, ⇛ rm, 🖃 📺 ☎ ✆ ♿ 🅿 – 🛐 600. Ⓜⓒ ᴬᴱ Ⓞ
𝑉𝐼𝑆𝐴 𝐉𝐂𝐁. 🞨   p. 14 AQ c
The Tenth (℘ (0171) 361 1910) : **Meals** *(closed Saturday lunch, Sunday, 2 weeks August
and Bank Holidays)* 21.00 **t.** (lunch) and a la carte 20.50/38.70 **t.** 🗍 13.75 – **Park Terrace** :
Meals 14.95 **t.** (lunch) and a la carte 18.15/31.20 **t.** 🗍 13.75 – ⬚ 16.50 – **385 rm**
195.00/295.00, 15 suites.

🏛 **Copthorne Tara,** Scarsdale Pl., W8 5SR, ℘ (0171) 937 7211, Fax (0171) 937 7100 –
🛗, ⇛ rm, 🖃 📺 ☎ ♿ 🅿 – 🛐 500. Ⓜⓒ ᴬᴱ 𝑉𝐼𝑆𝐴 𝐉𝐂𝐁. 🞨   FY u
Brasserie : **Meals** 19.00 **st.** and a la carte 🗍 6.50 – **Jerome K. Jerome** : **Meals** *(closed
Sunday, July and August)* (dinner only) a la carte 19.00/31.00 **st.** 🗍 6.50 – ⬚ 13.50 –
815 rm 170.00/185.00 **st.**, 10 suites – SB.

🏛 **Halcyon,** 81 Holland Park, W11 3RZ, ℘ (0171) 727 7288, Fax (0171) 229 8516 – 🛗 🖃
📺 ☎ ✆. Ⓜⓒ ᴬᴱ Ⓞ 𝑉𝐼𝑆𝐴 𝐉𝐂𝐁. 🞨   EX u
Meals (see **The Room** below) – ⬚ 14.00 – **40 rm** 175.00/270.00 **st.**, 3 suites – SB.

🏛 **The Milestone** without rest., 1-2 Kensington Court, W8 5DL, ℘ (0171) 917 1000,
Fax (0171) 917 1010, 🎞, 🇸 – 🛗 🖃 📺 ☎ ✆. Ⓜⓒ ᴬᴱ Ⓞ 𝑉𝐼𝑆𝐴. 🞨   p. 14 AQ u
⬚ 15.00 – **47 rm** 220.00/270.00 **st.**, 5 suites.

🏛 **London Kensington Hilton,** 179-199 Holland Park Av., W11 4UL, ℘ (0171) 603 3355,
Fax (0171) 602 9397 – 🛗, ⇛ rm, 🖃 📺 ☎ ✆ ♿ 🅿 – 🛐 300. Ⓜⓒ ᴬᴱ Ⓞ 𝑉𝐼𝑆𝐴 𝐉𝐂𝐁. 🞨
Meals 20.50 **t.** and a la carte 🗍 9.50 – **Hiroko** : **Meals** - Japanese - *(closed Monday)* 15.00 **t.**
(lunch) and a la carte 19.50/31.00 🗍 7.00 – ⬚ 14.95 – **400 rm** 190.00 **st.**   EX s

🏛 **Kensington Park Thistle,** 16-32 De Vere Gdns., W8 5AG, ℘ (0171) 937 8080,
Fax (0171) 937 7616 – 🛗, ⇛ rm, 🖃 📺 ☎ – 🛐 120. Ⓜⓒ ᴬᴱ Ⓞ 𝑉𝐼𝑆𝐴 𝐉𝐂𝐁. 🞨
Meals (buffet lunch) 16.00 **st.** and a la carte 🗍 10.00 – ⬚ 14.50 – **346 rm**
150.00/220.00 **t.**, 6 suites – SB.   p. 14 BQ e

Hilton National London Olympia, 380 Kensington High St., W14 8NL, ℰ (0171) 603 3333, Fax (0171) 603 4846, ₤ℰ, ⇌s – ⊠, ✻ rm, ▤ rest, ☑ ☎ ℗ – 🔬 450. ◉
AE ⓞ VISA JCB
EY
Meals a la carte 15.50/20.00 **st.** ⌀ 12.50 – ☕ 17.50 – **395 rm** 180.00/190.00 **st.**,
suites – SB.

Forte Posthouse Kensington, Wrights Lane, W8 5SP, ℰ (0171) 937 817
Fax (0171) 937 8289, ₤ℰ, ⇌s, ⊠, 🐎 – ⊠, ✻ rm, ▤ rest, ☑ ☎ ℗ – 🔬 180. ◉
ⓞ VISA JCB. ⊗
EY
Green's : **Meals** (closed Sunday lunch) 17.50 **t.** and a la carte – **Biancone** : **Meals** - Itali
- (dinner only) 17.50 **t.** and a la carte – ☕ 8.95 – **550 rm** 129.00 **st.** – SB.

Comfort Inn Kensington, 22-32 West Cromwell Rd, SW5 9QJ, ℰ (0171) 373 330
Fax (0171) 835 2040 – ⊠, ✻ rm, ▤ ☑ ☎ – 🔬 80. ◉ AE ⓞ VISA JCB. ⊗ EZ
Meals (bar lunch)/dinner a la carte 14.50/22.00 **st.** ⌀ 6.50 – ☕ 9.50 – **125 r**
83.50/110.00 **st.**

Holland Court without rest., 31-33 Holland Rd, W14 8HJ, ℰ (0171) 371 113
Fax (0171) 602 9114, 🐎 – ⊠ ☑ ☎. ◉ AE ⓞ VISA. ⊗
EY
22 rm ☕ 85.00/115.00 **st.**

The Room (at Halcyon H.), 129 Holland Park Av., W11 3UT, ℰ (0171) 221 541
Fax (0171) 229 8516, 🍽 – ▤. ◉ AE ⓞ VISA JCB
EX
closed Saturday lunch and Bank Holidays – **Meals** 26.00/43.00 **t.** and a la carte ⌀ 12.0

Clarke's, 124 Kensington Church St., W8 4BH, ℰ (0171) 221 9225, Fax (0171) 229 456
– ▤. ◉ AE VISA
EX
closed Saturday, Sunday, 2 weeks August and Christmas – **Meals** (set menu only at dinne
29.00/42.00 **st.** ⌀ 8.50.

Launceston Place, 1a Launceston Pl., W8 5RL, ℰ (0171) 937 691
Fax (0171) 938 2412 – ▤. ◉ AE VISA
p. 14 BR
closed Saturday lunch, Sunday dinner and Bank Holidays – **Meals** 17.50 **t.** and a la car
⌀ 6.00.

Belvedere in Holland Park, Holland House, off Abbotsbury Rd, W8 6LU, ℰ (017
602 1238, Fax (0171) 610 4382, 🍽, « 19C orangery in park » – ▤. ◉ AE ⓞ VISA
EY
closed Sunday dinner, 25 December and 1 January – **Meals** 21.50 **t.** (lunch) and a la car
20.50/32.50 **t.** ⌀ 5.75.

Arcadia, Kensington Court, 35 Kensington High St., W8 5EB, ℰ (0171) 937 429
Fax (0171) 937 4393 – ▤. ◉ AE ⓞ VISA
p. 14 AQ
closed Saturday lunch and 25 December – **Meals** 15.95 **t.** (lunch) and dinner a la car
16.75/24.70 **t.** ⌀ 6.95.

L'Escargot Doré, 2-4 Thackeray St., W8 5ET, ℰ (0171) 937 8508, Fax (0171) 937 850
– ▤. ◉ AE ⓞ VISA JCB
p. 14 AQR
closed Sunday, last 2 weeks August, 1 week Christmas and Bank Holidays – **Meals** - Frenc
- 16.50 **t.** (lunch) and a la carte 27.00/34.40 **t.** ⌀ 5.50.

Memories of China, 353 Kensington High St., W8 6NW, ℰ (0171) 603 695
Fax (0171) 603 0848 – ▤. ◉ AE ⓞ VISA
EY
closed Sunday lunch – **Meals** - Chinese - (booking essential) 20.00/25.00 **t.** and a la car
⌀ 11.00.

The Terrace, 33c Holland St., W8 4LX, ℰ (0171) 937 3224, Fax (0171) 937 3323, 🐎
– ▤. ◉ AE ⓞ VISA JCB
EY
closed Sunday dinner and 24 December-2 January – **Meals** 14.50 **t.** (lunch) and a la car
22.50/28.50 **t.** ⌀ 7.00.

Phoenicia, 11-13 Abingdon Rd, W8 6AH, ℰ (0171) 937 0120, Fax (0171) 937 7668
▤. ◉ AE ⓞ VISA JCB
EY
closed 24 and 25 December – **Meals** - Lebanese - (buffet lunch) 16.80 **t.** (lunch) and a
carte 18.60/23.75 **t.** ⌀ 5.80.

Kensington Place, 201 Kensington Church St., W8 7LX, ℰ (0171) 727 318
Fax (0171) 229 2025 – ▤. ◉ AE VISA
p. 16 AZ
closed 25 and 26 December – **Meals** (booking essential) 14.50 **t.** (lunch) and a la car
24.25/32.50 **t.** ⌀ 5.50.

Novelli W8, 122 Palace Gardens Terr., W8 4RT, ℰ (0171) 229 402
Fax (0171) 243 1826, 🍽 – ▤. ◉ AE ⓞ VISA
p. 16 AZ
closed Monday lunch – **Meals** (booking essential) a la carte 24.50/35.00 **t.**

Cibo, 3 Russell Gdns., W14 8EZ, ℰ (0171) 371 6271, Fax (0171) 602 1371 – ◉ AE ⓞ
VISA JCB
EY
closed Saturday lunch, Sunday dinner and Christmas – **Meals** - Italian - 12.50 **t.** (lunch) an
a la carte 25.00/31.50 ⌀ 6.95.

Malabar, 27 Uxbridge St., W8 7TQ, ℰ (0171) 727 8800 – ◉ VISA
p. 16 AZ
closed last week August and 4 days Christmas – **Meals** - Indian - (booking essential) (buffe
lunch Sunday) 17.25 **st.** and a la carte 15.80/31.40 **st.** ⌀ 4.75.

North Kensington – ✉ W2/W10/W11 – *Except where otherwise stated see pp. 4-7.*

Pembridge Court, 34 Pembridge Gdns., W2 4DX, ℘ (0171) 229 9977, *Fax (0171) 727 4982,* « Collection of antique clothing » – |≑|, ▤ rest, TV ☎. MC AE ⓪ VISA
p. 16 AZ n
Meals (residents only) (restricted menu) (dinner only) a la carte approx. 25.00 ⓑ 4.95 – **20 rm** ⌷ 115.00/180.00 **st.**

Abbey Court without rest., 20 Pembridge Gdns., W2 4DU, ℘ (0171) 221 7518, *Fax (0171) 792 0858,* « Victorian town house » – ⍁ TV ☎. MC AE ⓪ VISA JCB. ❄
⌷ 9.50 **22 rm** 88.00/175.00 **st.**
p. 16 AZ u

Leith's, 92 Kensington Park Rd, W11 2PN, ℘ (0171) 229 4481, *Fax (0171) 221 1246* –
▤. MC AE ⓪ VISA JCB
EV e
closed lunch Saturday and Monday, Sunday, 2 weeks Christmas-New Year, Bank Holidays and restricted opening in August – **Meals** 24.25/35.00 **t.** and dinner a la carte 34.50/47.75 **t.** ⓑ 8.00
Spec. Marinated scallops with avocado and clear gazpacho jelly. Noisette of roast pork, sweetbreads, bacon and potato rösti, truffle jus. Gooseberry and candied ginger soufflé.

Chez Moi, 1 Addison Av., Holland Park, W11 4QS, ℘ (0171) 603 8267, *Fax (0171) 603 3898* – ▤. MC AE ⓪ VISA
p. 8 EX n
closed Saturday lunch, Sunday and Bank Holidays – **Meals** - French - 15.00 **t.** (lunch) and a la carte 22.25/34.25 **t.** ⓑ 10.50.

Pharmacy, 150 Notting Hill Gate, W11 3QG, ℘ (0171) 221 2442, *Fax (0171) 243 2345* – ▤. MC AE ⓪ VISA
p. 16 AZ a
closed 25 December and 1 January – **Meals** 15.50 **t.** (lunch) and a la carte 20.80/35.00 **t.**

Orsino, 119 Portland Rd, W11 4LN, ℘ (0171) 221 3299, *Fax (0171) 229 9414* – ▤. MC AE VISA
p. 8 EX x
closed 24 and 25 December – **Meals** - Italian - (booking essential) 15.50 **t.** (lunch) and a la carte 27.00/31.00 **t.** ⓑ 6.00.

Woz, 46 Golborne Rd, W10 5PR, ℘ (0181) 968 2200, *Fax (0181) 968 0550* – MC AE VISA JCB
EU n
closed Monday lunch, Sunday dinner, Easter Saturday, 24 to 30 December and Bank Holidays – **Meals** (set menu only at dinner) 22.95 **t.** and lunch a la carte approx. 16.70 **t.** ⓑ 6.45.

South Kensington – ✉ SW5/SW7/W8 – *pp. 14 and 15.*

Millenium Gloucester, 4-18 Harrington Gdns., SW7 4LH, ℘ (0171) 373 6030, *Fax (0171) 373 0409,* ⍧ – |≑|, ⍁ rm, ▤ TV ☎ Ⓟ – ⚎ 650. MC AE ⓪ VISA JCB. ❄
BS r
South West 7 : Meals (dinner only) a la carte 17.50/21.95 **t.** ⓑ 8.50 – **Bugis Street Brasserie :** Meals 10.75 **t.** and a la carte – ⌷ 15.00 – **602 rm** 225.00/275.00 **st.,** 8 suites.

Pelham, 15 Cromwell Pl., SW7 2LA, ℘ (0171) 589 8288, *Fax (0171) 584 8444,* « Tastefully furnished Victorian town house » – |≑| ▤ TV ☎. MC AE VISA. ❄ CS z
Kemps : Meals *(closed Sunday lunch and Saturday)* 12.95/15.95 **t.** and a la carte 19.95/23.95 **t.** ⓑ 11.00 – ⌷ 13.50 – **46 rm** 145.00/225.00 **s.,** 2 suites.

Blakes, 33 Roland Gdns., SW7 3PF, ℘ (0171) 370 6701, *Fax (0171) 373 0442,* « Antique oriental furnishings » – |≑|, ▤ rest, TV ☎ ✆ Ⓟ. MC AE ⓪ VISA. ❄ BU n
Meals a la carte 35.50/48.00 **t.** ⓑ 11.00 – ⌷ 17.00 – **46 rm** 130.00/300.00, 5 suites.

Harrington Hall, 5-25 Harrington Gdns., SW7 4JW, ℘ (0171) 396 9696, *Fax (0171) 396 9090,* ⍧, ⊜ – |≑|, ⍁ rm, ▤ TV ☎ ✆ – ⚎ 250. MC AE ⓪ VISA JCB. ❄
BT n
Wetherby's : Meals 20.00 **st.** and a la carte ⓑ 14.00 – ⌷ 13.95 – **200 rm** 160.00/195.00 **st.**

Bailey's, 140 Gloucester Rd, SW7 4QH, ℘ (0171) 373 6000, *Fax (0171) 370 3760,* ⍧ – |≑|, ⍁ rm, ▤ TV ☎ ✆ – ⚎ 460. MC AE ⓪ VISA. ❄
BS a
Olives : Meals (dinner only) a la carte 18.70/27.70 **t.** ⓑ 6.50 – ⌷ 12.95 – **212 rm** 135.00/265.00 **st.**

Rembrandt, 11 Thurloe Pl., SW7 2RS, ℘ (0171) 589 8100, *Fax (0171) 225 3363,* ⍧, ⊜, ▨ – |≑|, ⍁ rm, ▤ rest, TV ☎ – ⚎ 250. MC AE ⓪ VISA JCB. ❄ DS x
Meals 17.95 **st.** and a la carte ⓑ 6.00 – ⌷ 11.95 – **195 rm** 165.00/220.00 **st.**

Swallow International, Cromwell Rd, SW5 0TH, ℘ (0171) 973 1000, *Fax (0171) 244 8194,* ⍧, ⊜, ▨ – |≑|, ⍁ rm, ▤ TV ☎ ✆ – ⚎ 200. MC AE ⓪ VISA. ❄
AS c
closed 23 to 27 December – **Blayneys :** Meals (dinner only) 22.50 **st.** and a la carte – **Hunter's :** Meals 18.00 **st.** and a la carte – ⌷ 13.00 – **419 rm** 145.00/165.00 **st.,** 2 suites.

Jury's Kensington, 109-113 Queen's Gate, SW7 5LR, ℰ (0171) 589 630(Fax (0171) 581 1492 – 🛗, ⇔ rm, 🖭 TV ☎ – 🕉 80. 🖭 AE ① VISA. 🛠 — closed 24 to 26 December – **Meals** (bar lunch)/dinner 20.50 **st.** and a la carte ⓘ 7.50 – ☕ 14.00 – **172 rm** 170.00/300.00 **st.**

CT

Regency, 100 Queen's Gate, SW7 5AG, ℰ (0171) 370 4595, Fax (0171) 370 5555, 🛏 ⇔ – 🛗, ⇔ rm, 🖭 TV ☎ 📞 – 🕉 100. 🖭 AE ① VISA JCB. 🛠 — **Meals** (closed lunch Saturday and Sunday) (carving lunch) 18.50 **st.** and a la carte ⓘ 6.0(– ☕ 15.00 – **204 rm** 147.00 **s.**, 6 suites – SB.

CT

Holiday Inn Kensington, 100 Cromwell Rd, SW7 4ER, ℰ (0171) 373 222; Fax (0171) 373 0559, 🛠, ⇔, 🏊 – 🛗, ⇔ rm, 🖭 TV ☎ 🕭 – 🕉 130. 🖭 AE ① VI! JCB. 🛠 — **Meals** (closed lunch Saturday and Sunday) 14.50/14.95 **st.** and a la carte ⓘ 7.95 – ☕ 12.5 – **143 rm** 175.00/195.00 **st.**, 19 suites.

BS

Gore, 189 Queen's Gate, SW7 5EX, ℰ (0171) 584 6601, Fax (0171) 589 812; « Attractive decor » – 🛗, ⇔ rm, TV ☎. 🖭 AE ① VISA JCB — closed 25 and 26 December – **Bistrot 190** : **Meals** (only members and residents may bool a la carte 17.95/23.75 **t.** (see also **Downstairs at One Ninety** below) – ☕ 9.50 – **54 r** 135.00/302.00 **st.**

BR

John Howard, 4 Queen's Gate, SW7 5EH, ℰ (0171) 581 3011, Fax (0171) 589 8403 🛗, ⇔ rest, 🖭 TV ☎. 🖭 AE ① VISA JCB. 🛠 — **Meals** (closed Sunday) (dinner only) 20.00 **t.** and a la carte ⓘ 6.50 – ☕ 11.50 – **43 r** 89.00/119.00 **st.**, 9 suites.

BQ

Cranley, 10-12 Bina Gdns., SW5 0LA, ℰ (0171) 373 0123, Fax (0171) 373 949; « Antiques » – 🛗 🖭 TV ☎. 🖭 AE ① VISA JCB. 🛠 — **Meals** (room service only) – ☕ 13.95 – **33 rm** 120.00/160.00 **st.**, 4 suites.

BT

Number Sixteen without rest., 16 Sumner Pl., SW7 3EG, ℰ (0171) 589 523; Fax (0171) 584 8615, « Attractively furnished Victorian town houses », 🛏 – 🛗 TV ☎ 🖭 AE ① VISA. 🛠 — ☕ 8.00 – **36 rm** 90.00/200.00 **st.**

CT

Five Sumner Place without rest., 5 Sumner Pl., SW7 3EE, ℰ (0171) 584 758(Fax (0171) 823 9962 – 🛗 TV ☎. 🖭 AE VISA JCB. 🛠 — **13 rm** ☕ 88.00/150.00 **st.**

CT

Aster House without rest., 3 Sumner Pl., SW7 3EE, ℰ (0171) 581 588; Fax (0171) 584 4925, 🛏 – ⇔ TV ☎. 🖭 VISA JCB. 🛠 — **12 rm** ☕ 60.00/155.00 **st.**

CT

Bombay Brasserie, Courtfield Rd., SW7 4UH, ℰ (0171) 370 4040, Fax (0171) 835 166! « Raj-style decor, conservatory » – 🍴. 🖭 AE ① VISA — closed 25 and 26 December – **Meals** - Indian - (buffet lunch)/dinner a la cart 23.40/34.70 **t.** ⓘ 7.50.

BS

Hilaire, 68 Old Brompton Rd, SW7 3LQ, ℰ (0171) 584 8993, Fax (0171) 581 2949 – 🍴 🖭 ① VISA — closed Saturday lunch, Sunday, 4 days Easter, 1 week August, 10 days Christmas and Ban Holidays – **Meals** (booking essential) 23.00/36.50 **t.** ⓘ 9.50.

CT

Downstairs at One Ninety (at Gore H.), 190 Queen's Gate, SW7 5EU, ℰ (017' 581 5666, Fax (0171) 581 8172 – 🍴. 🖭 AE ① VISA JCB — closed Sunday and 25-26 December – **Meals** - Seafood - (booking essential) (dinner only a la carte 25.20/35.90 **t.**

BR

Café Lazeez, (first floor), 93-95 Old Brompton Rd, SW7 3LD, ℰ (0171) 581 999; Fax (0171) 581 8200 – 🍴. 🖭 AE ① VISA JCB — **Meals** - North Indian - 5.75/14.50 **t.** and a la carte.

CT

Delhi Brasserie, 134 Cromwell Rd, SW7 4HA, ℰ (0171) 370 7617, Fax (0171) 244 863. – 🍴. 🖭 AE ① VISA — closed 25 and 26 December – **Meals** - Indian - 6.95/15.95 **t.** and a la carte.

AS

Khan's of Kensington, 3 Harrington Rd, SW7 3ES, ℰ (0171) 581 2900 Fax (0171) 581 2900 – 🍴. 🖭 AE ① VISA — closed 25 and 26 December – **Meals** - Indian - 7.95/14.50 **t.** and a la carte ⓘ 4.95.

CS

Cambio de Tercio, 163 Old Brompton Rd, SW5 0LJ, ℰ (0171) 244 897(Fax (0171) 373 8817 – 🖭 AE VISA — **Meals** - Spanish - a la carte approx. 19.25 **t.** ⓘ 6.50.

BT

Pasha, 1 Gloucester Rd, SW7 4PP, ℰ (0171) 589 7969, Fax (0171) 581 9996 – 🍴. 🖭 AE ① VISA — closed Sunday except September, 25 December and Bank Holidays – **Meals** - Morocca - 14.50 **t.** (lunch) and dinner a la carte 15.25/26.25 **t.**

BR

Memories of India, 18 Gloucester Rd, SW7 4RB, ℰ (0171) 589 6450 Fax (0171) 584 4438 – 🍴. 🖭 AE ① VISA JCB — closed 25 December – **Meals** - Indian - 15.50 (dinner) and a la carte 12.90/17.20.

BR

LAMBETH *pp. 10 and 11.*

Lambeth – ⊠ *SE1.*

 **Novotel London Waterloo,** 113 Lambeth Rd, SE1 7LS, ℰ (0171) 793 1010, *Fax (0171) 793 0202,* 🏋, ≘s – 🛗, ✵ rm, 🖪 🖸 ☎ ✆ ♿ ❦ ⇔ – 🕿 40. ⦿ 🆎 ⓪ 𝗩𝗜𝗦𝗔. ✵
Meals *(closed lunch Saturday and Sunday)* 15.95 **st.** and a la carte 🍶 7.00 – ☲ 11.50 –
185 rm 123.00/137.00 **st.,** 2 suites. LYZ a

Waterloo – ⊠ *SE1.*

Channel Tunnel : Eurostar information and reservations ℰ (0990) 186186.

🏨 **London Marriott H. County Hall,**, SE1 7PB, ℰ (0171) 928 5200, *Fax (0171) 928 5300,*
≤, 🏋, ≘s, ⊠, ▨ – 🛗 🖪 🖸 ☎ ✆ ❦ – 🕿 70. ⦿ 🆎 ⓪ 𝗩𝗜𝗦𝗔 𝗝𝗖𝗕. ✵ LY a
***County Hall* : Meals** a la carte 27.50/33.00 **t.** 🍶 10.50 – ☲ 13.95 – **195 rm**
205.00/225.00, 5 suites.

🏠 **London County Hall Travel Inn Capital,** Belvedere Rd, SE1 7PB, ℰ (0171)
902 1600, *Fax (0171) 902 1619* – 🛗 ✵, 🖪 rest, 🖸 ☎ ❦. ⦿ 🆎 ⓪ 𝗩𝗜𝗦𝗔. ✵ MX u
Meals (grill rest.) – **312 rm** 55.00 **t.**

XX **People's Palace,** Level 3, The Royal Festival Hall, SE1 8XX, ℰ (0171) 928 9999,
Fax (0171) 928 2355, ≤ Victoria Embankment and River Thames – 🖪. ⦿ 🆎 ⓪ 𝗩𝗜𝗦𝗔
Meals 17.00 **t.** (lunch) and a la carte 23.00/30.25 **t.** 🍶 5.75. p. 26 MX e

XX **RSJ,** 13a Coin St., SE1 8YQ, ℰ (0171) 928 4554, *Fax (0171) 401 2455* – 🖪. ⦿ 🆎 ⓪ 𝗩𝗜𝗦𝗔
closed Saturday lunch, Sunday and Christmas – **Meals** 16.95 **t.** and a la carte. NX e

MERTON

Wimbledon – ⊠ *SW19.*

🏰 **Cannizaro House** ⌂, West Side, Wimbledon Common, SW19 4UE, ℰ (0181) 879 1464,
Fax (0181) 879 7338, ≤, « 18C country house in Cannizaro Park », 🚗 – 🛗, ✵ rm, 🖸
☎ ℗ – 🕿 60. ⦿ 🆎 ⓪ 𝗩𝗜𝗦𝗔 𝗝𝗖𝗕. ✵
Meals 28.75 **t.** and a la carte 🍶 15.00 – ☲ 13.50 – **44 rm** 182.00/282.00 **t.,** 2 suites – SB.

SOUTHWARK *pp. 10 and 11.*

Bermondsey – ⊠ *SE1.*

🏨 **London Bridge,** 8-18 London Bridge St., SE1 9SG, ℰ (0171) 855 2200,
Fax (0171) 855 2233 – 🛗, ✵ rm 🖪 🖸 ☎ ✆ ❦ – 🕿 80. ⦿ 🆎 ⓪ 𝗩𝗜𝗦𝗔 𝗝𝗖𝗕. ✵ PX a
Meals (see *Simply Nico* below) – ☲ 11.95 – **119 rm** 150.00/175.00 **st.**

XXX **Le Pont de la Tour,** 36d Shad Thames, Butlers Wharf, SE1 2YE, ℰ (0171) 403 8403,
Fax (0171) 403 0267, ≤, 🌱, « Thames-side setting » – 🖪. ⦿ 🆎 ⓪ 𝗩𝗜𝗦𝗔 𝗝𝗖𝗕 PX c
closed Saturday lunch and dinner 24 to 28 December – **Meals** 28.50 **t.** (lunch) and dinner
a la carte 32.00/46.00 **t.** 🍶 10.00.

XXX **Bengal Clipper,** Cardamom Building, Shad Thames, Butlers Wharf, SE1 2YR, ℰ (0171)
357 9001, *Fax (0171) 357 9002* – 🖪. ⦿ 🆎 ⓪ 𝗩𝗜𝗦𝗔 𝗝𝗖𝗕 PX e
Meals - Indian - 8.75/28.00 **t.** and a la carte 🍶 8.95.

XX **Tentazioni,** 2 Mill St., Lloyds Wharf, SE1 2BD, ℰ (0171) 237 1100, *Fax (0171) 237 1100.*
⦿ 🆎 ⓪ 𝗩𝗜𝗦𝗔 𝗝𝗖𝗕
closed Saturday lunch, Sunday, 1 week August, Christmas and Bank Holidays – **Meals** -
Italian - 26.00 **t.** (dinner) and a la carte 23.50/27.50 **t.**

XX **Simply Nico** (at London Bridge H.), 8-18 London Bridge St., SE1 9SG, ℰ (0171) 407 4536,
Fax (0171) 407 4554 – 🖪. ⦿ 🆎 ⓪ 𝗩𝗜𝗦𝗔 𝗝𝗖𝗕 PX a
Meals 25.00/27.00 **st.** and a la carte 🍶 8.00.

X **Blue Print Café,** Design Museum, Shad Thames, Butlers Wharf, SE1 2YD, ℰ (0171)
378 7031, *Fax (0171) 357 8810,* 🌱, « Thames-side setting, ≤ Tower Bridge » – ⦿ 🆎
⓪ 𝗩𝗜𝗦𝗔 𝗝𝗖𝗕 PX u
closed Sunday dinner and Christmas – **Meals** a la carte 23.00/29.00 **t.**

X **Butlers Wharf Chop House,** 36e Shad Thames, Butlers Wharf, SE1 2YE, ℰ (0171)
403 3403, *Fax (0171) 403 3414,* « Thames-side setting, ≤ Tower Bridge » – ⦿ 🆎 ⓪
𝗩𝗜𝗦𝗔 𝗝𝗖𝗕 PX n
closed Saturday lunch, Sunday dinner, dinner 26 December and 1 to 3 January – **Meals**
22.50 **t.** (lunch) and dinner a la carte 24.75/40.25 **t.** 🍶 11.95.

X **Cantina Del Ponte,** 36c Shad Thames, Butlers Wharf, SE1 2YE, ℰ (0171) 403 5403,
Fax (0171) 403 0267, ≤, 🌱, « Thames-side setting » – ⦿ 🆎 ⓪ 𝗩𝗜𝗦𝗔 PX c
closed 25 and 26 December – **Meals** - Italian-Mediterranean - a la carte 15.75/27.15 **t.**
🍶 6.50.

Dulwich – ⊠ SE19.

XX **Belair House,** Gallery Rd, Dulwich Village, SE21 7AB, ✆ (0181) 299 9788, Fax (0181) 299 6793, 🍽, « Georgian summer house », 🌳 – 🅿. ⓶ⓒ ᴀᴇ ① VISA JCB
Meals 15.50/24.95 **t.** and dinner a la carte 🍷 10.50.

XX **Luigi's,** 129 Gipsy Hill, SE19 1QS, ✆ (0181) 670 1843, Fax (0181) 670 1396 – ▤. ⓶ⓒ A ① VISA JCB
Meals - Italian - 14.90 **t.** (lunch) and a la carte 16.20/24.65 **t.** 🍷 5.00.

Rotherhithe – ⊠ SE16.

🏨 **Holiday Inn at Nelson Dock,** 265 Rotherhithe St., Nelson Dock, SE16 1EJ, ✆ (0171) 231 1001, Fax (0171) 231 0599, ≤, 🍽, « Riverside setting », ⛱, ≘s, 🏊, 🎾 – ⏐
✺ rm, ▤ rest, ⓣⓥ ☎ 📞 ᴄ 🅿 – 🛏 350. ⓶ⓒ ᴀᴇ ① VISA JCB. ⅍
closed 22 to 29 December – **Three Crowns** : Meals (bar lunch)/dinner a la cart 19.85/27.85 **t.** – **Columbia's** : Meals (dinner only) 15.00 **st.** 🍷 8.00 – ☕ 10.50 – **364 rr** 121.00/143.00 **st.**, 4 suites.

Southwark – ⊠ SE1.

🏨 **Holiday Inn Express** without rest., 103-109 Southwark St., SE1 0JQ, ✆ (0171) 401 2525, Fax (0171) 401 3322 – ⏐, ✺ rm, ▤ rest, ⓣⓥ ☎ ᴄ. ⓶ⓒ ᴀᴇ ① VISA JCB. ⅍
90 rm 85.00 **st.**
OX

XXX **Oxo Tower,** (8th floor), Oxo Tower Wharf, Barge House St., SE1 9PH, ✆ (0171) 803 3888, Fax (0171) 803 3838, ≤ London skyline and River Thames, 🍽 – ⏐ ▤. ⓶ⓒ A ① VISA JCB
NX
closed Saturday lunch and 25-26 December – Meals 26.50 **t.** (lunch) and dinner a la cart 35.00/48.00 **t.** 🍷 22.50 (see also **Oxo Tower Brasserie** below).

X **Oxo Tower Brasserie** (at Oxo Tower), (8th floor), Oxo Tower Wharf, Barge House St SE1 9PH, ✆ (0171) 803 3888, Fax (0171) 803 3838, ≤ London skyline and River Thames 🍽 – ⏐ ▤. ⓶ⓒ ᴀᴇ ① VISA JCB
NX
closed 25 and 26 December – Meals a la carte 19.00/32.00 **t.** 🍷 8.50.

TOWER HAMLETS

Docklands – ⊠ E14.

🏨 **Travelodge,** A 13 Coriander Rd, E14 2AA, ✆ (0171) 531 9705, Fax (0171) 515 9178 Reservations (Freephone) 0800 850950 – ⏐, ✺ rm, ⓣⓥ ☎ ᴄ 🅿. ⓶ⓒ ᴀᴇ ① VISA. ⅍
Meals (cafe bar) – **132 rm** 39.95/59.95 **t.**

Canary Wharf – ⊠ E14.

XX **MPW,** Second Floor, Cabot Place East, E14 4QT, ✆ (0171) 513 0513, Fax (0171) 513 055 – ▤. ⓶ⓒ ᴀᴇ VISA
closed Christmas and Bank Holidays – Meals 16.95 **t.** (dinner) and a la carte 24.00/36.00

Whitechapel – ⊠ E1.

XX **Cafe Spice Namaste,** 16 Prescot St., E1 8AZ, ✆ (0171) 488 9242 Fax (0171) 488 9339 – ▤. ⓶ⓒ ᴀᴇ ① VISA JCB
closed Saturday lunch, Sunday, 24 December-1 January and Bank Holiday Monday – Meal - Indian - a la carte 17.75/24.40 **t.** 🍷 6.90.

WANDSWORTH p. 9.

Battersea – ⊠ SW8/SW11.

🏨 **Travelodge** without rest., 200 York Rd, SW11 3SA, ✆ (0171) 228 5508 Fax (0171) 228 5508, Reservations (Freephone) 0800 850950 – ⏐ ✺ ⓣⓥ ☎ ᴄ 🅿. ⓶ⓒ ᴀᴇ ① VISA JCB. ⅍
80 rm 39.95/59.95 **t.**

XX **Ransome's Dock,** 35-37 Parkgate Rd, SW11 4NP, ✆ (0171) 223 1611 Fax (0171) 924 2614, 🍽 – ⓶ⓒ ᴀᴇ ① VISA JCB
HZ
closed Sunday dinner, 1 week Christmas and August Bank Holiday – Meals a la cart 19.95/30.50 **t.** 🍷 6.50.

XX **Cafe Spice Namaste,** 247 Lavender Hill, SW11 1JW, ✆ (0171) 738 1717 Fax (0171) 738 1666 – ▤ rest. ⓶ⓒ ᴀᴇ ① VISA JCB
closed Monday to Wednesday lunch and 25-26 December – Meals - Indian - 10.00 **st.** (lunch and a la carte 16.70/24.70 🍷 6.90.

XX **Chada,** 208-210 Battersea Park Rd, SW11 4ND, ✆ (0171) 622 2209, *Fax (0171) 924 2178* – 🖥. 🅜 🆎 ⓪ *VISA* JCB
closed Saturday lunch and Bank Holidays – **Meals** - Thai - a la carte 16.40/31.40 st.

🍴 **Duke of Cambridge,** 228 Battersea Bridge Rd, SW11 3AA, ✆ (0171) 223 5662, *Fax (0171) 801 9684,* 🌳 – 🅜 *VISA*
Meals a la carte 11.40/20.40 t. 🍷 7.50.

Putney – ✉ SW15.

XX **Putney Bridge,** Lower Richmond Rd, SW15 1LB, ✆ (0181) 780 1811, *Fax (0181) 780 1211,* ≼, « Riverside setting » – 🅜 🆎 ⓪ *VISA* JCB
Meals 17.50 **t.** (lunch) and a la carte 18.30/34.00 **t.** 🍷 5.50.

XX **Royal China,** 3 Chelverton Rd, SW15 1RN, ✆ (0181) 788 0907 – 🖥. 🆎 ⓪
closed 24 to 26 December – **Meals** - Chinese - 20.00/26.00 **t.** and a la carte.

XX **The Phoenix,** Pentlow St., SW15 1LY, ✆ (0181) 780 3131, *Fax (0181) 780 1114* – 🖥. 🅜 🆎 ⓪ *VISA*
closed Saturday lunch September-May and Bank Holidays – **Meals** 12.00 **t.** (lunch) and a la carte 18.25/26.00 **t.**

Wandsworth – ✉ SW12/SW17/SW18.

XX **Tabaq,** 47 Balham Hill, SW12 9DR, ✆ (0181) 673 7820, *Fax (0181) 673 2701* – 🖥. 🅜 🆎 ⓪ *VISA* JCB
closed Sunday and 25 December – **Meals** - Indian - a la carte 18.90/29.95 **t.** 🍷 4.75.

X ✿ **Chez Bruce** (Poole), 2 Bellevue Rd, SW17 7EG, ✆ (0181) 672 0114, *Fax (0181) 767 6648* – 🖥. 🅜 🆎 ⓪ *VISA*
closed Sunday dinner, 24 to 30 December and Bank Holidays – **Meals** 18.00/25.00 **t.** 🍷 7.00
Spec. Boudin noir with caramelised apple and grain mustard sauce. Assiette of rabbit with ceps, Puy lentils and red wine. Crème brûlée.

X **Bombay Bicycle Club,** 95 Nightingale Lane, SW12 8NX, ✆ (0181) 673 6217, *Fax (0181) 673 9100* – 🅜 🆎 ⓪ *VISA*
closed Sunday and Christmas – **Meals** - Indian - (dinner only) a la carte 20.50/26.00 **t.** 🍷 7.50.

WESTMINSTER (City of)

Bayswater and Maida Vale – ✉ W2/W9 – *Except where otherwise stated see pp. 16 and 17.*

🏨 **Royal Lancaster,** Lancaster Terr., W2 2TY, ✆ (0171) 262 6737, *Fax (0171) 724 3191,* ≼ – 🛗, ✱ rm, 🖥 📺 ☎ 📞 🅟 – 🔬 1400. 🅜 🆎 ⓪ *VISA* JCB. ⚘   DZ e
Park : Meals (*closed Saturday lunch and Sunday*) 23.50 **st.** and a la carte – **Pavement Cafe :** Meals 13.50 **st.** (lunch) and a la carte 17.30/24.30 **st.** 🍷 6.00 (see also **Nipa** below) – ☕ 15.00 – **396 rm** 215.00/290.00, 20 suites.

🏨 **Stakis Metropole,** Edgware Rd, W2 1JU, ✆ (0171) 402 4141, *Fax (0171) 724 8866,* ≼, 🛠, ≘s, 🏊 – 🛗, ✱ rm, 🖥 📺 ☎ – 🔬 1200. 🅜 🆎 ⓪ *VISA*. ⚘   p. 5 GU c
Meals (buffet rest.) 21.95 **t.** (see also **Aspects** below) – ☕ 16.50 – **723 rm** 185.00/250.00 **st.,** 26 suites – SB.

🏨 **The Hempel** 🕊, Hempel Garden Sq., 31-35 Craven Hill Gdns., W2 3EA, ✆ (0171) 298 9000, *Fax (0171) 402 4666,* « Minimalist », 🚐 – 🛗 🖥 📺 ☎ 📞 ⅍ 🅟 – 🔬 40. 🅜 🆎 ⓪ *VISA* JCB. ⚘   CZ a
I-Thai : Meals - Thai-Italian - a la carte 30.45/52.75 **t.** 🍷 16.00 – ☕ 17.00 – **41 rm** 220.00/255.00 **s.,** 6 suites.

🏨 **Thistle Whites,** Bayswater Rd, 90-92 Lancaster Gate, W2 3NR, ✆ (0171) 262 2711, *Fax (0171) 262 2147* – 🛗, ✱ rm, 🖥 📺 ☎ 🅟 – 🔬 30. 🅜 🆎 ⓪ *VISA* JCB. ⚘   CZ v
Meals (*closed lunch Saturday and Bank Holidays*) 18.50/22.00 **t.** and a la carte 🍷 8.60 – ☕ 14.50 – **52 rm** 195.00/245.00 **st.,** 2 suites – SB.

🏨 **Stakis Hyde Park,** 129 Bayswater Rd, W2 4RJ, ✆ (0171) 221 2217, *Fax (0171) 229 0557* – 🛗, ✱ rm, 🖥 rest, 📺 ☎ 📞 – 🔬 40. 🅜 🆎 ⓪ *VISA* JCB. ⚘   BZ c
Meals (bar lunch Saturday and Sunday) 15.95 **t.** and a la carte – ☕ 10.95 – **128 rm** 145.00/205.00 **st.,** 1 suite – SB.

🏨 **Jarvis London Embassy,** 150 Bayswater Rd, W2 4RT, ✆ (0171) 229 1212, *Fax (0171) 229 2623* – 🛗, ✱ rm, 🖥 rest, 📺 ☎ 📞 🅟 – 🔬 100. 🅜 🆎 ⓪ *VISA*   BZ o
Meals (carving rest.) 15.95 **st.** and a la carte 🍷 7.00 – ☕ 9.50 – **212 rm** 135.00/155.00 **st.,** 1 suite.

UNITED KINGDOM

Mornington without rest., 12 Lancaster Gate, W2 3LG, ℘ (0171) 262 7361, Fax (0171) 706 1028 – 📶 ✂ TV ☎. MC AE ⓘ VISA JCB. ✄   DZ
66 rm ☕ 105.00/170.00.

Commodore, 50 Lancaster Gate, W2 3NA, ℘ (0171) 402 5291, Fax (0171) 262 108 – 📶, ✂ rm, TV ☎. MC AE ⓘ VISA JCB. ✄   CZ
Meals - Spanish - (closed 25 December) 15.00/20.00 **st.** and a la carte 🍷 6.50 – ☕ 7.00 – **90 rm** 85.00/110.00 **st.**

Miller's without rest., 111A Westbourne Grove, W2 4UW, ℘ (0171) 243 1024, Fax (0171) 243 1064, « Antique furnishings » – TV ☎. MC AE VISA JCB. ✄   AZ
7 rm ☕ 115.00/130.00 **s.** – SB.

Aspects (at Stakis Metropole H.), Edgware Rd, W2 1JU, ℘ (0171) 402 4141, Fax (0171) 724 8866, ≼ London – 🔳. MC AE ⓘ VISA   p. 5 GU
closed Saturday lunch and Sunday – **Meals** 24.15/33.00 **t.** and a la carte 🍷 10.50.

Nipa (at Royal Lancaster H.), Lancaster Terr., W2 2TY, ℘ (0171) 262 6737, Fax (0171) 724 3191 – 🔳 P. MC AE ⓘ VISA JCB   DZ
closed Saturday lunch and Sunday – **Meals** - Thai - 26.00 **st.**

Al San Vincenzo, 30 Connaught St., W2 2AE, ℘ (0171) 262 9623 – MC VISA   EZ
closed Saturday lunch, Sunday and 1 week Christmas – **Meals** - Italian - (booking essential) a la carte 22.50/32.00 **t.** 🍷 8.00.

Poons, Unit 205, Whiteleys, Queensway, W2 4YN, ℘ (0171) 792 2884 – 🔳. MC AE ⓘ VISA JCB   BZ
closed 25 and 26 December – **Meals** - Chinese - 15.00/25.00 **t.** and a la carte 🍷 13.00

Jason's, Blomfield Rd, Little Venice, W9 2PD, ℘ (0171) 286 6752, Fax (0171) 266 4332, ☘, « Canalside setting » – MC AE ⓘ VISA JCB   p. 4 FU
closed Sunday dinner, 25-26 December and 1 January – **Meals** - Seafood - a la carte 28.75/39.85 **t.** 🍷 4.95.

Royal China, 13 Queensway, W2 4QJ, ℘ (0171) 221 2535, Fax (0171) 792 5752 – 🔳 MC AE ⓘ VISA   BZ
closed 25-26 December – **Meals** - Chinese - 23.00 **t.** (dinner) and a la carte 20.50/80.50 **t.**

Assaggi, 39 Chepstow Pl., W2 4TS, ℘ (0171) 792 5501 – MC AE ⓘ VISA JCB AZ
closed Sunday, 2 weeks Christmas and Bank Holidays – **Meals** - Italian - 35.00 **t.** and a la carte.

L'Accento, 16 Garway Rd, W2 4NH, ℘ (0171) 243 2201, Fax (0171) 243 2201, ☘ MC AE VISA JCB   BZ
Meals - Italian - 15.50 **t.** and a la carte 20.50/25.00 **t.** 🍷 8.00.

Belgravia – ✉ SW1 – *Except where otherwise stated see pp. 14 and 15.*

The Lanesborough, Hyde Park Corner, SW1X 7TA, ℘ (0171) 259 5599, Fax (0171) 259 5606, 🛁 – 📶, ✂ rm, 🔳 TV ☎ 📞 ⅋ P – 🏛 90. MC AE ⓘ VISA JCB
The Conservatory : Meals 24.50/29.50 **st.** and a la carte 🍷 8.75 – ☕ 17.00 – **86 rm** 275.00/320.00 **s.**, 9 suites.   p. 9 IY

The Berkeley, Wilton Pl., SW1X 7RL, ℘ (0171) 235 6000, Fax (0171) 235 4330, 🛁, ⛱ 🔲 – 📶, ✂ rm, 🔳 TV ☎ 📞 🚗 – 🏛 220. MC AE ⓘ VISA JCB. ✄   FQ
Meals (see *La Tante Claire* and *Vong* below) – ☕ 19.50 – **132 rm** 255.00/465.00 **s.**, 26 suites.

The Halkin, 5 Halkin St., SW1X 7DJ, ℘ (0171) 333 1000, Fax (0171) 333 1100, ❀ « Contemporary interior design » – 📶, ✂ rm, 🔳 TV ☎ P – 🏛 25. MC AE ⓘ VISA JCB ✄   p. 16 AV
Stefano Cavallini Restaurant at The Halkin : Meals - Italian - (closed lunch Saturday and Sunday and 25-26 December) (booking essential) 25.00 (lunch) and a la carte 42.00/55.00 **st.** 🍷 9.50 – ☕ 16.00 – **36 rm** 255.00/325.00, 5 suites
Spec. Stuffed gnocchi with artichoke, white wine and ginger sauce. Mashed cod with potatoes and olive oil, roasted quail, broccoli sauce. Partridge with pomegranate, turnip confit and celeriac purée.

Sheraton Belgravia, 20 Chesham Pl., SW1X 8HQ, ℘ (0171) 235 6040, Fax (0171) 259 6243 – 📶, ✂ rm, 🔳 TV ☎ 📞 ⅋ P – 🏛 50. MC AE ⓘ VISA JCB. ✄
Chesham's : Meals (closed Sunday and Bank Holidays) (dinner only) 30.00 **t.** and a la carte – ☕ 17.00 – **82 rm** 260.00/360.00 **s.**, 7 suites.   FR

Lowndes, 21 Lowndes St., SW1X 9ES, ℘ (0171) 823 1234, Fax (0171) 235 1154 – 📶 ✂ rm, 🔳 TV ☎ 📞 P – 🏛 25. MC AE ⓘ VISA JCB. ✄   FR
Brasserie 21 : Meals 17.00 **st.** and a la carte – ☕ 14.50 – **77 rm** 235.00/245.00 **s.**, 1 suite.

La Tante Claire (Koffmann) (at The Berkeley H.), Wilton Pl., SW1X 7RL, ℘ (0171) 823 2003, Fax (0171) 823 2001 – 🔳. MC AE ⓘ VISA   FQ
closed Saturday lunch, Sunday and Christmas-1 January – **Meals** - French - (booking essential) 28.00 **t.** (lunch) and a la carte 51.50/77.00 **t.** 🍷 12.00
Spec. Coquille St.Jacques à l'encre. Pied de cochon farci aux morilles. Soufflé aux pistaches.

UNITED KINGDOM

Zafferano (Locatelli), 15 Lowndes St., SW1X 9EY, ℰ (0171) 235 5800, Fax (0171) 235 1971 – ▤. **MO** **AE** **VISA** **JCB**   FR i
closed Sunday, 2 weeks August, 2 weeks Christmas and Bank Holidays – **Meals** - Italian - 20.50/30.50 **t.** ⌀ 9.50
Spec. Tortelli ai gamberi. Filetto d'agnello primaverile alla griglia con peperonata. Tiramisu.

Vong (at The Berkeley H.), Wilton Pl., SW1X 7RL, ℰ (0171) 235 1010, Fax (0171) 235 1011 – ▤. **MO** **AE** **①** **VISA** **JCB**   FQ e
Meals - French-Thai - 20.00 **t.** (lunch) and a la carte 23.75/45.00 **t.** ⌀ 11.50.

Al Bustan, 27 Motcomb St., SW1X 8JU, ℰ (0171) 235 8277, Fax (0171) 235 1668 – ▤. **MO** **AE** **①** **VISA**   FR z
Meals - Lebanese - 13.00 **t.** (lunch) and a la carte 18.50/23.50 ⌀ 6.50.

Hyde Park and Knightsbridge – ✉ SW1/SW7 – pp. 14 and 15.

Mandarin Oriental Hyde Park, 66 Knightsbridge, SW1X 7LA, ℰ (0171) 235 2000, Fax (0171) 235 4552, ≤, ℔ – ⧍, ⇺ rm, ▤ **TV** ☎ ✆ ঙ – ⅍ 250. **MO** **AE** **①** **VISA** **JCB**. ⌗   FQ x
The Park : **Meals** 23.50/27.00 **t.** and a la carte ⌀ 17.50 – ⌸ 18.95 – **179 rm** 260.00/290.00 **s.**, 19 suites.

Knightsbridge Green without rest., 159 Knightsbridge, SW1X 7PD, ℰ (0171) 584 6274, Fax (0171) 225 1635 – ⧍ ▤ **TV** ☎ ✆. **MO** **AE** **①** **VISA**. ⌗   EQ z
closed 24 to 26 December – ⌸ 9.50 – **16 rm** 105.00/140.00 **st.**, 12 suites 165.00 **st.**

Mr. Chow, 151 Knightsbridge, SW1X 7PA, ℰ (0171) 589 7347, Fax (0171) 584 5780 – ▤. **MO** **AE** **①** **VISA** **JCB**   EQ a
closed 24 to 26 December and 1 January – **Meals** - Chinese - 9.50 **t.** (lunch) and a la carte 30.00/35.00 **t.**

Mayfair – ✉ W1 – pp. 12 and 13.

Dorchester, Park Lane, W1A 2HJ, ℰ (0171) 629 8888, Fax (0171) 409 0114, ℔, ⌂s – ⧍, ⇺ rm, ▤ **TV** ☎ ✆ ঙ ⇔ – ⅍ 550. **MO** **AE** **①** **VISA** **JCB**. ⌗   BN a
Meals (see **The Oriental** and **Grill Room** below) – ⌸ 20.50 – **197 rm** 255.00/315.00 **s.**, 47 suites.

Claridge's, Brook St., W1A 2JQ, ℰ (0171) 629 8860, Fax (0171) 499 2210, ℔ – ⧍, ⇺ rm, ▤ **TV** ☎ ✆ ঙ – ⅍ 200. **MO** **AE** **①** **VISA** **JCB**. ⌗   BL c
Restaurant : **Meals** 29.50/39.00 **st.** and a la carte 46.00/64.00 **st.** ⌀ 9.50 – ⌸ 18.50 – **137 rm** 265.00/375.00 **s.**, 60 suites.

Four Seasons, Hamilton Pl., Park Lane, W1A 1AZ, ℰ (0171) 499 0888, Fax (0171) 493 1895, ℔ – ⧍, ⇺ rm, ▤ **TV** ☎ ✆ ⇔ – ⅍ 500. **MO** **AE** **①** **VISA** **JCB**. ⌗   BP a
Lanes : **Meals** 32.00/30.50 **st.** and a la carte ⌀ 18.00 – ⌸ 18.75 – **185 rm** 260.00/315.00 **s.**, 35 suites.

Le Meridien Piccadilly, 21 Piccadilly, W1V 0BH, ℰ (0171) 734 8000, Fax (0171) 437 3574, ℔, ⌂s, ▨, squash – ⧍, ⇺ rm, ▤ **TV** ☎ ঙ – ⅍ 250. **MO** **AE** **①** **VISA** **JCB**. ⌗   EM a
Terrace Garden : **Meals** 21.50 **t.** and a la carte ⌀ 10.50 (see also **The Oak Room Marco Pierre White** below) – ⌸ 17.50 – **248 rm** 325.00, 18 suites – SB.

Grosvenor House, Park Lane, W1A 3AA, ℰ (0171) 499 6363, Fax (0171) 493 3341, ℔, ⌂s, ▨ – ⧍, ⇺ rm, ▤ **TV** ☎ ঙ ⇔ – ⅍ 1500. **MO** **AE** **①** **VISA** **JCB**. ⌗   AM a
Café Nico : **Meals** (closed Monday) 29.50 **t.** – **The Italian Restaurant** : **Meals** - Italian - (closed Saturday, Sunday, Easter, 2 weeks August and Christmas) a la carte 31.50/38.50 **t.** (see also **Chez Nico at Ninety Park Lane** below) – ⌸ 18.50 – **382 rm** 225.00/245.00 **s.**, 72 suites – SB.

London Hilton on Park Lane, 22 Park Lane, W1Y 4BE, ℰ (0171) 493 8000, Fax (0171) 493 4957, « Panoramic ≤ of London », ℔ – ⧍, ⇺ rm, ▤ **TV** ☎ ✆ ঙ – ⅍ 1000. **MO** **AE** **①** **VISA** **JCB**. ⌗   BP e
Trader Vics (ℰ (0171) 208 4113) : **Meals** (dinner only) a la carte 20.00/70.00 **t.** ⌀ 7.50 – **Park Brasserie** : **Meals** 21.50 **t.** and a la carte ⌀ 7.50 (see also **Windows** below) – ⌸ 17.00 – **394 rm** 270.00/350.00, 52 suites.

Connaught, Carlos Pl., W1Y 6AL, ℰ (0171) 499 7070, Fax (0171) 495 3262 – ⧍ ▤ **TV** ☎ ✆. **MO** **AE** **①** **VISA** **JCB**. ⌗   BM e
The Restaurant : **Meals** (booking essential) 29.00/60.00 **t.** and a la carte 26.60/69.20 **t.** ⌀ 15.00 – **Grill Room** : **Meals** (closed Saturday lunch) (booking essential) 29.00/39.00 **t.** and a la carte 26.60/69.20 **t.** ⌀ 15.00 – ⌸ 21.00 – **66 rm** 250.00/365.00 **s.**, 24 suites – SB.
Spec. Pâté de turbot froid au homard, sauce pudeur. Filet de bœuf en croûte légère ''Strasbourgeoise''. Crème brûlée au parfum saisonnier.

47 Park Street, 47 Park St., W1Y 4EB, ℘ (0171) 491 7282, *Fax (0171) 491 7281* –
■ TV ☎ ℃ MO AE ① *VISA* JCB. ⋪
AM
Meals (room service) (see also **Le Gavroche** below) – ☲ 20.00, **52 suites** 260.00/530.00 s.

Brown's, Albemarle St., W1X 4BP, ℘ (0171) 493 6020, *Fax (0171) 493 9381* – |$| TV
℃ – ᠕ 70. MO AE ① *VISA*. ⋪
DM
Meals (see **1837** below) – ☲ 18.00 – **112 rm** 250.00/345.00, 6 suites – SB.

Park Lane, Piccadilly, W1Y 8BX, ℘ (0171) 499 6321, *Fax (0171) 499 1965* – |$|, ⋈ rm
■ TV ☎ Ⓟ – ᠕ 300. MO AE ① *VISA* JCB. ⋪
CP
Brasserie on the Park (℘ (0171) 290 7364) : **Meals** 23.50/25.50 t. and a la carte ▮ 10.00
– ☲ 18.50 – **286 rm** 260.00/280.00 s., 20 suites.

Britannia, Grosvenor Sq., W1A 3AN, ℘ (0171) 629 9400, *Fax (0171) 629 7736*, ‮Ιδ
|$|, ⋈ rm, ■ TV ☎ – ᠕ 450. MO AE ① *VISA* JCB. ⋪
BM
Meals 16.50 t. (lunch) and a la carte 26.00/30.75 t. (see also **Shogun** below) – ☲ 16.5
– **302 rm** 150.00/215.00, 12 suites.

May Fair Inter-Continental, Stratton St., W1A 2AN, ℘ (0171) 629 7777
Fax (0171) 629 1459, Ιδ, ⇌s, ◪ – |$|, ⋈ rm ■ TV ☎ ৬ – ᠕ 290. MO AE ① *VISA* JC
⋪
DN
May Fair Café (℘ (0171) 915 2842) : **Meals** (closed Sunday) (lunch only) 15.00 t. and
la carte (see also **Opus 70** below) – ☲ 17.00 – **275 rm** 269.00/289.00 s., 12 suites.

Inter-Continental, 1 Hamilton Pl., Hyde Park Corner, W1V 0QY, ℘ (0171) 409 313
Fax (0171) 493 3476, ≤, Ιδ, ⇌s – |$|, ⋈ rm, ■ TV ☎ ৬ ⇔ – ᠕ 1000. MO AE ①
VISA. ⋪
BP
Meals 22.75/26.50 and a la carte (see also **Le Soufflé** below) – ☲ 20.00 – **416 rm**
280.00/350.00, 42 suites.

Athenaeum, 116 Piccadilly, W1V 0BJ, ℘ (0171) 499 3464, *Fax (0171) 493 1860*, Ιδ
⇌s – |$|, ⋈ rm, ■ TV ☎ ℃ – ᠕ 55. MO AE ① *VISA* JCB
CP
Bulloch's at 116 : **Meals** (closed lunch Saturday and Sunday) a la carte 35.90/45.95
▮ 11.00 – ☲ 17.95 – **122 rm** 255.00/325.00 s., 33 suites.

The Metropolitan, Old Park Lane, W1Y 4LB, ℘ (0171) 447 1000, *Fax (0171) 447 110*
≤, « Contemporary interior design », Ιδ – |$|, ⋈ rm, ■ TV ☎ ℃ ⇔. MO AE ① *VI*
JCB. ⋪
BP
Met Bar : **Meals** (residents and members only) (light lunch) a la carte 16.00/40.50 st. (se
also **Nobu** below) – ☲ 15.00 – **152 rm** 210.00/260.00, 3 suites.

Westbury, Bond St., W1A 4UH, ℘ (0171) 629 7755, *Fax (0171) 495 1163* – |$|, ⋈ rm
■ TV ☎ ℃ – ᠕ 110. MO AE ① *VISA* JCB
DM
Meals (closed Saturday and Sunday lunch) 19.50/21.50 t. and a la carte ▮ 12.00 – ☲ 16.7
– **231 rm** 210.00/270.00 s., 13 suites.

London Marriott Grosvenor Square, Duke St., Grosvenor Sq., W1A 4AW, ℘ (017
493 1232, *Fax (0171) 491 3201*, Ιδ – |$|, ⋈ rm, ■ TV ☎ – ᠕ 600. MO AE ① *VISA* JC
⋪
BL
Diplomat : **Meals** (closed Saturday lunch) 19.50/12.95 s. and a la carte – ☲ 12.95
210 rm 185.00/260.00, 11 suites.

Chesterfield, 35 Charles St., W1X 8LX, ℘ (0171) 491 2622, *Fax (0171) 491 4793* – |$
⋈ rm, ■ rest, TV ☎ – ᠕ 110. MO AE ① *VISA* JCB. ⋪
CN
Butlers : **Meals** (closed Saturday lunch) 10.50 t. (lunch) and a la carte 22.40/32.85 t.
☲ 16.50 – **106 rm** 155.00/252.00, 4 suites.

Washington, 5-7 Curzon St., W1Y 8DT, ℘ (0171) 499 7000, *Fax (0171) 495 6172* –
⋈ rm, ■ TV ☎ ℃ – ᠕ 80. MO AE ① *VISA* JCB. ⋪
CN
Meals a la carte 20.40/28.40 t. ▮ 6.95 – ☲ 13.95 – **169 rm** 190.00 s., 4 suites – SB

Holiday Inn Mayfair, 3 Berkeley St., W1X 6NE, ℘ (0171) 493 8282, *Fax (0171) 629 282*
– |$|, ⋈ rm, ■ TV ☎ ℃ – ᠕ 60. MO AE ① *VISA* JCB. ⋪
DN
Meals (closed Saturday lunch) a la carte 19.00/32.00 st. ▮ 8.00 – ☲ 13.95 – **181 rm**
190.00 st., 4 suites.

Flemings, 7-12 Half Moon St., W1Y 7RA, ℘ (0171) 499 2964, *Fax (0171) 629 4063*
|$| ■ TV ☎ – ᠕ 50. MO AE ① *VISA* JCB. ⋪
CN
Meals 12.50/23.50 st. and a la carte ▮ 9.00 – ☲ 13.00 – **120 rm** 150.00/180.00, 10 suite

Green Park, Half Moon St., W1Y 8BP, ℘ (0171) 629 7522, *Fax (0171) 491 8971* –
⋈ rm, ■ TV ☎ – ᠕ 130. MO AE ① *VISA* JCB. ⋪
CN
Meals 12.95 st. (lunch) and a la carte 24.00/40.00 st. ▮ 9.00 – ☲ 11.95 – **160 rm**
150.00/199.00 s., 1 suite – SB.

London Mews Hilton, 2 Stanhope Row, W1Y 7HE, ℘ (0171) 493 722
Fax (0171) 629 9423 – |$|, ⋈ rm, ■ TV ☎ ⇔ – ᠕ 50. MO AE ① *VI*
JCB. ⋪
BP
Meals (dinner only) 18.50 t. and a la carte – ☲ 14.50 – **72 rm** 188.00/237.00 t.

XXXXX ❀❀❀ **The Oak Room Marco Pierre White** (at Le Meridien Piccadilly H.), 21 Piccadilly, W1V OBH, ✆ (0171) 437 0202 – 🖥. 💳 AE VISA   EM a
closed Saturday lunch, Sunday, last 2 weeks August and 2 weeks Christmas-New Year – **Meals** (booking essential) 29.50/80.00 **t.** 🍷 25.00
Spec. Aspic of oysters with watercress en gelée de Champagne. Pigeon from Bresse en vessie, sauce Albufera. Soufflé chocolat, glace de lait.

XXXXX ❀❀❀ **Chez Nico at Ninety Park Lane** (Ladenis) (at Grosvenor House H.), Park Lane, W1A 3AA, ✆ (0171) 409 1290, *Fax (0171) 355 4877* – 🖥. 💳 AE VISA   AM e
closed Saturday lunch, Sunday, 4 days at Easter, 10 days at Christmas and Bank Holiday Mondays – **Meals** - French - (booking essential) 34.00/64.00 **t.**
Spec. Seared escalope of foie gras with brioche and caramelised orange. Grilled scallops with buttered leeks. Fillet of beef with celeriac and truffle.

XXXX ❀❀ **Le Gavroche** (Roux), 43 Upper Brook St., W1Y 1PF, ✆ (0171) 408 0881, *Fax (0171) 409 0939* – 🖥. 💳 AE ⓞ VISA JCB   AM c
closed Saturday, Sunday, Christmas-New Year and Bank Holidays – **Meals** - French - (booking essential) 40.00 **st.** (lunch) and a la carte 64.80/90.70 **st.** 🍷 19.00
Spec. Foie gras chaud et pastilla de canard à la cannelle. Râble de lapin et galette au parmesan. Le palet au chocolat amer et praline croustillant.

XXXX ❀ **The Oriental** (at Dorchester H.), Park Lane, W1A 2HJ, ✆ (0171) 317 6328, *Fax (0171) 409 0114* – 🖥. 💳 AE ⓞ VISA JCB   BN a
closed Saturday lunch, Sunday and 3 to 31 August – **Meals** - Chinese (Canton) - 29.50/42.00 **st.** and a la carte 43.00/72.50 **st.** 🍷 12.00
Spec. Roasted Peking duck. Double boiled shark's fin with chicken and Chinese cabbage. Stir-fried beef with lemon grass and black pepper.

XXXX **Grill Room** (at Dorchester H.), Park Lane, W1A 2HJ, ✆ (0171) 317 6336, *Fax (0171) 409 0114* – 🖥. 💳 AE ⓞ VISA JCB   BN a
Meals - English - 29.50/39.50 **st.** and a la carte 38.00/58.00 **st.** 🍷 12.00.

XXXX ❀ **Les Saveurs de Jean-Christophe Novelli,** 37a Curzon St., W1Y 7AF, ✆ (0171) 491 8919, *Fax (0171) 491 3658* – 🖥. 💳 AE ⓞ VISA JCB   BN o
closed Saturday lunch, Sunday and Monday – **Meals** - French - 18.50/31.50 **t.** 🍷 15.00
Spec. Tian of smoked salmon and crab with asparagus and confit tomatoes. Baked sea bream with polenta, piperade and basil cappuccino. Caramelised apple Tatin with caramel ice cream.

XXXX **Windows** (at London Hilton on Park Lane), 22 Park Lane, W1Y 4BE, ✆ (0171) 208 4021, « Panoramic ⋜ of London » – 🖥. 💳 AE ⓞ VISA JCB   BP e
closed Saturday lunch and Sunday dinner – **Meals** 39.50/44.00 **t.** and dinner a la carte.

XXXX **1837** (at Brown's H.), Albemarle St., W1X 4BP, ✆ (0171) 408 1837, *Fax (0171) 493 9381* – 💳 AE ⓞ VISA JCB   DM e
closed Saturday lunch and Sunday – **Meals** 27.00/45.00 **t.** and a la carte.

XXX ❀❀ **The Square** (Howard), 6-10 Bruton St., W1X 7AG, ✆ (0171) 495 7100, *Fax (0171) 495 7150* – 🖥. 💳 AE ⓞ VISA   CM v
closed lunch Saturday and Sunday, 25-26 December and 1 January – **Meals** 45.00 **t.** (dinner) and lunch a la carte 34.50/36.00 **t.** 🍷 13.50
Spec. Roast foie gras with caramelised endive and late picked Muscat grapes. Loin of lamb with artichoke, confit of garlic and rosemary. "A tasting of coffee".

XXX **Mirabelle,** 56 Curzon St., W1Y 8DL, ✆ (0171) 499 4636, *Fax (0171) 499 5449,* 🍃 – 🖥. 💳 AE VISA   CN x
Meals 17.95 **t.** (lunch) and a la carte 28.50/35.50 **t.** 🍷 12.75.

XXX **Sartoria,** 20 Savile Row, W1X 1AE, ✆ (0171) 534 7000, *Fax (0171) 534 7070* – 🖥. 💳 AE ⓞ VISA JCB   DL c
closed Sunday dinner and 25-26 December – **Meals** - Italian - a la carte 32.50/48.00 **t.** 🍷 10.25.

XXX **Goodes at Thomas Goode,** 19 South Audley St., W1Y 6BN, ✆ (0171) 409 7242, *Fax (0171) 629 4230* – 🖥. 💳 AE ⓞ VISA JCB   BM c
closed Saturday, Sunday, first 3 weeks August and 1 week Christmas – **Meals** (lunch only) 32.50 **t.** 🍷 15.20.

XXX **Le Soufflé** (at Inter-Continental H.), 1 Hamilton Pl., Hyde Park Corner, W1V 0QY, ✆ (0171) 409 3131, *Fax (0171) 409 7460* – 🖥 🚗. 💳 AE ⓞ VISA   BP o
closed Monday – **Meals** 29.50/35.00 and a la carte.

XXX **Morton's - The Restaurant,** 28 Berkeley Sq., W1X 5HA, ✆ (0171) 493 7171, *Fax (0171) 495 3160,* – 🖥 ⓟ. 💳 AE ⓞ VISA   CM a
closed lunch Saturday and Sunday and 24 to 27 December – **Meals** 19.50/29.50 **t.** and a la carte 🍷 9.75.

XXX **Princess Garden,** 8-10 North Audley St., W1Y 1WF, ✆ (0171) 493 3223, *Fax (0171) 629 3130* – 🖥. 💳 AE ⓞ VISA JCB   AL z
closed 23 to 26 December – **Meals** - Chinese (Peking, Szechuan) - 30.00 **t.** (dinner) and a la carte 29.00/45.00 **t.** 🍷 9.50.

UNITED KINGDOM

XXX **Opus 70** (at May Fair Inter-Continental H.), Stratton St., W1A 2AN, ☎ (0171) 915 2842,
Fax (0171) 629 1459 – 🍴. ⓶ⓢ Ⓐ Ⓞ VISA JCB   DN
closed Saturday lunch – **Meals** 20.00 **t.** (lunch) and dinner a la carte 28.00/32.50 **t.** 🍷 7.00

XXX **Scotts**, 20 Mount St., W1Y 6HE, ☎ (0171) 629 5248, Fax (0171) 499 8246 – 🍴. ⓶ⓢ Ⓐ
Ⓞ VISA JCB   BM
Meals - Seafood - 24.50 **t.** (lunch) and dinner a la carte 26.25/53.50 **t.** 🍷 9.50.

XX **Nobu** (at The Metropolitan H.), 19 Old Park Lane, W1Y 4LB, ☎ (0171) 447 4747,
✿ Fax (0171) 447 4749, ≼ – 🍴. ⓶ⓢ Ⓐ Ⓞ VISA JCB   BP
closed lunch Saturday and Sunday – **Meals** - New style Japanese with South American
influences - a la carte 45.00/90.00 **t.** 🍷 11.25
Spec. Toro tartar with caviar. Black cod with miso. Tiradito.

XX **L'Odéon**, 65 Regent St., W1R 7HH, ☎ (0171) 287 1400, Fax (0171) 287 1300 – 🍴. ⓶ⓢ
Ⓐ Ⓞ VISA JCB   EM
closed Sunday June-August, 25 to 27 December and Bank Holidays – **Meals** 19.50 **t.** (lunch)
and a la carte 28.50/45.95 **t.** 🍷 7.50.

XX **Tamarind**, 20 Queen St., W1X 7PJ, ☎ (0171) 629 3561, Fax (0171) 499 5034 – ⓶ⓢ Ⓐ
Ⓞ VISA JCB   CN
closed Saturday lunch, 25-26 December and Good Friday – **Meals** - Indian - 16.50 **st.** (lunch)
and a la carte 27.60/35.05 **t.** 🍷 10.00.

XX **Greenhouse**, 27a Hay's Mews, W1X 7RJ, ☎ (0171) 499 3331, Fax (0171) 499 5368
🍴. ⓶ⓢ Ⓐ Ⓞ VISA   BN
closed Saturday lunch, 25-26 December and Bank Holidays – **Meals** a la carte
24.40/39.50 **t.** 🍷 12.50.

XX **Bentley's**, 11-15 Swallow St., W1R 7HD, ☎ (0171) 734 4756, Fax (0171) 287 2972 – 🍴
⓶ⓢ Ⓐ Ⓞ VISA JCB   EM
closed Sunday, 25 December and 1 January – **Meals** - Seafood - 19.50 **t.** and a la carte
30.40/44.45 **t.** 🍷 13.50.

XX **Nicole's**, 158 New Bond St., W1V 9PA, ☎ (0171) 499 8408, Fax (0171) 409 0381 – 🍴
⓶ⓢ Ⓐ Ⓞ VISA JCB   DM
closed Saturday dinner, Sunday, 25-26 December, 1 January and Bank Holidays – **Meal**
a la carte 26.20/32.75 **t.** 🍷 11.50.

XX **Teca**, 54 Brooks Mews, W1Y 2NY, ☎ (0171) 495 4774, Fax (0171) 491 3545 – 🍴. ⓶ⓢ
Ⓐ VISA   CL
Meals - Italian - a la carte 24.00/30.00 **t.** 🍷 12.00.

XX **Langan's Brasserie**, Stratton St., W1X 5FD, ☎ (0171) 491 8822, Fax (0171) 493 830
– 🍴. ⓶ⓢ Ⓐ Ⓞ VISA JCB   DN
closed Saturday lunch, Sunday, Easter, 25-26 December, 1 January and Bank Holidays i
May and August – **Meals** a la carte 20.75/29.85 **t.** 🍷 7.50.

XX **Marquis**, 121A Mount St., W1Y 5HB, ☎ (0171) 499 1256, Fax (0171) 493 4460 – ⓶ⓢ Ⓐ
Ⓞ VISA JCB   BM
closed Saturday lunch, Sunday, 22 August-5 September, 24 December-6 January and Ban
Holidays – **Meals** 17.50 **t.** and a la carte 🍷 6.30.

XX **Chor Bizarre**, 16 Albemarle St., W1X 3HA, ☎ (0171) 629 9802, Fax (0171) 493 7756
« Authentic Indian decor and furnishings » – ⓶ⓢ Ⓐ Ⓞ VISA JCB   DM
closed 25 and 26 December – **Meals** - Indian - 14.95/23.00 **t.** and a la carte 🍷 7.95.

XX **Benihana**, 37 Sackville St., Piccadilly, W1X 2DQ, ☎ (0171) 494 2525,
Fax (0171) 494 1456 – 🍴. ⓶ⓢ Ⓐ Ⓞ VISA JCB   EM
closed 25 December – **Meals** - Japanese (Teppan-Yaki) - 8.50/14.00 **t.** and a la carte.

XX **Shogun** (at Britannia H.), Adams Row, W1Y 5DE, ☎ (0171) 493 1255,
Fax (0171) 629 7736 – 🍴. ⓶ⓢ Ⓐ Ⓞ VISA JCB   BM
closed Monday – **Meals** - Japanese - (dinner only) 28.50 and a la carte.

X **Coast**, 26B Albemarle St., W1X 3FA, ☎ (0171) 495 5999, Fax (0171) 495 2999 – ⓶ⓢ Ⓐ
Ⓞ VISA   DM
closed 31 December lunch, 25 December, 1 January and Bank Holidays – **Meals** a la cart
25.50/43.50 **t.**

Regent's Park and Marylebone – ✉ NW1/NW6/NW8/W1 – *Except where otherwis*
stated see pp. 12 and 13.
🛈 *Basement Services Arcade, Selfridges Store, Oxford St., W1* ☎ (0171) 824 8844.

🏨 **Landmark London**, 222 Marylebone Rd, NW1 6JQ, ☎ (0171) 631 8000,
Fax (0171) 631 8080, « Victorian Gothic architecture, atrium and winter garden », 🛎, ≋
📺 – 🛗, 🛏 rm, 🍴 📺 ☎ 🚻 🚗 – 🛎 350. ⓶ⓢ Ⓐ Ⓞ VISA JCB. 🛑   p.5 HU
The Dining Room : **Meals** (*closed Saturday lunch and Sunday dinner*) 26.00/36.95 **st.** an
a la carte 🍷 14.00 – *Winter Garden* : **Meals** 23.35 **st.** and a la carte 🍷 15.00 – 🍵 18.0
– **288 rm** 270.00/290.00 **s.**, 9 suites.

Churchill Inter-Continental, 30 Portman Sq., W1A 4ZX, ℘ (0171) 486 5800, *Fax (0171) 486 1255*, ※ – |⧢|, ↹ rm, ▤ TV ☎ ☏ ℗ – 🛉 200. ⓂⒸ AE Ⓞ VISA JCB. ※ AJ x
Clementine's : Meals *(closed Saturday lunch)* 23.00 **t.** and a la carte ⓑ 8.00 – ⌣ 17.75
– **415 rm** 280.00/290.00, 33 suites.

Langham Hilton, 1 Portland Pl., Regent St., W1N 4JA, ℘ (0171) 636 1000, *Fax (0171) 323 2340*, ⌶, ⇌s – |⧢|, ↹ rm, ▤ TV ☎ ⅙ – 🛉 250. ⓂⒸ AE Ⓞ VISA JCB.
※   p. 5   JU e
Memories : Meals 27.00 **st.** (lunch) and a la carte 25.00/46.00 **st.** ⓑ 9.50 – *Tsar's* : Meals
(closed Saturday lunch, Sunday and Bank Holidays) a la carte 26.50/36.00 **st.** ⓑ 9.50 –
⌣ 18.00 – **359 rm** 280.00 **s.**, 20 suites.

Selfridge, Orchard St., W1H 0JS, ℘ (0171) 408 2080, *Fax (0171) 629 8849* – |⧢|, ↹ rm,
▤ TV ☎ – 🛉 220. ⓂⒸ AE Ⓞ VISA JCB. ※   AK e
Fletchers : Meals 19.50 **t.** and a la carte – *Orchard* : Meals 12.50/16.50 **t.** and a la carte
ⓑ 9.95 – ⌣ 14.50 – **290 rm** 180.00/200.00 **t.**, 4 suites.

The Leonard, 15 Seymour St., W1H 5AA, ℘ (0171) 935 2010, *Fax (0171) 935 6700*,
« Attractively furnished Georgian town houses », ⌶ – |⧢| ▤ TV ☎ ☏ – 🛉 30. ⓂⒸ AE
Ⓞ VISA JCB. ※   AK n
Meals (room service only) – ⌣ 16.00 – **6 rm** 170.00/190.00 **s.**, **20 suites** 240.00/410.00 **s.**

Radisson SAS Portman, 22 Portman Sq., W1H 9FL, ℘ (0171) 208 6000, *Fax (0171) 208 6001*, ⌶, ⇌s, ※ – |⧢|, ↹ rm, ▤ TV ☎ ☏ – 🛉 350. ⓂⒸ AE Ⓞ VISA
JCB. ※   AJ o
Portman Corner : Meals (buffet lunch) 16.50 **t.** (lunch) and a la carte 19.75/32.50 **t.**
ⓑ 9.50 – ⌣ 16.50 – **272 rm** 226.00/245.00 **s.**, 7 suites.

Montcalm, Great Cumberland Pl., W1A 2LF, ℘ (0171) 402 4288, *Fax (0171) 724 9180*
– |⧢|, ↹ rm, ▤ TV ☎ – 🛉 80. ⓂⒸ AE Ⓞ VISA JCB   p. 17 EZ x
Meals (see *The Crescent* below) – ⌣ 17.95 – **110 rm** 210.00/300.00 **t.**, 10 suites.

London Regent's Park Hilton, 18 Lodge Rd, NW8 7JT, ℘ (0171) 722 7722, *Fax (0171) 483 2408* – |⧢|, ↹ rm, ▤ TV ☎ ☏ ℗ – 🛉 150. ⓂⒸ AE Ⓞ VISA JCB. ※
Minsky's : Meals 20.50/21.95 **t.** and a la carte ⓑ 8.50 – *Kashinoki* : Meals - Japanese
- *(closed Monday)* 15.00/32.00 **t.** and a la carte – ⌣ 16.50 – **376 rm** 180.00/235.00 **st.**,
1 suite – SB.   p. 5   GT v

Clifton Ford, 47 Welbeck St., W1M 8DN, ℘ (0171) 486 6600, *Fax (0171) 486 7492* –
|⧢| ▤ TV ☎ ⅙ 🚗 – 🛉 150. ⓂⒸ AE Ⓞ VISA. ※   BH a
Meals 24.50/26.00 **st.** and a la carte ⓑ 14.00 – ⌣ 16.00 – **184 rm** 180.00/200.00 **s.**,
2 suites.

Berners, 10 Berners St., W1A 3BE, ℘ (0171) 666 2000, *Fax (0171) 666 2001* – |⧢|,
↹ rm, ▤ rest, TV ☎ ⅙ – 🛉 150. ⓂⒸ AE Ⓞ VISA JCB. ※   EJ r
Meals (carving lunch) 16.95/10.25 **t.** and a la carte ⓑ 6.50 – ⌣ 14.95 – **214 rm**
160.00/240.00 **st.**, 3 suites.

London Marriott Marble Arch, 134 George St., W1H 6DN, ℘ (0171) 723 1277, *Fax (0171) 402 0666*, ⌶, ⇌s, ▧ – |⧢|, ↹ rm, ▤ TV ☎ ⅙ ℗ – 🛉 150. ⓂⒸ AE Ⓞ VISA
JCB. ※   p. 17 EZ i
Meals a la carte 23.95/32.40 **st.** ⓑ 6.50 – ⌣ 13.95 – **240 rm** 190.00/215.00 **s.**

Berkshire, 350 Oxford St., W1N 0BY, ℘ (0171) 629 7474, *Fax (0171) 629 8156* – |⧢|,
↹ rm, ▤ TV ☎ – 🛉 40. ⓂⒸ AE Ⓞ VISA JCB. ※   BK n
Meals 22.50/24.00 **st.** and a la carte – ⌣ 15.00 – **145 rm** 205.00/245.00 **s.**, 2 suites.

Forte Posthouse Regent's Park, Carburton St., W1P 8EE, ℘ (0171) 388 2300, *Fax (0171) 387 2806* – |⧢|, ↹ rm, ▤ rest, TV ☎ ☏ ⅙ – 🛉 320. ⓂⒸ AE Ⓞ VISA JCB.
※   p. 5   JU i
Meals *(closed lunch Saturday and Sunday)* a la carte 16.35/22.85 **t.** ⓑ 7.95 – ⌣ 12.95 –
324 rm 149.00/169.00 **st.**, 1 suite – SB.

Saint Georges, Langham Pl., W1N 8QS, ℘ (0171) 580 0111, *Fax (0171) 436 7997*, ≼
– |⧢|, ↹ rm, TV ☎ – 🛉 25. ⓂⒸ AE Ⓞ VISA JCB   p. 5   JU a
Meals 15.00/21.50 **st.** and a la carte ⓑ 7.85 – ⌣ 13.95 – **84 rm** 165.00/205.00 **st.**,
2 suites – SB.

Dorset Square, 39-40 Dorset Sq., NW1 6QN, ℘ (0171) 723 7874, *Fax (0171) 724 3328*,
« Attractively furnished Regency town houses », ▨ – |⧢| ▤ TV ☎ ☏. ⓂⒸ AE VISA. ※
The Potting Shed : Meals *(closed Sunday lunch and Saturday)* 14.95/18.95 **t.** and a la
carte ⓑ 9.00 – ⌣ 13.75 – **38 rm** 98.00/215.00 **s.**   p. 5   HU s

Durrants, 26-32 George St., W1H 6BJ, ℘ (0171) 935 8131, *Fax (0171) 487 3510*,
« Converted Georgian houses with Regency façade » – |⧢|, ▤ rest, TV ☎ – 🛉 100. ⓂⒸ
AE VISA. ※   AH e
Meals 19.50 **t.** and a la carte ⓑ 9.50 – ⌣ 12.50 – **89 rm** 97.50/145.00 **st.**, 3 suites.

Savoy Court, Granville Pl., W1H 0EH, ℘ (0171) 408 0130, *Fax (0171) 493 2070* – |⧢|,
↹ rm, TV ☎ – 🛉 40. ⓂⒸ AE Ⓞ VISA JCB. ※   AK i
Meals 12.00 **st.** and a la carte ⓑ 12.00 – ⌣ 12.00 – **108 rm** 125.00/150.00 **s.**

Langham Court, 31-35 Langham St., W1N 5RE, ℰ (0171) 436 6622, Fax (0171) 436 2303 – 🛗, ⇔ rm, 📺 ☎ 📞 – 🛐 80. 🆎 ⬆ ①, *VISA* JCB. ⚡
p. 5 JU
Meals 19.75 **st.** and a la carte 🍷 6.00 – ⊑ 14.50 – **56 rm** 139.00/159.00 **st.**

Stakis London Harewood, Harewood Row, NW1 6SE, ℰ (0171) 262 2707, Fax (0171) 262 2975 – 🛗, ⇔ rm, 🍽 rest, 📺 ☎. 🆎 ⬆ ①, *VISA*. ⚡ p. 5 HU
Meals (bar lunch)/dinner 16.50 and a la carte – ⊑ 10.50 – **92 rm** 125.00/184.00 **st.** SB .

Rathbone without rest., Rathbone St., W1P 2LB, ℰ (0171) 636 2001, Fax (0171) 636 3882 – 🛗 ⇔ 🍽 📺 ☎. 🆎 ⬆ ①, *VISA* JCB. ⚡ p. 6 KU
closed 24 to 26 December – ⊑ 13.50 – **72 rm** 150.00/225.00 **st.**

Orrery, 55 Marylebone High St., W1M 3AE, ℰ (0171) 616 8000, Fax (0171) 616 8080, « Converted 19C stables, contemporary interior » – 🛗 🍽. 🆎 ⬆ ①, *VISA* JCB
closed 25 December and Easter Sunday – **Meals** (booking essential) 26.50 **t.** (lunch) and dinner a la carte 33.50/46.00 **t.** p. 5 IU

Interlude, 5 Charlotte St., W1P 1HD, ℰ (0171) 637 0222, Fax (0171) 637 0224 – 🍽
🆎 ⬆ ①, *VISA* JCB p. 6 KU
closed Saturday lunch, Sunday, last 2 weeks August, 1 week Christmas and Bank Holidays – **Meals** 24.50/34.50 **st.** and dinner a la carte 24.50/34.50 **t.**
Spec. Langoustine ravioli with crushed coriander. Cumin roasted loin of lamb on smoked aubergine. Chocolate tart with prune and Armagnac ice cream.

The Crescent (at Montcalm H.), Great Cumberland Pl., W1A 2LF, ℰ (0171) 402 4288, Fax (0171) 724 9180 – 🍽. 🆎 ⬆ ①, *VISA* JCB p. 17 EZ
closed Saturday lunch and Sunday – **Meals** 19.00/24.00 **t.**

Nico Central, 35 Great Portland St., W1N 5DD, ℰ (0171) 436 8846, Fax (0171) 436 3455 – 🍽. 🆎 ⬆ ①, *VISA* JCB DJ
Meals 25.00/27.00 **st.** 🍷 9.00.

La Porte des Indes, 32 Bryanston St., W1H 7AE, ℰ (0171) 224 0055, Fax (0171) 224 1144 – 🍽. 🆎 ⬆ ①, *VISA* JCB AK
closed Saturday lunch, 25, 26 and 31 December – **Meals** - Indian - 22.00/31.00 **t.** and la carte 🍷 5.50.

Stephen Bull, 5-7 Blandford St., W1H 3AA, ℰ (0171) 486 9696, Fax (0171) 490 3126 – 🍽. 🆎 ⬆ ①, *VISA* BH
closed Saturday lunch, Sunday, 1 week Christmas-New Year and Bank Holidays – **Meals** la carte approx. 27.00 **t.** 🍷 7.00.

Caldesi, 15-17 Marylebone Lane, W1M 5FE, ℰ (0171) 935 9226, Fax (0171) 929 0927 – 🍽. 🆎 ⬆ ①, *VISA* JCB BJ
closed Saturday lunch, Sunday, 25 December and Bank Holidays – **Meals** - Italian - a la carte 17.00/26.00 **t.** 🍷 8.00.

Oceana, Jason Court, 76 Wigmore St., W1H 9DQ, ℰ (0171) 224 2992, Fax (0171) 486 1216 – 🍽. 🆎 ⬆ ①, *VISA* JCB BJ
closed Saturday lunch, Sunday, 25 December and Bank Holidays – **Meals** a la carte 19.25/29.00 **t.** 🍷 8.00.

Bertorelli's, 19-23 Charlotte St., W1P 1HP, ℰ (0171) 636 4174, Fax (0171) 467 8902 – 🍽. 🆎 ⬆ ①, *VISA* JCB p. 6 KU
closed Saturday lunch, Sunday, 25-26 December and Bank Holidays – **Meals** - Italian - la carte 17.50/26.75 🍷 7.75.

Asuka, Berkeley Arcade, 209a Baker St., NW1 6AB, ℰ (0171) 486 5026, Fax (0171) 224 1741 – 🆎 ⬆ *VISA* JCB p. 5 HU
closed Saturday lunch, Sunday, Christmas-New Year and Bank Holidays – **Meals** - Japanese - 14.50/23.90 **t.** and a la carte 🍷 13.95.

Gaylord, 79-81 Mortimer St., W1N 7TB, ℰ (0171) 580 3615, Fax (0171) 636 0860 – 🍽 🆎 ⬆ ①, *VISA* JCB p. 6 KU
Meals - Indian - 16.95 **t.** and a la carte 🍷 5.95.

Mash, 19-21 Great Portland St., W1M JD8, ℰ (0171) 637 5555, Fax (0171) 637 7333 🍽. 🆎 ⬆ ①, *VISA* DJ
closed 25 December – **Meals** a la carte approx. 31.50 **st.**

Ard-Ri at the O'Conor Don, (first floor), 88 Marylebone Lane, W1M 5FJ, ℰ (0171) 935 9311, Fax (0171) 486 6706 – 🆎 ⬆ *VISA* BJ
closed Saturday lunch, Sunday, Easter, 25-26 December and Bank Holidays – **Meals** - Irish - 19.00 **t.** (lunch) and a la carte 22.70/27.30 **t.**

Ibla, 89 Marylebone High St., W1M 3DE, ℰ (0171) 224 3799, Fax (0171) 486 1370 – 🆎 *VISA* p. 5 IU
closed Sunday, 25-26 December, 4 days January and Bank Holidays – **Meals** - Italian - 17.00/25.00 **t.**.

St. James's – ✉ W1/SW1/WC2 – *pp. 12 and 13.*

Ritz, 150 Piccadilly, W1V 9DG, ℘ (0171) 493 8181, *Fax (0171) 493 2687*, 🏮, ⌂ – |≡|, ⇥ rm ≡ TV ☎ ✆ – 🔒 50. MC AE ① VISA JCB. ✄
DN a
Italian Garden : Meals (summer only) 35.00/45.00 **st.** and a la carte 🍾 18.00 (see also *The Restaurant* below) – ☕ 23.50 – **115 rm** 245.00/290.00 **s.**, 15 suites – SB.

Dukes ⓢ, 35 St. James's Pl., SW1A 1NY, ℘ (0171) 491 4840, *Fax (0171) 493 1264* –
|≡| ≡ TV ☎ ✆ – 🔒 50. MC AE ① VISA JCB. ✄
EP x
Meals (residents only) a la carte 20.50/41.00 **st.** 🍾 7.50 – ☕ 12.50 – **73 rm** 185.00/205.00 **s.**, 8 suites.

Stafford ⓢ, 16-18 St. James's Pl., SW1A 1NJ, ℘ (0171) 493 0111, *Fax (0171) 493 7121* – |≡| ≡ TV ☎ ✆ – 🔒 35. MC AE ① VISA JCB. ✄
DN u
Meals *(closed Saturday lunch)* 25.50/29.00 **st.** and a la carte 🍾 8.50 – ☕ 15.50 – **76 rm** 199.00/310.00 **s.**, 5 suites – SB.

Cavendish, 81 Jermyn St., SW1Y 6JF, ℘ (0171) 930 2111, *Fax (0171) 839 2125* – |≡|, ⇥ rm, ≡ rest, TV ☎ ⇔ – 🔒 80. MC AE ① VISA JCB. ✄
EN i
Meals *(closed lunch Saturday and Sunday)* 21.25 and a la carte 🍾 6.95 – ☕ 14.50 – **249 rm** 165.00/195.00 **s.**, 2 suites – SB.

22 Jermyn Street, 22 Jermyn St., SW1Y 6HL, ℘ (0171) 734 2353, *Fax (0171) 734 0750* – |≡| ≡ TV ☎ ✆. MC AE ① VISA JCB
FM e
Meals (room service only) – ☕ 16.50 – **6 rm** 199.00 **s.**, **13 suites** 265.00/300.00 **s.**

Pastoria, 3-6 St. Martin's St., off Leicester Sq., WC2H 7HL, ℘ (0171) 930 8641, *Fax (0171) 925 0551* – |≡|, ⇥ rm, ≡ rest, TV ☎ – 🔒 60. MC AE ① VISA JCB. ✄
GM v
Meals 17.00 and a la carte 🍾 12.50 – ☕ 12.00 – **58 rm** 175.00/200.00 **s.**

Thistle Trafalgar Square, Whitcomb St., WC2H 7HG, ℘ (0171) 930 4477, *Fax (0171) 925 2149* – |≡|, ⇥ rm, TV ☎. MC AE ① VISA JCB. ✄
GM r
Meals 13.95/16.95 **st.** and a la carte 🍾 5.95 – ☕ 13.50 – **108 rm** 150.00/180.00 **st.** – SB.

Thistle Piccadilly without rest., 39 Coventry St., W1V 7EH, ℘ (0171) 930 4033, *Fax (0171) 925 2586* – |≡| ⇥ TV ☎. MC AE ① VISA JCB. ✄
FGM a
☕ 13.50 – **92 rm** 150.00/190.00 **st.**

The Restaurant (at Ritz H.), 150 Piccadilly, W1V 9DG, ℘ (0171) 493 8181, *Fax (0171) 493 2687*, 🏮, « Elegant restaurant in Louis XVI style » – ≡. MC AE ① VISA JCB
DN a
Meals (dancing Friday and Saturday evenings) 35.00/45.00 **st.** and a la carte 49.00/59.50 **st.** 🍾 18.00.

Suntory, 72-73 St. James's St., SW1A 1PH, ℘ (0171) 409 0201, *Fax (0171) 499 0208* – ≡. MC AE ① VISA JCB
EP z
closed lunch Sunday and Bank Holidays, Easter and Christmas-New Year – **Meals** - Japanese - a la carte 35.50/89.20 **st.** 🍾 12.00.

L'Oranger, 5 St. James's St., SW1A 1EF, ℘ (0171) 839 3774, *Fax (0171) 839 4330*, 🏮 ❀ – ≡. MC AE ① VISA JCB
EP a
closed Saturday lunch, Sunday and 1 week Christmas – **Meals** 23.50/33.50 **t.** 🍾 15.00
Spec. Goat's cheese parcels in a bouillon of artichoke, hazelnut oil and basil. Roast loin of veal, sautéed girolles, foie gras and truffle sauce. Coconut parfait with pistachio ice cream.

Quaglino's, 16 Bury St., SW1Y 6AL, ℘ (0171) 930 6767, *Fax (0171) 839 2866* – ≡. MC AE ① VISA JCB
EN r
Meals (booking essential) 19.00 **t.** and a la carte 26.00/50.50 **t.** 🍾 6.00.

Criterion Brasserie Marco Pierre White, 224 Piccadilly, W1V 9LB, ℘ (0171) 930 0488, *Fax (0171) 930 8190*, « 19C Neo-Byzantine decor » – MC AE VISA
FM c
closed Christmas – **Meals** 17.95 **t.** (lunch) and a la carte 26.65/29.25 **t.** 🍾 9.00.

Le Caprice, Arlington House, Arlington St., SW1A 1RT, ℘ (0171) 629 2239, *Fax (0171) 493 9040* – ≡. MC AE ① VISA
DN c
closed 25-26 and 31 December, 1 January and 30 August – **Meals** a la carte 22.00/44.25 **t.** 🍾 8.75.

Cave (at Caviar House), 161 Piccadilly, W1V 9DF, ℘ (0171) 409 0445, *Fax (0171) 493 1667* – ≡. MC AE ① VISA
DN s
closed Sunday, 25-26 December and 1 January – **Meals** a la carte 27.95/79.95 **t.**

The Avenue, 7-9 St. James's St., SW1A 1EE, ℘ (0171) 321 2111, *Fax (0171) 321 2500* – ≡. MC AE ① VISA
EP e
closed 25 and 26 December – **Meals** 19.50 **t.** (lunch) and dinner a la carte 23.15/40.65 **t.**

Matsuri, 15 Bury St., SW1Y 6AL, ℘ (0171) 839 1101, *Fax (0171) 930 7010* – ≡. MC AE ① VISA JCB
EN r
closed Sunday and Bank Holidays – **Meals** - Japanese (Teppan-Yaki, Sushi) - 14.00/40.00 **t.** and a la carte 🍾 12.50.

Soho - ✉ W1/WC2 - *pp. 12 and 13.*

Hampshire, Leicester Sq., WC2H 7LH, ℘ (0171) 839 9399, *Fax (0171) 930 8122*,
↑6 – |♣|, ⇔ rm, 🗏 📺 ☎ 📞 – 🛐 80. 🅜🅒 🆎 ⑩ *VISA* 🄹🄲🄱. 🕸   GM
Meals 22.50 **st.** and a la carte ⇞ 15.25 – ⬭ 15.00 – **119 rm** 280.00 **s.**, 5 suites.

Hazlitt's without rest., 6 Frith St., W1V 5TZ, ℘ (0171) 434 1771, *Fax (0171) 439 1524*
« Early 18C town houses » – 📺 ☎. 🅜🅒 🆎 ⑩ *VISA* 🄹🄲🄱. 🕸   FK
closed Christmas – ⬭ 7.25 – **22 rm** 125.00/163.00, 1 suite.

The Café Royal Grill, 68 Regent St., W1R 6EL, ℘ (0171) 437 1177
Fax (0171) 439 7672, « Rococo decoration » – 🗏. 🅜🅒 🆎 *VISA*   EM
closed Saturday lunch and Sunday – **Meals** 24.50 **st.** (lunch) and a la carte 70.00/90.00 **st.**
⇞ 11.50
Spec. Mousseline of lobster, beurre Champagne. Fillet of sea bass with scallops, ratatouille
of aubergine and tomato. Bresse pigeon en vessie, ravioli of wild mushrooms, fumet of
ceps.

L'Escargot, 48 Greek St., W1V 5LQ, ℘ (0171) 437 2679, *Fax (0171) 437 0790* – 🗏. 🅜🅒
🆎 ⑩ *VISA* 🄹🄲🄱   GK
Ground Floor : **Meals** *(closed Saturday lunch, Sunday and Christmas)* 17.95 **t.** (lunch) and
a la carte 25.65/31.65 **t.** ⇞ 10.50 – **Picasso Room** : **Meals** *(closed Saturday lunch, Sunday,
Monday, August, Christmas and Bank Holidays)* 27.50/42.00 **t.** ⇞ 10.50
Spec. Tartlet of snails, wild mushrooms, red wine poached eggs. Goosnargh duck, fondant
potato, mulled shallots and young vegetables. Iced caramel and apricot crumble.

Quo Vadis, 26-29 Dean St., W1A 6LL, ℘ (0171) 437 9585, *Fax (0171) 434 9972* – 🗏
🅜🅒 🆎 *VISA*   FK
closed lunch Saturday and Sunday and Christmas – **Meals** 17.95 **t.** (lunch) and a la carte
25.45/72.90 **t.**

Richard Corrigan at Lindsay House, 21 Romilly St., W1V 5TG, ℘ (0171) 439 0450
Fax (0171) 437 7349 – 🗏. 🅜🅒 🆎 ⑩ *VISA*   GL
closed Saturday lunch, Sunday, 2 weeks in summer and 1 week Christmas – **Meals**
26.00/38.00 **t.** ⇞ 16.00
Spec. Chilled lobster with tomato juices, avocado and basil. Saddle of rabbit stuffed with
black pudding with root vegetable juices. Marinated cherries with goat's cheese sorbet.

Teatro, 93-107 Shaftesbury Av., W1V 8BT, ℘ (0171) 494 3040, *Fax (0171) 494 3050*
– 🗏. 🅜🅒 🆎 ⑩ *VISA* 🄹🄲🄱   GL
closed Saturday lunch, Sunday and 25 to 30 December – **Meals** 18.00 **t.** (lunch) and a la
carte 25.75/38.75 ⇞ 11.00.

The Sugar Club, 21 Warwick St., W1R 5RB, ℘ (0171) 437 7776, *Fax (0171) 437 7778*
– ⇔ 🗏. 🅜🅒 🆎 ⑩ *VISA*   EL
closed 25-26 December and 1 January – **Meals** a la carte 24.10/33.10 **t.**

Circus, 1 Upper James St., W1R 4BP, ℘ (0171) 534 4000, *Fax (0171) 534 4010* – 🗏. 🅜🅒
🆎 ⑩ *VISA*   EL
closed Sunday dinner, 25-26 December and 1 January – **Meals** a la carte 20.50/34.50 **t.**

Red Fort, 77 Dean St., W1V 5HA, ℘ (0171) 437 2115, *Fax (0171) 434 0721* – 🗏. 🅜🅒
🆎 ⑩ *VISA*   FJK
Meals - Indian - (buffet lunch) a la carte 24.50/32.35 **t.**

Mezzo, Lower ground floor, 100 Wardour St., W1V 3LE, ℘ (0171) 314 4000
Fax (0171) 314 4040 – 🗏. 🅜🅒 🆎 ⑩ *VISA* 🄹🄲🄱   FK
closed Saturday lunch and 25-26 December – **Meals** 15.50 **t.** (lunch) and a la carte
23.00/30.25 **t.**

Soho Soho, (first floor), 11-13 Frith St., W1V 5TS, ℘ (0171) 494 3491
Fax (0171) 437 3091, – 🗏. 🅜🅒 🆎 ⑩ *VISA* 🄹🄲🄱   FK
closed Saturday lunch and Sunday – **Meals** a la carte 26.50/35.50 **t.** ⇞ 5.50.

Lexington, 45 Lexington St., W1R 3LG, ℘ (0171) 434 3401, *Fax (0171) 287 2997* – 🗏
🅜🅒 🆎 ⑩ *VISA* 🄹🄲🄱   EK
closed Saturday lunch, Sunday and Bank Holidays – **Meals** 15.00 **t.** (dinner) and a la carte
20.45/25.70 **t.** ⇞ 5.00.

Gopal's, 12 Bateman St., W1V 5TD, ℘ (0171) 434 0840, *Fax (0171) 434 0840* – 🗏. 🅜🅒
🆎 *VISA*   FK
closed 25 and 26 December – **Meals** - Indian - a la carte 13.95/19.50 **t.**

Gay Hussar, 2 Greek St., W1V 6NB, ℘ (0171) 437 0973, *Fax (0171) 437 4631* – 🗏. 🅜🅒
🆎 ⑩ *VISA*   GJ
closed Sunday and Bank Holidays – **Meals** - Hungarian - 17.50 **t.** (lunch) and a la carte
19.05/27.05 **t.** ⇞ 7.50.

Leith's Soho, 41 Beak St., W1R 3LE, ℘ (0171) 287 2057, *Fax (0171) 287 1767* – 🗏
🅜🅒 🆎 ⑩ *VISA* 🄹🄲🄱   EL
closed Sunday, 2 weeks Christmas and Bank Holidays – **Meals** 19.50 **t.** (lunch) and a la carte
18.50/32.50 **t.** ⇞ 5.75.

✗ **dell 'Ugo,** 56 Frith St., W1V 5TA, ✆ (0171) 734 8300, Fax (0171) 734 8784 – **M©** **AE**
① **VISA**
FK z
closed Saturday lunch, Sunday, 25-26 December and Bank Holidays – **Meals** 12.50 **t.** and
a la carte 23.35/27.35 **t.**

✗ **Sri Siam,** 16 Old Compton St., W1V 5PE, ✆ (0171) 434 3544, Fax (0171) 287 1311 –
▣. M© AE ① VISA
GK r
closed Sunday lunch, 25-26 December and 1 January – **Meals** - Thai - 12.95/19.95 **t.** and
a la carte ⌀ 7.75.

✗ **Soho Spice,** 124-126 Wardour St., W1V 3LA, ✆ (0171) 434 0808, Fax (0171) 434 0799
– **M© AE ① VISA**
FJ e
Meals - Indian - 15.95 **t.** and a la carte.

✗ **Alastair Little,** 49 Frith St., W1V 5TE, ✆ (0171) 734 5183 – **M© AE VISA JCB**   FK o
closed Saturday lunch, Sunday and Bank Holidays – **Meals** (booking essential)
25.00/33.00 **t..**

✗ **Wok Wok,** 10 Frith St., W1V 5TZ, ✆ (0171) 437 7080, Fax (0171) 437 3121 – **▣. M©**
AE ① VISA JCB
FK c
closed lunch Saturday and Sunday and 25 December – **Meals** - South East Asian - (bookings
not accepted) a la carte 13.65/19.65 **t.**

✗ **Fung Shing,** 15 Lisle St., WC2H 7BE, ✆ (0171) 734 0284, Fax (0171) 734 0284 – **▣.**
M© AE ① VISA
GL a
closed Bank Holiday lunch and 24 to 26 December – **Meals** - Chinese (Canton) - 16.00 **t.**
and a la carte ⌀ 6.00.

✗ **Saigon,** 45 Frith St., W1V 5TE, ✆ (0171) 437 7109, Fax (0171) 734 1668 – **▣. M© AE**
① VISA
FGK x
closed Sunday, Easter, 25-26 December and Bank Holidays – **Meals** - Vietnamese - a la carte
approx. 16.25 **t.**

✗ **Jen,** 7 Gerrard St., W1V 7LJ, ✆ (0171) 287 8193, Fax (0171) 734 9845 – **▣. M© AE VISA**
Meals - Hong Kong cuisine - 5.50/9.00 **t.** and a la carte.
GL e

Strand and Covent Garden – ✉ WC2 – p. 17.

🏨 **The Savoy,** Strand, WC2R 0EU, ✆ (0171) 836 4343, Fax (0171) 240 6040, ⅙, ≘s, 🔲
– |⚡|, ⇴ rm, ▣ TV ☎ ✆ 🚗 – 🔏 500. **M© AE ① VISA JCB.** ✄   DEY a
Grill : **Meals** (closed Saturday lunch, Sunday and August) a la carte 40.00/70.00 **t.** ⌀ 9.95
River : **Meals** 28.50/39.50-43.50 **st.** and a la carte 55.00/75.50 **st.** ⌀ 9.50 – ☕ 18.75 –
154 rm 270.00/325.00 **s.,** 48 suites – SB.

🏨 **Le Meridien Waldorf,** Aldwych, WC2B 4DD, ✆ (0171) 836 2400, Fax (0171) 836 7244
– |⚡|, ⇴ rm, ▣ rm, TV ☎ – 🔏 450. **M© AE ① VISA JCB**   EX x
Palm Court : **Meals** 23.50 **t.** (dinner) and a la carte 26.00/43.00 **st.** ⌀ 13.00 – **Aldwych
brasserie** : **Meals** (closed Sunday dinner) 15.50 **t.** and a la carte 14.40/19.40 **t.** ⌀ 9.50
– ☕ 17.00 – **286 rm** 225.00/315.00 **s.,** 6 suites – SB.

🏨 **The Howard,** Temple Pl., WC2R 2PR, ✆ (0171) 836 3555, Fax (0171) 379 4547, ≼ –
|⚡|, ⇴ rm, ▣ TV ☎ ✆ 🚗 – 🔏 100. **M© AE ① VISA JCB.** ✄   EX e
Meals a la carte 31.95/63.50 **st.** ⌀ 10.50 – ☕ 19.50 – **133 rm** 255.00/285.00 **st.,** 2 suites.

🏨 **One Aldwych,** WC2B 4BZ, ✆ (0171) 300 1000, Fax (0171) 300 1001, « Contemporary
interior », ⅙, ≘s, ⊒, 🔲 – |⚡|, ⇴ rm, ▣ TV ☎ ✆ ⅙ – 🔏 100. **M© AE ① VISA JCB.**
✄   EX r
Indigo : **Meals** a la carte 20.25/34.75 **t.** ⌀ 9.00 (see also **Axis** below) – ☕ 16.50 – **96 rm**
245.00/265.00 **s.,** 9 suites.

✗✗✗ **Ivy,** 1 West St., WC2H 9NE, ✆ (0171) 836 4751, Fax (0171) 497 3644 – **▣. M© AE ①**
VISA
p. 13 GK z
closed 25, 26 and 31 December, 1 January and 30 August – **Meals** a la carte 23.75/46.25 **t.**
⌀ 8.75.

✗✗✗ **Axis,** 1 Aldwych, WC2B 4BZ, ✆ (0171) 300 0300, Fax (0171) 300 0301 – **▣. M© AE ①**
VISA JCB
EX r
Meals (closed Saturday lunch, Sunday and Bank Holidays) 18.95 **t.** and a la carte ⌀ 10.00.

✗✗ **Rules,** 35 Maiden Lane, WC2E 7LB, ✆ (0171) 836 5314, Fax (0171) 497 1081, « London's
oldest restaurant with collection of antique cartoons, drawings and paintings » – **M© AE**
① VISA
DX n
closed 5 days Christmas – **Meals** - English - a la carte 26.45/31.65 **t.** ⌀ 6.00.

✗✗ **Bank,** 1 Kingsway, Aldwych, WC2B 6UA, ✆ (0171) 379 9797, Fax (0171) 379 9014 – **M©**
AE ① VISA JCB
EX s
closed 25, 27 and 28 December, 1 January and Bank Holidays – **Meals** 17.50 **t.** and a la
carte.

✗✗ **Christopher's,** 18 Wellington St., WC2E 7DD, ✆ (0171) 240 4222, Fax (0171) 836 3506
– **▣. M© AE ① VISA JCB**
EX z
closed Christmas – **Meals** a la carte 22.50/41.50 **t.**

XX **L'Estaminet,** 14 Garrick St., off Floral St., WC2 9BJ, ☎ (0171) 379 1432, Fax (0171) 379 1530 – MO AE VISA JCB
DX
closed Sunday, Easter, 25 December and Bank Holidays – **Meals** - French - a la cart 20.00/31.40 **t.** ⓘ 8.00.

XX **Sheekey's,** 28-32 St. Martin's Court, WC2N 4AL, ☎ (0171) 240 2565, Fax (0171) 240 8114 – ▤. MO AE ① VISA
DX
Meals - Seafood - a la carte 35.00/60.00 **t.** ⓘ 9.00.

XX **Bertorelli's,** 44a Floral St., WC2E 9DA, ☎ (0171) 836 3969, Fax (0171) 836 1868 – ▤
MO AE ① VISA JCB
DX
closed 24 December dinner, Sunday and 25-26 December – **Meals** - Italian - 14.00 **t.** (lunch and a la carte 16.85/24.95 **t.** ⓘ 9.25.

XX **Corney and Barrow,** 116 St. Martins Lane, WC2 4AZ, ☎ (0171) 655 9800, Fax (0171) 655 9801 – ▤. MO AE ① VISA JCB
DY
closed Sunday and 25-26 December – **Meals** a la carte 14.95/26.20 **t.**

X **Stephen Bull St. Martin's Lane,** 12 Upper St. Martin's Lane, WC2 H9DL, ☎ (0171) 379 7811 – ▤. MO AE ① VISA
DX
closed Saturday lunch, Sunday, 1 week Christmas-New Year and Bank Holidays – **Meals** la carte approx. 27.50 **t.** ⓘ 7.00.

X **Le Café du Jardin,** 28 Wellington St., WC2E 7BD, ☎ (0171) 836 8769, Fax (0171) 836 4123 – ▤. MO AE ① VISA JCB
EX
closed 25 December – **Meals** 13.50 **t.** and a la carte ⓘ 4.50.

X **Magno's Brasserie,** 65a Long Acre, WC2E 9JH, ☎ (0171) 836 6077, Fax (0171) 379 6184 – ▤. MO AE ① VISA JCB
DV
closed Saturday lunch, Sunday and 25-26 December – **Meals** - French - 16.95 **t.** and a l carte ⓘ 12.50.

X **Livebait,** 21 Wellington St., WC2E 7DN, ☎ (0171) 836 7161. MO AE ①
VISA JCB
EX
closed Sunday, 1 week Christmas and Bank Holidays – **Meals** - Seafood - a la cart 21.70/29.85 **t.**

X **Joe Allen,** 13 Exeter St., WC2E 7DT, ☎ (0171) 836 0651, Fax (0171) 497 2148 – ▤
MO AE VISA
EX
closed 24 and 25 December – **Meals** 13.00 **t.** (lunch) and a la carte 19.00/25.00 ⓘ 6.00.

Victoria – ✉ SW1 – *Except where otherwise stated see p. 16.*
🛈 *Victoria Station Forecourt, SW1V 1JU* ☎ (0171) 824 8844.

🏰 **St. James Court,** 45 Buckingham Gate, SW1E 6AF, ☎ (0171) 834 6655, Fax (0171) 630 7587, Ⅰ6, ⇆s – 🛗, ⇷ rm, ▤ TV ☎ ☏ – 🛠 180. MO AE ① VIS
JCB. ⌘
CX
Café Mediterranée : Meals a la carte 18.50/26.50 **t.** – **Inn of Happiness** : Meals Chinese - *(closed Saturday lunch)* 16.50/18.50 **t.** (see also **Auberge de Provence** below) – ☕ 16.00 – **372 rm** 229.00 **st.**, 18 suites.

🏰 **Thistle Royal Horseguards,** 2 Whitehall Court, SW1A 2EJ, ☎ (0171) 839 3400, Fax (0171) 925 2263, Ⅰ6 – 🛗, ⇷ rm, ▤ TV ☎ ☏ – 🛠 180. MO AE ① VIS
JCB. ⌘
p. 10 LX
Meals 24.00 **st.** and a la carte ⓘ 7.50 – ☕ 15.00 – **277 rm** 220.00/325.00 **st.**, 3 suite – SB.

🏰 **Stakis London St. Ermin's,** Caxton St., SW1H 0QW, ☎ (0171) 222 7888, Fax (0171) 222 6914 – 🛗, ⇷ rm, ▤ rest, TV ☎ – 🛠 250. MO AE ① VIS
JCB. ⌘
CX
Cloisters brasserie : Meals *(closed lunch Saturday and Sunday)* 18.95/20.95 **st.** and la carte – **Caxton Grill** : Meals *(closed Saturday lunch, Sunday and Bank Holidays)* a la cart 19.30/28.75 **st.** ⓘ 7.25 – ☕ 12.95 – **283 rm** 195.00/245.00 **st.**, 7 suites – SB.

🏨 **Goring,** 15 Beeston Pl., Grosvenor Gdns., SW1W 0JW, ☎ (0171) 396 9000, Fax (0171) 834 4393 – 🛗 ▤ TV ☎ – 🛠 50. MO AE ① VISA. ⌘
BX
Meals 27.00/35.00 **st.** ⓘ 14.00 – ☕ 15.00 – **71 rm** 160.00/195.00 s 4 suites.

🏨 **Thistle Grosvenor,** 101 Buckingham Palace Rd, SW1W 0SJ, ☎ (0171) 834 9494, Fax (0171) 630 1978 – 🛗, ⇷ rm, TV ☎ – 🛠 200. MO AE ① VISA JCB. ⌘
BX
Meals *(carving rest.)* 18.00 **st.** and a la carte ⓘ 7.00 – ☕ 14.00 – **363 rr** 140.00/203.00 **st.**, 3 suites.

🏨 **Thistle Royal Westminster,** 49 Buckingham Palace Rd, SW1W 0QT, ☎ (0171) 834 1821, Fax (0171) 931 7542 – 🛗, ⇷ rm, ▤ TV ☎ – 🛠 180. MO AE ① VIS
JCB. ⌘
BX
Meals 11.95/13.95 **t.** and a la carte ⓘ 6.00 – ☕ 13.95 – **134 rm** 165.00/195.00 **st.**

Dolphin Square, Dolphin Sq., Chichester St., SW1V 3LX, ℘ (0171) 834 3800, Fax (0171) 798 8735, ⅃₅, ≘s, ▨, ☞, ※, squash – |៛|, ↳ rm, ☰ rest, ⊺ᵥ ☎ ᒼ ⇔ Ⓟ – 🕹 50. 𝖬𝖢 𝖠𝖤 ⓪ 𝑽𝑰𝑺𝑨. ⅏   p. 10   KZ a
Meals 12.95 **t.** and a la carte ₰ 5.00 (see also ***Rhodes in the Square*** below) – ☕ 12.95 – **15 rm** 100.00/135.00 **st., 136 suites** 180.00 **st.**

Rubens, 39-41 Buckingham Palace Rd, SW1W 0PS, ℘ (0171) 834 6600, Fax (0171) 828 5401 – |៛|, ↳ rm, ☰ rest, ⊺ᵥ ☎ – 🕹 75. 𝖬𝖢 𝖠𝖤 𝑽𝑰𝑺𝑨 𝖩𝖢𝖡. ⅏   BX n
Meals (closed Sunday lunch) (carving lunch) 17.95 **st.** and dinner a la carte ₰ 10.00 – ☕ 13.00 – **174 rm** 130.00/210.00 **s.**

Rochester, 69 Vincent Sq., SW1P 2PA, ℘ (0171) 828 6611, Fax (0171) 233 6724 – |៛|, ☰ rest, ⊺ᵥ ☎ ᒼ – 🕹 60. 𝖬𝖢 𝖠𝖤 ⓪ 𝑽𝑰𝑺𝑨 𝖩𝖢𝖡. ⅏   CY e
Meals 19.75 **st.** and a la carte ₰ 6.00 – ☕ 14.50 – **80 rm** 159.00/175.00 **st.**

Holiday Inn London Victoria, 2 Bridge Pl., SW1V 1QA, ℘ (0171) 834 8123, Fax (0171) 828 1099, ⅃₅, ≘s, ▨ – |៛|, ↳ rm, ☰ ⊺ᵥ ☎ ᒼ – 🕹 180. 𝖬𝖢 𝖠𝖤 ⓪ 𝑽𝑰𝑺𝑨 𝖩𝖢𝖡. ⅏   BY i
Meals 17.95/19.50 **t.** and a la carte ₰ 7.50 – ☕ 12.75 – **212 rm** 170.00/190.00 **st.**

Rhodes in the Square (at Dolphin Square H.), Dolphin Sq., Chichester St., SW1V 3LX, ℘ (0171) 798 6767, Fax (0171) 798 5685 – ☰. 𝖬𝖢 𝖠𝖤 ⓪ 𝑽𝑰𝑺𝑨 𝖩𝖢𝖡   p. 10   KZ a
closed Saturday lunch and Bank Holidays – Meals 19.50 **t.** (lunch) and a la carte 27.10/38.40 **t.** ₰ 12.50.

Auberge de Provence (at St. James Court H.), 45 Buckingham Gate, SW1E 6AF, ℘ (0171) 821 1899, Fax (0171) 630 7587 – ☰. 𝖬𝖢 𝖠𝖤 ⓪ 𝑽𝑰𝑺𝑨 𝖩𝖢𝖡   CX i
closed Saturday lunch, Sunday, 2 weeks January, 2 weeks August and Bank Holidays – **Meals** - French - a la carte 26.50/31.50 **t.**

L'Incontro, 87 Pimlico Rd, SW1W 8PH, ℘ (0171) 730 6327, Fax (0171) 730 5062 – ☰. 𝖬𝖢 𝖠𝖤 ⓪ 𝑽𝑰𝑺𝑨 𝖩𝖢𝖡   p. 15   FT u
closed lunch Saturday and Sunday and 25-26 December – **Meals** - Italian - 20.50 **t.** (lunch) and a la carte 27.50/51.50 **t.** ₰ 12.50.

Santini, 29 Ebury St., SW1W 0NZ, ℘ (0171) 730 4094, Fax (0171) 730 0544 – ☰. 𝖬𝖢 𝖠𝖤 ⓪ 𝑽𝑰𝑺𝑨 𝖩𝖢𝖡   ABX v
closed lunch Saturday and Sunday and 25-26 December – **Meals** - Italian - 19.75 **t.** (lunch) and a la carte 25.00/51.75 **t.** ₰ 9.00.

Shepherd's, Marsham Court, Marsham St., SW1P 4LA, ℘ (0171) 834 9552, Fax (0171) 233 6047 – ☰. 𝖬𝖢 𝖠𝖤 ⓪ 𝑽𝑰𝑺𝑨 𝖩𝖢𝖡   p. 10   LZ z
closed Saturday, Sunday, Easter, summer Bank Holidays, 25-26 December and 1 January – **Meals** - English - (booking essential) 23.95 **t.** ₰ 14.75.

Roussillon, 16 St. Barnabas St., SW1W 8PB, ℘ (0171) 730 5550, Fax (0171) 824 8617 – ☰. 𝖬𝖢 ⓪ 𝑽𝑰𝑺𝑨 𝖩𝖢𝖡   p. 9   IZ c
closed Sunday, 15 to 29 August, 25-26 December and Bank Holidays – **Meals** 16.00/24.00 **t.** and a la carte.

Simply Nico, 48a Rochester Row, SW1P 1JU, ℘ (0171) 630 8061, Fax (0171) 828 8541 – ☰. 𝖬𝖢 𝖠𝖤 ⓪ 𝑽𝑰𝑺𝑨 𝖩𝖢𝖡   CY a
closed Saturday lunch, Sunday, 25-26 December and Bank Holidays – **Meals** (booking essential) 25.00/27.00 **st.**

Tate Gallery, Tate Gallery, Millbank, SW1P 4RG, ℘ (0171) 887 8877, Fax (0171) 887 8902, « Rex Whistler murals » – ☰. 𝖬𝖢 𝖠𝖤 ⓪ 𝑽𝑰𝑺𝑨   p. 10   LZ c
closed 25 December – **Meals** (booking essential) (lunch only) 18.50 **t.** and a la carte ₰ 8.50.

The Atrium, 4 Millbank, SW1P 3JA, ℘ (0171) 233 0032, Fax (0171) 233 0010 – ☰. 𝖬𝖢 𝖠𝖤 ⓪ 𝑽𝑰𝑺𝑨   p. 10   LY s
closed Saturday, Sunday, Christmas, Easter and Bank Holidays – **Meals** a la carte 17.40/29.40 **t.**

Ken Lo's Memories of China, 67-69 Ebury St., SW1W 0NZ, ℘ (0171) 730 7734, Fax (0171) 730 2992 – ☰. 𝖬𝖢 𝖠𝖤 ⓪ 𝑽𝑰𝑺𝑨 𝖩𝖢𝖡   AY u
closed Sunday lunch, 24 December-1 January and Bank Holidays – **Meals** - Chinese - 19.00/25.00 **t.** and a la carte.

Hunan, 51 Pimlico Rd, SW1W 8NE, ℘ (0171) 730 5712, Fax (0171) 730 8265 – 𝖬𝖢 𝖠𝖤 𝑽𝑰𝑺𝑨   p. 9   IZ a
closed Sunday, 4 days Christmas and Bank Holidays – **Meals** - Chinese (Hunan) - a la carte 11.70/43.80 **t.** ₰ 10.00.

Olivo, 21 Eccleston St., SW1W 9LX, ℘ (0171) 730 2505, Fax (0171) 824 8190 – ☰. 𝖬𝖢 𝖠𝖤 𝑽𝑰𝑺𝑨   AY z
closed lunch Saturday and Sunday, 25 December and Bank Holidays – **Meals** - Italian - 17.00 **t.** (lunch) and a la carte 24.50/31.00 **t.** ₰ 7.50.

La Poule au Pot, 231 Ebury St., SW1W 8UT, ℘ (0171) 730 7763, Fax (0171) 259 9651, ☂ – ☰. 𝖬𝖢 𝖠𝖤 ⓪ 𝑽𝑰𝑺𝑨 𝖩𝖢𝖡   p. 9   IZ e
Meals - French - 13.95 **t.** (lunch) and a la carte 26.00/36.35 ₰ 5.75.

UNITED KINGDOM

Bray-on-Thames *Berks. West : 34 m. by M 4 (junction 8-9) and A 308* **404** *R 29 – pop. 8 12* – ⊠ *Maidenhead.*

XXXX **Waterside Inn** (Roux) with rm, Ferry Rd, SL6 2AT, ℰ (01628) 620691
✿✿✿ *Fax (01628) 784710,* « ≼ *Thames-side setting* » –, 🛈, 🍽 rest, 📺 ☎ **P**. **MO** **AE** **①** **VISA** JCB. 🛇
closed 5 to 8 April and 26 December-28 January – **Meals** - French - *(closed Tuesday lunch Sunday dinner from October-April and Monday)* 29.50-44.50/67.50 **t.** and a la carte 59.30/88.50 **t.** 🍷 11.00 – **8 rm** 140.00/170.00 **st.**, 1 suite
Spec. Tronçonnettes de homard poêlées minute au Porto blanc. Filets de lapereau grillé aux marrons glacés. Soufflé chaud aux framboises.

Reading *Berks. at Shinfield West : 43 m. by M 4 and A 329 on A 327* **403** **404** *Q 29 – pop. 213 474*
🛈 *Town Hall, Blagrave St., RG1 1QH* ℰ *(01734) 566226.*

XXX **L'Ortolan** (Burton-Race), The Old Vicarage, Church Lane, RG2 9BY, ℰ (01189) 883783
✿✿ *Fax (01189) 885391,* 🍃 – **P**. **MO** **AE** **①** **VISA**
closed Sunday dinner and Monday – **Meals** - French - 23.00/42.00 **t.** *(except Saturday dinner)* and a la carte 46.00/64.50 **t.** 🍷 10.00
Spec. Queue de homard rôti, sauce Sauternes. Filet de veau et ses béatilles aux deux saveurs. Assiette chocolatière.

Oxford *Oxon. at Great Milton Northwest : 49 m. by M 40 (junction 7) and A 329* **403** **404** *Q 28* – *pop. 118 795* – ⊠ *Great Milton.*
🛈 *The Old School, Gloucester Green, OX1 2DA* ℰ *(01865) 726871.*

 filly **Le Manoir aux Quat' Saisons** (Blanc) 🦶, Church Rd, OX44 7PD, ℰ (01844) 278881
✿✿ *Fax (01844) 278847,* ≼, « *Part 15C and 16C manor house, gardens* », *park* – 🛇 rest
🍽 rest, 📺 ☎ **P** – 🔬 35. **MO** **AE** **①** **VISA** JCB. 🛇
Meals - French - 32.00 **st.** (lunch) and a la carte 70.00/88.50 **st.** 🍷 14.00 – ☕ 14.50
21 rm 210.00/310.00 **st.**, 6 suites – SB
Spec. Macaroni in a truffle jus with pan-fried langoustine. Roast rib of milk-fed veal with garden vegetables. Apricot fondue and poached meringue in a nougatine cassolette.

BIRMINGHAM *W. Mids.* **403** **404** *O 26* **Great Britain G.** – *pop. 965 928.*
See : *City★ – Museum and Art Gallery★★* JZ M^2 – *Barber Institute of Fine Arts★★ (a Birmingham University)* EX – *Cathedral of St. Philip (stained glass portrayals★)* KYZ.
Envir. : *Aston Hall★★* FV M.
Exc. : *Black Country Museum★, Dudley, NW : 10 m. by A 456 and A 4123.*
🏌 *Edgbaston, Church Rd* ℰ *(0121) 454 1736* FX – 🏌 *Hilltop, Park Lane, Handsworth* ℰ *(0121) 554 4463* – 🏌 *Hatchford Brook, Coventry Rd, Sheldon* ℰ *(0121) 743 9821* HX – 🏌 *Brand Hall, Heron Rd, Oldbury, Warley* ℰ *(0121) 552 2195* – 🏌 *Harborne Church Farm Vicarage Rd, Harborne* ℰ *(0121) 427 1204* EX.
✈ *Birmingham International Airport :* ℰ *(0121) 767 5511, E : 6 ½ m. by A 45.*
🛈 *Convention & Visitor Bureau, 2 City Arcade, B2 4TX* ℰ *(0121) 643 2514, Fax (0121) 616 1038 – Convention & Visitor Bureau, National Exhibition Centre, B40 1NT* ℰ *(0121) 780 4321 – Birmingham Airport, Information Desk, B26 3QJ,* ℰ *(0121) 767 7145/7146 130 Colmore Row, B3 3AP* ℰ *(0121) 693 6300.*
London 122 – Bristol 91 – Liverpool 103 – Manchester 86 – Nottingham 50.

Plans on following pages

filly **Hyatt Regency,** 2 Bridge St., B1 2JZ, ℰ (0121) 643 1234, Fax (0121) 616 2323, ≼
🏋, ≘s, 🏊 – 🕩, 🍽 rm, 🍽 📺 ☎ 🔥 🚗 – 🔬 250. **MO** **AE** **①** **VISA** 🛇 JZ
Number 282 : **Meals** *(closed Sunday and Bank Holidays)* 16.00 **t.** (lunch) and a la carte 23.25/28.25 **t.** 🍷 7.50 – ☕ 12.00 – **308 rm** 155.00/180.00 **st.**, 11 suites.

filly **Swallow,** 12 Hagley Rd, B16 8SJ, ℰ (0121) 452 1144, Fax (0121) 456 3442, 🏋, 🏊
🕩, 🍽 rm, 🍽 📺 ☎ 🔥 **P** – 🔬 25. **MO** **AE** **①** **VISA**. 🛇 FX
Langtrys : **Meals** a la carte 20.90/32.45 **t.** 🍷 9.00 (see also **Sir Edward Elgar's** below) – **94 rm** ☕ 160.00/200.00 **st.**, 4 suites – SB.

filly **Crowne Plaza Birmingham,** Central Sq., Holliday St., B1 1HH, ℰ (0121) 631 2000
Fax (0121) 643 9018, 🏋, ≘s, 🏊 – 🕩, 🍽 rm, 🍽 📺 ☎ 🔥 🔥 **P** – 🔬 150. **MO** **AE** **①**
VISA JCB JZ
Meals *(closed Saturday lunch)* (carving rest.) 14.95/18.95 **st.** and dinner a la carte – ☕ 12.50 – **281 rm** 125.00/135.00 **st.**, 3 suites – SB.

filly **Copthorne,** Paradise Circus, B3 3HJ, ℰ (0121) 200 2727, Fax (0121) 200 1197, 🏋, ≘s
🏊 – 🕩, 🍽 rm, 🍽 rest, 📺 ☎ 🔥 **P** – 🔬 180. **MO** **AE** **①** **VISA**. 🛇 JZ
Goldsmiths : **Meals** (dinner only except Sunday) a la carte approx. 26.95 **st.** 🍷 7.50 – *Goldies :* **Meals** a la carte 17.50/25.95 **st.** 🍷 7.50 – ☕ 12.75 – **209 rm** 130.00/170.00 **st.** 3 suites – SB.

The Burlington, Burlington Arcade, 126 New St., B2 4JQ, ℰ (0121) 643 9191, Fax (0121) 643 5075, 上ć, ≘s – ∣≜∣, ⇥ rm, ▤ rest, 🆃🆅 ☎ 🕾 – 🛦 400. 🝏🝎 🝁🝆 ⓪ 𝚅𝙸𝚂𝙰. ⋇
KY a
closed 25 December – **Berlioz** : Meals (closed lunch Saturday and Sunday) 13.95/21.95 **t.** and a la carte – ⊇ 12.50 – **107 rm** 110.00/120.00 **st.**, 5 suites.

Jonathan's, 16-24 Wolverhampton Rd, Oldbury, B68 0LH, West : 4 m. by A 456 ℰ (0121) 429 3757, Fax (0121) 434 3107, « Authentic Victorian furnishings and memorabilia » – ⇥, ▤ rest, 🆃🆅 ☎ 🅿 – 🛦 100. 🝏🝎 🝁🝆 ⓪ 𝚅𝙸𝚂𝙰
Boulton Watt Bistro : Meals 8.95 **t.** and a la carte – **Victorian Restaurant** : Meals - English - (closed Saturday lunch and Sunday dinner) (booking essential) 15.90 **t.** (lunch) and a la carte 22.30/47.30 **t.** ⅓ 6.80 – **44 rm** ⊇ 88.00/150.00 **st.** – SB.

Birmingham Grand Moathouse, Colmore Row, B3 2DA, ℰ (0121) 607 9988, Fax (0121) 233 1465 – ∣≜∣, ⇥ rm, ▤ rest, 🆃🆅 ☎ – 🛦 500. 🝏🝎 🝁🝆 ⓪ 𝚅𝙸𝚂𝙰   JKY c
Chamberlains : Meals (closed Saturday lunch and Sunday) 16.50 **st.** and a la carte ⅓ 5.75 – **Hugo's** : Meals a la carte 9.20/20.10 **st.** ⅓ 5.75 – ⊇ 10.50 – **170 rm** 115.00/135.00 **st.**, 3 suites – SB.

Forte Posthouse Birmingham City, Smallbrook, Queensway, B5 4EW, ℰ (0121) 643 8171, Fax (0121) 631 2528, 上ć, ≘s, 🏊, squash – ∣≜∣, ⇥ rm, ▤ 🆃🆅 ☎ 🅿 – 🛦 630. 🝏🝎 🝁🝆 ⓪ 𝚅𝙸𝚂𝙰 🅹🅲🅱
KZ o
Meals (carving rest.) 12.95/17.75 **t.** ⅓ 5.75 – ⊇ 9.95 – **250 rm** 95.00 **st.**, 1 suite – SB.

Plough and Harrow, 135 Hagley Rd, Edgbaston, B16 8LS, ℰ (0121) 454 4111, Fax (0121) 454 1868, ⛟ – ∣≜∣ ⇥ 🆃🆅 ☎ 🅿 – 🛦 70. 🝏🝎 🝁🝆 ⓪ 𝚅𝙸𝚂𝙰 🅹🅲🅱   EX a
Meals (closed Saturday lunch and dinner Bank Holiday Monday) 15.95 **st.** (lunch) and a la carte 20.20/31.15 **st.** ⅓ 6.95 – ⊇ 10.75 – **42 rm** 95.00/115.00 **st.**, 2 suites – SB.

Thistle Strathallan, 225 Hagley Rd, Edgbaston, B16 9RY, ℰ (0121) 455 9777, Fax (0121) 454 9432 – ∣≜∣, ⇥ rm, ▤ rest, 🆃🆅 ☎ 🅿 – 🛦 170. 🝏🝎 🝁🝆 ⓪ 𝚅𝙸𝚂𝙰 EX i
Meals (bar lunch Saturday) a la carte 15.25/25.05 **st.** ⅓ 7.25 – ⊇ 11.00 – **148 rm** 108.00/131.00 **st.**, 3 suites – SB.

Novotel, 70 Broad St., B1 2HT, ℰ (0121) 643 2000, Fax (0121) 643 9796, 上ć, ≘s – ∣≜∣, ⇥ rm, ▤ rest, 🆃🆅 ☎ 🕾 ⅋ 🚗 – 🛦 300. 🝏🝎 🝁🝆 ⓪ 𝚅𝙸𝚂𝙰   FV e
Meals 15.00 **t.** (dinner) and a la carte 15.40/23.35 **t.** – ⊇ 9.95 – **148 rm** 95.00 **st.**

Chamberlain, Alcester St., B12 0PJ, ℰ (0121) 606 9000, Fax (0121) 606 9001 – ∣≜∣ ⇥, ▤ rest, 🆃🆅 ☎ 🚗 – 🛦 400. 🝏🝎 🝁🝆 ⓪ 𝚅𝙸𝚂𝙰. ⋇
p. 4 FX r
Meals (closed Saturday lunch) (carving rest.) 6.00/10.00 **st.** – **250 rm** ⊇ 35.00/80.00 **st.**

Sir Edward Elgar's (at Swallow H.), 12 Hagley Rd, B16 8SJ, ℰ (0121) 452 1144, Fax (0121) 456 3442 – ▤ 🅿. 🝏🝎 🝁🝆 ⓪ 𝚅𝙸𝚂𝙰   FX c
Meals 21.50/27.00 **t.** and a la carte ⅓ 9.00.

Gilmore, 27 Warstone Lane, Hockley, ℰ (0121) 233 3655, « Former rolling mill » – 🝏🝎 🝁🝆 ⓪ 𝚅𝙸𝚂𝙰 🅹🅲🅱   FV r
closed Saturday lunch, Sunday, Monday, 1 week Easter, 2 weeks August and 1 week January – Meals 14.50/19.50 **t.** ⅓ 5.00.

Henry's, 27 St. Paul's Sq., B3 1RB, ℰ (0121) 200 1136, Fax (0121) 200 1190 – ▤. 🝏🝎 🝁🝆 ⓪ 𝚅𝙸𝚂𝙰   JY a
closed Sunday, 25-26 December and Bank Holidays – Meals - Chinese (Canton) - 15.00 **t.** and a la carte ⅓ 5.00.

Leftbank, 79 Broad St., B15 1AH, ℰ (0121) 643 4464, Fax (0121) 643 5793 – 🝏🝎 🝁🝆 ⓪ 𝚅𝙸𝚂𝙰   FV a
closed Saturday lunch, Sunday, 25 December-2 January and Bank Holidays – Meals 14.50 **t.** (lunch) and a la carte 24.40/34.50 **t.** ⅓ 8.90.

Shimla Pinks, 214 Broad St., B15 1AY, ℰ (0121) 685 0366, Fax (0121) 643 6383 – ▤. 🝏🝎 🝁🝆 ⓪ 𝚅𝙸𝚂𝙰   FX n
closed lunch Saturday and Sunday, 25 and 26 December and 1 January – Meals - Indian - 6.95/12.95 **t.** and a la carte.

at Hall Green Southeast : 5 ¾ m. by A 41 on A 34 – ✉ Birmingham :

Mizan, 1347 Stratford Rd, B28 9HW, ℰ (0121) 777 3185 – ▤. 🝏🝎 🝁🝆 𝚅𝙸𝚂𝙰   GX a
closed lunch Friday to Tuesday – Meals - Indian - 4.75/13.50 **t.** and a la carte.

at Birmingham Airport Southeast : 9 m. by A 45 HX – ✉ Birmingham :

Novotel, Passenger Terminal, B26 3QL, ℰ (0121) 782 7000, Fax (0121) 782 0445 – ∣≜∣, ⇥ rm, 🆃🆅 ☎ ⅋ – 🛦 35. 🝏🝎 🝁🝆 ⓪ 𝚅𝙸𝚂𝙰
closed 24 and 25 December – Meals (closed lunch Saturday and Sunday) 12.00/18.75 **st.** and a la carte – ⊇ 9.95 – **195 rm** 92.50 **st.**

Forte Posthouse Birmingham Airport, Coventry Rd, B26 3QW, on A 45 ℰ (0121) 782 8141, Fax (0121) 782 2476 – ⇥ rm, 🆃🆅 ☎ ⅋ 🅿 – 🛦 130. 🝏🝎 🝁🝆 ⓪ 𝚅𝙸𝚂𝙰
Meals (closed Sunday) a la carte 14.35/23.35 **st.** ⅓ 7.50 – ⊇ 9.95 – **141 rm** 115.00/135.00 **st.** – SB.

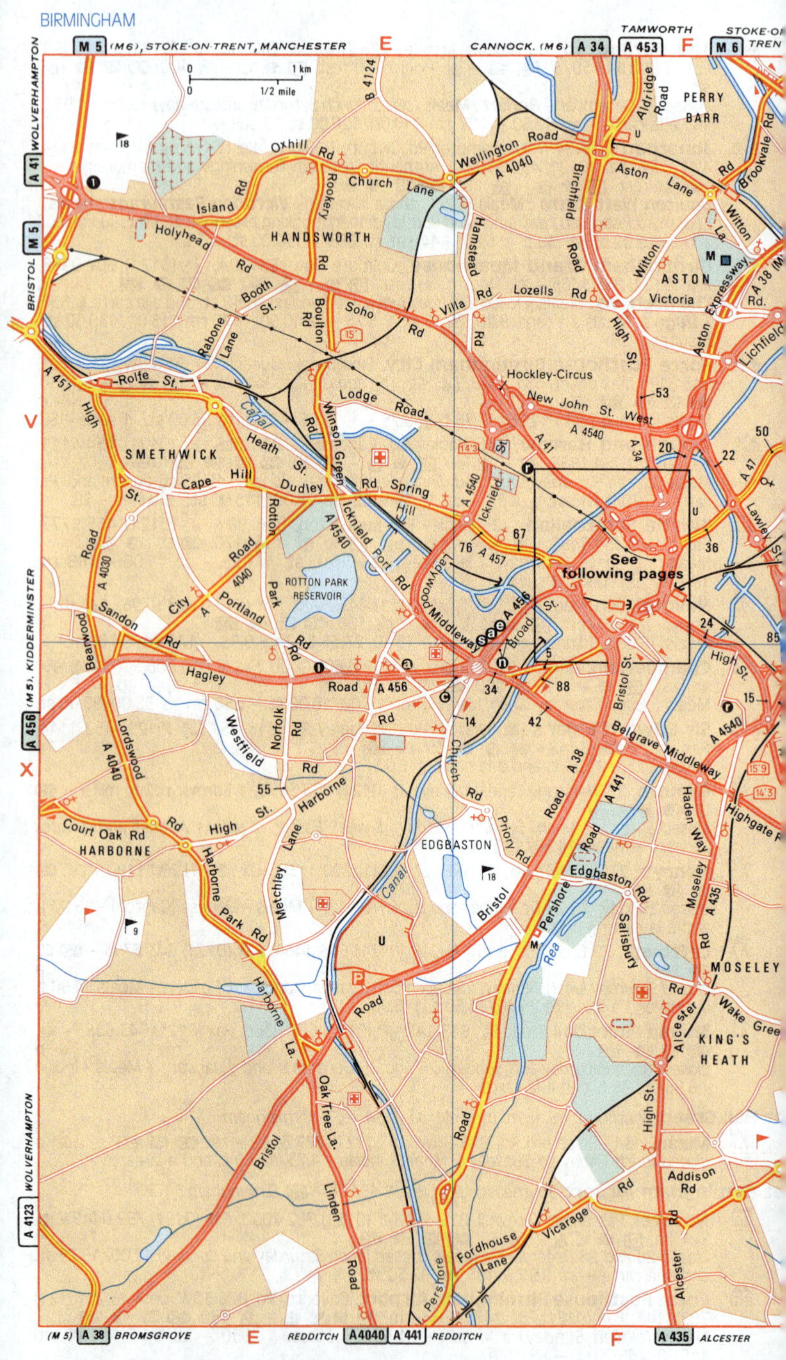

BIRMINGHAM
M 5 (M 6), STOKE-ON-TRENT, MANCHESTER
E
CANNOCK. (M 6) A 34 A 453
TAMWORTH
F
STOKE-ON-TRENT
M 6
WOLVERHAMPTON
A 41
BRISTOL
M 5
A 457
V
0 1 km
0 1/2 mile
B 4124
PERRY BARR
Oxhill Rd
Church Lane
Wellington Road
A 4040
Aston Lane
Rd
Aldridge Road
Witton
Brookvale Rd
Rookery Rd
Rd
Island
Holyhead
HANDSWORTH
Hamstead Rd
Birchfield Road
Aston
Witton La.
Rd
Booth St.
Boulton Rd
Soho
Villa Rd
Lozells Rd
Witton
Victoria
ASTON
M
Aston Expressway
Rabone Lane
Rolfe St.
High
Canal
Lodge Road
Winson Green Rd
Spring Hill
Hockley-Circus
New John St. West
A 4540
A 41
High St.
Lichfield
Lichfield Rd
A 38
SMETHWICK
Cape Hill
Heath St.
Dudley
Icknield Port Rd
Icknield
A 4540
A 457
67
76
A 34
20
22
50
A 47
Lawley St.
36
St.
Rd
Rotton
Road
A 4040
A 4030
City A Portland
Sandon Rd
ROTTON PARK RESERVOIR
Park
Rd
Ladywood Middleway
Broad St.
See following pages
Bristol St.
24
85
High St.
Bearwood
Road
Hagley
Road A 456
Westfield
Norfolk Rd
Rd
Rd
55
Harborne
High St.
Lane
Belgrave Middleway
A 4540
15
r
A 456
A 4040
Lordswood
Court Oak Rd
HARBORNE
Harborne Park Rd
Metchley
Canal
EDGBASTON
Bristol
Priory Rd
Church Rd
A 38
A 441
Pershore Road
Edgbaston Rd
Haden Way
Highgate
Moseley Rd
A 435
Rea
Salisbury Rd
MOSELEY
Alcester Rd
Wake Green Rd
U
Harborne La.
Road
Oak Tree La.
Bristol
Linden Road
KING'S HEATH
High St.
Fordhouse Lane
Vicarage Rd
Addison Rd
Alcester Rd
WOLVERHAMPTON
A 4123
(M 5) A 38 BROMSGROVE
E
REDDITCH A 4040 A 441 REDDITCH
F
A 435 ALCESTER

648

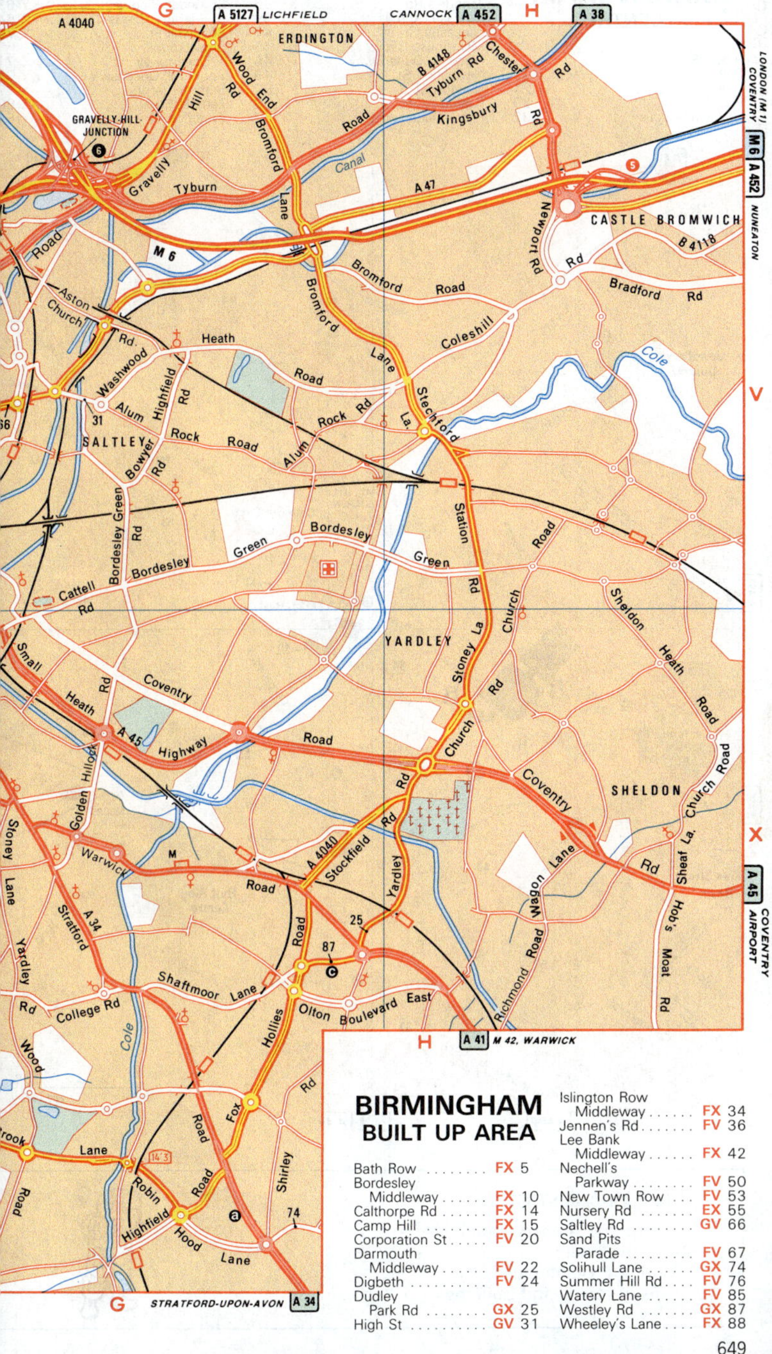

BIRMINGHAM
BUILT UP AREA

BIRMINGHAM
CENTRE

Albert St. .... KZ 2
Bull St. .... KY 13
Dale End .... KZ 21
Hall St. .... JY 29
Holloway Circus .... JZ 32

James Watt Queensway .. KY 35
Jennen's Rd .... KY 36
Lancaster Circus .... KY 39
Lancaster St. .... KY 41
Masshouse Circus ...... KY 43
Moor St. Queensway .... KZ 46
Navigation St. .... JZ 49
Newton St. .... KY 52
Paradise Circus .... JZ 56
Priory Queensway ...... KY 57

St. Chads Circus .... JKY 62
St. Chads Ringway .... KY 63
St. Martin's Circus .... KZ 64
Shadwell St. .... KY 70
Smallbrook
  Queensway .... KZ 71
Snow Hill Queensway .... KY 73
Summer Row .... JY 77
Temple Row .... KZ 80
Waterloo St. .... JZ 84

GREEN TOURIST GUIDES

Picturesque scenery, buildings
Attractive route
Touring programmes
Plans of towns and buildings.

STREET INDEX TO BIRMINGHAM TOWN PLANS

Pleasant hotels and restaurants
are shown in the Guide by a red sign.

Please send us the names
of any where you have enjoyed your stay.

Your **Michelin Guide** will be even better.

at National Exhibition Centre *Southeast : 9 ½ m. on A 45 HX* – ✉ *Birmingham :*

🏨 **Stakis Birmingham Metropole,** Bickenhill, B40 1PP, ✆ (0121) 780 4242, *Fax (0121) 780 3923,* ⮖, ≦s, ⊠ – ⮆, ⥲ rm, 🖩 📺 ☎ ♿ ❷ – 🛏 2000. 🅜 🅐🅔 ⓞ **VISA**
closed 24 to 30 December – **Meals** (carving rest.) 27.25 **st.** – ***Primavera* : Meals** - Italia
- *(closed Sunday and Bank Holidays)* a la carte 30.00/42.00 **st.** – **779 rm**
☕ 187.00/235.00 **t.,** 15 suites – SB.

at Acocks Green *Southwest : 5 m. by A 41* – ✉ *Birmingham*

🏨 **Westley,** Westley Rd, B27 7UJ, ✆ (0121) 706 4312, *Fax (0121) 706 2824* – 📺 ☎ ❷
– 🛏 80. 🅜 🅐🅔 ⓞ **VISA**. ⥲
GX
closed 25 December – **Meals** (bar lunch Monday to Saturday)/dinner 13.95 **t.** and a la carte
🍾 6.50 – ☕ 7.95 – **36 rm** 68.95/94.00 **st.**

at Kings Norton *Southwest : 7 m. on A 441 EX* – ✉ *Birmingham :*

🏨 **Mill House,** 180 Lifford Lane, B30 3NT, ✆ (0121) 459 5800, *Fax (0121) 459 8553,* ⮖
– ⥲ 📺 ☎ ❷. 🅜 🅐🅔 ⓞ **VISA**. ⥲
closed 1 to 16 January – **Meals** (see **Lombard Room** below) – **8 rm** ☕ 98.00/120.00 **st.**
1 suite – SB.

🍴 **Lombard Room,** 180 Lifford Lane, B30 3NT, ✆ (0121) 459 5800, *Fax (0121) 459 8553*
🍽, 🌿 – ⥲ 🖩 ❷. 🅜 🅐🅔 ⓞ **VISA**
closed lunch Monday and Saturday, Sunday dinner and 1 to 16 January – **Meal**
17.85/26.50 **st.** 🍾 7.00.

at Great Barr *Northwest : 6 m. on A 34 FV* – ✉ *Birmingham :*

🏨 **Forte Posthouse Birmingham,** Chapel Lane, B43 7BG, ✆ (0121) 357 7444, *Fax (0121) 357 7503,* ⮖, ≦s, ⊠ – ⥲ rm, 📺 ☎ ❷ – 🛏 120. 🅜 🅐
ⓞ **VISA**
Meals a la carte 12.05/26.90 **st.** 🍾 7.50 – ☕ 9.95 – **192 rm** 85.00 **st.**

at West Bromwich *Northwest : 6 m. on A 41 EV* – ✉ *Birmingham :*

🏨 **Moat House Birmingham,** Birmingham Rd, B70 6RS, ✆ (0121) 609 9988, *Fax (0121) 525 7403,* ⮖ – ⮆, ⥲ rm, 🖩 rest, 📺 ☎ ❷ – 🛏 180. 🅜 🅐🅔 ⓞ
VISA
Meals a la carte 16.15/26.60 **st.** 🍾 5.75 – ☕ 8.95 – **168 rm** 105.00/120.00 **st.** – SB.

BATH *Bath & North East Somerset* 🌐🌐🌐🌐 *M 29* – *pop. 85 202.*
🛈 Abbey Chambers, Abbey Churchyard, BA1 1LY ✆ (01225) 477101.
London 119 – Birmingham 98.

🍴 **Lettonie** (Blunos) with rm, 35 Kelston Rd, BA1 3QH, ✆ (01225) 446676, *Fax (01225) 447541,* ≤, 🌿 – ⥲ 📺 ☎ ❷. 🅜 🅐🅔 ⓞ **VISA**. ⥲
❀❀ *closed Sunday, Monday, 2 weeks January and 2 weeks August-September* – **Meal**
25.00/44.50 **t.** 🍾 9.20 – **5 rm** 95.00/165.00 **st.**
Spec. Breast of quail with foie gras and chicken mousse on onion marmalade. Pan-frie
fillet and honey glazed belly of pork with a sage sauce. Assiette of apple.

CHAGFORD *Devon* 🌐🌐🌐 *I 31* – *pop. 1 417.*
London 218 – Bath 102 – Birmingham 186.

🏨 **Gidleigh Park** ⮥, TQ13 8HH, *Northwest : 2 m. by Gidleigh Rd* ✆ (01647) 432367, *Fax (01647) 432574,* ≤ Teign Valley, woodland and Meldon Hill, « Timbered country house
❀❀ water garden », ⮥, park, 🍴 – ⥲ rest, 📺 ☎ ❷. 🅜 ⓞ **VISA**
Meals (booking essential) 22.00-60.00/60.00-65.00 **st.** 🍾 10.00 – **13 rm** ☕ (dinner inclu
ded) 235.00/440.00 **st.,** 2 suites
Spec. Roast langoustines with leek salad and langoustine butter sauce. Fillet of local bee
with roast shallots and red wine sauce. Poached cherries with cherry and Kirsch ic
cream.

Don't confuse :

Comfort of hotels : 🏨 … 🏠
Comfort of restaurants : 🍴🍴🍴🍴🍴 … 🍴
Quality of the cuisine : ❀❀❀, ❀❀, ❀, 🅐 **Meals**

EDINBURGH *Edinburgh City* **401** *K 16 Scotland G. – pop. 418 914.*

See : *City*★★★ *Edinburgh International Festival*★★★ *(August) – National Gallery of Scotland*★★ *DY* M⁴ *Royal Botanic Garden*★★★ *The Castle*★★ *AC DYZ : Site*★★★ *– Palace Block (Honours of Scotland*★★★*) St. Margaret's Chapel (*✳*★★★) Great Hall (Hammerbeam Roof*★★*) ⇐★★ from Argyle and Mill's Mount DZ – Abbey and Palace of Holyroodhouse*★★ *AC (Plasterwork Ceilings*★★★*, ✳★★ from Arthur's Seat) – Royal Mile*★★ *: St. Giles' Cathedral*★★ *(Crown Spire*★★★*) EYZ Gladstone's Land*★ *AC EYZ A – Canongate Talbooth*★ *EY B – New Town*★★ *(Charlotte Square*★★★ *CY* **14** *Royal Museum of Scotland*★★ *EZ M² – The Georgian House *★ *AC CY D – Scottish National Portrait Gallery*★ *EY M³ – Dundas House*★ *EY E) – Scottish National Gallery of Modern Art*★ *Victoria Street*★ *EZ* **84** *Scott Monument*★ *(⇐★) AC EY F – Craigmillar Castle*★ *AC – Calton Hill (*✳*★★★ AC from Nelson's Monument) EY.*

Envir. : *Edinburgh Zoo*★★ *AC – Hill End Ski Centre (*✳*★★) AC, S : 5 ½ m. by A 702 – The Royal Observatory (West Tower ⇐★) AC – Ingleston, Scottish Agricultural Museum*★*, W : 6 ½ m. by A 8.*

Exc. : *Rosslyn Chapel*★★ *AC (Apprentice Pillar*★★★*) S : 7 ½ m. by A 701 and B 7006 – Forth Bridges*★★*, NW : 9 ½ m. by A 90 – Hopetoun House*★★ *AC, NW : 11 ½ m. by A 90 and A 904 – Dalmeny*★ *(Dalmeny House*★ *AC, St. Cuthbert's Church*★ *- Norman South Doorway*★★*) NW : 7 m. by A 90 – Crichton Castle (Italianate courtyard range*★*) AC, SE : 10 m. by A 7 and B 6372.*

ᵢ₈, ᵢ₈ *Braid Hills, Braid Hills Rd ℘ (0131) 447 6666 –* ᵢ₈ *Craigmillar Park, 1 Observatory Rd ℘ (0131) 667 2837 –* ᵢ₈ *Carrick Knowe, Glendevon Park ℘ (0131) 337 1096 –* ᵢ₈ *Duddingston Road West ℘ (0131) 661 1005 –* ᵢ₈ *Silverknowes, Parkway ℘ (0131) 336 3843 –* ᵢ₈ *Liberton, 297 Gilmerton Rd ℘ (0131) 664 3009* ᵢ₈*,* ᵢ₈ *Dalmahoy Hotel C.C., Kirknewton ℘ (0131) 333 4105/1845 –* ᵢ₉ *Portobello, Stanley St. ℘ (0131) 669 4361.*

✈ *Edinburgh Airport : ℘ (0131) 333 1000, W : 6 m. by A 8 –* **Terminal :** *Waverley Bridge.*

🛈 *Edinburgh & Scotland Information Centre, 3 Princes St., EH2 2QP ℘ (0131) 557 1700 – Edinburgh Airport, Tourist Information Desk ℘ (0131) 333 2167.*

Glasgow 46 – Newcastle upon Tyne 105.

Plan on next page

Balmoral, Princes St., EH2 2EQ, ℘ (0131) 556 2414, Fax (0131) 557 3747, *Ⅰб*, ≘ₛ, 🖾 – 🛗 ⇔ ▤ TV ☎ & ⇔ – 🛆 350. 🆗 🆎 ⓪ *VISA* ⑆   EY n
Meals *(see* **Number One** *and* **Hadrian's** *below) –* ☕ 15.00 – **168 rm** 180.00/215.00 **st.**, 21 suites.

Caledonian, Princes St., EH1 2AB, ℘ (0131) 459 9988, Fax (0131) 225 6632, *Ⅰб*, ≘ₛ, 🖾 – 🛗, ⇔ rm, ▤ rest, TV ☎ ☏ & ⓟ – 🛆 300. 🆗 🆎 ⓪ *VISA*. ⌀   CY n
Carriages : **Meals** *(bar lunch Sunday)* a la carte 28.75/41.00 **st.** ⌀ 6.95 *(see also* **La Pompadour** *below) –* ☕ 15.95 – **233 rm** 147.00/315.00 **t.**, 13 suites.

Sheraton Grand, 1 Festival Sq., EH3 9SR, ℘ (0131) 229 9131, Fax (0131) 229 6254, *Ⅰб*, ≘ₛ, 🖾 – 🛗, ⇔ rm, ▤ TV ☎ ☏ & ⓟ – 🛆 485. 🆗 🆎 ⓪ *VISA* ⑆. ⌀   CDZ v
Terrace : **Meals** 20.50 **t.** and a la carte *(see also* **Grill Room** *below) –* ☕ 15.00 – **244 rm** 190.00/270.00 **t.**, 17 suites – SB.

Marriott Dalmahoy H. & Country Club ⑤, Kirknewton, EH27 8EB, *Southwest : 7 m. on A 71* ℘ (0131) 333 1845, Fax (0131) 333 1433, ⇐, « *Part Georgian mansion* », *Ⅰб*, ≘ₛ, 🖾, ᵢ₈, ⟝, park, ⛷ – 🛗 ⇔, ▤ rest, TV ☎ & ⓟ – 🛆 400. 🆗 🆎 ⓪ *VISA*. ⌀
Pentland : **Meals** *(closed Sunday lunch)* 15.00/25.00 **st.** and dinner a la carte ⌀ 6.00 –
Long Weekend : **Meals** *(grill rest.)* a la carte 10.75/19.25 **st.** ⌀ 6.00 – **150 rm** ☕ 130.00/145.00 **st.**, 1 suite – SB.

George Inter-Continental, 19-21 George St., EH2 2PB, ℘ (0131) 225 1251, Fax (0131) 226 5644 – 🛗 ⇔ rm, TV ☎ – 🛆 200. 🆗 🆎 ⓪ *VISA*. ⌀   DY z
Le Chambertin : **Meals** *(closed Saturday lunch and Sunday)* a la carte 26.00/37.50 **st.** ⌀ 12.50 – **Carvers** *(℘ (0131) 459 2305)* : **Meals** 16.50/19.50 **st.** and a la carte ⌀ 8.50 – ☕ 13.85 – **192 rm** 165.00/215.00 **st.**, 3 suites – SB.

Carlton Highland, North Bridge St., EH1 1SD, ℘ (0131) 472 3000, Fax (0131) 556 2691, *Ⅰб*, ≘ₛ, 🖾, squash – 🛗, ⇔ rm, ▤ rest, TV ☎ & ⓟ – 🛆 350. 🆗 🆎 ⓪ *VISA* ⑆   EY s
Quills : **Meals** *(closed Sunday and Monday)* *(dinner only)* 25.00 **t.** and a la carte ⌀ 8.95 –
Eureka : **Meals** *(carving rest.)* 10.95/18.95 **t.** and a la carte ⌀ 6.50 – ☕ 12.50 – **193 rm** 119.00/184.00 **st.**, 4 suites – SB.

Swallow Royal Scot, 111 Glasgow Rd, EH12 8NF, *West : 4 ½ m. on A 8* ℘ (0131) 334 9191, Fax (0131) 316 4507, *Ⅰб*, ≘ₛ, 🖾 – 🛗, ⇔ rm, ▤ rest, TV ☎ ⓟ – 🛆 300. 🆗 🆎 ⓪ *VISA*
Meals 22.50 **st.** *(dinner)* and a la carte 22.50/33.00 **st.** ⌀ 11.00 – **255 rm** ☕ 110.00/145.00 **st.**, 4 suites – SB.

The Howard, 34 Great King St., EH3 6QH, ℘ (0131) 557 3500, Fax (0131) 557 6515, « *Georgian town houses* » – 🛗 TV ☎ ⓟ – 🛆 40. 🆗 🆎 ⓪ *VISA* ⑆. ⌀   DY s
Meals *(see* **36** *below) –* **15 rm** ☕ 130.00/280.00 **st.** – SB.

EDINBURGH

UNITED KINGDOM

300 m / 300 yards

Map labels (grid): A 1 · A 900 · A 90 · A 8 · A 71

Map labels:
Royal Terrace Gardens · Calton Hill · Regent Road · Holyrood Road · Holyrood Park · London Road · Leith Walk · Broughton Street · York Place · St. James Centre · Waverley Market · Canongate · Cowgate · South Bridge · Jeffrey St. · Nicolson · Pleasance · St. Leonard's · Clerk Street · Buccleuch St. · Potterrow · Central Area Campus · East Meadow Park · Middle Meadow Walk · West Meadow Park · Melville Drive · Princes Street Gardens · CASTLE · St. Giles · Market St. · West Port · Lauriston · George Street · Queen Street · Hanover · Frederick St. · Castle St. · Heriot Row · Dundas Street · Great King Street · Howe St. · King St. Row · Gardens · Drummond Pl. · Royal Circus · St. Stephen St. · Dean · Comely Bank Avenue · Queensferry Road · Water of Leith · Dean Park Cres. · Brae · Orchard · Comely Bank · Ainslie Pl. · Moray Pl. · Queensferry St. · Lothian Rd. · International Conference Centre · Morrison · Grove St. · Haymarket Ter. · Palmerston Pl. · Belford · Dalry Road · Fountainbridge · Union Canal · Gilmore Place · Viewforth · Dundee · Street Place

EDINBURGH

654

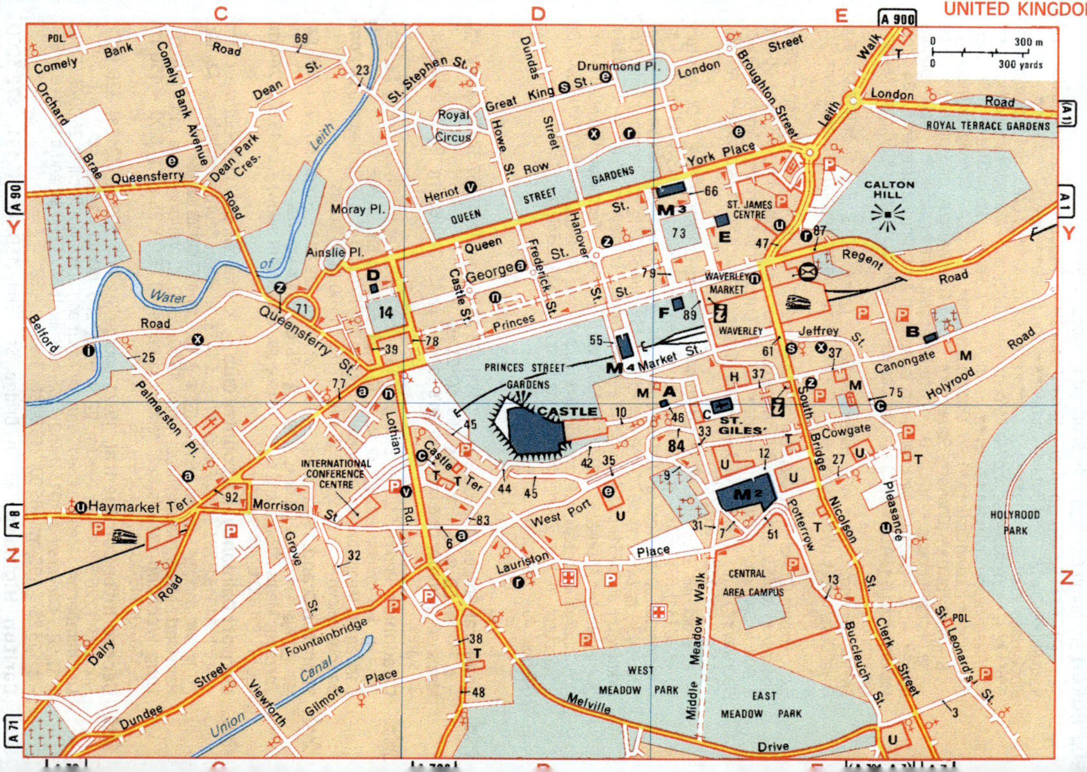

UNITED KINGDOM

The Bonham, 35 Drumsheugh Gdns., EH3 7RN, ℘ (0131) 226 6050, *Fax (0131) 226 6080*, « Contemporary interior design » – ⊞, ⇼ rm, 🖵 ☎ ✆ ⅋ – 🛦 50. 🅜🅒 🅐🅔 ⑩ 𝘝𝘐𝘚𝘈. ⅋   CY **z**
closed 24 to 28 December – **Meals** (light lunch)/dinner a la carte 16.00/22.00 **t.** 🍶 8.00 – ⊂⊃ 4.75 – **46 rm** 120.00/190.00, 2 suites – SB.

Crowne Plaza, 80 High St., EH1 1TH, ℘ (0131) 557 9797, *Fax (0131) 557 9789*, 🛋, ⇌, 🅢 – ⊞, ⇼ rm, 🖵 ☎ ✆ ⅋ 🅟 – 🛦 200. 🅜🅒 🅐🅔 ⑩ 𝘝𝘐𝘚𝘈 🅙🅒🅑. ⅋   EY **z**
Meals (buffet Saturday lunch and Sunday) a la carte 16.45/27.70 **st.** – ⊂⊃ 13.50 – **229 rm** 170.00/195.00 **st.**, 9 suites.

Channings, 12-16 South Learmonth Gdns., EH4 1EZ, ℘ (0131) 315 2226, *Fax (0131) 332 9631*, « Edwardian town houses » – ⊞ ⇼ 🖵 ☎ – 🛦 35. 🅜🅒 🅐🅔 ⑩ 𝘝𝘐𝘚𝘈 🅙🅒🅑. ⅋   CY **e**
Meals (bar lunch Saturday) 14.00/21.00 **t.** and a la carte 🍶 5.50 – **47 rm** ⊂⊃ 105.00/155.00 **st.**, 1 suite – SB.

Malmaison, 1 Tower Pl., Leith, EH6 7DB, *Northeast : 2 m. by A 900* ℘ (0131) 468 5000, *Fax (0131) 468 5002*, « Contemporary interior », 🛋 – ⊞ 🖵 ☎ ⅋ 🅟 – 🛦 55. 🅜🅒 🅐🅔 ⑩ 𝘝𝘐𝘚𝘈. ⅋
Meals - Brasserie - a la carte 20.45/25.25 **t.** 🍶 9.95 – ⊂⊃ 10.50 – **60 rm** 95.00/130.00 **st.**

Thistle King James, 107 Leith St., EH1 3SW, ℘ (0131) 556 0111, *Fax (0131) 557 5333* – ⊞, ⇼ rm, 🖵 ☎ ⅋ 🅟 – 🛦 250. 🅜🅒 🅐🅔 ⑩ 𝘝𝘐𝘚𝘈 🅙🅒🅑. ⅋   EY **u**
Meals (bar lunch Saturday and Sunday) a la carte approx. 10.95 🍶 5.50 – ***Craig's* :** **Meals** 9.75/19.50 **st.** and dinner a la carte 🍶 5.50 – ⊂⊃ 11.50 – **138 rm** 120.00/170.00 **st.**, 5 suites – SB.

Prestonfield House 🦢, Priestfield Rd, EH16 5UT, ℘ (0131) 668 3346, *Fax (0131) 668 3976*, ≼, « Part 17C country house », 🏌, 🐎, *park* – ⊞, ⇼ rm, 🖵 ☎ ✆ 🅟 – 🛦 650. 🅜🅒 🅐🅔 ⑩ 𝘝𝘐𝘚𝘈 🅙🅒🅑
Meals 20.00/27.00 **t.** and a la carte 🍶 7.00 – **31 rm** ⊂⊃ 185.00/375.00 **t.**

Royal Terrace, 18 Royal Terr., EH7 5AQ, ℘ (0131) 557 3222, *Fax (0131) 557 5334*, « Georgian town houses », 🛋, ⇌, 🅢, 🌿 – ⊞ ⇼ 🖵 ☎ – 🛦 80. 🅜🅒 🅐🅔 ⑩ 𝘝𝘐𝘚𝘈. ⅋
Meals (light lunch)/dinner 19.50 **st.** – ⊂⊃ 12.50 – **104 rm** 125.00/185.00 **st.**, 3 suites.   EY **i**

Forte Posthouse Edinburgh, Corstorphine Rd, EH12 6UA, *West : 3 m. on A 8* ℘ (0131) 334 0390, *Fax (0131) 334 9237* – ⊞ ⇼, 🍽 rest, 🖵 ☎ ✆ 🅟 – 🛦 120. 🅜🅒 🅐🅔 ⑩ 𝘝𝘐𝘚𝘈 🅙🅒🅑. ⅋
Meals a la carte 20.00/30.00 **t.** – ⊂⊃ 10.95 – **295 rm** 99.00 **st.** – SB.

Point, 34 Bread St., EH3 9AF, ℘ (0131) 221 9919, *Fax (0131) 221 9929* – ⊞, ⇼ rm, 🖵 ☎. 🅜🅒 🅐🅔 ⑩ 𝘝𝘐𝘚𝘈   DZ **a**
closed 25 and 26 December – **Meals** (closed Sunday) 7.90/10.90 **st.** – ⊂⊃ 8.00 – **94 rm** 80.00/130.00 **st.**, 1 suite – SB.

Edinburgh Residence without rest., 7 Rothesay Terr., EH3 7RY, ℘ (0131) 226 3380, *Fax (0131) 226 3381*, ≼, « Georgian town houses » – 🖵 ☎ ⅋ 🅟. 🅜🅒 🅐🅔 ⑩ 𝘝𝘐𝘚𝘈. ⅋
21 rm ⊂⊃ 175.00/275.00 **st.**, 8 suites.   CY **x**

Stakis Edinburgh Grosvenor, Grosvenor St., EH12 5EF, ℘ (0131) 226 6001, *Fax (0131) 220 2387* – ⊞ 🖵 ☎ – 🛦 500. 🅜🅒 🅐🅔 ⑩ 𝘝𝘐𝘚𝘈 🅙🅒🅑. ⅋   CZ **a**
Meals (bar lunch Sunday) 13.75 **t.** and dinner a la carte – ⊂⊃ 9.50 – **187 rm** 130.00/170.00 **st.**, 2 suites – SB.

Hilton National, 69 Belford Rd, EH4 3DG, ℘ (0131) 332 2545, *Fax (0131) 332 3805* – ⊞, ⇼ rm, 🖵 ☎ ⅋ 🅟 – 🛦 130. 🅜🅒 🅐🅔 ⑩ 𝘝𝘐𝘚𝘈   CY **i**
Meals (bar lunch)/dinner 18.50 **st.** and a la carte 🍶 6.50 – ⊂⊃ 12.00 – **144 rm** 125.00/190.00 **st.**

Edinburgh Capital Moat House, Clermiston Rd, EH12 6UG, ℘ (0131) 535 9988, *Fax (0131) 334 9712*, 🛋, ⇌, 🅢 – ⊞ ⇼ 🖵 ☎ ⅋ 🅟 – 🛦 300. 🅜🅒 🅐🅔 ⑩ 𝘝𝘐𝘚𝘈
Meals (bar lunch)/dinner 12.95 **t.** and a la carte 🍶 5.75 – ⊂⊃ 10.50 – **111 rm** 95.00/125.00 **t.** – SB.   by A 8 CZ

Jarvis Ellersly House, 4 Ellersly Rd, EH12 6HZ, ℘ (0131) 337 6888, *Fax (0131) 313 2543*, 🌿 – ⊞ ⇼ 🖵 ☎ 🅟 – 🛦 70. 🅜🅒 🅐🅔 ⑩ 𝘝𝘐𝘚𝘈   by A 8 CZ
Meals (closed Saturday lunch) 10.95/14.95 **t.** and a la carte 🍶 7.00 – ⊂⊃ 8.50 – **57 rm** 115.00/135.00 **t.** – SB.

Simpsons without rest., 79 Lauriston Pl., EH3 9HZ, ℘ (0131) 622 7979, *Fax (0131) 622 7900* – ⊞ ⇼ 🖵 ☎ ⅋. 🅜🅒 🅐🅔 𝘝𝘐𝘚𝘈 🅙🅒🅑. ⅋   DZ **r**
57 rm 80.00/100.00 **st.**, 1 suite.

Holiday Inn Garden Court, 107 Queensferry Rd, EH4 3HL, ℘ (0131) 332 2442, *Fax (0131) 332 3408*, ≼, 🛋 – ⊞ ⇼, 🍽 rest, 🖵 ☎ ⅋ 🅟 – 🛦 60. 🅜🅒 🅐🅔 ⑩ 𝘝𝘐𝘚𝘈 🅙🅒🅑
Meals (carving lunch)/dinner 15.50 **st.** and a la carte – ⊂⊃ 10.50 – **118 rm** 95.00/126.00 **st.**, 1 suite.   by A 90 CY

Apex International, 31-35 Grassmarket, EH1 2HS, ℰ (0131) 300 3456
Fax (0131) 220 5345 – |‡|, ↬ rm, ▤ rest, TV ☎ ℰ P – 🏊 225. MC AE ① VISA. ❄   DZ
Meals (bar lunch)/dinner 11.00 **st.** – ☕ 6.95 – **175 rm** 89.95 **st.**

Frederick House without rest., 42 Frederick St., EH2 1EX, ℰ (0131) 226 1999
Fax (0131) 624 7064 – |‡| TV ☎ ℰ. MC AE ① VISA JCB. ❄   DY
45 rm ☕ 40.00/130.00 **st.**

Apex European, 90 Haymarket Terr., EH12 5LQ, ℰ (0131) 474 3456
Fax (0131) 474 3400 – |‡|, ↬ rm, TV ☎ ℰ & – 🏊 70. MC AE ① VISA. ❄   CZ
Meals 9.90/11.00 **st.** and lunch a la carte – ☕ 7.95 – **66 rm** 79.95 **st.**

Parliament House without rest., 15 Calton Hill, EH1 3BJ, ℰ (0131) 478 4000
Fax (0131) 478 4001 – |‡| TV ☎ ℰ. MC AE ① VISA. ❄   EY
☕ 11.50 – **53 rm** 95.00/160.00 **st.**

Maitland without rest., 23-33 Shandwick Pl., EH2 4RG, ℰ (0131) 229 1467
Fax (0131) 229 7549 – |‡| ↬ TV ☎. MC AE ① VISA JCB. ❄   CY
65 rm ☕ 75.00/135.00 **st.**

Jurys Edinburgh Inn, 43 Jeffrey St., EH1 1DG, ℰ (0131) 200 3300
Fax (0131) 200 0400 – |‡|, ↬ rm, TV ☎ ℰ & – 🏊 50. MC AE ① VISA. ❄   EY
closed 4 days Christmas – **Meals** (bar lunch)/dinner 15.00 and a la carte 🍷 4.75 – ☕ 7.00
– **186 rm** 80.00/90.00 **t.**

Sibbet House without rest., 26 Northumberland St., EH3 6LS, ℰ (0131) 556 1078
Fax (0131) 557 9445, « Georgian town house » – ↬ TV ☎ ℰ. MC VISA. ❄   DY
4 rm ☕ 65.00/100.00, 1 suite.

27 Heriot Row without rest., 27 Heriot Row, EH3 6EN, ℰ (0131) 225 9474
Fax (0131) 220 1699, « Georgian town house », 🚗 – ↬ TV ☎ ℰ. MC VISA. ❄   DY
3 rm ☕ 50.00/100.00 **st.**

Drummond House without rest., 17 Drummond Pl., EH3 6PL, ℰ (0131) 557 9189
Fax (0131) 557 9189, « Georgian town house » – ↬. MC VISA. ❄   DY
closed Christmas and restricted opening in winter – **4 rm** ☕ 75.00/110.00 **t.**

17 Abercromby Place without rest., 17 Abercromby Pl., EH3 6LB, ℰ (0131) 557 8036
Fax (0131) 558 3453, « Georgian town house » – ↬ TV ☎ P. MC VISA. ❄   DY
7 rm ☕ 60.00/100.00 **t.**

Number One (at Balmoral H.), 1 Princes St., EH2 2EQ, ℰ (0131) 556 6727
Fax (0131) 557 3747 – ▤. MC AE ① VISA JCB   EY
closed lunch Saturday and Sunday – **Meals** 18.00/32.00 **t.** and a la carte 🍷 11.00.

La Pompadour (at Caledonian H.), Princes St., EH1 2AB, ℰ (0131) 459 9988
Fax (0131) 225 6632 – P. MC AE ① VISA   CY
closed Sunday and Monday – **Meals** (dinner only) a la carte 29.50/43.50 **t.** 🍷 9.25.

Grill Room (at Sheraton Grand H.), 1 Festival Sq., EH3 9SR, ℰ (0131) 221 6423
Fax (0131) 229 6254 – ▤ P. MC AE ① VISA JCB   CDZ
closed Saturday lunch and Sunday – **Meals** 27.50/35.50 **st.** and a la carte 🍷 10.00.

Bonars, 56 St. Mary's St., EH1 1SX, ℰ (0131) 556 5888, Fax (0131) 556 2588 – ↬ ▤
MC AE ① VISA   EYZ
Meals 14.95/24.95 **t.** and a la carte 🍷 5.80.

Martins, 70 Rose St., North Lane, EH2 3DX, ℰ (0131) 225 3106 – ↬. MC AE ① VISA
JCB   DY
closed Saturday lunch, Sunday, Monday, 1 week in spring, 1 week in autumn, and 24 December-20 January – **Meals** (booking essential) a la carte 18.55/33.00 **t.** 🍷 6.00.

Hadrian's (at Balmoral H.), 2 North Bridge, EH1 1TR, ℰ (0131) 557 5000
Fax (0131) 557 3747 – ▤. MC AE ① VISA JCB   EY
Meals a la carte 14.50/18.50 **t.**

36 (at The Howard H.), 36 Great King St., EH3 6QH, ℰ (0131) 556 3636, Fax (0131) 556 3663
« Contemporary decor » – ↬ ▤ P. MC AE ① VISA JCB   DY
closed Saturday lunch – **Meals** 14.00 **t.** (lunch) and dinner a la carte 20.50/27.50 **t.** 🍷 6.00.

(fitz)Henry, 19 Shore Pl., Leith, EH6 6SW, ℰ (0131) 555 6625, Fax (0131) 554 6216
« Part 17C warehouse » – MC AE VISA   by A 900 EY
closed Sunday, 25, 26 and 31 December and 1 January – **Meals** 15.00/22.00-27.00 **t.**
🍷 8.50.

Haldanes (at Albany H.), 39A Albany St., EH1 3QY, ℰ (0131) 556 8407, 🌳 – ↬. MC
AE ① VISA JCB   EY
closed Saturday and Sunday lunch – **Meals** 12.50/25.25 **t.** 🍷 7.00.

The Rock, 78 Commercial St., Leith, EH6 6LX, ℰ (0131) 555 2225, Fax (0131) 555 1116
– P. MC AE VISA   by A 900 EY
closed 25 December and 1-2 January – **Meals** 12.75 **t.** (lunch) and dinner a la carte
17.50/28.50 **t.** 🍷 4.90.

XX **Vintners Room,** The Vaults, 87 Giles St., Leith, EH6 6BZ, ℰ (0131) 554 6767, Fax (0131) 467 7130 – 🍴. ⓂⓒⒶⒺ 𝖵𝖨𝖲𝖠   by A 900   EY
closed Sunday and 2 weeks Christmas-New Year – **Meals** 14.50 t. (lunch) and dinner a la carte 23.25/30.75 t. 🍾 5.00.

XX **The Marque,** 19-21 Causewayside, EH9 1QF, ℰ (0131) 466 6660, Fax (0131) 466 6661 – Ⓜⓒ 𝖵𝖨𝖲𝖠   by A 701   EZ
closed Monday, 25-26 December and 1 to 7 January – **Meals** 14.50 t. (lunch) and dinner a la carte 19.25/25.75 t. 🍾 6.00.

XX **Kelly's,** 46 West Richmond St., EH8 9DZ, ℰ (0131) 668 3847, Fax (0131) 668 3847 – 🍴. Ⓜⓒ 𝖵𝖨𝖲𝖠   EZ u
closed Sunday to Tuesday, 25-26 December and 1 January – **Meals** 15.00/25.00 t. 🍾 7.50.

XX **Yumi,** 2 West Coates, EH12 5JQ, ℰ (0131) 337 2173, Fax (0131) 337 2818 – 🍴 Ⓟ. Ⓜⓒ Ⓓ 𝖵𝖨𝖲𝖠 𝖩𝖢𝖡
closed Sunday and Christmas-New Year – **Meals** - Japanese - (dinner only) 23.00 t. and a la carte 🍾 5.00.

X **Atrium,** 10 Cambridge St., EH1 2ED, ℰ (0131) 228 8882, Fax (0131) 228 8808 – ▤. Ⓜⓒ ⒶⒺ Ⓓ 𝖵𝖨𝖲𝖠   DZ c
closed Sunday and 1 week Christmas – Meals a la carte 16.50/30.00 t. 🍾 10.50.

at Bonnyrigg (Midlothian) Southeast : 8 m. by A 7 on A 6094 EZ – ✉ Edinburgh :

🏰 **Dalhousie Castle** ⤴, EH19 3JB, Southeast : 1 ¼ m. on B 704 ℰ (01875) 820153, Fax (01875) 821936, ⩽, « Part 13C and 15C castle with Victorian additions », 🚗 – 🍴 ⓉⓋ ☎ Ⓟ – 🎖 120. Ⓜⓒ ⒶⒺ Ⓓ 𝖵𝖨𝖲𝖠 𝖩𝖢𝖡. 🦌
closed mid-late January – **Dungeon** : Meals (booking essential to non-residents) 25.50 st. (dinner) and a la carte 15.00/21.50 🍾 7.50 – **34 rm** � 125.00/200.00 st., 1 suite – SB.

at Edinburgh International Airport West : 7 ½ m. by A 8 CZ – ✉ Edinburgh :

🏰 **Stakis Edinburgh Airport,** EH28 8LL, ℰ (0131) 519 4400, Fax (0131) 519 4422 – 🛗, 🍴 rm, ▤ rest, ⓉⓋ ☎ ⅙ Ⓟ – 🎖 220. Ⓜⓒ ⒶⒺ Ⓓ 𝖵𝖨𝖲𝖠
Meals (grill rest.) 5.95/14.00 st. and a la carte – ☕ 9.75 – **134 rm** 130.00/170.00 st. – SB.

at Ingliston West : 7 ¾ m. on A 8 CZ – ✉ Edinburgh :

🏰 **Norton House** ⤴, EH28 8LX, on A 8 ℰ (0131) 333 1275, Fax (0131) 333 5305, ⩽, 🚗 – 🍴 rm ⓉⓋ ☎ Ⓟ – 🎖 300. Ⓜⓒ ⒶⒺ Ⓓ 𝖵𝖨𝖲𝖠. 🦌
Meals (closed Saturday lunch) 26.00 t. (dinner) and a la carte approx. 28.00 t. 🍾 7.50 – **46 rm** � 120.00/165.00 t., 1 suite – SB.

GLASGOW Glasgow City 𝟦𝟢𝟣 𝟦𝟢𝟤 H 16 Scotland G. – pop. 662 853.

See : City★★★ – Cathedral★★★ (⩽★) DZ – The Burrell Collection★★★ – Hunterian Art Gallery★★ (Whistler Collection★★★ – Mackintosh Wing★★★ AC) CY **M4** – Museum of Transport★★ (Scottish Built Cars★★★, The Clyde Room of Ship Models★★★) – Art Gallery and Museum Kelvingrove★★ CY – Pollok House★ (The Paintings★★) – Tolbooth Steeple★ DZ **A** – Hunterian Museum (Coin and Medal Collection★) CY **M1** – City Chambers★ DZ **C** – Glasgow School of Art★ AC CY **B** – Necropolis (⩽★ of Cathedral) DYZ.

Envir. : Paisley Museum and Art Gallery (paisley Shawl Section★), W : 4 m. by M 8.

Exc. : The Trossachs★★★, N : 31 m. by A 879, A 81 and A 821 – Loch Lomond★★, NW : 19 m. by A 82.

🏌18 Littlehill, Auchinairn Rd ℰ (0141) 772 1916 – 🏌18 Deaconsbank, Rouken Glen Park, Stewarton Rd, Eastwood ℰ (0141) 638 7044 – 🏌 Linn Park, Simshill Rd ℰ (0141) 637 5871 – 🏌18 Lethamhill, Cumbernauld Rd ℰ (0141) 770 6220 – 🏌9 Alexandra Park, Dennistown ℰ (0141) 556 3991 – 🏌9 King's Park, 150a Croftpark Av., Croftfoot ℰ (0141) 556 1294 – 🏌9 Knightswood, Lincoln Av. ℰ (0141) 959 6358 🏌9 Ruchill, Brassey St. ℰ (0141) 946 7676.

Access to Oban by helicopter.

Erskine Bridge (toll).

🛫 Glasgow Airport : ℰ (0141) 887 1111, W : 8 m. by M 8 – **Terminal** : Coach service from Glasgow Central and Queen Street main line Railway Stations and from Anderston Cross and Buchanan Bus Stations 🛫 Prestwick International Airport : ℰ (01292) 479822 **Terminal** : Buchanan Bus Station.

🛈 35 St. Vincent Place ℰ (0141) 204 4400 – Glasgow Airport, Tourist Information Desk, Paisley ℰ (0141) 848 4440.

Edinburgh 46 – Manchester 221.

BOTANIC GARDENS
116
A 81
A 82
300 m
300 yards
Wilton
Street
128
Raeberry
Street
Maryhill
Garscube
Trossachs St.
Hopehill
Road
Road
Ellesmere
North
Woodside
Road
Great
Napiershall Street
Western
Road
Road
B 808
HILLHEAD
Great
Western
Road
Belmont
St.
Bank
Street
KELVINBRIDGE
Rd
West
George's
Road
GLASGOW
M 2
Gibson
105
Park
Prince's
ST. GEORGE'S
CROSS
UNIVERSITY
M 4
50
140
Street
Way
Woodlands
Saint
Kelvin
Park
Quadrant
Road
U
35
KELVINGROVE
MUSEUM AND
ART GALLERY
KELVINGROVE
PARK
108
17
M
107
34
143
e
47
Royal
Terrace
Woodside Place
141
18
Sauchiehall
Scott
Street
Argyle
Sauchiehall
42
Street
B
Street
95
Street
Berkeley
Street
Bath
St.
St.
West
St.
Kelvinhaugh
Street
Street
Kent
Road
Newton
C
West
Eldersile St.
North
a
T
Elmbank
POL.
Street
A 814
Saint
Vincent
e
Douglas
Street
West
Str
Stobcross
Road
Street
S
SCOTTISH
Street
Pitt
Z
Waterloo
EXHIBITION
Clydeside
Expressway
North
Campbel
r
CENTRE
Finnieston
A 814
Lancefield
Street
Hydepark Street
a
Argyle
Street
A 814
West
St.
Lancefield
Lancefield
Quay
M 8
V
120
CLYDE
Anderston
Quay
Broomielaw
85
Govan
Road
Road
St.
35
Govan
Paisley
A 8
Road
Kingston
22
93
West
Admiral St.
Seaward
St.
h
20
Morrison
Street
A 8
Nelson Street
A 8
KINNING
PARK
39
Milnpark
Street
100
West
M 8
(M 8)

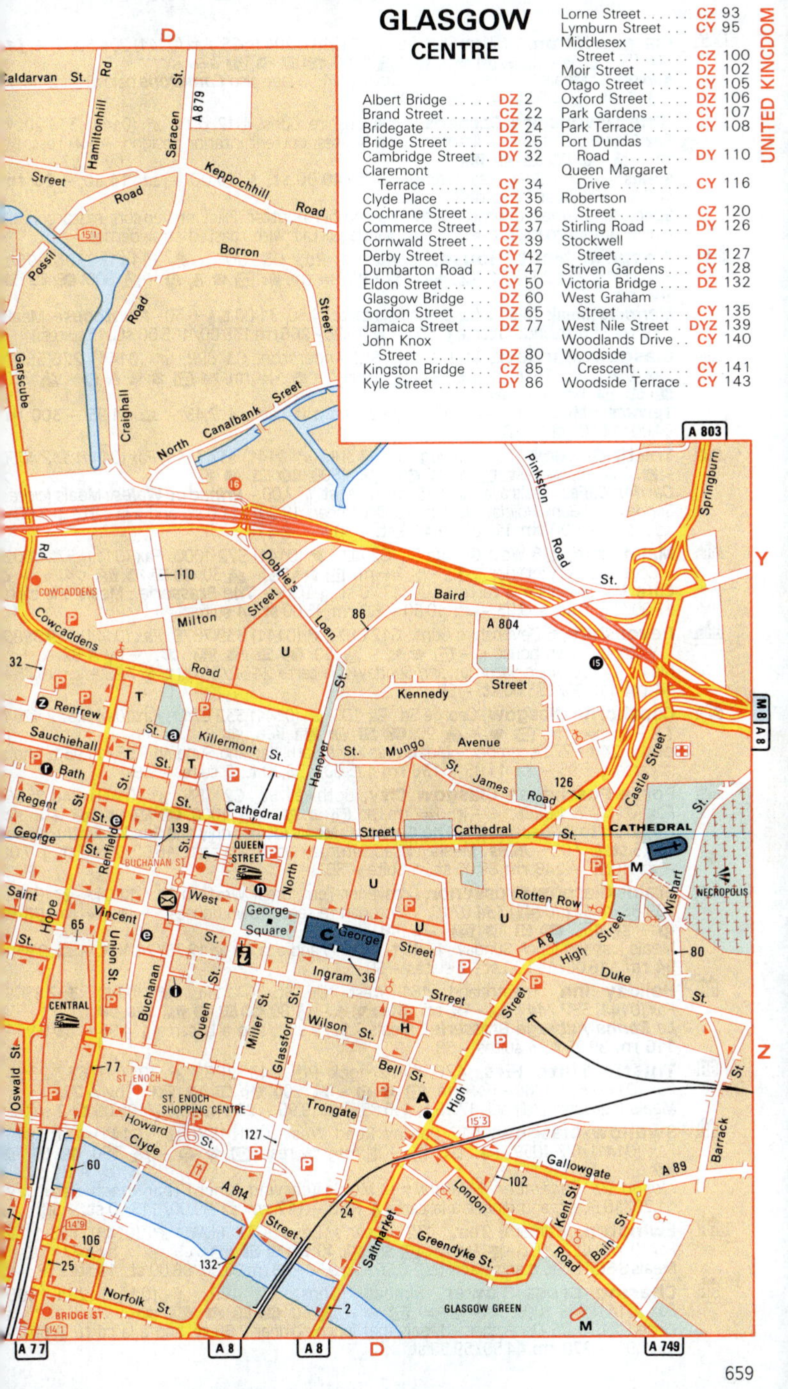

GLASGOW
CENTRE

Albert Bridge ..... DZ 2
Brand Street ...... CZ 22
Bridgegate .... DZ 24
Bridge Street ..... DZ 25
Cambridge Street.. DY 32
Claremont
  Terrace .... CY 34
Clyde Place ...... CZ 35
Cochrane Street ... DZ 36
Commerce Street.. DZ 37
Cornwald Street ... CZ 39
Derby Street ..... CY 42
Dumbarton Road .. CY 47
Eldon Street ...... CY 50
Glasgow Bridge ... DZ 60
Gordon Street .... DZ 65
Jamaica Street .... DZ 77
John Knox
  Street .... DZ 80
Kingston Bridge ... CZ 85
Kyle Street .... DY 86

Lorne Street...... CZ 93
Lymburn Street ... CY 95
Middlesex
  Street .... CZ 100
Moir Street ...... DZ 102
Otago Street ..... CY 105
Oxford Street .... DZ 106
Park Gardens .... CY 107
Park Terrace ..... CY 108
Port Dundas
  Road .... DY 110
Queen Margaret
  Drive .... CY 116
Robertson
  Street .... CZ 120
Stirling Road ..... DY 126
Stockwell
  Street .... DZ 127
Striven Gardens ... CY 128
Victoria Bridge ... DZ 132
West Graham
  Street .... CY 135
West Nile Street . DYZ 139
Woodlands Drive .. CY 140
Woodside
  Crescent ...... CY 141
Woodside Terrace . CY 143

UNITED KINGDOM

Caldarvan St.
Hamiltonhill Rd
Saracen St.
A 879
Keppochhill Road
Street
Borron
Road
Possil
Craighall Road
Garscube
North Canalbank Street
A 803
Pinkston Road
Springburn
Y
COWCADDENS
Cowcaddens
P
110
Milton Street
Dobbie's Loan
86
Baird
A 804
Street
St.
15
M 8 A 8
32
Renfrew
Sauchiehall
Bath
Regent
George
Saint
Hope
65
St.
Killermont St.
Cathedral
U
Kennedy Street
St. Mungo Avenue
St. James Road
126
Cathedral Street
Cathedral St.
CATHEDRAL
NECROPOLIS
Wishart St.
M
QUEEN STREET
BUCHANAN ST.
Renfield
North St.
West
George Square
Vincent
C George Street
Ingram 36
U
U
Rotten Row
High Street
Castle Street
A 8
Duke Street
80
CENTRAL
Buchanan
Queen St.
Miller St.
Glassford St.
Wilson St.
H
Bell St.
A
High Street
77
ST. ENOCH
ST. ENOCH SHOPPING CENTRE
Howard St.
Clyde St.
127
Trongate
Gallowgate
A 89
Barrack St.
Oswald St.
60
A 814
Street
24
Saltmarket
Greendyke St.
London Road
102
Kent St.
Bain St.
Norfolk St.
106
25
132
BRIDGE ST.
2
GLASGOW GREEN
M
A 77
A 8
A 8
D
A 749
14'1
14'9
15'1
15'3
16

Glasgow Hilton, 1 William St., G3 8HT, ✆ (0141) 204 5555, *Fax (0141) 204 5004*, ≼, Ⅰ₄, ⊆s, ℤ – |₺|, ⇔ rm, 🖩 TV ☎ Ġ ℗ – 🛦 1000. MO AE ① VISA JCB. ℘ CZ s
Minsky's : Meals 21.50 **st.** and a la carte 🍾 11.50 (see also *Camerons* below) – ⌹ 14.50
– **315 rm** 181.00 **st.**, 4 suites – SB.

One Devonshire Gardens, 1 Devonshire Gdns., G12 OUX, ✆ (0141) 339 2001,
Fax (0141) 337 1663, « Victorian town houses, opulent interior design » – ⇔ rest, TV
☎ – 🛦 50. MO AE ① VISA   by A 82 CY e
Meals *(closed Saturday lunch)* 25.00/40.00 **st.** 🍾 15.00 – ⌹ 14.50 – **25 rm**
140.00/190.00 **st.**, 2 suites
Spec. Home smoked lobster with lime and herb butter. Fillet of venison, macaroni and
truffle gratin, roasted celeriac. Iced vanilla parfait with roasted strawberries.

Glasgow Moat House, Congress Rd, G3 8QT, ✆ (0141) 306 9988,
Fax (0141) 221 2022, ≼, Ⅰ₄, ⊆s, ℤ – |₺|, ⇔ rm, 🖩 TV ☎ Ġ ℗ – 🛦 800. MO AE ①
VISA. ℘   CZ c
Mariners :Meals 16.50 **t.** (lunch) and a la carte 24.50/31.00 **t.** 🍾 6.50 – *Pointhouse* : Meals
18.95/22.95 **st.** and a la carte 🍾 5.75 – ⌹ 10.95 – **268 rm** 135.00/165.00 **st.**, 15 suites.

Glasgow Marriott, 500 Argyle St., Anderston, G3 8RR, ✆ (0141) 226 5577,
Fax (0141) 221 7676, ≼, Ⅰ₄, ⊆s, ℤ, *squash* – |₺|, ⇔ rm, 🖩 TV ☎ ℘ Ġ ℗ – 🛦 720.
MO AE ① VISA JCB. ℘   CZ a
Terrace : **Meals** *(dinner only)* 18.95 **t.** and a la carte 🍾 7.45 – ⌹ 11.95 – **300 rm**
94.00/145.00 **st.** – SB.

Thistle Glasgow, 36 Cambridge St., G2 3HN, ✆ (0141) 332 3311, *Fax (0141) 332 4050*
– |₺|, ⇔ rm, 🖩 rest, TV ☎ ℘ ℗ – 🛦 1500. MO AE ① VISA   DY z
Garden Cafe : Meals a la carte 13.00/23.00 **st.** 🍾 7.00 – *Prince of Wales* : Meals *(closed
Sunday and Bank Holidays except 25 December)* 18.00/22.00 **st.** and a la carte 🍾 7.00 –
⌹ 13.95 – **300 rm** 117.00/164.00 **st.** – SB.

Malmaison, 278 West George St., G2 4LL, ✆ (0141) 572 1000, *Fax (0141) 572 1002*,
« Contemporary interior », Ⅰ₄ – |₺|, ⇔ rm, TV ☎ ℘ Ġ – 🛦 30. MO AE ① VISA. ℘ CY c
Cafe Mal : Meals a la carte 10.00/17.70 **st.** 🍾 9.95 – *The Brasserie* : Meals a la carte
17.00/21.50 **st.** 🍾 9.95 – ⌹ 10.50 – **68 rm** 95.00 **st.**, 4 suites.

Devonshire, 5 Devonshire Gdns., G12 OUX, ✆ (0141) 339 7878, *Fax (0141) 339 3980*,
« Victorian town house » – TV ☎ ℘ – 🛦 50. MO AE ① VISA. ℘   by A 82 CY e
Meals *(closed lunch Saturday and Sunday)* a la carte 24.50/35.00 **t.** 🍾 7.25 – ⌹ 10.75 –
14 rm 115.00/185.00 **st.** – SB.

Copthorne Glasgow, George Sq., G2 1DS, ✆ (0141) 332 6711, *Fax (0141) 332 4264*,
Ⅰ₄ – |₺|, ⇔ rm, TV ☎ – 🛦 90. MO AE ① VISA JCB. ℘   DZ r
closed 24 to 27 December – **Meals** (bar lunch Saturday and Sunday) 9.95/11.95 **t.** and a
la carte 🍾 5.95 – ⌹ 11.95 – **136 rm** 125.00/135.00 **t.**, 5 suites – SB.

Forte Posthouse Glasgow City, Bothwell St., G2 7EN, ✆ (0141) 248 2656,
Fax (0141) 221 8986, ≼ – |₺|, ⇔ rm, 🖩 TV ☎ ℗ – 🛦 1000. MO AE ① VISA JCB. ℘
closed 24 to 27 December – *The Carvery* : Meals *(dinner only and Sunday lunch)*/dinner
15.75 **st.** 🍾 7.00 – *Jules* : Meals *(closed Saturday lunch)* a la carte 18.00/28.00 **st.** 🍾 7.00
– ⌹ 10.95 – **246 rm** 89.00 **st.**, 1 suite – SB.   CZ z

Stakis Glasgow Grosvenor, Grosvenor Terr., Great Western Rd, G12 OTA, ✆ (0141)
339 8811, *Fax (0141) 334 0710*, « Victorian terraced town houses » – |₺|, ⇔ rm, TV ☎
℗ – 🛦 450. MO AE ① VISA JCB. ℘   CY s
Meals (carving lunch Sunday) 15.00 **t.** (dinner) and a la carte 12.75/24.40 **t.** – ⌹ 9.95 –
94 rm 116.00/151.00 **st.**, 2 suites – SB.

Holiday Inn, Theatreland, 161 West Nile St., G1 2RL, ✆ (0141) 352 8305,
Fax (0141) 332 7447, Ⅰ₄ – ⇔ rm, TV ☎ ℘ Ġ – 🛦 80. MO AE ① VISA JCB. ℘   DY u
La Bonne Auberge Brasserie : Meals 7.95/9.95 **t.** and a la carte 🍾 4.95 – ⌹ 9.95 –
110 rm 89.95 **t.**, 3 suites – SB.

Thistle Tinto Firs, 470 Kilmarnock Rd, G43 2BB, ✆ (0141) 637 2353,
Fax (0141) 633 1340 – ⇔ rm, TV ☎ ℗ – 🛦 200. MO AE ① VISA   by A 77 DZ e
Meals (bar lunch)/dinner 17.95 **t.** 🍾 5.85 – ⌹ 9.95 – **25 rm** 85.00/105.00 **t.**, 2 suites.

Swallow Glasgow, 517 Paisley Road West, G51 1RW, ✆ (0141) 427 3146,
Fax (0141) 427 4059, Ⅰ₄, ⊆s, ℤ – |₺| ⇔, 🖩 rest, TV ☎ ℗ – 🛦 350. MO AE ①
VISA   by A 8 CZ x
closed 23 December-1 January – **Meals** (carving lunch) (bar lunch Saturday)
11.20/18.50 **st.** and dinner a la carte 🍾 8.00 – **117 rm** ⌹ 99.00/115.00 **st.** – SB.

Ewington, Balmoral Terr., 132 Queen's Drive, G42 8QW, ✆ (0141) 423 1152,
Fax (0141) 422 2030 – |₺|, ⇔ rm, TV ☎ – 🛦 40. MO AE ① VISA JCB   by A 77 DZ a
Meals 8.50/17.95 **t.** and a la carte 🍾 6.50 – ⌹ 9.50 – **43 rm** 80.00/98.00 **st.**, 1 suite – SB.

Charing Cross Tower, Elmbank Gdns., G2 4PP, ✆ (0141) 221 1000,
Fax (0141) 248 1000, ≼ – |₺| ⇔ TV ☎ – 🛦 60. MO AE ① VISA. ℘   CY a
closed 24 to 26 December – **Meals** (bar lunch)/dinner 7.50 **st.** and a la carte 🍾 6.00 –
⌹ 6.95 – **278 rm** 44.50/59.50 **st.**

XXXX **Camerons** (at Glasgow Hilton H.), 1 William St., G3 8HT, ✆ (0141) 204 5511, Fax (0141) 204 5004 – 🖵 🅿. 🝳 🄰🄴 🅾 *VISA* 🄹🄲🄱   CZ s
Meals *(closed Saturday lunch and Sunday)* 24.50 **t.** (lunch) and a la carte 33.50/44.00 **t.** 🍷 11.50.

XXX **Buttery**, 652 Argyle St., G3 8UF, ✆ (0141) 221 8188, Fax (0141) 204 4639 – 🅿. 🝳 🄰🄴 🅾 *VISA* 🄹🄲🄱   CZ e
closed Saturday lunch, Sunday, 25-26 December, 1-2 January and Easter Monday – **Meals** 16.85 **t.** (lunch) and dinner a la carte 28.00/35.75 **t.** 🍷 9.80.

XXX **Yes,** 22 West Nile St., G1 2PW, ✆ (0141) 221 8044, Fax (0141) 248 9159 – 🖵. 🝳 🄰🄴 🅾 *VISA*   DZ e
closed Sunday and Bank Holidays – **Meals** 15.95/22.95 **st.**

XXX **Rogano**, 11 Exchange Pl., G1 3AN, ✆ (0141) 248 4055, Fax (0141) 248 2608, « Art Deco » – 🖵. 🝳 🄰🄴 🅾 *VISA* 🄹🄲🄱   DZ i
closed 25 December and 1 January – **Meals** - Seafood - 16.50 **t.** (lunch) and a la carte 27.15/39.15 **t.** 🍷 7.00.

XX **Nairns** with rm, 13 Woodside Cres., G3 7UP, ✆ (0141) 353 0707, Fax (0141) 331 1684 – 📺 ☎. 🝳 🄰🄴 🅾 *VISA*. 🛇   CY e
closed 25-26 December and 1-2 January – **Meals** *(closed Monday)* 17.00/23.50 **t.** 🍷 9.50 – 🍵 7.50 – **4 rm** 90.00/125.00 **t.**

XX **Puppet Theatre,** 11 Ruthven Lane, G12 9BG, *off Byres Rd* ✆ (0141) 339 8444, Fax (0141) 339 7666 – 🝳 🄰🄴 🅾 *VISA* 🄹🄲🄱   on B 808 CY
closed Saturday lunch, Monday, 26 December and 1-2 January – **Meals** 14.50/27.95 **t.** 🍷 9.95.

XX **Papingo,** 104 Bath St., G2 2EN, ✆ (0141) 332 6678, Fax (0141) 332 6549 – 🝳 🄰🄴 🅾 *VISA*   DY r
closed lunch Sunday and Bank Holidays and 1 January – **Meals** 12.90/19.95 **t.** 🍷 6.95.

XX **Ho Wong,** 82 York St., G2 8LE, ✆ (0141) 221 3550, Fax (0141) 248 5330 – 🖵. 🝳 🄰🄴 🅾 *VISA*   CZ v
closed Sunday lunch and 3 days Chinese New Year – **Meals** - Chinese (Peking) - 8.50/25.00 **t.** and a la carte 🍷 6.95.

XX **Amber Regent,** 50 West Regent St., G2 2QZ, ✆ (0141) 331 1655, Fax (0141) 353 3398 – 🖵. 🝳 🄰🄴 🅾 *VISA* 🄹🄲🄱   DY e
closed Sunday, 1 January and 3 days Chinese New Year – **Meals** - Chinese - a la carte 18.65/26.75 **t.** 🍷 5.95.

X **Ubiquitous Chip,** 12 Ashton Lane, G12 8SJ, *off Byres Rd* ✆ (0141) 334 5007, Fax (0141) 337 1302 – 🝳 🄰🄴 🅾 *VISA*   by A 808 CY
closed 25 and 31 December and 1 January – **Meals** 23.60/31.60 **t.** 🍷 5.45.

at Stepps *(North Lanarkshire) Northeast : 5 ½ m. by M 8 DY on A 80* – ✉ *Glasgow*

🏨 **Garfield House,** Cumbernauld Rd, G33 6HW, ✆ (0141) 779 2111, Fax (0141) 779 9799 – 🛌 📺 ☎ ♿ 🅿 – 🔬 150. 🝳 🄰🄴 🅾 *VISA*
closed 1 January – **Meals** *(closed Saturday lunch and Sunday)* 12.50/18.45 **t.** and a la carte 🍷 6.40 – **46 rm** 🍵 75.00/102.00 **t.** – SB.

at Busby *(East Renfrewshire) South : 7 ¼ m. by A 77 DZ on A 726* – ✉ *Glasgow*

🏨 **Busby,** 1 Field Rd, Clarkston, G76 8RX, ✆ (0141) 644 2661, Fax (0141) 644 4417 – 🛗, 🛌 rm, 📺 ☎ 🅿 – 🔬 200. 🝳 🄰🄴 🅾 *VISA* 🄹🄲🄱. 🛇
Meals 9.95/16.45 **t.** and a la carte 🍷 6.00 – **32 rm** 🍵 66.00/94.00 **t.** – SB.

at Glasgow Airport *(Renfrewshire) West : 8 m. by M 8 CZ* – ✉ *Paisley*

🏨 **Forte Posthouse Glasgow Airport,** Abbotsinch, PA3 3TR, ✆ (0141) 887 1212, Fax (0141) 887 3738 – 🛗, 🛌 rm, 🖵 📺 ☎ 🅿 – 🔬 250. 🝳 🄰🄴 🅾 *VISA* 🄹🄲🄱
The Junction : **Meals** *(closed Saturday lunch and Bank Holiday Monday)* a la carte 10.25/28.60 🍷 7.50 – 🍵 10.95 – **295 rm** 95.00 **st.**, 2 suites – SB.

ULLAPOOL *Highland* 🄰🄾🄸 E 10 – *pop. 1 231.*
🛈 *Argyle St., IV26 2UR* ✆ *(01854) 612135 (April-November).*
Edinburgh 215 – Glasgow 225 – Inverness 59 – Aberdeen 168.

🏨 **Altnaharrie Inn** *(Gunn Eriksen)* 🛇, IV26 2SS, *Southwest : ½ m. by private ferry* ✆ (01854) 633230, « *Former drovers' inn on banks of Loch Broom*, ≼ *Ullapool* », 🚣 – 🛌. 🝳 *VISA*. 🛇
mid April-late October – **Meals** *(set menu only) (booking essential) (residents only) (dinner only)* 75.00 **st.** 🍷 6.60 – **8 rm** 🍵 *(dinner included)* 180.00/410.00 **st.**
Spec. Young turbot and summer truffles with caramelised baby fennel and carrots. Soup and mousseline of asparagus with taste of foie gras and langoustine. Ravioli of lobster with three sauces.

LEEDS *W. Yorks.* **402** P 22 **Great Britain G.** – *pop. 424 194.*

See : *City★ – City Art Gallery★ AC* **GY M.**

Envir. : *Kirkstall Abbey★ AC, NW : 3 m. by A 65* **FY** *– Templenewsam★ (decorative arts★ AC, E : 5 m. by A 64 and A 63.*

Exc. : *Harewood House★★ (The Gallery★) AC, N : 8 m. by A 61.*

Temple Newsam, Temple Newsam Rd, Halton ℘ (0113) 264 5624 – Gotts Park, Armley Ridge Rd ℘ (0113) 234 2019 – Middleton Park, Ring Rd, Beeston Park, Middleton ℘ (0113) 270 9506 – Moor Allerton, Coal Rd, Wike ℘ (0113) 266 1154 – Howley Hall, Scotchman Lane, Morley ℘ (01924) 472432 – Roundhay, Park Lane ℘ (0113) 266 2695.

Leeds - Bradford Airport : ℘ (0113) 250 9696, NW : 8 m. by A 65 and A 658.

The Arcade, City Station, LS1 1PL ℘ (0113) 242 5242.

London 204 – Liverpool 75 – Manchester 43 – Newcastle upon Tyne 95 – Nottingham 74.

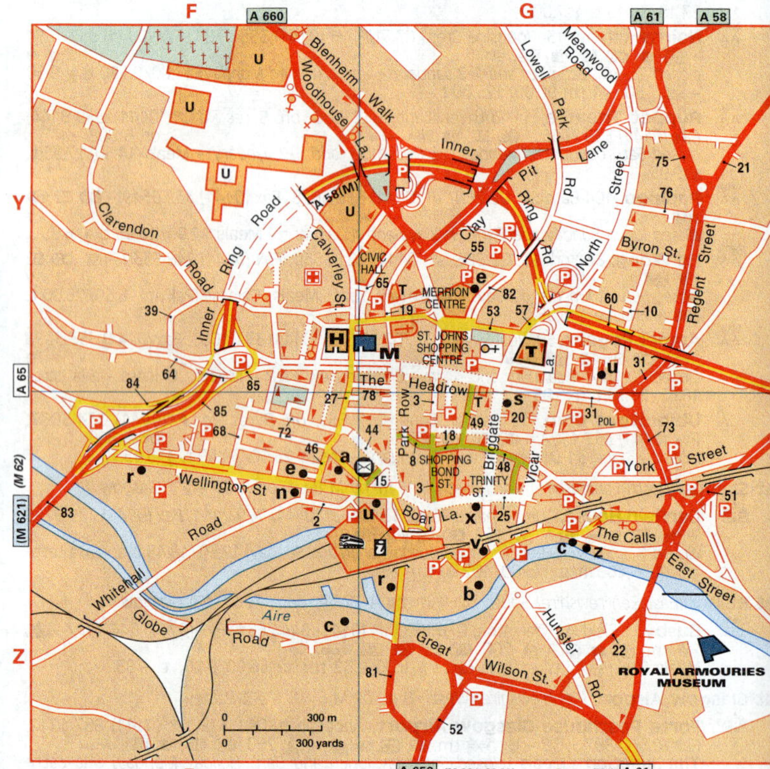

Oulton Hall, Rothwell Lane, Oulton, LS26 8HN, *Southeast : 5 ½ m. by A 61 and A 639 on A 654* ✆ (0113) 282 1000, *Fax (0113) 282 8066*, ≤, « Part Victorian mansion », ⅃ふ, ≋s, ⃞, 18, 9, ⚑ – 劇 ⅙ rm, ▤ rest, TV ☎ ⅙ P – 益 330. ⅏ ⅍ ⓪ VISA
Bronte : Meals *(closed Saturday lunch)* 15.00/23.00 st. and dinner a la carte ⌇ 8.95 – *Blayd's :* Meals 18.00 st. ⌇ 8.95 – **150 rm** ⌤ 130.00/150.00 t., 2 suites – SB.

Leeds Marriott, 4 Trevelyan Sq., Boar Lane, LS1 6ET, ✆ (0113) 236 6366, *Fax (0113) 236 6367,* ⅃ふ, ≋s, ⃞ – 劇, ⅙ rm, ▤ TV ☎ ⅙ P – 益 300. ⅏ ⅍ ⓪ VISA JCB. ⅊ GZ x
Dyson's (✆ *(0113) 236 6444) :* Meals *(dinner only and Sunday lunch)/dinner* 15.95 st. and a la carte 16.90/21.90 t. ⌇ 7.50 – **John T's :** Meals 15.95/18.95 st. and a la carte – ⌤ 11.95 – **244 rm** 99.00/105.00 st., 4 suites – SB.

Leeds Crown Plaza, Wellington St., LS1 4DL, ✆ (0113) 244 2200, *Fax (0113) 244 0460,* ⅃ふ, ≋s, ⃞ – 劇, ⅙ rm, ▤ TV ☏ ⅙ P – 益 200. ⅏ ⅍ ⓪ VISA JCB. ⅊ FZ r
Meals 14.95/17.95 st. – *Buongiorno's :* Meals - Italian - a la carte 16.45/27.45 st. ⌇ 5.95 – ⌤ 12.50 – **130 rm** 135.00 st., 5 suites – SB.

42 The Calls, 42 The Calls, LS2 7EW, ✆ (0113) 244 0099, *Fax (0113) 234 4100*, ≤, « Converted riverside grain mill » – 劇 TV ☎ ✆ ⇔ – 益 55. ⅏ ⅍ ⓪ VISA. ⅊ GZ z
closed 5 days Christmas – Meals *(see* **Pool Court at 42** *below) (see also* **Brasserie Forty Four** *below)* – ⌤ 11.50 – **38 rm** 98.00/150.00 st., 3 suites – SB.

Queen's, City Sq., LS1 1PL, ✆ (0113) 243 1323, *Fax (0113) 242 5154* – 劇, ⅙ rm, TV ☎ ⅙ ⇔ – 益 600. ⅏ ⅍ ⓪ VISA JCB GZ u
Harewood : Meals *(closed Saturday lunch)* 12.50/17.50 st. and a la carte ⌇ 8.95 – **The Carvery :** Meals *(carving rest.)* 12.50/15.50 st. ⌇ 7.95 – ⌤ 11.95 – **194 rm** 99.00/130.00 st., 5 suites.

Hilton National Leeds, Neville St., LS1 4BX, ✆ (0113) 244 2000, *Fax (0113) 243 3577,* ⅃ふ, ≋s, ⃞ – 劇, ⅙ rm, ▤ TV ☎ ⅙ P – 益 400. ⅏ ⅍ ⓪ VISA JCB GZ r
Meals 11.95/16.95 t. and dinner a la carte ⌇ 6.50 – ⌤ 11.95 – **176 rm** 120.00/130.00 st., 30 suites.

Weetwood Hall, Otley Rd, LS16 5PS, *Northwest : 4 m. on A 660* ✆ (0113) 230 6000, *Fax (0113) 230 6095,* ⅃ふ, ≋s, ⃞, ⚑ – 劇 ⅙, ▤ rest, TV ☎ ⅙ P – 益 150. ⅏ ⅍ ⓪ VISA JCB. ⅊
Meals *(bar lunch Saturday)* 12.95/17.50 st. and dinner a la carte ⌇ 6.95 – ⌤ 9.75 – **108 rm** 89.00/140.00 st. – SB.

Village H. and Leisure Club, Otley Rd, Headingley, LS16 5PR, *Northwest : 3 ½ m. on A 660* ✆ (0113) 278 1000, *Fax (0113) 278 1111,* ⅃ふ, ≋s, ⃞, *squash* – 劇 ⅙ ▤ TV ☎ ✆ ⅙ P – 益 250. ⅏ ⅍ ⓪ VISA. ⅊
Meals *(grill rest.)* a la carte 10.05/22.20 t. ⌇ 3.90 – **94 rm** ⌤ 88.00/119.00 t.

Haley's, Shire Oak Rd, Headingley, LS6 2DE, *Northwest : 2 m. off Otley Rd (A 660)* ✆ (0113) 278 4446, *Fax (0113) 275 3342* – ⅙ TV ☎ P – 益 25. ⅏ ⅍ ⓪ VISA JCB. ⅊
closed 26 to 30 December – Meals *(closed Sunday dinner to non-residents) (dinner only and Sunday lunch June-August)/dinner a la carte* 23.70/29.70 st. ⌇ 6.75 – **29 rm** ⌤ 105.00/140.00 st. – SB.

Metropole, King St., LS1 2HQ, ✆ (0113) 245 0841, *Fax (0113) 242 5156* – 劇 ⅙ TV ☎ ⅙ P – 益 200. ⅏ ⅍ ⓪ VISA. ⅊ FZ e
Meals *(closed Sunday lunch)* 12.95/15.95 st. and a la carte ⌇ 6.50 – ⌤ 11.95 – **117 rm** 99.00/119.00 st., 1 suite – SB.

Merrion, Merrion Centre, 17 Wade Lane, LS2 8NH, ✆ (0113) 243 9191, *Fax (0113) 242 3527* – 劇 ⅙ ▤ TV ☎ P – 益 80. ⅏ ⅍ ⓪ VISA JCB GZ e
Meals 14.95 st. and a la carte ⌇ 5.10 – ⌤ 10.50 – **109 rm** 109.00/129.00 t. – SB.

Golden Lion, 2 Lower Briggate, LS1 4AE, ✆ (0113) 243 6454, *Fax (0113) 242 9327* – 劇, ⅙ rm, TV ☎ P – 益 120. ⅏ ⅍ ⓪ VISA JCB GZ v
Meals *(bar lunch)/dinner* 15.95 st. and a la carte ⌇ 5.50 – **89 rm** ⌤ 99.00 st. – SB.

XXX **Pool Court at 42** (at 42 The Calls H.), 44 The Calls, LS2 7EW, ✆ (0113) 244 4242, *Fax (0113) 234 3332,* ⌸, « Riverside setting » – ▤. ⅏ ⅍ ⓪ VISA GZ z
closed Saturday lunch, Sunday, Christmas and Bank Holidays – Meals 17.00/29.50 t. ⌇ 9.15
Spec. Salad of caramelised sweetbreads with mint and basil. Nage of wild salmon, scallops and oysters. Poached squab pigeon in a fumet of ceps and Madeira.

XX **Rascasse** (Gueller), Canal Wharf, Water Lane, LS11 5BB, ✆ (0113) 244 6611, *Fax (0113) 244 0736,* ≤, « Converted grain warehouse, canalside setting » – ▤. ⅏ ⅍ ⓪ VISA FZ c
closed Saturday lunch, Sunday, 1 week after Christmas and Bank Holiday Monday – Meals 17.00 t. *(lunch)* and a la carte 22.00/35.00 t. ⌇ 7.00
Spec. Potage of scallops and oysters, leeks and truffles. Paupiettes of squab pigeon and foie gras with thyme jus. Caramelised lemon tart, cassis sorbet.

UNITED KINGDOM

XX **Marcell's,** 300 Harrogate Rd, LS17 6LY, *North : 3 ¾ m. following signs for A 58 and Chapeltown area* ℰ (0113) 236 9991, *Fax (0113) 236 9940,* « *Collection of contemporary local art* » – ⑁. ⓂⒸ ⒶⒺ Ⓞ *VISA* JCB
closed Monday and 1 to 14 January – **Meals** (booking essential) (dinner only and Sunday lunch)/dinner 15.40/16.40 **t.**

XX **Leodis,** Victoria Mill, Sovereign St., LS1 4BJ, ℰ (0113) 242 1010, *Fax (0113) 243 0432* ⑁, « Converted riverside warehouse » – ⓂⒸ ⒶⒺ Ⓞ *VISA* GZ b *closed lunch Saturday and Bank Holidays, Sunday, 25-26 December and 1 January* – **Meals** 13.95 **t.** and a la carte 20.20/26.70 **t.** ⚱ 6.85.

XX **Brasserie Forty Four** (at 42 The Calls H.), 44 The Calls, LS2 7EW, ℰ (0113) 234 3232 *Fax (0113) 234 3332* – ▤. ⓂⒸ ⒶⒺ Ⓞ *VISA* GZ *closed Saturday lunch, Sunday, Christmas and Bank Holidays* – **Meals** 12.95 **t.** (lunch) and a la carte 17.20/22.90 **t.** ⚱ 7.70.

XX **Fourth Floor** (at Harvey Nichols), 107-111 Briggate, LS1 6AZ, ℰ (0113) 204 8000 *Fax (0113) 204 8080* – ▤. ⓂⒸ ⒶⒺ Ⓞ *VISA* JCB GZ s *closed dinner Monday to Wednesday, Sunday and 25-26 December* – **Meals** (lunch booking not accepted) 15.00/15.95 **t.** and a la carte ⚱ 7.50.

XX **Lucky Dragon,** Templar Lane, LS2 7LP, ℰ (0113) 245 0520, *Fax (0113) 245 0520* – ▤ ⓂⒸ ⒶⒺ Ⓞ *VISA* JCB GY u *closed 25 December* – **Meals** - Chinese (Cantonese) - 16.50 **t.** and a la carte ⚱ 4.75.

XX **Maxi's,** 6 Bingley St., LS3 1LX, *off Kirkstall Rd* ℰ (0113) 244 0552, *Fax (0113) 234 3902* « Pagoda, ornate decor » – ▤ Ⓟ. ⓂⒸ ⒶⒺ Ⓞ *VISA* by Burley Rd FY *closed 25 and 26 December* – **Meals** - Chinese (Canton, Peking) - 17.50 **t.** and a la carte

X **Shears Yard,** The Calls, LS2 7EY, ℰ (0113) 244 4144, *Fax (0113) 244 8102* – ▤. ⓂⒸ ⒶⒺ *VISA* JCB GZ a *closed Sunday, Bank Holiday Monday, 1 January and 25 to 30 December* – **Meals** 10.00 **t.** (lunch) and a la carte 15.45/24.10 **t.** ⚱ 5.75.

X **L'Escapade,** (basement of Wellesley H.) Wellington St., LS1 4HJ, ℰ (0113) 245 8856 *Fax (0113) 242 6112* – ▤. ⓂⒸ ⒶⒺ *VISA* FZ r *closed Saturday lunch and Sunday* – **Meals** - French - 12.50 **t.** and a la carte ⚱ 4.80.

X **The Calls Grill,** Calls Landing, 38 The Calls, LS2 7EW, ℰ (0113) 245 3870 *Fax (0113) 243 9035,* « Converted riverside warehouse » – ▤. ⓂⒸ ⒶⒺ Ⓞ *VISA* JCB GZ c *closed Sunday lunch and Christmas-New Year* – **Meals** (grill rest.) 8.75 **t.** (dinner) and a la carte 17.20/25.70 **t.** ⚱ 6.50.

X **Est, Est, Est,** 151 Otley Old Rd, LS16 6HN, *Northwest : 4 ½ m. by A 660 off Cookridge rd* ℰ (0113) 267 2100, *Fax (0113) 267 2100* – ▤ Ⓟ. ⓂⒸ ⒶⒺ Ⓞ *VISA* *closed 25 and 26 December* – **Meals** - Italian - a la carte approx. 19.00 **t.**

X **Sous le nez en ville,** the basement, Quebec House, Quebec St., LS1 2HA, ℰ (0113) 244 0108, *Fax (0113) 245 0240* – ⓂⒸ ⒶⒺ *VISA* FZ a *closed Sunday, 25-26 December and Bank Holidays* – **Meals** 14.95 **st.** (dinner) and a la carte 16.10/27.00 **st.** ⚱ 6.50.

at Seacroft *Northeast : 5 ½ m. at junction of A 64* GY *with A 6120* – ✉ *Leeds :*

🏨 **Stakis Leeds,** Ring Rd, LS14 5QF, ℰ (0113) 273 2323, *Fax (0113) 232 3018* – 📶, ⑁ rm ▣ ☎ Ⓟ – 🚶 250. ⓂⒸ ⒶⒺ Ⓞ *VISA* **Meals** (*closed Saturday*) a la carte 17.00/26.90 **st.** – ☕ 9.95 **101 rm** 99.00/124.00 **st.** – SB.

at Garforth *East : 6 m. by A 64* GY *and A 63 at junction with A 642* – ✉ *Leeds :*

XX **Aagrah,** Aberford Rd, LS25 1BA, *on A 642* ℰ (0113) 287 6606 – Ⓟ. ⓂⒸ ⒶⒺ *VISA* JCB *closed 25 December* – **Meals** - Indian (Kashmiri) - (booking essential) (dinner only) a la carte 13.70/17.05 **t.**

at Pudsey *West : 5 ¾ m. by M 621* FZ *and A 647* – ✉ *Leeds :*

XX **Aagrah,** 483 Bradford Rd, LS28 8ED, *on A 647* ℰ (01274) 668818, *Fax (01274) 669803* – ▤ Ⓟ. ⓂⒸ ⒶⒺ *VISA* JCB *closed 25 December* – **Meals** - Indian (Kashmiri) - (booking essential) (dinner only) a la carte 13.70/17.05 **t.**

at Horsforth *Northwest : 5 m. by A 65* FY *off A 6120* – ✉ *Leeds :*

X **Paris,** Calverley Bridge, Calverley Lane, Rodley, LS13 1NP, *Southwest : 1 m. by A 6120* ℰ (0113) 258 1885, *Fax (0113) 239 0651* – ▤ Ⓟ. ⓂⒸ ⒶⒺ Ⓞ *VISA* *closed Saturday lunch* – **Meals** 13.95 **t.** and a la carte 14.30/28.40 **t.** ⚱ 6.25.

at **Bramhope** *Northwest : 8 m. on A 660* **FY** – ⊠ *Leeds :*

 **Forte Posthouse Leeds/Bradford,** Leeds Rd, LS16 9JJ, ℘ (0113) 284 2911, *Fax (0113) 284 3451*, ⬿, ⌊ᴅ, ⊜s, ⃞, ⬚, *park* – ⧈, ⤬ rm, ⊤ᵛ ☎ ℗ – ⅍ 160. ⫿⊙ ⒜ꜝ ⑩ 𝘝𝘐𝘚𝘈
Meals a la carte 16.85/27.15 **t.** ⟊ 7.50 – ⊑ 10.95 – **123 rm** 99.00 **t.,** 1 suite – SB.

 **Jarvis Parkway H. and Country Club,** Otley Rd, LS16 8AG, *South : 2 m. on A 660* ℘ (0113) 267 2551, *Fax (0113) 267 4410*, ⌊ᴅ, ⊜s, ⃞, ⬚, ⤬ – ⧈ ⤬ ⊤ᵛ ☎ ⅄ ℗ – ⅍ 300. ⫿⊙ ⒜ꜝ ⑩ 𝘝𝘐𝘚𝘈 ᴊᴄʙ
Meals *(carving lunch) (bar lunch Saturday)* 12.50/16.80 **t.** and dinner a la carte ⟊ 7.95 – ⊑ 10.50 – **116 rm** 99.00/109.00 **t.** – SB.

WINTERINGHAM *North Lincolnshire* 402 *S 22 – pop. 4 714 –* ⊠ *Scunthorpe.*
London 176 – Leeds 62.

 **Winteringham Fields** *(Schwab)* with rm, Silver St., DN15 9PF, ℘ (01724) 733096, *Fax (01724) 733898,* « *Part 16C manor house* » – ⤬ ⊤ᵛ ☎ ℗. ⫿⊙ ⒜ꜝ 𝘝𝘐𝘚𝘈 ⬚
closed first week March and August and 2 weeks Christmas – **Meals** *(closed Sunday and Monday)* 20.00/29.00 **st.** and a la carte 49.40/58.70 **st.** ⟊ 6.75 – ⊑ 9.50 – **9 rm** 70.00/105.00 **st.,** 1 suite
Spec. Millefeuille of lobster and truffle oil polenta, morel and lobster sauce. Pig's trotter stuffed with veal sweetbreads and chicken mousse, merlot sauce. Winteringham corn tart.

LIVERPOOL *Mersey.* 402 403 *L 23* **Great Britain G.** *– pop. 481 786.*
See : *City★ - Walker Art Gallery★★* **DY** **M²** *– Liverpool Cathedral★★ (Lady Chapel★)* **EZ** *– Metropolitan Cathedral of Christ the King★★* **EY** *– Albert Dock★* **CZ** *(Merseyside Maritime Museum★ AC* **M¹** *- Tate Gallery Liverpool★).*
Exc. : *Speke Hall★ AC, SE : 8 m. by A 561.*
ⓡ₈, ⓡ₉ *Allerton Municipal, Allerton Rd* ℘ (0151) 428 1046 – ⓡ₈ *Liverpool Municipal, Ingoe Lane, Kirkby* ℘ (0151) 546 5435 – ⓡ₉ *Bowring, Bowring Park, Roby Rd, Huyton* ℘ (0151) 489 1901.
Mersey Tunnels (toll).
✈ *Liverpool Airport :* ℘ (0151) 486 8877, *SE : 6 m. by A 561 –* **Terminal :** *Pier Head.*
⛴ *to Isle of Man (Douglas) (Isle of Man Steam Packet Co. Ltd) 1-3 daily (2 h 30 mn) – to Northern Ireland (Belfast) (Norse Irish Ferries Ltd) weekly (10 h 30 mn) daily.*
⛴ *to Birkenhead (Mersey Ferries) – to Wallasey (Mersey Ferries).*
🛈 *Merseyside Welcome Centre, Clayton Square Shopping Centre, L1 1QR* ℘ (0151) 709 3631 – *Atlantic Pavilion, Albert Dock, L3 4AA* ℘ (0151) 708 8854.
London 219 – Birmingham 103 – Leeds 75 – Manchester 35.

Plans on following pages

 **Swallow,** One Queen Sq., L1 1RH, ℘ (0151) 476 8000, *Fax (0151) 474 5000,* ⌊ᴅ, ⊜s, ⃞ – ⧈ ⤬ ▤ ⊤ᵛ ☎ 🖦 ⅄ ℗ – ⅍ 250. ⫿⊙ ⒜ꜝ ⑩ 𝘝𝘐𝘚𝘈. ⬚   **DY** e
Meals *(closed Saturday lunch)* 22.00 **st.** (dinner) and a la carte 21.50/34.00 **st.** ⟊ 6.50 – **143 rm** ⊑ 105.00/120.00 **st.,** 3 suites – SB.

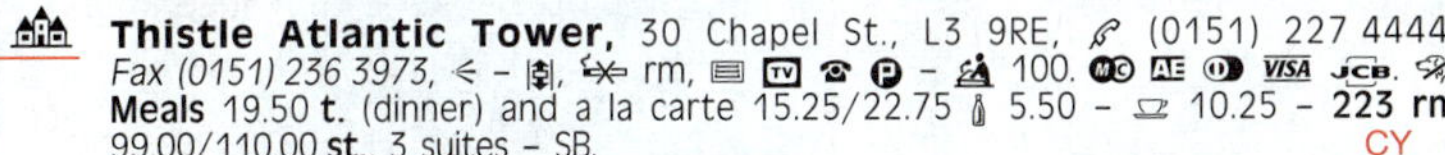 **Liverpool Moat House,** Paradise St., L1 8GT, ℘ (0151) 471 9988, *Fax (0151) 709 2706,* ⌊ᴅ, ⊜s, ⃞ – ⧈, ⤬ rm, ▤ ⊤ᵛ ☎ ℗ – ⅍ 400. ⫿⊙ ⒜ꜝ ⑩ 𝘝𝘐𝘚𝘈
Meals 8.95/16.50 **st.** and dinner a la carte ⟊ 5.75 – ⊑ 9.50 – **249 rm** 95.00/120.00 **st.,** 2 suites – SB.   **DZ** n

Thistle Atlantic Tower, 30 Chapel St., L3 9RE, ℘ (0151) 227 4444, *Fax (0151) 236 3973,* ⬿ – ⧈, ⤬ rm, ▤ ⊤ᵛ ☎ ℗ – ⅍ 100. ⫿⊙ ⒜ꜝ ⑩ 𝘝𝘐𝘚𝘈 ᴊᴄʙ. ⬚
Meals 19.50 **t.** (dinner) and a la carte 15.25/22.75 ⟊ 5.50 – ⊑ 10.25 – **223 rm** 99.00/110.00 **st.,** 3 suites – SB.   **CY** r

Devonshire House, 293-297 Edge Lane, L7 9LD, *East : 2 ¼ m. on A 5047* ℘ (0151) 280 3903, *Fax (0151) 263 2109,* ⬚ – ⧈ ⊤ᵛ ☎ 🖦 ⅄ ℗ – ⅍ 300. ⫿⊙ ⒜ꜝ ⑩ 𝘝𝘐𝘚𝘈
Meals *(closed Saturday lunch)* 13.95/16.95 **st.** and dinner a la carte – **54 rm** ⊑ 80.00/90.00 **st.** – SB.

The Park - Premier Lodge, Dunningsbridge Rd, L30 6YN, *North : 6 ¾ m. by A 59 on A 5036* ℘ (0151) 525 7555, *Fax (0151) 525 2481,* Reservations *(Freephone)* 0800 118833 – ⧈, ⤬ rm, ⊤ᵛ ☎ ℗ – ⅍ 200. ⫿⊙ ⒜ꜝ ⑩ 𝘝𝘐𝘚𝘈. ⬚
Meals *(grill rest.)* 7.25/12.95 **st.** and a la carte ⟊ 5.40 – ⊑ 6.95 – **60 rm** 43.95 **st.**

Travel Inn, Northern Perimeter Rd, L30 7PT, *North : 6 m. by A 59 on A 5036* ℘ (0151) 531 1497, *Fax (0151) 520 1842* – ⤬ rm, ▤ rest, ⊤ᵛ ⅄ ℗. ⫿⊙ ⒜ꜝ ⑩ 𝘝𝘐𝘚𝘈. ⬚
Meals *(grill rest.)* – **43 rm** 38.00 **t.**

LIVERPOOL
CENTRE

Great Britain and Ireland is now covered by an Atlas at a scale of 1 inch to 4.75 miles.

Three easy to use versions: Paperback, Spiralbound, Hardback.

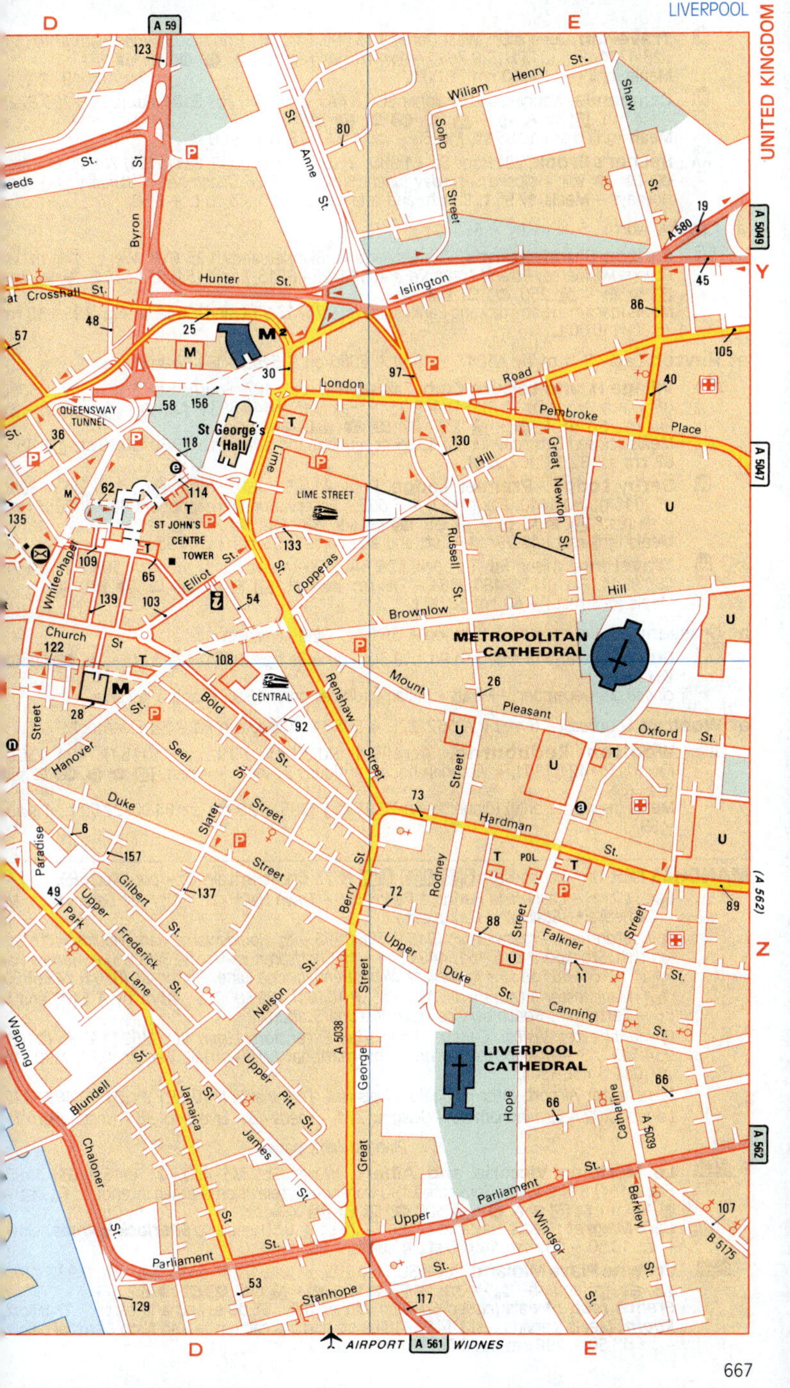

LIVERPOOL
UNITED KINGDOM
D
A 59
E
123
William Henry St.
Soho
Shaw
St.
Anne St.
80
Street
St.
19
A 580
A 5049
45
Hunter St.
Islington
Y
86
at Crosshall St.
105
48
25
30
London
97
Road
40
Queensway Tunnel
58 156
St George's Hall
130
Pembroke
Place
A 5047
36
St John's
114
Lime
T
Hill
Great Newton St.
U
57
62
M²
M
118
LIME STREET
135
T
St
St.
Copperas
Russell St.
Hill
St JOHN'S CENTRE TOWER
133
U
109
65
Elliot St.
Brownlow
139 103
54
METROPOLITAN CATHEDRAL
U
Church St
108
122
Mount
26
Pleasant
Oxford St.
28
CENTRAL
92
Renshaw Street
U
T
Whitechapel
Hanover
Bold St.
Street
U
a
U
Duke
Slater
Street
Street
73
Hardman
St.
Paradise
6
St.
Berry St.
Rodney Street
T POL
T
U
Gilbert
157
Street
72
88
Falkner
89
49
137
Upper Frederick St.
Street
11
Park Lane
Nelson St.
Upper Duke St.
Canning St.
66
LIVERPOOL CATHEDRAL
Wapping
Blundell
Jamaica St
Upper Pitt St.
George Street
A 5039
66
Berkley
107
Chaloner St.
James St.
Hope
Catharine
B 5175
A 562
A 5038
Great
Parliament
Windsor
Upper
53
Stanhope
117
St.
D
AIRPORT A 561 WIDNES
E
667

Travel Inn, Queens Dr., West Derby, L13 0DL, *East : 4 m. on A 5058 (Ringroad)* ℰ (0151) 228 4724, *Fax (0151) 220 7610* – ⊷ rm, ▤ rest, ⓣⓥ ⅃ ℗. ⓜⓒ ⒶⒺ ⓪ *VISA*. ⌁
Meals (grill rest.) – **40 rm** 38.00 **t.**   *by A 5049* EY

Campanile, Wapping and Chaloner St., L3 4AJ, ℰ (0151) 709 8104, *Fax (0151) 709 872*
– ⊷ rm, ⓣⓥ ☎ ⅃ ℗ – ⚒ 30. ⓜⓒ ⒶⒺ ⓪ *VISA*   CZ
Meals (grill rest.) 10.85 **st.** ⌁ 6.60 – ⌕ 4.50 – **78 rm** 38.00 **st.**

Becher's Brook, 29a Hope St., L1 9BQ, ℰ (0151) 707 0005, *Fax (0151) 708 7011* – ⊷
ⓜⓒ ⒶⒺ ⓪ *VISA* – *closed Saturday lunch, Sunday, 25-26 December, 1 January and Ban*
Holidays – Meals 17.95 **t.** (lunch) and a la carte 20.75/43.00 **t.** ⌁ 8.50.   EZ

at Crosby *North : 5 ½ m. by A 565* CY :

Carlton Blundellsands, The Serpentine, Blundellsands, L23 6YB, *West : 1 ¼ m. vi*
College Rd, Mersey Rd and Agnes Rd ℰ (0151) 924 6515, *Fax (0151) 931 5364* – 🛗, ⊷ rm
ⓣⓥ ☎ ℗ – ⚒ 250. ⓜⓒ ⒶⒺ *VISA*. ⌁
Meals (bar lunch Saturday and Bank Holidays) 9.75/13.95 **t.** and a la carte – ⌕ 8.95 – **30 rm**
75.00/110.00 **t.**

at Huyton *East : 8 ¼ m. by A5047* EY *and A 5080 on B 5199* – ✉ Liverpool :

Village H. and Leisure Club, Fallows Way, L35 1RZ, *Southeast : 3 ¼ m. by A 5080*
off Windy Arbor Rd ℰ (0151) 449 2341, *Fax (0151) 449 3832*, Ⅰ₅, ≘s, ▨, squash – 🛗
⊷ rm, ⓣⓥ ☎ ⅃ ℗ – ⚒ 250. ⓜⓒ ⒶⒺ ⓪ *VISA* ⌊CB⌋. ⌁
Meals (closed Saturday lunch) 15.95 **st.** (lunch) and a la carte 18.50/30.00 **st.** ⌁ 6.45 –
62 rm ⌕ 82.00/107.00 **st.**

Derby Lodge - Premier Lodge, Roby Rd, L36 4HD, *Southwest : 1 m. on A 5080*
ℰ (0151) 480 4440, *Fax (0151) 443 0932*, Reservations (Freephone) 0800 118833,
– ▤ rest, ⓣⓥ ☎ ⅃ ℗ – ⚒ 35. ⓜⓒ ⒶⒺ ⓪ *VISA* ⌊CB⌋ ⌁
Meals (grill rest.) 10.95/12.95 **st.** and a la carte – **53 rm** ⌕ 44.95 **st.**

Travel Inn, Wilson Rd, Tarbock, L36 6AD, *Southeast : 2 ¼ m. on A 5080* ℰ (0151
480 9614, *Fax (0151) 480 9361* – ⊷ rm, ▤ rest, ⓣⓥ ⅃ ℗. ⓜⓒ ⒶⒺ ⓪ *VISA*. ⌁
Meals (grill rest.) – **40 rm** 38.00 **t.**

at Grassendale *Southeast : 4 ½ m. on A 561* EZ – ✉ Liverpool :

Gulshan, 544-548 Aigburth Rd, L19 3QG, *on A 561* ℰ (0151) 427 2273 – ▤. ⓜⓒ ⒶⒺ ⓪
VISA ⌊CB⌋
closed 25 December – Meals - Indian - (dinner only) 16.95 **t.** and a la carte.

at Woolton *Southeast : 6 m. by A 562* EZ , *A 5058 and Woolton Rd* – ✉ Liverpool :

Woolton Redbourne, Acrefield Rd, L25 5JN, ℰ (0151) 421 1500
Fax (0151) 421 1501, « Victorian house, antiques », ⌁ – ⊷ rest, ⓣⓥ ☎ ℗. ⓜⓒ ⒶⒺ ⓪
VISA ⌊CB⌋
Meals (residents only) (dinner only) 22.95 **t.** ⌁ 8.95 – **25 rm** ⌕ 63.00/92.00 **t.**, 1 suite
– SB.

MANCHESTER *Gtr. Manchester* 402 403 404 N 23 *Great Britain G.* – *pop. 402 889.*
See : *City*⋆ – *Castlefield Heritage Park*⋆ CZ – *Town Hall*⋆ CZ – *City Art Gallery*⋆ CZ M
– *Cathedral*⋆ *(Stalls and Canopies*⋆*)* CY.
Ⅰ₈ *Heaton Park, Prestwick* ℰ (0161) 798 0295 – Ⅰ₈ *Houldsworth Park, Houldsworth St.*
Reddish, Stockport ℰ (0161) 442 9611 – Ⅰ₈ *Chorlton-cum-Hardy, Barlow Hall, Barlow Ha*
Rd ℰ (0161) 881 3139 – Ⅰ₈ *William Wroe, Pennybridge Lane, Flixton* ℰ (0161) 748 8680
⌖ *Manchester International Airport :* ℰ (0161) 489 3000, *S : 10 m. by A 5103 and M*
56 - Terminal : *Coach service from Victoria Station.*
🛈 *Manchester Visitor Centre, Town Hall Extension, Lloyd St., M60 2LA* ℰ (0161*
234 3157/8 – Manchester Airport, International Arrivals Hall, Terminal T1, M90 3NY
ℰ (0161) 436 3344.
Manchester Airport, International Arrivals Hall, Terminal 2, M90 4TU ℰ (0161) 489 6412
London 202 – Birmingham 86 – Glasgow 221 – Leeds 43 – Liverpool 35 – Nottingham 72

Plan on next page

Le Meridien Victoria and Albert, Water St., M3 4JQ, ℰ (0161) 832 1188
Fax (0161) 834 2484, « Converted 19C warehouse, television themed interior », Ⅰ₅, ≘s –
🛗, ⊷ rm, ▤ ⓣⓥ ☎ ⅃ ℗ – ⚒ 300. ⓜⓒ ⒶⒺ ⓪ *VISA* ⌊CB⌋. ⌁   *by Quay St.* CZ
Cafe Maigret : Meals a la carte 22.25/27.25 **st.** ⌁ 8.50 (see also **Sherlock Holmes** below
– ⌕ 10.50 – **152 rm** 149.00 **st.**, 4 suites – SB.

Crowne Plaza Midland, Peter St., M60 2DS, ℰ (0161) 236 3333, *Fax (0161) 932 4100*
Ⅰ₅, ≘s, ▨, squash – 🛗, ⊷ rm, ▤ ⓣⓥ ☎ ⅃ ⅃ ℗ – ⚒ 600. ⓜⓒ ⒶⒺ ⓪ *VISA* ⌊CB⌋   CZ x
French rest. : Meals (closed Sunday) (dinner only) 35.00 **t.** and a la carte – **Trafford**
Room : Meals (carving rest.) 14.95/18.95 **st.** and a la carte (see also **Nico Central** below
– ⌕ 13.50 – **296 rm** 120.00/190.00, 7 suites.

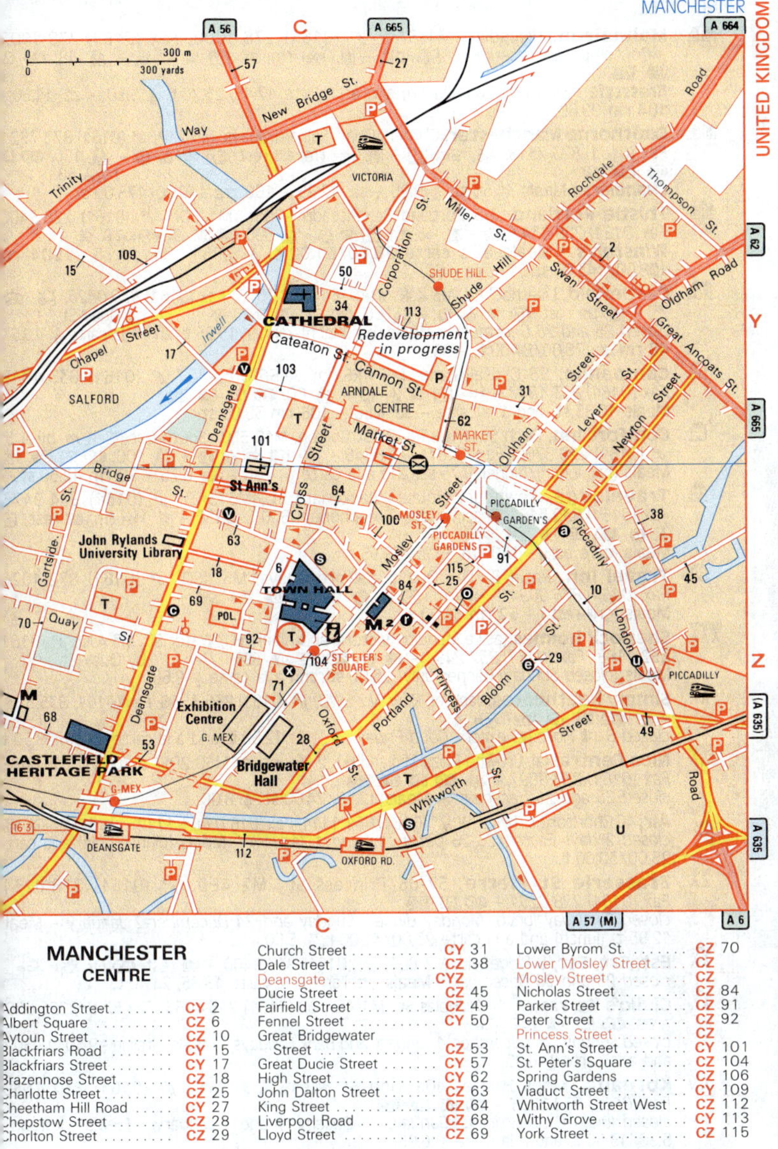

MANCHESTER
CENTRE

Ramada, Blackfriars St., Deansgate, M3 2EQ, ☎ (0161) 835 2555, *Fax (0161) 835 3077* – 🛗, ✻ rm, 🍽 rest, 📺 ☎ ♿ 🅿 – 🏛 400. MC AE ① VISA JCB. ✼   CY v
Meals *(closed Sunday dinner)* 15.50/21.50 **st.** and a la carte 🍷 7.25 – ☕ 11.50 – **196 rm** 116.00 **st.**, 4 suites.

Palace, Oxford St., M60 7HA, ☎ (0161) 288 1111, *Fax (0161) 288 2222*, « Victorian Gothic architecture, former Refuge Assurance building » – 🛗 ✻ 📺 ☎ – 🏛 850. MC AE ① VISA ✼   CZ s
Waterhouses : **Meals** *(closed Sunday lunch)* 12.95/17.95 **st.** and dinner a la carte 🍷 7.95 – ☕ 11.95 – **161 rm** 139.00/165.00 **st.**, 10 suites – SB.

Malmaison, Piccadilly, M1 3AQ, ℰ (0161) 278 1000, Fax (0161) 278 1002
« Contemporary interior », ₤6, ⇔s – ⌷, ☒ rm, ▤ TV ☎ ℄ ₺ – ▲ 48. MO A
⑩ VISA   CZ
Brasserie : Meals 12.50 **t.** (lunch) and a la carte 17.45/25.70 **t.** ⬦ 3.50 – ☕ 11.50
104 rm 99.00, 8 suites.

Copthorne Manchester, Clippers Quay, Salford Quays, M5 2XP, ℰ (0161) 873 732
Fax (0161) 873 7318, ₤6, ⇔s, ☒ – ⌷, ☒ rm, ▤ rest, TV ☎ ₺ ℗ – ▲ 150. MO A
⑩ VISA. ✕   by A 56 CZ
Chandlers : Meals 31.50 **st.** ⬦ 9.95 – ☕ 12.25 – **166 rm** 140.00/175.00 **st.**

Thistle Portland, 3-5 Portland St., Piccadilly Gdns., M1 6DP, ℰ (0161) 228 3400
Fax (0161) 228 6347, ⇔s – ⌷, ☒ rm, TV ☎ ℗ – ▲ 300. MO AE ⑩ VISA JCB. ✕   CZ
Winston's : Meals a la carte 20.00/31.00 **t.** ⬦ 6.95 – ☕ 11.75 – **204 rm**
108.00/143.00 **st.**, 1 suite – SB.

Castlefield, Liverpool Rd, M3 4JR, ℰ (0161) 832 7073, Fax (0161) 839 0326, ₤6, ⇔s
☒ – ⌷, ▤ rest, TV ☎ ₺ ℗ – ▲ 60. MO AE ⑩ VISA. ✕   by Quay St. CZ
closed 25 and 26 December – **Meals** (bar lunch)/dinner 15.95 **t.** and a la carte ⬦ 4.15
48 rm ☕ 78.00/84.00 **t.** – SB.

Campanile, 55 Ordsall Lane, M5 4RS, *by A 56 off A 57* ℰ (0161) 833 1845
Fax (0161) 833 1847 – ☒ TV ☎ ₺ ℗ – ▲ 60. MO AE ⑩ VISA
Meals 10.85 **st.** and a la carte – ☕ 4.50 – **105 rm** 38.00 **st.**

Comfort Inn, Birch St., Hyde Rd, West Gorton, M12 5NT, *Southeast : 2 ½ m. by A 5*
ℰ (0161) 220 8700, Fax (0161) 220 8848 – ☒ TV ☎ ₺ ℗ – ▲ 100. MO AE ⑩ VIS
Meals (bar lunch)/dinner 9.75 **st.** and a la carte ⬦ 4.50 – ☕ 6.75 – **90 rm** 42.50 **st.**

Travelodge, Townbury House, Blackfriars St., M3 5AB, ℰ (0161) 834 9476
Fax (0161) 839 5181, Reservations (Freephone) 0800 850950 – ⌷, ☒ rm, ▤ rest, TV
₺ ℗. MO AE ⑩ VISA. ✕   CY
Meals (cafe bar) – **160 rm** 39.95/59.95 **t.**

Travel Inn, Basin 8, The Quays, Salford Quays, M5 4SQ, ℰ (0161) 872 4026
Fax (0161) 876 0094 – ☒ rm, TV ₺ ℗. MO AE ⑩ VISA. ✕
Meals (grill rest.) – **52 rm** 38.00 **t.**

XXX **Sherlock Holmes** (at Le Meridien Victoria and Albert H.), Water St., M3 4JQ, ℰ (0161
832 1188, Fax (0161) 832 2484 – ▤ ℗. MO AE ⑩ VISA   by Quay St. CZ
Meals *(closed Sunday)* (dinner only) 25.00 **st.** and a la carte ⬦ 9.60.

XX **Simply Heathcotes,** Jackson Row, M2 5WB, ℰ (0161) 835 3536, Fax (0161) 835 353
– ▤. MO AE ⑩ VISA JCB   CZ
closed Bank Holidays except Good Friday – **Meals** 12.50 **t.** and a la carte 22.50/28.50 **t.**

XX **Nico Central** (at Crowne Plaza Midland H.), 2 Mount St., M60 2DS, ℰ (0161) 236 6488
Fax (0161) 236 8897 – ▤. MO AE ⑩ VISA   CZ
closed 25 and 26 December – **Meals** 12.50/24.00 **st.** ⬦ 8.00.

XX **Air,** 40 Chorlton St., M1 3HW, ℰ (0161) 661 1111, *Fax (0161) 661 1112* – ▤. MO AE ⑩ VIS
closed 2 days Easter, 25-26 December and 1 January – **Meals** (dinner only) a la cart
25.00/30.00 **t.**   CZ

XX **Brasserie St Pierre,** 57-63 Princess St., M2 4EQ, ℰ (0161) 228 0231
Fax (0161) 228 0231 – MO AE VISA   CZ
closed Saturday lunch, Monday dinner, Sunday and 24 December-2 January – Meal
12.95 **t.** (lunch) and a la carte 23.00/32.00 **t.** ⬦ 5.50.

XX **Est, Est, Est,** 5 Ridgefield, M2 6EG, ℰ (0161) 833 9400 – ▤ rest. MO AE VISA JCB
closed 25 and 26 December – **Meals** - Italian - a la carte 18.85/21.40 **t.**   CZ

XX **Giulio's Terrazza,** 14 Nicholas St., M1 4EJ, ℰ (0161) 236 4033, Fax (0161) 228 650
– ▤. MO AE ⑩ VISA JCB   CZ
closed Sunday, 25 December, 1 January and Bank Holidays – **Meals** - Italian - 9.50/12.50 **t**
and a la carte ⬦ 6.90.

XX **Koreana,** Kings House, 40a King St. West, M3 2WY, ℰ (0161) 832 4330
Fax (0161) 832 2293 – MO AE ⑩ VISA   CZ
closed lunch Bank Holidays, Sunday, 25 December and 1 January – **Meals** - Korean -
5.50/13.50 **t.** and a la carte ⬦ 6.95.

XX **Royal Orchid,** 36 Charlotte St., M1 4FD, ℰ (0161) 236 5183, Fax (0161) 236 8830
MO AE ⑩ VISA   CZ
closed lunch Monday and Saturday, Sunday, 25 December and 1 January – **Meals** - Tha
- 7.50/23.00 **t.** and a la carte.

X **Market,** 104 High St., M4 1HQ, ℰ (0161) 834 3743, Fax (0161) 834 3743 – MO AE ⑩
VISA JCB – *closed Sunday to Tuesday, 1 week Easter, August and 1 week Christmas* – Meal
- Bistro - (dinner only) a la carte 17.05/24.55 **t.** ⬦ 5.95.   CY

X **Mash,** 40 Chorlton St., M1 3HW, ℰ (0161) 661 6161, Fax (0161) 661 6060 – ▤. MO A
⑩ VISA   CZ
Meals a la carte 15.00/20.00 **t.**

at Northenden *South : 5 ¼ m. by A 57 (M) CZ and A 5103 –* ✉ *Manchester :*

Forte Posthouse Manchester, Palatine Rd, M22 4FH, ℰ (0161) 998 7090, *Fax (0161) 946 0139 –* 📶, ✻ rm, 📺 ☎ Ⓟ – 🍴 150. 🆖 �æ ⓪ *VISA* 🆓
Meals (bar lunch) a la carte 10.95/20.00 **st.** 🍷 7.50 – ☕ 8.95 – **190 rm** 75.00/115.00 **t.** – SB.

at Manchester Airport *South : 9 m. by Lower Mosley St. CZ and A 5103 off M 56 –* ✉ *Manchester :*

Manchester Airport Hilton, Outwood Lane (Terminal One), M90 4WP, ℰ (0161) 435 3000, *Fax (0161) 435 3040,* 🏋, ≘s, 🏊 – 📶, ✻ rm, 🖥 📺 ☎ 🚪 Ⓟ – 🍴 300. 🆖 �æ ⓪ *VISA*
Meals 18.50 **st.** and a la carte 🍷 7.50 – *Portico :* **Meals** *(closed Sunday)* (dinner only) 30.00 **st.** and a la carte 🍷 8.50 – ☕ 15.00 – **222 rm** 150.00/175.00 **st.,** 1 suite.

Forte Posthouse Manchester Airport, Outwood Lane (Terminal One), M90 3NS, ℰ (0161) 437 5811, *Fax (0161) 436 2340,* 🏋, ≘s, 🏊 – 📶, ✻ rm, 🖥 📺 ☎ Ⓟ – 🍴 75. 🆖 �æ ⓪ *VISA* 🆓. ✄
Meals (bar lunch Monday to Saturday)/dinner 22.50 **st.** and a la carte 🍷 5.00 – ☕ 11.95 – **284 rm** 119.00 **st.,** 1 suite – SB.

Etrop Grange, Thorley Lane, M90 4EG, ℰ (0161) 499 0500, *Fax (0161) 499 0790 –* ✻ rm, 📺 ☎ 📞 🚪 Ⓟ – 🍴 40. 🆖 �æ ⓪ *VISA* 🆓
Meals *(closed lunch Saturday and Bank Holidays)* 17.00/29.00 **st.** 🍷 6.95 – ☕ 12.50 – **37 rm** 120.00/190.00 **st.,** 2 suites – SB.

Holiday Inn Garden Court, Outwood Lane, M90 4HL, ℰ (0161) 498 0333, *Fax (0161) 498 0222 –* 📶, ✻ rm, 📺 ☎ 🚪 Ⓟ. 🆖 �æ ⓪ *VISA* 🆓. ✄
closed 31 December – **Meals** (bar lunch)/dinner 13.95 **t.** and a la carte – ☕ 8.00 – **163 rm** 65.00 **t.**

Moss Nook, Ringway Rd, Moss Nook, M22 5WD, ℰ (0161) 437 4778, *Fax (0161) 498 8089 –* Ⓟ. 🆖 �æ *VISA*
closed Saturday, Sunday, Monday and 2 weeks Christmas – **Meals** 18.50/29.95 **t.** and a la carte 🍷 7.00.

at Worsley *West : 7 ¼ m. by A 6 CY, A 5063, M 602 and M 62 (eastbound) on A 572 –* ✉ *Manchester :*

Novotel Manchester West, Worsley Brow, M28 2YA, *at junction 13 of M 62* ℰ (0161) 799 3535, *Fax (0161) 703 8207,* 🏊 heated – 📶, ✻ rm, 🖥 rest, 📺 ☎ 📞 🚪 Ⓟ – 🍴 220. 🆖 �æ ⓪ *VISA*
Meals 16.00 **st.** and a la carte 🍷 7.95 – ☕ 8.95 – **119 rm** 69.00 **st.**

Tung Fong, 2 Worsley Rd, M28 4NL, *on A 572* ℰ (0161) 794 5331, *Fax (0161) 727 9598* – 🖥. 🆖 �æ ⓪ *VISA*
closed lunch Saturday and Sunday – **Meals** - Chinese (Peking) - 6.50/16.50 **st.** and a la carte 🍷 5.50.

at Pendlebury *Northwest : 4 m. by A 6 CY on A 666 –* ✉ *Manchester :*

Henry Boddington - Premier Lodge, 219 Bolton Rd, M27 8TG, ℰ (0161) 736 5143, *Fax (0161) 737 2786, Reservations (Freephone) 0800 118833 –* 📺 ☎ 🚪 Ⓟ. 🆖 �æ ⓪ *VISA*. ✄
Meals (grill rest.) 7.25/10.95 **st.** and a la carte – ☕ 5.95 – **30 rm** 44.95 **st.**

at Swinton *Northwest : 4 m. by A 6 CY , A 580 and A 572 on B 5231 –* ✉ *Manchester :*

New Ellesmere - Premier Lodge, East Lancs Rd, M27 8AA, *Southwest : ½ m. on A 580* ℰ (0161) 728 2791, *Fax (0161) 794 8222, Reservations (Freephone) 0800 118833* – ✻ rm, 📺 ☎ 📞 🚪 Ⓟ. 🆖 �æ ⓪ *VISA*. ✄
Meals (grill rest.) 🍷 4.25 – ☕ 5.95 – **27 rm** 44.95 **st.** – SB.

Calendar of main tradefairs and other international events in 1999

AUSTRIA

Vienna	Wiener Festwochen	7 May to 20 June
Salzburg	Salzburg Festival (Festspiele)	27 March to 5 April
		24 July to 31 August

BENELUX

Amsterdam	Holland Festival	June
Bruges	Ascension Day Procession	Ascension
Brussels	Guild Procession (Ommegang)	first Thursday of July and the previous Tuesday
	Holiday and Leisure Activities International Show	Late March 2000
	Belgian Antique Dealers Fair	February 2000
	Eurantica (Antiques Show)	Late March 2000

CZECH REPUBLIC

Prague	Prague's Spring International Music Festival	12 May to 3 June

DENMARK

Copenhagen	International Fashion Fair	9 to 11 August
	Scandinavian Furniture Fair	26 to 30 August

FINLAND

	International Fashion Fair	22 to 24 August
	Helsinki Festival	20 August to 5 Sept.
	Helsinki Motor Show	22 to 24 December

FRANCE

Paris	Paris Fair	28 April to 9 May
	Motorcycle Show	1 to 11 October
Cannes	International Film Festival	12 to 23 May
Lyons	Lyons Fair	19 to 29 March 99
Marseilles	Marseilles Fair	24 Sept. to 4 Oct.

GERMANY

Berlin	*Berlin Fair (Grüne Woche)*	*22 to 31 January*
Frankfurt	*International Fair*	*19 to 23 Feb. and*
		27 to 31 August
	Frankfurt Book Fair	*13 to 18 October*
Hanover	*Hanover Fair*	*19 to 24 April*
Leipzig	*International Book Fair*	*25 to 28 March*
Munich	*Beer Festival (Oktoberfest)*	*18 Sept. to 3 Oct.*

GREECE

Athens	*Athens Festival*	*June to Sept.*

HUNGARY

Budapest	*Spring Festival (Music, Arts)*	*12 to 28 March*
	Travel 98 (International Tourism Exhibition)	*24 to 28 March*
	International Jazz Festival	*4 and 5 July*
	International Fashion Fair	*29 to 31 August*
	International Wine Festival	*7 to 12 Sept.*
	International Motor Exhibition	*29 Sept. to 3 Oct.*

IRELAND

Dublin	*Dublin film Festival*	*15 to 25 April*
	International Music Festival	*30 April to 3 May*
	Dublin Horse Show	*4 to 8 August*

ITALY

Milan	*Bit (International Tourism Exchange)*	*24 to 28 February*
	Fashion Fair (Moda Milano)	*26 February to 2 March*
		1 to 5 October
	SMAU (International Exhibition of Information and Communication Technology)	*30 Sep. to 4 October*
Florence	*Pitti Bimbo*	*18 to 20 June*
	Fashion Fair (Pitti Immagine Uomo)	*24 to 27 June*
Turin	*International Book Fair*	*13 to 18 May*
Venice	*International Film Festival*	*Late August to early September*
	The Carnival	*5 to 16 February*

NORWAY

Oslo	*Fashion Fair*	*13 to 15 August and*
		18 to 20 February 2000

POLAND

Warsaw	*International Book Fair*	*May*
	Mozart Festival	*15 June to 26 July*
	Jazz Jamboree	*21 to 24 October*
	International Chopin Year	*All year*

PORTUGAL

Lisbon	*Motorexpo*	*11 to 20 June*
	International Handicraft Exhibition	*3 to 11 July*

SPAIN

Madrid	*Fitur*	*26 to 30 Jan. 2000*
	International Fashion Week	*15 to 20 Feb.*
	Madrid Motor Show	*26 May to 4 June*
Barcelona	*International Tourism Show in Catalonia*	*20 to 23 April 2000*
Sevilla	*April Fair*	*2 to 7 May 2000*
Valencia	*Fallas*	*15 to 19 March*
	International Fair	*26 Dec. to 3 Jan.*

SWEDEN

Stockholm	*Stockholm Water Festival*	*6 to 14 August*
	International Fashion Fair	*28 to 30 August*
	Strindberg Cultural Festival	*28 Aug. to 5 Sept.*
	International Art Fair	*11 to 14 March*
Gothenburg	*International Horse Show*	*22 to 25 April*
	International Book & Library Fair	*16 to 19 Sep.*

SWITZERLAND

Berne	*BEA : Exhibition for Handicraft, Agriculture, Trade and Industry*	*24 April to 3 May*
Basle	*European Watch, Clock and Jewellery Fair*	*29 April to 6 May*
Geneva	*International Exhibition of inventions, new technologies and products*	*7 to 16 April 2000*
	International Fair for travel and languages	*28 April to 2 May*
	International Motor Show	*9 to 19 March 2000*
Zürich	*Züspa : Zurich Autumn Show for Home and Living, Sport and Fashion*	*24 Sept. to 3 Oct.*

London	London International Bookfair	*28 to 30 March*
	Fine Art and Antiques Fair	*3 to 13 June*
	International Motor Show	*20 to 31 October*
	International Film Festival	*2 weeks November*
Birmingham	International Classic Motor Show	*1 and 2 May*
	International Motorcycle Show	*2 weeks November*
Edinburgh	Book Festival	*14 to 30 August*
	International Film Festival	*15 to 29 August*
	Edinburgh International Festival	*15 Aug. to 4 Sept.*
Leeds	International Film Festival	*2 weeks October*

International Dialling Codes

Note : when making an international call, do not dial the first "0" of the city codes (except for calls to Italy).

Indicatifs Téléphoniques Internationaux

Important : Pour les communications internationales, le zéro (0) initial de l'indicatif interurbain n'est pas à composer (excepté pour les appels vers l'Italie).

from \ to	A	B	CH	CZ	D	DK	E	FIN	F	GB	GR
A Austria		0032	0041	00420	0049	0045	0034	00358	0033	0044	0030
B Belgium	0043		0041	00420	0049	0045	0034	00358	0033	0044	0030
CH Switzerland	0043	0032		00420	0049	0045	0034	00358	0033	0044	0030
CZ Czech Republic	0043	0032	0041		0049	0045	0034	00358	0033	0044	0030
D Germany	0043	0032	0041	00420		0045	0034	00358	0033	0044	0030
DK Denmark	0043	0032	0041	00420	0049		0034	00358	0033	0044	0030
E Spain	0043	0032	0041	00420	0049	0045		00358	0033	0044	0030
FIN Finland	0043	0032	0041	00420	0049	0045	0034		0033	0044	0030
F France	0043	0032	0041	00420	0049	0045	0034	00358		0044	0030
GB United Kingdom	0043	0032	0041	00420	0049	0045	0034	00358	0033		0030
GR Greece	0043	0032	0041	00420	0049	0045	0034	00358	0033	0044	
H Hungary	0043	0032	0041	00420	0049	0045	0034	00358	0033	0044	0030
I Italy	0043	0032	0041	00420	0049	0045	0034	00358	0033	0044	0030
IRL Ireland	0043	0032	0041	00420	0049	0045	0034	00358	0033	0044	0030
J Japan	00143	00132	00141	001420	0149	00145	00134	001358	00133	00144	00130
L Luxembourg	0043	0032	0041	00420	0049	0045	0034	00358	0033	0044	0030
N Norway	0043	0032	0041	00420	0049	0045	0034	00358	0033	0044	0030
NL Netherlands	0043	0032	0041	00420	0049	0045	0034	00358	0033	0044	0030
PL Poland	0043	0032	0041	00420	0049	0045	0034	00358	0033	0044	0030
P Portugal	0043	0032	0041	00420	0049	0045	0034	00358	0033	0044	0030
RUS Russia	81043	81032	81041	810420	81049	81045	*	009358	81033	81044	*
S Sweden	00943	00932	00941	00920	00949	00945	00934	00958	00933	00944	00930
USA	01143	01132	01141	011420	01149	01145	01134	011358	01133	01144	01130

** Direct dialing not possible** ** Pas de sélection automatique*

Internationale Telefon-Vorwahlnummern

Wichtig : bei Auslandsgesprächen darf die Null (0) der Ortsnetzkennzahl nicht gewählt werden (ausser bei Gesprächen nach Italien).

国際電話国別番号

H	I	IRL	J	L	N	NL	PL	P	RUS	S	USA	
0036	0039	00353	0081	00352	0047	0031	0048	00351	007	0046	001	**Austria A**
0036	0039	00353	0081	00352	0047	0031	0048	00351	007	0046	001	**Belgium B**
0036	0039	00353	0081	00352	0047	0031	0048	00351	007	0046	001	**Switzerland CH**
0036	0039	00353	0081	00352	0047	0031	0048	00351	007	0046	001	**Czech CZ Republic**
0036	0039	00353	0081	00352	0047	0031	0048	00351	007	0046	001	**Germany D**
0036	0039	00353	0081	00352	0047	0031	0048	00351	007	0046	001	**Denmark DK**
0036	0039	00353	0081	00352	0047	0031	0048	00351	007	0046	001	**Spain E**
0036	0039	00353	0081	00352	0047	0031	0048	00351	007	0046	001	**Finland FIN**
0036	0039	00353	0081	00352	0047	0031	0048	00351	007	0046	001	**France F**
0036	0039	00353	0081	00352	0047	0031	0048	00351	007	0046	001	**United GB Kingdom**
0036	0039	00353	0081	00352	0047	0031	0048	00351	007	0046	001	**Greece GR**
	0039	00353	0081	00352	0047	0031	0048	00351	007	0046	001	**Hungary H**
0036		00353	0081	00352	0047	0031	0048	00351	*	0046	001	**Italy I**
0036	0039		0081	00352	0047	0031	0048	00351	007	0046	001	**Ireland IRL**
00136	00139	001353		001352	00147	00131	00148	001351	*	00146	0011	**Japan J**
0036	0039	00353	0081		0047	0031	0048	00351	007	0046	001	**Luxembourg L**
0036	0039	00353	0081	00352		0031	0048	00351	007	0046	001	**Norway N**
0036	0039	00353	0081	00352	0047		0048	00351	007	0046	001	**Netherlands NL**
0036	0039	00353	0081	00352	0047	0031		00351	007	0046	001	**Poland PL**
0036	0039	00353	0081	00352	0047	0031	0048		007	0046	001	**Portugal P**
81036	*	*	*	*	*	81031	81048	*		*	*	**Russia RUS**
00936	00939	00953	00981	00952	00947	00931	00948	009351	0097		0091	**Sweden S**
01136	01139	011353	01181	011352	01147	01131	01148	011351	*	01146		**USA**

*Automatische Vorwahl nicht möglich

Notes
Notizen

Notes
Notizen

Notes

Notizen

Benelux • Deutschland •
España & Portugal • Europe • France •
Great Britain & Ireland • Ireland • Italia •
London • Paris • Portugal •
Suisse / Schweiz / Svizzera

Manufacture française des pneumatiques Michelin

Société en commandite par actions au capital de 2 000 000 000 de francs
Place des Carmes-Déchaux – 63 Clermont-Ferrand (France)
R.C.S. Clermont-Fd B 855 200 507

Michelin et Cie, propriétaires-éditeurs, 1999
Dépôt légal : mars 99 – ISBN 2.06.970999.X

**No part of this publication may be reproducted in any form
without the prior permission of the publisher.**

Printed in the EU – 3.1999

Illustrations : Nathalie Benavides, Patricia Haubert, Cécile Imbert/MICHELIN
Narratif Systèmes/Genclo p. 9, 11, 13, 15, 17, 19, 20, 21, 23, 26, 27, 31, 55, 62
64, 103, 110, 133, 143, 153, 161, 279, 287, 359, 367, 377, 391, 465, 483, 497
555, 571, 597, 617.
Rodolphe Corbel p. 182, 186, 188, 193, 197, 203, 207, 209, 213, 217, 221, 473